Abhidharmakośa-Bhāṣya of Vasubandhu

The Treasury of the Abhidharma and its (Auto) commentary

Translated into French by

Louis de La Vallee Poussin

Annotated English Translation by

Gelong Lodrö Sangpo

With a New Introduction by

Bhikkhu KL Dhammajoti

Volume I

MOTILAL BANARSIDASS PUBLISHERS
PRIVATE LIMITED • DELHI

First Edition : Delhi, 2012
Translated from L' Abhidharmakosa de Vasubandhu
First edition 1823-1931, Paris, Paul Geuthner
Second edition 1971, Bruxelles, Institute Belga des Hautes Ètudes Chinoises

ISBN : 978-81-208-3608-2 (Vol. I)
978-81-208-3609-9 (Vol. II)
978-81-208-3610-5 (Vol. III)
978-81-208-3611-2 (Vol. IV)
978-81-208-3607-5 (Set)

MOTILAL BANARSIDASS
41 U.A. Bungalow Road, Jawahar Nagar, Delhi 110 007
8 Mahalaxmi Chamber, 22 Bhulabhai Desai Road, Mumbai 400 026
203 Royapettah High Road, Mylapore, Chennai 600 004
236, 9th Main III Block, Jayanagar, Bangalore 560 011
Sanas Plaza, 1302 Baji Rao Road, Pune 411 002
8 Camac Street, Kolkata 700 017
Ashok Rajpath, Patna 800 004
Chowk, Varanasi 221 001

Printed in India

by RP Jain at NAB Printing Unit,
A-44, Naraina Industrial Area, Phase I, New Delhi–110028
and published by JP Jain for Motilal Banarsidass Publishers (P) Ltd,
41 U.A. Bungalow Road, Jawahar Nagar, Delhi-110007

Dedicated

To my Esteemed

Teachers

Volume I

- Summary and Discussion of the *Abhidharmakośa-bhāṣya*
  by Bhikkhu KL Dhammajoti
- Preface to the 1971 edition of *"L'Abhidharmakośa de Vasubandhu"*
  by Étienne Lamotte
- Bibliographical Addendum
  by Hubert Durt
- Preface
  by Louis de La Vallée Poussin
- Introduction
  by Louis de La Vallée Poussin
- Remarks of the Translator
- Abbreviations
- Outline of Chapter One
- Chapter One: Exposition of the Elements (*Dhātunirdeśa*)
- Endnotes to Chapter One
- Outline of Chapter Two
- Chapter Two: Exposition of the Faculties (*Indriyanirdeśa*)
- Endnotes to Chapter Two

Summary and Discussion of the *Abhidharmakośa-bhāṣya*

by

Bhikkhu KL Dhammajoti

A. Abhidharma as primarily a soteriology 1
B. The predecessors of the *Abhidharmakośa-bhāṣya* as a manual 2
C. The organizational structure of the *Abhidharmakośa-bhāṣya* 6
D. The affiliation of the *Abhidharmakośa-bhāṣya* 9
E. Summaries and discussion on the chapters 10
EA. Chapter one: *Dhātu-nirdeśa* 10
EB. Chapter two: *Indriya-nirdeśa* 15
EBA. On the *indriya*-s 16
EBB. One the co-nascence of material atoms 17
EBC. On the *citta-caitta*-s 17
EBD. On the disjoined conditionings 19
EBE. On causes, conditions and fruits 21
EC. Chapter three: *Loka-nirdeśa* 23
ECA. Constitution of the physical universe and its inhabitants 24
ECB. Formation and dissolution of the universe 25
ECC. Conditioned co-arising 25
ED. Chapter four: *Karma-nirdeśa* 28
EE. Chapter five: *Anuśaya-nirdeśa* 34
EF. Chapter six: *Mārgapudgala-nirdeśa* 40
EG. Chapter seven: *Jñāna-nirdeśa* 46
EH. Chapter eight: *Samāpatti-nirdeśa* 51
EI. Chapter nine: **Pudgalavāda-pratiṣedha* 56
F. Abbreviations 61

Abhidharma as primarily a soteriology

The term "*abhidharma*", as it occurs in the *sūtra*-s, means either "pertaining to (/about) the Doctrine", or the "excellent Doctrine". It is important to realize that although the northern Abhidharma tradition preserves the meaning of "*abhi-*" as "facing" (*abhimukha*), hence, also "pertaining", the signification of the two components (*abhi* + *dharma*) is profoundly different from that in the *sūtra*-s. In the developed Abhidharma system represented by the period of the Abhidharma treatises, firstly, "*abhi-*" in the sense of *abhimukha* signifies direct realization (*abhisamaya*) into the true nature of *dharma*-s. This is the meaning of the definition that "*abhidharma* is outflow-free (*anāsrava*) or pure *prajñā*",[1] where both *abhidharma* and *prajñā* are defined as "investigation/discernment of *dharma*-s" (*dharma-pravicaya*). Secondly, "*dharma*" here does not mean "Doctrine", but refers either to the ultimate reals, each having a unique intrinsic nature (*svabhāva*) and being uniquely experienced as an intrinsic characteristic (*svalakṣaṇa*), or to *Nirvāṇa* as the *Dharma par excellence*.[2] (Also *cf.* Section EA). In the MVŚ, the Sarvāstivāda master Buddhapālita explains the signification of "*abhi-*" thus:

> "*abhi-*" is a prefix signifying "*abhimukha*" (顯現). This *dharma* is called *abhidharma* because it induces all skillful *dharma*-s—the factors conducing to Enlightenment (*bodhi-pakṣa-dharma*)—to manifest directly.[3]

The signification of "*abhisamaya*" is in fact explicitly shown in one of the Ābhidharmikas' definitions:

> It is called *abhidharma* because it can directly realize the *dharma*-s.[4]

This spiritual significance (as opposed to a mere intellectual one) is also succinctly brought out by Saṃghabhadra:

> Now, why is it that only the outflow-free *prajñā* alone is called *abhidharma*? Because, when the characteristics of *dharma*-s have been directly realized (現觀; *abhi-sam-√i*) through it, one will no longer be deluded [therein].[5]

It is true that in the course of development of the Ābhidharmika exegetical methodology, there unavoidably came to be some distinctive elements of what might be called "scholasticism". But in view of the above consideration, I, for one, am very disinclined to adopt "scholasticism" as a formal rendering of "Abhidharma". Perhaps the term is best left in its Sanskrit form.

B. The predecessors of the *Abhidharmakośa-bhāṣya* as a manual

1. Like many other Buddhist schools, the Sarvāstivāda came to be a fully established school through a gradual process, and it is hardly possible to pinpoint an exact date of its founding or a particular person as its founder. This is especially so since the Sarvāstivāda is a broad lineage embracing, besides the Ābhidharmika masters, various masters and communities, some of whom—such as the early Dārṣṭāntikas—are basically anti-Ābhidharmika. Nevertheless, inasmuch as the Ābhidharmikas, constituting the mainstream Sarvāstivādins as they do, came to uphold the *Jñānaprasthāna* (*ca.* 150 B.C.) as the supreme authority on Abhidharma doctrines, its author Kātyāyanīputra came to be generally regarded by tradition as the school's effective founder. Eventually the orthodox Sarvāstivādins based in Kaśmīra composed the *Abhidharma-mahāvibhāṣā*, a gigantic commentary (translated by Xuan

Zang into 200 fascicles) on the *Jñānaprasthāna*, with the purpose of defining the Sarvāstivāda orthodoxy and purging all other views not compatible with those expressed by Kātyāyanīputra. Subsequent to this, these Kaśmīrian masters assumed the position of orthodox Sarvāstivādins and, conforming to the collectively sanctioned views arrived at in this commentary, came to be known as the Vaibhāṣikas. The *Mahāvibhāṣā*, now extant only in Chinese, was undoubtedly a great achievement to be proud of, representing the collective wisdom through a process of continuous effort of devoted study, careful analysis and articulation on the part of these Ābhidharmikas. Traditional accounts speak of it as being guarded as a great treasure, not to be transmitted outside the Kaśmīrian orthodoxy.

2. Be that as it may, it is certain that the text in due course came to be widely known by the other Sarvāstivādins outside Kaśmīra, including the so-called "western" (Pāścāttya) or "outside" (Bāhyaka/Bāhyābhidharmika) masters. These latter masters, based mainly in the Gandhāra region, while also respecting the *Jnānaprasthāna*, did not submit themselves to the dictation of the authority of this text or its huge commentary. In fact, many of them seemed to be much more influenced by Vasumitra's *Prakaraṇa-pāda*, another canonical Abhidharma text of the school. In respect of doctrinal exposition, one of major influences of the *Prakaraṇa* on these western masters was the tendency towards succinctness and organization — a tendency especially discernible in the exposition of its *Pañcavastuka* chapter which streamlines for the first time the classification of the totality of *dharma*-s into the five categories of *rūpa*, *citta*, *caitasika*, *viprayukta-saṃskāra* and *asaṃskṛta*.

3. The *Mahāvibhāṣā*, in contrast, encyclopedic as it is, in respect of organization leaves much to be desired as a text for a systematic comprehension of the Sarvāstivāda doctrines. This partly results from its structure being dictated by that of the *Jñānaprasthāna*, which is little organized, and partly owing to the compilers' style of branching off too frequently from one topic to another in discussing a given doctrinal position. This fact, coupled with a reaction on the part of some masters—mainly Gandhāra based—to its excessive adherence to the *Jñānaprasthāna* orthodoxy, led to the subsequent compilation of various Abhidharma manuals exhibiting the tendency towards succinctness and systematic organization.

i. The first of these appeared shortly after the *Mahāvibhāṣā*, entitled the **Amṛtarasa-śāstra* 甘露味論 (T no. 1553), a small treatise (two fascicles in Chinese tr.) by Ghoṣaka[6] who evidently consulted and often synthesized the views in the *Jñānaprasthāna*, *Prakaraṇa-pāda* as well as *Mahāvibhāṣā*. The influence from the

Prakaraṇa-pāda is particularly visible in the chapter on the *saṃskāra*-s which Ghoṣaka divides into *saṃprayukta*- (the *caitasika*-s) and *viprayukta-saṃskāra*-s (comprising fifteen *dharma*-s, just as the *Pañcavastuka* chapter of the *Prakaraṇa-pāda* does. Ghoṣaka also follows the *Pañcavastuka* in enumerating four non-defined roots (*avyākṛta-mūla*) and ten *jñāna*-s.[7] The *Amṛta-rasa*, though having the merit of succinctness and a distinctive emphasis on praxis, suffers from a lack of breadth and depth in terms of doctrinal elucidation.

ii. The next manual in this direction of development was Dharmaśrī's *Abhidharma-hṛdaya* 阿毘曇心論 (T no. 1550), around the latter part of the third century C.E.[8] This was basically a revision and enlargement (four fascicles in Chinese tr.) of the *Amṛta-rasa*. Its main contribution was the innovation of the style of expounding Abhidharma doctrines in verses, followed by prose elaboration. The verses very effectively summarize the doctrines and greatly facilitate their memorization. In terms of organization, it also shows a further improvement: it underscores the Abhidharma emphasis on the investigation of the intrinsic and common characteristics of *dharma*-s by making the "exposition on *dhātu*-s" the very first chapter. This is immediately followed by the second chapter on the "*saṃskāra*-s" (行品)—expounding the dynamic inter-relationship among the *dharma*-s—replacing chapters six, seven and eight of the *Amṛta-rasa*. In this way, the first two chapters fully accomplish the task of a general exposition on what the ultimate reals are and their dynamic functions. The remaining chapters are then devoted to the individual expositions on the specific cause-effect relations of these reals from different perspectives. Such an organization came to be consistently adopted by the later manuals, including the *Abhidharmakośa* and its *bhāṣya*. A significant doctrinal dissention from the Kaśmīrian orthodoxy in this text concerns the non-information (*avijñapti*) *karma*: it teaches that the non-information is unreal, speaking of it as a seed that arises in the doer's mind (whose serial continuity fluctuates in moral nature: sometimes skillful, sometimes unskillful and sometimes neutral) when it has been projected by a strong information *karma*.[9] It also asserts that "mental *karma* is exclusively of the nature of non-information *karma*, since the *cetanā* continues subtly as a series without manifesting itself".[10] Both assertions are contrary to the *Jñānaprasthāna-Mahāvibhāṣā* orthodoxy.

iii. The *Abhidharma-hṛdaya* sets the style of exposition and the structural trend for the subsequent Abhidharma manuals, and appears to have been very influential. Various commentaries,[11] extant now only in Chinese, came to be written on it, some with the intent of aligning more with the *Jñānaprasthāna-Mahāvibhāṣā* orthodoxy, while others dissent to varying degrees. One, by Upaśānta, entitled 阿毘曇心論,

apparently the same title as **Abhidharmahṛdaya*, or 阿毘曇心論經 (T no. 1551), probably **Abhidharmahṛdaya-bhāṣya* in its original Sanskrit, was translated in 555–561 C.E. This text adds two stanzas to those of the *Abhidharmahṛdaya*, modifies some of its stanzas and revises its expositions with an attempt to restore them to the *Jñānaprasthāna-Mahāvibhāṣā* orthodoxy.

iv. The **Abhidharmahṛdaya-vyākhyā* (or **Miśra-abhidharmahṛdaya* 雜阿毘曇心論, T no. 1552), composed around 350 C.E. by Dharmatrāta, another Gandhāra master, follows Upaśānta's commentary in this direction. Many scholars have long considered it as a direct reference of Vasubandhu when he composed the *Abhidharmakośa*.[12] This text contains 596 stanzas, twice as many as the *Abhidharmahṛdaya*, and in this way is better suited for more extensive doctrinal exposition. It also added a chapter on "discernment/investigation (擇品). But while aligning his views with those in the *Mahā-vibhāṣā*, the author often retains some variant Vaibhāṣika views. Besides following Upaśānta in rectifying Dharmaśrī's non-orthodox exposition, he also shows some attempt at more precise definitions. For instance, Dharmaśrī defines "with-outflow" (*sāsrava*) thus:

> The noble ones define "with-outflow" as that which generates defilement.[13]

Upaśānta follows this, though slightly modifying Dharmaśrī's stanza and offering a little elaboration:

> The noble ones define "with-outflow" as that wherein defilement is generated.[14]

Dharmatrāta's definition, on the other hand, is more articulate:

> The noble ones define "with-outflow" as that wherein defilement is intensified.[15]

Towards the end of the chapter on "discernment", he states that he finds it necessary to modify Dharmaśrī's stanza and explanation, not out of arrogance or a desire to become famous, but in the hope that his exposition would contribute to the propagation of the doctrinal legacy (of the ancient masters). Taking the definition on "with-outflow" as an example, he explains:

> For instance, he (Dharmaśrī) states that "the noble ones define 'with-outflow' as that which generates defilement". [But] cessation (*nirodha*) and the path (*mārga*) too generate defilement; yet they are not with-outflow. This is because they are adverse (非分; **apakṣa*) to the increase (/intensification) of the defilement. A defilement that takes an outflow-free object (*anāsrava-ālambanaḥ kleśaḥ*) diminishes rather than intensifies. ... Hence, I say "is intensified".[16]

v. Following the style of Dharmatrāta, Vasubandhu (*ca*. fourth century C.E.), another Gandhārian, composed the *Abhidharma-kośa* in verse. He skillfully summarizes the Vaibhāṣika doctrines, occasionally inserting the word "*kila*" where he dissents from the Vaibhāṣika orthodoxy. In his own prose commentary, the *Abhidharmakośa-bhāṣya*, he reviews the Vaibhāṣika tenets, often criticizing them from the Sautrāntika perspective. Vasubandhu's brilliant critique of the Vaibhāṣika doctrines was answered by the equally brilliant Saṃghabhadra, his contemporary and a staunch Vaibhāṣika, in the **Nyāyānusāra* which is now extant only in Xuan Zang's translation. Other more concise manuals followed, such as Skandhila's *Abhidharmāvatāra* (extant in both Tibetan and Chinese translations) which aims at expounding the totality of the Sarvāstivāda doctrines in a scheme of eight categories (*padārtha*)—five aggregates (*skandha*) and the three unconditioned (*asaṃskṛta*)—while steering clear of sectarian disputations.

C. The organizational structure of the *Abhidharmakośa-bhāṣya*

1. Vasubandhu's *Abhidharmakośa-bhāṣya* may be considered the culmination in the western-based development of Abhidharma manuals, influenced by the *Prakaraṇa-pāda*'s tendency towards succinctness and systematic exposition. In fact, like many western masters, he appears to respect the *Prakaraṇa* as much as the *Jñānaprasthāna*.

The structural similarity between the AKB and the AHV should be clear from the following table of comparison:

AKB	AHV
1. *Dhātu-nirdeśa* 界品	1. 界品 (**Dhātu-nirdeśa*)
2. *Indriya-nirdeśa* 根品	2. 行品 (**Saṃskāra-nirdeśa*)
3. *Loka-nirdeśa* 世間品	
4. *Karma-nirdeśa* 業品	3. 業品 (**Karma-nirdeśa*)
5. *Anuśaya-nirdeśa* 隨眠品	4. 使品 (**Anuśaya-nirdeśa*)
6. *Mārgapudgala-nirdeśa* 賢聖品	5. 賢聖品 (**Mārgapudgala-nirdeśa*)
7. *Jñāna-nirdeśa* 智品	6. 智品 (**Jñāna-nirdeśa*)
8. *Samāpatti-nirdeśa* 定品	7. 定品 (**Samāpatti-nirdeśa*)
	8. 修多羅品 (**Sūtra-nirdeśa*)
	9. 雜品 (**Kṣudraka/prakīrṇaka*)
	10. 擇品 (**Viniścaya*)
	11. 論品 (**Sāmkathya/*praśna-kathā*)

It can be seen that Vasubandhu deleted the last four chapters of the AHV, of which eight, nine and eleven were inherited from the *Abhidharmahṛdaya*. Since these four chapters do not contain specifically representative doctrines under their titles, Vasubandhu deleted them, though incorporated some of their content into his chapters. On the other hand, he added the *loka-nirdeśa* (chapter three) which then provides a proper venue for the Abhidharma exposition of cosmological doctrines; various discussions pertaining thereto are found scattered in different places of the AHV. Chapter two of the AHV is renamed as "*indriya-nirdeśa*"—perhaps also not a very suitable choice of title—because this chapter in his AKB begins by discussing the twenty-two *indriya*-s. Pu Guang[17] justifies Vasubandhu's deviation from Dharmatrāta here: "*indriya*" decisively signifies "function". On the other hand, the term "*saṃskāra*" (as in the AHV), while denoting constructive activity or conditioning (造作), also signifies procession or temporal flow (遷流; *sam-√kram*); the signification of function/activity is thus not decisive.[18]

As we have remarked above, the AKB inherited the scheme of exposition, set by the *Abhidharma-hṛdaya*: the first two chapters expound generally the ultimate reals as well as their mutual interactions; the remaining chapters deal separately with the specific aspects of their cause-effect relationship. In the first chapter of the AKB, Vasubandhu retains the title "*dhātu-nirdeśa*", subsuming all *dharma*-s into two fundamental species: with-outflow and outflow-free; these are correlated to the four Noble Truths.[19]

A ninth chapter on *Ātmavāda-pratiṣedha* is appended to the eight chapters of the AKB. In style, it is distinctively different from the previous chapters in being purely in prose, without the *kārikā*-s. At the end of chapter eight, Vasubandhu already says that he has finished expounding the Abhidharma doctrines. It is to be noted in this connection that Saṃghabhadra's **Nyāyānusāra* also ends with chapter eight on *samāpatti* and does not say a word on the ninth chapter. Nevertheless, Vasubandhu must have had this chapter in mind when composing the AKB, as he refers to it within this text.[20]

2. Pu Guang, takes all this into consideration in explaining the overall structure of the AKB. He firstly points out that all Indian treatises have as their aim the elucidation of the Buddha's teachings of the three insignia: (i) "All conditionings are impermanent" (*sarve saṃskārā 'nityāḥ*); (ii) "all *dharma*-s are without a self" (*sarve dharmā'nātmānaḥ*); (iii) "*Nirvāṇa* is quiescent" (*nirvāṇaṃ śāntam*). Some texts elucidate one; other, another. The AKB, he says, aims at elucidating no-self-ness, because by doing so, the no-self-ness of all *dharma*-s, whether conditioned or unconditioned, is demonstrated.[21] He then gives the outline structure of the whole text thus:

This treatise has a total of nine chapters, elucidating [the teaching] in the *sūtra*-s that "all *dharma*-s are without a self". The first eight chapters expound [as their proper concern][22] the *dharma*-s as [non-self] entities (事) … . The last chapter expounds [as its proper concern] the principle (理) of no-self-ness… .

Among the first eight chapters, the first two expound generally the with-outflow and outflow-free; the last six expound separately [the specific aspects of] the with-outflow and outflow-free… .

In the general exposition, the *dhātu-nirdeśa* elucidates [as its proper concern] the essential natures of the *dharma*-s; the *indriya-nirdeśa* elucidates [as its proper concern] the functions/efficacies of the *dharma*-s. … The essential natures constitute the bases, hence the *dhātu*-s are first expounded. The efficacies arise with the essential natures as support-bases, hence the *indriya*-s are next expounded.

Among the six chapters of separate expositions, the first three elucidate [as their proper concern] the with-outflow *dharma*-s; the last three elucidate [as their proper concern] the outflow-free *dharma*-s… .

Among the separate expositions of the with-outflow *dharma*-s, there are three chapters—*loka*, *karma* and *anuśaya*—which elucidate the sequence of the fruits, the causes and the conditions (*pratyaya*): The *loka-nirdeśa* [as its proper concern] elucidates the with-outflow fruits; they are expounded first because their characteristics are gross and are easy to be disgusted with… . The *karma-nirdeśa* [as its proper concern] elucidates the causes of the retributions; the fruits necessarily arise from the causes and their powers must be dominant, hence they are expounded next… . The *anuśaya-nirdeśa* elucidates [as its proper concern] the conditions for the *karma*-s. The *karma*-s by themselves cannot effectuate fruition, and must rely on the conditions; and in the production of the fruits, the *anuśaya*-s are relatively inferior [as a contributing factor], hence they are elucidated last.

Among the separate expositions of the outflow-free *dharma*-s, there are three chapters—*mārga-pudgala*, *jñāna* and *samāpatti*—which elucidate the sequence of the fruits, the causes and the conditions: The *mārga-pudgala-nirdeśa* [as its proper concern] elucidates the outflow-free fruits; they are elucidated first because their characteristics are manifest and easy to be delighted in. The *jñāna-nirdeśa* elucidates [as its proper concern] the causes for the realization of the fruits. The fruits necessarily depend on their causes, which are strong [as a contributory factor] to the realization of the fruits, hence they are elucidated next. The *samāpatti-nirdeśa* elucidates the conditions for the *jñāna*-s. The *jñāna*-s by themselves alone cannot [lead to] the realization of the fruits, they must rely on the *samāpatti*-s as conditions; and the *samāpatti*-s are comparatively inferior [as a contributory factor] to the fruits, hence they are elucidated last.[23]

Pu Guang's description of the organizational structure of the AKB can be summarized by the following chart:

<table>
<tr><th></th><th>CHAPTER</th><th>ELUCIDATION</th><th></th><th></th></tr>
<tr><td rowspan="8">Non-self dharma-s</td><td>1. Dhātu</td><td>Essential nature of dharma-s</td><td rowspan="2">With-outflow & outflow-free: general exposition</td><td rowspan="2"></td></tr>
<tr><td>2. Indriya</td><td>Functions of dharma-s</td></tr>
<tr><td>3. Loka</td><td>With-outflow fruits</td><td rowspan="6">With-outflow & outflow-free: separate expositions</td><td rowspan="3">Separate expositions on with-outflow</td></tr>
<tr><td>4. Karma</td><td>Causes of retribution</td></tr>
<tr><td>5. Anuśaya</td><td>Conditions for the karma-s</td></tr>
<tr><td>6. Mārga-pudgala</td><td>Outflow-free fruits</td><td rowspan="3">Separate expositions on outflow-free</td></tr>
<tr><td>7. Jñāna</td><td>Causes for the realization of the fruits</td></tr>
<tr><td>8. Samāpatti</td><td>Conditions for the jñāna-s</td></tr>
<tr><td>No-self doctrine</td><td>9. Ātmavāda-pratiṣedha</td><td>Principle of non-self-ness</td><td></td><td></td></tr>
</table>

The affiliation of the *Abhidharmakośa-bhāṣya*

1. Besides its culminating achievement in streamlining the overall structure of the whole exposition, Vasubandhu's AKB is also unmatched by any of the preceding manuals in respect to its comprehensiveness, incorporating all the important Vaibhāṣika doctrines since the *Vibhāṣā*, to its excellent skill in definition and elucidation, and to its ability to clarify the difficult points involved in doctrinal disputations. Added to these is its great value as a brilliant critique and insightful re-evaluation of all the fundamental Sarvāstivāda doctrines developed up to its time. Since its appearance, it had been used in India as a standard textbook for the understanding of not only the Abhidharma doctrines but fundamental Buddhist doctrines in general. Pu Guang tells us that in India, it was hailed as the "Book of Intelligence" (聰明論):

> [This treatise] gathers the essential teachings of the six "feet[-treatises]" without leaving out anything. Although the master, when discussing the Sarvāstivāda doctrines, at times rectifies them from the perspective of the Sautrāntikas, he [in fact] affiliates himself with whatever accords with truth and harbors no sectarian bias. Accordingly, the ninety-six heretical schools without exception enjoy studying this text, and all the eighteen [Hīnayāna] sects equally delight in it as an esoteric treatise (祕典)... . Hence, students in India hail it as the "Book of Intelligence".[24]

In China, Japan and the Far-East, too, the AKB has generally been highly treasured as a textbook of fundamental importance for Buddhist studies. In Japan, there is a popular saying: "Eight years of the *Kośa* and three years of the *Vijñaptimātra* [—for the mastery of Buddhist philosophy]".

2. Vasubandhu states that he, in the main, follows the Kaśmīrian Vaibhāṣikas in expounding the Sarvāstivādin doctrines. However, in many places, he is explicitly oriented towards the doctrinal standpoints of the Sautrāntikas, together with whom he repudiates even the fundamental Sarvāstivāda tenet of the tri-temporal existence of *dharma*-s. In his exposition on *karma* (including the doctrine of the *avijñapti*), the process of spiritual transformation (*āśraya-parivṛtti*) and no-self-ness, etc., he is seen to clearly favor the Sautrāntika theory of *bīja*. To this extent, he could be labeled as a Sautrāntika. But in many cases, he also advocates the Sarvāstivāda-Vaibhāṣika positions: notably, the doctrine of simultaneous causality (*sahabhū-hetu*), the *citta-caitta* doctrines in general (here he generally refrains from siding with the Sautrāntikas), and the system of spiritual praxis and its stages of progress. Moreover, he never in a sectarian manner rejects the doctrines of the Abhidharma texts—his composition of the AKB is a clear point in case. At the end of chapter eight, he states:

> This *abhidharma* proclaimed by us is for the most part established according to the principles of the Kaśmīrian Vaibhāṣikas (*kāśmīra-vaibhāṣikāṇāṃ nīti-siddhaḥ*). Whatever herein has been badly grasped by us is our fault. But then, with regard to the principle of the True Doctrine, the Buddha and the sons of the Buddha alone are the authority (*pramāṇa*).[25]

On the whole, therefore, concerning Vasubandhu's affiliation, the description by the Chinese commentators seems most appropriate: he affiliates himself with whatever accords with truth (以理勝為宗, 據理為宗). The following is expressed by Fa Bao, a student of Xuan Zang:

> The stanzas in this treatise are composed mostly in accordance with the *Vibhāṣā*. In the prose, [the author] affiliates with whatever excels in truthfulness, and is not partial to any particular school. Nevertheless, within [the prose commentary], he mostly takes the Sautrāntika doctrines as the correct ones.[26]

E. Summaries and discussion on the chapters

EA. Chapter one: *Dhātu-nirdeśa*

As we saw above, the title of this chapter is inherited from the *Abhidharma-hṛdaya*, and this first chapter has as its main purpose the exposition on the entities qua ultimate reals. Although this chapter also investigates these reals under the scheme of the *skandha*-s and *āyatana*-s, the term "*dhātu*" is chosen because it has a similar signification as "*dharma*" when understood in the sense of an ultimate real source. Thus, the Great Elements (*mahā-bhūta*) are also called *dhātu*-s with the definition: "they are *dhātu*-s because they sustain their intrinsic characteristics and the derived *rūpa*-s".[27] While the part concerning their sustaining the derived matter is to be expected, the first part of the definition—"sustain intrinsic characteristics"—is most instructive. It is the same definition as that for "*dharma*": "It is *dharma* because it sustains its intrinsic characteristic."[28] Moreover, when explaining "*dhātu*" in "*loka-dhātu*", etc. (chapter three), Vasubandhu again gives the gloss: "*svalakṣaṇa-dhāraṇād dhātuḥ*".[29] We may further note that in fact the Vaibhāṣikas—as represented by Saṃghabhadra—take "*dharmatā*" ("nature of *dharma*") as a synonym for "*dhātu*".[30] In this connection, we should also note that in his **Nyāyānusāra*, Saṃghabhadra names this chapter as "The Fundamental Entities" (本事品; **dravya-nirdeśa*) which confirms that "*dhātu*" in the title of this chapter of the AKB is indeed intended to signify the ultimate or fundamental reals.

This chapter offers definitions of the central concepts of Abhidharma, and discusses its most fundamental topics, some in outline, some in considerable detail.

1. Firstly, "*abhidharma*" is stated to be the outflow-free *prajñā*. In fact, both "*abhidharma*" and "*prajñā*" are glossed as "discernment/investigation of *dharma*-s." In a broader sense, *abhidharma* can be said to comprise all the five outflow-free *skandha*-s that constitute its "retinue" (*anucara*). This is *abhidharma* in the highest sense (*pāramārthika*). In the conventional sense, the term further connotes all that serves as the means for the acquisition of this outflow-free *prajñā*: the with-outflow *prajñā* derived from listening, from reflection and from cultivation, or innately acquired, as well as the Abhidharma texts.

"*Abhidharma*" is also etymologically defined as "face to face (*abhimukha*) with the *dharma*-s". A "*dharma*" is a unique, ultimate real entity "which sustains its intrinsic characteristic (*svalakaṣaṇa-dhāraṇād dharmaḥ*). This "*dharma*" is also said to refer to *Nirvāṇa*, the "*dharma* qua the absolute entity (*paramārtha-dharma*)". These explanations taken together mean that Abhidharma in the true sense is that which directly realizes the true nature of all *dharma*-s and hence also that which leads to the realization of *Nirvāṇa*.

2. The definitional identification of "*abhidharma*" with "*prajñā*" spells out the central importance of the latter as both the means and the ultimate aim of *abhi-*

dharma investigation. This is more explicitly shown in the definition of *prajnā* in the *Abhidharmadīpa-prabhāvṛtti*[31] and Skandhila's *Abhidharmāvatāra*:

> Understanding (*prajñā*) is the discernment of *dharma*-s. It is the examination (*upalakṣaṇa*), as the case may be, of the following eight kinds of *dharma*-s: inclusion (*saṃgraha*), conjunction (*saṃprayoga*), endowment (*samanvāgama*), causes (*hetu*), conditions (*saṃgraha*), effects (*phala*), intrinsic characteristic (*svalakṣaṇa*), common characteristic (*sāmānya-lakṣaṇa*).[32]

The eight items enumerated constitute the fundamental topics as well as methodological devices of the Ābhidharmikas.

"Intrinsic characteristic" and "common characteristic" constitute the core concern of *dharma-pravicaya*. "Conjunction" studies the dynamic relationship between the simultaneously existing mental factors.

"Inclusion" is an important device for determining the nature of *dharma*-s in terms of their intrinsic natures:

> For instance, the visual faculty is subsumed under the matter-aggregate, by the visual abode (*cakṣur-āyatana*) and the visual element (*cakṣur-dhātu*), and the truths of unsatisfactoriness and origin. This is because they constitute its intrinsic nature. It is not [subsumed under] the other aggregates, etc., for it is distinct in nature from them.[33]

Every *dharma* is both a cause/condition for other *dharma*-s and is also caused/conditioned by other *dharma*-s; the study of causality ("causes", "conditions" and "effects") is therefore of fundamental importance.

Last, "endowment"—a modality of acquisition (*prāpti*)—is a special topic, also of fundamental importance to the Sarvāstivāda system (*cf.* also Section EB).

3. Vasubandhu gives us the Vaibhāṣika view that the Abhidharma was taught by the Buddha himself for the purpose of emancipation from *saṃsāra*. But he also indicates his disgreement with the marker word "*kila*" ("it is said..."). Yaśomitra comments that Vasubandhu intends here to convey the Sautrāntika stance that "Abhidharma" refers to the teachings in certain types of *sūtra*-s such as the *Arthaviniścaya*, etc.[34]

4. The totality of *dharma*-s is subsumed as those that are with-outflow ("impure") and those that are outflow-free ("pure"). "Outflow" is a synonym for defilement; but it has the important signification of that which retains one (*āsayati*) in *saṃsāra*. A with-outflow (*sāsrava*) *dharma* is that which conduces to or is favorable for the

growth or intensification of a defilement. Even a skillful act, such as giving, however sincere, may be with-outflow unless done through spiritual insight, because it may retain us in some form of saṃsāric existence. This category comprises all the conditioned (*saṃskṛta*) *dharma*-s of the truths of unsatisfactoriness (*duḥkha*) and its origin (*samudaya*).

The truth of the path (*mārga*) and the three types of unconditioned (*asaṃskṛta*) *dharma*-s—Space (*ākāśa*), cessation through deliberation (*pratisaṃkhyā-nirodha*) and cessation independent of deliberation (*apratisaṃkhyā-nirodha*)—are outflow-free (*anāsrava*) because they do not conduce to the growth of a defilement. An outflow-free skillful act, such as the practice of an aspect of the noble eightfold path, leads one further and further away from *saṃsāra*.

Space has non-obstruction (*anāvaraṇa*) as its intrinsic nature. *Pratisaṃkhyā-nirodha* is a cessation—a real entity—arisen through an effort of discrimination. *Apratisaṃkhyā-nirodha* is a cessation acquired without specific effort, but owing to the mere deficiency in the conditions for a *dharma*'s arising; this too is a real entity (not a mere absence of conditions) efficacious in absolutely preventing the re-arising of the ceased *dharma*.

5. The conditioned *dharma*-s are etymologically defined as those "compounded by an assemblage of conditions" (*samety saṃbhūya pratyayaiḥ kṛtā iti saṃskṛtāḥ*). They are explained as comprising the five *skandha*-s:

i. Matter (*rūpa*), defined as that which is resistant and subject to deterioration, comprising the four Great Elements (*mahābhūta*) and the derived matter (*upādāya-rūpa*). A special type of matter called the non-information (*avijñapti*) matter is briefly explained as that which is projected by a physical or vocal *karma*. Although of the nature of *rūpa*, it is invisible and non-resistant; once projected, it continues serially even when the doer's thought is of a different moral nature than that when it was projected, and even when no mental activity occurs in him. (*Avijñapti* is discussed in detail in chapter four.)

ii. Sensation (*vedanā*) is of three species, pleasurable, unpleasurable and neutral.

iii. Ideation (*saṃjñā*) is that which grasps a sign: "male", "female", "green", "yellow", etc.

iv. Conditionings (*saṃskāra*) comprise all conditioned *dharma*-s other than matter, sensation, ideation and consciousness. They include both the conjoined (*samprayukta*) and the disjoined (*viprayukta*) conditionings (*cf.* Section EB).

v. Consciousness (*vijñāna*) is defined as the cognition of its specific object-domain as a whole (*viṣayaṃ viṣayaṃ prati vijñaptir upalabdhir vijñāna-skandhaḥ*).

6. We thus see that this chapter discusses all the five fundamental categories of *dharma*: (i) *rūpa*, (ii) *citta*, (iii) *caitasika*, (iv) *viprayukta-saṃskāra*, (v) *asaṃskṛta*; though ii–iv are only briefly mentioned. This five-category classification of *dharma*-s, originally innovated in Vasumitra's *Prakaraṇa-pāda*, served as the standard Sarvāstivādin classification throughout the ages.

7. The six internal faculties (visual, auditory, olfactory, gustatory, tactile and mental) and the six corresponding objects are also subsumed under the scheme of the "twelve abodes/entrances" (*āyatana*). All *dharma*-s are also subsumable under the scheme of the "eighteen elements" (*dhātu*).

"*Skandha*" is glossed as "heap"; "*āyatana*" as "gate of entry (*āya-dvāra*) of thoughts and thought-concomitants; "*dhātu*" as "clan" (*gotra*), in the sense of "mine" (*ākara*), like iron-mine, gold-mine, etc. — the source-origin. Whereas the Vaibhāṣikas take all these three categories as existent, the Sautrāntikas would only accept the *dhātu*-s as existent. Vasubandhu himself accepts the *āyatana*-s and the *dhātu*-s as existent.

8. The *dharma*-s—the eighteen elements—are further investigated from various doctrinal perspectives. Pu Guang counts a total of twenty-two perspectives in this chapter: (1) visible (*sa-nidarśana*), invisible (*anidarśana*); (2) resistant (*sa-pratigha*), non-resistant (*apratigha*) (3) skillful (*kuśala*), unskillful (*akuśala*), non-defined (*avyākṛta*); (4) connected with/pertaining to (*pratisaṃyukta*) sensuality sphere, to fine-materiality sphere, to non-materiality sphere; (5) with-outflow, outflow-free; (6) with-reasoning (*savitarka*), with-investigation (*savicāra*); (7) with cognitive object (*sa-ālambana*), without cognitive object (*anālambana*); (8) appropriated (*upātta*), non-appropriated (*anutpātta*); (9) Great Elements (*bhūta*), derived from Great Elements (*bhautika*); (10) accumulated (*saṃcita*), non-accumulated (*asaṃcita*); (11) that which cuts (*chinatti*), that which is cut (*chidyate*); (12) that which burns (*dāhaka*), that which is burnt (*dahyate*); (13) that which weighs (*tulayati*), that which can be weighed (*tulya*); (14) the five species: retribution-born (*vipākaja*), accumulative (*aupacayika*), emanational (*naiḥṣyandika*), yoked with a real entity (*dravya-yukta*), momentary (*kṣaṇika*); (15) acquisition (*prāpti/pratilambha*), endowment (*samanvāgama*); (16) external, internal; (17) participative/active (*sabhāga*), non-participative/facsimile (*tat-sabhāga*); (18) abandonable through seeing/vision (*darśana-heya*), abandonable through cultivation (*bhāvanā-heya*), not to be abandoned (*aheya*); (19) view (*dṛṣṭi*), not view; (20) consciousness (*vijñāna*), object of consciousness (/the cognized; *vijñeya* — i.e., what elements are cognized by which consciousness); (21) permanent, impermanent; (22) faculties (*indriya*), non-faculties.[35] Such an investigation from the various perspectives constitutes a fundamental methodology of *dharma-pravicaya*.

i. In discussing how many of the *dhātu*-s are views (*dṛṣṭi*), how many are not views, a controversy arises as to "what sees". The Vaibhāṣikas maintain that it is the visual faculty that sees; the Vijñānavāda, consciousness. The Sautrāntikas finally appear on the scene and ridicule the disputants as trying to chew empty space:

> Conditioned by the eye and *rūpa*-s, visual consciousness arises. Therein, what sees and what is seen? It is devoid of any operation; it is mere-*dharma* qua cause and effect... .[36]

ii. In the final discussion on how many *dhātu*-s are faculties (*indriya*), how many are not, twenty-two faculties are enumerated: 1–5. the five sensory faculties; 6. mental; 7. male; 8. female; 9. vital; 10. pleasure (*sukha*-); 11. displeasure (*duḥkha*-); 12. joyousness (*saumanasya*-); 13. distress (*daurmanasya*-); 14. even-mindedness (*upekṣā*-); 15. faith; 16. vigor; 17. mindfulness; 18. equipoise (*samādhi*-); 19. understanding (*prajñā*-); 20. "I shall know what has not been known" (*anājñātam-ājñāsyāmi*-); 21. full-knowledge (*ājñā*-); 22. possessing full-knowledge (*ājñātāvi*-).

Chapter two: *Indriya-nirdeśa*

We saw that Vasubandhu changed the title of the second chapter of AHV from "*saṃskāra*", and Pu Guang, observing that this chapter is intended to expound the dynamic activities vis-à-vis the ultimate reals, argues that "*indriya*" is a more appropriate title because it more decisively signifies "function/activity" (Section C). We may note here that Vasubandhu does gloss "*indriya*" as "dominance" (*ādhipatya*; see below), a term also used to define the "condition of dominance" (*adhipati-pratyaya*) and the "efficient cause" (*kāraṇa-hetu*), both signifying a cause/condition exercising a force of dominance over the arising of other *dharma*-s. On the other hand, this title may also simply be due to the fact that this chapter picks up from the enumeration of the *indriya*-s at the end of chapter one, and they are the first topic of discussion here. Nevertheless, it is possible that in choosing "*indriya*", Vasubandhu has actually simultaneously taken all these into consideration.

Probably not finding the title entirely satisfactory, Saṃghabhadra changes it to "Distinctive Varieties" (差別品; **Prabheda-nirdeśa*), which he perhaps thinks better indicates the varieties of modes that the ultimate reals can function in mutual interaction. Pu Guang, however, defends Vasubandhu's choice, and shows his preference for it over "Conditionings" and "Distinctive Varieties".[37]

This chapter comprises the following major sections: (a) on the twenty-two *indriya*-s; (b) on the co-nascence of material atoms, (c) on the *citta-caitta*-s, (d) on the conditionings disjoined from thought; (e) on causes, conditions and effects.

EBA. On the *indriya*-s

The chapter begins with the grammarian definition of the term "*indriya*": "The root *idi* is in the sense of 'supreme dominion' (*idi paramaiśvarye*). The *indriya*-s are so called because they exercise power (*indantīti indriyāṇi*)." It then states that *indriya* means "dominance" (*ādhipatya*).[38] E.g., the eye is an *indriya* since it exercises a dominant function in the arising of visual consciousness and its conjoined thought-concomitants, etc.

The last three outflow-free *indriya*-s are, in nature, spiritual insight at progressively higher levels of spiritual attainment and, in terms of intrinsic nature, they are, in each case, constituted by nine faculties: *manas*, *sukha*, *saumanasya*, *upekṣā*, *śraddhā*, *vīrya*, *smṛti*, *samādhi* and *prajñā*. The first of these three, called the faculty of "I shall know what has not been known" exercises dominance with regard to the cessation of the defilements abandonable through insight (*darśana-heya*). The second, the faculty of "full knowledge", exercises dominance with regard to the cessation of the defilements abandonable through cultivation (*bhāvanā-heya*). The third, the faculty of "possessing full knowledge" exercises dominance with regard to the state of bliss in the present and constitutes the path of liberation in the acquisition of the fruit of *arhat*-hood.

The definition of "*indriya*" in terms of "dominance" serves the purpose of a unifying concept for the twenty-two *indriya*-s whose members have occurred in different contexts in the *sūtra*-s (and *śāstra*-s) with different emphases. But this leads to the question as to why these twenty-two alone are considered *indriya*-s when many other *dharma*-s too exercise a dominant influence in the arising or functioning of other *dharma*-s. Vasubandhu presents the Vaibhāṣika explanation on the essential characteristics of the *indriya*-s: They firstly (1–6) refer to the six faculties of consciousness, visual to mental, which constitute the sixfold support-basis of thought (*citta-āśraya*), that is, the six internal *āyatana*-s which are the fundamental constituents (*maulaṃ sattva-drayam*) of a sentient being. They furthermore refer to what differentiates this six-fold basis as being male and female (7–8), to what sustains it for a period of duration (9), to what causes its pollution (*saṃkleśa*) (10–14), to what serves as requisites for its purification (*vyavadāna*) (15–19), and to what accomplishes its purification (20–22).

Vasubandhu does not raise any objection to these Sarvāstivāda-Vaibhāṣika explanations, and in fact refutes the claim by some, namely, that the defining characteristic of "dominance" results in having to admit that the hands, feet, etc., too, are "*indriya*-s".[39]

On the co-nascence of material atoms

In the Buddhist system, nothing can arise by itself. In the Abhidharma analysis, this means that whenever a *dharma* arises, it necessarily does so with a number of co-nascent *dharma*-s. In the case of material *dharma*-s, the Ābhidharmikas combine—apparently not so perfectly—the doctrine of the Great Elements with the relatively later theory of atoms (*paramāṇu*) coming from outside of Buddhism (probably from the Vaiśeṣika). At least by the time of the MVŚ, they had articulated their own version of the atomic theory to a large extent. Sometime after this, they came to stipulate that in the sensuality sphere a minimum of eight substances—constituting the subtlest aggregate, "aggregate-atom" (*saṃghāta-paramāṇu*)—are necessarily co-nascent. This theory is clearly proposed here in this chapter, mentioning the "octad molecule" as comprising the four Great Elements plus visible, odor, taste and touch. This is the case where no sound is produced and no sense faculty is involved. Where sound is generated, one has a nonad molecule; so also is the case of the bodily faculty, comprising the basic eight plus an atom of the bodily faculty. Where another faculty such as the eye is involved, the minimum is ten: the basic eight, plus an atom of the bodily faculty plus an atom of the eye. It should be noted that prior to the AKB, the *Abhidharma-hṛdaya*, in its second chapter, has already mentioned this doctrine:

> In a *rūpa* which is not a faculty, there are eight types of atom.
>
> Question: To the atoms of which sphere do these refer?
>
> Answer: They refer to [where there is] odor; odor exists in the sensuality sphere.[40]

On the *citta-caitta*-s

1. Vasubandhu expounds in great detail the Vaibhāṣika teachings on thoughts and thought-concomitants, and generally without repudiating them. For instance, he straightforwardly describes the Vaibhāṣika doctrine on *citta*, *manas* and *vijñāna* being one and the same object (*ekārtha*), even though having different significations, and then he proceeds to present, in a matter of fact manner, the Vaibhāṣika doctrine of the five-fold equality of two mental factors that are said to be in conjunction (*saṃprayoga*): same time, same support-basis, same cognitive object, same mode of activity (*ākāra*), same singularity of substance (*dravya*; i.e., one thought is conjoined with only one species of sensation, etc.). Here there is not the slightest indication of his objection to the doctrine.

Contrary to the Sarvāstivada-Vaibhāṣika model of simultaneous arising of mental factors, the Dārṣṭāntika-Sautrāntikas maintain that they arise sequentially.

2. Vasubandhu first states that there are five classes (*mahābhūmika*, etc.) of thought-concomitants; but in the end, he speaks of certain *dharma*-s that cannot be fitted into any of the five. Thus he effectively proposes six classes, comprising forty-six *dharma*-s. This is clearly an improvement on the basis of the classification in the MVŚ, which enumerates fifty-eight *dharma*-s subsumed under seven classes, with some items being repeated in several of these classes.[41] Significantly here, he does not seem to have been influenced by the classification in the *Prakaraṇa-pāda* which does not explicitly group the *caitta*-s under specific classes.

Among Vasubandhu's six classes, the "indeterminate thought-concomitants"class (*aniyata-dharma*) is most likely his innovation. Concerning this group of *dharma*-s, he comments: "There are also other [*caitta*-s than those of the preceding five classes], that are indeterminate [in respect of their scope of occurrence, moral nature, etc.]: reasoning (*vitarka*), investigation (*vicāra*), regret (*kaukṛtya*), sleep (*middha*), etc."[42] The last word, "etc.", led to some controversies among later commentators, such as Yaśomitra, Sthiramati and the Xuan Zang tradition, as to what exactly these other indeterminate *dharma*-s should be.

3. At the start of the enumeration of the ten universal (*mahābhūmika*) *dharma*-s, Vasubandhu inserts the usual "*kila*" ("it is said") to indicate some reservation on his own part. Nevertheless, he proceeds to define each of them without complaint. At the end of these definitions, he simply states:

> The differences among the *citta-caitta*-s are indeed subtle. This is difficult to discern even with regard to a serial flow (*pravāha*) of them, how much more so with regard to them [when co-existing] in each given moment... .[43]

No doubt, subsequently, he does cite the Sautrāntika questioning some of the thought-concomitants: e.g., how can two factors contradictory in nature, equanimity (*upekṣā*) and mental application (*manaskāra*), co-exist in a single thought? But we can observe that in such cases, Vasubandhu seems to do little more than record the arguments, without taking any side. Likewise, Vasubandhu records the Sautrāntikas' view that *vitarka* and *vicāra* are nothing more than the grossness and subtleness, respectively, of thought. In contrast, the Vaibhāṣikas assert that the two are distinct, real entities which are the causes, respectively, for the grossness and subtleness. Saṃghabhadra[44] refutes the Sautrāntika arguments, but nowhere puts any blame on Vasubandhu (as he often does in other contexts). It is, therefore, likely that Vasubandhu generally accepts the *citta-caitta* doctrines of the Vaibhāṣikas—most importantly the doctrine of their simultaneous arising—but in the case of some individual *caitta*-s, as regards their definitions and natures, he intends to subject them to a reassessment from the Sautrāntika perspective.

His alignment with the Ābhidharmika position is also discernible on the question of the existence or otherwise of a *citta* in the cessation meditation (*nirodha-samāpatti*). He prefers the view of the ancient masters (*pūrvācārya*) that the body and thought are mutually seeds to each other, rather than the Sautrāntika view of a subtle *citta* still remaining in the meditation. This is because, from the Ābhidharmika standpoint, it is not possible to have a *citta* without any *caitta*, or to have contact (*sparśa*) without sensation and ideation.[45]

On the disjoined conditionings

1. The "conditionings disjoined from thought" is an important doctrinal innovation of the Sarvāstivāda. They refer to forces in the universe that are neither mental nor physical, but nonetheless can operate on *dharma*-s of both domains. Unlike in the case of the *citta-caitta*-s, Vasubandhu is seen here to clearly side with the Sautrāntikas in their repudiation of these disjoined forces—one by one—as real entities. This seems to be an inheritance from the position of the Sarvāstivādin Dārṣṭāntikas in the MVŚ.

2. We may consider the example of the disjoined conditioning called "acquisition" (*prāpti*) which, in many ways, is of fundamental importance for the Sarvāstivāda system. It is considered the *sine qua non* for relating a *dharma*—which, in the Sarvāstivāda system has always been existing in its intrinsic nature—to a given sentient being. He is bound by a defilement thanks to this force which links the defilement to him; he is liberated from the bondage when the serial continuity linking this defilement to him from moment to moment is severed. Acquisition is equally a *sine qua non* for the distinction between an ordinary worldling (*pṛthagjana*) and an *ārya* (a Buddhist saint). The former, even when he generates a skillful thought, still remains a worldling on account of his still having the acquisitions of craving, etc. A trainee (*śaikṣa*), such as a stream entrant (*srota-āpanna*), remains an *ārya* even when certain defilements arise in him, on account of the continuous existence of the acquisitions of the *ārya-dharma*-s within him. In fact, it is possible for a sentient being in the conditioned domain to attain *Nirvāṇa*, an unconditioned, precisely by virtue of the arising of the acquisition of *Nirvāṇa*.

In the AKB, Vasubandhu presents the Sautrāntika view that "acquisition" is nothing more than a notion (*prajñapti*) for a being's possession of a *dharma*. The distinction between a worldling and an *ārya* is explained in terms of the Sautrāntika theory of seeds: the former still possesses the seeds of defilements; the latter, does not. In this connection Vasubandhu also introduces the important Sautrāntika conception of the "transformation of the basis" (*āśraya-parivṛtti*, *āśraya-parāvṛtti*): When a practitioner, through spiritual practice, is transformed into an *ārya*, his whole personal being or basis (*āśraya*) undergoes a transformation — a new basis free from any seed of defilement (*abījībhūta*) replaces the old one. (See also Section EBE.3).

Vasubandhu presents the arguments from both sides, the Vaibhāṣikas and the Sautrāntikas, but clearly gives more space for the latter's arguments. At the very end, he presents, as the final statement, the Sautrāntika argument and conclusion that both acquisition as well as non-acquisition (*aprāpti*, *asamanvāgama*), a force opposite in nature and function to acquisition, are not real entities. Immediately after this, Vasubandhu sums up:

> However, the Vaibhāṣikas consider both of them to be definitely real entities. Why? "Because this is our established tenet" (*siddhānta*).[46]

This is obviously a sarcastic remark meant to ridicule the Vaibhāṣikas: it is meant to imply that the Vaibhāṣikas can offer no more counter-arguments; all they can respond is that the two *dharma*-s must be real because their school holds that they are real. Xuan Zang's version here shows Vasubandhu's ridicule even more interestingly:

> The Vaibhāṣikas assert that both are distinct real entities. Both alternative positions (lit: "both paths") are proper assertions. Why? Because [one] does not contradict logical reasoning, [the other] is our tenet.[47]

3. Another important controversy concerns the two disjoined conditionings called "cessation meditation" (*nirodha-samāpatti*) and "ideationless meditation" (*asaṃjñi-samāpatti*). For the Vaibhāṣikas, they are in each case a real entity capable of preventing the arising of mental activities. When they are induced to arise, the meditator enters into a meditative state completely devoid of thought and thought-concomitants. The question arises as to how, after a long period of interruption, the meditator's thought comes to re-arise.

The Vaibhāṣikas' answer that it re-arises in dependence on the previous "thought of entry into the meditative attainment" (*samāpatti-citta*), which, though having become past, is capable of serving as the equal-immediate condition (*samanantara-pratyaya*) for the re-arising thought.

Vasumitra explains that there is still a subtle thought in this meditative attainment so that the re-arising poses no problem. But this is rejected by Ghoṣaka who points out that given the existence of any consciousness (= *citta*), there would necessarily be contact (*sparśa*) on account of which there would be sensation and ideation.

Vasubandhu rejects these two *dharma*-s as real existents. He favors the explanation by the "ancient masters" (*pūrvācārya*) that the body and thought are mutually seed to each other (*anyonya-bījaka*), so that, when the meditator emerges from the meditation, his thought arises from his body. Saṃghabhadra alleges that Vasubandhu aligns with this view. In fact, in this connection, he further alleges that Vasubandhu actually seems to align with "some masters" who hold that several consciousnesses arise simultaneously within a single body. For, "if it is held that consciousness arises simply in dependence on the body possessing the faculties (*sendriya-kāya*), without having to depend on the causal conditions pertaining to its own species (**svajātīya*), what, for him, prevents the simultaneous arising of consciousnesses of all object-domains in all stages?"[48]

On causes, conditions and fruits

1. Both the theories of the four conditions (*pratyaya*) and the six causes are presented. The former—comprising (i) condition qua cause (*hetu-pratyaya*), (ii) condition qua object (*ālambana-*), (iii) equal-immediate condition (*samanantara-*), (iv) condition of dominance (*adhipati-*)—was an earlier theory of causality attributed to the Buddha. The latter, i.e., the six causes—comprising (i) efficient cause (*kāraṇa-hetu*), (ii) homogeneous cause (*sabhāga-*), (iii) universal cause (*sarvatraga-*), (iv) co-existent cause (*sahabhū-*), (v) conjoined cause (*saṃprayuktaka-*), (vi) retribution (/maturation) cause (*vipāka-*)—was innovated by Kātyānīputra for the first time in his *Jñānaprasthāna*.

2. Of the six causes, the co-existent cause—of which the conjoined cause is a subset—is the most important. Vasubandhu describes it thus:

> The co-existent [causes] are those that are reciprocally effects.... For example: the four Great Elements are co-existent [causes] mutually among themselves; so also, thought and the *dharma*-s that are thought-accompaniments (*cittānuvarttin*); .... [The case of the co-existent cause] is like the staying in position of three sticks through their mutual strength/support — this establishes the causal relationship (*hetuphalabhāva*) of the co-existents.[49]

Co-nascence is a necessary, but not a sufficient, condition for two or more *dharma*-s to be co-existent causes. Saṃghabhadra does not give any suggestion that Vasubandhu is opposed to this doctrine; he only criticizes that the scope of this cause, as specified by Vasubandhu ("reciprocally effects..."), is not broad enough. Saṃghabhadra articulates that this causal category obtains in only three cases:

> [i] among those that share the same effect; or [ii] that are reciprocally effects; or [iii] where by the force of this, that *dharma* can arise. Such co-nascent [*dharma*-s] have a cause-effect relationship, [i.e., are co-existent causes].[50]

For the Sarvāstivādins, the fact of direct perception (*pratyakṣa*) cannot be established without the type of simultaneous causality represented by the co-existent cause. This is because, given that a sensory faculty and its object last for only one single moment (a doctrine commonly accepted by all Abhidharma schools with the exception of the Sāṃmitīya, etc.), if the corresponding consciousness (*qua* effect) were to arise in the second moment (as claimed by the Sautrāntikas and others), it would not have an existent object. If direct perception cannot be established, then inferential knowledge too would be impossible — and this would result in the absolute impossibility of any knowledge of the external world!

More importantly, the co-existent cause serves as the only valid paradigm of causation. In general, if *A* causes *B*, both *A* and *B* must be existent at the same time (an utter void or a non-existent cannot be causally efficacious) — although they may belong to different time periods with respect to their own temporal frame of reference. That is: *A* may be past or present or future, and *B* may also be past or present or future — *but they must co-exist, although not necessarily be co-nascent.* To borrow Dharmatrāta's terminology, they are both existent, but not necessarily of the same "mode of existence" (*bhāva*). Where *A* and *B* are necessarily co-nascent, i.e., both existing at the same *present* moment, it reduces to the category known as the co-existent cause.

In fact, according to the Sarvāstivāda conception of the tri-temporal existence of *dharma*-s, all *dharma*-s in their essential nature have always been existent; it is only a matter of inducing their arising through causes and conditions. This is the fundamental principle underlining the Sarvāstivāda doctrine of causality. Past and future *dharma*-s are also endowed with efficacies including that of actually giving an effect, although it is only a present *dharma* that has "activity" (*kāritra*; *cf.* Section EE) — the efficacy of establishing the specific causal relationship with the *dharma* to be produced as its effect.

3. The five fruits are: (i) disconnection fruit (*visaṃyoga-phala*), (ii) virile fruit (*puruṣakāra*-), (iii) fruit of dominance (*adhipati*-), (iv) emanational fruit (*niṣyanda*-), (v) retribution fruit (*vipāka*-). They are correlated to the conditions and causes as follows:

4 CONDITIONS	6 CAUSES	5 EFFECTS
hetu-pratyaya	*sahabhū-hetu* *saṃprayuktaka-hetu*	*puruṣakāra-phala*
	sabhāga-hetu *sarvatraga-hetu*	*niṣyanda-phala*
	vipāka-hetu ⟶	*vipāka-phala*
samanantara-pratyaya		
ālambana-pratyaya		
adhipati-pratyaya ——	*kāraṇa-hetu* ⟶	*adhipati-phala*
		visaṃyoga-phala (not a fruit of any of the 6 causes)

The unconditioned *dharma*-s, being transcendent to space and time, are neither causally produced nor do they operate as causes. However, they can serve as "condition qua object" (*ālambana-pratyaya*) inasmuch as they can be apprehended as cognitive objects. The Sarvāstivāda Ābhidharmikas would also concede that in some special sense and in conformity to worldly parlance, it is permissible to speak of the unconditioned *dharma*-s as "efficient causes" inasmuch as they do not hinder the arising of other *dharma*-s. Although not causally produced, the cessation through deliberation may also be expediently spoken of as a "disconnection-fruit" inasmuch as it is acquired (*pra-√āp*) through the efficacy of the noble path — even though it is not directly produced by it.[51]

In this discussion, the Sautrāntikas declare that all the three types of unconditioned proposed by the Sarvāstivādins are not real entities. But they do not assert that unconditioned things do not exist. Thus, *Nirvāṇa* is certainly a true spiritual attainment — albeit not an ontological entity. They explain this in terms of the doctrine of transformation of the basis (see above, Section EBD.2):

> *Nirvāṇa* is said to have been attained as a result of the obtaining—by virtue of the counteragent—of a basis which is absolutely opposed to the generation of defilements and rebirth.[52]

Chapter three: *Loka-nirdeśa*

This chapter deals with cosmological doctrines: the universe as the fruition of with-outflow[53] *karma*, its constitution (sentient and non-sentient), and the processes involved in its formation and dissolution. It also expounds the causal principles governing conditioned existence: conditioned co-arising (*pratītya-samutpāda*).

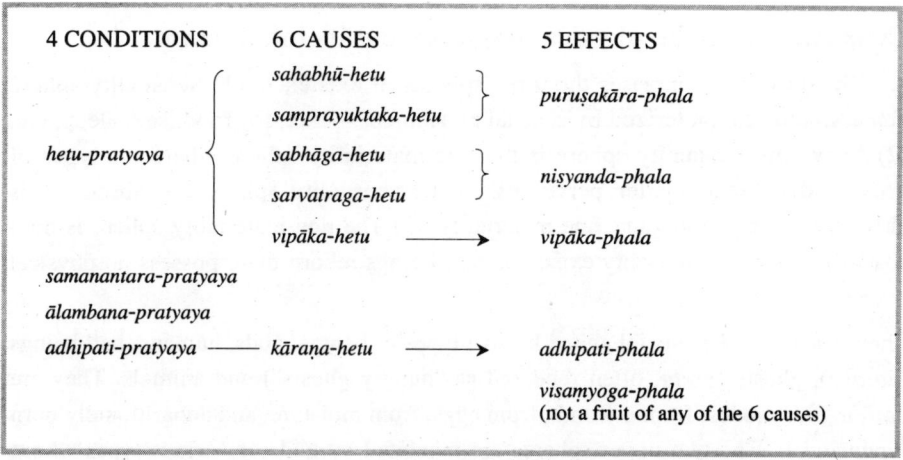

ECA. **Constitution of the physical universe and its inhabitants**

1. The universe comprises the three spheres of existence: (1) Sensuality sphere (*kāma-dhātu*) characterized by sensual attachment — i.e., for food, sex, sleep, etc. (2) Above the sensuality sphere is the fine-materiality sphere where the types of gross and unclean matter pertaining to the sensuality sphere are absent; it is characterized by subtle and fine materiality. (3) The non-materiality sphere is non-spatialized, as no materiality exists therein. Beings reborn there possess no physical bodies.

The sensuality sphere is inhabited by five types of beings: gods, humans, hell beings (*naraka*), ghosts (*preta*; often rendered as "hungry ghosts") and animals. They are born in four modes: from a womb, from eggs, from moisture, and apparitionally born (*upapāduka*). The two upper spheres are inhabited by gods of various types whose *karma*-s of meditative praxis are retributed therein; they are all apparitionally born.

2. A question arises: In a material sphere, thought exists/operates (*pra-√vṛt*) with the physical body as its support. How does thought in the non-materiality sphere exist/operate? The Vaibhāṣikas hold that it exists or operates with the two disjoined forces, group-homogeneity (*nikāya-sabhāga*) and vital principle (*jīvitendriya*) as support. The latter two, in turn, exist through mutual support. Vasubandhu raises several objections and states that thought and thought-concomitants exist through mutual support. He then cites the Sautrāntika explanation with which he ostensibly seeks to align himself: A thought in the non-materiality sphere does not have a support outside the mental series. In a material sphere, there is greed for matter, hence the thought will be reborn with matter and is necessarily dependent on matter. But a thought in the non-materiality sphere is freed from the greed for matter, hence it will be reborn without matter and will exist independent of matter.[54]

3. The whole of saṃsāric existence is characterized by greed (*rāga*). The greed of beings in the sensuality sphere who have not been detached (*vīta-rāga*) from this sphere (i.e. from the *dharma*-s pertaining to this sphere) is called "sensual greed" (*kāma-rāga*). The same applies to the greed pertaining to the fine-materiality-sphere as "materiality greed" (*rūpa-rāga*), and to greed pertaining to the non-materiality sphere as "non-materiality greed" (*ārūpya-rāga*). Or rather, sensual greed is greed in the stage (*bhūmi*) of non-equipoise (*asamāhita*); fine-materiality greed is greed in the stages of the four meditations (*dhyāna*); non-materiality greed is greed in the stages of the four non-materiality meditative attainments (*samāpatti*). Those *dharma*-s with regard to which the sensual or fine-materiality or non-materiality greed adhere and grow (*anuśerate*) are said to be, respectively, "connected with (i.e., pertaining to) the

sensuality sphere" (*kāmadhātu-pratisaṃyukta*), "connected with the fine-materiality sphere" (*rūpadhātu-pratisaṃyukta*) and "connected with the non-materiality-sphere" (*ārūpyadhātu-pratisaṃyukta*).

Formation and dissolution of the universe

1. The whole physical universe is called the "receptacle-world" (*bhājana-loka*), in contradistinction to the "world of sentient beings" (*sattva-loka*). The physical universe is centered around Mount Sumeru. At the beginning of the period of formation of the world system, on account of the force of dominance (*ādhipatya*) of sentient beings' *karma*, wind comes to arise in the empty space. This wind gradually increases in intensity, forming a great Wind Disc supported by space. The force of *karma* further gives rise to storms pouring onto the Wind Disc to form the Water Disc. Again by the force of *karma*, violent wind is generated striking this water so that its upper part coagulates as the Gold Disc. On this Gold Disc, further storms arise to result in huge billows which push some parts of it to form mountains, and other parts, oceans. In this way, the universe with Mount Sumeru as the center—comprising nine mountains, with eight oceans in between them—comes to be formed.

2. The whole process from the formation of the universe to its destruction involves four stages: (i) period of formation (*vivarta*), (ii) period of duration (*vivarta-sthāyin*), (iii) period of involution (*saṃvarta*), (iv) period of being emptied (*saṃvarta-sthāyin*). Each of these takes twenty small *kalpa*-s (*antarakalpa*), which together constitute one intermediate *kalpa*; thus, the whole process takes eighty intermediate *kalpa*-s, which together constitute a great *kalpa* (*mahākalpa*). A small *kalpa* is the time taken when the human lifespan decreases from 80,000 years to ten years, or that when human lifespan increases from ten years to 80,000 years.

Conditioned co-arising

1. Vasubandhu's exposition of the twelve-limbed conditioned co-arising is essentially based on explanations in the Sarvāstivāda canonical Abhidharma texts and the MVŚ. The distribution of the twelve limbs over three lives has been taught in the *Jñānaprasthāna*.[55] In fact, such an explanation is already discernible in the *Dharmaskandha* in its exposition of "conditioned by consciousness is name-and-form", and on "conditioned by being (*bhava*) is birth": It states that "consciousness" here refers to the last thought of the *gandharva* and it relinks at birth;[56] "being" is "*karma*-being" on account of which one will be reborn according to the *karma* incurred in the present existence.[57]

An interesting point to note in Vasubandhu's discussion on the individual limbs is that he does not particularly favor the Sautrāntikas; occasionally, he even seems to side with the Vaibhāṣikas or at least gives them the last say. For instance, on ignorance (*avidyā*), he joins the Vaibhāṣikas in establishing that it is a distinct force, not just a mere absence of knowledge (*vidyā*) as argued by the Dārṣṭāntika-Sautrāntikas. On contact (*sparśa*), he does not side with any party, but finishes off the dispute—and this, without any of the type of the sarcasm that we noted in the controversies on the disjoined forces— by stating the Vaibhāṣika view that it is a real entity. Likewise, in the dispute on the simultaneity of consciousness, contact, sensation, etc.

2. In the MVŚ, a question is posed: In the twelve-limbed exposition, there is no mention of the cause of ignorance or the effect of old-age-and-death. Does this not lead to the consequence that either there should be thirteen or fourteen limbs, or that ignorance and old-age-and-death are unconditioned? Among the explanations offered by the MVŚ compilers, by way of clearing away this difficulty, we find the doctrines of "defilement–*karma*–suffering" and of "defilement–*karma*–object-base".[58] The AKB poses the same question, albeit in a somewhat different form, and as a response, Vasubandhu expounds the doctrine of "defilement–*karma*–object-base" and asserts that this is the principle established for the existence-limbs (*eṣa nayo vyavasthito bhavāṅgānāṁ*). This triad is elaborated as follows:

Defilement ⇒ defilement

craving ⇒ clinging.

Defilement ⇒ *karma*

clinging ⇒ being; ignorance ⇒ conditionings.

Karma ⇒ object-base

conditionings ⇒ consciousness; being ⇒ birth.

Object-base ⇒ object-base

consciousness ⇒ name-and-form; name-and-form ⇒ 6-fold abode;

6-fold abode ⇒ contact; contact ⇒ sensation; birth ⇒ old-age-and-death.

Object-base ⇒ defilement

sensation ⇒ craving.[59]

The above elaboration is meant to indicate that, since ignorance and old-age-and-death are of the nature of being defilement and object-base, respectively; (a) ignorance is the effect of either a defilement or an object-base, and (b) old-age-and-death is the cause for an object-base or a defilement.

This is further explained thus: When the effects (= object-base) of the future are compared to the effects of the present, we have:

birth ~ consciousness;
old-age-and-death ~ name-and-form, six-fold abode, contact and sensation.

Since craving is conditioned by sensation, it is to be understood that ignorance (comparable to craving) is conditioned by old-age-and-death (comparable to sensation).

Moreover, name-and-form (one of the four object-bases comparable to old-age-and-death) conditions the six-fold base which conditions contact which conditions sensation. Thus, it is shown that old-age-and-death as object-base is a cause.

Accordingly, ignorance is the effect of old-age-and-death qua object-base and defilement.

In this way, according to the Sarvāstivāda, the Buddha intends his teaching of the twelve-limbed conditioned co-arising to represent sentient existence as being like a revolving wheel, without an absolute beginning, but capable of coming to an end: The first limb, ignorance, is the effect of defilement and an object-base, and the final limb, old-age-and-death, is the cause of defilement and an object-base. The two are causally related, the resulting cyclic existence coming to an end only when ignorance is absolutely eradicated.

Vasubandhu concludes that the enumeration of the twelve limbs in the *sūtra* is complete. Its sole intention is to clear the doubt of those deluded with regard to the saṃsāric process (*pravṛtti-saṃmūḍha*): how the present existence results from the previous existence, and how the next existence will proceed from the present existence.

3. Vasubandhu also explains the Vaibhāṣika theory of the fourfold conditioned co-arising:

   i. "Momentary" (*kṣaṇika*). All the twelve limbs are embraced within a single moment. E.g.: The craving generated in killing is conjoined with consciousness, volition, ignorance, contact, sensation, the enwrapment which is clinging, the information *karma* which is name-and-form and the six *āyatana*-s, the bodily and vocal *karma*-s which are being (*bhava*). The very arising of all these *dharma*-s is birth; their maturing is old-age; their perishing is death.[60]

ii. "Prolonged" (*prākarṣika*). When the process of karmic retribution is seen as extending over several existences, the perspective is described as "prolonged".

iii. "Connective" (*saṃbandhika*). "[This] refers to the fact that cause and effect, of a homogeneous or heterogeneous nature, arise in an immediate cause-effect connection. As it is said in the Sūtra, "With ignorance as cause, greed is generated; with wisdom (*vidyā*) as cause, no greed is generated. Again, it is said in the Sūtra: "Immediately from the skillful, a defiled [or] non-defined (*kliṣṭāvyākṛta*) is generated, or conversely."[61]

iv. "Pertaining to stage" (*āvasthika*). The twelve limbs comprise twelve distinctive stages. At the stage of each limb, all the five aggregates are present; but that particular limb is prominent and representative at that stage. E.g., in a given stage, if ignorance is prominent, then the five aggregates of that stage are collectively called "ignorance".[62]

Vasubandhu states, with his usual marker of skepticism, "*kila*", that the Vaibhāṣikas take the "pertaining to stage" perspective as the intended perspective in the Buddha's own exposition.

The Sūtra expounds conditioned co-arising as pertaining to sentient existence, whereas the *Prakaraṇa-pāda* states that the doctrine applies to all conditioned *dharma*-s. This difference, Vasubandhu states, is due to the fact that whereas the *sūtra* exposition is intentional (*ābhiprāyika*), the *abhidharma* is definitive (*lākṣaṇika*).[63]

ED.

Chapter four: *Karma-nirdeśa*

In chapter three, it was mentioned that the whole universe comes to assume its shape and appearance as a result of the dominance of the *karma* of sentient beings. Indeed, the Sarvāstivāda view—essentially in agreement with those of all Buddhists—is that the whole universe, with all its planets, mountains and oceans, etc., is the result, i.e., the fruit of dominance, of the collective *karma* of the totality of beings inhabiting therein.[64] It begins with the winds endowed with special power born of this collective *karma*.[65] The exhaustion of this collective *karma* brings about the dissolution of the universe through three great calamities: of fire, water and wind.[66] The fact that the *karma*-s of beings in this world are mixed—some good, some bad—accounts for the existence of beautiful and pleasant external things such as fragrant flowers, etc., on the one hand, and human bodies with all their impurities, on the other. In the case of the gods (*deva*), their exclusively skillful *karma*-s result in the equal beauty of both their internal bodies and external objects of enjoyment.[67] Chapter four begins by stating that all the variegatedness of the sentient world and the receptacle world is on account of sentient beings' *karma*-s, not the intelligent design of a creator God.

1. i. *Karma* is broadly twofold: volition (*cetanā*) and that which is generated after the volitional act (*cetayitvā*). The former is mental *karma*. The latter is bodily and vocal, and hence matter in nature, and is divisible as information (*vijñapti*) and non-information (*avijñapti-karma*). The following chart shows this classification:

two-fold	three-fold	*vijñapti/avijñapti*
cetanā-karma	mental *karma*	no *vijñapti* or *avijñapti*
cetayitvā-karma	bodily *karma*	bodily *vijñapti*
		bodily *avijñapti*
	vocal *karma*	vocal *vijñapti*
		vocal *avijñapti*

Information *karma* is so called because it is an action that informs others of the doer's mental state. A bodily *karma* has as its intrinsic nature the configuration-matter (*saṃsthāna-rūpa*) in the doer's body at the final moment of accomplishment of a serial bodily action (e.g., killing). For a vocal *karma*, it is the sound matter at the final moment of an utterance.

At the final moment of an information bodily or vocal action, the karmic efficacy is serially continued as an invisible force. Since this does not inform others of the doer's mental state, it is called non-information *karma*. Its intrinsic nature is matter since it is projected by an information *karma* that is matter in nature. Skandhila's definition below shows the set of simultaneous causal factors in dependence on which it is projected:

> Projected from a specific [set of] information *karma*, thought and [tetrad of] Great Elements, there arises [in the doer] a continuous series of skillful or unskillful matter, which is non-cumulative and which persists in the states of [sleep, wakefulness,] distracted (*vikṣipta*) thought, non-distracted thought

or "unconsciousness" (*acittaka*). It is the cause for the establishing of the *bhikṣu*, etc.[68]

Firstly, the above definition shows that it is non-cumulative, unlike the ordinary matter which is resistant. Secondly, its generation is dependent on a thought — i.e., one that is conjoined and conditioned by the volition involved in the action. Thus, although the information and non-information *karma*-s are considered as matter and not the volition itself, the thought/volition is nonetheless their *sine qua non*. From this perspective—notwithstanding their distinction of the *cetayitvā karma* from the *cetanā karma*—the Sarvāstivādins, like other Buddhists, equally uphold the primacy of the karmic role of volition: all three types of *karma* are originated (*samutthita*) by volition.

The information or non-information matter comes to acquire a particular moral nature and content on account of the thought/volition which constitutes its origination-cause (*samutthāna-hetu*): it is skillful or unskillful through origination (*samutthānena*). This is also how the disjoined conditionings come to be morally definable.[69] The notion of the origination-cause for bodily and vocal *karma*-s and the disjoined conditionings was already present in the early canonical texts.[70] It came to be articulated in the MVŚ as being twofold: origination qua cause (*hetu-samutthāna*) and simultaneous origination (*(tat)kṣaṇa-samutthāna*), explained as the initial propellant (*pravartaka*) and the subsequent propellant (*anuvartaka*), respectively.[71] Vasubandhu explains likewise, comparing the first origination cause to the hand that propels the rolling of a wheel and the second to the floor that sustains its motion from moment to moment. The MVŚ also mentions several views on whether the five sensory consciousnesses can serve as both types of cause. The compilers comment that they cannot serve as origination qua cause; only mental consciousness can serve as both.[72] Vasubandhu explains in the same manner.[73]

ii. *Karma* is also classifiable as (a) experiencible in this existence (*dṛṣṭa-dharma-vedanīya*), (b) experiencible in the next existence (*upapadya-vedanīya*), (c) experiencible in an existence after the next (*aparaparyāya-vedanīya*). These three types belong to the category of "determinate *karma*". To these is added a category of (d) "indeterminate *karma*" (*aniyata-vedanīya*) — i.e., that which may not actually be retributed.

Xuan Zang's translation here seems to suggest that Vasubandhu endorses the above classification of fourfold *karma*: "This explanation is good".[74] In the MVŚ, this fourfold *karma* is ascribed to "some [Sarvāstivāda] masters".[75] "[The first three types] cannot be transformed. Those *karma*-s whose retribution are indeterminate can be transformed. It is precisely for the sake of transforming this fourth type of *karma* that one observes the precepts and vigorously practises the spiritual life (*brahmacarya*), making the aspiration: 'May I be able to transform this *karma* by virtue of this'."[76]

iii. The notion of indeterminate *karma* is an interesting one, and subject to different interpretations. Some other Sarvāstivāda masters[77] arrive at five types of *karma* by subdividing it as (a) those determinate as regards retribution and (b) those indeterminate as regards retribution.

iv. Yet other masters arrive at eight types of *karma*: each of the four (*dṛṣṭa-dharma- … aniyata-vedanīya*) is divisible as being determinate or indeterminate in regard to retribution. These masters give a fourfold alternative (*catuḥkoṭi*)[78] as in the AKB: (a) determinate in regard to the period of retribution, but indeterminate in regard to retribution; (b) conversely; (c) determinate in regard to both period and retribution; (d) indeterminate in both respects. But it is interesting that Vasubandhu, likewise Saṃghabhadra,[79] ascribes this eightfold classification to the Dārṣṭāntikas, and Yaśomitra here states that "the Dārṣṭāntikas are the Sautrāntikas";[80] whereas the MVŚ ascribes it to "some other [Sarvāstivāda] masters".[81] In fact the compilers do not at all criticize any of these different classifications. We may note that Vasubandhu's expositions on these and the subsequent topics—i.e., "Is there a case where one generates all three types of *karma* (*dṛṣṭa-dharma- … aparaparyāya-*) at once", "How many types can project *nikāya-sabhāga*", etc.—also follow the sequence of exposition in the MVŚ.[82]

2. Among other things, the notion of indeterminate *karma* shows that the Buddhist doctrine of *karma* is not one of absolute determination. In this context, the Dārṣṭāntikas in the MVŚ are the most radical here. For them, all *karma*-s—including the fivefold gravest evil (*ānantarya*: patricide, etc.)—can be transformed. Thus, a *dṛṣṭadharma-vedanīya karma*, for instance, is not necessarily retributed in the present existence.[83]

3. Another noteworthy point repeatedly emphasized by the MVŚ compilers in this discussion is that "all skillful or unskillful *karma*-s must depend on a serial continuity or go beyond a serial continuity before they come to be retributed."[84] "There is definitely no *karma* that can be retributed/matured in the very same moment of it being done or in the immediately next moment".[85] This emphasis, coupled with the acknowledgement of the indeterminateness of certain karmic retributions, must imply that, in the process of maturation in the serial continuity, the status of the efficacy of a *karma* is subject to continuous adjustment. And the latter presupposes a

serially continuous karmic force which is always present in the serial continuity of the doer. Indeed, the Vaibhāṣikas teach that a *karma* done (*kṛta*), but not accumulated (*upacita*), is not necessarily retributed. Saṃghabhadra explains in what sense a *karma* is not necessarily retributed:

> ... [By indeterminate *karma*-s, the *sūtra* refers to] *karma*-s that are not necessarily experienced. If one can vigorously cultivate the precepts pertaining to the body, the thought (*citta*) and understanding (*prajñā*), these *karma*-s ought to be experienced in the human world. [However,] as a result of not cultivating the precepts pertaining to the body, the thought and understanding, one falls into *naraka* through these *karma*-s. ...
>
> Alternatively, the meaning [is] thus: There are *karma*-s that are, although done, not accumulated. If they are allowed to follow their own course, they would be retributed in the present life. If, [however,] one subsequently further commits *karma*-s that are retributable in the hells, nourishing the *karma* and causing it to be accumulated, one will proceed to experience it in the hells... .[86]

4. The *avijñapti* doctrine is a major doctrine innovated by the Sarvāstivādins. It is true that given their tenet of the tritemporal existence of the *dharma*-s, a past *karma*, though having assumed the past mode, is still causally efficacious and thus capable of yielding fruit. Accordingly, the Sarvāstivādins should have no difficulty in accounting for the preservation of the efficacy from a past *karma*. However, in the MVŚ, we see them considering certain situations that call for a more fine-tuned mechanism. For instance, when a person sends an emissary to murder another, at the time when the victim is actually killed, the informative *karma* of the instigator is no more. Besides, this informative *karma*—vocal in nature—cannot be one that constitutes the principal act of killing. It is, in fact, only part of the preparation for the killing. There arises in him at this time, however, a non-information *karma* of killing. It is this invisible karmic force at this present moment that causally effects the transgression of a murderer.[87] Another consideration: Given that a physical or vocal *karma* is momentary, if there were no non-information *karma*, there would be no legitimate establishment of the differences among those abiding in restraint (*saṃvara*), non-restraint (*asaṃvara*) and neither-restraint-nor-non-restraint (*naiva-saṃvara-na-asaṃvara*).[88] Restraint refers to the ordination vows taken by a *bhikṣu*, etc; non-restraint, to the commitment of a butcher or hunter to kill for his whole life, etc; neither-restraint-nor-non-restraint refers to all willful understandings outside the former two contexts. This notion of the *avijñapti* qua restraint in fact came to be greatly emphasized in the Sarvāstivāda development.

Vasubandhu also presents both the above considerations of the Sarvāstivāda. He in fact enumerates eight reasons proposed by the Vaibhāṣikas for establishing the *avijñapti* doctrine. The Sautrāntikas, who maintain that all *karma* is volition, vehemently reject this doctrine and repudiate all the eight reasons.[89] Instead, they enunciate the doctrine of the seed (*bīja*) and explain the process of the preservation of karmic efficacy culminating in the retribution fruit as a "distinctive transformation of the serial continuity" (*saṃtati-pariṇāma-viṣeśa*): The volition is like the seed. The karmic efficacy projected from it undergoes a process of transformation in the serial continuity of the *citta-caitta*-s. At the culminating point of the karmic maturation, when the required conditions obtain, a corresponding fruit is generated.

In the Sautrāntika refutation of the *avijñapti* doctrine, we once again come across their doctrine of the "transformation of the basis" (see sections EBD.2, EDE.3). The Vaibhāṣikas argue that if there were no *avjñapti*, when an *ārya* enters into *samādhi*, he would not have "proper speech", "proper activity" and "proper livelihood" — these three being incompatible with *samādhi*. That even in this state he does possess them is because they exist as *avijñapti*. The Sautrāntikas, however, explain that, when the *ārya* enters into the path (*mārga-samāpanna*), he obtains an intention (*āśaya*) and a basis (*āśraya*) of such a kind that he is enabled to generate these three factors on coming out of the meditation.[90] Yaśomitra comments that the basis here refers to the transformation of the basis.[91]

In another context, Vasubandhu enumerates five fields of merit relating to which the *karma* is retributed in the present existence. Among them, two are: (1) the person who emerges from the path of vision and (2) the person who emerges from the path of cultivation — i.e., who has just acquired the *arhat-phala*. In both cases, there is said to be the obtaining of the transformation of the basis and a new (*pratyagra*), pure (*nirmala*, *śuddha*) serial continuity.[92]

5. From the above discussion, we can discern how the *avijñapti* doctrine serves as a fine-tuning mechanism in the Sarvāstivādin *karma* theory. The *avijñapti*, being continuously present in the serial continuity of the doer, renders it possible for him to continuously modify its status — e.g., in the case of an evil *karma*, he can do so through such subsequent (*pṛṣṭha*) actions as repentance, etc. It is taught that the *avijñapti* serial flow will terminate owing to several conditions. One is when the *karma* is retributed; another, when the doer dies. In the latter case, the karmic force which has come to acquire a particular final status, though having become past, will nonetheless still be causally efficacious and give a fruit in some future time.

In this process of karmic maturation as taught by the Sarvāstivāda, involving the *avijñapti*, we can see some of the important features of the Sautrāntika seed theory, i.e., (i) continuation from the originating volition; (ii) a serial continuity whose karmic status is continuously updated; (iii) a process of transformation. To be sure, the seed theory differs importantly from the *avijñapti* theory, particularly since the former is a complete theory of *karma*, and it works on the principle of perfuming (*vāsanā*). But it seems possible that the historically earlier *avijñapti* theory had provided at least some raw doctrinal ingredients to the seed theory of the Dārṣṭāntika-Sautrāntikas who, after all, had come from the broad Sarvāstivāda tradition. In this connection, we may also note Saṃghabhadra's claim that it is in fact the Sarvāstivāda—rather than the Sautrāntika—doctrine of *karma* that can be said to accord with the causal principle of the sequential growth of a plant from its seed.[93]

6. Vasubandhu[94] clearly favors the Sautrāntika stance and endorses their seed theory. He states:

> There is not any hatred [on our part in rejecting the *avijñapti* doctrine]. But to say that through a bodily undertaking following a thought, there arises in the instigator, at the accomplishment of the action, a distinct *dharma* separate from the two (thought and body) — such an assertion does not give delight. On the other hand, delight arises in the assertion that the accomplishment of the action, brought about when the undertaking is completed, is the transformation of the serial continuity—caused by that [undertaking]—which arises in this very person (the instigator). This is also because the arising of the fruit in the future occurs from the *citta-caitta* serial continuity.[95]

EE. Chapter five: *Anuśaya-nirdeśa*

Our saṃsāric existence is the result of *karma*, and *karma* comes into operation on account of defilements (*kleśa*). Hence, after chapters three and four, this fifth chapter is devoted to defilements. *Anuśaya*, which we may render as proclivity, is one of the major synonyms for defilements. Besides "defilement" and "proclivity", the AKB enumerates the following synonymous terms: fetter (*saṃyojana*), bondage (*bandhana*), envelopment (*paryavasthāna*), outflow (*āsrava*), flood (*ogha*), yoke (*yoga*), clinging (*upādāna*) and corporeal tie (*kāya-grantha*).

Vasubandhu's choice of "*anuśaya*" as the chapter title is probably influenced by the fact that, since the *Abhidharmahṛdaya*, the chapter on defilements had been regularly entitled "*anuśaya*".[96] He begins the chapter by stating that the proclivities are the root of existence (*bhavasya mūlam*); without them, *karma*-s are incapable of effectuating existences.[97]

1. Six fundamental proclivities are enumerated; but they can be further divided into seven or ten, as shown in the following chart:

6 fundamental kinds	7 kinds (in the *sūtra*)	10 kinds (in the *Jñānaprasthāna*)
1. greed (*rāga*)	1. sensual greed (*kāmarāga*) 2. existence-greed (*bhavarāga*)	1. greed
2. hostility (*pratigha*)	3. hostility	2. hostility
3. ignorance (*avidyā*)	4. ignorance	3. ignorance
4. conceit (*māna*)	5. conceit	4. conceit
5. doubt (*vicikitsā*)	6. doubt	5. doubt
6. view (*dṛṣṭi*)	7. view	6. Self-view (*satkāya-dṛṣṭi*) 7. extreme-grasping view (*antagrāha-dṛṣṭi*) 8. false view (*mithyā-dṛṣṭi*) 9. attachment to view (*dṛṣṭi-parāmarśa*) 10. irrational attachment to religious vows and observances (*śīla-vrata-parāmarśa*)

Sensual greed is greed with regard to the sensuality sphere. Existence-greed is greed for the subtler forms of existence in the fine-materiality and non-materiality spheres. When view is subdivided into the fivefold views, we have a total of ten proclivities as given in the *Jñānaprasthāna*.

Besides the fundamental defilements, the AKB also enumerates a total of nineteen secondary defilements: non-diligence (*pramāda*), slackness (*kauśīdya*), faithlessness (*āśraddhya*), torpor (*styāna*), restlessness (*auddhatya*), immodesty (*āhrīkya*), shamelessness (*anapatrāpya*), anger (*krodha*), enmity (*upanāha*), dissimulation (*śāṭhya*), jealousy (*īrṣya*), depravity (*pradāśa*), concealment (*mrakṣa*), avarice (*mātsarya*), deceptiveness (*māyā*), pride (*mada*), harmfulness (*vihiṃsā*), remorse (*kaukṛtya*) and drowsiness (*middha*). The last two are grouped with the indeterminate *dharma*-s (*cf.* Section EB); the rest comprises the defiled *dharma*-s.

2. Vasubandhu, following the *Prakaraṇa-pāda*, gives four meanings of "*anuśaya*":

   i. *aṇu*: meaning "fine", "subtle": A pseudo-etymological interpretation of the prefix *anu* — stressing the difficulty in detecting the arising of the defilements which are subtle in nature.

ii. *anu* + √*bandh* ("bind"): They "bind along with" (*anu*-√*bandh*), i.e., they proceed together with the psycho-physical series (*saṃtati*). "It is extremely difficult to be separated from them... . According to some, this means that their *prāpti*-s always follow along."[98]

iii. *anu* + √*gam* or *anu* + √*saj*: Vasubandhu explains in the sense of *anu* + √*saj*: "They adhere through adhesion of their *prāpti*-s".[99] Saṃghabhadra: from beginningless time, one is followed along by the *prāpti*-s arising in one's serial continuity.[100]

iv. *anu* + √*śī*: They grow or become intensified in accord with (*anu*-√*śī*): They become nourished by (a) the objects they take (*ālambanato 'nuśerate*) and (b) the thought concomitants with which they are conjoined (*saṃprayogato'nuśerate*).[101] Saṃghabhadra explains that the first way (a) is like the case of an enemy seeking a weak point; the second way (b) is like the case of a heated ball that heats up the water. Like a foster mother who causes the growth of an infant, both the object taken and the conjoined mental *dharma*-s cause the series of the defilement to grow and accumulate.[102]

Out of the four senses given above, the MVŚ gives only three, i.e., without that of *anu*-√*gam*. It attributes the explanation in terms of the four senses to the foreign masters.[103]

3. Vasubandhu describes the controversy concerning the nature of the proclivities. For the Sautrāntikas, a proclivity is a seed—i.e., dormant efficacy—from which a corresponding defilement manifests given the right conditions. Since the seed is a mere concept, it is neither conjoined with (*saṃprayukta*) nor disjoined from (*viprayukta*) thought; when manifested, the defilement is called an enwrapment. For the Vaibhāṣikas, proclivity and enwrapment are both synonyms for defilement; there is no contrast of a dormant proclivity as opposed to a manifested enwrapment. A proclivity is therefore conjoined with thought and is an existent entity. Vasubandhu explicitly endorses the Sautrāntika view.[104]

In the MVŚ, the Vibhajyavādins' view is similar to the Sautrāntikas', except that they consider the proclivity as being conjoined with and the enwrapment as being disjoined from thought.[105] However, we know that some early Dārṣṭāntika masters, like Aśvaghoṣa, already proposed some form of a seed theory and contrasted the proclivity with the enwrapment in a similar manner.[106]

4. Those defilements of the nature of a cognitive error are abandonable through insight (*darśana-(pra)heya*) into the four truths. A defilement whose cognitive object

(*ālambana*) is abandonable through insight into a particular truth (e.g., unsatisfactoriness) is one abandonable through that truth.[107] This definition follows from the consideration that when an insight into a particular truth arises with regard to a given object, then the particular defilement which is a cognitive error with regard to that same object, with respect to that particular truth, has ceased.

The other defilements, of a more obstinate nature and not—or not entirely—of the nature of cognitive error, are to be abandoned through cultivation (*bhāvanā-(pra)-heya*), i.e., through a process of repeated practice.

The doctrine of the abandonment of defilements is correlated with the Sarvāstivādin cosmological view: To transcend saṃsāric existence, one must progressively abandon the defilements pertaining to the three spheres. A total of eighty-eight forms of the ten fundamental kinds of defilements are to be abandoned through insight — thirty-two pertaining to the sensuality sphere; twenty-eight each, pertaining to the two upper spheres. Ten forms are to be abandoned through cultivation: four pertaining to the sensuality sphere; three each, pertaining to the two upper spheres. (*Cf.* Section EF for more details.)

5. The central Sarvāstivāda doctrine of the tritemporal existence of *dharma*-s (*sarvāstivāda*, *sarvāstitva*) is discussed in this chapter. It is significant that both the beginning and end of this lengthy discussion are marked by the same spiritual concern: the validity of the process of bondage and emancipation. This section first gives the statement of its purpose as being the investigation into the kind of object-base (*vastu*) to which a person is bound by a past, present or future proclivity. The question is soon raised as to whether the so-called "past" and "future" (*dharma*-s) exist. Towards the end of the debate, the Vaibhāṣikas ask: If the past and the future are non-existent, how does one come to be yoked to a particular defilement? Indeed, how is the fact of liberation from bondage possible? This suggests that the Sarvāstivāda doctrine of tritemporal existence most probably originated in the context of such a fundamental spiritual concern.

i. As in the MVŚ, the four major versions of the theory are presented here, all purporting to explain how—given that all *dharma*-s are always existent—their temporal distinction can nonetheless be accounted for: (a) Dharmatrāta's theory of "change in the mode of being" (*bhava-anyathika*); (b) Ghoṣaka's "change in characteristic" (*lakṣaṇa-anyathika*); (c) Vasumitra's "change in state" (*avasthā-anyathika*); (d) Buddhadeva's "change in [temporal] relativity" (*anyathā-anyathika*). All of them state that when conditioning forces (= *dharma*-s) operate in time, there is no change in their intrinsic natures. Dharmatrāta says that only their modes of being—future, present and past modes—change. Ghoṣaka says that only their temporal characteristics change. Vasumitra says that only their temporal states/ positions change. Buddhadheva says that they are "future", "present" or "past" relative to that which precedes or that which succeeds.

Vasubandhu, following the MVŚ, states that Vasumitra's theory is considered the best, as it explains temporal differences in terms of activity (*kāritra*), without confusion: when a *dharma* has not yet exercised its activity, it is "future"; when the activity is being exercised, it is "present"; when it has exercised it, it is "past". Dharmatrāta's theory is rejected as being similar to the Sāṃkhya theory of *pariṇāma*. The other two are also rejected for reason of confusion. Saṃghabhadra, however, defends Dharmatrāta's theory as being in keeping with the Vaibhāṣika system. He himself in fact often uses it along with Vasumitra's and finds it indispensible for demonstrating the Vaibhāṣika doctrines. (See below.)

ii. The Sautrāntikas raise various objections to this theory of tritemporal existence of *dharma*-s. Concerning the explanation in terms of activity, they ask: "What is the activity of a present facsimile (*tat-sabhāga*) visual faculty?" A facsimile eye is one similar to an active present eye; but unlike the latter, it does not see (e.g., the eyes of a blind person). The Vaibhāṣikas answer that such an eye has the activity of "grasping a fruit" (*phala-parigraha*) and "giving a fruit" (*phala-dāna*); the former referring to a *dharma*'s causally determining its corresponding fruit to be generated in the future, the latter, its actually yielding its fruit subsequently. But the Sautrāntikas then point out that since a past *dharma* can have the activity of giving a fruit, it would have to be semi-present!

Moreover, if a *dharma*'s intrinsic nature is always existent, what prevents it from exercising its activity at all times? Various other objections are raised by the Sautrāntikas, and finally the Vaibhāṣikas have to state that the activity is not different from the *dharma*. But this only invites further objections. For instance, if the two are identical, then the activity, like the *dharma*, must also be always existent — how then can one speak of it as being past or future?

iii. In Saṃghabhadra's response, he articulates as follows:

a. When the Vaibhāṣikas assert that all *dharma*-s—future, present and past—are existent, an existent is defined as "that which can serve as an object-domain to generate a cognition (*buddhi*)". These existents may be either absolute or relative (based on the absolute reals). Absolute non-existents (*atyanta-abhāva*) are, for example, a horse's horns, etc.

b. The past and future *dharma*-s are not relative reals conceptualized upon the present *dharma*-s as real entities. They are real entities in themselves. But they do not exist in the same manner as the present *dharma*-s; the modes of existence of the tritemporal *dharma*-s are different.[108] (See below.)

c. "Activity" does not refer to any generic efficacy, such as an eye's efficacy for vision. It refers very specifically to the efficacy of "grasping a fruit", but not "giving a fruit". Thus, the charge of "semi-presentness" does not apply. This activity, also called "projecting a fruit" (*phala-ākṣepa*), is the efficacy of a present *dharma* to project its own arising (its own fruit) in the immediately following moment. A present facsimile eye does not have the efficacy of seeing; but it too necessarily has this activity. Since this activity is unique to a present *dharma*, it uniquely distinguishes it from a past or a future *dharma*.[109]

d. A *dharma*'s activity is neither identical with nor different from the *dharma* itself. It is momentary and is generated only when an assemblage of conditions obtains. The same is true for a *dharma*'s mode of being.[110]

iv. Back to the AKB, the Sautrāntikas go on to ridicule the Vaibhāṣika position with the following stanza:

> The intrinsic nature (*svabhāva*) exists always,
> but the mode of being (*bhāva*) is not conceded as permanent,
> nor is the mode of being [conceded as] different from the intrinsic nature.
> – This is clearly an act of the Almighty (*īśvara*) [who can state as he likes].[111]

This ridicule alludes to the apparent contradiction—as in Dharmatrāta's theory on *sarvāstivāda*—that a *dharma*'s *bhāva* changes, but not its *sva-bhāva*. Saṃghabhadra retorts:

> The intrinsic nature of a *dharma* remains always; its mode of being (*bhāva*) changes: When a conditioned *dharma* traverses in time, it gives rise to its activity (*kāritra*) in accordance with conditions, without abandoning its intrinsic nature; immediately after this, the activity produced ceases. Hence it is said that the *svabhāva* exists always and yet it is not permanent, since its *bhāva* changes.
>
> The Ābhidharmikas are entitled to ridicule thus: [The Sautrāntikas] acknowledge tritemporal existence and yet deny the reality of the past and the future. Such an assertion is wonderful! While asserting that the past is what has existed and the future is what will exist, they are only talking about the existence of the present in different words (from different perspectives); this has nothing to do with the past and the future.[112]

Towards the final part of the debate in the AKB, Vasubandhu comments that the Vaibhāṣika exposition of "all-exist" is not a proper one within the Dispensation (*na śāsane sādhur bhavati*). A proper assertion of "all-exist" should be in the manner of the *sūtra* statement that "all" refers to the twelve *āyatana*-s. Nothing exists outside these twelve *āyatana*-s. Or rather: "past" means what has been; "future", what will be. He then makes the following concluding remark, put into the Vaibhāṣikas' mouth:

> The Vaibhāṣikas assert: "The past and the future definitely exist". What cannot be comprehended must therein be thus understood by one who is self-respecting.[113]
>
> The nature of *dharma* is indeed profound.
>
> It is not necessarily capable of being proved through logical reasoning.[114]

On this, Saṃghabhadra sternly protests:

> I here must say that you have yourself stealthily fabricated the assertions which you deceivingly label as "Vaibhāṣika". The genuine Vaibhāṣikas would never utter such words.
>
> Moreover, they would not, like him, arbitrarily claim that the past and the future exist truly in the manner as the present, for the tritemporal [*dharma*-s] which exist as real entities have distinctive modes of being (*bhāva*). It is clear that he intends to bring about a disaster to the noble teachings, cunningly fabricating false words to vilify those who expound properly. But how can our tenets be harmed by such fabricated vilifying words? ... It appears that he has not studied the true Vaibhāṣika [teachings]... .[115]

In fact, throughout the very lengthy debate in the Ny, Saṃghabhadra exposes Vasubandhu, on every count, as framing all the arguments we have mentioned above as being "Sautrāntika". At the end, Saṃghabhadra states that he has confronted the Kośakara squarely on the issue of tritemporal existence, questioning and repudiating all his assertions and claims which have been worded to the best of Vasubandhu's ability. In this process, he has also briefly repudiated Śrīlāta's views.[116]

Chapter six: *Mārgapudgala-nirdeśa*

Xuan Zang gives the title of this chapter as "The Chapter on the Noble Sages" or "The Chapter on the Sages and the Noble Ones" (賢聖品).[117] Pu Guang comments that this chapter comes after the previous three which expound the with-outflow. This, together with the next two, expounds the outflow-free. As for the sequence, this exposition on the outflow-free fruits comes first, since the fruits are relatively more conspicuous; chapter seven expounds their causes; chapter eight, their conditions.[118]

1. Since the whole scheme of spiritual praxis in the Abhidharma is centered around the doctrinal framework of the four noble truths, the chapter begins with an examination of these truths: their meaning, nature, order of exposition, etc. In this context, there are a couple of controversial points.

One point concerns the nature of the truth of origin (*samudaya*). The Sarvāstivādins think that the five *upādāna-skandha*-s comprise both unsatisfactoriness (*duḥkha*) and its origin (*samudaya*): the former is the *skandha*-s in their effect aspect; the latter, in their cause aspect. The Sautrāntikas—such as Śrīlāta[119]—and others maintain that, as taught in the *sūtra*, craving (*tṛṣṇā*) alone is the origin of unsatisfactoriness. Vasubandhu provides the Vaibhāṣikas with much greater space for their defense, which includes the statement—uncontested by Vasubandhu—that the *sūtra* explanation is intentional (*ābhiprāyika*) whereas the Abhidharma explanation is definitive.

Another point concerns the pleasurable sensation (*sukhā vedanā*). The Sautrāntikas and others argue that there is no pleasurable sensation. Vasubandhu endorses the Vaibhāṣika position that there is, praising it as being a reasonable one.[120]

2. The next discussion concerns the path of spiritual progress. The essential components of the Sarvāstivāda path structure are: (i) the stage of preliminary practices; (ii) the stage or path of preparatory efforts (*prayoga-mārga*); (iii) the stage or path of vision/insight into the truths (*darśana-mārga*); (iv) the stage or path of repeated practice or cultivation (*bhāvanā-mārga*); (v) the stage or path of the non-trainee (*aśaikṣa-mārga*).

i. Although there seems to be no specific appellation in the Sarvāstivāda texts for the first stage, it may well be called the "stage of requisites" (*saṃbhāra*)—as in the Yogācāra—since they obviously serve as requisites for the *prayoga-mārga*. In the MVŚ, for instance, the preliminary practices at the stage of an ordinary worldling—the *bodhisattva* and a universal monarch (*cakravartin*)—are often emphasized as the "requisites of merits and knowledge" (**puṇya-jñāna-saṃbhāra*).[121] The Ny also speaks of the preliminary practices as "requisites" to be readied/accumulated before one embarks on meditation practices such as the mindfulness of breathing and the contemplation on the loathsome.[122] The AKB prescribes these preliminaries as the observance of precepts and development of the threefold understanding (*śrutamayī-*, *cintāmayī*, *bhāvanāmayī-prajñā*). For success of meditation, one must withdraw from non-conducive conditions and evil companions, and practice contentment that enables one to abide in the four "noble lineages" (*āryavaṃśa*): contentment with

(i) clothing, (ii) food, (iii) bed and seat, and (iv) delight in the abandonment of defilements and spiritual cultivation.

ii. This stage comprises two sub-stages: (a) The part conducing to liberation (*mokṣa-bhāgīya*) which essentially comprises the twofold meditative praxis of tranquillity (*śamatha*) and insight (*vipaśyanā*); the former refers mainly to mindfulness of breathing (*ānāpāna-smṛti*) and the meditation on the impure/loathsome (*aśubhā*), the latter, to the fourfold abiding of mindfulness (*smṛty-upasthāna*). It should be noted that although *śamatha* and *vipaśyanā* form two distinctive types of praxis, the Sarvāstivāda also stresses their complementarity. The following passage in the *Saṅgītiparyaya* is a good illustration:

> What is *śamatha*? The skillful one-pointedness of mind.
>
> What is *vipaśyanā*? The discernment ... operation of understanding (*prajñā-cāra*)—conjoined with *śamatha*—with regard to a *dharma*... . As the Bhagavat has said:
>
> > There is no *dhyāna* for one without *prajñā*; and no *prajñā* for one without *dhyāna*. Only he who has *dhyāna* and *prajñā* can realize *Nirvāṇa*.[123]
>
> "There is no *dhyāna* for one without *prajñā*": – If one has such a *prajñā*, then one has attained a corresponding category of *dhyāna*. If one does not have such a *prajñā*, then one has not attained such a *dhyāna*.
>
> "No *prajñā* for one without *dhyāna*": – If one has *prajñā* which is born of *dhyāna* and has *dhyāna* as its origination, this category of *prajñā*[124] is projected by *dhyāna*. If one has such a category of *dhyāna*, then there can be the attainment of such a category of *prajñā*. If one does not have such a *dhyāna*, then one cannot attain such a *prajñā*... .[125]

(b) The part conducing to penetration (*nirvedha-bhāgīya*) or decisive insight (into the four truths). This consists of repeated contemplation, by means of the mundane (with-outflow) understanding, on the four truths, resulting in the tangible attainments—albeit still with-outflow—of warmth (*uṣmagata*, *ūṣman*), summits (*mūrdhan*), receptivities (*kṣānti*) and supreme worldly *dharma*-s (*laukika-agra-dharma*). These four are also called skillful roots because they constitute the foundation for the arising of the outflow-free *prajñā*.

The above stages already suffice to show that the Abhidharma tradition is fundamentally concerned with spiritual praxis. Abhidharma studies, no doubt, are given their due place. They are indispensable as a preparation for the development of true spiritual insight:

> At the stage of preparatory effort, one may either mostly cultivate the

> requisite (*saṃbhāra*) of *śamatha* or mostly cultivate the requisite of *vipaśyanā*. One who mostly cultivates the requisite of *śamatha* is one who, at the stage of preparatory effort, always delights in solitude and quietness, fears disturbance and sees the faults of socialization; he always stays within his hermitage. When he enters into the noble path, he is called the *śamatha*-type of practitioner. One who mostly cultivates the requisite of *vipaśyanā* is one who, at the stage of preparatory effort, always delights in studying and reflecting on the *tripiṭaka*. He repeatedly examines the specific and general characteristics of all *dharma*-s. When he enters into the noble path, he is called the *vipaśyanā*-type of practitioner.[126]

iii. Immediately after the single moment of the thought and thought-concomitants collectively known as the "supreme worldly *dharma*-s", the practitioner sails into the path of vision. He enters into a sixteen-moment process of true spiritual (as opposed to intellectual) insight into the four truths, known as "direct realization" (*abhisamaya*), and emerges as an *ārya*.

This doctrine of *abhisamaya*—which, as we have seen above, defines the very nature of *abhidharma* itself—is of central importance. No matter how much an ordinary worldling has struggled and succeeded in intellectual understanding and abandoning defilements, he cannot become spiritually transformed into an *ārya* without going through the process of *abhisamaya* in which he progressively acquires insight into the four truths. For each truth, the insight first arises pertaining to the sensuality sphere, and next, pertaining to the two upper spheres together. The former insight is called "*dharma*-knowledge" because he acquires, for the very first time in his saṃsāric faring, this outflow-free understanding of the nature of *dharma*-s from the perspective of that particular truth. That pertaining to the two upper spheres is called "subsequent knowledge" since it arises, in a similar manner, subsequent to the *dharma*-knowledge — though nonetheless also a direct perception (*cf.* Section EG).[127] When each truth is so directly realized, a corresponding number of defilements are abandoned. For the abandoning of each defilement, two moments are necessarily involved: The first, called the "unhindered path" (*ānantarya-mārga*), is when the defilement is actually being abandoned; the second, called "liberation path" (*vimukti-mārga*), is when the cessation (*nirodha*) of the defilement arises. The former is also called the moment of receptivity (*kṣānti*); the latter, the moment of knowledge. In all, a total of eighty-eight *darśana-heya* defilements are abandoned through this process: twenty-eight under *duḥkha*, nineteen under *samudaya*, nineteen under *nirodha* and twenty-two under *mārga*.

All the above essential features of the *abhisamaya* doctrine are already discernible in the *Prakaraṇa-pāda*[128] and the *Jñānaprasthāna*;[129] but it is perhaps in the MVŚ that the doctrine becomes systematically articulated for the first time.[130] It may also be mentioned here that the Sarvāstivāda masters concede that, although *abhisamaya* in the true sense is an outflow-free insight, some conventional knowledges that are capable of clear discernment—such as that with which the *bodhisattva*, before his enlightenment, discerned truly that conditioned by birth there was old-age-and-death—can also qualify as *abhisamaya*.[131]

In contrast to the Sarvāstivādins who maintain that the direct realization into the truths is a gradual process, other schools—such as the Mahāsāṃghika,[132] the Mahīśāsaka, the Dharmaguptaka,[133] the Vibhajyavādins[134] in general (including the Theravāda) and certain Dārṣṭāntika-Sautrāntikas[135]—hold it to be an abrupt one.

Śrīlāta teaches an eight-moment *abhisamaya* process:

> ...next he generates the *duḥkha-dharmajñāna*; this is called the first thought (moment) of stream-entry. At that very time he is able to abruptly abandon the three fetters, for he is able to absolutely abandon their old pursuant elements (*purāṇa-anudhātu*). From this time onwards, he generates the *duḥkha-anvayjñāna*, etc. Thus there are definitely eight thoughts in the *abhisamaya*.[136]

The eight moments are thus: 1. *duḥkha-dharmajñāna* (which abruptly eliminates three fetters); 2. *duḥkha-anvayajñāna*; 3. *samudaya-dharmajñāna*; 4. *samudaya-anvayajñāna*; 5. *nirodha-dharmajñāna*; 6. *nirodha-anvayajñāna*; 7. *mārga-dharma-jñāna*; 8. *mārga-anvayajñāna*.

It is noteworthy that Vasubandhu does not follow this Dārṣṭāntika-Sautrāntika doctrine but prefers to stick to the Vaibhāṣika exposition. This is most likely in consideration of the fact that in respect of praxis, the Sarvāstivāda has had a long tradition of tested experiences to which no novel doctrine of any individual master can compare.[137] Saṃghabhadra in fact remarks that Śrīlāta has here arbitrarily proposed his doctrine in contradiction with the truth regarding *abhisamaya* established by the tradition of hundreds of thousands of *yogācāra*-s on the basis of genuine direct perception.[138]

iv. The path of vision lasts fifteen moments of the *abhisamaya* process during which time the practitioner is a candidate (*pratipannaka*)—he is on his way—for the fruit of stream-entry (*srotaāpatti-phala*). At the sixteenth moment, he has acquired the fruit of stream-entry and emerges to embark on the next stage, the path of cultivation, which can last as long as seven births. At this stage, he repeatedly contemplates on the four truths on the basis of the spiritual insight he has gained at the preceding stage. He must work further on the affective aspects of the four defilements: greed, hostility, ignorance and conceit, which, in respect to the three spheres, yield a total of ten species. In this process, he progressively attains the higher fruits of a once-returner (*sakṛdāgamin*), non-returner (*anāgāmin*) and *arhat*.

An important notion of the *bhāvanā-mārga* is that it can be either mundane (*laukika*) or supramundane (*lokottara*). Through the former, an ordinary worldling can also abandon defilements; but such abandonments can truly take effect only when the practitioner enters into the *abhisamaya* process. The principle here is that once a defilement is abandoned—even if it is through a mundane path—it does not need to be abandoned again. But the acquisition of disjunction (*visaṃyoga-prāpti*) can take place repeatedly. This means that following the arising of a superior path (*viśeṣa-mārga*), a superior acquisition of disjunction from the defilement arises.[139] It is only with an outflow-free path—outflow-free knowledge as counteragent—that the acquisition which arises comes to be of sufficient strength to ensure absolute abandonment of the defilement.

The above description of the sequential attainment of fruits applies to the case of one who begins without having yet abandoned any defilement — he is an ordinary worldling "who is fully bound" (*sakala-bandhana*). For one who has beforehand abandoned some defilements through the mundane *bhāvanā-mārga*, he may emerge from the *abhisamaya* process either as a once-returner or a non-returner, depending on the amount of defilements he has previously abandoned. But this mundane *bhāvanā-mārga* is incapable of abandoning the defilements pertaining to the stage (*bhūmi*) of the sphere of neither-ideation–nor-nonideation (*naiva-saṃjñā-nāsaṃjñā-āyatana*).

v. The final (ninth) unhindered path which absolutely eliminates all remaining defilements is called the diamond-like *samādhi*. At this point, the *ārya* is called a non-trainee (*aśaikṣa*), in contrast to those who acquire the preceding fruits who are called trainee (*śaikṣa*) since they still need further training for the final fruit of *arhat*-hood. The final liberation path that follows is called the "exhaustion-knowledge" (*kṣaya-jñāna*), a canonical term which occurs together with the "knowledge of non-arising" (*anutpāda-jñāna*) in the *sūtra* description at the time of the attainment of *arhat*-hood.

In the Sarvāstivāda scheme of the process of liberation, the arising of the knowledge of non-arising signifies the attainment of the highest, non-retrogressive (*aparihāṇa-dharman*) grade of *arhat*-hood — also called a "non-circumstantially liberated" (*asamaya-vimukta*) *arhat*. Such a practitioner has started off as a "doctrine-pursuer" (*dharmānusārin*). Accordingly, this knowledge does not follow the moment of the exhaustion-knowledge in the case of those *arhat*-s who are susceptible to retrogression (*parihāṇa-dharman*), also called those who are "circumstantially liberated" (*samaya-vimukta*), who have started off as "faith-pursuers" (*śraddhānusārin*).

There are a total of six types or grades of *arhat*-s: *parihāṇa-dharman*, *cetanā-dharman*, *anurakṣaṇā-dharman*, *sthita-akampya-dharman*, *prativedhanā-dharman* and *akopya-dharman* ("of the nature of being unshakable"). Only the last is non-retrogressive; but a retrogressive type can be elevated to be non-retrogressive through the process of "elevation/sublimation of the faculties" (*indriya-uttāpana*, *indriya-saṃcāra*). Some schools—like the Mahāsāṃghika,[140] and the Vibhajya-vādins[141] in general—hold that an *arhat* cannot retrogress. Vasubandhu also endorses the Sautrāntikas who hold a similar view.[142]

The *ārya-pudgala*-s are divisible into seven types: 1. *śraddhānusārin*; 2. *dharma–anusārin*; 3. *śraddhā-vimukta*; 4. *dṛṣṭi-prāpta*; 5. *kāya-sākṣin*; 6. *prajñā-vimukta*; 7. *ubhayatobhāga-vimukta*.

(3) and (4) started as (1) and (2) respectively, and become so called after emerging from the *darśana-mārga*.

(5) The "body-witness", who has realized through his body the cessation meditative attainment (*nirodha-samāpatti*).

(6) The "understanding-liberated", who is one liberated from the defilement-hindrance (*kleśa-āvaraṇa*) through understanding alone. He has not been able to enter into the cessation meditation (*nirodha-samāpatti*).

(7) The "doubly liberated", who is one who, besides being liberated from the defilement-hindrance, is also liberated from the *vimokṣa-āvaraṇa*. He is liberated from all hindrances to meditative attainments.[143] According to Saṃghabhadra, the intrinsic nature of this *vimokṣa-āvaraṇa* is the non-defiled nescience (*akliṣṭa-ajñāna*) which is still capable of manifestation in the *arhat*.[144]

EG.

Chapter seven: *Jñāna-nirdeśa*

This chapter discusses (1) the intrinsic nature and functions of the different types of knowledge, (2) their classification, (3) their modes of activities (*ākāra*) and (4) their excellent qualities (*guṇa*). The flow of this chapter from the last is described at the beginning of Saṃghabhadra's commentary thus:

> In this way, the *ārya-pudgala*-s have been designated on the basis of the differences in the paths. In [discussing] these paths, it has been mentioned that proper view and proper knowledge are called the non-trainee factors (*aśaikṣa-aṅga*). We should therefore now consider whether, in designating the two separate factors of view and knowledges, there are *prajñā*-s that are

> views but not knowledges, and *prajñā*-s that are knowledges and not views... .[145]

1. *Prajñā* is one of the most important terms in the Abhidharma. For the Sarvāstivāda, it can be of different moral species and operate in different modes for which various names are given. For this reason, we generally render it generically as "understanding". This chapter mainly distinguishes its modes of operation as (i) receptivity (*kṣānti*), (ii) knowledge (*jñāna*) and (iii) view (*dṛṣṭi*).

i. "Receptivity" is the stage of understanding that precedes knowledge proper. It is judgmental in nature (*saṃtīraṇātmaka*) and is receptive to a fact even though it has not been fully ascertained. But it is not a decisive understanding, for it arises together with the acquisition (*prāpti*) of the doubt that it is to abandon, i.e., so long as it has not abandoned the doubt, its understanding is non-decisive. It is the seeing (*darśana*) of a fact for the first time.

ii. "Knowledge" is an understanding that is decisive or definite (*niścita*), free from doubt; the process of judgmental investigation has come to cease. It is also said to be that which repeatedly discerns the object-domains, and it is from this perspective that all the with-outflow *prajñā*-s can be subsumed as knowledges,[146] since they have been discerning their object-domains repeatedly from beginningless time. As for the outflow-free understandings, those that repeatedly discern are called knowledges; but the outflow-free receptivities with regard to the four noble truths are not called knowledges on account of their not having made any repeated discernment.[147] The "exhaustion-knowledge" and the "knowledge of non-arising" are knowledges, but not views, because they arise after the ceasing of judgmental investigation.

iii. "View" is also judgmental in nature. This is also part of Vasumitra's definition of "view, which requires judgment and investigation".[148] Elsewhere in the MVŚ, four characteristics of view are mentioned: seeing, being judgmental, firm attachment, and penetrating into the cognitive objects.[149] Among the with-outflow *prajñā*-s, six are also views (besides being knowledges): the five defiled views comprising Self-view (*satkāya-dṛṣṭi*), etc., and the mundane proper view (*laukikī samyag-dṛṣṭi*).

2. Vasubandhu enumerates ten knowledges. This classification comes from the *Prakaraṇa-pāda*; the *Jñānaprasthāna*[150] enumerates eight. But Vasubandhu probably simply follows the ten-fold classification known since the *Amṛta-rasa*. These ten, with their different modes of activity (*ākāra*), are as follows:

(i) *Dharma*-knowledge. It operates with the sixteen *ākāra*-s of the four truths pertaining to the sensuality sphere (four for each truth). The sixteen *ākāra*-s are: (a) truth of unsatisfactoriness — impermanent, unsatisfactory, empty, non-self;

(b) truth of origin — cause (*hetu*), origin (*samudaya*), generation (*prabhava*), condition (*pratyaya*); (c) truth of cessation — cessation (*nirodha*), quiescent (*śānta*), excellent (*praṇīta*), exit (*niḥsaraṇa*); (d) truth of the path — path (*mārga*), propriety (*nyāya*), practice (*pratipat*), transcendent (*nairyāṇika*).

(ii) Subsequent knowledge. It operates with the sixteen *ākāra*-s of the four truths pertaining to the two upper spheres.

Saṃghabhadra objects to the view—probably shared by Vasubandhu[151]—that this subsequent knowledge is an inferential knowledge. Firstly, the *sūtra*-s speak of it as being a case of truly knowing the noble truths; true knowledge cannot be inferential. Moreover, if it were so, it would mean that an *ārya* can have no knowledge which takes cessation as object, since cessation is not an entity directly seen. Here he offers an important explanation on the Sarvāstivāda doctrine of direct perception (*pratyakṣa*) which is said to be threefold: (a) faculty-based (**indriyāśrita-pratyakṣa*) — direct grasping of the external object-domain by a sensory faculty; (b) direct perception of experience (**anubhava-pratyakṣa*) — when sensation, ideation, etc., are coming into the present; (c) direct perception of comprehension (**buddhi-pratyakṣa*) — the realization of a *dharma*'s intrinsic or common characteristic accordingly as the case may be. "Herein, if we say from the perspectives of (a) and (b) that the object-domain of *anvaya-jñāna* is not an entity directly seen, then there also ought not to be the *dharma-jñāna* of cessation, since cessation is not the domain of (a) and (b). If we consider from the perspective of (c), we should not say that the cognitive object of *anvayajñāna* is the object-domain of an inferential knowledge. Thus, all properly derived (**yoga-vihita*) ascertainment (*viniścaya*) of the reals are knowledge of direct perception (*pratyakṣa-jñāna*); the *anvayajñāna* being so, should pertain to direct perception".[152]

(iii) Conventional knowledge (*saṃvṛti-jñāna*). This takes all *dharma*-s as cognitive objects. At the stages of warmth, summits and receptivities (see Section EF), it operates with the sixteen *ākāra*-s of the four truths; at the stage of the upper grade of receptivity and the supreme worldly *dharma*-s, it operates with the *ākāra*-s of the truth of unsatisfactoriness alone; in the practice of *śamatha* and *vipaśyanā*, it has the intrinsic and common characteristics of *dharma*-s as its *ākāra*-s.

(iv)–(vii) Knowledge of unsatisfactoriness, knowledge of origin, knowledge of cessation, knowledge of the path. Each has the four *ākāra*-s of the particular truth concerned.

(viii) Knowledge of others' thoughts (*paracitta-jñāna*). This can be both outflow-free and with-outflow. In the former case, it is subsumed under the truth of the path, and thus operates with the four *ākāra*-s of the path. In the latter case, its *ākāra*-s relate to the intrinsic characteristics of the *citta-caitta*-s—but only one entity at a time—that it cognizes.

(ix)–(x) Exhaustion-knowledge and knowledge of non-arising. Each of them operates with fourteen *ākāra*-s — i.e., the sixteen minus *śūnya* and *anātman*. According to the Kaśmīrian masters: They are realized in an *arhat*'s contemplation and are thus outflow-free; but when he emerges from the contemplation, two conventional knowledges qua "subsequently obtained knowledges" (*pṛṣṭhalabdha-jñāna*) follow consecutively, through which he knows: "*duḥkha* has been known by me…" and "*duḥkha* has been known by me, and is no longer to be known…"[153] — such thoughts of "me", which then become possible, exclude the *śūnya* and *anātman ākāra*-s.

Of these knowledges, the conventional knowledge is with-outflow. The knowledge of others' thoughts are both with-outflow and outflow-free. The rest are all outflow-free. Although liberation must ultimately depend on the outflow-free knowledges, the conventional knowledges—derived from listening (*śrutamayī*), from reflection (*cintā-mayī*; note that this already involves meditative praxis), from cultivation (*bhāvanā-mayī*) and from birth (*upapatti-prātilambhikā*; i.e., innate)—are also emphasized in the Abhidharma, and in this emphasis, abhidharmic investigation (of intrinsic and common characteristics) is once again given its due place:

> Question: What kinds of conventional knowledge are also called "knowledge qua complete knowledge" (*jñāna-parijñā*)?
>
> Answer: Excepting the conventional knowledges which are conjoined with resolve (*adhimokṣa*), the other [conventional knowledges] derived from listening, reflection and cultivation which are exceedingly clear can also be called "direct realization" (*abhisamaya*; see Section EF.2.b.iii and note 125) as well as "knowledges qua complete knowledge". Those derived from listening examine the eighteen elements with regard to their intrinsic characteristics and common characteristics, etc. Those derived from reflection comprise the mindfulness of breathing and the fourfold abiding of mindfulness, etc. Those derived from cultivation comprise warmth, summits, receptivities and the supreme worldly *dharma*-s, etc. These as well as the outflow-free knowledges are called knowledges qua complete knowledge. …[154]
>
> Innate understanding is that which studies, recites and thoroughly propagates the twelve-division teachings of the *tripiṭaka*. On the basis of this, the understanding derived from listening comes into being. On the basis of this, the understanding derived from reflection comes into being. On the basis of this, the understanding derived from cultivation comes into being; this eradicates defilements and realizes *Nirvāṇa*. It is like the case that the

sprout is generated on the basis of the seed; the stem, on the sprout; the branches, leaves, flowers and fruits successively, on the stem.[155]

3. For the Vaibhāṣikas, *ākāra* refers to *prajñā*. Vasubandhu, however, endorses the Sautrāntika view that it is a mode of apprehending cognitive objects (*ālambana-grahaṇa-prakāra*) by the *citta-caitta*-s.[156] Saṃghabhadra rebukes him:

> Here, the Sūtrakāra leans towards the tenet of others... . It must be considered what is meant by the "object-grasping-mode". If it refers to the different modes/species (*prakāra*) of the form of the object, then the notion that all [*citta-caitta*-s] can assume the image-form (能像) [of the object] cannot be established at all, for an object has various forms, skillful, permanent, etc. Or rather, the *rūpa-dharma*-s are to be subsumed under *ākāra*, since *rūpa-dharma*-s can also assume the images of the forms of others. If it refers to the ability to grasp the distinctive characteristic of the object, then *ākāra* ought not to be possible for the five [sensory] consciousnesses, since they are not capable of grasping the specific characteristic of the object — since only a discriminative (*sa-vikalpaka*) consciousness is capable of grasping the specific characteristic of the object [in the form:] "it is blue, not green", etc. However, this is not what is conceded [by his definition]. Hence [his definition] is logically invalid.[157]

4. In the section on the excellent qualities (*guṇa*) of the knowledges, there is much buddhological discussion. These include: (i) qualities unique to the Buddha — his eighteen unique qualities (*āveṇika-dharma*), i.e., his ten powers, fourfold self-confidence (*vaiśāradya*), threefold abiding in mindfulness, great compassion; (ii) qualities also shared by other trainees — e.g., non-disputation (*araṇā*): the ability to prevent others' defilements from arising with respect to them; (iii) qualities also shared by the *śrāvaka*-s or the ordinary worldlings — e.g., the supernormal knowledges (*abhijñā*).

On the Buddha's ten powers, the AKB states that the Buddha's knowledges—such as knowing the possible and the impossible (*sthāna-asthāna*), etc.—are called powers because they know all objects without any hindrance. This results from the fact that he alone has abandoned all outflows together with all their traces (*vāsanā*). In this connection, the story is told of Śāriputra's refusal to a seeker for ordination because of Śāriputra's inability to see the seeds of liberation planted by this seeker in the remote past. This same example occurs in the Vy[158] to illustrate that an *arhat* still has the non-defiled type of nescience (*akliṣṭa-ajñāna*).

The Buddha's threefold accomplishment (*saṃpad*)—of cause (*hetu*), result (*phala*) and benefit (*upakāra*)—is also discussed. Under the accomplishment of result, the aspect of the accomplishment in respect to abandoning (*prahāṇa-saṃpad*) is said to be fourfold: (a) he has abandoned all defilements; (b) he has abandoned them absolutely (*atyanta-prahāṇa*); (c) he has abandoned them along with their traces; (d) he has abandoned all hindrances to meditative attainment.[159] This last aspect refers to the abandoning of the non-defiled nescience. Saṃghabhadra explains that an *arhat* still has to overcome the hindrance to the complete mastery of meditative attainment on account of the fact that his non-defiled nescience can still manifest (*sam-ud-ā-√car*) in him.[160] (See also, Section EF). This is fully abandoned and rendered incapable of manifestation only in the case of a Buddha — and this is why his wisdom surpasses those of the *pratyekabuddha*-s and the *śrāvaka*-s.

Chapter eight: *Samāpatti-nirdeśa*

1. This chapter expounds the meditative attainments as the causal conditions forming the basis for the generation of knowledges, particularly the outflow-free knowledges which effectuate emancipation. At the outset, it states that meditations (*dhyāna*) are twofold: (i) as rebirth (*upapatti*) states; i.e., as states of birth effectuated by the *karma* of meditative praxis; (this aspect has been dealt with in chapter three); (ii) as meditative attainment, *samāpatti*.

The experiences in these two aspects are not quite the same. For instance, for the *dhyāna*-s qua meditations:

- in the first *dhyāna*, there are *vitarka*, *vicāra*, *prīti*, *sukha* and *samādhi*;
- in the second, *prīti*, *sukha*, *samādhi* and *adhyātma-saṃprasāda*;
- in the third, *sukha*, *samādhi*, *saṃskāropekṣā*, *smṛti*, *saṃprajñāna*;
- in the fourth, *samādhi*, neutral sensation, *upekṣā-pariśuddhi*, *smṛti-pariśuddhi*.

But the sensations (*vedanā*) for the *dhyāna*-s qua existences are listed as follows:

- in the first, there are *sukha-vedanā* associated with visual, auditory and bodily consciousnesses, *saumanasya* associated with mental consciousness and *upekṣā* associated with visual, auditory, bodily and mental consciousnesses;
- in the second, *saumanasya* and *upekṣā* associated with the mind;
- in the third, *sukha* and *upekṣā* associated with the mind;
- in the fourth, only *upekṣā vedanā*.[161]

2. The term *samāpatti*, literally meaning "even attainment" (Xuan Zang's rendering of 等至 conveys this sense), is one of the key terms referring to meditation. It can refer to any of the *dhyāna*-s, the four *ārūpya*-s and the two non-conscious meditative

attainments (*acittaka samāpatti*). The verb from *sam-ā-√pad* is used technically to mean "enter into meditation". It is often used synonymously with *samādhi*. For some early masters like Bhadanta Dharmatrāta, the two terms in fact mean the same in the context of meditation — but he is also aware that *samāpatti* has a broader connotation outside the context of meditation.[162]

Samāpatti-s may be superior or inferior in accordance with the *gotra* (the particular type of *ārya*; sharp-faculty, weak-faculty, retrogressive, non-retrogressive, etc.) and *prajñā* of the meditators: the *śrāvaka*-s and *pratyekabuddha*-s cannot know even the names of the Buddha's *samāpatti*-s; those of Śāriputra cannot be known by other *śrāvaka*-s; and so on; when attaining *parinirvāṇa*, the Buddha entered into the *samāpatti* of "immovable radiance",[163] whereas Śāriputra entered into the *siṃha-vijṛmbhita-samāpatti* and Maudgalyāyana entered into the *gandhahasti-vijṛmbhā-samāpatti*; etc.[164]

3. Another term generally connoting "meditation" is *samādhi*: "holding (*√dhā*) evenly", "equipoise". It is one of the ten universal thought-concomitants (*mahā-bhūmika-dharma*) of the Sarvāstivāda system, defined very simply by Vasubandhu as "one-pointedness of thought" (*cittasyaikāgratā*) in chapter two. The MVŚ explains it thus:

> It sustains (*ā-√dhā*) various types of skillful *citta-caitta*-s making them continue evenly as a series; hence called *samādhi*. ... It is *samādhi* because it holds evenly ..., it holds various excellent even *dharma*-s.[165]

Various opinions distinguishing between *samādhi* and *samāpatti* are given in the MVŚ: (i) the former is of a single entity (*dravya*), the latter comprises the five *skandha*-s; (ii) the former, momentary, the latter, in a serial continuity; (iii) all *samādhi*-s are *samāpatti*-s, but some *samāpatti*-s are not *samādhi*-s; (iv) some *samādhi*-s are not *samāpatti*-s — viz, the *samādhi* conjoined with a non-concentrated (*asamāhita*) thought.[166]

4. The English word "meditation" is perhaps best reserved for *dhyāna*.[167] Vasubandhu brings out the important point of the Vaibhāṣika system that it involves equally the aspects of concentration and contemplation — or *śamatha* and *vipaśyanā*:

> [*Dhyāna*] is that through which they meditate (*dhyāyanty aneneti*); this means "they understand truly" (*prajānanti*), because one who is concentrated understands truly (i.e., there is necessarily an element of insight in a concentrated mind; see Section EG). This root (*√dhyai*) is in the sense of reflection (*cintana*) which, according to the accepted tenet of the school (Sarvāstivāda), refers to *prajñā*.

> If so, it amounts to that all *samādhi* is *dhyāna*.
>
> No. The name ["*dhyāna*"] is given to a *samādhi* endowed with excellences (*prakarṣa*)... . But what [*samādhi*] is endowed with excellences?
>
> That *samādhi* which is endowed with the *dhyāna*-factors. For, being bound by the pair of *śamatha* and *vipaśyanā* (*śamatha-vipaśyanābhyāṃ yuga-naddhaḥ*), it is called an "abode of happiness in the present life" (*dṛṣṭa-dharma-vihāra*) or the path of ease (*sukhā pratipad*) [for liberation]: with it, [the practitioners] meditate at ease.[168]

For this reason, while all the nine meditative attainments can be called *samāpatti*, only the first four meditative attainments are called *dhyāna*. This agrees with the explanations in the MVŚ:

> Only when both senses are fulfilled can it be called a *dhyāna* — [the sense of] abandoning fetters and of proper seeing (*sam-anu-√paś*). The sensuality-sphere *samādhi*-s, although capable of proper seeing, cannot abandon the fetters; the non-material-sphere *samādhi*-s, although capable of abandoning fetters, cannot see properly. Hence, [both] are not *dhyāna*. ... Further, the non-material-sphere *samādhi*-s have quiescence, but no contemplation; the sensuality-sphere *samādhi*-s have contemplation, but no quiescence. The *rūpa samādhi*-s have both, hence they are called quiescent contemplation (*dhyāna*):[169] quiescent in the sense of being concentrated (*samāhita*); contemplation in the sense of insight (*vidarśana/vipaśyanā*).[170]

5. The nine meditative attainments are: (i) the four *dhyāna*-s pertaining to the *rūpadhātu*, (ii) the four *ārūpya* attainments—*ākāśānantya-āyatana*, *vijñānānantya-āyatana*, *ākiṃcanya-āyatana*, *naiva-saṃjñā-nāsaṃjñā-āyatana*—and (iii) the cessation meditative attainment (*nirodha-samāpatti*). These are called the "nine sequential meditative attainments" (*nava-anupūrva-samāpatti*), because they have to be mastered in sequence. But once mastered, they can be entered into in any order. Of these, on the whole, it is the four *dhyāna*-s that Vasubandhu discusses in greatest detail. Indeed, the four *dhyāna*-s constitute the fundamental emphasis on Buddhist meditation praxis. Proper equipoise (*samyak-samādhi*) is defined in terms of the *dhyāna*-s,[171] and they are the meditation praxis praised by the Buddha himself.[172] As the *bodhisattva*, the Buddha was said to have been instructed in and gained mastery over the attainment of the *ākiṃcanya-āyatana* and *naiva-saṃjñā-nāsaṃjñā-āyatana*; but he did not find them efficacious in bringing about enlightenment. The MVŚ in fact states that all *buddha*-s, more numerous than the sands of river Gangā, without exception, relied on the fourth *dhyāna* to attain supreme perfect enlightenment.[173] In attaining *parinirvāṇa* too, the Buddha—and for that matter the great disciples like Śāriputra and Maudgalyāyana—passed away after emerging from the fourth *dhyāna*. The *dhyāna*-s are emphasized as the "predominant thought-concomitant" (*adhi-*

caitasika), as the "abode of happiness in the present life" (*dṛṣṭadharma-vihāra*) and as the "path of ease" (*sukhā pratipad*) (see above) in which a more and more subtle form of comfort and bliss (*prasrabdhi*; "lightness", "pliability", "fitness") is experienced:

> There is no *samādhi* like the four fundamental *dhyāna*-s which, possessing great power and being highly efficacious, can accomplish great things. For this reason, they alone are called the *adhi-caitasika*. Moreover, in the four *dhyāna*-s there are immeasurable kinds of excellent qualities of the *adhi-caitasika*... . Moreover, on the basis of the four *dhyāna*-s, the *yogācāra*-s experience the *caitasika* bliss through immeasurable ways. ... Furthermore the four *dhyāna*-s are included as "paths of bliss/ease", hence they alone are called the *adhi-caitasika*.[174]

6. Other forms of meditative praxis discussed in this chapter include (i) the threefold *samādhi* and (ii) the threefold-threefold *samādhi*, (iii) the eight liberations (*vimokṣa*), (iv) the eight spheres of conquest (*abhibhv-āyatana*) and (v) the ten pervasive spheres (*kṛtsna-āyatana*), etc.

i. The threefold *samādhi* is (a) emptiness-*samādhi* (*śūnyatā-samādhi*), so called because it contemplates the *śūnya* and *anātman ākāra*-s of the truth of unsatisfactoriness, conducing to the realization of the emptiness of the self and of what pertains to the self; (b) characteristicless-*samādhi* (*ānimitta-samādhi*), so called because it takes as its cognitive object *Nirvāṇa*, which is free from the ten characteristics of the five sensory objects, male, female and the three characteristics of the conditioned; (c) aspirationless-*samādhi*, so called because, contemplating the *duḥkha* and *anitya ākāra*-s of *duḥkha-satya* and the four *ākāra*-s of the truth of origin, it comes to aspire for no *dharma* at all. These three may be with-outflow and outflow-free, and the latter are also called gateways of liberation (*vimokṣa-mukha*) as they are efficacious in leading to *Nirvāṇa* — thus spelling out their importance as methods of meditative praxis.

ii. The threefold-threefold *samādhi*-s are emptiness-emptiness-*samādhi*, characteristicless-characteristicless-*samādhi*, aspirationless-aspirationless-*samādhi*; each takes its respective threefold *samādhi* as object. E.g., an *arhat* first contemplates, by means of his outflow-free knowledge, the emptiness and no-self-ness of all *dharma*-s, generating the emptiness-*samādhi*. He further contemplates, by means of the with-outflow knowledge, the preceding knowledge of emptiness as being empty, generating dispassion towards it; this is emptiness-emptiness-*samādhi*. Saṃghabhadra explains thus:

> This is like the case of using a stick to turn around the corpse that is being burned; when the corpse has become extinct, the stick too must be burned. Likewise, having burned the defilements by means of the emptiness [-*samādhi*], one further generates the emptiness-emptiness-*samādhi* in order to generate dispassion toward the preceding emptiness.[175]

iii. The eight liberations (*vimokṣa*) are: (*1*) "possessing matter, he sees [external] matter"; (*2*) "internally without the ideation of matter, he sees matter externally"; (*3*) "having realized through the body and fully attained the beautiful liberation (*śubha-vimokṣa*), he abides therein"; (*4*) – (*7*) "the four *ārūpya samāpatti*-s; (*8*) the *nirodha-samāpatti.* These liberations, cultivated sequentially, are for the purpose of rendering defilements more distant and gaining mastery over the *samāpatti*-s — with these liberations the practitioner can bring about qualities like non-disputation (*araṇā*; see Section EG), etc., and psychic power for such activities as prolonging and shortening the life-span.[176]

iv. As for the spheres of conquest (*abhibhv-āyatana*), the first two are the same as the first liberation; the next two are the same as the second liberation; the next four are the same as the third liberation. However, there is a difference: In cultivating the liberations, one is only able to "turn one's back" on the defilements — i.e., one is only "liberated". Subsequently, in cultivating these "spheres of conquests", one is able to also conquer the cognitive object: one can view the object in any manner that one delights in, without any defilement being provoked by it.

v. The eight liberations conduce to the eight spheres of conquest which in turn conduce to the ten pervasive spheres (*kṛtsna-āyatana*). The latter are: earth, water, fire, wind (four Great Elements), blue, yellow, red, white (four primary colours), *ākāśa-ānantya-āyatana* and *vijñāna-ānantya-āyatana* (first two *ārūpya* meditative attainments). These ten are so called "because their cognitive objects pervade extensively and their resolve (*adhimukti*) is boundless".[177] The MVŚ elaborates as follows:

> The first eight pervasive spheres pertain to the fine-materiality spheres, the last two pertain to the non-materiality sphere... . This is because, the "beautiful liberation" is in the fourth *dhyāna*. From this [the practitioner] can enter into the last four spheres of conquest; from these last four spheres of conquest he can further enter into the first eight pervasive spheres. Herein, the liberation can only apprehend generically the mark of the beautiful, it cannot distinguish blue, yellow, red and white; although the last four spheres of conquest can distinguish blue, yellow, red and white, they cannot exercise the mode of understanding (*ākāra*) of being boundless. The first four pervasive spheres not only distinguish blue, yellow, red and white; they can also exercise the mode of understanding of being boundless. That

> is: [the practitioner] contemplates on blue, etc., being each boundless, and further reflects: "What are the support-bases (*āśraya*) of green, etc?" Having known that they have the Great Elements as support-basis, he next contemplates earth, etc., being in each case boundless. He further reflects: "On account of what does this cognized *rūpa* become extensive?" Having known that it is on account of space, he next generates the *ākāśa-ānantya-āyatana*. He further reflects: "What is the support basis of this cognizing awareness (*buddhi*)?" Having known that it has the extensive consciousness as support-basis, he next generates the *vijñāna-ānantya-āyatana*. This consciousness qua support-basis being without another support-basis, the [stages] further up are not designated as pervasive spheres.[178]

7. At the end of the chapter, Vasubandhu states that he has completed his exposition of the Abhidharma doctrines in this text, basing himself mostly on the established tenets of the Kaśmīrian Vaibhāṣikas (*prayeṇa hi kāśmīravaibhāṣikāṇāṃ nītyādisiddha…*). He adds: "Whatever, herein, has been wrongly grasped by us is our fault."

EI. Chapter nine: **Pudgalavāda-pratiṣedha*

Unlike the previous eight chapters, this chapter does not contain any stanzas (not counting the couple of verses quoted within the whole prose text). Samghabhadra's commentary ends with chapter eight at the end of which, as we saw, Vasubandhu states that he has completed his exposition of the AKB. It is therefore clear that this chapter forms an appendix to the AKB.

As to its title, we may first note that Vasubandhu refers to this chapter twice, once as *pudgalavāda-pratiṣedha*[179] ("refutation of the *pudgala*") and another time as *ātma-vāda-pratiṣedha*[180] ("refutation of the *ātman*"). On the first, Yaśomitra comments: "*pudgalavāde* pudgala-pratiṣedha-prakaraṇe";[181] on the second: "*ātmavāda-pratiṣedha* iti śāstrāvasāne vātsīputrīya-matạ-pratiṣedhe".[182] It thus appears that the title must have been either *pudgalavāda-pratiṣedha* or *ātmavāda-pratiṣedha*, and, as Yaśomitra suggests, it is mainly for the refutation of the Vātsīputrīya doctrine of the *pudgala*. However, the doctrines of the Sāṃkhyas, Vaiśeṣikas and the Grammarians (*vaiyākaraṇa*)—in this regard—are also refuted.

1. Vasubandhu begins the chapter by stating that outside the Buddhist teaching there can be no liberation. This is because those outside of Buddhism differ from the Buddhists in being deeply attached to the view of the *ātman* (*ātmadṛṣṭi-niviṣta*). They falsely conceptualize the *ātman* as a real entity (*dravya-antara*) distinct from the *skandha*-s, and all defilements are generated through the power of this clinging to the *ātman*.

2. Succinctly speaking, the previous eight chapters constitute a doctrine of the *dharma*-s demonstrating the truth of no-self-ness (*cf.* Pu Guang's explanation in Section C). This is the common concern of all the Abhidharma traditions other than the Pudgalavādins, such as the Vātsīputrīya and its off-shoots. The following discussion in the introductory chapter of the *Jñānaprasthāna* illustrates this:

> Question: How is the merit (*ānuśaṃsa*) of this treatise to be characterized?
>
> Answer: It accords with liberation, eradicates bondages and conforms to emptiness and non-self-ness. It elucidates the truth of no-self-ness, repudiates the *pudgala*, ... turns away from pollution (*saṃkleśa*) and tends towards purification, ... establishes all the true doctrines of the *Buddha-dharma*.[183]

But, after the eight chapters, the most pressing problems still remain to be explained. Since Buddhism denies the *ātman* and the Abhidharma teaches the doctrine of momentariness, how is moral responsibility to be established? What is the agent of action and the recipient of an action? On this, Vasubandhu finds the need, in the chapter on *karma*, to refer the readers to our chapter (see first reference, p. 56, bottom). Again, in the context of discussing the process of karmic retribution— i.e., how a subsequent result can be derived from a previous *karma* which lasted for only a single moment—Vasubandhu denies the need and validity to resort to the theory of tri-temporal existence of *dharma*-s. He briefly mentions the Sautrāntika doctrine that the result comes from a distinctive state of the serial continuity of thought (*citfasaṃtāna-viśeṣa*), but again finds the need to refer the readers to our chapter for details (see second reference, page 56, bottom). We can therefore see that the purpose of this chapter nine is mainly to establish in detail the Sautrāntika doctrine of *karma* in terms of *bīja* and *saṃtati-pariṇāma-viśeṣa*, without *sarvāstitva* and *pudgalavāda*. In other words, while the previous chapters have shown the working of *dharmavāda*—from the perspectives of both the Sarvāstivāda and the Sautrāntika—it remains for Vasubandhu to refute *pudgalavāda* and to establish in detail how the validity of karmic "agency", moral responsibility, "agent" of *saṃsāra* and the fact of memory can all be satisfactorily explained in terms of the Sautrāntika model. He probably feels that without such an exposition the preceding accounts on the operations of the *dharma*-s, however detailed, would not be convincing enough for the practitioners.

These are in fact the very concerns of the Vātsīputrīyas and the Ātmavādins. The Vātsīputrīyas ask: "If in that case the *pudgala* does not exist, who is it that goes around in *saṃsāra*? For, it is not possible that *saṃsāra* itself goes around in *saṃsāra*".[184] And, "If in that case the *ātman* does not exist in any way whatsoever, how does memory or recognition of a long experienced object occur in the thoughts which are momentary?"[185] Similarly, the Vaiśeṣikas ask: "There being no *ātman*, who is the agent(/doer) of *karma*-s? Who comes to be the experiencer (*bhoktṛ*) of the fruits?"[186]

4. The Vātsīputrīyas branched off quite early from the Sarvāstivāda, which is said to have occurred during the third century after the Buddha's *mahā-parinirvāṇa*. Devaśarman's *Vijñāna-kāya* already contains a detailed disputation between the Sarvāstivādins—called the Śūnyatāvādins in that context—and the Pudgalavādins. The following is an example of its denial of the *pudgala* as a real entity:

> There are six consciousnesses: visual … mental consciousness. Conditioned by the eye and visible forms, visual consciousness arises. This visual consciousness can only cognize the visibles, not the *pudgala*. This *pudgala* is not cognizable by visual consciousness; only the visibles are cognizable by visual consciousness. Thus, this visual consciousness is not the *pudgala*. …
>
> Further, conditioned by the eye and visible forms, visual consciousness arises. From the coming together of the three, there is contact. Conditioned by contact there is sensation. This sensation generated by visual contact can only sense the visibles, not the *pudgala*. This *pudgala* is not sensed by the sensation generated by visual contact; only the visibles are sensed by the sensation generated by visual contact. Thus, this sensation generated by visual contact is not a sensation generated by the *pudgala*. …
>
> Hence, the *pudgala* does not exist. As with visual consciousness, the same is true for the cases of auditory, olfactory, gustatory, bodily and mental consciousnesses.[187]

5. In the present chapter, Vasubandhu expounds the Vātsīputrīyas' conception of the *pudgala* as being ineffable in respect to its nature. They teach a distinctive doctrine of the five categories of *dharma*: (i) the future; (ii) the present; (iii) the past; (iv) the unconditioned; (v) the ineffable, to which the *pudgala* belongs. It can only be stated that this *pudgala* is in a necessary relation to the five *skandha*-s, being neither identical with nor different from the latter. However, it should be noted that for the Vātsīputrīyas, the *pudgala* is a designation (*prajñapti*) based on the *skandha*-s, though cognizable by the six consciousnesses.

Vasubandhu presses the Vātsīputrīyas to be precise: Is the *pudgala* existent as a real entity or non-existent? If it is an existent, it should be known through either direct perception or inference — but this is not the case. If it is a non-existent and a mere concept, then it does not differ from our notion of the *pudgala*. But the Vātsīputrīyas complain that their doctrine is misunderstood; the *pudgala* is ineffable as to its being identical with or different from the *skandha*-s. It is a dynamic reality designated on the presently existing appropriated *skandha*-s. Nevertheless, ontologically it is neither purely a non-existent nor, for that matter, an existent entity:

> It indeed does not exist as a real entity (*dravya*) or as a [mere] concept [in the manner that you are suggesting]. ... The *pudgala* is designated on the basis of the internal appropriated *skandha*-s existing at the present.[188]

That the Vātsīputrīyas explain the *pudgala* as a designation on the basis of the *skandha*-s is also confirmed by their other texts, such as the **Tridharmaka-śāstra* (三法度論)[189] and the **Sāṃmitīya-śāstra*. For instance, the **Tridharmaka* defines the "nescience (*ajñāna*) of the ineffable" (不可說不知)—i.e., the non-understanding concerning the ineffable *pudgala*—as the nescience with regard to the following threefold designation:

i. designation of the appropriated (受施設; **upātta-prajñapti*):[190] "Sentient beings, having appropriated (*upātta*) the *skandha*-s, *dhātu*-s and *āyatana*-s, come to (falsely) consider [the sentient being] (= the *pudgala*) as being identical with or different from [the appropriated *skandha*-s, *dhātu*-s and *āyatana*-s]";[191]

ii. designation of the past: It is an expression based on the past *skandha*-s, *dhātu*-s and *āyatana*-s, such as: "In the past, I was named Govinda";

iii. designation of the ceased: This refers to the designation of the *skandha*-s, etc., that have ceased—i.e., designation of the non-appropriated (**anupādatta*) *skandha*-s, etc.—such as: "The Bhagavat enters into *parinirvāṇa*."

In other words, the ineffable *pudgala* is designated from the above three perspectives. This threefold designation of the *pudgala* is said to counteract, respectively, the three false views: non-existence, annihilation, existence/eternalism.[192] Thus, it becomes clear that: (a) the *pudgala* is to be designated on the basis of the *skandha*-s, etc; (b) that the *pudgala*—the sentient being mentioned in (i)—must not be understood as being identical with or different from the *skandha*-s, etc.; (c) the notion of the *pudgala* must also steer clear from the false views of existence, non-existence, eternality, annihilation. To that extent, it is different from the Brahmanical notion of the *ātman*, on the one hand, and a mere concept of the Sarvāstivādins, Sautrāntikas and others, on the other.

6. Vasubandhu also refutes the doctrine of "a certain heretic" (*ekīyas tīrthikaḥ*)[193]—identified by both Yaśomitra[194] and Pu Guang[195] as the Vaiśeṣika—that consciousness necessarily arises from the *ātman*. It claims that the observed variation in the consciousness arising in the different moments and the lack of a fixed order of arising is due to the conjunction (*saṃyoga*) of the *ātman* with the *manas*.

Vasubandhu argues that a conjunction necessarily occurs at a particular localized spot, which implies that the two things in conjunction are localized. Moreover, the Vaiśeṣikas define conjunction as "a meeting-together preceded by a non-meeting-together" (*aprāptipūrvikā prāptiḥ saṃyogaḥ*). Now, *manas* possesses activity and moves; when it does so, the *ātman* which meets with it must also move. All this contradicts the claim of an omnipresent, non-limited, non-moving *ātman*.

In response to the Vaiśeṣika question as to how, in the absence of the *ātman*, a past *karma* which has perished can subsequently generate an effect, Vasubandhu expounds the distinctive Sautrāntika theory of *saṃtati-pariṇāma-viśeṣa*:

> Just as it is said [in the world], "a fruit arises from the seed". But it does not arise from the perished seed nor does it arise immediately. How then? It [arises] from the distinctive [culminating moment] in the serial transformation (*saṃtati-pariṇāma-viśeṣa*) of that [seed]: from the final stage of the flower, generated successively from the sprout to the stem to the leaves, etc. But as for that which is generated from the flower, why is it said to be the fruit of the seed? Because the efficacy [for generating the fruit] existing in the flower was induced by it through a succession from it. ... It is thus that the fruit is said to arise from the *karma*. And it is not the case that it arises from the *karma* that has perished, nor [does it arise] immediately [after the *karma*]. ... It is from the distinctive [culminating moment] in the serial transformation of that [*karma*].[196]

7. Some [like the Grammarians[197]] claim (*yo 'py āha*)[198] that the *ātman* exists, since a state of existence (*bhāva*) depends on an existent agent (*bhavitṛ*), just as Devadatta's walking depends on Devadatta qua the agent of walking (*gantṛ*). Likewise, consciousness—and for that matter any action—depends on an agent of cognition (*vijñātṛ*).

Vasubandhu replies that if by such an "agent" is meant a real *ātman*, its existence remains to be proved (and in fact it has already been disproved). If it is a person in the conventional usage of the term (*vyavahāra-puruṣa*), it refers simply to a name given to a serial continuity of conditionings (*saṃskāra*). As to the *sūtra* statement that consciousness cognizes (*vijñānaṃ vijānāti*), Vasubandhu explains that in the cognitive process consciousness in fact does nothing (it is not a true, independent agent):

> It does nothing. Nevertheless, just as an effect, though doing nothing whatsoever, is said to correspond (*anuvidhīyate*) to the cause on account of its acquiring its existence (*ātma-lābha*) resembling (*sādṛṣyena*) [the cause]; likewise, consciousness, though doing nothing whatsoever, is said to be conscious [of the object] on account of its acquiring its existence resembling [the object]. Now, what is its resemblance? The fact of having the

form or aspect (*ākāra*) of that [object] (*tadākāratā*). For this very reason, although it is arisen through the sense faculty as well, it is said to cognize the object-domain, not the sense faculty. Or rather, the statement "consciousness cognizes" is also faultless from this perspective: because of the fact of the serial continuity of consciousness being the cause for the consciousness [that arises in each moment with regard to the object-domain] (because, in the serial continuity of consciousness, the preceding moment of consciousness is the cause for the succeeding one).[199]

8. The religiosity of this great scholar monk, Vasubandhu, shows up unmistakably in various places in the AKB. In this chapter too, on several occasions, he stresses that the true nature of things concerning the operation of consciousness and the process of *karma* are truly profound, fully comprehensive by the Buddha alone.

Abbreviations

AKB = Pradhan, P. (ed.), 2nd edition. *Abhidharmakośabhāṣyam of Vasubandhu.* (1975, Patna).

AHV = **Abhidharmahṛdaya-vyākhyā (/Miśra-abhidharmahṛdaya).* 雜阿毘曇心論. T28, no. 1552.

MVŚ = *Abhidharma-mahāvibhāṣā* 阿毘達磨大毘婆沙論. T29, no. 1545.

Study = Yin Shun, 說一切有部為主論書與論師之研究 (*A Study of the Śāstras and Ācāryas of the Sarvāstivāda and Other Schools*). (1968, Taipei).

Ny = **Nyāyānusāra.* T29, no. 1562.

Vy = Wogihara, U (ed.), *Sphuṭārthā Abhidharmakośavyākhyā.* (1936, 1971, 1989, Tokyo).

Endnotes

1 *Cf.* AKB, 2: *prajñāmalā sānucarābhidharmaḥ* | *tatra prajñā dharma-pravicayaḥ* (= *abhidharma*) |

2 AKB, 2.

3 MVŚ, 4b22–25.

4 MVŚ, 4a15–16.

5 Ny, T29, 329b. See also the third meaning of *abhidharma* according to the Ābhidharmikas in MVŚ, 4a15–16.

6 La Vallée Poussin takes him to be the same Ghoṣaka mentioned frequently in the MVŚ (see LVP's Introduction). Yin Shun, however, points out that they cannot be the same person since their views differ, and the *Amṛta-rasa* was compiled after the MVŚ (*Study*, 486).

7 See *Study*, 479 *ff.*

8 Some scholars, including La Vallée Poussin (see his Introduction), misinterpreted Dao An's preface to the older translation of the *Mahāvibhāṣā* (T no. 1546) to suggest that the *Abhidharmahṛdaya* was composed before the *Mahāvibhāṣā*. So, also, Erich Frauwallner, *Studies in the Abhidharma Literature and the Origins of Buddhist Philosophical Systems*. English tr. by Sophie Francis Kidd (1995), 152. Yin Shun (*Study*, 472–74), however, shows convincingly that the Chinese narration in this preface in fact indicates that the *Abhidharmahṛdaya* post-dated the *Mahāvibhāṣā*.

9 T28, 812c3–4.

10 T28, 812c6–7.

11 But as Yin Shun (*Study*, 511 *f*) remarks, the *Abhidharmahṛdaya* does not have any real commentary properly so called; partly because its content is too concise, and partly on account of its tendency to deviate from the orthodox doctrinal positions. Accordingly, the "commentators" felt it necessary to revise and supplement its content.

12 For e.g., see Hirakawa, A., *et. al.*, (1973), *Index to the Abhidharmakośabhāṣya, Part One*, p. XXX.

13 T28, 809b10: 若生諸煩惱, 是聖說有漏.

14 T28, 834b14: 若處生煩惱, 是聖說有漏.

15 T28, 871a15: 若增諸煩惱, 是聖說有漏.

16 T28, 963c8–13.

17 Pu Guang, a close pupil of Xuan Zang, is an important commentator on the *Abhidharmakośabhāṣya*. For twenty years, from the very inception (645 C.E.) of the Translation Bureau established with Xuan Zang as the head until Xuan Zang's death in 664 C.E., Pu Guang followed and learned the AKB and other texts from the teacher. In fact, most of Xuan Zang's translations were written down in Chinese by him. Pu Guang wrote the *Notes on the Abhidharmakośabhāṣya* (俱舍論記, T no. 1821) which is a record of the explanations on the text he received from Xuan Zang during the translation process.

18 T41, no. 1821, 55c.

19 AKB, 3.

20 *Cf.* AKB, 300: ...*ity ātmavādapratiṣedhe sampravedayiṣyāmaḥ* |

21 T41, no. 1821, 1b12–24.

22 This phrase in square brackets (likewise below) paraphrases Pu Guang's qualification: "Although [this chapter] also elucidates the principle, this is so stated from the point of view that this is mostly the case or that [the elucidation of the principle] is not its proper concern."

23 T41, no. 1821, 1c10–2a19.

24 T41, 1a15–22.

25 AKB, 460.

26 T41, no. 1822, 458a29–b2.

27 AKB, 8: *ete catvāraḥ svalakṣaṇopādāyarūpadhāraṇād dhātavaś catvāri mahābhūtānīty ucyante* |

28 AKB, 2: *svalakṣaṇa-dhāraṇād dharmaḥ* |

29 AKB, 112.

30 *Cf.* Ny, 747b.

31 Jaini, *op. cit.*, 70: *dhiḥ prajñā dharmasaṃgrahādy-upalakṣaṇa-svabhāvā* |

32 See Dhammajoti, KL (2008), *Entrance into the Supreme Doctrine*, 83.

33 AKB, 12.

34 Vy, 11.

35 T41, 34b6–44c11.

36 AKB, 31: *nirvyāpāraṃ hīdaṃ dharmamātraṃ hetuphalamātraṃ ca* |. For a detailed account and discussion of this controversy, see Dhammajoti, KL (2007). *Abhidharma Doctrines and Controversies on Perception*. 3rd ed. Hong Kong, 51–91.

37 T41, 55c24–56a1.

38 AKB, 38.

39 Vasubandhu also presents the explanation of some other Sarvāstivādin masters; likewise, he does not show any objection (*cf.* AKB, 40). Saṃghabhadra also refutes such a claim (Ny, 397a–b).

40 T28, 811b11–13.

41 MVŚ, 220a–b.

42 AKB, 57.

43 AKB, 54.

44 Ny, 394a–c.

45 See *Study*, 680. – Also *ibid.*, 681: "On questions pertaining to the *citta-caitta*-s, Vasubandhu, the author of the *Abhidharmakośabhāṣya*, is very prudent and discreet; it is more correct to say that Vasubandhu respects the Abhidharma tradition, rather than that he approves of the Sautrāntikas."

46 AKB, 64.

[47] T29, no. 1558, 22c.

[48] Ny, 403c24–404a9: 經主於此, 引異釋言: 由前定心能為遮礙. ... 唯不轉位, 假立為定, 無別實體. ... 若爾, 後心從何而起? 彼說, 此依有根身起; 以有根身與心, 展轉為種子故. 何有此理? 應一切時, 一切境識俱時起故. ... 若執不待自類因緣, 待有根身, 識便起者; 彼一切位, 一切境識, 何法為礙, 起不俱時? 聞有餘師, 起如是見: 執有多識, 一身俱起. 今觀仁者, 似已稟承, 故說此言, 欲符彼執.

[49] *Cf.* AKB, 83–85.

[50] Ny, 419c.

[51] *Cf.* AKB, 91.

[52] AKB, 93.

[53] In chapter one, AKB, 5, "the world" (*loka*) and "existence" (*bhava*) are given as two among the various synonyms for the with-outflow *dharma*-s.

[54] AKB, 112.

[55] T26, 921b.

[56] T26, 507b–c.

[57] T26, 512c.

[58] MVŚ, 121c24–122b17.

[59] AKB, 134 *f.*

[60] MVŚ, 118c; AKB, 133.

[61] Ny, 494b.

[62] *Cf.* AKB, 133: *yady aṅgam aṅgaṃ pañca skandhāḥ kiṃ kāraṇam avidyādīn eva dharmān kīrttayati sma* | ... *avidyāpradhānām avasthām avidyāṃ jagāda saṃskārapradhānāṃ saṃskārān yāvaj jarāmaraṇam ity adoṣaḥ* |

[63] AKB, 133.

Vasubandhu, in showing the difference, gives here: "*tathā āvasthikaḥ kṣaṇikaḥ prākarṣikaḥ sāṃbandhikaḥ sattvākhyo'sattvākhyaś ceti bhedaḥ*". That is, he conveys the sense that both the *sūtra* exposition and the *abhidharma* exposition involve the fourfold perspective (*āvasthika*, etc.). Since he is skeptical about the Vaibhāṣika view that the Buddha's exposition is intended to be *āvasthika*, it seems very probable that Vasubandhu here is giving his own view when he says that the *sūtra* is intentional whereas the *abhidharma* is definitive. This, then, is yet another indication that Vasubandhu cannot be straightforwardly assigned to be a Sautrāntika.

[64] MVŚ, 41b, 106c, 692c.

[65] AKB, 157 *f*, 189: *sattvānāṃ karmajaḥ prabhāva-viśiṣṭo vāyur bījam* |. *Cf.* MVŚ, 691b; Ny, 216b.

[66] MVŚ, 690a *ff.*

[67] AKB, 192.

[68] See Dhammajoti, KL (2008), *Entrance Into the Supreme Doctrine* (2nd edn), 76, 214. Hong Kong.

69 AKB, 202.

70 E.g., *Dharmaskandha*, T26, 503c11–13: "Hostility, and the *vedanā, saṃjñā, saṃskāra*-s conjoined with it, as well as the bodily and vocal *karma*-s and disjoined conditionings originated (*sam-utthita*) [by it], are collectively called the hostility-element (*pratigha-dhātu*)."

71 MVŚ, 610a.

72 MVŚ, 610a.

73 AKB, 205.

74 T29, 82a4: 是說為善. It may be possible that Vasubandhu is here merely stating the Sarvāstivāda-Vaibhāṣika stance — since he does not refute the other alternative explanations in this context. *Cf.* AKB, 230: *niyatam eva tu dṛṣṭadharmādi-vedanīyam aniyatam cathurtham iti varṇayanti*. But, of course, neither does it particularly advocate the Dārṣṭāntika-Sautrāntika explanations.

75 MVŚ, 593b.

76 MVŚ, 593b23.

77 MVŚ, 593b28: 復有餘師 (**apare punar āhuḥ*, **anye ācāryāḥ punar āhuḥ*).

78 MVŚ, 593c6–15.

79 Ny, 570c27–28.

80 Vy, 392: *dārṣṭāntikāḥ sautrāntikāḥ* |

81 The Dārṣṭāntikas in the MVŚ were also Sarvāstivāda masters so that the two ascriptions need not be contradictory. However, it is also to be observed that in this very same context, the MVŚ introduces the specific Dārṣṭāntika theory that all *karma* is transformable.

82 MVŚ, 592a–594a.

83 MVŚ, 593b9–16.

84 E.g., MVŚ, 592a26–27: 諸善惡業要待相續, 或度相續, 方受異熟.

85 MVŚ, 592b1–2: 必無有業, 此剎那造, 則此及次剎那熟義.

86 Ny, 569c.

87 *Cf.* MVŚ, 635a, 636c; AKB, 196, 238.

88 MVŚ, 634c24–26.

89 AKB, 196 *ff.*

90 AKB, 198.

91 Vy, 357: *āśraya āśraya-parāvṛttiḥ* |

92 AKB, 232. Saṃghabhadra (Ny, 572a) does not object here to the mention of the transformed basis, but he himself avoids using that term in his exaplanation.

93 Ny, 535b.

94 Xuan Zang gives here: "But both this [theory of *saṃtati-pariṇāma-viśeṣa*] and that [theory of the *avijñapti*] are difficult to understand. … [We] do not have hatred therein … ." This understanding is supported in the Vy, 357: *tathaivāsaṃjñāyamāna* iti

yathaivāvijñaptir duravabodhā | *tathaiva* saṃtati-pariṇāma-viśeṣo 'pīti | … tatprayoga-nimittaḥ *saṃtati-pariṇāmo bhavatīti bhavati paritoṣo* 'smākam iti vākya-śeṣaḥ |. Pu Guang (T41, 208b16–20) also conveys the same understanding.

95 AKB, 198: *na khalu kaścit pradveṣaḥ | kiṃtu cittānvaya-kāyaprayogeṇa kriyāpari-samāptau tābhyāṃ pṛthagbhūtaṃ dharmāntaraṃ prayojayitur utpadyata iti notpadyate paritoṣaḥ | yatkṛtaprayoga-saṃbhūtā tu kriyāparisamāptis tasyaiva tannimittaḥ saṃtati-pariṇāmo bhavatīti bhavati paritoṣaḥ | cittacaitta-saṃtānāc ca āyatyāṃ phalotpatteḥ |*

96 "使品"; 使 being the older rendering for *anuśaya*. The *Amṛta-rasa* has "結使", which is also likely to have been a rendering for *anuśaya*.

97 AKB, 255.

98 Ny, 641c.

99 AKB, 308.

100 Ny, 641c.

101 AKB, 308; Ny, 641c.

102 Ny, 641c.

103 MVŚ, 257a–b.

104 AKB, 278: *evaṃ tu sādhu yathā sautrāntikānām* |

105 MVŚ, 313a.

106 See Dhammajoti, KL (2007), *Abhidharma Doctrines and Controversies on Perception*, 14–18. Hong Kong.

107 AKB, 280: *ye yaddarśanaheyālambanās te taddarśanaheyā avaśiṣṭā bhāvanāheyāḥ* |

108 For points (i) and (ii), see Ny, 621c10–22, etc.

109 Ny, 409c.

110 Ny, 633a–b, especially, a28–b2.

111 AKB, 298.

112 Ny, 633c24–634a1.

113 I follow here Honjō's emendation given in Odani Nobuchiyo and Honjō Yoshihumi (2007) 俱舍論原典研究 — 隨眠品 (Kyoto), 144, note 46: *yan na … tatrātmakāmenaivaṃ …*

114 AKB, 301.

115 Ny, 634c22–635a1.

116 Ny, 635a2–4.

117 Paramārtha's rendering, "分別聖道果人品", corresponds well with the Sanskrit.

118 T41, 332c7–11.

119 Ny, 659c1–5.

120 AKB, 330: *asty evety ābhidharmikāḥ | eṣa eva nyāyaḥ* |. Vasubandhu's endorsement here is also confirmed by Yaśomitra (Vy, 518).

121 MVŚ, 159b–c, 363c.

122 Ny, 670c28–671a.

123 T26, 375b. *Cf. Dhammapada*, 372. Udv XXXI, 25.

124 定 here seems to be an error for 慧.

125 T26, 375b–c.

126 MVŚ, 148a23–29.

127 Ny, 735c. See also *infra*, Section EG.

128 E.g., T26, 719c14–27: eighty-eight *darśana-heya*, ten *bhāvanā-heya*. T26, 694a14–17: *duḥkha-dharmajñāna-kṣānti*, *duḥkha-anvayajñāna-kṣānti*, etc. T26, 712c3–5: "There are six [kinds of] *dharma*-s: *duḥkhadarśana-heya*, *samudayadarśana-heya*, *nirodhadarśana-heya*, *mārgadarśana-heya*, *bhāvanā-heya*, *aheya*."

129 E.g., T26, 918a27–b9: "In entering into *samyaktva*, one first directly realizes the *duḥkha* pertaining to the sensuality sphere as *duḥkha*, then directly realizes, collectively, the *duḥkha* pertaining to the *rūpa-* and *ārūpya-dhātu* as *duḥkha*...". T26, 940a13–18: "*duḥkha-dharmajñāna-kṣānti*, ... *samudaya-dharma-jñāna*, *duḥkha-anvayajñāna-kṣānti*, ... *mārgadharma-jñāna*, *mārga-anvayajñāna-kṣānti*, ..." T26, 957b26–c1: "What is *duḥkha-jñāna*? That which, with regard to the conditionings, operates with the *ākāra*-s of *duḥkha*, *anitya*, *śūnya*, *anātman*. ... What is *mārga-jñāna*? That which, with regard to the counteracting path of the conditionings, operates with the *ākāra*-s of *mārga*, *nyāya*, *pratipat*, *nairyāṇika*. T26, 930c20–22: "Among the ninety-eight *anuśaya*-s, twenty-eight are *duḥkhadarśana-heya*, nineteen are *samudayadarśana-heya*, nineteen are *nirodha-darśana-heya*, twenty-two are *mārgadarśana-heya*, ten are *bhāvanā-heya*."

130 In any case, it is unlike the claim by Erich Frauwallner and others that the *abhisamaya* doctrine was innovated in Dharmaśrī's *Abhidharmahṛdaya*. See Erich Frauwallner, *op. cit.*, 153 *ff*.

131 MVŚ, 175a25–b2. See *Nidāna-saṃyutta*, 10.

132 T49, 15c; but also *cf.* T49, 16a. Also according to Pu Guang, T41, 351c.

133 Vy, 542.

134 MVŚ, 533a.

135 *Cf.* **Catuḥsatya-śāstra* 四諦論, T32, 378a, 379a.

136 Ny, 684b21–24.

137 See also, *Study*, 567 *f*.

138 Ny, 684a24–26.

139 See AKB, 321:

sarveṣāṃ hi kleśānāṃ
sakṛt kṣayaḥ
yasya yaḥ prahāṇa-mārgas tenaiva tasya kṣayaḥ |
visaṃyoga-lābhas teṣāṃ punaḥ punaḥ |

140 T49, 15c; T41, 375a.

141 MVŚ, 312b.

142 AKB, 375.

143 Vy, 650: *sarva-samādhi-samāpatty-āvaraṇa-prahāṇam* ity ubhayato-bhāga-vimukteḥ |

144 Ny, 724b.

145 Ny, 735a25–28.

146 AKB, 391.

147 See MVŚ, 547c6–10.

148 MVŚ, 490c–491a.

149 MVŚ, 744a18–20.

150 T26, 957b19.

151 Vasubandhu explains this as *tad-anvayāt* (AKB, 350), and Yaśomitra (Vy, 542) says this means: "it has [the *dharmajñāna*] for its cause": *taddhetukatvād ity arthaḥ*. See also *infra*, summary on chapter six.

152 Ny, 736c7–17.

153 AKB, 394.

154 MVŚ, 175b2–8

155 MVŚ, 217b12–16.

156 AKB, 401: *evaṃ tu yuktaṃ syāt* …|. Yaśomitra (Vy, 629) comments: *evaṃ tu yuktaṃ syād iti sautrāntika-matam* |

157 Ny, 741b. In brief: "The term *ākāra* is a synonym of *prajñā*. The term *ākārayati* is a synonym for the grasping of an object (*viṣaya-grahaṇa*); this word *ākārayati* does not exclusively denote *prajñā*. The term *ākāryate* applies to all *dharma*-s." (*loc. cit.*)

158 Vy, 5.

159 AKB, 416.

160 Ny, 724b.

161 AKB, 437 *f*, 442.

162 Including *dvaya-dvaya-samāpatti* referring to sexual copulation, MVŚ, 539a.

163 不動明, **aninjyā prabhā* (?). This must be the same as the "immovable quiescent *samādhi*" 不動寂靜定, MVŚ, 1024a2.

164 MVŚ, 821b19–c1.

165 MVŚ, 539a.

166 MVŚ, 821c.

167 Not "absorption", "ecstasy", "trance", etc.

168 AKB, 433.

169 Xuan Zang's tr. of *dhyāna* as 靜慮 ("quiescence-contemplation") reflects these two senses.

170 MVŚ, 412a.

171 *Majjhima*, iii.252.

172 *Gopaka-moggallāna-sutta*, *Majjhima*, iii.13 *f*.

173 MVŚ, 881b.

174 MVŚ, 417c–418a.

175 Ny, 766c15–17.

176 Ny, 773b–c.

177 MVŚ, 727a23–24.

178 MVŚ, 440b24–c9.

179 AKB, 243.

180 AKB, 300.

181 Vy, 405.

182 Vy, 476.

183 T26, 4c12–17.

184 AKB, 471.

185 AKB, 472.

186 AKB, 476.

187 T26, 545b24–c18. MVŚ, 596b3–7, cites this.

188 AKB, 461: *naiva hi dravyato 'sti nāpi prajñaptitaḥ* | … *ādhyātmikān upāttān varttamānān skandhān upādāya pudgalaḥ prajñapyate* |

189 Yin Shun, *Study*, 458 *f*, shows that this is a Vātsīputrīya text, and its notion of the 受施設 (**upātta-prajñapti*), etc., represents this doctrine.

190 That 受 here translates *upātta* is suggested by the following elaboration: 於中受者: 陰界入二種自受他受. 不受者: 草木牆壁比。於中若他受、若不受者, 是當知不受: "Herein, appropriated (受) refers to being appropriated by oneself or by others. The non-appropriated is such as vegetation, the wall, etc. Among them, that appropriated by others and that which is not appropriated is to be known as 'non-appropriated' (*anupātta*)".

191 T25, no. 1506, 24b2–3: 受施設者: 眾生已受陰界入, 計一及餘.

192 T25, 24b5–8.

193 AKB, 475.

194 Vy, 715.

195 T4, 449a26–27.

196 AKB, 477.

197 Vy, 712. But according to Pu Guang, T41, 448a26–27, this is the Sāṃkhya.

198 AKB, 473.

199 AKB, 473.

Preface to the 1971 edition of "*L'Abhidharmakośa de Vasubandhu*"

by Étienne Lamotte

The *Abhidharmakośa* or *The Treasury of Scholasticism* is an exposition of Buddhist scholasticism as the Vaibhāṣika school of Kaśmir taught it at the beginning of our era. The work was composed by the Indian master Vasubandhu some time around the fifth century. It consists of two parts:

1. the *Karikās*, "memorial verses", where the author impartially sets forth the *orthodox* system of the school;
2. the *Bhāṣya*, "commentary" in prose, inserted between each verse, where the same author explains the *Kārikās* almost word for word, states and criticizes the opinions of other Buddhist schools and finally gives his own personal opinion which often departs from the Vaibhāṣika interpretation.

From its publication onward, the *Abhidharmakośa* was very successful, not only in India but in all of the Far East, where it is universally considered to be the indispensable basis for all Buddhist studies. It was the object of many translations into Chinese, Tibetan, and Uigur and gave its name to the *Kiu-chö* school, which saw the light of day in China at the end of the sixth century, and to the *Kusha* school, officially recognized in Japan in 793. Even in our times, the *Abhidharmakośa* is taught in all the great Japanese universities.

In the West, the importance of this work was recognized towards the middle of the nineteenth century. Eugène Burnouf comments that its author, Vasubandhu, was rightly held to be the "Sage similar to a second Buddha". Nevertheless, western Indologists hesitated for a long time to undertake the study of a text the technical nature of which presented insurmountable difficulties for them. Moreover, the original Indian text being lost, the work could be approached only by means of the Chinese and Tibetan translations.

Louis de La Vallée Poussin, who towered masterfully over the major Buddhist languages—Pāli, Sanskrit, Chinese and Tibetan—dedicated the last half of his life to a French translation of the *Abhidharmakośa*, the anastatic reproduction of which will be found here. The work, which was published between 1923 and 1931, consists of six volumes:

- Vol. I (chapters 1 and 2)
- Vol. II (chapter 3)
- Vol. III (chapter 4)
- Vol. IV (chapters 5 and 6)
- Vol. V (chapters 7, 8 and 9)
- Vol. VI (introduction, index, and addenda)

The French version relies on the following sources:

1. The original Sanskrit text of the *Kārikā*s for the first three chapters and the beginning of the fourth chapter.
2. The two Chinese translations of the *Kārikās* and the *Bhāṣya* made by Paramārtha between 563 and 567 (Taishō edition, no. 1559) and by Hiuan-tsang between 651 and 654 (Taishō edition, no. 1558), respectively.
3. A Tibetan translation of the *Kārikās* and the *Bhāṣya* made at the beginning of the ninth century by Jinamitra and Dpal-brtsegs.
4. The *Sphuṭārthā Abhidharmakośavyākhyā, Exegesis of Clear Meaning of the Abhidharmakośa*. This refers to an exegetical treatise in Sanskrit composed in the seventh century by the Indian master Yaśomitra. It is a treasure-mine of precious information, but in no way does it constitute an uninterrupted commentary: "By itself it is a very inefficient tool for the study of the *Abhidharmakośa*." Louis de La Vallée Poussin knew it from copies of the manuscript, but the work was published later in 1933–1936 by Unrai Wogihara (Publishing Association of Abhidharmakośavyākhyā, Tokyo).

It was in this way, using indirect sources, that the Belgian scholar undertook the study of an intrinsically difficult text. Actually, Vasubandhu—the author of the *Abhidharmakośa*—called upon Indian and Buddhist concepts familiar to him, but which are and remain foreign to the western world's way of thinking. These ideas are expressed in technical terms with very precise meaning that, however, have no exact equivalents in the western philosophical vocabulary.

In order to make this text understandable without thereby misrepresenting the Indian mind, Louis de La Vallée Poussin had recourse to a skillful stratagem. Although French in terms of syntax, his translation is Indian in terms of vocabulary, in the sense that the technical terms are retained in their original Sanskrit form. Disconcerting as this may be for the uninitiated reader, this method proves to be the one most valuable to the specialists, for it alone, in its specificity and its subtleties, allows one to grasp the Buddhist mind.[1]

Some have wished to see in it an easy method, but this criticism has no basis. Indeed, as soon as a new technical term comes up in the exposition, Louis de La Vallée Poussin proposes a French equivalent, an equivalent that, although it does not exhaust the Indian notion in its comprehension and its extension, gives at the very least a close idea of it. This being done, the Belgian scholar subsequently keeps the Indian original term. More than anyone else, he has contributed to establishing the

---

[1] *Lodrö Sangpo* (*LS*): To also accommodate the "uninitiated reader", in most cases I will translate the Sanskrit technical terms but also maintain them in brackets.

French vocabulary of Buddhist philosophy and, with the exception of slight modifications, this is the vocabulary that the majority of translators are now using.

In his *Abhidharmakośa*, Vasubandhu continually appeals to the canonical and post-canonical scriptures, namely, the doctrinal teachings of the Buddha, codes of religious discipline, scholastic manuals, collections of stories and legends, great treatises of philosophy, in short, a literature stretching over almost ten centuries. But according to the custom of the times, Vasubandhu refers to these sources without giving precise references. In the many notes added onto his translation, Louis de La Vallée Poussin has succeeded in identifying almost all. This precision in information somehow doubles the value of Vasubandhu's work and makes the French translation of the *Abhidharmakośa* the most instructive book of early Buddhism (Small Vehicle).

While Louis de La Vallée Poussin was working in this way on what was to be the great work of his life, he held as irremediably lost the Sanskrit text of the *Abhidharmakośa*. But in 1935, three years before the death of the Belgian scholar, Rāhula Sāṃkṛtyāyana discovered the text in question in the Tibetan monastery of Ngor. As far as I know, this refers to a manuscript in Nāgarī characters dating from the twelfth to thirteenth centuries approximately. Louis de La Vallée Poussin had no awareness of this sensational discovery that certainly would have filled him with joy. The second World War and the troubles it brought about slowed the publication of the manuscript until recently. The *Text of the Abhidharmakośakārikā of Vasubandhu* was published by V.V. Gokhale in the Journal of the Bombay Branch, Royal Asiatic Society, XXII, 1946, pp. 73–102; the complete text of the *Abhidharmakośa* (*Kārikās* and *Bhāṣya*) was published by P. Pradhan in the Jayaswal Research Institute of Patna, 1967.

I was not surprised to notice that the French translation of Louis de La Vallée Poussin, based mainly on the Chinese version of Hiuan-tsang, adhered literally to the original Indian text. The honor of such an exceptional success must be given both to the Chinese master of the seventh century and the Belgian master of the twentieth century who, on different accounts but with the same talent, labored hard to render Vasubandhu's mind faithfully.

I will go even further. By its conciseness and abstractness, an Indian philosophical text demands from its reader an effort of sustained attention and, in order to be understood in all its nuances, must be reread several times. The inconvenience, if there be any inconvenience, disappears in the French version as well as in the Chinese translation, which, by their analytical nature, can be more directly assimilated.

This is why the *Abhidharmakośa* of Vasubandhu and its French translation by Louis de La Vallée Poussin are today inseparably united for the greatest benefit to Buddhist studies.

But now it is more than thirty years that the French translation has been out of print and if we do not wish to lose one of the finest jewels of Belgian Sinology, its new edition is needed most urgently.

Desirous of paying a last tribute to the memory of Louis de La Vallée Poussin who at one time was its finest collaborator, the Institut Belge des Hautes Études Chinoises has been very happy to take on this task. Our gratitude is especially addressed to his distinguished president, M. Henri Lavachery who, by this happy initiative, adds a new kind deed to the innumerable services he had rendered to science as professor in the Université Libre of Brussels, chief conservator of the Musées Royaux d'Art et d'Histoire, permanent secretary of the Académie Royale de Belgique and general secretary of the Union Académique Internationale.

With a dedication both efficient and discreet, MM. Hubert Durt and Marcel Van Velthem, librarians at the Institut, have successfully carried out the multiple procedures involved in the realization of the project.

The relatives of M. Louis de La Vallée Poussin have enthusiastically welcomed the initiative of the Institut and authorized, completely free of charge, the reproduction of this work. This gesture of rare elegance is within the lineage of the illustrious scholar who devoted his entire life to science.

Bibliographical Addendum

by Hubert Durt

Here we will note only the editions of texts and works relative to the *Abhidharmakośa* that have been published subsequent to the first publication of the present work (1923–1931).

SANSKRIT:

V.V. Gokhale, "The Text of the Abhidharmakośakārikā of Vasubandhu". *Journal of the Bombay Branch of the Royal Asiatic Society*, N.S., Vol. 22, 1946, pp. 73–102.

P. Pradhan, *Abhidharmakośabhāṣya of Vasubandhu.* 2d ed. Tibetan Sanskrit Works Series 8. Patna: Kashi Prasad Jayaswal Research Institute, 1975.

Swami Dwarikadas Shastri, *Abhidharmakośa & Bhāṣya of Acharya Vasubandhu with Sphuṭārthā Commentary of Ācārya Yaśomitra*, Part I (I and II *Kośasthāṇa*), critically edited, Bauddha Bharati, Varanasi, 1970.

Unrai Wogihara, *Sphuṭārthā Abhidharmakośavyākhyā*, 2 vols., Tokyo, 1933–1936. Anastatic reproduction, Tōkyō, 1971.

TIBETAN:

Otani University, *The Tibetan Tripiṭaka*, Peking edition, vol. 115 (no. 5590) to vol. 119 (no. 5597). Suzuki Research Foundation, Tokyo, 1962.

CHINESE:

J. Takakusu, K. Watanabe, *The Tripiṭaka in Chinese*, vol. 29 (no. 1558–1563). The Taishō Issai-kyō kanko kwai, Tōkyō, 1926.

Otani University, *Index to the Taishō Tripiṭaka*, no. 16, Bidon-bu III (vol. 29). Research Association for the Terminology of the Taishō Tripiṭaka, Tōkyō, 1962.

S. and I. Funahashi, *Kandō Abidatsuma Kusharon Sakuin*, Kyōto, 1956. (This index is based on the Chinese version used by Louis de La Vallée Poussin; Kyokuga Saeki, Kandō Kusharon, 30 vols., Kyōto, 1887).

Preface

by

Louis de La Vallée Poussin

1. By the kind generosity of Sylvain Lévi, this sixth and last volume of the *Kośa* is enriched by the text of the *kārikā*s of the first three chapters according to a Nepalese manuscript of the thirteenth to fourteenth centuries. For the *kārikā*s of the other chapters, fragments of which appear in the *Vyākhyā* or which can be safely restored, see the notes to the translation. The Tibetan text of the *kārikā*s of the third chapter are mentioned in *Cosmologie bouddhique*.

2. Four indexes have been created:

   i. a general index;
   ii. *gāthā*s or *kārikā*s cited in the text or in the notes;
   iii. the first words of the citations of *sūtra*s or *śāstra*s;
   iv. names, scholars, sects, books, Sūtras, Abhidharma.

The words Meru, Jambudvīpa, Trāyastriṃśas, etc., are placed in the general index.[2]

3. The *Additions and Corrections*[3] contain the notes that I marked haphazardly in my working copy. I have not undertaken either the accumulation of a complete documentation, clearly impossible, or a conscientious revision of the translation.

4. The *Introduction* does not contain everything that I wanted to put in it.

a. It lacks the summary of the doctrines of the *Kośa*. The recent study by René Grousset, *Analyse de l'Abhidharmakośaśāstra*,[4] can favorably substitute for what I might have written. Besides, I had started to examine various problems of general interest which the *Kośa* clarifies: *Nirvāṇa* (1925), *Morale bouddhique* (1927), *Dogme et philosophie du Bouddhisme* (1930). I plan a *Chemin de Nirvāṇa* (*Kośa*,

---

[2] Royal names and the huge numbers in the third chapter, which are cited in the Index of *Cosmologie bouddhique*, have been omitted. The *Vyākhyā* has not been studied systematically.

[3] *LS*: Since I have incorporated most of the additions and corrections into the footnotes of the translation, they have not been translated separately.

[4] In *Philosophies indiennes* (1931), i, pp. 153–99 [*LS*: See *Electronic Appendix*]. In the same work, vol. ii, pp. 10–130 and 404–14, there is an analysis of the large treatises and the important questions of the Vijñānavāda. – Sometimes biased, but evidence of a serious attempt at interpretation, see the works of Stcherbatski and Rosenberg, cited below in the *Introduction*, p. xvii.

chap. v–viii) and a *Histoire de l'Abhidharma* (Sūtras; *Kośa*; *Siddhi*) which will explain what the Sarvāstivāda added to the early Abhidhamma.[5]

The materials gathered together for the study of some points, either important or difficult, make up a very considerable amount. They are in the course of publication under the title *Documents d'Abhidharma*. The first part, on the Asaṃskṛtas (according to the *Vibhāṣā* and Saṃghabhadra), is published in the *Bulletin de l'École Française d'Extrême-Orient*. It will be followed by notes on the authenticity of the Scriptures and the sacred nature of the Abhidharma; the doctrine of the refuges and the purity of the body of the perfected being (*arhat*); the controversy on time, the moment and the atom; the two, the four and the three truths; the possessions (*prāpti*) and the traces (*vāsanā*); the Dārṣṭāntikas-Sautrāntikas; the Yogasūtras and the Abhidharma.

b. One will find here [in my *Introduction*], along with the bibliography of the *Kośa*, only the beginnings of a study on Vasubandhu's sources[6]:

A. Annotated edition of the comments that appear in the foreword to *Cosmologie bouddhique* (1913): the place of the Abhidharma in the old literature of Buddhism, the place of the *Kośa* in the Abhidharma literature; pp. vi–xvi
B. Bibliography of the *Kośa* and its commentaries, European sources, Sanskrit sources, etc.; pp. xvii–xxiii
C. The question of the date of Vasubandhu; pp. xxv–xxviii
D. The seven canonical treatises of the Abhidharma; pp. xxix–xlii

---

[5] The historic relationships of orthodox or Brahmanic philosophy and Buddhist philosophy are not clear. But it is easy to see (1) that the Sarvāstivādin theory of the homogenous character (*sabhāgatā*), if not merged with the Vaiśeṣika theory, resembles it greatly (AKB ii, F 198); (2) that the thesis of the *word manifested by the voice* has a Mīmāṃsa air; (3) that Dharmatrāta's explanation of *all exists* has similarities to the Sāṃkhya (v, F 53).

I think I have shown that the Yogasūtras depend upon the Sarvāstivāda (*Ac. de Belgique*, Nov. 1922: 520–26); but who would claim that Buddhist Yoga has not been influenced by Brahmanic Yoga? (See the note on Nirvāṇa in *Mélanges Raymonde Linossier*, 1931).

[6] AKB iv, F 189, cites the *Saundarananda* of Aśvaghoṣa, which the *Vyākhyā*, in turn, cites several times. Aśvaghoṣa's poem should be mentioned among the works that depend closely on the Abhidharma. The spiritual progress of Nanda, for example, is described with technical precision. – Verse xiii, 44 (which is reminiscent of *Sumaṅgalavilāsinī*, i, 12) is Nāgārjunian by changing the last *pāda*: *bhūtadarśī vimucyate*; see *Index of kārikās*

The study of the *Vibhāṣā*, facilitated particularly by the references of Saeki Kiokuga (ed. of the *Kośa*), and the study of the old Abhidharma treatises show clearly all that Vasubandhu owes to the Sarvāstivādin sources: Vasubandhu speaks the truth when he says that this book is an explanation of the doctrines of the Vaibhāṣikas of Kaśmīr; the *Kośa* is, by definition, a judicious and well-ordered analysis of the *Vibhāṣā*. But the *Kośa*, as we know, is also the refutation of several essential doctrines of the *Vibhāṣā*. Vasubandhu, who the orthodox Vaibhāṣika Saṃghabhadra calls "the Sautrāntika", sets the view of the Sautrāntikas or his own views against the views of the Sarvāstivādin-Vaibhāṣikas: here we have very little information on the sources that he uses; he makes use of data foreign to and undoubtedly later than the *Vibhāṣā*, the Darṣṭāntikas–Bhadanta–Dharmatrāta cited by the *Vibhāṣā*. We will see more clearly when we have read Saṃghabhadra who gathers information on Śrīlāta, who must be one of the Sautrāntika sources of Vasubandhu.[7]

My task is to offer to my colleagues the information—such as it is and in all its simplicity—that I have available. The *Kośa* and the Abhidharma remind one of the definition the poet gave of the boar, *animal propter convivia natum* ("an animal created for conviviality"). Concerted and numerous efforts are required to sort out, if not the theories—too free of metaphysics, more complicated than profound—then at least the history of the theories and books.

---

7 Another authority of Vasubandhu is the Vasumitra who is the author of the *Paripṛcchāśāstra*; see *Index* s.v. Sautrāntika. I have not found any information on the *Netrīpadaśāstra*, ii, 205.

Introduction

by

Louis de La Vallée Poussin

A. The three baskets (*piṭaka*) & the *Abhidharmakośabhāṣya* 80
AA. The two baskets of the Vinaya and Dharma & the first Mātṛkās 80
AB. The Pāli school & the third basket of the Abhidhamma 81
AC. The school of the Sarvāstivādins and Vaibhāṣikas & the *Jñānaprasthāna* and its six feet, and the *Vibhāṣā* 83
AD. The school of the Sautrāntikas & the *Abhidharmakośa* and *Bhāṣya* 85
ADA. The importance of the *Abhidharmakośa* and its *Bhāṣya* for the study of canonical philosophy and scholasticism 86
ADB. Why the study of the *Abhidharmakośa* and its *Bhāṣya* was deferred for so long 89
B. Bibliography of the *Kośa* 91
C. The question of the date of Vasubandhu. – Vasubandhu-the-Ancient 97
CA. Bibliography related to the date of Vasubandhu 97
CB. The dating of Vasubandhu in dependence on the date of Asaṅga and the question of the historicity of Maitreyanātha 98
CC. Difficulties regarding the biography of Vasubandhu, the expression *pūrvācārya*, etc. 99
CD. Vasubandhu-the-Ancient 100
D. The seven canonical treatises of the Abhidharma 102
DA. *Jñānaprasthāna* 102
DB. *Prakaraṇa* of Vasumitra 106
DC. *Vijñānakāya* 107
DD. *Dharmaskandha* 111
DE. *Prajñāptiśāstra* 111
DF. *Dhātukāya* 115
DG. *Saṃgītiparyāya* 116
E. Some masters of the *Vibhāṣā* 118
EA. Vasumitra 119
EB. Ghoṣaka and the *Abhidharmāmṛtaśāstra* 121
EC. Buddhadeva 123
ED. Dharmatrāta 124
EE. Bhadanta, Dharmatrāta 125
F. Some schools of the *Vibhāṣā* 130
FA. Dārṣṭāntikas and Sautrāntikas 130
FB. Vibhajyavādins 134
FC. Yogācāras 138
G. The Śāriputrābhidharma 140
GA. Dharmadhātu 141
GB. Nirodhasatya 141
H. The *Abhidharmasāra* 143
HA. Obstructions, AKB iv, F 201–12; *Vibhāṣā*, 115, p. 599 146
HB. Non-informative action (*avijñapti*), AKB iv, F 4, 14 147

A. *THE THREE BASKETS (PIṬAKA) & THE ABHIDHARMAKOŚA-BHĀṢYA*[8]

AA. *The two baskets of the Vinaya and Dharma & the first Mātṛkās*

The oldest literature of Buddhism is divided into two parts or baskets:

1. Vinaya: the rule and procedures of monastic discipline, history of and commentary on the discipline;
2. Dharma:[9] since then called Sūtra, the collection of discourses that explain the Dharma, that is to say, all that directly or indirectly concerns the path of salvation: to some extent the moral law, incapable though it may be of definitively releasing from unsatisfactoriness; but above all the Eightfold Noble Path, the methods of contemplation and of meditation that lead to the definitive release from unsatisfactoriness, i.e., to *nirvāṇa*: this is the essential thing, for *the sole flavor of the True Doctrine is the flavor of release.*

The Sūtra or Dharma cannot be practiced exclusively. Greed (*lobha*) and hatred (*dveṣa*) are combated effectively only by destroying delusion (*moha*); the most humble moral law implies right view (*samyagdṛṣṭi*), right view concerning life after death and ripening of action. All the more so, the elimination of defilements and their most subtle traces, indispensable for the liberation from the cycle of transmigrations, implies penetrating insight into the nature of phenomena, into their accidental and transient characteristics. The *sūtras* always contained, one may believe, much psychology or ontology.[10] When catechesis, {i.e., oral instruction by the method of question and answer,} developed, <vii> numerous "discourses of the Buddha" that are enumerations, endowed with glosses, of

---

[8] [This first section, pp. vi–xvi, formed originally the main section of the Foreword to "Cosmologie bouddhique",] printed 1913, published 1919, Mémoires in-4° de l'Académie royale de Belgique (Luzac, London), which contains the reconstruction of the verses (*kārikā*) of the third chapter of the *Kośa*, the Tibetan *kārikās*, the version of the *Bhāṣya*, the text of the *Vyākhyā*: in the appendix, the summary of the *Lokaprajñāpti* and of the *Kāraṇaprajñāpti*.

Lodrö Sangpo (LS): Besides a few additions and corrections that were added by LVP in square brackets, the Foreword is reproduced nearly unchanged.

[9] *Cullavagga*, XI, 1, 8. – [For a more exact exposition, J. Przyluski, *Concile de Rājagṛha*, pp. 341, 345, 349.]

[10] Oldenberg, *Buddha*..., 6th ed. p. 202; transl. Foucher, 2nd ed. p. 177. – [Psychology, yes; but ontology is doubtful.]

technical terms were edited. This is what an old tradition calls *mātṛkās* or indices.[11] The *Aṅguttara*[12] and the *Dīgha* 33–34, where the categories are classified according to the increasing number of terms, have conserved for us an early type of this literature. [One of the most notable *mātṛkās* is the *Saṃgītisuttanta*. The Pāli canon considers it a *sūtra*, which it places in the *Dīgha*. Under the name of *Saṃgītiparyāya*, this *mātṛkā* ranks among the seven canonical Abhidharmas of the Sarvāstivāda.][13]

The Pāli school & the third basket of the Abhidhamma

A very famous school, perhaps the first to constitute the standardized baskets of Vinaya and of Sūtra, the Pāli school, was also the first to compile a third basket. Whereas the first catechisms had been incorporated into the Sūtra, to the new and more systematic catechisms the name of *Abhidharma* was given, a term that designated a special manner of expounding the Dharma, and their authenticity was asserted, if not historically at least doctrinally, by grouping them in one *basket* on an equal footing with the baskets of Vinaya and Sūtra. <viii> [For a discussion concerning the authenticity of the *Abhidhammapiṭaka*, see, for example, *Atthasālinī*, p. 35.]

---

11 M. Kern (*Manual*, p. 3) thinks that in the *Divya*, i.e., a Sarvāstivādin work where we find the expressions *sūtrasya vinayasya mātṛkāyāh*: "the monks ask about the Sūtra, the Vinaya, the Mātṛkā" (p. 18, 15), and *sūtraṃ mātṛkā ca*, equivalent to *āgama-catuṣṭayam* (p. 333, 7), the term *mātrīkā* is used "as synonymous with *abhidharma*". It cannot, however, refer to the Abhidharmas of the Sarvāstivādins of which we shall speak below on p. x, which are treatises; it fits the Abhidhammas a little less poorly, without being satisfactory. Does it designate lists "omitting all the explanations and other details" (Childers, 243), tables of contents which belong to the Āgama (Scripture) and are not specifically Abhidharma? The Sautrāntikas, who deny the existence of a basket of the Abhidharma as distinct from Sūtra, certainly had *indices*, just like the Sarvāstivādins of the period (previous to the Abhidharmas) to which we date the expressions of the *Divya*. – Does it designate the expositions, in the manner of the *sūtras*, as those that constitute the *mātikās* of the *Vibhaṅga*? In this book, whatever is peculiar to the Abhidharma is often a type of commentary in the form of glosses.

12 See the article of Rhys Davids in Hastings' *Encyclopedia*.

13 [Development of the Abhidharma, *Dogme et philosophie*, p. 123; J. Przyluski, *Concile*, third chapter and 179, 353, *Açoka*, 322, *Funérailles*, 49; Lévi, *Seize Arhats*, 20, 39.]

Mrs. Rhys Davids says:

> Let it, then, be clearly understood that our present knowledge of such philosophy as is revealed in the Buddhist Pāli canon would be practically undiminished if the whole of the Abhidhamma *piṭaka* were non-existent... . The burden, then, of Abhidhamma is not any positive contribution to the philosophy of early Buddhism, but analytic and logical and methodological elaboration of what is already given... . The chief methods of that [Abhidhamma] training were:
>
> - first, the definition and determination of all names or terms entering into the Buddhist scheme of culture;
> - secondly, the enunciation of all doctrines, theoretical and practical, as formulas, with co-ordination of all such as were logically interrelated; and
> - finally, practice in reducing all possible heterodox positions to an absurdity... .[14]

Nevertheless, as an example will make clear, the word Abhidharma took on a higher scope: the ban on drinking intoxicating liquor is a precept of the Vinaya; but to examine whether the transgression of drinking intoxicating liquor is a transgression by nature or a transgression of disobedience is to create a pure theory about the Vinaya; it is *to refine the Vinaya*, this is called the Abhivinaya. In the same way, the Abhidharma does not remain foreign to scientific and philosophical research; it embraces questions the relationships of which with the Dharma proper are rather loose. This tendency is very pronounced in the most recent of the Pāli treatises of the Abhidharma, the *Kathāvatthu* (*Points of Controversy*), which tradition dates back to the council of Aśoka.[15] This is a book on heresies [or controversial issues] that lays down the [diverse] positions very clearly in regards to a mass of purely speculative issues: the long work of exegesis of which the Sūtra has been the object may be noticed here.

---

[14] In Hastings' *Encyclopedia*, I, 19f. [*LS*: This is not a direct translation from the French. I have replaced it with the original English text.] – Winternitz, *Geschichte*, 134. – Scholastic definitions of the Abhidharma: *Atthasālinī*, 48–50 and following; *Sūtrālaṃkāra*, XI, 3.

[15] Tradition knows, however, that the author of the *Kathāvatthu* foresaw and refuted in advance the future heresies; see *Atthakathā*, pp. 6–7. – The remark is by Minayef and the observations of H. Oldenberg (*Buddh. Studien*, pp. 633, 676) do not prove that the *Kathāvatthu* has not been amplified in the course of time.

The Pāli Abhidharmas do not belong to the early patrimony common to all the sects—which does not mean that they are Singhalese! Whereas any surveys made in the purely Indian Buddhist canonical literature show us Vinayas and Sūtras dependent on Pāli literature or closely related to that literature, nothing there indicates the presence of *replicas* of Pāli Abhidhammas in them.[16] <ix>

Moreover, according to the tradition itself, the *Kathāvatthu* belongs solely to a certain philosophical school, the Vibhajjavādins, *those who distinguish*.[17] To the old question discussed in the *sūtras*: "Does everything exist?",[18] these philosophers answered by distinguishing (*vibhajya*):

> The present and the past that has not yet given forth its effect, exist; the future and the past that has given forth its effect, do not exist.[19]

The school of the Sarvāstivādins and Vaibhāṣikas & the Jñānaprasthāna and its six feet, and the Vibhāṣā

Opposed to this school—presumably from early times—was the school of *All exists*, *sarvāstivāda*, Sarvāstivādins, Sabbatthivādins. This school, which also was a sect endowed with a special Vinaya and its own canon, and which was sanskritized,[20] also

---

16 [*LVP*: This is not correct. The *Saṃgītiparyāya* is just the *Saṃgītisuttanta*. The second part of the *Dhātukāya* has close relations with the *Dhātukathāprakaraṇa*. A careful study will show other points of contact and it may be seen that the Sarvāstivādins have simply enriched the early material of the Abhidhamma by their inventions (theory of the *viprayuktas*, i.e., the formations dissociated from thought, of the *mahābhūtas*, i.e., the generally permeating mental factors, etc.).]

17 The account of Buddhaghosa, *Kathāvatthu-Atthakathā*, p. 6, is valid at least in that the Vibhajjavādins are the orthodox.

18 This is one of the aspects of the problem of *kiriyavāda*.

LS: PTS: *kiriyavāda*: promulgating the (view of a) consequence of action, believing in merit and demerit, usually combined with *kammavāda*.

19 This definition of the two [?] schools is borrowed from the *Abhidharmakośa*, v. 25; see *Kathāvatthu*, I, 8 (which does not entirely confirm our interpretation). ["La controverse du temps et du pudgala dans le Vijñānakāya", *Études Asiatiques*, 1925.]

20 [*LVP*: Geography of the Sarāvastivādin sect, J. Przyluski, *Açoka*.]

I know that the sinologists, notably Takakusu, are not sure about the language in which the first of the Abhidharmas of the Sarvāstivādins, the *Jñānaprasthāna*, was written:

looked closely into the Dharma. <x> Besides the *casuists*,[21] i.e., the Vinayadharas, this school had *philosophers*, i.e., the Ābhidhārmikas. [Its Devaśarman, follower of the existence of past–future, opposed Mo-lien or Moggaliputta.] Long labor, on which we have little information,[22] led to the redaction of numerous works, among which are the seven books of the Abhidharma, Treatises (*śāstra*) or Works (*prakaraṇa*): the *Jñānaprasthāna* and its six *feet* (*pāda*), i.e., *Dharmaskandha*, etc. [see below].

> In what language, however, the original text was composed we have no means of ascertaining. All we can say is that the text brought by Saṃghadeva and Dhammapiya [Dharmapriya] from Kaçmīra [A.D. 383] seems to have been in a dialect akin to Pāli, whereas the text used by Hsüan-tsang [A.D. 657], as in other cases, seems to have been in Sanskrit. But this supposition rests solely on the phonetic value of Chinese ideographs employed in these translations, and is not corroborated by any other evidence... . It seems to me more than probable that the *Jñānaprasthāna* at least was written in some dialect: one thinks naturally of the dialect of Kaçmīra, but we really have no certainty that the *Jñānaprasthāna* was not composed in Kosala (*JPTS*, 1905, pp. 84, 86).

We possess a fragmentary quotation of the Sarvāstivādin Prātimokṣa which proves that the old forms, Pāli or dialect, remained in use: "In the Poṣadha ceremony, when the Vinayadhara asks: 'Are you pure?' (*bhikṣupoṣadhe hi kacci ttha pariśuddhā iti vinayadhareṇānuśrāvite*), if any Bhikṣu does not confess his transgression..." (*Abhidharmakośavyākhyā ad* IV, 75; compare the introduction of the Pātimokkha and the remarks of Rhys Davids, *Dialogues*, II, p. 257). [See L. Finot, "Prātimokṣasūtra des Sarvāstivādins", *JA*, 1913, 2, pp. 477–79.]

But we possess a fragment of the *Jñānaprasthāna*, cited in the *Abhidharmakośavyākhyā* (ad i, 46): *katamad buddhavacanaṃ tathāgatasya yā vāg vacanaṃ vyavahāro gīr niruktir vākpatho vāgghoṣo vākkarma vāgvijñaptiḥ* ‖ *buddhavacanaṃ kuśalaṃ vaktavyam athāvyakṛtaṃ vaktavyam* | *syāt kuśalaṃ syād avyākṛtam* ‖ *katarat kuśalam* | *kuśalacittasya tathāgatasya vācaṃ bhāṣamāṇasya yā* [*vāg*]*vijñaptiḥ* ‖ *katarad avyākṛtam* | ...*pūrvavat* ‖ *punas tatraiva–anantaram uktam* | *buddhavacanaṃ ka eṣa dharmaḥ* | *nāmakāyapadakāyavyañjana-kāyānāṃ yānupūrvavacanā anupūrvasthāpanā anupūrvasamāyoga iti* |

[21] *LS*: Webster Deluxe Unabridged Dictionary (Second Edition): Casuist: one who studies and resolves questions of right and wrong in conduct.

[22] [*LVP*: The invention of the possessions (*prāpti*); the group homogeneity (*sabhāgatā*); the existence of past and future factors; the different types of cause; the cessation not due to deliberation (*apratisaṃkhyānirodha*); not to speak of the stages conducive to penetration (*nirvedhabhāgīya*), etc.]

There were philosophers who held themselves to this first layer of scholarly literature.[23] But the speculative work continued and, toward the end of the first century of our era (Council of Kaniṣka),[24] a commentary was written on the *Jñāna-prasthāna*, the *Vibhāṣā*,[25] a collective work that gave its name to all the scholars who adopted it. The Vaibhāṣikas are the philosophers who claim to adhere to the *Vibhāṣā* (Watters, i, 276). The center of the school appears to be Kaśmīr, although there were Sarvāstivādins outside of Kaśmīr—Bahirdeśakas, i.e., scholars of a foreign country, Pāścāttyas, i.e., Westerners [relative to Kaśmīr], Aparāntakas, i.e., scholars of the western border—and Kaśmīrians who are not Vaibhāṣikas. <xi>

The school of the Sautrāntikas & the Abhidharmakośa and Bhāṣya

The Sarvāstivādins and the Vaibhāṣikas think that the Abhidharmas are the words of the Buddha. But there were scholars who did not recognize the authenticity of these books. When it was brought to the attention of these scholars that there is no "Abhidharma basket" outside the Abhidharmas of the Sarvāstivādins and that everyone knows that the word of the Buddha involves "three baskets", they answer that the Buddha taught the Abhidharma in the Sūtra itself—which is quite accurate; they recognize only the authority of the Sūtra, and they take on the name of Sautrāntikas.[26]

But one should not be mistaken about their attitude. Although formally opposed to some of the theses of the *Vibhāṣā* and of the Vaibhāṣikas, and although, for their part, they had a fairly modernistic speculation and perhaps buddhology, they do not combat systematically their adversaries, who were, without doubt, their predecessors. Of the system of the Vaibhāṣikas they assert everything of which they have no formal reason to deny.

---

[23] The *Abhidharmakośavyākhyā* speaks of Ābhidhārmikas *who read only the Abhidharma with its six feet* (*saṭpādābhidharmamātrapāṭhinas*), which could mean: *who do not read the Vibhāṣā*. – These are Sarvāstivādins; but not all Sarvāstivādins are *adherents of the Vibhāṣā* (Vaibhāṣikas). We know, for example, that there are four ways of understanding *All exists*, those of the Sarvāstivādins (1) Dharmatrāta, (2) Ghoṣaka, (3) Vasumitra and (4) Buddhadeva: the Vaibhāṣikas of Kaśmīr condemn the first, the second and the fourth; they condemn the first for the serious reason that it merges with the heresy of the Sāṃkhyas.

[24] [*LVP*: Better, "after the reign of Kaniṣka", *Inde sous les Mauryas*..., p. 328].

[25] *LS*: EIP.VII.511–68.

[26] [See this *Introduction*, Dārṣṭāntikas, and *Index*, Sautrāntikas.]

[To speak more cautiously:] this at least is the attitude of our author, Vasubandhu.[27]

His work, the *Abhidharmakośa*, a collection of about 600 verses, is portrayed as "an exposition of the Abhidharma as the Vaibhāṣikas of Kaśmīr teach it". This does not mean that Vasubandhu is a Vaibhāṣika; he is not a Sarvāstivādin; he has evident sympathies for the Sautrāntikas; he utilizes the opinions of the "ancient masters", i.e., the "Yogācāras, headed by Asaṅga"—but without a doubt, in his opinion, the system of the Vaibhāṣikas is in fact indispensable: the Vaibhāṣikas are *the School.* Nowhere else is there a body of doctrine as coordinated and as complete as theirs. <xii> However they sometimes make mistakes, and on important points. Therefore Vasubandhu supplements his collection of technical verses, an impartial exposition of the Vaibhāṣika system, with his prose commentary, the *Abhidharmakośabhāṣya*, where his personal opinion, his objections, the opinion of different schools or of different scholars are set out on the occasion of numerous theses defended by the School.[28] We know that he was himself, in his turn, combated and refuted by the orthodox Vaibhāṣikas.

But it matters little to us whether he was always right! The essential point, for us as for the scholars who followed after him, is that his book and his *Bhāṣya* are truly a treasury (*kośa*).

ADA. *The importance of the Abhidharmakośa and its Bhāṣya for the study of canonical philosophy and scholasticism*

From the point of view of dogmatics, the *Abhidharmakośa*, with the *Bhāṣya*, is perhaps the most instructive book of the old Buddhism (Small Vehicle). I think that it is destined to render a great service in the study of canonical philosophy and the study of actual scholasticism.

It would not be accurate to say that we do not know the philosophy of canonical Buddhism: we know the essentials, the principles, and the broad outline, and many details. (On the other hand,) the history of this philosophy, of its origins, of its birth, of its developments, is less clear, even though one could think that Buddhism, like

---

27 [*LVP*: I remove here the rather long note where the bibliography regarding the *dating* of Vasubandhu was summarized, and where the texts establishing the existence of an "older Vasubandhu" (see below pp. xxvii.f.) were gathered together.]

28 All the opinions, or almost all the opinions, marked in the *Kośa* or in the *Bhāṣya* by the adverb *kila* ("indeed", "so said", "so reported", [Tib.] *grags so*), are erroneous opinions of the Vaibhāṣikas. The true translation is: "The School says, wrongly, that…".

the Buddha himself, from its birth took many steps and these in all directions. But it is fair to say of [Buddhism] and encouraging to repeat that, although the history of the canonical philosophy has not been done, the picture that scholars such as Rhys Davids and Oldenberg have provided of this philosophy either remains definitive or calls for only slight alterations. We may think, nevertheless, that we do not know any part of [this philosophy] thoroughly, because we know very imperfectly the scholasticism that certainly enriched it, <xiii> that perhaps deformed it, but that certainly derived from it; (the scholasticism) that, moreover, should be, by its methods and its tendencies, very similar to the original speculation from which the canonical philosophy itself emerged. This philosophy is made up of the old layers of a speculation that continues within the actual scholasticism, both in Pāli and in Sanskrit.

The awareness of a gap in our knowledge becomes very strong when we read, better, when we attempt to read the old works such as the *Dhammasaṅgaṇi* or the *Kathāvatthu*; when we seek to determine the meaning of the *sūtra*s themselves, word by word (*avayavārtha*), with some rigor. How many terms there are the exact significance of which escapes us! It is easy and often correct to observe (1) that these terms originally did not have a precise meaning; (2) that the general orientation of Buddhist thought alone deserves to interest us; (3) that—though not knowing that which is exactly the four meditations (*dhyāna*) and the four formless meditative attainments (*ārūpyasamāpatti*), initial inquiry (*vitarka*) and investigation (*vicāra*), form (*rūpa*), the fruits (*phala*), and the candidates of the fruit (*pratipannaka*)—we nevertheless have a sufficient idea of the goal and the methods of Buddhist saintliness; (4) that the candidates of the fruit should be concerned with the details of the Eightfold Noble Path, but not the western historians. – Some think that scholasticism is not interesting; that throughout Buddhist history it remained foreign to the actual religion, as it was in fact to the original doctrine. This is wrong: "If one thinks thus, no, for this is in contradiction with the Sūtra!" (*iti cen na sūtravirodhataḥ*). Buddhism is born complicated and verbose; the scholastic classifications are often pre-Buddhist; it is our good fortune to be able to examine them closely, in sources older than Buddhaghosa; and the *Abhidharmakośa* bestows on us this fortune to the extent that we have the courage to be worthy of it.

The example is set by the Buddhists themselves.

The *Abhidharmakośa* has had a great plane of existence: "This work... had an enormous influence. From the time of its appearance, it was indispensable for all, friends and adversaries, we are told; and there is reason to believe this, for the same fortune followed it everywhere, first in China with Paramārtha, Hsüan-tsang and his disciples, <xiv> then in Japan, where today specialized Buddhist studies still begin with the *Kośaśāstra*."[29]

The author asserts that we will find in his book an accurate summary of the doctrine of the Vaibhāṣikas; but however close his dependence on the ancient masters of the Abhidharma may be, we think that he says it better than what they had said. When the *Kośa* had appeared, the old works of the Sarvāstivādins, Abhidharmas, and *Vibhāṣā* doubtlessly lost part of their practical interest: for while the Chinese translated them, the Lotsavas did not consider it relevant to put them into Tibetan, with the sole exception of the *Prajñāpti*.[30] And this is undoubtedly so because the *Abhidharmakośa*, in accordance with the wish of Vasubandhu, constituted a veritable comprehensive survey, embraced all problems—ontology, psychology, cosmology, discipline and the doctrine of action, theory of the fruits, mysticism, and arhathood—and treated them with sobriety and in clear language, with every method of which the Indians are capable. Ever since Vasubandhu, the Buddhists of the North—to whatever school they belong, whether they adhere to the Great Vehicle or not—learn the basic elements of Buddhism from the *Kośa*. – All schools, in fact, agree about a great number of fundamental data, the same as are accepted by Pāli orthodoxy, the same, we may add, as are often subjacent to the *sūtra*s themselves. These data, which the Vaibhāṣikas had elucidated, were nowhere as wisely presented as in the *Abhidharmakośa*. This sufficiently explains the reputation of the author and the popularity of the book.

While Vasubandhu is an excellent teacher of Buddhism, of Buddhism without epithet of sect or of school, he also renders precious service by initiating us into the systems of these schools. He constructs before us the spacious edifice of the dogmatic Vaibhāṣikas; <xv> he shows its gaps; he explains what the Sautrāntikas say, what the Vaibhāṣika answer, and what he himself thinks. Like many philosophical treatises, and like the best of them, the *Abhidharmakośa* is a circumstantial work, written *sub specie aeternitatis* ["under the forms of eternity"]. We find in it

---

29 N. Péri. "À propos de la date de Vasubandhu", *Bulletin de l'École Française d'Extrême-Orient* (*BEFEO*), 1911, p. 374. – The Tibetan Siddhāntas also take great advantage of the *Kośa*. – Note that it was translated into Chinese only in 563; the Tibetan version, of Jinamitra and Śrīkūṭarakṣita, at the time of Ral-pa-can (816–38).

30 The *Prajñāpti* does not exist *in extenso* in Chinese (*Journal of the Pali Text Society* [*JPTS*], 1905, p. 77). – This is the treatise the first two parts of which are analysed in the Appendix of *Cosmologie bouddhique*.

many proper names, many allusions to contemporary debates.[31] This is not a boring book.

We find in it also a great number of quotations elsewhere shortened. In that way, the *Kośa* is a precious testimony for the study of the oldest literature.[32] Its quotations add to the numerous fragments of the Sanskrit canon which the sands of Turkestan have given us or which we discover under the modernistic prose of the *Divyāvadāna* and of the *sūtra*s of the Great Vehicle. [The quotations] most often revolve around texts of a doctrinal nature and enlighten us as to the dogmatic, if not the historical, relationships of the canon.

ADB. *Why the study of the Abhidharmakośa and its Bhāṣya was deferred for so long*

The importance of the *Kośa* was long ago recognized by the European scholars, and first of all by Burnouf. Let us look into why the study of it was deferred for so long.

The work of Vasubandhu consists of two distinct parts:

- the *Abhidharmakośa*, the *Kārikā*, a collection of about 600 verses, and
- the [auto]commentary or *Bhāṣya*.

The Sanskrit verses and *Bhāṣya* [were not available to scholars until 1946 and 1967].[33]

And of the vast exegetical literature that fills eight volumes of the Tibetan canon, the Nepalese scribes have preserved for us only a single document, the commentary on the *Bhāṣya* by Yaśomitra, the *Abhidharmakośavyākhyā*, which is called *Sphuṭārthā*, "of clear meaning".

This commentary of Yaśomitra is not a complete commentary; it quotes on occasion the verses of Vasubandhu; it elucidates a given passage of the *Bhāṣya*, indicating it by the first words of the passage in question, following the custom of commentators: "The subject itself", says Burnouf, "is difficult to follow here because of the form of the commentary, which considers each word of the text separately, develops it or

---

31 The *Vyākhyā*, the commentary on the *Bhāṣya* by Yaśomitra, adds many details.

32 It is from this point of view that M. Oldenberg recommends the study of the *Abhidharmakośa*, "Buddhistische Studien", *Zeitschrift der Deutschen Morgenländischen Gesellschaft* (*ZDMG*), LII, p. 644 (1898).

33 *LS*: See above Étienne Lamotte's comments on this topic in his "Preface to the New Edition of the Abhidharmakośa of Vasubandhu".

submerges it in a gloss which is usually very extended. It is only very rarely possible to distinguish the text from these comments in the midst of which it is found."[34] Let us add that Yaśomitra passes over in silence anything that appears to him easy or without interest, and introduces the reader abruptly into the discussions of which the data and the *positions* are not pointed out. In the first chapter, he explains just about every word of the text. Elsewhere he aims at only the points with respect to which he has something important to say.

The commentary of Yaśomitra is thus, as Burnouf said, "an inexhaustible mine of precious teachings" (*Introduction*, p. 447); we read thousands of interesting things in it; but it is, by itself, a very ineffective instrument for the study of the *Abhidharmakośa*.

This is why this work has been neglected for such a long time. Or rather, why, although it attracted the attention of several researchers, no-one has yet put his hand to the work. The knowledge of Sanskrit is not enough; one must join with it the knowledge of Tibetan or Chinese, for [until 1946 and 1967][35] it is solely in the Tibetan and Chinese versions that the book of Vasubandhu, *Kārikā* and *Bhāṣya*, was available in full. <xvii>

---

34 *LS*: In Wogihara's edition, "the original text" is now italicized.

35 *LS*: See note 35.

BIBLIOGRAPHY OF THE KOŚA[36]

1. Burnouf, *Introduction*, 34, 46, 447 ("the importance of the AKB"), 563; Wassiliew, *Buddhismus*, 77, 78, 108, 130, 220; S. Lévi, *La science des religions et les religions de l'Inde* (École des Hautes-Études, programme 1892); Hasting's *Encyclopaedia*, i, 20 (1908); Minayef, *Recherches et Matériaux*, 1887, trans. 1894.

J. Takakusu, "On the Abhidharma Literature", *JPTS*, 1905.

Noël Péri, "À propos de la date de Vasubandhu", *BEFEO*, 1911.

La Vallée Poussin, *Cosmologie bouddhique, Troisième chapitre de l'Abhidharmakośa, kārikā, bhāṣya et vyākhyā, avec* [*une introduction et*] *une analyse de la Lokaprajñāpti et de la Kāraṇaprajñāpti de Maudgalyāyana*, 1914–19; Paul Demiéville, review of the *Kośa* i–ii, *BEFEO*, 1924, p. 463; O. Rosenberg, *Probleme der buddhistischen Philosophie*, 1924, translation of the work published in Russian in 1918 (the appendix contains a bulky bibliography of Abhidharma literature, Chinese sources and Japanese sources); Th. Stcherbatsky: (a) *The Central Conception of Buddhism and the Meaning of the Word "Dharma"*, 1923 (the first appendix is a translation of *Kośa* v, F 48–65; the second is a table of seventy-five *dharma*s enriched by substantial notes); (b) an English translation of the *Pudgalapratiṣedhaprakaraṇa*, or ninth chapter of the *Kośa*, Acad. of Petrograd, 1918.

Yamakami Sōgen, *Systems of Buddhist Thought*, Calcutta, 1912, chap. iii, "Sarvāstivādins". – Bibliography of contemporary Japanese memoirs in Péri, Demiéville, Rosenberg, and in particular in Funabashi Suisai, *Kusha tetsugaku*, Tokyo, 1906.

2. *Kośa* and commentaries, Sanskrit, Tibetan, and Chinese sources:

i. *Abhidharmakośavyākhyā, Bibliotheca Buddhica, Sphuṭārthā Abhidharmakośavyākhyā*, the work of Yaśomitra, first *Kośasthāna*, edited by Prof. S. Lévi and Prof. Stcherbatsky, 1st fasc., Petrograd, 1918; 2nd fasc. by Wogihara, Stcherbatsky and Obermiller, (part of the 2nd chapter), Leningrad, 1931. <xviii>

Text of the third chapter, *kārikā*s and *vyākhyā*, in *Bouddhisme, Cosmologie...* by Louis de La Vallée Poussin [with the collaboration of Dr. P. Cordier], Brussels, 1914–1919.

ii. Tibetan translation of the *Abhidharmakośakārikāḥ* and of the *Abhidharmakośabhāṣya* of Vasubandhu, ed. by Th. I. Stcherbatsky, 1st fasc. 1917, 2nd fasc. 1930.

---

36 *LS*: See also the bibliography at the end of the translation.

3. Tibetan sources, Palmyr Cordier, *Catalogue du fonds tibétain de la Bibliothèque Nationale*, third part, Paris 1914, pp. 394 and 499.

   i. *Abhidharmakośakārikā* and *Bhāṣya* of Vasubandhu, *Mdo* 63, fols. 1–27, and fol. 28 – *Mdo*, 64, fol. 109.
   ii. *Sūtrānurūpā nāma abhidharmakośavṛttiḥ* of Vinītabhadra, 64, fols. 109–304.
   iii. *Sphuṭārthā nāma abhidharmakośavyākhya* of Yaśomitra, 65 and 66. This is the commentary preserved in Sanskrit.
   iv. *Lakṣaṇānusāriṇī nāma abhidharmakośaṭīkā* of Pūrṇavardhana, student of Sthiramati, master of Jinamitra and of Śīlendrabodhi, 67 and 68.
   v. *Upāyikā nāma abhidharmakośaṭīkā* of Śamathadeva, 69 and 70, fols. 1–144.
   vi. *Marmapradīpo nāma abhidharmakośavṛttiḥ* of Dignāga, 70, fols. 144–286.
   vii. *Lakṣaṇānusāriṇī nāma abhidharmakośaṭīkā*, abridged recension of the *Bṛhaṭṭīkā*, (see above iv,) 70, fols. 286–315.
   viii. *Sārasamuccayo nāma abhidharmāvatāraṭīkā*, anonymous, 70, fols. 315–93.
   ix. *Abhidharmāvatāraprakaraṇa*, anonymous, 70, fols. 393–417.
   x. *Tattvārtho nāma abhidharmakośabhāṣyaṭīkā* of Sthiramati, 129 and 130.

4. *Abhidharmakośaśāstra*, of Vasubandhu, translated by Paramārtha, 564–67, *Nanjio* 1269, *Taishō* 1559, vol. 29, pp. 161–309; trans. by Hsüan-tsang, 651–54, *Nanjio* 1267, *Taishō* 1558, vol. 29, pp. 1–160. <xix>

The references in our translation are to the edition of Saeki Kiokuga, Kyoto 1891, *Kandō Abidatsumakusharon*, the pages of which correspond to those of the Ming edition, a remarkable work that notably contains, besides the interlinear notes of the editor, copious extracts of (1) the two great Chinese commentaries, (2) the *Vibhāṣā*, (3) the commentary of Saṃghabhadra, (4) the work of K'uei-chi on the *Thirty Verses*.

5. Among the Chinese commentaries on the *Kośa*:[37]

   i. Shen-t'ai, the author of a *Shu*, [i.e., the *Chü-she lun shu*, originally in twenty Chinese volumes, today only volumes 1, 2, 4, 5, 6, 7 and 17 are extant; *Manji Zoku-zōkyō* I.83.3–4].[38]
   ii. P'u-kuang, the author of a *Chi* [i.e., the thirty-volume *Chü-she lun Chi*; *TD* 41, number 1821], which quotes Shen-t'ai, edited by Saeki Kiokuga.
   iii. Fa-pao, the author of a *Shu* [i.e., *Chü-she lun Shu*; *TD* 41, number 1822], which quotes Shen-t'ai and P'u-kuang, edited by Saeki Kiokuga.

---

[37] According to P. Demiéville, *BEFEO*, 1924, p. 463.

[38] *LS*: The comments in the following square brackets are by Pruden.

Two other disciples of Hsüan-tsang, Huai-su and K'uei-chi, have written commentaries on the *Kośa* which are lost.

P'u-kuang has also written a small treatise on the doctrine of the *Kośa*.

iv. Yuan-hui, with a preface dated before 727 by Chia-ts'eng, has written a *Shu*, [i.e., the *Chü-she lun sung Shu*, preserved in *TD* volume 421, number 1823], on the *kārikā*s of the *Kośa*, a *Shu* that was "commented upon several times in China and widely used in Japan; it is from this intermediary that the Mahāyānists generally draw their knowledge of the *Kośa*. But from the point of view of Indology, it does not offer the same interest as the three preceding commentaries."

Hsüan-tsang dictated his version of Saṃghabhadra to Yuan-yu. There exist fragments of a commentary attributed to him.

6. Guṇamati and the *Lakṣaṇānusāra*.

Guṇamati is known through his commentary on [Vasubandhu's] *Vyākhyāyukti*; several fragments of this commentary are quoted in the *Chos-'byung* of Bu-ston, translated by Obermiller, 1931.

Guṇamati is mentioned four times by Yaśomitra in the *Abhidharmakośavyākhyā*.

i. Introductory verses: Guṇamati has commented on the *Kośa*, as has also Vasumitra; Yaśomitra follows this commentary when it is good.

ii. Guṇamati and his disciple Vasumitra say that the word *namas* is constructed with the fourth case. But when the word *namas* is not independent, we have the accusative. <xx> This is why this master (Vasubandhu), in the *Vyākhyāyukti*, says: "Bowing to the Muni with my head..." (*Kośa*; *Vyā.*, i, p. 7).

iii. Guṇamati asserts that the *Kośa* teaches wrongly: "Conditioned phenomena, with the exception of the path, are *in a relationship with the fluxes* (*sāsrava*), (AKB i, F 6)", for all factors (*dharma*), without exception, can be taken as object by the fluxes (*āsrava*) (*Vyā.*, i, p. 13).

iv. Concerning the continuity of the mental stream, "the master Guṇamati, with his disciple the master Vasumitra, being fond of the doctrine of his own group (*nikāya*), instead of confining himself to explaining the *Kośa*, refutes it" (AKB iii, F 34, note).

N. Péri (*Date*, 41) reminds us that Burnouf has pointed out, based on Yaśomitra, the commentary of Guṇamati. He adds: "An author very rarely quoted. His *Lakṣaṇa–anusāraśāstra* (*Nanjio* 1280 = *Taishō* 1641) belongs to the Canon where it is classed among the Hīnayānist works. He summarizes there the ideas of the *Kośa*, then sets out his own particular ideas on a few issues. The *Hsi-yü-chi*, after having cited him amongst the celebrated monks of Nālandā, k. 9, tells us that he left the monastery in which he lived in order to establish Valabhī, k. 11."

The *Nanjio* 1280, *Taishō* 1641, is only an extract of the treatise of Guṇamati, the chapter which examines the sixteen aspects of the truths (AKB vii, F 30–39):

> Are we dealing here with sixteen real entities or sixteen names? The masters of the *Vibhāṣā* say that sixteen names are established because there are sixteen real entities. But the *sūtra-upadeśa*-masters say that there are sixteen names, but only seven real entities, four real entities for the first truth, one real entity for each of the three others. Originally, the Buddha promulgated the *Upadeśasūtra*. After the death of the Buddha, Ānanda, Kātyāyana, etc., read/recited what they had heard. In order to explain the meaning of the *sūtra*, as disciples [do], they composed a *śāstra* explaining the *sūtra*, which is thus called *sūtra-upadeśa*. From what is found in [this] *upadeśa*, the *Vibhāṣā* then extracted an *upadeśa* [exposition]; since it originates only indirectly [from the Sūtra], it is not called *sūtra-upadeśa*.

Guṇamati continues as in AKB vii, F 31: "According to the first exegesis, impermanent (*anitya*) because of arising in dependence on conditions (*pratyaya-adhīnatvāt*)." And he comments: "Conditioned phenomena, without power, do not arise by themselves...".

The first book ends: "The thesis of Vasubandhu is similar to what the *sūtra-upadeśa*-masters meant."

The second begins: "The author says: I will express now the explanation of what I believe. <xxi> Impermanent (*anitya*), because of having arising, having destruction. Conditioned entities, having arising and destruction, are not permanent. Birth is existence... .

The treatise touches on various philosophical issues, absence of self (*ātman*), etc. In it we find very interesting notes, for example (*Taishō*, 168b9): "In the Small Vehicle, hungry ghosts (*preta*) are superior to animals; in the Great Vehicle, the opposite. In fact, hungry ghosts are enveloped in flames... ."

It is curious that the title of Guṇamati's work, literally *Lākṣaṇānusāraśāstra*, is exactly the same as the book attributed to Pūrṇavardhana in the Tanjur. – We have Guṇamati, the master of Sthiramati, and Pūrṇavardhana, the student of Sthiramati.[39]

---

39 As for Guṇamati, consult H. Ui, *Studies in Indian Philosophy*, fifth vol., pp. 136–40.

7. Sthiramati, a student of Guṇamati, defended the *Kośa* against Saṃghabhadra. "His commentary on the *Kośa* is mentioned on several occasions by Shen-t'ai, P'u-kuang and Fa-pao in their works on the same text. The precise manner in which they quote it, in which they comment on it and discuss the opinions, makes us think that Hsüan-tsang must have brought it back to China and perhaps they as well were able to read it" (N. Péri, *Date*, 41). Sthiramati, the author of *Tsa-chi*, is one of the great scholars of the *Vijñaptimātratā*.

There is (*Taishō* 1561) a small treatise of Sthiramati (transcription and translation) entitled *Kośatattvārthaṭīkā* or *Abhidharmakośaśāstratattvārthaṭīkā*, which is doubtless an extract of the voluminous work of the same name and by the same author preserved in Tibetan, Cordier, 499.

We notice, at the beginning, the commentary on the seven points indicated in the introductory verse of the *Kośa*.

On the knowledge of the Buddha, superior to that of the noble ones, the author quotes the *Kalpanāmaṇḍitikā* verse[40] (Huber, *Sūtrālaṃkāra*), AKB i, F 2 and vii, F 72; and reminds us of Maudgalyāyana's ignorance of the place of rebirth of his mother, AKB i, F 2.

In order to demonstrate the thesis of the *Kośa* that the faculty of faith (*śraddhā-indriya*) can be impure, ii, F 119, the author quotes at length the *sūtra* on the request of Brahmā to the Buddha (setting in motion the wheel [of the teachings]), a *sūtra* briefly pointed out by Vasubandhu. <xxii>

The work ends with comments on the duration of life: The verse says: "Among the Kurus, life is always 1,000 years; half of this in the West and the East; in this [i.e., our] continent, it is not determined: at the end, ten years; at the beginning, incalculable" (AKB iii, F 171–72).

There are indeed in this world sentient beings who have meritorious actions to spare and who wish: "May I have a long life!", without wishing precisely: "May I live 100 years, ninety years, eighty years!" Or else, venerable persons, parents and friends, say: "May you live a long time!" without saying precisely how much time. That one makes similar wishes is because the actions committed by humans of this continent are associated with thoughts of desire.

The Sūtra says: "Know, *bhikṣus*, that the life-span was 8,000 years long under Vipaśyin, 20,000 years under Kāśyapa; the life-span is now 100 years; few exceed

40 *LS*: *mokṣabījam ahaṃ hy asya susūkṣmam upalakṣaye | dhātupāṣāṇavivare nilīnam iva kāñcanam* ||

this, many stay less than that." If the duration of life is not determined, why does the Fortunate One (Bhagavat) express himself in this way? ... – The treatise concludes with the well-known verse: *sucīrṇabrahmacarye 'smin...* (AKB vi, F 269).

8. Saṃghabhadra has written two works.

The first, the title of which is transcribed in Chinese as *Abhidharmanyāyānusāra-śāstra*—or perhaps better *Nyāyānusaro nāma Abhidharmaśāstram*—is a commentary which reproduces, without modifications, the *kārikā*s of the *Abhidharmakośa*. But this commentary criticizes those *kārikā*s which set out the Vaibhāṣika doctrine by marking them with the word *kila*, which signifies *the School says*; it refutes the *Bhāṣya*, the auto-commentary of Vasubandhu, when it presents views opposite to those of the Vaibhāṣikas, corrects it when it attributes to the Vaibhāṣikas views that are not theirs.

The title of the second treatise is not completely transcribed: *Abhidharmasamaya-hsien-śāstra* or *Abhidharmasamaya-kuang-śāstra*. J. Takakusu proposes *Abhidharma-samayapradīpikāśāstra*, which is not bad; however *pradīpa*, lamp, is always (Ch.) *teng*, and we have for (Ch.) *hsien* the equivalents of *prakāśa* and *dyotana*.

This is an extract of the *Nyāyānusāra*, from which all controversy is excluded and which is thus a simple exposition of the system (*samaya*) of the Abhidharma. It differs from the *Nyāyānusara* by the presence of a fairly long introduction, in seven verses and prose, and as well by the manner in which it treats the *kārikā*s of Vasubandhu: these *kārikā*s are either removed (ii. 2–3) or corrected (i. 11, 14) when they express false doctrines or when they cast suspicion on the true doctrines by adding the word *kila*.[41] <xxiii>

Saṃghabhadra innovates, and K'uei-chi distinguishes the old and the new Sarvāstivādins: *Siddhi*, 45: theory of atoms (in relation to the cognitive object condition [*ālambanapratyaya*]); *Siddhi*, 65: the characteristics (*lakṣaṇa*) of the *conditioned*; *Siddhi*, 71: the factor dissociated from thought (*viprayukta*) called (Ch.) *ho-ho* (*saṃketa*, *samavāya*, etc.); *Siddhi*, 147: sensation (*vedanā*): (*viṣaya-vedanā*; *svabhāva-vedanā*); *Siddhi*, 311: divergent Sarvāstivādins on resolve (*adhi-mokṣa*). <xxiv>

---

[41] Missing in the two treatises of Saṃghabhadra, the *āryā* quoted in *Vyākhyā*, i, 31, who is the critic of AKB i, k. 11.

In the two treatises of Saṃghabhadra, the first chapter is called *mūlavastunirdeśa*, the second *viśeṣanirdeśa*, the third *pratītyasamutpādanirdeśa*. And of course, the *Pudgalapratiṣedhapra-karaṇa*, the annex of the *Kośa*, is ignored.

THE QUESTION OF THE DATE OF VASUBANDHU. – VASUBANDHU-THE-ANCIENT

Here we will not undertake the bibliography of Vasubandhu.[42]

But his treatise, *Pratītyasamutpādavyākhyā*, Cordier, iii, 365, requires the attention of the reader of the *Kośa*. G. Tucci has published fragments of this work (*Journal of the Royal Asiatic Society of Great Britain and Ireland* [*JRAS*], 1930, pp. 611–23) where the twelve members of the chain are explained in detail, with numerous quotations from scriptures.

G. Tucci intends to publish the *Trisvabhāvakārikā*[43] and parts of the commentary of the *Madhyāntavibhāga*.

With regard to the "definition of direct perception by Vasubandhu" (*vāsubandhava pratyakṣalakṣaṇa*), known through the *Tātparyaṭīkā*, 99, and the *Vādavidhi* attributed to Vasubandhu, see the articles by G. Tucci (*JRAS*, 1929, p. 473); A.B. Keith (*Ind. Hist. Quarterly*, 1928, pp. 221–27); R. Iyengar (*Ind. Hist. Quarterly*, 1929, pp. 81–86); Stcherbatsky, *Logic*, ii, 161, 382; G. Tucci, *Maitreya[nātha] et Asaṅga*, 70–71; and finally *Pramāṇasamuccaya*, chap. i, by R. Iyengar, pp. 31–35. It seems that Dignāga denies the authorship to Vasubandhu despite the common opinion, and the *ṭīkā* quotes the AKB ii, *kārikā* 64, which contradicts the aforesaid definition of direct perception (*pratyakṣa*).

There are also numerous passages of the *Vyākhyāyukti* in the *Chos-'byung* of Bu-ston (see above p. xix).

A. *Bibliography related to the date of Vasubandhu*

- Wassiliew, *Buddhismus*, 235 (1860): life of Vasubandhu.
- Kern, *Geschiedenis*, trans. Huet, ii, 450.
- S. Lévi, *Journal Asiatique* (*JA*), 1890, 2, 252; *Théatre indien*, 1890, i, 165; ii, 35; "Date de Candragomin", *BEFEO*, 1903, p. 47; *Sūtrālaṃkāra*, translation, preface, 1911, pp. 2–3.
- Bühler, *Alter der indischen Kunst-Poesie*, 1890, p. 79.
- J. Takakusu, "Life of Vasubandhu", *T'oung-pao*, 1904; "A Study of Paramārtha's Life of Vasu-bandhu and the Date of Vasu-bandhu", *JRAS*, 1905; "Sāṃkhyakārikā", *BEFEO*, 1904.

---

42 *LS*: On the question of which works can reasonably be attributed to Vasubandhu the Kośakāra, see section 5, ii, a in my *Remarks by the Translator*.

43 He has been preceded by Susumu Yamaguchi [September 1931].

- Wogihara, *Asaṅga's Bodhisattvabhūmi*, 14, Strasbourg thesis, Leipzig, 1908.
- Noël, Péri, "À propos de la date de Vasubandhu", *BEFEO*, 1911, pp. 339–92. <xxv>
- Pathak, Bhandraka, *Indian Antiquary*, 1911–12 (V. Smith, *History*, 3rd ed., 328; 4th ed., 346).
- B. Shiiwo, Dr. Takakusu and Mr. Péri on the date of Vasubandhu (270–350), *Tetsugaku Zasshi*, Nov.–Dec. 1912.
- Winternitz, *Geschichte*, ii, 256 (1913); iii, 694 (1922).
- H. Ui, "On the author of the *Mahāyānasūtrālaṃkāra*", *Zeitschrift für Indologie und Iranistik* (*ZII*), vi, 1928, pp. 216–25.

A group of articles, several of which are summaries of papers written in Japanese, in *Mélanges Lanman* (Indian Studies in Honor of Charles Rockwell Lanman), 1929:

- J. Takakusu, *Date of Vasubandhu, the Great Buddhist Philosopher.*
- T. Kimura, *Date of Vasubandhu Seen from the Abhidharmakośa.*
- G. Ono, *Date of Vasubandhu Seen from the History of Buddhist Philosophy.*
- H. Ui, *Maitreya as a Historical Personage.*

In addition, information on the opinions of B. Shiiwo, S. Funabashi, E. Mayeda, S. Mochizuki.

CB. *The dating of Vasubandhu in dependence on the date of Asaṅga and the question of the historicity of Maitreyanātha*

"H.P. Śāstrī pointed out the historicity of Maitreyanātha from the colophon of *Abhisamayālaṃkārakārikā*, which is a commentary, from the Yogācāra point of view, on *Pañcaviṃśatisāhasrikā-prajñā-pāramitā-sūtra* by Maitreyanātha" (Kimura, *Origin of Mahāyāna Buddhism*, Calcutta, 1927, p. 170).

The date of Vasubandhu is linked to that of Asaṅga, his brother.[44] Now, parts of the *Yogaśāstra*, the work of Asaṅga, were translated into Chinese in 413–21 and in 431. – However, the opinion is widespread among Japanese scholars that the works attributed to Asaṅga, written under the inspiration of the future Buddha Maitreya, were in reality works of a Master Maitreya, a teacher (*ācārya*), "a historical personage". This thesis allows us to remove from Asaṅga one collection of books of which we thought him to have been the devout editor, and to place him, with his

---

[44] *LS*: On the issue of the alternative hypotheses of one or two Vasubandhus, his life time, his relationship to Asaṅga, the problems of the information available on the relevant Gupta dynastic history, see section 5, ii, b in my *Remarks by the Translator*.

brother Vasubandhu, back into the middle or the end of the fifth century, or—why not?—into the sixth century. "If a scholar named Maitreya be found to be the author of those works hitherto attributed to Asaṅga, then the date of the latter ought to be shifted later, at least by one generation, if not more. The ground for an earlier date for Vasubandhu should give way altogether" (Takakusu, *Mélanges Lanman*, 85). <xxvi>

H. Ui, in the *Philosophical Journal of the Imperial University Tokyo*, n° 411, 1921 (or 1922?), has put forward the arguments, developed since then in his *Studies of Indian Philosophy*, i, 359, summarized in *Mélanges Lanman*.

[But these arguments] appear weak to me and, I really think, to be nonexistent (*Note bouddhique xvi: Maitreya et Asaṅga*, Ac. royale de Belgique, January 1930). I do not think that they gain any strength from the observations of G. Tucci ("On some aspects of the doctrines of Maitreya[nātha] and Asaṅga", *Calcutta Lectures*, 1930). The tradition of the Vijñaptimātratā school establishes, as G. Tucci observes, the succession Maitreyanātha–Asaṅga–Vasubandhu; but Maitreyanātha is not a name of a man: "Who has Maitreya as protector"; *nātha* is synonymous with *buddha* or, more exactly, with *bhagavat* (lord).[45] The commentary of the *Abhisamayālaṃkāra* (p. 73 of Tucci's edition) gives to Maitreya the title of *bhagavat* in a passage where it explains how "Asaṅga, in spite of his scriptural erudition and his *insight* (*labdhādhigamo 'pi*, AKB viii, F 220), did not understand the *Prajñāpāramitā* and was in despair. Then the Bhagavat Maitreya explained the *Prajñāpāramitā* for the sake of [Asaṅga] (*tam uddiśya*) and composed the treatise that is called *Abhisamayālaṃkārakārikā*." It is with the name Maitreyanātha that Śāntideva designates the noble one who, in the *Gaṇḍavyūha*, explains the virtues of the *thought of Bodhi* to the wanderer Sudhana (*Bodhicaryāvatāra*, i, 14; Rājendralāl Mitra, *Buddhist Nepalese Literature*, 92). If the school holds the treatises of Asaṅga as sacred, as *āryā deśanā* [instructions of a noble one], it is because the Bhagavat Maitreya revealed them. That the Tibetan-Chinese tradition varies in its attributions, naming as author sometimes a revealing deity, sometimes an inspired master, does not present any difficulty.

Difficulties regarding the biography of Vasubandhu, the expression pūrvācārya, etc.

The biography of Vasubandhu (Paramārtha) is not without difficulties. – The *Kośa* gave rise to criticism by Saṃghabhadra who, in the bulky *Nyāyānusāra*, notes the

---

45 See AKB i, F 1. – Obermiller, in the preface of the translation of the *Uttaratantra* (*Asia Major*, 1931), dismisses the thesis of H. Ui.

innumerable heresies of Sautrāntika flavor that mar the work of Vasubandhu. <xxvii> We are told that Vasubandhu refused to accept a debate: "I am now already old. You may do as you please" (Version of Takakusu). But it is also ascertained that Vasubandhu was then converted to the Mahāyāna by his brother Asaṅga, considered cutting out his tongue in order to punish it for not confessing the Mahāyāna sooner and, better advised, wrote numerous treatises wherein the doctrine of the Mahāyāna is learnedly elaborated.

Yaśomitra, the commentator on the *Kośa*, says that the expression *pūrvācārya* (i.e., ancient masters) of the *Kośa* refers to "Asaṅga, etc." (*asaṅgaprabhṛtayaḥ*; WOG.281.27f.). N. Péri thought that Yaśomitra means to refer to the school of the Pūrvācāryas by their most illustrious name, and does not say that Asaṅga is indeed *ancient* (*pūrva*) in relation to Vasubandhu (*Cosmologie bouddhique*, footnote on p. ix).

The *Kośa* was translated [into Chinese] only in 563, whereas the work of Dharmatrāta, an imperfect draft of the *Kośa*, was translated in 397–418, 426–31, 433–42. J. Takakusu observes: "If the *Kośa* had existed, why would so many translators linger over the book of Dharmatrāta?" (*Mélanges Lanman*). And it is difficult to reply pertinently to this question.[46]

But it seems almost impossible to believe that Paramārtha, the biographer of Vasubandhu, the first translator of the *Kośa*, arriving in China in 548, is in error when he makes the author of the *Kośa* the contemporary and brother of Asaṅga. It is a hopeless hypothesis to identify the brother and the convert of Asaṅga with Vasubandhu-the-Ancient.

CD. *Vasubandhu-the-Ancient*

We must accept the existence and "ābhidhārmic" activity of an ancient Vasubandhu. The problem which I had tackled in the Foreword to *Cosmologie bouddhique* (see above p. xi, [as well as the footnote on p. viii in *Cosmologie bouddhique*: "We have to distinguish Vasubandhu, the author of the *Kośa*, from Vasubandhu-the-Ancient who likewise worked in the field of Abhidharma."]) has been taken up by Taiken Kimura, "Examen lumineux de l'Abhidharma" (table in *Eastern Buddhist*, iii, p. 85), fifth part: "Sur les sources du *Kośa*": we will see a summary of his conclusion in *Mélanges Lanman*. <xxviii> Since then has appeared *Note bouddhique xvii:*

---

46 Maybe because the work of Dharmatrāta has long since enjoyed a great reputation; maybe because, in the eyes of the Sarvāstivādins, the *Kośa* was, with good reason, regarded as heretical and tendentious.

Vasubandhu l'ancien, Acad. de Belgique; and a note by Paul Pelliot in *JA*, (July 1931).

Yaśomitra—in three places: AKB i, F 26, iii, F 70 and iv, F 7—recognizes a "Sthavira Vasubandhu, a master of Manoratha",[47] an "ancient master Vasubandhu" (*vṛddhācārya-vasubandhu*), as a master who was refuted by Vasubandhu, i.e., the author of the *Kośa* and disciple of Manoratha according to Hsüan-tsang. P'u-kuang (Kimura, *Mélanges Lanman*, 91) confirms Yaśomitra, and refers to the master in question under the name "ancient Vasubandhu, a dissident Sarvāstivādin Master".

On the other hand, the gloss of the initial five verses of Dharmatrāta's treatise [SAH.2], the new edition of the *Abhidharmasāra* of Dharmaśrī,[48] attributes an edition of the same book in 6,000 verses to Vasubandhu. These verses and this gloss are not very clear. Kimura has studied them (*Mélanges Lanman*); I have amended his interpretation (*Note bouddhique* xvii); Paul Pelliot, finally, draws from it what can be drawn from it. <xxix>

---

47 Quoted iii. 152, on the explanation of the word *neighboring hell* (*utsada*).

48 See below.

D. *THE SEVEN CANONICAL TREATISES OF THE ABHIDHARMA*

The Sarvāstivādins recognize the authority of seven Abhidharma treatises, "the word of the Buddha". Among the Sarvāstivādins, there are the Ābhidhārmikas "who read only the Abhidharma with its six feet",[49] who are distinct from the Vaibhāṣikas "who read the Abhidharma".

The Abhidharma with its six feet[50] is the great treatise of Kātyāyanīputra—entitled *Jñānaprasthāna*, of which the *Vibhāṣā* is the long commentary—and the six treatises, the order and authorship of which vary somewhat according to the sources. To follow the order of the *Abhidharmakośavyākhyā*:

1. *Prakaraṇapāda* of Vasumitra;
2. *Vijñānakāya* of Devaśarman;
3. *Dharmaskandha* of Śāriputra (or of Maudgalyāyana, Chinese sources);
4. *Prajñāptiśāstra* of Maudgalyāyana;
5. *Dhātukāya* of Pūrṇa (or of Vasumitra, Chinese sources);
6. *Saṃgītiparyāya* of Mahākausṭhila (or of Śāriputra, Chinese sources).

We should note that the Tibetans name the *Dharmaskandha* first and the *Jñānaprasthāna* only as sixth: "The Tibetans seem to regard the *Dharmaskandha* as the most important of all." This is also the opinion of Chin-mai (664 A.D.), the author of the Chinese colophon (Takakusu, 75, 115).

J. Takakusu, in "On the Abhidharma Literature" (*JPTS*, 1905), collects a number of details on these seven books, which Burnouf was the first to name; he gives a table of the chapters of each of them. The comments that follow are an addition to this fine work.

DA. *Jñānaprasthāna*[51]

1. According to Hsüan-tsang, Kātyayanīputra composed this *śāstra* in the monastery of Tāmasavana, 300 years after the Nirvāṇa (fourth century).[52] <xxx>

---

49 *ṣaṭpādābhidharmamātrapāṭhinas*, a good reading of AKB v, F 45 (note).

50 Account of the council in *Ta-chih-tu-lun*. Przyluski, *Concile de Rājagṛha*, p. 72.

51 Translated in 383 by Gotama Saṃghadeva of Kaśmīr, and by Hsüan-tsang.

LS: See SBS.221–29; EIP.VII.108–10; 417–49.

52 Watters, i. 294; S. Lévi, *Catalogue géographique des Yakṣas*, 55; J. Przyluski, *Açoka*, 263.

However, the *Vibhāṣā*, 5, p. 21 at the end, commenting on the *Jñānaprasthāna*, 1, p. 918, says: "When the Bhadanta composed the *Jñānaprasthāna*, he was residing in the East, and this is why he quotes the five rivers [i.e., Gaṅgā, Yamunā, Sarayū, Aciravatī, Mahī] known in the East as examples." (AKB iii, F 147)

2. We know through the quotations of Yaśomitra that the chapters are called *skandhaka* (*indriyaskandhaka*, *samādhiskandhaka*) and that the work he uses is composed in Sanskrit.

However, the first translation has as its title *Śāstra of eight chien-tu*; in Paramārtha, *Śāstra of eight ch'ien-tu*; we might think of *khaṇḍa*, but Paramārtha explains that *ch'ien-tu* is equivalent to *ka-lan-ta*, which is obviously *grantha*. S. Lévi thought that (Ch.) *ch'ien-tu* is the Prākrit *gantho*. – J. Takakusu concludes: "All we can say is that the text brought by Saṃghadeva seems to have been in a dialect akin to Pāli.... But this supposition rests solely on the phonetic value of Chinese ideographs."[53]

3. The *Jñānaprasthāna*, a very poorly composed work, begins with the study of the worldly supreme factors (*laukikāgradharma*).[54]

"What are the worldly supreme factors? (1) The thought and thought-concomitants that are immediately followed by entry into the assurance of the eventual attainment of enlightenment (*samyaktvanyāma*) (see AKB vi, F 180). (2) There are those who say to this: "The five (praxis-oriented) faculties (*indriya*: faith, etc.) that are immediately followed by entry into the assurance of the eventual attainment of enlightenment are what are called the *worldly supreme factors*." The text continues: "Why are these thought and thought-concomitants so called...?"

---

[53] On the language in which the *Jñānaprasthāna* was written, Takakusu, pp. 82, 84, 86. – See above p. ix.

LS: Hirakawa (IA.XXIX) states that the *Jñānaprasthāna* "consists of eight chapters, and the *Mahāvibhāṣā*, which is the commentary on the *Jñānaprasthāna*, also consists of eight chapters and forty-four *vargas* as follows:

1. *Kṣudrakagrantha* (8 *vargas*); 2. *Anuśayagrantha* (4 *vargas*); 3. *Jñānagrantha* (5 *vargas*); 4. *Karmagrantha* (5 *vargas*); 5. *Mahābhūtagrantha* (4 *vargas*); 6. *Indriyagrantha* (7 *vargas*); 7. *Samādhigrantha* (5 *vargas*); 8. *Dṛṣṭigrantha* (6 *vargas*)."

[54] On the *laukikāgradharmas*, AKB vi, F 167, and "Pārāyaṇa quoted in the *Jñānaprasthāna*", *Mélanges Linossier* (where we see that the *Jñānaprasthāna* sets out the problem of the stages conducive to penetration [*nirvedhabhāgīya*] very poorly).

The *Vibhāṣā*, 2, p. 7c,[55] reproduces the two definitions from the *Jñānaprasthāna*, and explains: "Who are the people who say that the worldly supreme factors are the five (praxis-oriented) faculties? – The ancient Ābhidhārmikas. – Why do they express themselves in this way? – In order to refute another school: they do not mean that the worldly supreme factors consist solely of the five (praxis-oriented) faculties. But the Vibhajyavādins maintain that the five (praxis-oriented) faculties are solely pure (*anāsrava*) (see AKB ii, F 118).... To refute this doctrine, the ancient Ābhidhārmikas say that the worldly supreme factors consist of the five (praxis-oriented) faculties. <xxxi> Now, these factors (*dharma*) occur in an ordinary worldling (*pṛthagjana*): thus it is established that the five (praxis-oriented) faculties can be impure."

The significance of this commentary is that it distinguishes (1) Kātyāyanīputra and the *Jñānaprasthāna* from (2) the "ancient Ābhidhārmikas".

4. One of the last verses of the last chapter is the verse (*śloka*) on the meaning of which, according to Vasumitra (*Sectes*, Masuda, p. 57), the Vātsīputrīyas disagreed with each other: hence the separation of the four schools, Dharmottarīyas, etc.

5. But, if the *Jñānaprasthāna* is the work of Kātyānīputra, how can the Sarvāstivādins consider this treatise to be the word of the Buddha?

The *Vibhāṣā* answers this question.[56]

> Question: – Who has composed this Treatise [that is, the *Jñānaprasthāna*]?
>
> Answer: – The Buddha Bhagavat. For the nature of the factors (*dharma*) to be known is very profound and very subtle: apart from the Buddha Bhagavat, who could know it and expound it?
>
> [Question:] – If that is so, who, in this Treatise, asks the questions, and who answers?
>
> [Answer:] – There are several opinions:
>
> 1. the Sthavira Śāriputra asks the questions and the Fortunate One (*bhagavat*) answers;
> 2. the 500 *arhat*s ask the questions and the Fortunate One answers;
> 3. the gods ask the questions and the Fortunate One answers;
> 4. miraculously manifested (*nirmita*) *bhikṣu*s ask the questions and the Fortunate One answers: it is the law (*dharmatā*; [Ch.] *fa-erh*) of the

55 Same text, *Small Vibhāṣā*, p. 5b, toward the end.

56 Compare AKB i, F 5–6, and *Documents d'Abhidharma*; *Vibhāṣā*, 46, p. 236b.

> Buddhas that they should expound to the world the nature of the factors to be known. But if there is no questioner? In that case the Fortunate One creates *bhikṣus* with a proper countenance and appearance, agreeable to be seen, shaven-headed, dressed in robes; he causes these beings to ask the questions and he answers... .

Question: – If that is so, why does tradition attribute the composition of the Treatise to the Ārya Kātyāyanīputra?

Answer: – Because this Ārya has written and published this treatise in such a way that it became widespread; this is why it is said to be by him. But the Treatise has been spoken by the Fortunate One. However, according to another opinion, this Treatise is the work of the Ārya Kātyāyanīputra.

Question: – Did we not say above that no one, with the exception of the Buddha, is capable of knowing and expounding the nature of the factors? How is the Ārya able to compose this Treatise?

Answer: – Because the Ārya also possesses a subtle, profound, ardent, skilful intelligence; knows well the particular inherent and common characteristics of the factors; penetrates the meaning of the texts from beginning to end (*pūrvāparakoṭi*); <xxxii> knows the three baskets well; has abandoned the stains of the three realms (*dhātu*); is in possession of the three clear knowledges (*vidyā*; AKB vii, F 108); is endowed with the six super-knowledges (*abhijñā*) and the eight liberations (*vimokṣa*); has obtained the unhindered knowledges (*pratisaṃvid*); has obtained the cognition resulting from a resolve (*praṇidhijñāna*); in past times, has practiced the religious life under 500 Buddhas of the past; has developed the resolution: "In the future, after the Nirvāṇa of Śākyamuni, I shall compose the Abhidharma." This is why it is said that this Treatise is his work. – In the multitude of disciples of all the Tathāgata-Samyaksaṃbuddhas, it is the law (*dharmatā*) that there are two great masters (*śāstrācārya*) who uphold (*dhātar*; AKB viii, F 219) the True Doctrine (Saddharma): just like Ārya Śāriputra in the lifetime of the Tathāgata and Ārya Kātyāyanīputra after his Nirvāṇa. – Therefore, this Ārya, through the power of his vow, has seen that which is of use to the Dharma and has composed this Treatise.

Question: – If that is so, how can you say that it is the Buddha who speaks the Abhidharma?

Answer: – The Fortunate One, when he was in this world, explained and expounded the Abhidharma in different places by means of various theoretical presentations (lit. *vāda-patha*). Either after the Nirvāṇa or when the Fortunate One was still in this world, the Ārya-disciples, by means of cognition resulting from a resolve (*praṇidhijñāna*), compiled and collected [these presentations], arranging them into sections. Therefore after the departure of the Fortunate One, Kātyāyanīputra also, by means of cognition resulting from a resolve (*praṇidhijñāna*), compiled, collected and composed the *Jñānaprasthāna*. Amongst the theoretical presentations of the Fortunate One, Kātyāyanīputra set up the gates of a book (*vākyadvāra*); he worked out verse-summaries, he composed various chapters to which he gave the name *Skandhaka*. He collected various presentations drawing from disparate subjects and from them composed (1) the *Miscellaneous-Skandhaka*, [i.e., *Saṃkīrnaka-skandhaka*]. The presentation relating to (2) the fetters (*saṃyojana*), (3) cognitions (*jñāna*), (4) actions (*karman*), (5) fundamental material elements (*mahābhūta*), (6) faculties (*indriya*), (7) concentrations (*samādhi*) and (8) views (*dṛṣṭi*) constituted the *Saṃyojanaskandhaka*, etc. – Likewise, all the *Udānagāthā*s have been spoken by the Buddha: the Buddha Bhagavat spoke them, in various places, in response to various persons, according to the circumstances. After the Buddha left the world, the Bhadanta Dharmatrāta, who knew [the *Udānagāthā*s] from tradition, compiled and collected them and gave the name *varga* [to the groups]. He collected the *gāthā*s relating to impermanence and composed the *anityavarga*, and so forth from them.

The Abhidharma is originally the word of the Buddha; it is also a compilation of the Ārya Kātyāyanīputra.

Whether the Buddha spoke [the Abhidharma] or whether the disciple spoke it does not contradict the Dharmatā, for all the Buddhas want the *bhikṣus* to uphold [the Abhidharma]. Thus this Ārya—whether he knows the Abhidharma from tradition or whether he sees and examines it thanks to the cognition resulting from a resolve—has composed this Treatise in order that the True Doctrine remain for a long time in the world... .

DB. *Prakaraṇa of Vasumitra*[57]

It is also called *Prakaraṇagrantha* or *Prakaraṇapādaśāstra*. An important work which is not very systematic (for many things have been amassed in the chapter of *The Thousand Questions*) but frequently quoted in the *Kośa* (for example, i, F 12, 15; ii, F 200, 251, 269...). <xxxiii>

---

57 *LS*: See SAL.32–36; SBS.212–21; EIP.VII.106–8; 375–79.

[The *Prakaraṇa*] differs from the classical Vaibhāṣikavāda on one important issue: it ignores the unwholesome permeating mental factors (*akuśalamahābhūmika*; iii, F 105). Sometimes it expresses itself in terms that must be interpreted rather heavily to make them fit (ii, F 229, 259; iii, F 14, 128). It differs from the *Jñānaprasthāna*, v, F 28.

Ignorance of the unwholesome permeating mental factors (*akuśalamahābhūmika*) category seems to prove that the *Prakaraṇa* is earlier than the *Jñānaprasthāna*.

However, the authors of the *Vibhāṣā* (45, p. 231c) are uncertain:

> Why does this treatise (that is to say, the *Jñānaprasthāna*) say *pṛthagjanatva* and not *pṛthagjanadharma*, whereas the *Prakaraṇapāda* says *pṛthagjanadharma* and not *pṛthagjanatva*? ... This treatise having said *pṛthagjanatva*, the *Prakaraṇapāda* does not repeat it; this treatise not having said *pṛthagjanadharma*, the *Prakaraṇapada* says *pṛthagjanadharma*. This indicates that the latter was composed after this one. There are people who say: That treatise having said *pṛthagjanadharma*, this treatise does not repeat it...; this indicates that that treatise was composed before this one.

The *Prakaraṇa* does not enumerate the faculties (*indriya*) in the same order as the Sūtra, the *Jñānaprasthāna*, the early Pāli scholasticism, AKB i, F 101.

Vijñānakāya[58]

This is a work that the Chinese sources (quoted in Takakusu) date 100 years after the Nirvāṇa; it is attributed to Devaśarman or to *lha-skyid* (Devakṣema?). About the author, who has the title of Arhat in Hsüan-tsang, see Wassiliew in *Tāranātha*, 296, Hiouen-thsang [= Hsüan-tsang], *Vie*, 123, Watters, i, 373.

The significance of this book, not very great from the doctrinal point of view, is noteworthy from the point of view of history. The first chapter, *Maudgalyāyanaskandhaka*, and the second chapter, *Pudgalaskandhaka*, relate to the two great controversies, the existence of past and future [factors] and the existence of the person (*pudgala*), [respectively].[59] <xxxiv>

---

58 *LS*: See SAL.28–31; SBS.197–205; EIP.VII.104–6; 367–74.

59 "La Controverse du Temps and du Pudgala dans le Vijñānakāya", in *Études Asiatiques*, 1925, I, pp. 343–76; *Inde sous les Mauryas*, 1930, p. 138; *Note bouddhique ii: Le Vijñānakāya et le Kathāvatthu*, Ac. Belgique, Nov. 1922, pp. 516–20.

[First chapter:] – Devaśarman refutes the doctrine of Mu-lien or Maudgalyāyana who denies the existence of past and future [factors], just as Tissa Moggaliputta in the Pāli ecclesiastical history denied it.

We have here, from the Sarvāstivādin point of view, the controversy which gave rise to the council of Aśoka. [On the other hand,] according to the legend that Buddhaghosa has caused to be believed in Ceylon and in London, the king ascertained that the Buddha was a *follower of those who distinguish* (*vibhajya-vādin*)—that is to say, probably, did not accept as a whole *the existence of all* (*sarvāstivāda*); then [the king] gave to Tissa Moggaliputta, that is to say, I think, our Mu-lien, the responsibility of presiding over a council where only the opponents of past and future [factors] were admitted.[60]

[Second chapter:] – There is no close relationship between the *Maudgalyāyana-skandhaka* and the work of Tissa (*Katthāvatthu*, i, 6 and following). This is not surprising since the two books represent opposing doctrines and present their own side as prevailing over their opponent.

On the contrary, the *Pudgalaskandhaka* presents close analogies with the *Kathā-vatthu*, i, 1, even down to the identity of phrases.

Devaśarman has two scholars speaking, the follower of the person (*pudgala-vādin*),[61] who admits a vital principle or living being, a kind of soul or self (*pudgala*), and the follower of emptiness (*śūnyatāvādin*), i.e., the negator of the self (*ātman*), the orthodox Buddhist who does not recognize a permanent principle.

The fourth volume of the Japanese translation of the Abhidharma just reached me (September 1931). It contains the *Vijñānakāya*. The translator, B. Watanabe, in a short preface, deals with the philosophical significance of the book, its *compilation*, and its relationship to the Abhidhammas.

60 We must clarify the comments of Barth (ii, 355): to tell the truth, the editors of the *Dīpavaṃsa* are alone in knowing a Tissa Moggaliputta "who must have presided over the council of Aśoka and composed the *Kathāvatthu*." But the Sarvāstivādin tradition knows a Mu-lien to whom it attributes—in the controversy of the past and future [factors]—the position that the *Dīpavaṃsa* assigns to Tissa. There is certainly much legend in the Singhalese hagiography.

61 The enigmatic Gopāla of Hsüan-tsang? – Our sources agree in attributing the doctrine of the *pudgala* to the Sammitīyas, to the Vātsīputrīyas. See *Madhyamakavṛtti*, pp. 275–76.

1. The thesis of the *pudgalavādin* is formulated in terms that are partly identical to those which the *puggalavādin* of the *Kathāvatthu*[62] uses. <xxxv>
2. The arguments are partly the same:
    i. Argument taken from the passage from one plane of existence to another (compare *Kathāvatthu*, i, 1, 158–61).
    ii. Argument taken from the passage from one stage of nobleness to another (i, 1, 221).
    iii. Connections between the doer of the action and the "eater of the fruit" (i, 1, 200).
    iv. Is unsatisfactoriness *caused by oneself* or *caused by another*? (i, 1, 212)
    v. The *pudgala* is not perceived by any of the six consciousnesses; the consciousnesses arise from well-known causes, without intervention from the *pudgala* (*Kathāvatthu, passim*).
3. The method of argumentation is the same in the Sanskrit source as in the Pāli source. The negator of the *pudgala* puts the follower of the *pudgala* into contradiction with the Sūtra, i.e., into contradiction with [the *pudgalavādin*] himself—for the follower of the *pudgala* recognizes that the Buddha has indeed said all that he said.

> The Pudgalavādin says: – There is a self (*ātman*), a sentient being (*sattva*), a living being (*jīva*), a being who is born (*jantu*), a being who is nourished (*poṣa*), an individual (*puruṣa*), a person (*pudgala*).[63] Because there is a person (*pudgala*), he performs actions that must bear an agreeable (*sukhavedanīya*), disagreeable, or neither disagreeable nor agreeable fruit.
>
> The Śūnyatāvādin asks him: – Yes or no, is it the same person who does the action and experiences the sensation?
>
> The Pudgalavādin answers: – No.

---

[62] *Kathāvatthu*: *saccikaṭṭhaparamaṭṭhena puggalo upalabbhati*. – The Sanskrit phrase is not reconstructed with certainty. We have *tattvārthataḥ* (*satyārthataḥ*?) *paramārthataḥ pudgala upalabhyate sākṣīkriyate saṃpratividyate* (?) *saṃvidyate*. – Devaśarman's version, more developed than that of Tissa, appears more modern.

[63] The Sanskrit sources are fond of the expression *puruṣapudgala*. For example, the Sanskrit edition of *Majjhima*, iii, 239 (*chadhāturo ayam puriso*) has *ṣaḍdhātur ayaṃ puruṣapudgalaḥ*. – See *Madhyamakavṛtti*, pp. 129, 180, etc.

> [Reply:] – Recognize the contradiction into which you fall![64] <xxxvi> If there is a self, a person (*pudgala*), and if, because there is a person (*pudgala*), he performs actions and experiences the just retribution of them, then one must say that it is the same person who does the action and who experiences the sensation: thus your answer is illogical. If you now deny that it would be the same person who does the action and experiences the sensation, then one cannot say that there is a self, a living being and so on. To say that is illogical.
>
> If the Pudgalavādin answers: – "It is the same person who does the action and who experiences the sensation", one must ask him: Yes or no, is what the Fortunate One says in the Sūtra well-said, well-defined, well-declared, namely: "Brahmin, to say that it is the same person who does the action and who experiences the sensation is to fall into the extreme view of permanence"[65]?
>
> The Pudgalavādin answers: – Yes, that is well said.
>
> [Reply:] – Recognize the contradiction into which you fall... .

The relationship of the Pāli treatises and the Sanskrit Abhidharma is close. The comparison of the *Prakaraṇa* and the *Dhātukāya* with the *Dhammasaṅgaṇi*, like that of the *Vijñānakāya* with the *Kathāvatthu*, supplies numerous testimonies of the unity of scholasticism. The controversy of the *pudgala* is, without a doubt, one of the controversies (*kathāvatthu*), one of the oldest subjects of discussion. Expounded, in Pāli or in Sanskrit, according to the same principles, with often the same arguments and striking coincidences in phraseology—clearer in Devaśarman, older, it seems to me, in Tissa—it cannot fail to throw light to some extent on the history of the most

---

64 The expression that I translate: "Recognize the contradiction into which you fall", (Ch.) *ju t'ing tuo fu*, corresponds to a Sanskrit original *ājānīhi nigraham*. *Tuo fu* is indeed translated by *nigraha sthāna* in a vocabulary (*Tetsugaku daijisho*, Tokyo 1912) examined in detail by Rosenberg ("Introduction to the study of Buddhism", i, *Vocabulary*, Tokyo, 1916). – We have therefore the exact equivalent here of the phrase *ājānāhi niggaham* of the *Kathāvatthu* and of *Milinda*.

65 The doctrine of the Fortunate One is a path between two extremes. It avoids the extreme theory of permanence, by saying that he who eats the fruit of action is not the same person who has committed the action (*sa karoti so' nubhavati*?): it avoids the theory of annihilation by denying that he who eats the fruit is a person other than the one who has committed the action. – Compare *Saṃyutta*, ii, p. 23.

serious conflict that had troubled ancient Buddhism. We may be surprised that the Pudgalavādin of Devaśarman does not cite the *Sūtra on the Bearer of the Burden* (*Bhārahārasūtra*), the *sūtra* that is one of the principal authorities of Vasubandhu's Pudgalavādin, AKB ix.

As for the *Kathāvatthu*, it is not ill-advised to think that this book is made up of bits and pieces. Certain parts are old, other parts are suspect. <xxxvii>

Dharmaskandha[66]

J. Takakusu wonders whether the compilation having this name is the work of Śāriputra (Yaśomitra) or Maudgalyāyana (Chinese title). This is a somewhat futile concern.

It is a collection of *sūtras*, promulgated in Jetavana, addressed to *bhikṣus*, preceded by two verses: "Homage to the Buddha… . The Abhidharma is like the ocean, the great mountain, the great earth, the great sky. I will try to expound in brief the treasures of the Dharma found therein."

The author indeed comments most often on the *sūtra* that he quotes by citing other *sūtras*: "Among these four, what is stealing? – The Fortunate One says… ."

Without a doubt, the author is a scholarly man and well-informed about the most subtle doctrines of the Sarvāstivāda: "The Fortunate One, in Jetavana, says to the *bhikṣus*: There are four noble fruits of religious praxis (*śrāmaṇyaphala*). What are the four? The fruit of the stream-enterer (*śrotaāpanna*)… . What is the fruit of the stream-enterer? It is twofold, conditioned (*saṃskṛta*) and unconditioned (*asaṃskṛta*). Conditioned, namely, the acquisition of the fruit and that which is acquired by this acquisition, the morality of those in training (*śaikṣa*), … all the factors (*dharma*) of those in training. Unconditioned, namely, the cutting off of the three fetters…" (comp. AKB vi, F 242, 297).

Prajñāptiśāstra[67]

a. The Tibetan *Prajñāptiśāstra*:

The Tibetan *Prajñāptiśāstra* is made up of three parts: (1) *lokaprajñāpti* (world); (2) *kāraṇaprajñāpti* (reasons); (3) *karmaprajñāpti* (action).

The first two are described and analyzed in *Cosmologie bouddhique*, pp. 295–350.

---

66 *LS*: See SAL.15–21; SBS.181–89; EIP.vii.103; 179–87.

67 *LS*: See SBS.189–96; EIP.VII.104; 217.

The third is of the same style. The text [of this part] is divided into chapters preceded by a summary. Here is the beginning:

> Summary: (1) intentional (action); (2) intention; (3) past; (4) wholesome; (5) object; (6) realm of desire; (7) verse; (8) summary of actions.
>
> 1. Thus have I heard. The Fortunate One resided in Jetavana in the park of Anāthapiṇḍada; he said to the *bhikṣus*: "I teach the retribution of intentional action, action done and assumed, retribution in this life...". Thus spoke the Fortunate One. <xxxviii>
>
> 2. There are two actions: the action of intention (*cetanā-karman*), the action subsequent to intention (*cetayitvā-karman*). What is the first? It says: *cetanā*, *abhisaṃcetanā*, *cintanā*, *cetayitatva*, *cittābhisaṃskāra*, *mānasa karman*, that is called *action of intention*... .
>
> 3. The action of intention is past, future, present. What is past action of intention? That which is *jāta*, *utpanna*, *abhinirvṛtta*, ...*abhyatīta*, *kṣīṇa*, *niruddha*, *vipariṇata*, *atītasaṃgṛhīta*, *atītādhvasaṃgṛhīta*... .
>
> 4. Action of intention is wholesome, unwholesome, non-defined... .
>
> 5. Is the object of good intention wholesome...?
>
> 6. The action of intention is of the three realms (*dhātu*). What is that of the realm of desire (*kāma*)?
>
> 7. A verse in honor of the Buddha who teaches the different types of action.
>
> 8. One action, all actions being action (literally: *ekahetuna karmaṇaṃ saṃgrahaḥ karmeti*). Two actions: intention and action subsequent to intention. Three actions: bodily, vocal, mental. Four actions: of Kāma, of Rūpa, of Ārūpya, not belonging to the realms (*dhātu*). Five actions: (i–ii) the defined and non-defined actions that are abandoned by the path of insight; (iii–iv) the defined and non-defined actions that are abandoned by the path of cultivation; (v) that action which is not to be abandoned (*aheya*)... . And so on up to: Twelve [actions].

Almost all the theories expounded in AKB iv are treated, with long quotations from the *sūtras*.

Several details are worth mentioning. For example: "False speech arising from delusion (*moha*) (AKB iv, F 148). Asked by the hunter whether he has seen the gazelle, he thinks: 'It is not appropriate for the hunter to kill the gazelle', and he answers that he has not seen it (compare the story of Kṣāntivādin, Chavannes, *Cinq cents contes*, i, 161). Asked by the king's army whether he has seen the group of bandits... . Asked by the group of bandits whether he has seen the king's army... ." And above all, this case of frivolous speech that arises from greed (*lobha*): "Or else, through the attachment to the examination of the word of the Buddha."

Chapter xi is interesting from another point of view. After the definition of death through the exhaustion of life (*āyus*) or of merit (*puṇya*), the story of the naked ascetic Kāśyapa (*Saṃyutta*, ii, 19–22) is quoted with long expositions:

> Shortly after he had left the Fortunate One, he was killed by a cow. At the time of his death, his faculties became very clear; the color of his face became very pure; the color of his skin became very brilliant.

It should also be noted that Kāśyapa was welcomed as a lay practitioner (*upāsaka*):

> Master, I go forth to the Fortunate One, Master, I go forth to the Sugata. Master, I take refuge in the Fortunate One, I take refuge in the Dharma and in the Saṃgha. May the Fortunate One recognize me (*dhāretu*) as a lay practitioner having renounced killing..." (compare *Saṃyutta*, ii, 22 and *Dīgha*, i, 178). <xxxix>

Then: "The acquisition of *karman* is of four types. They are enumerated as in *Saṃgītiparyāya*." – Three paragraphs on *giving* follow: "Four givings: it happens that the giver is pure and the recipient impure... and so on as in *Saṃgītiparyāya*. Eight givings: the giving to those near (*āsadya*; AKB iv, F 239), and so on as in *Saṃgītiparyāya*. Eight givings: it happens that the person with little faith gives little, to immoral people, for a short period of time... ."

b. The Chinese *Prajñāptiśāstra*:

The Chinese *Prajñāptiśāstra* is incomplete. The edition of the first part merely gives the title: "In the great *Abhidharmaśāstra*, the first part is called *Lokaprajñāpti*", and a gloss says that the Indian original is missing. The title of the second part immediately follows: *Kāraṇaprajñāpti*.

The text continues as follows: "In the *śāstra*, the question is posed: For what reason does the Cakravartin have the royal treasure (*ratna*) of the queen...?" Comparing this with the Tibetan *Kāraṇaprajñāpti*, we see that the Chinese text omits the first chapter on the characteristics (*lakṣaṇa*) of the Bodhisattva; in the second chapter, it omits the enumeration of the royal treasures and the essays on the wheel (*cakra*), the elephant (*hasti*), the horse (*aśva*) and the jewel (*maṇi*).

The third chapter, in Chinese as well as in Tibetan, is composed of verses on the Buddha, a king like the Cakravartin, and the jewels of the Buddha: the Dharma is a wheel; the bases of supernormal power (*ṛddhipāda*) are an elephant. The Tibetan tells us that these verses are the *Śailagāthās*. This concerns a recension which departs from the *Suttanipāta* where the single verse 554 has two quarter-verses (*pāda*) corresponding to the Tibetan: "Śaila, I am a king, a sublime king of the Dharma; in the circle (*maṇḍala*) of the earth, I set in motion the wheel of Dharma; like a Cakravartin king, consider the Tathāgata as merciful, full of pity, a Muni useful to the world."

The Chinese text has fourteen chapters; the last, dealing with meteorological issues (rain, etc.), corresponds closely, as do the others, to the Tibetan text. The latter has four supplementary chapters: the four planes of existence (*gati*), the five modes of birth (*yoni*), to which mode of birth the sentient beings of the various planes of existence belong, etc. It is likely that Vasubandhu had this chapter in front of him, when he includes, like the Tibetan *Prajñāpti*, the story of the *pretī* who eats ten children every day, the stories of Śaila, Kapotamālinī, etc. (AKB iii, F 28–29; *Vibhāṣā*, 120). <xl>

J. Takakusu has ingeniously assumed that the *Lokaprajñāpti*—omitted *either by mistake or on purpose* in the Chinese *Prajñāptiśāstra* of which it should be the first *gate*—occurs in fact in the *śāstra Nanjio* 1297, *Taishō* 1644, entitled *Li-shih*: "*Nanjio* translated *Loka-sthiti*(?)-*abhidharmaśāstra*. But *li* signifies *constructing*, *establishing* and is *practically* equivalent to *shi-she* or *prajñāpti*." Thus J. Takakusu translates *Lokaprajñāpty-abhidharmaśāstra*.

We may note that the *śāstra* 1297, *Taishō* 1644, shows the characteristics of a *sūtra*. In some editions the title is preceded by "spoken by the Buddha".

The text begins: "As the Buddha Bhagavat and Arhat spoke, thus have I heard. The Buddha resided in Śrāvastī, in the monastery of the *upāsikā* Mṛgāramātar Viśākhā, with many *bhikṣus*, all perfected beings (*arhat*)... with the exception of Ānanda. Then the earth shook. And Pūrṇa Maitrāyaṇīputra asked... ." The chapters begin usually: "Then the Buddha spoke", "The Buddha spoke to *bhikṣu* Pūrṇa", "The Buddha spoke to the *bhikṣus*", and end: "This is what the Buddha spoke; thus have I heard."

The table of the chapters, established by J. Takakusu, shows that, although [the *śāstra* 1297] deals with the [same] subject as that with which the Tibetan *Lokaprajñāpti* deals, the former has nothing to do with this *Lokaprajñāpti*. In the latter, there is nothing that corresponds to the 1297 chapter on the *yakṣas* and notably to the conversation of Sātāgira and Hemavata (the verses of the *Hemavatasutta* of the *Suttanipāta*, *Uragavagga*, *Taishō*, p. 177). The *Lokaprajñāpti* has only a brief summary on the heavenly gardens, on which the *Nanjio* 1297 has long expositions. But in both works there is the battle of the gods (*sura*) and the demi-gods (*asura*), the movements of the sun and moon, the durations of life, the hells, the three small and the three great calamities. The order, however, differs.

Sometimes the titles of the chapters of 1297 do not give an exact idea of the contents of the book.

For example, in the first chapter, we have (1) the two causes of earthquakes (movement of the wind, water; magical powers of the noble ones who "consider the earth as small, the water as large"). – (2) After two verses on earthquakes, the Buddha then says to Pūrṇa: "There are winds called Vairambhas..." (AKB vi, F 155). On this circle (*maṇḍala*) of wind, there is the water and the earth, the thickness and width of which are determined as in the *Kośa* (iii, F 138). – The Buddha explains the great hell called Black Darkness which is between the universes (which is not mentioned in the *Kośa*), and the ten cold hells (AKB iii, F 150, n. 2).... <xli> A little later, Ānanda shows his admiration for the Buddha and his power. Udāyin reprimands him and is, in turn, reprimanded by the Master. This is a recension of the famous *Suttanta* (*Aṅguttara*, i, 278) which differs from the Pāli by the prophecy: "Aquatic beings are many, terrestrial beings are few.... The circumstantially liberated (*samayavimukta*; AKB vi, F 251) Arhats are many, the non-circumstantially liberated (*asamayavimukta*) Arhats are few, are difficult to meet in this world: and I declare that Ānanda will become a non-circumstantially liberated Arhat."

Dhātukāya[68]

1. At the beginning, we find here the enumeration and definition of the factors (*dharma*) of the Sarvāstivādins: ten generally permeating mental factors (*mahābhūmika*); ten afflicted permeating mental factors (*kleśamahābhūmika*), ten mental factors of defilement of restricted scope (*parīttakleśa*), five defilements (*kleśa*), five afflicted views (*dṛṣṭi*), five factors (*dharma*)....

The wholesome permeating mental factors (*kuśalamahābhūmika*) are missing, as are the unwholesome permeating mental factors (*akuśalamahābhūmika*).

The five defilements make up an unfamiliar list: *kāmarāga*, *rūparāga*, *ārūpyarāga*, *pratigha*, and *vicikitsā*.

More interesting is the list of five factors: initial inquiry (*vitarka*), investigation (*vicāra*), consciousness (*vijñāna*; meaning the six consciousnesses, i.e., visual, etc.), non-modesty (*āhrīkya*) and shamelessness (*anapatrāpya*).

---

68 *LS*: See SAL.21–28; SBS.206–12; EIP.VII.104; 345–58.

We may believe that this book is from the old Sarvāstivāda.

2. The second part deals with association (*saṃprayoga*), inclusion (*saṃgraha*).

"With how many of the six faculties of sensation (*vedanendriya*: pleasure, etc.) is the sensation (*vedanā*) that belongs to the generally permeating mental factors associated? With how many is it not associated? ... and so on up to: With how many of the faculties of sensation is the affection arisen through mental contact associated? With how many is it not associated?"

"In what is that which is associated with sensation included (*saṃgṛhīta*)? – In the thought and thought-concomitants, eight elements (*dhātu*), two sense-spheres (*āyatana*), three aggregates (*skandha*). – What is it that is left out? – Sensation (*vedanā*), form (*rūpa*), the unconditioned factors (*asaṃskṛta*), the formations dissociated from thought (*viprayuktasaṃskāra*), i.e., eleven elements, ..."

This is exactly the kind of questions that the *Dhātukathāpakaraṇa* examines: *sukhindriyam ... kehici saṃpayuttaṃ kathīhi vippayuttam...*? These are the same questions: *vedanākkhandena ye dhammā saṃpayuttā te dhammā katīhi khandhehi katīhāyataneḥi katīhi dhātūhi saṃgahītā? te dhammā tīhi khandhehi dvīhāyatanehi aṭṭhahi dhātūhi saṃgahītā* (Section xii). <xlii>

3. We can therefore affirm the close relationship of the *Dhātukāya* and the *Dhātukathāpakaraṇa*. The first, in its second part, is merely a Sarvāstivādin recension (theory of the generally permeating mental factors, of the formations dissociated from thought...) of an old book of academic exercises on the factors.

DG. *Saṃgītiparyāya*[69]

The *Saṃgītiparyāya* is a recension of the *Saṃgītisuttanta* which is part of the *Dīghanikāya*.

Same *nidānā*: the Buddha at Pāvā; the death of the Nirgrantha; Śāriputra invites the monks to chant the Dharma and the Vinaya together so that, after the Nirvāṇa of the Tathāgata, his sons would not quarrel. Then follow the chapters on the single factors (*dharma*), the pairs of factors, ... the decades of factors. Finally, the eulogy of Śāriputra: *sādhu sādhu*, by the Fortunate One: "You have well collected and recited with the *bhikṣus* the *Ekottaradharmaparyāya* taught by the Tathāgata...".

The close relationship of the Pāli and of the Sanskrit does not exclude some variants. Thus among the octads, the Abhidharma omits the eight false factors (*mithyātva*; the

---

[69] *LS*: See SAL.14–15; SBS.177–81; EIP.VII.102–3; 203–16.

first of the Pāli list) and adds the eight liberations (*vimokṣa*; omitted in the Pāli list, but which appear in the *Dasa-uttara*). The order differs also. On the one hand, *mārgāṅga, pudgala, dāna, kausīdyavastu, ārabhyavastu, puṇyotpatti, parṣad, loka-dharma, vimokṣa, abhibhvāyatana*, on the other hand, *micchatta, sammatta, puggala, kusītavatthu, ārabbhavatthu, dāna, dānuppatti, parisā, lokadhamma, abhibhāyatana*. Notice that *puṇyotpatti* is better than *dānuppatti*.[70]

Yaśomitra and Bu-ston attribute the *Saṃgītiparyāya* to Mahākauṣṭhila; the Chinese sources name Śāriputra. Is it possible that in one recension, that known by Yaśomitra, Mahākauṣṭhila was given the role that the Pāli and Chinese texts assign to Śāriputra?

J. Takakusu says that the *Saṃgītiparyāya*, in books 15 and 18, quotes the *Dharma-skandhaśāstra*. I have not come across these quotations. The *Prajñāptiśāstra* refers the reader to the *Saṃgītiparyāya*. <xliii>

---

70 The edition of the *Dīrgha* has only four octads: *vimokṣa*, *abhibhū*, *lokadharma* and *samyag-mārga* (which recalls the Pāli *samattas*).

E. *SOME MASTERS OF THE VIBHĀṢĀ*

The *Vibhāṣā* frequently quotes the opinions of masters and of various schools, often divergent opinions. This presentation is often followed by the opinion of P'ing or of the P'ing-chia: "The P'ing-chia says that the first opinion is good." Elsewhere the commentators simply state: "there is no *p'ing-chia*" (AKB iii, F 49, 61, 124; *Siddhi*, 552, 690).[71]

A good specimen of the methods of the *Vibhāṣā*: "whether there is a pure understanding (*prajñā*) outside of the sixteen aspects or modes of activity (*ākāra*)" (AKB vii, F 27–30; *Vibhāṣā*, 102, p. 529): "If yes, why does the *Vijñānakāya* not say this...? If no, why do the *Prakaraṇa* and the *Saṃgītiparyāya*, and this very treatise of the *Vibhāṣā*, say that...? And how does one explain such a *sūtra*? – It should be said that there is no pure understanding outside of the sixteen aspects or modes of activity. – In this case, one understands the *Vijñānakāya*, but how does one explain the *Prakaraṇa*...? – ... There are five reasons that justify this text... ."

Among the masters of the *Vibhāṣā*, we find:

- Pārśva—frequently quoted—who, with several anonymous authors, comments on the *Brahmajāla*, *Vibhāṣā*, 98, p. 508 (note also *Vibh.*, 175, p. 881, on the Śuddhāvāsikas; *Vibh.*, 177, p. 889, on the number of characteristics [*lakṣaṇa*]);
- Pūrṇāśa, *Kośa* iii, F 74; *Vibh.*, 23, p. 118b;
- Śamadatta (?), iii, F 49; *Vibh.*, 118c;
- Saṃghavasu, *Vibh.*, 19, p. 97a; 106, p. 547a; 142, p. 732a (only six faculties [*indriya*] in the absolute sense: the vitality faculty [*jīvita*] and the group of five, i.e., eye, etc., because these six are the root of a sentient being (*sattvamūla*; AKB ii, F 111);

and, in the same passage:

- Kuśavarman, who admits only one faculty, the mental faculty (*manas*), a doctrine which leans toward the *Vijñānavāda*.

---

[71] [LVP, iii, F 61: One should, it seems to me—without having the *Vibhāṣā* at hand—understand by (Ch.) *p'ing-chia* the group of philosophers who edited the *Vibhāṣā* and formulated a critical judgment on the opinons of various masters. Saeki notes that, on such and such a point, the *Vibhāṣā* is content with enumerating opinions: "There is no *p'ing-chia*", it says. – In regard to other points, four *p'ing-chia*.]

Vasumitra[72]

1. Vasumitra is one of the great masters of the *Vibhāṣā*, one of the leaders of the Sarvāstivādin school. His theory on *the existence of all* is, Vasubandhu says, preferable to that of the three other masters, Dharmatrāta, Ghoṣaka and Buddhadeva (AKB v, F 52).

One searches in vain in the two Abhidharmas (within the collection of the seven treatises) attributed to Vasumitra, i.e., the *Prakaraṇapāda* and the *Dhātukāya*, for an allusion to this theory. Tāranātha says, moreover, that the author of the *Prakaraṇa* has nothing to do with the Vasumitra of the *Vibhāṣa* (p. 68).

2. The Āryavasumitrabodhisattva gives his name to the treatise *Nanjio* 1289 [**Āryavasumitrabodhisattvasaṅgītiśāstra*, *Taishō* 1549]. According to the preface, this would be the Vasumitra who, after Maitreya, <xliv> will be the Siṃhatathāgata, the Vasumitra to whom the fathers refused entrance into the Council because he was not a perfected being (*arhat*), and who later became the president of the Council (*Hiuan-tsang*, Watters, i, 271). Watters does not claim that he is the great master of the *Vibhāṣā*; in fact, the thirteenth chapter of 1289, entitled *Sarvāsti-khaṇḍa*, does not contain any reference to Bhadanta Vasumitra's system of difference of state (*avasthānyathātva*). This is all that I will venture to say about this very intricate chapter.

The theory of the time periods is found in the second book (p. 780, 2), where the following text is discussed: "The past and the future are impermanent, all the more so, the present." Why does the Fortunate One say: "all the more so, the present"? Six explanations follow (among which the fifth: "In days of old the length of life was 80,000 years; it will again become 80,000 years"); then: "The Bhadanta says: The present appears for a short period of time; the past and the future do not reside permanently but come and go in turn. That is what is in accord with the *sūtra*."

The paragraph devoted to ignorance (*avidyā*; p. 722) does not express the opinion of the author. It is only: "It is said", notably the opinion of the Mahīśāsakas. Is it the non-cognition (*ajñāna*), the five hindrances (*nīvaraṇa*), incorrect mental application (*ayoniśomanaskāra*), mistaken view (*viparyāsa*), etc? (See AKB iii, F 88). It

---

72 On the various Vasumitras, see Watters, i. 274–75; Masuda's Preface to Vasumitra's treatise on the origins and doctrine of early Indian Buddhist schools, *Asia Major*, ii, p. 7; Tāranātha, 174.

seems, from the silence of S. Kiokuga, the editor of the *Kośa*, that the *Vibhāṣā* does not deal with this point.

The problem of intoxicating liquor is dealt with in 8, p. 786; AKB iv, F 83; *Vibhāṣā*, 124, p. 645.

The discussion on acquisition (*lābha*) and cultivation (*bhāvanā*) (AKB vii, F 63), in which Vasumitra takes part (according to the *Vyākhyā*), should refer to *Nanjio* 1289, for Vasumitra is not named in *Vibhāṣā*, 107, p. 554b.

The same comment applies to the erroneous opinion of Vasumitra on the loss of the stages conducive to penetration (*nirvedhabhāgīya*), AKB vi, F 171.

The verse (*śloka*) on the eight undetermined (*aniyata*) mental factors (AKB ii, F 165) is not in *Nanjio* 1289.

For the discussion: "Does it happen that the factor (*dharma*) which is the causal condition (*hetupratyaya*) of a factor, is not the causal condition of this factor?", see *Nanjio* 1289, 9, at the beginning, compare the *Jñānaprasthāna* in AKB ii, F 258.

Regarding the survival beyond the *kalpa*, p. 782, 2; *manodaṇḍa*, schism, p. 785, classical doctrines.

3. Vasubandhu (ii, F 212) quotes the *Paripṛcchā*, the work of a Vasumitra who is other than the Vasumitra of the *Vibhāṣā*,[73] and who also wrote a *Pañcavastuka* (*Vyākhyā*). <xlv>

The *Paripṛcchā* teaches a doctrine which is clearly Sautrāntika (that the attainment of cessation [*nirodhasamāpatti*] is accompanied by a subtle thought). Also, K'uei-chi (*Siddhi*, 211) says that this Vasumitra is a divergent Sautrāntika master.

As for the *Pañcavastuka*,[74] we possess a commentary, the *Pañcavastukavibhāṣā*, attributable to Dharmatrāta (*Nanjio* 1283, *Taishō* 1555). – The five *vastus* are the *vastus* explained in AKB ii, F 286–87 (*vastu* in the sense of a specific entity [*svabhāvavastu*], *vastu* in the sense of cognitive object of consciousness [*ālambana-vastu*], ...).

---

73 Who (*Vibhāṣā*, p. 152a) declares that any thought–thought-concomitant (*citta-caitta*) disappears in the attainment of cessation (*nirodhasamāpatti*)?

74 Maybe *Taishō* 1556, anonymous: *Sarvāstivādasamaya-pañcavastuka*, notable for its enumeration of the formations dissociated from thought (*viprayukta*), 997c): *prāpti, asaṃjñisamāpatti, nirodhasamāpatti, āsaṃjñika, jīvitendriya, sabhāgatā, deśaprāpti* (?), *āyatanaprāpti, jāti, jarā, sthiti, anityatā, nāma-pāda-vyañjanakāyas*.

This work does not seem to contain Sautrāntika opinions;[75] it is divided into three chapters: *Rūpavibhāga* (material form), *Cittavibhāga* (thought), and *Caittavibhāga* (thought-concomitants).

Vasubandhu takes from it the demonstration of the "vision by two eyes" by means of the argument of perceiving two moons (AKB i, F 86; *Pañcavastukavibhāṣā*, end of first book, p. 991c).

He probably also takes from it the theory (i, F 71): the five consciousnesses (*vijñāna*) are *of retribution* (*vipākaja*) and *of equal outflow* (*naiṣyandika*), and that the sixth is also *of a moment* (*kṣaṇika*) (*Pañcavastuka*, p. 933c).

The demonstration of the existence of the agreeable (*sukha*; AKB vi, F 127) is very similar to the demonstration established in the *Pañcavastuka*[*vibhāṣā*],[76] p. 994c.

As for the treatise of the sects, (Sarvāstivādin thesis, 28), K'uei-chi indicates the opinion of the *Pañcavastuka* (Tokyo, 24, 1, 25a8) on the nature of the particular inherent characteristic (*svalakṣaṇa*) that is the object of the consciousnesses (*vijñāna*; AKB i, F 19). <xlvi>

Ghoṣaka and the Abhidharmāmṛtaśāstra

A Tho-gar or Tukhāra who, after the Council and the death of Kaniṣka, was invited with Vasumitra by a ruler of the country of Aśmaparānta, located to the west of Kaśmīr and close to Tukhāra (Tāranātha, 61); he was the patron of a theory that *all exists*, which was not good; he is frequently quoted in the *Vibhāṣā*; he was also the author of the *Abhidharmāmṛtaśāstra* (*Nanjio* 1278, *Taishō* 1553).[77]

---

[75] It quotes the Abhidharma-ācāryas. It admits the generally permeating mental factors (*mahābhūmika*, p. 994b3,) and also the non-informative (*avijñapti*, p. 992c), which it explains, along with the restraints (*saṃvara*), in exactly the same way as the *Kośa*. – But the phrase: "There are two gates to the deathless (*amṛta*), the meditation on the repulsive and the regulation of the breath", is worth noting, p. 989b.

[76] *LS*: LVP has *Pañcavastuka*, but Kritzer comments (RCYA.131) that "La Vallée Poussin seems to have made a slip in referring to it as the *Pañcavastuka* when it is, in fact, Dharmatrāta's commentary, the *Pañcavastukavibhāṣā*, but he gives the correct *Taishō* reference: T. 1555: 994c6–995b28".

[77] *LS*: Dessein (SBS.278) comments that Fukuhara, Frauwallner, Mochizuki, Lin and Kritzer agree with this attribution; he himself, however, and Dhammajoti disagree with it. Dhammajoti states (SA.IV.107f.):

This treatise is a small, truly ambrosial book, very readable (in spite of the early date of its translation: 220–65 A.D.), very complete (for example, chap. vi, the doctrine of the primary characteristics [*lakṣaṇa*] and secondary characteristics [*anulakṣaṇa*], AKB ii, F 222), but brief: where, nevertheless, we find some well-chosen details (for example, the enumeration of the fields of merit: father, mother, an old person, a sick person…).

The list of the formations dissociated from thought (*viprayukta*, p. 970) is similar to that of the *Prakaraṇa* (AKB ii, F 178): *prāpti*, *jāti*, *sthiti*, *anityatā*, *asaṃjñisamāpatti*, *nirodhasamāpatti*, *asaṃjñi-āyatana*, *nānādeśaprāpti* (?), *vastuprāpti* (?), *āyatana-prāpti* (?), the three *kāyas*, *pṛthagjanatva*.

The *Kośa* (ii, F 212f.) reproduces the essentials of a discussion between Ghoṣaka and the Sautrāntika Vasumitra, the author of the *Paripṛcchā* (see above p. xliv), on the

---

> The *Jñānaprasthāna-śāstra* (JPŚ) and the *Mahāvibhāṣā-śāstra* (MVŚ), magnificent as they are, lack sufficient unity and systematization as a whole. … Such a state of affairs eventually brought about a significant reaction from some of the more progressive doctors of the Sarvāstivāda, and this led to a new line of development. These doctors deviated to varying degrees from the Kāśmīrian orthodoxy—known after the MVŚ as the Vaibhāṣika—and began to compose manuals aimed at being concise, lucid and systematic.
>
> The earliest of such manuals that we possess in Chinese is the *Abhidharmāmṛta-rasa-śāstra* (AmRŚ) by a certain Ghoṣaka, which effectively serves as an introduction to the JPŚ and MVŚ. Its Chinese translation comprises 16 short chapters in two fascicles. There is clear evidence that while AmRŚ derives its material from the JPŚ, MVŚ, *Abhidharmaprakaraṇa-śāstra* (PrŚ) and other sources, it is basically inclined toward PrŚ and the Gāndhāra school. As Bhadanta Ghoṣaka, one of the "four great Sarvāstivāda Ābhidharmikas", was pre-MVŚ, the author of the AmRŚ must be a different Ghoṣaka whose date is probably not far from the completion of the MVŚ.

Likewise, Van den Broeck, in his Foreword to his *La saveur de l'immortel* (*A-p'i-t'an Kan Lu Wei Lun*). *La version chinoise de l'Amṛtarasa de Ghoṣaka*, states (p. 21; transl.: Migme Chödrön):

> It seems logical to conclude that the *Amṛta* should be the work of another Ghoṣaka, since not only the theses of the Bhadanta Ghoṣaka are not mentioned in it, but also the text contradicts them in certain cases and, lastly, seems to belong to a later period than that of the Bhadanta cited in the *Vibhāṣā*.

existence of thought in the attainment of cessation (*nirodhasamāpatti*). – The *Vibhāṣā*, it seems, ignores the author of the *Paripṛcchā*.

Among the opinions of Ghoṣaka, indicated in the *Vibhāṣā* and found in the *Kośa*, the most notable is that "visible forms are seen by understanding (*prajñā*) associated with the visual consciousness", an opinion that departs from orthodoxy (*Vibhāṣā*, 13, beginning; AKB i, F 83).

Elsewhere Ghoṣaka is very orthodox,[78] or else his divergences, which are minimal, indicate a progress, for example, AKB vi, F 167, 170, 301. – The references iv, F 26, 174 and v, F 112 deserve to be examined.

Vibhāṣā, 77, p. 397b, is interesting: <xlvii>

> Ghoṣaka says: The five aggregates (*skandha*) that belong to one's own stream, to the stream of another, that belong to sentient beings and that do not belong to sentient beings, are *unsatisfactoriness* and the *truth of unsatisfactoriness*. At the direct realization (*abhisamaya*), the meditators see only that the five aggregates of their own stream are unsatisfactoriness; they do not see that the [aggregates of] others are unsatisfactoriness. Why? Because unsatisfactoriness is understood under the aspect of *torment*: yet, the aggregates of the stream of another... do not torment one's own stream.

Buddhadeva

S. Lévi wonders (*JA*, 1896, 2, p. 450, compare Barnett, *JRAS*, 1913, p. 945) whether the Buddhadeva of the *Vibhāṣā* should be identified with the Ārya Buddhadeva, a Sarvāstivādin, the Lion of Mathurā. The same Lion indicates the Sarvāstivādin Budhila who seems to have a relationship with the Mahāsāṃghikas and who is perhaps the Fo-t'i-lo of Hsüan-tsang,[79] the author of the *Chi-chin-lun* (*Tattvasamuccayaśāstra*) for use in the Mahāsāṃghikas (?) (Lévi, *ibid.*; Watters, i, 82).

In Konow (*Kharoshṭhī Inscriptions*, 44–49) we will find the most recent comments on these difficult inscriptions. – There is nothing wrong with Buddhadeva being quite earlier than the *Vibhāṣā*. The Sarvāstivādins owe their name to the theory that *all exists*, which Buddhadeva is probably one of the first to have explained.

---

[78] On the never-returner (*anāgāmin*), *Vibhāṣā*, 175, p. 879b; on the meaning of existence (*bhava*), (192, p. 960b); on the meditative attainments that follow a good thought of the realm of desire (192, p. 961c).

[79] A gloss says that the word signifies *Bodhi-taking*, which would give Bodhilāta.

In addition to his theory that *all exists* (AKB v, F 54), Buddhadeva is unique in maintaining that derived matter (*bhautika*) is merely a state (*avasthā*) of the fundamental material elements (*mahābhūta*) (i, F 64), that the thought-concomitants (*caitta*: sensation, ideation, intention) are merely states of thought (*citta*, *vijñāna*) (ii, F 150; ix, F 262; *Siddhi*, 395; *Vibhāṣā*, 127, beginning; 142, p. 730, 2)—a doctrine which connects Buddhadeva with Dharmatrāta and with the Dārṣṭāntikas-Sautrāntikas.[80]

ED. *Dharmatrāta*

There are at least two Dharmatrātas:

1. The Bodhisattva who compiled the *Udānavarga*. <xlviii> The *Vibhāṣā*, followed by the *Kośa*, quotes it to show that a work may be the *word of the Buddha* even though composed by a master. According to the preface of *Nanjio* 1321, *Taishō* 212 (399 A.D.), this Dharmatrāta was the maternal uncle of Vasumitra (Chavannes, *Cinq cents contes*, iii, 297).[81]

2. The master quoted in the *Vibhāṣā*, the patron of a theory of *all exists* (AKB v, F 53), which seemed to the Vaibhāṣikas to be too akin to the system of the heterodox, [i.e., Sāṃkhya].

3. This master of the *Vibhāṣā* is also the author of a *Abhidharmasāra* [see p. xliii], which bears his name (*Taishō* 1552),[82] a commentary and a new edition of the

---

[80] The Dārṣṭāntikas deny the thought-concomitants (*caitta*); the Sautrāntikas admit the thought-concomitants but differ on their number.

[81] *LS*: On Dharmatrāta, the compiler of the *Udānavarga*, see Dessein (2003.293f.) and Dhammajoti (1995; 2007) and Lin (1949). Dessein comments that "this Bhadanta Dharmatrāta of the *Ch'u Yao Ching* [**Udāna*] is generally accepted to be a Dārṣṭāntika, and is also referred to in the **Saṃyuktābhidharmahṛdaya*, i.e., as the *Dharmatrāta of former times*. [Lin (1949) dates this Dārṣṭāntika Dharmatrāta around the second century B.C.]. See also Dhammajoti ADCP.51–53.

[82] *LS*: Note that both Dhammajoti (ADCP.51–53) and Paul Dessein (EIP.VIII.314) disagree with LVP on the authorship of this text. Dessein himself distinguishes (1999.xxii.f) between three kinds of Dharmatrāta:

1. a Bhadanta Dharmatrāta, Dārṣṭāntika, and one of the four masters of the **Mahāvibhāṣā*, author of the *Ch'u yao Ching*, of the second century A.D.

2. a Dharmatrāta, author of the **Saṃyuktābhidharmahṛdaya*, and possibly commentator of Vasumitra's *Pañcavastuka*. He was a Sarvāstivādin of the beginning of the fourth century.

Abhidharmasāra of *Dharmaśrī* (*Nanjio* 1288, *Taishō* 1550). As a matter of fact, the Dharmatrāta of the *Vibhāṣā* (74, p. 383, 2) denies the material form (*rūpa*) that is part of the sense-sphere of factors (*dharmāyatana*), i.e., the non-informative form (*avijñaptirūpa*); we find the same negation, somewhat more veiled but clear nevertheless, in the *Sāra*, chapter on action, p. 888, (see below).

4. There is nothing to oppose [the idea] that this same Dharmatrāta is the commentator on the *Pañcavastuka* of Vasumitra (the Sautrāntika), *Nanjio* 1283, *Taishō* 1555, the *Pañcavastukavibhāṣā*.[83]

Bhadanta and Dharmatrāta

The *Vibhāṣā*, it seems, ignores Kumāralāta and Śrīlāta, who are the heads of the Sautrāntika school (*Siddhi*, 221, teachings by K'uei-chi). The Sautrāntika school—more exactly the school that ought to take the name of Sautrāntika—is represented in the *Vibhāṣā* by the Dārṣṭāntikas and by two masters: (1) Dharmatrāta, a divergent Sarvāstivādin, and (2) the master whom the *Vibhāṣā* calls simply "Bhadanta", whom the *Vyākhyā* of the *Kośa* calls the "Sautrāntika Bhadanta" (AKB viii, F 151), who is at the "top of the list of Sautrāntikas" (viii, F 222), and who adheres to or leans toward the Sautrāntika system (i, F 36).[84]

(Dessein elaborates that the **Saṃyuktābhidharmahṛdaya* takes the *Abhidharmahṛdayaśāstra* of Dharmaśreṣthin as its fundament, and that all doctrinal deviations in it are adaptations of the *Mahāvibhāṣā*, which makes the work posterior to the *Mahāvibhāṣā*.)

3. a Dharmatrāta, Dhyāna master of the beginning of the fifth century, whose name is linked to the *Ta-mo-to-lo Ch'an Ching*.

See Dessein's *Dharmas Associated with Awarenesses and the Dating of the Sarvāstivāda Abhidharma Works.* (1996) and Dessein's Introduction (SAH.xix–lxxxv) to his translation of the **Saṃyuktābhidharmahṛdayaśāstra* (1999), as well as Dessein (2003).

[83] See above p. xlv.

LS: Dhammajoti comments (ADCP.51ff.) that since Dharmatrāta, the author of the *Pañcavastuka-vibhāṣā*, upholds the Vaibhāṣika view, which consistently and explicitly insists that "the eye sees", it is unlikely that he is the same one as Bhadanta Dharmatrāta of the *Mahāvibhāṣā*, since the *Mahāvibhāṣā* tells us that the latter holds the "consciousness sees" theory. Dhammajoti dates the author of the *Pañcavastuka-vibhāṣā* around the fourth century A.D. and attributes to him also the **Abhidharma-hṛdaya-vyākhyā* (T no. 1552), which Dessein names **Saṃyuktābhidharmahṛdayaśāstra*.

[84] *Sautrāntikā Bhadantādayaḥ*; *sautrāntikadarśanavalambin*.

As for Hsüan-tsang, P'u-kuang and Bhagavadviśeṣa, they sometimes recognize in the "Bhadanta" of the *Vibhāṣā* the Sthavira or Bhadanta Dharmatrāta (AKB i, F 36; iv, F 22). <xlix> – Yaśomitra states that Bhagavadviśeṣa is mistaken: "Bhadanta is the philosopher whom the *Vibhāṣā* mentions under the simple name of *Bhadanta*, a philosopher who adheres to the Sautrāntika system or leans toward this system; whereas Dharmatrāta, whom the *Vibhāṣā* calls by his name, is a Sarvāstivādin, the author of one of the four theories of the Sarvāstivāda (AKB i, F 36)." – Moreover, "the first version of the *Vibhāṣā* gives the name of this master [i.e., Bhadanta] in transcription and precedes this, like those of the other masters, with the title of venerable: [the doctrine of venerable Bhadanta says]" (note based on N. Péri, in *Cosmologie bouddhique*, 276).

Be that as it may, "Dharmatrāta" expresses opinions on major issues which clearly depart from the system of the *Vibhāṣā*, from the orthodox Sarvāstivādin system; the same, by the way, is true for Buddhadeva.

1. The Bhadanta does not accept that the eye sees: it is the visual consciousness that sees (i, F 83);
   - he has a specific theory on the non-contact of atoms (Wassiliew, 279), which Vasubandhu accepts and which Saṃghabhadra discusses (i, F 91);[85]
   - he admits three thought-concomitants (*caitta*) (ii, F 150, Add.), which distinguishes him from the Dārṣṭāntikas;
   - he denies, with the Sarvāstivādins, that material form (*rūpa*) is a condition as the equivalent and immediate antecedent (*samanantarapratyaya*; ii, F 301);
   - he admits the prolonged existence of intermediate existence (*antarābhava*), against the Sarvāstivādins (iii, F 48);
   - he has a specific opinion on *pratītyasamutpāda* and *samutpanna* (iii, F 74);
   - he denies the non-informative (*avijñāpti*), which is clearly anti-Sarvāstivādin (iv, F 22);
   - he has a very orthodox doctrine on the four ways in which factors are wholesome (*kuśala*), (iv, F 33);
   - he maintains that intelligent animals (iv, F 205) are capable of committing a transgression with an immediately successive retribution (*ānantarya*);
   - he gives an explanation of the word *liberation* (*vimokṣa*; viii, F 207);
   - he mixes the meditations (*dhyāna*), and the pure abodes (*śuddhāvāsika*) (*Vibhāṣā*, 175, p. 881c);

---

[85] According to Wassiliew, 279, Saṃgharakṣita differs a little. We do not know this master, nor the Bhūmisena of p. 280.

- he deals with the last thought of the perfected being (*arhat*) (*Vibhāṣā*, 191, p. 954, 1);
- he deals with annihilation (*uccheda*) and eternality (*śāśvata*) (*Vibhāṣā*, 200, p. 1003, 3);
- he deals with the meaning of *alpa*, *sulabha*, *anavadya*, and with the praise of the disciples by the Buddha (*Vibhāṣā*, 181, p. 909, 1, and 179, p. 900, 2, where he differs from Vasumitra).[86] <l>

The Bhadanta is very clear on "investigation–initial inquiry" (*vicāra-vitarka*),[87] *Vibhāṣā*, 145, p. 744b (and 52, p. 269; AKB ii, F 174 and viii, F 183):

> The author of the *Jñānaprasthāna* wants to refute what the Dārṣṭāntika says. The latter says: "There is initial inquiry–investigation (*vitarka-vicāra*) from Kamadhātu up to Bhavāgra (summit of cyclic existence). – Why? – Because the Sūtra says that grossness of thought is initial inquiry, that subtleness of thought is investigation: but grossness and subtleness of thought exist up to Bhavāgra."
>
> The Bhadanta says: "The masters of the Abhidharma say that initial inquiry–investigation are grossness–subtleness of thought. But grossness and subtleness are relative things and exist up to Bhavāgra. However, these masters accept initial inquiry and investigation only in Kamadhātu and in the Brahmaloka. This is poorly said, this is not well said."
>
> The masters of the Abhidharma say: "What we say is well said, not poorly said. In fact… ."

2. Vasubandhu (AKB vii, F 73) attributes to the Bhadanta Dharmatrāta an opinion on the strength of the body of the Fortunate One which is the opinion of the Bhadanta according to *Vibhāṣā*, 30, p. 155c.

In the *Vibhāṣā* (13, beginning), Dharmatrāta says that visible form is seen by the visual consciousness (*cakṣurvijñāna*): an opinion that the *Kośa* attributes to a Vijñānavādin (i, F 82), and which differs from that of the Bhadanta (*Vibhāṣā*, 13, p. 3b): the eye sees because of light…, the *manas* knows because of mental application (*manaskāra*).

---

86 The opinions on seeing by means of the visual consciousness, on the number of the thought-concomitants (*caitta*), on the non-existence of the non-informative (*avijñāpti*), are clearly non-Vaibhāṣika. Moreover, the *Vibhāṣā* carefully points out the opinions of the Bhadanta.

87 See also *Vibhāṣā*, p. 219.

3. *Vibhāṣā*, 127, beginning, p. 661c16.

The *Jñānaprasthāna* wants to refute what the other masters say. In this school there are two masters, the first is Buddhadeva, the second, Dharmatrāta:

i. Buddhadeva says that material form (*rūpa*) is solely the four fundamental material elements (*mahābhūta*), that the thought-concomitants (*caitta*) are thought (*citta*). Derivative material form (*upādāyarūpa*) is solely the particular fundamental material elements (*mahābhūtaviśeṣa*); the thought-concomitants (*caitta*) are solely the particular thought (*cittaviśeṣa*). – The *sūtra*s that are put forward in support of this theory:

a. "Everything that is in the eye, [the ball of flesh (*māṃsapiṇḍa*),] is solid, [humid, etc.]" (AKB i, F 65);

b. "Concentration (*samādhi*) is application of thought to a single object (*cittaikāgrya*)…" (viii, F 128).

How does Buddhadeva establish the elements (*dhātu*), the sense-spheres (*āyatana*) and the aggregates (*skandha*)? … The Abhidharmācāryas say: "The *sūtra*s that are put forward do not have this meaning…".

ii. Dharmatrāta accepts derivative material form (*rūpa*) apart from primary material form (*rūpa*; i.e., the fundamental material elements), and thought-concomitants (*caitta*) apart from thought (*citta*). But he maintains that derivative tangibles and the material form (*rūpa*) that is part of the sense-sphere of factors (*dharmāyatana*) do not exist. In this way he wants to establish the existence of the elements, sense-spheres, aggregates, just as the Abhidharma system has done. <li> But the derivative tangibles [LS: do not??] exist apart, as the other derivative material forms do; but if the material form of the sense-sphere of factors does not exist, then the non-informative (*avijñāpti*) does not exist (AKB i, F 64; iv, F 14).

4. *Vibhāṣa*, 74, p. 383b.

The Abhidharma says: "What is the aggregate of material form (*rūpaskandha*)? Ten sense-spheres of material form (*rūpāyatana*) and the material form (*rūpa*) included in the sense-sphere of factors (i.e., the non-informative)." – What system does [the Abhidharma] want to refute? – It wants to refute the Dārṣṭāntikas, for they deny any material form included in the sense-sphere of factors.

Dharmatrāta also says: "Everything that is material form is either support or object of consciousness (*vijñāna*). How could there be material form which is neither one nor the other?" It is in order to refute these opinions that the above-mentioned definition of the aggregate of material form is given. – But if the material form which is included within the sense-sphere of factors is real, how can one explain what Dharmatrāta says? – It is not necessary to explain it, for this is not in the *Tripiṭaka*. Or, if one must explain it, one can say… that the material form included within the sense-sphere of factors—arising from the fundamental material elements (*mahābhūta*) which are the object of the body—can be considered to be the object of tactile consciousness. Thus the statement of Dharmatrāta is without error.

5. *Vibhāṣā*, 142, p. 730b:

   Among the twenty-two controlling faculties (*indriya*) (AKB i, F 101), how many are real entities on their own and how many are only names? – The Ābhidhārmikas say that for twenty-two names there are seventeen real entities, since the two sexual faculties (parts of the body sense-faculty) and the three pure faculties (combinations of faith, etc.) are not real entities on their own (AKB ii, F 108, 116).

   Dharmatrāta accepts only fourteen real entities: the first five faculties (eye, etc.), the vitality faculty (*jīvitendriya*), the faculty of sensation of equanimity (*upekṣendriya*) and the (praxis-oriented) faculty of concentration (*samādhi–indriya*) are not real entities. In fact, the vitality faculty is one of the formations dissociated from thought (*viprayuktasaṃskāra*) (AKB ii, F 215) and these are not real.[88] There is no sensation apart from the agreeable and the disagreeable: thus the sensation of equanimity is not a real entity. There is no concentration, apart from thought.

   Buddhadeva says that only a single controlling faculty is real, namely the mental faculty (*mana-indriya*): "Conditioned phenomena (*saṃskṛta*), he says, are of two types: fundamental material elements (*mahābhūta*) and thoughts (*citta*)…".

The *Name Index* [see *Appendix*] contains the information, nearly complete, of the references to the Bhadanta in the *Vibhāṣā*. <lii>

---

88 However, Dharmatrāta, in *Abhidharmasāra*, 2, p. 885, explains the causes of the formations dissociated from thought (*viprayukta*).

F. *SOME SCHOOLS DISCUSSED IN THE VIBHĀṢĀ*[89]

FA. *Dārṣṭāntikas and Sautrāntikas*

The history of this school, being long, is not yet clear. The notes of K'uei-chi (*Siddhi*, 221–24;[90] Masuda, "Sects", *Asia Major*, ii, 67; Lévi, *Dṛṣṭāntapaṅkti*, p. 97) show that Hsüan-tsang was not very well informed. Takakusu (*Abhidharma Literature*, 131) says that the *Vibhāṣā* speaks of the Sautrāntikas, but rarely, in any case, for I have found only a single reference to the Sautrāntikas; we can say that the *Vibhāṣā* knows only the Dārṣṭāntikas.

There has been some thought about establishing a relationship between this name and the book of Kumāralāta, the *Dṛṣṭāntapaṅkti*; one may wonder if the Dārṣṭāntikas are characterized by the use of *comparisons*, as the Tibetans say (Wassiliew, 274, according to whom Sautrāntika = Dārṣṭāntika); nevertheless, the meaning of the word *dṛṣṭānta* is not established with certainty. J. Przyluski thinks that the Dṛṣṭānta is contrasted with scripture.[91] This way of looking at it is confirmed, I believe, by the *Vibhāṣā*, 154, beginning.

It is said in the traditional *Dṛṣṭānta*:[92]

> He who gives alms to a person who has come out of the attainment of cessation (*nirodhasamāpatti*) is endowed with an action that bears an effect in this life.
>
> Why? – There is no good reason to explain this text.
>
> Why? – Because this is neither Sūtra, nor Vinaya, nor Abhidharma, but only stated in the traditional *Dṛṣṭānta*. That which is said in the traditional *Dṛṣṭānta* may be true or not true. If, however, one wishes to explain it, one should say that this alms-giver obtains the effect in this life or obtains great

---

89 See the references to the Mahāsāṃghikas, the Vātsīputrīyas, the Mahīśāsakas, and the Dharmaguptas in the *Index*.

90 *LS*: See appendix to *Introduction*.

91 *LS*: Przyluski: *Dārṣṭāntika, Sautrāntika and Sarvāstivādin*, 1940, p. 250: "In literature, the *dṛṣṭānta* is then opposed to the *sūtra* or *sūtrānta*, to which it is a kind of complement, or illustration".

See SA.IV.74.

92 (Ch.) *ch'uan-yü*; *ch'uan* translates *āgama* or *avavāda*.

effects. The text mentions only the first alternative because it pleases the people of the world.[93] <liii>

We may speak of a Dārṣṭāntika-Sautrāntika school: in looking at it more closely, the *Vibhāṣā* ascribes to its Dārṣṭāntikas almost all of the theses that the *Kośa* ascribes to the Sautrāntikas.

Here are the more important disagreements between the Sarvāstivādins and the Dārṣṭāntikas-Sautrāntikas:

1. The Abhidharmas of the Sarvāstivādins are not authoritative (AKB i, F 5; ii, F 104; vii, F 22).
2. The unconditioned factors (*asaṃskṛta*) do not have a real existence (ii, F 52).
3. The formations dissociated from thought (*viprayukta*; ii, F 178) do not have a real existence: negation of the possessions (*prāpti*), of the vitality faculty (*jīvitendriya*), etc.
4. Past and future factors do not have a real existence (v, F 52).
5. The existence of past factors allows the Sarvāstivādins to explain the play of causality; the possessions render the same service. Negating past factors, the possessions, etc., the Dārṣṭāntika-Sautrāntika school accepts a subtle thought or seeds (*bīja*) or traces (*vāsanā*; perfuming), and thus takes into account the modes of the stream (ii, F 185, 246; iv, F 173; ix, F 295...).
6. Destruction does not have a cause; things do not have a duration (*sthiti*): the moment (*kṣaṇa*) is of a size that tends toward zero (iv, F 4). (See *Rocznik*, vol. viii).
7. Notable divergences with respect to action: negation (i) of the non-informative (*avijñapti*; iv, F 14), (ii) of bodily action (iv, F 12), (iii) of the unavoidable character of the retribution of a transgression with an immediately successive retribution (*ānantarya*) (*Vibhāṣā*, 69, p. 359b).
8. On the thought-concomitants (*caitta*) and the derived material elements (*bhautika*): opinions that depart from the Sarvāstivādin system (ii, F 150).
9. Explanation of the three categories (*rāśi*) (AKB iii, F 137) that exist from hell to Bhavāgra: (i) beings having the factors (*dharma*) of Nirvāṇa; (ii) beings not having them; (iii) indetermined beings (*Vibhāṣā*, 186, p. 930c); compare the *Siddhi* and its families (*gotra*).

---

93 Vasubandhu, AKB iv, F 123—and also Saṃghabhadra, 40, p. 572, which is rather surprising—do not take the second alternative into account and follow the doctrine of the (Ch.) *ch'uan-yü*.

10. The body of perfected beings (*arhat*) is pure, being produced through *understanding* (i, F 4; Saṃghabhadra, 1, p. 331b).
11. Simultaneity of the Buddhas (iii, F 199).

The references which follow—completed in the *Name Index* (*see entries* Dārṣṭāntika, Sautrāntika in the *Appendix*]—are listed according to the order of the material in the *Kośa*:

1. The Dārṣṭāntika rejects certain *sūtra*s: how does he claim the name of Sautrāntika? Saṃghabhadra, 1, p. 332a.

   The consciousnesses (*vijñāna*), including the mental consciousness (*manovijñāna*), have a special object, see AKB ix, F 242; *Vibhāṣā*, 87, p. 449, 1.

   Whether the eye sees the visible form, see AKB i, F 82; *Vibhāṣā*, 13, beginning.

2. The Sthavira (= Śrīlāta) and all the other Dārṣṭāntika masters deny space (*ākāśa*), see Saṃghabhadra, 3, p. 347b.

   Negation of possession (*prāpti*), of cessation not due to deliberation (*apratisaṃkhyānirodha*), see *Vibhāṣā*, 93, beginning; 157, p. 796; 186, p. 931b. <liv>

   The characteristics (*lakṣaṇa*) of the *conditioned*, Dārṣṭāntikas, Vibhajyavādins, Saṃtānasābhāgikas..., see *Vibhāṣā*, 38, p. 198ab.

   The condition (*pratyayatā*) is not real, see *Vibhāṣā*, 131, p. 690b.

   There is no ripening cause (*vipākahetu*) outside of the intention (*cetanā*), no ripened effect (*vipākaphala*) outside of the sensation (*vedanā*), see *Vibhāṣā*, 19, p. 96a.

   Material form (*rūpa*) is not a homogeneous cause (*sabhāgahetu*) of material form (*rūpa*), the opinion of the Dārṣṭāntika according to the gloss of Saeki Kyokuga, see AKB ii, F 256; but, according to the *Vibhāṣā*, 17, p. 87c), the opinion of the Bahirdeśakas.

   "Among the Sautrāntikas, the Bhadanta Dārṣṭāntika holds sensation-ideation-intention (*vedanā-saṃjñā-cetanā*) to be existing on their own; Buddhadeva adds contact (*sparśa*) and mental application (*manasikāra*): the other thought-concomitants (*caitta*) are only thought (*citta*); the master Śrīlāta considers the unconditioned factors (*asaṃskṛta*) and the formations dissociated from thought (*viprayukta*) as nominal existents" (Wassiliew, 281, [309], corrected).

   There is a subtle thought in the attainment of cessation (*nirodhasamāpatti*) and in the attainment of non-ideation (*asaṃjñisamāpatti*) (as also maintained by the Vibhajyavādins), AKB ii, F 212; viii, F 208; *Vibhāṣā*, 152, p. 774a; 151, p. 772c.

   Negation of the reality of the dream, see *Vibhāṣā*, 37, p. 193. col. 2.

The thought-concomitants (*caitta*) arise in succession, the Dārṣṭāntikas and likewise the Bhadanta, see *Vibhāṣā*, 95, p. 493c and 145, p. 745a; thought cannot be accompanied by cognition (*jñāna*) and non-cognition (*ajñāna*), 106, p. 547.

Initial inquiry (*vitarka*) and investigation (*vicāra*) in the three realms (*dhātu*), see AKB ii, F 174; viii, F 183; *Vibhāṣā*, 52, p. 269b; 145, p. 744b.

3. The intermediate existence (*antarābhava*) and miraculous emanation (*nirmita*), see *Vibhāṣā*, 135, p. 700a.

Contact (*sparśā*) is not a real entity in itself, see *Vibhāṣā*, 149, beginning.

4. Arising depends on the causal condition (*hetupratyaya*) but not destruction, the Dārṣṭāntikas against the Ābhidhārmikas, see AKB iv, F 5; *Vibhāṣa*, 21, p. 105a.

Negation of the material form of the sense-sphere of factors (*dharmāyatanarūpa* = the non-informative [*avijñapti*]), Dharmatrāta, the Dārṣṭāntikas, see *Vibhāṣā*, 74, p. 383b.

On the four and eight types of actions from the point of view of their being determined, Dārṣṭāntikas, or Sautrāntikas according to *Vyākhyā* (AKB iv, F 116); *Vibhāṣā*, 114, p. 593b: all actions can be *reversed*; action of the intermediate existence (*antarābhava*) (AKB iii, F 47); the transgression with an immediately successive retribution (*ānantarya*); the action in *bhavāgra*; action in the attainment of non-ideation (*asaṃjñisamāpatti*, *Vibhāṣā*, 69, p. 359b; 152, p. 773c.

That covetousness (*abhidhyā*), malice (*vyāpāda*) and false view (*mithyādṛṣṭi*) are actions, opinion of the Dārṣṭāntikas, see AKB iv, F 136, 169; of the Vibhajyavādinikāya, *Vibhāṣā*, 113, p. 587a.

5. All the defilements (*kleśa*) are unwholesome, Dārṣṭāntikas, see *Vibhāṣā*, 50, p. 259c; contra, AKB v, F 42.

Adhering (*anuśayana*), see *Vibhāṣā*, 22, beginning; AKB v, F 37.

In conventional cognition (*saṃvṛtijñāna*), the ordinary worldling (*pṛthagjana*) does not cut off the defilements (*kleśa*); Dārṣṭāntikas and the Bhadanta, see *Vibhāṣā*, 51, p. 264 col. 2; 144, p. 741c.

The object of attachment and the person (*pudgala*) are unreal, Dārṣṭāntikas (compare the doctrine of thought only [*cittamātravāda*]); the object of attachment, attachment, and the person (*pudgala*) are real, Vātsīputrīyas, see *Vibhāṣā*, 56, p. 288.

Reincarnation solely because of desire and hatred, see *Vibhāṣā*, 60, p. 309a (in fact, because of any defilement [*kleśa*]). <lv>

On the time periods, see *Vibhāṣā*, 183, p. 919b.

6-7. Definition of the truths, see AKB vi, F 122; opinion of the Ābhidhārmikas, Dārṣṭāntikas, Vibhajyavādins, Ghoṣaka, Pārśva..., see *Vibhāṣā*, 77, p. 397b.

On receptivity (*kṣānti*) and cognition (*jñāna*), see AKB vii, F 1, 2, 50, 52; Dārṣṭāntikas, the Bhadanta, *Vibhāṣā*, 95, beginning.

Purity of the body of the perfected being (*arhat*), see AKB i, F 6; iv, F 19; Dārṣṭāntikas, according to Saṃghabhadra, 1, p. 331b.

8. Doctrine of meditation (*dhyāna*), the Bhadanta-Dārṣṭāntikasautrāntika, see AKB viii, F 151–57.

The stages of the preliminary concentration (*sāmantaka*) are wholesome, Dārṣṭāntikas, see AKB viii, F 180; *Vibhāṣā*, 164.

Mixed meditation (*dhyāna*), (AKB vi, F 221, 259; vii, F 55) explained by perfuming, Dārṣṭāntikas and Yogācārins, see *Vibhāṣā*, 175, p. 879c; compare *Siddhi*.

The retrogression from the attainment of non-ideation (*asaṃjñisamāpatti*), Dārṣṭāntikas, see *Vibhāṣā*, 152, p. 773c.

The miraculous emanation (*nirmita*) is not real, Dārṣṭāntikas and the Bhadanta, see *Vibhāṣā*, 135, p. 700a.

Vibhajyavādins

They are clearly defined as *those who distinguish* and admit the existence of a certain kind of past factor and a certain kind of future factor (AKB v, F 52; P'u-kuang quotes AKB v, F 24, and Vinītadeva, *Traité sur les Sectes*).

However, the information that we possess on the Vibhajyavādins is confused: the Vibhajyavādins are the Mahāsāṃghikas, the Ekavyavahārikas, the Lokottaravādins, the Kaukkuṭikas (K'uei-chi; *Siddhi*, 109).

1. Vasumitra, in his treatise on the sects, does not mention them. Vinītadeva, expounding the theories of the historical account of the Sarvāstivādins, makes them the seventh Sarvāstivādin school. Bhavya (the Sthavira theory) makes them a division of the Sarvāstivādins, and (the Mahāsāṃghika theory) the third mother-school. According to Bhikṣvagra, they are the fourth Mahāsāṃghika school.

2. Here is the note by Kyokuga (edition of the AKB xix, fol. 14a–b).[94]

---

[94] A note translated inaccurately in AKB v, F 24 (note).

K'uei-chi, commentating on the *Siddhi* [iv, 1, 35, p. 179 of the French translation], says: "Those who were called Vibhajyavādins are now called Prajñāptivādins." <lvi> [This should be taken to mean: Paramārtha, in his version of the *Treatise of Vasumitra*, has written "Vibhajyavādin", whereas] Vasumitra [in the version of Hsüan-tsang] says: "In the second century, a school called the Prajñaptivādins came out of the Mahāsāṃghikas." On that, the commentator Fa-pao says: "According to these two translations, the Vibhajyavādins make up only one school [with the Prajñaptivādins]."[95] In the *Vibhāṣā*, 23, p. 116, the Mahāsāṃghikas, etc., are called Vibhajyavādins [that is to say: the *Vibhāṣā* attributes to the Vibhajyavādins an opinion that we know to be the opinion of the Mahāsāṃghikas, see AKB iii, F 77]. Therefore, the *Arthapradīpa*, 3, p. 48, says, "The Vibhajyavādins are either some divergent masters of the Great Vehicle or all the schools of the Small Vehicle are called Vibhajyavādins: these are not a specific school. Therefore, in the *Mahāyānasaṃgraha* (*Nanjio* 1183, *Taishō* 1593), the Vibhajyavādins are explained as Mahīśāsakas; in the *Vibhāṣā*, as Sāṃmitīyas."[96]

3. In several texts, the meaning of the word Vibhajyavādin is clearly defined.

   i. Bhavya: [The Sarvāstivādins] are called by the name of Vibhajyavādin when they distinguish (*vibhaj*) by saying, "Among these factors, some exist, namely, the former action the effect of which has not occurred; some do not exist, namely, the former action the effect of which has been consumed, and future factors."
   ii. AKB v, F 52: Those who affirm (a) the existence of the present [factors] and of one part of the past [factors], i.e., the action which has not given forth its effect, and (b) the non-existence of the future [factors] and of one part of the past [factors], i.e., the action which has given forth its effect, are regarded as Vibhajyavādins, *followers of those who distinguish.* They do not belong to the school of the Sarvāstivādins.
   iii. P'u-kuang, 20, fol. 4. (AKB v, F 42): They say that there is no opinion that is completely right; that [factors are] in part existence and in part non-existence [or: in part true, in part false]: one should thus distinguish. Thus they are called Vibhajyavādins. <lvii>
   iv. The Kāśyapīyas (Vasumitra, thesis 1 and 2) take up a clearly Vibhajyavādin position: "The action the effect of which has ripened does not exist;

---

95 The truth is that Paramārtha wrote one word for another.

96 This is obscure; the *Saṃgraha* quotes the *āgama* of the Mahīśāsakas and ignores the Vibhajyavādins; the *Vibhāṣā*, it seems, ignores the Sāṃmitīyas.

the action the effect of which has not ripened exists." Now Buddhaghosa (*Kathāvatthu*, i, 8) attributes to the Kassapikas, a branch of the Sarvāstivādins, the opinion that one part of the past factors and of the future factors exists: this is the second Vibhajyavādin thesis of the summary of Vinītadeva. Yet the Theravādin, who should be a Vibhajyavādin like the Buddha, denies and refutes this.

4. Elsewhere: Vibhajyavādins are called those who distinguish, i.e., accept that the aggregates (*skandha*) are real, and the sense-spheres (*āyatana*) and the elements (*dhātu*) are of nominal existence.

5. *Vibhāṣā*, 110, p. 571c and elsewhere, opposes the Vibhajyavādin and the Yuktavādin.

6. Vinītadeva attributes to the Vibhajyavādins the following theses:

   a. The person (*pudgala*) exists *absolutely*;

   b. the past factor does not exist, except the cause the effect of which has not ripened; the future factor does not exist, except the effect;[97] the present factor which is a non-concordant type (*rigs mi mthun pa* ?) does not exist;[98]

   c. the factor (*dharma*) does not become an equivalent and immediate antecedent cause (*samanantarahetu*);[99]

   d. material form (*rūpa*) does not have a homogeneous cause (*sabhāgahetu*), like the Dārṣṭāntikas (AKB ii, F 256).

7. More notable is the note of Hsüan-tsang (*Siddhi*, 179) which associates the Vibhajyavādins and the Sthaviras with the belief in *bhavāṅgavijñāna*.

   And also: pure (*viśuddha*) thought, *Siddhi*, 109–11; persistence of a subtle thought in the attainment of cessation (*nirodhasamāpatti*) (with the Dārṣṭāntikas), 207; see also 770.

8. References to: *Kośa–Vibhāṣā*, completed in the *Index*:

   i. Sound is *of retribution* (with the Vātsīputrīyas), see AKB i, F 69; *Vibhāṣā* 18, beginning; *Siddhi*, 190.

   The body of birth (*janmakāya*) of the Buddha is *pure* (with the Mahāsāṃghikas), see *Vibhāṣā*, 173, p. 871c; *Siddhi*, 769–70.

---

97 *Bareau*: The effect [which has not yet ripened]. SBPV.180

98 *Bareau*: The meaning of this thesis is obscure. SBPV.180

99 *Bareau*: *Kośa*, ii, F 300–6. SBPV.180

ii. Faith (*śraddhā*), etc., are pure, see AKB ii, F 118; *Vibhāṣā*, 2, p. 7.

Life is a thought-associate (*cittānuvartin*), see AKB ii, F 248; *Vibhāṣā*, 151, p. 770, 3 (refuted by Vasumitra). Therefore, there is a subtle thought in the attainment of non-ideation (*asaṃjñisamāpatti*) and in the attainment of cessation (*nirodhasamāpatti*), AKB viii, F 207; *Vibhāṣā*, 151, p. 772, 3; 152, p. 774, 1.

iii. Negation of intermediate existence (*antarābhava*), see AKB iii, F 32; *Vibhāṣā*, 69, p. 356, 3; 135, p. 700, 1. – Whence the complicated explanation of the never-returner who is destined to obtain Nirvāṇa in the intermediate existence (*antarāparinirvāyin*), AKB iii, F 39; *Vibhāṣā*, 69, p. 357, 2. <lviii>

Dependent origination (*pratītyasamutpāda*) is an unconditioned factor (*asaṃskṛta*), likewise the path, see AKB iii, F 77; *Vibhāṣā*, 23, p. 116, 3; 93, p. 479 (like the Mahāsāṃghikas and the Mahīśāsakas).

iv. Covetousness (*abhidhyā*), malice (*vyāpāda*) and false view (*mithyādṛṣṭi*) are *action*, see *Vibhāṣā*, 113, p. 587, 1 (AKB iv, F 136: Dārṣṭāntikas).

Definition of *wholesome through their intrinsic nature* (as *jñāna*), of *wholesome through association* (*as vijñāna*), *of wholesome through their arousing cause* (as action of the body...) (AKB iv, F 33: Dārṣṭāntika); ix, 248; *Vibhāṣā*, 144, p. 741, 1.

The thought of the Fortunate One is always in concentration, see AKB iv, F 40; *Vibhāṣā*, 79, p. 410, 2.

v. The craving for non-existence (*vibhavatṛṣṇā*) is abandoned through cultivation (*bhāvanā*), see AKB v, F 29; *Vibhāṣā*, 27, p. 138, 3.

On mistaken views (*viparyāsa*), see *Kośa* v, F 23, *Vibhāṣā*, 104, beginning.

vi. Definition of the truths, see AKB vi, F 123; *Vibhāṣā*, 77, p. 397, 2.

Direct realization of the truths at once, see AKB vi, F 185, *Vibhāṣā*, 103, p. 532, 1.

The perfected being (*arhat*) does not retrogress, see AKB vi, F 264; *Vibhāṣā*, 60, p. 312, 2.

Forty-one factors conducive to enlightenment (*bodhipākṣika*), see AKB vi, F 281; *Vibhāṣā*, 96, at the end; 97, p. 499.

vii. Material form (*rūpa*) in the realm of immateriality, see AKB viii, F 135, 141; *Vibhāṣā*, 83, at the end.

Only the first meditation (*dhyāna*) has members (*aṅga*), see *Vibhāṣā*, 160, p. 813, at the beginning.

The noble one (*ārya*) of the fourth *ārūpya* obtains the quality of a perfected being (*arhat*) without the assistance of the path, see *Vibhāṣā*, 185, p. 929, 2. (This is thesis 12 of the Mahīśāsakas in the treatise of Vasumitra).

FC. *Yogācāras*

Or *yoga-ācāryas*, as the Chinese reads; we also have *yogācāracitta* (AKB ii, F 149; *Vyākhyā*, ii, 49).

1. People who practice *yoga* or the contemplation of *yogins*;[100] see AKB iv, F 18, note, and the *Vibhāṣā*, *passim*: they seek the truth of cessation (*nirodhasatya*) (103, p. 534a), practice the concentration of emptiness (*śūnyatāsamādhi*) (104, p. 540, 3), are disgusted with sensation (*vedanā*; the realm of fine-materiality) and ideation (*saṃjñā*; the realm of immateriality) (152, p. 775, 2); also 7, p. 35, 2; 102, p. 529, 2; 165, p. 832, 1. – The *Ratnarāśisūtra* (*Śikṣāsamuccaya*, 55) examines the obligations of the monk who does service (*vaiyāvṛtyakara*[101] *bhikṣu*), i.e., the steward and secretary (?) of the monastery, toward (i) the forest-dwelling monk (*āraṇyaka*), (ii) begging monk (*piṇḍacārika*), (iii) the contemplative monk (*yogācārin bhikṣu*), (iv) the student who is devoted to erudition (*bāhuśrutye 'bhiyukta*), (v) the preacher (*dharmakathika*).

2. Devoted to *yoga*, to breathing exercises, to meditation (*dhyāna*), etc., the *yogācāra* becomes, as the Chinese say, a *master of yoga* (*yogācārya*): he has theories on the control of breath (*prāṇāyāma*), on the concentration of emptiness (*śūnyatāsamādhi*), ... <lix> The AKB iv, F 18–19, indicates a thesis of this school of contemplatives on material form (*rūpa*) that arises through the power of concentration.

3. [This school of contemplatives became a philosophical school, the Yogācāra school, when, under the influence of Maitreya–Asaṅga, it became devoted to the old phrase of the *Daśabhūmika*: "The threefold world is only thought." We can clearly see the relationship between the theories of meditation and idealism, we can clearly see how the study of the attainment of non-ideation (*asaṃjñisamāpatti*) ends up in the assertion of a subtle thought.... Asaṅga utilizes Dārṣṭāntika–Sautrāntika speculations.]

Below are the references of the *Kośa* to the Yogācāras:

- They explain mixed meditation (*dhyāna*; AKB vi, F 221) by perfuming, see *Vibhāṣā*, 175, p. 879, 3, (like the Dārṣṭāntikas do).

---

100 This is the meaning of *yogācāra* in the *Saundarananda*, in the *Mahāvastu*.

101 Or *vaiyāpṛtya*, *Avadānaśataka*, ii, 235.

- They have connections with the Sautrāntikas, see AKB ii, F 177; *Vyākhyā*: "of the opinion of the Sautrāntika or the Yogācāra".
- The Yogācāracitta accepts that an agglomerate can be formed from a single fundamental material element (*mahābhūta*): a lump of dry earth; from two fundamental material elements: the same, but wet..., see AKB ii, F 149; *Vyākhyā*, ii, 49.
- In the system of the Yogācāra (*yogācāradarśana*), there is an element of the mental faculty (*manodhātu*) distinct from the six consciousnesses (*vijñāna*) *Vyākhyā*, i, 40, ad i, 32; compare the Tāmraparṇīyas.
- [The Vijñānavādin denies that the eye sees, AKB i, F 82].
- The Yogācāracitta defines resolution (*adhimukti*), see AKB ii, F 154; *Vyākhyā*, ii, 51.
- According to the Yogācāras, the attainments of non-ideation (*asaṃjñi-samāpatti*) are endowed with thought due to the store-consciousness (*ālaya-vijñāna*), see *Vyākhyā* ad ii, 211. – Yaśomitra speaks here of the school of Asaṅga; likewise AKB iii, F 3; *Vyākhyā*, ad v, F 21 (the 128 defilements [*kleśa*] of the Yogācāras).
- [The *ancient masters* of the AKB ii, F 212, should be the Dārṣṭāntikas].
- Elsewhere, the *Vyākhyā* explains the *ancient masters* of the *Bhāṣya* as being "the Yogācāras" or "the Yogācāras, Asaṅga, etc.", see *Vyākhyā* ad iii, F 53; iv, F 162; vi, F 141. <lx>

G. *THE ŚĀRIPUTRĀBHIDHARMA*

This book, *Nanjio* 1268, *Taishō* 1548, is divided into four parts, (1) *sapraśnaka*, (2) *apraśnaka*, (3) *saṃprayukta-saṃgraha* (three titles that correspond to the first four sections of the Abhidharma according to the Dharmaguptas-Haimavatas, J. Przyluski, *Concile*, 179, 353–54, and remind us of the *Dhātukāya–Vibhaṅga–Dhātukathā*, above p. xli), and (4) succession (*krama* or *nidāna*??).

This is, strictly speaking, a *śāstra*, without the usual *sūtra* introduction: "Thus have I heard... ." It was compiled by Śāriputra, either while the master was alive (*Ta-chih-tu-lun*) or after his Nirvāṇa, to set up a barrier to heresy, for some "counterfeited the Dharma" (*dharmapratirūpaka*).

However that may be, it is a very extensive and archaic treatise, much in the style of the Pāli *Vibhaṅga*.

The *Ta-chih-tu lun* establishes the relationship between the Abhidharma of Śāriputra and the Vātsīputrīyas.[102] But in the book of Śāriputra I have not found any mention of the person (*pudgala*) in the Vātsīputrīya sense of the word.

Saeki Kyokuga, AKB viii, F 135, points out that the *Śāriputrābhidharma* accepts the existence of material form (*rūpa*) in the realm of immateriality (*ārūpyadhatu*). See indeed 4, p. 552a, at the end of the chapter on the aggregates (*skandha*). This material form is the non-informative (*avijñapti*). The book accepts the non-informative, which is a Sarvāstivādin invention.

But it is not an orthodox Sarvāstivādin position. It believes that the proclivity (*anuśaya*) is dissociated from thought (26, p. 690 and AKB v, F 3). It contains nothing about the existence of the past–future factors,[103] or about *unconditioned* space. <lxi> It explains the element of abandonment (*prahāṇadhātu*): "that which should be abandoned" (576c and AKB vi, F 301). Its system of the conditions (*pratyaya*), which is very developed (25, at the beginning), and its list

---

[102] "Some say: 'When the Buddha was in this world, Śāriputra, in order to explain the words of the Buddha, compiled the *Abhidharma*. Later, the monk Vātsīputrīya recited [this work]. Up to now, this is what is called the *Abhidharma of Śāriputra*'," J. Przyluski, *Concile*, p. 73.

The only book of the Abhidharma that teaches the doctrine of the person (*pudgala*) seems to be *Nanjio* 1281, *Taishō* vol. 32, no. 1649, the *Sāṃmitīya-nikāya-śāstra*, AKB ix, F 229, 261, 270f.

[103] "The past is that which has arisen and is destroyed; the future is that which has not arisen, has not appeared", 3, at the beginning.

of the sense-spheres (*dhātu*) (7, p. 575) have nothing of the Sarvāstivādin position.

We will have some idea of the style of Śāriputra by comparing (2) the description of the aggregate of material form (*rūpaskandha*; 3, at the beginning, p. 543) with AKB i, F 35 and *Vibhaṅga*, 1 and following; (2) the definition of the element of factors (*dharmadhātu*; 2, p. 535) with *Vibhāṅga*, 89; (3) the definition of the truth of cessation (*nirodhasatya*; 4, p. 553) with *Vibhaṅga*, 103.

Dharmadhātu

The element of factors (*dharmadhātu*) is defined first as being identical with the sense-sphere of factors (*dharmāyatana*); then, as being made up of the aggregate of sensation (*vedanāskandha*), the aggregate of ideation (*saṃjñāskandha*), the aggregate of formations (*saṃskāraskandha*), the invisible (*anidarśana*) and non-resistant (*apratigha*) material form (*rūpa*), and the unconditioned factors (*asaṃskṛta*) (compare *Vibhaṅga*, 86). A third definition enumerates, after sensation (*vedanā*) and ideation (*saṃjñā*), the series of the formations (*saṃskāra*) associated with thought (beginning with intention [*cetanā*] and ending with defilement–proclivity [*kleśa–anuśaya*]); the series of the formations dissociated from thought (*viprayukta*; see 3, p. 547b): *jāti, jarā, maraṇa … nirodhasamāpatti*; finally: *pratisaṃkhyā-nirodha, apratisaṃkhyānirodha, niyamadharma-sthiti*(*tā*), *ākāśāyatana, vijñāna–āyatana, ākiṃcanyāyatana, naivasaṃjñānāsaṃjñāyatana,*[104] [i.e., the list of the unconditioned factors (*asaṃskṛta*)]: "this is what is called the *element of factors*".

On the one hand, the formations dissociated from thought are not those of the Sarvāstivādins; although one may have doubts about the equivalences of the translators (Dharmagupta and Dharmayaśas, 414 A.D.), the group of names (*nāmakāya*)... are missing.

On the other hand, the unconditioned factors of Śāriputra remind one of those of the Mahāsāṃghikas and the Mahīśāsakas (see *Siddhi*, p. 78).

Nirodhasatya

To the question: "What is the noble truth of the cessation of unsatisfactoriness (*duḥkhanirodha āryasatya*)?", our text answers in canonical terms: *yo tassā yeva taṅhāya asesavirāganirodho cāgo patinissaggo mutti anālayo* (*Vibhaṅga*, 103, *PTS*

---

[104] For the last terms, compare the variant p. 526c: the Sanskrit reading is doubtful: *ākāśa-āyatanajñāna…* and *ākāśyāyatanapratyaya*[*jñāna*].

No. 39: "That which is the entire dispassionate cessation of, the forsaking of, the discarding of, the freedom from, the non-attachment to that same craving"), and adds: "Already cut off, not to arise again: this is what is called the *noble truth of the cessation of unsatisfactoriness*."

The question is repeated: "What is the noble truth of the cessation of unsatisfactoriness? The cessation due to deliberation (*pratisaṃkhyānirodha*) is called the *noble truth of the cessation of unsatisfactoriness.* <lxii> This noble truth of the cessation of unsatisfactoriness is, in truth, like that, not not like that, not different, not a different thing. As the Tathāgata has well expressed the truths of the noble ones (*ārya*), it is the noble truth (*āryasatya*)."

But, "What is the cessation due to deliberation (*pratisaṃkhyānirodha*)?" The question is repeated three times: "If a factor (*dharma*) is destroyed when one obtains the noble (*ārya*) path, the destruction of this factor is called *cessation due to deliberation.*" ... "The four noble fruits of religious praxis (*śrāmaṇyaphala*) are called *cessation due to deliberation*."

"What is the fruit of the stream-enterer (*srotaāpannaphala*)? If the three defilements (*kleśa*) to be cut off by the path of insight are cut off; if the afflicted view of self (*satkāyadṛṣṭi*), the doubt (*vicikitsā*) and the 'overesteeming of (such things as) morality and certain spiritual practices' (*śīlavrata*) are exhausted, this is called the *fruit of the stream-enterer*."[105] Śāriputra repeats: "What is the fruit of the stream-enterer? The three defilements (*kleśa*) to be cut off by the path of insight being cut off—the afflicted view of self, the doubt and 'the overesteeming of (such things as) morality and certain spiritual practices' being exhausted, if one obtains immortality (*amṛta*), this is what is called the *fruit of the stream-enterer*."

It seems that we may have found here a terminology foreign to the Abhidharma and to the Sarvāstivāda. <lxiii>

---

[105] Compare the doctrine of the *Dhammasaṅgaṇi*, AKB v, F 10 (note).

THE ABHIDHARMASĀRA[106]

1. Several masters, before Vasubandhu, undertook to summarize the doctrines of the Abhidharma. We possess notably three works:

   i. The *Abhidharmasāra* of Dharmaśrī in ten chapters, made up of *kārikās* (probably in *āryan* strophe)[107] and a commentary;
   ii. a second edition of this same *Sāra* by Upaśānta,[108] to which the Chinese give the name of *Abhidharmasāra-ching*: the same *kārikās* with a more developed commentary; and
   iii. a third edition of the *Sāra*, the *Tsa Abhidharma-ching*, by Dharmatrāta,[109] which is, in fact, a new work containing a new chapter and many new *kārikās*.[110]

2. The preface to the *Vibhāṣā* (*Nanjio* 1264, *Taishō* 1546)[111] by Tao-yen places the work of Dharmaśrī before the *Jñānaprasthāna*: "After the cessation (*nirodha*) of the Buddha, the *bhikṣu* Dharmaśrī composed the four books of the *Abhidharmasārā*. Then Kātyāyanīputra composed the Abhidharma in eight books... ."

3. The work of Dharmaśrī contains ten chapters (*varga*):

   i. *Dhātuvarga* (Elements)
   ii. *Saṃskāravarga* (Formations)
   iii. *Karmavarga* (Action)
   iv. *Anuśayavarga* (Proclivities)
   v. *Āryavarga* (Nobility)
   vi. *Jñānavarga* (Cognition)
   vii. *Samādhivarga* (Concentration)
   viii. *Sūtravarga* (Scriptural Texts)

---

106 *Taishō* volume 28, numbers 1550, 1551, 1552, *Abhidharmahṛdaya*; see above p. xxviii.

107 We have the Sanskrit text of one of the *kārikās*, AKB v, F 5–6.

LS: See Charles Willemen's translation: *The Essence of Scholasticism. Abhidharmahṛdaya. T 1550.* Delhi, 2006. See also SAL.128–33; SBS.255–49; EIP.VII. 451–70.

108 *LS*: SBS.259–60; EIP.VIII.228.

109 *LS*: See Bart Dessein's translation: *Saṃyuktābhidharmahṛdaya. Heart of Scholasticism with Miscellaneous Additions.* Delhi, 1999. See also EIP.VIII.314–19.

110 For example, the ninth chapter: Dharmatrāta takes up twenty verses (*kārikā*) of Dharmaśrī and inserts six new verses; he continues with twenty-two new verses.

111 Mentioned by Takakusu, p. 128.

ix. *Tsavarga* (*Prakīrṇakavarga*; Miscellaneous Matters)
x. *Śāstravarga* or *Vādavarga* (*Dharmakathā*; Discussion)

4. The *Pravicayavarga* (Investigations) of Dharmātrāta's **Saṃyuktabhidharma-hṛdaya* (SAH):

Between the ninth and the tenth chapter of Dharmaśrī, Dharmatrāta places a new chapter, the *Pravicayavarga* (Investigations), which indeed seems to constitute an independent work.

There is an introductory verse (SAH 500) [to the *Pravicayavarga*]: "Although many factors (*dharma*) have already been spoken of, their meaning remains confused..."[112] and four concluding verses:[113] "The author has composed this book based on the book of Dharmaśrī, not because of conceit (*māna*) or in order to acquire a reputation (*yaśas*)...".

The chapter [of the *Pravicayavarga*] begins (SAH 501) with an investigation of the wheel of the doctrine (*dharmacakra*): "The Muni proclaimed that the path of insight (*darśanamārga*) is called wheel of the doctrine either because it penetrates into the thought of others (*paracitta*)..." (AKB vi, F 245, 249). <lxiv>

Then comes the investigation of the wheel of Brahma (*brahmacakra*; SAH 502; AKB vi, F 244; vii, F 74), the *upāsaka* (SAH 503; AKB iv, F 69), the four parts of morality (*śīla*; SAH 504; AKB iv, F 67), the *prātimokṣa* (SAH 505).... Later (p. 959, 2), cosmology is investigated: the periods of weapons, etc. (SAH 556; AKB iii, F 207), the destruction by fire, etc. (SAH 557; AKB iii, F 216); and then follows the theory of the three types of retrogressing (*parihāṇi*) (SAH 559; AKB vi, F 267) and the definition of the Bodhisattva (SAH 561; AKB iv, F 220).

All of a sudden, the question is asked (SAH 562): "How many types of Sarvāstivāda are there?" Presentation of the four doctrines (AKB v, F 52) without mentioning the names of the four masters. The second and the fourth masters are bad because they mix up the time periods. The first (i.e., difference in mode of existence [*bhāva*], translated [Ch.] *fen*): "One should know that this is the *Sarvāstivāda of transformation* (*pariṇāma-sarvāstivāda*)."[114]

---

[112] *LS*: SAH 500: "Although many factors have already been spoken of, and [although] there is certainty about all the many miscellaneous meanings, one further has to investigate the essence regarding these unlimited objects."

[113] *LS*: See SAH 568.

[114] The third doctrine, difference of state (*avasthā*), (trans. [Ch.] *fen-fen*).

There is a variety of opinions as to whether the truths are seen at the same time (SAH 563; AKB vi, F 185): the Sarvāstivādins and Vātsīputrīyas on the one hand, Dharmaguptakas on the other. The investigation [in regards to the existence of the] intermediate existence (*antarābhava*; SAH 564; AKB iii, F 38). Then (SAH 565–66) the explanation of Sarvāstivāda. And at the end of verse 566, the discussion "whether the Buddha is part of the *saṃgha* [of listeners (*śrāvaka*)]". – Finally, the concluding verses (SAH 567–70).

5. The *Saṃskāravarga* (Formations) deals (i) with the simultaneous arising of thought and thought-concomitants (*citta-caitta*) and of the atoms (AKB ii, F 144), (ii) with the four characteristics (*lakṣaṇa*) of the *conditioned* (AKB ii, F 222), (iii) with the causes (*hetu*) and the conditions (*pratyaya*) (AKB ii, F 255, 299).

The *Sūtravārga* (Scriptural Texts) is a collection of notes: the three realms (*dhātu*) and a calculation of the places that they contain: sixteen in the realm of fine-materiality, but, according to some, seventeen (AKB iii, F 2): the abidings of beings (*sattvāvāsa*; AKB iii, F 22), the stations of consciousness (*vijñānasthiti*; AKB iii, F 16); the three courses (*vartman*) of dependent origination (*pratītyasamutpāda*; AKB iii, F 60, 68), the twelve members; the fundamental material elements (*mahā-bhūta*), the truths, the fruits of the noble ones (*ārya*), etc.

The *Tsavarga* (*Prakīrṇakavarga*; Miscellaneous Matters) defines the thought–thought-concomitants as associated (*saṃprayukta*), having a basis (*sāśraya*), etc. (AKB ii, F 177); it enumerates the formations dissociated from thought (*viprayukta*): the state of ideation (*āsaṃjñika*), the two non-conscious attainments, the [group] homogeneity (*sabhāgatā*), the collection of names, etc. (*nāmakāyādayas*), the vitality faculty (*jīvitendriya*), the possession of factors (*dharmaprāpti*), the nature of an ordinary worldling (*pṛthagjanatva*), four characteristics (*lakṣaṇa*) (compare AKB ii, F 178); it ends with half a verse on the four existences (*bhava*; AKB iii, F 43, 45) and a verse on *disgust* and *detachment* (AKB vi, F 302).

The *Śāstravarga* (or *Vādavarga*; *Dharmakathā*: Discussion) is made up of questions put into verse, followed by answers in prose, related to restraint (*saṃvara*; AKB iv, F 53), to the fruits, etc. Dharmatrāta adds sixteen questions.

6. In order to assess the nature of the treatises of Dharmaśrī, Upaśānta and Dharmatrāta, and the indebtedness of Vasubandhu to Dharmatrāta, which seems noteworthy, <lxv> we can look at how two categories of factors (*dharmaparyāya*),

---

LS: See Dessein (2003, vol. 2, p. 314).

i.e., the subject of the three obstructions (*āvaraṇa*) and that of the non-informative action (*avijñapti*), are dealt with by the different masters.

HA. *Obstructions, AKB iv, F 201–12; Vibhāṣā, 115, p. 599*

Dharmaśrī, 1, p. 815:

> The Fortunate One proclaimed that there are three obstructions (*āvaraṇa*): (1) action (*karman*), (2) defilement (*kleśa*) and (3) retribution (*vipāka*). What is their definition?
>
> > (1) Actions entailing an immediately successive retribution (*ānantarya*) that are without remedy, (2) developed defilements, and (3) unwholesome action experienced in the unfortunate planes of existence: those are the obstructions.
>
> These three make an obstacle to the Dharma; they hinder the gaining of the factors of a noble one (*ārya*); they are thus called *obstructions.* – Which is the gravest action?
>
> > The action which divides the Saṃgha is said to be the gravest.
>
> This action is the worst. The guilty one remains for one aeon (*kalpa*) in Avīci hell. – Which is the best action?
>
> > The intention (*cetanā*) of the summit of cyclic existence (*bhavāgra*) is the greatest.
>
> The perception-sphere of neither-ideation-nor-non-ideation (*naiva-saṃjñāna-asaṃjña-āyatana*) is the summit of cyclic existence (*bhavāgra*). The intention which belongs to the domain of this stage is the greatest and finest: its effect is a life of some 80,000 aeons in length.

Upaśānta, p. 843bc, has the same two verses, but a fuller commentary:

> The term *obstruction* is used for that which hinders the path of the noble ones and the means (*upāya*) of this path.
>
> Action as obstruction is the five actions entailing an immediately successive retribution, namely, patricide, etc., … . He who commits such an action is immediately and necessarily reborn in Avīci: therefore the action is immediately successive (*ānantarya*). Patricide and matricide destroy the benefactor, whence Avīci hell. The other three transgressions undermine a field of merit.
>
> Defilement as obstruction is the (1) *agitated* defilement and (2) *sharp* defilement: the first is the habitual defilement; the second is the dominant

defilement. This is a matter of *current* defilements, not of defilements that one *possesses* (i.e., that one has as potential), for all sentient beings *possess* all the defilements… .

There is a variant to the second verse: "False speech which divides the Saṃgha…; the intention of the summit of cyclic existence, among wholesome actions, has the greatest effect", which is better. The commentary notes the differences in the two schisms (*cakrabheda, karmabheda*).

Dharmatrāta is longer, 3, pp. 898b–899c, and very close to Vasubandhu:

After the first verse of Dharmaśrī, he has:

2. defilement as obstruction is the worst; the action as obstruction, mediocre; and retribution as obstruction, the least; <lxvi>

3. the schism of the Saṃgha, by nature, is non-harmony; this is a formation dissociated from thought (*viprayukta saṃskāra*) of the unobscured-non-defined (*anivṛta-avyākṛta*) class;

4. schism is a matter of the Saṃgha; the transgression is with him who divides the Saṃgha; he experiences, in Avīci, a retribution for one aeon (*kalpa*);

5. the *bhikṣus* are divided in their opinion of who is the Master, what is the path: this is the schism of the Saṃgha which was united. He who divides it is an *intellectual* (*dṛṣṭicarita*);

6. in three continents, a minimum of eight persons is required for the schism of formal ecclesiastical action (*karmabheda*); in Jambudvīpa, a minimum of nine persons is required for the breaking of the wheel (*cakra-bheda*);

7. the breaking of the wheel is impossible during six periods: (i) when the parish has no boundaries; (ii) at the beginning; (iii) at the end; (iv) when the Muni has passed into Nirvāṇa; (iv) before the appearance of the *abscess*; (v) before the appearance of the pair of chief disciples (six quarter-verses [*pāda*]);

8. false speech which divides the Saṃgha is the worst of actions; the intention of the summit of cyclic existence is said to bear the greatest effect.

HB. *Non-informative action (avijñapti), AKB iv, F 4, 14*

Dharmaśrī (i, p. 812c):

Bodily action is informative action (*vijñapti*) and non-informative action (*avijñapti*).

> The bodily informative action is the movement of the body, wholesome, unwholesome or non-defined: wholesome when it arises from a wholesome thought... .
>
> As for non-informative action: when one does an action in a firm manner, thought can change, but the seed remains. If, for example, a person undertakes the precepts, his thought can afterwards be unwholesome or non-defined: nevertheless, morality continues... . Mental action is solely non-informative action... because this action is not visible... . Informative action is wholesome, unwholesome or non-defined; the same for the non-informative action which belongs to the mind (*manas*). The other non-informative actions are never non-defined.

Upaśānta (2, p. 840) adds a few things. The bird-catcher is considered as being free from bodily non-informative action. Mental action is called *non-informative action* because it does not inform others. Some say that it is called *informative action* because it is discourse (*jalpa*?).

Dharmatrāta (3, p. 888b) replaces the terms informative action (*vijñapti*) and non-informative action (*avijñapti*) with *doing* (*karaṇa*) and *not doing* (*akaraṇa*) (AKB iv, F 14):

> Bodily action is of two types: (1) *karaṇasvabhāva*, (2) *akaraṇasvabhāva*.
>
> *Doing* (*karaṇa*): movement of the body, exercise[115] of the body is the *doing of the body*.
>
> *Not doing* (*akaraṇa*, [Ch.] *wu-tso*): when the movement of the body has ended, the nature (wholesome or unwholesome) of this [movement, of this action which is the movement], <lxvii> continues to arise, simultaneous with thoughts of a different nature. Just as wholesome morality produced through undertaking (*kuśalasamādānaśīla*) continues to arise even when unwholesome or non-defined thoughts (*citta*) are present. Just as with the immoral person (*dauḥśīlya-puruṣa*): even when wholesome or non-defined thoughts are present, the immorality continues to arise.
>
> ... Mental action is intention (*cetanā*) by nature... .
>
> *Not doing* is also called *nirati* (? *Vyut.*, 21, 114), *virati*, *upekṣā*, *akriyā* (Tib. *pu-tso*). Because it does not do, it is called *not doing*. If one says that

---

115 We have [Ch.] *fang-pien*, which should translate *vyāyāna* (see Demiéville, *Milinda*), instead of *upāya*.

this is not an action (*karman*), this is not correct, because it *does.* [Even though] the wholesome does not do the unwholesome, the unwholesome does not do the wholesome: there is here also an action. Just as the equanimity (*upekṣā*) limb of enlightenment (*bodhyaṅga*) is not equanimity according to what is called *equanimity*; because the practice of the path, stopping other things, is called *equanimity.* The same here. – Furthermore, in *doing* the cause, one *does* the effect: therefore, one can call the effect according to the cause: ...*not doing* is not material form (*rūpa*), but the *doing* [which is the cause of the *not doing* or the non-informative] is material form; *not doing* is thus called *material form.* Likewise, *not doing* is action.[116]

[116] See above p. xlviii.

Remarks by the Translator

The following was originally written as the first endnote to chapter 1, but has been extracted due to its length. It has been placed here since its content is meant to be merely complementary to what has already been discussed in the preceding prefaces and introduction by Étienne Lamotte and Louis de La Vallée Poussin (LVP), and, to a lesser extent, in the new introduction by Bhikkhu KL Dhammajoti, i.e., his *Summary and Discussion of the Abhidharmakośa-bhāṣya*, which was received just prior to publication. The topics of my *Remarks* can be outlined as follows:

(1) a brief outline of what has been discussed so far by Lamotte, La Vallée Poussin (LVP) and Dhammajoti; (2) the new additions in our publication and some helpful new sources; (3) the influences on our translation and its endnotes; (4) the stratagems of Hsüan-tsang's, LVP's and our translation, as well as biographical data on Hsüan-tsang and La Vallée Poussin. Next we will focus on (5) "what further needs to be addressed", i.e., (i) the life of Vasubandhu according to Paramārtha and (ii) some issues surrounding Vasubandhu as discussed by contemporary scholarship: (a) Vasubandhu's other texts, (b) his life and (c) some thorny issues related to the schools of the Sarvāstivāda, Dārṣṭāntika, Sautrāntika and Yogācāra, and their relationship to each other and to Vasubandhu; (6) LVP's "additional" attributions in his translation and Kritzer's identified passages, and finally (7) the structure of the *Abhidharmakośabhāṣya* as well as (8) a more detailed outline of this endnote and (9) the obligatory yet heartfelt acknowledgements and thanks.

1. *Brief outline of what was has been discussed so far by Lamotte, La Vallée Poussin and Dhammajoti*:

Since Étienne Lamotte in his *Preface* and Louis de La Vallée Poussin (LVP) in his *Preface* and *Introduction*, as well as Bhikkhu KL Dhammajoti in his *Summary*, have already covered much of the introductory ground necessary for the reading of our translation, we would like to briefly review these topics to get a clearer picture regarding what still needs to be added or would be helpful for the reader of our translation.

i. Étienne Lamotte first points out the two parts of the *Abhidharmakośabhāṣya* (AKB), i.e., the Kārikās and the Bhāṣya, and their great success in all of the Far East. He then addresses the reception of the AKB in the West and the publication of the first French edition (1923–1931), which is unchanged from the second French edition (1971), except that LVP's *Introduction* has been moved from vol. VI into vol. I. Lamotte then goes on to list the sources upon which LVP's French translation relied and to describe the "skillful stratagem" LVP used in his translation. Lamotte notes that most of the canonical and post-canonical scriptures used by Vasubandhu were successfully identified by LVP. He then informs us that the original Sanskrit text of the AKB, considered to be lost, was not available to LVP, but was discovered by Rāhula Sāṃkṛtyāyana in the Tibetan monastery of Ngor in 1935, three years before La Vallée Poussin's death. Lamotte closes his Preface by saying that "the *Abhidharmakośa* of Vasubandhu and its French translation by Louis de La Vallée Poussin are today inseparably united for the greatest benefit to Buddhist studies" since the Chinese translation and its French version (with its cross references)—being more analytical in nature than the original Sanskrit text—can be more directly assimilated by the reader than the Sanskrit original.

ii. Lamotte's Preface is followed by Hubert Durt's Bibliographical Addendum, listing the Sanskrit, Tibetan and Chinese editions of texts and works relative to the AKB published subsequent to the first 1923–1931 edition.

iii. LVP himself, in his Preface, points to the items included in Vol. VI (first edition), i.e., the four indices (the general index of which we have divided and expanded into a Sanskrit-English Index and English-Sanskrit Index) and the *Additions and Corrections*. Since nearly all of the latter have been incorporated into the endnotes of our translation, they have not been translated separately. In his *Introduction*, LVP makes the following important comments (pp. iii–v): it "does not contain everything that I wanted to put in it. (a) It lacks the summary of the doctrines of the *Kośa*. ... (b) One will find here [in my *Introduction*], along with the bibliography of the *Kośa*, only the beginnings of a study on Vasubandhu's sources." He lists the eight main sections of his *Introduction* and states that "the *Kośa* is, by definition, a judicious and well-ordered analysis of the *Vibhāṣā*".. LVP's study of the *Vibhāṣā* was particularly facilitated by the references of Saeki Kiokuga's annotated edition (1887) of Hsüan-tsang's Chinese translation of the *Kośa* (see further comments below). LVP makes reference to the old Abhidharma treatises and the Sautrāntikas as sources for Vasubandhu, but points out in regard to the latter that, besides "the Dārṣṭāntikas—Bhadanta—Dharmatrāta cited by the *Vibhāṣā*", we know only little about what sources Vasubandhu used; he puts his hopes on a future reading of Saṃghabhadra who had gathered information on "Śrīlāta, who must be one of the Sautrāntika sources of Vasubandhu". – As for the topics of LVP's *Introduction*, consult its table of contents.

iv. The masterly *Summary* by Bhikkhu KL Dhammajoti—Glorious Sun Professor of Buddhist Studies (University of Hong Kong)—gives us the missing summary: it first discusses Abhidharma as being primarily a soteriology, the predecessors of the AKB as a manual, the organizational structure of the AKB and the affiliation of the AKB, before giving a brief summary of the main doctrines and content of each of the nine chapters, while highlighting Vasubandhu's doctrinal positions.

2. *The new additions in our publication and helpful new sources*:

i. Before the missing summary of the chapters and their doctrines was available to us, LVP had suggested filling the gap by referring to René Grousset's *Analyse de l'Abhidharmakośaśāstra* and to his own already published articles and books, as well as to further materials he planned to publish. Since these articles and books are at present not easily available, we have put some of them in PDF format on the webpage of the Chökyi Gyatso Translation Committee, which also includes other source materials pertinent to our translation. See *Electronic Appendix*:

http://gampoabbey.org/translation-committee.php

In regard to summaries, there are now also a few other helpful sources available, for example, Chaudhuri's *Analytical Study of the Abhidharmakośa*, which, however, is more of a synoptic listing of the topics rather than a discussion of the meaning and implications of the doctrines; the same applies to Anacker's summary in Potter's *Encyclopedia of Indian Philosophies*, Volume VIII.

As for our annotated translation, in our endnotes we will present summaries, overviews, additional important information and source materials drawn mainly from the work of contemporary scholars in the field, including La Vallée Poussin, as well as many cross-references in the AKB, and we hope this will prove to be helpful to the general reader. This explains the many additional endnotes, but also why the endnotes occasionally will be quite lengthy, the latter being very much in line with LVP's own method of including longer overview footnotes at pertinent places. The first two chapters have more endnotes than the later ones, simply due to their being beginning chapters and their topics.

We will say a little more below about the main sources on which the endnotes rely; as for the nature of these endnotes, we would like to point out that they are mainly intended to remain within the framework of what other contemporary scholars have accomplished with their hard work, i.e., the reader should not expect to find, in these endnotes, any new research of our own beyond what these scholars have published. Choices had to be made and discussions of topics had to be abbreviated, sometimes greatly; but we hope that we are presenting their work fairly and correctly.

ii. In addition to the bibliography of the *Kośa* in LVP's *Introduction*, we have provided an updated bibliography in three parts: (A) Primary Sources (Sanskrit, Pāli, Chinese, Tibetan); (B) Indices; (C) Secondary Sources. The list of the primary sources is based on the more detailed bibliography in *Disputed Dharmas. Early Buddhist Theories on Existence*, by Collett Cox, pp. 417–23. The list of the secondary sources includes the books referred to in the endnotes of our translation and, as such, provides a record of the influences on our translation. For good additional bibliographies of secondary sources, particular by the Japanese, see *Disputed Dharmas*, pp. 423–40, and *Sarvāstivāda Buddhist scholasticism*, by Charles Willemen, Bart Dessein, Collett Cox, pp. 294–311. Unfortunately Japanese Abhidharma studies had only a minimal influence on this annotated translation, with the exception of those written in English or mediated through scholars such as Cox, Kritzer, etc.

A list of text abbreviations used in our translation and endnotes has been added after the *Remarks of the Translator*.

iii. We have created (and inserted) section headlines for each chapter, a step which was greatly influenced by Karmapa Wangchung Dorje's outline (*sa bcad*) for his commentary on the root verses of the *Abhidharmakośa* (*chos mngon pa mdzod kyi rnam bshad gzhon nu rnam rol zhes bya ba'i sa bcad bzhugs so*), kindly provided by David Karma Choephel. Many clues also came from the parallel reading of the two *Hṛdaya*s on which the AKB is structurally based, namely, Charles Willemen's translation of Dharmaśreṣṭhin's *The Essence of Scholasticism. Abhidharmahṛdaya. T1550* (2006), and Bart Dessein's translation of Dharmatrāta's *Saṃyuktābhidharmahṛdaya. Heart of Scholasticism with Miscellaneous Additions* (1999), as well as a close reading of the AKB itself. Gedun Drup's outline in his *Clarifying the Path to Liberation* has also been consulted to some extent. The fact that we had to create an outline for LVP's entire *Bhāṣya* and not just for the root verses (*kārikās*) has caused our outline to be more detailed than Wangchuk Dorje's. As for chapter 9, its outline and its numbering system is mainly taken over from James Duerlinger's work.

Based on the section headlines, we then generated a table of contents (TOC) and inserted it at the beginning of each chapter. For easier access and overview of the material, we have also frequently inserted into the translation itself brief outlines of subsections of the text; these inserts are differentiated from the main text by left and right indents, as well as smaller point size.

The work on the outline or "map" was one of the more interesting and challenging aspects of the translation, and it is our hope that it will help the reader as much as it did us in the process of accessing and grasping the main train of thoughts and structure of the text. In general, we would advise the readers, before reading a chapter, to first familiarize themselves with the TOC, since it is easy to lose the overview in the wealth of all the material presented by Vasubandhu and in his sometimes lengthy discussions on a topic. Any shortcomings of the outlines have naturally to be blamed on us.

iv. We have inserted into the endnotes the rediscovered original Sanskrit text of the *kārikās*, which was published by V.V. Gokhale in the Journal of the Bombay Branch, Royal Asiatic Society, XXII, 1946, pp. 73–102. By doing so we have mostly replaced LVP's renderings and reconstructions of them. At the same time we have inserted next to the Sanskrit *kārikās* the entire Tibetan translation of the *kārikās* (reprinted by permission of Nitartha International).

Moreover, since the complete text of the AKB (i.e., *Kārikās* and *Bhāṣya*) was published in 1967 by P. Pradhan in the Jayaswal Research Institute of Patna and since Hirakawa published his detailed and very helpful *Index to the Abhidharmakośabhāsya (P. Pradhan Edition)*: Part 1 (1973) Sanskrit–Tibetan–Chinese. Part 2 (1977) Chinese–Sanskrit. Part 3 (1978) Tibetan–Sanskrit, we were now able without too much difficulty to trace and insert into the text many of the original technical Sanskrit terms to which LVP did not have direct access during his translation. With the help of electronic search, we were also able to identify many of LVP's Sanskrit text passages in his footnotes as stemming from Yaśomitra's *Sphuṭārthā Abhidharmakośavyākhyā*. While doing so we not only specified page and line numbers but also separated out "the original text" (in italics) and the "commentary" (in non-italics) according to Wogihara's 1971 edition (= WOG). As for identifying canonical citations in the AKB, see Bhikkhu Pāsādika's *Kanonische Zitate im Abhidharmakośabhāṣya des Vasubandhu* (find URL in our Bibliography).

We have also taken over the Taishō Canon references from Pruden, as well as his Wade-Giles renderings. In the few instances where Pruden was unable to find the Taishō Canon references, the references have been kept as given by LVP.

Here we might also mention that we have inserted numbers (1, 2, 3; i, ii, iii; a, b, c; etc.) into the text (as does LVP himself). These are intended to make the logic of the text easier to follow and to avoid ambiguities since English has only genderless articles (a, the) and relative pronouns (which, that). The numbers are often not meant to suggest official lists, but are merely intended as help in reading. Also, we have added drawings and charts for illustrative and didactic reasons.

3. *Influences on our translation and its endnotes*:

i. As will be seen from the endnotes, besides LVP's additional writings (see our Bibliography), the main influence on the translation and its endnotes comes from Bhikkhu KL Dhammajoti's and Collett Cox's writings (see our Bibliography), both of whom have kindly given us permission to quote freely from their work. In particular, Dhammajoti's *Sarvāstivāda Abhidharma* (fourth revised edition, Hong Kong 2009; SA.IV), which is probably the most comprehensive discussion of the major

Sarvāstivāda doctrines and topics within a single volume to date, and which has a very helpful Sanskrit-English Glossary, has had the greatest impact on the translation and its endnotes, especially since we had the good fortune to proofread and edit its third edition. In this process we were able to clear up many of our questions and to "squeeze in" a few directly AKB related issues (giving Professor Dhammajoti plenty of opportunity to practice patience!). Here we reproduce its chapter headings (fourth edition) with the hope that it will give the reader a glimpse of an overview of the major Sarvāstivāda doctrines and topics (as presented in his book):

Chapter 1: Abhidharma – Its Origin, Meaning and Function
Chapter 2: The Ābhidharmika – Standpoint, Scope and Methodology
Chapter 3: The Sarvāstivāda School and Its Notion of the Real
Chapter 4: The Abhidharma Treatises of the Sarvāstivāda
Chapter 5: *Sarvāstitva* and Temporality
Chapter 6: Theory of Causality I: The Six Causes
Chapter 7: Theory of Causality II: The Four Conditions and the Five Fruits
Chapter 8: The Category of Matter (*rūpa*)
Chapter 9: The Category of Thought and Thought-concomitants (*citta-caitta*)
Chapter 10: Theories of Knowledge
Chapter 11: The Category of the Conditionings Disjoined from Thought (*citta-viprayukta-saṃskāra*)
Chapter 12: Defilements
Chapter 13: The Doctrine of *Karma*
Chapter 14: *Karma* and the Nature of its Retribution
Chapter 15: The Path of Spiritual Progress
Chapter 16: The Unconditioned (*asaṃskṛta*) *Dharma*-s

Further, we have included in the endnotes many passages from Dhammajoti's translation of Skandhila's *Abhidharmāvatāra*, which not only succinctly summarizes all the basic categories of the Sarvāstivāda doctrines but "its presentation parallels that of the AKB to which therefore it can serve also as an excellent introduction" (ESD.2).

When quoting from Dhammajoti's works, we have emphasized selecting passages from the *Abhidharma-mahāvibhāṣā* (MVŚ) and Saṃghabhadra's **Nyāyānusāra* (Ny), which should be of great interest to scholars and students unable to read Classical Chinese.

As for La Vallée Poussin's additional writings, unfortunately many of them are only available in French right now, but it is our hope to publish a collection of a great number of them (mainly Abhidharma related, but also other topics) in the near future.

In addition to these three main influences (LVP, Dhammajoti, Cox), this translation is generally influenced by specific works focusing on the AKB's individual chapters or topics. To mention just a few: for chapter 1, Bruce Cameron Hall's *Vasubandhu on "Aggregates, Spheres, and Components": Being Chapter One of the Abhidharmakośa*; for chapter 2, Collett Cox's *Disputed Dharmas. Early Buddhist Theories on Existence*; for chapter 3, Akira Sadakata's *Buddhist Cosmology. Philosophy and Origins* and Susan C. Stalker's *A Study of Dependent Origination: Vasubandhu, Buddhaghosa, and the Interpretation of "Pratītyasamutpāda"*; for chapter 4, Alexander von Rospatt's *The Buddhist Doctrine of Momentariness. A Survey of the Origins and Early Phase of this Doctrine up to Vasubandhu*; for the later chapters, Étienne Lamotte's *Le Traité de la Grande Vertu de Sagesse de Nāgārjuna (Mahāprajñāpāramitāśāstra)* (unpublished English translation by Migme Chödrön). Chapter 9 is particularly influenced by James Duerlinger's *Indian Buddhist Theories of Persons. Vasubandhu's "Refutation of the Theory of a Self"*. Professor Duerlinger kindly gave us permission to use his outline for the translation. In addition, Geshe Jampa Gyatso's general commentary on the *Treasury of Manifest Knowledge*, on the basis of Gedun Drup's *Clarifying the Path to Liberation: An Explanation of the "Treasury of Manifest Knowledge"*, has also been consulted.

ii. Another major influence on our translation comes from the English translations of two of the *Hṛdaya* treatises, which in turn—as we have seen in LVP's and Dhammajoti's *Summary*—had a great influence on the structure and content of Vasubandhu's AKB, namely, Dharmaśreṣṭhin's *Abhidharmahṛdaya* (= AH) and Dharmatrāta's *Saṃyuktābhidharmahṛdaya* (= SAH). We have therefore cross-referenced these two texts in our endnotes, following mainly Dessein's cross-references in his endnotes.

4. *Various translation stratagems and biographical data on Hsüan-tsang and La Vallée Poussin*:

i. LVP's general stratagem for translation has been described by Lamotte in his Preface: "although French in terms of syntax, his translation is Indian in terms of vocabulary, in the sense that the technical terms are retained in their original Sanskrit form". As for LVP's more specific method of translation, Robert Kritzer (2003a.203) comments: "Although [La Vallée Poussin's translation of the *Abhidharmakośabhāṣya*] is a masterpiece that must always be consulted, La Vallée Poussin often inserts, without comment, explanations from the *Abhidharmakośavyākhyā*. Furthermore, he sometimes attributes a statement to, for example, Sautrāntika, even when neither the Chinese nor Tibetan translation (the Sanskrit text was not available to him) does so. As we mention below, the attributions are usually actually those of the seventh-century Chinese commentators, and they continue to circulate, unidentified, in the scholarly literature."

ii. As for ourselves, we have modified LVP's general stratagem, thinking it advisable, as far as possible, to translate the Sanskrit terms into English, so that the text is more accessible to a wider readership. On the other hand, we have maintained the technical Sanskrit terms in brackets.

We also preferred not to make too literal a translation of the French. Instead we have often chosen our English terms for technical Sanskrit terms from the "tested" English Abhidharma terminology used by leading modern Abhidharma scholars, in particular, Dhammajoti, but also Cox and Schmithausen, and then tried to apply the chosen terms consistently throughout the translation, as LVP did. As an aside, may I say that this method is quite different from the method we used in our translation of Frauwallner's *The Philosophy of Buddhism*, where we tried to stay as close as possible to the German original.

Putting all of what has been said up until now together—i.e., what has been newly added and helpful new sources; influences on our translation and its endnotes; our own translation stratagem—we can add to Lamotte's above statement that "the *Abhidharmakośa* of Vasubandhu and its French translation by Louis de La Vallée Poussin are today inseparably united for the greatest benefit to Buddhist studies", etc., that the analytical nature has further increased in our publication, but that, at the same time, certain aspects of it have moved closer to the rediscovered Sanskrit original.

iii. Because La Vallée Poussin himself did not have the advantage of having access to the Sanskrit text of the *Abhidharmakośabhāṣya*, which was considered to be lost, and since his translation is mainly based on Hsüan-tsang's Chinese translation, it might be valuable here to also provide some information in regard to the resources available to Hsüan-tsang and his method of translation, which we will do by reproducing a section from Collett Cox's *Disputed Dharmas*, pp. 59f:

> Both Saṅghabhadra's **Nyāyānusāra* and his **Abhidharmasamayapradīpikā* were translated into Chinese by Hsüan-tsang, who also translated many other Sarvāstivādin Abhidharma texts. Among the texts translated by Hsüan-tsang are Vasubandhu's *Abhidharmakośakārikā* and *Bhāṣya*, which had been translated previously in 563 A.D. by Paramārtha.[a] Hsüan-tsang began his translation of both the **Abhidharmasamayapradīpikā* and the *Abhidharma-*

kośabhāṣya in 651 A.D. Completing his translation of the **Abhidharma-samayapradīpikā* in 652 A.D., Hsüan-tsang began the translation of the **Nyāyānusāra* in 653 A.D. and finished both the **Nyāyānusāra* and the *Abhidharmakośabhāṣya* in 654 A.D. The multiple Chinese translations of the *Abhidharmakośabhāṣya*, the existence of the Sanskrit text of the *Abhidharmakośabhāṣya*, and the consistency of Hsüan-tsang's translation of technical terms provide a basis for the study of the Abhidharma texts like the **Nyāyānusāra* not extant in Sanskrit or Tibetan translation.

The method of translation employed by Hsüan-tsang was the product of several centuries of development. In the earliest period of the translation of Buddhist texts, translation involved oral recitation of a text from memory by a foreign monk who would explain (often in Chinese) the meaning to a Chinese collaborator who would then "translate" the text into Chinese. By Hsüan-tsang's period during the T'ang dynasty, translations were produced in well-funded bureaus that could support highly specialized collaborators. Since Hsüan-tsang had studied Sanskrit, he could himself combine the roles of reciter and translator. Following the traditional method of oral translation, Hsüan-tsang translated each text aloud, but now from a written text. These oral translations were then written down by a scribe-translator (*pi shou*), whose tasks included not only taking dictation but also checking the meaning of the Chinese translation with the Sanskrit original and finally ensuring the intelligibility of the translation and its doctrinal consistency with Buddhist teaching. The translated text then passed through several stages of editing and correction, including primary editors (*cheng i*), who verified the choice of Chinese translations in order to prevent mistakes in meaning, stylists (*chui wen*), who refined the Chinese composition, editors of transliteration (*tzu hsüeh*), who checked transliterations from Sanskrit, and the Sanskrit editors (*cheng fan-yü fan-wen*), who ensured consistency of the Chinese translation of terms with the Sanskrit.

Among these various specialists, the role of scribe-translator (*pi shou*) and primary editor (*cheng i*) were most important; both roles demanded a thorough knowledge of Buddhist doctrine and some knowledge of Sanskrit. Among these scribe-translators and primary editors of translations of Abhidharma texts were several disciples of Hsüan-tsang who were later to write commentaries on the *Abhidharmakośabhāṣya* and **Nyāyānusāra*. P'u-kuang, a scribe-translator, Shen-t'ai, a primary editor, and Fa-pao, a disciple of Hsüan-tsang who was later to serve as a primary editor, all wrote commentaries on the *Abhidharmakośabhāṣya*. Yüan-yü, the primary scribe-translator for both the *Abhidharmakośabhāṣya* and the **Nyāyānusāra*, also wrote a commentary on the **Nyāyānusāra*. Since Shen-t'ai, Fa-pao, and P'u-kuang worked closely with Hsüan-tsang, their commentaries undoubtedly contain interpretations of the *Abhidharmakośabhāṣya* and **Nyāyānusāra* offered by Hsüan-tsang himself and may well represent interpretations that Hsüan-tsang received in India. In an attempt to clarify the points of disagreement between Vasubandhu and Saṅghabhadra, the commentaries on the *Abhidharmakośabhāṣya* also cite the **Nyāyānusāra* frequently, often referring to Yüan-yü's own commentary on it. Thus, they are a valuable source for the study of the **Nyāyānusāra*.

[a] Paramārtha's translation is very literal, following both the syntax as well as the verse and commentary divisions of the extant Sanskrit. Hsüan-tsang combines the parts of each verse, which in the Sanskrit had been interspersed with commentary, and includes summary or introductory sentences to ease transitions in the commentary from one verse section to another. He also frequently adds explanatory sentences and references that present his understanding of assumptions underlying doctrinal arguments.

iv. For biographical data on Hsüan-tsang and La Vallée Poussin, see our translation of Lamotte's *Biographical Note on Louis de La Vallée Poussin* as well as Samuel Beal's translations *Si-yu-ki. Buddhist Records of the Western World. Translated from the Chinese of Hiuen Tsiang* (*A.D. 629*), and the *Life of Hsüan-tsang*, all found in the *Electronic Appendix*. For further data on Hsüan-tsang, see the references in Der Huey Lee's entry: "Xuanzang (Hsüan-tsang) (602–664 C.E.)" in *The Internet Encyclopedia of Philosophy* (http://www.iep.utm.edu/xuanzang/).

5. *What further would be good to address:*

We mentioned above LVP's comment that we find in his *Introduction* "only the beginnings of a study on Vasubandhu's sources" and that regarding Sautrāntikas "we have little information of the sources that he uses". In regard to these issues, what progress has been made by Buddhist research? And in terms of our introductory remarks—even though LVP, Lamotte and Dhammajoti already provided a lot of the necessary information so that the reader can more readily access the content of this translation and its endnotes—what would still be good to further address?

As for the latter, although in his *Introduction* LVP has discussed the question of the date of Vasubandhu and the bibliography related to it, as well as a few difficulties within Paramārtha's biography of Vasubandhu, not much was said about the life of Vasubandhu himself. It seems thus worthwhile and appropriate here to say first a few words about the life of the author of the AKB, Vasubandhu, and then address further the issues surrounding his person, information pertinent to the above-mentioned questions.

i. *The life of Vasubandhu according to Paramārtha*

The oldest and basic source for the biography of Vasubandhu is *The Life of Vasubandhu* (*P'o-sou-p'an-tou Fa-shi chuan*) by Paramārtha (499–569 A.D.), translated by Takakusu (1904; see *Electronic Appendix*). There are also other accounts by Hsüan-tsang (596/600–664), Vāmana (ca. 800), Bu-ston (1290–1364), Tāranātha (1575–1634), etc., that provide important additional but also sometimes differing information.

According to Paramārtha, Vasubandhu was born at Puruṣapura ("Territory of the Hero"; Peshāwar) in Gandhāra, as the second of three brothers, his father being the Brahman Kauśika, a court priest, his mother, Viriñci. His youngest brother was called Viriñci-vatsa (son of Viriñci), his oldest brother was the famous Asaṅga ("Without Attachment") who (according to Tāraṇatha's *History*, p. 167) became a Buddhist monk one year before Vasubandhu's birth. Paramārtha comments that "Vasu means 'God' and Bandhu 'Kinsman'," and Bu-ston writes (HB.II.145) that "he was possessed of the wealth (*vasu*) of the Highest Wisdom and, having propagated the Doctrine out of mercy, had become the friend (*bandhu*) of the living beings". Sarao (http://www.iep.utm.edu/vasubandhu/) comments that "during the formative years of his life, Vasubandhu may have been introduced by his father not only to the Brahmanical tradition but also to the postulates of classical Nyāya and Vaiśeṣika, both of which had influence on his logical thought".

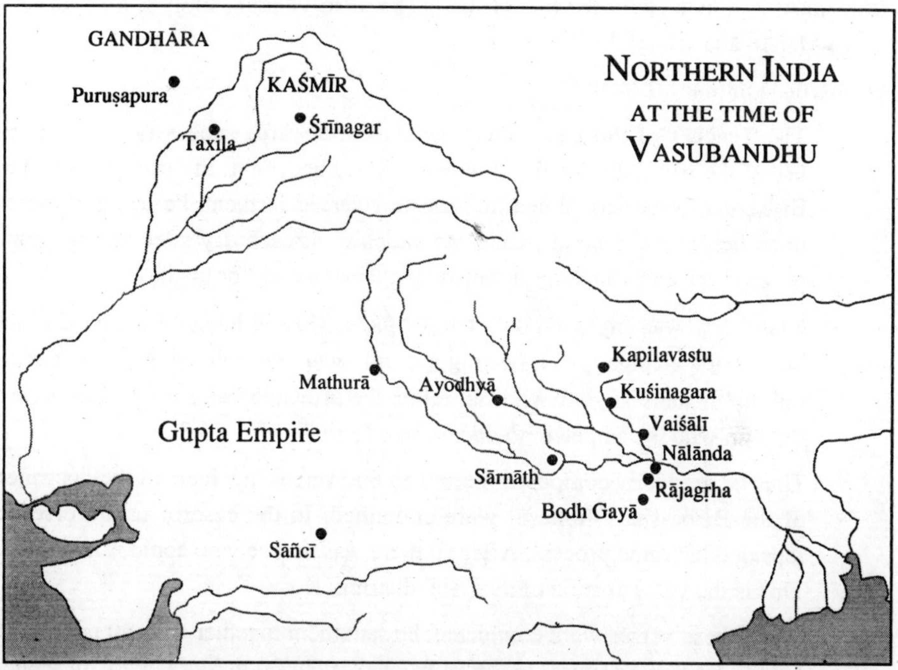

Gandhāra was known as the seat of the "Western masters" of Abhidharma, that is, the Pāścātyas, and was the birth place of the Sarvāstivāda masters Dharmaśrī (or Dharmaśreṣṭhin) and Bhadanta Dharmatrāta, but the main Sarvāstivāda movement in force in Gandhāra were the Vaibhāṣikas, taking the *Mahāvibhāṣā* as their authoritative text. Vasubandhu became a Sarvāstivādin monk, studying primarily the scholastic system of the Vaibhāṣikas. Hsüan-tsang states (Si.105ff.) that Vasubandhu was the disciple of Manorhita (or Manoratha) but Paramārtha mentions (LV.284) that his teacher was a certain Buddhamitra who resided in Ayodhyā (central Gangetic valley; now located in Uttar Pradesh, far removed from Gandhāra and Kashmir).

According to Paramārtha, "Vasubandhu's first apparent place of significant activity was Ayodhyā". He speaks of the arrival of the Sāṃkhya teacher Vindhyavāsin in Ayodhyā who—while Vasubandhu is "absent travelling in other countries"—is victorious over Vasubandhu's teacher Buddhamitra. Upon Vasubandhu's return, he composed the *Paramārthasaptati* ["Treatise on the Seventy Verses on the Truth"] in which, although not encountering his opponent in person, he completely confuted Vindhyavāsin. The King (Vikramāditya) (LV.286f.) "gave him three lacs (*lakṣa*) of gold as a prize. This amount he divided into three portions with which he built three monasteries in the country of A-yu-ja (Ayodhyā): 1. a monastery for pi-ku-ni (Bhikṣuṇī); 2. a monastery for the Sat-ba-ta (Sarvāsti-vāda) school; 3. a monastery for the Mahā-yāna school."

Paramārtha continues (LV.287f.):

> The Teacher of the Law (Vasu-bandhu) afterwards successively re-established the true Law (of the Buddha). He studied, first, the principles of the Bi-ba-sha (Vibhāṣā). When he was well versed in them, he lectured thereupon before the general public. At the close of each day's lecture, he composed a verse in which he summed up his exposition for the day.
>
> Each verse was engraved on a copper plate. This he hung on the head of an intoxicated elephant, and, beating a drum, made the following public declaration: "Is there anyone who can refute the principles set forth in this verse? Let him who is competent to do so come forth."
>
> Thus he gradually composed more than 600 verses in which all the doctrines of the Bi-ba-sha (Vibhāṣā) were contained. In the case of each verse he repeated the same process. After all there was no one who could refute them. This is the verse portion of the (Abhidharma) Kośa.
>
> When these verses were completed, he sent them together with 50 pounds of gold to Ki-pin (Kaśmīra) to the Bi-ba-sha (Vibhāṣā) masters, who, on seeing them, were all exceedingly pleased, thinking that the true Law held by themselves would now be widely promulgated. The words of the verses, however, were so abstruse in meaning that they could not understand them all. They therefore added 50 pounds of gold to the sum received from Vasubandhu, thus raising the amount to 100 pounds altogether, and sent it back to him, requesting him to write a prose explanation of the verses. Thereupon he composed the prose portion of the Abhidharma-kośa, which is a commentary upon them. He thus established the tenets of the Sat-ba-ta (Sarvāstivāda) school; but whenever he found a doctrine pushed to an extreme in that school, he refuted it by the principles of the Sautrāntika school. This work was called the A-bi-dat-ma-ku-sha (Abhidharma-kośa). When he had completed the work he forwarded it to the Bi-ba-sha (Vibhāṣā) teachers of Ki-pin (Kaśmīra), who, on seeing their own opinions therein refuted, were grieved.

Although Cox and Sarao think that, according to Paramārtha, the AKB was written in Ayodhyā, Hsüan-tsang in his *Si-yu-ki* states (LV.105) that the AKB was composed in Puruṣapura (Gandhāra): "To the east of Pārśvika's chamber is an old building in which Vasubandhu Bodhisattva prepared the '*O-pi-ta-mo-ku-she-lun* (*Abhidharma-kosha Śāstra*); men, out of respect to him, have placed here a commemorative tablet to this effect." Also, according to Hsüan-tsang's disciples P'u-kuang and Fa-pao (SBS.271), "Vasubandhu had gone to Kaśmīra in disguise and studied the *Abhidharma* literature for four years under the instruction of Skandhila with the purpose of preparing a thorough criticism of the **Mahāvibhāṣā*. Afterwards Skandhila discovered his real intention and thereupon Vasubandhu returned to Gandhāra."

Paramārtha continues (LV.288):

> In former days the King (Vikramāditya) sent the Crown Prince [namely, Bālāditya] to Vasu-bandhu to receive his instruction. The Queen too went forth from her family and became his pupil. – When the Crown Prince succeeded to the throne, he and the Queen-mother invited their teacher to settle in Ayodhyā and accept the Royal support. He accepted the invitation.

Next Paramārtha relates that the grammarian Vasurāta, living in Ayodhyā and well-versed in Pāṇini's *Vyākāraṇa*, attacked the construction of the words and sentences of the *Abhidharmakośa*; Vasubandhu responded by writing a treatise refuting the thirty-two chapters of the *Vyākāraṇa*. Thereupon king Bālāditya and the Queen-mother lavished three lacs of gold on Vasubandhu with which he built three temples, one in Ayodhya, one in Puruṣapura and one in Kaśmīr. Paramārtha then continues (LV.289f.):

> The heretic [i.e., Vasurāta] was angry and ashamed, and, resolving to vanquish the Buddhist teacher, sent a messenger to Tien-chu (Central India) to invite the Buddhist priest, "Sang-ka-ba-da-la" (Saṅgha-bhadra) to come to Ayodhyā in order to compile a treatise and refute the Kośa. This teacher of the Law came and compiled two *śāstra*s. One, entitled the "Samaya of Light" [**Samayapradīpikā*], contained 10,000 verses, which merely explain the doctrines of the "Bi-ba-sha" (*Vibhāṣā*). "Samaya" means "Groups of meanings". The other bore the name "Conformity to the Truth" [**Nyāya-anusāra*], and contained 120,000 verses. It refutes the Kośa in favour of the Vibhāṣā. When these treatises were completed, he invited Vasu-bandhu to meet him in person and have a decisive debate.
>
> The latter, knowing that, in spite of his attempted refutation, his opponent had not been able after all to overthrow the doctrine of the Kośa, was not inclined to debate with him in person. He said: "I am now already old. You

> may do as you please. I formerly composed the *śāstra* to refute the doctrines of the Vibhāṣā. There is no need to enter further upon a decisive debate with you. You have now composed two *śāstras*. What is the use of challenging me? Any person endowed with knowledge will himself judge which party is in the right and which is in the wrong?"

This account, however, differs in detail from other accounts. See Collett Cox's discussion (DD.53ff.), who distinguishes three basic versions of biographical information concerning Saṅghabhadra and his two works as well as his relationship with Vasubandhu: (a) Paramārtha (LV.287–90), (b) Hsüan-tsang (Si.192–96) and (c) Buston (HB.142–47).

Paramārtha then ends this section of Vasubandhu's biography, creating a link to his conversion to the Mahāyāna (LV.290–93), by commenting:

> The Teacher of the Law (Vasu-bandhu) was versed in all the principles of the eighteen schools (of Buddhism) and thoroughly understood the Hīna-yāna. It was the Hīna-yāna that he held firmly to be right. He did not believe in the Mahā-yāna thinking that the "Ma-ka-yen" (Mahā-yāna) was not the Buddha's own teaching.

Hall summarizes (VASC.15): Vasubandhu "wrote numerous Hīnayāna treatises until his brother Asaṅga converted him to Mahāyāna. Thereafter he wrote numerous Mahāyāna treatises and commentaries, and became, along with Asaṅga, the co-founder of the Yogācāra-Vijñānavāda school. He enjoyed the patronage of two rulers of Ayodhyā (Vikramāditya and Bālāditya), where he died at the age of eighty."

See below more on the life of Vasubandhu.

ii. *Various issues surrounding Vasubandhu as discussed by contemporary scholarship*

In regard to the issues "what progress has been made by Buddhist research", etc., some of that has already been addressed by Dhammajoti in his *Summary* and will be further discussed by us in relation to specific and concrete topics in our endnotes to the nine chapters of the actual translation. Thus even though there does not seem to be a need to add much more to this, it might still be worthwhile to present/select some perspectives of contemporary scholarship regarding the following three themes that are not directly related with specific topics discussed in the AKB but with its author and his relationship with the various Buddhist schools, which then naturally has its impact on the reading and translation of the specific topics discussed in the AKB:

a. Which works can reasonably be attributed to Vasubandhu the Kośakāra?
b. The alternative hypotheses of one or two Vasubandhus, his life time, his relationship to Asaṅga, the problems of the information available on the relevant Gupta dynastic history.
c. Vasubandhu's relationship to the Sarvāstivādins/Vaibhāṣikas, Dārṣṭāntikas, Sautrāntikas and the Mahāyāna/Yogācāra. To what school did he belong when he was writing the AKB? Who were these schools? How did they interact or influence each other?

The opinions expressed in the following are admittedly and maybe also unavoidably selective and sometimes also partial; for further detail and opposing views, the reader can find the references and details in the works of the scholars mentioned.

a. In regard to "which works can reasonably be attributed to Vasubandhu the Kośakāra", Peter Skilling presents two useful criteria (VVL.298f.):

> The first is cross-references in the works of Vasubandhu himself or those of his commentators. These establish that the works are related: that they were known to and accepted by Vasubandhu, or held by representatives of his lineage to be his own compositions.
>
> The second criterion is style. Vasubandhu's prose style is distinctive: it is confident and learned, replete with citations and allusions to canonical and other literature, and to the opinions of different teachers or schools. It often employs debate: an "opponent" raises an objection, which is resolved through recourse to reasoning or scripture. Vasubandhu's prose cannot be mistaken for that of, say, Asaṅga or Candrakīrti. His verse is terse: compact, concise, mnemonic, it could not be mistaken for that of Nāgārjuna or Śāntideva.
>
> Applying these criteria, I classify the works into two groups:
>
> 1. Works shown to be by the Kośakāra on the evidence of internal cross-references or references by Vasubandhu's commentators, and confirmed by style, sources used, methodology, and development of ideas: the *Vyākhyāyukti*, the *Karmasiddhiprakaraṇa*, the *Pratītyasamutpādādivibhaṅganirdeśa*, and the *Pañcaskandhaprakaraṇa*;
> 2. Works that may be accepted as by the Kośakāra on the evidence of style, sources used, methodology, and development of ideas: the *Gāthāsaṃgraha* texts (and their excerpt, the *Ekagāthābhāṣya*), the *Viṃśatikā*, the *Triṃśikā*, and the *Trisvabhāvanirdeśa*.

Similar conclusions were reached by Deleanu (CMP.235) following Schmithausen who limits Vasubandhu's corpus to the following works (= first group): *Abhidharmakośabhāṣya, Vyākhyāyukti, Karmasiddhi, Pratītyasamutpādavyākhyā, Pañcaskandhaka, Viṃśatikā* and *Triṃśikā*, and prefers (AV.263) "to treat the Vasubandhu commentaries on *Madhyāntavibhāga, Dharmadharmatāvibhāga, Mahāyānasaṃgraha* and *Mahāyānasūtrālaṃkāra* ... as well as the *Trisvabhāvanirdeśa* ... as a separate group, because in these certain central doctrinal peculiarities of the comparable parts of the first group seem to be lacking (or at best marginal). This procedure should not, however, be misunderstood as a commitment with regard to the authorship problem." See in this context also Kritzer, VY.xxvi. On the full list of works attributed to Vasubandhu in different traditions, see Mejor 1991, pp. 7–13.

b. In regard to "the alternative hypotheses of one or two Vasubandhus, his life time, etc.", some scholars have suggested that there were two or even three or more, while some others would preserve the traditional view of a single Vasubandhu. Still others felt that, due to insufficient evidence, the issue could not be settled. On the other hand, Deleanu (2006) has presented a seemingly well-balanced discussion (CMP.186–96) of the issues that seems to solve some of the pitfalls of previous proposals by suggesting that Vasubandhu the Kośakāra lived between ca. 350 and 430, was the half-brother of Asaṅga (ca. 330–405), composed the *Abhidharmakośabhāṣya* sometime between or around 380–390, converted to the Mahāyāna sometime in his forties, thus starting off his creative Mahāyāna period sometime after ca. 390, and wrote his *Triṃśikā*, often considered to be his latest work, or at least one of the latest, sometime between 410–430. Deleanu also assumes that the *Yogācārabhūmi* "must have already assumed more or less its present form before 380", and that "Vasubandhu knew and drew inspiration from [the *Yogācārabhūmi*] or, at least, was familiar with the doctrinal tradition which had produced it". He does, however, not "rule out the possibility that a part of the works traditionally attributed to 'Vasubandhu' might have been written by another person or even persons". This basic argument for the dates is based on Schmithausen's analysis which states that two passages in the *Laṅkāvatārasūtra* (LAS) clearly appear to presuppose Vasubandhu's *Triṃśikā*, and since "both passages form part of the LAS text already in the earliest extant Chinese translation, viz. that by Guṇabhadra, dated 443 A.D." (NV.392f.), the most likely explanation is that the *Triṃśikā* must have been composed before this date.

Yet Deleanu's proposed dates bring into question the passage of Paramārtha's biography, cited above: "In former days the King (Vikramāditya) sent the Crown Prince [i.e., Bālāditya] to Vasu-bandhu to receive his instruction...". Frauwallner and other scholars had opted to identify these two kings as Skandagupta (ca. 456–467) and Narasiṃhagupta (ca. 467–473), who was actually Skandagupta's nephew. But Deleanu questions this identification "mainly because Narasiṃhagupta's date and order of ascending the throne is far from being clear" and he attempts to make a case, taking his clues again from Anacker (1984) and Schmithausen (1992), that Vikramāditya refers to Candragupta II (375–413/415) and Bālāditya to Kumāragupta I/ Govindagupta. For more details see Deleanu's lengthy discussion in CMP.186–94.

c. La Vallée Poussin had stated that his *Introduction* was only the "beginnings of a study on Vasubandhu's sources" and that in regard to Sautrāntikas "we have little information of the sources that [Vasubandhu] uses". He hoped that future research, particularly connected with Saṃghabhadra, would throw light on these issues.

This brings up some thorny issues which modern scholarship is still busy with, namely: What is Vasubandhu's relationship to the Sarvāstivādins/Vaibhāṣikas, the Dārṣṭāntikas, the Sautrāntikas and the Mahāyāna/Yogācāra? Who were these schools? How did they interact or influence each other? More specifically: What school did Vasubandhu belong to when he was writing the AKB?

These issues will be addressed in three sections:

- α. The traditional presentation of the four representative schools of Buddhism.
- β. The origins of the (*1.*) Sarvāstivādins and (*2.*) Dārṣṭāntikas and Sautrāntikas, and what defines them.
- γ. Vasubandhu's relationship to the Sarvāstivādins/Vaibhāṣikas, Dārṣṭāntikas, Sautrāntikas and Mahāyāna/Yogācāra. What school did he belong to when he was writing the AKB?

α. *The traditional presentation of the four representative schools of Buddhism*:

While the Sarvāstivāda, Sautrāntika and Yogācāra have traditionally been presented in the relatively later texts as three distinct schools, often mentioned together with the Madhyamaka as the four representative schools of Buddhism, contemporary scholarship has seriously questioned this simplistic framework in recent years (see VY.xi; JIABS.26.225). The historical relationship between these three schools has been a keen subject of investigation among some Japanese and Western scholars. We will first briefly look at each of these three schools separately and mention some of the works of modern scholarship (Western language) in regard to them:

1. As for the Sarvāstivāda, for whom there is a wealth of data available, much work has been done in screening all their texts and tenets as can be seen, for example, in Erich Frauwallner's *Studies in Abhidharma Literature and the Origins of Bud-*

dhist Philosophical Systems (English translation: 1995), in Collett Cox's *Disputed Dharmas. Early Buddhist Theories on Existence* (1995), in *Sarvāstivāda Buddhist scholasticism* by Charles Willemen, Bart Dessein and Collett Cox (1998), and in Dhammajoti's *Sarvāstivāda Abhidharma*, his *Abhidharma Doctrines and Controversies on Perception* and his many articles related to Sarvāstivāda. Regarding the various stages of the development of these texts, see LVP's *Introduction* and Dhammajoti's *Summary*, as well as Dhammajoti's chapter 4 (SA.IV.83–116), which is outlined in the following way:

- 4.1. Seven canonical treatises
  - 4.1.1. Treatises of the earliest period
    - 4.1.1.1. *Dharmaskandha-śāstra* (DSŚ)
    - 4.1.1.2. *Saṃgītiparyāya-śāstra* (SgPŚ)
    - 4.1.1.3. *Prajñapti-śāstra* (PjŚ)
  - 4.1.2. Later, more developed texts
    - 4.1.2.1. *Vijñānakāya-śāstra* (VKŚ)
    - 4.1.2.2. *Jñānaprasthāna-śāstra* (JPŚ)
    - 4.1.2.3. *Prakaraṇapāda-śāstra* (PrŚ)
    - 4.1.2.4. *Dhātukāya-śāstra* (DKŚ)
- 4.2. Development of the Sarvāstivāda manuals
  - 4.2.1. *Abhidharma-mahāvibhāṣā* (MVŚ)
  - 4.2.2. Development of the more concise manuals
    - 4.2.2.1. **Abhidharmāmṛta(-rasa)-śāstra* (T no. 1553), by Ghoṣaka, 2 fasc., translator unknown.
    - 4.2.2.2. **Abhidharmahṛdaya* (T no. 1550) by Dharmaśrī, 4 fasc., tr. by Saṃghadeva *et. al.*
    - 4.2.2.3. **Abhidharmahṛdaya-sūtra* (? T no. 1551) by Upaśānta, 2 fasc., tr. by Narendrayaśas.
    - 4.2.2.4. **Abhidharmahṛdayavyākhyā* (? T no. 1552), by Dharmatrāta, 11 fasc., tr. by Saṃghabhūti.
    - 4.2.2.5. *Abhidharmakośa-mūla-kārikā* (T no. 1560) by Vasubandhu, 1 fasc., tr. by Xuan Zang.
    - 4.2.2.6. *Abhidharmakośabhāṣyam* (T no. 1558) by Vasubandhu, 1 fasc., tr. by Xuan Zang; (there is also an earlier translation by Paramārtha: T no. 1559).
    - 4.2.2.7. **Abhidharmakośaśāstra-tattvārthā-ṭīkā* (T no. 1561) by Sthiramati, 2 fasc., translator unknown.
    - 4.2.2.8. **Abhidharma-nyāyānusāra* (T no. 1562) by Saṃghabhadra, 40 fasc., tr. by Xuan Zang.

4.2.2.9. **Abhidharma-samayapradīpikā* (T no. 1563) by Saṃghabhadra, 40 fasc., tr. by Xuan Zang.

4.2.2.10. **Abhidharmāvatāra* (T no. 1554) by Skandhila, 2 fasc., tr. by Xuan Zang.

As an important source on the Buddhist sects of the *Śrāvakayāna*, we should now also mention André Bareau's *Les Sectes Bouddhiques du Petit Véhicule* (1955).

2. As for the Sautrāntika, scholars nowadays still think, as LVP eighty years ago, that it is not that clear who the Sautrāntikas were, in particular the Sautrāntikas to whom Vasubandhu refers in his AKB. But as is shown in JIABS volume 26, Number 2, 2003: "The Sautrāntikas" (which covers also Japanese scholarship) and Dhammajoti's books *Sarvāstivāda Abhidharma* (Fourth Revised Edition: 2009) and *Abhidharma Doctrines and Controversies on Perception* (Third Revised Edition: 2007) as well as his articles *The Citta-caitta Doctrine of Śrīlāta* and *Śrīlāta's anudhātu doctrine* (relying on Saṃghabhadra's **Nyāyānusāra*), some progress has been made, even though no consensus has been reached among scholars; but more on that later.

3. As for the Yogācāra—in the context of Vasubandhu—some research was done on the *Yogācārabhūmi*, a fairly comprehensive work (comprising about 2,000 pages in an English translation) that can be regarded as the foundational work of the Yogācāra school (see Kritzer's brief overview of it in his *Vasubandhu and the Yogācārabhūmi. Yogācāra Elements in the Abhidharmakośabhāṣya*, 2005, pp. xii–xx). Lambert Schmithausen makes the following interesting comment in his lecture *Yogācāra School and the Tathāgatagarbha Schools of Thought* (1998; prepublished English translation):

> The work [i.e., the *Yogācārabhūmi*] is attributed sometimes to the founder of the school, Asaṅga, and sometimes to the mythical Bodhisattva Maitreya (the future Buddha). It is, however, more likely a collective work in which (apparently in several passes) in the 3rd or 4th century, the traditions or body of thought of a specific group or movement was compiled or worked over. Although the underlying canon is that of the Mūlasarvāstivādins throughout, it seems, however, that connections to other Schools also existed, in particular to the Mahīśāsakas. ...
>
> The *Yogācārabhūmi* is indeed regarded as a Mahāyāna text, but only certain parts, in particular the chapter *Bodhisattvabhūmi* ("Stage of the Bodhisattva"), are specifically dedicated to the path of salvation in the spirit of the Mahāyāna, ... Alongside this, there is also a chapter, "Stage of the Hearer" (*Śrāvakabhūmi*), which describes the traditional path of salvation

> of the "Hīna"- or Śrāvakayāna. The other parts of the text as well contain predominantly materials which remain within the scope of "traditional" Buddhism, that is, the Śrāvakayāna, or which are at least so formulated as to be acceptable to both schools of thought. The text thus apparently is derived from a milieu in which both schools of thought coexisted. Similar things hold true for a few additional texts, in particular the *Abhidharmasamuccaya*, the "Compendium of the Abhidharma", a work whose title already makes clear that it is drawing on the systematics of the older tradition, but which nonetheless also contains mahāyānistic elements.
>
> Other early Yogācāra works are, by contrast, decidedly mahāyānistic: for instance the *Mahāyānasūtrālaṃkāra* ("Ornament of the Mahāyāna Discourses"), ascribed to the Bodhisattva Maitreya, or the *Mahāyānasaṃgraha*, ("Summary of the Mahāyāna"), composed by Asaṅga. These works too, however, definitely recognize the goal of salvation of the Śrāvakayāna, ...

As will be mentioned below, Kritzer finds it very likely that the *Yogācārabhūmi* was available to Vasubandhu in a form similar to the one we know.

Work has also been done in mapping out the general development of the thought of the Yogācāra school and its representatives, and in showing Vasubandhu's involvement in it, for example, in the long Yogācāra section of Erich Frauwallner's *The Philosophy of Buddhism* (2010), p. 280–437 and in his article *Amalavijñāna and Ālayavijñāna. A Contribution to the Epistemology of Buddhism*, which is appended to *The Philosophy of Buddhism.*

β. *The origins of the (1.) Sarvāstivādins and (2.) Dārṣṭāntikas and Sautrāntikas, and what defines them*:

To provide a better basis for the discussion of Vasubandhu's relationship to the Sarvāstivādins, Dārṣṭāntikas, Sautrāntikas and Yogācārins—as traditionally seen and as seen by more modern scholarship—we will first briefly look into the origins of some of these schools, what defines them and what distinguishes them from other schools.

1. As for the origins of the Sarvāstivādins and what defines them, Collett Cox writes (DD.23f.):

> The causes and pattern of the emergence of distinct groups within the developing Buddhist community continue to be the subject of much scholarly disagreement. Nevertheless, despite variation in the traditional sources as to the date of what is generally accepted as the initial division between the Mahāsaṅghika and the Sthavira *nikāya*s, most scholars would agree that

> even though the roots of these earliest recognized Buddhist groups predate Aśoka, their actual separation did not occur until after his death.
>
> The Sarvāstivādin sect emerged at a later point from within the Sthavira group, and therefore, represents the phase of the secondary proliferation of sects and schools. This secondary proliferation undoubtedly resulted from a variety of conditions, different in each case, including external social conditions or geographical separation, as well as internal reasons such as differences in disciplinary codes or doctrinal interpretation. The traditional reason given for the recognition of the Sarvāstivādins as a distinct sect is their doctrinal position that "everything exists", a position reflected in their name that distinguishes the Sarvāstivādins from other groups. [...]
>
> Scholars have proposed the second or first century B.C. as the date for the emergence of the Sarvāstivādins as a distinct group. [...]
>
> Of particular interest both for the origin of the Sarvāstivādin sect and its later textual development is the identity of the various groups that the Sarvāstivādins comprise, specifically those mentioned in the later Abhidharma treatises: [1] those referred to by the terms "Sarvāstivādin" and "Mūlasarvāstivādin" [see DD.25ff.]; [2] the various presumably Sarvāstivādin groups such as the Westerners [*pāścātya*], the Foreign Masters [*bahirdeśaka*], the Sarvāstivādins of Kaśmīra or of Gandhāra [see DD.27f.]; and, finally, [3] the various masters such as Ghoṣaka, Dharmatrāta, Vasumitra, and Buddhadeva [see DD.28]. [...]
>
> In scholarly attempts to determine the sectarian or geographical identification of these [four] masters, ... the primary issue is their affiliation with a non-Kāśmīra Sarvāstivādin lineage or their association with the incipient Dārṣṭāntika faction within the Sarvāstivādin school.

Dhammajoti adds (ADCP.5f.):

> At the outset, it must be emphasized that "Sarvāstivāda", "Vaibhāṣikā", and the "*Mahāvibhāṣā* orthodoxy" do not have the same connotations. The Sarvāstivāda remained the most powerful and influential school in Northwestern India from around the beginning of the Christian era to about the 7th century A.D., initially established in Mathurā and expanding in the north where Kaśmīra became its centre of orthodoxy. [...]
>
> The Sarvāstivādins represent a fairly broad spectrum of people who are united by their categorical doctrine that *dharma*-s persist (*sarvadā asti* [= all exists, i.e., *dharma*-s always, *sarvadā*, exist, whether future, present or past]) through the three periods of time. This doctrinal stance is opposed

to that of the Vibhajyavādins (the Distinctionists). The latter are so called because they hold that the status of existence of the *dharma*-s in the three periods of time has to be distinguished: only the present, or those *karma*-s which have not given fruit exist; all other past *dharma*-s as well as future ones are not existent. [...] [SA.IV.56: It is noteworthy that in the *Vijñāna-kāya-śāstra*, the Sarvāstivādins never call themselves as such. When arguing against the Vibhajyavādins, they refer to themselves as the Yukta-vādins ("those who accord with (or emphasize) logical reasoning"); against the Pudgalavādins, as the Śūnyatā-vādins ("those who proclaim the doctrine of emptiness").]

Since the compilation of the *Mahāvibhāṣā-śāstra*, the adherents of the *Mahāvibhāṣā*, based mainly in Kaśmīra, came to be known as the "Vaibhāṣika". But even this orthodox and conservative group of Sarvāstivādins are not entirely unanimous in what they uphold as the true doctrines of the MVŚ. [SA.IV.57: This fact is reflected in the post-MVŚ works, such as the **Satya-siddhi-śāstra*, the **Abhidharmahṛdaya* (T no. 1550) and its commentaries (T no. 1551, no. 1552), the AKB and its commentaries, the *Abhidharmadīpa* and the **Nyāyānusāra*.]

In the **Nyāyānusāra* (ADCP.28; SA.IV.60), Saṃghabhadra provides an additional requirement to the definition of Sarvāstivāda given above:

Only [those who] believe in the existence of the tri-temporal [*dharma*-s] and the three types of truly existent *asaṃskṛta* can claim to be Sarvāstivāda. For it is only on account of their holding the existence of these *dharma*-s that they are acknowledged as Sarvāstivāda. The others are not; because they either superimpose/add on, or subtract from, [the *dharma*-s recognized by the Sarvāstivāda]. [1] The Superimposers [Samāropavādins = Pudgalavādins] assert that there exist the *Pudgala* and the previous *dharma*-s. [On the other hand], [2] the Vibhajyavādins assert the existence of only the present and those past *karma*-s that have not yet given fruit. [3] The Kṣaṇikavādins[a] assert the existence of only the 12 *āyatana*-s in the single moment of the present. [4] The Prajñaptivādins assert that the *dharma*-s of the present too are mere *prajñapti*-s [designations]. [5] The Vaināśika-s assert that all *dharma*-s are completely without any *svabhāva* like *ākāśa-puṣpa*-s [sky-flowers]. All of them are not Sarvāstivāda.

[a] The Sautrāntika, here referred to as Kṣaṇikavādins, and are singled out by Saṃghabhadra [Ny, 630c–631a] who denies that they qualify as Sarvāstivādins, for their view "differs from the Vaināśikas by just a mere *kṣaṇa* [moment]!"

2. *As for the origins, history and factions of the Dārṣṭāntika and Sautrāntika and what defines them*, things are more complicated, particularly their relationship, and scholars have different views. We will discuss this in more detail, while emphasizing Dhammajoti's views.

i. *In regard to the founding fathers*, Cox states (DD.40f.):

> The founding of the Dārṣṭāntikas (and Sautrāntikas if they are identified with one another) is traditionally attributed to Kumāralāta. ... However, by analyzing positions attributed to Kumāralāta, Katō concludes that the Kumāralāta who is associated with the Dārṣṭāntikas must have lived after the **Mahāvibhāṣā*. In that case, the traditional identification of Kumāralāta as the teacher of Harivarman, the author of the **Tattvasiddhiśāstra*, is plausible. However, admitting this late third century A.D. date for Kumāralāta leaves the origins of the Dārṣṭāntika group cited in the *Vibhāṣā* obscure.[a] Nevertheless, it would appear that they emerged just prior to the composition of the *Vibhāṣā* compendia not as a distinct ordination lineage or sect, but rather as a dogmatically distinguished group or school that objected to Sarvāstivādin doctrinal interpretations.
>
> Traditional descriptions portray Śrīlāta as the second Sautrāntika master; he is credited with the composition of a "**Sautrāntikavibhāṣā*" and is identified with the Sthavira cited frequently in Saṅghabhadra's **Nyāyānusāra*. If one accepts the identity of Sthavira as Śrīlāta, the frequent and lengthy citations of this Sthavira in the **Nyāyānusāra* not only verify the existence of some source text, but also provide a detailed, and indeed the only account of its contents. Indeed, these citations in the **Nyāyānusāra* would suggest that Sthavira's text was itself a detailed exegetical treatise that, despite Sautrāntika claims to the contrary, must have been at least stylistically similar to Abhidharma texts. By noting the biographical comments in the references to Sthavira in the **Nyāyānusāra*, Katō concludes that Śrīlāta was from a region to the east of that of Saṅghabhadra. This would suggest that in Saṅghabhadra's period, the area of primary opposition to the Kāśmīra Sarvāstivādins had shifted from the west, as it had been several centuries earlier, to the east. Given the often personal nature of Saṅghabhadra's criticisms, Katō also concludes that Śrīlāta must have been an older contemporary of both Vasubandhu and Saṅghabhadra. Concerning the relation among these roughly contemporaneous figures, Katō suggests that Kumāralāta was the teacher of both Harivarman and Śrīlāta and that Śrīlāta was the direct teacher of Vasubandhu.

[a] LS: See below Dhammajoti's view on the Dārṣṭāntikas.

Dhammajoti dates Kumāralāta (SA.IV.341) as "a Dārṣṭāntika leader of *ca.* late 2nd or early 3rd century C.E.".

As for Śrīlāta, Dhammajoti states at the beginning of his *Śrīlāta's anudhātu Doctrine* (ŚAD):

> Śrīlāta (*circa* 4th century C.E.), a senior contemporary of both Vasubandhu and Saṃghabhadra, was a leading Dārṣṭāntika-Sautrāntika master. According to Xuan Zang, he composed the **Sautrāntika-vibhāṣā* (經部毘婆沙論) in ancient Ayodhyā. Saṃghabhadra as well mentions his writing(s), though unfortunately without giving any title. In the **Nyāyānusāra*, Saṃghabhadra calls him "the Sthavira", and, when refuting the Dārṣṭāntika-Sautrāntika tenets, makes him his main target of attack.

ii. *As for the term and definition of Sautrāntika*, Yaśomitra states the following (WOG.11.29f.): "What is the meaning of 'Sautrāntika'? Those who take the *sūtra* as the authority, and do not take the *śāstra* as the authority." However, Dhammajoti (SD.202f.) and Katō show (DD.40) that this definition is not intended to be a sufficient one, since the distinction between the Sarvāstivāda and the Sautrāntika is not merely one pertaining to the attitude with regard to the *Abhidharma śāstra*, but entails the central Sarvāstivādin tenet of *sarvāstitva*, which is rejected by the Sautrāntikas.

Katō thinks (DD.38f.) that the earliest evidence of the Sautrāntikas as a distinct group is in the AKB where it occurs nineteen times, whereby Vasubandhu almost always agrees, whereas the Dārṣṭāntikas occur only three times, whereby Vasubandhu disagrees in all three cases. But (DD.40) "Katō notes that there are passages attributed to the Sautrāntikas in the *Abhidharmakośabhāṣya* that do not agree with Śrīlāta's own views. Therefore, Katō concludes that it is best not to construe the appellation 'Sautrāntika' as entailing either a distinct ordination lineage or a defined set of doctrinal positions." He suggests instead that the appellation "Sautrāntika" could have been used to encompass a broad range of individual opinions that conform to the general guidelines mentioned above.

iii. *As for the origin and significance of the "term" Dārṣṭāntika*, commentators interpret it differently (DD.37): "K'uei-chi, whose opinion became definitive in the Chinese and Japanese commentarial traditions, suggests that it derives either from comparisons—*dṛṣṭānta* drawn between Kumāralāta, the reputed founder of the Dārṣṭāntikas, and the light of the sun, or from the name of his text, the **Dṛṣṭānta-paṅkti*. Yaśomitra also explains the name 'Dārṣṭāntika' as indicating their practice of employing examples (*dṛṣṭānta*)." The earliest references to the Dārṣṭāntikas occurs in the *Vibhāṣā* compendia, where the term occurs eighty-six times. Some scholars think that the connotation of the term is pejorative used in contempt by an opponent, for example, the Kāśmīra Sarvāstivādins in the **Mahāvibhāṣā*, to refer to those who rely incorrectly upon the invalid authority of conventional examples.

Cox comments (DD.39) that as a result of his investigations, "Katō corroborates the view of Jean Przyluski that the terms 'Dārṣṭāntika' and 'Sautrāntika' simply represent different perspectives from which the same group can be seen: the term 'Dārṣṭāntika' has a negative connotation and is used by opponents, such as the Kāśmīra Sarvāstivādins, to suggest the group's reliance upon the invalid authority of conventional examples; the term 'Sautrāntika' has a positive connotation and is used by the group itself to refer to its own views". On the other hand, Saṃghabhadra, who uses predominantly "Dārṣṭāntika", though also frequently "Sautrāntika", seems to be, according to Katō, the first to identify the two terms with one another, as does also Yaśomitra several centuries later, though then with no negative connotation.

Dhammajoti, on the other hand, does not agree with the view (influenced by Przyluski's theory) that "the term Dārṣṭāntika in itself" has a derogatory or pejorative implication in the *Vibhāṣā*. He states (SD.185):

> My objections to Przyluski's view can be summarized as follows:
>
> a. They are quoted as "Venerable Dārṣṭāntika masters" (譬喻尊者)—hardly pejorative;
> b. they are not the only group objected to as regards the use of similes;
> c. the Vaibhāṣika-s themselves use similes quite frequently as doctrinal proofs;
> d. as Jayatilleke argues [in his *Early Buddhist Theory of Knowledge*, 381f.], Przyluski is topsy-turvy in claiming that in the Buddhist tradition, *dṛṣṭa* [LS: "what is seen"] (> *dṛṣṭānta* > *dārṣṭāntika*) is inferior to *śruta* [LS: "what is heard"];
> e. the interchangeable use of "Sautrāntika" and "Dārṣṭāntika" is attested only around Vasubandhu's time.
> f. Very recently, it has further been pointed out that the Dārṣṭāntika leader, Kumāralāta entitled his own book as *Dṛṣṭāntapaṅkti*, and it is hardly imaginable that he would have chosen such a title had *dṛṣṭānta/Dārṣṭāntika* been treated by his opponents as a pejorative term.

iv. Furthermore, Dhammajoti (SD.186f.) distinguishes (1) the early Dārṣṭāntikas, with Dharmatrāta and Buddhadeva as the most eminent, and (2) the later Dārṣṭāntika-Sautrāntikas of the post-*Mahāvibhāṣā-śāstra* period, and he states that the key factor in considering their relationship is the doctrinal position concerning *sarvāstitva* and that the latter are indisputably Vibhajyavādins while the former are Sarvāstivādins [see our discussion of these schools above]. He goes on:

> Xuan Zang's tradition tells us that Kumāralāta was the "original master" of the Sautrāntika. But even this Dārṣṭāntika *guru* of the post-*Vibhāṣā* era[a] holds the *sarvāstitva* standpoint [or the view of tri-temporal existence].[b] Harivarman, the author of **Tattvasiddhi*, who, according to tradition, was his pupil, had, on the other hand, become a Vibhajyavādin. From this fact, we should learn to be more cautious not to hastily equate the early with the later Dārṣṭāntika-s. Moreover, Buddhadeva and Dharmatrāta, two early Dārṣṭāntika masters, are well known to subscribe to the *sarvāstitva* doctrine.

[a] ADCP.33: "The Dārṣṭāntika leader Kumāralāta must have been instrumental in the final stage of the transition from the Dārṣṭāntika to the Sautrāntika."

[b] Cf. *Abhidharmadīpa*, 277, and also Frauwallner's comments on this passage, SAL.207f.

Dhammajoti continues (SD.189):

> [But,] there had indeed been some confusion—even on the part of the ancients—concerning the sectarian affiliation of "the Bhadanta". In the MVŚ, this term generally refers to Dharmatrāta whom everybody knew as a Dārṣṭāntika leader. But because a major section of the later-time Sautrāntika—such as that led by Śrīlāta—advocated doctrines derived from or heavily influenced by him, some commentators seemed to think of him as a Sautrāntika or "one leaning toward the Sautrāntika". Secondly, for others, the Bhadanta Dharmatrāta—and for that matter the Dārṣṭāntika-s in the MVŚ—was a Vaibhāṣika/Sarvāstivādin, sharing the thesis of *sarvāstitva*. Thus, to say the least, it is certain that the ancient did not indiscriminatively equate "Dārṣṭāntika" with "Sautrāntika".

v. To give a clearer presentation of Dhammajoti's views on the development of the various factions of the above mentioned two groups (i.e., earlier and later Dārṣṭāntikas) in the context of the Sarvāstivādins, in the following longer quote we will reproduce various pertinent sections from his SA.IV.74ff:

> The early Dārṣṭāntika masters were known for their active effort in popularizing the Buddha's teachings, employing poetry and possibly other literary devices in the world in the process, and were particularly skilled in utilizing similes and allegories in demonstrating the Buddhist doctrines. It was most probably for this reason that they came to be known as the Dārṣṭāntikas. They were also noted as meditators and proponents of meditation. At the same time, we see in the MVŚ some of their masters—such as

Dharmatrāta and Buddhadeva—as being engaged in controverting the Ābhidharmika doctrines. It is therefore conceivable that, broadly speaking, there existed two sections of the early Dārṣṭāntikas—one more pre-occupied with popular preaching and meditation, the other with doctrinal disputation. It was probably from the latter section that the Sautrāntika evolved. In this process of disputation, they also seem to have contributed to the development of Buddhist logic, as the Vaibhāṣikas, themselves proud of being in conformity to logic, spoke of the Sautrāntikas as being arrogant in their logical skill (*tarkābhimāna*). [...]

From the beginning, divergent viewpoints within the [Sarvāstivāda] school were found and even tolerated—as long as they did not directly contravene the thesis of Sarvāstivāda. To take just a few examples: Dharmatrāta, Buddhadeva, Vasumitra and Ghoṣaka—the so called "four great Ābhidharmikas of the Sarvāstivāda"—each offered a different explanation as to how, given the theory that a *dharma* exists as an everlasting *dravya*, the difference in the three periods of time can be accounted for. [...]

But since the compilation of the *Jñānaprasthāna-śāstra* (JPŚ), the Kāśmīrian Sarvāstivādins upheld the supreme authority of the JPŚ system and raised this work to the status of being the Buddha's words. As time went on, they assumed the position of orthodoxy and became increasingly dogmatic and intolerant toward all other views not compatible with the JPŚ system. Partly to consolidate their position as the orthodox Sarvāstivādins, they eventually compiled the encyclopedic MVŚ which purports to be a commentary on JPŚ. In it, besides their own views, those of the following Sarvāstivāda schools of thought were also cited and usually criticized and rejected: The Dārṣṭāntikas, the western masters (*pāścātya*; also called "the Venerables of the west" 西方尊者; and "the western *śramaṇa*-s"), the foreign masters (*bahirdeśaka*; also called "the masters outside Kaśmīra", and the "Gāndhārian masters"). Even the so-called "old Kāśmīrian masters" were not spared.

Subsequent to the compilation of the MVŚ, the orthodox Kāśmīrians who based themselves on it were known as the Vaibhāṣikas. ... The term "Vaibhāṣikas" eventually came to connote the orthodox Sarvāstivādins, based mainly—but not exclusively—in Kāśmīra. ...

This dogmaticism and intolerance of the Vaibhāṣikas inevitably brought about a reaction from the other Sarvāstivādins. On the one hand, it resulted in the split of the Sarvāstivāda school into two major camps—the eastern one representing the Kāśmīrian school and the western one representing the

> Gāndhārian school—although it would seem that not all Kāśmīrian Ābhidharmikas were as orthodox or dogmatic as the professed Vaibhāṣikas. On the other hand, it compelled the *sūtra*-centered Dārṣṭāntikas to co-operate with other holders of heterodox views, including the Mahāyāna Śūnyatāvādins, prevailing around the first and second centuries C.E., and finally to change over to the "present-only-exist" standpoint. ... It was in this process that, a section among their radicals, the Dārṣṭāntika, eventually evolved into the Sautrāntika.
>
> Although the appellations "Gāndhārian masters", "western masters" and "foreign masters" may suggest a considerable difference in the geographical locations of these masters, in actual fact, they refer mainly to the Sarvāstivāda masters west of Kāśmīra—the western masters—of Gāndhāra and Parthia, with Gāndhāra as the center. ...
>
> The western masters too studied JPŚ, although with a more critical attitude than the Kāśmīrians. They too, being Sarvāstivādin Ābhidharmikas, were not really opposed to the Kāśmīrians in a sectarian sense. The MVŚ compilers held them in considerable regard, calling them "the honored ones of the west". ...
>
> But the work which most deeply influenced the basic attitude of these western masters was the *Prajñapti-śāstra* (PrŚ) whose importance for the Sarvāstivādins was next only to the JPŚ. A new trend of development was inherited from the tradition of the PrŚ, tending toward organization, the essential and conciseness.

γ. We should now be in a better position to deal with the second part of our thorny issue, namely: Vasubandhu's relationship to the Sarvāstivādins/Vaibhāṣikas, Dārṣṭāntikas, Sautrāntikas and the Mahāyāna/Yogācāra. What school did he belong to when he was writing the AKB?

First of all, when looking at the above discussions regarding the Sarvāstivādins, Dārṣṭāntikas, Sautrāntikas, and to a lesser degree the Yogācāras, it should now be clearer that answering these questions from the perspective of the traditional framework of neatly distinguished schools is too simplified, both (1) when looking at each school (and their representatives) separately, as well as (2) when looking at the borders and interrelationship between the schools (and their representatives), particularly in a historical context. In other words, we would have to be more specific about what kind of Sarvāstivādins/Vaibhāṣikas, Dārṣṭāntikas, etc., we are talking about.

But even if we would accept this traditional framework, modern scholarship is running into further problems in regard to the views most commonly held in the past regarding Vasubandhu's own philosophical beliefs and relation to the mentioned schools, which Hirakawa (1973–1978, v. 1: xi–xii) summarizes as follows:

> It is generally accepted among scholars that the author of the *Kośa* was ordained in the Sarvāstivāda School, but his thoughts were closer to those of the Sautrāntika School. The doctrine of the Sautrāntika School is based on "the *prajñapti*" [provisional factor or provisional designation] which includes the teaching of *bīja*; therefore, the developed form of this doctrine can be related to the doctrine of Vijñānavāda. It does not necessarily mean that the Sautrāntika School itself developed into the Vijñānavāda, but it can be easily assumed that the author of the *Kośa* belonged to the Sautrāntika school [and] later changed to the Vijñānavāda, for there is a certain common ground between the doctrines.

Robert Kritzer comments (RCYA.198) that "according to this way of thinking, Vasubandhu wrote the *Abhidharmakośabhāṣya* when he was a Sautrāntika, the *Triṃśikā* when he was a Yogācāra, and texts like the *Karmasiddhiprakaraṇa* and the *Pratītyasamutpādavyākhyā* at some time in between, while he was presumably in the process of conversion from Sautrāntika to Yogācāra".

1. This account has been put into question by some modern scholars in the last twenty years who think, for example Kritzer, that they have found evidence that already in the AKB we find positions identified in the Sanskrit text as Sautrāntika the majority of which have correspondences in the *Yogācārabhūmi*, which is supposedly to be a Mahāyāna text. Thus Kritzer states (JIABS.26.2, p. 373):

> I assume that the *Yogācārabhūmi* was available to Vasubandhu in a form similar to the one we know, i.e., with at least the *Maulībhūmi* and the *Viniścayasaṃgrahaṇī* included in one text. If Vasubandhu was not familiar with the *Yogācārabhūmi*, then we would have to assume that he learned his Sautrāntika ideas from the same sources as the authors of the corresponding passages in the *Yogācārabhūmi*. As we have seen [previously in my article] written records of these sources, if they ever existed, are no longer extant.

Kritzer acknowledges (VY.xxxvii) that "with the exception of *bīja*, one can find none of the characteristic terms of the Yogācāra among the above correspondences [between the *Abhidharmakośabhāṣya* and the *Yogācārabhūmi*, as discussed in his article]: words such as *ālayavijñāna*, *vijñaptimātra*, and *trisvabhāva* simply do not appear. Nor is there any explicit statement of Mahāyāna themes, such as the emptiness of *dharma*s or the three bodies of the Buddha."

But his research brings him to the following conclusion (RCYA.19f.):

> Vasubandhu is famous for upholding the Sautrāntika position when it differs from Sarvāstivāda. However, the fact that opinions that he identifies as Sautrāntika can often be found in the *Yogācārabhūmi* has not been remarked upon until recently. Moreover, in at least several cases, when he does favor Sarvāstivāda over Sautrāntika (or Dārṣṭāntika), the *Yogācārabhūmi* position also is in agreement with Sarvāstivāda.... I [Kritzer] suspect that Vasubandhu's so-called Sautrāntika opinions are, in fact, Yogācāra *abhidharma* in disguise. If this is true, it raises questions about the meaning of the terms Sautrāntika and Yogācāra as well as about the definition of Mahāyāna.

Furthermore (2005.xxix):

> [O]ne explanation for the correspondences between Vasubandhu's Sautrāntika positions and passages in the *Yogācārabhūmi* is that the authors of both texts rely on a common source that represented an intermediate stage between Sarvāstivāda and fully developed Yogācāra, based on the concept of *ālaya-vijñāna*. ... My own [Kritzer's] conclusion is that in the *Abhidharmakośa-bhāṣya* Vasubandhu uses the term Sautrāntika to designate positions in the *Yogācārabhūmi* that he prefers to those of orthodox Sarvāstivāda. As I argue elsewhere (1999: 203–4; 2003b), Vasubandhu in the *Abhidharmakośabhāṣya* adjusts the traditional Sarvāstivādin *abhidharma* so that it no longer conflicts with the central theories of *Yogācāra*. Unlike in the Yogācāra texts attributed to him, his purpose in the *Abhidharmakośabhāṣya* is not to propound or defend these theories. Therefore, he does not mention *ālayavijñāna*, ...

2. Kritzer's view does not go unchallenged. Dhammajoti, who very much welcomes the new research, has a more conservative approach since he does not find the "new" results all that compelling yet. He thinks that the cases put forth by Kritzer could be interpreted differently.

For example, in regard to Kritzer's contention (JIABS.26.2, p. 379f.) that the *ālaya-vijñāna* doctrine is to be expounded only at the highest level of truth, whereas the *bīja* doctrine, at the provisional level, Dhammajoti comments (SD.205) that in this context Kritzer also refers to the distinction made by Vasubandhu between *abhi-dharma* in the conventional sense and in the absolute sense (*pāramārthika*), suggesting (JIABS.26.2, p. 379f.) that "from Vasubandhu's point of view, although most of the Sarvāstivāda *abhidharma* that he describes without criticism in the *Abhidharmakośabhāṣya* is conducive to pure wisdom, it is not necessarily a statement of all that is known by pure wisdom".

But Dhammajoti replies (SD.205) that even the Vaibhāṣika would have no problem with this observation and that "the said distinction is in fact not Vasubandhu's own, but [it is] based on the explanations given in the *Vibhāṣā* [MVŚ, 2c, 3b], and [that] Saṃghabhadra [T 29, 329a–b] expounds on it without the slightest protest". He thus sees no justification for the assertion that Vasubandhu intentionally avoids the *ālayavijñāna* doctrine and prefers to think that Vasubandhu himself, in fact, did not believe in it at the stage of composing the AKB. But he does not leave it there and proceeds to specify his own views:

> Yin Shun [*Study*, 678ff.] explains Vasubandhu's initial reluctance to accept the *ālayavijñāna* doctrine as follows: Vasubandhu basically accepted the Ābhidharmika doctrines pertaining to the *citta-caitta*. At the initial stage of the development of the *ālayavijñāna*, it did not seem acceptable to Vasubandhu that the *ālayavijñāna* as a *vijñāna* could be without associated *caitta*-s. It is in fact out of the same kind of consideration that he preferred the doctrine of the mutual seeding of *nāma* and *rūpa*, rather than the Dārṣṭāntika-Sautrāntika doctrine that in *nirodhasamāpatti* there can be a *citta* without any *caitta*. But when later on (at the stage of the *Karmasiddhi*) it came to be articulated that the *ālaya-vijñāna* too had associated *caitta*-s, the doctrine became acceptable to him.

Similarly, in regard to many of the other passages discussed in Kritzer's *Sautrāntika in the Abhidharmakośabhāṣya* article, which Dhammajoti discusses in his *Sarvāstivāda, Dārṣṭāntika, Sautrāntika and Yogācāra—Some Reflections on Their Interrelation*, Dhammajoti states (SD.198) that "Vasubandhu's sources in most cases could very well be the MVŚ or some other sources that are now no more extant, rather than necessarily the *Yogācārabhūmi-śāstra*".

3. But in the context of the identity of the Sautrāntika, Dhammajoti also pursues the following issue in his article (SD.206): "If the Sautrāntika cannot be considered to belong to the Sarvāstivāda school and is a relatively independent school in its own right, why is it that, as Lamotte points out, no Sautrāntika monastery has ever been attested?" He replies by referring to Yin Shun's interesting views that the Sautrāntikas failed to establish their organized monastic strongholds for the following reasons (SD.206):

> i. They emerged too late (to be properly established as a distinct sect), [while] the Buddhist sects with their *sūtra-vinaya* as basis were continuing to thrive after flourishing for some 500 years, having long established their specific area of propagation and monastic system. The fact that the Vinaya was not the Sautrāntika emphasis also did not help in this regard.

ii. Doctrinally, they tended to (a) be liberal, resulting in the lack of unity and stability; (b) merge with other sects in the process of breaking away from the Sarvāstivāda, which in turn added to the inconsistency in their tenets; (c) be transformed by the then well-flourishing Mahāyāna thoughts of the Śūnyatāvāda and Yogācāra, given the compatibility of some of their tenets with those of the Mahāyāna—especially Yogācāra that was nearing doctrinal maturation.

iii. The early Dārṣṭantika-s and the Ābhidharmika-s were at first mutually benefiting, and each in their own way—the former being influential religious preachers and meditation masters, and the latter, articulate and thorough theorists—contributing to the common cause of the Sarvāstivāda. But once the later Dārṣṭāntika themselves had turned into full-fledged theorists claiming to be *sūtra-prāmāṇika* and were constantly engaged in anti-*Ābhidharmika* confrontation, they began to lose the charisma that they once had in the hearts of the devotee whose support was needed in establishing regional strongholds of their own.

4. But then again, even though Dhammajoti is more conservative in regard to the Yogācāra influence on Vasubandhu in the AKB, Dhammajoti agrees with Nobuyoshi Yamabe's suggestion (see JIABS.26.2, p. 243) that "the Dārṣṭāntika or Sautrāntika tradition was fairly closely linked to meditative traditions". He also agrees, in the main, with Yamabe's provisional conclusions, namely, that "the Yogācāra tradition and the Sautrāntika-like elements were almost inseparably interconnected long before the compilation of the *Yogācārabhūmi*". He then specifies (SD.195):

> The early Dārṣṭāntika-s and (Sarvāstivādin) Yogācāra-s all belonged to the same Sarvāstivāda tradition originally. The term Yogācāra master (瑜伽師) occurs about 140 times in MVŚ. These masters are the meditators whose primary concern is spiritual praxis and realization, generally well respected by even the Ābhidharmika-s. ... Against this backdrop, we may understand that Vasubandhu would have been familiar with doctrines propagated within the larger Sarvāstivāda lineage, some of which later developed into the so-called Sautrāntika doctrines, and others, [into] Yogācāra doctrines. Of course, being within the same milieu, the Dārṣṭāntika-Sautrāntika and the Mahāyānic Yogācāra—particularly those who are praxis-oriented—must have been mutually influenced doctrinally. Accordingly, it should not be surprising to find doctrinal parallels between what Vasubandhu identifies as Sautrāntika doctrines in AKB on the one hand, and some of the doctrines in the *Yogācārabhūmi* on the other.

He then comments that this does not necessarily imply that Vasubandhu bases his Sautrāntika doctrines on the *Yogācārabhūmi* and that "while not ruling out the possibility entirely at this stage, and not contesting that Vasubandhu was probably familiar with the *Yogācārabhūmi*", he concludes that the parallels presented so far are mostly unconvincing.

5. *What school did Vasubandhu belong to when he was writing the AKB?*

Dhammajoti answers as follows (SD.200):

> The Yogācāra-s at least in part evolved from the praxis-oriented Sautrāntika-s who in turn evolved from the early Dārṣṭāntika-s. In this process, it is possible that, given the attitude of openness to non-orthodox doctrines among the early Dārṣṭāntika-s—as witnessed in the MVŚ—and their predilection toward the authority of meditation experience, some of them had been influenced (and reacted to) the then flourishing Mahāyāna tenets such as *Śūnyatā*, becoming perhaps the early members of the "Mahāyānic" Yogācāra. But judging by the earliest portion of the *Yogācārabhūmi-śāstra* (*maulī bhūmi*), even these early "Mahāyānic Yogācārins" were still realists. ...
>
> Others within the Sautrāntika lineage, who were in some way more "resilient" to the new doctrines and ideals, remained as "Hīnayāna" Sautrāntika-s, holding on in particular to their form of realism. This latter group seemed to have been greatly influenced by Bhadanta Dharmatrāta (and later on also by Kumāralāta and others), and in Vasubandhu's time had Śrīlāta as a prominent leader. It is this group that preserved—sometimes with slight modification (e.g., Śrīlāta's doctrine that there are only the three *caitta*-s *vedanā*, *saṃjñā* and *cetanā*; all the other *caitta*-s being *cetanā-viśeṣa*)—many of the Dārṣṭāntika doctrines in the MVŚ.
>
> In the AKB, Vasubandhu himself seems to be generally partisan to this latter Hīnayāna group. But he too was evidently open-minded, of which fact the AKB is a testimony, and accordingly did not seem to have become exclusively partisan to the tenets of any group as such—be it those of Hīnayāna or Yogācāra Sautrāntika or Sarvāstivāda. ... As another illustration, Vasubandhu is known to accept some of the Sarvāstivāda *caitta*-s, and the notion of *saṃprayoga* of *citta-caitta*-s—differing from Śrīlāta. This also necessarily means that he accepts the *sahabhū-hetu* doctrine, which Śrīlāta rejects. Furthermore, he disagrees with a Sautrāntika view—held also by Śrīlāta—that a subtle *citta* exists in the *nirodhasamāpatti*, and endorses the *Pūrva-ācārya*-s' view of the mutual seeding of *nāma* and *rūpa*, a view that is found

in YBŚ. Yet at times, Saṃghabhadra has to protest that he is partisan to Śrīlāta.

Dhammajoti summarizes (SD.201):

> The Vasubandhu of AKB [...] belonged to the Hīnayāna Sautrāntika school of thought, while also maintaining allegiance to certain acceptable Sarvāstivādin tenets, and at the same time was open to the developing Yogācārin tenets. This is not surprising considering his own doctrinal background, as well as the fact that the Yogācāra evolved from the broad Sarvāstivāda lineage. He must have been quite well exposed to the evolving Yogācāra tenets in North-western India where he had been active.

Moreover (SD.202):

> Vasubandhu, subscribing to the Vibhajyavādin standpoint as he does, cannot qualify as a Sarvāstivādin.

For Vasubandhu's specific views held in the AKB, see Dhammajoti's *Summary.*

6. *LVP's additional attributions and Kritzer's identified passages.*

Since modern scholarship is still in the midst of sorting out who is who, who says what and who influenced whom, and since La Vallée Poussin—often basing himself on Saeki Kiokuga, who in turn draws his attributions mainly from those of the seventh-century Chinese commentators, for example, P'u-kuang, etc.—sometimes attributes a statement to, for example, Sautrāntika, when neither the Chinese nor Tibetan translation does so, based on the Pradhan Sanskrit edition we decided to identify these added attributions by round brackets.

For similar reasons, we also endnoted all of Kritzer's identified passages from his systematic comparative study of the AKB and the *Yogācārabhūmi.*

7. *The structure of the Abhidharmakośabhāṣya*

This will be discussed in the first endnote at the beginning of section B of chapter 1: "Discernment of the factors *(dharma)*; F 6–102; chapters one to nine." See also Dhammajoti's *Summary.*

8. *Outline of this introductory endnote:*

   1. Brief outline of what has been discussed so far by Lamotte, La Vallée Poussin and Dhammajoti.
   2. The new additions in our publication and helpful new sources:

i. Summary of the doctrines: Grousset, LVP's articles and books, *Electronic Appendix*, our endnotes and their sources, etc.
ii. New updated bibliography.
iii. The newly inserted outline and headlines and their sources.
iv. Further additions to the translation and endnotes: Gokhale's Sanskrit root verses; Tibetan root text; inserted original technical Sanskrit terms; inserted numbers.

3. Influences on our translation and its endnotes:
   i. The three main influences and secondary influences.
   ii. The specific influence from Willemen's and Dessein's translations of two *Hṛdaya* treatises.
4. The stratagems of LVP's translation, of our translation and of Hsüan-tsang's translation. Biographical data on Hsüan-tsang and La Vallée Poussin.
5. What further needs to be addressed to facilitate further access for the reader of this annotated translation:
   i. The life of Vasubandhu according to Paramārtha.
   ii. Various issues surrounding Vasubandhu as discussed by contemporary scholarship.
      a. Which works can reasonably be attributed to Vasubandhu the Kośakāra?
      b. The alternative hypotheses of one or two Vasubandhus, his life time, his relationship to Asaṅga, the problems of the information available on the relevant Gupta dynastic history.
      c. Vasubandhu's relationship to the Sarvāstivādins/Vaibhāṣikas, the Dārṣṭāntikas, the Sautrāntikas and the Mahāyāna/Yogācāra. What school did Vasubandhu belong to when he was writing the *Abhidharmakośabhāṣya* (AKB)? Who were these schools? How did they interact or influence each other?
         α. The traditional presentation of the four representative schools of Buddhism:
            1. The Sarvāstivādins.
            2. The Sautrāntikas.
            3. The Yogācāras.
            4. [The Mādhyamikas (omitted)]
         β. The origins of (*1.*) the Sarvāstivādins and (*2.*) Dārṣṭāntikas and Sautrāntikas, and what defines them.
         γ. Vasubandhu's relationship to the Sarvāstivādins/Vaibhāṣikas, Dārṣṭāntikas, Sautrāntikas and the Mahāyāna/Yogācāra. What school did he belong to when he was writing the AKB?

6. LVP's additional attributions and Kritzer's identified passages.
7. The structure of the *Abhidharmakośabhāṣya.*
8. Outline of this introductory endnote.

9. *Acknowledgements and Thanks*

It has been a great honor and learning experience to work on this translation which started more than ten years ago. It goes without saying that such an undertaken cannot be done alone. Being a very good example of the "less gifted ones", it is thus time for me to say thanks to the people who at the various stages of this project have inspired me, encouraged me to go on and supported me in their own unique way to bring this project to completion.

Despite deceiving outside looks, but actually not being much of a religious person, I would not be of much use as a monk without the ongoing spiritual support (sometimes better called "babysitting") of my teachers. I therefore would first of all like to thank my root teacher, the late Venerable Trungpa Rinpoche, for the very original inspiration to start this project, the Venerable Khenchen Thrangu Rinpoche, my abbot, for encouraging me in this inspiration and my present personal teacher, Dzogchen Pönlop Rinpoche, for his modern-day pith instruction: "Back things up!"

Next, I would like to acknowledge my deep gratitude towards Bhikkhu KL Dhammajoti with whom I have been in contact since 2006 and whose writings have helped to raise this translation to a completely new level.

Further I would like to thank Collett Cox, Ernst Steinkellner, Alexander von Rospatt, Anne MacDonald, James Duerlinger, Paul Dessein, Peter Skilling, Bill Waldrön and Karl Brunnhölzl for being true Professor Bodhisattvas, willing to help and support where there was need.

In terms of hands-on-help, there is no real way that I can thank Bhikṣuṇī Migme Chödrön, my friend and editor, i.e., "partner-in-crime", for so many years, who when still doing research as a Chemist at the University of Alberta acquired all these great French translations of Buddhist texts, including La Vallée Poussin's AKB.

I also want to thank Bhikṣuṇī Lodrö Palmo, member of the Chökyi Gyatso Translation Committee, for always being ready to help with some of the "French puzzles" of the translation; Mildred Carrigan, my interlibrary loans "fairy"; Ane Sangmo, who helped with some of the proofreading; Mike Peters, computer "god" in Sydney; Stephanie Johnston, for cover design tips, and my Shedra students for being guinea pigs for testrunning parts of the translation.

Last but not least, I would like to thank my late father and mother and my family as well as my monastic community of Gampo Abbey for "letting me get away" with who I am and with this work.

May it be of benefit!

Abbreviations

A	*Atthasālinī*: Buddhaghosa
ACP	*The Abhidharma Controversy on Perception*: KL Dhammajoti
AD	*Abhidharmadīpa with Vibhāṣāprabhāvṛtti*: Jaini
ADCP	*Abhidharma Doctrines and Controversies on Perception*: KL Dhammajoti
ADP	*Ākāra and Direct Perception*: *Vaibhāṣika versus Sautrāntika*: KL Dhammajoti
ADV	*Abhidharmadīpa* (with *Vibhāṣāprabhāvṛtti*)
AH	*Abhidharmahṛdaya*: Dharmaśrī
AHV	*Abhidharmahṛdaya-vyākhyā*: Dharmatrāta
AIP	*Ākāra and Immediate Perception*: KL Dhammajoti
AKB	*Abhidharmakośabhāṣya*: Vasubandhu
AKB(C)	Chinese translation of AKB by Xuan Zang (T 1558)
AKBh	*Abhidharmakośabhāṣya*: Vasubandhu
AKBP	*Abhidharmakośabhāṣyam by Louis de La Vallée Poussin*: Leo M. Pruden
A.K.V.	*Sputârthā Abhidharmakośavyākhyā*: Yaśomitra
AKVy	*Sputârthā Abhidharmakośavyākhyā*: Yaśomitra
AmRŚ	**Abhidharmāmṛta-rasa-śāstra* (T 1553)
AMS	*The aśubhā meditation in the Sarvāstivāda*: KL Dhammajoti
AMSV	*The Apramāṇa Meditation in the Sarvāstivāda*: KL Dhammajoti
AMVŚ	*Abhidharmamahāvibhāṣāśāstra*
AN	*Aṅguttaranikāya*
AS	*Abhidharmasamuccaya*: Asaṅga
ASA	*Analytical Study of the Abhidharmakośa*: Sukomal Chaudhuri
ASB	*Ābhidharmika Schools of Buddhism*: Collett Cox
ATA	*Attainment through Abandonment*: Collett Cox
ATV	*The Atomic Theory of Vasubandhu*: Kajiyama
AV	*Ālayavijñāna*: Lambert Schmithausen
Avatāra	**Abhidharmāvatāra*: Skandhila
BC	*Buddhist Cosmology*: W. Randolph Kloetzli
BCO	*Buddhist Cosmology. Philosophy and Origins*: Akira Sadakata
BD	*Buddhist Dictionary*: Ñyanatiloka
BDB	*The Bodhisattva Doctrine in Buddhist Sanskrit Literature*: Har Dayal
BDE	*A Buddhist Doctrine of Experience*: Thomas A. Kochumuttom
BDM	*The Buddhist Doctrine of Momentariness*: Alexander von Rospatt
BE	*Buddhist Ethics*: Jamgön Kongtrül Lodrö Thayé
BEFEO	*Bulletin de l'École Française d'Extrême-Orient*
BHSD	Buddhist Hybrid Sanskrit Grammar and Dictionary: Franklin Edgerton
BL	*Buddhist Logic, Vol. I & II*: Theodore Stcherbatsky
BM	*Buddhist Doctrine of Momentariness* (Routledge): Alexander von Rospatt

BMC	*The Buddhist Monastic Code I*: Ṭhānissaro Bhikkhu
BPUF	*Buddhist Philosophy of Universal Flux*: Satkari Mookerjee
Brethren	*Psalms of the Brethren* (*Theragātha*): C.A.F. Rhys Davids
BSOS	*Bulletin of the School of Oriental Studies*
BTAC	*Buddhist Thought and Asian Civilization*: Ed.: Leslie S. Kawamura and Keith Scott (ed.)
BTI	*Buddhist Thought in India*: Edward Conze
BU	*The Buddhist Unconscious*: William Waldron
CBN	*Conception of Buddhist Nirvāṇa*: Theodore Stcherbatsky
CC	*Cosmogony and Cosmology* (*Buddhist*): Louis de La Vallée Poussin
CCB	*Central Conception of Buddhism*: Theodore Stcherbatsky
CDŚ	*The Citta-caitta Doctrine of Srīlāta*: KL Dhammajoti
CEGS	*Ceaseless Echoes of the Great Silence*: Khenpo Palden Sherab, Rinpoche
Ch.	Chinese
CM.6	*Crystal Mirror, Volume VI*: Dharma Publishing
CMP	*The Chapter on the Mundane Path* (*Laukikamārga*) *in the Śrāvakabhūmi*: Florin Deleanu
Compendium	*Compendium of Philosophy* (*Abhidhammattha-sangaha*): Shwe Zan Aung and C.A.F. Rhys Davids
CPBS	*Collected Papers on Buddhist Studies*: Padmanabh S. Jaini
CPL	*Clarifying the Path to Liberation*: Gedun Drup
CT	*Collected Topics*: Āchārya Tenpa Gyaltsen
CTA	*Cutting Through Appearances*: Jeffrey Hopkins
CWSL	*Ch'eng Wei-Shih Lun*: Hsüan Tsang, transl. Wei Tat
DA	*Documents d'Abhidharma*: *La Controverse du Temps*: Louis de La Vallée Poussin
DAE	*The Defects in an Arhat's Enlightenment*: KL Dhammajoti
DB	*The Connected Discourses of the Buddha* (*Saṃyutta Nikāya*): Bhikkhu Bodhi
DCO	*Demonstration of Consciousness Only*, in: *Three Texts on Consciousness Only*: Francis H. Cook
DD	*Disputed Dharmas. Earliest Buddhist Theories on Existence*: Collett Cox
DDSA	*Digital Dictionaries of South Asia*: *The Pāli Text Society's Pali-English Dictionary*.
DEBCK	*Development in the Early Buddhist Concept of Kamma/Karma*: James Paul McDermott
DhCPS	*Dharmacakrapravartanasūtra*
Dhp	*Dhammapada*
Dialogues	*Dialogues of the Buddha* (translation of *Dīgha Nikāya*): C.A.F. Rhys-Davids
DIS	*Dignāga on the Interpretation of Signs*: Richard P. Hayes

DKB	*The Doctrine of Karma in Buddhism*: *A Study*: Y. Krishan, in *Amalā Prajñā*
DKŚ	**Dhātu-kāya-śāstra,* 阿毘達磨界身足論 (T 1540)
DN	*Dīgha Nikāya*: Maurice Walshe
DO	*Dependent Origination*: *Its Elaboration in Early Sarvāstivādin Abhidharma Texts*: Collett Cox
DOP	*Dignāga*, *On Perception*: Masaaki Hattori
DS	*The Doctrine of the Six-stage Mindfulness of Breathing*: K.L. Dhammajoti
DSŚ	**Dharma-skandha-śāstra,* 阿毘達磨法蘊足論 (T 1537)
EBP	*Early Buddhist Philosophy*: Alfonso Verdu
EBT	*The Early Buddhist Tradition and Ecological Ethics*: Lambert Schmithausen
EEPR	*Encyclopedia of Eastern Philosophy and Religion*
EIP	*Encyclopedia of Indian Philosophies*: Ed.: Karl Potter
EIP.II	EIP: Indian Metaphysics and Epistemology: The Tradition of Nyāya-Vaiśeṣika up to Gaṅgeśa: (Ed.) Karl P. Potter
EIP.III	EIP: Advaita Vedānta up to Śaṃkara and His Pupils: (Ed.) Karl P. Potter
EIP.IV	EIP: Sāṃkhya. A Dualist Tradition in Indian Philosophy: (Ed.) Gerald James Larson and Ram Shankar Bhattacharya
EIP.V	EIP: The Philosophy of the Grammarian: Harold G. Coward and K. Kunjunni Raja
EIP.VI	EIP: Indian Philosophical Analysis. Nyāya-Vaiśeṣika from Gaṅgeś to Raghunātha Śiromaṇi: (Ed.) Karl P. Potter and Ram Shankar Bhattacharya
EIP.VII	EIP: Abhidharma Buddhism to 150 A.D.: (Ed.) Karl P. Potter with Robert E. Buswell, jr, Padmanabh S. Jaini and Noble Ross Reat
EIP.VIII	EIP: Buddhist Philosophy from 100 to 350 A.D.: (Ed.) Karl P. Potter
EIP.IX	EIP: Buddhist Philosophy from 350 to 600 A.D.: (Ed.) Karl P. Potter
EMA	*Essence of Metaphysics. Abhidharmahṛdaya*: Charles Willemen
EPL	*Elucidating the Path to Liberation*: David Patt
EPS	*Rangjung Yeshe Wiki Dharma Dictionary*
ER	*Encyclopedia of Religion*: Ed.: Mircea Eliade
ESA	*Essence of Scholasticism. Abhidharmahṛdaya*: Charles Willemen
ESD	*Entrance into the Supreme Doctrine. Skandhila's Abhidharmāvatāra*: KL Dhammajoti
EV	*The Entrance to the Vinaya*: Vajirañāṇavarorasa
F	French page number
FCO	*From Category to Ontology*: *the Changing Role of Dharma in Sarvāstivāda Abhidharma*: Collett Cox
FDP	*Foundations of Dharmakīrti's Philosophy*: John D. Dunne
FRC	*From Reductionism to Creativity*: Herbert V. Guenther
G	*The Text of the Abhidharmakośakārikā of Vasubandhu*: V.V. Gokhale

GGB	*Gewalt und Gewaltlosigkeit im Buddhismus: Zur Einführung*: Lambert Schmithausen
GIP	*Geschichte der indischen Philosophie*: Erich Frauwallner
HB	*History of Buddhism by Bu-ston*: E. Obermiller
HIB	*History of Indian Buddhism*: Hirakawa Akira. Transl. and ed.: Paul Groner
HIP	*History of Indian Philosophy*: Erich Frauwallner
HoIB	*History of Indian Buddhism*: Étienne Lamotte
IA	*Index to the Abhidharmakośabhāṣya*: Hirakawa
IBP	*Researches in Indian & Buddhist Philosophy* (Ed.: Ram Karan Sharma)
IBTP	*Indian Buddhist Theories of Persons*: James Duerlinger
IMM	*In the Mirror of Memory*: Ed.: Janet Gyatso
IP	*Sourcebook in Indian Philosophy*: Sarvepalli Radhakrishnan
ISBP	*The inner science of Buddhist practice*: *Vasubandhu's* Summary of the Five Heaps with commentary by Sthiramati: Artemus B. Engle
IT	*Impermanence and Time. The Contemplation of Impermanence (anityatā) in the Yogācāra Tradition of Maitreya and Asaṅga*: Alexander von Rospatt
JA	*Journal Asiatique*
JAOS	*Journal of the American Oriental Society*
J.As.	*Journal Asiatique*
JASB	*Journal of the Asiatic Society of Bengal*
JIABS	*Journal of the International Association of Buddhist Studies*
JIP	*Journal of Indian Philosophy*
JPŚ	*Jñānaprasthāna-śāstra*, 阿毘達磨發智論 (T 1544)
JPTS	*Journal of the Pali Text Society*
JRAS	*Journal of the Royal Asiatic Society of Great Britain and Ireland*
K	*Karma*: Louis de La Vallée Poussin, in: Encyclopaedia of Religion and Ethics
KA	*Kuśala and Akuśala* (forthcoming): Lambert Schmithausen
KJ	*mKhas 'jug*: Lama Mipham, Rinpoche
KL	*Knowledge and Liberation*: Anne Klein
KvU	*Kathāvatthu*
LA	*Logic in the Abhidharma-mahāvibhāṣā*: KL Dhammajoti
LAS	*Laṅkāvatārasūtra*
LI	*On some Aspects of Descriptions or Theories of "Liberating Insight" and "Enlightenment" in Early Buddhism*: Lambert Schmithausen
LM	*Later Mādhyamikas on Epistemology and Meditation*: Yuichi Kajiyama
LO	*Lorik*: Āchārya Sherab Gyaltsen
Lotus	*Le Lotus de la bonne loi, traduit du sanscrit, accompagné d'un commentaire et de vingt et un mémoires relatifs au buddhisme*: Eugène Bournouf

LPEB	*The Literature of the Personalists of Early Buddhism*: Bhikshu Thich Thiện Châu
LS	*Lodrö Sangpo*
LV	*The life of Vasu-bandhu by Paramārtha* (*A.D. 499–569*): Takakusu Junjirō
LVP	*Louis de La Vallée Poussin*
MAS	*The Mahā-vibhāṣā arguments for Sarvāstivāda*: David Bastow
MB	*La Morale Bouddhique*: Louis de La Vallée Poussin
MBP	*Mind in Buddhist Psychology*: Herbert Guenther
MBPC	*A Manual of Buddhist Philosophy*: *Cosmology*: William Montgomery McGovern
MCB	*Mélanges Chinois et Bouddhiques*
MCIY	*Memory in Classical Indian Yogācāra*: Paul J. Griffiths (in: IMM)
MDA	*The Meaning of "Dharma" and "Abhidharma"*: Akira Hirakawa
MDB	*The Middle Length Discourses of the Buddha*: Bhikkhu Bodhi
Mel. As.	*Mélanges Asiatiques*
MF	*Mind and its Functions*: Geshe Rabten
MM	*Mindfulness and Memory*: Collett Cox, in *In the Mirror of Memory*, ed.: Janet Gyatso
MN	*Majjhima Nikāya*
MOE	*Meditation on Emptiness*: Jeffrey Hopkins
MPN	*The Mind and its Place in Nature*: C.D. Broad
MPPŚ	*Mahāprajñāpāramitāśāstra*: Nāgārjuna (translated by Étienne Lamotte)
$MPPU_L$	*Mahāprajñāpāramitāśāstra*: Nāgārjuna (translated by Étienne Lamotte)
MSA	*Mahāyānasūtrālaṅkara*
MSABh	*Mahāyānasūtrālaṅkara-bhāṣya*: Vasubandhu
MSADC	*Materials for the Study of Āryadeva, Dharmapāla and Chandrakīrti*: Tom J.F. Tillemans
MS(S).	manuscript(s)
MVB	*Mahāvibhāṣā*
MVŚ	**Abhidharma-mahā-vibhāṣā-śāstra*, 阿毘達磨大毘婆沙論 (T 1545)
MVyut	*Mahāvyutpatti*
MW	*Sanskrit-English Dictionary*: M. Monier-Williams
MWBC	*Myriad Worlds. Buddhist Cosmology in Abhidharma, Kālacakra, and Dzog-chen*: Jamgön Kongtrül Lodrö Thaye
NA	**Nyāyānusāraśāstra*: Saṃghabhadra, transl. Hsüan-tsang
Nanjio	*Bunyiu Nanjio, A Catalogue of the Chinese Translation of the Buddhist Tripiṭaka, the Sacred Canon of the Buddhists in China and Japan*
NAS	**Nyāyānusāraśāstra*: Saṃghabhadra, transl. Hsüan-tsang
NS	*The Nyāya-Sūtras of Gautama*: (Tr.) Gaṅgānātha Jhā
NTB	*Nirvāṇa in Tibetan Buddhism*: E. Obermiller

NV	*A Note on Vasubandhu and the Laṅkāvatārasūtra*: Lambert Schmithausen
Ny	* *Abhidharma-nyāyānusāra*, 阿毘達磨順正理論 (T 1562): Saṃghabhadra
OAO	*On the Abhidharma Ontology*: Paul M. Williams
OB	*On the Buddhist Doctrine of the Threefold Unsatisfactoriness*: Lambert Schmithausen
OBB	*On Being Buddha*: Paul J. Griffiths
OBM	*On Being Mindless*: Paul Griffiths
OD	*On the Date of the Buddhist Master of the Law Vasubandhu*: Erich Frauwallner
OLD	*On-line discussion*: with Richard Hayes, etc.
OP	*On the Possibility of a Nonexistent Object of Consciousness*: *Sarvāstivādin and Dārṣṭāntika Theories*: Collett Cox
OTED	*Online Tibetan English Dictionary*: Rangjung Yeshe Publications
PB	*The Philosophy of Buddhism*: Erich Frauwallner
PDVA	*Prajñā and Dṛṣṭi in the Vaibhāṣika Abhidharma*: Padmanabh S. Jaini
PED	*Pāli-English Dictionary*: (eds.) R.W. Rhys-Davids and W. Stede
PIPB	*Passions and Impregnations of the Passions in Buddhism*: Étienne Lamotte
PjŚ	*Prajñapti-śāstra*, 施設論 (T 1538)
PoB	*The Philosophy of Buddhism*: Alfonso Verdu
PPA	*Philosophy and Psychology of the Abhidharma*: Herbert V. Guenther
PPP	*Mind and Mental Factors*: Āchārya Sherab Gyaltsen (in: *Profound Path of Peace*, No. 16)
PrŚ	*Abhidharmaprakaraṇa-śāstra*, 阿毘達磨品類足論 (T 1542)
PS	*Pañcaskandhaka*: Vasubandhu (original Sanskrit text)
PSME	*Progressive Stages of Meditation on Emptiness*: Ḳhenpo Tsültrim Gyamtso
PTS	*Pali Text Society*
PuB	*Pudgalavāda Buddhism*: Leonard C.D.C. Priestley
RCYA	*Rebirth and Causation in the Yogācāra Abhidharma*: Robert Kritzer
RHR	*Revue de l'Histoire des Religions*
RR	*Recognizing Reality*: Georges Dreyfus
RSS	*Realism of the Sarvāstivāda School*: Yuichi Kajiyama
RT	*Reason's Traces*: Matthew T. Kapstein
RTC	*From Reductionism to Creativity*: Herbert Guenther
SA.IV	*Sarvāstivāda Abhidharma* (fourth revised edition): KL Dhammajoti
ŚAD	*Śrīlāta's anudhātu doctrine*: KL Dhammajoti
SAH	*Saṃyuktābhidharmahṛdaya*, Vol. I: Bart Dessein
SAHN	*Saṃyuktābhidharmahṛdaya*, Vol. II, Notes: Bart Dessein
SAL	*Studies in Abhidharma Literature and the Origins of Buddhist Philosophical Systems*: Erich Frauwallner
SatŚ	**Satyasiddhi-śāstra*

SAVSN	*The sect-affiliation of the Arthaviniścaya-nibandhana*: KL Dhammajoti
SBAT	*The Sautrāntika Background of the* Apoha *Theory*: Massaki Hattori (in: BTAC)
SBE	*Sacred Books of the East*
SBP	*Studies in Buddhist Philosophy*: Yuichi Kajiyama
SBPV	*Les Sectes Bouddhique du Petit Véhicule*: André Bareau
SBS	*Sarvāstivāda Buddhist Scholasticism*: Charles Willemen
SD	*Sarvāstivāda, Dārṣṭāntika, Sautrāntika and Yogācāra*: KL Dhammajoti
SDO	*A Study of Dependent Origination*: *Vasubandhu, Buddhaghosa, and the Interpretation of Pratītyasamutpāda*: Susan C. Stalker
SDS	*The Sarvāstivāda Doctrine of Simultaneous Causality*: KL Dhammajoti
SE	*Zur Struktur der erlösenden Erfahrung im Indischen Buddhismus*: Lambert Schmithausen
SgPŚ	*Abhidharma-saṅgīti-paryāya-śāstra,* 阿毘達磨異門足論 (T 1536)
SH	*Satyasiddhiśāstra of Harivarman*. Vol. II. Translator: N. Aiyaswami Sastri
Si	*Si-yu-ki. Buddhist Records of the Western World*: Samuel Beal
Siddhi	*Vijñaptimātratāsiddhi*. Translator: Louis de La Vallée Poussin
Skt.	Sanskrit
SM	*Śāntarakṣita's Madhyamakālaṃkāra*: Masamichi Ichigō
SMB	*The Sixteen-mode Mindfulness of Breathing*: KL Dhammajoti
SN	*The Connected Discourses of the Buddha* (*Saṃyutta Nikāya*): Bhikkhu Bodhi (Tr.)
SPPT	*Spirituelle Praxis und Philosophische Theorie im Buddhismus*: Lambert Schmithausen
SPrŚ	**Abhidharma-samaya-pradīpikā-śāstra* (T 1563)
SS	*Saṅgītisūtra*: Maurice Walshe (in: DN)
STB	*The Sautrāntika Theory of Bīja*: Padmanabh S. Jaini
Study	*A Study of the Śāstras and Ācāryas of the Sarvāstivāda and Other Schools*: Yin Shun
SWV	*Seven Works of Vasubandhu*: Stefan Anacker
T	*Taishō Shinshū Daizōkyō* or *Taishō Isaikyō*
TD	*Taishō Shinshū Daizōkyō*
TFT	*The two, the four, the three truths*: Louis de La Vallée Poussin
Tib.	Tibetan
TS	*Tattvasaṃgraha*: Śantarakṣita
TSP	*Tattvasaṃgrahapañjikā*: Kamalaśīla
TT	*Time and Temporality in Sāṃkhya-Yoga and Abhidharma Buddhism*: Braj M. Sinha
TTVM	*Treatise in Thirty Verses on Mere-Consciousness*: Swati Ganguly
TVB	*Triṃśikāvijñaptibhāṣya*: Ed.: Sylvain Lévi.

TYDS	*Tibetan Yogas of Dream and Sleep*: Tenzin Wangyal, Rinpoche
UM	*Understanding Mind*: Geshe Kelsang Gyatso
V	*The Book of Analysis* (*Vibhaṅga*): Sayadaw U Thittila (Tr.)
VA	*Vasubandhu's Abhidharmakośa and the Commentaries preserved in the Tanjur*: Marek Mejor
VAR	*Vasubandhu on the Avijñapti-Rūpa*: Thomas Lee Dowling
VASC	*Vasubandhu on 'Aggregates, Spheres, and Components': Being Chapter One of the 'Abhidharmakośa'*: Bruce Cameron Hall
VEE	*Versenkungspraxis und erlösende Erfahrung in der Śrāvakabhūmi*: Lambert Schmithausen
VKA	*Die vier Konzentrationen der Aufmerksamkeit*: Lambert Schmithausen
VKŚ	*Abhidharma-vijñāna-kāya-śāstra*, 阿毘達磨識身足論 (T 1539)
VM	*Visuddhimagga*: Buddhaghosa
YP	*Youthful Play: An Explanation of the Treasury of the Abhidharma*: Karmapa Wangchuk Dorje
VRTS	*Vasubandhu's 'Refutation of the Theory of Selfhood'* (*Ātmavādapratiṣedha*): James Duerlinger
VVL	*Vasubandhu and the Vyākhyāyukti Literature*: Peter Skilling
Vy	*Sputârthā Abhidharmakośavyākhyā*: Yaśomitra
VY	*Vasubandhu and the Yogācārabhūmi*: Robert Kritzer
Vyā.	*Vyākhyā*: Yaśomitra
Vyut.	*Mahāvyutpatti*
W	*Saṃyuktābhidharmahṛdaya*: Bart Dessein
WB	*Why Buddhas can't remember their previous lives*: Paul J. Griffiths
WE	*Ways of Enlightenment*: Nyingma Institute
WMFG	*Wohlwollen, Mitleid, Freude und Gleichmut*: Mudagamuwe Maithrimurthi
WOG	*Sputârthā Abhidharmakośavyākhyā by Yaśomitra*: Edited by Unrai Wogihara
WPT	*The Words of My Perfect Teacher*: Patrül Rinpoche
WZKS	*Wiener Zeitschrift für die Kunde Südasiens*
YBŚ	*Yogācārabhūmi-śāstra*
YIF	*Yoga. Immortality and Freedom*: Mircea Eliade
ZDMG	*Zeitschrift der Deutschen Morgenländischen Gesellschaft*
ZF	*Zur zwölfgliedrigen Formel des Entstehens in Abhängigkeit*: Lambert Schmithausen
ZII	*Zeitschrift für Indologie und Iranistik*

Chapter One:

Exposition of the Elements

(*Dhātunirdeśa*)

Outline of Chapter One:

Exposition of the Elements
(*Dhātunirdeśa*)

A. General introduction ... 203

B. Discernment of the factors (*dharma*) ... 208

BA. Twofold classification of factors: impure (*sāsrava*) & pure (*anāsrava*) ... 208

BB. Threefold classification of factors: five aggregates (*skandha*), twelve sense-spheres (*āyatana*), eighteen elements (*dhātu*) ... 214

BBA. Aggregate of material form (*rūpaskandha*) ... 214

BBA.1. Eleven types of material form ... 214

BBA.1.1. Five sense-faculties (*indriya*) ... 215

BBA.1.2. Five object-referents (*artha*) ... 216

BBA.1.3. The non-informative (*avijñapti*) ... 222

BBA.2. Four fundamental material elements (*mahābhūta*) or elementary substances (*dhātu*) & large scale matter ... 223

BBA.3. Definitions of material form (*rūpa*) ... 225

BBA.4. Ten sense-spheres and ten elements & aggregate of material form ... 228

BBB. Aggregate of sensation (*vedanāskandha*) ... 229

BBC. Aggregate of ideation (*saṃjñāskandha*) ... 229

BBD. Aggregate of formations (*saṃskāraskandha*) ... 230

BBE. Sense-spheres and elements & the aggregates of sensation, ideation and formations & the object of mental consciousness ... 231

BBF. Aggregate of consciousness (*vijñānaskandha*) ... 231

BBG. Discussion of various issues related to the threefold classification of factors ... 232

BBG.1. Element of the mental faculty and its relation to the six consciousnesses ... 233

BBG.2. Element of the mental faculty (*manas*) ... 233

BBG.3. Inclusion (*saṃgraha*) & an abbreviated presentation of the aggregates, sense-spheres and elements ... 234

BBG.4. Twofold sense-faculties & enumeration of too many elements ... 235

BBH. Meaning of the terms "aggregate", "sense-sphere" and "element" ... 236

BBI. Ontological status of aggregates, sense-spheres and elements ... 238

BBJ. Need for giving the threefold instructions ... 240

BBK. Definite number of the aggregates ... 241

BBL. Reasons for the set order and progression of the aggregates, sense-spheres and elements ... 243

BBM. Reasons for the names of *rūpa-āyatana* and *dharma-āyatana* ... 246

BBN. Classification of other aggregates, other sources and other elements ... 247

BC. Twenty-two doctrinal perspectives on the eighteen elements 253
BCA. 1. Visible (*sanidarśana*) and invisible (*anidarśana*) 253
BCB. 2. Resistant (*sapratigha*) and non-resistant (*apratigha*) 254
BCC. 3. Wholesome (*kuśala*), unwholesome (*akuśala*), non-defined (*avyākṛta*) 257
BCD. 4. Realm of desire, realm of fine-materiality and realm of immateriality 258
BCE. 5. Impure (*sāsrava*) and pure (*anāsrava*) 262
BCF. 6. Associated with initial inquiry and investigation (*savitarka-savicāra*) – free from initial inquiry but associated with investigation (*avitarka-savicāra*) – free from initial inquiry and from investigation (*avitarka-avicāra*) 262
BCG. 7. Having a cognitive object (*sālambana*) and not having a cognitive object (*anālambana*) 265
BCH. 8. Appropriated (*upātta*) and non-appropriated (*anupātta*) 266
BCI. 9. Primary matter (*bhūtasvabhāva*) and secondary matter (*bhautika*) 267
BCJ. 10. Aggregated (*saṃcita*) and non-aggregated (*asaṃcita*) 269
BCK. 11. How many cut off (*chinnati*), are cut off (*chidyate*); burn (*dahati*), are burned (*dahyate*); weigh (*tulayati*), are weighed (*tulyate*) 270
BCL. 12. Effect of retribution (*vipākaja*), effect of accumulation (*aupacayika*), effect of equal outflow (*naiṣyandika*) 271
BCM. 13. Containing the [permanent] real (*dravyayukta*) 274
BCN. 14. Momentary (*kṣaṇika*) 274
BCO. 15. Acquiring accompaniment (*samanvāgamaṃ pratilambhate*) and accompaniment (*samanvāgama*) 275
BCP. 16. Internal (*ādhyātmika*) and external (*bāhya*) 277
BCQ. 17. Homogeneous (*sabhāga*) and partially homogeneous (*tatsabhāga*) 279
BCR. 18. Abandoned by insight (*darśanaheya*) and by cultivation (*bhāvanāheya*), and not to be abandoned (*aheya*) 282
BCS. 19. View (*dṛṣṭi*) and not view (*na dṛṣṭi*) 285
BCT. 20. Cognized (*vijñeya*) by consciousness 306
BCU. 21. Eternal (*nitya*) and non-eternal (*anitya*) 306
BCV. 22. Controlling faculties (*indriya*) and not controlling faculties (*nendriya*) 306

ABHIDHARMAKOŚA-BHĀṢYA

The Treasury of the Abhidharma
and its (Auto)commentary
by
Vasubandhu

Chapter One:

EXPOSITION OF THE ELEMENTS

(*Dhātunirdeśa*)

OṂ NAMO BUDDHĀYA

GENERAL INTRODUCTION;[1] *F 1–6*

Homage and pledge to compose;[2] *F 1–3*

1. **He, [i.e., the Buddha Bhagavat,] has, in every respect, destroyed all darkness; he has drawn out the world from the mire of cyclic existence: I pay homage to him, to this teacher of truth, before propounding the treatise called *Abhidharmakośa*.**[3]

Desiring to compose a treatise for the purpose of making known the greatness [*māhātmya*][4] of his teacher [*śāstṛ*], the author begins by rendering homage [*namaskāra*] to him, having first declared his qualities [*guṇa*].

AAA. *Homage;* F 1–3

AAA.1. *Qualities for the benefit of the Buddha himself;* F 1–2

– "He, [i.e., the Buddha Bhagavat], has destroyed all darkness" [*sarvahatāndhakāra*], that is to say: the darkness in regard to everything, in regard to all knowable objects (*jñeya*),[5] is destroyed by him or for him.

– "Darkness" [*andhakāra*], i.e., ignorance or not-knowing [*ajñāna*], for ignorance hinders [*pratibandha*] the seeing of things as they are [*bhūtārtha*].

– "In every respect" [*sarvathā*],[6] i.e., of such a kind that [darkness] could no longer rearise. <2>[7]

By this, the Buddha Bhagavat[8] {1 b}[9] is sufficiently designated, for he alone, through the possession of the counter-agent [*pratipakṣa*] to ignorance (v. 60), has definitely destroyed all ignorance.

Granted [*kāmam*], the self-enlightened ones (Pratyekabuddha) and the listeners (Śrāvaka)[10] have also destroyed all darkness, for all ignorance defiled by the defilements or defiled ignorance (*kliṣṭasaṃmoha*) is completely absent [*atyanta vigama*] in them; but they have not destroyed the darkness in every respect [*sarvathā*], for the ignorance in which defilements are absent or undefiled ignorance [*akliṣṭam ajñānam*] is active or manifests in them; they do not know:[11]

1. the qualities [*dharma*] belonging [uniquely] to the Buddha (vii. 28);[12]
2–3. objects very distant [*ativiprakṛṣṭa*] in space [*deśa*] or in time [*kāla*] (vii. 55);[13]
4. the infinite variety and divisions [*anantaprabheda*] of things.[14]

AAA.2. *Qualities for the benefit of others;* F 2–3

Having thus praised the Fortunate One (Bhagavat) from the point of view of his [completely accomplished] qualities for the Fortunate One's own benefit [*ātma-hita-pratipatti-saṃpad*], the author then praises him from the point of view of his [completely accomplished] qualities for the benefit of others [*para-hita-pratipatti-saṃpad*].

– "He has drawn out the world from the mire of cyclic existence" [*saṃsāra-paṅkāj jagad ujjahāra*]: cyclic existence[15] is a mire [*paṅka*], because the world remains stuck in it or attached to it [*āsaṅga*], because it is difficult to cross over [*duruttara*] cyclic existence. The Fortunate One, having compassion [*anukampamāna*] for the world which finds itself drowned in this mire without recourse, has drawn the people of the world out as far as possible,[16] by extending to each one the hands of the teaching of the True Doctrine [*saddharma-deśanā*].[17] <3>

– "I pay homage", by respectfully bowing my head, "to this teacher of truth" [*tasmai namaskṛtya yathā'rthaśāstre*]:[18] teacher of truth, because he teaches, without error [*aviparīta*], in conformity with reality or with that which exists [*yathārtha*].

By thus qualifying the Fortunate One, the author shows the method [*upāya*] by which the Fortunate One benefits others. It is by the teaching [*śāsana*] of what is truly real [*yathābhūta*] that the Fortunate One, the teacher, has drawn the world out from the mire of cyclic existence, {2 a} and not by virtue [*prabhāva*] of the supernormal accomplishments [*ṛddhi*] or of the granting of boons [*varapradāna*].[19]

Pledge to compose; F 3

After having paid homage to this teacher of truth, what will the author do?

– "I shall propound a treatise" [*śāstraṃ pravakṣyāmy*]. That which forms and teaches [*śāsana*] disciples [*śiṣya*] is called *treatise*.[20]

Which treatise?

– The "*Abhidharmakośa*".

Explanation of the name of the treatise; F 3–5

What does the name *Abhidharma* refer to?

Three types of Abhidharma;[21] *F 3–4*

.1. *Abhidharma in the absolute sense: pure understanding; F 3–4*

2a. **The Abhidharma, [in the absolute sense (*pāramārthika*),] is stainless understanding with its following [i.e., the five pure aggregates].**[22]

Understanding (*prajñā*), which will be defined below (ii. 24; vii. 1), is the discernment of factors [*dharmapravicaya*].[23]

Stainless (*amala*) understanding is pure understanding [or understanding without a (positive) relationship with the fluxes (*anāsravaprajñā*; vi. 25c, etc.)].[24]

That which is called the *following* (*anucara*) of understanding is its retinue (*parivāra*), namely, the five pure aggregates (*skandha*; i. 7a) which coexist with understanding.[25] <4>

Such, in the absolute sense [*pāramārthika*],[26] is the Abhidharma.

ABA.2. *Abhidharma in the conventional sense: impure understanding & Abhidharma as Treatise; F 4*

2b. [The Abhidharma] is also any understanding and the Treatise which make one obtain stainless understanding.[27]

1. In common usage [*sāṃvyavahārika*], the word Abhidharma also designates any understanding (*prajñā*) which makes one obtain the Abhidharma in the absolute sense: the impure (*sāsrava*) understanding, whether it is[28]

i. innate or natural or acquired at birth (*upapattipratilambhika*; ii. 53b, 71b),[29] or

ii–iv. derived from an effort, i.e., from listening, reflection, cultivation (*śruta-cintā-bhāvanā-mayī*; vi. 5c–25b) (ii. 71c),

receives, with its following, the name Abhidharma, by convention.[30]

2. The name Abhidharma is also given to the Treatise [*śāstra*],[31] for the Treatise also makes one obtain the pure understanding: it is thus a requisite [*saṃbhāra*] for the Abhidharma in the absolute sense.

ABB. *Etymological explanation of* dharma *and* abhi-dharma; *F 4*

[Etymologically,] *dharma* signifies: that which upholds or sustains (*dhāraṇa*) its own characteristic or a particular inherent characteristic (*svalakṣaṇa*).[32]

The Abhidharma[33] is called *abhi-dharma* because it envisages or is face to face with or is directed toward (*abhimukha*; *pratyabhimukha*) the factors (*dharma*), i.e.,

1. toward the supreme factor [*paramārthadharma*], namely, Nirvāṇa,[34] [which is absolute or supreme in the sense of] being the object-referent of supreme cognition [*paramasya jñānasyārthaḥ*]; or else,
2. toward the characteristics of the factors [*dharmalakṣaṇa*], namely, (i) the particular inherent characteristics or specific characteristics [*svalakṣaṇa*] and (ii) the common characteristics [*sāmānyalakṣaṇa*].[35] (See vi. 14cd). {2 b}

ABC. *Meaning of* Abhidharma-kośa; *F 4–5*

Why is the present treatise [*śāstra*] called *Abhidharmakośa*?

2cd. The present treatise is called the *Abhidharmakośa* (1) because the Abhidharma enters through its meaning into [our treatise]; or else, (2) because the Abhidharma constitutes its basis.[36] <5>

1. The Treatise bearing the name Abhidharma, namely the *Abhidharmapiṭaka*[37] (see i. 2b), enters [*antarbhūta*] through its meaning [*artha*], through what is most important [*pradhāna*], into this [our] treatise,[38] which is, therefore, "[like] the sheath

(or case or treasury [*kośasthānīya*]) of [the meaning and what is most important of] the Abhidharma" (*Abhidharmakośa*).

2. Or else, as the Abhidharma is the basis [*āśraya*] of this [our] treatise, it can be said that this treatise is drawn from or extracted from the Abhidharma as from a sheath [or case or treasury]; [our treatise] is thus called the *Abhidharmakośa*, "the treatise which has the Abhidharma for its sheath [or case or treasury]".

Purpose for composing the Abhidharmakośa *& the need for the Abhidharma and its first teacher;*[39] *F 5–6*

[Question:] – (1) For what purpose [*artha*] have the elaborative expositions (*upadeśa*)[40] of the Abhidharma [been uttered]? (2) By whom was the Abhidharma originally taught?

[Reply:] – The answer to these two questions will tell us why the author [*ācārya*; *śāstra-kāra*] respectfully [*ādriyate*] undertakes the composition of the *Abhidharmakośa*.

3. **Since, apart from the discernment of factors, there is no method to appease the defilements—and it is on account of the defilements that people wander in this ocean of existence [*bhavārṇava*]—it is with a view to this discernment, it is said [by the Vaibhāṣikas] [*kila*], that the Abhidharma has been expounded by the Teacher.**[41]

Apart from the discernment of factors, there are no existing methods [*upāya*] to appease [*upaśama*] the defilements [*kleśa*; v. 1],[42] and it is the defilements which cause the people [*loka*] {3 a} to wander in this great ocean [*mahārṇava*] of cyclic existence [*saṃsāra*]. <6> This is why, the Vaibhāṣikas say [*kila*],[43] the Teacher [*śāstṛ*], the Buddha Bhagavat, has uttered the Abhidharma for the purpose of the discernment of factors [*dharmapravicaya*]. For without the elaborative expositions [*upadeśa*] of the Abhidharma, the disciples would be incapable to discern the factors.

However, the Vaibhāṣikas explain that the Fortunate One uttered the Abhidharma in a scattered way [*prakīrṇa*]. And in the same way that the Sthavira Dharmatrāta made a collection of the Udānas [Sayings] dispersed throughout the Scriptures, i.e., the *Udānavarga*,[44] so the Bhadanta Kātyāyanīputra and others established the Abhidharma by collecting it in the seven Abhidharmas.[45]

B. *DISCERNMENT OF THE FACTORS (DHARMA);*[46] *F 6–102; CHAPTERS ONE TO NINE*

A. Twofold classification of factors: impure (*sāsrava*) & pure (*anāsrava*); F 6

B. Threefold classification of factors: five aggregates (*skandha*), twelve sense-spheres (*āyatana*), eighteen elements (*dhātu*); F 14

C. Twenty-two doctrinal perspectives on the eighteen elements; F 51–102

BA. *TWOFOLD CLASSIFICATION OF FACTORS: IMPURE (SĀSRAVA) & PURE (ANĀSRAVA);*[47] *F 6–14*

BAA. *Brief exposition;*[48] *F 6*

What are the factors (*dharma*) of which the Abhidharma teaches the discernment [*pravicaya*]?

4a. **The factors are "impure", "in a [positive] relationship with the fluxes" (*sāsrava*), or "pure", "without a [positive] relationship with the fluxes" (*anāsrava*).**[49]

[This is a brief exposition (*samāsanirdeśa*) of all factors.]

BAB. *Extensive exposition;*[50] *F 6–14*

What are the impure factors [*sāsrava*]?

4bd. **The conditioned factors, with the exception of the (noble) path, are impure; they are impure because the fluxes adhere to or grow concordantly in them [*samanuśerate*].**[51] {3 b} <7>

As for what is understood by a conditioned factor (*saṃskṛta*),[52] see i. 7a; ii. 45cd. For the fluxes (*āsrava*), see v. 40.[53]

Granted [*kāmaṃ*] that certain fluxes, for example, false view [*mithyādṛṣṭi*], can have [the truth of] the (noble) path (*mārgasatya*) or the unconditioned factors (*asaṃskṛta*; the truth of cessation [*nirodhasatya*]) for their cognitive object.[54] Still, it does not follow that the (noble) path or these factors are "impure", "in a [positive] relationship with the fluxes" (*sāsrava*), because the fluxes do not become installed in them, do not adhere to [or grow concordantly in] them [*anuśerate*]. This point is explained in the fifth chapter (i.e., EXPOSITION OF THE PROCLIVITIES, *Anuśayanirdeśa*; v, F 34–40, 70f., 78f.).[55]

[The impure factors have been discussed.] What are the pure factors [*anāsrava*]?

5ab. **The truth of the (noble) path [vi. 2a, 25d; vii. 3b] and also the three unconditioned factors are pure.**[56]

B.1. *Extensive exposition of the unconditioned factors (asaṃskṛta);*[57] *F 7–10*

What are the three kinds of unconditioned factors [*asaṃskṛta*; ii. 45cd, 55cd (F 275ff.)]?[58] <8>

5c. [The three unconditioned factors are] space (*ākāśa*) and the two cessations [i.e., cessation due to deliberation and cessation not due to deliberation].[59]

[Question: – What are the two cessations (*nirodha*)?]

[Answer:] – They are the cessation due to deliberation (*pratisaṃkhyānirodha*) and the cessation not due to deliberation (*apratisaṃkhyānirodha*).

The three unconditioned factors and [the factors constituting] the truth of the (noble) path are the pure (*anāsrava*) factors because the fluxes do not adhere to them.

B.1.1. *Space (ākāśa);*[60] *F 8*

5d. Space is that which does not hinder [matter or material form; and that which is not hindered by matter or material form].[61]

Space is in its intrinsic nature [non-obstruction (*anāvaraṇa*), in that it] (1) does not hinder (*āvṛṇoti*) matter or material form (*rūpa*), which, in fact, takes place freely in space; and also (2) is not hindered (*āvriyate*) by matter or material form, for space is not turned away by matter or material form.[62]

AB.1.2. *Cessation due to deliberation (pratisaṃkhyānirodha);*[63] *F 8–9*

6ab. Cessation due to deliberation is disconnection [from the impure factors], each disconnection taken separately.[64]

Cessation due to deliberation (*pratisaṃkhyā-nirodha*) or *nirvāṇa* is disconnection (*visaṃyoga*; ii. 57d) from the impure factors. (See ii. 55cd; vi. 2a). <9>

Pratisaṃkhyāna or *pratisaṃkhyā* means a specific kind of understanding [*prajñā-viśeṣa*], [i.e.,] the pure [*anāsrava*] understanding, the deliberation of the noble truths [of unsatisfactoriness, etc.].

The cessation (*nirodha*) of which one takes possession by means of this understanding is called *cessation due to deliberation* (*pratisaṃkhyā-nirodha*): we could say *pratisaṃkhyā-prāpya-nirodha, cessation to be possessed due to deliberation*, but the middle word (i.e., *prāpya*) is elided, {4 a} as in the expression *ox-cart*, and not *cart yoked to or drawn by oxen* (*go-ratha* = *go-yukta-ratha*).

[Question:] – Does this mean that there is only one single [*eka*] cessation due to deliberation for all the impure factors?[65]

[Answer:] – No: each disconnection taken separately is cessation due to deliberation. There are as many things subject to connection (*saṃyogadravya*) as there are things subject to disconnection (*visaṃyogadravya*).[66]

If it were otherwise, if the cessation due to deliberation were single, a person who has obtained, i.e., realized (*sākṣātkar*), the cessation of the defilements [*kleśanirodha*] which are abandoned by insight into the truth of unsatisfactoriness would have obtained or actualized at the same time the cessation of the defilements which are abandoned by insight [*darśana*] into the other truths and by cultivation [*bhāvanā*], [i.e., the cessation of all the defilements (*sarvakleśa*)]. It would be futile [*vaiyarthya*] then for the practitioners to cultivate the part of the (noble) path which counteracts these [remaining (*śeṣapratipakṣa*)] defilements (MVŚ, 164c16).

[Objection:] – But is it not said that "cessation (*nirodha*) is non-similar or non-homogeneous (*asabhāga*)"?

[Answer:] – This does not mean that cessation would be single [*eka*], that there would not be a cessation homogeneous to another cessation. This means that cessation does not have a homogeneous cause (*sabhāgahetu*) and is not a homogeneous cause to any effect (ii. 52; see discussion at ii. 55d).[67] <10>

[Cessation due to deliberation has been discussed.]

BAB.1.3. *Cessation not due to deliberation (apratisaṃkhyānirodha);*[68] *F 10*

6cd. **A different type of cessation, which consists of the absolute hindering of the arising [of future factors], is called *cessation not due to deliberation.***[69]

The cessation which is different from disconnection and which consists of the absolute hindering [*ātyantavighnabhūta*] of the arising of future factors[70] is the cessation not due to deliberation. (This cessation) is called thus because it is obtained, not by the deliberation [*pratisaṃkhyā*] of the truths, but by the deficiency of the [necessary] causes and conditions of arising (*pratyayavaikalyāt*).

For example, when the eye sense-faculty and the mental faculty are occupied with a certain visible form (*rūpa*), other visible forms, sounds, odors, tastes and tangibles pass from the present into the past. It follows that the five sensory consciousnesses, i.e., the visual consciousness, etc., which would have other visible forms, sounds, odors, tastes and tangibles for their cognitive object, cannot arise: for the sensory consciousnesses are not capable of seizing their own object-field when this object-field is past. There is thus an *absolute hindering of the arising of the said consciousnesses*, because of deficiency of the [necessary] causes and conditions of arising.[71] {4 b}

Here we have a fourfold alternative [tetralemma[72] between *cessation due to deliberation* and *cessation not due to deliberation*] (MVŚ, 164c16):

1. solely cessation due to deliberation of the impure factors which are past, present, destined to arise (*utpattidharman*);
2. solely cessation not due to deliberation of pure conditioned factors which are not destined to arise (*anutpattidharman*);
3. cessation due to deliberation and cessation not due to deliberation of the impure factors which are not destined to arise;
4. neither cessation due to deliberation nor cessation not due to deliberation of the pure factors which are past or present or destined to arise.[73]

[The three kinds of unconditioned factors have been discussed.] <11>

AB.2. *Extensive exposition of the conditioned factors (saṃskṛta);*[74] *F 11–14*

We have said (i. 4b) that "the conditioned factors, with the exception of the (noble) path, are impure".

What are the conditioned factors (*saṃskṛta*)?[75]

7ab. [On the other hand,] the conditioned factors are the fivefold aggregates: material form, etc.[76]

(1) The aggregate of material forms (*rūpaskandha*), (2) the aggregate of sensations (*vedanāskandha*), (3) the aggregate of ideations (*saṃjñāskandha*), (4) the aggregate of formations (or conditioning forces) (*saṃskāraskandha*), (5) the aggregate of consciousnesses (*vijñānaskandha*), [these are the conditioned factors].

AB.2.1. *Etymological meaning of* saṃskṛta;[77] *F 11*

Saṃskṛta, conditioned factor, is explained etymologically as "that which has been made (*kṛta*) by causes or conditions [*pratyaya*] co-existing in assemblage (*sametya, saṃbhūya*)".[78] There is no factor which can be engendered by one single cause or condition [*ekapratyaya*; ii. 64].

The expression *saṃskṛta*, although it signifies "that which has been made...", also applies (1) to future factors, (2) to present factors, as well as (3) to past factors; in fact, a factor (*dharma*) does not change its nature or type [*jātīyatvāt*][79] by changing its time period.

In the same way, the milk in the udder [i.e., that which has not yet been drawn] is called *dugdha*, i.e., "that which has been drawn"; the tree [i.e., that which has not yet been kindled] is called *indhana*, i.e., "kindling". <12>

BAB.2.2. *Synonyms for* conditioned factors;[80] *F 12–13*

7cd. The conditioned factors are (1) the course or time periods; they are (2) the ground of discourse; they are (3) endowed with escape; (4) endowed with causes.[81]

1. Conditioned factors are the course [*adhvan*][82]—that is to say, the time periods, i.e., the past, the present and the future—because (conditioned factors) have for their nature [*bhāva*] having gone, {5 a} presently going, shall be going. In the same way, it is said that a path led, that it leads, that it will lead, to the town.

Or rather, conditioned factors are called *time period* because they are devoured (*adyante*) by impermanence [*anityatā*; ii. 45c].

2. By discourse (*kathā*) is meant speech, discourse (*vākya*); and discourse has for its ground (*vastu*) the name or word (*nāman*; ii. 36).[83]

[Question:] – Should the definition given by the stanza be taken literally and say that conditioned factors are the words?

[Answer:] – No. *Ground of discourse* (*kathāvastu*) means "the ground of discourse, i.e., the words (*nāman*), together with that which the words signify [*artha*]". To understand by *ground of discourse* the words alone, one would be in conflict with the *Prakaraṇapāda*,[84] which says: "The grounds of discourse (*kathāvastu*) are included within the eighteen elements (*dhātu*)" (MVŚ, 74a20).[85]

3. *Niḥsāra* signifies "necessary (*avaśyam*) escape (*sāra* = *niḥsaraṇa*)", the *nirvāṇa* (*nirupadhiśeṣanirvāṇa* = *nirvāṇa* without remainder) of all conditioned factors. As one should leave conditioned factors, they are qualified as *endowed with escape* [*saniḥsāra*].[86] <13>

4. Conditioned factors depend on causes (*sahetuka*); they are thus qualified as *savastuka*, i.e., *endowed with causes*.[87] – The Vaibhāṣikas say [*kila*] that, in the expression *savastuka*, *vastu* signifies "cause" (*hetu*).[88]

Such are the diverse synonyms [*paryāya*] for conditioned factors [*saṃskṛta dharma*].

BAB.2.3. *Synonyms for impure conditioned factors;*[89] *F 13*

BAB.2.3.1. *Appropriative aggregates (upādānaskandha);*[90] *F 13*

8ab. When [the conditioned factors] are impure, they are appropriative aggregates.[91]

The impure (*sāsrava*) conditioned factors constitute the five appropriative aggregates (*upādānaskandha*). Everything that is an appropriative aggregate is an aggregate (*skandha*); but the pure [*anāsrāva*] conditioned factors included within the aggregates are not included within the appropriative aggregates (MVŚ, 387a9). {5 b}

The graspings (*upādāna*) are the defilements (*kleśa*; v. 38).

B.2.3.1.a. *Three reasons for the name* upādānaskandha; *F 13*

The *upādānaskandha*s are thus called:[92]

1. because they proceed [*saṃbhūta*] from the defilements, as we say *grass fire* [*tṛṇāgni*], *straw fire* [*tuṣāgni*]; or rather
2. because they are governed [*vidheyatva*] by the defilements, as we say the *king's man* [*rāja-puruṣa*]; or rather
3. because they give rise [*saṃbhavanti*] to defilements, as we say the *flower-bearing tree* [*puṣpa-vṛkṣa*], *fruit-bearing tree* [*phala-vṛkṣa*].

B.2.3.2. *Endowed with conflict (saraṇa);*[93] *F 13–14*

[These same impure factors are spoken of as follows:]

8c. [Impure factors] are also called *endowed with conflict*.[94] <14>

The defilements [*kleśa*] are conflict (*raṇa*) because they harm oneself and others [*ātmapāravyābādhana*]. The impure conditioned factors are qualified as *endowed with conflict* or *in a relationship with conflict* (*saraṇa*) because the defilements or conflicts adhere to them. In the same way, as we have seen, they are qualified as *impure* or *endowed with impurity* (*sāsrava*), because the fluxes (*āsrava*) become attached to them.

B.2.3.3. *Other synonyms of* impure factors;[95] *F 14*

8cd. [Impure factors] are also (1) unsatisfactoriness, (2) the origin, (3) the world, (4) the locus of afflicted views, (5) existence.[96]

1. Unsatisfactoriness [*duḥkham*],[97] because they are inimical or adverse [*pratikūla*] to the noble ones [*ārya*; vi. 2f.].

2. The origin [*samudaya*], because unsatisfactoriness originates [*samudeti*] from them (vi. 2).

3. The world [*loka*], because they are in the process of decomposition [*lujyate*].[98]

4. The locus of afflicted views[99] [*dṛṣṭisthānam*], because the five afflicted views abide in them (*tiṣṭhati*) and become attached to them [*anuśayana*; v. 7] (*Prakaraṇa*, 33b7).

5. Existence [*bhava*], because they exist.[100]

[Such are the synonyms, according to their meaning (*anvartha*), of the impure factors (*sāsravāṇāṃ dharmāṇām*).]

BB. ## *THREEFOLD CLASSIFICATION OF FACTORS: FIVE AGGREGATES (SKANDHA), TWELVE SENSE-SPHERES (ĀYATANA), EIGHTEEN ELEMENTS (DHĀTU);*[101] *F 14–51*

A. Aggregate of material form (*rūpaskandha*); F 14
B. Aggregate of sensation (*vedanāskandha*); F 27
C. Aggregate of ideation (*saṃjñāskandha*); F 28
D. Aggregate of formations (*saṃskāraskandha*); F 28
E. Sense-spheres and elements & the aggregates of sensation, ideation and formations & the object of mental consciousness; F 30
F. Aggregate of consciousness (*vijñānaskandha*); F 30
G. Discussion of various issues related to the threefold classification of factors; F 31
H. Meaning of the terms "aggregate", "sense-sphere" and "element"; F 35
I. Ontological status of aggregates, sense-spheres and elements; F 37
J. Need for giving the threefold instructions; F 39
K. Definite number of the aggregates; F 40
L. Reasons for the set order and progression of the aggregates, sense-spheres and elements; F 42
M. Reasons for the names of *rūpa-āyatana* and *dharma-āyatana*; F 45
N. Classification of other aggregates, other sources and other elements; F 46–51

We have seen that there are five aggregates[102] (i. 7). We will first study the aggregate of material form (i. 9–14b).

BBA. ### *Aggregate of material form (rūpaskandha);*[103] *F 14–27*

1. Eleven types of material form, F 14
2. The four fundamental material elements (*mahābhūta*) or elementary substances (*dhātu*) & derivative material elements and large scale matter, F 21
3. Definitions of material form (*rūpa*), F 24
4. The ten sense-sources and ten sense-elements & aggregate of material form; F 27

BBA.1. #### *Eleven types of material form;*[104] *F 14–21*

9ab. Matter or material form is (1–5) the five sense-faculties, (6–10) the five object-referents [or object-fields of the five sense-faculties], and (11) the non-informative.[105]

1.–5. The five sense-faculties [*indriya*; i. 9cd, 36ac, 44–47]:[106] {6 a}

1. eye sense-faculty (*cakṣurindriya*);
2. ear sense-faculty (*śrotrendriya*);

3. nose sense-faculty (*ghrāṇendriya*);
4. tongue sense-faculty (*jihvendriya*);
5. body sense-faculty (*kāyendriya*). <15>

6.–10. The five object-referents [*artha*], object-fields [*viṣaya*] (i. 10)[107] of the five sense-faculties:

6. visible form (*rūpa*);
7. sound [*śabda*];
8. odor [*gandha*];
9. taste [*rasa*];
10. tangible (*spraṣṭavya*).

11. The non-informative (*avijñapti*;[108] i. 11, 13, 15bd; iv. 4–44).

Such is the aggregate of material form.

1.1. *Five sense-faculties (indriya);*[109] *F 15*

We have enumerated five object-referents (*artha*): visible form, sound, etc.

9cd. The bases of the consciousnesses of these [five object-fields], namely the subtle material elements [*rūpaprasāda*], are the five sense-faculties, i.e., the sense-faculty of the eye, etc.[110]

The five [sense-faculties] which are the basis [*āśraya*] of the consciousnesses (1) of visible form, (2) of sound, (3) of odor, (4) of taste and (5) of the tangible, and which are of the nature of suprasensible [*atīndriya*] subtle material elements, are, respectively, the sense-faculty (1) of the eye, (2) of the ear, (3) of the nose, (4) of the tongue and (5) of the body.

The Fortunate One says, in fact:

> The eye, O *bhikṣus*, is the internal sense-sphere [*ādhyātimikāyatana*], subtle matter derived from the four fundamental material elements… .[111]

Or else, it can be understood as:[112]

[9cd.] The bases of the consciousnesses of these [sense-faculties], namely…

The bases of the visual consciousness (*cākṣurvijñāna*), etc. – This interpretation complies with the *Prakaraṇa* (692c12), which says:

> What is the eye sense-faculty? – It is the subtle matter [*rūpaprasāda*] which is the basis of the visual consciousness. {6 b}

[The five sense-faculties have been discussed.]

BBA.1.2. *Five object-referents (artha); F 15–20*

BBA.1.2.1. *Visible form (rūpa);*[113] *F 16–17*

Let us now discuss the five object-referents beginning with visible form, i.e., the sense-sphere of visible form or sense-sphere of material form (*rūpāyatana*; see i. 24). <16>

10a. **[Vaibhāṣikas:] – Visible form is (1) of two types, (2) of twenty types.**[114]

BBA.1.2.1.a. *Two types;*[115] *F 16*

Visible form is [twofold]:

1. color [*varṇa*] and
2. shape [*saṃsthāna*; iv, F 4–12].[116]

1. Color is fourfold:

   i. blue [*nīla*],
   ii. yellow [*pīta*],[117]
   iii. red [*lohita*],
   iv. white [*avadāta*].

The other colors are substitutes or subdivisions [*bheda*] of the fourfold color.

2. Shape (iv. 3c) is eightfold:

   i. long [*dīrgha*; iv, F 10–12],
   ii. short [*hrasva*],
   iii. square [*vṛtta*],[118]
   iv. round [*parimaṇḍala*],[119]
   v. high (*unnata*),[120]
   vi. low (*avanata*),[121]
   vii. even [or regular] [*sāta*],
   viii. uneven [or irregular] [*visāta*].

BBA.1.2.1.b. *Twenty types; F 16*

This will give us twenty types:

1–4. primary colors;
5–12. eight shapes;
13–20. eight colors:

   13. cloud [*abhra*],
   14. smoke [*dhūma*],

15. dust [*rajaḥ*],
16. mist [*mahīkā*],
17. shadow [*chāyā*],
18. sun-light [*ātapa*],
19. light [*āloka*],
20. darkness [*andhakāra*].

Some make one [additional] color out of the firmament (*nabhas*), which appears as a wall [*bhitti*] of lapis-lazuli [*vaiḍūrya*]; this would give us the number twenty-one.[122]

[Among these,]

7. even (*sāta*) signifies regular shape [*samasthāna*];
8. uneven (*visāta*) is the opposite, irregular shape [*visamasthāna*];
16. mist [*mahikā*] is vapor [*nihāra*], which rises from the ground and from water;
18. sun-light (*ātapa*) is the radiance of the sun [*sūryaprabhā*];
19. light (*āloka*) is the radiance [*prabhā*] of the moon [*candra*], of the stars [*tāraka*], of fire [*agni*], of herbs [*oṣadhi*] and of gems [*maṇi*];
17. shadow [*chāyā*]—arisen from an obstruction to light [by an object]—is where visible forms [*rūpa*] remain visible [*darśana*];
20. darkness [*andhakāra*] is the contrary to this [i.e., where there is no visibility at all]. {7 a}

The other terms do not call for any separate explanation as they are easy to understand [*sugamatva*].

.1.2.1.c. *Visible form & its relationship to color and shape; F 16*

[There are three alternatives (trilemma):] The sense-sphere of visible form

1. can be [*vidyate*] color without being shape:[123] blue, yellow, red, white, shadow, sun-light, light, darkness;
2. can be shape without being color: that part [*pradeśa*] of long, of short, etc., which constitutes [*svabhāva*] the bodily informative action (*kāyavijñapti*)[124] (iv. 2);
3. can be both [*ubhayathā*], color and shape: all remaining categories of the sense-sphere of visible form.

Other scholars maintain that only sun-light [*ātapa*] and light [*āloka*] are exclusively color, for blue, yellow, etc., appear to the view [*dṛśyate*] under the aspects [*pariccheda*] of long, short, etc.

BBA.1.2.1.d. *(Sautrāntika:) A single real entity cannot be twofold; F 16–17*

(Objection by the Sautrāntikas:[125]) – But how could a single [*eka*] real entity [*dravya*] [i.e., the sense-sphere of visible form] be (*vidyate*) both or twofold [*ubhayathā*], color and shape together? For—in the system of the Vaibhāṣikas—color and shape are established as distinct real entities [*dravyāntara*] (see iv. 3 [F 8–12]). <17>

[Vaibhāṣikas:] – [The sense-sphere of visible form is both] because color and shape are known (*prajñāna*) in a single real entity [i.e., the sense-sphere of visible form]. The root *vid* here (in *vidyate*: "is found, is known, occurs") has the meaning of *to know, to perceive* [*jñānārtha*], and not the meaning of *to be, to exist* [*sattārtha*].

[The Sautrāntikas:] – But (then) you should admit that bodily informative action [i.e., the second alternative] is also both color and shape.

[The sense-sphere of visible form has been discussed.]

BBA.1.2.2. *Sound (śabda);*[126] *F 17*

BBA.1.2.2.a. *Eight types;*[127] *F 17*

10b. Sound is eightfold.[128]

1. [Sound (*śabda*)] is fourfold:
   i. having for its cause appropriated [*upātta*] [i.e., animated][129] fundamental material elements forming part of the sense-faculties (*upāttamahābhūta-hetuka*; i. 34cd): first category: sound caused by the hand [*hasta*], by the voice [*vāc*];
   ii. having for its cause unappropriated [*anupātta*] [i.e., inanimate] fundamental material elements (*anupāttamahābhūtahetuka*; i. 34cd): second category: sound of the wind [*vāyu*], of the forest [*vanaspati*], of flowing water [*nadī*];
   iii. included among factors indicative of sentient beings (*sattvākhya*):[130] third category: {7 b} sound of vocal informative action [*vāgvijñapti*; iv. 3d];
   iv. included among factors non-indicative of sentient beings (*asattvākhya*):[131] fourth category: any other sound [*anya*].

Each of these four categories can be (a) agreeable [*manojñā*] or (b) disagreeable [*amanojñā*].

2. According to other scholars, a sound can belong to the first two categories at one and the same time, for example, the sound produced when the hand is in conjunction with or beats [*saṃyoga*] the drum [*mṛdaṅga*]. But the School (MVŚ, 663c12) does not accept that one atom of color (*varṇaparamāṇu*) would have for its cause two tetrads of fundamental material elements [*bhūtacatuṣka*]; thus one cannot accept that

one atom of sound is produced by the four fundamental material elements of the hand and the four fundamental material elements of the drum.

[Sound has been discussed.]

.1.2.3. *Taste (rasa);*[132] *F 17*

.1.2.3.a. *Six types;*[133] *F 17*

10bc. Taste is of six types.[134]

[Taste (*rasa*) is of six types, because of the distinction (*bheda*) between]

1. sweet [*madhura*],
2. sour [*amla*],
3. salty [*lavaṇa*],
4. pungent [*kaṭuka*],
5. bitter [*tikta*],
6. astringent [*kaṣāya*]. <18>

.1.2.4. *Odor (gandha);*[135] *F 18*

.1.2.4.a. *Four types;*[136] *F 18*

10c. Odor is fourfold.[137]

[Odor (*gandha*) is fourfold because] good odor [*sugandha*] and bad odor [*durgandha*] are either (1) excessive (*sama* [even] = *utkaṭa*) or (2) non-excessive (*viṣama* [uneven] = *anutkaṭa*).

According to the *Prakaraṇa* (692c22), however, odor is threefold: (1) good [*sugandha*], (2) bad [*durgandha*], (3) even or neutral [*samagandha*].[138]

.1.2.5. *Tangible (spraṣṭavya);*[139] *F 18–19*

.1.2.5.a. *Eleven types;*[140] *F 18*

10d. The tangible consists of eleven types.[141]

Eleven real entities are tangible real entities (*spraṣṭavyadravya*) [in their intrinsic nature (*svabhāva*)]:[142]

1–4. the four fundamental material elements (*mahābhūta*),[143]
5. smoothness [*ślakṣṇatva*],[144]
6. roughness [*karkaśatva*],
7. heaviness [*gurutva*],
8. lightness [*laghutva*],
9. coldness [*śīta*],

10. hunger [*jighatsā*],
11. thirst [*pipāsā*].

Among those,

1–4. the fundamental material elements (*mahābhūta*) will be explained below (i. 12);
5. smoothness (*ślakṣṇatva*) is the softness [*mṛdutā*];
6. roughness (*karkaśatva*) is the harshness [*paruṣatā*];
7. heaviness (*gurutva*) is that in accordance with which bodies or things [*bhāva*] are susceptible of being weighed [*tulyante*; i. 36];
8. lightness (*laghutva*) is the contrary;
9. coldness (*śīta*) is that which produces the desire for heat [*uṣṇābhilāsakṛt*];
10. hunger (*bubhukṣā*; *jighatsā*) is that which produces the desire for food [*bhojanābhilāṣakṛt*];
11. thirst (*pipāsā*) is that which produces the desire for drink.

In fact, the words *hunger* and *thirst* designate the tangible which produces hunger and thirst: by hypallage [*upacāra*],[145] the cause [*kāraṇa*] is designated by the name of its effect [*kārya*]. In the same way, it is said: {8 a}

> The appearance [*utpāda*] of the Buddhas is [the cause of] happiness [*sukha*]; the teaching of the religion [*dharmasya deśanā*] is [the cause of] happiness; the concord [*sāmagrī*] of the community [*saṃgha*] is [the cause of] happiness; the austerity [*tapas*] of the monastics who live in concord is [the cause of] happiness.[146]

BBA.1.2.5.b. *Realm of fine-materiality & the tangible;*[147] *F 18–19*

In the realm of fine-materiality [*rūpadhātu*],[148] hunger and thirst are absent, but the other tangibles occur there.

It is true that the garments [*vastra*] of the gods of the realm of fine-materiality weigh nothing individually [*ekaśas*]; but gathered together [*saṃcita*], they have weight.

It is true that harmful coldness [*upaghātaka*] is absent in the realm of fine-materiality, but favorable or refreshing coldness (*anugrāhaka*) occurs there: such <19> at least is the opinion of the Vaibhāṣikas [*kila*]. [For us, it is concentration [*samādhi*] which refreshes [*anugrāha*] the gods, not the coldness.]

BBA.1.2.5.c. *From how many real entities do the various consciousnesses arise? F 19*

[It has been said that visible form is manifold:]

1. It may happen[149] that visual consciousness arises from one single [*eka*] real entity (*dravya*), from one single category of visible form: when the characteristic [*prakāra*] of this real entity (blue, etc.) is distinguished or discerned separately [*vyavaccheda*].

2. In other cases, (visual) consciousness is produced by many real entities: when such a distinction is lacking; for example, when one sees from afar [*dūrāt*] the multiple [*aneka*] colors and shapes of an army [*senāvyūha*] or a pile of jewels [*maṇisamūha*] all together.

The same comment applies to the ear consciousness, the nose consciousness, etc.

But a tactile consciousness arises from five tangibles [*spraṣṭavya*] at most, namely, the four fundamental material elements [*mahābhūta*] and one of any other tangible: smoothness, roughness, etc. Such is the opinion of certain scholars, yet, according to another opinion, a tactile consciousness can arise from the eleven tangibles at the same time.

.1.2.6. *Do the five sensory consciousnesses have particular inherent or common characteristics for their object?* F 19

Objection:[150] – According to what you say, each of the five sensory consciousnesses bears on an ensemble or compound [*samasta*]; for example, the visual consciousness bears on blue, yellow, etc.; consequently, the sensory consciousnesses would have for their object-field the common characteristic (*sāmānyalakṣana*) and not, as Scripture teaches, the particular inherent characteristic (*svalakṣaṇa*). {8 b}

The Vaibhāṣika (MVŚ, 65c12) answers: – [There is no fault (*adoṣa*).] By particular inherent characteristic, the Scripture understands, not the particular inherent characteristic of real entities [*dravyasvalakṣaṇa*], but the particular inherent characteristic of the sense-sphere [*āyatanasvalakṣaṇa*; ii. 62c].[151] <20>

.1.2.7. *Which consciousness arises first?* F 20

[Question:] – When the body and tongue sense-faculty attain or reach [*prāpta*] their object-field at the same time [*yugapad*] (i. 43cd), which consciousness is the first to arise?[152]

[Answer:] – The one whose object is the more energetic [*paṭīyāṃs*]. But if the energy of the two object-fields is equal [*sama*], the gustatory consciousness arises first, because the desire for food dominates.

We have discussed the object-referents [*artha*] of the five sense-faculties of the sensory consciousnesses and how these object-referents are seized or apprehended [*grahaṇa*].

BBA.1.3. *The non-informative (avijñapti);*[153] *F 20–21*

BBA.1.3.1. *Definition; F 20–21*

We will now discuss the non-informative (*avijñapti*; see also i. 13, 15bd and iv. 3d–44), which is the eleventh category of the aggregate of material form (*rūpa-skandha*).

11. **[Vaibhāṣikas:] – Even in a person whose thought is distracted, or who is [for a certain time] without thought, there exists a serial continuity, good or bad, in reliance upon the fundamental material elements: that, indeed, is what is called *non-informative*.**[154]

– "(A person) whose thought is distracted (*vikṣipta*)" means (a person) who has a thought different from the thought which has induced the non-informative; for example, an unwholesome thought when the non-informative has been induced by a wholesome thought.[155] <21>

– "(A person) who [for a certain time] is without thought (*acittaka*)" means (a person) who has entered into one of the [two] attainments of non-consciousness called (1) the attainment of non-ideation (*asaṃjñisamāpatti*) and (2) the attainment of cessation (*nirodhasamāpatti*) (ii. 42).

– "Even in a person… [*api*]" means that the word *even* indicates that the non-informative also exists in a person whose thought is not distracted, in a person whose thought is not immersed in the two attainments.[156]

– "A serial continuity (*'yo anubandha*)" means a flux or stream (*pravāha*).

– "Good or bad (*śubha*, *aśubha*)" means wholesome or unwholesome (*kuśala*, *akuśala*), [i.e., not non-defined (*avyākṛta*); see iv. 7a].[157] [But in what is wholesome and what is unwholesome, the flux or stream of possession (*prāptipravāha*) is like this (*īdṛśa*) also.[158]]

– "In reliance upon the fundamental material elements (*mahābhūta upādāya*)": this is in order to distinguish [*viśeṣaṇa*] the stream called *non-informative* (*avijñapti*) from the stream of the possessions [*prāpti*][159] (ii. 36). [The Vaibhāṣikas hold that the meaning of *upādāya*, "in reliance upon", is the same as that of *hetu*, "cause".[160]] The non-informative exists in reliance upon the fundamental material elements, because those are (1) its generating cause [*jananahetu*],[161] (2) its reliance cause [*niśrayahetu*], etc., [(3) its supporting cause (*pratiṣṭhāhetu*), (4) its maintaining cause (*upastambha-hetu*) and (5) its growth cause (*upabṛṃhaṇahetu*; *vṛddhihetu*)] (ii. 65; MVŚ, 663a26). (See i. F 26–28; iv, F 26–31.)

– "That, indeed [*hi*], is what (is called) *non-informative* [*sa hyavijñapti*]": {9 a} [the word *hi* is used] in order to indicate the reason [*karaṇa*] for the name *avijñapti*.

Although this serial continuity is in its intrinsic nature [*svabhāva*] material form (*rūpa*; i. 13 [F 26]) and action [or function] [*kriyā*; iv. 2a]—like bodily and vocal informative action (*vijñapti*)—nevertheless, it does nothing to inform another (*vijñapayati*), as does informative action. [Hence it is called the *non-informative.*]

– "Is called [*ucyata*]", in order to indicate that the author is showing the opinion of the Vaibhāṣikas [*ācārya*], not his own here.[162]

In short, the non-informative is a material form (*rūpa*; i. 13 [F 25]), wholesome or unwholesome [*kuśalākuśala*],[163] arisen [*saṃbhūta*] from informative action (*vijñapti*)[164] or from concentration [*samādhi*].[165]

..2. *Four fundamental material elements (mahābhūta) or elementary substances (dhātu) & large scale matter;*[166] *F 21–24*

..2.1. *Four types of fundamental material elements & the reasons for calling them* dhātu *and* mahā; *F 21–22*

[It has been said above: "in reliance upon the fundamental material elements (*mahābhūta upādāya*)". What are these elements (*bhūta*; see also i, F 49f.)?]

12ab. **The elements, i.e., the great or fundamental material elements, are (1) the elementary substance earth, (2–4) the elementary substances water, fire and wind.**[167] <22>

These four fundamental material elements are the four elementary substances or *dhātu*, so called because they uphold or sustain (*dhāraṇa*)[168] both

1. their own characteristic or particular inherent characteristic [*svalakṣaṇa*] and
2. the secondary or derivative material form (*upādāyarūpa*; derivative material elements [*bhautika*]).

They are called *great* or *fundamental* (= primary) [*mahā*]: they are fundamental or great [or greatness; *mahattvam*] either

1. because they are the basis [*āśrayatva*] for all derivative material form, or else
2. because they assemble on a large scale [*mahāsaṃniveṣa*] in the mass [*skandha*] of earth, water, fire and wind, where their modes of efficacy or function (*vṛtti*) come forth together (MVŚ, 681a17, 663a11).[169]

..2.2. *Efficacies of the four elementary substances; F 22*

Through what efficacies [*karma*] are these elementary substances (*dhātu*) established or accomplished [*saṃsiddha*]?

12c. **[The elementary substances (1) earth, (2) water, (3) fire and (4) wind] are established or accomplished, by the efficacies of (1) supporting, [(2) cohesion, (3) heating or maturation, and (4) expansion, respectively].**[170]

The elementary substances (1) earth [*pṛthivī*], (2) water [*ap*], (3) fire [*tejas*] and (4) wind [*vāyu*] are established or accomplished {9 b} by the efficacies of (1) supporting [*dhṛti*], (2) cohesion (*saṃgraha*), (3) heating or maturation (*pakti*),[171] and (4) expansion (*vyūhana*), respectively.

By *expansion* one should understand increasing (*vṛddhi*) and displacement or locomotion (*prasarpaṇa*).

Such are their efficacies [*karma*].

BBA.2.3. *Intrinsic nature of the four elementary substances; F 22–23*

What is the intrinsic nature [*svabhāva*] of these elementary substances (*dhātu*)?

12d. **[(1) Earth, (2) water, (3) fire, (4) wind] are [in their intrinsic nature] (1) solidity, (2) humidity, (3) heat and (4) mobility, [respectively].**[172]

As for their intrinsic nature, (1) the elementary substance earth [*pṛthivīdhātu*] is solidity [*khara*], (2) the elementary substance water [*abdhātu*] is humidity [*sneha*]; (3) the elementary substance fire [*tejodhātu*] is heat [*uṣṇatā*]; (4) the elementary substance wind [*vāyudhātu*] is mobility [*īraṇā*].[173] <23>

By *mobility* [*īraṇā*] one should understand that which brings it about that the stream of states that constitute an element [*bhūtasrotas*] will reproduce itself in different places;[174] just as one speaks of the mobility of a flame [*pradīpīraṇavat*] (iv. 2cd).

The *Prakaraṇas*[175] and the Sūtra[176] say:

> What is the elementary substance wind? – Lightness (*laghutva*) [or the quality of lightly setting into motion (*laghusamudīraṇatva*)].

The *Prakaraṇas* also say:

> Lightness (*laghu*) is a derivative material form [*upādāyarūpa*].

Consequently, the factor (*dharma*) which has mobility for its intrinsic nature (*īraṇātmaka*; *irāṇāsvabhāva*) is the elementary substance wind [*vāyudhātu*]:[177] its intrinsic nature (i.e., lightness) is manifested by its efficacy of mobility (*īraṇākarman*).

A.2.4. *Difference between the elementary substance earth & earth, etc.;*[178] *F 23–24*

What is the difference between the elementary substance earth [*pṛthivīdhātu*] and earth [*pṛthivī*], between the elementary substance water [*abdhātu*] and water [*ap*], etc?

13. **In common usage [*lokasaṃjñā*], the word *earth* signifies [actually] color and shape; the same for [the common usage of the words] *water* and *fire*, [i.e., they signify actually color and shape]. [The common usage of the word] *wind* [signifies] either the elementary substance wind, or else, color and shape.**[179] {10 a} <24>

[Just as *earth*, in common usage, signifies color and shape, so also does *wind*]. In fact, one speaks of *blue wind* [*nīlika vātyā*] and of *circular or whirling wind* [*maṇḍalikā vātyā*]; but what one commonly [*loke*] calls *wind* is also the elementary substance wind.

A.3. *Definitions of material form (rūpa);*[180] *F 24–27*

A.3.1. *Definition according to the meaning of* rūpaṇa (breaking *or* oppression)*; F 24*

[Question:] – Why do all these factors, from visible form to the non-informative, receive the name *material form* (*rūpa*)? Why do they together constitute the aggregate of material form (*rūpaskandha*)?

[Answer:] – [Because of being subject to "breaking" (*rūpaṇa*).]

The Fortunate One said [in the *Saṃyuktāgama*]:

> Because it is subject to being broken [*rūpyate*], O *bhikṣus*, one calls it *appropriative aggregate of material form* (*rūpa upādānaskandha*). By what is it broken? – As soon as it is touched by the hand, it is broken, … .[181]

[Here] "is broken" (*rūpyate*) signifies being oppressed, troubled or disturbed (*bādhyate*), which is brought out in a stanza of the *Arthavargīyas*, in the *Kṣudraka–āgama* (*Aṭṭhakavagga*, i. 2):[182]

> A person who ardently searches out the objects of desire [*kāma*][183] is broken [= oppressed, disturbed] (*rūpyate*) if the objects of desire are lacking, just as someone who is pierced by an arrow [*śalyaviddha*].[184] (Compare Mbh., xiii. 193, 48.)

[Question:] – But what oppression (*bādhanā*) does material form have?

[Answer:] – [An oppression] which is of the nature of transformation or change in arising (*vipariṇāmotpādana*), i.e., which is of the nature of being disfigurement or deterioration (*vikriyotpādana*). {10 b}

BBA.3.2. *Definition according to the meaning of* rūpaṇa ("the nature of being rūpa"): *as impenetrability, physical resistance, obstruction; F 24–25*

According to other scholars, the quality that constitutes material form (*rūpa*), namely, *rūpaṇa*, is not breaking, [oppression,] deterioration (*bādhanarūpaṇa*, *rūpaṇa* in the sense of deterioration), but rather impenetrability, physical resistance, or obstruction (*pratighāta*; i. 29bc), the obstacle which a material form opposes to its place being occupied by another material form (see i. 43cd).[185] <25>

BBA.3.3. *Various objections to the definitions; F 25–27*

BBA.3.3.1. *An atom as a monad would not be material form; F 25*

[Objection:] – If this is so, the material form which constitutes a single atom, a *monad* [*paramāṇurūpa*, i.e., *dravyaparamāṇu*; see ii, F 144] will not qualify as material form, for the monad [*niravayavatva*], not susceptible to deterioration [*bādhana*], not susceptible to offering obstruction (*pratighāta*; i. 29bc), is free from *rūpaṇa*.

[Answer:] – Without a doubt, the monad is free from *rūpaṇa*; but a single material form as a monad (*paramaṇuṛūpa*) never exists in an isolated state [*pṛthak*];[186] [however,] in the state of a composite (*saṃghātastha*), i.e., being in aggregation (*saṃcita*), it is susceptible to deterioration and to offering resistance (MVŚ, 390a1) (iii, F 213).

BBA.3.3.2. *Past and future material form would not be material form; F 25*

[Objection:] – The material forms of the past and of the future would not qualify as material form, for it cannot be said that they are actually in a state of resistance (*rūpyante pratihanyanta iti*).

[Answer:] – Without a doubt, but they have been, they will be in this state. Whether past or future, they are of the same nature as the factor that is actually in a state of resistance. In the same way one calls *kindling* (*indhana*) not only the actually burning wood, but also the [non-burning] wood or fuel (see i. 7ab).[187]

BBA.3.3.3. *The non-informative would not be material form; F 25–27*

[Objection:] – The non-informative (*avijñapti*; see i. 11) would not qualify as material form (*rūpa*), for it is devoid of resistance.

[Answer:] – Without a doubt, but the quality of material form attributed to the non-informative can be justified, [as may be seen from the following discussion]. <26>

.3.3.3.a. *The non-informative is material form because bodily and vocal informative action from which it proceeds are material form;* F 26

[First explanation.] – The informative (*vijñapti*), i.e., bodily or vocal informative action, from whence proceeds the non-informative (*avijñapti*), is material form (*rūpa*); thus the non-informative is [also] material form, just as a [tree's] shadow [*chāyā*] follows the movement of the tree [*vṛkṣa*].

Reply: – No, because the non-informative is not subject to modifications [*avikārāt*]; besides, if the comparison is supposed to be accurate, then the non-informative should perish when the informative perishes (iv. 4cd), as is the case for the shadow and the tree.[188]

.3.3.3.b. *The non-informative is material form because the fundamental material elements which constitute its basis are material form;* F 26–27

Second explanation.[189] – The non-informative is material form, for the fundamental material elements which constitute its basis [*āśraya*] are material form.

Objection. – According to this principle, the five sensory consciousnesses would be material form, for their basis (the eye sense-faculty, etc.) is material form.

[First attempt to refute the objection:][190] – This response is not valid. The non-informative exists based [*āśritya*] on the fundamental material elements, just as the shadow exists based on the tree and as the light or glitter [*prabhā*] of the gem [*maṇi*] exists based on the gem. [However,] the visual consciousness does not exist based on the sense-faculty, which is merely the [external] cause of its arising [*utpattinimitta*].

Reply [to the first attempt]: – That the shadow exists based on the tree and that the light or glitter exists based on the gem is a hypothesis not in conformity with the principles of the Vaibhāṣikas (MVŚ, 63c22). {11 a} [First of all,] the Vaibhāṣikas admit that any one of the color atoms [*vārṇaparamāṇu*] constituting the shadow and the light or glitter exists based on a tetrad of fundamental material elements. But even if you suppose that: "The shadow exists based on the tree, for the shadow exists based on the fundamental material elements which are particular to it, and these exist based on the tree"—the comparison of the shadow and of the non-informative would (still) be inadmissible. [This is so because] the Vaibhāṣika admits that the non-informative does not perish when the fundamental material elements which serve as its basis perish (iv. 4cd). Consequently your refutation [*parihāra*] ("This response is not valid. The non-informative...") is without value.

[Second attempt:] – We say: But we can refute the objection:[191] "According to this principle, the five sensory consciousnesses would be material form." <27>

In fact, the basis of the visual consciousness, [etc.,] is twofold:

1. the eye sense-faculty, [etc.,] which are subject to being broken or resistant [*rūpyate*; *sapratigha*, i. 29b], which are material form;
2. the mental faculty (*manas*; i. 44cd) [which is not in a state of encounter], which is not material form.

Now the same does not hold for the non-informative whose basis is exclusively material form. Thus, from the fact that the non-informative is called *material form* because the basis is material form, one cannot conclude, [as maintained in the objection,] that the visual consciousness should be called *material form*. Thus, the second explanation is good.[192]

BBA.4. *Ten sense-spheres and ten elements & the aggregate of material form; F 27*

14ab. **(The sense-faculties and the object-referents which have been defined as aggregate of material form,) these same[193] sense-faculties and object-referents are regarded as being ten sense-spheres, ten elements.[194]**

1. Considered as *āyatana*, i.e., as origin of thought and thought-concomitants (i. 20), [the sense-faculties (*indriya*) and object-referents (*artha*)] are ten sense-spheres (*āyatana*):

i. sense-sphere of the eye (*cakṣurāyatana*);
ii. sense-sphere of visible form or sense-sphere of material form (*rūpāyatana*; i. 24);
iii. sense-sphere of the ear (*śrotrāyatana*);
iv. sense-sphere of sound (*śabdāyatana*);
v. sense-sphere of the nose (*ghrāṇāyatana*);
vi. sense-sphere of odor (*gandhāyatana*);
vii. sense-sphere of the tongue (*jihvāyatana*);
viii. sense-sphere of taste (*rasāyatana*);
ix. sense-sphere of the body (*kāyāyatana*);
x. sense-sphere of the tangible (*spraṣṭavyāyatana*).

2. Considered as *dhātu*, i.e., as minerals (i. 20), [the sense-faculties and object-referents (i. 48)] are ten elements (*dhātu*):

i. element of the eye (*cakṣurdhātu*);
ii. element of visible form or element of form (*rūpadhātu*; i. 24);
iii. element of the ear (*śrotradhātu*);
iv. element of sound (*śabdadhātu*);

v. element of the nose (*ghrāṇadhātu*);
vi. element of odor (*gandhadhātu*);
vii. element of the tongue (*jihvādhātu*);
viii. element of taste (*rasadhātu*);
ix. element of the body (*kāyadhātu*);
x. element of the tangible (*spraṣṭavyadhātu*).

We have discussed the aggregate of material form (*rūpaskandha*) {11 b} and how it is distributed among the sense-spheres (*āyatana*) and elements (*dhātu*).

We have to explain the other aggregates.

. *Aggregate of sensation (vedanāskandha);*[195] *F 27*

.1. *Definition; F 27*

14c. Sensation is affect or experience that is unpleasant, [pleasant, or neither-unpleasant-nor-pleasant].[196]

.2. *Three types; F 27*

The aggregate of sensation is the threefold mode of sensing or experiencing (*anubhava, anubhūti, upabhoga*),[197]

1. unpleasant sensation [*duḥkha*; vi. 3],
2. pleasant sensation [*sukha*; vi. 3: F 128–136],
3. neither unpleasant-nor-pleasant sensation [*aduḥkhāsukha*].

.3. *Six types; F 27*

Six groups of sensations [*vedanākāya*] can also be distinguished (ii. 7ff; iii. 101):

1–5. [bodily sensations:] those that arise from contact [*saṃsparśa*] of the five material sense-faculties: the eye sense-faculty [*cakṣus*], etc., with their object;

6. [mental sensations:] those that arise from contact with the mental faculty. <28>

. *Aggregate of ideation (saṃjñāskandha);*[198] *F 28*

.1. *Definition; F 28*

14cd. Ideation consists of the seizing or apprehension of signs.[199]

The seizing or apprehending [*udgrahaṇa*] of [the signs or marks (*nimitta*)], of the diverse intrinsic natures (*svabhāva*), i.e., perceiving that this is blue [*nīla*], yellow [*pīta*], long [*dīrgha*], short [*hrasva*], male [*puruṣa*], female [*strī*], friend (*mitra*; *śāta*), enemy (*amitra*; *aśāta*), agreeable [*sukha*], disagreeable [*duḥkha*], etc., is the aggregate of ideation (see i. 16a).

BBC.2. *Six types;* F 28

Six groups of ideation [*saṃjñākāya*], according to the sense-faculty, as with sensation, can also be distinguished.

BBD. *Aggregate of formations (saṃskāraskandha);*[200] F 28–29

BBD.1. *Definition;* F 28

15ab. The aggregate of formations (or conditioning forces) is the conditioning forces [*saṃskāra*] different from the other four aggregates.[201]

The conditioning forces (*saṃskāra*) are everything that is conditioned (*saṃskṛta*; i. 7a); but the name *aggregate of formations* (or *conditioning forces*)[202] (*saṃskāraskandha*) is reserved for those conditioning forces (*saṃskāra*) which do not fit either in the aggregates of material form (*rūpa*), sensation (*vedanā*), ideation (*saṃjñā*), explained above, or in the aggregate of consciousness (*vijñāna*), explained below (i. 16).

BBD.1.1. *Are formations only intention?*[203] F 28–29

It is true that the Sūtra says:

> The aggregate of formations is the six groups of intention (*cetanākāya*);[204] <29>

and this definition excludes from the aggregate of formations:

1. all formations dissociated from thought (*viprayukta-saṃskāra*; ii. 35),
2. the formations associated with thought (*saṃprayuktasaṃskāra*; ii. 23b, 34) with the exception of intention itself.

But the Sūtra expresses itself in this way because of the capital importance or predominance [*prādhānya*] of intention, which, being action [*karma*] by nature [*svarūpatva*], is of capital importance [*prādhāna*] for modeling, conditioning or creating (*abhisaṃskar*) the future existence.[205] Therefore the Fortunate One said:

> The appropriative aggregate (*upādānaskandha*) called *formations* (*saṃskāra*) is so called because it conditions (*abhisaṃskar*) the conditioned factors (*saṃskṛta*),[206]

that is to say, because it creates and determines the five aggregates of the future existence.[207] {12 a}

To understand the exposition [*nirdeśa*] of the Sūtra literally, one would come to the conclusion that the mental factors (*caitasika*; *saṃprayukta*), with the exception of intention, and all the factors of the dissociated (*viprayukta*) class (ii. 35) are not included in any aggregate (*skandhāsaṃgraha*). They would thus not be included in the truths of unsatisfactoriness and of the origin: one would neither have to know (*parijñā*) them nor to abandon (*prahāṇa*) them. But the Fortunate One said:

> If one has not completely known or mastered [*aparijñāya*], has not known [*anabhijñāya*] even a single factor, I declare that one cannot put an end to unsatisfactoriness (vi. 33).[208]

And furthermore:

> If one has not abandoned even a single factor… (*Saṃyukta*, 8, 22).

Thus the whole of the thought-concomitants (*caitta*) and of the dissociated factors [see ii. 23–48] is included in the aggregate of formations (*saṃskāraskandha*).[209] <30>

Sense-spheres and elements & the aggregates of sensation, ideation and formations & the object of mental consciousness;[210] *F 30*

15bd. **These three aggregates [i.e., (1) sensation, (2) ideation and (3) formations,] along with (4) the non-informative and (5–7) the unconditioned factors, are [called] *the sense-sphere of factors*, the *element of factors*.**[211]

(1) The aggregate of sensation, (2) the aggregate of ideation, (3) the aggregate of formations, along with (4) the non-informative (i. 11; iv, F 16)[212] and (5–7) the three unconditioned factors (i. 5b), [i.e., space and the two kinds of cessations,] are seven real entities [*dravya*] which are called the *sense-sphere of factors* (*dharmāyatana*), the *element of factors* (*dharmadhātu*). (i. 24; 39bc, 48a)

Aggregate of consciousness (vijñānaskandha);[213] *F 30–33*

Definition of consciousness in general; F 30

16a. **[The aggregate of] consciousness is that which makes known [*vijñapti*], [i.e., the apperception,] relative to each [object-field].**[214]

The aggregate of consciousness (ii. 34) is that which makes known (*vijñapti*),[215] [i.e.,] the "naked or bare or generic apperception" (*upalabdhi*),[216] relative to each object-field (*viṣayaṃ viṣayaṃ prati*).[217]

BBF.2. *Classification of consciousness; F 30–31*

The aggregate of consciousness is, [again, (as with sensation, ideation and intention),] six groups of consciousnesses [*vijñānakāya*]:[218] <31>

1. visual consciousness or consciousness of the eye [*cakṣurvijñāna*];
2. auditory consciousness or consciousness of the ear [*śrotravijñāna*];
3. olfactory consciousness or consciousness of the nose [*ghrāṇavijñāna*];
4. gustatory consciousness or consciousness of the tongue [*jihvāvijñāna*];
5. tactile consciousness or consciousness of the body [*kāyavijñāna*];
6. mental consciousness or consciousness of the mental faculty [*manovijñāna*].

BBF.3. *Sense-spheres and elements & the aggregate of consciousness;[219] F 31*

16b. **(Considered as sense-sphere [*āyatana*; i. 20a], the aggregate of consciousness) is the sense-sphere of the mental faculty (*mana-āyatana*).**[220]

16cd. **(Considered as element [*dhātu*; i. 20a], the aggregate of consciousness) is seven elements, namely, (1–6) the six consciousnesses and (7) the mental faculty (*manas*).**[221]

That is to say:

1. the element of the visual consciousness (*cakṣurvijñānadhātu*),
2. the element of the auditory consciousness (*śrotravijñānadhātu*),
3. the element of the olfactory consciousness (*ghrāṇavijñānadhātu*),
4. the element of the gustatory consciousness (*jihvāvijñānadhātu*),
5. the element of the tactile consciousness (*kāyavijñānadhātu*),
6. the element of the mental consciousness (*manovijñānadhātu*),
7. the element of the mental faculty (*manodhātu*) (i.e., the *manas*, the mental faculty).

BBG. *Discussion of various issues related to the threefold classification of factors;[222] F 31–34*

In this way, we have shown [*nirdiṣṭa*] that there are five aggregates, twelve sense-spheres, eighteen elements.

1. The aggregate of material form is ten sense-spheres, ten elements, plus the non-informative.

2. The aggregates of sensation, ideation and formations, plus the non-informative, plus the [three] unconditioned factors, are the sense-sphere of factors (*dharma-āyatana*), the element of factors (*dharmadhātu*).

3. The aggregate of consciousness is the sense-sphere of the mental faculty (*mana-āyatana*); it is seven elements (*dhātu*), namely, the six groups of consciousness (*vijñānakāya* = *vijñānadhātu*) and the element of the mental faculty (*manodhātu*) or mental faculty (*manas*).

3.1. *Element of the mental faculty and its relation to the six consciousnesses; F 31*

[Objection:] – [But surely it has been said that the six groups of consciousness constitute the aggregate of consciousness.] Now what could be the mental faculty or element of the mental faculty which is distinct from the six groups of consciousness, distinct from the sensory consciousnesses and of the mental consciousness?

[Answer:] – There is no mental faculty (*manas*) distinct from the consciousnesses.[223]

.2. *Element of the mental faculty (manas); F 31–33*

[Objection: – In that case, what is the element of the mental faculty?]

.2.1. *Definition; F 31–32*

17ab. **Of these six consciousnesses, the consciousness which has just passed away is the mental faculty (*manas*, i.e., *manodhātu*).**[224] <32>

All consciousness which has just perished [*samanantaraniruddha*] is given the name of *element of the mental faculty* (*manodhātu*): {13 a} in the same way, the same man is the son [*putra*] [of one person] and the father [*pitṛ*] [of another], or the same vegetable element is the fruit [*phala*] [of one plant] and the seed [*bīja*] [of another].

.2.2. *Enumeration of the eighteen elements & the mental faculty;*[225] *F 32–33*

Objection. – If the six consciousnesses which make up six elements (*dhātu*) constitute the mental faculty (*manas*) and if the mental faculty is not an entity distinct from the six consciousnesses, there would be either seventeen elements, by excluding the mental faculty which is made redundant [*itaretarāntarbhāva*] by the six consciousnesses, or twelve elements, by excluding the six consciousnesses which are made redundant by the mental faculty—supposing, of course, that you want to enumerate distinct real entities and not mere designations. [Why then are those elements classified as eighteen?]

17cd. **(Answer: – Even though that is so, nevertheless) eighteen elements are counted with the view of assigning a basis to the sixth consciousness.**[226]

The first five consciousnesses have the five material sense-faculties, i.e., the eye sense-faculty, etc. (see i. 44cd) for their basis; the sixth consciousness, i.e., the mental consciousness (*manovijñānadhātu*), does not have a similar basis, [i.e., has no other (*anya*) basis]. <33>

Therefore, with a view of attributing a basis to this [mental] consciousness, *manas* (mental faculty) or *manodhātu* (element of the mental faculty), or furthermore, the *mana-āyatana* (sense-sphere of the mental faculty) and *mana-indriya* (mental faculty) is called that which serves as basis, i.e., any one of the six consciousnesses.

In this way there are (1) six bases [*āśraya*] or sense-faculties, (2) six consciousnesses based on these six bases and (3) six cognitive objects (*ālambana*), [and thus the elements come to be eighteen in number].

BBG.2.3. *Last thought of a perfected being & the mental faculty;*[227] *F 33*

Objection. – If the consciousness or thought is called *mental faculty* (*manas*) when, having ceased, it is the basis of another consciousness, then the last (*carama*) thought (*citta*) of a perfected being (*arhat*) would not be a mental faculty, since (this last thought) is not followed by a thought of which it would be the immediately preceding cause and the basis (i. 44cd).

[Reply:] – [This is not so, since] this last thought has indeed the nature of the mental faculty, the nature of basis. If it is not followed by a new thought, namely, the consciousness-at-conception (*pratisaṃdhivijñāna*) of a new existence (*punarbhava*), this is not related to its nature but results from the absence or deficiency [*vaikalya*] of the other causes, i.e., actions [*karma*] and defilements [*kleśa*], necessary for the production of a new consciousness [*uttaravijñānasambhūti*].

BBG.3. *Inclusion (saṃgraha) & an abbreviated presentation of the aggregates, sense-spheres and elements;*[228] *F 33*

All the conditioned factors (*saṃskṛta*) are included [*saṃgrah*]) in all [*sarva*] of the aggregates (i. 7); all the impure (*sāsrava*) factors are included in all of the appropriative aggregates (i. 8); all the (conditioned and unconditioned) factors are included in all of the sense-spheres and of the elements (i. 14). {13 b}

18ab. **(But in short, it should be known that) all the factors are included in one aggregate [i.e., the aggregate of material form], plus one sense-sphere [i.e., the sense-sphere of the mental faculty], plus one element [i.e., the element of factors].**[229]

[One should understand that all of the factors are included (*saṃgraha*)] in the aggregate of material form (*rūpaskandha*), the sense-sphere of the mental faculty (*mana-āyatana*) and the element of factors (*dharmadhātu*).

.3.1. *Meaning of* inclusion;[230] *F 33–34*

18cd. A factor is included by that which has the same intrinsic nature [*svabhāva*], for it is distinct from other-nature [*parabhāva*].[231]

[A factor is distinct from other-nature (i.e., from that which is not itself). Therefore it is not reasonable that] a factor (*dharma*) is included (*saṃgrah*) in that from which it is distinct [*viyukta*]. <34>

For example, the eye sense-faculty is included (1) in the aggregate of material form (*rūpaskandha*), its intrinsic nature being material form;[232] (2) in the sense-sphere of the eye (*cakṣurāyatana*), in the element of the eye (*cakṣurdhātu*), for it is the sense-sphere of the eye, the element of the eye [in its intrinsic nature]; (3) in the truths of unsatisfactoriness and of the origin, for [their intrinsic nature] is unsatisfactoriness and origin; but the eye sense-faculty is not included in the other aggregates, sense-spheres, etc., for it is distinct in its intrinsic nature from that which it is not.

Without a doubt, [it is said that the four] assemblies (*parṣad*)[233] are included, i.e., won over or attracted (*saṃgrah*), by giving [*dāna*] and the other [three] bases for gathering [an audience] [*saṃgrahavastu*]:[234] thus there is *saṃgraha* of one thing by another. But this *saṃgraha* is occasional (*kadācitka*) and, consequently, not real but [merely] conventional (*sāṃketika*).

.4. *Twofold sense-faculties & the enumeration of too many elements;*[235] *F 34*

[Possible objection:] – But there are two sense-faculties in regard to the eye, the ear, the nose: therefore, one should count twenty-one elements.

19. [Answer:] – The sense-faculties of the eye, the ear and the nose, although twofold, constitute, in pairs, only one element, for their (1) type, (2) experiential domain and (3) consciousness are common [*sāmānya*]. It is for beauty's sake that they are twofold.[236] {14 a}

The two sense-faculties of the eye have

1. commonality of type [*jātisāmānya*], for both of them are an eye sense-faculty in their intrinsic nature [*svabhāva*];
2. commonality of experiential domain [*gocarasāmānya*], for they both have visible form (*rūpadhātu*) for their object-field [*viṣaya*];

3. commonality of consciousness [*vijñānasāmānya*], for both of them are the basis [*āśraya*] of a single visual consciousness (*cakṣurvijñānadhātu*).

Therefore, the two eye sense-faculties make up only one element.

The same holds for the sense-faculties of the ear and of the nose.

Although (the sense-faculties) make up only one element, these sense-faculties are produced in pairs for the sake of the beauty [*śobhārtha*] of the body [*āśraya*]. [Otherwise,] with a single [physical seat (*adhiṣṭhāna*)] of the eye or ear, or with a single nostril [*nāsikāvila*], one would be very ugly [*vairūpya*][237] (ii. 1a; i. 43, 30). {14 b} <35>

[The aggregates, sense-spheres and elements have been discussed.]

BBH. *Meaning of the terms* aggregate, sense-sphere *and* element;[238] *F 35–39*

What should be understood by the terms *skandha*, *āyatana*, *dhātu*?

20ab. **(i) *Skandha* signifies heap [*rāśi*], (ii) *āyatana* signifies gate of arrival or gate of arising [*āyadvāra*] [of thought and thought-concomitants (*cittacaitta*; ii. 23)], and (iii) *dhātu* signifies lineage [or genus] [*gotra*].**[239]

BBH.1. *Meaning of* skandha;[240] *F 35–37*

In the Sūtra, *skandha* signifies heap or group or mass (*rāśi*):[241]

> Whatever material form (*rūpa*) there is, (1) past [*atīta*] or future [*anāgata*] or present [*pratyutpanna*], (2) internal [*ādhyātmika*] or external [*bāhya*], (3) gross [*audārika*] or subtle [*sūkṣma*], (4) inferior [*hīna*] or superior [*praṇīta*], (5) distant [*dūra*] or near [*antika*], if all this material form—that which is past, etc.—is grouped together into one heap [*aikadhyam abhisaṃkṣipya*], this is called *aggregate of material form.*[242]

BBH.1.1. *The Sūtra passage according to the Vaibhāṣikas; F 35–36*

According to the Vaibhāṣikas, [this passage means that]:

1. past material form is the material form destroyed by impermanence [*anityatā*],[243] future material form is the material form which has not yet arisen [*anutpanna*], present material form is the material form which has arisen and which has not been destroyed [*utpannāniruddha*];

2. [as for material form being internal or external, there are two hypotheses:]

  i. material form is internal (*ādhyātmika*) when it forms part of the life-stream (*saṃtāna*) called "me" (i. 39); any other material form is external [*bāhya*]; or rather,
  ii. the terms internal and external are understood from the point of view of the sense-sphere (*āyatana*):[244] the eye sense-faculty is internal because it forms part of my life-stream or of the life-stream of another; <36>

3. [as for material form being gross or subtle, there are two hypotheses:]
  i. material form is gross [*audārika*] when it is susceptible to offering resistance [*sapratigha*; i. 29b]; it is subtle [*sūkṣma*] when it is not susceptible to offering resistance [*apratigha*], (see iv. 4a);[245] or rather,
  ii. these two designations, [i.e., gross and subtle,] are established relative to each other [*āpekṣika*] and not ultimately.

[Objection:] – In this second hypothesis, the gross and the subtle are not established, since the same material form is gross or subtle according to whether it is compared to a material form more subtle or more gross.

[Answer:] – The objection is invalid, for the terms of comparison do not vary: when a material form is gross relative to another material form, it is not subtle relative to this same other material form: just as the case of father and son;

4. inferior [*hīna*] material form is defiled (*kliṣṭa*) material form; {15 a} superior [*praṇīta*] material form is non-defiled [*akliṣṭa*] material form;

5. past or future material form is distant [*dūra*]; present material form is near [*antika*].[246]

The same for the other aggregates (*skandha*), with this difference:
  i. gross consciousness is that which has the five sense-faculties for its basis [*aśraya*]; subtle consciousness is the mental consciousness;[247] or rather,
  ii. the consciousness is gross or subtle according to whether it belongs to a lower or higher stage [*bhūmi*].

.2. *The Sūtra passage according to the Bhadanta;* F 36–37

According to the Bhadanta, [the Sūtra passage means]:[248]

1. gross [*audārika*] material form is that which is perceived [*grāhya*] by the five sense-faculties; all other material form is subtle [*sūkṣma*];

2. inferior [*hīna*] signifies unpleasant (*amanāpa*); superior [*praṇīta*] signifies pleasant [*manāpa*];

3. distant [*dūra*][249] material form is that which occurs in a place that is not visible [*adṛśyadeśa*]; near [*antika*] material form is that which occurs in a place that is visible [*dṛśyadeśa*]: the Vaibhāṣika explanation [of distant and near] is bad, for past material form, etc., has already been referred to under its own name [*svaśabda*]. <37>

The same for sensation [and the other aggregates (*vedanādi*)]: they are distant or near depending on whether their bases are invisible or visible [*adṛśyāśraya*; *dṛśyāsraya*]; they are gross or subtle depending on whether they are bodily or mental (ii. 7).

BBH.2. *Meaning of* āyatana;[250] *F 37*

Āyatana signifies the gate of arrival or gate of arising (*āyadvāra*) of thought and thought-concomitants (*cittacaitta*; ii. 23). Etymologically [*nirvacana*], that which extends [or makes the gate wider or prepares a way for] (*tanvanti*) the arising (*āya*) of thought and thought-concomitants is called *āyatana*.[251]

BBH.3. *Meaning of* dhātu;[252] *F 37*

Dhātu signifies *gotra* (family, race, lineage, mine, genus).[253]

1. Just as the place, namely a mountain [*parvata*], where many families [*gotra*] of minerals: iron, copper, silver, gold, etc., occur, is said *to have numerous dhātus*, in the same way, in the single human complex (*āśraya*) or life-stream (*saṃtāna*), eighteen kinds of families occur which are called the *eighteen elements*. That which is signified by *gotra* {15 b} is thus a mine [or source] (*ākara*).[254]

[Question:] – Of what is the eye sense-faculty (*cakṣurdhātu*) the mine [or source]? Of what are the other elements the mine [or source]?

[Answer:] – The elements are the mine [or source] of their own genus (*svasyā jāteḥ*): the eye, being a homogeneous cause (*sabhāgahetu*; ii. 52) of the later moments of the existence of the eye, is the mine [or source] (*dhātu*) of the eye.

[Objection:] – But then how could the unconditioned factors, which are eternal, be considered to be an element?

[Answer:] – In that case, let us say that (unconditioned factors) are the mine [or source] of thought and thought-concomitants.

2. According to another opinion, *dhātu* signifies genus (*jāti*). The specific nature or genus of the distinct eighteen factors [*aṣṭādaśadharmāṇāṃ jātayaḥ svabhāvā*] is what is understood by the eighteen elements.

BBI. *Ontological status of aggregates, sense-spheres and elements; F 37–39*

Objections:[255] <38>

1. If *skandha* signifies heap (*rāśi*), then aggregates (*skandha*) exist only as a provisional or nominal entity (*prajñaptisat*) and not as a real entity (*dravyasat*), for the aggregation (*saṃcita*), the collection [*samūha*], is not one [*aneka*] thing: for example, a heap of grain [*rāśi*], or the person (*pudgala*).[256]

The Vaibhāṣika: – No, for [even a single] atom or monad (*dravyaparamāṇu*) is a *skandha*.[257]

[Reply:] – In this hypothesis, since the monad cannot have the quality of being a heap [*rāśitva*], you cannot say that *skandha* signifies heap.

2. According to another opinion (MVŚ, 407c9), (i) *skandha* signifies that which carries the load, namely, its effect [*kārya bhārodvahana*].[258]

Or else, (ii) *skandha* signifies part, section (*praccheda, avadhi*):[259] as one commonly says: "I will lend money to you, if you promise to return it in three sections or installments (*skandha*)."[260]

[Reply:[261]] – These two explanations do not conform to the Sūtra.[262] The Sūtra [passage mentioned above (F 35)], in fact, attributes to *skandha* the meaning of heap [only] and no other meaning:

> Whatever material form there is, past or future or present, ... if one puts together all this material form... .

3. The Vaibhāṣika says: – The Sūtra teaches that all material form, i.e., past material form, future material form, etc., is, individually [*pratyeka*], called *skandha*—in the same way {16 a} that it teaches that hairs, etc., are the elementary substance earth (below, F 49, note)—thus each [*ekaśas*] "real" (atomic) element of past material form, future material form, etc., is given the name of *skandha*. Thus the aggregates (*skandha*) do exist as a real entity [*dravyasat*] and not as a provisional or nominal entity [*prajñaptisat*]. <39>

[Reply:] – This interpretation is inadmissible, for the Sūtra (above F 35) says:

> ...if one puts together all this material form, this is called aggregate of material form.

[Hence, the aggregates, too, exist as a nominal entity just as the heap does.[263]]

4. (The Sautrāntika:[264]) – If this is the case, then the material sense-spheres (*āyatana*), i.e., the sense-faculties and the objects of the five sensory consciousnesses, must also exist only as a provisional or nominal entity, for the quality of being a "gate of arising [*āyadvāra*] of thought and thought-concomitants [*citta-caitta*]" does not belong to atoms taken one by one, which alone are real, but to

the collections [*bahu*] of atoms which constitute the eye sense-faculty, the visible object, etc.

Reply: – Each of these atoms possesses individually the quality of being a "gate of arising of thought", of being the cause [*kāraṇabhāva*] of consciousness (*compare* i. 44ab: section "invisibility"), If you do not accept this doctrine, you deny to the sense-faculty—considered in its totality—the quality of being a cause of consciousness, for it does not produce the consciousness by itself and without the cooperation of the object-field [*viṣayasahakāritva*].

5. On the other hand, the MVŚ (384a18) expresses itself thus:

> When the Abhidharma scholars[265] take into consideration the fact that the term *skandha* is only the designation [*prajñapti*] for a heap [*rāśi*],[266] they point out that the atom is a part [*pradeśa*] of one element, one sense-sphere, one aggregate;
>
> when they do not take this fact into consideration, they point out that the atom is one element, one sense-sphere, one aggregate.[267]

In fact, one designates the part [*pradeśa*] by the whole [*pradeśin*] metaphorically [*upacāra*]; for example: "The garment [*paṭa*] is burned", for: "One part of the garment is burned."

BBJ. *Need for giving the threefold instructions;*[268] *F 39–40*

[Question:] – Why did the Fortunate One give this threefold instruction [*deśanā*] of the factors (*dharma*): as aggregates (*skandha*), sense-spheres (*āyatana*) and elements (*dhātu*)? {16 b} <40>

[Answer: – Because of the disciples (*vineya*).]

20cd. The instructions on the aggregates, [sense-spheres and elements were given,] because (1) delusion, (2) faculty or ability, (3) preference are [each] threefold.[269]

1. The delusion or bewilderment (*moha, saṃmoha*) [of sentient beings (*sattva*)] is threefold:

   i. the first category of disciples are deceived by considering the mental factors (*caitta*) as together [*piṇḍa*] constituting a self (*ātman*);[270]
   ii. the second category of disciples is deceived similarly with respect to the material elements (*rūpa*) [alone];
   iii. the third category of disciples is deceived similarly with respect to both the material and mental elements [*rūpacitta*].

2. The (praxis-oriented) faculties [*indriya*; faith, etc.; ii. 3cd], the faculty of understanding (*prajñendriya*), are also of three categories,[271]

   i. sharp [*tīkṣṇa*],
   ii. mediocre [*madhya*],
   iii. dull [*mṛdu*].

3. The preference [or resolve] (*ruci*; *adhimokṣa*) is also threefold:

   i. the first category of disciples apply themselves to that which is said in an abbreviated [*saṃkṣipta*] way;
   ii. the second to that which is said normally [*madhya*];
   iii. the third to that which is said at great length (*vistīrṇa*; *vistara*).[272]

(a) The instruction on the aggregates addresses itself to the first category of disciples, to those who are deceived with regard to mental factors, who have sharp faculties, who are fond of abbreviated teachings; (b) the instruction on the sense-spheres addresses itself to the second category; (c) the instruction on the elements addresses itself to the third category.[273]

Definite number of the aggregates;[274] *F 40–42*

1. *Why sensation and ideation constitute separate aggregates;*[275] *F 40–41*

Sensation (*vedanā*) and ideation (*saṃjñā*) each constitute a separate aggregate (*skandha*): all the other mental factors (ii. 24) are placed in the aggregate of formations (*saṃskāraskandha*; i. 15). Why?

21. The two thought-concomitants, i.e., sensation and ideation, are defined as distinct aggregates [separate from other mental factors] (1) because they are, [respectively,] the [predominant] causes of the [two] roots of dispute [i.e., attachment to pleasures and attachment to views], (2) because they are the causes of cyclic existence and also (3) because of the causes that justify the order of the aggregates.[276] <41>

1. There are two roots of dispute (*vivāda*):[277]

   i. attachment (*adhyavasāya*, *abhiṣvaṅga*) to pleasures or objects of desire [*kāma*];
   ii. attachment to views (*dṛṣṭi*).

Sensation and ideation are, respectively, the predominant cause [*pradhānahetu*] of these two roots. In fact, if one becomes attached to pleasures, it is because one enjoys (*āsvāda*) the sensation; if one becomes attached to views, it is because of mistaken ideation (*viparītasaṃjñā*; v. 9). {17 a}

2. Sensation and ideation are [also] the predominant causes of cyclic existence [*saṃsāra*]: the person who is greedy (*gṛddha*) to enjoy sensation and in whom ideations are mistaken transmigrates.

3. The reasons justifying the order [*krama*] of the aggregates will be explained below (i. 22bd).

BBK.2. *Why the unconditioned factors do not form part of the aggregates;*[278]

F 41–42

[First, however,] why do the unconditioned factors (*asaṃskṛta*), which are part of the sense-sphere of factors (*dharmāyatana*) and of the element of factors (*dharmadhātu*) (i. 15d), not form part of the aggregates?

22ab. The unconditioned factors are not named with respect to the aggregates because they do not correspond to the meaning [of *skandha*].[279]

1. The unconditioned factors cannot be placed within any of the five aggregates, for they are neither matter or material form, nor sensation... [nor consciousness].

2. Nor can one speak of the unconditioned factors as a sixth aggregate [*ṣaṣṭhaḥ skandha*], because it does not correspond to the meaning of *skandha*, since *skandha* signifies heap [*rāśi*], susceptible of being put together. What the Sūtra says of material form (see F 35), one cannot say of the unconditioned factors, like: "If one puts together all the unconditioned factors—that which is past, etc.—one has what is called the *aggregate of the unconditioned factors* (*asaṃskṛtaskandha*)", for the distinctions of past, etc., do not exist with respect to unconditioned factors. <42>

3. Furthermore, by the expression *appropriative aggregate* (*upādānaskandha*; i. 8a) the assemblage [*vistara*] of that which is the cause [*vastu*] of pollution (*saṃkleśa*) is designated; by the expression *aggregates* (*skandha*) the assemblage of that which is the cause of pollution (i.e., impure conditioned factors) and the cause of purification (*vyavadāna*) (i.e., pure conditioned factors: the noble path) is designated. Thus the unconditioned factors, which are neither the cause of defilement nor the cause of purification, {17 b} cannot be classified either among the *appropriative aggregates* or among the *aggregates*.

4. According to one opinion, just as the end or ceasing (*uparama*) of a jug [*ghaṭa*] is not a jug, in the same way the unconditioned factor, which is the end or ceasing of the aggregates, cannot be an aggregate (*skandha*) (MVŚ, 385b18).[280]

[Reply:] – But, to reason like that, the unconditioned factors would be neither a sense-sphere (*āyatana*) nor an element (*dhātu*).[281]

L. ## *Reasons for the set order and progression of the aggregates, sense-spheres and elements;*[282] *F 42–46*

L.1. ### *Set order of the five aggregates;*[283] *F 42–43*

We have defined the aggregates. We have now to explain the order [*krama*] in which the aggregates are enumerated.

22bd. The order of the aggregates is justified by (1) their [relative] grossness, (2) [the causes of the progression of] pollution, (3) the characteristic of the pot, [food, seasoning, cook, consumer,] and also (4) from the point of view of [the predominance in] the realms of existence.[284]

1. [Relative grossness (*audārika*; F 36):] – (i) Material form (*rūpa*), being susceptible to offering resistance [*sapratighatva*; i. 29b], is the most gross of [all] the aggregates. Among the non-material (*arūpin*) aggregates, (ii) sensation is the most gross, because of the grossness of its operation [*pracāra*; *samudācāra*]: in fact, sensation is localized in one's hand, in one's foot, etc. (iii) Ideation (*saṃjñā*) is more gross than the last two aggregates. (iv) The aggregate of formations is more gross than (v) the aggregate of consciousness.[285]

The aggregates are thus arranged in the order of their diminishing grossness (*audārikatara*).

2. [Causes of the progression (*anukramahetu*) of pollution (*saṃkleśa*):] – In the course of eternal [or beginningless (*anādimat*)] cyclic existence [*saṃsāra*], men and women [*strīpuruṣa*] are mutually (i) enamoured by their bodies (*rūpa*) because they are (ii) attached to the enjoyment [*āsvāda*] of sensation (*vedanā*). This attachment proceeds from (iii) mistaken ideations (*saṃjñā-viparyāsa*), which are due to (iv) the defilements (*kleśa*) which are formations (*saṃskāra*). {18 a} And it is (v) thought (*citta*, *vijñāna*) which is defiled by the defilements [*kleśa*].

The aggregates are thus arranged according to the progression of pollution (*saṃkleśa*). <43>

3. [Analogy (*bhājanādyārtha*):] – (i) Matter or material form is [figuratively] the pot [*bhājana*], (ii) sensation is the food [*bhojana*], (iii) ideation is the seasoning [*vyañjana*], (iv) formations are the cook [*paktṛ*] and (v) consciousness or thought is the one who eats [*bhoktṛ*]. – We have here a third reason for the order [*krama*] of the aggregates.

4. [Predominance in the three realms (*dhātu*):] – Finally, to consider the aggregates on the one hand, the realms of existence (*dhātu*) (ii. 14) on the other hand, it is seen that:

i. the realm of desire (*kāmadhatu*; iii. 1) is distinguished, specified, dominated (*prabhāvita, prakarṣita*) by matter or material form, namely, by the five objects of sense enjoyments or of desire (*kāmaguṇa*; *Dharmaskandha*, 5, 10; MVŚ, 376; comp. *Kathāvatthu*, viii. 3);
ii. the realm of fine-materiality (*rūpadhātu*; iii. 2), i.e., the four meditations (*dhyāna*), is distinguished by sensation (faculties of pleasure, satisfaction and equanimity, viii. 12);
iii. the first three [of the four] stages of the realm of immateriality (*ārūpya-dhātu*; iii. 3) are distinguished by ideation [alone]: ideation of infinite space, (infinite consciousness, and nothingness, viii. 4);
iv. the fourth stage of the realm of immateriality, the summit of cyclic existence (*bhavāgra*), is distinguished by intention (*cetanā*), the formation *par excellence* [*saṃskāramātra*], which creates an existence of 80,000 cosmic aeons (iii. 81c);
v. these diverse stages are the stations of consciousness (*vijñānasthiti*; iii. 6): it is in these places that the consciousness resides.

[The progression (*anukrama*) of the aggregates is for the sake of showing that] the first four aggregates constitute the field [*kṣetra*] and the fifth the seed [*bīja*].

There are thus five aggregates, no more, no less.

We see how the reasons which justify the order of the aggregates also justify the doctrine that makes sensation and ideation separate [*pṛthak*] aggregates: (1) they are more gross than the other formations; (2) they are the cause of the progression of pollution; (3) they are [figuratively] the food and the seasoning; (4) they dominate two realms of existence.

BBL.2. *Set progression of the sense-spheres and elements; F 43–45*

Now we will explain the progression [*anukrama*] in which the six sense-spheres (*āyatana*) or elements (*dhātu*) which are the six sense-faculties of consciousness, i.e., the eye sense-faculty, etc., are enumerated; the progression in dependence on which the object-field (*viṣaya*) and the consciousnesses that correspond to these sense-faculties (*rūpadhātu, cakṣurvijñānadhātu*...) are arranged. {18 b}

23a. The first five [of the six sense-faculties, beginning with the eye sense-faculty,] are the first because their object-referent [*artha*] is present.[286] <44>

Five [sense-faculties], beginning with the eye sense-faculty, are called *the first*, because they bear only on present or simultaneous [*vartamāna*] object-fields.

On the contrary, the object-field of the mental faculty (*manas*; i. 39ab) [is undetermined [*aniyata*]; i.e., it] can be either (1) simultaneous [*vartamāna*] to this sense-faculty; (2) previous or past [*atīta*]; (3) later or future [*anāgata*]; (4) tritemporal [*try-adhva*], i.e., simultaneous, previous and later; (5) outside of time [*anadhva*].

23b. The first four [of these five sense-faculties] are the first because their object-referent is solely derivative or secondary matter.[287]

The sense-faculties of the eye, ear, nose and tongue do not attain the fundamental material elements (i. 12), but only the derivative material elements or derivative material forms (*bhautika, upādāyarūpa*; ii. 50a, 65).

The object-field (*viṣaya*) of the body (*kāyendriya*) is undetermined [*aniyata*; i. 35ab; 10d]: (1) sometimes the fundamental material elements [*bhūta*], (2) sometimes the derivative material elements [*bhautika*], (3) sometimes both at the same time [*ubhaya*].

23c. These [first] four [sense-faculties] are arranged according to the range and speed of their function.[288]

[The first four sense-faculties are listed progressively because] they function [*vṛtti*] (1) at a distance [*dūra*], (2) at a greater distance [*dūratara*], (3) with greater speed [*āśutara*].

1. The eye sense-faculty and the ear sense-faculty function with regard to a distant object-field (i. 43cd). They are thus named first.
2. The eye sense-faculty functions at a greater distance than the ear sense-faculty, for one may see a river [*nadī*] but not hear its sound. The eye sense-faculty is thus named before the ear sense-faculty.
3. Neither the nose nor the tongue perceive at a distance. But the nose functions quicker than the tongue, for the nose perceives the odor of food before the tongue perceives the taste. {19 a}

23d. Or rather, the sense-faculties are arranged according to their position [in the body].[289]

[In this body (*śarīra*),] the physical seat [*adhiṣṭhāna*] of the eye sense-faculty, i.e., the eye, is located uppermost; below it is the physical seat of the ear sense-faculty; below it, the physical seat of the nose sense-faculty; below it, the physical seat of the tongue sense-faculty. <45> As for the physical seat of the body sense-faculty, i.e., the body (*kāya*), for the most part it is lower than the tongue. As for the mental faculty, it is not material (i. 44ab).[290] [Thus, the order (*krama*) of these (six sense-faculties) would be according to their (physical) position (*sthāna*).]

BBM. *Reasons for the names of* rūpa-āyatana *and* dharma-āyatana;[291] *F 45–46*

Among the ten sense-spheres included in the aggregate of material form, only one receives the name *rūpa-āyatana* (sense-sphere of material form). Although all sense-spheres are factors (*dharma*), only one is called *dharma-āyatana* (sense-sphere of factors). Why?

24. **(1) In order to distinguish it from the other [sense-spheres], because of its predominance, one single sense-sphere is called *rūpa-āyatana* (sense-sphere of material form). (2) With a view to distinguish it from the other [sense-spheres], because it includes many of the factors, [i.e., sensations, ideations, etc.] and the best factor [i.e., *nirvāṇa*], one single sense-sphere is called *dharma-āyatana* (sense-sphere of factors).**[292]

[Question: – Why is it "in order to distinguish it" (*viśeṣaṇārtha*)?]

[Answer:] – 1. The ten material sense-spheres (i. 14ab) are, each separately [*pratyeka*], one sense-sphere: five being the subject [*viṣayitva*], five being the object [*viṣayatva*] of certain consciousnesses. They are not, when put together [*samasta*], one single sense-sphere of consciousness, which one would call *rūpa-āyatana*.

Nine sense-spheres are individualized by specific names: sense-sphere of the eye (*cakṣurāyatana*), sense-sphere of the ear (*śrotrāyatana*), sense-sphere of sound (*śabdāyatana*)… .

The sense-sphere which does not bear any of these nine names and yet is matter or material form (*rūpa*), is designated sufficiently by the expression *rūpa-āyatana* (sense-sphere of material form), without there being any need to give it another name. {19 b}

[Question:] – But the other nine sense-spheres are also both sense-sphere (*āyatana*) and material form (*rūpa*): why is the name of *rūpa-āyatana* given in preference to the object of the eye sense-faculty?

[Answer:] – Because of its predominance [*prādhānya*] [in three ways]. (Visible form) is material form (*rūpa*), in fact:

first, because of being *rūpaṇa* in the sense of deterioration (*bādhanalakṣaṇa-rūpaṇa*; i. 13, F 24): on account of it offering resistance [*sapratighatva*]; visible form is broken by the touch of the hand [*pāṇisaṃsparśa*], etc.;

second, because of being *rūpaṇa* as being visible in a particular place (*deśa-nidarśana-rūpaṇa*: i. 13, F. 25): [on account of its visibility (*sanidarśanatva*),] one can indicate visible form [as being "this" (*idam*),] as being "here" [*iha*], as being "there" [*amutra*])] third, because of common usage [*loka*]: that which is commonly [*loke*] understood by *rūpa*, is the visible form: color and shape. <46>

2. The sense-sphere of factors (*dharmāyatana*; i. 15bd) is sufficiently distinguished from the other sense-spheres by the name of *dharmāyatana* (sense-sphere of factors). Same explanation as above, i.e., because the sense-sphere of factors includes:

i. numerous [*bahu*] factors, such as sensation, ideation, etc.;
ii. the best [*agra*] factor (*dharma*), i.e., *nirvāṇa*.

This is why the general name, *dharma-āyatana*, is attributed to [this sense-sphere] *par excellence.*

* * *

According to another opinion (Dharmatrāta),[293] visible form is called *rūpāyatana* (sense-sphere of material form) (1) because [of its grossness (*audārikatva*) in that] it includes twenty varieties [*prakāra*] [of visible form, i.e., blue, etc.], (2) because it is the domain [*gocara*] of the three kinds of eyes: the fleshly eye (*māṃsacakṣus*), the divine eye (*divyacakṣus*), the wisdom eye (*prajñācakṣus*) (*Itivuttaka*, 61).[294]

N. *Classification of other aggregates, other sources and other elements;*[295] *F 46–51*

[Question:] – The Sūtras name other *skandhas*, other *āyatanas*, other *dhātus*. Are these included (*saṃgraha*) in the aggregates, sense-spheres and elements, described above, [or are they separate (*vyatireka*)]? {20 a}

[Answer: They are included, not separate.]

N.1. *Other* skandhas;[296] *F 46–47*

N.1.1. *80,000 aggregates of* dharmas;[297] *F 46–47*

N.1.1.1. *Aggregates of* dharmas *& their inclusion in the aggregates;*[298] *F 46*

25. **The 80,000 aggregates of *dharmas* which the Muni promulgated, according to whether one regards them (1) as voice or (2) as name, are included in (1) the aggregate of material form or (2) the aggregate of formations, [respectively].**[299]

1. For the philosophers who say that the Buddha-word [*buddhavacana*] is in its intrinsic nature *voice* (*vāc*), these [80,000] aggregates are included in the aggregate of material form (*rūpaskandha*).

2. For those who consider the Buddha-word as being *name* (*nāman*) [in its intrinsic nature,] these [80,000] aggregates are included in the aggregate of formations (*saṃskāraskandha*; ii. 36, 47ab).

BBN.1.1.2. *Dimension or measure of the* dharmaskandha;[300] *F 46–47*

What is the dimension or measure [*pramāṇa*] of the *aggregate of dharmas* (*dharmaskandha*)?[301] <47>

BBN.1.1.2.a. *Various interpretations of the aggregate of* dharmas;[302] *F 47*

26a. According to some, the aggregate of *dharmas* is of the dimension or measure of the Treatise [known as *Dharmaskandha*].[303]

That is to say, of the dimension of the Treatise of Abhidharma known by the name of *Dharmaskandha*, comprising 6,000 stanzas.[304]

26b. [According to another opinion,] the expositions on aggregates, [sense-spheres, elements, dependent origination,] etc., constitute as many *aggregates of dharmas*.[305]

According to another opinion, the expositions (*kathā*, *ākhyāna*) on the aggregates (*skandha*), sense-spheres (*āyatana*), elements (*dhātu*), dependent origination (*pratītyasamutpāda*), truths (*satya*), sustenances (*āhāra*; iii. 38d), meditations (*dhyāna*), {20 b} immeasurables (*apramāṇa*), formless meditative attainments (*ārūpya*), liberations (*vimokṣa*), perception-spheres of mastery (*abhibhvāyatana*), perception-spheres of totality (*kṛtsnāyatana*), factors conducive to enlightenment (*bodhipakṣika*), superknowledges (*abhijñā*), unhindered knowledges (*pratisaṃvid*), cognition resulting from a resolve (*praṇidhijñāna*), concentration of being without conflict (*araṇā*), etc., are each separately [*pratyeka*] as many *aggregates of dharmas* (*dharmaskandha*).

BBN.1.1.2.b. *True interpretation of the aggregate of* dharmas;[306] *F 47*

26cd. In fact, [however,] each aggregate of *dharmas* has been preached in order to cure or counteract a certain category [of behavior] of the faithful.[307]

With respect to their behavior [*carita*; ii. 26], sentient beings are 80,000 in number: some are dominated or distinguished [*bheda*] (1) by attachment [*rāga*], others (2) by hatred [*dveṣa*], (3) by delusion [*moha*], (4) by conceit [*māna*], etc.[308] 80,000 *aggregates of dharmas* have been uttered by the Fortunate One in order to cure or counteract these [behaviors].

.2. *Other* skandhas, āyatanas, dhātus *& their inclusion within the aggregates, sense-spheres, elements;*[309] *F 47–51*

27. **[Just as the 80,000 *aggregates of dharmas* are included in (the aggregates, i.e.,) the aggregate of material form or the aggregate of formations,] so also the other *skandhas*, *āyatanas* and *dhātus* [mentioned in other Sūtras] should be suitably arranged within the aggregates, sense-spheres and elements as described above, by taking into account the specific characteristics attributed to them.**[310] <48>

The other *skandhas*, *āyatanas* and *dhātus* mentioned in other Sūtras should be arranged within the five aggregates, twelve sense-spheres and eighteen elements, by taking into account the specific characteristics [*svalakṣaṇa*] attributed to them in this treatise [*śāstra*].

.2.1. *Five pure groups;*[311] *F 48*

There are five pure groups (*skandha*),[312]

1. morality (*śīla*; iv. 13),
2. concentration (*samādhi*; vi. 68),
3. superior knowledge (*prajñā*; ii. 25), {21 a}
4. liberation (*vimukti*; vi. 76a); and
5. cognition–insight of liberation (*vimuktijñānadarśana*):

the first is included in the aggregate of material form (*rūpaskandha*); the others (i.e., 2–5.) are included in the aggregate of formations (*saṃskāraskandha*) (*Saṃyutta*, i. 99; *Dīgha*, iii. 279; *Dharmasaṃgraha*, 23).

2.2. *Other spheres (āyatana);*[313] *F 48–49*

The first eight [of the ten] perception-spheres of totality (*kṛtsnāyatana*) (viii. 36) being non-greed (*alobha*) in their intrinsic nature are included in the sense-sphere of factors (*dharmāyatana*). If they are considered along with their following (*parivāra*), they are the five aggregates (*skandha*) in their intrinsic nature, and they are included in the sense-sphere of the mental faculty (*mana-āyatana*) and the sense-sphere of factors (*dharmāyatana*).

The same holds for the [eight] perception-spheres of mastery (*abhibhvāyatana*) (viii. 35).

The last two [of the ten] perception-spheres of totality (*kṛtsnāyatana*), [i.e., the infinite perception-spheres of space and of consciousness,] and the four formless perception-spheres (*ārūpyāyatana*; viii. 2c) are in their intrinsic nature the four aggregates (*skandha*), with the exclusion of material form (*rūpa*). They are included in the sense-sphere of the mental faculty (*mana-āyatana*) and the sense-sphere of factors (*dharmāyatana*).

The five gates of arrival into liberation (*vimuktyāyatana*)[314] are in their intrinsic nature speculative knowledge or understanding (*prajñā*); they are thus included in the sense-sphere of factors (*dharmāyatana*). If they are considered along with their following, they are included in the sense-sphere of sound (*śabdāyatana*), the sense-sphere of the mental faculty (*mana-āyatana*) and the sense-sphere of factors (*dharmāyatana*).

Two other *āyatana*s remain to be mentioned:[315]

1. the gods without ideation (*asaṃjñisattva*; ii. 41bd), included in the ten sense-spheres (*āyatana*), with the exception of odors and tastes; <49>
2. the approachers of the perception-sphere of neither-ideation-nor-non-ideation (*naivasaṃjñānāsaṃjñāyatanopaga*), included in the sense-sphere of the mental faculty (*mana-āyatana*) and the sense-sphere of factors (*dharma-āyatana*).

BBN.2.3. *Other elements (dhātu);*[316] *F 49–51*

BBN.2.3.1. *Sixty-two elements;*[317] *F 49*

In the same way, the sixty-two elements (*dhātu*) enumerated in the *Bahudhātuka* should be included within the eighteen elements by taking into account their nature [*yathāyogaṃ saṃgraha*].[318]

BBN.2.3.2. *Six elementary substances;*[319] *F 49–51*

Among the six elementary substances (*dhātu*)[320] of which the *Bahudhātukasūtra*[321] speaks,

1. elementary substance earth [*pṛthivīdhātu*],
2. elementary substance water [*abdhātu*],
3. elementary substance fire [*tejodhātu*],
4. elementary substance wind [*vāyudhatu*],
5. elementary substance space (*ākāśadhātu*),
6. elementary substance consciousness (*vijñānadhātu*),

the last two have not yet been defined.

2.3.2.a. *Elementary substance space (ākāśadhātu);*[322] *F 49–50*

[Question:] – Should we understand that the elementary substance space [*ākāśa-dhātu*] is the same factor as space (*ākāśa*), the first unconditioned factor (i. 5c)? {21 b}

[Answer: – No.]

28ab. Cavity or empty space is what is called the elementary substance space; according to the School [*kila*], [empty space or elementary substance space] is *light* and *darkness*.[323]

(1) The cavity or empty space [*chidra*] of the gate [*dvāra*], the window [*vātāyana*], etc., is the external (*bāhya*) elementary substance space; (2) the cavity of the mouth (*mukha*), the nose (*nāsikā*), etc., is the internal (*ādhyātmika*) elementary substance space.[324] <50>

According to the School (*kila*), empty space or the elementary substance space is light [*āloka*] and darkness [*tamas*] (i. 10), i.e., a certain category of color (*varṇa*), of matter or material form (*rūpa*; i. 9b), for what is perceived in a cavity is light or darkness. Being light or darkness in its intrinsic nature, empty space will be day and night in its intrinsic nature [*rātriṃdivasvabhāva*].[325]

Empty space is called *aghasāmantaka rūpa* (i.e., material form that is proximate to *agha*) (MVŚ, 388b5).

Agha, some say [*kila*], is explained etymologically as that which is exceedingly obstructive (*atyarthaṃ ghātāt*): "because it is exceedingly obstructive or obstructed".[326] *Agha* should thus be understood as solid, agglomerated matter or material form (*saṃcita rūpa*; *citastha rūpa*). Empty space is thus a type of matter that is proximate (*sāmantaka*) to *agha*.

According to another opinion, according to us, *agha* signifies "free from being obstructive" (*a-gha*). Empty space is *agha* because other matter is not obstructed by it [*apratighāta*]; it is, at the same time, proximate (*sāmantaka*) to other matter; it is thus *agha* and *sāmantaka*.

2.3.2.b. *Elementary substance consciousness (vijñānadhātu);*[327] *F 50–51*

[Question:] – Should we understand that all consciousness is the elementary substance consciousness?

[Answer: – No.]

28cd. The elementary substance consciousness is an impure consciousness, because it is the basis [*niśraya*] of the arising [of the *thought at conception* and of all existence until the *mind at death*].[328]

The impure (*sāsrava*) consciousness, i.e., the mind that does not form part of the (noble) path.

The six elementary substances are presented in the Sūtra (F 49, note) as basis [*sādhāraṇa*], as the *raison d'être* of the arising, i.e., of the *thought at conception* (*pratisaṃdhicitta*) and all of existence until the *thought at death* (*maraṇacitta*; *cyuti-citta*). <51>

The pure (*nirāsrava*) factors are opposed to arising, to existence. Thus the five sensory consciousnesses, which are always impure, and the mental consciousness, when it is impure, give us the elementary substance consciousness (MVŚ, 389a8).

Of these six elementary substances, [i.e., (1) elementary substance earth, (2) elementary substance water, (3) elementary substance fire, (4) elementary substance wind, (5) elementary substance space and (6) elementary substance consciousness,] the first four are included within the tangible (*spraṣṭavyadhātu*), the fifth is included within visible form (*rūpadhātu*), the sixth within the seven elements (*dhātu*) enumerated in i. 16c, [i.e., the six consciousnesses and the mental faculty].

TWENTY-TWO DOCTRINAL PERSPECTIVES ON THE EIGHTEEN ELEMENTS;[329] *F 51–102*

1. visible (*sanidarśana*) – invisible (*anidarśana*); F 51
2. resistant (*sapratigha*) – non-resistant (*apratigha*); F 51
3. wholesome (*kuśala*) – unwholesome (*akuśala*) – non-defined (*avyākṛta*); F 53
4. connected with/pertaining to (*pratisaṃyukta*) the realm of desire, realm of fine-materiality, realm of immateriality; F 54
5. impure (*sāsrava*) – pure (*anāsrava*); F 58
6. associated with initial inquiry and investigation (*savitarka-savicāra*) – free from initial inquiry but associated with investigation (*avitark-savicāra*) – free from initial inquiry and from investigation (*avitarka-avicāra*); F 62
7. having a cognitive object (*sālambana*) – not having a cognitive object (*anālambana*); F 62
8. appropriated (*upātta*) – non-appropriated (*anupātta*); F 62
9. primary matter (*bhūta*) – secondary matter (*bhautika*); F 63
10. aggregated (*saṃcita*) – non-aggregated (*asaṃcita*); F 66
11. that which cuts off (*chinnati*), is cut off (*chidyate*); that which burns (*dāhaka*), is burned (*dahyate*); that which weighs (*tulayati*), can be weighed (*tulya*); F 67
12. effect of retribution (*vipākaja*) – effect of accumulation (*aupacayika*) – effect of equal outflow (*naiṣyandika*); F 68
13. yoked with a [permanent] real (*dravyayukta*); F 70
14. momentary (*kṣaṇika*); F 71
15. acquiring accompaniment (*samanvāgamaṃ pratilambhate*) – accompaniment (*samanvāgama*); F 71
16. internal (*ādhyātmika*) – external (*bāhya*); F 73
17. homogeneous (*sabhāga*) – partially homogeneous (*tatsabhāga*); F 74
18. abandoned by insight (*darśanaheya*) – abandoned by cultivation (*bhāvanāheya*) – not to be abandoned (*aheya*); F 78
19. view (*dṛṣṭi*) – not view (*na dṛṣṭi*); F 80
20. consciousness (*vijñān*), object of consciousness/the cognized (*vijñeya*); F 100
21. permanent (*nitya*) – impermanent (*anitya*); F 100
22. controlling faculties (*indriya*) – not controlling faculties (*nendriya*); F 100–2

1. Visible (sanidarśana) and invisible (anidarśana) & the eighteen elements;[330] *F 51*

{ii 1 a}[331] Among the eighteen elements (*dhātu*), how many are visible or susceptible to be pointed at with the finger (*sanidarśana*)? [How many are invisible (*anidarśana*)?]

29ab. **[Among the eighteen elements,] the one element of visible form (*rūpadhātu*) is visible.**[332]

One can indicate its location and say "this one" [*idam*], "here" [*iha*], "there" [*amutra*]. The remaining [seventeen] elements are invisible.

BCB. *2. Resistant (sapratigha) and non-resistant (apratigha) & the eighteen elements;*[333] *F 51–53*

How many of the elements are resistant (*sapratigha*)? How many are non-resistant (*apratigha*)?

29bc. **The ten elements which are exclusively material (*rūpiṇaḥ*) are resistant.**[334]

The ten elements included in the aggregate of material form (*rūpaskandha*) are resistant (i. 13).[335] {1 b}

BCB.1. *Three types of obstruction (pratighāta);*[336] *F 51–52*

[Resistance (*pratigha*) means obstruction (*pratighāta*).[337]]

Obstruction (*pratighāta*, or *abhighāta*) is of three types:

1. obstruction qua obstacle (*āvaraṇapratighāta*);
2. obstruction qua object-field (*viṣayapratighāta*);
3. obstruction qua cognitive object (*ālambanapratighāta*) (MVŚ, 391c6).

BCB.1.1. *Obstruction qua obstacle (āvaraṇapratighāta);*[338] *F 51*

Obstruction qua obstacle (or "common" physical resistance) is the quality belonging to a body making a hindrance [*pratibandha*] to the arising of another body in its own place, the impenetrability.[339]

[For instance,] when the hand [*hasta*] encounters a hand or a rock [*upala*], or when the rock encounters a rock or a hand, it is obstructive, it is repelled (*pratihanyate*).

BCB.1.2. *Obstruction qua object-field (viṣayapratighāta);*[340] *F 51–52*

Obstruction qua object-field is the obstruction of the sense-faculty (*viṣayin*), [such as the eye, etc.] when it encounters its object-field (*viṣaya*), [such as visible form, etc.].[341] <52>

According to the *Prajñapti*:[342]

1. There is an eye, an eye sense-faculty, that is encountering (= is struck by) [*pratihanyate*] [its object-field, i.e., a visible form,] in water [*jala*] but not on land [*sthala*], namely, the eye of a fish [*matsya*].

2. There is an eye that encounters [its object-field] on land but not in water, namely, the eye of humans in general [*manuṣya*] (with the exclusion of fishermen).

3. There is an eye that encounters [its object-field] both in water and on land, namely, the eye of the crocodile [*śiśumāra*], frog [*maṇḍūka*], crab [or demon (*piśāca*)], of the fishermen [*kaivartta*].

4. There is an eye that encounters [its object-field] neither in water nor on dry land, namely, the eye which is none of the preceding categories (for example, the eye of sentient beings who perish in the womb).

[Moreover:]

1. There is an eye that encounters [its object-field] at night [*rātri*] [but not during the day (*divā*)], namely, the eye of the bat [*titīla*], owl [*ulūka*], etc.

2. There is an eye that encounters [its object-field] during the day, namely, the eye of humans in general (with the exclusion of thieves, etc.).

3. There is an eye that encounters [its object-field] at night and during the day, namely, the eye of the dog [*śvan*], jackal [*śṛgāla*], horse [*turaga*], leopard [*dvīpin*], cat [*mārjāra*], etc.

4. There is an eye that encounters [its object-field] neither at night nor during the day, namely, the eye which is none of the preceding categories.[343] {2 a}

:B.1.3. *Obstruction qua cognitive object (ālambanapratighāta);*[344] *F 52*

Obstruction qua cognitive object is the encounter of thought and thought-concomitants (*citta, caitta*) with their cognitive object (*svālambana*) (ii. 62c).[345]

:B.1.4. *Difference between object-field (viṣaya) and cognitive object (ālambana);*[346] *F 52*

What is the difference between (1) the object-field (*viṣaya*) and (2) the cognitive object (*ālambana*)?

1. By *viṣaya*, one understands that place where [the eye, ear, etc.,] exercises its operation [*kāritra*],[347] i.e., seeing, hearing, etc.[348]

2. By *ālambana*, one understands that which is grasped by thought and thought-concomitants [*cittacaitta*].[349]

Thus, whereas thought and thought-concomitants have an object-field and a cognitive object, the eye, the ear, etc., have only an object-field.

BCB.1.5. *Meaning of pratighāta in viṣayapratighāta and ālambanapratighāta; F 52*

Why is the issuing forth (*pravṛtti*) or operation (*kāritra*) of the sense-faculty or of the thought with respect to its [own] object-field (*viṣaya*) or its [own] cognitive object (*ālambana*) called *obstruction* (*pratighāta*)?[350]

1. Because the sense-faculty does not issue forth [*apravṛtti*], is not active, beyond the object-field: thus it is obstructed by the object-field [for, in common usage, it is said that one is obstructed by a wall beyond which one cannot "proceed"].

2. Or rather, by *obstruction* one understands "encounter, meeting, or the arrival there" (*nipāta, nipatana*): this is the issuing forth or operation (*pravṛtti* = *kāritra*) of the sense-faculty with respect to its own object-field. <53>

BCB.2. *Ten elements and obstruction qua obstacle; F 53*

When we say that ten elements are resistant (*sapratigha*), "characterized by obstruction (*pratighāta*)", we are speaking of the obstruction qua obstacle (*āvaraṇa-pratighāta*): these are bodies that are mutually impenetrable, susceptible of collision.

BCB.3. *Tetralemma between* obstruction qua object-field & obstruction qua obstacle; *F 53*

You may ask if the factors that are resistant (*sapratigha*) in terms of obstruction qua object-field (*viṣayapratighāta*) are also resistant in terms of obstruction qua obstacle (*āvaraṇapratighāta*).

Four alternatives (tetralemma):

i. the seven elements of thought (*cittadhātu*; i. 16c) and one part of the element of factors (*dharmadhātu*), namely, the associated factors (*saṃprayukta*; ii. 23), are resistant only in terms of obstruction qua object-field;
ii. the five object-fields, i.e., visible form, etc., (i. 9), are resistant only in terms of obstruction qua obstacle;
iii. the five sense-faculties, i.e., the eye, etc., (i. 9), are resistant from two points of view [i.e., qua object-field and qua obstacle];
iv. one part of the element of factors, namely, the dissociated factors (*viprayukta*; ii. 35), is not resistant (*sapratigha*).

BCB.4. *Relationship between "obstruction qua object-field" & "obstruction qua cognitive object"; F 53*

You may ask if the factors that are resistant in terms of obstruction qua object-field [*viṣayapratighāta*] are also resistant in terms of obstruction qua cognitive object (*ālambanapratighāta*). {2 b}

We answer by speaking of that which accords with the latter (and not the former) alternative (*paścātpādaka*), namely, the factors that are resistant in terms of obstruction qua cognitive object are also resistant in terms of obstruction qua object-field. But there are factors that are resistant in terms of obstruction qua object-field without at the same time being resistant in terms of obstruction qua cognitive object, namely, the five sense-faculties.

.5. Sapratigha *and* apratigha *according to Kumāralābha; F 53*

The Bhadanta Kumāralābha says:

1. We call *sapratigha* that in which [i.e., the sense-faculty] and with regard to which [i.e., the object-field] a consciousness or mental faculty (*manas*) can be obstructed from arising by a foreign [body];
2. in the contrary case, it is *apratigha*.[351]

[*Resistant* and *non-resistant* have now been discussed.]

3. Wholesome (kuśala), unwholesome (akuśala), non-defined (avyākṛta) & the eighteen elements;[352] *F 53–54*

Among the eighteen elements, how many are wholesome (*kuśala*), unwholesome (*akuśala*), non-defined (*avyākṛta*) (iv. 8, 9, 45)?[353] <54>

29cd. **Eight elements [among the ten elements that are exclusively material] are (morally) non-defined, namely, the preceding [ten elements] minus visible form and sound.**[354]

The ten elements spoken of as resistant (*sapratigha*; i. 29bc), minus visible form (*rūpa*) and sound (*śabda*)[355]—i.e., the eight elements: the five material sense-faculties; odor; taste; and the tangible—are non-defined, because of not being defined as wholesome or unwholesome,[356] or else, according to another opinion, because of not being defined from the point of view of [karmic] ripening (*vipāka*).

30a. **The other [ten of the eighteen elements] are of three types [i.e., wholesome, unwholesome, or non-defined].**[357]

The other ten [of the eighteen] elements are, according to the case, [either] wholesome, unwholesome, or non-defined (iv, F 33ff.). [Among these ten elements,]

1–7. the seven elements [of thought] (*cittadhātavaḥ*; i. 16c) are:

i. wholesome when they are associated with the three wholesome roots [i.e., non-greed (*alobha*); non-hatred (*adveṣa*); non-delusion (*amoha*); ii, F. 160; iv. 8],

ii. unwholesome when they are associated with the unwholesome roots [i.e., greed, hatred, delusion; v. 20ab],
iii. non-defined in all other cases;[358] {3 a}

8. the element of factors (*dharmadhātu*; i. 15cd) includes:

i. the wholesome roots, factors associated with these roots, factors arisen from these roots,[359] the cessation due to deliberation (*pratisaṃkhyānirodha*) or *nirvāṇa* [see iv. 8bc], [which are all wholesome];
ii. the unwholesome roots, factors associated with these roots, factors arisen from these roots, [which are all unwholesome];
iii. the other factors, for example, space [*ākāśa*], which are non-defined;

9–10. the element of visible form (*rūpadhātu*) and the element of sound (*śabdadhātu*) are:

i–ii. wholesome or unwholesome when they are included in bodily or vocal action (iv. 26; 3d) arisen from a wholesome or unwholesome thought;
iii. non-defined in all other cases.

[Wholesome, unwholesome and non-defined have now been discussed.]

BCD. *4. Connected with (pratisaṃyukta) the realm of desire, realm of fine-materiality and realm of immateriality & the eighteen elements;*[360] *F 54–58*

Among the eighteen elements, how many exist in each of the realms of existence, i.e., the realm of desire, the realm of fine-materiality, the realm of immateriality (iii. 1–3)?[361]

.BCD.1. *Realm of desire & the eighteen elements;*[362] *F 54–55*

30ab. All [eighteen elements] exist in the realm of desire.[363] <55>

All the elements are connected with or pertain to (*pratisaṃyukta*) the realm of desire, not dissociated from the realm of desire (MVŚ, 746c1).

BCD.2. *Realm of fine-materiality & the fourteen elements;*[364] *F 55–57*

30b-d. Fourteen elements exist in the realm of fine-materiality, with the exception of odor, taste, olfactory consciousness, gustatory consciousness.[365]

BCD.2.1. *Odor and taste are lacking because they are material food;*[366] *F 55*

Odor and taste are lacking there, for they constitute material food [*kavadīkāra-āhāratva*; iii. 39], and no one is born into the realm of fine-materiality who is not detached [*vītarāga*] from this kind of food.[367] [Since the cognitive objects (*ālambana*), i.e.,] odor and taste are lacking, the olfactory and the gustatory consciousness are also lacking.

Objection: – The tangible (*spraṣṭavyadhātu*) should also be lacking, for it also constitutes material food.

[Answer:] – No, for the tangible is not exclusively food. The tangible which is not food [in its intrinsic nature] does exist in the realm of fine-materiality. {3 b}

Objection: – One can reason in the same way in regard to odor and taste.

[Answer:] – No. The tangible has a useful function (*pariviṣṭi*) apart from food:

1. it serves as a basis of the sense-faculties (*āśrayabhāva*);
2. it serves as a support in general (*ādhārabhāva*);
3. it serves as garment [*prāvaraṇabhāva*].

Outside of consumption (*āhārābhyavahāra*), odor and taste have no use (*paribhoga*): they have no utility [*niṣprayojana*] for sentient beings detached [*vītarāga*] from food.

D.2.2. *Śrīlābha: Odor and taste are lacking because of a certain tangible;* F 55

Śrīlābha gives a different explanation. – When persons in the realm of desire enter into meditative attainments [*samāpatti*], enter into meditation (*dhyāna*), they see visible forms; they hear sounds; their body is favored, comforted (*anugrah*) by a certain tangible that accompanies the bodily pliancy (*praśrabdhi*) produced by the meditation (viii. 9b).[368] It can be concluded from this fact that, in the celestial abodes of the realm of fine-materiality which bear the name *meditation* (*dhyāna*; i.e., meditation as birth [*upapattidhyāna*], iii. 2; viii. 1), there are [only] visible form, sound, tangible, but not taste and odor. <56>

D.2.3. *Vasubandhu & the number of elements in the realm of fine-materiality;*[369] F 56–57

[Vasubandhu:[370]] – We think that, if odor and taste are absent in the realm of fine-materiality, the nose and the tongue sense-faculties should also be absent there, for they have no utility [*niṣprayojana*] there. Thus there would be only twelve elements in the realm of fine-materiality.

Answer by a scholar who substitutes for the Vaibhāṣikas (*vaibhāṣikadeśīya*): – The nose and the tongue sense-faculties have a utility in the realm of fine-materiality, for, without them, [respectively,] bodily beauty [*āśrayaśobhā*] and elocution or communication [*vyavahāra*] could not occur.

[Vasubandhu:] – The nose, i.e., the physical seat [*adhiṣṭhāna*] of the subtle matter which constitutes the nose sense-faculty, suffices for beauty [*śobhā*], leaving aside subtle matter (i. 44); the tongue, i.e., the physical seat of the tongue sense-faculty, suffices for elocution [*vacana*], leaving aside subtle matter which constitutes the tongue sense-faculty.

The *Vaibhāṣikadeśīya*: – The physical seat, i.e., the nose and the tongue, which supports the sense-faculty, cannot be without this sense-faculty. There is no nose, no tongue where the subtle matter, which constitutes the nose or the tongue sense-faculty, is lacking. In the same way, the male sexual organ is always invested with this special body sense-faculty called *male sexual faculty* (*puruṣendriya*) (i. 44a; ii. 2cd).

[Vasubandhu:] – One can very well conceive that the sexual organ is absent when the sexual faculty is absent, for, being left without this faculty, the sexual organ has no utility; but [the physical seats of] the nose and the tongue have a utility independent of the nose and tongue sense-faculties. Thus [the physical seats of] the nose and tongue exist in the realm of fine-materiality although the corresponding sense-faculties are absent there. Thus there would be only twelve elements in the realm of fine-materiality.

Answer by the Vaibhāṣika: – A sense-faculty can arise without having any utility, for example, the sense-faculties of sentient beings destined to perish in the womb.

[Vasubandhu:] – Agreed! The arising of a sense-faculty can be without utility: but it is never without a cause [*nirhetuka*]. {4 a} What is the cause of the arising of a sense-faculty, if not a certain [past] action [*karmaviśeṣa*] commanded by craving [*tṛṣṇā*] related to this sense-faculty? But whoever is without craving [*vitṛṣṇa*] for the object-field, odor, is also without craving for the sense-faculty, the nose sense-faculty. Thus, there is no reason for the nose and tongue sense-faculties to appear among sentient beings who are reborn in the realm of fine-materiality, since these sentient beings are detached from [the object-fields, i.e.,] odors and tastes. Or else, tell us, why is the sexual faculty absent in the realm of fine-materiality? <57>

Answer by the Vaibhāṣika: – The sexual faculty is a cause of ugliness [*aśobhākaratva*; ii. 12].

[Vasubandhu:] – Is it not beautiful among the sentient beings who possess the marks of the Mahāpuruṣas?[371] Moreover, it is not because of its utility that the sexual faculty arises, but rather because of its cause [*svakaraṇa*]. The cause being given, it will arise, even if it is ugly.

D.2.3.1. *Vaibhāṣika: argument from scriptural authority and logical reasoning that there are fourteen elements;* F 57

Argument from authority.

Vaibhāṣika: – To maintain that the nose and tongue sense-faculties are absent in the realm of fine-materiality is to contradict the Sūtra. The Sūtra[372] teaches that sentient beings of the realm of fine-materiality possess all of the sense-faculties (*ahīna–indriya*), all sense-faculties in a complete or unimpaired way (*avikalendriya*): they are never one-eyed (*kāṇa*) or one-eared (*kuṇṭha*) (iii. 98a).

[Reply:] – This text teaches that sentient beings of the realm of fine-materiality possess, completely, the faculties that [actually do] exist in the realm of fine-materiality. If the Vaibhāṣikas do not understand it in this way, [it would entail that] they should attribute the sexual faculty to these sentient beings.

Answer [based on logical reasoning] and conclusion by the Vaibhāṣika: – Although odor and taste are absent there, the nose and tongue sense-faculties [do indeed] exist in the realm of fine-materiality.

In fact, the persons who are detached from odor retain the attachment in regard to the nose sense-faculty as being part of the person (*ātmabhāva, svasaṃtāna*). Craving enters into action with regard to these six sense-faculties of consciousness, not because of the object-field of these six sense-faculties, but because of the persons themselves (*ātmabhāvamukhena*). Thus the arising of the nose and tongue sense-faculties has a cause, even if one were detached from odors and tastes.

The same does not hold for the sexual faculty. The craving related to this faculty is in regard to craving for the tactile consciousness of sexual union.[373] But sentient beings who will be reborn in the realm of fine-materiality are detached from the aforementioned consciousness; thus they have not accomplished the action commanded by craving related to the sexual faculty, and therefore this faculty is absent in the realm of fine-materiality.[374] {4 b} <58>

[Thus, it has been established that there are fourteen elements that exist in the realm of fine-materiality.]

D.3. *Realm of immateriality & the three elements;*[375] F 58

31ab. **In the realm of immateriality, there are [only] (1) the mental faculty (*manodhātu*), (2) the object of the mental consciousness (*dharmadhātu*), (3) the mental consciousness (*manovijñānadhātu*).**[376]

Sentient beings detached [*vītarāga*] from matter (*rūpa*) arise in the realm of immateriality.

The ten elements that are material form in their intrinsic nature, namely, the five sense-faculties and their object-referents, and the five consciousnesses that have a material element for their basis [*āśraya*] and for their cognitive object [*ālambana*] are thus absent in Ārūpya (viii. 3c).

BCE. *5. Impure (sāsrava) and pure (anāsrava) & the eighteen elements;*[377] *F 58*

How many elements are impure [*sāsrava*]? How many are pure [*anāsrava*]?

31cd. **The three elements which have just been named, [i.e., the mental faculty, the object of the mental consciousness, the mental consciousness,] are [either] (1) pure [when they are part of the truth of the path or of the unconditioned] or (2) impure [in the opposite case].**[378]

They are:

1. pure (*anāsrava*) when they are part of the truth of the path [*mārgasatya*] or of the unconditioned [*asaṃskṛta*];
2. impure [*sāsrava*] [in the opposite case (i. 4)].

31d. **The other elements, [fifteen in number,] are [solely] impure.**[379]

The other elements, fifteen in number, are solely impure.[380] <59>

BCF. *6. Associated with initial inquiry and investigation (savitarka-savicāra) – free from initial inquiry but associated with investigation (avitarka-savicāra) – free from initial inquiry and from investigation (avitarka-avicāra) & the eighteen elements;*[381] *F 59–61*

How many elements are (1) associated with initial inquiry and with investigation [*savitarkāḥ savicārāḥ*; ii. 28, 33], (2) free from initial inquiry but associated with investigation [*avitarkā vicāramātrāḥ*], (3) free from initial inquiry and investigation [*avitarkā vicārāḥ*]?[382]

BCF.1. *Associated with initial inquiry and investigation & the first five consciousnesses;*[383] *F 59*

32ab. **[Vaibhāṣikas: – The first] five [of the seven] consciousness-elements always (*hi*) involve initial inquiry and investigation.**[384] {5 a}

[The first five of the seven consciousness-elements] are always [*nityam*] associated with initial inquiry (*vitarka*) and with investigation (*vicāra*), for these [consciousnesses] are gross, being turned toward the outside.[385] The word *hi*, "always", ["indeed",] indicates restriction [*avadhāraṇa*]: they are exclusively factors involving initial inquiry and investigation.

2. *Three kinds & the last three elements;*[386] *F 59–60*

32c. The last three [of the eighteen] elements, [i.e., the mental faculty, the object of mental consciousness and the mental consciousness,] are of three kinds [that is, (1) associated with initial inquiry and with investigation, (2) free from initial inquiry but associated with investigation, (3) free from both initial inquiry and investigation].[387]

These elements are the mental faculty (*manodhātu*), the factors, i.e., the object of mental consciousness (*dharmadhātu*), the mental consciousness (*manovijñānadhātu*). [These three elements are of three kinds (*prakāra*).]

1. In the realm of desire and in the first meditation (*dhyāna*; viii. 7, 11), (i) the mental faculty (*manodhātu*, (ii) the element of mental consciousness (*manovijñānadhātu*), (iii) that part of the element of factors (*dharmadhātu*) which is associated with thought (ii. 23), except for initial inquiry and investigation themselves, are *associated with initial inquiry and with investigation.*

2. In the intermediate meditation (*dhyānāntara*) (viii. 22d), these same elements are *free from initial inquiry but associated with investigation.*

3. In the higher stages (*bhūmi*), [i.e., beginning with the second meditation] up to and including the last stage (*naivasaṃjñānāsaṃjñāyatana*; *bhavāgra*), these same elements are *free from both initial inquiry and investigation* (viii. 23cd).

4. The part of the elements of factors which is dissociated from thought (ii. 35) and the investigation of the special meditation [*dhyānāntara*] are also *free from both initial inquiry and investigation.* <60>

5. As for initial inquiry [itself], it is always accompanied by investigation and it is always free from initial inquiry, in view of the impossibility of two simultaneous initial inquiries.[388]

But investigation [itself], in the realm of desire and in the first meditation, are not included within any of the three kinds: in fact, there it is always associated with initial inquiry and is never accompanied by investigation, in view of the impossibility of two simultaneous investigations.

Thus we say that, in the stages (*bhūmi*) involving both initial inquiry and investigation (viii. 7), there are four categories (*prakāra*):

i. factors associated with thought, except for initial inquiry and investigation, are *associated with initial inquiry and investigation*; {5 b}
ii. initial inquiry is *free from initial inquiry but associated with investigation*;
iii. factors dissociated from thought are *free from initial inquiry and investigation*;
iv. investigation is *free from investigation but associated with initial inquiry.*

BCF.3. *Free from initial inquiry and investigation & the other ten elements;*[389] *F 60*

32d. The other elements [i.e., the ten material elements] are free from both [i.e., initial inquiry and investigation].[390]

The other elements are the ten material (*rūpin*) elements. Not being associated with thought, they are [always] free from initial inquiry (*vitarka*) and investigation (*vicāra*).

BCF.4. *Associated with initial inquiry and investigation & free from conceptualizing activity (avikalpaka);*[391] *F 60–61*

But, if the [first] five sensory consciousnesses are always associated with initial inquiry and investigation, how are they defined as *free from conceptualizing activity* (*avikalpaka*)?

33ab. [The first five sensory consciousnesses] are *free from conceptualizing activity* insofar as they are free from conceptualizing activity consisting of examining and from conceptualizing activity consisting of recollecting, [but they include conceptualizing activity in its intrinsic nature].[392]

BCF.4.1. *Three types of conceptualizing activity (vikalpa);*[393] *F 60–61*

According to the Vaibhāṣika [*kila*],[394] conceptualizing activity (*vikalpa*) is of three kinds:[395]

1. conceptualizing activity in its intrinsic nature (*svabhāvavikalpa*);
2. conceptualizing activity consisting of examining (*nirūpaṇā*; *abhinirūpaṇā*);[396]
3. conceptualizing activity consisting of recollecting (*anusmaraṇa*).[397] <61>

The five sensory consciousnesses involve the first kind of conceptualizing activity but not the other two kinds.[398] This is why they are said to be *free from conceptualizing activity* [*avikalpaka*], as when a horse has only one foot [*ekapādaka*], it is said that it has no feet [*apādaka*].

The conceptualizing activity in its intrinsic nature or by definition [*svabhāvavikalpa*] is the initial inquiry (*vitarka*), which we will study in the chapter on the thought-concomitants (*caitta*) (ii. 33).[399]

As for [the intrinsic nature (*svabhāva*) of] the other two conceptualizing activities:

33cd. **(1) Dispersed mental understanding [is the conceptualizing activity consisting of examining or of defining]; (2) [all] mental recollection, whatever it may be, [is the conceptualizing activity consisting of recollecting].**[400]

1. Mental understanding (*prajñā*; ii. 24), i.e., the discernment of the factors associated with the mental consciousness [only, i.e., not with the sensory consciousnesses], when dispersed (*vyagra*), {6 a} i.e., non-concentrated (*asamāhita*), not in the state of meditating [*bhāvanā*; viii. 1], is the conceptualizing activity consisting of examining [*nirūpaṇā*] or of defining (*abhinirūpaṇāvikalpa*).[401]

2. All "mental" recollection (*smṛti*), when either concentrated [*samāhita*] or non-concentrated, is the conceptualizing activity consisting of recollecting (*anusmaraṇa-vikalpa*).[402] <62>

7. Having a cognitive object (sālambana) and not having a cognitive object (anālambana) & the eighteen elements;[403] *F 62*

How many elements are *having a cognitive object* (*sālambana*), i.e., are the subject-matter of the consciousness? [How many are *not having a cognitive object* (*an-ālambana*)?]

34ab. **Seven [elements, i.e.,] the elements of thought, are *having a cognitive object.***[404]

(1–5) The elements of the visual, auditory, olfactory, gustatory and tactile consciousness, (6) the element of the mental consciousness and (7) the mental faculty [*mano-dhātu*], [these seven elements of thought (*cittadhātu*)] are *having a cognitive object* (*sālambana*) only, because they always seize their object-field (*viṣaya*).

34b. **And also one part of the element of factors [is *having a cognitive object*].**[405]

That part [of the element of factors (*dharmadhātu*)] which consists of the factors associated with thought [or related to thought] [*caitasikasvabhāva*; ii. 23], [is *having a cognitive object* (*sālambana*)].

The other elements, namely, the ten material elements and the part of the element of factors which is not associated with thought (ii. 35), are *not having a cognitive object* [*anālambana*].

BCH. *8. Appropriated (upātta) and non-appropriated (anupātta) & the eighteen elements;*[406] *F 62–63*

How many elements are non-appropriated (*anupātta*)? How many are appropriated [*upātta*]?

34cd. Nine [of the eighteen elements] are non-appropriated, namely, the eight elements which have just been mentioned, [i.e., the seven elements of thought and one part of the element of factors,] and sound.[407]

(1–7) The seven elements of thought [*cittadhātu*; i. 16c] [said to have cognitive objects (*sālambana*)], (8) [one part of] the element of factors (*dharmadhātu*; i. 15c) and (9) sound (*śabdadhātu*) are never appropriated, [i.e., are non-appropriated].

34d. The other nine [of the eighteen elements] are of two kinds [i.e., sometimes appropriated, sometimes non-appropriated].[408] {6 b}

They are sometimes appropriated [*upātta*] and sometimes non-appropriated [*anupātta*]. (1) The five sense-faculties of the sensory consciousness (i.e., element of the eye, etc.), when they are present, are appropriated. (2) Those sense-faculties, when they are future and past, are non-appropriated. <63>

1. The four object-fields—visible form, odor, taste and tangible—when they are present, when they are not separated from or are an integral part of the sense-faculties (*indriyābhinna, indriyāvinirbhāga*), are appropriated.
2. Any other visible form, any other odor, any other taste, any other tangible, is non-appropriated; for example:
   - i. the visible form—color and shape—of head hair [*keśa*], body hair [*roma*], nails [*nakha*] and teeth [*danta*], with the exception of their roots [*mūla*], which are tied up with the body or the body sense-faculty;
   - ii. the color and shape of excrement [*viṣ*], urine [*mūtra*], saliva [*kheṭa*], mucus [*siṅghāṇaka*], blood [*śoṇita*], etc.;
   - iii. the color and shape of earth [*bhūmi*], water [*udaka*], fire, etc.

BCH.1. *Meaning of the expression* appropriated *(upātta);*[409] *F 63*

[Question:] – How should the expression *upātta*, appropriated, be explained?

[Answer:] – That which thought and thought-concomitants seize (*upagṛhīta*) and appropriate (*svīkṛta*) to themselves in the quality of a support or physical seat (*adhiṣṭhāna*) is called *appropriated.* Organic matter, i.e., the matter which constitutes the five sense-faculties of consciousness, as well as the matter not separable from the organic matter, is *appropriated*, is *made one's own*, by thought: this results from the fact that, in the case of well-being [or benefit; *anugraha*] or of sickness [or injury; *upaghāta*], there is a reciprocal reaction [*anyonānuvidhāna*] between thought and this matter. The matter called *appropriated* by the Abhidharma is, in the common language [*loka*], called *sacetana* (animate matter), *sajīva* (living matter).[410]

I. *9. Primary matter (bhūtasvabhāva) and secondary matter (bhautika) & the eighteen elements;*[411] *F 63–66*

How many elements (*dhātu*) are primary matter or fundamental material elements [in their intrinsic nature (*bhūtasvabhāva*)]? How many are secondary matter or derivative material elements [*bhautika*]?[412] {7 a} <64>

35ac. **The tangible is of two kinds [i.e., primary matter and secondary matter]. The other nine material elements are solely secondary matter, as is also the part of the element of factors [i.e., the non-informative] that is material.**[413]

(1) The four fundamental material elements (themselves): solidity [*khara*], humidity [*sneha*], heat [*uṣṇatā*] and mobility [*īraṇā*] (i. 12), and (2) the sevenfold secondary matter: smoothness [*ślakṣṇatva*], roughness [*karkaśatva*], [heaviness (*gurutva*), lightness (*laghutva*), coldness (*śīta*), hunger (*jighatsā*) and thirst (*pipāsā*) (i. 10d),] are tangibles.

The other nine material elements (i. 15cd), i.e., the five sense-faculties, the object-fields of the first four sense-faculties, are solely secondary matter.

Likewise the part of the element of factors (*dharmadhātu*; i. 15cd) that is called the *non-informative* [*avijñaptisaṃjñaka*; i. 11] [is solely secondary matter].

The [remaining seven] elements of thought [*cittadhātu*; i. 16c] are neither primary matter nor secondary matter.

Likewise the element of factors (*dharmadhātu*), except for the non-informative (*avijñapti*), [is neither primary matter nor secondary matter].

.1. *Refutation of Bhadanta Buddhadeva's view that the ten sense-spheres are solely primary matter; F 64–65*

According to the Bhadanta Buddhadeva, the [first] ten sense-spheres (*āyatana*), i.e., the five sense-faculties of consciousness and their object-fields, are solely primary matter [*bhūtamātra*].[414]

[Reply:] – An inadmissible opinion. The Sūtra teaches, in a restrictive manner [*avadhāraṇa*], that there are four fundamental material elements and defines them in a restrictive manner as being solid, humid, etc. (i. 12d). But solidity, humidity, etc., are tangibles and tangibles only: hardness [*kāṭhinya*] is not perceived by the eye sense-faculty. Besides, each sense-faculty attains the secondary matter suitable to it: color [*varṇa*] is not perceived by the body sense-faculty.[415] <65>

Furthermore, that the tangible is primary matter (*bhūta*) and secondary matter (*upādāya rūpa*), that the other nine material sense-spheres are [not the primary matter itself, but] secondary matter only, is clearly shown by the very words of the Sūtra:

> The eye, O *bhikṣu*, is the internal [*ādhyātmika*] sense-sphere of the consciousness (i. 39), {7 b} subtle matter [*rūpaprasāda*] derived from the four fundamental material elements [*upādāya*), material [*rūpin*], invisible [*anidarśana*], resistant [*sapratigha*],

and so on with respect to the other four material sense-faculties which are described in the same terms.

With respect to that which concerns the first four object-fields:

> Visible forms (*rūpāṇi*), O *bhikṣu*, are the external [*bāhya*] sense-sphere of the consciousness, derived from the four fundamental material elements, material, visible [*sanidarśana*], resistant.
>
> Sound, O *bhikṣu*, is the external sense-sphere of the consciousness, derived from the four fundamental material elements, material, invisible, resistant.

The same for that which concerns odor and taste. But, with respect to the tangible:

> The tangibles, O *bhikṣu*, are the external sense-sphere of the consciousness, the four fundamental material elements and matter derived from the four fundamental material elements, material, invisible, resistant.[416]

BCI.2. *Interpretation of various Sūtra passages; F 65–66*

[Objection:] – One can maintain that the five sense-faculties are primary matter, for the Sūtra (*Saṃyukta*, 11, 1) says:[417]

> Everything that is in the eye, the ball of flesh (*māṃsapiṇḍa*), is solid, resistant... (*khakkhaṭa, kharagata*...).

Answer: – Here the Sūtra refers to the ball of flesh which is not separable from the eye sense-faculty, and does not refer to the actual sense-faculty itself. <66>

[Objection:] – So be it. But the *Garbhāvakrāntisūtra* (F 49 note) states:

> The person consists of six elementary substances (*dhātu*),[418]

i.e., (1) the elementary substance earth [*pṛthivīdhātu*], (2) the elementary substance water [*abdhātu*], (3) the elementary substance fire [*tejodhātu*], (4) the elementary substance wind [*vāyudhātu*], (5) the elementary substance space [*ākāśadhātu*] and (6) the elementary substance consciousness [*vijñānadhātu*]. Thus, in the embryonic state [*kalala*], the body is primary matter, not secondary matter.

[Answer:] – No. For, in this first sentence: "The person consists of six elementary substances", the Sūtra wants to describe the fundamental substances making up a person (*maulasattvadravya*)[419] and does not pretend to give an exhaustive definition. In fact, the Sūtra later says that the person consists of the six bases or sense-spheres of the mental factor called *contact* (ii. 24) (*sparśa–āyatana*), i.e., the six sense-faculties.[420] Besides, to take the definition "The person consists of six elementary substances" literally would entail the non-existence of the thought-concomitants (*caitta*; ii. 24, 34), for the thought-concomitants are not included within the element of consciousness (*vijñānadhātu*), which is thought.

[Objection:] – Could one not maintain that the thought-concomitants are thought [*citta*] and, therefore, are included in the element of consciousness?

[Answer:] – No, for the Sūtra says:

> Sensation [*vedanā*] and ideation (*saṃjñā*) are mental factors (*dharma*), i.e., factors related to thought (*caitasika*), {8 a} having thought for their basis;

and the Sūtra speaks of "thought that is with attachment" (*sarāgacitta*; vii. 11d); thus attachment, which is a thought-concomitant, is not thought.

It is thus established that [the ten material elements consist of fundamental material elements and derivative material elements, and that] our definitions (i. 35ac) are correct.[421]

10. Aggregated (saṃcita) and non-aggregated (asaṃcita) & the eighteen elements; F 66–67

How many elements (*dhātu*) are aggregated [*saṃcita*]? [How many are non-aggregated (*asaṃcitā*)?] <67>

35d. The ten material elements are aggregated.[422]

The five sense-faculties [*indriya*] of the sensory consciousness and their object-fields [*viṣaya*] are [aggregated because they are] agglomerations or composites of atoms (*paramāṇusaṃghāta*; accumulations of atoms [*paramāṇusaṃcaya*]) (ii. 22).

[This establishes that the remaining eight elements are not-aggregated.[423]]

BCK. *11. That which cuts off (chinnati), is cut off (chidyate); that which burns (dāhaka), is burned (dahyate); that which weighs (tulayati), can be weighed (tulya) & the eighteen elements;*[424] *F 67–68*

BCK.1. *That which cuts off (chinnati), is cut off (chidyate); F 67*

Among the eighteen elements, how many cut off [*chinnati*], how many are cut off [*chidyate*]; how many burn [*dahati*], how many are burned [*dahyate*]; how many weigh [*tulayati*], how many are weighed [*tulyate*]?

36ab. Four external elements [i.e., visible form, odor, taste, tangible] cut off [when they bear the name of axe, etc.] and are cut off [when they bear the name of wood, etc.].[425]

Visible form [*rūpa*], odor [*gandha*], taste [*rasa*] and tangible [*spraṣṭavya*] cut off when they bear the name of axe [*paraśu*], etc., and they are cut off when they bear the name of wood [*dārva*], etc.

[Question:] – What is the factor called *cutting off* [*cheda*]?

[Answer:] – To produce the sectioning [*vibhaktotpādana*] of the stream consisting of a composite[426] [*saṃghātasrotas*] the nature of which is to arise continuously [*saṃbandhotpādin*]. {8 b} The axe cuts off a piece of wood which is a "stream" and makes it into two "streams" which exist and develop separately.

The sense-faculties cannot be cut off. For example, the body sense-faculty [*kāya-indriya*] [itself]—when cutting off all the members [of the fleshly body] [*nir-avaśeṣāṅgaccheda*]—is, for all this, not duplicated or multiplied [*advaidha*]: the members that have been cut off, i.e., amputated from the trunk, do not possess the body sense-faculty.

Moreover, the sense-faculties do not cut off because of their translucidity or transparency (*acchatva*),[427] just like the light or glitter of a [luminescent] gem [*maṇi-prabhā*].

BCK.2. *That which burns (dāhaka), is burned (dahyate); that which weighs (tulayati), can be weighed (tulya); F 67–68*

36c. In the same way, [four external elements, i.e., visible form, odor, taste and tangible,] are burned and weigh.[428]

The same holds for being burned [*dāhyate*] and for weighing [*tulayati*] as for cutting off and for being cut off.

The [same] four external elements are burned. The same weigh, for example, when they constitute a scale. Not so the sense-faculties, because of their translucidity or transparency [*acchatva*], just like the light or glitter of a [luminescent] gem [*maṇi-prabhā*].

Sound does not cut, is not cut off, is not burned, does not weigh, because it [perishes momentarily (*uccheditva*) and] does not exist in a [continuous] stream (*apravāha-vartitva*).

36d. **There is no agreement with respect to what burns and what is weighed.**[429] <68>

According to some, the same four external elements burn and are weighed.

According to others, only the elementary substance fire (*tejodhātu*) burns, namely when it manifests its particular manner of being in flames; only heaviness (*gurutva*), which is one type of secondary matter (i. 10d), is weighed, but lightweight factors, light, etc., cannot be weighed, although material form (*rūpa*) manifests its particular manner of being in them.

12. *Effect of retribution (vipākaja), effect of accumulation (aupacayika), effect of equal outflow (naiṣyandika) & the eighteen elements;*[430] *F 68–70*

Among the eighteen elements (*dhātu*), how many are an effect of retribution (*vipākaja*), an effect of accumulation (*aupacayika*), an effect of equal outflow (*naiṣyandika*)?[431]

37–38a. **(1) The five internal [*adhyātma*] elements, [i.e., the five sense-faculties, except for the mental faculty,] are an effect of retribution and an effect of accumulation; (2) [the external element] sound is not an effect of retribution; (3) the eight elements free from resistance [i.e., the seven elements of thought and the element of factors,] are an effect of equal outflow and also an effect of retribution; (4) the others, [i.e., the external elements of visible form, odor, taste and tangible,] are of three types [i.e., an effect of retribution, of accumulation and of equal outflow].**[432] {9 a}

..1. *Definitions; F 68–69*

..1.1. *Definition of effect of retribution (vipākaja); F 68–69*

Vipākaja,[433] [effect] of retribution; literally, "arisen from retribution" stands for *arisen from the ripening cause or cause of retribution* (*vipākahetuja*) (ii. 54cd), by omission of the middle word, in the same way that we say: "ox-cart" [*goratha*] for *ox-drawn-cart* [*gobhir yukto ratho*].

Or else, in the expression *vipākaja*, "arisen from *vipāka*", the word *vipāka* designates, not retribution (as above), but action [*karma*], namely, the ripened action, i.e., the action reaching the time period when it gives forth its effect or fruit [*phalakālaprāpta*], [thus taking *vipāka* in the sense of *what is brought to fruition* (*vipacyata iti kṛtvā*)].[434] That which arises [*jāta*] from ripened action, namely, the fruit or effect or retribution, is called *arisen from vipāka*. Furthermore, the effect or fruit [*phala*] is also called *vipāka*, because it is [the very fact of] being well ripened [*vipakti*].[435]

Or else, the expression *vipākaja*, "arisen from retribution", signifies *arisen from the cause of retribution*; but, [in contrast to the above interpretation,] one should not say that the word *cause* is omitted. In fact, the cause [*hetu*] is often designated [metaphorically] [*upacāra*] by the name of its effect [*phala*], in the same way that the effect is often designated by the name of its cause,[436] as in: <69>

> These present six sense-faculties, i.e., sense-spheres of contact, are known to be *old action*[437] (*Ekottara*, 14, 5; *Saṃyutta*, ii. 65; iv. 132; below ii. 28).

BCL.1.2. *Definition of effect of accumulation (aupacayika); F 69*

Aupacayika, [effect] of accumulation,[438] i.e., "that which is accumulated on the side or increased (*upacita*)" by a certain sustenance or food [*āhāra*; iii. 39], a certain grooming [*saṃskāra*; bathing (*snāna*), etc.], a certain sleep [*svapna*], a certain concentration [*samādhi*; iv. 6c].[439]

According to one opinion,[440] celibacy (*brahmacarya*) is also a cause of accumulation [or increase]; but in reality, celibacy brings it about that there is [no damage or] diminution (*upaghāta, apacaya*); it is not a cause of increase (*upacaya*).[441]

The stream of the effect of accumulation [*aupacayasaṃtāna*] protects [*ārakṣa*] the stream of the effect of retribution [*vipākasaṃtāna*] {9 b} like a rampart [*pratiprākāra*], by surrounding it.

BCL.1.3. *Definition of effect of equal outflow (naiṣyandika); F 69*

Naiṣyandika, [effect] of equal outflow, i.e., effect of equal outflow (*niṣyandaphala*; ii. 57), "that which is produced by a cause similar to its effect".

BCL.2. *The three effects and the eighteen elements;[442] F 69*

BCL.2.1. *The five sense-faculties: not an effect of equal outflow;[443] F 69*

Five sense-faculties or internal elements, except for the mental faculty, are an effect of retribution and an effect of accumulation. They are not an effect of equal outflow, for there is no outflow [of the sense-faculties] [*niṣyandābhāva*] apart [*vyatirikta*] from [them being] the effect of retribution and the effect of accumulation.[444]

L.2.2. *Sound: not an effect of retribution;*[445] *F 69–70*

Sound is an effect of accumulation, for the voice is weak when the body is emaciated [*anupacita*].[446] It is also an effect of equal outflow. It does not arise from a ripening cause, for the voice proceeds from a [current effort (*iha*) or] desire to act [*icchā*; *chanda*] (ii. 24).[447]

Objection: The *Prajñaptiśāstra* says:

> The mark of the great man (*mahāpuruṣa*; iii. 98) called *intonation of Brahmā*[448] (*brahmasvaratā*) results from the perfect practice [*subhāvitatva*] of abstinence from harsh speech [*pāruṣya*; iv. 76c].[449] <70>

Thus sound is retribution.

[Answer:[450]] – Etiology (i.e., science of causes) of sound:

First opinion: – Three moments should be distinguished: (1) action [*karma*]; (2) fundamental material elements [*bhūta*] arisen from this action and which are retribution; (3) the sound which arises from the fundamental material elements. [Thus, sound is the third step in the series (*paraṃparā*).]

Second opinion: – Five moments should be distinguished: (1) action; (2) fundamental material elements as effect of retribution; (3) fundamental material elements as effect of accumulation; (4) fundamental material elements as effect of equal outflow; and (5) sound. [Thus, sound is the fifth step in the series.]

Thus sound is not an effect of retribution because it does not directly proceed from action. (*Vibhāṣā*)

Objection. – To reason thus, bodily sensation (ii. 7), not being produced directly through action but being directly produced by the fundamental material elements arisen from [past] action (iii. 32), will not qualify as ripened effect.

Reply. – But sensation is not induced by the desire [*icchā*] to experience such a sensation, whereas sound is induced by the desire to speak. If sensation were induced by desire, it would not qualify as ripened effect.

..2.3. *The eight elements not susceptible to offering resistance: not an effect of accumulation;*[451] *F 70*

The eight elements not susceptible to offering resistance (i. 29b), namely the seven elements of thought [*cittadhātu*] and the element of factors (*dharmadhātu*), are an effect of equal outflow and an effect of retribution:

1. an effect of equal outflow[452] when they are produced by the homogeneous cause (*sabhāgahetu*) (ii. 52) or the pervasive cause (*sarvatragahetu*) (ii. 54);
2. an effect of retribution when they are produced by the ripening cause (*vipākahetu*) (ii. 54c).

They are not an effect of accumulation because the non-material elements have nothing in common with accumulation (*saṃcaya*).[453] {10 a}

BCL.2.4. *The other elements are of three types;*[454] *F 70*

The other elements, that is to say, the four not mentioned above, i.e., visible form, odor, taste, tangible, are of three kinds: (1) an effect of retribution when they are not separable from organic matter [*indriyāvinirbhāga*; i. 34], (2) an effect of accumulation and (3) an effect of equal outflow.

BCM. *13. Yoked with a [permanent] real (dravyayukta) & the eighteen elements;*[455] *F 70–71*

[Among the eighteen elements, how many are *yoked with a* [*permanent*] *real* (*dravyayukta*)?]

38a. One single element [i.e., the element of factors] is *yoked with a* [*permanent*] *real.*[456]

The unconditioned (*asaṃskṛta*), on account of being permanent, essential or indestructible (*sāratvāt = avināśat*), is a real entity (*dravya*). <71>

The unconditioned is part of the element of factors (*dharmadhātu*; i. 15); the element of factors is thus the only element that is *yoked with a* [*permanent*] *real* (*dravyavat*; *dravyayukta*).

BCN. *14. Momentary (kṣaṇika) & the eighteen elements;*[457] *F 71*

[Among the eighteen elements, how many are *momentary* (*kṣaṇika*)?]

38b. The last three elements [of the moment called *receptivity to the cognition of the factors with regard to unsatisfactoriness,*] are [called] *momentary.*[458]

The last three [of the eighteen] elements are (1) the mental faculty (*manodhātu*), (2) the object of the mental consciousness (*dharmadhātu*), (3) the mental consciousness (*manovijñāna-dhātu*).

In the range of factors of the moment called *receptivity to the cognition of the factors with regard to unsatisfactoriness* (*duḥkhe dharmajñānakṣānti*), which is the first moment in the path of insight into the truths (vi. 25) and, therefore, the first moment that is pure (*anāsrava*), these [last] three elements are "not produced by the homogeneous cause" (*sabhāgahetu*) (ii. 52), for—in the stream which constitutes the person under consideration—no pure factor (*dharma*) has yet appeared that would be the homogeneous cause of the receptivity to the cognition of the factors with regard to unsatisfactoriness. This is why these three elements are called *momentary* (*kṣaṇika*), because, for a moment, they do not proceed from this kind of cause [and are "not an effect of equal outflow" (*anaiṣyandika*)].

In the range under consideration [*tatra*],

i. thought [*citta*] to which this receptivity (*kṣānti*) is associated constitutes [two of the last three elements, i.e.,] the element of the mental faculty and the element of mental consciousness;
ii. the factors which coexist (*sahabhū*; ii. 51) with this thought constitute the [third element, i.e.,] the element of factors: pure restraint (iv. 13c); sensation, ideation, intention and other thought-concomitants; possessions (*prāpti*; ii. 36) and characteristics of the conditioned (*saṃskṛtalakṣaṇa*; ii. 46).

•. *15. Acquiring accompaniment (samanvāgamaṃ pratilambhate) and accompaniment (samanvāgama) & the eighteen elements;*[459]

F 71–73

There is a problem to be examined: Those who acquire accompaniment (*samanvāgamaṃ pratilabhate*) (ii. 36b) of the eye sense-faculty (*cakṣurdhātu*) when previously they were not accompanied with it (*asamanvāgata*), do they also acquire accompaniment of the visual consciousness (*cakṣurvijñānadhātu*)? Those who acquire accompaniment of the visual consciousness when they were previously not accompanied by it, do they also acquire accompaniment of the eye sense-faculty? <72>

38cd. **Those [who were not accompanied by the eye sense-faculty, who were not accompanied by the visual consciousness,] can have acquisition (*lābha*) of the eye sense-faculty and the visual consciousness (1) separately [*pṛthak*] and also (2) together [*saha*].**[460] {10 b}

).1. *Acquisition separately: acquisition as acquiring accompaniment;* F 72

[As for the "acquisition separately", there is a tetralemma between acquiring accompaniment of the eye sense-faculty and acquiring accompaniment of the visual consciousness:][461]

1. Persons who are not accompanied by the eye sense-faculty acquiring accompaniment of it without at the same time [*pṛthak*] acquiring accompaniment of the visual consciousness:

   i. beings of the realm of desire (*kāmadhātu*) whose sense-faculties progressively appear (ii. 14): for, before the eye sense-faculty appears in them, they already have accompaniment of their past visual consciousness (intermediate existence; iii. 14) and their future visual consciousness (on *possession*; ii. 36b);

   ii. beings who die in the realm of immateriality (*ārūpyadhātu*), [where the visual consciousness and the eye sense-faculty are absent,] and are reborn in the heavens of the second to fourth meditations (*dhyāna*), where the visual consciousness is absent, although the eye sense-faculty exists (viii. 13ac).

2. Persons who are not accompanied by the visual consciousness acquiring accompaniment of it without at the same time acquiring accompaniment of the eye sense-faculty:

   i. beings born in the heaven of the three higher meditations can manifest (*sammukhīkurvāṇa*) a visual consciousness of the stage of the first meditation (viii. 13): they do not acquire accompaniment of the eye sense-faculty which they already possess;

   ii.* beings who fall from [*pracyuta*] one of the three higher meditations and are reborn below, [i.e., the first meditation or the realm of desire].

3. Persons who are not accompanied by the two acquire accompaniment [*samanvāgamaṃ pratilabhate*] of the two [at the same time (*saha*)]:

   i. beings who fall from the realm of immateriality and are reborn, either in the realm of desire or in the first meditation (i.e., world of Brahmā).

4. [Persons may acquire neither: those situations apart from these three categories.[462]]

BCO.2. *Acquisition together: acquisition as acquiring accompaniment and as accompaniment; F 72–73*

We have up to now understood the term *lābha*, "acquisition", which the stanza uses, in the sense of *pratilambha*, "acquiring accompaniment"; but one can also understand it in the sense of *prāpti*, "possession" [*samanvāgama*, "accompaniment"; ii. 36b].

[Question:] – Those who are already accompanied (*samanvāgata*) with the eye sense-faculty, are they also accompanied with the visual consciousness?

[Answer:] – Four alternatives are possible [tetralemma between possessing the eye sense-faculty and possessing the visual consciousness]:

1. beings born in a heaven of the three higher meditations necessarily possess the eye sense-faculty, but possess the visual consciousness only when they manifest a visual consciousness of the stage of the first meditation [*dhyāna*]; <73>
2. beings of the realm of desire who have not taken possession [*alabdha*] of the eye sense-faculty in the course of embryonic life or who become blind [*vihīna*]: they remain in possession of the visual consciousness acquired in the course of the intermediate existence (iii. 14) or at conception;
3. (i) beings of the realm of desire who have taken possession [*labdha*] of the eye sense-faculty and have not lost it [*avihīna*]; (ii) beings born in the heaven of the first meditation; (iii) beings born in a heaven of the three higher meditations who manifest a visual consciousness of the stage of the first meditation: these three categories of beings are accompanied with the sense-faculty and with the consciousness;
4. any other beings, the beings of the realm of immateriality, are not accompanied with the eye sense-faculty and with the visual consciousness.

* * *

The acquiring of accompaniment (*pratilambha*) and the accompaniment (*samanvāgama*), simultaneously or not simultaneously, of the eye sense-faculty (*cakṣurdhātu*) {11 a} and of visible form (*rūpadhātu*), of the visual consciousness (*cakṣurvijñānadhātu*) and of visible form, of the ear sense-faculty (*śrotradhātu*) and of sound (*śabdadhātu*), etc., will be defined as is fitting in each case.

16. Internal (ādhyātmika) and external (bāhya) & the eighteen elements;[463] *F 73–74*

Among the eighteen elements, how many are personal or internal (*ādhyātmika*)? How many are external (*bāhya*)?

39ab. **Twelve elements are internal or personal, [i.e., the six sense-faculties and the six consciousnesses,] with the exception of [the elements of] visible form, [sound, odor, taste, tangible and factors].**[464]

1. Twelve elements, i.e., the six sense-faculties [*āśraya*] and the six consciousnesses, are internal or personal [*ādhyātmika*].

2. Six elements, i.e., the six object-fields of the consciousness, that is, visible form, etc., are external [*bāhya*].

BCP.1. ### *Sense-faculties and consciousnesses as basis of the mind (ātman);*[465] *F 73–74*

[Question:] – But how can you speak of internal or personal elements or of external elements since there is no *ātman*, i.e., no self or person? <74>

[Answer:[466]] – The mind [*citta*] is the object or basis [*saṃniśraya*] of the notion of self [*ahaṃkāra*], the mind is what people falsely imagine to be their self. This mind thus receives, metaphorically [*upacaryate*], the name of *ātman.*

This can be seen, for example, by comparing these two lines from Scripture:

> By means of the well-tamed [*sudānta*] *ātman*, the teacher [*paṇḍita*] obtains heaven,

and:

> It is good to tame thought [*citta*]; the tamed [*dānta*] thought brings happiness [*sukha*].[467] {11 b}

But the sense-faculties and consciousnesses are close (*pratyāsanna*, *abhyāsanna*) to the thought [*citta*] to which is given the name of *ātman*: they are in fact the basis (*āśraya*) of it; thus they are qualified as "internal", "personal" (*ādhyātmika*), whereas visible form, etc., are held to be "external" (*bāhya*) because of being object-fields of the consciousness.[468]

BCP.2. ### *Can the consciousnesses as the past mental faculty be the basis of thought? F 74*

[Objection:] – But can you say that the six consciousnesses [as elements] are the basis [*āśraya*] of thought [*citta*]? They are the basis of thought only when, having perished, they acquire the quality of mental faculty (*manodhātu*; i. 17). Thus they are not "personal" [*ādhyātmika*].

[Reply:] – This objection is without value. When the consciousnesses become the basis of thought by having perished, it is indeed these very same consciousnesses that become a basis: thus, having become a basis, they do not exceed [*atovartamte*] [their characteristic or nature (*lakṣaṇa*),] their quality of basis. They are thus "personal" because of their future quality of basis.

Otherwise, the mental faculty would be past only; it would not be either future or present. But it is well understood that the eighteen elements belong to the three time periods.

Further, if the future or present consciousness did not have the characteristic or nature [*lakṣaṇa*] of the mental faculty, it would be absurd to attribute this characteristic or nature to it once it is past. For a factor (*dharma*) does not change or deviate from [*vyabhicāra*] its (defining) characteristic or nature in the course of time [*adhvan*] (v. 25; MVŚ, 109a18, 200b2).

CQ. *17. Homogeneous (sabhāga) and partially homogeneous (tatsabhāga) & the eighteen elements;*[469] *F 74–78*

Among the eighteen elements, how many are "homogeneous", "active", "participating", "in mutual assistance" (*sabhāga*; see below F 77)? How many are "partially homogeneous", "non-participating" (*tatsabhāga*)[470]? <75>

CQ.1. *The element of factors is homogeneous;*[471] *F 75*

39bc. **The element called *factors* is [always] homogeneous.**[472]

An object-field of consciousness (*viṣaya*) is qualified as "homogeneous", "active", "in mutual assistance" {12 a} when the consciousness of which it constitutes the particular object-field has arisen [*utpanna*] or is destined to arise [*utpatti*] in regard to it.

But there is no factor in regard to which mental consciousness, being without limit (*ananta manovijñāna*), has not arisen or is not destined to arise. All noble ones [*āryapudgala*], in fact, necessarily produce the thought: "All factors are non-self" [*sarvadharmā anātmāna*; vii. 13a]. Now it is true that this thought bears neither on itself [*svabhāva*] nor on the factors which are co-existing (*sahabhū*; ii. 50b) with it; but this [(first) moment (*kṣaṇa*)] of thought and the factors co-existing with it are the cognitive object [*ālambana*] of a second moment of thought which sees that all factors are non-self; thus "all factors" are indeed included within the cognitive object of these two moments of thought (vii. 18cd).[473] – Therefore the element of factors (*dharmadhātu*; i. 15bd), i.e., the particular cognitive object of the mental consciousness, is in its entirety always [*nitya*] homogeneous or active as a cognitive object.

BCQ.2. *The other elements are homogeneous and partially homogeneous;*[474] *F 75–77*

39cd. **The other elements are also partially homogeneous.**[475]

The word "also" shows that they are homogeneous (*sabhāga*) and partially homogeneous (*tatsabhāga*).

When are they partially homogeneous?

39d. **When [the other elements] do not perform their particular task, [they are partially homogeneous].**[476]

This implies the definition: they are homogeneous when they perform their particular task [*svakarmakṛt*].

BCQ.2.1. *Six sense-faculties & homogeneous and partially homogeneous;*[477] *F 75–76*

[In that regard,] the eye sense-faculty (*cakṣurdhātu*) which has seen, sees or will see visible form is qualified as *homogeneous.*

The same with respect to the other sense-faculties, [including the mental faculty,] by indicating for each its own object-field (*viṣaya*) and its own particular activity (*kāritra, puruṣakāra*; ii. 58).

According to the Vaibhāṣikas of Kaśmīr, the eye sense-faculty is *partially homogeneous* in four cases:

1–3. the eye sense-faculty which has ceased, ceases, will cease, without having seen, and

4. the eye sense-faculty not destined to arise (*anutpattidharman*) (v. 24). {12 b} <76>

According to the Westerners (*pāścātya*), [there are five cases since] the eye sense-faculty not destined to arise constitutes two categories according to whether or not it is accompanied (*samāyukta* = *saṃbaddha*) by visual consciousness.[478]

The same with respect to the other sense-faculties, [including the body (*kāya*),] of the sensory consciousness.

As for the mental faculty (*manodhātu*), it is partially homogeneous [only] when it is not destined to arise; in fact, when it does arise, it always has an object-field, [i.e., it is homogeneous].[479]

BCQ.2.2. *The other five objects & homogeneous and partially homogeneous;*[480] *F 76*

Visible forms which have been seen, which are seen or which will be seen by the eye sense-faculty are *homogeneous.*

They are *partially homogeneous* [in four cases]:

1–3. when they have ceased, cease, or will cease: without having been seen, and

4. when they are not destined to arise.

The same with respect to the other object-fields, [including the tangible,] of the sensory consciousness by indicating for each the sense-faculty [*indriya*] and the activity [*kāritra*] that correspond to them.

2.2.3. *The unshared sense-faculties and the shared object-fields & homogeneous and partially homogeneous;*[481] *F 76–7*

The eye sense-faculty which is homogeneous or partially homogeneous is such for everyone, i.e., for the person to whom this sense-faculty belongs and for other persons [who have the sense-faculty]. The same for the other sense-faculties, [including the mental faculty].

But a certain visible form is homogeneous for the person who sees it, partially homogeneous for the person who does not see it. In fact, the visible form which a person sees can be seen by many, for example, the moon [*candra*], exhibitions [*prekṣā*] of dance [*naṭa*] or wrestling [*malla*], whereas two persons cannot see by means of one and the same eye sense-faculty. <77>

1. Therefore it is in relation to one person [*saṃtāna*] that the eye sense-faculty, not being shared [*asādhāraṇa*], is qualified as *homogeneous* or *partially homogeneous*: the eye sense-faculty is homogeneous when it sees a visible form. {13 a}

2. On the contrary, visible form is shared [*sādhāraṇa*]: visible form is qualified as *homogeneous* and *partially homogeneous* from the point of view of numerous persons: it is homogeneous in relation to those who see it, partially homogeneous in relation to those who do not see it. The same holds for sound, odor, taste and tangible as holds for visible form.[482]

2.2.3.1. *Are odor, taste and the tangible shared? F 77*

[Objection:] – So be it in regard to that which concerns sound, which, like visible form, is perceived at a distance [*dūra*] and can be perceived by many people (i. 43cd). But odor, taste and the tangible are not perceived at a distance, they are perceived only when they enter into a close relationship [*prāptagrahaṇa*] with the sense-faculty;[483] thus the odor that one person perceives is not perceived by another. Thus these objects are not shared [*asādhāraṇa*], and we should rank them with the sense-faculties in regard to the qualification of "homogeneous", "partially homogeneous": when they are homogeneous for one person, they are homogeneous for everyone.

We answer: – We regard these object-fields as shared [*sādhāraṇa*] because there is the possibility of them being so. It is possible, in fact, that odor—the same atomic group of odor—which produces the olfactory consciousness in one person, is also perceived by another.[484] But this does not hold in the same way for the sense-faculties. Therefore, odors, tastes and the tangibles should be ranked together with visible forms and sounds.

BCQ.2.4. *Six consciousnesses; F 77*

As for the six consciousnesses, they are homogeneous or partially homogeneous according to whether they are (1) destined to arise, (2) not destined to arise. This is as in the case of the mental faculty.

BCQ.3. *Meaning of the expressions* sabhāga *and* tatsabhāga;[485] *F 77–78*

1. What is the meaning of the expression *sabhāga*, [literally, "having a share in common"]? <78>

"Share" (*bhāga*) designates the mutual sharing, i.e., the mutual services (*anyonya-bhajana*) which the sense faculties, the object-fields and the consciousnesses render one another, in their quality of basis of the consciousness (*āśraya*), of object-field of the consciousness (*viṣaya*), of consciousness relying on the sense-faculty (*āśrayin*).

Or else, "share" signifies sharing or possession (*bhajana*) of the activity (*kāritra*): (i) the activity of the sense-faculties is to see (*darśana*), etc.; (ii) the activity of the object-field is to be the object of the consciousness (*viṣaya, ālambana*), of being seen, etc.; (ii) the activity of the consciousness is to be the subject of the consciousness, to be the cognizer (*vijñātṛtva*).

Therefore *sabhāga* is called the factors (*dharma*) which possess (*sa-*) the share (*bhāga*), i.e., the sense-faculties, object-fields and consciousnesses which are endowed with their particular activity (*kāritrabhajana*), or else, the sense-faculties, objects-fields and consciousnesses which render mutual services to one another (*anyonya-bhajana*). Or else, the factors which have for their effect the same contact (*sparśa-samānakāryatva*): the encounter of the eye, of the visible form, of the visual consciousness; etc., are *sabhāga* (iii. 22).[486]

2. What is the meaning of the expression *tatsabhāga*, [literally, "homogeneous to those"]?

That which is not homogeneous (*sabhāga*) but nevertheless is partially homogeneous is called *tatsabhāga*, that is, "partially (*sabhāga*)—[in the sense of belonging to the same kind (*jātisāmānya*)]—to those [elements] (*tat*) [that are homogeneous (*sabhāga*) (in the strict sense)]", that is, "partially homogeneous" (*sabhāga-sabhāga*).[487]

BCR. *18. Abandoned by insight (darśanaheya) and by cultivation (bhāvanāheya), and not to be abandoned (aheya) & the eighteen elements;*[488] *F 78–80*

How many elements can be abandoned (*hā, prahā*; v. 28; vi. 1) by insight into the truths, in other words, by the path of insight (*darśanamārga*) or by insight (*darśana*;

vi. 25b)? How many can be abandoned by cultivation or repeated consideration (*bhāvanā*) of the truths, in other words, by the path of cultivation (*bhavanāmārga*) or by cultivation (*bhavanā*)? {13 b} How many elements are not to be abandoned, cannot be abandoned [*aheya*]?[489]

R.1. *The first fifteen elements and the last three elements;*[490] *F 78–80*

40ab. **(1) The ten [material elements] and the five [sensory consciousnesses] are abandoned by cultivation. (2) The last three [elements] are, [from the point of view of abandoning them,] of three kinds [i.e., abandoned by insight, abandoned by cultivation, not abandoned].**[491] <79>

1. The ten material elements, i.e., the sense-faculties and object-fields, and the five sensory consciousnesses are abandoned by cultivation [*bhāvanāheya*].

2. The last three [of the eighteen] elements, i.e., the mental faculty [*manodhātu*], the mental object [*dharmadhātu*] and the mental consciousness [*manovijñāna*], from the point of view of abandoning them, involve factors of three kinds:

i. eighty-eight [of the ninety-eight] proclivities (*anuśaya*; v. 4);

   a. with the coexisting (*sahabhū*) factors—whether these coexisting factors are of the associated (*saṃprayukta*) class or of the dissociated (*viprayukta*) class (ii. 46; characteristics [*lakṣaṇa*] and secondary characteristics [*anulakṣaṇa*]);
   b. with the possessions (*prāpti*; ii. 36) of the said proclivities and the said coexisting factors;
   c. with the following (i.e., secondary possessions [*anuprāpti*] and characteristics [*lakṣaṇa*]) of the said possessions,

are abandoned by insight [*darśanaheya*];

ii. the other impure [*sāsrava*] factors:

   a. ten proclivities (v. 5) with the coexisting factors, possessions, etc.;
   b. the wholesome-impure (*kuśalasāsrava*) and unobscured-non-defined (*anivṛta-avyākṛta*) (ii. 66) formations (*saṃskāra*);[492]
   c. the impure non-informative (*avijñapti*) with its following (iv. 13),

are abandoned by cultivation [*bhāvanaheya*];

iii. the pure [*anāsrava*] factors:

   a. the unconditioned factors and
   b. the factors which are part of the (noble) path,

cannot be abandoned [*apraheya*].

BCR.1.1. *Objection by the Vātsīputrīyas; F 79*

Objection of the Vātsīputrīyas: – We believe that not only the eighty-eight [of the ninety-eight] proclivities (*anuśaya*), but also some other factors are abandoned by insight:

1. the status of the ordinary worldling [*pṛthagjanatva*][493] is a factor which is unobscured-non-defined: you classify it among the factors abandoned by cultivation;
2. unwholesome bodily or vocal action [*kāyavākkarma*], retributed by an unfortunate plane of existence [*āpāyika*], is material form (*rūpa*): you classify it also in the second category.

The status of the ordinary worldling and the action which causes an unfortunate plane of existence are in contradiction with the (noble) path, with the path of insight into the truths (*darśanamārga*). Thus, according to us, both are abandoned by insight.

BCR.1.2. *Refutation of the objection made by the Vātsīputrīyas; F 79–80*

In order to refute the thesis of the Vātsīputrīyas, the author says in brief:

40cd. **Neither the (1) non-defiled nor (2) that which is material form, nor (3) that which has arisen from the non-sixth, [i.e., that which has arisen from the five sense-faculties),] are abandoned by insight into the truths.**[494] <80>

1–2. Nothing of that which is non-defiled (*akliṣṭa*), i.e., of that which is neither unwholesome (*akuśala*) nor obscured-non-defined (*nivṛtāvyākṛta*) (ii. 66), and nothing of that which is material form, can be abandoned by insight into the truths. {14 a}

But the status of the ordinary worldling [*pṛthagjanatva*] is non-defiled[-non-defined (*akliṣṭāvyakṛta*)]: it can belong to a person who has cut off the wholesome roots [*samucchinnakuśalamūla*; iv. 79] or it can belong to a person who is detached (*vītarāga*).

But bodily action and vocal action are material form (*rūpa*).

Thus the status of the ordinary worldling and bodily or vocal action are not contradictory (*vipratipatti*) to the truths, for the first is not defiled by the defilements (*kleśa*) and is not a consciousness, a factor which has a cognitive object (*anālambaka*); for the second is not a factor which has a cognitive object. Thus, neither the one nor the other are abandoned by insight into the truths.

Besides, if the status of the ordinary worldling were abandoned by insight, it would follow that it would exist at the first stage of the path of insight [*duḥkhe dharma-jñānakṣānti*; vi. 26.]—which is incorrect.[495]

3. By "sixth" one should understand [the sense-sphere of] the mental faculty [*manāyatana*]. *Arisen from the non-sixth* (*aṣaṣṭhaja*) is called that which has arisen from a sense-faculty different from the sixth sense-faculty, i.e., that which has arisen from the other five sense-faculties, i.e., the eye sense-faculty, etc. It refers to the visual consciousness, etc.

This also is not abandoned by insight.

19. View (dṛṣṭi) and not view (na dṛṣṭi) & the eighteen elements;[496] *F 80–100*

1. Eight views within the element of factors; F 80
   - Definition of view (*dṛṣṭi*) as judgment after contemplation; F 81
2. Eye sense-faculty; F 81
   - 2.1. Different views on whether the eye sense-faculty or the visual consciousness sees; F 81
   - 2.2. Are visible forms seen by one eye or by two eyes? F 86
   - 2.3. Perception of the object with or without reaching it with the sense-faculty; F 87
   - 2.4. Insert: Do atoms touch one another or not? F 89
     - 2.4.1. Vaibhāṣikas: atoms do not touch one another; F 89
     - 2.4.2. Bhadanta (and Vasubandhu): atoms do touch one another metaphorically; F 91
   - 2.5. Size of the sense-faculties and their object-fields; F 92
   - 2.6. Issues related to the atoms of the sense-faculties: their arrangement, etc.; F 93
   - 2.7. Simultaneity and non-simultaneity of the object-field or sense-faculty with its consciousness; F 94
   - 2.8. Sense-faculties as the basis (*āśraya*) of consciousness; F 95
   - 2.9. Sense-faculties as the basis for naming the consciousnesses; F 96
   - 2.10. Stages (*bhūmi*) & the sense-faculties, body, object-fields and consciousnesses of the eighteen elements; F 97–100

Among the eighteen elements, how many are view (*dṛṣṭi*)? [How many are *not view* (*na dṛṣṭi*)?]

41ab. **The eye sense-faculty [i.e., the element of the eye] and eight parts of the element of factors are view.**[497]

BCS.1. *Eight views within the element of factors;*[498] *F 80–81*

[Question:] – What are these eight parts[499] of the element of factors (*dharma-dhātu*)?

[Answer:] – 1–5. The five afflicted views (*dṛṣṭi*; v. 7): (1) the afflicted view of self (*satkāyadṛṣṭi*), [(2) the afflicted view of holding to an extreme (*antagrāhadṛṣṭi*); (3) the false view (*mithyādrsti*); (4) the esteeming of (such things as bad) views (*dṛṣṭiparāmarśa*); (5) the overesteeming of (such things as) morality and certain types of spiritual practices (*śīlavarataparāmarśa*)]. They will be defined in the chapter Exposition of the Proclivities (*anuśayanirdeśa*) (v. 7). <81>

6. The mundane (*laukikī*) right view (*samyagdṛṣṭi*), i.e., understanding (*prajñā*; ii. 24) associated with the mental consciousness, wholesome (*kuśala*), but impure (*sāsrava*).[500]

7. The (right) view of those in training (*śaikṣī dṛṣṭi*), i.e., the pure view [or understanding] that is particular to the noble one who is not a perfected being (*arhat*).

8. The (right) view of those beyond training (*aśaikṣī dṛṣṭi*), i.e., the pure view [or understanding] particular to the perfected being (vi. 50).

These eight factors that are part of the element of factors (*dharmadhātu*) are view (*dṛṣṭi*). [There is no (other) view left over (*avaśiṣṭa*).]

BCS.1.1. *Fourfold classification with their comparisons of the eight views;*[501] *F 81*

Comparison. Just as visible forms are seen [differently] by night [*rātri*] or by day [*diva*], with a cloudy sky [*samegha*] or with a clear sky [*amegha*], in the same way the factors are seen [differently]

1. by the defiled [*kliṣṭa*] mundane view—the five afflicted views;
2. by the non-defiled [*akliṣṭa*] mundane view or right mundane view;
3. by the view of those in training (*śaikṣī*);
4. by the view of those beyond training (*aśaikṣī*).[502]

BCS.1.2. *Definition of view;*[503] *F 81*

Why is mundane right view spoken of only as understanding (*prajñā*) associated with the mental consciousness?

41cd. **The understanding [*dhī*] which arises with the five sensory consciousnesses is not view because it is not judgment after contemplation.**[504]

View [*dṛṣṭi*] is judgment after contemplation (*tīraṇa*, *saṃtīraṇa*), i.e., judgment [*niścaya*] preceding from contemplation (*upadhyāna* = *upanidhyāna*, "knowing exactly") of the object-field [*viṣaya*].[505]

But understanding (*prajñā*) which arises with the five sensory consciousnesses does not have this characteristic. Thus, it is not view. – For the same reason, it happens that [other] understanding, even though mental, whether defiled [*kliṣṭa*] or non-defiled [*akliṣṭa*], is not [necessarily] view, namely, when it is purely intuitive [i.e., cognition of exhaustion and non-arising (*kṣayānutpādajñāna*)] (vii. 1).[506]

.2. *Eye sense-faculty;*[507] *F 81–100*

[Objection:] – But the eye sense-faculty does not possess a "judgment preceding from contemplation of the object" (*saṃtīraṇa*). How can you say that it is view (*dṛṣṭi*)? {15 a}

[Answer:] – "View" is understood here as the seeing (*ālocana*) of visible forms (*rūpa*).[508]

.2.1. *Different views on whether the eye sense-faculty or the visual consciousness sees;*[509] *F 81–86*

1. Vaibhāṣika: the eye sense-faculty and not the visual consciousness sees; F 81
    a. Vaibhāṣika: the homogeneous eye sense-faculty sees; F 82
    b. Vaibhāṣika argument through logical reasoning: because concealed visible form is not seen; F 83
    c. Vaibhāṣika argument from scriptural authority: the eye sense-faculty sees; F 83
    d. Vaibhāṣika argument through logical reasoning: visual consciousness cannot see and cognize at the same time; F 84
2. Opinions of other schools; F 85
    a. Vijñānavāda (Vātsīputrīya) argument in regard to the relationship between the agent of seeing and the action of seeing; F 85
    b. Vijñānavāda (Dharmaguptaka) argument from the conventional worldly point of view; F 85
    c. Sautrāntika: the play of causes and effects & the use of metaphors; F 86
3. Vaibhāṣika of Kaśmīr: the eye sense-faculty sees, the mental faculty cognizes; F 86

.2.1.1. *Vaibhāṣika: the eye sense-faculty and not the visual consciousness sees;*[510] *F 81–82*

42. (1) It is the eye sense-faculty, when it is homogeneous (*sabhāga*), [i.e., when it is conjoined with the visual consciousness,] that sees visible forms. (2) It is not the consciousness of which this sense-

faculty is the basis [that sees], for concealed visible form is not seen. Such is the opinion of the Vaibhāṣikas [*kila*].[511] <82>

BCS.2.1.1.a. *Vaibhāṣika: the homogeneous eye sense-faculty sees;*[512] *F 82–83*

The Vijñānavādin (Vij)[513] is a scholar who attributes *view*, not to the eye sense-faculty, but to visual consciousness.

[Vij:] – If it were the eye sense-faculty that sees, then even the [eye] sense-faculty of a person who is occupied with an auditory or tactile consciousness should see (i. 6cd).[514]

[Vaibhāṣika (Vai):] – We do not say that every eye sense-faculty sees. The eye sense-faculty sees [only] when it is homogeneous (*sabhāga*; i. 39), i.e., when it is conjoined with the visual consciousness [*savijñānaka*].[515]

BCS.2.1.1.b. *Vaibhāṣika argument through logical reasoning: because concealed visible form is not seen; F 83*

[Vij:] – But then that which sees is indeed the consciousness based on the eye sense-faculty.[516] <83>

[Vai:] – No, for the visible form, concealed or separated [*vyavahita*] by a wall [*kuḍya*] or any other screen, is not seen. But the consciousness is non-material [*amūrti*], not susceptible to offering resistance or to being repelled (*apratigha*; i. 29b). [Some masters:] Thus, if the visual consciousness were to see, it should see even the visible forms concealed or screened [*āvṛta*] by a wall.

The Vijñānavādin replies: – The visual consciousness does not arise in regard to concealed or screened visible forms; not arising in regard to them, it does not see them [or how can there be seeing? (*katham drakṣyati*)[517]].

[Vai:] – But why does it not arise in regard to these [concealed or screened] visible forms?[518] We—the Vaibhāṣikas who attribute *view* to the sense-faculty and who accept that the sense-faculty, being susceptible to offering resistance or to being stopped (*sapratigha*),[519] cannot exercise its activity with regard to concealed visible or separated forms—can easily explain why the visual consciousness does not arise in regard to concealed or separated visible forms: the visual consciousness, in fact, [cannot arise] since it must exercise its activity on the same object-field as its basis [i.e., the sense-faculty]. But if you think that the consciousness sees, how would you explain the fact that it does not arise in regard to concealed visible forms?

The author (*ācārya*; Vasubandhu) takes on the opinion of the Vijñānavādin and responds [on behalf of the Vijñānavādin] to the last reply of the Vaibhāṣika:

Do you maintain that the eye sense-faculty sees its object-field by entering into a close relationship or "reaching" its object-field [*prāptaviṣaya*], in the way that the body sense-faculty experiences a tangible (i. 43cd)?[520]

In this hypothesis, I would understand that, because of being susceptible to offering resistance or to being stopped, the eye sense-faculty does not see the concealed or screened [*āvṛta*] visible forms. But you, (i.e., the Vaibhāṣika,) maintain that the eye sense-faculty sees at a distance (i. 43cd): thus, you must not say that, being susceptible of being stopped, it does not see the separated or concealed visible forms.

Besides, visible forms which are separated [*antarita*] by glass [*kāca*], a veil of clouds [*abhrapaṭala*], crystal [*sphaṭika*], and water [*ambu*] can be seen: how would you explain this fact? {15 b} [Therefore, it is not because of being susceptible to offering resistance or to being stopped that the eye sense-faculty does not see screened or concealed visible forms.[521]]

Thus, [from the point of view of the Vijñānavādin,] I would say that the visual consciousness sees; it arises [even] in regard to screened or concealed visible forms when the screen does not form an obstacle to light [*ālokasyāpratibandha*]; it does not arise in the contrary case.[522]

.2.1.1.c. *Vaibhāṣika argument from scriptural authority: the eye sense-faculty sees;*[523] *F 83–84*

The Vaibhāṣika makes an appeal to Scripture: – The Sūtra says:

> Having seen visible forms with the eye sense-faculty.[524]

Thus the sense-faculty sees, not the visual consciousness. <84>

[Answer by the Vijñānavādin:] – The Sūtra intends to say: "Having seen the visible forms by means of the eye sense-faculty as basis (*tena āśrayeṇa*), by relying (*āśritya*) on the eye sense-faculty." In fact, the same Sūtra says:

> Having cognized (*vijñāya*) the factors with the mental faculty (*manas*).[525]

But this sense-faculty, because of being past (i. 17), cannot cognize [factors]; it is actually with the mental consciousness (*manovijñāna*) that one cognizes; thus, if the text says: "with the mental faculty", it means to say: "by relying on the mental faculty, the basis of the mental consciousness". The same for seeing and the eye sense-faculty.

One can also accept that the Sūtra [metaphorically] attributes to the basis, to the sense-faculty, the action which belongs to that which seizes the basis, i.e., to the consciousness. One commonly says: "the benches cry" [*mañcāḥ krośanti*]; the "benches" are the persons seated on the benches.

This manner of speaking is common in Scripture. We read:

> Visible forms, agreeable [*iṣṭa*] and attractive [*kānta*], are cognized (*vijñeya*) by the eye sense-faculty.

But you do not maintain that the eye sense-faculty cognizes. You attribute the cognition to the consciousness whose eye sense-faculty is the basis.

The Sūtra (*Saṃyukta*, 9, 20) also says:

> The eye sense-faculty, O Brahman, is the gate (*dvāra*) just for the seeing (*darśanāya*) of visible forms.[526]

This text proves that the visual consciousness sees by way of this gate which is the eye sense-faculty. You would not maintain that the *gate* signifies the *seeing*, for it would be absurd to say: "The eye sense-faculty is the seeing for the seeing of visible forms." {16 a}

BCS.2.1.1.d. *Vaibhāṣika argument through logical reasoning: visual consciousness cannot see and cognize at the same time;*[527] *F 84*

Objection by the Vaibhāṣika: – If the visual consciousness sees (*paśyati*), what is it that cognizes (*vijānāti*)[528] (i. 48a)?

[Answer by the Vijñānavādin:] – What is the difference between these two functions of seeing and cognizing that would bring it about that the same factor could not see and cognize at the same time? [The very cognizing of a visible form is the seeing of it.] Is it not accepted that a certain type of understanding (*prajñā*; *darśanātmika*; vii. 1) sees (*paśyati*) as well as understands (*prajānāti*)?[529] In the same way, a certain consciousness, i.e., the visual consciousness, sees as well as cognizes. Here there is just one single function designated by two names.[530] <85>

BCS.2.1.2. *Opinions of other schools; F 85–86*

BCS.2.1.2.a. *Vijñānavāda (Vātsīputrīya) argument in regard to the relationship between the agent of seeing and the action of seeing; F 85*

Certain followers of the thesis: "The visual consciousness sees", namely, the Vātsīputrīyas, object: – If the eye sense-faculty sees, what then is the action of seeing (*dṛśikriyā*), existing separate (*anyā*) [from the eye sense-faculty], which you attribute to this sense-faculty, the agent [*kartṛ*] of this action?

[Reply by the Vaibhāṣikas:] – The objection cannot be made. Just as you can have it that the consciousness cognizes (*vijānāti*), without accepting a difference between the agent [*kartṛ*] and the action [*kriyā*], in the same way we accept that the sense-faculty sees.

2.1.2.b. *Vijñānavāda (Dharmaguptaka) argument from the conventional worldly point of view;* F 85

According to another opinion, that of the Dharmaguptakas, it is the visual consciousness which sees; but, as the eye sense-faculty is the basis of this consciousness, one says that it also sees. In the same way one says "the bell rings" [*ghānta nadati*], because it is the basis of the resounding (*nāda*).

[Reply:] – But, according to this principle, one should also say that the eye sense-faculty cognizes (*vijānāti*), for it is the basis of the visual consciousness (*vijñāna*).

[Dharmaguptakas:] – No. For, in the world, it is conventional [*rūḍha*] to give the name of seeing (*darśana*) to the visual consciousness; in fact, when this consciousness occurs, it is said that visible form has been *seen* (*dṛṣṭa*); one does not say that the visible form has been *cognized* (*vijñāta*). And the MVŚ (489c19) confirms:

> That which is reached by the eye sense-faculty or falls within its range (*cakṣuḥsaṃprāpta* = *cakṣurābhāsagata*) and that which is perceived (*anubhūta*) by the consciousness is said to be seen.

Thus, in the world we say that the eye sense-faculty sees, because it is the basis of the visual consciousness that sees; we do not say that it cognizes, because the activity attributed to the visual consciousness is seeing and not cognizing.

On the other hand, when we say that the consciousness (*vijnāna*) cognizes, we do not mean that it cognizes insofar as it would be the basis of a certain cognizing, as we understand that the eye sense-faculty sees because it is the basis of the visual consciousness. It is understood that the consciousness cognizes by itself or its mere presence [*sānnidhyamātra*], that it is itself cognizing. In the same way, we say that the sun is the maker of the day [*sūryo divasakara*] [when it rises by its mere presence].[531] {16 b} <86>

2.1.2.c. *Sautrāntika: the play of causes and effects & the use of metaphors;* F 86

Opinion of the Sautrāntika:[532] – Are you not devouring empty space here![533] The Sūtra teaches: "Dependent on the eye sense-faculty and visible forms, there arises the visual consciousness"; there is neither a sense-faculty that *sees* nor a visible form that *is seen*; here there is no function of seeing [*nirvyāpāra*], no agent that sees; it is [a mere play of factors (*dharmamātra*),] a mere play of causes and effects [*hetuphalamātra*].[534] In conformity with ordinary discourse [*vyavahāra*], we speak, if we like, of this process by using metaphors [*upacāra*]: "The eye sees [*cakṣuḥ paśyati*], the consciousness cognizes [*vijñānaṃ vijānāti*]." But [the wise ones] should not be attached [*abhiniveṣṭavya*] to these metaphors, for the Fortunate One has said:

One should not obstinately be attached to the manner of speaking of the people or the country [*janapadanirukta*], nor should one [unnecessarily] insist on the expressions [*saṃjñā*] used in the world [*loka*].[535]

BCS.2.1.3. *Vaibhāṣika of Kaśmīr: the eye sense-faculty sees, the mental faculty cognizes; F 86*

According to the system [*siddhānta*] of the Vaibhāṣikas of Kaśmīr, the eye sense-faculty *sees*, the ear sense-faculty hears, the nose sense-faculty smells, the taste sense-faculty tastes, the body sense-faculty touches, the mental faculty *cognizes*.[536]

BCS.2.2. *Are visible forms seen by one eye or by two eyes? F 86–87*

[Then, if the eye sense-faculty sees,] are the visible forms seen by one eye or by two eyes?

43ab. Visible forms are seen also with the two eyes, as the clarity of sight demonstrates.[537]

There is no fixed rule [*niyama*]: one sees with one eye; one also sees with both eyes.

The Ābhidhārmikas[538] say: "[Visible forms are] seen also with the two eyes; the two eyes being open, the view is clearer [*pariśuddhatara*]."

Besides,[539] when one eye is open [*unmīlita*] {17 a} and the other is half-closed [*ardhanimīlita*], one perceives two moons [*dvicandra*], but not when one completely closes or half-closes that eye that was open, or when one opens or closes completely the eye that was half-closed. <87>

From the fact that its basis [*āśraya*] is twofold [*viccheda*], it should not be concluded that the visual consciousness is twofold, for the consciousness is not material like material form [*rūpa*]; not having a mass (*amūrta*), it is not situated in a [particular] place (*deśāpratiṣṭhita*).

BCS.2.3. *Perception of the object with or without reaching it with the sense-faculty & the eighteen elements;*[540] *F 87–89*

We have said that the eye sense-faculty sees; that the sense-faculties of the ear, the nose, the tongue, the body, each perceive their object-field; that the mental faculty cognizes. Do these sense-faculties reach or directly touch (*prāp*; *prāpta*) their object-field [or not (*aprāpta*)]?

43cd. The eye sense-faculty, the ear sense-faculty and the mental faculty know their object-field without reaching [*aprāptaviṣaya*] it. For the other three sense-faculties, the opposite.[541]

.2.3.1. *Perception of the object-field without reaching it: the eye, ear and mental sense-faculties;*[542] *F 87–88*

(1) The eye sense-faculty [*cakṣus*] [sees visible form from a distance [*dūra*], but it does not see the eye-salve [*añjana*] placed [directly] on the eye [*akṣistha*]; (2) the ear sense-faculty [*śrota*] hears the distant sound; (3) the mental faculty [*manas*], being non-material, does not enter into a close relationship with its object-field.[543] <88>

If the eye and ear sense-faculties were to enter into a close relationship with their object-field [*prāptaviṣaya*], then practitioners in meditation (*dhyāyin*) would not be endowed with the divine eye [*divyacakṣus*], the divine ear [*divyaśrotra*], just as they do not possess a divine nose, [etc.] (vii. 42).

Objection: – If the eye sense-faculty has an object-field with which it is not in a close relationship, why does it not see [all] visible forms [with which it is not in a close relationship, including] what is too distant [to be seen] [*dūra*] or what is concealed [*tīraskṛta*]?[544]

Answer: – Why does the magnet [*ayaskānta*] not draw *all* iron [with which it is not in a close relationship (*aprapta*)]? {17 b}

Besides, supposing that the sense-faculty enters into a close relationship with the object-field [*viśaya*], the same difficulty remains: why does the eye sense-faculty not see *all* the object-fields with which it is in a close relationship, such as the eye-salve [*añjana*] and the little rod [used for painting the eye-salve; *śalākā*)]?

Or else, let us say that the same rule should apply to the eye sense-faculty and the nose and tongue sense-faculties: [for example,] the nose sense-faculty smells only the odor with which it is in a close relationship, but it does not smell the odor that constitutes the sense-faculty itself (*sahabhū*).

In the same way, the eye sense-faculty sees only distant visible form [with which it is not in a close relationship], but it does not see *all* distant visible forms.

[The mental faculty, however, not being material, is incapable of entering into a close relationship at all.[545]]

According to certain scholars, however, from the fact that one can hear sounds even [of what is] inside the ear [*karṇābhyantara*], one can conclude that the ear sense-faculty [*śrotra*] can hear sounds with which it is in a close relationship, as it also can hear distant sounds.[546]

BCS.2.3.2. *Perception of the object with reaching it: the nose, tongue and body sense-faculties;*[547] *F 88–89*

The other three sense-faculties, i.e., nose, tongue and body, perceive an object-field with which they are in close relationship. For the nose, [for example,] this results from the fact that in-breathing is necessary for the perception of the odor.[548]

BCS.2.3.2.a. *Meaning of the expressions "reach" and "non-separation"; F 88–89*[549]

[Question:] – What should one understand by the expression "to reach" (to enter into a close relationship) (*prāp*; *prāpti*)? What does it mean when one says that the sense-faculty *reaches* its object-field, knows its object-field *after having reached it*?

[Answer:] – *To reach* is *to arise in non-separation* [*nirantarotpatti*].[550] The object-field, which renews itself from moment to moment (iv. 2cd), occurs by arising in the state of non-separation with the sense-faculty and *vice versa*. <89>

[What should one understand by the state of non-separation (*nirantaratva*)?

1. According to the Bhadanta, immediate juxtaposition, absence of interval (see below).[551]

2. According to the Vaibhāṣika, immediate vicinity, absence of an interposed body (see below).[552]]

BCS.2.4. *Insert: Do atoms touch one another or not? F 89–92*

The question is then whether the atoms [*paramāṇu*] do or do not touch [*spṛśanti*] one another.[553]

1. Vaibhāṣikas: atoms do not touch one another; F 89
    a. Objections; F 89
        - If atoms do not touch, then how does sound occur? F 89
        - If atoms do not touch, why does the aggregation not fall to pieces when being struck; F 89
    b. Non-separation and reaching as absence of an interposed body; F 90
    c. Composites can touch one another, but atoms do not; F 90
2. Bhadanta (and Vasubandhu): atoms do touch one another metaphorically; F 91
    a. Non-separation as absence of interval; F 91
    b. The composites are nothing other than the atoms; F 92
    c. Spatial division of the atom; F 92

BCS.2.4.1. *Vaibhāṣikas: atoms do not touch one another; F 89–91*

The Vaibhāṣikas of Kaśmīr (MVŚ, 683a24) say that atoms do not touch one another:

1. if the atoms were to touch one another in their totality [or with their whole self; *sarvātman*], the real entities (*dravya*), i.e., the different atoms, would "blend into one another" [*miśrībhaveyuḥ*], i.e., they would occupy only one place;
2. if the atoms were to touch one another in one spot [*ekadeśa*], they would thus have parts (*avayava*): but the atoms do not have parts or are partless [*niravayava*].[554]

5.2.4.1.a. *Objections; F 89–90*

5.2.4.1.aa. *If atoms do not touch, then how does sound occur? F 89*

[Objection:] – But if there is no contact between the atoms, how then is sound produced?

[Answer:] – For this very reason that there is no contact, sound is possible: {18 a} if the atoms touched one another, the hand [*hasta*] in collision (*abhyāhata*) with the hand would merge [*sajyeta*] into it, the stone [*upala*] in collision with the stone would merge into it, just as plant gum [*jatu*] merges into or sticks to plant gum. And the sound would not occur.

5.2.4.1.ab. *If atoms do not touch, why does the aggregation not fall to pieces when being struck; F 89–90*

[Objection:] – But if the atoms do not touch, why does the aggregation (*saṃcita*; *cita*) or the composite of atoms not fall to pieces [*viśīryate*] when it is struck [*pratyāhata*]? <90>

[Answer:] – Because the wind element (*vāyudhātu*) concentrates it or holds it together [*saṃdhāraṇa*]:

1. a certain wind element has dispersion [*vikiraṇāya*] for its function, for example, the wind at the aeon of the dissolution [*saṃvartakalpa*] of the world;
2. a certain wind element has concentration or holding together [*saṃdhāraṇāya*] for its function, for example, the wind at the aeon of creation [*vivartakalpa*] [of the world] (iii. 91, 100).

5.2.4.1.b. *Non-separation and reaching as absence of an interposed body; F 90*

[The Vaibhāṣikas continue the exposition of their doctrine.]

Of three sense-faculties, [i.e., nose, tongue and body,] it is said that they reach [*prāpta*] their object-field because their object-field is with them in a state of non-separation (*nirantaratva*).

[Question:] – What does non-separation consist of?

[Answer:] – [The state of non-separation] consists of the fact that there is nothing in the middle between the two (*tad evaiṣāṃ nirantaratvaṃ yan madhye nāsti kiṃ cit*).

This is also what is meant by "to reach".

BCS.2.4.1.c. *Composites can touch one another, but atoms do not; F 90–91*

Furthermore, as the composites (*saṃghāta*) have parts, there is no problem [*doṣa*] in composites touching one another. And from this point of view, the definitions of the MVŚ (684) are justified:

> Does the thing-in-contact [*spṛṣṭa*] arise having a thing-*in*-contact [*spṛṣṭa-hetuka*] for its cause or does it arise having a thing-*outside-of*-contact [*aspṛṣṭahetuka*] for its cause? <91>

The same question in regard to that which concerns the thing-*outside-of*-contact.

> This cannot be answered in an absolute manner:
>
> 1. sometimes the thing-*outside-of*-contact arises from the thing-*in*-contact when the thing-*in*-contact falls to pieces [*viśīryate*];
> 2. sometimes the thing-*in*-contact arises from the thing-*outside-of*-contact when the thing-*outside-of*-contact becomes compounded [*cayaṃ gaccchati*];
> 3. sometimes the thing-*in*-contact {18 b} arises from the thing-*in*-contact when there is a compounding of compounds [*cayavatāṃ caya*];
> 4. sometimes the thing-*outside-of*-contact arises from the thing-*outside-of*-contact, for example, the dust particles moving suspended in the empty space of the window [*vātāyanarajas*].

The Bhadanta Vasumitra says:

> If atoms touched one another, then they would abide for two moments [*uttarakṣaṇāvasthāna*].[555]

[(Therefore), they do not touch.]

BCS.2.4.2. *Bhadanta (and Vasubandhu): atoms do touch one another metaphorically; F 91–92*

[Opinions of Vasubandhu:[556]]

BCS.2.4.2.a. *Non-separation as absence of interval; F 91*

The Bhadanta says:[557]

> There is, in reality, no contact. Metaphorically it is said that the atoms touch one another when they are juxtaposed without interval (*nirantaratva*). (Quoted in MVŚ, 684a2, see note F 90).[558]

This opinion [*mata*] is the correct one.[559] In fact, if the atoms were to allow an interval between themselves [*sāntarā*], this interval being empty [*śūnya*], what would prevent the movement [*gati*] of atoms into this interval that leaves the atoms separated (*sāntara*)? It is accepted that atoms are impenetrable (*sapratigha*).[560] <92>

.2.4.2.b. *The composites are nothing other than the atoms; F 92*

[Since those atoms are admitted to possess resistance (*sapratigha*), and since] the composites (*saṃghāta*) are nothing other than the atoms, they are the very atoms which, in a state of aggregation [i.e., as composites], are contacted [*spṛśyante*]; just as they are material form (*rūpa*; i. 13).[561] It is thus absurd to deny that the atoms touch one another, and admit that agglomerates touch one another.

2.4.2.c. *Spatial division of the atom; F 92*

1. If you admit the spatial division (*digbhāgabheda*) of the atom, [i.e., the division of the atom into different portions in different directions,] then the atom certainly has parts [*sāvayavatva*] whether it enters into contact or not (*spṛṣṭa, aspṛṣṭa*).

2. If you deny it, it is hard to see why the atom, even if it enters into contact, would have parts.[562]

2.5. *Size of the sense-faculties and their object-fields;*[563] *F 92–93*

Should we think that the sense-faculties seize only an object-referent [*artha*] of their own size [*parimāṇa*]? I.e., if it is thought that one sees the extended object-referent [*mahatā*] all at once [*sakṛt*], for example, a mountain [*parvata*], then that is by way of an illusion, because we see quickly [*āśuvṛtti*] the parts of the mountain: this is obviously so when we see the circle of fire drawn by a whirling torch [*alātacakra*]. <93>

Or should we think that the sense-faculties seize an object-field of their own [*tulya*] size and of a different [*atulya*] size indiscriminately? {19 a}

44ab. **The three sense-faculties, of which the nose sense-faculty is the first, [i.e., the nose, tongue and body sense-faculties,] seize an object-field of their own size.**[564]

A given number of atoms [*paramāṇu*][565] of the sense-faculty, reaching the same number of atoms of an object-field, produce the consciousness.

1–3. This holds for the nose, the tongue and the body in this way. (ii. 22)

4–5. But, there is no rule [*aniyama*] for [the sense-faculties of] the eye and the ear.

[As for the eye:]

i. sometimes the object-field is smaller than the sense-faculty, as when one sees the tip of a hair [*vālāgra*];
ii. sometimes the same as the sense faculty, as when one sees a grape [*drākṣā*];
iii. sometimes larger than the sense-faculty, as when one sees a great mountain [*parvata*] in a mere glance [*unmiśitamātra*].

The same for sound or noise [*ghoṣa*], [i.e., it is smaller, larger, etc.]: one hears the buzzing of a mosquito [*maśaka*], the roaring of a thundering cloud [*megha*], etc.

6. In regard to that which concerns the mental faculty which is non-material [*amūrti*], the question [of dividing it according to size (*parimāṇapariccheda*)] does not arise.

BCS.2.6. *Issues related to the atoms of the sense-faculties; F 93–94*

Here some problems arise relative to the sense-faculties.

BCS.2.6.1. *Arrangement of the atoms of the sense-faculties; F 93–94*

How are the atoms [*paramāṇu*] of the different sense-faculties arranged?[566]

1. The atoms of the eye sense-faculty are arranged on the pupil of the eye [*akṣi-tārakā*] like cumin flowers (*ajājipuṣpavat, kālajirakapuṣpa*), i.e., on one surface [*ekatala*]; they are covered by a membrane or shield of translucent color (*varṇa; acchacarmāvacchādita*) which prevents them from dispersing.[567]

According to another opinion, they are arranged in depth or one on top of the other [*adharauttarya*] like a pill or ball [*piṇḍavat*]; being translucent, like the crystal [*sphaṭikavat*], they do not obscure or obstruct one another.

2. The atoms of the ear sense-faculty are arranged in the interior [*abhyantara*] of the *bhūrja*, a kind of birch-bark leaf found in the [inner] ear [*karṇa*].

3. The atoms of the nose sense-faculty {19 b} are arranged like two needles [*śalākāvat*] in the interior of the nostrils (*ghāṭā, nāsāpuṭī*). <94>

These first three sense-faculties form a garland [or are arranged like a garland (around the head)] [*mālāvat*].[568]

4. The atoms of the tongue sense-faculty are arranged on the upper surface of the tongue like a half-moon [*ardhacandravat*]. That is, in the middle of the tongue, a

space, the size of the tip of a hair [*vālāgramātra*], is not occupied [*astṛta*; *asphuṭa*, *avyāpta*] by the atoms of the sense-faculty. Such is the opinion expressed in the Scripture.[569]

5. The atoms of the body sense-faculty are arranged like the form of the body itself [*kāyavat*].

6. The atoms of the female sexual faculty are arranged like the bowl of a drum [*bherīkaṭāhavat*].

7. The atoms of the male sexual faculty are arranged like a thumb [*aṅguṣṭhavat*].

2.6.2. *Homogeneous and partially homogeneous & the atoms of the sense-faculties;* F 94

1. As for the atoms [*paramāṇu*] of the eye sense-faculty, sometimes they can be all homogeneous (*sabhāga*; i. 39); sometimes all partially homogeneous (*tatsabhāga*); sometimes some homogeneous and some partially homogeneous.

2–4. The same for the atoms of the ear, nose and tongue sense-faculties.

5. But in regard to that which concerns the body sense-faculty, it is not the case that its atoms are all homogeneous: even when the body is enveloped in the flames of the Pratapana hell (iii. 58), an infinite number of atoms [of the body sense-faculty] are partially homogeneous, because, the School says, the body [*āśraya*] would fall to pieces [*viśiryate*] if all the atoms of the body sense-faculty were to work at the same time.

2.6.3. *Aggregations as sense-faculties (basis) and cognitive objects of the sensory consciousnesses & the invisibility of real-entity atoms;* F 94

It does not happen that consciousness is produced by one single atom of a sense-faculty [*indriyaparamāṇu*], by one single atom of an object-field [*viṣayaparamāṇu*]. In fact, the five categories of consciousness have the aggregations (*saṃcita*) for their basis and their cognitive object.[570] {20 a}

The result of this is that atoms [by themselves] are not seen [*adṛśyatva*]; they are therefore qualified as invisible (*anidarśana*; i. 29ab; iv. 4).[571]

2.7. *Simultaneity and non-simultaneity of the object-field or sense-faculty with its consciousness & the eighteen elements;* F 94–95

[There are these six elements of consciousness that have been discussed, from visual consciousness through mental consciousness.] The object-field [*viṣaya*] of the first five consciousnesses is [present, i.e.,] simultaneous [*vartamāna*] with them;[572] the object-field of the sixth consciousness is either prior to it, simultaneous with it, or later than it; in other words, it is past, present, or future (i. 23).

Does the same hold for the basis [*āśraya*] of the consciousnesses? <95>

44cd. Relative to the consciousnesses, (1) the basis of the sixth consciousness is past [only]; (2) the basis of the first five [consciousnesses] is also simultaneous [*sahaja*], [i.e., both earlier than and simultaneous with the consciousness].[573]

1. The sole basis of the mental consciousness is the mental faculty (*manodhātu*), i.e., the consciousness which has just perished (i. 17).

2. The basis of five consciousnesses is also simultaneous with them: that is to say, it is prior to and simultaneous with the consciousness. In fact, the basis of these consciousnesses is twofold:

- i. the sense-faculty, i.e., the eye sense-faculty, etc., which is simultaneous with the consciousness;
- ii. the mental faculty, which is past at the moment when consciousness arises.

The five consciousnesses thus have two sense-faculties as their basis.

[For this very reason] the question is posed: {20 b} Is that which is the basis of the visual consciousness at the same time the condition as the equivalent and immediate antecedent (*samanantarapratyaya*; ii. 62) of this consciousness?

Four alternatives (tetralemma):

- i. the eye sense-faculty, which is the basis only;
- ii. the totality of the thought-concomitants, i.e., sensation, etc. (ii. 24), which have just perished [*samanantarātītaś caitasiko dharmadhātu*]: they are the condition as the equivalent and immediate antecedent only;
- iii. the consciousness which has just perished, or the mental faculty, which is at the same time the basis and the condition as the equivalent and immediate antecedent;
- iv. the other factors which are neither one or the other.[574]

The same for the auditory, olfactory, gustatory and tactile consciousnesses.

In regard to the mental consciousness, [is that which is the basis of the mental consciousness at the same time the condition as the equivalent and immediate antecedent of mental consciousness?] The answer is in accord with the former (and not the latter alternative) of the question [*pūrvapādaka*]: that which is the basis of the mental consciousness is always the condition as the equivalent and immediate antecedent of this consciousness; but the inverse is not true: [the totality of] the thought-concomitants which just have perished is not a basis.

2.8. *Sense-faculties as the basis (āśraya) of consciousness & the eighteen elements; F 95–96*

The visual consciousness depends on both the eye sense-faculty and on the visible form. Why is only the sense-faculty considered as the basis (*āśraya*) of the consciousness to the exclusion of the object-field? <96>

45ab. The basis of the consciousness is the sense-faculty, for the consciousness changes or is modified [*vikāra*] according to any change or modality [*vikāritvā*] of the sense-faculty.[575]

When the eye sense-faculty is the object of medical care (*anugraha*; application of eye salve, etc.); when it is injured [*upaghāta*] by dust [*reṇu*], etc.; when it is sharp (*paṭu*); when it is dull and weak (*manda*), the consciousness reproduces its change or modality [*vikāra*]: it is accompanied by pleasure [*sukha*] or by pain [*duḥkha*], it is sharp or weak.

[The change or modality of] the object-field, on the contrary, has no influence on the change or modality of the consciousness. {21 a}

Therefore, it is the sense-faculty and not the object-field that is [more properly (*sādhiyas*)] the basis of consciousness (ii. 2ab).

2.9. *Sense-faculties as the basis for naming the consciousnesses & the eighteen elements; F 96*

The consciousness knows the object-field. Why is it designated by the name of the sense-faculty: consciousness of the eye (*cakṣurvijñāna*)... consciousness of the mental faculty (*manas*), and not by the name of the object-field: consciousness of the visible form (*rūpavijñāna*)... consciousness of the factors (*dharmavijñāna*)?

45cd. (1) For the reason [that the sense-faculty is the basis of the consciousness], and (2) also because [the sense-faculty] is "its own or not shared", it is the sense-faculty that gives its name to the consciousness.[576]

1. Because the sense-faculty is its basis, the consciousness takes the name of the sense-faculty.

2. Because the sense-faculty is "its own or not shared" [*asādhāraṇatva*]: the eye sense-faculty of a given person is the basis of (i) the visual consciousness only, (ii) of just this one person.

Visible form, on the contrary, is shared [*sādhāraṇa*], for a certain visible form is perceived (i) by the visual consciousness and by the mental consciousness, (ii) by one person and by another person.

The same observation for the (other) sense-faculties: ear, nose, tongue and body, and for the (other) object-fields: sound, odor, taste and tangible.

We conclude that the consciousness is named after the sense-faculty, (1) because the sense-faculty is its basis and (2) because the sense-faculty is its own or not shared. The same does not hold for the object-field. [Just so,] it is said commonly "the sound of the drum" [*bherīśabda*], and not "the sound of the stick" [*daṇḍaśabda*]; "the sprout of barley" [*yavāṅkura*], and not "the sprout of the field" [*kṣetrāṅkura*]. <97>

BCS.2.10. *Stages (bhūmi) & the sense-faculties, body, object-fields and consciousnesses of the eighteen elements;*[577] *F 97–100*

Beings are born in a certain stage of the world (*bhūmi*), in the realm of desire, in the first meditation (*dhyāna*), etc.; they are of this stage, and their body (*kāya*) is also of this stage. They see—by means of the eye sense-faculty—visible forms.

Question: – Do the body, the eye sense-faculty, the visible forms and the consciousness belong to the same stage or to different stages?

Answer: – All can belong to different stages.

BCS.2.10.1. *Eye sense-faculty & the body, sense-faculty, visible form and consciousness;*[578] *F 97–98*

BCS.2.10.1.a. *Eye sense-faculty, body, etc., in the realm of desire;*[579] *F 97*

When beings who have arisen in the realm of desire see—by means of the eye sense-faculty of their stage—the visible forms of their stage, then (1) the body, (2) the sense-faculty, (3) the visible forms and (4) the consciousness are of the same stage.

When these beings see—by means of the eye sense-faculty of the *first* meditation (*dhyāna*)—the visible forms of this stage (i.e., the realm of desire), then (1) the body and (3) the visible forms are of the realm of desire, (2) the sense-faculty and (4) the consciousness are of the *first* meditation {21 b}. If these beings see—by means of the same sense-faculty—the visible forms of the *first* meditation, then (1) the body alone is of the realm of desire; (2–4) the other three are of the *first* meditation.

When these beings see—by means of the eye sense-faculty of the *second* meditation—the visible forms of the realm of desire, then (1) the body and (3) the visible forms are of the realm of desire, (2) the sense-faculty is of the *second* meditation, (4) the consciousness is of the *first* meditation. [If these beings see—by means of the same sense-faculty—the visible forms of the *first* meditation, then (4) the consciousness and (3) the visible forms are of the *first* meditation, (1) the body is of the realm of desire, and (2) the sense-faculty is of *the second* meditation.[580]] If these beings see—by means of the same sense-faculty—the visible forms of the *second*[581] meditation, then (1) the body is of the realm of desire, (2) the sense-faculty and (3) the visible forms are of the *second* meditation, (4) the consciousness is of the *first* meditation. (viii. 13ac)

The cases where beings who have arisen in the realm of desire see—by means of the eye sense-faculty of the *third* or of the *fourth* meditation—the visible forms of these same stages or of a lower stage can be explained in the same way.

S.2.10.1.b. *Eye sense-faculty, body, etc., in the first meditation;*[582] *F 97–98*

When beings who have arisen in the *first* meditation see—by means of the eye sense-faculty of their stage—the visible forms of their stage, then (1) the body, (2) the sense-faculty, (3) the visible forms and (4) the consciousness are of the same stage. If these beings see—by means of the same sense-faculty—the visible forms of the lower stage, then (1) the body, (2) the sense-faculty and (4) the consciousness are of their stage, the *first* meditation.

When these beings see—by means of the eye sense-faculty of the *second* meditation—the visible forms of their stage—then three (i.e., (1) the body, (3) the visible forms and (4) the consciousness) are of their stage (*first* meditation), (2) the sense-faculty is of the *second* meditation. <98> If these beings see—by means of the same sense-faculty—the visible forms of the realm of desire, then (1) the body and (4) the consciousness are of their stage (*first* meditation), (3) the visible forms are of the lower stage, (2) the sense-faculty is of the *second* meditation. If these beings see—by means of the same sense-faculty—the visible forms of the *second* meditation, then (1) the body and (4) the consciousness are of their stage (*first* meditation), (2) the sense-faculty and (3) the visible forms of the *second* meditation.

The cases where beings arisen in the *first* meditation see—by means of the eye sense-faculty of the *third* or of the *fourth* meditation—the visible forms of these stages or of a lower stage can be explained in the same way.

CS.2.10.1.c. *Eye sense-faculty, body, etc., in the second, third and fourth meditation;*[583] *F 98*

According to the same principles, we can explain the cases where beings who have arisen in the *second* meditation, the *third* meditation or the *fourth* meditation, see—by means of the eye sense-faculty of their stage or of a different stage—the visible forms of their stage or of a different stage. {22 a}

BCS.2.10.2. *General rules;*[584] *F 98–100*

BCS.2.10.2.a. *General rule related to the eye sense-faculty;*[585] *F 98–99*

The rule is the following:

46. (1) The eye sense-faculty is never of a [stage] lower than the body, [i.e., it can also be of a higher stage]; (2) the visible form is never of a [stage] higher than the sense-faculty; (3) the consciousness is also not [of a stage higher than the sense-faculty]; (4) the visible form—in relation to the consciousness—and the visible form as well as the consciousness—in relation to the body—are of all types [i.e., equal, higher, lower].[586]

The body, the eye sense-faculty, the visible form can belong to five stages: the realm of desire, four meditations (*dhyāna*).

The visual consciousness is of two stages only: the realm of desire and the first meditation (viii. 13ac).

Having said all this, (1) the eye sense-faculty which a certain being employs can be of the same stage [*tadbhūmika*] to which the body of this being belongs, i.e., of the stage where this being is arisen; it can be of a higher stage [*ūrdhvabhūmika*]; it is never of a lower stage [*adharabhūmika*].

(2–3) The visible form and the consciousness—in relation to the sense-faculty—are either of the same stage or of a lower stage, never of a higher stage. A visible form of a higher stage cannot be seen by an eye sense-faculty of a lower stage. A visual consciousness of a higher stage cannot arise from a sense-faculty of a lower stage.

(4) The visible form—in relation to the visual consciousness—is either equal, higher, or lower. <99>

The visible form and the visual consciousness—in relation to the body—are as visible form is in relation to the consciousness, i.e., equal, higher, lower.

BCS.2.10.2.b. *General rule related to the ear sense-faculty;*[587] *F 99*

47a. The same holds for the ear sense-faculty.[588]

(1) The ear sense-faculty is not lower than the body. (2–3) Sound is not higher than the ear sense-faculty, nor is the auditory consciousness. (4) Sound—in relation to the auditory consciousness—and sound and the consciousness—in relation to the body—can be of any type. {22 b}

.2.10.2.c. *General rule related to the nose, tongue and body sense-faculties;*[589] *F 99*

47ab. [With respect to the] three sense-faculties [of the nose, of the tongue and of the body,] all, [i.e., the body, the sense-faculty, the object-field and the consciousness,] belong [exclusively] to their own stage.[590]

With respect to what concerns the nose, tongue and body sense-faculties, (1) the body, (2) the sense-faculty, (3) the object-field and (4) the consciousness belong exclusively to their own stage, to the stage in which the beings under consideration have arisen.

.2.10.2.ca. *Exception: tactile consciousness;*[591] *F 99*

Having formulated this general rule [*utsarga*], the author indicates an exception [*apavāda*]:

47cd. The tactile consciousness is of its own stage or a lower stage.[592]

The body (*kāya*), the body sense-faculty (*kāyadhātu*) and the tangible [*spraṣṭavya*] are always of the stage in which the beings under consideration have arisen. But the tactile consciousness (1) is of its own stage, in the case of beings who have arisen in the realm of desire or in the first meditation; (2) is of a lower stage (first meditation), in the case of beings arisen in the second meditation or higher.

2.10.2.d. *General rule for the mental faculty;*[593] *F 99–100*

47d. There is no restriction with respect to that which concerns the mental faculty.[594]

1. Sometimes the mental faculty is of the same stage [*samānabhūmika*] as the body, the element of factors (*dharmadhātu*) and the mental consciousness.

2. Sometimes (the mental faculty) is of a lower or a higher stage [*ūrdhvādho-bhūmika*]. <100>

The body belonging to the first five stages, i.e., the realm of desire and the four meditations, the mental faculty, the element of factors and the mental consciousness can, in meditative attainment (*samāpatti*) or at conception (*pratisaṃdhi*; *upapatti*), be of whatever stage—all the stages, in addition, not being the same in each case. This will be explained in the eighth chapter: EXPOSITION OF THE MEDITATIVE ATTAINMENTS (*Samāpattinirdeśa*; viii. 19cd]. To avoid making this treatise too long, we will not discuss this here; little purpose [*prayojana*] would be served, and the pains [*śrama*] would be great.

BCT. *20. Consciousness (vijñāna), object of consciousness/the cognized (vijñeya) & the eighteen elements;*[595] *F 100*

There are eighteen elements and six consciousnesses. Which element is cognized [*vijñeya*] by which consciousness (*vijñāna*)?

48a. The five external elements are cognized by two consciousnesses, [that is, by a sensory consciousness and by the mental consciousness].[596]

(1) Visible forms, (2) sounds, (3) odors, (4) tastes and (5) tangibles are known (*anubhūta*) by the consciousnesses (1) of the eye, (2) of the ear, (3) of the nose, (4) of the tongue and (5) of the body, respectively.

They are all [also] cognized (*vijñeya*) by the mental consciousness [*manovijñāna*].[597] Each of these external elements is thus cognized by two consciousnesses.

The other thirteen elements, not being of the object-field [*viṣaya*] of the [five groups of] sensory consciousness, are cognized by the mental consciousness alone.

BCU. *21. Permanent (nitya) and impermanent (anitya) & the eighteen elements;*[598] *F 100*

[Question:] – How many elements are permanent [*nitya*] [and how many are impermanent (*anitya*)]?

[Answer:] – No element is permanent in its totality.

48b. (But) the unconditioned factors [which form a part of the element of factors] are permanent.[599]

The unconditioned factors (i. 5b) form a part of the element of factors (*dharmadhātu*; i. 15c). Thus one part of the element of factors is permanent, [the remaining ones are impermanent[600]].

BCV. *22. Controlling faculties (indriya) and not controlling faculties (nendriya) & the eighteen elements;*[601] *F 100–2*

How many of the elements are controlling faculties (*indriya*), i.e., rulers (ii. 1), [and how many are not controlling faculties (*nendriya*)]?

48cd. (1) The twelve internal elements and (2) a part of the element of factors are controlling faculties.[602] <101>

BCV.1. *Enumeration of the twenty-two controlling faculties;*[603] *F 101*

The Sūtra[604] enumerates twenty-two controlling faculties (*indriya*):

1. eye sense-faculty (*cakṣurindriya*);
2. ear sense-faculty (*śrotendriya*);
3. nose sense-faculty (*ghrāṇendriya*);
4. tongue sense-faculty (*jihvendriya*);
5. body sense-faculty (*kāyendriya*);
6. mental faculty (*mana-indriya*);
7. male sexual faculty (*puruṣendriya*);
8. female sexual faculty (*strīndriya*);
9. vitality faculty (*jīvitendriya*);
10. faculty of sensation of pleasure (*sukhendriya*);
11. faculty of sensation of displeasure (*duḥkha–indriya*);
12. faculty of sensation of satisfaction (*saumanasya–indriya*);
13. faculty of sensation of dissatisfaction (*daurmanasya-indriya*);
14. faculty of sensation of equanimity (*upekṣa–indriya*);
15. (praxis-oriented) faculty of faith (*śraddhendriya*);
16. (praxis-oriented) faculty of vigor (*vīryendriya*);
17. (praxis-oriented) faculty of mindfulness (*smṛtīndriya*);
18. (praxis-oriented) faculty of concentration (*samādhīndriya*);
19. (praxis-oriented) faculty of understanding (*prajñendriya*);
20. faculty of coming to know what is not yet known (*anājñātamājñāsyāmi–indriya*);
21. faculty of perfect knowledge (*ājñendriya*);
22. faculty of final and perfect knowledge (*ājñātāvīndriya*) (see F 117).

The Ābhidhārmikas (*Prakaraṇapāda*, fol. 31b) do not take into account the group constituted by the six sense-faculties of consciousness (*āyatana*), i.e., (1–5) the eye, ear, nose, tongue and body sense-faculties and (6) the mental faculty, and thus do not place the mental faculty after the body sense-faculty but after the vitality faculty, because the mental faculty, just like the faculties of sensation (10–14), has a cognitive object (*ālambana*; i. 29bc) and not only an object-field (*viṣaya*) as the sense-faculties of the sensory consciousness (1–5).[605] {23 b} <102>

CV.2. *One part of the external element of factors & the twenty-two controlling faculties;* F 102

Among the twenty-two controlling faculties,

i. eleven controlling faculties, namely, the vitality faculty (9), the five faculties of sensation (10–14), the five (praxis-oriented) faculties (15–19), and
ii. a part of the last three controlling faculties (20–22),

form a part of the element of factors (*dharmadhātu*).[606]

BCV.3. *Twelve internal elements & the twenty-two controlling faculties; F 102*

The twelve internal elements are (1) the five sense-faculties of sensory consciousness, which form five elements (*dhātu*) and the (first) five controlling faculties, [being called by their own names (*svanāmokta*)], (2) the mental faculty (i. 16c), i.e., the sixth controlling faculty, which makes up seven elements of thought [*cittadhātu*], and (3) a part of [the body sense-faculty, i.e., male and female sexual faculties (*strīpuruṣendriye kāyadhātupradeśa*)[607]].

BCV.4. *The remaining five external elements & the twenty-two controlling faculties;*[608] *F 102*

(1) The five remaining [external] elements, [i.e., visible form, sound, odor, taste and the tangible], and (2) a part of the element of factors (*dharmadhātu*; i. 15bd) are not controlling faculties [*indriya*].

* * *

This concludes the

First Chapter (*Kośasthāna*)

called

EXPOSITION OF THE ELEMENTS (*Dhātunirdeśa*)

in the

Abhidharmakośa-Bhāṣya.

Endnotes to Chapter One

[1] *Lodrö Sangpo* (*LS*): AH 1; SAH 1.

As for a brief discussion of chapter 1, see Dhammajoti's *Summary and Discussion of the Abhidharmakośa-bhāṣya* (from now onwards: *Summary*), which also briefly addresses the usage of *dhātu* in its title: *Dhātunirdeśa.*

[2] *LS*: Ibid.

[3] *Gokhale*: [1] *yaḥ sarvathā sarvahatā'ndhakāraḥ* | *saṃsārapaṅkāj jagad ujjahāra* | *tasmai namaskṛtya yathā'rthaśāstre* | *śāstraṃ pravakṣyāmy abhidharmakośam* ||

Tib.: [1] *gang zhig kun la mun pa gtan bcom zhing* | *'khor ba'i 'dam las 'gro ba drangs mdzad pa* | *don bzhin ston pa de la phyag 'tshal nas* | *chos mngon mdzod kyi bstan pcos rab bshad bya* ||

[4] *LS*: This "greatness" refers, according to Yaśomitra (WOG.2.6f.), to the "completeness of his accomplishment for the benefit of himself and others" (*svaparārtha-pratipatti-sampat*) (VASC.40).

[5] *LS*: I.e., all twelve sense-spheres (*āyatana*) (WOG.4.2f; VASC.41).

[6] *LS*: According to the *Vyākhyā*, "in every respect" refers to all modes, i.e., to the absence of the defiled and undefiled darkness: sarveṇa prakāreṇa sarva-hataṃ *sarvathā sarva-hatam.* [...] *sarveṇa prakāreṇêti* kliṣṭākliṣṭāndhakāra-vigamataḥ [WOG.3.31ff.].

In his footnotes to the *Abhidharmakośabhāṣya* (hereafter AKB), La Vallée Poussin (LVP) often quotes from Yaśomitra's *Sphuṭārthā Abhidharmakośavyākhyā* (hereafter *Vyākhyā* or WOG) but does not italicize the original text. At the same time, he often does not identify his Sanskrit quotes. With the help of electronic search. I attempted to identify the WOG Sanskrit passages and was able to trace many, which are now indicated, for example, as [WOG.5.15ff.]. While doing so, I separated out "the original text" (in italics) and the "commentary" (in non-italics) according to Wogihara's 1971 edition. On the other hand, the texts sometimes show slight differences. When these differences were greater, the commentary was not separated out and the passages were then referenced as: "cf. WOG" or "see WOG".

[7] *LS*: I.e., LVP, page 2. The numbers in angle brackets hereafter refer to the page numbers in LVP's 1923–1931 edition, which are the same page numbers as in the unchanged 1971 edition. As already mentioned in our *Remarks by the Translator* (hereafter *Remarks*), the difference between the two editions is that the 1923–1931 edition contains LVP's *Preface* and *Introduction* in vol. 6, whereas in the 1971 edition they are found in vol. 1. The 1923–1931 edition has also a brief introduction (2 pages) where LVP outlines his plans for the various volumes and the sources he utilized, which—although omitted in the 1971 edition—we have included in our *Electronic Appendix* (see URL in our *Remarks*). The 1971 edition adds Étienne Lamotte's "Préface à la Réédition" (5 pages) and an "Addendum Bibliographique" (1 page) by Hubert Durt.

[8] *La Vallée Poussin* (*LVP*): The authors of the *Vinayavibhāṣā* say [tetralemma]:

1. there is a Buddha who is not a Fortunate One (Bhagavat), namely, the Pratyeka-

buddhas (self-enlightened ones), because they are self-arisen ones (*svayambhū*), i.e., because they have obtained Bodhi by themselves, because they have not completed the task of the perfection of generosity (*dānapāramitā*), etc. (vii. 34);

2. there is a Fortunate One who is not a Buddha, namely, the Bodhisattva in his last existence;
3. there is a Buddha Bhagavat;
4. there are persons who are neither a Buddha nor a Fortunate One [cf. WOG.3.5ff.].

One can also say that the Śrāvakas, i.e., the listeners or [enlightened] disciples, are Buddhas (Āryadeva, *Śataka*, 270), for they obtain Bodhi (enlightenment; vi. 67).

LS: 1. There are various traditional epithets given to the Buddha, ten of which form a traditional formula of praise: *bhagavāṃs tathāgato 'rhaṃ samyaksaṃbuddho vidyācarana-saṃpannaḥ sugato lokavid anuttaraḥ puruṣadamyasārathiḥ śāsta devamanuṣyāṇāṃ buddho bhagavāṃ*. For the etymological explanations of the various epithets of the Buddha, see *Visuddhimagga*, I, pp. 198–213 and MPPŚ, I, pp. 115–37.

2. As for "Bhagavat" and our translation "Fortunate One", the *Visuddhimagga* (I, pp. 224–27) states:

> Blessed (*bhagavant*) is a term signifying the respect and veneration accorded to him as the highest of all beings and distinguished by his special qualities. ... It may be known that he [can also] be called "Blessed (*Bhagavā*)" when he can be called "fortunate (*bhāgyavā*)" owing to the fortunate-ness (*bhāgya*) of having reached the further shore [of the ocean of perfection] of giving, virtue, etc., which produce mundane and supramundane bliss. ... And by his fortunate-ness (*bhāgyavatā*) is indicated: the excellence of his material body that bears a hundred characteristics of merit; ... the esteem of worldly [people]...; that he is fit to be relied on by laymen.

The MPPŚ states (I, pp. 116f.):

> 1. In the word *bhagavat*, *bhāga* means quality (*guṇa*) and *vat* indicates its possession: "the one who possesses qualities". 2. Furthermore, *bhāga* means analysis (*vibhāga*) and *vat* indicates skill (*kuśala*). Skillful in analyzing the specific and common characteristics (*svasāmānyalakṣaṇa*) of the *dharmas*, he is called Bhagavat. 3. Furthermore, *bhāga* means glory (*yaśas-*) and *vat* indicates its possession. Thus this word means "the one who possesses glory". ... 4. Furthermore, *bhāga* means to break (*bhaṅga*) and *vat* indicates the ability. The person who can break desire or attachment (*rāga*), hatred (*dveṣa*) and delusion (*moha*) is called Bhagavat.

9 *LS*: I.e., Hsüan-tsang, i, fol. 1b. The numbers in curly brackets hereafter refer to the page references in the Kandō edition of the *Abhidharmakośabhāṣya* [*A-p'i-ta-mo chü-she-shih lun*]; Vasubandhu, trans. Hsüan-tsang. See also Hirakawa's helpful concordance chart (IA.III.317–22; see *Electronic Appendix*) of the various editions: Pradhan, Shastri, Taishō, Kandō, Peking, Derge.

10 *LS*: Dhammajoti comments (SA.IV.257): "*śrāvaka* (i.e., 'disciple', referring in this context mainly to an *arhat*), ...".

11 *LVP*: In fact, the self-enlightened ones as well as the listeners have abandoned (*prahīṇa*) the undefiled ignorance (*akliṣṭam ajñānam*) just as they have abandoned the eye sense-faculty,

etc., by abandoning all predilection-attachment (*chandarāga*) with respect to it. But this undefiled ignorance, just like the eye sense-faculty, remains active or manifest in them (*samudācarati*) even though it is abandoned.

Such is not the case for the Buddha: this is why the author says that he has destroyed (*hata*) the darkness in such a manner that it can not rearise.

LS: 1. In this beginning passage of the AKB, Vasubandhu discusses the distinction between the Buddha and the two *yānas*, i.e., the *śrāvaka* and the *pratyekabuddha*, only with regard to undefiled ignorance (*akliṣṭājñāna*). Later in chapter 7, however, when discussing the eighteen unique factors (*aveṇikadharma*) of the Buddha, we find also two brief references to "traces" (*vāsanā*) (see SA.IV.360):

i. vii. 32cd: "The eighteen *āveṇika-dharma*-s of the Buddha are *āveṇika* (unique) because He has abandoned the defilements along with their *vāsanā* (*sa-vāsanam*)."

ii. vii. 34: "The Buddha's perfection as regards the abandoning of defilements (*prahāṇa-saṃpad*) is fourfold: (i) He has abandoned all defilements (*sarvakleśa-prahāṇa*); (ii) He has abandoned them absolutely (*atyanta-prahāṇa*); (iii) He has abandoned them along with their *vāsanā* (*savāsanaprahāṇa*); (iv) He has abandoned all hindrances to the attainment of *samādhi* (*sarva-samādhi-samāpattyāvaraṇaprahāṇa*)." Dhammajoti comments that the last (iv) aspect refers, for the Vaibhāṣikas, to the abandoning of *akliṣṭa-ajñāna*.

See our detailed endnote on *akliṣṭa-ajñāna* and *vāsanā* at vii. 32d.

2. Dhammajoti comments (SA.IV.257): "While both the Buddha and Śāriputra can correctly understand all that is subsumable under the 12 *āyatana*-s, the Buddha has both omniscience (*sarvajñā/sarvajñatā*) and 'wisdom of all modes' (*sarva-ākāra-jñāna/sarvathā-jñāna*), and knows them with regard to both their common and intrinsic characteristics. Śāriputra has only *sarvajñā* which knows only their common characteristics. A supreme-perfect Buddha (*anuttara-samyak-sambuddha*) alone, as a result of having absolutely abandoned all defiled (*kliṣṭa*) and non-defiled (*akliṣṭa*) ignorance (*ajñāna*), understands all knowables, both conventional and absolute."

[12] *LVP*: Śāriputra does not cognize the five [pure] aggregates (*skandha*; i, F 48) [i.e., morality (*śīla*), concentration (*samādhi*), superior knowledge (*prajñā*), liberation (*vimukti*), and cognition-insight of liberation (*vimuktijñānadarśana*)] of the Tathāgata.

LS: Dhammajoti comments (SA.IV.258; WOG.4.32f.) that the self-enlightened ones and listeners have *ajñāna* with regard to the Buddha qualities (the eighteen unique qualities, etc.) on account of their being extremely subtle and profound in nature (*svabhāva-parama-sūkṣma-gambhīratvāt*). The eighteen unique qualities (*āveṇika dharma*), discussed at vii. 28, are: (1–10) the ten powers (*daśabala*), (10–14) the four fearlessnesses (*vaiśāradya*); (15–17) the three mindful equanimities (*smṛtyupasthāna*) and (18) great compassion (*mahākaruṇā*).

[13] *LVP*: [With regard to things far remote in space,] Maudgalyāyana does not see that his mother is reborn in Marīcilokadhātu.

[With regard to things or events extremely distant in time,] Śāriputra does not perceive the wholesome roots of a candidate for ordination (*mokṣabhagīya-kuśala-mūla-adarśana*); see vii. 30: Śāriputra refused a person who asked for admission into the Order (*pravrajyāprekṣa-*

puruṣapratyākhyāna); but the Buddha pointed out:

> *mokṣabījam aham hy asya susūkṣmam upalakṣaye |*
> *dhātupāṣāṇavivare nilīnam iva kāñcanaṃ* || [see WOG.5.6ff.]

Compare Huber, *Sūtrālaṃkāra*, p. 286.

LS: Dhammajoti comments (SA.IV.258; WOG.5.3ff.): "The two *yāna*s [i.e., *pratyekabuddha* and *śrāvaka*] in fact cannot know visible matter composed of atoms [*rūpiṇaḥ paramāṇu-saṃcitāḥ*] which are extremely distant, or invisible, non-material things [*avijñapty-arūpiṇaḥ*] belonging to far away places on account of their being many world systems away [*aneka-loka-dhātv-antarita-deśatvāt*]."

14 *LVP*: As the stanza says (see ix, F 284; WOG.5.16f.):

> *sarvākāraṃ kāraṇam ekasya mayūracandrakasyāpi*
> *nāsarvajñair jñeyaṃ sarvajñajñānabalaṃ hi taj-jñānam*
>
> The [generative] causes in all their various aspects for even a single eye in a peacock's tail (*mayūracandraka*), is not to be known by those without omniscience (*asarvajña*): for it is the power (*bala*) of the cognition of the Omniscient One (*sarvajña*) to know [a thing in all its modes/aspects].

LS: Dhammajoti comments (SA.IV.258) that this refers to things difficult to perceive, such as the divisions of realms (*dhātu*), planes of existence (*gati*), mode of births (*yoni*) and births (*upapatti*) [WOG.5.14f.]. For a discussion of these divisions see chapter 3.

15 *LS*: Hall translates (VASC.43) Yaśomitra's gloss of *saṃsāra* [WOG.5.28f.]: "*Saṃsāra* (transmigration) is the 'wandering about' (*saṃsaraṇa*), the back and forth succession of birth and death. Or, Saṃsāra is that in which sentient beings transmigrate ('wander together', *saṃ-sṛ*), namely the three realms (*dhātu*) of desires, forms, and formless states."

16 *LVP*: "As far as possible" (*yathābhavyam*). This is obvious, as in the case when one says: "He will give the Brahmins something to eat."

17 *LVP*: We read in the *Vyākhyā* [WOG.56.5], *saddharmadeśanāhastapradānaiḥ*. We have the plural because the persons to save are numerous.

18 *LVP*: Expression of Āryadeva, *Śataka*, 265.

19 *LVP*: *na tu ṛddhi-vara-pradāna-prabhāvena*. First explanation: through the power of supernormal accomplishments (*ṛddhi*; vii. 48), like Viṣṇu; through the power of giving, like Maheśvara.

Second explanation: through supernormal accomplishments, through giving, through their power (*prabhāva*) (vii. 34).

It is true that the Buddhas perform miracles (*ṛddhi-prātihārya*) in order to attract the faithful (*āvarjanamātra*); but it is through the miracle of the teaching (*anuśāsanī-prātihārya*) that they save the world by destroying the fluxes (vii. 47ab).

20 *LS*: The words *śāstra* (treatise), *śāsana* (teaching) and *śiṣya* (disciple, student) all derive from the root *śās* (teach) (VASC.44).

21 *LS*: 1. Wangchuk Dorje (YP.11f.) distinguishes between absolute *abhidharma*, path *abhidharma* and textual *abhidharma*. Hirakawa, in turn, states (MDA.168) that "in short, the

three types of *abhidharma* given in the *Kośa* are (i) the wisdom that realizes *nirvāṇa*; (ii) the wisdom of ordinary people that cognizes *dharmas*; and (iii) abhidharmic treatises". See also VASC.1–12 and Dhammajoti's *Summary*, p. 1f., 10f.

2. In regard to the endeavor of Abhidharma analysis, see in particular Collett Cox's *From Category to Ontology: the Changing Role of Dharma in Sarvāstivāda Abhidharma.* Regarding the purpose of "*dharmic*" analysis, she points out (FCO.549):

> The early, emergent scholasticism of Sāṃkhya, Vaiśeṣika, and Buddhism was all directed by a similar intention: that is, a refusal to accept the world as it presents itself to untutored, common sense and a desire to analyze experience into its salient, functional constituents… . Initially the primary concern is immediately soteriological and is directed toward supplanting defiling or ensnaring *dharmas* with those conducive to liberation.

She then comments that this soteriologically motivated analysis is succinctly reflected in the term *dharmapravicaya,* the discernment of factors, that plays a significant role throughout the history of Buddhist praxis, particularly as one of the seven members of enlightenment (*bodhyaṅgadharma*) included within the thirty-seven factors conducive to enlightenment (*bodhipakṣyadharma*; vi, F 281ff.). *Dharmapravicaya,* as can be seen in the following sections of the AKB, (1) is linked with understanding (*prajñā*) and *abhidharma,* (2) discerns factors according to their intrinsic nature (*svabhāva*), or according to their particular inherent (*svalakṣaṇa*) and common characteristics (*sāmānyalakṣaṇa*), and (3) provides the only method to extinguish the defilements due to which the world wanders in cyclic existence and experiences unsatisfactoriness.

3. See also the sections 1.1. Character and Function of Abhidharma; 1.2. Origin of Abhidharma Texts; and 1.3. Methods of Abhidharma Exegesis, in Collett Cox's *Disputed Dharmas,* pp. 3–19. Likewise, chapter 1. *Abhidharma* – Its Origin, Meaning and Function, and chapter 2: The Ābhidharmika – Standpoint, Scope and Methodology, in Dhammajoti's SA.IV.1–54.

For numerous explanatory definitions of the term *abhidharma,* see section "Definitions of *abhidharma*" in Dhammajoti's SA.IV.6–10.

[22] *Gokhale*: [2a] *prajñā 'malā sā'nucarā 'bhidharmas* |

Tib.: [2a] *chos mngon shes rab dri med rjes 'grang bcas* |

[23] *LVP*: The factors (*dharma*) are mixed together (*saṃkirṇa*) as in the case of flowers; they are discerned (*pravicīyante*) and sorted (*uccīyante*) into bouquets: these are pure (*anāsrava*), these are impure (*sāsrava*), [these possess material form (*rūpiṇa*), these do not possess material form (*arūpiṇa*)] [see WOG.127.27ff.].

In this operation, a certain factor associated with thought (*caitta, caitasika,* ii. 23) called understanding (*prajñā*) plays the primary role. Consequently, *understanding* is defined as "discernment of factors".

LS: 1. The definition of understanding in Skandhila's *Avatāra* is typically abhidharmic in emphasis (SA.IV.219; ESD.83):

> Understanding is the discernment (*pravicaya*) of *dharma*-s. It is the examination (*upalakṣaṇa*), as the case may be, of the following eight kinds of *dharma*-s: inclusion

(*saṃgraha*), conjunction (*saṃprayoga*), endowment (*samanvāgama*), causes (*hetu*), conditions (*pratyaya*), fruitions (*phala*), specific-characteristic (*sva-lakṣaṇa*), common-characteristic (*sāmānya-lakṣaṇa*).

2. Various modes of pure and impure understanding are later discussed in great detail in the AKB:

At first it is explained within the context of cessation due to deliberation (*pratisaṃkhyā-nirodha*; i. 6ab) and then, as weak and strong understanding, in the context of the five sensory consciousnesses or the mental consciousness and the three types of conceptualizing activities, in particular the conceptualizing activity consisting of examining (*abhinirūpaṇāvikalpa*) (i. 33). As view (*dṛṣṭi*), understanding is discussed and defined within the context of the eighteen elements in i. 41; as one of the five praxis-oriented controlling faculties it is explained within the context of the last four controlling faculties (i. 48cd and beginning of chapter 2), i.e., the praxis-oriented faculty of understanding (*prajñendriya*) and the three pure controlling faculties: the faculty of coming to know what is not yet known (*anājñātam-ājñāsyāmīndriya*), the faculty of perfect knowledge (*ājñendriya*) and the faculty of final and perfect knowledge (*ājñātāvīndriya*).

Understanding is defined at ii. 24 in the context of it being one of the ten generally permeating factors (*mahābhūmika*); as such it can be either wholesome (*kuśala*), unwholesome (*akuśala*) or non-defined (*avyākṛta*), pure (*anāsrava*) or impure (*sāsrava*), right (*samyañc*) or wrong (*mithyā*), weak (*mṛdu*) or sharp (*tīkṣṇa*).

The importance of understanding as defilement (*kleśa*), i.e., the five afflicted views (*dṛṣṭi*), is discussed in chapter 5 (EXPOSITION OF THE PROCLIVITIES), particularly at v, F 15–26.

The pure *prajñā*s and their interrelationship are explained in chapter 7 as view (*dṛṣṭi*), as receptivity (*kṣānti*), as cognition (*jñāna*), i.e., as cognition of the factors (*dharmajñāna*), as subsequent cognition (*anvayajñāna*), as cognition of destruction (*kṣayajñāna*), as cognition of non-arising (*anutpādajñāna*). In chapter 7 (vv. 12c–13) we also find a discussion of the sixteen aspects or modes of activities (*ākāra*) of pure understanding as related to the sixteen common characteristics (*sāmānyalakṣaṇa*) of the four noble truths and likewise (vv. 3–11) a detailed exposition of the ten cognitions, including mundane conventional cognition (*lokasaṃvṛti-jñāna*), cognition of another's mind (*paracittajñāna*).

As one of the five praxis-oriented controlling faculties it is naturally addressed throughout chapter 6 (EXPOSITION OF THE PATH AND THE PERSONS IN WHOM THE NOBLE PATH ARISES), as well as in chapter 8 (EXPOSITION OF THE MEDITATIVE ATTAINMENTS).

24 *LVP*: Stain (*mala*) is a synonym for *flux* (*āsrava*). – We will translate *anāsrava* as *pure*. – The fluxes are defined in v. 35. – See below i. 4.

LS: 1. Gedun Drup comments (CPL 1, p. 17) that the three pure paths of insight, cultivation and those beyond training, as the subject, are ultimate *abhidharma* because they are stainless understanding together with its following.

2. In regard to pure *prajñā* and its relation to direct perception (*pratyakṣa*) and conceptualized perception, see Dhammajoti's discussion (ADCP.137ff.) of the "three types of direct perception" (according to Saṃghabhadra), i.e.:

i. that which is dependent on the sense faculty (*indriyaśrita*), i.e., the direct grasping, supported by the five sense faculties, of the five types of external objects, *rūpa*, etc.;

ii. that which is experience (*anubhava*), i.e., the coming into the present of the *citta-caitta-dhamma*-s;

iii. that which is discernment (**buddhi*), i.e., the direct realization (*sākṣāt-√kṛ*) of the specific or common characteristic (*sva-sāmānya-lakṣaṇa*)—accordingly as the cases may be—of *dharma*-s.

Dhammajoti comments (ADCP.139):

> Saṃghabhadra's articulation above, that the **buddhi-pratyakṣa* is the direct realization of either *svalakṣaṇa* or *sāmānyalakṣaṇa* accordingly as the case may be, can be comprehended as follows: So long as the contribution from the co-nascent *caitta*-s are still weak, it too, like the preceding consciousness, can only apprehend the mere object, e.g., a blue color; it is therefore a grasping of a *svalakṣaṇa*. But when the contribution is strong enough and it can apprehend, using name, "it is blue", etc., it is apprehending universals—i.e., *sāmānya-lakṣaṇa*. This is then not a case of *pratyakṣa*. The mode of activity (*ākāra* = *prajñā*) that functions at this time can be erroneous.
>
> However, in the case of spiritual realization—"realization-knowledge" (證智; *pratyakṣa-buddhi*, **pratyaksa-jñāna*, *adhigama-jñāna*)—the meditator apprehends directly, truly as they are, the universal characteristics of all *dhamma*-s—unsatisfactoriness, impermanence, etc. The modes of activity in this case differ not the slightest from the true nature of the *dharma*-s being examined. This is a case of direct seeing *par excellence* (真現量; **bhūta-pratyakṣa*, **tattva-pratyakṣa*)—without any conceptualization—and therefore a case of *pratyakṣa* even though *sāmānya-lakṣaṇa* is involved. For this reason the Sarvāstivāda identifies the 16 modes of activity pertaining to the four noble truths with *prajñā*—i.e., *prajñā* in the sense of spiritual insight. The MVŚ [217a] states that "outside the 16 modes of activity, there is no other outflow-free *prajñā*". "The *prajñā*-s not subsumed under the 16 modes of activities mostly discern *svalakṣāṇa*-s; the *prajñā*-s subsumed under the 16 modes of activities discern only *sāmānya-laksaṇa*-s."

For more detail, see iii. 30cd (F 89) (endnote) and vii. 13.

[25] *LVP*: The name *Abhidharma* designates not only the pure consciousness that discerns the nature of factors, but also all pure elements of the psychological moment in which this consciousness occurs: sensation, etc. (i. 14c). One of these elements is material (*rūpa*): this is what is called *pure restraint* (*anāsrava saṃvara*; iv. 13c).

LS: 1. The *Vyākhyā* [WOG.8.23ff.] mentions the aggregates of material form [specifying pure restraint (*anāsrava saṃvara*)], sensation, ideation, formations and consciousness. – See i. 27 for a discussion of a different set of five kinds of pure *skandhas*—also referred to as the five-membered (*pañcāṅga*) or five-part (*pañcabhāga*) *dharmakāya* (AKB vi, F 297; *Siddhi* 767)—which do not seem to be the same five pure *skandhas* as the ones mentioned in the *Vyākhyā* since, from the Vaibhāsika point of view (vi, F 297f.), they all can be included in two aggregates, as stated in AKB i, F 48: "There are five pure groups (*skandha*), (i) morality (*śīla*), (ii) concentration (*samādhi*), (iii) superior knowledge (*prajñā*), (iv) liberation (*vimukti*), and

(v) cognition-insight of liberation (*vimuktijñānadarśana*): the first is included in the aggregate of material form (*rūpaskandha*), (ii–v) the others are included in the aggregate of formations (*saṃskāraskandha*)."

Gedun Drup comments (CPL 1, p. 19): "Question: How many aggregates are there when [uncontaminated wisdom] is together with its retinue? Response: Since in the retinue of uncontaminated wisdom there is (i) the non-revelātory form included in the uncontaminated vow, it has five aggregates because, in addition, there are (ii) mental happiness in dependence on the first two concentrations, happiness of mind in dependence on the third, and equanimity feeling in dependence on any of the other levels of equanimity; (iii) the discrimination aggregate and (iv) the mental factors—the compositional factors aggregate—that arise in the retinue of mental consciousness and any non-associate compositional factors, together with (v) the mental consciousness."

2. Hall comments (VASC.45) that, due to its predominance, understanding (*prajñā*) rather than thought (*citta*) is depicted here as the "king" (*rāja*); the other factors accompanying it are depicted as its "following" or "retinue" [WOG.8.16].

26 *LVP*: *Vyākhyā* [WOG.8.27ff.]: paramārtha eva *pāramārthikaḥ* | paramārthe vā bhavaḥ *pāramārthikaḥ* | paramārthena va dīvyati caratīti vā *pāramārthikaḥ*.

27 *Gokhale*: [2b] *tatprāptaye yā 'pi ca yac ca śāstram* |

Tib.: [2b] *de thob bya phyir gang dang bstan bcos gang* |

28 *LS*: SA.IV.436 provides a chart of the preparatory stages that lead to the attainment of perfect *prajñā* (= Abhidharma in the absolute sense), namely: (1) studying the Buddha's teachings with the support of the understanding derived from birth (the impure [*sāsrava*] *upapatti-pratilambhika-prajñā*); (2) studying the Abhidharma—analyzing the characteristics of *dharma*-s (the impure *śrutamayi-prajñā*); (3) meditations such as meditation on the loathsome and mindfulness of breathing (the impure *cintamayī prajñā*); (4) heat, summit, receptivity, and supreme mundane factors (= the impure *bhāvanāmayī prajñā*), and (5) the attainment of pure *prajñā* or *prajñā* "without a relationship with the fluxes" (*anāsrava*) [= Abhidharma in the absolute sense] as final destination.

See AKB i. 4–5b for a brief clarification of the notions of *sāsrava* and *anāsrava*. It has to be kept in mind, that the scope of the impure (*sāsrava*) factors (*dharma*) is greater than that of the unwholesome (*akuśala*) factors, since it can also include wholesome (*kuśala*) and non-defined (*avyākṛta*) factors. See AKB iv. 8b–9d for the various ways of defining *kuśala*, *akuśala* and *avyākṛta* factors.

29 *LS*: Hall comments (VASC.46) that this kind of conventional understanding "is dependent on one's birth (*upapatti*) in a specific realm (*dhātu*), world (*loka*), plane of existence (*gati*), and so on".

30 *LVP*: *sāṃketika*, *sāṃvyavahārika abhidharma*. [Cf. WOG.8.29].

31 *LVP*: The Treatise, i.e., either

1. the *Abhidharmaśāstra*, the *Abhidharmapiṭaka*. In which case, (i) some think that we should not understand: "The Treatise, *with its following*, receives the name of Abhidharma", for a book does not have a retinue; (ii) some believe that the following

is constituted by the characteristics (*lakṣaṇa*; ii. 45cd); or else,

2. the *Jñānaprasthāna*, considered as the body (*śarīra*) of the Abhidharma, having the six books: *Prakaraṇapāda, Vijñānakāya, Dharmaskandha, Prajñāptiśāstra, Dhātukāya, Saṃgītiparyāya* (Burnouf, *Introduction*, p. 448), for its feet (and "following") (*ṣaṭpāda*).

LS: 1. Collett Cox comments (DD.29) that the Sarvāstivāda sect possessed a canon in four sections containing *sūtra* (doctrinal discourses), *vinaya* (disciplinary codes and discourses), *abhidharma* and *kṣudraka* (miscellaneous) collections, and, among these, emphasized and valued most the exegesis of the Abhidharma containing seven texts that came in the tradition to be referred to collectively as the "Abhidharma with six feet" (*ṣaṭpādābhidharma*). Cox explains (SBS.139, 173f.) that these seven treatises make up the early Sarvāstivāda Abhidharma canonical materials that primarily are available only through their Chinese translations.

Chinese translations also preserve (i) the later Sarvāstivāda Abhidharma materials such as the voluminous *Vibhāṣā* compendia, which are commentaries on one of the earlier Sarvāstivāda texts and reflect the emergence of full sectarian self-consciousness, expressed in a polemical style of exposition, and which enumerate the positions of contending groups when expounding each doctrinal point, and (ii) the even "later polemical, summary digests such as Saṅghabhadra's *Nyāyānusāra* and the *Abhidharmadīpa*, products of a single author, that attempt to defend Kāśmīra Sarvāstivāda-Vaibhāṣika orthodoxy in the fact of the challenge raised by Vasubandhu's *Abhidharmakośabhāṣya*" and that "adopt an organization of topics that attempts to present all aspects of the teaching according to a well-reasoned structure, in which virtually the entirety of Buddhist doctrine is cogently summarized in the form of verse and autocommentary.

2. As for the "origin of Abhidharma", Collett Cox states (DD.8) that the majority of Western scholars (for example, Lamotte and Frauwallner) find it in *mātṛkā*s, whereas most Japanese scholars (for example, Kimura Taiken) seem to think that Abhidharma originated from "dialogues concerning the doctrine (*abhidharmakathā*) or monastic discussions in catechetical style characterized by an exchange of questions and interpretative answers intended to clarify complex or obscure points of doctrine".

In regard to *mātṛkā*, Frauwallner writes (SAL.3ff.) that the oldest Buddhist tradition had no Abhidharmapiṭaka but only comprehensive lists (*mātṛka*) that were meant to collect and preserve the doctrinal concepts found scattered in the Buddha's many discourses (*sūtra*) and out of which the Abhidharma later developed. Of particular importance in this context were the lists of the fundamental concepts, such as the five aggregates (*skandha*), twelve sense-spheres (*āyatana*), eighteen elements (*dhātu*), into which one attempted to subsume all the various factors (*dharma*s). Next to these fundamental concepts, there occasionally also appear the five appropriative aggregates (*upādānaskandha*) and the six elementary substances (*dhātu*), as well as frequently the twenty-two controlling faculties. These lists were intended to serve as a basis for teaching and thus were accompanied by explanations, at first delivered orally but later also in written form.

Besides this simple method, quite early on, a separate method to explain the lists of factors was developed, which Frauwallner dubbs "attribute-*mātṛkas*" and which consisted mainly of dyads, such as: having a material form (*rūpa*) and not having material form (*arūpa*); visible (*sanidarśana*) and invisible (*anidarśana*); resistant (*sapratigha*) and non-resistant (*apratigha*); impure (*sāsrava*) and pure (*anāsrava*); conditioned (*saṃskṛta*) and unconditioned (*asaṃskrta*), etc., and triads, such as: past (*atīta*), future (*anāgata*) and present (*pratyutpanna*); wholesome (*kuśala*), unwholesome (*akuśala*) and non-defined (*avyākṛta*); etc.

But in addition to explaining the nature of the factors collected in these lists, their relationship to each other was also discussed, which included questions about (i) which factors are included (*saṃgraha*) in which factors, (ii) which factors were associated (*saṃprayoga*) with which factors, and (iii) which factors were the center or bearer of which factors, i.e., which factors were accompanied (*samanvāgama*) by which factors. Questions such as these led to a consistent systematization of the factors. Thus, besides the small number of fundamental doctrinal statements, such as the Four Noble Truths, dependent origination and the description of the path of liberation, it is from these lists and methods that the Abhidharma developed, and these are for Frauwallner the most important ways in which the Abhidharma treats the traditional doctrinal material. [Leaving the issue of the "origin" aside, many of these lists and methods can easily be detected, particularly throughout chapter 1.] "The sole aim was to preserve safely what the Buddha had taught and to illuminate it from a variety of different angles."

3. As for "mature Abhidharma" exegesis, Collett Cox comments (SBS.168f.) that it is characterized stylistically by two methods: one is the practice of formulating matrices (*mātṛkā*) or categorizing lists of all topics found in the traditional teaching, a practice that results in taxonomies arranged according to both numeric and qualitative criteria; the other is doctrinal discussions (*abhidharmakathā*) in catechetical style held among monks in order to clarify complex or obscure points of doctrine. These two methods are present, to varying degrees, in virtually every Abhidharma text, where the taxonomies were used to record or preserve a doctrinal outline that was then elaborated through a pedagogical question and answer technique."

For more detail on the standard, scope and methodology of the Ābhidharmika, see chapter 2 in SA.IV.

4. For general examinations of the Sarvāstivādin Abhidharma literature, their dating and their doctrinal development, see section D "The seven canonical treatises of the Abhidharma", pp. xxx–xliii, in LVP's *Introduction*, and also the chapter "The Canonical [Abhidharma] Works [of the Sarvāstivāda School]" and the chapter "The Origin of the Buddhist Systems", pp. 119–34 in Erich Frauwallner's SAL, as well as the section "The Abhidharmapiṭaka", pp. 179–91 in Lamotte's HOIB; see also chapter 3: "Kaśmīra: Vaibhāṣika Orthodoxy" (Collett Cox) and chapter 4: Bactria and Gandhāra" (Paul Dessein) in SBS, and Dhammajoti's discussion (SA.IV.83–103) of the seven canonical treatises of the Sarvāstivāda.

Dhammajoti states (SA.IV.85) that the *Dharmaskandha-śāstra*, *Saṃgītiparyāya-śāstra* and the *Prajñapti-śāstra* are generally accepted to be the treatises of the earliest period: "They all exhibit features similar to the 'abhidharmic' discourses in the *sūtra-piṭaka*, and generally show little organization and doctrinal articulation. There is also the absence of explicit definition or establishment of the thesis of *sarvāstitva*. Furthermore, these three texts are noticeably attributed by tradition to the immediate disciples of the Buddha. We may note here that the Sarvāstivāda tradition enumerates these three texts by name as part of the *abhidharma-piṭaka*."

SA.IV.91: "In contrast to the above three treatises, the remaining four are clearly more developed in terms of organization and doctrinal concepts. Moreover, some divergence notwithstanding, they all contain sectarian doctrines which can be regarded as specifically Sarvāstivādin. In addition, as regards authorship, all traditions agree in ascribing them to the *abhidharma* masters subsequent to the Buddha's time." Though there are various views on this, Dhammajoti states: "the following enumeration reflects only a probable relative chronology of these four treatises:" Vijñānakāya-śāstra; Jñānaprasthāna-śāstra; Prakaraṇa-śāstra; and *Dhātukāya-śāstra.*

32 *LVP*: *svalakṣaṇadhāraṇa*, *Madhyamakavṛtti*, 457; see *Siddhi*, 4, 568. – "the supreme *dharma*" or *paramārtha.*

LS: 1. Pradhan.2.9f. has: *nirvacanaṃ tu svalakṣaṇādhāraṇād dharmaḥ | tadayaṃ paramārtha-dharmaṃ vā nirvāṇaṃ dharmalakṣaṇaṃ vā pratyabhimukho dharma ityabhidharmaḥ | ukto 'bhidharmaḥ ||*

The *Vyākhyā* has [WOG.9.18ff.]: *tad ayam* iti. *tad* iti vākyopanyāse. *ayam* iti *svalakṣaṇa-dhāraṇatvena* niruktaḥ pāramārthikaḥ sāṃketiko 'bhidharmaḥ. *paramārtha-dharmam* iti. paramasya jñānasyārthaḥ *paramārthaḥ*. paramo vā 'rthaḥ *paramārthaḥ* sarva-dharmāgratvāt *paramārthaḥ*. paramārthaś cāsau dharmaś ca *paramārtha-dharmaḥ*. *dharma-lakṣaṇaṃ* veti. sva-sāmānya-lakṣaṇaṃ khakkhaṭalakṣaṇaḥ pṛthivī-dhātur anityaṃ duḥkham iti-evam-ādi. *tat pratyabhimukhaḥ*... .

2. *The AKB definition of dharma and its source*:

Cox comments (FCO.558f.): "Neither the early Sarvāstivāda, canonical Abbidharma texts nor the *Vibhāṣā* compendia contain an abstract definition of *dharma*s as such. A definition is found, however, in Upaśānta's and Dharmatrāta's commentaries on the **Abhidharmahṛdaya*, and is transmitted in the *Abhidharmakośabhāṣya* and subsequent texts: that is, *dharma* means upholding, [namely], upholding intrinsic nature (*svabhāva*)." The AKB uses *svalakṣaṇa* in place of *svabhāva* in Upaśanta's definition, but Yaśomitra [see above] distinguishes between particular inherent characteristics (*svalakṣaṇa*), such as solidity in the case of earth, and generic characteristics (*sāmānyalakṣaṇa*), such as impermanence and suffering in the case of all conditioned *dharmas*. Cox comments that this definition of *dharma* does not appear in either Saṃghabhadra's **Nyāyānusāra* or **Abhidharmasamayapradīpikā*, but resembles the exposition in Dharmaśreṣthin's **Abhidharmahṛdaya.*

3. *Soteriological and epistemological aspects of the 75 dharmas theory*:

Dhammajoti writes (SA.IV.242.): "Like all other forms of Buddhism, Sarvāstivāda Abhidharma is primarily concerned with the problem of knowledge: Given that we are bound to *saṃsāra* through ignorance (*avidyā*), how can we overcome the topsy-turvy way of cognizing things (*viparyāsa*) and acquire the liberating insight (*prajñā*) which sees things truly as they are (*yathābhūtam*)? With this central soteriological concern and starting from an epistemological investigation, the school arrives at a list of roughly 75 types of ultimate reals known as *dharma*-s. This central concern and fundamental methodology of investigation are summarily reflected in what the school underscores as Abhidharma in the absolute sense: i.e., pure *prajñā* defined as *dharma-pravicaya.*

A *dharma*—whether, physical, mental, neither physical nor mental, or even unconditioned—is a unique force, possessing a unique, intrinsic characteristic, that has impact on the human experience, and it is discovered by a valid means of knowledge (*pramāṇa*), either direct perception (including spiritual realization) or inference having its ultimate basis on direct experience."

4. *The relation of dharma and svalakṣaṇa/svabhāva*:

He also states (SA.IV.19):

> For a *dharma* to be a *dharma*, its characteristic must be sustainable throughout time [see i. 18ab and 39a; v. 25]: A *rūpa* remains as a *rūpa* irrespective of its various modalities. It can never be transformed into another different *dharma* (such as *vedanā*). Thus, a uniquely characterizable entity is a uniquely real (in the absolute sense) entity, having a unique intrinsic nature (*svabhāva*): "To be existent as an absolute entity is to be existent as an intrinsic characteristic (*paramārthena sat svalakṣaṇena sad ityarthaḥ*)."
>
> As the MVŚ explains, this is on account of the fact that "the entity itself is [its] characteristic, and the characteristic is the entity itself; for it is the case for all *dharma*-s that the characteristic cannot be predicated apart from the *dharma* itself". [MVŚ, 777a. Cf. Ny, 432b: *lakṣaṇa = svarūpa/svabhāva*]. This is no doubt quite in keeping with the fundamental Buddhist stance which consistently rejects any substance-attribute dichotomy. By accounting for the *svalakṣaṇa* of a *dharma*—its phenomenologically cognizable aspect—its very ontological existence as a *svabhāva/dravya* is established. Ultimately these two are one [MVŚ, 196c].

5. *Tri-temporal existence of impermanent and conditioned dharmas and their activities*:

Vasubandhu explains v, F 50, that "the Vaibhāṣikas maintain that past and future factors really exist (*dravya*); the conditioning forces, however, are not eternal, for they are endowed with the characteristics (*lakṣaṇa*) of the conditioned (ii. 45cd)".

Dhammajoti states (SA.IV.148f.):

> In the Sarvāstivāda perspective, all *dharma*-s have always been existing. As a matter of fact, time is an abstraction on our part derived from their activities [MVŚ, 393c]. A *dharma* exists throughout time and yet is not permanent as it "courses in time" (*adhva-saṃcāra*). But as MVŚ explains, "conditioned *dharma*-s are weak in their intrinsic nature, they can accomplish their activities only through mutual dependence".
>
> > We declare that the causes have the activities as their fruits, not the entities in themselves (*svabhāva/dravya*). We further declare that the effects have the activities as their causes, not the entities in themselves. The entities in themselves are eternally without transformation, being neither causes nor effects. [MVŚ, 105c]
>
> Moreover,
>
> > the tri-temporal *dharma*-s exist throughout time as entities in themselves; there is neither increase nor decrease. It is only on the basis of their activities that they are said to exist or not exist [as phenomena]. [MVŚ, 396a]

But, in turn, their activities necessarily depend on causes and conditions [MVŚ, 108c]:

> Being feeble in their *svabhāva*-s, they have no sovereignty (*aiśvarya*). They are dependent on others, they are without their own activity and unable to do as they wish. [MVŚ, 283b]

6. *Dharmas as conditioned forces* (*saṃskṛta*) *and as conditioning forces* (*saṃskāra*):

Dhammajoti further explains (SA.IV.24): "All *dharma*-s in phenomenal existence are *pratītya-samutpanna*—dependently originated from an assemblage of conditions. In this respect, they are often called *saṃskṛta*-s, 'the compounded/conditioned'. In the Sarvāstivāda conception, *dharma*-s are distinct ontological entities that, in their intrinsic nature, abide throughout time, totally unrelated to one another and totally devoid of any activities. Given such a theory, it is of fundamental importance that the school has an articulated causal doctrine good enough to account for the arising of dharma-s as phenomena and their dynamic inter-relatedness in accordance with the Buddha's teaching of *pratītya-samutpāda*. Moreover, for the establishment of each of the *dharma*-s as a real entity, a conditioning force (*saṃskāra*), its causal function in each case must be demonstrated. It is probably for this reason that the Sarvāstivāda was also known as Hetuvāda—a school specifically concerned with the theory of causation."
Further (SA.IV.146): "A *dharma* ... is a real on account of it being a real force—of having a causal efficacy—in other words, on account of it being a cause. It is for this reason that *dharma*-s are also called *saṃskāra*-s—conditioning forces. Failure to prove an alleged existent's causal efficacy is tantamount to failure to prove its very existence/reality. Accordingly, if *saṃskāra-dharma*-s are asserted to be real tri-temporally, they must be established to belong to one category of *hetu* or another."

7. For more detail on *dharma*, see Hirakawa's *The Meaning of "Dharma" and "Abhidharma"*. See also Collett Cox's *From Category to Ontology: the Changing Role of Dharma in Sarvāstivāda* Abhidharma which discusses how the term *dharma* was used within Abhidharma—specifically within the Sarvāstivāda Abhidharma literature—and its relationship to other terms used to explain and elaborate it, such as *bhava, svabhāva, dravya, prajñapti, svalakṣaṇa, sāmānyalakṣaṇa*, etc.

[33] *LS*: Hirakawa comments (MDA.167, footnote): "There are two interpretations regarding the word *abhidhamma.* One takes it as meaning "as regards the *dhamma*", and the other sees it as meaning "excellent *dhamma*" (*dhammātireka, dhammavisesa*: *Aṭṭhasālinī*, p. 2, line 2). In the *Abhidharma-Mahāvibhāṣā* (*Amv*), altogether 25 different views on the meaning of "*abhidharma*" are given, including the two given above: .... *Kośa* adopts from among these 25 that of "regarding the *dharma*" (*pratyabhimukho dharma ity abhidharmaḥ*: *Kośa*, p. 2, lines 9–10). Various scholars have brought forth studies on the original meaning of the word: cf. *Geiger*, pp. 118ff; Horner, I.B., "Abhidhamma Abhivinaya in the First Two Piṭakas of the Pali Canon". *Indian Historical Quarterly* XVII (1941), pp. 291–310; Lamotte, Etienne. *Histoire du bouddhisme indien.* Louvain: 1958, p. 197; etc."

For a translation of the *Abhidharma-Mahāvibhāṣā* definitions, see Dhammajoti's SA.IV.6ff.

[34] *LS*: SA.IV.532 (Glossary): "*nirvāṇa*: The goal of the Buddhist spiritual life, explained in Buddhism as the extinction/blowing out of the fire of *rāga* [attachment], *dveṣa* [hatred] and

moha [delusion]. It is the state of perfect bliss, and transcendence of all *duḥkha* [unsatisfactoriness] and births. In Sarvāstivāda, this is not a mere absence of *duḥkha*, but a positive entity acquired when a defilement is abandoned, which serves to prevent the further arising of the defilement. It is a synonym for *pratisaṃkhyā-nirodha* [cessations through deliberation]."

Thus there are many *pratisaṃkhyānirodha*s (see i. 6ab), starting from the path of insight (*darśanamārga*) upwards.

35 *LS*: Dhammajoti comments that of all the Ābhidharmika studies, the examination of intrinsic characteristic and common characteristic may be considered as the most important one. We therefore cover this topic here in somewhat greater detail by reproducing sections from Cox and Dhammajoti.

1. *The move towards an epistemological ontology*:

Collett Cox, putting *svalakṣaṇa* and *sāmānyalakṣaṇa* into a bigger context, writes (FCO.574ff.) that from the period of the *Vibhāṣā* compendia onward an epistemologically grounded type of causal functioning became dominant.

> This epistemological emphasis is evident both in a shift in the terminology used to describe the character of *dharma*s and in the later definitions offered for existence in the abstract. The shift in terminology is indicated by the terms "particular inherent characteristic" (*svalakṣaṇa*) and "generic characteristic" (*sāmānyalakṣaṇa*), which come to be used in conjunction with and, in the case of the particular inherent characteristic, often in place of intrinsic nature (*svabhāva*). These terms do not appear in the canonical Sarvāstivāda Abhidharma texts, ... *Lakṣaṇa* appears prominently ... in both Dharmaśreṣṭhin's **Abhidharmahṛdaya* and in Upaśānta's commentary, as well as in Dharmatrāta's **Miśrakābhidharmahṛdayaśāstra*, where the particular inherent and generic characteristics are explicitly defined and contrasted. [...]
>
> In general terms, a single *dharma* is marked by many characteristics: that is, every *dharma* is marked by (at least) one particular inherent characteristic reflecting its intrinsic nature and by multiple generic characteristics, which are shared with other *dharma*s and hence signify the larger categories to which it belongs. The distinction between the particular inherent and the generic characteristics thus discriminates levels in the apprehension or discernment of *dharma*s that serve to clarify the ambiguity encountered in the application of the term *svabhāva* to both individual *dharma*s and to categorical groups [see more on this below]. [...] The two methods of analytical description, either by intrinsic nature (*svabhāva*) or by characteristics are separated by one important difference: whereas intrinsic nature acquires its special significance in the context of exegetical categorization, the starting point for the characteristics lies in perspectivistic cognition. Ontology is a concern for both systems, but the shift in terminology from intrinsic nature to the characteristics reflects a concurrent shift from a category-based abstract ontology to an epistemological ontology [that] is experientially or cognitively determined.
>
> And indeed, we find in the mature Sarvāstivāda exegesis of Saṅghabhadra, a definition of existence in the abstract that expresses this new epistemological emphasis. For Saṅghabhadra, as for all Sarvāstivādins, existence is causally grounded, but

his definition of existence suggests that this causal efficacy is specifically cognitive: "To be an object-field that produces cognition (*buddhi*) is the true characteristic of existence" [NA 50 p. 621c21].

2. *Distinction between intrinsic characteristic and common characteristic*:

The *Mahāvibhāṣā* states (SA.IV.19):

> The analysis of the characteristic (*lakṣaṇa*) of a single entity (*dravya*) is the analysis of intrinsic characteristic. The analysis of the characteristic of numerous entities [collectively] is the analysis of common characteristic.
>
> Furthermore, the analysis of an individual aggregate (*skandha*), etc., is an analysis of intrinsic characteristic. The analysis of two, three aggregates, etc., is an analysis of common characteristic. [MVŚ, 217a]

It further states (MVŚ, 179b):

> The intrinsic nature (*svabhāva*) of a *dharma* is the intrinsic characteristic of a *dharma*. Homogeneity in nature is common characteristic. (Cf. Ny, 675b: "The contemplation of *svalakṣaṇa* is the analysis that a given *dharma* is different from the other *dharma*-s. The contemplation of *sāmānyalakṣaṇa* is the analysis that a given dharma is not different from the other *dharma*-s.")

Dhammajoti comments (SA.IV.20):

> Thus, all *rūpa*-s, *vedanā*-s, *saṃjñā*-s, etc., have the nature of being impermanent. This impermanent nature is a common characteristic.
>
> Whereas a sensory consciousness cognizes only the intrinsic characteristic of a dharma, the mental consciousness with its ability of abstraction can cognize the common characteristic. Thus, the latter pertains to the domain of inference (*anumāna*), the former to direct perception (*pratyakṣa*).
>
> However, distinguishing the understanding (*prajñā*) that examines intrinsic characteristic from that which examines common characteristic, MVŚ, 217a, also states:
>
> > Furthermore, the understanding derived from listening (*śruta-mayī*) and reflection (*cintā-mayī*) mostly analyze intrinsic characteristics. The understanding derived from cultivation (*bhāvanā-mayī*) mostly analyze common characteristics.
> >
> > The understanding not subsumed under the 16 modes of understanding mostly analyzes intrinsic characteristics; the understanding subsumed under the 16 modes of understanding analyzes only common characteristics.
> >
> > Furthermore, the understanding that apprehends (√*car*, lit: "courses") the [four] truths mostly discerns intrinsic characteristics; the understanding at the time of direct realization (*abhisamaya*) discerns only common characteristics.
>
> This statement is to be understood as follows: The 16 modes of understanding (*ākāra*) are those pertaining to the four noble truths (four each): unsatisfactory, impermanent, etc., for the truth of unsatisfactoriness, etc. These are no doubt the common characteristics of *dharma*-s. But they are the non-erroneous universal characteristics (principles) discernible only by spiritual insight as direct perception

par excellence in direct realization.

3. *Relativity as regards the notions of intrinsic characteristic and common characteristic*:

In this connection Dhammajoti comments (SA.IV.21):

> Thus, among various *rūpa*-s—different colors, different shapes—there is the common nature of being resistant and subject to deterioration. Accordingly, this intrinsic characteristic of a *rūpa* is distinct from a *vedanā*, etc. But, at the same time, it is also the common characteristic of these various types of *rūpa*-s. ...
>
> The Sarvāstivāda Ābhidharmikas distinguish two kinds of distinctive characteristic: The first, *dravya-svalakṣaṇa*, is the intrinsic characteristic of the *dharma* as a unique entity in itself; for instance, that of a particular color, say, blue. The second, *āyatana-svalakṣaṇa*, refers to the intrinsic characteristic of the *dharma* as a member of a unique class—an *āyatana*—of which it is a member; for instance, the particular blue color as a unique class of *dharma*-s known as "visibles" (*rūpa*), i.e., the *rūpa-āyatana*. We can see from this example that, in this context, the *āyatana-svalakṣaṇa* is, in a sense, a common characteristic in relation to the *dravya-svalakṣaṇa*. It is for this reason that MVŚ, 65a, states:
>
>> From the point of view of *dravya-svalakṣaṇa*, the five sensory consciousnesses (*pañca-vijñāna-kāya*) also take common characteristic as their cognitive object (*ālambana*). But from the point of view of *āyatana-svalakṣaṇa*, the five sensory consciousnesses take intrinsic characteristic alone as their object.

[36] *Gokhale*: [2cd] *tasyā 'rthato 'smin samanupraveśāt | sa v āśrayo 'sy ety abhidharmakośaḥ ||*
Tib.: [2cd] *'dir de don du yang dag chud phyir ram | 'di yi gnas de yin pas chos mngon mdzod ||*

[37] *LS*: As for the three *piṭakas*, Dhammajoti comments (SA.IV.9): "The nature and characteristics of the *abhidharma* are distinguished from those of the other two *piṭaka*-s as follows [MVŚ, 1c–2a]: The Sūtra is the emanation (*niṣyanda*) of the Buddha's power (*bala*), for none can refute the doctrines therein. The Vinaya is the emanation of Great Compassion (*mahākaruṇā*), for it advocates morality (*śīla*) for the salvation of those in the unfortunate planes of existence (*durgati*). The Abhidharma is the emanation of fearlessness, for it properly establishes the true characteristics of *dharma*-s, answering questions and ascertaining fearlessly."

The MVŚ states (SA.IV.18): "The meanings of the *abhidharma-piṭaka* should be understood by means of 14 things: (1–6) the six causes (*hetu*), (7–10) the four conditions (*pratyaya*), (11) subsumption/inclusion (*saṃgraha*), (12) conjunction (*saṃprayoga*), (13) endowment (*samanvāgama*), (14) non-endowment (*asamanvāgama*). Those who, by means of these 14 things, understand the *abhidharma* unerringly, are called Ābhidharmikas, not [those who] merely recite and memorize the words." Other masters add skillfulness (*kauśalya*) with regard to intrinsic characteristic (*svalakṣaṇa*) and common characteristic (*sāmānyalakṣaṇa*). For a discussion of these categories see SA.IV.19–25.

[38] *LS*: Hall translates: "Abhidharma designated [in 2b] as 'Śāstra' (text or corpus of texts) has been included in this [present text] essentially—in accordance with a direct meaning [of the word 'Abhidharma', or,] in terms of what is most important [in the Abhidharma

corpus]." He refers (VASC.47) to Yaśomitra's "double interpretation of *yathāpradhānam*: (1) 'Abhidharma-Śāstra' is included here because it is one of three explicit (*pradhāna*) meanings of the word 'Abhidharma' (in k. 2ab). (2) The 'Abhidharma-Śāstra' is included, in that its main points (*pradhāna*) are included, in the present text."

39 *LS*: AH 1.

40 *LS*: SA.IV.524/546 (Glossary): *upadeśa*: "Teaching", "elaborative exposition"; the last member of the twelvefold classification of the Words of the [Buddha] Dharma (*dvādaśāṅga-dharma-pravacana*):

1. *sūtra*, 2. *geya*, 3. *vyākaraṇa*, 4. *gāthā*, 5. *udāna*, 6. *nidāna*, 7. *avadāna*, 8. *itivṛttaka/ ityuktaka*, 9. *jātaka*, 10. *vaipulya*, 11. *adbhuta-dharma*, 12. *upadeśa*.

In a specific sense, it is synonymous with Abhidharma. In Saṃghabhadra's words, "*upadeśa* refers to the non-erroneous revealing, answering of objections and ascertainment of the preceding [eleven] members".

See Dhammajoti's *Abhidharma and Upadeśa* (2005).

41 *Gokhale*: [3] *dharmāṇāṃ pravicayam antareṇa nā 'sti | kleśānāṃ yata upaśāntaye 'bhyupāyaḥ | kleśaiś ca bhramati bhavā'rṇave 'tra lokas | taddhetor ata uditaḥ kil aiṣa śāstrā ||*

Tib.: [3] *chos rnams rab tu rnam 'byed med par nyon mongs rnams | gang phyir nye bar zhi bar bya ba'i thabs med la | nyon mongs pas kyang 'jig rten srid mtsho 'dir 'khyams te | de bas de phyir 'di ni ston pas gsungs so lo ||*

LVP: The first two lines are cited, with the reading *yad upaśāntaya*, in a commentary (*Amṛta-kaṇikā*) on the *Nāmasaṃgīti*, 130; the third is cited in the *Vyākhyā* [WOG.11.2].

42 *LS*: Dhammajoti comments (SA.IV.329) that in the *abhidharma* scheme of explanation, *duḥkha* results from *karma*, and *karma* arises from defilements, and that, without defilements, *karma*s are incapable of producing new existences. See in his SA.IV the sections 12.4: "Defilements as the root of existence" (SA.IV.329–30) and 12.5: "Ābhidharmika investigation of defilements" (SA.IV.331–32), where Dhammajoti translates Saṃghabhadra's sixteen functions performed by a defilement and renders thirty-three essential taxonomical topics for the investigation of defilements (dharmapravicaya). In summary, Saṃghabhadra states [Ny, 596b]: "It is after having properly understood the nature of the *anuśaya*-s in this way that one can decisively eliminate them." As for the elimination of defilements, Dhammajoti further clarifies (SA.IV.345): "For the Sarvāstivādins, defilements cannot be 'destroyed' in an ontological sense since like all other *dharma*-s, their *svabhāva*-s exist perpetually. Abandonment in the proper sense means the severing of the acquisition (*prāpti*) linking the defilement to the individual series."

43 *LVP*: *kila paramatadyotane*. The word *kila* ["it is said"] shows that here Vasubandhu explains an opinion, the opinion of the Vaibhāṣikas, which he does not accept. For the Sautrāntikas and for Vasubandhu, the Abhidharmas are not the word of the Master. The problem of the authenticity of the Abhidharmas is studied in [La Vallée Poussin's] *Introduction.*

Contradiction of the Sūtra and the Abhidharmas, for example, iii, 104; vii, 22.

LS: 1. Yaśomitra [WOG.11.25ff.] comments (*JIABS*, vol. 26, no. 2, p. 322; translation by Yoshifumi Honjō):

> The word *kila* indicates the statement of others. It means, "This is what is understood by the Ābhidhārmikas, not by us Sautrāntikas", since the authors [other than the Buddha] of the Abhidharmaśāstras are handed down to us; i.e., the author of the *Jñānaprasthāna* is Ārya Kātyāyanīputra, the author of the *Prakaraṇapāda* is Sthavira Vasumitra, [the author] of the *Vijñānakāya* is Sthavira Devaśarman, [the author] of the *Dharmaskandha* is Ārya Śāriputra, [the author] of the *Prajñaptiśāstra* is Ārya Maudgalyāyana, [the author] of the *Dhātukāya* is Pūrṇa, [the author] of the *Saṅgītiparyāya* is Mahākauṣṭhila.

Yaśomitra then adds (AD.47; translation Jaini):

> [Question:] – What is meant by the term Sautrāntika?
>
> [Answer:] – Those who hold the *sūtra*s as authentic and not the *śāstra*s, are called Sautrāntika.
>
> [Question:] – If they do not accept the *śāstra*s as authentic, how do they explain the division of the canon in the three Piṭakas? Is it not a fact that the *sūtra*s know the term "Abhidharma-piṭaka", as for instance in an expression "a *tripiṭaka* monk"?
>
> [Answer:] – That does not matter. For a certain kind of Sūtras themselves, dealing with the determination of meanings and characteristics of *dharma*s are called Abhidharma.

Dhammajoti comments (SA.IV.2) that according to the Theravāda tradition, Śāriputra transmitted the *abhidhamma* to the disciples, but that the Sarvāstivāda tradition accepts that their canonical *abhidharma* works were compiled by the disciples. He adds (SA.IV.16f.):

> For the Ābhidharmikas, the *abhidharma* doctrines are not speculative philosophy or intellectual inventions; they are *the buddha-vacana* ("words of the Buddha") *par excellence.* Their opponents, the Sautrāntikas, repudiate this claim. Saṃghabhadra analyses the Sautrāntika disagreement as being threefold:
>
> i. They were said to be composed by Kātyāyanīputra and others.
> ii. The Buddha never mentioned that *abhidharma* is a reliance (*pratiśaraṇa*) [but exhorted Ānanda to take the *sūtra*-s as *pratiśaraṇa*].
> iii. The tenets of the different *abhidharma* schools vary.

2. Our *kila* passage here is the first of Kritzer's fifteen passages discussed in relation to chapter 1.

As referred to in our *Remarks of the Translator*, Kritzer—in his major study *Vasubandhu and the Yogācārabhūmi. Yogācāra Elements in the Abhidharmakośabhāṣya* (2005), a systematic comparison of the *Abhidharmakośabhāṣya* and the *Yogācārabhūmi*—attempts to show the extent of Vasubandhu's dependence on the *Yogācārabhūmi*:

i. For a general description, issues of composition and authorship and doctrinal content of the *Yogācārabhūmi,* see VY.xii–xx.

ii. For a general description of the *Abhidharmakośabhāṣya*, a discussion of Vasubandhu's career and the question of Sautrāntika, see VY.xx–xxx.

iii. For Kritzer's (a) methodology and (b) results in his systematic comparison, see VY.xxxi–xxxvii.

But we also already mentioned that Kritzer's views do not go unchallenged. Dhammajoti who very much welcomes the new research has a more conservative approach since he does not find the "new" results all that compelling yet, i.e., he thinks that the cases put forth by Kritzer could also be interpreted differently.

In regard to the first eight chapters, Kritzer lists 174 passages (= 1.15 + 2.44 + 3.18 + 4.42 + 5.33 + 6.13 + 7.6 + 8.3)—indicated by Saṃghabhadra in his **Nyāyānusāra*—that are attributed to Vasubandhu and for which he searched in the *Yogācārabhūmi* for similar passages. Throughout the endnotes to the first eight chapters of the AKB, we will, in general, only mark the places of the 174 passages without reproducing them.

44 *LVP*: The Tibetan version of the *Udānavarga* (Mdo XXVI) has been translated by W. Rockhill (London 1883) and published by H. Beck (Berlin 1911). A good part of the original has been rediscovered in Turkestan (*JRAS*, 1912, pp. 355–77; *J. As.*, 1912, I. p. 311, showing the correspondence with the Pāli sources). – S. Lévi, *J. As.*, 1912, II, pp. 215–22. – See LVP's *Introduction*, F xxxii.

LS: SA.IV.545 (Glossary): *udāna*: "Breathing out", inspirational verses said to be uttered spontaneously by the Buddha; one of the twelvefold classification of the "Words of the [Buddha] Dharma".

45 *LVP*: J. Takakusu, "On the Abhidharma Literature of the Sarvāstivādins", *JPTS*, 1905, p. 75.

46 *LS*: After having set the agenda for the remainder of the text, namely, the discernment of factors, we have arrived at the actual beginning of the text. Even though having already looked to some extent at the doctrinal affiliations of Vasubandhu in LVP's *Introduction* and Dhammajoti's *Summary*, at this point it seems appropriate to first briefly

1. address/repeat once more (but using different sources) the overall "structure" of the entire text and where this structure comes from,

but then in particular to

2. examine specifically the "structure" of the first two chapters.

1. *The overall "structure" of the entire text and where this structure comes from*:

i. The AKB is structurally closely based on the **Abhidharmahṛdaya* (AH) and the **Saṃyuktābhidharmahṛdaya* (SAH). Dessein writes (SBS.257) that Chiao-ching, when commenting on the overall structure in his preface to the SAH in the *Ch'u San-tsang Chi Chi*, describes the SAH as corresponding to the four noble truths, namely:

I. truth of unsatisfactoriness (*duḥkhasatya*):
   1. Elements (*dhātuvarga*)
II. truth of the origin (*samudayasatya*):
   2. Formations (*saṃskāravarga*)
   3. Action (*karmavarga*)
   4. Proclivities (*anuśayavarga*)

III. truth of cessation (*nirodhasatya*):
  5. Nobility (*āryavarga*)
IV. truth of the path (*mārgasatya*):
  6. Cognition (*jñānavarga*)
  7. Concentration (*samādhivarga*)

Dessein renders chapter 8: Scriptural texts (*sūtravarga*), chapter 9: Miscellany (*prakīrṇavarga*), chapter 10: Investigations (*pravicayavarga*) and chapter 11: Discussion (*dharmakathā*) as: V. additional chapters.

On the other hand, Dessein comments that Wanabe and Mizuno (1932) give chapters 1 and 2 as *duḥkhasatya*, chapters 3 and 4 as *samudayasatya*, chapter 5 as *nirodhasatya*, and chapters 6 and 7 as *mārgasatya*.

Since Dharmatrāta's SAH is structurally based on Dharmaśrī's **Abhidharmahṛdaya* (AH), and the AKB on the AH and the SAH—as we have seen in LVP's *Introduction* and as we will see further just below—the above given "four noble truths" classifications also applies to the AH and the AKB. [As for the chapters 3 and 9 of the AKB, Dessein renders them as V. additional chapters.]

A classification in three parts, based on Pūrṇavardhana, can also be found in some Tibetan commentaries on the AKB (cf. also Pu Guang's explanation in Dhammajoti's *Summary*). For example, Jampaiyang comments (translation Coghlan, unpublished, p. 167ff.):

> The master Pūrṇavardhana states that the eight chapters are enumerated from the perspective of extensively explaining the abbreviated meaning of "contaminated and uncontaminated *dharmas*". The first two chapters teach in general the contaminated and uncontaminated. Three chapters are (enumerated) from the perspective of teaching the contaminated in detail: (The third chapter of) the *Abhidharmakośa* teaching the mundane, teaches who is completely afflicted, i.e., the sentient beings of the three realms and five migrations, and where they are completely afflicted, i.e., the mundane environment, and how they are completely afflicted, i.e., the four abodes of birth and the twelve links of dependent arising. (The chapters 4 and 5 of) the *Abhidharmakośa* teaching *karma* and the *anuśaya*, teach what completely afflicts.
>
> The last three chapters (are enumerated) from the perspective of teaching the uncontaminated in detail. (The chapter 6 of) the *Abhidharmakośa* teaching path and person teaches what person is purified, in what realm they are purified and the order of realization (marking) how they are purified. (The chapter 7 of) the *Abhidharmakośa* teaching wisdom (teaches) by what (means) purification (is achieved). (The chapter 8 of) the *Abhidharmakośa* teaching equilibrium teaches the support of wisdom. (The master Pūrṇavardhana explains it in that way) because that is the principle of (their) relationship.

As for chapter 9, Kritzer comments (2005, p. xxii) that it is often characterized as an appendix. It is entirely prose whereas the first eight chapters consist of verses and commentary on each verse. He states that although many commentaries cover all nine chapters, Saṃghabhadra's **Nyāyanusāra* ends with chapter 8. Stefan Anacker thinks (SWV.17) that it "may be the only extant work by Vasubandhu written prior to the *Kośa*. This seems likely in view of the fact that its arguments and solutions are less developed. It was originally an independent treatise, but was finally attached by Vasubandhu to the *Kośa* as its last chapter." That chapter 9 is a kind of appendix to the eight chapters can also be seen from the concluding sentence of the *Kośa* at the end of the eighth chapter. Further, none of the previous works have a parallel to this ninth chapter.

ii. Since Erich Frauwallner has researched in depth the structure and development of thought within the above mentioned Abhidharma treatises in his *Studies in Abhidharma Literature and the Origins of Buddhist Philosophical Systems*, here we will reproduce two pages from his chapter *The Origin of Buddhist Systems*, pp. 128f. [Bracketed text is inserted by LS.]

> [The *Abhidharmakośa*] is a description of the Sarvāstivāda system and is one of the most important descriptions of a Buddhist philosophical system that we possess. It is, however, not entirely new in that it is based on the works of a number of predecessors. The earliest of these works available to us (and probably the earliest of them all) is the Abhidharmasāra of a certain Dharmaśrī,* which gives a brief description in verse explicated by an accompanying prose text. This text long enjoyed high standing: new commentaries were repeatedly written and the verse text supplemented and extended until Vasubandhu eventually wrote a new verse text and commentary in his Abhidharmakośa. Yet only the form is completely new: in all essentials [Vasubandhu] bases his work on that of Dharmaśrī.
>
> It is, of course, obvious that if we want to explain the origin of the Sarvāstivāda system we must start with the earliest work, Dharmaśrī's *Abhidharmasāra*. This work consists of ten chapters; [see LVP's *Introduction*, pp. lxiii–lxv:
>
> 1. *Dhātuvarga* (Elements)
> 2. *Saṃskāravarga* (Formations)
> 3. *Karmavarga* (Action)
> 4. *Anuśayavarga* (Proclivities)
> 5. *Āryavarga* (Nobility)
> 6. *Jñānavarga* (Cognition)
> 7. *Samādhivarga* (Concentration)
> 8. *Sūtravarga* (Scriptural Texts)
> 9. *Tsavarga* (*Prakīrṇakavarga*; Miscellaneous Matters)
> 10. *Śāstravarga* or *Vādavarga* (*Dharmakathā*; Discussion).]
>
> Its structure will be clearer if we differentiate between two parts. The first part, consisting of chapters 1 to 7, contains a systematic description of the doctrinal concepts. The second part, chapters 8 to 10, contains all the other transmitted material that Dharmaśrī was unable to accommodate elsewhere in his work. Later, Vasubandhu composed a further chapter on the structure of the world and incorporated this into the systematic description [as his chapter 3], so that his version comprises eight chapters. He also integrated the contents of the last three chapters into this description. However, what his work now possessed in compactness, it lacked in clarity and lucidity of exposition [Übersichtlichkeit].
>
> If we now look more closely at the systematic description in Dharmaśrī's work, the

following structure emerges: [Chapter 1:] following the 5 groups (*skandhāḥ*), he first discusses the constituent elements of which, according to old canonical doctrine, the phenomenal world consists. [Chapter 2:] Proceeding from the realization that things never come into being in isolation, he goes on to discuss the various kinds of mental elements, briefly mentions the theory of atoms and afterwards deals with the different temporal states and the doctrine of causality; that is, the four kinds of conditions (*pratyayāḥ*) and the six causes (*hetavaḥ*). Vasubandhu subsequently inserted a description of the Buddhist conception of the world as consisting of various spheres. There then follows [Chapter 3] a discussion of the doctrine of *karma*; how good or evil actions determine the fate of beings in the cycle of existence. This is followed [Chapters 4 and 5] by the doctrine of liberation, a discussion of the propensities (*anuśayāḥ*) that determine entanglement in the cycle of existence and the knowledge by which these propensities can be eliminated. Finally [Chapters 6 and 7] there is a description of the different kinds of knowledge (*jñānāni*) and concentration (*samādhiḥ*).

The systematic structure of this description is striking. [1–2] It begins with a type of theory of first principles. Then follow the conception of the world, [3] the laws which determine the fate of beings in the vicissitudes of the world and finally [4–5] the doctrine of liberation. The fact that [6] knowledge and [7] concentration are then dealt with separately can be explained in that the idiosyncratic treatment of the doctrine of liberation, to which I have given the name Abhisamayavāda, gives the customary form of these concepts too little emphasis. On the whole, however, we can say that this constitutes a real system that covers all the principal doctrinal concepts and presents them in a consistent, logically connected structure.

Nevertheless, however uniformly constructed and complete this work would seem to be, it is not entirely original. Closer examination reveals that in all essential points it was composed from older material, particularly that from the earlier sections of the *Abhidharmapiṭaka* mentioned above [see also LVP's *Introduction*, pp. xxix–xlii]. [1] The beginning of the theory of principles is based on a Pañcaskandhaka. [2] The discussion of the mental elements is modeled on that of the *Dhātukāya*. The doctrine of causality takes the four conditions (*pratyayāḥ*) from the *Vijñānakāya* and the six causes (*hetavaḥ*) from the *Jñānaprasthāna*. [3] The doctrine of *karma* is modelled on the 3rd part of [the *Prajñaptiśāstra*,] the *Lokaprajñapti*. [4–5] The doctrine of liberation (at least in its first part) can be attested in the *Prakaraṇa* in the doctrine of the propensities (*anuśayāḥ*) and elsewhere, and [6–7] the sections on knowledge and concentration are again based on the *Jñānaprasthāna*.

* See LVP's *Introduction*, p. lxiii, but also notice that Dhammajoti thinks (based on *Yin Shun*; see *Summary*, note 8) that the *Abhidharmasāra* or *Abhidharmahṛdaya* post-dates the *Mahāvibhāṣā*.

Frauwallner finishes this brief overview regarding the general structure by commenting that "here a scholar with an appreciation of logical connections and an understanding of systematic thought has built up an edifice and thus a real philosophical system. His work also stood the test of time: as I have pointed out, all later standard descriptions of the Sarvāstivāda system, up to those of Vasubandhu and Saṃghabhadra, are based on this work."

In a similar vein, Collett Cox writes (DD.xxii): "Despite its later importance as the text representative of northern Indian Abhidharma, one cannot assume that the *Abhidharmakośa* is an original work that represents the culmination of Sarvāstivāda-Vaibhaṣika thought. Certainly, the *Abhidharmakośa* is a monument of Vasubandhu's genius in organization, critical analysis, and clear exegesis. But the structure that Vasubandhu adopts bears the influence of earlier digests and the views that he expresses, whether his own, those of the Sarvāstivāda-Vaibhāṣikas, or those of other masters, are usually traceable to the *Vibhāṣā* compendia. Therefore, the role as representative or as the final determinant of Sarvāstivāda-Vaibhāṣika orthodoxy should more appropriately be accorded to the *Vibhāṣā* compendia, or to the works of Vasubandhu's opponent, Saṅghabhadra."

Now from a less abstract point of view, we also should point out that the fairly close structural dependence of the first eight chapters of the AKB (T 1558) on Dharmaśrī's *Abhidharmasāra* (T 1550), but also on Dharmatrāta's *Saṃyuktābhidharmahṛdayaśāstra* (T 1552), can be clearly and easily seen in the detailed Concordance Chart assembled by Bart Dessein in his SAH.III, pp. 413–61.

2. *The structure of the first two chapters*:

Since not all scholars agree on the classification of the first two chapters in relation to the four noble truths, we present in the following the outlines of their specific structure together:

i. Within the overall context of the discernment of factors, Vasubandhu starts out discussing (section BA.) the twofold classification of factors: impure (*sāsrāva*) and pure (*anāsrava*), which is no surprise since he had just determined the purpose of the AKB as the appeasement of defilements (verse i. 3). But then he inserts into this classification immediately a discussion of the conditioned and unconditioned factors, which is based on the "Miscellaneous" chapter of the AH and SAH, and deals more in detail with the three unconditioned factors: space (*ākāśa*), cessation due to deliberation (*pratisaṃkhyānirodha*) and cessation not due to deliberation (*apratisaṃkhyānirodha*). He returns to his theme of impure factors by providing synonyms for impure conditioned factors and there, among others, mentions the appropriative aggregates (*upādānaskandha*), unsatisfactoriness (*duḥkha*) and origin (*samudaya*).

After this fairly brief section, Vasubandhu turns (section BB.) to the threefold classification of factors: five aggregates (*skandha*), twelve sense-spheres (*āyatana*), eighteen elements (*dhātu*), which is a longer section mainly dealing with the five aggregates—the aggregate of material form (rūpa) receiving the most detailed treatment—but also the relationship between the aggregates, sense-spheres and elements.

For the remainder of chapter 1 (section BC.), he continues with a presentation of twenty-two doctrinal perspectives on the eighteen elements, i.e., not on the aggregates as one could have expected from the previous section, ending with a doctrinal perspective that lists the twenty-two controlling faculties (*indriya*).

ii. Chapter 2, entitled *Indriyanirdeśa*, picks up the preceding theme from chapter 1 by giving a detailed discussion (= section A) of the twenty-two controlling faculties, which is clearly an insert based on the additional chapters of the AH and SAH. As for the name of this chapter, see Dhammajoti's comments in his *Summary*. Vasubandhu then presents a new classification

(= section B), namely, the five-group (*pañca-vastu*) classification of factors:

a. matter or material form (*rūpa*);
b. thought (*citta*);
c. thought-concomitants (*caitta*; *caitasika*) or factors (*dharma*) [or formations (*saṃskāra*)] associated with thought;
d. formations dissociated from thought (*cittaviprayukta*);
e. unconditioned factors (*asaṃskṛta*).

However, he does not give a detailed presentation. This new classification, representing the most developed form of the classifications of the Vaibhāṣikas (see endnote in chapter 2), is again an insert resulting indirectly from the "Miscellaneous" chapter of the AH and SAH. It is introduced in the context of a discussion on the "genesis or origin" of the factors, how factors come into existence, i.e., whether the five aggregates, etc., that have been discussed so far arise independently from each other or if certain ones of them necessarily arise together, which constitutes the beginning of the *Saṃskāravarga* in the AH and SAH. But the new classification is not presented in full as one might expect, for example, since unconditioned factors do not arise, they are never discussed. On the other hand, based on the "Miscellaneous" chapter of the AH and SAH, the presentation of the formations dissociated from thought is inserted after the presentation of the thought-concomitants (*caitta*) (or formations associated with thought). As for the issue of the simultaneous arising of factors, it seems to be dropped after the detailed presentation of the thought-concomitants.

The chapter ends with a new classification (= section C), namely, the very detailed classification of factors according to causes (*hetu*), effects (*phala*) and conditions (*pratyaya*).

iii. If we glance briefly at the topics discussed in chapters 1 and 2, it becomes more apparent why certain scholars classify chapter 2 as belonging to the truth of the origin while others classify it as still being part of the truth of unsatisfactoriness. On the other hand, the brief outline also gives us a better sense of the "work method" of Vasubandhu in the AKB, which is closely scrutinized by Frauwallner in his discussion of the structure of the first two chapters in his *Pañcaskandhaka and Pañcavastuka* (SAL, pp. 135–47).

What Frauwallner dubs as "Pañcaskandhaka" is the "standard form being used [at an early period of Buddhism, at the time of the old Abhidharma,] to represent comprehensively the elements of being that were the material of the dogmatics". It contains, often after a brief beginning assignment of all factors to the categories of undefiled (sāsrava) or defiled (*anāsrava*), the following main elements:

a. discussion of the aggregates, sense-sources and elements and their relationship, with the emphasis, however, on the aggregates (*skandha*);
b. discussion of a list of attributes or doctrinal perspectives on the aggregates (or elements);

to which could be added, as in chapter 2 of AH and SAH:

c. discussion of the arising of factors;
d. discussion of the doctrine of causality: causes (*hetu*) and conditions (*pratyaya*).

As for the emphasis on the aggregates, Frauwallner thinks (SAL.147) that "the skandhāḥ seemed to have assumed more importance as the fields of matter and the mental elements can thus be more easily distinguished. I believe it also possible that even at this early stage of development, matter was dealt with fairly extensively".

As for the list of attributes, Frauwallner shows (SAL.141ff.) that the lists used by various scholars are not necessarily identical, for example, the list in the *Jñānaprasthāna* has only ten items, whereas Vasubandhu has twenty-two.

In the above mentioned article, Frauwallner raises the question of why Vasubandhu did not base his discussion "on the structure most obviously suited to a systematic description", i.e., the five-group classification or Pañcavastuka, even though it constitutes the main content of Vasubandhu's discussion in the first two chapters. As we have seen, Frauwallner distinguishes two distinct stages of development in the dogmatics of the early Abhidharma (SAL.147): "The initial stage, which found expression in the Pañcaskandhaka, is a first attempt at philosophical systematics. The second, represented by the Pañcavastuka, is an attempt at a comprehensive and systematic doctrine of principles", independently of the old canonical categorization of all factors according to *skandhas*, *āyatanas* and *dhātus*. Frauwallner concludes that although the Pañcavastuka signified an important advance, it was not generally adopted since the old Pañcaskandhaka was already too deeply rooted in the tradition. Yet since its innovations could not be ignored, they were somehow "forced" into the old framework, which prevailed "until the end of the Abhidharma period and the last, authoritative reworking of the dogmatics in the works of Vasubandhu".

47 *LS*: AH 4–6, 225; SAH 4–6, 458–59.

48 *LS*: AH 4; SAH 4.

49 *Gokhale*: [4a] *sāsravā'nāsravā dharmāḥ*

Tib.: [4a] *zag bcas zag pa med chos rnams* |

LS: *Āsrava* (lit. "flowing out/toward") is a synonym of *kleśa* (defilement). For the doctrinal perspective *sāsrava–anāsrava* in regard to the eighteen elements (*dhātu*), see i. 31cd. For a discussion of the three fluxes, see v. 35–36; for an explanation of the term *āsrava*, see v. 40.

Dhammajoti comments in his Glossary (SA.IV.514, 542):

> *anāsrava*: Outflow-free ("pure" in the sense that such a *dharma* does not conduce to the saṃsāric process).
>
> *sāsrava*: With-outflow. A with-outflow object is one by taking which the defilement adheres to it and grows. It is also one whose effect is to retain us in *saṃsāra*.

50 *LS*: AH 4–6.

51 *Gokhale*: [4bd] *saṃskṛtā mārgavarjitāḥ* | *sāsravā āsravās teṣu yasmāt samanuśerate* ||

Tib.: [4bd] *lam ma gtogs pa'i 'dus byas rnams* | *zag bcas gang phyir de dag la* | *zag rnams kun tu rgyas par 'gyur* ||

LVP: The conditioned factors, with the exception of those that are part of the (noble) path, are called *sāsrava*, "in a [positive] relationship with the fluxes".

How and why are they *in a [positive] relationship with the fluxes*?

1. One cannot say: because they are associated (*saṃprayukta*) with the fluxes, for only the

thought and the thought-concomitants that are defiled (*kliṣṭa*) are associated with the fluxes (i. 23).

2. One cannot say: because they coexist (*sahotpāda*) with the fluxes. In this hypothesis, (i) neither the external (*bāhya*; i. 39a) factors, (ii) nor the five appropriative aggregates (*upādānaskandha*; i. 8) of a person within whom thc fluxes are not presently active would be *in a relationship with the fluxes.*

3. One cannot say: because they are the support (*āśraya*) of the fluxes, for only the six sense faculties of the consciousness are the support of the fluxes.

4. One cannot say: because they are the cognitive object (*ālambana*) of the fluxes: in this hypothesis, *nirvāṇa* (= *nirodhasatya*) would be *in a [positive] relationship with the fluxes*, for there can be false views with regard to Nirvāṇa; in this hypothesis, a higher stage would be *in a relationship with the fluxes* by the fact of the fluxes of a lower stage that take this higher stage as their cognitive object (opinions condemned; v. 18).

The author thus explains that a factor is called *in a [positive] relationship with the fluxes* because the fluxes adhere (*anuśerate*) to it, i.e., grow in it (*puṣṭim labhante*) or take their dwelling or support (*pratiṣṭhā*) in it, as a foot can stand on earth but not on red-hot fire. The proclivities (*anuśaya*) develop (*saṃtāyante*) by taking their growth or support in and on the factors *in a [positive] relationship with the fluxes*.

According to another opinion, just as one says: "This food suits me" (*mama anuśete*), in order to say: "This food agrees with me, is favorable to me (*anuguṇībhavati*)", so the fluxes "suit these factors", "are favorable to these factors". Thus those factors to which the fluxes are favorable, namely, the conditioned factors with the exception of the (noble) path are called *in a [positive] relationship with the fluxes*: in fact, the conditioned factors are created by the actions aroused by the fluxes; the fluxes are thus favorable to them (*Vyākhyā*). See v. 1, 18, 29, 39, 40.

The schools are not in agreement in regard to whether the body of the Buddha is *in a [positive] relationship with the fluxes.* See i. 31d.

LS: 1. As for the notion of "adhere and grow", Ny, 637c7ff. (ATA.79), referring to the *Jñānaprasthāna*, states:

> What is "adhering" or "growing" (*anuśerate*)? It refers to the fact that contaminants are associated with this [moment of] thought, are dependent upon thought, and not yet abandoned.
>
> What is "not adhering" or "not growing" (na anuśerate)? It refers to the fact that contaminants are [still] associated with this [moment of] thought, and yet one has already attained complete abandonment [of them].

2. As for the notion "growing concordantly", (i) a defilement can grow concordantly with the conascent defiled *citta-caitta* associated with it, by way of conjunction (*saṃprayogatas*). (ii) It can also grow concordantly by way of taking a [with-outflow] object (*ālambanatas*).

i. As for "*anuśayana* by way of conjunction", Ny, 637c, elaborates on it as a threefold operation (SA.IV.344):

a. inducing the acquisition (*prāpti*) [of the defilements];
b. obstructing the thought series (*citta-santati*);
c. serving as the homogeneous cause for the emanation of the subsequent moment in

the series.

ii. As for "*anuśayana* by way of taking an object", Ny, 616b, explains this to mean that "the *anuśaya* adheres along and grows in the *(sāsrava) dharma*, i.e., it binds concordantly and increases stagnation therein". Saṃghabhadra explains further (Ny, 616b; SA.IV.343):

> This is like the adherence of dust on a wet garment, or the growth of seeds in an irrigated field. The *anuśaya*-s that take the *anāsravadharma*-s—*nirvāṇa* or the path—or a higher sphere (than the one to which they belong) as objects, do not operate in this mode, because these objects are not appropriated as the Self or what pertains to the Self either through Self-view (*ātmadṛṣṭi*) or craving (*tṛṣṇā*). As a matter of fact, the wish for the attainment of the pure *dharma*-s or a higher sphere is not a greed as such but a predilection or aspiration for the good (*kuśala-dharma-chanda*). Besides, the pure objects as well as the *dharma*-s belonging to a higher sphere are in nature opposed to the *anuśaya*-s that take them as objects, and hence not supportive of their growth. As such, the *anuśaya*-s cannot find a footing in them, just as the sole of a foot cannot stay when placed on a heated rock.

For further examples for the phenomena of *anuśayana* given by the *pūrvācārya*-s and "some others", see SA.IV.344f.

52 *LS*: The *Vyākhyā* glosses [WOG.12.22]: hetu-pratyaya-janitā rūpa'ādayaḥ *saṃskṛtāḥ*.

53 *LS*: As for the fluxes, v. 40 states: "The proclivities fix, keep (*āsayanti*) beings in cyclic existence (*saṃsāra*); they [cause beings to] flow around (āsravanti, gacchanti) from the highest heaven (summit of cyclic existence [*bhavāgra*] = *naivasaṃjñānāsaṃjñāyatana*; iii. 3, 81) to the hell of ceaseless torture (*avīci*; iii. 58); they discharge or ooze (*kṣar*) through the six wound-like entrances (*āyatana*; i.e., the sense-faculties). They are thus called *fluxes* (*āsrava*)."

54 *LS*: Pradhān has *nirodhamārgasatyālambana*.

55 *LS*: As an example for acts that are wholesome or skillful (*kuśala*) but may still be with-outflow (*sāsrava*), Dhammajoti mentions (SA.IV.42) that "one may practice generosity in the hope of having a favorable rebirth in the future". Thus the scope of the "with-outflow" is greater than that of the unwholesome or unskillful (*akuśala*).

MVŚ, 444c–445a, mentions (SA.IV.43) a few examples given by the Venerable Vasumitra:

> When a proclivity arises having a with-outflow *dharma* as its cognitive object, the proclivity grows/waxes gradually. This is like the case of a man looking at the moon which helps the growth of his visual faculty. Thus, the with-outflow *dharma*-s accord with the growth of the proclivities.
>
> When a proclivity arises having an outflow-free *dharma* as its cognitive object, the proclivity wanes gradually. This is like the case of a man looking at the sun, which damages his visual faculty. Thus, the outflow-free *dharma*-s do not accord with the growth of the proclivities.

56 *Gokhale*: [5ab] *anāsravā mārgasatyaṃ trividhaṃ cā 'py asaṃskṛtam* |

Tib.: [5ab] *zag med lam gyis bden pa dang* | *'dus ma byas rnam gsum yang ste* |

LVP: The truth of the (noble) path is the totality of the factors that constitute the insight into and the cultivation of the truths (vi. 25d; vii. 3b).

On the unconditioned factors (*asaṃskṛta*), see i. 48b, ii. 55cd and the *Introduction* by LVP.

LS: The *Avatāra* states (ESD.110): "By outflow-free [*anāsrava*] *dharma*-s are meant the Truth of the Path (*mārga-satya*) and the three unconditioned *dharma*-s, as all of them do not belong to any of the three spheres (*apratisaṃyukta*)."

As for the "unconditioned factors", we have seen above in our note on the structure of the first two chapters of the AKB that the discussion of the unconditioned factors had no special place in the main elements of the Pañcaskandhaka, since the latter focused mainly on the *skandhas*, which do not include the unconditioned ones in contrast to the *āyatanas* and *dhātus*. Thus based on a Pañcavastuka where they form the fifth group, they were added by Dharmaśrī and Dharmatrāta to the "Miscellaneous" chapter of their AH and SAH. Frauwallner shows (SAL.136f.) that from the more advanced Pañcavastuka point of view, Vasubandhu's moving the discussion of the unconditioned factors into first place was due to his being bound by tradition, i.e., the Pañcaskandhaka, which often begins with a brief assignment of all factors to the categories of undefiled (*sāsrava*) or defiled (*anāsrava*), before discussing its main elements, i.e., the five aggregates, etc. Thus moving within the wider structure of the Pañcaskandhaka, the discussion of the three unconditioned factors was incorporated with the "undefiled", which gave them a prominent place as in the Pañcavastuka.

As for the "path", Jampaiyang (transl. Coghlan; p. 158) clarifies: "Here, the masters Guṇamati and Pūrṇavardhana state that since the term 'path' refers to both mundane and transcendent (paths), therefore doubt arises as to whether the mundane path is uncontaminated. To distinguish it from that, the term 'truth' is mentioned in the statement: 'The uncontaminated truth of path.' That is because the mundane path is only the path and not the truth of path because (the mundane path) is subsumed by the truths of unsatisfactoriness and the origin." And Geshe Jampa Gyatso quotes (p. 34) Gedun Drup: "True paths do not increase contaminations either by observing them or by being concomitant with them. True paths are the paths of seeing, meditation, and no-more-learning. Because the contaminations do not increase by observing them, they are uncontaminated."

57 *LS*: 1. As for the conditioned and unconditioned factors "in general", the MVŚ (392c–393a) distinguishes (SA.IV.38):

> A *dharma* is said to be conditioned if it has arising and ceasing, cause and effect, and acquires the characteristics of the conditioned.
>
> A *dharma* is said to be unconditioned if it has no arising and ceasing, no cause and effect, and acquires the characteristics of the unconditioned.

Dhammajoti explains that "the conditioned *dharma*-s have causes and conditions because they are weak in nature and must therefore depend on causes and conditions for their activities. The unconditioned *dharma*-s, on the other hand, are strong and therefore are not dependent on them. Moreover, the unconditioned *dharma*-s have no activities at all, hence no use of causes and conditions [MVŚ, 711a–b]."

2. As for the conditioned factors, according to the Vaibhāṣikas they are characterized by the characteristics of conditioned factors (*saṃskṛtalakṣaṇa*; ii. 45cd)—the four factors of (i) origination (jāti), (ii) deterioration (jarā), (iii) duration (sthiti) and (iv) impermanence (*anityatā*)—considered to be real entities belonging to the class of formations dissociated

from thought (*viprayuktasaṃskāra*).

3. As for the unconditioned factors, various schools interpret them and their ontological status differently:

i. The "orthodox" Vaibhāṣikas teach that all unconditioned factors—having no activities and not being conditioned by causes and conditions—are not conditioned or accompanied by the four characteristics of origination, duration, deterioration and impermanence (ii. 45cd), and they accept the three factors mentioned in our root verse. Collett Cox discusses their ontological status (FCO.558):

> The **Mahāvibhāṣā* specifies that unconditioned *dharma*s function not only as sovereign conditions (*adhipatipratyaya*), but also as comprehensive non-obstructing causes (*kāraṇahetu*) and as object-support conditions (*ālambanapratyaya*). Their function as comprehensive non-obstructing causes is identical to their function as sovereign conditions: that is, as in the case of all *dharma*s, unconditioned *dharma*s also function not to obstruct the arising of *dharma*s other than themselves. And in this function as non-obstructing causes, unconditioned *dharma*s do not exert any generative causal efficacy: that is to say, they are not active in producing an effect. As object-support conditions, unconditioned *dharma*s function as objects of mental perceptual consciousness, but here also they do not function as the generative causes for its arising. Hence, unconditioned *dharma*s are said to have no cause, since they do not arise, and no effect, since they do not function as generative causes in producing their own effect. Nevertheless, even though unconditioned *dharma*s lack generative activity, they do have a function, and this functioning, as in the case of conditioned *dharma*s, makes known their characteristic nature and mandates their existence as distinct *dharma*s.

Dhammajoti explains (SA.IV.474) that the essential characteristic of the unconditioned factors is that they are neither temporalized nor spatialized, and since they are "beyond the space-time dimensions, they can neither arise nor cease, and accordingly are not directly involved in any causal process".

In this context see the longer discussion at ii. 55d.

ii. For the Sautrāntika (SA.IV.472), the unconditioned is simply a concept (*prajñapti*) of that which is opposed to the conditioned. The AKB ii, F 278ff., states that all the unconditioned are not real or non-entities (*sarvam evāsaṃskṛtam adravyam*), for they do not exist as distinct or real entities (*bhāvāntara*) as are *rūpa*, *vedanā*, etc. Thus cessation due to deliberation or *nirvāṇa*, for example, would be nothing more than the absolute absence of unsatisfactoriness (*duḥkha*). Or space as an unconditioned factor would be merely the absence of tangible things (*spraṣṭāvyābhāva-mātra*), as when people in darkness say that there is space when they do not encounter any obstacles.

iii. Dhammajoti adds (SA.IV.472f.):

> Even within the Sarvāstivāda school itself, opinions differ as regards the ontological status of these unconditioned *dharma*-s. It appears that at the early stages, the Sarvāstivāda did not elaborate on the ontological status of the unconditioned *dharma*-s. In the JPŚ, the canonical text upheld as the supreme authority by the

orthodox Sarvāstivādins, one finds only the mention of *pratisaṃkhyā-nirodha* and *apratisaṃkhyā-nirodha*, but not *ākāśa*. In the MVŚ, the various *ācārya*-s hold contradictory views. Thus, Buddhadeva accepts the realities of all three; the Bhadanta (= Dharmatrāta?) denies the reality of *ākāśa*; the Dārṣṭāntika denies the ontological status of all three. Probably in response to the denial by the Dārṣṭāntika and the Sautrāntika, in the post AKB period there had consistently been an additional requirement in the definition of "Sarvāstivāda": A Sarvāstivādin must accept not only the tri-temporal existence of *dharma*, but also the reality of all three kinds of unconditioned *dharma*-s.

58 *LVP*: Certain philosophers, the Vātsīputrīyas, say that there is only one unconditioned factor (*asaṃskṛta*), namely, *nirvāṇa*. The Vaiśeṣikas assert many unconditioned factors: the atoms (*paramāṇu*), etc. (WOG.15.2ff.). – Some assert three unconditioned factors; others consider emptiness (*śūnyatā*), which is the characteristic or nature of suchness (*tathatā-lakṣaṇā*) (*Madhyamaka*, vii, 33, p. 176), as an unconditioned factor. – Wassilief, pp. 264, 282; *Kathāvatthu*, ii. 9; vi. 1–6; xix, 5; Bhāvaviveka, *Nanjio* 1237, 2, p. 275c.

LS: Thích Thiên Châu (LPEB.202f.) and Bareau (SBPV.120; *L'Absolue en philosophie bouddhique*, p. 260–61)—seemingly all based on LVP and Yaśomitra—repeat the view that the Vātsīputrīyas say that there is only one unconditioned factor (*asaṃskṛta*), this view does not seem to be corroborated by the Chinese sources. For example, it is not mentioned in the *Tridharmakhaṇḍaka* and the *Sāṃmitīyanikāyaśāstra*; it is also not mentioned in Vasumitra's *Samayabhedoparacaṇa-cakra* ("Wheel of statements of the dissensions of doctrines"), where, if the *asaṃskṛtas* were different from the Sarvāstivāda presentation, one would expect it to be mentioned as it is with the Mahāsāṃghikas and Mahīśāsakas; likewise, Dhammajoti (private communication) points out that Fa Bao (Pu Guang's fellow student) states in his AKB commentary (T 41, 470a): "although the schools designate the *asaṃskṛtas* differently, the various [Hīnayāna] schools all have these three *asaṃskṛtas*. Mahāyāna adds six..., Mahāsāṃghika, etc., adds six..., Mahīśāsaka...".

59 *Gokhale*: [5c] *ākāśaṃ dvau nirodhau ca*

Tib.: [5c] *nam mkha' dang ni 'gog pa gnyis* |

LVP: On the two cessations (*nirodha*), i. 6; ii. 55c; on the five cessations, i. 20ab.

60 *LS*: AH 225; SAH 458.

61 *Gokhale*: [5d] *tatr ākāśaṃ anāvṛtiḥ* ||

Tib.: [5d] *de la nam mkha' mi sgrib pa'o* ||

LVP: On *ākāśa*, see "Documents d'Abhidharma", *BEFEO*, 1930 [see *Electronic Appendix*]; see ii, 279; iii, 139, Add.

62 *LVP*: On the difference between space (*ākāśa*) and the elementary substance space (*ākāśadhātu*), i. 28; on the nonexistence of the unconditioned factor (*asaṃskṛta*) called *space* (Sautrāntika theory), see ii. 55cd. – *Kathāvatthu*, vi. 6–7.

The opinion of the Mādhyamika on space and the other unconditioned factors, an opinion identical to that of the Sautrāntika, is explained by Āryadeva, *Śataka*, ix. 3 (*Madhyamakavṛtti*, 505; *Catuḥśatikā*, 202, As. Soc. of Bengal, iii. p. 483, 1914): "Where there is no matter (*rūpa*), nothing opposes the arising of material factors: the absence of matter receives the name *ākāśa*, because the factors shine brightly there (*bhṛśam asyāntaḥ kāśante bhāvāḥ*). The Vaibhāṣikas assume in the Abhidharmaśāstra that space is a reality (*vastu*), not seeing that the Scripture contents itself to giving a name to a non-reality, to a pure nothingness (*avastusato kiṃcanasya*)… ."

LS: 1. The *Avatāra* states (ESD.124):

> Space (*ākāśa*) has the characteristic of accommodating resistant things; as it is by the dominant (*adhipati*) force of this that they are capable of being produced, and as it is the nature of Space to be accommodative. If it were non-existent, there ought not to be the production of resistant things, since there would be nothing to accommodate them.
>
> Thus, the Bhagavat has said, "O *brāhmaṇa*, Wind is supported by Space." The *brāhmaṇa* asked, "By what is Space supported?" The Buddha further told him, "Your question is unreasonable. Space is immaterial (*arūpin*), invisible (*anidarśana*) and non-resistant (*apratigha*); what can be its support? Nevertheless, Space can be known [to exist] on account of the existence of light."

2. But space as an unconditioned factor must be distinguished from the conditioned elementary substance space (*ākāśa-dhātu*; i. 28), the latter (i) being empty space that is visible in between objects occupying space, for example, the cavity of the door, mouth, etc., and (ii) being "of the nature of material form (*rūpa*)—more specifically of the nature of light and darkness (*āloka-tamaḥ-svabhāva*), as what we perceive in such cavities is light or darkness" (SA.IV.491).

Cox comments (FCO.556) that the **Mahāvibhāṣā* "contends that traditional sources do not clearly distinguish space as an unconditioned *dharma* from space as a conditioned, material element (*ākāśadhātu*). Scriptural passages using the simple term 'space' (*ākāśa*) actually describe space as a material element, and the *Prakaranapāda* also uses the 'gross' characteristics of space as a material element to indicate the 'subtle' unconditioned *dharma* space." Since the *Jñānaprasthāna* as well as Dharmatrāta, for example, do not mention or accept *ākāśa* as an unconditioned *dharma*, Dhammajoti suggests (SA.IV.491) that it is "possible that this category came to be regarded as one of the three unconditioned at a relatively later stage by the orthodox Sarvāstivādins".

The MVŚ, 388b, distinguishes the conditioned and unconditioned space as follows (SA.IV.491):

> The Ābhidharmikas assert thus: What is the space element? It is the *agha-sāmantaka rūpa*. By *agha* is meant agglomerated [matter] (*citastham rūpam*), i.e., a wall, etc. There exists a matter that is proximate to it, called *agha-rūpa*. Such space as found in the wall, in the forest, in the leaves, in the windows, among the fingers—they are called the space-elements. …
>
> What is the difference between Space and the space-element? Space is not matter; the space-element is matter. Space is invisible (*anidarśana*); the space-element is visible. Space is non-resistant (*apratigha*); the space-element is resistant (*sapratigha*). Space is outflow-free; the space-element is with-outflow. Space is unconditioned; the space-element is conditioned.

3. Dhammajoti remarks (SA.IV.492) that "Vasubandhu presents the Sautrāntika view that

Space is unreal [AKB ii. F 278f.]: It is merely the absence of tangible things (*spraṣṭavya-abhāva-mātra*). ... Saṃghabhadra informs us [Ny, 347b] that the Sautrāntika master Sthavira Śrīlāta and all the other Dārṣṭāntika masters hold the view that the space-element is nothing apart from Space; but Space does not exist as a real entity, hence thc space-element too is unreal."

[63] *LS*: AH 225; SAH 458.

[64] *Gokhale*: [6ab] *pratisaṃkhyānirodho yo visaṃyogaḥ pṛthak pṛthak* |

Tib.: [6ab] *so sor brtags pas 'gog pa gang* | *bral ba'o so so so so yin* |

LVP: Compare the discussion in *Kathāvatthu*, xix. 3.

The Sarvāstivādin considers that "disconnection from a defilement", "the cessation of future defilement or unsatisfactoriness" (*visaṃyoga, nirodha*), is a phenomenon in and of itself, a real factor, a real entity (*dravya*). *Disconnection* is not produced by causes, it is eternal. The possession (*prāpti*) of disconnection through *pratisaṃkhyā* (deliberation; comprehension of the truths) is obtained.

LS: 1. Dhammajoti states (SA.IV.471 and 476) that cessations due to deliberation represent the goal of Buddhist praxis and as such are the most important of the three unconditioned factors. For the Sarvāstivāda, these cessations are distinct positive entities (*dravyāntara*) and ontologically real forces acquired by the practitioner when a given defilement is completely abandoned, and they act to ensure that the possession of the defilement so abandoned will absolutely not be able to arise any more, "just like a dike holding back the water or a screen blocking the wind".

These cessations are not causes or conditions in the proper sense and as such cannot be said to have fruits (*sa-phala*) (see AKB ii. 55cd and 57d). "Nevertheless, in conformity with the *sūtra* tradition which speaks of the fruit of spiritual life (*śrāmāṇya-phala*) and conventional usage, it is permissible to call *pratisaṃkhyā-nirodha* a 'fruit of disjunction' (*visaṃyoga-phala*) without implying that it is causally produced, and it is also permissible to consider them as a 'condition qua object' (*ālambana-pratyaya*)—e.g., as an object of thought of a yogi, and 'fruit of (pre)-dominance' (*adhipati-pratyaya*)—making an indirect contribution by merely not obstructing."

2. In discussing *pratisaṃkhyānirodha*, Vasubandhu gives first its definition, which he then linguistically links to its three main components: (i) deliberation (*pratisaṃkhyā*), of which he provides a definition that is the same as the one given in the MVŚ, (ii) cessation (*nirodha*) and (iii) possession or acquisition (*prāpti*). The term *nirvāṇa*, which in the Sarvāstivāda is a synonym for *pratisaṃkhyānirodha*, is added by LVP. In the remainder of this section Vasubandhu then discusses whether *pratisaṃkhyānirodha* is plural or not. Later (see ii. 55d), in the context of discussing the five effects—including the effect of disconnection (*visaṃyoga-phala*)—Vasubandhu will venture into a longer discussion and debate on the ontological status of *pratisaṃkhyānirodha*, in which context he will then provide additional definitions of the three unconditioned factors given by the Sautrāntikas, who concede (ii. F 282) that these factors, as well as acquisition, exist but merely as provisional designations (*prajñaptisat*), (and definitions given by other schools), and also further synonyms for *nirvāṇa*.

i. In regard to deliberation, see the next endnote.

ii. In regard to types of cessation (*nirodha*), LVP lists (F 35) five types:

a. cessation by the characteristic (*lakṣaṇanirodha*) (ii. 45cd);
b. cessation by attainment (*samāpattinirodha*) (ii. 42f.);
c. cessation by birth (*upapattinirodha* = state of non-ideation [*āsaṃjñika*]; ii. 41b);
d. cessation due to deliberation (*pratisaṃkhyānirodha*) (i. 6ab);
e. cessation not due to deliberation (*apratisaṃkhyānirodha*) (i. 6cd).

iii. In regard to possession or acquisition, the important role that this factor plays—for the Vaibhāṣikas—in spiritual attainments is pointed out by Dhammajoti (SA.IV.481):

> [With regard to the questions in the MVŚ, 162a–b:] when sentient beings realize *pratisaṃkhyānirodha*, (a) do they together realize a common one or (b) do they individually realize a different (i.e., identical but distinct) one in each case? ... The MVŚ compilers answer:
>
> > When sentient beings realize *pratisaṃkhyā-nirodha*, they realize a common one. However, although *nirvāṇa* is in actual fact common as an entity, it is said to be non-common in respect to its acquisition since the *visaṃyoga-prāpti* arises separately in the series of each individual.
>
> It is only when the acquisition of *nirvāṇa* arises in a particular individual that he is said to have acquired/attained *nirvāṇa*. [...]
>
> Any religion or philosophy that posits a transcendental absolute needs to account for the way in which the empirical is related to the transcendental. In the Sarvāstivāda perspective, the relationship is effected by acquisition, a real force existing in its own right, which connects a *dharma* to a given series. The *dharma* then is one possessed by that particular individual. In abandoning a defilement, two final moments are involved: In the first moment known as *ānantarya-mārga* [unhindered path], the acquisition of the defilement is severed. In the second moment, known as *vimukti mārga* [path of liberation], the acquisition of the corresponding *pratisaṃkhyā-nirodha* arises, and the practitioner is said to have realized the *nirodha*.
>
> The notion of acquisition is also invoked to explain away the apparent contradiction involved in stating that the *nirvāṇa* is a *phala—visaṃyoga-phala*—although it is not causally produced by the spiritual path [cf. AKB ii, F 276f.]. ...

3. In regard to the *pratisaṃkhyānirodha* of our passage and the *nirvāṇa/nirodha* of a worldling, as well as the *prāpti*s related to them, Dhammajoti comments (private communication): "The AKB here clearly says that *pratisaṃkhyā-nirodha* is multiple. It is not a reference to 'the' Nirvāṇa; but to *nirvāṇa*-s. It also does not refer to the *nirvāṇa/nirodha* with which a worldling (*pṛthagjana*) can be endowed through the mundane path. The point to note is that the *nirodha* of a defilement acquired by a *pṛthagjana* is not a *pratisaṃkhyā-nirodha*; it will become such through *satya-abhisamaya*. I.e., a *pṛthagjana* can have the acquisition (*prāpti*) of the *pratisaṃkhyā-nirodha* of a *kleśa*; but the *pratisaṃkhyā-nirodha* cannot manifest in him until he becomes an *ārya*. The *prāpti* which was earlier *sāsrava* now becomes *anāsrava*. So, we can say that both a *pratisaṃkhyā-nirodha* and a *nirodha* acquired through a mundane path can be called a '*nirvāṇa*' (T27, 147b6–7). A *pṛthagjana*, through the mundane path, can have the '*prāpti* of *visaṃyoga*' arisen in him. (Note that the word *visaṃyoga* applies

also to such a *nirodha*.) This *prāpti* is neither-*śaikṣa*-nor-*aśaikṣa* (MVŚ, 170b7–11). After *abhisamaya*, the *prāpti* is transformed into the *śaikṣa* [trainee] type. But [this] *pratisaṃkhyā-nirodha* is necessarily acquired through an *anāsrava prajñā*. *Pratisaṃkhyā-nirodha* is *na-śaikṣa-nāśaikṣa*; but its *prāpti* can be either *śaikṣa*, *aśaikṣa* or neither-*śaikṣa*-nor-*aśaikṣa*. (MVŚ, 161b19–26). In brief: a *pratisaṃkhyā-nirodha* is a *nirodha/visaṃyoga*; but a *nirodha/visaṃyoga* is not necessarily a *pratisaṃkhyā-nirodha*."

4. In regard to the object of acquisition, moral quality, etc., of the *pratisaṃkhyānirodhas*, the MVŚ lists the following (SA.IV.488f.):

> The *pratisaṃkhyā-nirodha*-s are acquired with regard to the with-outflow *dharma*-s of the three periods of time; ...are skillful (*kuśala*) and so are their acquisitions; ...are outflow-free (*anāsrava*) and their acquisitions are either with-outflow or outflow-free; ...are not bound to any sphere of existence (*apratisaṃyukta*) and their acquisitions may be bound to the fine-material sphere (*rūpa-dhātu*) or the non-material sphere (*ārūpyadhātu*) or not bound to any sphere; ...are neither-trainee-nor-nontrainee (*naiva-śaikṣa-nāśaikṣa*) and their acquisitions may be trainee, non-trainee or neither-trainee-nor-nontrainee; ...are not to be abandoned (*aheya*) and their acquisitions are either to be abandoned by cultivation (*bhāvanā-heya*) or not to be abandoned; ...are non-defiled (*akliṣṭa*) and so are their acquisitions; ...are without retribution (*avipāka*) and their acquisitions are either with or without retribution; ...are fruits of the path (*mārga-phala*) and their acquisitions may be either paths and fruits of the path or neither paths nor fruits of the path; ...are subsumed under truth of cessation (*nirodha-satya*) and their acquisitions are subsumed under the other three truths.

65 *LVP*: Several *pratisaṃkhyānirodhas*, Vasumitra, Mahāsāṃghikas, thesis 34.

LS: 1. The unconditioned factors—with the exception of space—are pluralistic in nature. The *Avatāra* states (ESD.125f.):

> There are innumerable entities [of the cessations through deliberation], accordingly as the amount of abandonables which is innumerable. ... [T]here are as many cessations through deliberation as there are *dharma*-s with outflows, since this accords with logic.
>
> [However,] in accordance with the different [counteractive] paths, [the cessations through deliberation] are established as eighty-nine. In accordance with the [different] abandonment-knowledges (*prahāṇa-parijñā*) they are established as nine. In accordance with the five different classes [of abandonables] they are established as five. In accordance with the different fruits [of spiritual cultivation], they are said to be four—stream-entry, etc. In accordance with the three different elements—of abandonment, detachment and cessation (*prahāṇa-dhātu, virāga-dhātu, nirodha-dhātu*)—they are established as three. In accordance with the abandonment of unsatisfactoriness and the origin of unsatisfactoriness, and also accordingly as [the *nirvāṇa*] with or without remainder (*sopadhiśeṣa, nirupadhiśeṣa*), they are established as two. From the point of view of the abandonment of births and deaths collectively, it is established as one.

Comparing the cessations due to deliberation and not due to deliberation in terms of quantity, Dhammajoti comments (ESD.205) that the MVŚ, 164, explains the latter to be "more numerous because its quantity is in accordance with that of the *saṃskṛta dharma*-s, whereas the quantity of the former is only in accordance with that of the *sāsrava-dharma*-s".

2. In the context of the abandonment of the defilements (*kleśa*) and the plurality of the *pratisaṃkhyānirodhas* and its various synonyms (SA.IV.352f.), this then implies for the Vaibhāṣikas a gradual and systematic abandonment of the defilements and realization of the corresponding cessations (*nirodha*), i.e., not an "abrupt awakening", so that MVŚ, 465c, can state that "there are eighty-nine different stages in the abandonment of the defilements; for in all these stages there is the realization of *nirodha*". Thus depending on the specific stage of progress at which a corresponding amount of defilements is abandoned, MVŚ, 321b–322b, distinguishes between eight types of synonyms which may or may not apply in full in the different stages (SA.IV.353):

> The abandonment in its intrinsic nature [is given various names]—(1) "abandonment" (*prahāṇa*), (2) "disjunction" (*visaṃyoga*), (3) "cessation" (*nirodha*), (4) "truth" (*satya*), (5) "complete knowledge" (*parijñā*), (6) "fruit of the spiritual life" (*śrāmaṇya-phala*), (7) "sphere of *nirvāṇa* with a remnant of substratum" (*sopadhiśeṣa-nirvāṇa-dhātu*), and (8) "sphere of *nirvāṇa* without a remnant of substratum" (*nirupadhiśeṣa-nirvāṇa-dhātu*). ... Thus, when the receptivity to the knowledge of *dharma* with regard to *duḥkha* (*duḥkhe dharma-jñāna-kṣānti*) ceases and the knowledge of *dharma* with regard to *duḥkha* arises, that abandonment acquired is called "abandonment", "disjunction", "cessation", "truth"; [but] it is not yet called "complete knowledge", not yet called "fruit of the spiritual life", not yet called "sphere of *nirvāṇa* with a remnant of substratum", not yet called "sphere of *nirvāṇa* without a remnant of substratum". ...

66 *LVP*: The Fortunate One compares the impure object (*sāsrava*) to a post, i.e., the object to which the defilements, attachment, hatred, etc., can adhere; the defilements or fetters (*saṃyojana*) are the rope; the person (*pudgala*) is the animal. (Compare *Saṃyutta*, iv. 282). The impure object is the *place with binding* (*saṃyogavastu; saññojaniya*).

67 *LVP*: Dharmadinnā was questioned by her former husband, the householder Viśākha: *kiṃsabhāga ārye nirodhaḥ*? – She answered: *asabhāga āyuṣman viśākha*. (*Madhyamāgama*, fasc. 18, fol. 3; MVŚ, 162b11; 162a). – Compare *Majjhima*, i. 304: *nibbānassa pan' ayye kiṃ patibhāgo*... .

LS: Hall comments (VASC.54): "If 'non-homogeneous' (*a-sabhāga*) were taken literally it would mean 'having nothing similar to it' (*apratidiśa*). In that case there could be only one unique cessation of all defilements. Therefore 'non-homogeneous' is here taken to mean 'not having or being a homogeneous cause'. If 'cessation' had a homogeneous cause it would not be 'unconditioned'."

68 *LS*: AH 225; SAH 459.

69 *Gokhale*: [6cd] *utpādā'tyantavighno 'nyo nirodho 'pratisaṃkhyayā* ||

Tib.: [6cd] *skye la gtan du gegs byed pa* | *'gog gzhan so sor brtags min pas* ||

LS: In discussing *apratisaṃkhyānirodha*, Vasubandhu first gives its definition, then explains its name—related to the way it is acquired—before providing an example. In chapter 2, Vasubandhu will first clarify the relationship of possession (*prāpti*) and non-possession (*aprāpti*) with *apratisaṃkhyanirodha* (ii. F 179f.), and then determine (ii. F 275) that the *apratisaṃkhyānirodha* and *ākāśa* are not effects. Connected with the latter, he will also provide additional definitions of the three unconditioned factors given by the Sautrāntikas and other schools, and enter into a discussion on their ontological status.

1. In regard to its definition, Dhammajoti points out (ESD.44f.) that "the Vaibhāṣikas generally explain the *apratisaṃkhyā-nirodha* as an entity acquired owing to the deficiency in the conditions for a *dharma*'s arising", but that Saṃghabhadra defines it as a positive force—a notion that is not completely missing in the MVŚ—as follows (Ny, 434b):

> The *apratisaṃhkyā-nirodha* is not merely the deficiency in conditions. It is a distinct *dharma*, acquired by reason of the deficiency in conditions. This *dharma* has the special potency of obstructing the *dharma* which may [otherwise] be produced, causing it never to arise... .

2. In regard to its name and the way it is acquired, the MVŚ, 164b, explains [SA.IV.486]:

> It is called a cessation independent of deliberation because it is not acquired through deliberative understanding, not being an effect of deliberation. Furthermore, it is so called because it is not acquired through deliberation by means of necessary effort, necessary preparation or necessary exertion. Furthermore, ... because its acquisition does not require the repeated ascertaining of *duḥkha*, etc. ...
>
> It is [acquired] on account of the deficiency in conditions (*pratyaya-vaikalyāt*). Thus, when one is focused [on an object] in one direction, all the other objects—visible, sound, smell, taste and tangible—in the other directions cease. ...

3. In regard to the object of acquisition, moral quality, etc., of the *apratisaṃkhyānirodhas*, the MVŚ lists the following (SA.IV.488f.):

> The *apratisaṃkhyā-nirodha*-s are acquired with regard to the future conditioned *dharma*-s destined not to arise; ...are non-defined (*avyākṛta*), and so are their acquisitions; ...are outflow-free (*anāsrava*), and their acquisitions are with-outflow only; ...are not bound to any sphere, and their acquisitions are bound to the three spheres only; ...are neither-trainee-nor-nontrainee (*naiva-śaikṣa-nāśaikṣa*), and so are their acquisitions; ...are not to be abandoned, and their acquisitions are to be abandoned by cultivation only; ...may be either defiled or non-defiled, and so are their acquisitions; ...are without retribution, and so are their acquisitions; ...are neither paths nor fruits of the paths (*mārga-phala*), and their acquisitions are both; ...are not subsumed under the truths (*satya*), and their acquisitions are subsumed under two truths, namely the truths of unsatisfactoriness and of origin (*duḥkha-* and *samudaya-satya*).

4. As for the quantity of the cessations not due to deliberation, it is even greater than that of the cessations through deliberation, the former being as numerous as the conditioned *dharmas*, whereas the quantity of the latter is only in accordance with that of the with-outflow *dharmas*.

Verdu: EBP.134ff., 144f.

[70] *LS*: Hall comments (VASC.55): "Calling this the 'total' prevention of future arising rules out those meditative attainments (*asaṃjñi-* and *nirodha-samāpatti*) that, while they are in effect, temporarily inhibit the arisal of future thoughts and concomitants. The use of 'arising' rules out cessation-through-impermanence, which is the total prevention of the 'stability' (*sthiti*)—not the arising—of *dharmas*."

[71] *LVP*: MVŚ, 164b13. – The *Kathāvatthu*, ii. 11, attributes to the Mahiṃsāsakas (Wassilief, p. 282) and to the Andhakas the distinction of *cessation due to deliberation* and *cessation not due to deliberation* (*paṭisaṃkhānirodha* and *appaṭisaṃkhānirodha*). Śaṃkara discusses these two cessations ad ii. 2, 22 (see Album Kern, 111); he mixes up *cessation not due to deliberation* and *cessation of impermanence* (*anityatānirodha*) (i. 20ab).

LS: Hall comments (VASC.56): "According to Yaśomitra (WOG.17–18), among the four 'preconditions' (the *hetu-*, *samanantara-*, *ālambana-*, and *adhipati-pratyayas*), this instance shows a deficiency of the *ālambana-pratyaya* (of the cognitive object as a precondition for the arisal of future thought moments)."

[72] *LS*: The four alternatives (*catuṣ-koṭi*) have the following set-up:

1. *p* is true, not *q* (*pūrva-pādaka*);
2. *q* is true, not *p* (*paścat-pādaka*);
3. both *p* and *q* are true (*evaṃ-pādaka*);
4. neither *p* nor *q* is true (*naivam-pādaka*).

[73] *LVP*: This classification rests on two principles: (1) There can be cessation due to deliberation (*pratisaṃkhyānirodha*), (disconnection, detachment) from impure factors, of whatever time period they may be, whether they are or are not destined to arise. (2) There is cessation not due to deliberation (*apratisaṃkhyānirodha*) of all factors, pure or impure, that are not destined to arise: the future factors exist: they will arise when the causes of arising cause them to pass from the future into the present; they will not arise when one obtains their cessation not due to deliberation. For example, the noble ones, at a certain moment, obtain the impossibility of being reborn in an animal womb: they obtain the cessation not due to deliberation of the animal womb, which is henceforth *not destined to arise* (*anutpattidharman*) for them.

The Fortunate One says of the stream-enterer (*srotaāpanna*): "For them the hells, the animal wombs, the existences of the hungry ghosts (*preta*) are exhausted (*niruddha*)" (compare *Saṃyutta*, v. 356, *khīṇanirayo khīṇatiracchānayoniko*...). – The cessation not due to deliberation is a factor in and of itself that renders the arising of such and such a factor absolutely impossible for whoever possesses (*prāpti*) [this cessation]. This absolute non-arising does not result from the [mere] deficiency of the causes, for when later the necessary causes presented themselves, the factor would have to arise, [but this is not so]: it is thus the possession of the cessation not due to deliberation that renders the sufficient coming together of the causes and the arising definitively impossible.

See ii. 55cd and v. 24.

[74] *LS*: AH 5–6; SAH 5–7.

[75] *LS*: This question: *katame te saṃkskṛtāḥ*? refers to conditioned factors in general, i.e., both pure (*anāsrava*) and impure (*sāsrava*).

Dharmaśrī writes and comments (AH 6):

> 6. All the formed that is pure, free from afflictions, and all the various aggregates of grasping, are the aggregates, expounded by the noble. They are the five aggregates: form, feeling, perception, formation, and consciousness.
>
> I.e., the formed factors—because they are produced by causes—that are free from the afflictions: the view of individuality, etc., and that are free from the impurities, all these and the previously mentioned aggregates of grasping are all called aggregates.* They are the five aggregates: form, feeling, perception, formation, and consciousness.

* The *anāsrava saṃskṛta*s and the *sāsrava saṃskṛtas* (*upādānaskandhas*), i.e., all *saṃskṛtas* are called *skandhas*, aggregates.]

76 *Gokhale*: [7ab] *te punaḥ saṃskṛtā dharmā rūpādiskandhapañcakam* |

Tib.: [7ab] *'dus byas chos rnams de dag kyang* | *gzugs la sogs pa'i phung po lnga* |

LVP: The term *skandha* is explained in i. 20.

saṃkṛta, *Visuddhi*, 293.

LS: Gedun Drup says (p. 13) that "also" or "on the other hand" means: "Not only do the unconditioned have divisions, the conditioned also have divisions."

77 *LS*: AH 6.

78 *LS*: Dhammajoti comments (SA.IV.38): "What is conditioned is what is dependently originated (*pratītya-samutpanna*) and characterized by the four characteristics of the conditioned (*saṃskṛta-lakṣaṇāni*: *jāti, sthiti, jarā/anyathātva, anityatā/vyaya*) [see AKB ii. 45cd]. These four—each a distinct force—are real entities belonging to the class of *viprayukta-saṃskāra* which together cause a so-called conditioned *dharma* to be impermanent, nay, momentary (*kṣaṇika*)."

SA.IV.473: "In its aspect of being a dependently co-arisen (*pratītya-samutpanna*) existent, a conditioned *dharma* is called a *saṃskṛta*—'compounded', 'co-produced', 'conditioned'. In its other aspect of being a causally productive force, it is also called a *saṃskāra*—'conditioning' or 'conditioning force'."

79 *LS*: The *Vyākhyā* glosses [WOG.20.22f.]: *taj-jātīyatvāt* sva-lakṣaṇa-sādṛśyatvāt.

According to the Vaibhāṣikas, the *svalakṣaṇa* (= *svabhāva*) of a conditioned factor remains at all times, while its special activity (*kāritra*), which is neither different from nor completely identical with the *svabhāva* of a factor (*dharma*), arises and ceases.

Collett Cox summarizes Saṃghabhadra (EIP.VIII.652): "Future factors that have not yet arisen, and even those that will not arise, can still be said to be conditioned because they are of the same category as those present or past factors that have already arisen."

80 *LS*: AH 218; SAH 451.

81 *Gokhale*: [7cd] *ta evā 'dhvā kathāvastu saniḥsārāḥ savastukāḥ*

Tib.: [7cd] *de dag nyid dus gtam gzhi dang* | *nges par 'byung bcas gzhi dang bcas* ||

82 *LS*: Hall comments (VASC.58): "As Yaśomitra makes clear, the word *adhvan*, which

means 'extent in space' (course, road) and 'extent in time' (duration, tense), here indicates the 'three times'."

83 *LVP*: According to the Sūtra: *trīṇīmāni bhikṣavaḥ kathāvastūny acaturthāny apañcamāni yāny āśrityāryāḥ kathāṃ kathayantaḥ kathayanti | katamāni trīṇi | atītaṃ kathāvastu anāgataṃ kathāvastu pratyutpannaṃ kathāvastu.*

Compare *Aṅguttara*, i. 197.

Saṃghabhadra, 633c13.

84 *LVP*: xxiii. 10, fol. 44a4: "The three paths, the three grounds for discourse (*kathāvastu*) (1) are included in the eighteen elements, the twelve sense-spheres, the five aggregates; (2) are known by nine cognitions, excluding the cognition of cessation (*nirodhajñāna*); (3) are cognized by six consciousnesses; (4) are affected by all proclivities (*anuśaya*)."

85 *LVP*: Why is the unconditioned not a ground of discourse? – Because it is not the cause of discourse (ii. 55); because there is no history of the unconditioned, in the same way that one can say: "Dīpaṃkara was such...; Maitreya will be...; King Kapphina (?) is such." (WOG.21.21f.).

LS: Gedun Drup states (p. 14): "Although uncompounded phenomena are the objects of expression of names, they are not presented as being a basis for conversation due to not being causes and seldom being objects of expression."

86 *LVP*: According to *Prakaraṇa*, 716b23, we can reconstruct: *saniḥsārā dharmāḥ katame? sarve saṃskṛtā dharmāḥ.*

One should "leave" not only the impure factors but also the (noble) path. The *Vyākhyā* [WOG.21.25f.] cites the text on the abandonment of the raft, *Majjhima*, i. 135; *Vajracchedikā* § 6: *kolopamaṃ dharmaparyāyam ājānadbhir dharmā api prahātavyāḥ prāg evādharmā iti.* (Compare *Bodhicaryāvatāra*, ix. 33; *Kaṭha*, ii. 14).

kolopama, viii, F 186.

LS: Geshe Jampa Gyatso comments: "According to the Vaibhāṣikas when one attains a *nirvāṇa* without remainder one leaves all compounded phenomena behind. The Dharma aggregate—true paths—is likened to a boat because, just as a boat is necessary to cross an ocean but when the far shore is reached it is left behind, so too is the Dharma aggregate necessary when one is in cyclic existence but is left behind when one attains a *nirvāṇa* without remainder."

87 *LVP*: According to *Prakaraṇa*, 716a3: *savastukāḥ sapratyayā dharmāḥ katame? – saṃskṛtā dharmāḥ.* – See ii. 55 at the end.

88 *LVP*: *vastu* signifies cause (*hetu*) according to the etymology [WOG.21.29]: vasanty asmin prāk kāryāṇi paścāt tata utpattir iti.

Here the *Vyākhyā* cites a fragment of the *Bhāṣya* ad ii. 55 (at the end), on the five meanings of the word *vastu* in the Scripture (MVŚ, 980b12). – For Vasubandhu, *savastuka* signifies *real*: the conditioned factors are real; the unconditioned factors are unreal.

LS: Hall comments (VASC.59): "Here Yaśomitra interprets this 'so say' (*kila*) as Vasubandhu's tacit endorsement of the Sautrāntika view. The latter takes 'grounded' [*sa-vastu-ka*] to mean that the conditioned *dharmas* are 'substantially existent' (*savastuka* = *sasvabhāva* = *dravyasat*), while the unconditioned *dharmas* exist merely as designations (*prajñapti-sat*)."

89 *LS*: AH 5; SAH 5–6.

90 *LS*: Ibid.

91 *Gokhale*: [8ab1] *ye sāsravā upādānaskandhās te*

Tib.: [8ab1] *gang dag zag bcas nyer len pa'i | phung po'ang de dag*

92 *LVP*: The MVŚ, 386c12f. gives fourteen explanations of the term *upādānaskandha*. Vasubandhu cites the first three explanations.

On aggregate (*khanda*) and appropriative aggregate (*upādānakkhandha*), *Visuddhimagga*, xiv, *apud* Warren, p. 155.

93 *LS*: AH 5; SAH 5.

94 *Gokhale*: [8b2] *saraṇā api* |

Tib.: [8b2] *'thab bcas kyang* |

LVP: On *raṇa, saraṇa, araṇā* (vii. 35c), see *Muséon*, 1914, p. 35; Walleser, *Die Streitlosigkeit des Subhūti* (Heidelberg, 1917); *Majjhima*, iii, 235.

LS: Dharmatrāta comments (SAH.14): "There are three kinds of conflict (*raṇa*): conflict defilement, conflict aggregate and conflict dispute. Conflict defilement is one hundred and eight defilements; conflict aggregate is dying (*maraṇa*); conflict dispute is the one opposing the other. It should be known that [here] this conflict defilement is spoken of."

95 *LS*: AH 5, 236; SAH 5, 471.

96 *Gokhale*: [8cd] *duḥkhaṃ samudayo loko dṛṣṭisthānaṃ bhavaś ca te* ||

Tib.: [8cd] *sdug bsngal kun 'byung 'jig rten dang | lta gnas srid pa'ng de dag yin* ||

97 *LS*: See AV.66 and Schmithausen's *Zur Buddhistischen Lehre von der dreifachen Leidhaftigkeit* (1977).

98 *LVP*: *asminn eva rohita vyāyāmamātre kalevare lokaṃ prajñapayāmi lokasamudayaṃ ca* (*Aṅguttara*, ii. 48: *rohitassadevaputta*). – The Fortunate One further said: *luhyate praluhyate tasmāl lokaḥ* (*Saṃyutta*, iv. 52). – *Aṣṭasāhasrikā*, p. 256; *Mahāvyutpatti*, 154, 16 (Wogihara, *Bodhisattvabhūmi*, Leipzig 1908, p. 37). – The root is *luji*, not *loki*.

99 *LS*: Since other defilements also increase by having impure factors as their locus, Jampaiyang asks (p. 176) why impure factors are called "locus of afflicted views". He replies by quoting master Pūrṇavardhana:

> At all times and for all,
> view is without fragmentation and immutable.
> Accordingly, attachment, etc., and
> ignorance and doubt are not (that).

100 *LVP*: *bhavatīti bhavaḥ*. – *Vyākhyā* [WOG.23.13]: According to the text: *bhavaḥ katamaḥ* | *pañcopādānaskandhāḥ*.

Hsüan-tsang translates: "They are the threefold existence."

The source of Vasubandhu appears to be the *Prakaraṇa*, 715a9: "Which factors are existence (*bhava*)? The impure factors. Which factors are not existence? The pure factors."

bhava; viii, 141.

[101] *LS*: AH 7–9, 14; SAH 7–15, 17–26, 51–52, 411, 458–59.

As for the threefold classification, see our endnote (i. 4) regarding the overall structure of the first two chapters of the AKB.

The abhidharmic classifications or taxonomies of factors (*dharma*) into the five aggregates (*skandha*), twelve sense-spheres (*āyatana*) and eighteen elements (*dhātu*) were at first taken over from the *sūtras* by the Ābhidharmikas for the examination of factors (*dharma*) in terms of their intrinsic nature (*svabhāva*) by the methodological device of inclusion (*saṃgraha*; SA.IV.22f., 26–35; cf. AKB i. 18).

1. The five aggregates (*skandha*) constitute the totality of phenomenal existence—with emphasis on an ontological perspective—and this taxonomy is often employed in the *sūtras* to explain the Buddhist doctrine of no-Self (*nairātmya*). The AKB explains *skandha* as "heap or group of mass" (*rāśi*). The five aggregates do not include the three unconditioned factors, and thus include seventy-two *dharmas* in the Vaibhāṣika system.

2. The twelve sense-spheres comprise the six sense-faculties (*indriya*) and the six corresponding objects. The AKB explains *āyatana* as "gate of arising" (*āyadvāra*) of thought (*citta*) and thought-concomitants (*caitta*) and as such reflects the emphasis on an epistemological perspective. The twelve sense-spheres include the three unconditioned factors in the twelfth sense-sphere, i.e., the sense-sphere of factors (*dharmāyatana*), and thus include seventy-five *dharmas* in the Vaibhāṣika system.

3. The eighteen elements comprise the six sense-faculties, the six corresponding objects and the six corresponding consciousnesses, and as such reflect again an emphasis on an epistemological perspective. Dhammajoti points out again (SA.IV.30) that originally in the *sūtras*, "the 18-*dhātu* taxonomy was a pragmatic classificatory scheme mainly employed to underscore the Buddha's no-Self doctrine". The AKB explains *dhātu* as *gotra* (family, race, lineage, mine, source, genus). The eighteen elements include the three unconditioned factors in the twelfth element, i.e., the element of factors (*dharmadhātu*), and thus include seventy-five *dharmas* in the Vaibhāṣika system.

4. Dhammajoti finds some incongruities concerning the Sarvāstivāda explanations on *dharmāyatana* and *dharmadhātu*, which will be addressed later (i. 15bd; cf. SA.IV.32f.).

5. In further endnotes, we will also address the controversy regarding the ontological status or reality of *skandha*, *āyatana* and *dhātu* (cf. SA.IV.34f.).

[102] *LS*: *Skandha* will be explained (i. 20ab) by Vasubandhu as "heap" (*rāśi*), i.e., each of the five *skandhas* forms a heap of its own category which may be past, present or future, on the other hand, Saṃghabhadra maintains that *skandha* does not signify *heap*, but "that which is susceptible of being collected together in a heap". *Skandha* is also discussed (i. F 38) as that which carries a load or as a part. The five aggregates constitute the totality of phenomenal existence but do not include the three unconditioned factors (see i. 22ab), which, being beyond space and time, do not form such heaps. The import of this taxonomy will be brought out when Vasubandhu discusses dependent origination (*pratītyasamutpāda*), where he shows (iii. 18)

that phenomena are all dependently arisen—i.e., without any ontological status, as, for example, a permanent and independent self (*ātman*)—and all reducible to these five *skandhas* which alone are the ultimate reals forming the basis of our conceptual superimposition. The Vaibhāṣikas consider the *skandhas* to be real entities (*dravya*). See SA.IV.25f.

103 *LS*: AH 7; SAH 7–8, 15.

As for material form, Vasubandhu provides further detail at various places in the AKB, but in particular:

1. throughout his presentation of the twenty-two doctrinal perspectives on the eighteen sense-spheres (i. 29ff.): (*2*) resistant (*sapratigha*) – non-resistant (*apratigha*); (*9*) primary matter (*bhūta*) – secondary matter (*bhautika*); (*10*) aggregated (*saṃcita*) and non-aggregated (*asaṃcita*); (*16*) internal (*ādhyātimika*) – external (*bāhya*); (*19*) view (*dṛṣti*) – not view (*na dṛṣti*) [especially: Do atoms touch one another or not? Arrangement of the atoms of the sense-faculties?];
2. when discussing the simultaneous arising of material factors (ii. 22): real-entity atoms (*dravyaparamāṇu*) and the composite molecule (*saṃghātaparamānu*);
3. when presenting the units for calculating space (physical matter) from the smallest unit, i.e., the atom (*paramāṇu*), up to one league (*yojana*) (iii. 85b–88a);
4. when discussing the third member of the twelvefold dependent origination (*pratītya*-samutpāda; see iii. 18–38c), which is called name-and-form (nāmarūpa). For its definition and meaning within the four types of dependent origination, i.e., momentary (*kṣanika*), prolonged (*prākarṣikā*), connected (*sāṃbandhika*), pertaining to states (*āvasthika*), see chapter 3, as for the fourth type, i.e., within a three-life-times model, it is defined as: "Name-and-form (*nāmarūpa*) [is the five aggregates, in the womb,] (i) from this moment [i.e., existence-as-birth], (iii) until the (complete) arising of the six sense-spheres."

For a good discussion of (a) the general nature and definition of *rūpa*, (b) primary and derived matter and (c) atomic theory, see SA.IV.187–209.

104 *LS*: AH 7; SAH 7–8, 15.

105 *Gokhale*: [9ab] *rūpaṃ pañcendriyāṇy arthāḥ pañcā 'vijñaptir eva ca* |

Tib.: [9ab] *gzugs ni dbang po lnga dang don* | *lnga dang rnam rig byed min nyid* |

LVP: Compare the *Prakaraṇapāda*, chapter I (*Pañcavastuka*).

LS: Before discussing (i. F 24–27) more formal definitions of material form (*rūpa*) in terms of its self-characteristic (*svalakṣaṇa*) or intrinsic nature (*svabhāva*), Vasubandhu, in accordance with early *sūtra* and *abhidharma* custom, presents merely a delimitation-definition, i.e., a listing of eleven items, which are not only eleven derivative material elements (*upādāya-rūpa*) but include the four fundamental material elements (*mahābhūta*) among the tangible. Later (i, F 35), in the context of discussing the meaning of the term *skandha* as heap (*rāśi*), he adds the following *sūtra* based delimitation-definition:

> Whatever material form (*rūpa*) there is, (1) past [*atīta*] or future [*anāgata*] or present *pratyutpanna*], (2) internal [*ādhyātmika*] or external [*bāhya*], (3) gross [*audārika*] or subtle [*sūkṣma*], (4) inferior [*hīna*] or superior [*praṇīta*], (5) distant [*dūra*] or near

[*antika*], if all this material form—that which is past, etc.—is grouped together into one heap [*aikadhyam abhisaṃkṣipya*], this is called *aggregate of material form.*

By contrast, Vasubandhu's *Pañcaskandhaka* and Skandhila's *Avatāra* give only a delimitation-definition based on the division between *mahābhūta* and *upādāyarūpa*. See below the Sanskrit text based on the original Sanskrit text of Vasubandhu's *Pañcaskandhaka* (critically edited by Li Xuezhu and Ernst Steinkellner, 2008; words not attested by *Pañcaskandhakavibhāṣā* [Sthiramati] [= photostat copy of the Potala Ms, which has seven missing lines at the beginning] are in non-italics):

1. *rūpaṃ katamat* | yat kiñcid rūpam, sarvaṃ tac *catvāri mahābhūtāni catvāri ca mahābhūtāny upādāya* ||

1.1 catvāri mahābhūtāni katamāni | pṛthivīdhātur abdhātus tejodhātur vāyudhātuś ca || tatra pṛthivīdhātuḥ katamaḥ | khakkhaṭatvam | abdhātuḥ katamaḥ | snehaḥ | tejodhātuḥ katamaḥ | uṣmā | vāyudhātuḥ katamaḥ | laghusamudīraṇatvam |

1.2 *upādāyarūpaṃ katamat* | *cakṣurindriyaṃ* śrotrendriyaṃ ghrāṇendriyaṃ jihva–indriyaṃ kāyendriyaṃ rūpaṃ śabdo gandho rasaḥ spraṣṭavyaikadeśo 'vijñaptiś ca || tatra *cakṣurindriyaṃ katamat* | *varṇaviṣayo rūpaprasādaḥ* | *śrotrendriyaṃ katamat* | *śabdaviṣayo rūpaprasādaḥ* | ghrāṇendriyaṃ katamat | gandhaviṣayo rūpaprasādaḥ | jihvendriyaṃ katamat | rasaviṣayo rūpaprasādaḥ | kāyendriyaṃ katamat | spraṣṭavya-viṣayo rūpaprasādaḥ | rūpaṃ katamat | cakṣurviṣayaḥ – *varṇaḥ saṃsthānaṃ* vijñaptiś ca | *śabdaḥ katamaḥ* | *śrotraviṣayaḥ – upātto 'nupātta ubhayaś ca catvāri mahābhūtāny upādāya* | *gandhaḥ katamaḥ* | *ghrāṇaviṣayaḥ* – sugandho durgandhas tadanyac ca | *rasaḥ katamaḥ* | *jihvāviṣayaḥ* – madhuro 'mlo lavaṇaḥ kaṭukas *tiktaḥ kaṣāyaś ceti* | *spraṣṭavyaikadeśaḥ katamaḥ* | *kāyendriyasya viṣayo mahābhūtāni sthāpayitvā ślakṣṇatvaṃ karkaśatvaṃ gurutvaṃ laghutvaṃ śītaṃ jighatsā pipāsā ca* | *avijñaptiḥ katamā* | *vijñaptisamādhijaṃ rūpam anidarśanam apratigham* ||

Engle translates (ISBP.229f.):

1. What is form? It is all form whatsoever that is included in the four great elements and that is derived from the four great elements.

1.1 What are the four great elements? The earth constituent, the water constituent, the fire constituent, and the air constituent. [...]

1.2 What is derivative form? The eye-faculty, [visible] form, sound, smell, taste, a portion of tangible objects, and noninformative [form].

The *Avatāra* has (ESD.73):

Matter is of two kinds: The Great Elements (*mahābhūta*) and the derived matter (*upādāyarūpa/bhautika*).

106 *LS*: As for the five sense-faculties, in particular the eye sense-faculty, see Vasubandhu's detailed discussion (i. 41–47) of the 19th doctrinal perspective on the eighteen sense-spheres: view (*dṛṣṭi*) – not view (*na dṛṣṭi*). Here is a brief outline of most of the points discussed:

1. Different views on whether the eye sense-faculty or the visual consciousness sees.
2. Are visible forms seen by one eye or by two eyes?
3. Perception of the object with or without reaching it with the sense-faculty.

4. When the sense-faculty reaches the object-field, do atoms touch one another or not?
5. Size of the sense-faculties and their object-fields.
6. Atoms of the sense-faculties.
   6.1. Arrangement of the atoms of the sense-faculties.
   6.2. Homogeneous and partially homogeneous atoms of the sense-faculties
   6.3. Aggregations as sense-faculties and cognitive objects of the sensory consciousnesses & the invisibility of real-entity atoms.
7. Simultaneity and non-simultaneity of the object-field or sense-faculty with its consciousness.
8. Why is the sense-faculty the basis (*āśraya*) of consciousness and not the object-field?
9. Why are the sense-faculties the basis for naming the consciousnesses?

As for Vasubandhu's presentation of the underlying atomic structure of the sense-faculties, see ii. 22. But in regard to the atomic theory "in general", it is good to keep in mind Dhammajoti's following comment (SA.IV.198f.):

> Unlike the doctrine of the Great Elements, the Buddhist atomic theory is not discernable in the *sūtra*-s. It was likely to have been taken over from outside the Buddhist schools—probably from the Vaiśeṣika. However, no Buddhists—including the Sarvāstivāda Ābhidharmika-s—would conceive of atoms as being eternally immutable or permanent. ... Atoms are in fact momentary. ... At least by the time of MVŚ, the Buddhist Ābhidharmika-s had already articulated the theory to a large extent in their own way.

As for the different epistemological models (Vaibhāṣika, Śrīlāta, Vasubandhu) regarding sensory perception, see Vasubandhu's detailed discussion—in the context of his presentation of dependent origination (*pratītyasamutpāda*)—in iii. F 101–7, in connection with which we have written longer endnotes on the three types of direct perception (*pratyakṣa*) of the Vaibhāṣika and the representational perception of the Sautrāntika.

107 *LS*: As for the five object-referents (*artha*) or object-fields (*viśaya*), see Vasubandhu's discussion (1) of the 2nd doctrinal perspective on the eighteen sense-spheres: resistant (*sapratigha*) – non-resistant (*apratigha*), which includes a discussion of the three types of obstruction (*pratighāta*) and defines object-field (*viṣaya*) as that place where the eye, ear, etc., exercises its operation [*kāritra*], i.e., seeing, hearing, etc., and cognitive object (*ālambana*) as that which is grasped by thought and thought-concomitants (*cittacaitta*), (2) of the 7th doctrinal perspective: having a cognitive object (*sālambana*) and not having a cognitive object (*anālambana*), and (3) the 20th doctrinal perspective: cognized (*vijñeya*) by consciousness. See also the above given outline of the 19th doctrinal perspective.

As for Vasubandhu's presentation of the underlying atomic structure of the object-fields, see ii. 22.

108 *LS*: In general, the non-informative (*avijñapti*) can refer to non-informative form (*avijñapti-rūpa*) and non-informative action (*avijñapti-karma*). Cf. i. 11, 13 (F 25–27), 15bd; iv. 4–44.

The SA.IV.Glossary.520 describes them as follows:

> *avijñapti-rūpa*: Non-informative matter. This is a special type of matter (*rūpa*)

which constitutes a non-informative action (*avijñapti-karma*). It is non-resistant and invisible, and comes into existence in dependence on the force of a volition (*cetanā*), an informative action and a set of great elements (*mahābhūta*). It is a special type of derived matter (*upādāya-rūpa*) which is not comprised of atoms (*paramāṇu*).

avijñapti-karma: Non-informative action. Unlike an informative action (*vijñapti karma*) which informs us of the mental state of the doer, this is a karmic force which, once projected by a bodily or vocal action (*karma*), continues to exist as a series invisibly; hence, non-informative.

109 *LS*: SAH 15.

110 *Gokhale*: [9cd] *tadvijñānāśrayā rūpaprasādāś cakṣurādayaḥ* ||

Tib.: [9cd] *de dag rnams kyi rnam shes rten | mig la sogs gzugs dang ba rnams* ||

LVP: The five sense-faculties (*indriya*) are suprasensible (*atīndriya*), transparent (*accha*), distinct from the object of the sense-faculties, distinct from visible form, tangible, etc. It is through logical reasoning that we cognize their existence. They have for their support (*adhiṣṭhāna*) what common language calls the eye, etc. (i. 44ab).

On *pasādacakkhu, cakkhupasāda, Dhammasaṅgaṇi*, 616, 628.

The sense-faculties are *bhūtavikāraviśeṣa*.

LS: 1. As for transparency, AKB i. 36ac states: "The sense-faculties do not cut off because of their translucidity or transparency (*acchatva*), just like the light or glitter of a [luminescent] gem (*maṇiprabhā*)."

2. As for obstructiveness and resistance, the MVŚ (63a) explains (SA.IV.192):

> Because [the atoms of the sense-faculties] are transparent/clear in nature, they do not mutually obstruct one another. That is to say, for such a type of derived clear matter, even when a large number of them are accumulated together, there is no mutual obstruction. It is like the water in an autumn pond; on account of its clarity, even a needle that is dropped into it can be visible.

Even though the atoms of the sense-faculties do not obstruct one another, i. 29bc (F 51f.) states that they are resistant (*sapratigha*) when encountering their object-field.

3. As for *rūpaprasāda*, LVP renders it as "éléments matériels subtils". Dhammajoti—glossing (SA.IV.Glossary) *prasāda* as "clarity, translucence, sensitivity (said of the sense faculties)"—renders "clear matter" or "very subtle and perspicuous (*prasāda*) kinds of matter" or "translucent, sensitive matter".

Edgerton gives (p. 388): "(1) *faith* ... (2) *tranquillity* of the four physical elements (*dhātu*) in sense-organs, as resulting in the sensitivity of the organs and so in sense-perception: Śikṣ 250.14ff; cf. 251f, which by contrast with *kṣobha* (agitation) proves what *prasāda* means. ..."

Verdu, in his discussion of *rūpaskandha* (EPB.21–38), elaborates on this notion of tranquility or equilibrium (p. 24):

> The idea seems to suggest that, in the production of this subtle "translucent" matter (*rūpaprasāda*), the four activities that characterize the four *mahābhūta*s neutralize one another into a perfect state of equilibrium. ... Its *prasāda*-translucidity (*accha-*

tva) would allow the permeation of these five *prasāda-indriyāṇi* (sense-organs) by the subject-awareness seated in the *vijñāna-dharma* (fifth of the *skandhas*). Their being "not resistant" (*apratigha*) to the *dharma* of the subjective awareness (*vijñāna*) would make them suprasensitive (*atīndriya*) to the "grosser" resistance (*pratighāta*) offered to them by the other five derivative matters, i.e., the gross-matters or objects of sensation. These coarser matters derive from the four *mahābhūtas* according to the unbalanced combinations which would allow certain characteristics of the former to predominate upon the others. The absence of "tranquillity" or "equilibrium" (*aprasāda*) among the four elements—always entering into the composition of these coarse and external (*bāhya*) matters—would bring about the different physical determinations that these latter exhibit, either as "colors and shapes" or as "sounds", or as "smells", or as "tastes", or as "tactile" objects of sensation.

111 *LVP*: See the Sūtra cited i. 35. – Compare *Vibhaṅga*, 122; *Psychology*, 173.

112 *LVP*: The first interpretation according to the MVŚ, 369b21.

113 *LS*: SAH 15.

114 *Gokhale*: [10a] *rūpaṃ dvidhā viṃśatidhā*

Tib.: [10a] *gzugs rnam gnyis dang rnam nyi shu* |

LVP: MVŚ, 64a5; *Mahāvyutpatti*, 101; compare *Dhammasaṅgaṇi*, 617.

115 *LS*: SAH 15.

116 *LVP*: The Sautrāntikas deny that shape is anything other than color (iv, F 8–12).

LS: As for the ontological status of color and shape, Dhammajoti states (SA.IV.200) that although individual atoms of colors (such as blue, etc.) and shapes (such as long, etc.) are not directly perceivable by the eye and visual consciousness, in their collective and accumulative capacity they function as visible objects, for the Vaibhāṣikas, since "if there were no individual atoms of color and shape, an agglomeration of atoms would not, for instance, become green or long" (MVŚ, 64ab). For the Vaibhāṣikas, therefore, the individual atoms as well as the agglomeration of atoms of the same type as perceivable visible forms—in contrast to a unification of atoms of diverse species—are both real entities.

For the Sautrāntika, on the other hand, only color (*varṇa*) is a real entity (*dravya*), whereas shape (*saṃsthāna*) is merely a mental fabrication or provisional entity (*prajñapti*), i.e., the so-called shape atoms are simply the color atoms arranged in various ways. See Vasubandhu's proof in iv, F 8–12.

117 *LS*: LVP has: "blue, red, yellow, white", but Pradhan.6.12 and WOG.25.8f., as well as the Tibetan, have: "blue, yellow, red, white".

118 *LS*: *Avatāra* defines (ESD.74): "A square shape is that whose boundary is square."

119 *LS*: *Avatāra* defines (ibid.): "A round shape is one [whose boundary] is circular."

120 *LS*: Yaśomitra glosses [WOG.25.16f.]: *unnataṃ* sthūl'ādi-rūpaṃ.

121 *LS*: Yaśomitra glosses [WOG.25.17.]: *avanataṃ* nimna-rūpaṃ.

122 *LS*: *Avatāra* speaks (ESD.74) of twenty-one visible forms that are the object-fields (*viṣaya*) of the visual consciousness as well as the mental consciousness induced thereby.

[123] *LVP*: *Vijñānakāya*, xxiii. 9, 45b18; MVŚ, 390b24.

[124] *LVP*: *Dhammasaṅgaṇi*, 636.

[125] *LS*: LVP mentions the Sautrāntikas here, but they are not explicitly mentioned in Pradhan.

[126] *LS*: SAH 15.

[127] *LS*: ibid.

[128] *Gokhale*: [10b1] *śabdas tv aṣṭavidho*

Tib.: [10b] *sgra ni rnam pa brgyad yod de* |

LVP: *Dhammasaṅgaṇi*, 621.

[129] *LS*: LVP translates *upātta* here as *actuel*, as does Jha.

Avatāra comments (ESD.74): "What is integrated into the human organism (*ātmabhāva*) is said to be appropriated [by consciousness], which is to say conscious; otherwise they are said to be unappropriated."

[130] *LVP*: *sattvākhya* = *sattvam ācaṣṭe*. Any factor that denotes a sentient being is called *sattvākhya* ("indicative of sentient beings"). When we hear the sound that constitutes the vocal informative action (*vāgvijñapti*; iv. 3d), we know: "This is a sentient being."

LS: Articulate sound.

[131] *LVP*: Any sound different from speech is *asattvākhya* ("non-indicative of sentient beings").

LS: Inarticulate sound.

[132] *LS*: SAH 15.

Even though Vasubandhu presented the usual order: *rūpa*, *śabda*, *gandha*, *rasa* and *spraṣṭavya* in i. 9ab, here he explains *rasa* before *gandha*.

[133] *LS*: SAH 15

[134] *Gokhale*: [10b2c1] *rasaḥ* | *ṣoḍhā*

Tib.: [10c1] *ro ni rnam drug*

LVP: According to *Dharmaskandha*, 9, 9, of fourteen types. Compare *Dhammasaṅgaṇi*, 629.

LS: *Avatāra* comments (ESD.75): "All these six kinds are the objects of the gustatory consciousness and the mental consciousness induced thereby."

[135] *LS*: SAH 15.

[136] *LS*: Ibid.

[137] *Gokhale*: [10c2] *caturvidho gandhaḥ*

Tib.: [10c2] *dri rnam bzhi* |

LVP: *Dhammasaṅgaṇi*, 625.

Dharmatrāta comments (SAH.26): "The sense-field smell (*gandhāyatana*) is threefold: agreeable smells, disagreeable smells and neither-agreeable-nor-disagreeable smells."

[138] *LS*: *Avatāra* comments (ESD.75): "That which nourishes the Great Elements of the sense-faculties is said to be a good smell. That which does damage to them is said to be a bad smell.

That which does neither the one nor the other, is said to be neutral. All these three kinds of smell are the objects of the olfactory consciousness and of the mental consciousness induced thereby."

139 *LS*: SAH 15.

140 *LS*: Ibid.

141 *Gokhale*: [10d] *spṛśyam ekādaśātmakam* ||

Tib.: [10d] *reg bya bcu gcig bdag nyid do* |

LVP: MVŚ, 661c14ff. *Dhammasaṅgaṇi*, 648. – See i. 35.

For *middha* and *mūrchana* as being part of the tangible, see *Siddhi*, 410.

LS: The eleven tangibles consist of four fundamental material elements and seven derivative material elements (*bhautika*; *upādāyarūpa*). See ii. 65, where Vasubandhu discusses:

1. two ways in which fundamental material elements are a cause of fundamental material elements;
2. five ways in which the fundamental material elements are the enabling cause of derivative material elements;
3. three ways in which derivative material elements are a cause of derivative material elements;
4. one way in which derivative material elements are a cause of fundamental material elements.

See also below i. 12–13, where Vasubandhu discusses the fundamental material elements (*mahābhūta*) and elementary substances (*dhātu*), their efficacies, their intrinsic nature and the difference to common usages of earth, water, etc.

See further ii. 22, which discusses the four fundamental material elements within Buddhist atomic theory and how we can know that the molecule includes the four fundamental elements.

142 *LS*: Even though the orthodox Vaibhāṣikas hold that the eleven tangibles are real entities, LVP shows in his *Introduction* (p. xlvii; cf. also SA.IV.193) that among the four great masters of the Sarvāstivāda lineage Buddhadeva maintains that material form (*rūpa*) consists merely of fundamental material elements, i.e., that the derivative material elements (*bhautika*) are merely a state (*avasthā*) or specific types (*viśeṣa*) of the fundamental material elements (*mahābhūta*). Dharmatrāta, on the other hand, accepts the derivative material elements as distinct real entities, but holds that there are no derivative tangibles, i.e., that the tangibles consist only of the fundamental material elements. And Sthavira Śrīlāta also denies the existence of the derivative tangibles, which are for him nothing more than the specific configuration of the fundamental material elements.

143 *LS*: Earth, water, fire and wind are subsumed here under the tangibles (*spraṣṭavya*) because their functions (i.e., supporting, cohesion, heating or maturation, and expansion) can only be experienced through the body sense-faculty.

144 *LS*: Saṃghabhadra states (Ny, 333c) that each of the following seven derivative types of tangibles results from a predominance or difference in intensity of one of the four fundamental material elements. MVŚ, 665a, specifies (SA.IV.195):

5. water and fire for smoothness;
6. earth and wind for roughness;
7. earth and water for heaviness;
8. fire and wind for lightness;
9. water and wind for coldness;
10. wind for hunger;
11. fire for thirst.

Saṃghabhadra (Ny, 355b) criticizes Vasubandhu's explanation that the seven derivative tangibles are due to the predominance of effect, whereas the orthodox Vaibhāṣika view is that they are due to the predominance of substance.

On the other hand, since MVŚ, 682–683a, also explicitly maintains (SA.IV.196) that in a given mass of *rūpa* there can be a "quantitative" difference in the *mahābhūtas* without contradicting the principle of inseparability, it would follow that even though the four *mahābhūtas* always co-exist and are functionally interdependent, that they are not necessarily juxtaposed.

145 *Oxford English Dictionary* (Compact Edition): Hypallage = a figure of speech in which there is an interchange of two elements of a proposition, the natural relations of these being reversed.

146 *LVP*: *Dhammapada*, 194; *Udānavarga*, xxx. 23. – The appearance of the Buddhas is a cause of happiness, not happiness itself.

147 *LS*: SAH 15.

148 *LVP*: See i. 30b.

149 *LVP*: According to MVŚ, 64a11.

150 *LVP*: vii, F 17: Does one know the piece of cloth and the stain at the same time? – *dravyasvalakṣaṇa*, *āyatanasvalakṣaṇa*. Vasumitra, Sarvāstivādins, thesis 28.

LS: See our note on intrinsic characteristic and common characteristic, and their relativity, at i. F 4.

151 *LVP*: The mental consciousness (*manovijñāna*) seizes the totality of the objects of the sensory consciousnesses, i.e., visual consciousness (*cakṣurvijñāna*), etc.; this is why it is considered to have the common characteristic (*sāmānyalakṣaṇa*) for its sphere; in other words, it is not specialized with respect to its object.

When, likewise, one says that the visual consciousness seizes the totality of the four objects of the four visual consciousnesses bearing on blue, yellow, red and white, we should say that it has the common characteristic for its sphere, since the characteristics of visible form, the sense-sphere of visible form (*rūpāyatana*), are its object. The same for the auditory consciousness, the olfactory consciousness, etc. – But this is in opposition to the Scripture.

Answer: – When the Scripture teaches that each of the five sensory consciousnesses has a particular inherent characteristic (*svalakṣaṇa*) for its sphere, it refers to the particular or unique or self (*sva*) characteristic (*lakṣaṇa*) of the sense-spheres (*āyatana*), namely, the quality of being the sense-sphere of visible form (*rūpāyatana*), i.e., the quality of being cognizable by the visual consciousness, the quality of being the sense-sphere of sound (*śabdāyatana*), i.e., the quality of being cognizable by the auditory consciousness, etc. Scripture does not refer to the particular inherent characteristic of real entities, namely, the quality of having a blue aspect or the quality of being cognizable by a visual consciousness having a blue aspect, etc. It is not from the point of view of these particular inherent characteristics of the real entities that the five consciousnesses are said "to have the particular inherent characteristic for their sphere", in other words, are said "to be specialized in regard to their object".

152 *LS*: According to Vaibhāṣika doctrine, a gustatory and tactile consciousness cannot arise at the same time.

153 *LS*: SAH 8, 15.

154 *Gokhale*: [11] *vikṣiptā'cittakasyā 'pi yo 'nubandhaḥ śubhā'śubhaḥ | mahābhūtāny upādāya sa hy avijñaptir ucyate ||*

Tib.: [11] *g.yeng dang sems med pa yi yang | dge dang mi dge rjes 'brel gang | 'byung ba che rnams sgyur byas pa | de ni rnam rig byed min brjod ||*

LVP: *Avijñāpti* will be described in detail at iv. 3d, etc. – It may be translated as non-informative. This is an action that makes nothing known to another, in this way it resembles the mental action; but [this action] is matter (*rūpa*) and in this way it resembles the bodily and vocal informative action. – We shall see that the Sautrāntikas and Vasubandhu do not admit the existence of a certain factor called the *non-informative* (*avijñapti*).

Saṃghabhadra thinks that the definition of the non-informative, as Vasubandhu formulates it, is not in conformity with the doctrine of the Vaibhāṣika. His objections (*Nyāyānusāra*) are reproduced and refuted by Yaśomitra (WOG.30.31ff.). In the *Samayapradīpikā*, he substitutes a new verse (*kārikā*) for the verse of Vasubandhu which Yaśomitra cites [Ny, 335; WOG.32.21]:

> *kṛte 'pi visabhāge 'pi citte cittātyaye ca yat |*
> *vyākṛtāpratighaṃ rūpaṃ sā hy avijñaptir iṣyate ||*

LS: Vasubandhu's *Pañcaskandhaka* (2008) states:

> *avijñaptiḥ katamā | vijñaptisamādhijaṃ rūpam anidarśanam apratigham ||*
>
> What is noninformative [form]? It is form that is derived either from informative form or one-pointed concentration; and it is both not capable of being indicated and does not possess resistance. ISBP.230

As already mentioned and briefly glossed (i. 9ab), the non-informative (*avijñapti*) can refer to non-informative form (*avijñapti-rūpa*) and non-informative action (*avijñapti-karma*).

Here Vasubandhu gives his definition of the non-informative and, in his endnote, LVP provides a brief introduction to the informative, explaining why this factor is called *non-informative*, referring to Saṃghabhadra's "new verse", to which we will return below after first providing more context and information about the features and history of the non-informative.

1. Here is a map for Vasubandhu's other main discussions regarding the non-informative:

As for the threefold classification of factors, below (i. 13), within the context of giving definitions of material form (*rūpa*), he will discuss how the non-informative can be included within the aggregate of material form (*rūpaskandha*) even though it is qualified as being "non-resistant" (*apratigha*). Later (i. 15bd), he will include the informative with the sense-sphere of factors (*dharmāyatana*) and element of factors (*dharmadhātu*) rather than in the *rūpa-āyatana*.

At iv. 3d–44 (F 14–105), Vasubandhu will discuss the non-informative in its aspect as non-informative action in great detail:

First (F 14–25)—within the wider context of informative action (*vijñapti*) and non-informative action (*avijñapti*)—he will discuss the ontological status of the non-informative action, giving eight reasons by the Vaibhāṣikas for its existence and their refutation by the Sautrāntikas, and then he will present (F 43–53) the three types of non-informative action:

i. restraint (*saṃvara*),
ii. non-restraint (*asaṃvara*),
iii. neither-restraint-nor-non-restraint (*naivasaṃvaranāsaṃvara*),

whereby restraint is further divided into three types:

a. *prātimokṣa* restraint (*pratimokṣasaṃvara*),
b. restraint co-existent with meditation (*dhyānasaṃvara*),
c. pure restraint (*anāsravasaṃvara*).

This is followed by a discussion (F 53–59) of the possession of informative and non-informative action in regard to the time period to which these belong and by a discussion (F 59–103) on how the three types of non-informative action can be acquired and how they may be lost.

2. As for its specific features, even though it is classified as secondary matter (*bhautika*; i. 35ac), it is a special case of *rūpa*, since it is invisible (*anidarśana*; i. 29ab), non-resistant (*apratigha*; i. 29bc), does not occupy space or have the nature of *rūpaṇa* (i. 13; MVŚ, 395a) and is not atomic in nature (*asaṃcita*; i. 35d; *Samayapradīpikā*, 782a). It is said to be of the nature of *rūpa* (i. 13), since the fundamental material elements that constitute its basis (*aśraya*) are resistant material form. But, as already mentioned above, it is also included (i. 15bd) as a special case under *dharmāyatana* and *dharmadhātu*, rather than *rūpāyatana*, which is justified (iv. F 16: fifth reason) with the *Elephant-simile sūtra* reference to a specific *rūpa* included in the *dharmāyatana*. It can be cognized only by mental consciousness (*manovijñāna*) (ESD.78).

As for its moral quality (i. 30a), it is necessarily either wholesome (*kuśala*) or unwholesome (*akuśala*), as pointed out by Vasubandhu in verse 11.

As for its ontological status, as already stated, the orthodox Sarvāstivādins, basing themselves on scripture and reasoning, affirm its existence as a real entity (*dravya*), whereas the Sautrāntikas as well as the early Dārṣṭāntika masters (MVŚ, 383b), for example, Dharmatrāta and Buddhadeva, deny it.

In this context, Saṃghabhadra criticizes Vasubandhu's usage of "serial continuity" (*anubandha*), since it implies that *avijñapti* is not a real entity and would have certain other unwanted consequences. As LVP points out, Saṃghabhadra replaces it therefore with the following new verse (giving a word-by-word commentary in his *Samayapradīpikā*, 781c–782a; see SA.IV.379):

> That [morally] defined, non-resistant matter, which exists in the thought [*citta*] at the time of the action as well [as subsequently], which is of a dissimilar as well [as similar moral] species, and also in the thoughtless state—this is conceded as the non-informative [matter].

On the other hand, in his **Nyāyānusāra*, 335b, Saṃghabhadra also provides another definition (SA.IV.379):

> In brief, the non-informative [matter] is that non-resistant [*apratigha*] skillful [*kuśala*] or unskillful [*akuśala*] matter which arises in dependence on a specific corporeal or vocal informative [*vijñapti*] *karma*, and on a specific skillful or unskillful thought [*citta*], etc.

3. As for its "history", the term *avijñapti* is not directly mentioned in the *sūtras*, but is implied according to the orthodox Sarvāstivādins. Dhammajoti (SA.IV.381) points to the fact "that the *Dharmaskandha-śāstra*, one of the earliest Sarvāstivāda canonical *abhidharma* texts, also makes no mention of the *avijñapti* in all its discussion on matter", but (ESD.23) that since the time of the *Jñānaprasthāna*—including a whole section on *avijñapti* (with clear notions of *saṃvara*, etc., and *prātimokṣa-saṃvara*, etc.)—it has been one of the central tenets of the orthodox Sarvāstivāda.

Dhammajoti also points out a shift in emphasis over time (SA.IV.402):

> The *avijñapti* doctrine ... was probably first formulated out of a twofold consideration:
>
> i. There are situations—such as that of a murder committed through an emissary—in which an invisible force must be assumed, capable of preserving the karmic nature of the originating volition and serving as a completing cause to ensure the future arising of the retribution fruit.
>
> ii. The *avijñapti* as an invisible force—called "restraint" or "abstention"—preserving the essence of the ordination vows, serves as a legitimate cause for the distinction among the *bhikṣu*-s, *bhikṣuṇī*-s, etc.
>
> From this, the contrasting categories called non-restraint and neither-restraint-nor-non-restraint, as well as the categories of meditation and pure restraints came to be elaborated. It would seem that the monastic *abhidharma* scholiasts gradually shifted their focus of discussion on the *avijñapti* as restraint and its related categories.
>
> But this shift of emphasis [of non-informative matter *qua prātimokṣa-saṃvara*] has never obscured the nature of the *avijñapti* as a karmic force... .

For more detail on *avijñapti* as a karmic force, see SA.IV.389–402.

4. Returning now to LVP's endnote, as for the *avijñapti*'s name and its distinction from informative action, the *Avatāra* states (ESD.75f.):

> An action which can by itself inform (*vijñāpayati*) [others] of a specific variation (*pariṇāma-viśeṣa*) in the thought and thought-concomitants (*citta-caitta*) [of the doer], is one that is information (*vijñapti*).
>
> An action which is of the same species as the informing action—[being also material and an action]—but incapable of [such] an information, is one that is non-information (*avijñapti*).

5. As for Vasubandhu's verse definition, Gedun Drup (p. 25) mentions five attributes: (i) attribute of occasion: the three states of mind, i.e., distracted, non-distracted, without thought, (ii) attribute of entity: good or bad, (iii) attribute of time: serial continuity,

(iv) attribute of cause: fundamental material elements, (v) attribute of etymology: "non-informative".

6. Finally, see also Vasubandhu's discussion of *vijñapti* and *avijñapti* in his *Karmasiddhiprakaraṇa* (see our translation of Lamotte's introduction and translation in the *Electronic Appendix*).

[155] *LS*: Ny, 335a; ESD.134: "By distracted thought (*vikṣipta citta*) is meant the unwholesome (*akuśala-*) and non-defined thought (*avyākṛta-citta*); the other thoughts (*citta*) are non-distracted (*avikṣipta*)."

[156] *LS*: Cf. iv. 19–21b.

[157] *LS*: When Vasubandhu uses *śubha* and *aśubha* in the *Kośa* root verses, in general in his commentary he switches to *kuśala* and *akuśala*, but there are a few exceptions.

As for how informative and non-informative matter become wholesome or unwholesome, Dhammajoti comments (SA.IV.381):

> Informative and non-informative matter—being karmic forces—must necessarily be either skillful or unskillful. A neutral informative action—being weak in nature—cannot generate a karmic force (i.e., non-informative *karma*). In this case, the moral nature of the informative and non-informative *karma*-s is endowed by that of the volition and the thought conjoined with the volition. The latter becomes skillful or unskillful by virtue of their conjunction (*saṃprayoga*) with a thought-concomitant of either nature—e.g., greed or moral shame (*hrī*). The informative *karma*, on the other hand, though being matter in nature becomes morally defined by virtue of the morally defined volition that serves as the originating cause (samutthāna) for the informative *karma*, which in turn defines the moral nature of the non-informative *karma* that it generates.

In regard to Vasubandhu's discussion of *kuśala*, *akuśala* and *avyākṛta* in the context of the eighteen elements (*dhātu*), see i. 29c–30a; as for the number of associated thought-concomitants in regard to *kuśala*, *akuśala* and *avyakṛta* thoughts, see ii. 28–30d; as for the various classifications of *kuśala*, *akuśala* and *avyākṛta* factors, see iv. 8b–9c; as for the definitions of *kuśala*, *akuśala* and *avyākṛta* actions, see iv. 45ab; in regard to the definitions of *kuśala* and *akuśala* paths of action (*karmapatha*), see iv. 66bd.

In this context see also Lambert Schmithausen's article (forthcoming): "*Kuśala* and *Akuśala*: Reconsidering the Original Meaning of a Basic Pair of Terms of Buddhist Spirituality and Ethics and its Development up to Early Yogācāra."

[158] *LS*: Pradhan.8.5 has: *kuśalākuśale prāptipravāho'pyastīdṛśa.*

[159] *LVP*: I.e., possession (*prāpti*) is not associated with thought; it is not of the nature of form (*rūpa*); it is included within the aggregate of formations (*saṃskāraskandha*); being non-material, it resembles thought.

[160] *LS*: Pradhan.8.7 has *hetvartha upādāyārtha iti vaibhāṣikaḥ.*

[161] *LS*: AKB iv. 4cd discusses whether or not non-informative action is simultaneous with the fundamental material elements upon which it arises, and distinguishes a first moment and later moments of the arising of non-informative action. As for the later moments, it states:

"(1) (Specific) past fundamental material elements constitute—from the second moment onward—the basis (*āśraya*) of the non-informative action, for they are the cause of its issuing forth (*pravṛtti*), they are its projecting cause (*ākṣepakāraṇa*); (2) the fundamental material elements simultaneous with each of the moments, from the second moment onward, are the support (*saṃniśraya*) of the non-informative action, for they are the cause of its continuance (*anuvṛtti*), they are its supporting cause (*adhiṣṭhānakāraṇa*)."

162 *LS*: This is the second of Kritzer's fifteen passages discussed in relation to chapter 1 (see VY.4).

163 *LS*: The *Vyākhyā* glosses [WOG.30.16f.]: *kuśalaṃ* prātimokṣa-saṃvara-saṃgṛhītaṃ naiva-saṃvarana-saṃvarasaṃgṛhītaṃ ca. *akuśalaṃ* punar asaṃvara-saṃgṛhītaṃ naivasaṃvaraṇa-asaṃvarasaṃgṛhītaṃ ca.

See iv. 13.

164 *LS*: WOG.30.10f: kāya-vāk-vijñapti-sambhūtaṃ.

See iv. F 4–104.

165 *LS*: iv. 6cd, 9d, 13cd, 17–18b, 20b–21b, 67d–68.

166 *LS*: Before entering into the details regarding the fundamental material elements, we will look briefly at the historical development of this doctrine and its relation to the Buddhist atomic theory, and then at certain problems that result from it, particularly since this aspect is, in the main, only unfolded later in chapters 1, 2 and 3 (although it is also brought up in an objection below: i. F 25). Here are the pertinent points made by Dhammajoti in his section on "Atomic" theory (SA.IV.198–206):

> It would seem that at first the four *mahābhūta*-s were conceived of as being material qualities—Earth Element is solidity, etc. [see i. 12d]. They are real entities qua material qualities. When the atomic theory was introduced into the *abhidharma* system,* the notion that matter was constituted of atoms and that *mahābhūta*-s existed as atoms came to be developed. This led to a contradiction that seemed to have been quietly left unsettled: On the one hand [see iii. 85d–88a], the atomic theory requires that atoms are grouped as septuplets from which matter is derived. The smallest molecule, an *aṇu*, or *saṃghāta-paramāṇu*, consisting of just seven *paramāṇu*-s [*sapta paramāṇavo 'ṇuḥ*] is the smallest unit of matter that is perceivable—and even then not by an ordinary human being. On the other hand [see ii. 22], a new doctrine was then articulated that a molecule that can arise in the empirical world consists of a minimum of eight substances [*aṣṭadravyaka*]. Taking both doctrines into consideration, one commentarial opinion [see ii, F 148, note], in fact, arrives at 1,379 as the number of atoms that constitute a molecule of a visible! The contradiction, however, would not have necessarily arisen if the *mahābhūta*-s were conceived of as *dravya*-s in the sense of real material qualities—real forces—rather than atoms.

* It likely was taken over from outside the Buddhist schools. See Dhammajoti's qualifying comments in our endnote at i. 9ab.

167 *Gokhale*: [12ab] *bhūtāni pṛthivīdhātur aptejovāyudhātavaḥ* |

Tib.: [12ab] *'byung ba dag ni sa khams dang | chu dang me dang rlung khams rnams |*

LVP: See ii, F 144, 313.

Saṃghabhadra explains: Why are the fundamental material elements (*mahābhūta*) termed *dhātu*? – Because they are the place of origin of all material factors (*rūpadharma*); the fundamental material elements themselves have their origins in the fundamental material elements. But in the world, the place of origin receives the name of *dhātu*: it is thus that gold mines, etc., are called *dhātus* of gold, etc. – Or rather, they are called *dhātu* because they are the place of origin of the variety of sufferings. Examples as above.

Some say that they are called *dhātu* because they bear or maintain both the particular inherent characteristic of the fundamental material elements and the derivative material form (*rūpa*).

The *dhātus* also bear the name of *mahābhūta*. – Why *bhūta*? Why *mahābhūta*?

At the moment when the diverse types of derivative material form (blue, etc.,) arise, each of them comes forth under different aspects: this is why they are called *bhūta*.

According to other scholars, it is because of the dominant (*adhipati*) power of the action of sentient beings, in the course of eternal *saṃsāra*, that they always exist: this is why they are called *bhūta*. Or else, the appearance or arising (*utpāda*) of the factors is called *bhava*… .

LS: 1. Later (i. F 49–51), Vasubandhu presents also a list of six elementary substances (*dhātu*), that is, earth, water, fire, wind, space and consciousness, where space, according to the Vaibhāṣikas, refers to cavities or the empty space of the gate, window, etc., defined as being light (*āloka*) and darkness (*tamas*) in nature, i.e., refers to matter and not to unconditioned space (*ākāśa*). Thus the *Avatāra* must refer to the unconditioned space when delimiting the four fundamental material elements (ESD.73):

> [The four Great Elements] are called the Great Elements because of their being both great and having the nature of an Element (*bhūta*). Thus space [although great], is not included among the Great Elements, as by "Element" is meant the ability to produce its own fruit (*svaphala*).

2. As for the causal relationship of the four fundamental material elements among themselves, see ii. 50bd, where Vasubandhu discusses them as existing inseparably from one another, being co-existing causes (*sahabhūhetu*) but not associated causes (*saṃprayuktakahetu*). On the other hand, according to i. 51d (F 252) and 65c, some derivative material elements are not co-existent causes with one another, whereas others are.

As for the causal relationship of the four fundamental material elements to the derivative material elements, ii. 65b states:

> The four fundamental material elements are causes of derivative material elements (*bhautika*)—color, taste, etc.—in five ways [*prakāra*], "in the quality of (i) generating (*janana*) cause, (ii) reliance (*niśraya*) cause, (iii) supporting (*pratiṣṭhā*; *sthāna*) cause, (iv) maintaining (*upastambha*) cause and (v) growth (*upabṛṃhaṇa*) cause".

As for the reverse relationship, ii. 65d states that the derivative material elements are not a co-existent cause of the fundamental material elements.

3. As for the difference between the fundamental material elements and the derivative material elements, MVŚ, 665a, states that the fundamental material elements are invisible

(*anidarśana*), resistant (*sapratigha*), with-outflow (*sāsrava*), non-defined (*avyākṛta*), etc., whereas the derivative material elements are visible or invisible, resistant or non-resistant, with-outflow or outflow-free, skillful, unskillful, or non-defined, etc. For the entire list, see SA.IV.198.

For a discussion of primary matter (*bhūta*) versus secondary matter (*bhautika*) in the context of the eighteen elements, see i. 35ac.

4. As for the fundamental material elements and derivative material elements in the context of the atomic theory, see the discussion of atoms (*paramāṇu*) in ii. 22, which states:

> In the realm of desire, (i) the molecule (*paramāṇu*; i.e., *saṃghātaparamāṇu*) that does not involve sound and does not involve any sense-faculty, includes eight [kinds of] real entities (*dravya*): [i.e., the four fundamental material elements and the four derivative material elements: visible form, taste, odor, tangible]. (ii) When the body sense-faculty is involved in [the molecule, it includes] nine real entities. (iii) When any other sense-faculty is involved in [the molecule, it includes] ten real entities.

5. As for the question how—within the parameters of the atomic theory and the limitations resulting from being co-existent causes—the great diversity, in manifestation and experience, of material form (*rūpa*) could be explained, see the endnote to smoothness (i. 10d).

6. As for the ontological status of the *mahābhūtas* and *bhautikas*, even though all Sarvāstivādins accept the four fundamental material elements as real entities, not all of them (SA.IV.193) accept the eleven derivative material elements as real. For example, Dharmatrāta does not accept the non-informative form (*avijñaptirūpa*) and Buddhadeva even holds that all derivative material elements are just specific types of the fundamental material elements. Also, for the Sautrāntika Śrīlāta they are nothing more than the specific configuration of the fundamental material elements.

168 *LS*: Cf. the etymological explanation of *dharma* (i, F 4).

169 *LVP*: *tadudbhūtavṛttiṣu pṛthivyaptejovāyuskandheṣu teṣv eṣāṃ mahāsaṃniveśatvāt.*

The etymological explanation of *bhūtāni* is *bhūtaṃ tanvanti.*

170 *Gokhale*: [12c] *dhṛtyādikarmasaṃsiddhāḥ*

Tib.: [12c] *'dzin pa la sogs las su grub* |

LVP: Water (in the popular sense of the word) supports ships: thus the substantial element earth manifests its particular activity in it; it is warm; it moves; etc.

See ii. 22; *Dhammasaṅgaṇi*, 962–66; *Compendium*, *Appendix*, p. 268.

171 *MW*: *pakti*: cooking, preparing food; digesting; ripening, development, having results or consequences.

172 *Gokhale*: [12d] *kharasnehoṣṇateraṇāḥ* ||

Tib.: [12d] *sra gsher dro nyid g.yo ba rnams* ||

LS: See PB.101–4.

173 *LVP*: *Prakaraṇa*, 757a23. – The *Mahāvyutpatti* (101) has *khakkhaṭatva, dravatva, uṣṇatva, laghusamudīraṇatva.*

[174] *LVP*: *deśāntarotpādanasvabhāvā ... īraṇā*, compare the cited source in *Compendium*: *desantaruppattihetubhāvena*.

[175] *LVP*: The Sanskrit and the Tibetan have the plural. – Hsüan-tsang: *Prakaraṇapāda*; Paramārtha: *Fen-pieh tao-li lun*. – *Prakaraṇa*, 699c5: *vāyudhātuḥ katamah*? *laghusamudīraṇatvam*.

[176] *LVP*: The Sūtra in question (*Saṃyuktāgama*, 11, 1; MVŚ, 388a18) is perhaps the *Garbhāvakrāntisūtra* (*Majjhima*, III, 239; below, p. 49, n. 2). In the edition known through the *Śikṣāsamuccaya* (p. 244), there is: (1) for earth: *kakkhaṭatva kharagata* (compare *Mahāvastu*, i. 339), *Divyāvadāna*, 518, 2; *Dhammasaṅgaṇi*, 648; Harṣacarita, *JRAS*, 1899, p. 494); (2) for water: *āpas abgata aptva sneha snehagata snehatva dravatva*; (3) for fire: *tejas tejogata uṣmagata*; (4) for wind: *vāyu vāyugata laghutva samudīraṇatva*.

[177] *LVP*: That is to say: light (*laghu*) is derivative material form (*rūpa*); lightness (*laghutva*), which, in its intrinsic nature is mobility (*īraṇa*), is the elementary substance wind; the elementary substance wind is thus *laghusamudīraṇatva*: that which produces lightness and motion.

[178] *LS*: SAH 495.

[179] *Gokhale*: [13] *pṛthivī varṇasaṃsthānam ucyate lokasaṃjñayā | āpas tejaś ca vāyus tu dhātur eva tathā 'pi ca* ||

Tib.: [13] *'jig rten gyi ni tha snyad du | kha dog dbyibs la sa zhes brjod | chu me yang ngo rlung tshogs khams | nyid yin de dang 'dra ba'ng yin* ||

LVP: Such is the reading cited in the *Vyākhyā*, viii. 35; but, according to the Tibetan and the *Vyākhyā*, p. 35, the reading should be *vātya tu*... . – *Vātyā* = *vātānāṃ samūhaḥ*, according to Pāṇini, iv, 2, 42.

See viii. 36b (perception-sphere of totality of wind [*vāyukṛtsnāyatana*]). In regard to whether the wind is visible, there are two opinions in MVŚ, 441a, 689b3.

LS: As to how the great diversity—in manifestation and experience—of material form (*rūpa*) could be explained, see the endnote to "smoothness" (i. 10d).

As for "common usage" (*lokasaṃjñā*), see Vasubandhu's classical explanation of the difference between conventional truth and absolute truth, see at vi. 4, which Hirakawa summarizes (MDA.170) as follows:

> The own-being of *dharma*s is considered as absolutely real (*paramārtha-sat*) in the *Kośa*, while things the existence of which depends on assemblages of the real *dharmas* are called conventionally real (*saṃvṛti-sat*). For example, a vase or water visible to the eye are said to be conventionally existent; the vase, on being smashed apart, loses its existence. Yet even in the shards of the broken vase, the color remains. Smashing the vase's shards further, even pulverizing them to atoms, still the own-being of the color remains. Thus *dharma*s with own-being are absolutely real. In contrast, visible water consists of color, odor, taste, tangibility (i.e., temperature, weight, et cetera), which are analyzable. On analytic separation of these aspects, the perception of water is lost. Things like the vase and visible water that lose their perceptible existence on physical or analytical breaking up are said to be conventionally real. However, color, odor, and so on, the raw material of perception, cannot be further analyzed. [For] the Sarvāstivādins, not only color, but also odor and taste,

warmth (the great elementary quality fire), dampness (the great elementary quality water), and so forth, are all seen as made of atoms. In the case of "matter", the raw material of sense perception was thought to exist ... in the outer world as collective bodies of these atoms.

180 *LS*: Vasubandhu, in accordance with early *sūtra* and *abhidharma* custom, began his discussion of material form (*rūpa*; i. 9ab) with a mere delimitation-definition, but since the fundamental concern of *abhidharma* is the discernment of the particularly inherent and common characteristics of factors (*dharmapravicaya*, i. 2) (SA.IV.187), it was inevitable that the Ābhidharmikas eventually had to seek a more formal and articulate definition for it.

LVP: There are two roots:

1. *rup*, rumpere, λύπη, in Vedic Sanskrit: *rupyati*, *ropana*, etc.; in Pāḷi: *ruppati* (= *kuppati ghaṭṭiyati pīliyati domanassito hoti*); in Classic Sanskrit: *lup*, *lumpati*;
2. *rūp*, which gives *rūpa*, shape, color, beauty, *rūpya*, gold, etc.

LS: Dhammajoti elaborates (SA.IV.188):

> The AKB defines *rūpa* by the term *rūpaṇa/rūpaṇā*—which Xuan Zang renders as "change-obstruction" 變礙—understood in the sense of being subject to deterioration or disintegration. For the verb form, *rūpayati/rūpyate*, he also occasionally renders ... 變壞 ("deteriorate"). The term is evidently linked etymologically to the root √*rup* (connected to √*lup*)—"disturb", "violate", "break".
>
> But *rūpaṇa* is also often implicitly linked to √*rūp*, a denominative root from the noun *rūpa*, in which case *rūpaṇā* means no more than "the nature of being *rūpa*".

We can see this distinction between √*rup* and √*rūp* reflected in the first and second definition, as given by Vasubandhu.

181 *LVP*: *rūpyate rūpyata iti bhikṣavaḥ*... . [The Tibetan and Chinese sources demand, it seems, the translation: "What is it that is broken? As soon as it is touched by the hand... ."

Saṃyutta, iii, 86: *ruppatīti kho bhikkhave tasmā rūpaṃ ti vuccati* | *kena ruppati* | *sītena ... siriṃsapasampassena ruppati*. (See the interpretation of Shwe Zan Aung in *Compendium*: "form (*rūpa*) means that which changes its form under the physical conditions of cold... .")

The *Mahāvyutpatti* has: *rūpaṇād rūpam* (111, 3; 244, 1137, 1153, 1154).

LS: Bhikkhu Bodhi (DB.915) translates *Saṃyutta*, iii. 86 as:

> And why, *bhikkhus*, do you call it form? "It is deformed", *bhikkhus*, therefore it is called form. Deformed by what? Deformed by cold, deformed by heat, deformed by hunger, deformed by thirst, deformed by contact with flies, mosquitoes, wind, sun, and serpents. "It is deformed", *bhikkhus*, therefore it is called form.

The Chinese version of the *Saṃyuktāgama* reads (SA.IV.188):

> That which is susceptible to being obstructed and decomposed is called *rūpa-upādāna-skandha*. It is obstructed by the fingers. It is touched by the hand, or stone, or stick, or knife, or coldness, or heat, or thirst, or hunger, or insects such as mosquitoes, or wind or rain—this is called resistance by touch. Thus, resistance is [the characteristic] of the *rūpa-upādāna-skandha*. Furthermore, it is because this

rūpa-skandha is impermanent, unsatisfactory and subject to change.

182 *LVP*: The Sarvāstivādins understand: "Useful Chapters"; the Pāli signifies: "The Octades". (S. Lévi, *J. As.*, 1915, i. 412; 1916, ii. 34).

> *tasya cet kāmayānasya chandajātasya dehinaḥ |*
> *te kāmā na samṛdhyanti śalyaviddha iva rūpyate ||*

Mahāniddesa, p. 5. – Kern, *Verspreide Geschriften*, ii, 261 (La Haye 1913), illustrates the meaning of *rup* by *Jātaka* iii, 368; *Cariyapiṭaka*, 3. 6, etc.

183 *LS*: The *Vyākhyā* glosses [WOG.34.8f.] *kāma* as object-field (*viṣaya*).

184 *LS*: Whereas Yaśomitra in his *Vyākhyā* links this passage to the following question-and-answer and seems to want to explain away the subjective sense of "oppression" (*bādhanā*) by stating that "*rūpa* is unlike a pleasure-seeking human", Dhammajoti thinks (SA.IV.189) that "one may understand this as the Ābhidharmika attempt to relate *rūpyate* to the subjective sense encountered in the *sūtra*-s. ... Since [*rūpa*] is of the nature of being subject to resistance and impermanent, it is mutated or disfigured as it arises—visibly so in contrast to other *dharma*-s—and therefore it is ultimately disturbing to the experiencer."

185 *LVP*: 1. *rūpaṇaṃ pratighāta ity apare.* – *pratighāta* signifies *svadeśe parasyotpatti pratibandha.* – See below i, F 51.

Elsewhere, the *sapratigha* ("impenetrable/resistant") phenomenon is defined as that which *covers* a place, that which is extended.

We will see (i. 43) the kind of *pratighāta* that is referred to in *Dhammasaṅgaṇi*, 618–19:

> [618] What is that [material] form which is the sphere of visible shape?
>
> That [material] form which, derived from the Great Phenomena, is visible under the appearance of colour and reacting—is blue, yellow, red, white, black, crimson, bronze, green-coloured, of the hue of the mango-bud; is long, short, big, little, circular, oval, square, hexagonal, octagonal, hekkaidecagonal; low, high, shady, glowing, light, dim, dull, frosty, smoky, dusty; like in colour to the disc of moon, sun, stars, a mirror, a gem, a shell, a pearl, a cat's eye, gold or silver; or whatever other shape there is which, derived from the four Great Phenomena, is visible and reacting—on which shape, visible and reacting, the eye, invisible and reacting, has impinged, impinges, will, or may impinge—this which is visible shape, this which is the sphere of visible shape, the constituent element of visible shape—this is that form which is the sphere of visible shape.
>
> [619] What is that [material] form which is the sphere of visible shape?
>
> That [material] form which, derived from the Great Phenomena, is visible under the appearance of colour and produces impact—which form, visible and producing impact, has impinged, impinges, will, or may impinge on the eye that is invisible and reacting—this which is visible shape, this which is the sphere of visible shape, the constituent element of visible shape—this is that form which is the sphere of visible shape.

2. There is a third definition of *rūpaṇa*, *Madhyamakavṛtti*, 456, 9: *tatredam ihāmutreti nirūpaṇād rūpam* = "This is called *rūpa* because one can indicate it as being here or there",

and *Vyākhyā*, ad i. 24 [WOG.51.30ff.] *pāṇyādisaṃsparśair bādhanālakṣaṇād rūpaṇāt | idam ihāmutreti deśanidarśanarūpaṇāc ca*. – Compare *Mahāvyutpatti*, 245, 1139, *deśanirūpaṇa*.

We have thus: *rūpa*, that which is impenetrable, that which occupies a place; thus physical matter.

Saṃghabhadra furthermore has other explanations: the *rūpa* is thus called because it indicates a previous action: "This man has performed an action, anger, which has produced his malformation."

LS: As for the second definition, some Ābhidharmika masters interpret "the nature of being *rūpa*" (*rūpaṇa*) as referring to physical resistance (*pratighāta*), which is further specified by Vasubandhu (i. 29bc) as one of the threefold obstruction, namely, obstruction qua obstacle (*āvaraṇapratighāta*). But MVŚ, 389c–390a, also refers to Vasumitra's explanation, an elaborated version of this *rūpāna*, containing twelve characteristics (see SA.IV.189), which can be narrowed down to two: (1) visibility [= indicability] (*sanidarśanatva*) and (2) resistance (*sapratighātatva*), which, over time, seemed to be stressed primarily by the Ābhidharmikas, which can be seen from the fact that they form the first two members of the twenty-two doctrinal perspectives on the eighteen sense-elements as discussed by Vasubandhu (i. 29). Saṃghabhadra as well takes them to be the two qualities most distinctive of *rūpa* (NY, 346b) :

> On account of it being obstructive, it deteriorates as soon as it is touched by the hand, etc., and on account of it being visible, one can indicate it as being located differently—here, there.

Saṃghabhadra even argues (SA.IV.191) that visibility as an intrinsic characteristic of the category of *rūpa* must apply to even the smallest unit, i.e., an atom, since otherwise it would forfeit its very intrinsic nature as *rūpa*. On the other hand, Saṃghabhadra also gives three defining characteristics of *rūpa*: (1) indicatability of location, (2) susceptibility to deterioration through obstructive contact, (3) *rūpa* by designation, whereby the third refers to non-informative matter (*avijñapti*), a special type of matter, being devoid of the first two characteristics (i.e., visibility and resistance) and subsumed under the *dharmāyatana* rather than the *rūpa-āyatana*.

186 *LVP*: *na vai paramāṇurūpam ekaṃ pṛthagbhūtam asti*. – See i. 43cd and ii. 22.

187 *LVP*: *rūpa*s of the past, Saṃghabhadra, 636a8.

188 *LS*: This is the third of Kritzer's fifteen passages discussed in relation to chapter 1 (see VY.8f.). Saṃghabhadra [Ny, 338a9–14] comments that the analogy given is Vasubandhu's and not that of the Vaibhāṣika. On the other hand, Saṃghabhadra himself maintains (EIP.VIII.654) that the first explanation is unacceptable, "because in that case those types of unmanifest material form that arise in accordance with mental action and are not produced from manifest material form would not be classified as material form".

189 *LVP*: *āśrayabhūtarūpaṇāt* [WOG.35.20]. This formula has passed into the *Mahāvyutpatti*, 109, 2. The Japanese editor refers to MVŚ, 390a1.

The *Vyākhyā* instructs us that this second explanation is due to the Vṛddhācārya Vasubandhu.

On Vasubandhu the master of Manoratha, who in turn is the master of Vasubandhu the author of the *Kośa*, see *Bhāṣya*, iii. 27 and iv. 3a, and the sources discussed in the *Avant Propos de la Cosmologie Bouddhique*, p. viii (Londres, 1918).

190 *LS*: This is the fourth of Kritzer's fifteen passages discussed in relation to chapter 1 (see VY.10f.).

191 *LS*: Hall translates (VACS.79): "But others offer a solution to this."

192 *LS*: Hall translates (VACS.80): "It is demonstrated from this that something is form (*rūpa*) because of the 'striking' (*rūpaṇa*) of its [physical] basis (*āśraya*)" (*ata upapannametad āśrayarūpaṇād rūpamiti*).

193 *LS*: But not the non-informative (*avijñapti*).

194 *Gokhale*: [14ab] *indriyā'rthās ta ev eṣṭā daśāyatanadhātavaḥ* |

Tib.: [14ab] *dbang don de dag kho na la* | *skye mched dang ni khams bcur 'dod* |

LVP: Saṃghabhadra, in the *Samayapradīpikā*, reads: *ta evoktā*. – Vasubandhu uses the expression *iṣṭa*, "are regarded by the Vaibhāṣikas", because for him the aggregates (*skandha*) do not really exist (i. 20).

195 *LS*: AH 9; SAH 10.

196 *Gokhale*: [14c1] *vedanā 'nubhavaḥ*

Tib.: [14c1] *tshor ba myong ba'o*

LVP: ii. 7, 8, 24; iii. 32; *Saṃyutta*, iii. 96; *Dhammasaṅgaṇi*, 3; *Théorie de douze causes*, p. 23.

LS: The aggregates of sensation and ideation are not included among the other thought-concomitants in the aggregate of formations which would be their natural place. Instead they are treated as separate aggregates (*skandha*) because (i. 21) of their great importance as the predominant causes (*pradhānahetu*) (1) of the two roots of dispute (*vivāda*), i.e., attachment to pleasures (*kāma*) and attachment to views (*dṛṣṭi*), and (2) of cyclic existence (*saṃsāra*). But in spite of their great importance, in comparison to the fairly detailed discussion of the aggregate of material form, they, together with the fourth and fifth aggregates, are treated only rather briefly "at this stage" in the AKB. The reason for this seems to be related with the *Pañca-skandhaka* and *Pañcavastuka* as discussed in the introductory endnote at F 6.

1. As for a formal definition of sensation (*vedanā*), we have two, i.e., one of the aggregate of sensation (i. 14c), and the other of the generally permeating factor sensation (ii. 24):

> Sensation (*vedanā*; *tshor ba*) is the three kinds of sensation or experience or affect (*anubhava*), i.e., (i) pleasant (*sukha*), (ii) unpleasant (*duḥkha*) and (iii) neither-unpleasant-nor-pleasant (*aduḥkhāsukha*).

The seventh member of the twelvefold dependent origination (*pratītyasamutpāda*; see iii. 18–38c) is also called sensation (*vedanā*). For its definition and meaning within the four types of dependent origination, i.e., momentary (*kṣanika*), prolonged (*prākarṣikā*), connected (*sāṃbandhika*), pertaining to states (*āvasthika*), see chapter 3, but as for the fourth type, i.e., within a three-life-times model, it is defined as follows: "Sensation (*vedanā*; *vitti*) [is the five aggregates] before sexual union, [i.e., as long as attachment to sexual union is not in action]."

As for other texts, Vasubandhu's *Pañcaskandhaka* (2008) defines:

> 2. *vedanā katamā* | *trividho 'nubhavaḥ – sukho duḥkho 'duḥkhāsukhaś ca* | *sukho yasya nirodhe saṃyogacchando bhavati* | *duḥkho yasyotpādād viyogacchando bhavati* | *aduḥkhāsukho yasyotpādāt tadubhayaṃ na bhavati* ||

> 2. What is feeling? The three types of experience: pleasant, unpleasant, and neither pleasant nor unpleasant. A pleasant experience is one that you desire to be united with again when it ceases. An unpleasant experience is one that you desire to be separated from when it arises. An experience that is neither pleasant nor unpleasant is one for which you develop neither of those desires when it occurs. ISBP.231

The *Avatāra* (ESD.79) includes *vedanā*'s epistemological connection with the contact (*sparśa*) born of the coming together of the sense faculty, the object and the consciousness:

> There are three kinds of experience (*anubhava*): (i) pleasurable (*sukha*), (ii) unpleasurable (*duḥkha*) and (iii) neither pleasurable nor unpleasurable (*aduḥkha-asukha*). These are the experiencing of three results of contact (*sparśānubhavana*).

See also CEGS.51f; MBP.19; MF.56f; EBP.38ff.

2. As for classifications of *vedanā* itself, our i. 14c presents a threefold and six-fold classification. But it is also discussed as a single term and as threefold or six-fold classification at various places of Vasubandhu's extensive discussion of dependent origination (*pratītya-samutpāda*; iii. F 56–119), which also includes a detailed presentation of mental sensation as the eighteen types of mental-faculty–ponderings (*manopavicāra*; iii, F 107–16).

In addition, we also find (ii.7) a twofold classification: (i) bodily sensation and (ii) mental sensation, whereby bodily sensation is explained as the sensation "that relates to the body", that is associated with the five sensory consciousnesses, i.e., the visual consciousness, etc., and mental sensation as the sensation associated with the mental consciousness (*manovijñāna*).

But more importantly, there is also (i. 48cd; ii. 7–8) the following fivefold classification: (i) pleasure (*sukha*), (ii) displeasure (*duḥkha*), (iii) satisfaction (*saumanasya*), (iv) dissatisfaction (*daurmanasya*) and (v) equanimity (*upekṣa*), which is included and discussed within the context of the twenty-two controlling faculties (*indriya*). As controlling faculties, the sensations exercise controlling power not only with regard to pollution (*saṃkleśa*) because the proclivities (*anuśaya*), i.e., attachment (*rāga*), etc., become attached to the sensations and become lodged therein, but also with regard to purification (*vyavadāna*) because it supports concentration (*samādhi*), faith (*śraddha*), etc.,

On the other hand, within the context of discussing the first noble truth of unsatisfactoriness, Vasubandhu (vi. 128–36), based on scriptural authority and logical reasoning, (i) presents the opinion of certain masters—identified by the *Vyākhyā* and Saṃghabhadra as the Bhadanta Śrīlāta, etc., and by the gloss of the Japanese editor, as the Sautrāntikas, Mahāsāṃghikas, etc.—that denies agreeable sensation as a whole and affirms that all sensation is only painful, and (ii) presents its refutation by the Ābhidharmikas and also by Vasubandhu, who affirm that agreeable sensation is agreeable in nature and exists as a real entity.

3. As for its relation to other thought-concomitants (*caitta*), *vedanā* is listed as the first of the ten generally permeating mental factors (*mahābhūmika*) within the orthodox Vaibhāṣika system (ii. 24). As for the Dārṣṭāntika Dharmatrāta, it is also probably one of the thought-concomitants that he accepts as being real entities, as does the Sautrāntika Śrīlāta. On the other hand, Buddhadeva only accepts *citta* as a real entity and thus denies a real entity status to any of the thought-concomitants.

Even though *vedanā* is a *mahābhūmika*, there are states where, according to the Vaibhāṣikas, all *vedanās* and all other thought-concomitants and also thought itself cease, as indicated in the name "attainment of cessation of ideation and sensation" (*saṃjñāveditanirodhasamāpatti*), the term by which the attainment of cessation (*nirodhasamāpatti*) sometimes is referred to.

As for its relation to the other aggregates, i. 22bd describes the five aggregates from the point of view of (i) their relative grossness, (ii) their being causes of the progression of pollution, (iii) analogy, and (iv) their predominance in the three realms.

Vedanā is considered to be the most gross among the non-material aggregates, because of the grossness of its operation.

4. As for the question of whether sensation arises later or simultaneously with contact, this issue is discussed at iii. 32 [F 101–7], which includes also a long discussion regarding Śrīlāta's doctrine of perception.

5. As for the question of whether *vedanā* is a ripened effect (*vipākaphala*) or not, AKB ii. 10ac and iv. 57d argues that dissatisfaction is never a ripened effect for the Vaibhāṣikas (and seemingly also for Vasubandhu), whereas the other four of the five sensations are of two types, i.e., sometimes a ripened effect and sometimes not. Gedun Drup comments (p. 13) that dissatisfaction is not a fruition "because it is definitely either contaminated virtue or non-virtue. This is because when there is mental unhappiness in regard to a virtuous action it is non-virtuous, and when there is mental unhappiness in regard to a non-virtuous action it is virtuous".

On the other hand, iv. 57 discusses sensation not only as an element of retribution of action, but as the "essential or predominant" element of retribution.

6. *Vedanā* is often translated as feeling or sensation. We have chosen "sensation" since it seems to cover the momentary nature of *vedanā* somewhat better, whereas in ordinary parlance "feelings" can get mixed up quickly with all kinds of emotions and series of mental events, which fall "more" into the domain of the fourth aggregate. As for the functioning of *vedanā*, see the next endnote.

197 *MW*: *anubhava*: perception, apprehension, fruition; understanding; experience, impression on the mind not derived from memory.

LS: In the following, some of Dhammajoti's points (SA.IV.276–78), which clarify the role of *anubhava* and *vedanā* within sensory perception from the Vaibhāṣika point of view, are summarized. For more detail regarding the Vaibhāṣika and Sautrāntika doctrine of sensory perception, see Vasubandhu's long discussion regarding Śrīlāta's doctrine of perception (iii, F 102–7), at which time we will also provide longer endnotes on the subject, based on Dhammajoti's *Abhidharma Doctrines and Controversies on Perception* (2007).

> Saṃghabhadra [Ny, 736a] [enumerates three types of direct perception (*pratyakṣa*)]:
>
> 1. that which is dependent on the sense faculty (依根現量; *indriya–āśrita-pratyakṣa*);
> 2. that which is experience (領納現量; *anubhava-pratyakṣa*);
> 3. that which is discernment (覺了現量; **buddhi-pratyakṣa*).
>
> The first refers to the direct grasping (*pratyakṣaṃ* √*grah*?), supported by the five sense faculties, of the five types of external objects, *rūpa*, etc.

The second refers to the coming into the present of the *citta-caitta-dharma*-s, *vedanā*, *saṃjñā*, etc.

The third refers to the direct realization (*sākṣāt-√kṛ*) of the specific or common characteristic (*sva-sāmānya-lakṣaṇa*)—accordingly as the case may be—of *dharma*-s.

From this, it is clear that it is the visual consciousness, not the mere seeing by the eye, that is *indriya-pratyakṣa*.

The second type of *pratyakṣa* is intrinsically linked with the first in-as-much as these *caitta*-s become present at the first moment of the perceptual process together with visual consciousness, sensing and categorizing (albeit weakly), etc., on the very same object that is being grasped generically by visual consciousness.

The third type is mental consciousness that follows immediately from the first moment. It can still be considered a type of direct perception since it is a clear vivid perception directly induced by the immediately preceding sensory perception. [...]

Saṃghabhadra argues that *sahabhū* [co-existent] causality obtains in a sensory perception; the sensory faculty and the object as the causes and the sensory consciousness as the effect all arise in the same first moment. Moreover, *vedanā*, the instrumental force for *anubhava*, must be "conjoined with" consciousness—which entails not only simultaneity, but also that both take the same object, etc. In fact, a sensory consciousness necessarily has a present perceptual object, or it will not be possible for one to have the *pratyakṣa* experience. For, with regard to what is personally sensed, one experiences it and discerns it at different times. That is, the *anubhava-pratyakṣa* and *buddhi-pratyakṣa* are not simultaneous. Discernment occurs at the state of recollection, taking the experience—the *vedanā*—that has just ceased as its object. Accordingly, "a sensation—pleasurable, etc.—must first be experienced by the *anubhava-pratyakṣa* before a *pratyakṣa* discernment can arise having it as its perceptual object. Likewise, an external object must first be experienced by *indriyāśrita-pratyakṣa* before a *pratyakṣa* discernment can arise having it as the perceptual object, by virtue of the thrust of presentness." This is consistent with the Sarvāstivāda view that the *citta-caitta-dharma*-s cannot discern themselves or those conjoined or coexist with them.

198 *LS*: AH 9; SAH 10.

199 *Gokhale*: [14c2–d] *saṃjñā nimittodgrahaṇātmikā* ||

Tib.: [14c2–d] *'du shes ni* | *mtshan mar 'dzin pa'i bdag nyid do* ||

LVP: By *nimitta* (signs) one should understand *vastuno 'vasthāviśeṣa*, the diverse conditions or states of the phenomenon. *Udgrahaṇa* signifies *pariccheda* (determination, discernment).

The *Vijñānakāya*, 26a16, cited in the *Nyāyabindupūrvapakṣasaṃkṣepa* (*Mdo*, 111, fol. 108b) and in the *Madhyamakavṛtti* (p. 74), says that the visual consciousness knows blue (*nīlaṃ jānāti*), but does not know "This is blue" (*no tu nīlam iti*). – See the note ad i. 33ab. – It is through ideation (*saṃjñā*) that a name is given to the visual impression, to the external cause of the visual impression.

Objection: – Consciousness (*vijñāna*) and ideation (*saṃjñā*) are always associated (ii. 24); thus the visual consciousness will know the signs of the object. – Answer: The ideation accompanying the sensory consciousnesses is weak, indistinct, [i.e., includes only *conceptualizing activity in its intrinsic nature* (*svabhāvavikalpa*; *vitarka-vicāra*)]. Only the mental consciousness is accompanied by an efficacious ideation; it alone is (the three types of) *savikalpaka* (i. 32–33).

Compare *Saṃyutta*, iii. 86; *Atthasālinī*, 291; *Milinda*, 61.

Majjhima, i, 293; *Siddhi*, 148; the ten signs (*nimitta*), viii, F 185:

1–5. the five sense-spheres (*āyatana*), external sense-spheres of the sensory consciousnesses, color-shape (*rūpa*), sound, etc.;

6–7. male (*puruṣa*) and female (*strī*);

8–10. the three characteristics of the conditioned (*saṃskṛtalakṣaṇa*; ii. 45cd), (i) arising, (ii) duration-change, (iii) passing away.

LS: 1. The translation of *saṃjñā* continues to cause scholars great trouble. William Waldron (BU.198) comments:

> Usually translated as "perception", the Sanskrit form *saṃjñā* is composed of the prefix *saṃ*, "together", plus the root verb *jña*, "to know, perceive, understand", that is, a "knowing-together". *Saṃjñā* (*P. saññā*) thus means "conception, idea, impression, perception" (BHSD 551–52). Interestingly, it is etymologically parallel with "conscious": *com*, "together, with", plus *scire* "to know". *Saṃjñā* is formally the opposite of *vijñāna* (*P. viññāna*), which is composed of *vi-*, "*dis-*", plus the same root, *jña*. While *vijñāna* stresses disjunctive discernment, *saṃjñā* emphasizes a conjunctive construction of an image or idea that brings disparate sensations together into a whole, often connected with a name or concept. This is why *saṃjñā* is a *saṃskārā* (P. *sankhārā*) of mind, a construction or complex (*Saṃyutta*, IV 293: *saññā ca vedanā ca cittasankhāre ti*).

Waldron, as well as some other scholars suggest "apperception". We will use "ideation", following Dhammajoti, Deleanu, and also Schmithausen who uses it in some of his writings.

2. In our endnote to the aggregate of sensation, we have already alluded to the great importance of the aggregate of ideation, why it is treated as a separate aggregate (*skandha*) and why it is nevertheless discussed only briefly "at this point". If we search the remaining chapters of the AKB in regard to how the details are filled in, we find various perspectives that seem to fall into the following two bigger categories: (A) *saṃjñā* as a generally permeating factor and member of the five *upādānaskandha*s, and, as such, related to general psychology and epistemology—distinguishing between the five sensory consciousnesses and mental consciousness, and their moment by moment developments—and to the first noble truth; (B) *saṃjñā* in its role within meditation and the general Buddhist path to liberation, and, as such, related to soteriology and the second, third and fourth noble truths. We will try to address both categories in the following longer endnote.

A.1. *Definitions*: As for the first bigger category, we have two formal definitions of ideation, i.e., a definition of the aggregate of ideation (i. 14cd), providing more detail, and a definition of the generally permeating factor ideation (ii. 24), both of which are not explicit about the relationship to other generally permeating factors or to factors discussed in the other aggregates. Here is the one from ii. 24:

> Ideation (*saṃjñā*; *'du shes*) is conceiving (*saṃjñāna*), that which seizes or apprehends the signs (*nimitta*; male, female, etc.) of the object-field (*viṣayanimittagrahaṇa* = *viṣayaviśeṣarūpagrāha*).

Vasubandhu's definition in his *Pañcaskandhaka* (2008) is fairly similar (and also includes a reference to a threefold *saṃjñā* instead of a sixfold *saṃjñā* as in i. 14cd):

> 3. *sañjñā katamā | viṣayanimittodgrahaṇam | tat trividham – parīttaṃ mahadgatam apramāṇaṃ ca ||*
>
> 3. What is conception? The grasping of an object's sign, which is of three types: limited, great, and immeasurable. ISBP.231

As for *saṃjñā*'s specific activity and function in the relationship with other factors—within the wider psychological and epistemological context—i.e., its object and its connection with initial inquiry or reasoning (*vitarka*) and investigation (*vicāra*), name (*nāma*), etc., it is addressed in the definition of the *Avatāra* (ESD.80):

> This is that which comprehends, by combining conceptually (*saṃ-√jñā*) the appearance (*nimitta*), name (*nāma*) and the signified (*artha*) [of a *dharma*]. That is, with regard to matter like blue, yellow, long and short [figures], etc.; sounds like those of a conch-shell, a drum, etc.; smells like those of gharu-wood and musk, etc., tastes like those of saltiness and bitterness, etc., tangibles like those of hardness and softness, etc., *dharma*-s like males and females, etc.—it comprehends them, [in each case], by conceptually combining together (*eka-√jñā*) their appearances, names and [the signified]. It is the cause of reasoning (*vitarka*) and investigation (*vicāra*). Thus, this is named ideation.

Sthiramati's definition clarifies further some of its aspects (TVB.21):

> *Saṃjñā* is the grasping of the appearance of an object. The object is the cognitive object. [Its] appearance is its distinctiveness—the cause for establishing the cognitive object as a blue colour, a yellow colour, etc. The grasping of [this appearance] is the determination (*nirūpaṇā*) that "this is blue, not yellow".

As for "determination", Dhammajoti (ESD.139) refers to Saṃghabhadra's definition of *saṃjñā* (Ny. 384b):

> [...] that which causes the determination and grasping of the diverse forms (*nimitta*) of male, female, etc., is named ideation,

and explains that "determination" (see below) presupposes a proper investigation (*vicāra*) and understanding (*prajñā*), which is why the *Avatāra* calls ideation the cause of *vitarka* and *vicāra*.

The *Siddhi* (F 148f; ESD.139), on the other hand, clarifies *saṃjñā*'s relationship with speech as follows [bracketed inserts by LVP]:

> Ideation has, with regard to the objects, the grasping of forms as its nature [*viṣaya-nimitta-udgrahaṇa*], and [when it is mental (*mānasī*)] the designation of diverse manners of speech [names and words] as its function [*nānā-abhidhāna-prajñapti-karmikā*]. It is only after the determination ["This is blue; not non-blue"] of the

particular characteristics of the objects that there arise the diverse manners of speech [that correspond to these characteristics].

A.2. If we combine this now with Saṃghabhadra's enumeration of three types of *pratyakṣa* (see our endnote on *vedanā*), the following Vaibhāṣika model of perception emerges:

i. In the first moment, visual consciousness—as *indriyāśritapratyakṣa* and *anubhava-pratyakṣa*, when the contribution of the conascent thought-concomitants (*caitta*), including ideation (*saṃjñā*), is still weak—"directly perceives" the specific characteristics (*svalakṣaṇa*) of a visual object, for example, the blue (*nīlaṃ jānāti*), but does not know the common characteristic (*sāmānyalakṣaṇa*): "It is blue" (*no tu nīlam iti*).

ii. In the second moment, mental consciousness—as *buddhipratyakṣa*, but while the contribution of the conascent thought-concomitants (*caitta*) is still weak—"directly discerns" the particular inherent characteristic of the visual object, for example, the blue, i.e., takes the experience of the blue that has just ceased, in a state of recollection, as its object, but does not know yet: "It is blue" (*no tu nīlam iti*).

iii. In the third moment, mental consciousness—when the contribution of the conascent thought-concomitants (*caitta*), in particular ideation (*saṃjñā*), initial inquiry (*vitarka*) and investigation (*vicāra*), as well as understanding (*prajñā*), are strong enough, and being no longer direct perception (*pratyakṣa*)—knows the common characteristic of the visual object through a determination (*nirūpaṇā*), for example: "It is blue", by combining conceptually (*saṃ-√jñā*) the appearance (*nimitta*), name (*nāma*) and the signified (*artha*) of a *dharma*. The generally permeating factor understanding (*prajñā*) that functions at this time can be erroneous.

iv. In the fourth moment, there "might" arise diverse manners of actual speech, etc.

A.3. In the AKB, we find the parts of this wider context, i.e., the relationship to (i) *nāma* and (ii) *nirūpāna*, *vikalpa*, *vitarka* and *vicāra*, mentioned at various places, but never discussed as a whole:

i. As for name (*nāma*), ii. 47ab—discussing the collections of names, phrases and syllables—explains (translation LVP):

> By "names" or "words" (*nāman*) one should understand "that which causes ideation to arise" (*saṃjñākaraṇa*), for example, the words "color", "sound", etc.

However, Collett Cox makes the following important comment (DD.164):

> Both Vasubandhu and Saṅghabhadra define name in terms of concepts (*saṃjñā*). Vasubandhu identifies name simply as *saṃjñākaraṇa*, which Yaśomitra interprets [WOG.182.32ff.] in two ways. [1] It can be understood either as a dependent determinative compound (*tatpuruṣa*): that is, "[name is] the maker of concepts", or "that by which the mental factor, concept, is made or produced". Or, [2] the compound can be interpreted as a descriptive determinative (*karmadhāraya*) used exocentrically (*bahuvrīhi*): that is, "[name is] that of which the maker is concepts". In other words, Yaśomitra suggests a reciprocal functioning, whereby name is either the cause of concepts, or concepts are the cause of names. P'u-kuang cites both of these interpretations and adds a third, whereby name and concept are identified with one another. However, Yaśomitra observes that name and concept must be distinct "for if

name were said to be precisely concept, it would be possible for [name] to be a mental factor", and name is, instead, classified among the dissociated factors.

AKB iii. 30cd further clarifies the notion of name (*nāma*) and *saṃjñā*'s role within mental consciousness alluded to above:

> *Adhivacana* (designation) means *name* (*nāma*). Now, a name is the additional cognitive object or the cognitive object *par excellence* (*adhikam ālambana*) of contact associated with the mental consciousness. In fact, it is said:
>
> > Through visual consciousness, one knows blue; but one does not know: "This is blue"; through mental consciousness, one knows blue and one knows: "This is blue".

Saṃghabhadra explains (Ny, 506c) that it is "additional" because mental consciousness takes both *nāma* and *artha* as its object, whereas the five sensory consciousnesses, having only a weak *saṃjñā*, do not take *nāma* as their perceptual objects. In this context, Dhammajoti refers to a longer version of the above quote (*Vijñāna-kāya-śāstra*, T26, 559bc), which shows the first three moments of the moment-by-moment time line presented above:

> [a] The visual consciousness can only apprehend a blue colour (*nīlam*), but not "it is blue" (*no ti nīlam iti*). [b] Mental consciousness can also apprehend a blue colour. [But] so long as it is not yet able to apprehend its name, it cannot apprehend "it is blue". [c] When it can apprehend its name, then it can also apprehend "it is blue".

ii. As for the close relationship of ideation with determination (*nirūpaṇā*), conceptual construction (*vikalpa*), initial inquiry (*vitarka*) and investigation (*vicāra*), AKB i. 33ab clarifies the notion *abhinirūpaṇa-vikalpa* within its discussion of the doctrinal perspective "associated with initial inquiry (*vitarka*) and investigation (*vicāra*) & free from conceptual construction (*avikalpaka*)", which have already been mentioned as being part of the wider context of *saṃjñā*. AKB i. 33ab distinguishes three kinds of conceptual construction (*vikalpa*):

a. conceptualizing activity in its intrinsic nature (*svabhāvavikalpa*);
b. conceptualizing activity consisting of determination (*nirūpaṇā*; *abhinirūpaṇā*);
c. conceptualizing activity consisting of recollecting (*anusmaraṇa*).

The first refers to initial inquiry (*vitarka*), which will be studied at ii. 33, where it is defined together with investigation (*vicāra*) simply as grossness and subtleness of thought, respectively.

The second refers to "mental" understanding (*prajñā*; ii. 24), i.e., the discernment of the factors associated with the mental consciousness only [i.e., not with the sensory consciousnesses], when dispersed (*vyagra*) [i.e., non-concentrated (*asamāhita*), not in the state of meditating (*bhāvanā*; viii. 1)].

The third refers to all recollection (*smṛti*) that is exclusively "mental", when either concentrated (*samāhita*) or non-concentrated.

The five sensory consciousnesses, even though always associated with initial inquiry and investigation, as well as ideation (*saṃjñā*), are spoken of as being *free from conceptualizing activity* (*avikalpaka*) in the sense of being "free of the second and third conceptualizing activity", whereas mental consciousness involves all three. But as we have seen in the discussion above, the contribution of the conascent thought-concomitants (*caitta*)—in the context of sensory consciousnesses—is in general regarded as being weak, at least in contrast to conceptual mental consciousness. This layered approach seems to be reflected also in the explanation of *vitarka* and *vicāra* in the *Avatāra* (p. 83):

> Reasoning (*vitarka*) has the characteristic of causing thought to be gross with regard to an object (*cittaudāryalakṣaṇa*). It is also named discriminative reflection (*saṃkalpadvitvīyanāmā*). Struck by the wind of ideation (*saṃjñāpavanoddhata*), it operates (*vartate*) in a gross manner. It is this *dharma* which serves as the projecting cause (*pañcavijñāna-pravṛtti-hetu*) of the five consciousnesses.
>
> Investigation (*vicāra*) has the characteristic of causing thought to be subtle. It is this *dharma* which serves as the cause that accords with the operation of mental consciousness on its object (*manovijñāna-pravṛttyanukūla-hetu*).

Thus since *vitarka* is "more" related with the sensory consciousnesses and *vicāra* "more" with mental consciousness, it is now more apparent why Vasubandhu (i. 33a) as well as Saṃghabhadra (Ny, 349a, 350b) explain *svabhāvavikalpa* as *vitarka* only.

On a coarser temporal level or "stages" timeline, in contrast to a subtle temporal level or "moment-by-moment" timeline as presented above, we may now distinguish two main stages in which ideation plays a major role: (*1*) the initial stage and (*2*) the subsequent interpretive stage, which Dhammajoti seems to have in mind when stating (ADCP.103):

> In addition to grasping the mere object-substance, thanks to contribution from the conascent concomitants—particularly understanding (*prajñā*) and recollection (*smṛti*) and ideation (*saṃjñā*) which can function strongly therein—mental consciousness can also interpret a given perceptual data, and even abstractize and conceptualize on it. In Abhidharma terms, it can perceive both the specific as well as the common characteristics. This interpretive capability of mental consciousness is generically indicated by the term *vikalpa*, "discrimination". The Sarvāstivāda speaks of three types of *vikalpa*.

Returning now to our discussion of *abhinirūpaṇa-vikalpa* that is conjoined only with mental consciousness, it is equated (ADCP.104, 108) particularly with the aspect of judgmental investigation of *prajñā*, represented by *saṃtīraṇa*, when *prajñā* is called view (*dṛṣṭi*), whereby it is good to keep in mind that this non-concentrated *prajñā* "derives its name from the fact that it operates by way of determining (計度而轉; *abhirūpaṇayā pravartate*) the names of the corresponding [cognitive objects]". Dhammajoti stresses (ADCP.107–8) that—besides *prajñā*—ideation (*saṃjñā*) is also a contributing factor for the *abhinirūpaṇa* through its functioning as a synthetic comprehension of appearance (*nimitta*), name (*nāma*) and the signified (*artha*). As we have seen it is because of the contribution from *saṃjñā* that mental consciousness is able to operate by means of name (= *adhivacana*). The connection between *abhinirūpāna* and *saṃjñā* is also obvious in Sthiramati's definition of *saṃjñā* (TVB.21) given above.

Dhammajoti summarizes some of the main features of the role of *saṃjñā* in the following way (ADCP.108–9):

> According to the Sarvāstivāda, *saṃjñā* is the cause of *vitarka*, and *vitarka* is in turn the cause for the arising of a sensory consciousness. At this stage, there is a simple

inquiry or searching on the mere object grasped, in the form "what is it?". ... Some kind of inarticulate mental inquiry is involved here. The Sarvāstivāda perspective may be understood to conceive of this as a contribution coming from the co-nascent thought-concomitants, *saṃjñā*, *prajñā* and *smṛti*—which all operate weakly—and *vitarka*. ... At the same time, a sensory consciousness is said to be distinguished from mental consciousness by its lack of *abinirūpaṇā-vikalpa* on account of its not taking name as its object. This must then mean that, for the Sarvāstivāda, in a sensory perception, the "wind of *saṃjñā*" is strong enough only for a rudimentary determination, in a generic manner, of the object as a thing in itself, but not for conceptualization based on judgement and association. In other words, *saṃjñā* could be considered as the cause of the intrinsic discrimination (= *vitarka*) that is present in all acts of consciousness, but when *prajñā* and *smṛti* operate prominently in a mental consciousness, it also functions to assist in the conceptualizing act involving name. *Vitarka*, though not subsumed as a universal thought-concomitant, is nonetheless always present at the arising of a sensory perception. It is in fact considered the latter's cause, evidently in the sense that it makes the main contribution in such a rudimentary discrimination as regards the object's appearance (*nimitta*) that constitutes the grasping of an object by a sensory consciousness.

A.4. As for *saṃjñā*'s relation to the other aggregates, i. 22bd describes the five aggregates from the point of view of (i) their relative grossness, (ii) their being causes of the progression of pollution, (iii) analogy and (iv) their predominance in the three realms. As for the first, ideation is described as being less gross than the first two aggregates but more gross than the last two aggregates. As for the second, attachment to the enjoyment of sensation is described as proceeding from mistaken ideations (*saṃjñāviparyāsa*), which are due to the defilements (*kleśa*) that are formations (*saṃskāra*).

Before ending our comments on the first bigger category, we want to mention again that it is probable that for the Dārṣṭāntika Dharmatrāta *saṃjñā* is one of the three thought-concomitants that he accepts as being real entities, as does the Sautrāntika Śrīlāta. On the other hand, Buddhadeva accepts only *citta* as a real entity and thus denies a real entity status to any of the thought-concomitants.

B. Now as for the second bigger category, i.e., *saṃjñā* in its role within meditation and the general Buddhist path to liberation, etc., we must first refer again to AKB i. 21 which states that sensation and ideation are separate aggregates (*skandha*) because of their great importance as the predominant causes (*pradhānahetu*) (1) of the two roots of dispute (*vivāda*), i.e., attachment to pleasures (*kāma*) and attachment to views (*dṛṣṭi*), and (2) of cyclic existence (*saṃsāra*).

In this context we also must keep in mind that, in the third moment of our moment-by-moment time line—when the contribution of the conascent thought-concomitants (*caitta*) is strong enough, in particular initial inquiry (*vitarka*) and investigation (*vicāra*), understanding (*prajñā*) and recollection (*smṛti*), and when ideation conceptually combines (*saṃ-√jñā*) the appearance (*nimitta*), name (*nāma*) and the signified (*artha*) of a *dharma*—mental consciousness can become erroneous since the generally permeating factor understanding (*prajñā*) that functions at this time can be erroneous, particularly when influenced by defilements (*kleśa*). This is pointed out in i. 22bd, which states that attachment to the enjoyment of sensation is described as proceeding from mistaken ideations (*saṃjñāviparyāsa*), which are due to the defilements (*kleśa*) that are formations (*saṃskāra*).

From these points of view it is no surprise that we find in the Buddhist path specific practices such as calm abiding (*śamatha*) or an emphasis on the five praxis-oriented faculties, for example, concentration (*samādhi*), mindfulness (*smṛti*), understanding (*prajñā*), etc., in order to curb or completely eliminate (i) initial inquiry (*vitarka*) and investigation (*vicāra*), sensation (*vedanā*) and ideation (*saṃjñā*), and (ii) the "trouble" that they can cause when combined with defilements (*kleśa*).

As for *vitarka* and *vicāra*, there is the intermediate meditation (*dhyānāntara*), which is specified as being free from the manifestation of *vitarka*, and the second to eighth fundamental meditative attainments, specified as being free from the manifestation of *vitarka* and *vicāra* (viii. 23cd).

As for *saṃjñā*, there is the perception-sphere of neither-ideation-nor-non-ideation (*naiva-saṃjñānāsaṃjñāyatana*), which receives its name from the fact that ideation (*saṃjñā*) is very weak (*mṛdu*) in it, although not completely absent. In this connection, AKB viii. 4cd states:

> No doubt, one prepares oneself for this formless meditative attainment by considering: "Ideation (*saṃjñā*) is a disease! Ideation is a tumor! Ideation is an arrow! The state of non-ideation (*āsaṃjñika*; compare ii. 41b) is stupor (*saṃmoha*)! The perception-sphere of neither-ideation-nor-non-ideation (*naivasaṃjñānāsaṃjñāāyatana*) is calmness, is excellent!"

But we also find the tendency and desire to abandon the manifestation of *saṃjñā* completely, at least for an extended period of time, as in regard to (1–2) the two attainments (*samāpatti*), i.e., (i) the attainment of non-ideation (*asamjīsamāpatti*) and (ii) the attainment of cessation (*nirodhasamāpatti*) or the attainment of cessation of ideation and sensation (*saṃjñāvedita-nirodhasamāpatti*), and (3) the state of non-ideation (*āsaṃjñika*).

The "negative" role that *saṃjñā* plays in this context can be seen from the names given to some of these practices, attainments and states.

Since the AKB not only discusses the issues related to the second bigger category in detail but also fairly systematically in the entire chapter 8, entitled EXPOSITION OF THE MEDITATIVE ATTAINMENTS (*samāpattinirdeśa*), and in chapter 2, pp. F 198–214, there is no further need to discuss them here.

200 *LS*: AH 9; SAH 10, 12.

201 *Gokhale*: [15ab1] *caturbhyo 'nye tu saṃskāraskandha*

Tib.: [15a] *'du byed phung po bzhi las gzhan |*

LVP: On the *saṃskāras*, *Théorie des douze causes*, pp. 9–12 (see *Electronic Appendix*).

LS: 1. Vasubandhu's *Pañcaskandhaka* (2008) explains the *saṃskāras* as follows:

> 4. *saṃskārāḥ katame | vedanāsañjñābhyām anye caitasikā dharmāś cittaviprayuktāś ca ||*
>
> 4.1 *caitasikā dharmāḥ katame | ye dharmāś cittena samprayuktāḥ || te punaḥ katame |*

sparśo manaskāro vedanā sañjñā cetanā cchando 'dhimokṣaḥ smṛtiḥ samādhiḥ prajñā śraddhā hrīr apatrāpyam alobhaḥ kuśalamūlam adveṣaḥ kuśalamūlam amohaḥ kuśalamūlaṃ vīryaṃ praśrabdhir apramāda upekṣā 'vihiṃsā rāgaḥ pratigho māno 'vidyā dṛṣṭir vicikitsā krodha upanāho mrakṣaḥ pradāsa īrṣyā mātsaryaṃ māyā śāṭhyaṃ mado vihiṃsā āhrīkyam anapatrāpyaṃ styānam auddhatyam āśraddhyaṃ kausīdyaṃ pramādo muṣitasmṛtitā vikṣepo 'samprajanyaṃ kaukṛtyaṃ middhaṃ vitarko vicāraś ca ||

eṣāṃ pañca sarvatragāḥ pañca pratiniyataviṣayā ekādaśa kuśalāḥ ṣaṭ kleśā avaśiṣṭā upakleśāś catvāro 'nyathāpi || [...]

4.2 *cittaviprayuktāḥ saṃskārāḥ katame* | *ye rūpacittacaitasikāvasthāsu prajñapyante tattvānyatvataś ca na prajñapyante* || *te punaḥ katame* | *prāptir asañjñisamāpattir nirodhasamāpattir āsañjñikaṃ jīvitendriyaṃ nikāyasabhāgatā jātir jarā sthitir anityatā nāmakāyāḥ padakāyā vyañjanakāyāḥ pṛthagjanatvam ity evambhāgīyāḥ* | [...]

4. What are the formations? The mental factors other than feeling and conception, and the entities that do not accompany consciousness.

4.1 What are the mental factors? Those entities that are concomitants of consciousness. What are they? Contact, attention, [...] and reflection.

Among these, five are universal, five are limited to a particular object, eleven are virtues, six are [root] mental afflictions, the remaining ones are secondary mental afflictions, and four can also vary. [...]

4.2 What are the formations that do not accompany consciousness? They are [entities] that are nominally ascribed to a particular state of form, consciousness, or the mental factors. They are not [entities that are] ascribed to [form, consciousness, or the mental factors] themselves or to something distinct from them. What, then, are they? Acquirement, [...] as well as those [other entities] that are of the same kind. ISBP.231 and 237f.

2. As for the AKB, for a detailed and systematic explanation of all the factors included in the aggregate of formations, see chapter 2, pp. 150–244, which discusses:

i. Forty-six formations associated with thought (*cittasaṃprayuktsaṃskāra*) or thought-concomitants (*caitta*) included in the following six groups:

   a. ten generally permeating factors (*mahābhūmika*), those that accompany all thoughts (ii. 24);
   b. ten wholesome permeating factors (*kuśalamahābhūmika*), those that accompany every wholesome thought (ii. 25);
   c. six permeating factors of defilement (*kleśamahābhūmika*), those that accompany every defiled thought (ii. 26ac);
   d. two unwholesome permeating factors (*akuśalamahābhūmika*), those that accompany every unwholesome thought (ii. 26cd);
   e. ten factors of defilement of restricted scope (*parīttakleśabhūmika*), which have the restricted defilement for their stage (ii. 27);
   f. eight undetermined factors (*aniyata*) (ii. 27).

ii. Fourteen formations dissociated from thought (*cittaviprayuktasaṃskāra*; ii. 35–48).

As for the thought-concomitants intention (*cetanā*), defilements (*kleśa*), understanding (*prajñā*) and concentration (*samādhi*), they are, respectively, discussed further in great detail in chapter 4: EXPOSITION OF ACTION (*karmanirdeśa*); chapter 5: EXPOSITION OF THE PROCLIVITIES (*anuśaya-nirdeśa*); chapter 7: EXPOSITION OF THE COGNITIONS (*jñānanirdeśa*); chapter 8: EXPOSITION OF THE MEDITATIVE ATTAINMENTS (*samāpattinirdeśa*).

The five praxis-oriented faculties, but in particular mindfulness (*smṛti*) and understanding (*prajñā*), are discussed in great detail in chapter 6: EXPOSITION OF THE PATH AND THE NOBLE ONES (*mārgapudgalanirdeśa*).

The second member of the twelvefold dependent origination (*pratītyasamutpāda*; see iii. 18–38c) is called *karma*-formations (*saṃskāra*). For its definition and meaning within the four types of dependent origination, i.e., momentary (*kṣanika*), prolonged (*prākarṣikā*), connected (*sāṃbandhika*), pertaining to states (*āvasthika*), see chapter 3, but as for the fourth type, i.e., within a three-life-times model, it is defined as follows: "(*Karma-*)formations (*saṃskāra*) are, in a previous life, the state of [wholesome, unwholesome or non-defined] action [of the five aggregates]."

202 *LS*: In order to make the *saṃskāras* (when referring to the *saṃskāraskandha*) easier to distinguish from the *saṃskāras* (when referring to the conditioning forces in general), from now onwards we will translate the former as *formations* and the latter as conditioning forces.

203 *LS*: SAH 12.

204 *LVP*: *saṃskāraskandhaḥ katamaḥ | ṣac cetanākāyāḥ*. – Compare *Saṃyutta*, iii. 60 *katame ca bhikkhave saṃkhārā | chayime cetanākāyā | rūpasaṃcetanā ... dhammasaṃcetanā*; *Vibhaṅga*, p. 144; *Sumaṅgalavilāsinī*, p. 64.

LS: Bhikkhu Bodhi translates *Saṃyutta*, iii. 60, as follows: "And what, *bhikkhus*, are volitional formations? There are these six classes of volition: volition regarding forms, volition regarding sounds, volition regarding odours, volition regarding tastes, volition regarding tactile objects, volition regarding mental phenomena."

Collett Cox summarizes (EIP.VIII.655f.) the exchange in Saṃghabhadra's *Nyāyānusāra (338c):

> The conditioning aggregate [*saṃskāraskandha*] includes all conditioning factors—those associated with thought and those dissociated from both thought and material form—except for those included in the other four aggregates.
>
> Objection (by the Dārṣṭāntika teacher Śrīlāta): All [those] conditioning factors are merely varieties of thinking [*cetanā*].
>
> Answer: This interpretation is not justified. The aggregate of conditioning factors is often represented by thinking because thinking [*cetanā*] is the essence of action [*karma*], is predominant in the development of the effects of action, and therefore is the primary factor among the conditioning aggregates. However, the conditioning aggregate as a whole karmically prepares other conditioned and contaminating factors.
>
> Śrīlāta: "Karmically developing conditioning factors" means that thought creates conditioning factors that were originally nonexistent.

> Answer: We Abhidharma masters maintain that factors in their essential nature exist as actual entities. Only nominal entities can be said to exist after being originally nonexistent. "Developing" means projecting the production of an effect: though the effect already exists in its essential nature as an actual entity, its activity can be projected and then produced.

As for Dharmatrāta, even though MVŚ, 8c, states: "(b) The Venerable (尊者) Dharmatrāta asserts thus: the *citta-caitta*-s are specific [modes of] *cetanā*", such brief statements need interpretation. See in this context ADCP, chapter 7.1: The *citta-caitta* doctrine of Bhadanta Dharmatrāta, pp. 114–20, where Dhammajoti comments:

> [F]or Dharmatrāta, *cetanā* is the main terminology for the mind in activity, of which *citta* as well as *caitta*-s are specific modes. That is to say, *cetanā* in statement (b) does not seem to mean volition in the specific sense of the same term for one of the ten *mahābhūmika dharma*-s of the Ābhidharmikas. Rather, being derived from the same root ($\sqrt{}$*cit*) as *citta*, it seems to be taken to denote the sense of "consciousness", "awareness" or "activity of thinking". Accordingly, given Dharmatrāta's position that the *citta-caitta-dharma*-s arise successively, the statement that *citta-caitta*-s are specific [modes of] *cetanā*, coupled with the doctrine that *caitta*-s are not identical with *citta*, seems to mean: *citta* as it arises in the present moment is consciousness (*vijñāna*), and the *caitta*-s which arise subsequently in a succession are not identical with the consciousness in the first moment, but are distinct modes—just as consciousness/thought is a distinct mode—of the mental flow. However, given the general outlook of the Dārṣṭāntikas—of whom Dharmatrāta is a prominent member—it is probable that Dharmatrāta accepts *vedanā* and *saṃjñā* too as such distinct modes, since these two mental *dharma*-s are usually mentioned together with *cetanā* in the *sūtra*-s whose authority the Dārṣṭāntikas uphold.

205 *LVP*: Intention is action (iv. 1), the cause of birth (*upapatti*), in contrast with craving, the cause of the re-existence (*abhinirvṛtti*) (vi, F 137f.):

> [Question:] – (1) What should one understand by birth (*upapatti*)? (2) What should one understand by re-existence (*abhinirvṛtti*)?
>
> [Answer:] – 1. By birth, one should understand a birth or an existence characterized by a certain realm (*dhātu*; the realm of desire, etc.), a certain plane of existence (*gati*; god, human, etc.), a certain mode of birth (*yoni*; birth from the womb, from the egg), a certain gender, etc.
>
> 2. By re-existence, one should understand the re-existence without qualification.

LS: As we can see clearly from his endnote, LVP reads the whole section here as being oriented toward future birth, i.e., focusing mainly on *cetanā*'s more long term effect. Later, at ii. 24, *cetanā* is defined as a generally permeating factor, focusing mainly on the present thought (*citta*) as karmic cause:

> Intention (*cetanā*; *sems pa*) is that which instigates or causes thought to be [karmically] creative (*cittābhisaṃskāra*; *cittaprasyanda*); it is mental action (*manaskarma*).

Saṃghabhadra defines (SA.IV.217):

Cetanā is that which causes *citta* to do *kuśala*, *akuśala* and *avyākṛta* [*karma*], resulting in good, bad and neutral [*vipāka*]. On account of the existence of *cetanā*, the *citta* has the activity of moving forth (有動作用) with regard to the object. It is like a magnet, owing to the force of which iron can move forth.

According to the Vaibhāṣikas, every intention is action, but not every action is intention; for example, bodily and vocal action are not intention (iv. 1b).

As for the relationship of the ripening cause (*vipākahetu*) and action (*karma*) according to the Vaibhāṣikas, we could formulate the following tetralemma: (1) there are factors that are only action but not a ripening cause, for example, non-defined actions; (2) there are factors that are only a ripening cause but not action, for example, sensation associated with a wholesome intention; (3) there are factors that are both a ripening cause and action, for example, wholesome intention (*cetanā*) or wholesome bodily and vocal action; (4) there are factors that are neither, for example, space (*ākāśa*) or sensation associated with a non-defined intention.

206 *LVP*: That is to say: "Because it conditions that which should be conditioned", as one says: "Cook the porridge that should be cooked."

207 *LVP*: 1. *Saṃyutta*, iii. 87: *saṃkhatam abhisaṃkharontīti bhikkhave tasmā saṃkhārā ti vuccanti | kiñ ca saṃkhatam abhisaṃkharonti | rūpaṃ rūpattāya saṃkhatam abhisaṃkharonti | vedanaṃ vedanattāya*… .

2. *Saṃyutta*, v. 449: *jātisaṃvattanike 'pi saṃkhāre abhisaṃkharonti | jarāsaṃvattanike 'pi… | maraṇasaṃvattanike 'pi… | te jātisaṃvattanike 'pi samkhāre abhisaṃkharitvā … jātipapātam pi papatanti | …*

3. *abhisaṃskaraṇalakṣaṇāḥ saṃskārāḥ* (*Madhyamakavṛtti*, 343, 9); *cittābhisaṃskāramanaskāralakṣaṇā cetanā* (ibid. 311, 1); *raktaḥ san rāgajaṃ karmābhisaṃskaroti* (ibid. 137, 7; *Mahāvastu*, i. 26 and 391).

208 *LVP*: *nāham ekadharmam apy anabhijñāya aparijñāya duḥkhasyāntakriyāṃ vadāmi.*

<u>LS</u>: The *Vyākhyā* glosses [WOG.37.31ff.] that *anabhijñāya* and *aparijñāya* refer, respectively, either to the mundane path and supramundane path, or to the path of insight and path of cultivation.

209 <u>LS</u>: Cox writes (DD.68): "Th[e] newly established category of discrete factors dissociated from both thought and form presented a challenge to the traditional methods of classifying all experienced phenomena. The traditional lists of the five aggregates (*skandha*), the twelve sense spheres (*āyatana*), and name and form (*nāmarūpa*) were ill-suited to incorporate factors that are neither thought nor form, nor associated with either. […] The inclusion of these dissociated forces within the *saṃskāraskandha* contributed to a certain tension in the meaning of the term *saṃskāra* evident in later Abhidharma discussions of the term, … .

The challenge presented by these discrete dissociated forces to the traditional categories of factors contributed significantly to the creation of new taxonomies: specifically, the new fivefold taxonomy of form (*rūpa*), thought (*citta*), thought concomitants (*caitta*), dissociated forces (*cittaviprayuktasaṃskāra*), and unconditioned forces (*asaṃskṛtadharma*)." See ii. F 143.

210 <u>LS</u>: AH 9; SAH 10, 15.

211 *Gokhale*: [15b2–d] *ete punas trayaḥ | dharmāyatanadhātvākhyāḥ sahā 'vijñaptyasaṃ-*

skṛtaiḥ ||

Tib.: [15bd] *de gsum rnam rig byed min dang* | *'dus ma byas rnams bcas pa ni* | *chos kyi skye mched khams zhes bya* ||

LS: 1. Although the sense-sphere of factors (*dharmāyatana*) and the element of factors (*dharmadhātu*)—the object of mental consciousness (*manovijñāna*)—are here defined as being limited to seven factors, at other places in the AKB the object of mental consciousness is referred to as including all factors. For example, i. 48a, the twentieth doctrinal perspective, discusses which elements (*dhātu*) are cognized (*vijñeya*) by consciousness and states:

> (*1*) Visible forms, (*2*) sounds, (*3*) odors, (*4*) tastes and (*5*) tangibles are known (*anubhūta*) by the consciousnesses (*1*) of the eye, (*2*) of the ear, (*3*) of the nose, (*4*) of the tongue and (*5*) of the body, respectively. They are all [also] cognized (*vijñeya*) by the mental consciousness (*manovijñāna*). Each of these external elements is thus cognized by two consciousnesses.
>
> The other thirteen elements, not being of the object-field (*viṣaya*) of the [five groups of] sensory consciousness, are cognized by the mental consciousness alone.

Or, AKB ii. 62c, discussing the cognitive object condition (*ālambanapratyaya*), states:

> 62c. All factors are the cognitive object (*ālambana*) of consciousness [i.e., the cognitive object condition].
>
> All factors (*dharma*), i.e., the conditioned (*saṃskṛta*) as well as the unconditioned (*asaṃskṛta*) factors, are a cognitive object condition of thoughts and thought-concomitants (*cittacaitta*), accordingly as the case applies (*yathāyogaṃ*): for example, visual consciousness (*cakṣurvijñāna*) and the thought-concomitants, i.e., sensation, etc., associated with it, have all visible forms [*rūpa*] for their cognitive object; auditory consciousness, sounds; olfactory consciousness, odors; tactile consciousness, tangibles. [On the other hand,] mental consciousness (*manovijñāna*) and the thought-concomitants associated with it have all the factors [*sarvadharma*] for their cognitive object. [With respect to the mental faculty (*manas*), verse 62c is thus understood literally.]

But as for "all factors", i. 39bc comments:

> There is no factor in regard to which mental consciousness, being without limit (*ananta manovijñāna*), has not arisen or is not destined to arise. All noble ones (*āryapudgala*), in fact, necessarily produce the thought: "All factors are non-self" (*sarvadharmā anātmāna*; vii. 13a). Now it is true that this thought bears neither on itself (*svabhāva*) nor on the factors which are co-existing (*sahabhū*; ii. 50b) with it; but this [(first) moment (*kṣaṇa*)] of thought and the factors co-existing with it are the cognitive object [*ālambana*] of a second moment of thought which sees that all factors are non-self; thus "all factors" are indeed included within the cognitive object of these two moments of thought (vii. 18cd).

AKB vii. 18cd further specifies:

> When a moment of conventional cognition (*saṃvṛtijñāna*) cognizes all factors as not being a "self", that is by excluding, from the totality of factors,

i. itself, this same moment of conventional cognition, for the subject of cognition cannot be its own object (*viṣayiviṣayabhedāt*);
ii. the mental factors (*caitta*) associated with it, for they have the same cognitive object as it does (*ekālambanatvāt*);
iii. the factors dissociated from thought (*viprayukta*) which accompany it (*sahabhū*), for example, its characteristics (*lakṣaṇa*; ii. 45c), for they are too close.

Thus in the AKB we have two incongruent interpretations regarding the object of mental consciousness, one maintaining that it consists of seven *dharma*s and the other that it consists of all *dharma*s.

2. If we now look into the historical records regarding the *dharmadhātu*, Dhammajoti comments (SA.IV.30f.):

> We must remember that originally in the *sūtra*-s, the 18-*dhātu* taxonomy was a pragmatic classificatory scheme, mainly employed to underscore the Buddha's no-Self doctrine. This scheme was intended to show the correlation between the six faculties of a human being with their corresponding objects and the consciousnesses generated. It is essentially an epistemological consideration without any explicit ontological commitment. In this scheme, *dharma-dhātu* corresponded to the objects of the mind and mental consciousness just as the visibles corresponded to those of the eye and visual consciousness. When this scheme (together with those of the *skandha*- and *āyatana*-taxonomies) came to be adopted as a methodology of *dharma-pravicaya*, what is the Abhidharmic principle that it was made to represent? ... In the words of the MVŚ, "these 18 *dhātu*-s are established on the basis of (intrinsic) characteristic". ... The consideration in terms of intrinsic characteristic would mean, among other things, that the specific items assigned to each of the 18 *dhātu*-s must represent ultimate real existents (i.e., *dharma*-s in the proper Abhidharmic sense). Accordingly, even though the mind can think of all kinds of things, the *dharma-dhātu* cannot be said to comprise objects that are relatively real.

This is clear from the items enumerated [below] in the MVŚ, the *Vijñānakāya* and *Prakaraṇa-śastra* as objects cognized by mental consciousness (eye ... mental consciousness), which may be said to be still in keeping with the intent of the *sūtra*s.

MVŚ, 370c, as well as the earlier *Prakaraṇa-śāstra* (T 26, 699a), state:

> What is *dharmadhātu*? *Dharma*-s that have been, are being and will be cognized by the mind are called *dharmadhātu*.

Here *dharmadhātu* clearly refers to the mental objects as being cognized in the three times, which should include—for the orthodox Vaibhāṣikas—all possible "categories" of *dharma*s, as explicitly stated in the *Vijñāna-kāya-śāstra* (T 26, 546c):

> What does mental consciousness cognize? Mental consciousness cognizes: eye, visibles and visual consciousness; ear, sounds and auditory consciousness; nose, odors and olfactory consciousness; tongue, tastes and gustatory consciousness; body, tangibles and bodily consciousness; mind, *dharma*-s (mental objects) and mental consciousness.

Thus it includes even mind, objects of mind and mental consciousness.

But then, at least starting from the *Jñānaprasthāna*, *dharmadhātu* is referred to or implied as "seven *dharmas*" by the orthodox Vaibhāṣikas, seemingly influenced by their five-group taxonomy (*pañcavastuka*; SA.IV.35ff.) that had gradually become their standard classification of *dharmas*, which includes the *avijñapti-rūpa* and the three unconditioned factors.

Thus the *Jñānaprasthāna* (T 26, 1027b), as well as AKB i. 18ab, can state that all of the factors are included (*saṃgraha*) in the aggregate of material form (*rūpaskandha*), the sense-sphere of the mental faculty (*mana-āyatana*) and the element of factors (*dharmadhātu*), and not just in the *dharmadhātu*. On the other hand, the Sautrāntika Śrīlāta maintains that all *dharmas* are subsumed under the *dharmāyatana*. Although this is repudiated by Saṃghabhadra, he also seemed to speak at times explicitly—apparently under the shadow of the *sūtra* tradition—of the *dharmāyatana* as the cognitive objects corresponding to mental consciousness (Ny, 448b):

> The totality of *dharma*-s is just the twelve *āyatana*-s, i.e., the visual, auditory, olfactory, gustatory and mental consciousness, with their corresponding cognitive objects, the visibles, sound, odors, tastes tangibles and *dharma*-s.

3. But we also find in the above passages a second incongruity concerning the Sarvāstivāda explanation on *dharmāyatana* and *dharmadhātu*, namely, in regard to material form (*rūpa*), i.e., the sense-faculties (*indriya*), which in fact can be cognized only by thought but are not included among the "seven *dharmas*". Dhammajoti explains (SA.IV.33):

> The reason for this, however, is not far to seek. In keeping with the classification in the *sūtra*, the six faculties must be retained as the corresponding supporting bases (*āśraya*) of the six types of consciousness generated by the six corresponding types of object. This means that the *dharma*-s, constituting the *dharmāyatana* and *dharmadhātu*, must not be comingled with the five sensory faculties or the mental faculty (the mind). The five sensory faculties must be retained as five of the ten traditional subdivisions of matter. The mental faculty likewise has to be separated from the mental objects. The result is that the *dharmadhātu* then came to subsume all the remaining *dharma*-s qua mental objects excluding the five sensory objects, the six faculties and the six consciousnesses. It must of course further take in the non-information matter, the conditionings disjoined from thought and the three unconditioned which were newly established as real entities by the orthodoxy.

4. As for a discussion of the reasons why only the object of mental consciousness receives the name of *dharmāyatana* even though all *āyatanas* are *dharmas*, see AKB i. 24.

As for the *skandhas*, it is good to keep in mind, as later pointed out (i. 22ab), that even though Vasubandhu inserts here into his general discussion of the five aggregates a correlation of the *skandhas* with the *āyatanas* and *dhātus*, the scheme of the five aggregates does not include the three unconditioned factors.

212 *LS*: We have already mentioned above that even though *avijñapti* is classified as secondary matter (*bhautika*), it is a special case of *rūpa* since it is invisible (*anidarśana*), non-resistant (*apratigha*), does not occupy space, does not have the nature of *rūpaṇa* and is not atomic in nature. Although it is said to be of the nature of *rūpa* since the fundamental material

elements that constitute its basis (*aśraya*) are resistant material form, it is also included as a special case under *dharmāyatana* and *dharmadhātu*, rather than *rūpāyatana*, which is justified (iv. F 16: fifth reason) with the *Elephant-simile sūtra* reference to a specific *rūpa* included in the *dharmāyatana*. Further, it can only be cognized by mental consciousness (*manovijñāna*).

[213] *LS*: AH 8; SAH 9, 15, 20, 26.

[214] *Gokhale*: [16a] *vijñānaṃ prativijñaptir*

Tib.: [16a] *rnam shes so sor rnam rig pa* |

LVP: *citta* and *caitta*, see ii, F 177.

LS: As for the definitions of *vijñāna* in the *Pañcaskandhaka* and the *Avatāra*, see endnote to ii. 34ab.

Here Vasubandhu provides the often quoted definition of consciousness (*vijñāna*), before presenting the sixfold classification of consciousness and linking up the aggregate of consciousness with the sense-spheres (*āyatana*) and elements (*dhātu*). Since this is again only a fairly brief presentation on a very important subject, what other aspects does Vasubandhu discuss later in the AKB?

1. As for its relation to the other aggregates, i. 22bd describes the five aggregates from the point of view of (i) their relative grossness, (ii) their being causes of the progression of pollution, (iii) analogy and (iv) their predominance in the three realms. *Vijñāna* is considered to be the most subtle among the non-material aggregates.

2. As for its being included in other lists, AKB i. 28cd discusses *vijñāna* as the sixth member of the six elementary substances, namely as the elementary substance consciousness (*vijñāna-dhātu*), an impure consciousness that does not form part of the noble path.

Vijñāna is also listed as the third member of the twelvefold dependent origination (*pratītya-samutpāda*; see iii. 18–38c). For its definition and meaning within the four types of dependent origination, i.e., momentary (*kṣanika*), prolonged (*prākarṣikā*), connected (*sāṃbandhika*), pertaining to states (*āvasthika*), see chapter 3. But as for the fourth type, i.e., within a three-life-times model, it is defined as follows (iii. 21c): "Consciousness (*vijñāna*) is the (five) aggregates, (in the womb,) at conception (*pratisaṃdhi*)."

3. As for the mental faculty (*manas*; *mano-āyatana*; *manodhātu*), it is briefly discussed (i. 17ab):

> Of the six consciousnesses, the consciousness that has just passed away is the mental faculty.

4. As for the twenty-two doctrinal perspectives, Vasubandhu clarifies (i. 29bc) the distinction between the objects of the sense-faculties and the consciousnesses, wherein the consciousnesses are determined to have both an object-field (*viṣaya*) and a cognitive object (*ālambana*), whereas the sense-faculties can have only an object-field (*viṣaya*).

AKB i. 33a clarifies the difference between the five sensory consciousnesses and the mental consciousness (i) from the point of view of the three conceptual constructions (*vikalpa*), whereby the mental consciousness is described as involving all three and the sensory consciousness as involving only conceptual construction in its intrinsic nature (*svabhāvavikalpa*) and is thus declared to be "free from conceptual construction", i.e., from the second and third conceptual construction. This difference is also (i. 48a) further discussed (ii) from the point of view of which and how many elements (*dhātu*) are cognized (*vijñeya*) by which and by how many consciousnesses. The first five consciousnesses are described as cognizing, each, one element (*dhātu*) only, whereas mental consciousness is described as being able to cognize all eighteen elements. The same difference is, furthermore (i. 23a), discussed (iii) from the point of view of the time period to which the object-field of the sense-faculty and of the mental faculty (*manas*) belongs. Whereas the object-field of the first five sense-faculties can be only present or simultaneous, the object-field of the mental faculty (*manas*; i. 39ab)—depending on whether the *manas* is a sensory consciousness or a mental consciousness—can be either (i) simultaneous (*vartamāna*] to the *manas*; (ii) previous or past [*atīta*]; (iii) later or future [*anāgata*]; (iv) tritemporal [*try-adhva*], i.e., simultaneous, previous and later; (v) outside of time [*anadhva*].

Further, *vijñāna* is discussed at length when addressing (ii. 42) the question of whether it is the eye sense-faculty that sees, as maintained by the Vaibhāṣikas, or whether it is the visual consciousness. In this context Vasubandhu also addresses (ii. 44cd) (i) whether or not the object-field and sense-faculty occur simultaneous with the resulting consciousness, (ii) why the sense-faculty is considered to be its basis (*āśraya*) and not the object-field, (iii) why the sense-faculties are the basis for naming the consciousnesses.

As for the sense-faculties of the consciousnesses, i. 44cd specifies that the sole basis of the mental consciousness is the mental faculty, i.e., the consciousness that has just perished, whereas the basis of the five consciousnesses is twofold: (i) for example, the eye sense-faculty that is simultaneous with the visual consciousness; etc., and (ii) the mental faculty, which is past at the moment when one of these five consciousnesses arises.

5. In chapter 2, Vasubandhu continues his discussion of *vijñāna* within a detailed presentation of thought and thought-concomitants (ii. 23–34), which does not include another formal definition of *vijñāna*, but features a presentation of the etymology of *citta*, *manas* and *vijñāna*. These are treated as synonyms in the Vaibhāṣika system, although distinguished in terms of their different functional aspects of the mind they represent (ii. 34ab):

> 34ab. (i) Thought (*citta*), (ii) mind (*manas*) and (iii) consciousness (*vijñāna*), these names designate the same object-referent [*ekārtha*].
>
> i. The mind is named *citta* (T. *sems*; thought) because it accumulates or collects together (*cinoti*).
>
> ii. It is named *manas* (T. *yid*; mind) because it considers or thinks (*manute*).
>
> iii. It is named *vijñāna* (T. *rnam par shes pa*; consciousness) because it cognizes its cognitive object (*ālambanaṃ vijānāti*).

See MVŚ, 371ab, for a discussion of various other distinctions (SA.IV.212).

For the Yogācārins, however—but only those who maintain eight consciousnesses—*citta*, *manas* and *vijñāna* "also" take on a different significance (BU.226), i.e., *citta* can refer to the *ālaya-vijñāna*, *manas* to the *kliṣṭa-manas* and *vijñāna* to the traditional classification of six forms of sensory and mental consciousnesses.

6. As for the detailed exposition of thought and thought-concomitants, and their relationship,

in ii. 23–34, which occurs within the context of his discussion of the simultaneous arising of thought, thought-concomitants and formations dissociated from thought, Vasubandhu starts out by explaining that, within the orthodox Vaibhāṣika system, thought and thought-concomitants necessarily arise together or simultaneously. Later (ii. 50b–51 and 53cd), this relationship is further specified and discussed as associated cause (*saṃprayuktakahetu*) and as an exemplification of the co-existent cause (*sahabhūhetu*). He then continues (ii. 23c–33) with a very detailed discussion of the forty-six thought concomitants—i.e., the formations associated with thought (*cittasaṃprayuktasaṃskāra*), presenting them in six distinct groups (see chart at ii, F 143)—representing more or less the classic one by the Sarvāstivādins. This includes the discussion (ii. 28–30b) as to which and how many thought-concomitants arise in association with which thought. For example, in regard to the realm of desire (*kāmadhātu*):

i. wholesome (*kuśala*) thought;
ii–iii. unwholesome (*akuśala*) thought, according to whether it is:
– "independent" (*āveṇikī*), i.e., associated with ignorance (*avidyā*) alone, or
– associated with the other defilements, i.e., attachment (*rāga*), etc.;
iv–v. non-defined (*avyākṛta*) thought, i.e., thought that is unproductive in regard to retribution, according to whether it is:
– obscured (*nivṛta*), i.e., associated with the afflicted view of self (*satkāyadṛṣṭi*) or with the afflicted view of holding to an extreme (*antagrāhadṛṣṭi*) (v. 3), or
– unobscured (*anivṛta*), i.e., an effect of retribution (*vipākaja*), etc. (i. 37; ii. 71).

(i) The wholesome thought involves twenty-two thought-concomitants, i.e., ten generally permeating factors, ten wholesome permeating factors, initial inquiry and investigation; (ii–iii) the unwholesome thought, either twenty or twenty-one thought-concomitants; and (iv–v) the non-defined thought, eighteen or twelve thought-concomitants. But all involve ten generally permeating factors, which are therefore of special importance, being distinct forces that together make possible the operation of consciousness. Here it should be pointed out that the acceptance of the doctrine of the *mahābhūmika*s was far from being unanimous within the early Sarvāstivāda lineage; for example, for Dharmatrāta, the *citta-caitta* "arise successively and not simultaneously, like a group of merchants who pass through a narrow road one by one" (SA.IV.225), and for Buddhadeva, there is no *caitta* apart from the *citta*.

7. Vasubandhu ends his detailed exposition (ii. 23–34) by presenting the five equivalences (*samatā*; ii. 34d), due to which thought and thought-concomitants are associated:

i. equivalence with respect to basis [or sense-faculty] (*āśraya*; *rten*);
ii. equivalence with respect to cognitive object (*ālambana*; *dmigs*);
iii. equivalence with respect to aspect or a mode of activity (*ākāra*; *rnam pa*);
iv. equivalence with respect to time [of occurrence of the activity of thought and thought-concomitants] (*kāla*; *dus*);
v. equivalence with respect to the number of real entities [or the singular instance of the occurrence of a real entity or the status as real entities] (*dravya*; *rdzas*).

But although he ends his discussion with the five equivalences, Vasubandhu's discussion has shown the general differences between the first five and the sixth consciousnesses as well as a general difference in functionality between *citta* and *caitta*s (SA.IV.227f.):

> *Citta* or *vijñāna* is the general discernment or apprehension with respect to each individual object [AKB i. 16a]. This discernment is the mere grasping of the object itself, without apprehending any of its particularities. A *caitta*, on the other hand, apprehends the particularities of the object [cf. Vy, 38 and ESD.120]. Thus, in a visual perception, the *citta*, i.e., visual consciousness in this case, can only apprehend a blue object. It is only in conjunction with the *caitta* called *saṃjñā*, whose function it is to categorize, and *prajñā* whose function it is to discriminatively conceptualize, that the mind apprehends specifically: "This is blue." [...]
>
> The *Abhidharmadīpa* explains that while the *citta* is conascent with the *caitta*-s, it is distinguishable as the chief substance (*pradhāna-dravya*) inasmuch as it is the *citta* that grasps the mere object. The specifics pertaining to the object so apprehended are grasped simultaneously by a *caitta*—*saṃjñā* ideates, *smṛti* recollects, *prajñā* examines, etc. The implication is that without the raw or general grasping of the object to begin with, there cannot be the specific functioning of the *caitta*-s. Accordingly, the *caitta*-s are functionally subordinate to and dependent on the *citta* which is like the governor (*rāja-sthānīya*) in relation to the governed. It is by the *citta* that the fundamental essence of a being (*mūla-sattva-dravya*) is designated [ESD.120]. That the *citta* is the chief is also to be understood from the fact that the unenlightened are attached to it—not to the *caitta*-s—as the *Ātman*. [...]
>
> According to Xuan Zang's disciple [i.e., Pu Guang], there are four ancient schools or views on the functional relationship between the *citta* and the *caitta*-s: ... [For details see SA.IV.229].

8. In this context, Dhammajoti also raises the question of the original nature of thought (see SA.IV.232ff.) and summarizes the Sarvāstivāda position as presented by Saṃghabhadra (Ny, 733ab):

> When *citta* abides in its intrinsic nature, i.e., the neutral nature, it is necessarily pure—essentially agreeing with the Theravāda commentarial tradition. But when it abides in adventitious nature, it can be defiled.

See here also Vasubandhu's discussion of the two modes of wholesome factors (ii, F 184), i.e., "(1) the innate wholesome factors not produced through effort (*ayatnabhāvin*), which are [referred to as] those that are acquired at birth (*aupapattika*, *upapattilābhika*), and (2) the wholesome factors produced [only] through effort [*yatnabhāvin*], which are [referred to as] those that are acquired through preparatory effort (*prāyogika*, *prayogalābhika*; ii. 71b)", where we also find the comment that the wholesome factors can never have their roots completely cut off. See also Jaini's discussion of *kuśala-dharma-bīja* (AD.111–17).

9. Vasubandhu continues with a detailed discussion of the formations dissociated from thought (*cittaviprayuktasaṃskāra*; ii. 35–48). Saṃghabhadra comments (EIP.VIII.685) that these are conditioning factors (i) that necessarily arise simultaneously with other factors, and as such also with *vijñāna*, as for example: possession (*prāpti*), vitality (*jīvita*), the four conditioning characteristics (*lakṣana*; origination, duration, deterioration, impermanence), or (ii) that explicitly do not arise with *vijñāna*, as, for example, the state of non-ideation (*āsaṃjñika*), the attainment of non-ideation (*asaṃjñisamāpatti*) and the attainment of cessat-

ion (*nirodhasamāpatti*). These factors are conditioned, but cannot be classified with thought, thought-concomitants or material form (*rūpa*).

10. As for the life-force, it is determined (ii. 45ab) as the support of heat (*ūṣman*) and consciousness (*vijñāna*), i.e., it is the cause of the duration of their stream. The life-force itself, in turn, is supported by heat and consciousness.

11. At the end of chapter 2, Vasubandhu returns once more to a discussion of *vijñāna*, where he gives a specific explanation (ii. 66–73) of the immediate condition, i.e., the causal relationships between different thoughts (wholesome, unwholesome, obscured-non-defined, and unobscured-non-defined thought of the realm of desire; etc.) and different thoughts.

12. In chapter 9, Vasubandhu discusses consciousness in relation to the self, the person, memory, the agent and its action. "As to the *sūtra* statement that consciousness cognizes (*vijñānaṃ vijānāti*), Vasubandhu explains that in the cognitive process consciousness in fact does nothing (it is not a true, independent agent)" (see Dhammajoti's *Summary*, p. 57).

The above passages seem to cover the main points as presented by the AKB concerning *vijñāna* and its wider context.

215 *LS*: Schmithausen comments (SPPT.164; translation is by LS): "The Sanskrit word *vijñapti*—a causative form with the basic meaning 'making known', 'informing'—explains the aspect of the actual execution of cognition and the relatedness of cognizance to an object. In contrast to that, *citta* and *vijñāna* do not designate only the actual cognition as correlate to an object, but also, from a more ontological perspective, [1] the changing and intermittent stream of perceptions and cognitions in contrast to a substantial self, or [2] the mind in contrast to matter. *Citta* is used in particular in the latter sense." In this context see the usage of *vijñāna* in the twelvefold *pratītyasamutpāda* pertaining to states (*āvasthika*).

Hall comments (JIABS.9/1, p. 8): "In ordinary parlance *vijñapti* (Pāli *viññatti*) means 'information' or the act of informing someone, that is 'report' or 'proclamation', especially a report to a superior, and hence, 'request' or 'entreaty'. *Vijñapti* is a noun of action derived from the causative stem (*jñapaya-* or *jñāpaya-*) of the verb root *jñā* ("know") with the prefix *vi-*. Etymologically the term *vijñapti* would mean the act of causing [someone] to know [something] distinctly, or in a concrete sense, that which causes [one] to know distinctly."

216 *LVP*: The *Vyākhyā* explains *upalabdhi* by means of the gloss vastumātragrahaṇa [WOG.38.24], and adds *vedanādayas tu caitasikā viśeṣagrahaṇarūpāḥ*:

> The consciousness (*vijñāna*) or thought (*citta*) apprehends (*grahaṇa*) the specific entity, nothing more (*vastumātra*); the thought-concomitants (*caitasika*) or factors associated with consciousness (ii. 24), that is to say, sensation, etc. (*vedanā saṃjñā…*), apprehend particular characteristics, special conditions.

For example, the tactile consciousness (*kāyavijñāna*) apprehends unevenness, softness, etc. (i. 10d); it is associated with an agreeable sensation (*vedanā*) that apprehends a certain characteristic of unevenness or softness, the characteristic of being the cause of an agreeable sensation (*sukhavedanīyatā*). The visual consciousness [LS: LVP should say "mental consciousness"; see i. 14cd] apprehends color (blue, etc.,) and shape (*saṃsthāna*); it is associated with a certain thought-concomitant called *ideation* (*saṃjñā*), which apprehends a certain characteristic of the color and shape under consideration: "This is a man, this is a woman, etc."

This doctrine has been adopted by the school of Nāgārjuna. *Madhyamakavṛtti*, p. 65 *cittam arthamātragrāhi caittā viśeṣāvsthāgrāhiṇaḥ suhkhādayaḥ*; and by the school of Dignāga, *Nyāyabinduṭīkā*, p. 12, Tibetan version, p. 25.

The Japanese editor of the *Kośa* cites the *Kōki* and the *Vibhāṣā*, which indicate four opinions on this problem.

See ii. 34bd.

217 *LVP*: That is to say, according to Saṃghabhadra: "The visual consciousness, even though numerous material objects may be present, seizes solely visible form, not sound; it seizes blue, etc., but does not say that it is blue, etc., that it is agreeable, disagreeable, male, female, etc., a stump, etc. ...".

218 *LS*: As for the simultaneity of consciousnesses, Schmithausen states (AV.45f.): "Taking *ālayavijñāna* as a continuous entity ... inevitably implies that—apart from unconscious states like *nirodhasamāpatti*—one has to assume the simultaneous occurrence of at least two *vijñānas*: one or the other of the ordinary *vijñānas*, and *ālayavijñāna*. But this was problematic since there is explicit evidence showing that the pre-*ālayavijñānic* materials of the *Yogācārabhūmi* share the view of most Abhidharma schools [—especially Vaibhāṣikas (explicit statement: MVŚ, 47b29ff.), Sautrāntikas, and Theravādins, the only exception pointed out by the sources being the (or some) Mahāsāṅghikas—] that in one and the same stream-of-personality several *vijñānas* cannot arise simultaneously. ...

But a ... theory of simultaneous occurrence not only of a continuous subliminal form of mind with actual *vijñānas* but—given the necessary conditions—also of several actual *vijñānas* (occasionally even of all the six kinds) is, as is well-known, categorically affirmed in the Vth chapter of the *Saṃdhinirmocanasūtra*."

In this context, Dhammajoti mentions in his *Summary*, p. 20, that Saṃghabhadra alleges that Vasubandhu actually seems to align with "some masters" who hold that several consciousnesses arise simultaneously within a single body. For (Ny, 403c24–404a9), "if it is held that consciousness arises simply in dependence on the body possessing the faculties (*sendriyakāya*), without having to depend on the causal conditions pertaining to its own species (**svajātīya*), what, for him, prevents the simultaneous arising of consciousnesses of all object-domains in all stages?"

219 *LS*: AH 8; SAH 9.

220 *Gokhale*: [16b] *manaāyatanaṃ ca tat* |

Tib.: [16b] *yid kyi skye mched kyang de yin* |

221 *Gokhale*: [16cd] *dhātavaḥ sapta ca matāḥ ṣaḍ vijñānāny atho manaḥ* ||

Tib.: [16cd] *khams bdun dag tu'ang 'dod pa ste* | *rnam par shes pa drug dang yid* ||

222 *LS*: SAH 20–21, 26, 51–52.

223 *LVP*: The consciousnesses (*vijñāna*) succeed one another; they can be visual... mental. The consciousness that disappeared is the immediately preceding condition (ii. 62a), the basis (*āśraya*) of the consciousness which immediately follows. Under this aspect it receives the name of mental faculty (*manas*), of sense-sphere of the mental faculty (*mana-āyatana*), of element of the mental faculty (*manodhātu*), of the mental faculty (*mana-indriya*; ii. 1). It is to

the consciousness that follows it what the eye sense-faculty is for the visual consciousness.

[224] *Gokhale*: [17ab] *ṣaṇṇām anantarā'tītaṃ vijñānaṃ yad dhi tan manaḥ* |

Tib.: [17ab] *drug po 'das ma thag pa yi* | *rnam shes gang yin de yid do* |

LVP: See i. 39ab.

According to the *Vyākhyā* [WOG.39.25f.], the Yogācāras assert a *manodhātu*, a *manas* or mental faculty, distinct from the six consciousnesses.

The Tāmraparṇīyas, the scholars of Taprobane, imagine (*kalpayanti*) a material sense-faculty, the heart (*hṛdayavastu*), a basis of the mental consciousness. This heart exists also in the realm of immateriality, the nonmaterial sphere: these scholars assert, in fact, the existence of matter in this sphere (viii. 3c); they explain the prefix *ā* [in Ārūpyadhātu] in the sense of "a little", as in *āpiṅgala*, "a little red".

The Paṭṭhāna (cited in *Compendium of Philosophy*, p. 278) assigns a material basis (*rūpa*) to the mental consciousness, without giving to this basis the name *heart*, whereas it calls *eye* the basis of the visual consciousness. But the later Abhidhamma (*Visuddhimagga*; *Abhidhamma-saṅgaha*) considers the heart as the sense-faculty of thought.

The teaching of the *Vibhaṅga*, p. 88, is less clear: "From the consciousness of the eye, ear, ... body that has just perished arises the mind, the *manas*, the mental faculty (*mānasa* = *manas*), the heart (= the mind), the *manas*, the *manas* sense-faculty..." (*Atthasālinī*, 343).

LS: 1. Collett Cox, in her *On the Possibility of a Nonexistent Object of Consciousness: Sarvāstivādin and Dārṣṭāntika Theories*, comments (JIABS.11.35f.): "Mental perception differs from external perception in several significant respects. The mental organ (*manas*), which conditions the arising of a present moment of mental perceptual consciousness, is defined as the immediately preceding moment of perceptual consciousness, regardless of its types. That is to say, any of the six varieties of perceptual consciousness may be designated as the mental organ for a subsequent moment of mental perceptual consciousness. Unlike the other five externally directed sense organs, this mental organ, precisely because it is past, cannot be said to perform its distinctive activity ... of sensing or grasping the object-support of the present moment of perceptual consciousness. Instead it serves simply as the door, or immediately contiguous condition (*samanantarapratyaya*) for the arising of the present moment of mental perceptual consciousness, which then apprehends the object-support. Therefore, unlike the five externally directed sense organs and corresponding types of perceptual consciousness, the prior mental organ and its resultant present mental perceptual consciousness are not simultaneous, and do not necessarily share the same object-support. Nevertheless, the two requisite conditions for the arising of a present moment of mental perceptual consciousness, that is, a basis (*āśraya*) and an object-support (*ālambana*), are still provided through the past mental organ and the object-support."

See i. 44cd.

2. For Vasubandhu's discussion whether the last thought of the perfected being (*arhat*) is a *manas*, see ii, F 305.

[225] *LS*: SAH 20, 26.

[226] *Gokhale*: [17cd] *ṣaṣṭhāśrayaprasiddhyarthaṃ dhātavo 'ṣṭādaśa smṛtāḥ* ||

Tib.: [17cd] *drug pa'i rten ni rab bsgrub phyir | khams ni bco brgyad dag tu 'dod* ||

LVP: *hṛdayavastu*, *Compendium*, 122, 278; *JPTS*, 1884, 27–29; *Atthasālinī*, 140; Mrs. Rhys Davids, *Bulletin of the School of Oriental Studies*, iii, 353, cites *Comm. Jātaka*: ...*hadayamam-santare patiṭṭhitā paññā*; *Siddhi*, 281.

227 *LS*: SAH 20.

228 *LS*: SAH 52.

229 *Gokhale*: [18ac1] *sarvasaṃgraha ekena skandhen āyatanena ca | dhātunā ca*

Tib.: [18ab] *phung po dang ni skye mched dang | khams gcig gis ni thams cad bsdus* |

LVP: The non-informative (*avijñapti*) forms part of the aggregate of form (*rūpaskandha*) and of the element of factors (*dharmadhātu*).

230 *LS*: AH 14; SAH 51.

231 *Gokhale*: [18c2–d] *svabhāvena parabhāvaviyogataḥ* ||

Tib.: [18cd] *rang gi ngo bo nyid kyis te | gzhan gyi dngos dang mi ldan phyir* ||

LVP: The problem of inclusion (*saṃgraha*) is examined in *Dhātukathāpakaraṇa*; *Kathāvatthu*, vii. 1; *Dhātukāya*; *Prakaraṇa* (see below i. 20, F 39, note).

LS: 1. Dharmaśrī's root verse says (AH 14): "All factors are separated from factors of another nature. Everything dwells naturally on something of its own nature. Therefore they say that all factors are comprised (*saṃgraha*) within something of their own nature."

2. For a discussion of the historical development of the method of *saṃgraha* ("inclusion", "subsumption"), see the section "*Svabhāva* and the method of inclusion", pp. 558–65, in Collett Cox's *From Category to Ontology: The changing role of* Dharma *in Sarvāstivāda Abhidharma.* She writes (p. 560f.):

> [The] method of inclusion, integral to any taxonomic practice, is implicit within Abhidharma categorization in all periods. However, even though the earliest canonical Sarvāstivāda Abhidharma texts classify specific *dharmas* according to a method of simple inclusion, they do not utilize the intricate matrices typical of the *vibhāṣā* compendia, nor do they explicitly consider the meaning of "inclusion", its rationale, and its implications for the nature of the *dharmas* so classified, as evident in the controversy concerning intrinsic nature and other-nature... . The early method of simple inclusion is expanded in the canonical texts of the middle period such as the *Prakaṇapāda*, *Vijñānakāya*, and the *Jñānaprasthāna*, which relate entire categories rather than simply classifying individual *dharmas*, but which still do not explicitly discuss the rationale for the method of inclusion in terms of a fundamental contrast between intrinsic nature and other-nature. [...]
>
> [I]t is significant to note that the term *svabhāva* in the distinctive sense of the intrinsic nature of a category or of an individual *dharma* is not used in the earliest Sarvāstivāda canonical Abhidharma texts; it appears only in texts from the period of the early *vibhāṣā* compendia onward, that is, concurrent with the systematic development of the analytical method of categorization by inclusion. It is then plausible to infer that this sense of *svabhāva* as intrinsic nature, so important in later Sarvāstivāda

exegesis for the interpretation of the character of *dharmas per se*, first emerged through its function as the criterion determining categories of *dharmas*, specifically in the context of inclusion.

3. As for "other-nature", she points out that the topic of "inclusion" is raised to counter the view of the Vibhajyavādins (MVŚ, 306b12–14] that "*dharmas* are included on the basis of other nature (*parabhāva*), and not on the basis of intrinsic nature (*svabhāva*)", which they support by appealing to both scriptural authority and common usage in which "that which includes" and "that which is included" are clearly distinct from one another, as in the case of a householder who states "I possess land, domestic animals". Yet the **Mahāvibhāṣā* points out that these commonplace examples involve inclusion (*saṃgraha*) merely in a conventional sense, whereas Abhidharma analysis applies inclusion in the absolute sense (*pāramārthika*) by declaring (MVŚ, 306bc) that "all *dharma*-s are included with respect to intrinsic nature".

4. In this context, Dhammajoti (SA.IV.22) and Cox (p. 560) both refer to the passage in MVŚ, 308a, where inclusion/subsumption (*saṃgraha*) *vis-à-vis* intrinsic nature is explained:

> Because, *vis-à-vis* intrinsic nature, an intrinsic nature is existent, real, apperceivable (*upa-√labh*); hence it is called *saṃgraha*. Because, *vis-à-vis* intrinsic nature, an intrinsic nature is not different, not external, not separated, not distinct, not empty; hence it is called *saṃgraha*. [Cox: It is not the case that it has not existed, does not exist, or will not exist; it neither increases nor decreases. Inclusion by intrinsic nature does not involve one thing grasping another.] When *dharma*-s are subsumed *vis-à-vis* intrinsic nature, it is unlike the case of taking up food with the hand or that of nipping a garment with the fingers. Rather, each of them sustains itself so as not to be disintegrated; hence it is called *saṃgraha*. It is named *saṃgraha* in the sense of sustaining. Hence, *saṃgraha* in the absolute sense (*paramārtha*) is subsumption of intrinsic nature alone.

Dhammajoti then comments (SA.IV.22):

> The study of subsumption in terms of intrinsic nature is none other than the study of the intrinsic characteristics of all *dharma*-s. This analysis may be made between one single *dharma* and another *dharma*, or between one *dharma* and several other *dharma*-s, or between one category of *dharma*-s and another category, or between one category and several other categories.
>
> However, this should not be understood as an ambiguous application of the term intrinsic nature—to both individual *dharma*-s and categorical groups of *dharma*. Although the method of subsumption does serve to discriminate the different categorical-types, its fundamental function is to investigate into the essential or intrinsic nature of a given group of forces (phenomenal or unconditioned) which through having the same intrinsic nature are experienced by us in diverse modes or forms. This is the essential meaning of "subsumption in respect of intrinsic nature".

232 *LS*: Yaśomitra explains (cf. WOG.41.10ff; FCO.564) that "the smaller is to be included within the larger, and not the larger within the smaller. Hence, the smaller category of the visual controlling faculty, which constitutes merely one part of the material form aggregate, is to be included within the larger category of the material form aggregate, which includes all

varieties of material form. Yaśomitra explains that such inclusion based upon intrinsic nature is absolute (*paramārthika*), and not conventional or consensual (*sāṃketika*)."

233 *LS*: The *Vyākhyā* glosses [WOG.41.23]: catasraḥ *parṣadaḥ* bhikṣu-bhikṣuṇy-upāsakopāsikāḥ.

234 *LVP*: *Digha*, iii. 232: "four bases of sympathy (*saṃgaha-vatthūni*): generosity [*dāna*], pleasing speech [*priyavaditā*], beneficial conduct [*arthacaryā*], and impartiality [*sāmanārthatā*]" (Walshe). *Dharmasaṃgraha*, 19; *Mahāvyutpatti*, 35, etc.

LS: *Aṅguttara-nikāya* (PTS) iv. 218: "Lord, it is by those four bases of gatherings, which have been declared by the Exalted One, that I gather this following together. Lord, [1] when I realize that this man may be enlisted by a gift, I enlist him in this way; [2] when by a kindly word, then in that way; [3] when by a good turn, then so; or [4] when I know that he must be treated as an equal, if he is to be enlisted, then I enlist him by equality of treatment."

235 *LS*: SAH 21.

236 *Gokhale*: [19] *jātigocaravijñānasāmānyād ekadhātutā | dvitve 'pi cakṣurādīnāṃ śobhā'rthaṃ tu dvayodbhavaḥ ||*

Tib.: [19] *mig la sogs pa gnyis mod kyi | rigs dang spyod yul rnam par shes | 'dra ba'i phyir na khams gcig nyid | mdzes bya'i phyir na gnyis byung ngo |*

237 *LVP*: Great ugliness would result from the fact of having only one eye, one ear, one nostril. – But many animals: camels, cats, owls, etc., although having two eyes, etc., are not beautiful! – They are not beautiful in comparison with the other types of animals, but, among their fellow creatures, the individuals who have only one eye, etc., they are ugly.

Saṃghabhadra explains the meaning of beauty (*śobhārtham*) in the sense of *for supremacy's sake* (*ādhipatyārtham*; see ii. 1). Those who possess supremacy are beautiful, shine in the world. Individuals who have only one eye do not possess *supremacy*, i.e., the capacity for clear vision, for sight is not as clear with one eye as with two eyes... (i. 43).

238 *LS*: SAH 7, 24–25.

239 *Gokhale*: [20ab] *rāśyāyadvāragotrā'rthāḥ skandhāyatanadhātavaḥ |*

Tib.: [20ab] *spungs dang skye sgo rigs kyi don | phung po skye mched khams rnams yin |*

240 *LS*: SAH 7, 25.

241 *LVP*: *skándha*, *rāśi*, *Vibhāṣā*, 74, p. 383.

LS: Each of the five aggregates (*skandha*) forms a heap (*rāśi*) of its own category which may be past, present or future.

242 *LVP*: *Saṃyukta*, 15, 2: *yat kiṃcid rūpam atītānāgatapratyutpannam ādhyātmikaṃ vā bāhyaṃ vā audārikaṃ vā sūkṣmaṃ vā hīnaṃ vā praṇītaṃ vā dūraṃ vā antikaṃ vā tad ekadhyam abhisaṃkṣipya ayam ucyate rūpaskandhaḥ.*

Compare *Vibhaṅga*, p. 1.

The edition of the *Vyākhyā* has *aikadhyam* [WOG.42.32], but the *Mahāvyutpatti*, 245, 343 *ekadhyam abhisaṃkṣipya*. Wogihara indicates *ekadhye* in *Divya*, 35, 24; 40, 22.

243 *LVP*: *anityatāniruddha*, i.e., destroyed by impermanence, which is one of the characteristics of conditioned factors (ii. 45cd).

There are five types of cessation (*nirodha*):

1. cessation by the characteristic (*lakṣaṇanirodha*) (ii. 45cd), which is referred to here;
2. cessation by attainment (*samāpattinirodha*) (ii. 42f.);
3. cessation by birth (*upapattinirodha* = state of non-ideation [*āsaṃjñika*]; ii. 41b);
4. cessation due to deliberation (*pratisaṃkhyānirodha*) (i. 6ab);
5. cessation not due to deliberation (*apratisaṃkhyānirodha*) (i. 6cd).

If the text said: "Past, the destroyed *rūpa*", it could mean that it refers to the cessations 2–5. But cessations 2 and 3 are the destruction of the future thought and thought-concomitants; cessation 4 is the destruction of the impure thought and thought-concomitants; cessation 5 is the destruction of the future factors not destined to arise (*anutpattidharman*).

244 *LS*: Hall brackets: "... [and the organs are the internal spheres while their objects are the external spheres]".

245 *LS*: As for gross and subtle, the *Vyākhyā* [WOG.43.19f.] renders: *audārikaṃ sapratigham* iti. paramānu-saṃcaya-svabhāvaṃ. *sūkṣmam apratighaṃ*. avijñapti-rūpaṃ. Yaśomitra thus states that the gross form has the collection of atoms as its intrinsic nature and that subtle form refers to the non-informative form. See iv. 4a.

246 *LVP*: Āryadeva, *Śataka*, 258, shows that this definition contradicts the thesis of the existence of the future.

247 *LS*: Pradhan.13.13 has: *ayaṃ tu viśeṣaḥ | audārikaṃ pañcendriyāśrayaṃ sūkṣmaṃ mānasam.*

248 *LVP*: Hsüan-tsang translates: Bhadanta Dharmatrāta. But the *Vyākhyā* says [WOG.44.14ff.]: Bhadanta, i.e., a Sthavira Sautrāntika, or the Sthavira Sautrāntika of this name. (On the other hand,) Bhagavadviśeṣa (also) thinks that this refers to the Sthavira (or Bhadanta) Dharmatrāta. We object to this. Dharmatrāta is a follower of the existence of the past and of the future, thus a Sarvāstivādin, and we are concerned here in this passage (i, F 36) with a Sautrāntika, i.e., with a Dārṣṭāntika. For the Bhadanta Dharmatrāta has a Sarvāstivādin theory presented later (v. 25). The "Bhadanta" mentioned here is the philosopher whom the *Vibhāṣā* cites under the simple name of Bhadanta, a philosopher who adheres to the Sautrāntika system (*sautrāntika-darśanāvalambin*), whereas the *Vibhāṣā* calls the Bhadanta Dharmatrāta by his name. Thus we have here a certain Sthavira Bhikṣu Sautrāntika, different from Dharmatrāta. (See *Introduction*; p. xlviii.)

The Japanese editor refers to the MVŚ, 383b16, where it is said that Dharmatrāta does not assert that the sense-sphere of factors (*dharmāyatana*) includes material form (*rūpa*) (see iv. 4ab).

249 *LVP*: *dūratā*, *Kathāvatthu*, vii, 5.

250 *LS*: SAH 25.

251 *LVP*: The MVŚ, 379a12, presents twenty opinions on the meaning of the term *āyatana*. – *Atthasālinī*, 140–41. The definition of the *Kośa* is reproduced in the *Madhyamakavṛtti*, p. 552.

LS: As for "gate of arising", Dharmatrāta comments (SAH.38): "Because frustration and satisfaction pass through it." Moreover, MVŚ, 379a, comments (SA.IV.28):

> The meaning of *āyatana* is "gate of arising": Just as various things arise within a city on account of which the bodies of sentient beings are nourished, so, within the supporting bases (*āśraya*) and object-supports (*ālambana*)—[the two constituent

components of the *āyatana*-s]—various *citta-caitta-dharma*-s arise on account of which the defiled and pure serial continuities (*santati*) are nourished.

252 *LS*: SAH 24, 25.

253 *LVP*: MVŚ, 367c21, has eleven etymologies. We have here the first.

LS: Dhammoti comments (SA.IV.29):

The MVŚ enumerates the following senses of *dhātu*:

1. Family/kin/species (*gotra*)—like the different species of metals, gold, iron, etc., in a mountain.
2. Cluster/lump (段; *kavaḍa*?)—like a cluster of timbers etc., arranged in a certain order resulting in what is called a mansion, a house, etc.
3. Part/constituent (分; *bhāga*?)—like the 18 parts of a human body.
4. Piece/division (片)—like the 18 pieces/divisions of a human body.
5. Dissimilar—the eye-element is dissimilar to the other elements in a human; etc.
6. Demarcation/boundary—the demarcation of the eye-element is distinct from the other 17 elements.
7. Distinctive cause—that by virtue of which there is the eye-element is a cause distinctively for the eye-element alone, and not for other elements.
8. Running (√*dhāv*)—these elements run around *saṃsāra*.
9. Sustaining/holding (√*dhā*)—these elements each hold or sustain their own intrinsic nature.
10. Nourishing (√*dhā*)—they nourish other entities.

The last three meanings are attributed to the grammarians (*śābdika*). In the AKB, Vasubandhu gives the meanings of *dhātu* as species/family and as causal origin.

See Dhammajoti's chapter (ADCP.162–64): "The Sautrāntika doctrine that only the *dhātu*-s are real".

254 *LVP*: *gotra* signifies *mine* [*ākara*] in the expression *suvarṇagotra*, Asaṅga, *Sūtrālaṃkāra*, iii. 9 and note of the translator.

LS: Hsüan-tsang (ADCP.162f.) "renders *ākara* as 生本, 'birth-origin' or 'arising-source'. The *dhātu*-s are mines of their own species, each being the homogeneous cause of the later moments in the existence of a given *dharma*. This Sautrāntika interpretation of *dhātu*, which clearly has the connotation of causal efficacy, is rejected by Saṃghabhadra (Ny, 343c), as it is more in tune with the Sautrāntika *bīja* theory. He proposes instead that the eighteen *dhātu*-s are said to be *gotra*-s in the sense of being eighteen different species, each having its distinct essential nature."

255 *LVP*: 1. The Vaibhāṣika believes that the aggregates (*skandha*), the sense-spheres (*āyatana*) and the elements (*dhātu*) exist as real entities.

2. The Sautrāntika holds that the elements exist as real entities, but that the aggregates and the sense-spheres exist as provisional or nominal entities.

3. Vasubandhu holds that the aggregates exist as provisional or nominal entities, but that the sense-spheres and the elements exist as real entities.

LS: In the following we will elaborate on LVP's terse statement regarding the differences of these three important epistemological-ontological positions concerning the *skandhas*, *āyatanas* and *dhātus*, by amply quoting Kajiyama and Dhammajoti.

1. As for Vasubandhu, Kajiyama comments (ATV.23f.):

> Vasubandhu's approach to the problem of whether the *skandha*, *āyatana* and *dhātu* are real or not was epistemological. The *rūpa-skandha* means matter in general. Thus, the cognitive organ of the eye and the color-form as its object are both included in the same *rūpa-skandha*, although they are different in function—one being internal and organic, the other being external and mechanical. An existent material thing of the present time and an inexistent material thing of the past or future time belong to one and the same category of *rūpa-skandha*, though the former is real and the latter unreal [for Vasubandhu]. In the *rūpa-skandha*, things different in nature and function or things real and unreal are put into one kind. Vasubandhu could not find any principle by which he could distinguish one from the other. This is the reason why he declared the *skandha* as nominally existent and rejected it from epistemological categories.
>
> On the contrary, the *āyatana* of an eye and the *āyatana* of color-form cooperate to produce the same effect of visual perception. Therefore, it is reasonable to subsume these two under the category of cognition. However, the atoms of the internal and organic organ of an eye are homogeneous and have the same kind of causal efficiency of seeing, whereas the atoms of the *āyatana* of color-form have the causal efficiency of being seen, which is heterogeneous to that of the atoms of an eye. Therefore, these two kinds of atoms can be classified under two different subdivisions, i.e., as visual organ (*cakṣurāyatana*) and visual object (*rūpāyatana*).
>
> Thus, the material *āyatana* (*rūpīṇy āyatanāni*) is further classified into five cognitive organs and five cognitive objects: and the mental organ (*mana-āyatana*) and mental object (*dharmāyatana*) are differentiated from the above ten *āyatanas*. As for *dhātus*, the epistemological principle common to them and their classification into eighteen kinds are easily understood in a similar way.
>
> Vasubandhu's statement under *Abhidharmakośa* I, v. 20ab [that *skandha* means "heap" (*rāśi*) and that in the case of an *āyatana* the aggregate of atoms is a cause of cognition, each individual atom contributing to it,] purports the following significance:
>
> First, according to him, the theory that a sense-organ and its object form two different *āyatanas* means that the atoms constituting a sense-organ are of one kind and those constituting its object are of another. In other words, the same kind of atoms, when gathered together, form a real aggregate.
>
> Second, Vasubandhu seems to suggest that the atoms of a sense-organ and those of its object, though both are the same as a cause of sense-perception, differ in function. Vasubandhu thinks that in sense-perception knowledge is the effect of its object, a cause, and that knowledge appears resembling the object, i.e., in the form of it. Although a sense-organ is also a cause of sense-perception, it does not throw its form

into knowledge. Therefore the atoms of an object and the atoms of a sense-organ have different functions.

Third, the Sarvāstivādin says that an atom is not cognized* [i.e., is invisible] but only assembled atoms are the cause of cognition. Against this standpoint, Vasubandhu thinks that the atom of an eye has causal efficiency for perception, though it is very minute. Therefore, when many atoms of an eye gather together, the aggregate is efficient enough to produce a visual perception in cooperation with the aggregate of atoms of color-form and other conditions. The same thing can be said of the atoms of the object of perception. This can be understood only when we note that for Vasubandhu the criterion of reality or existence is causal efficiency (*kāraṇabhāva*, *śakti*). An atom and the aggregate of the same kind of atoms are both real because the two are different not in essence but only in grade.

* LS: Notice (see below), that Saṃghabhadra does disagree with this presentation.

2. As for the Sarvāstivādins and the Sautrāntikas, their positions will be discussed more in detail in chapter 3, in the context of Vasubandhu's discussion of Śrīlāta's theory of perception (F 101–7), but here is the gist of them.

i. The Sarvāstivādins maintain that the aggregates (*skandha*), sense-sphere (*āyatana*) and the elements (*dhātu*) really exist (ADCP.142):

> For the Sarvāstivādins, in a *pratyakṣa* [direct perception] experience, whether sensory or mental, the cognitive object as the *ālambana-pratyaya* is actually the object out there existing at the very moment when the corresponding consciousness arises. It is a real entity, just as a single atom is a real. Saṃghabhadra argues that a sensory consciousness necessarily takes a physical assemblage or agglomeration of atoms (和集; **saṃcaya*, **saṃghāta*, **samasta*) as its object. What is directly perceived is just these atoms assembled together in a certain manner, not a conceptualized object such as a jar, etc. The jug *per se* is never perceived by the visual consciousness; only the *rūpa* as agglomerated atoms of colour and shapes. This is direct perception. It is the succeeding mental consciousness, with its *abhinirūpaṇā* capability and using names, that determines that the object is a "jug". At this stage—as opposed to the initial stage immediately following the visual perception—it is no more an experience of *pratyakṣa*, but an inference.

ii. As for the Sautrāntikas, Saṃghabhadra summarizes (Ny, 350c) the view of Śrīlāta, the leading Dārṣṭāntika-Sautrāntika at the time, who maintains that *dhātu*, i.e., *anu-dhātu*, alone is real (ADCP.163):

> Herein, the Sthavira asserts thus: Both the supporting basis as well as the objects for the five sensory consciousness do not exist truly. For each individual atom by itself cannot serve as a supporting basis or an object; they can do so only in the form of a unified complex (和合); ... He and his disciples employ the simile of the blind in support of their doctrine. It is said that (*kila*—showing Saṃghabhadra's disagreement) each blind person by himself is devoid of the function of seeing visible forms; an assemblage (和集) of these blind persons likewise is devoid of the function of seeing. Similarly, each individual atom by itself is devoid of the function of being a

> supporting basis or an object; an assemblage of many atoms likewise is devoid of such functions. Hence, *āyatana* is unreal; *dhātu* alone is real.

For Śrīlāta the *dhātus* alone are real in the sense of being causally efficacious factors of existence (*dharmas*) existing only in the present moment of a *dharma*-series. Dhammajoti comments (SA.IV.35):

> In this sense, as Saṃghabhadra argues, *dhātu* has essentially the same significance as the Sautrāntika notion of seeds (*bīja*), the causal efficacy that is passed down in the series. This significance is well brought out by the term *anudhātu* or **pūrvānudhātu*, proposed by Śrīlāta, which is said to subsume all the karmic efficacies hitherto accumulated in a given moment of a series.

iii. Dhammajoti presents Saṃghabhadra's and Śrīlāta's various objections to each other and then makes the link to Vasubandhu (SA.IV.35):

> Saṃghabhadra, however, points out the difficulty in the *bīja* doctrine, since the Sautrāntika does not consider *bīja*—though real as a causal efficacy—as being an ontological entity. This causal efficacy—the *dharma*—is neither identical with nor different from the serial continuity itself, and the serial continuity is considered to be unreal (a mere concept); and yet, at the culminating moment of the serial transmission of the causal efficacy, is productive of a fruit!

Thus (ADCP.142f.):

> Saṃghabhadra rejects Śrīlāta's theory that the object of visual perception is a unified complex (合; **sāmagrī*, **saṃghāta*) of atoms.
>
> In return [as already mentioned above] Śrīlāta ridicules the Vaibhāṣika notion of assembled atoms as a cognitive object, comparing it to the case of a group of blind persons who, like an individual member, is incapable of vision.
>
> Saṃghabhadra answers this, and states that even an individual atom is in actual fact visible,* even though its visibility is almost nil, on account of its being very subtle for visual consciousness which can grasp only a gross object (取境麤故). In fact, it is conceded that each individual atom, in its own right, actually serves as a cognitive object (*ālambana*) or a supporting basis (*āśraya*). He argues that such a superimposed unity as proposed by Śrīlāta can only be grasped by *abhinirūpaṇā-vikalpa* [see AKB i. 33ab]. A sensory consciousness, lacking this capacity, can only take an existent—not a conceptualized unity—as its object. He further explains that a unified complex obtains where speech operates, as a result of the arising of an appellation (*adhivacana*) with regard to a multiplicity of *dharma*-s. It is on account of its non-discriminative nature that visual consciousness is incapable of discerning the extremely subtle form of an atom; only those endowed with the power of excellent wisdom can do so. In any case, he says, atoms are always found assembled, and thus are visible.
>
> As a matter of fact, Saṃghabhadra does not seem to be entirely alone or innovative in the way he considers the efficacy of the atoms. In the AKB [i.e., our section here], Vasubandhu argues for the reality of the *āyatana* (a dissent here from the Sautrāntika) by saying that an aggregate of atoms, constituting an *āyatana*, together

serve as the cause for cognition, each individual atom contributing to the causal efficacy (*ekaśāḥ samagrāṇāṃ kāraṇabhāva*).

On this, Yaśomitra comments that it is like the case of many people gathering sufficient strength to drag a log, each contributing his share of strength; and again like the case of many strands of hairs becoming sufficiently visible, each single piece of hair contributing to the visibility.

Surprisingly, such explanations coming from a professed Sautrāntika do not seem very different from what Saṃghabhadra says above. The common factor in this case, uniting these three masters of different sectarian affiliation, appears to be the criterion of causal efficacy being identified with reality. As far as Saṃghabhadra is concerned, he is being true to the Vaibhāṣika orthodoxy in maintaining that if an atom as well as an agglomeration of them constituting an object of perception are real substances, they must in each case be causally efficient.

* LS: Thus differing from Kajiyama's presentation above.

256 *LVP*: The doctrine of the persons (*pudgala*) is discussed in a supplement to the *Kośa*: Chapter 9.

LS: This is the fifth of Kritzer's fifteen passages discussed in relation to chapter 1 (VY.12f.): "Saṃghabhadra does not specify that this is the opinion of the *sūtra*-master, but he refutes it [Ny, 344a15–18], ... P'u-kuang attributes it to Vasubandhu and distinguishes it from the position of the Vaibhāṣikas, who say that *skandha*s, *āyatana*s, and *dhātu*s are all real, and that of the Sautrāntikas, who say that, since the *āyatana*s are also *prajñapti*, only the *dhātu*s are real. Comparison: There are a number of statements in the *Yogācārabhūmi* to the effect that the meaning of *skandha* is 'collection'."

257 *LVP*: Saṃghabhadra: This objection is without value. *Skandha* does not signify *heap*, but "that which is susceptible of being collected together in a heap", [i.e., the real *dharma*s that comprise the *skandha*s].

258 *LVP*: As, in the world, *skandha* signifies *shoulder*, so name-and-form (*nāmarūpa*) is the two shoulders that bear the six sense-spheres (*ṣaḍāyatana*; iii. 21).

259 *LVP*: The part that is material form (*rūpa*), the part that is sensation... .

260 *LVP*: Paramārtha: "I will return to you three *skandha*s." – Tibetan: *dbul bar bya ba'i phung po gsum dag tu dbul bar bya'o = deyaskandhatrayeṇa dātavyam* (?).

261 *LS*: This is the sixth of Kritzer's fifteen passages discussed in relation to chapter 1 (VY.14f.): "Saṃghabhadra [Ny, 344a13–18] comments only on the second of these definitions [i.e., being a 'part'], saying that the statement that it does not conform with *sūtra* is the opinion of the *sūtra*-master and criticizes it [Ny, 344a14–18], saying that Vasubandhu insists too strictly on *sūtra* in determining the meaning of *skandha*, when he should rely more on reason."

262 *LVP*: *utsūtra*, *Mahābhāṣya*, i. p. 12; Kielhorn, *JRAS*, 1908, p. 501.

263 *LS*: *tasmād rāśivad eva skandhāḥ prajñaptisantaḥ*.

Dhammajoti, referring to this section, comments (ESD.3) that Vasubandhu denies the reality of the *skandha*, as well as that of the *asaṃskṛta*.

[264] *LS*: LVP attributes the following remark to the Sautrāntikas but, according to Kajiyama (ATV.20), it is a counterattack by the Sarvāstivādin expressing the logical consequences of the aforementioned reply to the Vaibhāṣika statement. The term Sautrāntika is not mentioned in Pradhan.

[265] *LVP*: The Ābhidhārmika scholar is not always clearly distinguished from the Vaibhāṣika. – See the *Introduction* [by La Vallée Poussin].

[266] *LVP*: *skandhaprajñaptim apekṣate.*

[267] *LVP*: Compare *Prakaraṇapāda*, chapter vi (731c19): The element of the eye (*cakṣurdhātu*) is included in one element, one sense-sphere, one aggregate; it is known (*jñeya*) through seven cognitions (*jñāna*; see *Kośa*, vii.) excluding the cognition of another's mind (*paracittajñāna*), the cognition of cessation (*nirodhajñāna*), the cognition of the path (*mārgajñāna*); it is cognized by one consciousness (*vijñāna*); it exists in the realm of desire and in the realm of fine-materiality; it is affected by the proclivities (*anuśaya*) to be abandoned by cultivation (see *Kośa*, v.).

Dhātukathāpakaraṇa (PTS, 1892) p. 6: *cakkhudhātu ekena khandhena ekenāyatanena ekāya dhātuyā saṃgahitā.*

[268] *LS*: SAH 24.

[269] *Gokhale*: [20cd] *mohendriyarucitraidhāt tisraḥ skandhādideśanāḥ* ||

Tib.: [20cd] *rmongs dbang 'dod rnam gsum gyi phyir* | *phung po la sogs gsum bstan to* ||

LVP: According to MVŚ, 366c26.

LS: This is the seventh of Kritzer's fifteen passages discussed in relation to chapter 1 (VY.16f.): "Vasubandhu says that the teachings of the *skandha*s, *āyatana*s, and *dhātu*s are directed variously at people who have differing degrees of ignorance, faculties, and faith. [...] Saṃghabhadra [Ny, 344a24–27] says that the *sūtra*-master has abbreviated the explanation and gives an expanded explanation [Ny, 344a27–b2].

[270] *LVP*: *piṇḍātmagrahaṇatas.*

[271] *LS*: Jampaiyang (p. 213): "From the perspective of those of sharp faculty [who understand through a slight movement of the head, (they) comprehend] the five *skandha*s [and in addition, by themselves, the *āyatana*s and *dhātu*s]. From the perspective of those of intermediate (faculty) [who understand through elaboration, they comprehend] the twelve *āyatana*s [when taught, and in addition, (by themselves,) the *dhātu*s]. From the perspective of those of dull (faculty) [who (comprehend) through application,] the eighteen *dhātu*s are explained [for without extensive explanation they don't understand]."

[272] *LS*: The *Vyākhyā* glosses [WOG.48.10ff.]: śamatha-caritānāṃ *saṃkṣiptā ruciḥ*. śamatha-vipaśyanā-caritānāṃ *madhyā ruciḥ*. vipaśyanā-caritānāṃ *vistīrṇā rucir*.

[273] *LVP*: Teaching of the aggregates (*skandha*) to persons of sharp faculties (*prajñendriya*). Example: *yad bhikṣo na tvaṃ sa te dharmaḥ prahātavyaḥ* | *ājñātaṃ bhagavan* | *katham asya bhikṣo saṃkṣiptenoktārtham ājānāsi* | *rūpaṃ bhadanta nāhaṃ sa me dharmaḥ prahātavyaḥ* |

The three types of listeners, i.e., (1) *udghaṭitajña* (those who, during the course of a given explanation, come to penetrate the truth), (2) *avipañcitajña* (those who realize the truth after explanation), (3) *padaṃparama* (those for whom the words are the highest attainment) (*Puggalapaññatti*, p. 41; *Sūtrālaṃkāra*, transl. p. 145), correspond to the three classes of faculties.

274 *LS*: SAH 11, 23

275 *LS*: SAH 11.

276 *Gokhale*: [21] *vivādamūlasaṃsārahetutvāt kramakāraṇāt | caittebhyo vedanāsaṃjñe pṛthak skandhau niveśitau ||*

Tib.: [21] *rtsod pa'i rtsa bar gyur pa dang | 'khor ba'i rgyu phyir rim rgyu'i phyir | sems byung rnams las tshor ba dang | 'du shes logs shig phung por bzhag ||*

LVP: *Dharmaskandha*, 9, 10; MVŚ, 385a29.

277 *LVP*: Six roots of contention (*vivādamūla*) in *Dīgha*, iii. 246, etc.

LS: MVŚ, 775b9ff., states (DD.284): "Conception and feelings are able to give rise to two types of defilements: desires and [false] views. Desires arise through the power of feelings, [false] views, through the power of conception. All defilements have these two as their head." Cox comments: "Thus the two categories—desires and false views—represent all defilements; false views include all those defilements to be abandoned by the path of vision, and desires, those to be abandoned by the path of cultivation."

278 *LS*: SAH 23.

279 *Gokhale*: [22ab1] *skandheṣv asaṃskṛtam n oktam arthā'yogāt*

Tib.: [22ab] *phung po dag tu 'dus ma byas | don du mi rung phyir ma bshad |*

LVP: MVŚ, 385b15.

280 *LS*: Cox summarizes Saṃghabhadra (Ny, 345a; EIP.VIII.658): "Others suggest that, because the unconditioned factors are equivalent to the inactivity of the aggregates, they cannot themselves be aggregates. The inactivity of the aggregates results from the termination of the false imagination of self because the aggregates, in every case, serve as the basis for the imagination of self. The sense bases and elements, however, do not necessarily give rise to the idea of self. Therefore, the unconditioned factors can be included within the factor basis of the twelve sense bases, or the factor element of the eighteen elements."

281 *LS*: This is the eighth of Kritzer's fifteen passages discussed in relation to chapter 1 (VY.18f.): Saṃghabhadra (Ny, 345a10–11) identifies the objection as that of Vasubandhu and criticizes it (Ny, 345a11–20), justifying the simile of the pot.

282 *LS*: SAH 7, 17–18.

283 *LS*: SAH 7.

284 *Gokhale*: [22b2–d] *kramaḥ punaḥ | yathaudārikasaṃkleśabhājanādyarthadhātutaḥ ||*

LS: Gokhale has: "*yathaudarika-*".

Tib.: [22cd] *rim ni rags dang kun nyon mongs | snod sogs don khams ji bzhin no ||*

LVP: According to MVŚ, 384b1–6.

285 *LS*: Jampaiyang (p. 218): "Consciousness is the subtlest of all since cognizing the mere nature of the object is difficult to comprehend."

286 *Gokhale*: [23a] *prāk pañca vārtamānārthyād*

Tib.: [23a] *da lta'i don phyir dang po lnga* |

287 *Gokhale*: [23b] *bhautikārthyāc catuṣṭayam* |

Tib.: [23b] *'byung ba las gyur don phyir bzhi* |

288 *Gokhale*: [23c] *dūrāśutaravṛttyā 'nyad*

Tib.: [23c] *gzhan mi ches ring myur 'jug phyir* |

289 *Gokhale*: [23d] *yathāsthānaṃ kramo 'tha vā* ||

Tib.: [23d] *yang na ji ltar gnas bzhin rim* ||

LS: This is the ninth of Kritzer's fifteen passages discussed in relation to chapter 1 (VY.20f.): "Saṃghabhadra [Ny, 345c27–346a5] quotes this passage in a slightly expanded form, says that the *sūtra*-master is either speaking provisionally or following some 'other' interpretation, and points out that the organs of seeing, hearing, and smelling are arranged like a garland, with none higher or lower."

290 *LS*: Pradhan.16.12 has: *manaḥ punastānyeva niśritamadeśasthaṃ*. Hall translates as follows (VASC.104): "...while the mind (*manas*), although dependent on just those [organs], is not located in [one] place".

291 *LS*: SAH 17–18

292 *Gokhale*: [24] *viśeṣaṇā'rtham prādhānyād bahudharmā'grasaṃgrahāt* | *ekam āyatanaṃ rūpam ekaṃ dharmākhyam ucyate* ||

Tib.: [24] *bye brag don dang gtso bo'i phyir* | *chos mang ba dang mchog bsdus phyir* | *gcig ni gzugs kyi skye mched dang* | *gcig ni chos zhes bya bar brjod* ||

LVP: The MVŚ, 399c4–7, enumerates eleven reasons that justify the terms *rūpāyatana*, *dharmāyatana*.

LS: 1. Cox summarizes (EIP.VIII.659) Saṃghabhadra (Ny, 346b): "Though ten of the twelve sense bases have the nature of material form and all sense bases may be objects of mental perceptual consciousness, they are differentiated in order to enable disciples to distinguish their characteristics, that is, to distinguish those that *are* contents and those that are organs, i.e., *have* contents."

2. Saṃghabhadra highlights (Ny, 346b) visibility (*sa-nidarśanatva*) and resistance (*sa-pratighatva*) as constituting the distinctive nature of *rūpa*, yet, of the ten material elements (*dhātu*), only visible form has visibility and therefore is given the name *rūpa* as such, without being individuated by a specific name. See i. 29ac.

Although we have translated *rūpāyatana* so far by offering two translations, i.e., "sense-sphere of visible form" and "sense-sphere of material form", and since we have translated it in this verse—due to context—only as "sense-sphere of material form", we will, from the next verse onwards, translate it only as "sense-sphere of visible form", i.e., we will drop the subtlety presented in this verse since "sense-sphere of visible form" is more specific.

3. Cox summarizes (EIP.VIII.660) Saṃghabhadra (Ny, 346b): "Though the sense basis of factors (*dharmāyatana*) includes many different types of factors, including the factor of cessation through realization or *nirvāṇa*, their character as factors enables them to be placed in the same category."

[293] *LVP*: This is the opinion of Dharmatrāta (*Nanjio* 1287), i. 17.

[294] *LS*: Jampaiyang (p. 221): The *Vyākhyāyuktiṭīkā* states:

> The flesh eye is any that exists like ours. The divine eye is the eye of higher perception because it is the ground of the first absorption, etc. The wisdom eye of an Ārya is uncontaminated primordial awareness. The eye of *dharma* is transcendent post-equipoise primordial awareness because it fully differentiates any *dharma*. The Buddha eye comprehends all aspects of all objects of awareness.

[295] *LS*: SAH 13–14, 19, 22, 411.

[296] *LS*: SAH 13–14.

[297] *LS*: Ibid.

[298] *LS*: SAH 13.

[299] *Gokhale*: [25] *dharmaskandhasahasrāṇi yāny aśītiṃ jagau muniḥ | tāni vāṅ nāma v ety eṣāṃ rūpasaṃskārasaṃgrahaḥ ||*

Tib.: [25] *chos kyi phung po brgyad khri dag | gang rnams thub pas gsungs de dag | tshig gam ming yin de dag ni | gzugs dang 'du byed dag tu 'dus ||*

LVP: 1. [Yaśomitra states (WOG.52.10ff.):] (i) According to the Sautrāntikas, the speech of the Buddha (*buddhavacana*) is vocal informative action (*vāgvijñapti*; iv. 3d); (ii) according to another school (*nikāyāntarīya*), it is name (*nāman*). (iii) For the Ābhidhārmikas, it is, at the same time, speech or voice (*vāc*) and name (*nāma*).

2. In another canon, the Sūtra says that there are 84,000 *dharmaskandhas*. The Sūtra has Ānanda saying: "I have learned from the Fortunate One more than 80,000 *dharmaskandhas*": *sātirekāṇi me 'śītir dharmaskandhasahasrāṇi bhagavato 'ntikāt saṃmukham udrgṛhītāni*. (See Burnouf, *Introduction*, p. 34; *Sumaṅgalavilāsinī*, i. p. 24; *Theragāthā* 1024; *Prajñāpāramitā* in the *Akutobhaya* of Nāgārjuna, i. 8; *Avadānaśataka*, ii. 155).

Vasumitra, *Bahuśrutīyas*, thesis 1. – Nature of the teaching, Demiéville; *Milinda*, 52–57, 62; *Siddhi*, 795. – *Daśabhūmi*, 74: *caturaśītikleśacaritanānātvasahasra*.

On the 84,000, 2,000 are from Śāriputra.

LS: 1. Here is a translation of Burnouf, *Introduction*, p. 34:

> In a philosophical compilation, the *Abhidharmakośavyākhyā*, [...] I found a passage [WOG.52.24ff.] in regard to a certain tradition—[becoming generally widespread among the Buddhists of the North and of the South, a tradition that speaks on the whole of up to 84,000 texts of the law]—that proves that it is not just oral:
>
> > I have received from the mouth of the Fortunate One, says a sacred text (*sūtra*), 80,000 texts of the law (*dharmaskandha*) and more. Another collection (*nikāya–antara*), the commentary adds, says there are 84,000. The body of the law (*dharmaskandha*) consists of books (*śāstra*) that have authority (*pramāṇa*); now these books, according to some, are 6,000 in number, and they are designated with the title of *Dharmaskandha*, or body of the law. As for the 80,000 texts of the law, they are lost (*antarhita*); the only one that remains is the single (*eka*) body [of 6,000 volumes]. Others understand by *Dharmaskandha* each of the

> articles (*kathā*) of the law, and in this way there are 80,000.
>
> It is rather in the latter sense that one should understand the term *skandha*. If one were to admit [in the first sense] that there ever was such a voluminous collection, a fact which M. Hodgson rightly contests, one would be forced to imagine it as containing works of very diverse propoṙtions, from an actual treatise to a simple stanza, for in this way we know of a work on Buddhist metaphysics, the *Prajñāpāramitā*, of which there are two versions, one of 100,000 articles and the other of only one vowel, *multum in parvo* ["much in little", i.e., A, which contains all!]. The tradition that I have just spoken of is, moreover, old among the Buddhists. It might even have given the number 84,000 as a kind of blessing; for we know that [the Buddhists] have applied this number to other objects than their religious books.
>
> Whatever the case may be with these 84,000 texts of the law, in the reality of which one can believe, if by *texts* one understands *articles*, the books that remain today are divided into three classes, called collectively *Tripiṭaka*, that is to say, 'the three baskets or collections'. These three classes are the *Sūtrapiṭaka* or the Discourses of the Buddha, the *Vinayapiṭaka* or the Discipline, and the *Abhidharmapiṭaka* or the manifested laws, i.e., metaphysics."

2. Cox points out (DD.160f.) that in the *Saṅgītiparyāya* the Buddha's teachings (*dharma*) are defined as the three sets of name, phrase and syllable (see AKB ii. 47), and that that which is manifested, understood, indicated, and so on, by these three is called the referent (*artha*). The *Jñānaprasthāna*, on the other hand, offers the following two passages regarding the Buddha's teaching (WOG.52.15ff; SA.IV.309):

> What is *buddha-vacana*? That which is the Tathāgata's speech, words, talk, voice, explanation, vocal path, vocal sound, vocal action, vocal expression (*vagvijñapti*)... .
>
> What is this *dharma* that has just been spoken of as *buddha-vacana*? The sequential arrangement, sequential establishment, and sequential combination of the *nāma-kāya*, *pada-kāya*, and *vyañjana-kāya*.

MVŚ, 658c and 659c, explains that the motive of the first passage is to eliminate misconception regarding what *buddha-vacana* is and what it is not, and to establish what is spoken by the Buddha as true *buddha-vacana*, the nature of which is described by the compilers of the MVŚ as being vocal information (*vāg-vijñapti*). By contrast, the motive of the second passage is to show the function of *buddha-vacana*. Dhammajoti comments (SA.IV.309) that "the MVŚ also mentions here the opinion of some who assert that *buddha-vacana* has *nāma*, etc., as its nature. The compilers do not reject this view [although preferring the first as being vocal information by nature]; instead, they interpret it as referring to vocal speech as the successive cause—speech (*vāk*) gives rise to *nāma*; *nāma* manifests the *artha*. However, properly speaking, it has *vāg-vijñapti* as its nature."

3. Sāṃghabhadra—not objecting to either of the two positions—explains this position as follows (Ny, 346c; SA.IV.310):

> Some assert that *buddha-vacana* has *vāk* as its *svabhāva*. They assert that the *dharma-skandha*-s are all subsumed under the *rūpa-skandha*, for *vacana* has *śabda* as its *svabhāva*.

Some assert that *buddha-vacana* has *nāma* as its *svabhāva*. They assert that the *dharma-skandha*-s are all subsumed under the *saṃskāra-skandha*, for *nāma* is of the nature of a *viprayukta-saṃskāra*. [Now,] *vāk* and *vacana* being synonyms, *vacana* may be conceded as *vāk*; [but] *nāma* and *vāk* are distinct entities, how is the [*buddha*]*vacana nāma*? They explain thus: There must be *nāma* for it to be called *vacana*; hence the nature of *buddha-vacana* is none other than *nāma*. Why? It is called *buddha-vacana* because it conveys the *artha* truly; *nāma* can convey *artha*; hence *vacana* is *nāma*. Accordingly, *buddha-vacana* definitely has *nāma* as its *svabhāva*.

4. See in this context Collett Cox's discussion: "Origins of Language Analysis and the Nature of the Buddha's Teaching" (DD.160ff.) and Dhammajoti's "Word (*nāma*) and the nature of Buddha-word (*buddha-vacana*)" (SA.IV.309f.).

300 *LS*: SAH 14.

301 *LS*: Cox summarizes (EIP.VIII.660) Saṃghabhadra (Ny, 346c): "These 80,000 factor aggregates have been interpreted in various ways, [1] as the content of a specific text by that name, or [2] as the discourse on each of the topics of the teaching, but actually [3] they are antidotes to the 80,000 types of defiled behavior."

302 *LS*: SAH 14.

303 *Gokhale*: [26a] *śāstrapramāṇa ity eke*

Tib.: [26a] *ka cig bstan bcos tshad ces zer* |

LVP: MVŚ, 385c18: The *Dharmaskandhaśāstra* is 6,000 verses (*gāthā*) long.

See analysis of Takakusu, *JPTS*, 1905, p. 112.

304 *LVP*: The 80,000 *dharmaskandhas* have perished; a single *dharmaskandha* has been preserved [WOG.52.27ff.].

305 *Gokhale*: [26b] *skandhādīnāṃ kath aikaśaḥ* |

Tib.: [26b] *phung po la sogs gtam re yin* |

LVP: This is the explanation of Buddhaghosa, *Sumaṅgala*, i. 24.

306 *LS*: SAH 14.

307 *Gokhale*: [26cd] *caritapratipakṣas tu dharmaskandho 'nuvarṇitaḥ* ||

Tib.: [26cd] *spyod pa rnams kyi gnyen por ni* | *chos kyi phung po mthun par gsungs* ||

308 *LS*: The *Vyākhyā* has (WOG.53.8ff.): kecit sattva rāga-caritāḥ. kecid dveṣa-caritāḥ. kecin moha-caritaḥ. kecin māna-cāritāh. kecid dṛṣṭi-caritāḥ. kecid vicikitsā-caritāḥ. kecid rāga-dveśa-caritāḥ. kecid rāga-dveṣa-moha-caritāḥ. kecid rāg'āśayā dveṣa-prayogāḥ... .

309 *LS*: SAH 13, 19, 22, 411.

310 *Gokhale*: [27] *tathā 'nye 'pi yathāyogaṃ skandhāyatanadhātavaḥ* | *pratipādyā yathokteṣu saṃpradhārya svalakṣaṇam* ||

Tib.: [27] *de bzhin gzhan yang ci rigs par* | *phung po skye mched khams rnams ni* | *rang gi mtshan nyid legs dpyad de* | *ji skad bshad par bsdu bar bya* ||

LVP: Among the collections of *dhātus*, the Sūtra on the seven *dhātus*, *Vibhāṣā*, 85, p. 437:

vidyādhātu, śubhadhātu (?), *ākāśānantyadhātu* ... *nirodhadhātu*.

311 *LS*: SAH 13.

312 *LS*: This is also referred to as the five-membered (*pañcāṅga*) or five-part (*pañcabhāga*) *dharmakāya*; see AKB vi, F 297, *Siddhi*, 767.

1. LVP comments in his *Musīla and Nārada*, F 190, footnote (see *Electronic Appendix*):

> The theory of salvation is ... summarized in the list of three, four or five members (*aṅga*) (*Aṅguttara*, i. 162) or constitutive groups (*skandha*) of the perfected being (*arhat, aśaikṣa*): Three things are necessary: morality (*śīla*), concentration (*samādhi*), understanding (*prajñā*) [*Kośa*, i, F 3; *Vyākhyā*, 8; *Visuddhimagga* and its three divisions]. Understanding arises only in the moral and concentrated person. By means of understanding, the meditators attain liberation (*vimukti*), i.e., removal of the fluxes, which is the fourth and last member in *Dīgha*, II, 123, and III, 229. Finally, a fifth member was added, a consecutively acquired cognition (*Kośa*, Index: *pṛṣṭhalabdha*) that is the "cognition of liberation" (*vimuktijñāna*): "I have been liberated...".
>
> [A curious variant in the *Ekottarāgama*, J. Przyluski, *Funérailles*, 92: erudition (*bāhuśrutya*) is the fourth and last member].
>
> If two members are added to the three essential members, it is perhaps in order to establish parallelism between the five "normal" aggregates (*skandha*) (material form or body, sensation, ideation, formations, consciousness) and the five groups (*skandha*) that make up the perfected beings: supramundane (*lokottara*), pure (*anāsrava*), "dharmic" groups (*dharmaskandha*). – Again: "groups of the Victor" (*jinaskandha*), "*dharmakāya* of five parts (as morality, by itself, constitutes the *dharmakāya* of the mendicant)". – *Kośa*, vi, F 297; *Siddhi*, 764; *Pāli Text Dict.* s.v. *khandha*.
>
> But it should be noted:
>
> i. the path (or the cognition) that destroys the fluxes (*ānantaryamārga*) is followed by a path called "path of liberation" (*vimuktimārga*): it is one thing to chase the thief out of the house, another to close the door. This distinction is important in the Abhidharma (*Kośa*, Index: *vimuktimārga*). Liberation (*vimukti*), the work of understanding (*prajñā*), will make up a separate group (*skandha*) or member (*aṅga*);
>
> ii. it is one thing to be liberated, another to cognize that one has been liberated. The schools have discussed whether the perfected beings (*arhat*) cognize that they are perfected beings. We will see, *Musīla* F 220, that the acquisition of "liberation" and the acquisition of the "cognition of liberation" are not simultaneous.

2. Gedun Drup states: "According to the Vaibhāṣikas, they are included in the form and compositional factors aggregates because morality is the form of the seven abandonments of body and speech, while the others are mental factors that are other than feeling and discrimination [...]

The Sautrāntikas and so forth assert that the aggregate of morality is also an attribute of intention, therefore they assert all of them to also be included in the compositional factors aggregate."

313 *LS*: SAH 19.

314 *LVP*: The *Vyākhya* cites a Sūtra, a more developed recension of *Dīgha*, iii. 241, and *Aṅguttara*, iii. 21.

vimuktyāyatana = vimukter āyadvāram.

315 *LVP*: *rūpiṇaḥ santi sattvā asaṃjñino 'pratisaṃjñinaḥ tad yathā devā asaṃjñisattvāḥ | idaṃ prathamam āyatanam | arūpiṇaḥ santi sattvāḥ sarvaśa ākiṃcanyaāyatanaṃ samatikramya naivasaṃjñānāsaṃjñāyatanam upasaṃpadya viharanti | tadyathā deva naivasaṃjñānāsaṃjñā–āyatanopagāḥ | idaṃ dvitīyam āyatanam |*

316 *LS*: SAH 22.

317 *LS*: Ibid.

318 *LVP*: They oppose the sixty-two afflicted views (*dṛṣṭi*) (MVŚ, 376c6f.). – The *Bahudhātuka* (*Madhyama*, 48, 16; *Dharmaskandha*, chapter xx) is closely related to the *Majjhima*, iii. 61f. (41 *dhātus*). Compare Asaṅga, *Sūtrālaṃkāra*, iii. 2.

LS: Dessein lists (SAHN.62) the sixty-two elements: "sixty-two elements: six faculties, six objects, six forms of consciousness (18); the six elements earth, water, fire, wind, space and consciousness (24), the six elements greed, hatred, harmfulness, absence of greed, absence of hatred and kindness (30); the six elements satisfaction, frustration, contentedness, regret, equanimity and ignorance (36); the four elements feeling, conceptual identification, conditioning factors and consciousness (40); the three elements of the sensual, the material and the immaterial (43); the three elements of the material, the immaterial and cessation (46); the three elements of the three times (49); the elements good, bad and in between (52); the three elements good, bad and neutral (55); the three elements still having learning to do, having no more learning to do, and neither still having learning to do nor having no more learning to do (58); the two elements pure and impure (60); the two elements conditioned and unconditioned (62)".

319 *LS*: AH 182; SAH 411.

320 *LS*: Cox summarizes (EIP.VIII.660) Saṃghabhadra (Ny, 347a23): "This list [of six elements] indicates those components that serve as the basis of one lifetime from the moment of conception to death."

321 *LVP*: This refers to the Sūtra that explains the constitutive elements of the human individual: *ṣaḍdhātur ayaṃ bhikṣo puruṣaḥ*. Vasubandhu cites it (i. 35) under the name of *Garbhāvakrāntisūtra* (*Vinayasaṃyuktavastu*, § 11, *Nanjio* 1121; *Ratnakūṭa*, chap. 14; *Nanjio*, 23. 15). In the *Majjhima*, this Sūtra is called *Dhātuvibhaṅgasutta* (iii. 239); it is one of the sources of *Pitāputrasamāgama* of which we have extracts in *Śikṣāsamuccaya*, p. 244; *Bodhicaryāvatāra*, ix. 88; *Madhyamakāvatāra*, p. 269.

See i, F 23, note, F 63, note and *Prakaraṇapāda* cited in the note ad ii. 23cd.

On the six elementary substances (*dhātu*), see *Aṅguttara*, i. 176; *Vibhaṅga*, pp. 82–85; *Abhidharmahṛdaya*, viii. 7.

The *Vyākhyā* refers [WOG.56.32] to the *Bāhudhātuka*.

[322] *LS*: AH 182; SAH 411.

[323] *Gokhale*: [28ab] *chidram ākāśadhātvākhyam ālokatamasī kila* |

Tib.: [28ab] *bu ga nam mkha'i khams shes bya* | *snang dang mun pa dag yin lo* |

LS: See our endnote to i. 5d, which discusses the distinction between the conditioned and unconditioned space. At ii. F 278f., Vasubandhu explains the three unconditioned factors from the point of view of the Sautrāntikas who deny that they are real entities.

[324] *LVP*: MVŚ, 388a29; *Dharmaskandha*, 10, p. 503b. – Same definition in *Vibhaṅga*, p. 84: *katamā ajjhattikā ākāsadhātu? yaṃ ajjhattaṃ paccattam ākāso ākāsagataṃ aghaṃ aghagataṃ vivaro vivaragatam ... kaṇṇacchiddaṃ nāsacchiddaṃ...* .

[325] *LVP*: P'u-kuang (*Kō-ki*, 17/*TD* 41, p. 32c28): "It is said that the elementary substance space (*ākāśadhātu*) is light and darkness in order to show that it is a kind of color (*varṇa*) and a real entity." The author does not believe that the elementary substance space is a real entity, that is why he adds the word *kila* ["so said", "so reported"]. For Vasubandhu and the Sautrāntikas, the elementary substance space is just the absence of a resisting body (*sapratigha-dravyābhāvamātra*). See ii. 55cd.

MVŚ, 388b19: What difference is there between space (*ākāśa*) and the elementary substance space (*ākāśadhātu*)? – The first is non-material (*arūpin*), invisible (*anidarśana*), non-resistant (*apratigha*), pure (*anāsrava*), unconditioned (*asaṃskṛta*); the second is material... .

[326] *LVP*: The edition of the *Vyākhyā* reads *āgha*: *āghaṃ kila citasthaṃ rūpam* iti citasthaṃ saṃghātastham | *atyarthaṃ hanti hanyate ce*ty āgham | ...atyarthaśabdasya ākārādeśaḥ kṛto hanteś ca ghādeśaḥ [WOG.57.16]. But the Burnouf MS. reads: *agham ... akārādeśaḥ*; we have, ad iii. 72, *agha = citastharūpa* (aggregated matter or form); *Mahāvyutpatti*, 245, 162.

[327] *LS*: AH 182; SAH 411.

[328] *Gokhale*: [28cd] *vijñānadhātur vijñānaṃ sāsravaṃ janmaniśrayaḥ* ||

Tib.: [28cd] *zag dang bcas pa'i rnam shes ni* | *rnam shes khams yin skye ba'i rten* ||

[329] *LS*: AH 10–13; SAH 27, 30–38, 43–47, 49–50.

See Frauwallner's discussion (SAL.141ff.) of the development of this list of twenty-two doctrinal perspectives, which is part of what he dubs "Pañcaskandhaka" (see our endnote to Section B at ii. 4a).

Tibetan and Chinese sources, however, give different listings of the these twenty-two perspectives, although referring to the same listed items.

1. As for Pu Guang's listing (T41, no. 1821, 34b6–44c11), see Dhammajoti's *Summary*, p. 14. Dhammajoti adds (private communication) that another well-known master of the Chinese tradition, Yuan Hui, also belonging to the Tang Dynasty (but posterior to Pu Guang), states the same in his commentary on the *Kośa kārikā*: T41, no. 1823, 826b: "Yuan Hui is most likely influenced by Pu Guang; it is indeed the 'general Chinese tradition' (no doubt transmitted through the Xuan Zang school)."

2. Our list follows fairly well the one presented by Gedun Drup. Comparing Gedun Drup and Pu Guang, we find that the doctrinal perspectives (*1*) – (*10*) and (*15*) to (22) are the same,

but that Gedun Drup combines Pu Guang's doctrinal perspectives (*11*) – (*13*) into his doctrinal perspective (*11*), whereas Pu Guang combines Gedun Drup's doctrinal perspectives (*12*) – (*14*) into his doctrinal perspective (*14*).

3. Moreover, from the point of view of ease of expression, Gedun Drup's *Clarifying the Path to Liberation* groups the twenty-two doctrinal perspectives into the following categories:

i. The five, those that can be indicated and so forth (*1–5*)
ii. The division of those with investigation and with analysis and so forth (*6*)
iii. The five, those with observed objects and so forth (*7–11*)
iv. The classification of the three arisals (*12*)
v. The five, those having substance and so forth (*13–17*)
vi. The classification of those that are objects of abandonment of the path of seeing and so forth (*18*)
vii. The classification of those that are views and non-views (*19*)
viii. The three that are to be understood by the two and so forth (*20–22*)

4. But Tibetan sources also have different listings of the twenty-two doctrinal perspectives, see, for example, Mikyö Dorje's *Youthful Play*. He groups the twenty-two into the following seven topics (Gedun Drup's twenty-two perspectives are rendered first in italic numbers and then Mikyö Dorje's):

i. Classifying in two categories (*1–2*; two perspectives)
ii. Classifying in three categories (*3–4*; two perspectives)
iii. Whether they possess something or not (*5–7*; three perspectives)
iv. Classification of those with form (*8–11*; five perspectives)
v. Three modes of production (*12–14*; two perspectives)
vi. Distinctions of attainment (*15*; one perspective)
viii. Classifying as external, internal and so forth (*16–22*; seven perspectives)

330 *LS*: AH 10; SAH 27.

331 *LS*: Hsüan-tsang, ii, fol. 1a.

332 *Gokhale*: [29ab1] *sanidarśanam eko 'tra rūpaṃ*

Tib.: [29a] *bstan yod 'dir ni gzugs gcig pu* |

LS: 1. See iv. 4a, which quotes the Sūtra (cf. *Dighanikāya*, iii, 217) saying that material form (*rūpa*) is of three types:

> Material form is included in a threefold material form (*rūpasya rūpasaṃgrahaḥ*): (1) there is a material form that is visible [*sanidarśana*] and resistant [*sapratigha*] (visible form) (see i. 29ac); (2) there is a material form that is invisible [*anidarśana*] and resistant [*sapratigha*] (the eye, etc.) (see i. 29ac); (3) there is a material form that is invisible [*anidarśana*] and non-resistant [*apratigha*].

The Vaibhāṣikas state that besides the element of visible form, all other elements are invisible, which leaves us with nine material elements that are both invisible and resistant. As for the third type, they claim that it refers to non-informative action (*avijñapti*).

2. See also i. 24, which gives three reasons for the predominance of the sense-sphere of visible form (*rūpāyatana*): resistance (*sapratighatva*), visibility (*sanidarśanatva*) and common

usage (*loka*), the first two being singled out by Saṃghabhadra as constituting the distinctive nature of visible form (*rūpa*). He elaborates (Ny.348a; SA.IV.190) regarding being visible or "with seeing" (*sanidarśana*):

> This is in two senses:
>
> i. Matter is necessarily co-existent with seeing (*darśana*), hence said to be visible ("with-seeing", *sanidarśana*), for matter and the eye arise simultaneously; this is like [the sense of] "with companion".
>
> ii. Matter has indicatability, hence said to be visible, for it can be differently indicated as being here or being there; this is like [the sense of] "with-object" (*sa-ālambana*).

3. *Visibility and the theory of atoms*: Even though the Buddhist atom theory was not yet developed during the time of the Buddha, thus could not have been addressed in the Sūtram the Vaibhāṣikas (SA.IV.199) admit that an atom as the smallest unit of matter is known through mental analysis and is referred to as "conceptual atom" (**prajñapti-paramāṇu*). This conceptual atom is, however, based on the ultimately real atom having the intrinsic characteristic of matter (the visibles, etc.), which as individual *paramāṇu* cannot be directly observed by the human eye (cf. i, F 94) and thus cannot serve individually as the object of visual perception. As a physical assemblage (和集; *he ji*) (i. 35d; ii. 22), however, it can be known through direct perception (*pratyakṣa*) (Ny, 522a), as stated in AKB iii. F 213: "The atoms (*paramāṇu*), although suprasensible (*atīndriya*), become sensible (*pratyakṣatva*) when they are combined (*samasta*)."

The MVŚ, 702ab, gives the following descriptive definition of an "atom" (SA.IV.199):

> An atom (*paramāṇu*) is the smallest *rūpa*. It cannot be cut, broken, penetrated; it cannot be taken up, abandoned, ridden on, stepped on, struck or dragged. It is neither long nor short, square nor round, regular nor irregular, convex nor concave. It has no smaller parts; it cannot be decomposed, cannot be seen, heard, smelled, touched. It is thus that the *paramāṇu* is said to be the finest (*sarva-sūkṣma*) of all *rūpa*-s.
>
> Seven of these *paramāṇu*-s constitute an *aṇu*—the finest among all *rūpa*-s perceivable by the eye and visual consciousness. [However,] this [*aṇu*] can be seen by only three types of eyes: 1. the divine eye (*divya-cakṣus*), 2. the eye of a Universal Monarch (*cakravartin*), 3. the eye of a *bodhisattva* in his last birth. Seven *aṇu*-s constitute a *tāmra-rajas* ["Copper-dust"]. ... Seven *go-rajas*-s ["Cow-dust"] constitute a *vātāyana-rajas* ["Dust in the wind passage"] ... [in this way, the whole physical universe is composed].

Based on Saṃghabhadra (Ny, 383c), we can speak of two types of *paramāṇu*-s: (1) the "real-entity atom" (*dravya-paramāṇu*)—the smallest conceivable building block of matter that cannot be further divided into many parts by means of another matter or the intellect (*buddhi*)—which is the *parama-aṇu* in the proper sense of the term, i.e., the "ultimately small", since there can be no further part; (2) the "aggregate-atom" (*saṃghāta-paramāṇu*) in the sense of a molecule—a multitude of *dravya-paramāṇu*-s that are mutually combined and necessarily inseparable—which is the smallest unit of matter that can actually occur in the phenomenal world.

Now, although in the MVŚ passage, cited above, the human eye is said to be unable to perceive an atom (cf. also i. F 94), Saṃghabhadra argues that this does not mean (SA.IV.201) that an atom is invisible (*anidarśana*) in its intrinsic nature, but simply means that its visibility is extremely minute, i.e., virtually nil, since otherwise it would forfeit its very intrinsic nature (*svalakṣaṇa*) as visible form (*rūpa*), i.e., visibility (*sa-nidarśana*). Therefore, with regard to an atom of colour or shape, another passage in the MVŚ (64a; SA.IV.244) can state:

> There exists [an atom of green]; it is only that it is not grasped by visual consciousness. If a single atom is not green, an accumulation of numerous atoms cannot be green; likewise for yellow, etc., … .
>
> There exists [an atom of a long shape, etc.]; it is only that it is not grasped by visual consciousness. If a single atom is not long, etc., in shape, an accumulation of numerous atoms cannot be long, etc., in shape.
>
> Furthermore, there exist *rūpa*-s which are not visible on account of being extremely fine, not on account of being non-objects (*aviṣaya*).

According to Vaibhāṣika epistemology, an agglomeration of visible form atoms comes to be directly perceived and exists as an absolutely real entity (*paramārtha-sat*). Not being a superimposition on the real atoms, it is not a relatively real entity or conceptually existent entity (*prajñāpti-sat*), since (ADCP.147) "it is but the 'form' which is none other than the very atoms themselves—each atom is contributing in its own right and the collective contribution comes to be strong enough to generate a sensory consciousness. This is essentially the same as saying that a visible *rūpa* is as much a real entity (*dravya*) as an individual atom. But the assembled atoms directly perceived by a sensory consciousness—and only directly by a sensory consciousness—are not anything in the form of a jar etc., which can only be perceived by mental consciousness when superimposition takes place."

333 *LS*: AH 10; SAH 30.

334 *Gokhale*: [29b2–c1] *sapratighā daśa | rūpiṇo*

Tib.: [29b] *thogs dang bcas pa gzugs can bcu |*

LVP: See above i. 24ff.

LS: The *Siddhi* has (F 38): "The Foundational Vehicle distinguishes two types of form (*rūpa*): (i) resistant (*sapratigha*) form, which consists of atoms (*paramāṇumaya*), which includes the first ten sense-spheres (*āyatana*): eye and visible form, … body and tangible; (ii) non-resistant (*apratigha*) form, which does not consist of atoms, which includes one part of the sense-sphere of factors (*dharmāyatana*) (*Kośa*, iv, F 16). – In our language, material and immaterial form."

335 *LVP*: The element of factors (*dharmadhātu*) is eliminated: it includes the non-informative (*avijñapti*) that is material and not resistant.

336 *LS*: SAH 30.

337 *LS*: Pradhan.19.6 has *pratigho nāma pratighātaḥ*. Saṃghabhadra explains (Ny, 348a; SA.IV.190): "Resistance means obstruction. 'This has the obstruction by that' (i.e., this is obstructed by that), hence it is said to be 'with-resistance' [*sa-pratigha*]. Obstruction (*pratighāta*) is threefold: …".

Dessein thinks (JIABS, vol. 26, No. 2, 2003, p. 302f.) that, according to P'u-kuang, "in the early Abhidharma literature, 'resistance' was explained to be the relation between a faculty and its respective object. In the course of philosophical development, three forms of 'resistance' came to be distinguished: 'resisting by way of being an obstruction' (*āvaraṇapratighāta*), 'resisting of the object' (*viṣayapratighāta*), and 'resisting of the supporting object' (*ālambanapratighāta*). Of these, 'resisting of the object' corresponds to the interpretation of 'resisting' presented in early Abhidharma literature."

338 *LS*: SAH 30.

339 *LS*: Two material factors are mutually resistant or obstructive in this sense to each other (Ny, 348a; SA.IV.191).

340 *LS*: SAH 30.

341 *LS*: The contact between the sense-faculty, thought or thought-concomitants and the content or object-field is referred to as "resistance". When the sense-faculty meets with its corresponding object-field and "its efficacy of the sense-faculty (e.g., seeing) is exercised, then it is said to be obstructed by that object domain inasmuch as its sphere of vision is at that time confined to that object" (Ny, 348a; SA.IV.191).

342 *LVP*: See *Kāraṇaprajñaptiśāstra*, analyzed in **Cosmologie bouddhique**, p. 339.

343 *LVP*: Compare *Saṃyutta*, iv. 201: *puthujjano cakkhusmiṃ haññati manāpāmanāpehi rūpehi.*

344 *LS*: SAH 30.

345 *LS*: The sense of obstruction here refers to the thought and thought-concomitants being obstructed by—confined to—their cognitive object (Ny, 348a; SA.IV.191).

346 *LS*: SAH 30.

347 *LS*: Hsüan-tsang translates here *kāritra* as *gong neng*. In his **Nyāyānusāra* he translates *kāritra* very consistently as *zuo yong* (作用), and uses *gong neng* (功能), efficacy, for the terms denoting activities other than *kāritra*. See SA.IV.207.

348 *LS*: A *dharma*, *y*, is the object-field (*visaya*) of another *dharma*, *x*, if *x* exercises its efficacy (seeing, etc.) in *y*. The *Vyākhyā* glosses [WOG.59.4ff.]: *yasmiṃ yasya kāritraṃ. sa tasya viṣaya* iti. kāritraṃ puruṣa-kārāh. cakṣuḥ-śrotra'ādīnāṃ rūpa-śabda'ādiṣv ālocana-śravaṇ'ādi-kāritraṃ. tac ca sva citta-caittan praty āśraya-bhāva-śakti-viśeṣa-lakṣanaṃ veditavyaṃ.

349 *LS*: Dhammajoti comments (ADCP.41f.):

> The Sarvāstivāda distinction is that whereas an external object that is sensed by a sense faculty is called a *viṣaya*—the domain wherein it can exercise its activity—sometimes also called an *artha*; an object that generates a corresponding consciousness is called an *ālambana* (<*ā-√lamb*, "hang on to"). This latter is so called because it is that which is hung on to—i.e., is grasped (*gṛhyate*)—by a mental *dharma* so as to arise at the present. In its capacity of serving as one of the two necessary conditions for the arising of a consciousness, it is called an *ālambana-pratyaya*, "condition qua object". ... The *ālambana-pratyaya* subsumes all *dharma*-s —i.e., all the twelve *āyatana*-s—since all real entities known as *dharma*-s have this capacity.

[350] *LS*: Cox summarizes (EIP.VIII.661) Saṃghabhadra (Ny, 348a): "This contact between the sense-organ, awareness or awareness concomitants and the content or supporting object is referred to as 'resistance' because the sense organs, awareness and so on cannot operate with regard to anything else."

[351] *LVP*: *yatrotpitsor manasaḥ pratighātaḥ śakyate [paraiḥ] kartum | tad eva sapratighaṃ [tad] viparyayād apratigham iṣṭam.*

That is to say: the consciousness that arises having for its object-field (*viṣaya*) blue and for its support (*āśraya*) the eye, can be hindered from arising through the interposition of a foreign body between the eye and the blue object: the eye and the blue are thus resistant (*sapratigha*).

On the contrary, neither the mental faculty (*manodhātu*) functioning as the sense-faculty of the mental consciousness (*manovijñāna*) nor the element of factors (*dharmadhātu*) that is the particular object of the mental consciousness (e.g., sensation) are resistant (*sapratigha*): with respect to the element of factors, nothing can hinder—by making an *obstacle* or placing a *screen* (*āvaraṇa*)—the mental consciousness from arising by means of the mental faculty.

LS: Dessein translates (JIABS, vol. 26, No. 2, 2003, p. 299) the corresponding passage in the *A-p'i-t'an Hsin Lun Ching* (T. 1551: 835b27–28): "That which, at the moment an idea (*manas*) is about to arise, is resisting, should be known as 'resisting' (*sapratigha*). In the contrary case, it is unresisting (*apratigha*)." P'u-kuang comments (p. 302):

> When, in this stanza, "obstruction" (*āvaraṇa*) is mentioned, the idea is that it is so that because something is hindered by something else, it does not succeed in arising. When properly taking the specific object (*svaviṣaya*) as supporting object (*ālambana*), what is then said to be obstructing? It is as when visual consciousness (*cakṣurvijñāna*) wants to arise regarding matter (*rūpa*) as object (*viṣaya*), its arising would be hindered by such other things as sound (*śabda*). When it would be obstructed by other things, it should be known it is "resisting" (*sapratigha*); when properly taking matter as supporting object, it is said to be "unresisting" (*apratigha*).

[352] *LS*: AH 10, 222–23; SAH 27; 34.

[353] *LS*: 1. Regarding the meaning and etymology of the word *kuśala*, Buddhaghosa (*Atthasālinī*.48) states:

> The word "*kusala*" (moral) means "of good health", "faultless", "skilful", "productive of happy sentient results", etc. ...
>
> To come to word-definitions:
>
> *kusalas* are so called in that they cause contemptible things to tremble [from *ku*, "bad", + √*sal*, "to tremble"], to shake, to be disturbed, destroyed.
>
> Or, *kusa* are those (vices) which lie in a person under contemptible conditions [from *ku*, "bad", + √*sī*, to lie]. And *kusalas* (from *kusa*, so derived + √*lū*, to cut) are so called because they lop off, cut off what are known as immoralities (*a-kusala*).
>
> Or, knowledge is called *kusa* [from *ku*, "bad", + √*so*, to reduce] because of the reduction or eradication of contemptible things, and *kusala* [from *kusa*, so defined, + √*lā*, to take] is so called because things should be taken, grasped, set in motion by that *kusa*.

> Or just as the *kusa* grass cuts a part of the hand with both edges, so also certain things cut off the corrupt part in two portions, either what has arisen, or what has not arisen. Therefore *kusalas* are so called because they cut off the corruptions like the *kusa* grass.

2. MVŚ, 741a, provides, among others, the following definitions of the triad wholesome (*kuśala*), unwholesome (*akuśala*), non-defined (*avyākṛta*) (SA.IV.39):

> A *dharma* which is to be subsumed as being skillful, which effects a desirable fruit, and which is by nature secure (*kṣema*) is said to be *kuśala*. ... Some say: A *dharma* which can produce the germs of a desirable existence and of liberation is said to be *kuśala*.
>
> A *dharma* which cannot produce the germs of a desirable existence and of liberation is said to be *akuśala*.
>
> That which is opposed to these two classes is said to be *avyākrta*.

Vasubandhu deals with wholesome, unwholesome and neutral factors mainly in chapter 4: EXPOSITION OF ACTION (*karma*), where he defines (at iv. 8b–9c) *dharmas* as being wholesome or unwholesome in four ways:

i. absolutely (*paramārthatas*);
ii. through their intrinsic nature or in and of themselves (*svabhāvatas* = *ātmatas*);
iii. through association (*saṃprayogatas*);
iv. through their originating cause (*samutthānatas*);

at which occasion he also briefly explains "that which is absolutely non-defined".

But as for the "general" non-defined *dharmas* (*avyākṛta*), they are divided into two groups: (i) *nivṛta-avyākṛta* (veiled-non-defined or obscured-non-defined) and (ii) *anivṛta-avyākṛta* (non-veiled-non-defined or unobscured-non-defined) (SA.IV.40f.):

> i. A veiled-non-defined *dharma*, being weak in nature, is that which, though incapable of inducing an undesirable fruit, is nevertheless obstructive to the arising of the outflow-free understanding or the noble path. This fact of obstructiveness of the defiled *dharma*-s is what is meant by its being "veiled". An example of this is the "Self-view", *satkāya-dṛṣṭi*, which is a defiled *prajñā*.* ...
>
> ii. An non-veiled-non-defined *dharma* is that which is neither capable of inducing a retribution-fruit—desirable or undesirable—nor obstructing the arising of the noble path. Examples of this category are: the knowledge (a *prajñā*) of a particular art and craft (*śailpasthānika*), or the mind associated with a supernormal power (*abhijñā-phala*), or with deportment (*īryāpatha*). (a) Karmic retribution, and (b) physical matter—*rūpa*, *gandha*, *rasa* and *spraṣṭavya*—are also non-veiled-non-defined. The latter are in fact non-defined (*avyākṛta*) in their intrinsic nature (*svabhāvatas*). The two *asaṃskṛta*-s—*apratisaṃkhyā-nirodha* and *ākāśa*—are non-defined absolutely (*paramarthato'vyākṛta*), also belong to this category.

* MVŚ, 259c–260a [SA.IV..41], explains why *satkāya-dṛṣṭi* is not *akuśala*, but *avyākṛta* (*nivṛta*).

Saṃghabhadra gives the following definitions (Ny, 348c; SA.IV.39):

> A non-defined *dharma* is that which cannot be defined as being either skillful or unskillful, its nature being indistinct.
>
> A *dharma* is said to be (morally) defined (*vyākṛta*) if it is praise-worthy or contemptible, and definable as pertaining to the "black" or "white" (i.e., good or bad) species.
>
> A skillful *dharma* is that which is opposed to the unskillful, or that which sustains or is sustained by understanding (*prajñā*), or that which brings about the auspicious.
>
> The opposite to this is unskillful.

3. As for the definitions of *kuśala, akuśala* and *avyākṛta* actions (*karma*) in terms of their effect, see iv. 45ab.

4. As for the definitions of *kuśala* and *akuśala* paths of action (*karmapatha*), see iv. 66bd.

5. As for the number of associated thought-concomitants in regard to *kuśala, akuśala* and *avyākṛta* thoughts, see ii. 28–30d.

6. See also in particular Lambert Schmithausen's *Kuśala and Akuśala: Reconsidering the Original Meaning of a Basic Pair of Terms of Buddhist Spirituality and Ethics and its Development up to Early Yogācāra* (forthcoming).

354 *Gokhale*: [29c2–d] *'vyākṛtā aṣṭau ta evā 'rūpaśabdakāḥ* ||

Tib.: [29cd1] *lung ma bstan brgyad de dag nyid | gzugs sgra ma gtogs*

LVP: See ii. 9a; MVŚ, 263c12, 740b8.

355 *LS*: Visible form and sound—since they include bodily and vocal acts—belong to all three moral categories.

356 *LS*: Schmithausen comments (KA, section 3):

> One of the achievements of the canonical Abhidharma works is the attempt to fix the range of employment of the categories *kuśala* and *akuśala*, as one item within the scheme of properties applied to the list of *dharmas*—basic factors of existence established on the basis of the Sūtras and considered to comprise everything that exists—in order to determine their common and distinctive features. If *kuśala* and *akuśala* are to cover all *dharmas*, *akuśala* would have to be taken in the sense of a mere negation of *kuśala*, i.e., as "not wholesome". But in most if not all of its occurrences in the canon it is used in the sense of something opposed to *kuśala*, i.e., "unwholesome" = "detrimental", "baneful", implicitly admitting the possibility of factors that are neither *kuśala* nor *akuśala*. For this reason, most Abhidharmic traditions share the assumption of a third alternative, namely *avyākṛta*, "unexplained [as either *kuśala* or *akuśala*]",* "neutral".

* *kuśālākuśalabhāvenāvyākaraṇād avyākṛtāḥ*. Another explanation says: "because they are not explained with regard to (i.e., as entailing an agreeable or disagreeable) retribution (*vipākaṃ praty avyākaraṇād ity apare*)."

357 *Gokhale*: [30a1] *tridhā 'nye*

Tib.: [29d2] *gzhan rnam gsum* |

358 *LVP*: The Mahīśāsakas believe that the first four consciousnesses are all non-defined; the

tactile consciousness and the mental consciousness are of three types. The problem is discussed in *Siddhi*.

359 *LS*: The *Vyākhyā* has [WOG.60.16f.]: *dharma-dhātur* iti vistaraḥ. *alobh'ādi-svabhāvo* yo' 'yam uktaḥ. alobh'ādi-*saṃprayukto* vedan'ādiḥ. alobh'ādi-*samuttho* viprayuktaḥ. prāpti-jāty-ādiḥ. avijñaptiś ca.

360 *LS*: AH 11; SAH 31.

361 *LS*: The three realms (*dhātu*), i.e., the world (*loka*) and their related meditative attainments (*samāpatti*) are discussed in great detail later by Vasubandhu in chapter 3, EXPOSITION OF THE WORLD (*lokanirdeśa*), and chapter 8, EXPOSITION OF THE MEDITATIVE ATTAINMENT (*samāpattinirdeśa*).

Here is the outline of chapter 3:

A. The three realms (*dhātu*): the world of sentient beings & the receptacle world (vv. 1–3)
  - Realm of desire (*kāmadhātu*)
  - Realm of fine-materiality (*rūpadhātu*)
  - Realm of immateriality (*ārūpyadhātu*)
  - Definition of the three realms (*dhātu*)
  - Are the triple realms unique (single)?
  - The arrangement of the triple realms

B. The world of sentient beings (*sattvaloka*) (vv. 4–44)
  - The planes of existence (*gati*), modes of birth (*yoni*), intermediate beings (*antarābhava*), Process of reincarnation (*pratisaṃdhi*)
  - Dependent origination (*pratītyasamutpāda*) & refutation of the doctrine of self (*ātman*)
  - The enduring of sentient beings
  - Death and birth of sentient beings

C. The receptacle world (*bhājanaloka*) (vv. 45–74)

D. The measurements (*pramāṇa*) of the bodies and life-expectancy (*āyus*) of sentient Beings (vv. 75–89)

E. The great aeon (*mahākalpa*) of the world (vv. 90–102)
  - The four stages of dissolution, nothingness, creation and duration

362 *LS*: AH 11; SAH 31.

363 *Gokhale*: [30a2–b1] *kāmadhātvāptāḥ sarve*

Tib.: [30a] *'dod khams gtogs pa thams cad do* |

LVP: The factors that do not belong to any realm of existence, that are transcendent to existence (*adhātupatita, adhātvāpta, apariyāpanna*), are the unconditioned factors and the pure factors (*anāsrava*).

364 *LS*: AH 11; SAH 31.

365 *Gokhale*: [30b2–d] *rūpe caturdaśa* | *vinā gandharasaghrāṇajihvāvijñānadhātubhiḥ* ||

Tib.: [30bd] *gzugs kyi khams na bcu bzhi'o* | *dri dang ro dang sna dang ni* | *lce yi rnam shes khams ma gtogs* ‖

LVP: The examination of this problem is taken up again in ii. 12.

Compare *Kathāvatthu*, viii, 7.

366 *LS*: AH 11; SAH 31.

367 *LS*: Dharmatrāta comments (SAH.48): "[The realm of form] is without the nature of solid food: because the body is subtle (*sūkṣma*)."

368 *LVP*: The bodily well-being is *kāyakarmaṇyatā*.

369 *LS*: SAH 31.

370 *LS*: This is the tenth of Kritzer's fifteen passages discussed in relation to chapter 1 (VY.22f). Saṃghabhadra [Ny, 349b22–25] identifies the objection as Vasubandhu's.

371 *LVP*: *kośagatavastiguhya*.

LS: Hall translates literally: "Would it not be beautiful in the case of those [Buddhas and others] who have their private parts concealed in a sheath (*kośa-gata-vasti-guhya*)?" He comments (VASC.124) that "this is the tenth of the thirty-two marks of a great man (*mahā-puruṣā*—that is of a future Buddha or *cakravartin*) in the list given, for example, in the *Lakkhana-suttanta* of the *Dīgha-nikāya*".

372 *LVP*: Comp. *Dīgha*, i. 34, 186.

373 *LS*: Pradhan.21.19 has *maithunasparśamukhena*.

374 *LVP*: MVŚ, 746a4: "Do the male and female sexual faculties exist in the realm of fine-materiality? Neither of the sexual faculties exist there.

First opinion: it is because one wishes to abandon these faculties that one cultivates the meditations (*dhyāna*) and that one will be reborn in the realm of fine-materiality. If the sentient beings of the realm of fine-materiality did possess these faculties, one would not wish to be reborn in this realm.

Second opinion: these faculties are created by coarse food (iii. 39); the Sūtra (iii. 98c) says, in fact, that human beings at the beginning of the cosmic aeon did not possess these faculties, that they all had the same shape; later, when they ate the earth-juice, the two faculties arose, the difference between man and woman appeared; in the absence of coarse food, the two faculties are lacking.

Third opinion: the two faculties have a use in the realm of desire, but have no use in the realm of fine-materiality: thus they are lacking in the realm of fine-materiality... ."

On the gods of the realm of desire, see iii. 70.

375 *LS*: AH 11; SAH 31.

376 *Gokhale*: [31ab] *ārūpyāptā manodharmamanovijñānadhātavaḥ* |

Tib.: [31ab] *gzugs med gtogs pa yid dang ni* | *chos dang yid kyi rnam shes khams* |

377 *LS*: AH 11; SAH 31.

378 *Gokhale*: [31cd1] *sāsravā'nāsravā ete trayaḥ*

Tib.: [31c] *de gsum zag bcas zag pa med* |

LS: This is the twofold classification with which Vasubandhu starts out. For details and further AKB references, see i. 4. For its soteriological context see i. 3.

379 *Gokhale*: [31d2] *śeṣās tu sāsravāḥ* ||

Tib.: [31d] *lhag ma rnams ni zag bcas so* ||

380 *LVP*: The Mahāsāṃghikas and the Sautrāntikas maintain that the body of the Buddha is pure (*anāsrava*) (see iv. 4ab, discussion of the non-informative [*avijñapti*]). (Compare *Kathāvatthu*, iv. 3, xiv. 4). The MVŚ, 229a17, 391c27 and 871c11 [see *Siddhi*, 770]: Certain scholars maintain that the body of the Buddha is pure, namely the Mahāsāṃghikas who say: "Scripture says that the Tathāgata remains above the world, that he is not mundane, that he is not defiled; we know thus that the body of the Buddha is pure." In order to refute this opinion, it is shown that the body of the Buddha is impure. To say that it is pure is to contradict the Sūtra.

The body of the Buddha is not pure (*anāsrava*) because it can be the occasion for the defilement of another. MVŚ, 871c11; see *Siddhi*, 770: The body of the Buddha is the result of ignorance and of craving; thus it is not pure. The Sūtra says that ten *āyatana*s (the eye sense-faculty..., the visible form...) in their entirety, and two sense-spheres (*āyatana*) in part (*mana-āyatana*; *dharma*s) are impure.... If the body of the Buddha were pure, women would not have affection for him; the body would not produce, among others, desire, hatred, confusion, arrogance... .

Compare *Vyākhyā*, p. 14; see above, F 6.

381 *LS*: AH 12; SAH 32, 50.

382 *LVP*: Same question in *Vibhaṅga*, 97, 435. – Initial inquiry (*vitarka*) and investigation (*vicāra*) are defined ii. 28, 33.

383 *LS*: AH 12; SAH 32.

384 *Gokhale*: [32ab] *savitarkavicārā hi pañca vijñānadhātavaḥ* |

Tib.: [32ab] *nges par rtog dang rjes dran pa'i* | *rnam par rtog pas rnam mi rtog* |

385 *LS*: This is the eleventh of Kritzer's fifteen passages discussed in relation to chapter 1 (VY.24f.). Saṃghabhadra [Ny, 350a7–12] states that this is Vasubandhu's own reasoning and presents as the real reason why these five consciousnesses are always associated with *vitarka* and *vicāra* the fact that these kinds of consciousness arise only where both occur, i.e., in the realm of desire and the first meditation (*dhyāna*) (EIP.VIII.662).

386 *LS*: AH 12; SAH 32.

387 *Gokhale*: [32c] *antyās trayas triprakārāḥ*

Tib.: [32c] *tha ma gsum ni rnam gsum mo* |

388 *LS*: This is the twelfth of Kritzer's fifteen passages discussed in relation to chapter 1 (VY.26f.). Dhammajoti comments (private communication) that "Saṃghabhadra says that this is not the proper reason, because even if there were two simultaneous *vitarka*, no *vitarka* can be associated with itself. So the correct reason that should be given is: no *svabhāva* can be associated with itself."

389 *LS*: AH 12; SAH 32.

390 *Gokhale*: [32d] *śeṣā ubhayavarjitāḥ* ||

Tib.: [32d] *lhag ma rnams ni gnyis ka spangs* ||

391 *LS*: SAH 50.

392 *Gokhale*: [33ab] *nirūpaṇā'nusmaraṇavikalpenā 'vikalpakāḥ* |

Tib.: [33ab] *nges par rtog dang rjes dran pa'i* | *rnam par rtog pas rnam mi rtog* |

LVP: They are called *free from conceptualizing activity* (*avikalpaka*) according to the text: *cakṣurvijñānasamaṅgī nīlaṃ vijānāti no tu nīlam iti* (see above p. F 28, note).

See *Kośa*, iii, F 109; iv, F 39; *Siddhi*, 282, 389–91.

LS: 1. See our endnote to ideation (*saṃjñā*; i. 14cd), where we have discussed the relationship of ideation with determination (*nirūpaṇā*), conceptual construction (*vikalpa*), initial inquiry (*vitarka*) and investigation (*vicāra*).

2. Here, Vasubandhu emphasizes the difference between the non-conceptualizing or non-discriminative sensory consciousnesses and the conceptualizing or discriminative mental consciousnesses.

i. As for the difference regarding their object, Dhammajoti explains (ADCP.103):

> While all the six forms of consciousness are said to have the same intrinsic nature of being conscious, and all grasp in each case the object-substance generically [see AKB i. 16a], the Sarvāstivāda sees distinct differences as regards the functional nature between the five sensory consciousnesses on the one hand and mental consciousness on the other. ...
>
> To begin with, each sensory consciousness is confined to its specific object at the present moment only: visual consciousness can cognize only a single present visual object, auditory consciousness, only a single present sound; etc. Its object is always external; the sense faculties and the consciousnesses cannot become its objects. ...
>
> In contrast, mental consciousness can at once take multiple objects, including those of the five sensory consciousnesses, and its objects need not be confined to a single species or time period.

ii. As for the difference regarding their conceptualizing activity or discrimination (*vikalpa*) (ADCP.103):

> Moreover, in addition to grasping the mere object-substance, thanks to contribution from the co-nascent concomitants—particularly understanding (*prajñā*) and recollection (*smṛti*) and ideation (*saṃjñā*) which can function strongly therein—mental consciousness can also interpret a given perceptual data, and even abstractize and conceptualize on it. In Abhidharma terms, it can perceive both the specific as well as the common characteristics. This interpretive capability of mental consciousness is generically indicated by the term *vikalpa*, "discrimination".
>
> In the Sarvāstivāda explanation, the *smṛti* and *prajñā*—identified with the second and third *vikalpa*, respectively—conjoined with the five sensory consciousnesses are weak, and hence the latter two types of *vikalpa*-s are not operative. They are thus said to be without *vikalpa*, "non-discriminative" (*avikalpaka*)... .

> In contrast, because mental consciousness possesses all the three types of *vikalpa*, it is said to be *vikalpaka*, "discriminative". [...]

Samghabhadra elaborates further (Ny, 349a) as to why mental consciousness is said to be "discriminative" or "conceptualizing" (*vikalpaka*) and how it therefore can generate a stream of thoughts, and why the sensory consciousnesses are said to be "non-discriminative" or "non-conceptualizing" and do not have the ability to generate a stream of thoughts (SA.IV.265f.):

> If a consciousness can, within a single moment, grasp objects belonging to numerous species, and can, with regard to one given perceptual object, generate a stream of thoughts—a consciousness of such a nature is said to be discriminative. The five groups of *vijñāna*, on the other hand, grasp only present objects. No two moments [of thought] have the same perceptual object, for when the previous grasping of a perceptual object has ceased, there cannot be the arising of a repeated grasping [of the same object] by the consciousness in the second moment. Mental consciousness can take objects belonging to the three periods of time. [In this case,] a *dharma*, though having ceased, can still be its object, and a stream of thoughts can be generated with regard to the same object. For these reasons, only this [consciousness] is said to be discriminative. However, since the five *vijñāna-kāya*-s are always conjoined with *svabhāva-vikalpa*, they are also discriminative. The *sūtra*-s speak of them as being non-discriminative [only] in the sense of being without *anusmaraṇa*- and *abhinirūpaṇā-vikalpa*-s.

3. See in this context also our endnote below, regarding *anusmaraṇa*, and also Vasubandhu's discussion of *dṛṣṭi* (i. 41cd) which Vasubandhu explains as judgment after contemplation (*tīraṇa, saṃtīraṇa*), i.e., judgment (*niścaya*) preceding from contemplation (*upanidhyāna*) of the object-field, since, as Dhammajoti states (ADCP.104), it is particularly the aspect of judgmental investigation of *prajñā*, represented by *saṃtīraṇa*, that characterizes the function of *abhinirūpaṇāvikalpa*.

4. As for the co-nascent concomitant understanding (*prajñā* = *ākāra*) that is conjoined with a sensory consciousness, MVŚ, 490c, further specifies:

   i. it does not have a keen or sharp (*tikṣna, paṭu*) mode of activity (*ākāra*) and cannot penetrate deeply into the perceptual object;
   ii. it cannot discriminate;
   iii. it can have as their cognitive object only the *svalakṣaṇa*, but not the *sāmānya-lakṣaṇa*;
   iv. it has only present objects, whereas a view [*dṛṣṭi*] can have as objects *dharma*-s of all the three temporal periods as well as the unconditioned;
   v. a view can grasp an object repeatedly, but this *prajñā* can only grasp an object in a single moment;
   vi. unlike a view, it cannot cogitate and examine a perceptual object.

393 *LS*: SAH 50.

394 *LVP*: *kila* ["so said", "so reported"]: this is an opinion of the Vaibhāṣikas without support in the Sūtra.

The opinion of Vasubandhu is explained below, ii. 33. For him, as for the Sautrāntika, initial inquiry (*vitarka*) and investigation (*vicāra*) are thought (*citta*), the mental consciousness (*manovijñāna*), [i.e., (ii, F 174) by *vitarka* and *vicāra* one should not understand two distinct factors but rather the collection of thought and thought-concomitants that induce speech and that are sometimes gross, sometimes subtle].

395 *LS*: SAH.85f.

396 *MW*: *nirūpaṇa* = stating, defining, determining, examination, searching, investigation.

397 *LVP*: MVŚ, 219b7: Conceptualizing activity in its intrinsic nature (*svabhāvavikalpa*) is initial inquiry–investigation (*vitarka-vicāra*); conceptualizing activity consisting of recollecting (*anusmaraṇavikalpa*) is the recollection associated with mental consciousness; conceptualizing activity consisting of examining (*nirūpaṇāvikalpa*) is non-absorbed understanding (*prajñā*) of the sphere of the mental consciousness. In the realm of desire, the five consciousnesses have only the first type of conceptualizing activity (*vikalpa*), i.e., the conceptualizing activity in its intrinsic nature: they involve recollection but not conceptualizing activity consisting of recollecting, for they are not capable of recognition; they involve understanding (*prajñā*) but not conceptualizing activity consisting of examining, for they are not capable of examination.

Nyāyānusāra: The nature of conceptualizing activity in its intrinsic nature (*svabhāvavikalpa*) is initial inquiry (*vitarka*).

MW: *anusmaraṇa* = remembering, repeated recollection.

LS: See: *Cox*: JIABS.11.36f; Dhammajoti: SA.IV.229–32; ADCP.103–9.

398 *LVP*: Understanding (*prajñā*) and recollection are associated with the five sensory consciousnesses, but their function is reduced therein (Saṃghabhadra).

399 *LS*: Even though every sensory consciousness is accompanied by both initial inquiry (*vitarka*) and investigation (*vicāra*)—according to the Vaibhāṣikas—the AKB, as also Saṃghabhadra in this context, define *svabhāva-vikalpa* as *vitarka* only. The reason for this is that due to their opposing nature, these two thought-concomitants cannot be dominant simultaneously, as can be seen from their characteristics, i.e., *vitarka* causes thought to be gross with regard to an object whereas *vicāra* causes it to be subtle; *vitarka* is the projecting cause of the five sensory consciousnesses, whereas *vicāra* is the projecting cause of mental consciousness. This then implies that even though they both exist simultaneously, for the Vaibhāṣikas, *vitarka* is predominant in the sensory consciousnesses, whereas *vicāra* is predominant in the mental consciousnesses (cf. SA.IV.265f.)

400 *Gokhale*: [33cd] *tau prajñā mānasī vyagrā smṛtiḥ sarv aiva mānasī* ||

Tib.: [33cd] *de dag yid kyi shes rab gyeng* | *yid kyi dran pa thams cad nyid* ||

401 *LS*: The *Vyākhyā* has [WOG.65.1ff.]: *sā hy abhinirūpaṇāvikalpa* iti. sā mānasy asamāhitā prajñā śruta-cintā-mayy upapatti-pratilambhikā ca. sā hi manasi bhavā *mānasī*. *vyagrā* vividhā 'grā vyagrā vividh'ālambanety arthaḥ. vigata-pradhānā vā muhur-muhur ālambanāntara-āśrayaṇāt. vyagrā kasmād abhinirūpaṇā-vikalpa ity ucyate. tatra-tatr' ālambane nāmāpekṣayā 'bhipravṛtteḥ. rūpaṃ vedanā anityaṃ duḥkham ity-ādy-abhinirūpaṇāc ca. samāhitā tu bhāvanā-mayī nāmānapekṣy' ālambane pravartata iti. naiṣā 'bhinirūpaṇāvikalpa ity ucyate.

LVP: 1. Mental (*mānasī*) understanding (*prajñā*), i.e., *manasi bhavā*, whether it proceeds from listening to Scripture or from reflecting (*śrutacintāmayi*), or whether it is innate (*upapatti-prātilambhikā*); dispersed (*vyagrā*), i.e., non-concentrated, having different objects (*agra*), or else, "discrowned" (*vigatapradhānā*) by the fact that it successively seizes after different objects.

[Question:] – Why does one give the name of *abhinirūpaṇāvikalpa* (conceptualizing activity consisting of defining) to this understanding?

[Answer:] – Because it applies itself to a given object by taking into account its name (*nāmāpekṣayā*) and it examines (*abhinirūpaṇā*): "This is form (*rūpa*), sensation (*vedanā*), impermanent (*anitya*), unsatisfactory (*duḥkha*)", etc.

2. On the contrary, concentrated (*samāhitā*) understanding, proceeding from meditating (*bhāvanāmayī*), applies itself to the object without taking into account its name. Thus it is not conceptualizing activity consisting of defining (*abhinirūpaṇāvikalpa*).

LS: As for ideation (*saṃjñā*), which also is an important contributing factor for *abhinirūpaṇā*, see our endnote to ideation (i. 14cd).

402 *LS*: The *Vyākhyā* has [WOG.65.8ff.]: *mānasy eva sarvā smṛtir* iti. *samāhitā cāsamāhitā ca*. sā kila nāmānapekṣā anubhūtārtha-mātr'ālambanā pravartate. smṛtiḥ katamā. cetaso 'bhilāṣa iti lakṣaṇāt. paṃca-vijñāna-kāya-saṃprayuktā tu nānubhūta–arthābhilāṣapravṛtteti nānusmaraṇa-vikalpa itīṣyate.

LVP: 1. All mental mindfulness (*smṛti*), i.e., mental mindfulness whether *concentrated* or not. For, according to the School, the mental mindfulness has solely the phenomenon previously experienced for its object and does not take into account its name (*nāmānapekṣā*), according to the definition: "What is mindfulness? The expression of thought or mental speech (*cetaso 'bhilāpaḥ*)."

2. As for mindfulness connected with the five consciousnesses, its mode of existence is not an expression (*abhilāpa*) of the phenomenon previously experienced. It is thus not conceptualizing activity consisting of recollecting (*anusmaraṇavikalpa*) (WOG.65.10f.). See ii. 24; i. 33ab.

LS: In the AKB, *smṛti*, *smaraṇa*, etc., are discussed and translated variously according to different contexts (conceptualizing activity consisting of recollecting; mindfulness; applications of mindfulness; memory; etc.): see ii. 24; v, F 6f; vi. 14ff; ix, F 273–79.

As for *anusmaraṇa* (ADCP.105), it "presupposes the ability to examine the object (more correctly, object-series) clearly and for more than one moment. There must also be a clear mental noting of the object in the form 'it is such and such'—a kind of mental speech (*abhilapanā*). This means that the prominent functioning of *smṛti* here requires the assistance of *prajñā*, *vitarka* (and *vicāra*), and *saṃjnā*."

403 *LS*: AH 12; SAH 32.

404 *Gokhale*: [34ab1] *sapta sālambanāś cittadhātavo*

Tib.: [34a] *dmigs bcas sems kyi khams bdun no |*

LVP: On the meaning of cognitive object (*ālambana*), i. 29b.

Compare *Vibhaṅga*, p. 95.

LS: In this context Saṃghabhadra (Ny, 350b; EIP.VIII.663) presents a discussion with Śrīlāta, who maintains—while referring to the atom theory—that the sense-spheres (*āyatana*) as composite cognitive objects (*ālambana*) exist only as nominal designations (*prajñaptisat*) within the process of perception and that the respective elements (*dhātu*) alone exist as actual entities (*dravyasat*). To this thesis Saṃghabhadra replies that both sense-spheres and elements exist as real entities, that composite cognitive objects can only be perceived by conceptual mental consciousnesses and that no distinction can be drawn between those factors classified as sense-spheres and those classified as elements. For the details, see Vasubandhu's discussion concerning the ontological status of aggregates, sense-spheres and elements (i. F 37ff., and its endnotes).

405 *Gokhale*: [34b2] *'rdhaṃ ca dharmataḥ* |

Tib.: [34b1] *chos kyi phyed kyang*

406 *LS*: AH 13; SAH 33–34.

407 *Gokhale*: [34cd1] *navā 'nupāttās te cā 'ṣṭau śabdaś cā*

Tib.: [34b2c] *ma zin dgu* | *brgyad po de dag rnams dang sgra* |

408 *Gokhale*: [34d2] *'nye nava dvidhā* ||

Tib.: [34d] *dgu po gzhan ni rnam pa gnyis* ||

409 *LS*: SAH 33.

410 *LVP*: The Abhidhamma (*Vibhaṅga*, p. 96; *Dhammasaṅgaṇi*, 653, 1211, 1534) understands *upādinna* in the same sense. Modern commentators of the Abhidhamma translate *upādinna* as *issue of grasping*; they do not see that *upādā* = *upādāyarūpa* (derived form), *bhautika* (derived material element), and create great confusion.

Moreover, the *Vibhaṅga* does not classify the elements (*dhātu*) as does the Abhidharma. (See also *Suttavibhaṅga*, p. 113; *Mahāvyutpatti*, 101, 56; *Divyāvadana*, p. 54; *Bodhicaryāvatāra*, viii. 97, 101). And there is some wavering even in the Sanskrit sources. For example, *Majjhima*, iii. 240, reproduced in *Pitāputrasamāgama* (see above i, F 49, note), gives hair... excrement as *ajjhattaṃ paccattaṃ kakkhalaṃ upādinnaṃ*. But hair is not *upādinna*. The description of bodily matter (*ādhyātmika*; see *Majjhima*, iii. 90) has been confused with the description of organic matter (*upātta*).

Organic (*upātta*) matter, plus the mental faculty (*manas*), is given the name of basis (*āśraya*; see ii. 5). This is the subtle body of the non-faithful.

LS: Dhammajoti (ESD.132), basing himself on Karunadasa's *Buddhist Analysis of Matter*, pp. 103–7, disagrees here with LVP's statement that *upātta* and *anupātta* have the same meaning as the Pāli *upādinna*, and *anupādinna*, etc.

411 *LS*: SAH 36.

412 *LVP*: *bhūta*, *mahābhūta*; *upādāya rūpa*, *bhautika*; see i. 12, 23–24; ii. 12, 50a, 65. – *bhautika* = *bhūte bhava* = derived from the *bhūtas*.

413 *Gokhale*: [35ac] *spraṣṭavyaṃ dvividhaṃ śeṣā rūpiṇo nava bhautikāḥ* | *dharmadhātveka-deśaś ca*

Tib.: [35ac] *reg bya rnam pa gnyis yin te* | *lhag ma gzugs can dgu po ni* | *'byung gyur chos khams phyogs gcig kyang* |

LVP: Compare *Vibhaṅga*, p. 96.

414 *LVP*: MVŚ, 661c14: In this school, there are two masters, Buddhadeva and Dharmatrāta. Buddhadeva says: "Material form (*rūpa*) is only the fundamental material elements; thought-concomitants (*caitta*) are only thought (*citta*)." He says that "*upādāyarūpa* (secondary matter or derived material form) is a type of the fundamental material elements (*mahābhūtaviśeṣa*), that the thought-concomitants are a type of thought..." (compare *Kathāvatthu*, vii. 3). – MVŚ, 383c24: The Sūtra says: "Material form is the four fundamental material elements and that which derives from the four fundamental material elements." Which opinion does the Sūtra want to refute? It wants to refute the opinion of Buddhadeva. The Buddha sees that, in the future, there will be a master, Buddhadeva, who will say: "There is no distinct derivative material element outside of the fundamental material elements." In order to refute this opinion, Buddha says: "Material form is the four fundamental material elements...". – 142, 7: Buddhadeva says: "All conditioned factors are either the fundamental material elements or thought; outside of the fundamental material elements, there is no derived material form; outside of *citta* (thought), there is no *caitta* (thought-concomitant)."

On thought and thought-concomitants, see below F 66 and ii. 23c.

Buddhadeva is perhaps the master named in the inscription of the Mathurā lion.

LS: Cox summarizes (EIP.VIII.664f.) Saṃghabhadra's discussion with Śrīlāta (Ny, 352b):

> Śrīlāta: The tangible element consists only of the great elements because this so-called derivative material form is merely a distinctive arrangement of these four great elements. [...]
>
> Answer: [...] Since the activities of smoothness and so on belonging to derivative material form are recognized as distinct from the activities hardness and so on belonging to the four great elements, derivative material form and the four great elements must be admitted to exist separately. [...]
>
> Śrīlāta: Further, lightness and heaviness ... are established simply by mutual comparison and do not exist as actual entities.
>
> Answer: Though one thing may be light or heavy with respect to two different things, it is not light and heavy with regard to the same thing. Therefore, though the description of a thing may vary relative to other things, its nature as light or heavy is without alteration. Varying description does not constitute a reason for the unreality of the quality described.
>
> Śrīlāta: Coldness ... is simply a small degree of or the absence of the fundamental element fire.
>
> Answer: [...]
>
> Śrīlāta: Hunger and thirst have the mental factor called "interest" (*chanda*) as their nature and therefore do not exist as actual entities.
>
> Answer: [...]
>
> Śrīlāta: All types of derivative form are nothing other than the four great elements.

Answer: In that case, all material sensory objects would have the same characteristics of hardness and so on that define the four great elements, and the sensory range of all externally directed sense-organs would be identical.

Furthermore, the sense-organs and their objects would have the same inherent characteristic of hardness and so on, and would not be capable of being distinguished from one another.

415 *LVP*: Thus (1) the sense-faculties are not primary matter, not being solidness, etc.; (2) the tangible involves the primary matter, since solidness is perceived by the body; (3) the secondary matter perceived by the other sense-organs is not perceived by the body.

LS: Hall comments (VASC.133f.): "Each organ perceives different secondary characteristics of the elements, or rather of their derivatives. If all sense objects were only the elements themselves, then the eye should be able to see tangible qualities, the body be able to feel visible ones, and so on."

416 *LVP*: cakṣur bhikṣo ādhyātmikam āyatanaṃ catvāri mahābhūtāny upādāya rūpaprasādo rūpi anidarśanaṃ sapratigham | ...mano bhikṣo ādhyātmikam āyatanam arūpy anidarśanam apratigham | rūpāṇi bhikṣo bāhyam āyatanaṃ catvāri mahābhūtāny upādāya rūpi sanidarśanaṃ sapratigham | ...spraṣṭavyāni bhikṣo bāhyam āyatanaṃ catvāri mahābhūtāni catvāri ca mahābhūtāny upādāya rūpi anidarśanaṃ sapratigham | dharmā bhikṣo bāhyam āyatanam ekādaśabhir āyatanair asaṃgṛhītam arūpi anidarśanam apratigham | [WOG.58.12ff.]

417 *LVP*: *Vibhāṣā*, 127, p. 661.

418 *LS*: *ṣaḍdhāturayaṃ bhikṣo puruṣaḥ.*

419 *LVP*: See ii. 5. – The first four elementary substances (*dhātu*) (earth... wind) are *fundamental elementary substances* because the sense-faculties arise from these elementary substances; the elementary substance consciousness (*vijñānadhātu*) or element of the mental faculty (*manodhātu*) is *fundamental* because it gives rise to the *manaḥsparśāyatana*.

Or else, the first four fundamental elementary substances are *fundamental* because they give rise to the secondary matter; the elementary substance consciousness is *fundamental* because it gives rise to the thought-concomitants (*caitta, caitasika*).

420 *LVP*: Thus the first five *bases of contact*, the five sense-faculties of sensory consciousness, are *secondary matter*: otherwise, they would be included in the definition: "The person is made up of six fundamental elementary substances (*dhātu*)."

421 *LVP*: According to the Abhidhamma (*Dhammasaṅgaṇi*, 647), the derivative material form (*rūpa*) is not a tangible. Saṃghabhadra (Ny, 352c1) refutes this opinion, which is attributed to the Sthavira: "The ignorant Sthavira maintains that the tangible does not include derivative material form." On this subject, there is a discussion on the authenticity of the Sūtras in the *Introduction* of La Vallée Poussin. See *Documents d'Abhidharma.*

422 *Gokhale*: [35d] *saṃcitā daśa rūpinaḥ* ||

Tib.: [35d] *gzugs can bcu ni bsags pa'o* ||

LVP: MVŚ, 391c6.

423 *LS*: Pradhan.24.18f. has *śeṣā na saṃcitā iti siddhaṃ bhavati.*

[424] *LS*: SAH 494.

The three topics mentioned in Gedun Drup's eleventh doctrinal perspective form three separate doctrinal perspectives in Pu Guang's listing of the twenty-two doctrinal perspectives.

[425] *Gokhale*: [36ab] *chinatti cchidyate c aiva bāhyaṃ dhātucatuṣṭayam* |

Tib.: [36ab] *gcod byed gcad par bya ba nyid* | *phyi rol gyi ni khams bzhi yin* |

LVP: MVŚ, 689c5ff.

[426] *LS*: The *Vyākhyā* glosses [WOG.68.14]: *saṃghātasrota* rūp'ādi-saṃghāta-saṃtāna ity arthaḥ.

[427] *MW*: *accha* = pellucid, transparent, clear.

[428] *Gokhale*: [36c] *dahyate tulayaty evaṃ*

Tib.: [36c] *de bzhin bsreg bya 'jal byed pa'o* |

[429] *Gokhale*: [36d] *vivādo dagdhṛtulyayoḥ* |

Tib.: [36d] *sreg dang gzhal la mi mthun smra* ||

[430] *LS*: SAH 45.

[431] *LS*: Here Pradhan.25.6f. adds the categories 13 and 14: "How many are 'containing the [permanent} real'? How many are 'of a moment' (*kṣaṇika*)?" These questions are omitted by LVP, but we will add these below to our translation.

All factors can be classified into five groups according to their status as an effect: (1) effect of retribution (*vipākaja*), (2) effect of accumulation (*aupacayika*), (3) effect of equal outflow (*naiṣyandika*); (4) containing the [permanent] real entity (*dravyayukta*); (5) momentary (*kṣaṇika*). See DD.441 and SAH.75.

In the twenty-two doctrinal perspectives as listed by Pu Guang, these five form one doctrinal perspective; in Gedun Drup, they form three perspectives.

See chapter 2, for a discussion of (1) the ripened effect or effect of retribution (*vipākaphala*; ii. 56a, 57ab) and (2) the effect of equal outflow (*niṣyandaphala*; ii. 56c, 57c).

[432] *Gokhale*: [37–38a1] *vipākajaupacayikāḥ pañcā 'dhyātmaṃ vipākajāḥ* | *na śabdo 'pratighā aṣṭau naiṣyandikavipākajāḥ* || *tridhā 'nye*

Tib.: [37–38a] *rnam par smin las byung ba dang* | *rgyas las byung ba nang gi lnga* | *sgra ni rnam smin las skyes min* | *rgyu mthun las byung rnam smin skyes* || *thogs pa med brgyad gzhan rnam gsum* |

[433] *LS*: Dhammajoti points out (ADCP.99) an important difference in the understanding of the term "retribution-born" or "arisen from retribution" (*vipākaja*) between the Sarvāstivāda and Śrīlāta's school of thought.

1. The Sarvāstivāda defines *vipākaja* as "that which is born of retribution-cause" or "that born from the *karma* which has become matured" and considers the karmic cause as either skillful or unskillful, whereas the retribution-effect (ii. 54cd, 57ab; NY, 454b)—being projected by the force of previous *karma* and not by an effort—is always non-defined and unobscured (*anivṛtāvyākṛta*); thus being weak like rotten seeds, the retribution-effect is incapable of generating a skillful (or unskillful) *citta* of effort and cannot serve as a karmic cause.

2. Sthavira Śrīlāta, however, asserts [Ny, 359ab, 359c] that "retribution-born" signifies whatever is born of retribution and asserts that all twelve sense-spheres (*āyatana*) are retribution-born.

Śrīlāta's theory entails the following (ADCP.101):

i. All pertaining to the sentient serial continuity (the six *āyatana*-s) arise in each moment from the *anudhātu* (= *bīja*) within the being. These *anudhātu*-s have been possessed by the being since previous times. Their nature is ineffable, and is neither unitary nor differentiated—neither identical with nor different from the serial continuity.
ii. All *dharma*-s are arisen immediately in the present moment.
iii. The totality of empirical existence—the twelve *āyatana*-s—is *vipākaja*, which is to be distinguished from *vipāka* of the *karma* of a sentient being.

As for the *anudhātu* theory, it is meant to account "for the continuous manifestation of the totality of a sentient being's existence—the six *āyatana*-s—from one present moment to the next. The *anudhātu* is the causal efficacy within the sentient being's present serial continuity, and the next moment of the serial continuity is the effect."

From the above we can also see that Śrīlāta makes a distinction between what is retribution-born and what is properly termed the retribution of past *karma*, and since the former can serve as a cause generating *dharma*s of different moral species, it is possible in his system that *dharmas*, even though being *vipākaja*, can also be skillful or unskillful at the same time.

434 *LVP*: This is the etymology *vipacyata iti vipākaḥ*; *vipāka* is what has become ripe.

435 *LVP*: This is the etymology *vipāka* = *vipakti*.

LS: Hall translates (VASC.138): "However the 'fruit' (*phala*) is the very fact of coming to fruition (*vipakti*), in that sense it is [also called] fruition (*vipāka*)."

436 *LVP*: See ii, F 271.

437 *LS*: Hall adds in brackets (VASC.138): "[when 'prior action' is really the cause of these]".

438 *LVP*: See ii, F 301; *Vibhāṣā*, 118 at the beginning; *Siddhi*, 190.

439 *LS*: The *Vyākhyā* glosses [WOG.70.5ff.]: *āhāra-saṃskāra-svapna-samādhi-viśeṣair upacitā aupacayikā* iti. viśeṣa-śabdaḥ pratyekam abhisaṃbadhyata. tatr'āhāra-svapnau loke pratītau. saṃskāro 'bhyaṃgasnānānuvāsan'ādi-svabhāvaḥ. samādhiś cittaikāgratā-lakṣaṇaḥ.

Hall comments (VASC.138f.): "Yaśomitra takes *āhāra* (food, nourishment) and *svapna* (sleep) in their everyday meanings. He takes *saṃskāra*—elsewhere 'disposition'—here in the sense of 'cleansing' (compare the ritual sense of *saṃskāra* as a Hindu 'sacrament'). Here *samādhi* (concentration) has its technical, meditational sense of 'one-pointed-ness of thought'."

440 *LVP*: It seems that this is the opinion of Dharmatrāta, i. 45 (*Nanjio* 1287).

441 *LS*: Hall comments (VASC.139): "Chastity, continence, or restraint (*brahmacarya*) removes some causes that damage the organs, but does not directly nourish or foster them."

442 *LS*: SAH 45.

443 *LS*: Ibid.

444 *LVP*: See iv, F 29.

Let us consider a moment or state of existence of this subtle matter, which is the eye sense-faculty (*prasāda*-element). One part of this matter is the retribution of a former action; another part proceeds from food: all of this matter is the effect of equal outflow of the previous moment, or state, in the existence of the eye. But this previous moment or state is not, in and of itself, capable of generating the present moment: in fact, at death, the eye sense-faculty ceases to produce itself through equal outflow. Thus, by definition, the eye sense-faculty is not an effect of equal outflow. But consider, on the contrary, the flesh that makes up the body: it persists after death; it is thus an effect of equal outflow, the effect, in each of the moments of its existence, of the previous moment.

The *Kathāvatthu*, xii, 4, xvi. 8, does not hold that matter is retribution.

445 *LS*: SAH 45.

446 *LVP*: Nine reasons are enumerated at MVŚ, 612c. Vasubandhu cites the third.

LS: Yaśomitra glosses as follows [WOG.70.15f.]: *śabda aupacayika* ity anupacita-kāyasya śabda-sauṣṭhavādarśanāt.

447 *LVP*: The Vātsīputrīyas and the Vibhajyavādins maintain that sound is an effect of retribution.

LS: Cox summarizes Saṃghabhadra stating (Ny, 358a; EIP.VIII.666) that sound is not an effect of retribution because it is discontinuous and arises in accord with one's wish at any given time.

448 *LS*: Hall comments (VASC.139f.): "This 'intonation of Brahmā' is number 13 in the list of thirty-two marks of a great man in *Mahāvyutpatti* (248). It would seem to be a sound, which qualifies as the fruition of past action. However, it is only the great man's vocal organs, which are, strictly, fruitional. His vocal acts too are current deeds resulting from conscious effort."

449 *LVP*: Compare *Dīgha*, iii. 173, cited by the Mahāsāṃghikas in *Kathāvatthu*, xii. 2: *saddo vipāko*.

450 *LS*: Dharmatrāta comments (SAH.75f.):

> *Question*: Why is it that sound is not arisen by retribution?
>
> *Answer*: Because it arises by present effort (*vyāyāma*). Sound arises by present effort; retribution (*vipāka*) is what is produced by former action. Sound is what arises according to desire; retribution is not what arises according to desire.

451 *LS*: SAH 45.

452 *LS*: Hall comments (VASC.140): "The 'continuing' (*naiṣyandika*) components continue their moment to moment 'on-flow' (*niṣyanda*) even apart from karmic fruition and nutritive addition. An example is the bodily components that persist for some time after death."

453 *LS*: Cox summarizes Saṃghabhadra who states (Ny, 358a; EIP.VIII.666) that the eight elements are not the effects of accumulation because, unlike material form, they do not consist of collections of atoms, and therefore cannot be accumulated.

454 *LS*: SAH 45.

455 *LS*: AH 13; SAH 33, 45.

456 *Gokhale*: [38a2] *dravyavān ekaḥ*

Tib.: [38b1] *rdzas dang ldan gcig*

LS: Of the five groups: (1) effect of retribution (*vipākaja*), (2) effect of accumulation (*aupacayika*), (3) effect of equal outflow (*naiṣyandika*); (4) containing the [permanent] real entity (*dravyayukta*) and (5) momentary (*kṣaṇika*), the unconditioned element of factors (*asaṃskṛta dharmadhātu*) is only included in the fourth group.

Cox summarizes Saṃghabhadra stating (Ny, 358a; EIP.VIII.666f.) that some suggest that the element of factors (*dharmadhātu*) alone exists as an actual entity (*dravaysat*) because it contains the unconditioned factors, but that others suggest that all factors exist as actual entities.

457 *LS*: SAH 45.

458 *Gokhale*: [38b] *kṣaṇikāḥ paścimās trayaḥ* |

Tib.: [38b2–c1] *tha ma gsum* | *skad cig ma ste*

LS: Cox summarizes Saṃghabhadra stating (Ny, 358a; EIP.VIII.666f.; see also DD.411) that some suggest that (1) the element of the mental faculty (*manodhātu*), (2) the element of factors (*dharmadhātu*) and (3) the element of mental consciousness (*manovijñānadhātu*) that occur with the first moment of the noble path are said to be momentary (*kṣaṇika*) but others suggest that all factors, with the exception of the unconditioned factors, are momentary. Since these three are (1) not an effect of retribution (*vipākaja*) of previous action, (2) nor an effect of accumulation (*aupacayika*) because they are not material form and, therefore, are not composed of atoms, (3) nor are they the effect of equal outflow (*naiḥṣyandika*) resulting from a homogeneous cause (*sabhāgahetu*) in the previous moment, and finally, (4) since they are not unconditioned, they are not classified as existing only as real entities (*dravyavat*). They are, therefore, merely momentary (*kṣaṇika*).

459 *LS*: SAH 48.

460 *Gokhale*: [38cd] *cakṣurvijñānadhātvoḥ syāt pṛthag lābhaḥ sahā 'pi ca* ||

Tib.: [38c2–e] *mig dang ni* | *rnam shes khams dag so so dang* | *lhan cig tu yang 'thob pa yod* |

LVP: MVŚ, 823a20, 449a16; Dharmatrāta (*Nanjio* 1287), i. 48c.

461 *LS*: For understanding the tetralemma, Hall provides the following sketch (VASC.271):

1. realm of immateriality: here neither the eye sense-faculty nor visual consciousness exist;

2. realm of fine-materiality, i.e., second to fourth meditation: here the eye sense-faculty exists, but not the visual consciousness, except as a memory, etc., of lower levels;

3. realm of desire and first meditation of the realm of fine-materiality: here both the eye sense-faculty and visual cognition exist.

462 *LS*: Jampaiyang comments (p. 252): "The fourth is when born in the formless realm."

463 *LS*: SAH 36.

464 *Gokhale*: [39ab1] *dvādaś ādhyātmikā hitvā rūpādīn*

Tib.: [39ab1] *nang gi bcu gnyis gzugs la sogs* | *ma gtogs*

LVP: MVŚ, 714a7ff. The difference between the internal or personal (*ādhyātmika*) and external (*bāhya*) factors is threefold:

1. difference from the point of view of the stream (*saṃtāna*): the factors that occur in a particular person (*svātmabhāva*) are internal or personal; those that occur among others, and also those that are not indicative of sentient beings (*asattvākhya*; i. 10b), are external;

2. difference from the point of view of the sense-sphere (*āyatana*): the sense-spheres that are the basis (*āśraya*) of thought and thought-concomitants are internal or personal; those that are the cognitive object (*ālambana*) are external;

3. difference from the point of view of the sentient being: the factors indicative of sentient beings can be internal or personal; the others are external.

LS: At first sight. i. 39ab seems to suggest that thought-concomitants (*caitta*) in general, i.e., sensation, ideation, formations, etc.—being included in the sense-sphere of factors—would be considered to be external to thought! But the distinction of the *Vibhāṣā* seems to make it clear that whether they are considered to be external or internal is dependent on the point of view from which the thought-concomitants are considered, i.e., whether they are considered as being simultaneously associated with thought, having the same cognitive object, or whether they are considered as being the cognitive object of thought and thought-concomitants. See in this context also i. 39bc, as well as vii. 18cd which states:

> When a moment of conventional cognition (*saṃvṛtijñāna*) cognizes all factors as not being a "self", that is by excluding, from the totality of factors, (1) itself, this same moment of conventional cognition, for the subject of cognition cannot be its own object (*viṣayiviṣayabhedāt*); (2) the mental factors (*caitta*) associated with it, for they have the same cognitive object as it does (*ekālambanatvāt*); (3) the factors dissociated from thought (*viprayukta*) that accompany it (*sahabhū*), for example, its characteristics (*lakṣaṇa*; ii. 45c), for they are too close.

465 *LS*: SAH 36.

466 *LS*: This is the thirteenth of Kritzer's fifteen passages discussed in relation to chapter 1 (VY.28f.). Saṃghabhadra criticizes (Ny, 360b21c4; EIP.VIII.667) Vasubandhu's view that thought serves as the basis for the sense of self and can be referred to figuratively as the internal "self", while those factors that serve as its basis, i.e., the sense bases, should be internal, since this view leads to confusion as to whether or not certain factors act as the basis of thought. For example, why are thought-concomitants (*caitta*) that are simultaneous with and share the same effect as thought, not considered to be internal?

467 *LVP*: *ātmanā hi sudāntena svargaṃ prāpnoti paṇḍitaḥ…*
cittasya damanaṃ sādhu cittaṃ dāntaṃ sukhāvaham [WOG.74.27ff.]

See *Udānavarga*, xxiii; *Madhyamakavṛtti*, p. 354; *Dhammapada*, 160.

468 *LS*: LVP translates: "whereas visible form and other object-fields of consciousness are held to be external".

469 *LS*: SAH 37.

470 *LS*: Cox and Dessein translate *tatsabhāga*: partially homogeneous; *sabhāga*: homogeneous.

Dhammjoti glosses (SA.IV.545): "*tatsabhāga*—'Similar to that (which is presently active, although this itself is non-active)', a 'facsimile'."

Saṃghabhadra states (Ny, 362a; EIP.VIII.668; JIABS.11.73) that "those elements that have carried out their own activity, are carrying it out, or will carry it out together are called homogeneous because they share their function, depend for their functioning upon the functioning of others, or share the same contact. For example, when the eye and the object function as the conditions for the arising of visual perceptual consciousness, these three elements are homogeneous.

The elements that do not carry out their activity, [for example, those sense organs or object-fields that arise and pass away without performing their particular function of grasping or being grasped, as well as those future sense organs or object-fields that will never arise,] are partially homogeneous because they are of the same category as those elements that do function."

[471] *LS*: SAH 37.

[472] *Gokhale*: [39b2–c1] *dharmasaṃjñakaḥ | sabhāgas*

Tib.: [39b2–c1] *chos zhes bya ba ni | sten ba dang bcas*

LVP: *Prakaraṇa*, 699a3–28.

[473] *LS*: MVŚ, 42c–43a (SA.IV.253):

> There are some who hold that the *citta-caitta-dharma*-s can cognize their own intrinsic natures (i.e., themselves), like the Mahāsāṃghika which asserts: "Because knowledge, etc., has cognition as its intrinsic nature, it can cognize both itself and others. This is just like the case of a lamp; because it has illumination as its intrinsic nature, it can illuminate both itself and others."
>
> There are some, like the Dharmaguptaka which holds that the *citta-caitta-dharma*-s can cognize what are conjoined with them. It asserts thus: "*Prajñā* can cognize the sensation conjoined with it."
>
> There are some, like the Mahīśāsaka, which holds that the *citta-caitta-dharma*-s can cognize what are co-existent with them. They assert thus: "There are two types of *prajñā* which arise simultaneously: one is conjoined [with thought], the other not conjoined. The conjoined *prajñā* knows the unconjoined one; the unconjoined *prajñā* knows the conjoined one."
>
> There are some, like the Vātsīputrīya, which holds that the *pudgala* can cognize *dharma*-s. It asserts thus: "It is the *pudgala* that knows *dharma*-s, not knowledge (*jñāna*)...".

Dhammajoti comments (SA.IV.255):

> In later Indian treatises, the Sautrāntikas are described as holding the view of reflexive knowledge, denoted by the term *svasaṃvedana/svasaṃvitti* (also, *ātmasaṃvedana*) which means "self-awareness". In the MVŚ, as we have seen, the doctrine is attributed to the Mahāsāṃghikas, but not to the Dārṣṭāntikas who were the fore-runners of the Sautrāntikas. In the Ny, although there is no explicit attribution of such a theory under this term to the Sautrāntika-Dārṣṭāntikas, in a discussion on the latter's doctrine of direct perception, it is mentioned that they assert the simultaneous occurrence of "sensation as direct perception" (*anubhava-pratyakṣa*) and "awareness as direct perception" (*buddhi-pratyakṣa*). That is to say, one has awareness of what

one is directly sensing [Ny, 374c]: "One has the awareness of a direct perception (現量覺; **pratyakṣa-buddhi*) with regard to one's own sensation." This is clearly a doctrine of reflexive awareness. Śrīlāta argues there that unless this fact is accepted, we will not be able to account for the sense of vividness—as demanded by experience of direct perception—in the subsequent moment when one is completely convinced that "this is directly perceived by me" (*idaṃ me pratyakṣam iti*).

474 *LS*: SAH 37.

475 *Gokhale*: [39c2–d1] *tatsabhāgāś ca śeṣā*

Tib.: [39c2–d] *lhag ma ni | de dang mtshungs pa dag kyang yin |*

476 *Gokhale*: [39d2] *yo na svakarmakṛt ||*

Tib.: [39e] *gang zhig rang gi las mi byed ||*

477 *LS*: SAH 37.

478 *LS*: Jampaiyang (p. 256f.): "The Western Vaibhāṣikas say there would be five since the non-generated instances are two: possessing consciousness [in the Desire (Realm) and the first (absorption), for example,] and not possessing (consciousness) [in the second, etc.]."

479 *LVP*: MVŚ, 368a21: The sense-faculty that has seen, sees, or will see visible form (*rūpa*), and the partially homogeneous (*tatsabhāga*), (i.e., the sense-faculty that resembles this sense-faculty,) is the element of the eye (*cakṣurdhātu*). The sense-faculty that has seen is the past element of the eye; the sense-faculty that sees is the present element of the eye; the sense-faculty that will see is the future element of the eye. As for the partially homogeneous, the scholars of this country say that it is of four types: (1–3) the past, present, future partially homogeneous eye is the element of the eye that has perished, perishes, will perish, without having seen the visible form; (4) the element of the eye that will absolutely not arise should be added.

The foreign scholars (*bahirdeśaka*) say that it is of five kinds: (1) past, (2) present, (3) future, as above. In addition, the future element of the eye that absolutely will not arise is of two types: accordingly as it (4–5) is, or is not, associated with consciousness.

LS: Hall comments (VASC.149): "A homogeneous cause is that which actually at some time produces a homogeneous result, such as an eye that actually sees forms. A quasi-homogeneous eye could see, but does not happen to. Since the sense organs are material, one may infer their continued existence when not functioning. Not so mind (*manas*). One can imagine a non-existent mind (which might have come about under certain circumstances) but one cannot infer an existing but non-functioning mind, since something immaterial like mind does not exist apart from its activity. Therefore mind is either 'homogeneous', or is 'quasi-homogeneous' in the sense of possessing the nature of not actually arising."

480 *LS*: SAH 37.

481 *LS*: Ibid.

482 *LVP*: MVŚ, 368b13: Three opinions. – Can one see the visible form by means of the eye of another? – Who maintains such an opinion? – If one cannot see by means of the eye of another, how could the eye of a certain being be called *homogeneous* (*sabhāga*) in relation to other sentient beings? – Because the activity of the eye is determined: this activity consists of

seeing. When the eye, after having been active, has perished, it is called *homogeneous*: neither for the person him- or herself, nor for another, does this name *homogeneous* (*sabhāga*) change. In the same way… .

483 *LS*: Hall comments (VASC.151): "One such particle, of odor for instance, could not simultaneously touch different organs."

484 *LS*: Jampaiyang (p. 258): "Since it is possible that nose consciousness is produced for a minute worm living in the nose, it is not definite that touch with any nose power, etc., produces nose consciousness for just that (being)."

485 *LS*: SAH 37.

486 *LVP*: By explaining *bhāga* in the passive, *bhajyata iti bhāgaḥ*.

LS: Hall translates (VASC.152): "Or else it is that they are the common results of [the same] sense contact."

487 *LVP*: "The eye that perishes without having seen is similar to the eye that sees, etc."

The Mādhyamikas (*Vṛtti*, p. 32 and the note that should be corrected) take advantage of this theory: "In reality, the homogeneous eye does not see visible form because it is a sense-faculty, exactly like the partially homogeneous": *na paramārthataḥ sabhāgaṃ cakṣuḥ paśyati rūpāṇi, cakṣurindriyatvāt, tadyathā tatsabhāgam.*

488 *LS*: SAH 38.

489 *LVP*: Three categories: *darśanaheya, bhāvanāheya, aheya*. We should distinguish unqualified loss (vihāni) and retrogressing (parihāṇi), vi, 173. The pure factors (dharmas forming part of the path of vision) can be let go, but they are not abandoned, to be rejected by the path of insight or cultivation: they are the object of cessation due to deliberation (*apratisaṃkhyānirodha*), viii, F 209. – See Index *aheya*, *Vibhāṣā*, 364b, in *Documents d'Abhidharma* (on *niḥsaraṇa*) and *Siddhi*, 666.

490 *LS*: SAH 38.

491 *Gokhale*: [40ab] *daśa bhāvanayā heyāḥ pañca cā 'ntyās trayas tridhā* |

Tib.: [40ab] *bcu ni bsgom pas spang bya yin* | *lnga yang tha ma gsum rnam gsum* |

LVP: MVŚ, 265cb: The same problem is examined in *Vibhaṅga*, pp. 12, 16, 97; *Dhammasaṅgaṇi*, 1002, 1007, 1008.

492 *LS*: Dhammajoti comments (SA.IV.43): "Among the with-outflow (*sāsrava*) *dharma*-s, the *kuśala* and *avyākṛta* ones, not being defilements, are not really abandonable in the proper sense. However, when the defilement which takes a *kuśala* or an *avyākṛta dharma* as its object is destroyed, this *dharma* is said to be abandoned (*tadālambana-kleśa-prahāṇāt*); for at that time the *dharma* comes to be disconnected. In fact, having been 'abandoned', a *kuśala dharma* can still re-arise. Thus, this is not a case of abandonment in terms of the *dharma*'s intrinsic nature (*svabhāva-prahāṇa*)."

493 *LVP*: On the quality of the ordinary worldling (*pṛthagjana*), ii. 40c; vi. 26a, 28cd. – At MVŚ, 232c13–23, divergent explanations of Vasumitra, Bhadanta and Ghoṣaka. On *pṛthagjana*, see *Siddhi*, 639.

494 *Gokhale*: [40cd] *na dṛṣṭiheyam akliṣṭaṃ na rūpaṃ nā 'py aṣaṣṭhajam* ||

Tib.: [40cd] *nyon mongs can min mthong spang min | gzugs min drug pa min skyes min ||*

LVP: See ii. 13; iv. 11ab.

495 *LVP*: We will see that the first stage is the unhindered path (*ānantaryamārga*), the path that destroys the defilement; the second stage is the path of liberation (*vimuktimārga*), the path in which the defilement has been destroyed (vi. 28).

LS: As for the ceasing of the status of ordinary worldling in relation to the receptivity to the cognition of the factors with regard to unsatisfactoriness (*dhamrajñāna-kṣānti*), see vi. 26 (F 181f.).

496 *LS*: SAH 34–35, 43–44, 46–47.

497 *Gokhale*: [41ab] *cakṣuś ca dharmadhātoś ca pradeśo dṛṣṭir aṣṭadhā |*

Tib.: [41ab] *mig dang chos kyi khams phyogs ni | lta ba yin te rnam pa brgyad |*

LS: Cox summarizes Saṅghabhadra stating (Ny, 363c; EIP.VIII.668f.) that only two among all factors (*dharma*) have view (*dṛṣṭi*) as their essential nature: (1) the visual sense-faculty alone because it illumines visible form, opposes darkness and has an acute activity; (2) the internally directed understanding (*prajñā*) that is acute with respect to contemplation of the features of the mental object and judges it.

498 *LS*: SAH 34.

499 *LS*: Cox summarizes Saṃghabhadra stating (Ny, 363c; EIP.VIII.669) that these eight types of view represent stages in the cultivation of purity and clarity of understanding related to objects, whereby purity or clarity mainly resides in the view itself, "in the eye of the beholder", so to speak.

500 *LVP*: We do not think that the *Visuddhimagga*, 509, knows the mundane right view (*sammādiṭṭhi*); it knows only the *sammādiṭṭhi*, which is the member of the noble path (*maggaṅgga*), the member of enlightenment (*bojjhaṅga*) (*Kośa*, vi, 290).

501 *LS*: SAH 34.

502 *LS*: Dharmatrāta comments (SAH.54): "[1] Viewing factors with defiled wisdom (*vidūṣaṇā prajñā*) is as seeing colours in a dark night; [2] conventional view is as seeing colours in a clear night; [3] view of still having learning to do is as seeing colours on a dark day; [4] view of having no more learning to do is as seeing colours on a clear day."

503 *LS*: SAH 34.

504 *Gokhale*: [41cd] *pañcavijñānasahajā dhīr na dṛṣṭir atīraṇāt ||*

Tib.: [41cd] *rnam shes lnga dang mtshungs skyes blo | nges rtog med phyir lta ma yin ||*

LVP: *dhī* in place of *prajñā*, for prosodic reasons (ii. 57d).

LS: 1. As for our section here, Yaśomitra glosses [WOG.80.5f.]: *atīraṇād* iti asaṃtīraṇāt. saṃtīraṇaṃ punar viṣayopanidhyāna-pūrvakaṃ niścay'ākarṣaṇam.

2. MVŚ, 490c–491a, defines (SA.IV.250) view (*dṛṣṭi*)—other than the case of the eye—as "that which has the nature of judgment or decision (*saṃtīrakatva*), which is also part of Vasumitra's definition which requires judgment and investigation. Elsewhere [MVŚ, 744a], four characteristics of view are given, namely, seeing, judging, firm attachment, and pene-

trating into the objects of perception." But since for Sarvāstivāda it is the eye that sees—and not consciousness, as held by the Vijñānavādins—the eye is also "included as a view on account of its function of seeing (*ālocana*) in spite of its being non-epistemic".

3. *Dṛṣṭi* is also later defined (ii. 29ab)—as pointed out by Jaini in his *Prajñā and Dṛṣṭi in the Vaibhāṣika Abhidharma*—as *prajñāviśeṣa* ("a special kind of *prajñā*"), to which Yaśomitra adds the following (WOG.134.1f; CPBS.271):

> *santīrikā yā prajñā, sā dṛṣṭiḥ* ("*dṛṣṭi* is that kind of *prajñā* that involves judgement").

Jaini comments:

> Our translation of the word *santīrikā* ("involving judgement") requires some expansion here. This seems to have been a Buddhist technical term that, along with the related *santīraṇa*, denoted that stage of the cognitive process that followed perception and that comprised the making of discriminative decisions, i.e., "this is (an) *x* as opposed to (a) *y*". Now, it will be immediately apparent that the decision or judgement arrived at may be either incorrect or correct. In the former case we would have an example of *mithyādṛṣṭi*, "inaccurate view"; such views may be of various types, but as we have suggested earlier the term most often implies *satkāyadṛṣṭi*, belief in a permanent soul. (This is the most pernicious, hence most important, of *mithyādṛṣṭis*.) If, on the other hand, one's judgement is correct, i.e., made in accord with the Buddha's teachings ("that thing is nothing but the five *skandhas*; it is characterized by suffering; it is impermanent"; etc.), we have a *samyakdṛṣṭi*, "accurate view".

4. See vii, F 1 for a discussion of cognition (*jñāna*), understanding (*prajñā*) and view (*dṛṣṭi*) and also for a chart that indicates the relation between these three important terms. For *dṛṣṭi* and *upanidhyāna*, see also vii. 1 and viii. 1 (F 130f.). Further see our endnote to i. 33ab and specifically our comments to conceptual construction of examining (*abhinirūpaṇāvikalpa*), which is linked to *saṃtīraṇa*.

505 *LVP*: *upanidhyāna*, viii. 1 (F 130f.).

506 *LS*: Yaśomitra glosses [WOG.80.7f.]: *ata evā*saṃtīraṇād *anyā 'pi* mānasī *kliṣṭā* rāg'ādi-saṃprayuktā *akliṣṭā vā* kṣayānutpāda-jñānānivṛtāvyākṛtā prajñā *na dṛṣṭiḥ*.

507 *LS*: SAH 34–35, 43–44, 46–47.

508 *LS*: Ny, 364a, classifies it in this way for three reasons (ADCP.70): "(1) because it is considered in the world that the eye sees (*ā-√loc*) visible forms; (2) because it is opposed to darkness; and (3) because its activity is clear and sharp". As can be seen from the chart at vii. 1, the eye is not a member of the set of understanding (*prajñā*). Also, even though the Vaibhāṣikas maintain, as we will see, that it is the eye that sees and not visual consciousness, nevertheless, strictly speaking, the mere seeing by the eye is non-epistemic, since the proper operation of *prajñā* is not involved, whereas the simultaneously arising visual consciousness is "conscious seeing", better, discernment, and as such epistemic, since the operation of *prajñā* is involved; and the same applies to the subsequent moment of mental consciousness (*manovijñāna*), and so on.

Dhammajoti explains (SA.IV.262) that "in the **Nyāyānusāra*, Saṃghabhadra argues vehemently that it is absolutely necessary for the function of seeing visible forms to belong uniquely to the visual organ. ... This absolute necessity, of course, stems from the central Vaibhāṣika conception that in the persistence of all *dharma*-s in the three periods of time, each and every *dharma* is a distinct *dharma* by virtue of its specific nature and function."

509 *LS*: SAH 34–35.

Find a much more detailed presentation of the following debate in Dhammajoti's *Abhidharma Doctrines and Controversies on Perception*, chapter 5: "The 'What Sees' Debate in the AKB, Vy and Ny", pp. 69–91.

510 *LS*: SAH 34–35.

511 *Gokhale*: [42] *cakṣuḥ paśyati rūpāṇi sabhāgaṃ na tadāśritam | vijñānaṃ dṛśyate rūpaṃ na kilā 'ntaritaṃ yataḥ ||*

Tib.: [42] *mig gis gzugs rnams mthong sten bcas | de la brten pa'i rnam shes min | gang phyir bar du chod pa yi | gzugs ni mthong ba min phyir lo ||*

LVP: See *Nyāyabinduṭīkāṭippaṇī*, p. 26; *Bodhicaryāvatārapañjikā*, p. 520; *Atthasālinī*, p. 400; Warren (*Visuddhimagga*), p. 297; *Buddhist Psychology*, p. 351, note; Spence Hardy, *Manual*, p. 419. – *Kathāvatthu*, xviii. 9, or the thesis: "The eye sees", is attributed to the Mahāsāṃghikas. Compare *Samayabheda*, Wassilief, p. 262. Wassilief sums up the discussion of the *Kośa*, p. 308 (Read: "das Auge nicht das Maß des Sichtbaren *sieht*", and not "*ist*".)

MVŚ, 489b14: According to another opinion, all conditioned phenomena (*saṃskṛta*) are by their nature view (*dṛṣṭi*). That which one understands by view is the manifested characteristic of its manner of being (*paṭupracāra*). All conditioned phenomena possess this characteristic.

Others say that the cognition of the exhaustion of defilements and of non-arising (*kṣaya-anutpādajñāna*; vii. 1) is view.

MVŚ, 61c.ff:

1. Dharmatrāta claims that the visual consciousness (*cakṣurvijñāna*), [and not the eye,] sees visible forms. – If the visual consciousness sees visible forms, the consciousness would have seeing for its characteristic; but this is not the case: thus this opinion is false.

2. Ghoṣaka claims that the understanding (*prajñā*) associated with visual consciousness sees visible forms. – If the understanding associated with visual consciousness sees visible forms, the understanding associated with the auditory consciousness should also hear sounds; but the understanding does not have hearing for its characteristic: thus this opinion is false. [For more detail see ADCP.54]

3. The Dārṣṭāntika claims that the complete assemblage (*sāmagrī*) of causes [of *citta-caitta* (*Pañcavastuka*, 991bc; of the eye, etc. (*Abhidharmadīpa*, 31f.)] sees visible forms. – If the complete assemblage sees visible forms, one should always see visible forms, for the complete assemblage is always present.

4. The Vātsīputrīya claims that a single eye sees visible forms. – If one eye, and not both eyes, sees visible forms, the parts of the body would not experience tangibles at one and the same time: since the two arms, however distant they may be from each other, can simultaneously experience tangibles and produce one single tactile consciousness, what obstacle is there that the two eyes, however distant they may be from each other, simultaneously see and produce one single visual consciousness?

LS: 1. For a more elaborated form of this controversy, see Dhammajoti's translation (ADCP.52f.) of the related passage in the *Pañcavastuka-vibhāṣā* by a certain Dharmatrāta of about the fourth century A.D.

2. This is the fourteenth of Kritzer's fifteen passages discussed in relation to chapter 1 (VY.32f.): "In verse 42, Vasubandhu gives the accepted Vaibhāṣika opinion that it is the eye that sees *rūpa*, but, according to Saṃghabhadra, he uses the word *kila* to indicate that he disagrees. Vasubandhu then examines a number of other opinions found in the *Vibhāṣā*, most prominently that of Dharmatrāta, to the effect that it is the visual consciousness that sees *rūpa*. As Katō points out (1989: 24), the commentators think that Vasubandhu favors Dharmatrāta's opinion, but in fact Vasubandhu may just be using it to refute the Vaibhāṣikas.* At the end of the discussion, he ascribes to the Sautrāntikas the opinion that there is nothing that sees or is seen; consciousness simply arises in dependence on the organ and the object. [...] Comparison: The *Yogācārabhūmi* contains a number of statements to the effect that cognition is really the result of the laws of cause and effect, not of something seeing and something else being seen."

* LS: But see below the endnote at F 86, top, where Dhammajoti disagrees with Katō and Kritzer on this point.

512 *LS*: SAH 35.

513 *LS*: As for the Vijñānavāda or Vijñānavādins mentioned here in the following "What sees" debate, as well as in Yaśomitra's *Vyākhyā* and Saṃghabhadra's **Nyāyānusāra*, they do not refer to the Yogācāra Vijñānavāda and its followers but rather stand for the "consciousness sees" theory and its followers (cf. ADCP.69).

514 *LS*: The argument seems to assume that the "seeing" eye occurs simultaneously with visual consciousness, but the Vaibhāṣika tenet does not allow for two consciousnesses to occur at the same time.

515 *LS*: 1. Saṃghabhadra adds (Ny, 364ab; ADCP.62 and 70f.) that it is not the case that all the sense-faculties are simultaneously sustained by their respective consciousnesses. For example, it is only the *sabhāga-cakṣus* that sees its object when being assisted by the visual consciousness, i.e., the eye sense-faculty participating in the activity of seeing when being in the simultaneous (*sahabhū*) cause-effect relationship which obtains when the visual consciousness, the eye and other necessary conditions flash forth their individual functions in coordination to give rise to the seeing of a visible form. This is like the arising of the specific activity of fire when there is the support of the force of fuel, etc.

Dharmatrāta comments (SAH.55f.): "There is no vision at the moment [the eye] is together with another form of consciousness: because when together with another form of consciousness, it would be idle, and, the eye, [although] present, would not be homogeneous. Because of this reason, all objects are not acquired together. ... There are no two forms of consciousness that proceed together: because there is no second condition as direct antecedent (*samanantara-pratyaya*)."

2. In regard to the "seeing" of a visible form, visual consciousness is a cause (for the Vaibhāṣika), not an effect (seeing) (ADCP.62f.):

It serves as the proximate condition and as the support for the visual organ; it

> nourishes the co-nascent Great Elements (*mahā-bhūta*-s), causing the potent (*viśeṣa* —lit. specific: that is the *indriya* that has come to the stage of being capable of exercising its potency) sense organ to arise and see visible forms.

Dhammajoti comments that "this is in contrast to the Sautrāntika view that visual consciousness—which is the seeing of the object [for the Sautrāntika]—is an effect produced in the moment subsequent to that when the eye, the visible form, etc., were present."

516 *LS*: Dhammajoti adds (ADCP.71): "...since whether there is seeing or not depends on the presence or otherwise of visual consciousness".

517 *LS*: See Saṃghabhadra's reply to this counter-question (ADCP.76).

518 *LS*: Based on the *Vyākhyā* [WOG.80.19; ADCP.75] Dhammajoti comments: "Consciousness being not susceptible to obstruction, having penetrated the wall, etc., should arise, just as in the case where the object is not intervened."

519 *LS*: Ny, 365c, clarifies what the Vaibhāṣikas mean by "being susceptible to obstruction" (*sapratigha*) (ADCP.78): "We do not simply mean that the [visual organ], being susceptible to obstruction on account of hindrance (*āvaraṇa-pratighāta*), can only take objects that are in contact, and hence cannot take objects, which are screened. 'Being susceptible to obstruction' here also includes the meaning of being 'susceptible to obstruction on account of being confined to a given object (*viṣaya-pratighāta*)': When it is confined to a given object, it cannot exercise its activity on any other object, even if the object is not screened—how much more so if it is screened. This in fact applies to any *dharma*, which takes an object—it cannot simultaneously take all objects."

520 *LS*: The *Vyākhyā* states (WOG.80.30–81.2; ADCP.78): "Do you mean that like the tangible organ which, being susceptible to obstruction, cannot move over the screen which is obstructive, to reach the object, and thus cannot exercise its activity on the object: The eye cannot see in this case because it needs to move over the screen which it cannot do, being susceptible to obstruction to reach and see the object?"

521 *LS*: *tasmānna sapratighatvāccakṣuṣa āvṛtasya rūpasyādarśanam.*

522 *LVP*: This is the thesis of the Bhadanta (MVŚ, 63b23, c12).

LS: 1. McGovern (MBPC.121f.) tells us: "The later Buddhists distinguish between the eye and ear on one hand, and the nose, tongue and body on the other. The latter can sense only that which is in immediate contact with them, while the former can sense that which is at a distance.... (This distinction) is insisted upon by the Sarvāstivādins both in the Mahāvibhāṣā and the Abhidharma Kośa. Vasubandhu tells us, moreover [ii. 23c], that the scope of the eye is even greater than that of the ear. It is to be regretted that the Buddhists did not tell us more concerning the nature of the medium between the sense organ and the sense-object."

2. However, as for *āloka*, it is defined at i. 10 a:

> *18.* sun-light (*ātapa*) is the radiance of the sun (*sūryaprabhā*);
>
> *19.* light (*āloka*) is the radiance (*prabhā*) of the moon (*candra*), of the stars (*tāraka*), of fire (*agni*), of herbs (*oṣadhi*) and of gems (*maṇi*);
>
> *17.* shadow (*chāyā*)—arisen from an obstruction to light [by an object]—is where visible forms (*rūpa*) remain visible (*darśana*);

> *20.* darkness (*andhakāra*) is the contrary to this [i.e., where there is no visibility at all].

Further, i. 28ab states the following:

> According to the School (*kila*), empty space or the elementary substance space is light (*āloka*) and darkness [*tamas*] (i. 10), i.e., a certain category of color (*varṇa*), of matter or material form (*rūpa*; i. 9b), for what is perceived in a cavity is light or darkness. Being light or darkness in its intrinsic nature, empty space will be day and night in its intrinsic nature (*rātriṃdivasvabhāva*).

3. Dhammajoti, in his chapter 5 of his *Abhidharma Doctrines and Controversies on Perception* renders a section (ADCP.78ff.) from the **Nyāyānusāra*, 365c, presenting the debate between the Vaibhāṣika (Vai) and the Vijñānavāda (Vij) related to why objects obstructed by glass, crystal, etc., are visible even though the visual organ cannot see obstructed objects on account of its being obstructive. Unfortunately, this section is too long to reproduce here. We will therefore give here just the section that sheds more light on *āloka*:

> Vij: Why ... does the eye not see visible forms screened by a wall, etc?
>
> Vai: We do not explain as you do, that it is because there is no light herein, since in the world it is observed that there can be perception in the absence of light. Rather, this is because of the [different] ways accumulated forms (*saṃcita-rūpa*) constitute obstruction. Thus, light and darkness differ in the ways they constitute hindrance: Though darkness and light both belong to the category of material forms (*rūpa-āyatana*), we can see what is obstructed by light, but not what is obstructed by darkness. Nocturnal creatures, while capable of seeing forms obstructed by darkness as well, cannot see what is obstructed by a wall, etc. In this way, though the visual organ can see forms screened by a glass, etc., it cannot see those screened by a wall, etc. By virtue of the obstructive nature of accumulated forms, the visual organ can only see the wall, etc., and not the objects screened by the wall, etc.
>
> Such is the nature of *dharma*-s; it is not a matter for speculation. There are organs, though capable of taking objects in a distance, fail to take some such objects due to certain obstruction. There are organs, though capable of seeing objects in contact, fail to see some such objects. Thus, as regards the author's question mentioned above—"Do you mean that the visual organ, like the organ of touch, can take an object only when in contact, so that on account of its being susceptible to obstruction, it cannot see a screened object"—we may retort: Your assertion will be futile; unless it is the case that an organ capable of taking objects in contact can actually take all such objects, and one capable of taking objects in a distance can actually take all such objects.

Collett Cox summarizes Saṃghabhadra as follows (EIP.VIII.670):

> For those who accept the theory that the eye sees, the eye is incapable of seeing an obstructed object because that eye has resistance. Since visual perceptual consciousness proceeds in accordance with the same object as its locus, the eye, it cannot cognize obstructed objects. Vasubandhu maintains that visibility of an object obstructed by something transparent is due to the ability of light to pass through to

the object. I (Saṃghabhadra), however, claim that the visibility or invisibility of an obstructed object depends upon the degree of resistance offered by the atomic structure of the obstruction.

4. Cf. also Harivarman's *Tattvasiddhi* (SH.95f.):

The heretics say: In the eye the fire element is predominant because of equality in their action-cause. The eye is obtained by donation of the lamp. The eye sees in collaboration with the light. The light illuminates distant things. The eye also has contact with the distant thing because of its ray. ...

See also in particular the entire section 49: "Contact and non-contact between the sense and the object" (SH.101–6), which is a debate with the Nyāya-Vaiśeṣika masters, discussing among others, their theory that the ray of the eye travels to the object.

[523] *LS*: SAH 35.

[524] *LVP*: *cakṣuṣā rūpāṇi dṛṣṭvā*... cited in iii. 32d. – *Saṃyukta*, 13, 4; *Vibhaṅga*, p. 381; *Madhyamakavṛtti*, p. 137; *Dhammasaṅgaṇi*, 597. – This is the argument of the Mahāsāṃghikas, *Kathāvatthu*, xviii. 9.

LS: As for the visual organ, Cox summarizes Saṃghabhadra (Ny, 366; EIP.VIII.670): "The visual organ has two activities: (1) it acts as a door, or as the locus for the emerging of aspects within awareness and accompanying mental factors with regard to the object. (2) It is able to grasp the object, that is, it sees colored shapes. Now we maintain that visual perceptual consciousness supports the eye and enables it to see because the eye cannot see apart from visual perceptual consciousness. However, visual perceptual consciousness itself does not see because, if it did, all types of perceptual consciousness, which are not different in nature from one another, should be able to see. The difference in the perceptual activity of seeing, hearing and so on can only be accounted for by the distinctions among the various organs.

[525] *LS*: *cakṣurvijñeyāni rūpāṇīṣṭāni kāntāni.*

[526] *LS*: *cakṣur brāhmaṇa, dvāraṃ yāvad eva rūpāṇām rūpāṇāṃ darśanāya.*

[527] *LS*: SAH 35.

[528] *MW*: *vijānāti*: to distinguish, discern, observe, investigate, recognize, ascertain, know, understand.

paśyat: seeing, beholding.

[529] *LVP*: Compare the formula: *tasyaivaṃ jānata evaṃ paśyataḥ*... .

[530] *LS*: For Saṃghabhadra's reply, see ADCP.74–75

[531] *LVP*: *Bhāṣya*: *vijñānaṃ tu saṃnidhyamātreṇa* [*rūpaṃ vijānātītyucyate*] | *yathā sūryo divasakara iti*. – *Vyākhyā* [WOG.24ff.]: *vijñānaṃ tu sāṃnidhyamātreṇe*ti nāśrayabhāvayogeneti darśayati | *yathā sūryo divasakara* iti | yathā sāṃnidhyamātreṇa sūryo divasaṃ karotīty ucyate tathā vijñānaṃ vijānātīty ucyate | kasmāt | loke tathā siddhatvāt.

[532] *LS*: 1. This is the first place in Pradhan (31.12) where the term Sautrāntika is explicitly mentioned.

For Saṃghabhadra's reply see ADCP.88–90.

2. We have already mentioned above Katō's and Kritzer's view that Vasubandhu—even

though the commentators think that he favors Dharmatrāta's view that it is the visual consciousness (*cakṣurvijñāna*) and not the eye sense-faculty that sees visible forms—in fact may just be using it to refute the Vaibhāṣikas. Now here at the end of the discussion, Vasubandhu ascribes to the Sautrāntikas the opinion that there is nothing that sees or is seen.

Dhammajoti comments (SD.198f; ADCP.23f.):

> However, it does seem wiser to trust the commentators' opinion, not only because these ancient masters were much closer to the time of AKB, but also in consideration of the following fact: The Sautrāntika remark at the end effectively denies the reality of the *āyatana*-s—there is neither the internal *āyatana* as that which sees, nor the external *āyatana* as the object of vision. This is in line with Śrīlāta's position that "both the supporting bases (*āśraya*; i.e., the organs) and the objects (*ālambana*) of the five [sensory] consciousnesses do not exist truly; the *dhātu*-s alone are real existents". For him, even the consciousnesses themselves do not exist as real entities [Ny, 484b]:
>
> > When the *sūtra* speaks of consciousness as that which is conscious (*vijānātīti vijñānam*), it is not a discourse of *paramārtha*; it is a conventional one (*saṃvṛti-deśanā*). [...]
>
> In contrast, Vasubandhu is known to hold that the *āyatana*-s exist truly in as much as they are epistemic facts. According to Sthiramati, this view, contrary to the understanding of some scholars, is not Vasubandhu's own, but a Sautrāntika view. Accordingly, it is more reasonable to understand Vasubandhu as basically advocating the "consciousness sees" position, rather than the one that is in line with Śrīlāta's denial of the *āyatana*-s. There is some confusion concerning the holders of this "consciousness sees" position. In the MVŚ it is attributed to Dharmatrāta; in the *Abhidharmadīpa* (31), the Dārṣṭāntika-pakṣa, likewise in Ny (367b), in *Tattvārthā*, the Sautrāntika-s. [...]
>
> According to [the *Tattvārthā*] it is correct to attribute the "consciousness sees" view to the Sautrāntika(-Dārṣṭāntika), and also correct to attribute the concluding remark to the Sautrāntika. But the two Sautrāntika are not exactly identical. The former is the Hīnayāna Sautrāntika, [holding in particular to their form of realism,] and we might call them Dārṣṭāntika Sautrāntika; the latter, the Sautrāntika Yogācāra, who were probably Mahāyānists ... derived from the broad Sautrāntika lineage. [...]
>
> [The "Hīnayāna" Sautrāntika] group seemed to have been greatly influenced by Bhadanta Dharmatrāta (and later on also Kumāralāta and others), and in Vasubandhu's time had Śrīlāta as a prominent leader. It is this group which preserved—sometimes with slight modification (e.g., Śrīlāta's doctrine that there are only three *caitta*-s *vedanā*, *saṃjñā* and *cetanā*; all the other *caitta*-s being *cetanā-viśeṣa*)—many of the Dārṣṭāntika doctrines in the MVŚ. ...
>
> In the AKB, Vasubandhu himself seems to be generally partisan to this Hīnayāna group. But, he too was evidently open-minded, of which fact the AKB is a testimony, and accordingly did not seem to have become exclusively partisan to the tenets of any group as such—be it those of Hīnayāna or Yogācāra Sautrāntika or Sarvāstivāda.

Thus, in the context of the "what sees" debate, he seems to basically side [with] the view of Dharmatrāta; and yet at the same time probably senses the meaningfulness of the Yogācāra-Sautrāntika's concluding remark.

533 *LS*: Pradhan.31.12 has: *kimidamākāśaṃ khādyate*?

534 *LS*: Dhammajoti translates based on Pradhan (SA.IV.263):

> Conditioned by the visual organ and visible objects, visual consciousness arises. Therein, what is it that sees, and what is it that is seen? It is really devoid of any function (*nirvyāpāra*)—a mere play of *dharma*-s as cause and effect" (*nirvyāpāraṃ hīdaṃ dharmamātraṃ hetuphalamātraṃ ca*).

He comments (ADCP.162):

> Given its Dārṣṭāntika inheritance (see above), it is not difficult for the Sautrāntika to arrive at the conclusion that causality *per se*, as an abstract principle dictating a necessary relationship between two entities conceived as "cause" and "effect", is a mentally superimposed concept. [...]
>
> Obviously, it is not that the Sautrāntika denies the empirical fact of causal efficacy as such. But what we do experience—and *ipso facto* know to exist—are no more than the momentary flashing of *dharma*-s, now experienced as so-called "cause", now as so-called "effect". The Sautrāntika acknowledgement of causal efficacy as the only reality finds explicit expression in its view that, in the traditional threefold classification of *dharma*-s—*skandha*, *āyatana*, and *dhātu*—only *dhātu* can be considered as real.

535 *LVP*: Or rather: "The expressions or words used in the world should not be rejected for the reason that they do not correspond to the realities." – *janapadaniruktiṃ nābhiniveśeta saṃjñāṃ ca lokasya nātidhāvet*. (*Madhyama*, 43, 18; *Saṃyukta*, 13, 12). Compare *Majjhima*, iii. 230: *janapadaniruttiṃ nābhiniveseyya samaññaṃ nātidhāveyya*; *Saṃyutta*, iv. 230: *yaṃ ca sāmaṃ ñātaṃ taṃ ca atidhāvanti, yaṃ ca loke saççasaṃmataṃ taṃ ca atidhāvānti*. – *Itivuttaka*, 49.

LS: Dhammajoti comments (SA.IV.281): "In the last sentence, *nābhidhāvet* could also be rendered as 'not [unnecessarily] contravene (/find faults with)'."

Majjhima, iii. 224f. explains (Translation: Bhikkhu Bodhi):

> How, *bhikkhus*, does there come to be insistence on local language and overriding of normal usage? Here, *bhikkhus*, in different localities they call the same thing a *dish*, a *bowl*, a *vessel*, a *saucer*, a *pan*, a *pot*, a *mug*, or a *basin*. So whatever they call it in such and such a locality, one speaks accordingly, firmly adhering [to that expression] and insisting: "only this is correct; anything else is wrong". This is how there comes to be insistence on local language and overriding of normal usage.

536 *LS*: Dhammajoti comments (SA.IV.264f.):

> In terms of intrinsic efficacy, the Vaibhāṣika maintains that whereas the eye sees, consciousness cognizes (*vijānāti*). But, what exactly does consciousness do in the perceptual process? In the AKB [ix. F 280f.], Vasubandhu discusses this question:
>
> It is said in the *sūtra*, "consciousness cognizes". Herein what does consciousness do?

> It does nothing... . Although doing nothing, consciousness is said to cognize because of the obtaining of itself resembling [the object] (*sādṛśenātma-lābhād akurvad api kiṃcit*)—[i.e., with the object as its supporting condition, it simply arises as an effect resembling the object]. What is its resemblance [with the object]? This consists in having the form or aspect of that [object] (*tadākāratā*).

Given the proper context—especially Vasubandhu's usage of the term *ākāra* (equated with the resemblance of the object) here—this doctrine, as some scholars like La Vallée Poussin [*Siddhi*, F 445] assert, can be considered a Sautrāntika one. Nevertheless, even the Vaibhāṣika would have no objection to the statement that consciousness in this process does nothing in particular. Saṃghabhadra too accepts that it is only with regard to the specific nature of *dharma* that one speaks in conventional terms of an agent, so as to refute the view that apart from consciousness there exists a real agent which is conscious; consciousness actually does nothing in the perceptual process [Ny, 342a]:

> In what other situations does one see the reference of an agent as a conventional expression (*prajñapti*) to nothing more than the nature of a *dharma*? One sees in the world that people speak of a shadow as that which moves. In this case there is no movement; but when it arises in a different place in the following moment (*anantaram*), it is said to move. The same is true for the case of consciousness; when it arises serially with regard to a different object, it is said to be that which cognizes—i.e., it cognizes the object—even though there [really] is no action [on its part].

537 *Gokhale*: [43ab] *ubhābhyām api cakṣurbhyām paśyati vyaktadarśanāt* |

Tib.: [43ab] *mig ni gnyis ka dag gis kyang | mthong ste gsal bar mthong phyir ro* |

LVP: According to *Jñānaprasthāna*, 919c27; MVŚ, 62b1.

Against the Vātsīputrīyas. – See above note ad i. 42, at the end.

LS: Cox summarizes Saṃghabhadra (Ny, 368a; EIP.VIII.671):

> Both eyes can be said to see material form at the same time because the object appears clearer when both eyes are open. If the eyes saw in succession, there would be no difference between the clarity of an object seen with two eyes or one.
>
> Śrīlāta: The two eyes give rise to their activity successively. Perceptual consciousness produced by two eyes is clearer than that produced by one alone because the two successive moments of the visual organ exchange their activity producing a clearer perceptual consciousness.
>
> Answer: Whether one or two eyes are open in any given moment, only one moment of visual perceptual consciousness is produced. However, if two eyes, both open, acted successively, they would produce two distinct moments of visual perceptual consciousness. Finally, since awareness and accompanying mental factors, which include all varieties of perceptual consciousness, cannot be established in a particular place, the two spatially distinct sense-organs do not produce two spatially distinct instances of visual perceptual consciousness.

538 *LS*: "An Ābhidharmika is one who specializes in the *abhidharma* and takes the *abhidharma* as the final authority. For him, the *abhidharma* is definitive (*lākṣaṇika*) and represents the true intention of the Buddha, taught at the level of absolute truth (*paramārtha-satya*), with fully drawn out meanings (*nītārtha*). In contrast, the *sūtra*-s are implicit (*ābhiprāyika*) and do not represent the Buddha's true intention. They generally represent the expedient (*aupacārika*) teachings whose meanings are yet to be fully drawn out (*neyārtha*)." (SA.IV.15)

539 *LVP*: Argumentation of Vasubandhu, *Pañcavastuka*, i. 10.

540 *LS*: SAH 43.

541 *Gokhale*: [43cd] *cakṣuśrotramano 'prāptaviṣayaṃ trayam anyathā* ||

Tib.: [43cd] *mig dang yid dang rna ba ni* | *yul dang ma phrad gsum gzhan du* ||

LVP: Compare *Atthasālinī*, 629.

MVŚ, 63b14ff: It is said that the object is attained (*prāpta*) in a twofold sense:

1. either because it is *seized as object* or *perceived*;
2. or else because there is a juxtaposition (*nirantaratva*) of the object and the sense-faculty.

In the first sense, the six sense-faculties attain the object.

In the second sense, three sense-faculties only, i.e., the sense-faculties of the nose, of the tongue and of the body, attain the object; on the contrary, three sense-faculties, i.e., the sense-faculties of the eye, of the ear and of the mental faculty, perceive without attaining:

- the eye sense-faculty perceives visible form because of the light; when the visible form is close to the sense-faculty, it hinders the light: the sense-faculty does not see;
- the ear sense-faculty perceives sound because of space or the void; when the sound is close to the sense-faculty, it does not hinder the void: the sense-faculty hears...;
- the nose sense-faculty perceives because of the wind;
- the tongue sense-faculty perceives because of the water;
- the body sense-faculty perceives because of the earth;
- the mental faculty perceives because of mental application (*manaskāra*).

Fa-pao comments that the *rūpa* of the moon does not abandon the moon in order to juxtapose itself onto the eye.

Compare Āryadeva, *Śataka*, 288.

542 *LS*: SAH 43.

543 *LS*: Cox, summarizing Saṃghabhadra (Ny, 370a; EIP.VIII.672), adds: "Further, the eye can produce doubtful or erroneous visual perceptual consciousness; if it touched its object, all visual perceptual consciousnesses would be certain. The ear also does not touch its object because distinctions of direction, distance and clarity are noticed in the perception of sounds. The mind does not touch its object because it does not apprehend connected factors that are simultaneous with it. Further, the mind is not material form, and therefore cannot touch or be touched."

544 *LVP*: Objection by the Vaiśeṣikas.

LS: See also part 3 in our endnote regarding light (*āloka*) at i, F 83.

545 *LS*: Pradhan.32.7f. has: *manastvarūpitvāt prāptumevāśaktam.*

546 *LVP*: This doctrine is refuted by Saṃghabhadra; Tao-thai attributes it to the Sāṃmitīyas; Fa-pao, to certain masters of the *Vibhāṣā.*

547 *LS*: SAH 43.

548 *LVP*: Saṃghabhadra discusses this thesis.

549 *LVP*: In regard to the entire discussion of i, F 88–92, see Saṃghabhadra, Ny, 370b23ff., *Documents d'Abhidharma.*

550 *LVP*: Here and below (definition of the Bhadanta, F 91), our Tibetan version translates *nirantara* by *'dab chags pa.* But the Tibetan Siddhāntas analyzed by Wassilief (p. 307) contrast the *nirantara* of the Bhadanta (*bar med pa*) with the *nirantara* of the other scholars (*'dab chags pa*).

According to the *Bodhicaryāvatāra*, p. 516, the sense-faculty and the object cannot be either separated (*savyavadhāna, sāntara*) or contiguous (*nirantara*).

551 *LS*: Yaśomitra [WOG.85.9]: *nirantare tu spṛṣṭa-saṃjñeti Bhadantaḥ.*

552 *LVP*: Saṃghabhadra (Ny, 371c7): What is the meaning of *to reach*? When the object arises in proximity to the sense-faculty, the sense-faculty seizes it. To understand factors in this way, one can say that the nose, the tongue and the body seize the object that they reach; just as one says that the eye sense-faculty does not see the eyelid, the little rod, and the other visible forms that it reaches. The eyelid does not [actually] "touch" the eye sense-faculty: one says, nevertheless, that the eye sense-faculty "reaches" it. From the fact that the eyelid arises in proximity with the sense-faculty, one says that the sense-faculty reaches it. As the eye sense-faculty does not see the visible form reached in this way, one says that the eye sense-faculty seizes without reaching and not by reaching; moreover, it does not seize a very distant object. In this same way, even though the nose seizes the object that it reaches, it does not seize that which is very close.

553 *LVP*: According to the MVŚ, 683c24: Do the atoms touch one another? – They do not touch one another; if they did touch one another, they would touch one another (1) in their totality or (2) partially. If they did touch one another in their totality, they would form only one real entity; if they would touch one another partially, they would thus have parts. But the atoms do not have parts.

How is it that agglomerated factors, striking one another, do not separate? – They do not separate because the wind element (*vāyudhātu*) holds them together.

But does the wind element not separate? – (1) Sometimes it separates, for example, at the end of the cosmic aeon. (2) Sometimes it holds together, for example, at the beginning of the cosmic aeon.

If the atoms do not touch, how does striking produce sound? – For this same reason, sound is produced. For, if the atoms did touch one another, how could there be the production of sound? If the atoms did touch one another, the hand and the body that the hand strikes would blend, and there would be no free space, how could sound arise?

Vasumitra says: "The atoms do not touch one another: if they were to touch, they would thus last for a second moment."

The Bhadanta says: There is no real contact; through acquiescence to popular truth, one says that there is contact when the atoms arise in a union without interval (*nirantara*).

Does the real entity in contact arise having a real entity in contact for its cause? ...

LS: The *Siddhi* states (F 39): "We pose two dilemmas: (1) either the atoms are 'substantially repellent' [Ch.: *ti-tche-ngai*] or they are not; (2) either the atoms are 'extended', or they are not."

LVP comments:

> According to the Sautrāntikas, the atom is "extended", it involves spatial division (*digbhāgabheda* or *digvibhāga*); according to the Sarvāstivādins, the atom is 'unextended'; we would say that it is merely a point.
>
> Both schools maintain that the atom is "resistant" (*sapratigha*) through "obstruction qua obstacle" (*āvaraṇapratighāta*): that one atom cannot occur in the place where another atom is. But the two schools, as they are not agreeing on the extension of the atom, do not understand "obstruction qua obstacle" (*āvaraṇapratighāta*) in the same way, i.e., the Sautrāntikas admit that the atoms touch one another and that they "are resistant due to their extension" (*digdeśabheda-pratighāta*), whereas the Sarvāstivādins cannot admit that their atom-points touch one another (*Kośa*, i, F 89); they therefore attribute to them an obstruction (*pratighāta*) that is called, in Chinese, *ti-tche-ngai* or *tche-ngai* of which I [LVP] do not attempt to reconstruct the Sanskrit, and which, until something better turns up, I render as "substantial repellence", (a repellence due to which the atom-points resist or repel each other at a distance, which brings it about that nothing is able to enter in between them). – The Sautrāntikas do not accept the resistance called "substantial repellence" (*ti-tche-ngai*).

We have already previously noted that the Buddhist atomic theory is not discernable in the *sūtras* and that it was likely taken over from outside the Buddhist schools—probably from the Vaiśeṣika—though articulated in their own way. As for an overview of the Vaiśeṣika theories, see EIP.II.79–86: *Atomic Theory and Theory of* "*Cooking*", and EIP.II.115ff., which addresses whether atoms are non-locus-pervading or locus-pervading.

554 *LVP*: Compare the *Viṃśaka* of Vasubandhu, 12–14; *Bodhicaryāvatāra*, p. 503; Praśastapāda, p. 43, etc.

555 *LVP*: They should have arisen (first moment) in order to touch one another (second moment). Opinion of Vasumitra, cited by Kouei-ki, *Twenty Stanzas*, iii, 11b.

556 *LS*: This is the last of Kritzer's fifteen passages discussed in relation to chapter 1 (VY.34f.).

557 *LS*: Cox summarizes Saṃghabhadra (EIP.VIII.673): "One master proposes that atoms do not contact one another; instead, the idea of contact arises when there is no interval between atoms. This proposal can be accepted as long as a clear distinction is drawn between 'having no interval' and 'contact'. 'Having no interval' means that the atoms of the four fundamental elements arise in close proximity; it does not mean that atoms have contact and hence, parts. Nor does it mean that they have no resistance and hence abide in the same place."

558 *LS*: Pradhan.33.3 has *na spṛśanti* | *nirantare tu spṛṣṭasaṃjñeti bhadantaḥ* |. Jha translates:

"In case they do not touch, when there is no interval, that will be called contact—this is the opinion of Bhadanta."

559 *LVP*: Vasubandhu believes that the Bhadanta understands *juxtaposition without interval* in the sense that the atoms do not allow an interval between them. We will see that Saṃghabhadra is of a different opinion.

560 *LVP*: For Vasubandhu, the atoms are immediately juxtaposed; nevertheless they do not mingle one with another, for, being impenetrable, they remain distinct in spite of their contiguity.

Here is the essential point of the explanations of Saṃghabhadra.

Nyāyānusāra, i. 43cd (fol. 43a17):

The Bhadanta nevertheless says: "The atoms do not touch one another; it is said metaphorically that they touch one another, because they are juxtaposed without interval" (*nirantara*). The Sautrāntika (that is to say, Vasubandhu), indicating that this is the best theory, says: "This doctrine is the correct one; otherwise, the atoms would present intervals (*sāntara*); these intervals being empty, what would hinder the atoms from moving (one toward the other)? One admits that they are impenetrable (*sapratigha*)."

(Saṃghabhadra continues:) This theory of the Bhadanta should be neither approved nor censured; one should merely examine how there can be an absence of interval without it having contact: the reasoning not being explicit, this theory is difficult to understand.

One might say that the atoms are absolutely without intervals and yet do not blend with one another, it is necessary that they should have parts: a wrong opinion. Furthermore, if *nirantara* signifies *without interval* (*anantara*), how could the atoms not touch one another?

Consequently, the word *nirantara* signifies *close.* (1) The prefix *nis* signifies *certitude*. As there certainly is an interval, the atoms are *nirantara*, i.e., *with intervals*: the same way as *nirdahati* means "it burns". Or else, (2) the prefix *nis* signifies *absence*. The atoms are called *without interposition* (*nirantara*) because there is no *rūpa*-in-contact (*spṛṣṭa*) of the dimension of an atom between them. When the atoms of the fundamental material elements arise close to one another without *interposition*, it is said metaphorically that they touch one another.

To understand the Bhadanta in this way, we approve him... .

LS: Dhammajoti comments (SA.IV.206) that "the Vaibhāṣika position is a logical consequence of the doctrine that an atom has no spatial extension, and yet is aggregated with six other atoms in the six directions—north, east, south, west, above and below—with the given atom at the centre. This may imply that an atom has at least six sides—a point seized upon by the Vijñānavādins in their refutation of the Ābhidharmika notion of atom. To avoid this fallacy, atoms must be thought of as being aggregated in such a way that in between the atoms there must be gaps that are less than the size of a single atom."

561 *LVP*: *saṃghāte spṛśyante yathā rūpyante*.

562 *LVP*: Saṃghabhadra reproduces this paragraph (The Sautrāntika says: "If you admit...") and pursues:

> This is not correct. *To have parts*, and *to be spatially divided*: two expressions of the same idea. By the fact that it is said: "The atom does not have parts", it is said that it is foreign to all spatial division. How can you be in doubt with respect to this point

and say: "If you admit the spatial division..."? – Since the atoms are foreign to this division, how could they touch one another? We have explained that contact can only be total or partial; thus the atom, foreign to spatial division, cannot enter into contact. How can you thus say: "If you deny the spatial division, there will be no difficulty in the atoms touching one another." – Thus the atoms are called *nirantara*, "not separated", because there is no *rūpa*-in-contact (*spṛṣṭa*) of the dimension of an atom between them.

See ii. 22 and the *Introduction*.

563 *LS*: SAH 43–44.

564 *Gokhale*: [44ab] *tribhir ghrāṇādibhis tulyaviṣayagrahaṇam matam* |

Tib.: [44ab] *sna la sogs pa gsum gyis ni* | *yul ni mnyam pa 'dzin par 'dod* |

LVP: According to the MVŚ, 63c12.

565 *LS*: Discussing the *paramāṇus* of objects and sense-faculties, *Kośa* ii. 22 (F 144) states: "By *paramāṇu* one does not understand the atom (*paramāṇu*) here [in verse 22] in the strict sense, the real-entity atom (*dravyaparamāṇu*), the atom or monad that is a single real entity (*dravya*; i. 13); but rather the composite molecule (*saṃghātaparamānu*), i.e., the most subtle (*sarvasūkṣma*) among the composite matters (*rūpasaṃghāta*), since there is nothing more subtle than it among the composite matters."

In a footnote to ii. 22 (F 145), LVP comments: "The (composite) molecules that involve the body sense-faculty, the eye sense-faculty, etc., are the 'atoms' that are discussed in i. 44ab."

566 *LS*: Cox summarizes Saṃghabhadra (Ny, 373c; EIP.VIII. 673): "Since the atoms in these five externally directed organs cannot be seen, their arrangement is difficult to determine, but because they have resistance, and therefore occupy a particular place, they are arranged."

567 *LVP*: The opinion of the Sarvāstivādins.

568 *LVP*: *mālāvad avasthita* = maṇḍalena samapaṅktyāvasthita [WOG.86.7].

569 *LVP*: The text has *kila* ["so said", "so reported"]. As a general rule, Vasubandhu indicates, by the word *kila*, that the opinion in question is an incorrect opinion of the Vaibhāṣikas; but here the *Vyākhyā* says: āgamasūcanārthaḥ kilaśabdāḥ [WOG.86.8].

570 *LS*: For the Sarvāstivādins, the object of sensory perception (ADCP.142–44) is an assemblage or agglomeration of atoms (和集, *he-ji*; **saṃcaya*, **saṃghāta*, **samasta*), "capable of being seen by the eye", "a set of entities of the same species": "what is directly perceived is just these atoms assembled together in a certain manner, not a conceptualized object such as a jar, etc."

On the other hand, for the Sautrāntikas (including Śrīlāta, but not Vasubandhu; see i. 20ab, F 39), the object of sensory perception is a unified complex (和合, *he-he*; **sāmagri*, **samghāta*) of atoms, which is not a real entity.

As for Vasubandhu, see Dhammajoti's comment in the next endnote.

For a discussion of the important epistemological and ontological issues and implications underlying the Sarvāstivādin and Sautrāntika views regarding the object of sensory perception, see the long endnote at iii. F 104.

[571] *LS*: As for the visibility of atoms, see part 2.iii of our endnote at i, F 37, bottom.

Dhammajoti adds (ADCP.143f.):

> The Vaibhāṣika speaks summarily of two types of atoms, real (*dravyatas*) and conceptual (*prajñaptitas*) [Ny.522a]:
>
> > The real are the *svalakṣaṇa*-s of *rūpa*, etc., which are universally acknowledged (*prasiddha*); they are perceived through *pratyakṣa* at the assembled state (和集位; **saṃcitāvasthā*, **samastāvasthā*). The conceptual ones are those [arrived at] through analysis, and known through inference (*anumāna*).
>
> In a similar manner, Vasubandhu too, in his AKB [iii, F 213], when refuting the Vaiśeṣika, explains the Buddhist view that "in spite of the atoms being imperceptible by the senses [individually], there is the direct perception (*samastānāṃ pratyakṣatva*) of them in agglomeration". Moreover, it is also the doctrine of the MVŚ [63c] that the first five consciousnesses have, for their supporting bases and objects, an agglomeration of atoms, not the atoms singly.

See also Kajiyama's article *The Atomic Theory of Vasubandhu, the Author of the Abhidharmakośa*, SBP.171–76.

[572] *LS*: See our endnotes at iii, F 99 and 104.

[573] *Gokhale*: [44cd] *caramasy āśrayo 'tītaḥ pañcānāṃ sahajaś ca taiḥ* ||

Tib.: [44cd] *tha ma'i rten 'das lnga rnams kyi* | *de dag lhan cig skyes pa'ng yin* ||

LS: In terms of the discussion as to whether or not Vasubandhu accepts simultaneous causation (see for example ii. 50bd [F 253f.]), it should be noted that he does not object here to the simultaneity of object and sense-faculty in regard to the five sensory consciousnesses. As already mentioned in our introductory note, Dhammajoti states (SD.201) that "Vasubandhu is known to accept some of the Sarvāstivāda *caitta*-s, and the notion of *saṃprayoga* of *citta-caitta*-s—differing from Śrīlāta. This also necessarily means that he accepts the *sahabhū-hetu* doctrine which Śrīlāta rejects."

[574] *LS*: Yaśomitra glosses (WOG.86.21f.): koṭi-traya-muktā viprayuktā asaṃskṛt'ādayaḥ.

[575] *Gokhale*: [45ab] *tadvikāravikāritvād āśrayāś cakṣurādayaḥ* |

Tib.: [45ab] *de dag gyur pas 'gyur nyid phyir* | *rten ni mig la sogs pa yin* |

LVP: According to the MVŚ, 369c10ff.

[576] *Gokhale*: [45cd] *ato 'sādhāraṇatvāc ca vijñānaṃ tair nirucyate* ||

Tib.: [45cd] *de phyir thun mong ma yin phyir* | *de dag gis ni rnam shes bstan* ||

LS: Cox summarizes Saṃghabhadra (EIP.VIII.675): "Though the arising of perceptual consciousness depends upon many causes and conditions, the organ and the object are designated as the locus and supporting object because they are essential for its arising, in each and every case."

[577] *LS*: SAH 46–47.

[578] *LS*: SAH 46.

[579] *LS*: Ibid.

580 *LS*: This passage is missing in LVP. Pradhan.35.7f. has: *prathamadhyānabhūmīni paśyato vijñānarūpe tadbhūmike kāyaḥ kāmāvacaraścakṣurdvitīyadhyānabhūmikam.*

581 *LS*: LVP has second meditation, but Pradhan has *prathamadhyāna.* Jha has "first meditation".

582 *LS*: SAH 46.

583 *LS*: Ibid.

584 *LS*: Ibid.

585 *LS*: Ibid.

586 *Gokhale*: [46] *na kāyasyā 'dharaṃ cakṣur ūrdhvaṃ rūpaṃ na cakṣuṣaḥ | vijñānaṃ cā 'sya rūpaṃ tu kāyasy obhe ca sarvataḥ ||*

Tib.: [46] *lus la 'og ma'i mig ma yin | mig gi gong ma'i gzugs ma yin | rnam par shes pa'ng de yi gzugs | lus kyi'ng gnyis ka thams cad du ||*

LVP: See vii, F 107; viii, F 154.

587 *LS*: SAH 47.

588 *Gokhale*: [47a1] *tatha śrotraṃ*

Tib.: [47a1] *rna ba'ng de bzhin*

589 *LS*: SAH 47.

590 *Gokhale*: [47a2–b] *trayāṇāṃ tu sarvam eva svabhūmikam |*

Tib.: [47a2–b] *gsum dag ni | thams cad rang gi sa pa nyid |*

591 *LS*: SAH 47.

592 *Gokhale*: [47cd1] *kāyavijñānam adharasvabhūmy*

Tib.: [47cd1] *lus kyi rnam shes 'og dang ni | rang gi sa*

593 *LS*: SAH 47.

594 *Gokhale*: [47d2] *aniyataṃ manaḥ ||*

Tib.: [47d2] *yid ma nges te ||*

595 *LS*: SAH 49.

596 *Gokhale*: [48a] *pañca bāhyā dvivijñeyā*

Tib.: [48a] *gnyis kyi rnam shes phyi yi lnga |*

597 *LS*: See our endnote regarding the sense-sphere of factors (*dharmāyatana*) and the element of factors (*dharmadhātu*) at i. 15bd.

598 *LS*: SAH 37.

599 *Gokhale*: [48b] *nityā dharmā asaṃskṛtāḥ |*

Tib.: [48b] *'dus ma byas chos rtag pa'o |*

LVP: Unconditioned factors are eternal because they do not go from one time period to another time period (*adhvasaṃcārābhāvāt*; v. 25). – Unconditioned factor (*asaṃskṛta*; iv. 9), eternal factor (*nitya*), firm factor (*dhruva*; iv. 9) and real entity (*dravya*; inherent in the real entity [*dravyavat*], see i. 38a) are synonyms.

[600] *LS*: Pradhan.37.4 has *śeṣā anityāḥ*.

[601] *LS*: AH 203; SAH 36, 432.

[602] *Gokhale*: [48cd] *dharmā'rdham indriyaṃ ye ca dvādaś ādhyātmikāḥ smṛtāḥ* ||

Tib.: [48cd] *chos kyi phyed dang gang dag ni* | *bcu gnyis nang gir bshad dbang po* ||

LVP: According to another reading (*kecit paṭhanti*): *dharmārdham*... .

See *Dhammasaṅgaṇi*, 661.

[603] *LS*: AH 203; SAH 432.

[604] *LVP*: The *Vyākhyā* cites the conversation of the Brahmin Jātiśroṇa with the Bhagavat: indriyāṇīndriyāṇīti bho Gautama ucyante | kati bho Gautama indriyāṇi | kiyatā cendriyāṇāṃ samgraho bhavati... [WOG.90.29f.].

LS: Cox summarizes Saṃghabhadra (Ny, 377a; EIP.VIII.675f.):

> Concerning those elements (*dhātu*) that are controlling faculties [*indriya*], the five sense organs, the seven mental elements, part of the tactile organ element, and part of the factor element [*dharmadhātu*] are controlling faculties.
>
> The tactile organ element includes the masculine and feminine faculties, and the seven mental elements constitute the mental faculty.
>
> Those controlling faculties included within the factor element are the five feeling faculties of satisfaction, frustration, contentedness, irritation and equanimity; the five faculties of faith, energy, mindfulness, meditation and insight; the controlling faculty of vitality; and the three faculties of coming to know what is as yet unknown, understanding, and perfect knowledge.

[605] *LVP*: The order of the controlling faculties (*indriya*) is justified in ii. 5–6.

We have the order of our Sūtra in *Vibhaṅga*, p. 122; *Kathāvatthu*, transl. p. 16; *Visuddhimagga*, xvi; and also in the *Indriyaskandhaka*, sixth book of the *Jñānaprasthāna* (Takakusu, "Abhidharma Literature", *JPTS*, 1905, p. 93).

The small treatise of Anuruddha (*Compendium*, p. 175) follows the same order as the *Prakaraṇapāda.*

The *Mahāvyutpatti* (108) places the vitality faculty at the end.

LS: Collett Cox discusses a slightly different order of the twenty-two controlling faculties as follows (FCO.552):

> Early efforts to organize the multiplying categories of *dharma*s resulted in comprehensive taxonomic systems that combine both the "evaluative" and "descriptive" purposes. For example, the early comprehensive system of the twenty-two controlling faculties (*indriya*) subsumes earlier standard sets, which were reordered in large part to reflect these two purposes.
>
> It begins with a "descriptive" presentation of the five externally directed, corporeal sense organs (1–5), which are followed by the three controlling faculties (6–8)—namely, femininity, masculinity, and the life-force that further qualify the final corporeal sense organ of the body. The mental sense organ is listed next (9), and

is followed by the five varieties of feelings (10–14) that determine the affective quality of mental events.

Here the focus shifts to the "evaluative" or soteriological purpose represented by eight praxis-oriented controlling faculties, culminating in the controlling faculty of one possessed of complete knowledge (*ājñātāvīndriya*), which is tantamount to arhat ship or enlightenment.*

* *Dharmaskandha* (T.1737) 10 p. 498b12–499c24; *Prakaraṇapāda* (T.1542) 8 p. 723a24–c2. For a discussion of the 22 controlling faculties and their development throughout early Sarvāstivāda Abhidharma texts, see Saitō (2002). Saitō also examines the different orders in which the controlling faculties are enumerated and explores various related doctrinal and historical questions.

606 *LVP*: The last three controlling faculties (*indriya*) are made up of (1–3) three faculties of sensation; (4–8) the five (praxis-oriented) faculties; (9) the mental faculty: 1–8 are the element of factors (*dharmadhātu*). [See WOG.91.18f.].

607 *LS*: Here LVP has "(3) une partie des trois derniers souverains".

608 *LS*: SAH 36.

Chapter Two:

Exposition of the Faculties

(*Indriyanirdeśa*)

Outline of Chapter Two:
Exposition of the Faculties
(*Indriyanirdeśa*)

A. Controlling faculties (*indriya*) 463

AA. Name and meaning of *indriya* & the link between chapters 463

AB. Brief Vaibhāṣika explanation of the controlling power of each controlling faculty 464

AC. Brief Sautrāntika explanation of the controlling power of each controlling faculty 468

AD. Explanation of the enumeration and order of the twenty-two controlling faculties 470

AE. Detailed explanation of the intrinsic nature (*svabhāva*) of the twenty-two controlling faculties 473

AF. The different modes (*prakārabheda*) of the controlling faculties 478

AG. Original acquisition (*labha*) of the controlling faculties at conception & final discarding (*tyāga*) of the controlling faculties at death 491

AH. The obtaining (*prāpti*) of the fruits of the religious praxis & the number of controlling faculties 494

AI. The number of controlling faculties with which people are accompanied (*samanvāgata*) 499

B. The way conditioned factors (*saṃskṛta*) arise & five-group (*pañca-vastu*) classification of factors 505

BA. The simultaneous arising (*sahotpāda*) of factors 507

BAA. The simultaneous arising of atoms or molecules (*paramāṇu*) 507

BAB. The simultaneous arising of thought, thought-concomitants and formations dissociated from thought 511

BAB.1. The formations associated with thought (*cittasaṃprayukta-saṃskāra*): forty-six thought-concomitants 512

BAB.1.1. The five determined kinds and one undetermined kind 512

BAB.1.1.1. The ten generally permeating factors (*mahābhūmika*) 513

BAB.1.1.2. The ten wholesome permeating factors (*kuśalamahābhūmika*) 515

BAB.1.1.3. The six permeating factors of defilement (*kleśamahābhūmika*) 518

BAB.1.1.4. The two unwholesome permeating factors (*akuśalamahābhūmika*) 521

BAB.1.1.5. The factors of defilement of restricted scope (*parīttakleśabhūmika*) 521

BAB.1.1.6. The undetermined factors (*aniyata*) 522

BAB.1.2. Which thought-concomitants arise in association with which thought? 523
BAB.1.3. Drawing distinctions between similar thought-concomitants 528
BAB.1.4. Thought and thought-concomitants 534
BAB.2. The formations dissociated from thought (*cittaviprayukta-saṃskāra*): fourteen types 536
BAB.2.1. The name "formations dissociated from thought" 537
BAB.2.2. Possession (*prāpti*) & non-possession (*aprāpti*) 537
BAB.2.3. Group homogeneity (*nikāyasabhāgatā*) 555
BAB.2.4. State of non-ideation (*āsaṃjñika*) 559
BAB.2.5. The two attainments (*samāpatti*) 561
BAB.2.6. Vitality faculty (*jīvitendriya*) 575
BAB.2.7. Characteristics (*lakṣaṇa*) 583
BAB.2.8. Collections of names, phrases and syllables (*nāmakāya, padakāya, vyañjanakāya*) 599
BAB.2.9. The modes of group homogeneity, possessions, characteristics, two attainments, non-possession 605

C. Classification of factors according to causes (*hetu*), effects (*phala*), conditions (*pratyaya*) 607
CA. The six causes (*hetu*) 607
CAA. Efficient cause (*kāraṇahetu*) 608
CAB. Co-existent cause (*sahabhūhetu*) 610
CAC. Homogeneous cause (*sabhāgahetu*) 617
CAD. Associated cause (*saṃprayuktakahetu*) 630
CAE. Pervasive cause (*sarvatragahetu*) 631
CAF. Ripening cause (*vipākahetu*) 633
CAG. The six causes and the unconditioned factors & the three time periods 638
CB. The five effects (*phala*) 638
CBA. The correspondence of the effects with the causes 639
CBB. The defining characteristics of the five effects 652
CBB.1. Ripened effect (*vipākaphala*) 652
CBB.2. Effect of equal outflow (*niṣyandaphala*) 653
CBB.3. Effect of disconnection (*visaṃyogaphala*) 654
CBB.4. Effect of human action (*puruṣakāraphala*) 654
CBB.5. Effect of dominance (*adhipatiphala*) 655
CBC. Two stages of causing an effect 656
CBD. The four effects of the Westerners 660
CC. Topics related to causes and results 660

Chapter Two:

EXPOSITION OF THE FACULTIES

(*Indriyanirdeśa*)[1]

A. Controlling faculties (*indriya*); F 103

B. The way conditioned factors (*saṃskṛta*) arise & five-group (*pañca-vastu*) classification of factors: (1) matter or form (*rūpa*): atoms and molecules; (2) thought (*citta*); (3) thought-concomitants (*caitta*) or formations associated with thought (*cittasaṃprayukta*); (4) formations dissociated from thought (*cittaviprayukta*); (5) unconditioned factors (*asaṃskṛta*); F 143

C. Classification of factors according to causes (*hetu*), effects (*phala*) and conditions (*pratyaya*); F 244–331

CONTROLLING FACULTIES (INDRIYA);[2] *F 103–43*

AA. Name and meaning of *indriya*; F 103

AB. Brief Vaibhāṣika explanation of the controlling power of each controlling faculty; F 103

AC. Brief Sautrāntika explanation of the controlling power of each controlling faculty; F 107

AD. Explanation of the enumeration and order of the twenty-two controlling faculties; F 110

AE. Detailed explanation of the intrinsic nature (*svabhāva*) of the twenty-two controlling faculties; F 113

AF. The different modes (*prakārabheda*) of the controlling faculties; F 118

AG. Original acquisition (*labha*) of the controlling faculties at conception & final discarding (*tyāga*) of the controlling faculties at death; F 131

AH. The obtaining (*prāpti*) of the fruits of the religious praxis & the number of controlling faculties; F 134

AI. The number of controlling faculties with which people are accompanied (*samanvāgata*); F 138–143

NAME AND MEANING OF INDRIYA *& THE LINK BETWEEN CHAPTERS;*[3] *F 103*

In regard to the elements (*dhātu*; i. 48), we have enumerated the controlling faculties or *indriyas*.[4] What is the meaning [*artha*] of the word *indriya*?

The root *idi* signifies supremacy or supreme power or supreme dominion (*idi paramaiśvarya*) (*Dhātupāṭha*, i. 64). That which exercises supreme power is called *indriya*. Thus, in general, *indriya* signifies *adhipati* [sovereign, ruler, commander, regent, king; *ādhipatya*: sovereignty or controlling power or dominance].[5]

BRIEF VAIBHĀṢIKA EXPLANATION OF THE CONTROLLING POWER OF EACH CONTROLLING FACULTY;[6] *F 103–7*

What is the object of the controlling power [*ādhipatya*] of each controlling faculty?

1. **According to the School [i.e., the Vaibhāṣika]:**

   (1) five controlling faculties [i.e., the five sense-faculties of the sensory consciousnesses] exercise controlling power with regard to four things [*artha*] [i.e., beauty, protection, production, special mode of activity];

   (2) four controlling faculties [i.e., the two sexual faculties, vitality faculty, mental faculty] exercise controlling power with regard to two things [i.e., division and differentiation; forming an initial connection and supporting the *nikāyasabhāga*; connection at rebirth and continual domination];[7]

   (3) five controlling faculties [i.e., the faculty of sensation of pleasure, displeasure, satisfaction, dissatisfaction and equanimity] and eight controlling faculties [i.e., the praxis-oriented faculties of faith, vigor, mindfulness, concentration, understanding and the three pure controlling faculties] exercise controlling power with regard, [respectively,] to pollution [*saṃkleśa*] and purification [*vyavadāna*].[8]

The five sense-faculties & the object of the controlling power;[9] *F 103–4*

Each of the five controlling faculties of which the eye sense-faculty is the first—the five sense-faculties of the sensory consciousness—exercises controlling power [*ādhipatya*]:

1. with regard to the beauty of the person (*ātmabhāvaśobhā*),[10] <104>
2. with regard to the protection of the person (*ātmabhāvaparikarṣaṇa*), {1 b}[11]
3. with regard to the production of a consciousness (*vijñāna*) and of the thought-concomitants associated with this consciousness,
4. with regard to its particular or uncommon activity (*asādhāraṇakāraṇatva*) (MVŚ, 730a29).

BA.1. *The sense-faculty of the eye and the ear & the object of the controlling power;*[12] *F 104*

The sense-faculties of the eye and the ear exercise controlling power:

1. with regard to beauty, for the body in which they are missing is not beautiful (i. 19);
2. with regard to protection, for thanks to the eye and the ear, the person avoids that which is harmful or adverse (*viṣamaparihāra*);
3. with regard to production of two consciousnesses, i.e., of the visual consciousness and auditory consciousness, and of the mental factors which are associated with them;
4. with regard to their particular or uncommon activity: the seeing of visible forms, the hearing of sounds.

BA.2. *The sense-faculty of the nose, the tongue, the body & the object of the controlling power;*[13] *F 104*

The sense-faculties of the nose, tongue and body exercise controlling power:

1. with regard to beauty, as above;
2. with regard to protection, through the consumption of material food (*kavaḍīkārāhāra*; iii. 39);
3. with regard to the production of three consciousnesses;
4. with regard to their particular or uncommon activity [*asādhāraṇakāraṇatva*]: smelling odors, tasting tastes, touching tangibles.

BB. *The two sexual faculties, the vitality faculty, the mental faculty & the object of the controlling power;*[14] *F 104–5*

Four controlling faculties, namely, (1–2) the two sexual faculties, (3) the vitality faculty (*jīvitendriya*) and (4) the mental faculty (*mana-indriya*), each exercise controlling power with regard to two things [*artha*] [see the specifics below] (MVŚ, 731b12).

BB.1. *The two sexual faculties & the object of the controlling power;*[15] *F 104–5*

The sexual faculties exercise controlling power:

1. with regard to the (primary) distinction among sentient beings (*sattvabheda*): it is because of these two faculties that sentient beings form the categories of (i) male [*puruṣa*] and (ii) female [*strī*];
2. with regard to the differentiation (of secondary characteristics) among sentient beings (*sattvavikalpa*): because of these two faculties there are,

among the sexes, a difference [*anyathātva*] (i) of physical form (*saṃsthāna*), [breasts (*stana*), etc.,] (ii) of voice (*svara*) and (iii) of manner of being (*ācāra*).[16]

Other masters[17] do not admit this explanation. In fact, the sexes show differences (*sattvavikalpabheda*) among the gods of the realm of fine-materiality who do not possess the sexual faculties (i. 30), and the distinction into sexes results from these differences. <105> – Thus, if the sexual sense-faculties exercise controlling power from two points of view, they exercise controlling power with regard to pollution (*saṃkleśa*) and purification (*vyavadāna*): in fact, the three kinds of eunuchs [*ṣaṇḍha*, *paṇḍaka*] and hermaphrodites [*ubhayavyañjana*] {2 a} are alien to (1) the factors (*dharma*) of pollution (*sāṃkleśika*), non-restraint [*asaṃvara*; iv. 13b], transgression with an immediately successive retribution [*ānantārya*; iv. 103], the cutting off of the wholesome roots [*kuśalamulasamuccheda*; iv. 80] and (2) the factors of purification (*vaiyavadānika*), restraint [*saṃvara*; iv. 23]), acquisition of the fruits [*phalaprāpti*; vi. 51], detachment (*vairāgya*: vi. 45c) (see ii. 19cd).

ABB.2. *The vitality faculty & the object of the controlling power;*[18] *F 105*

The vitality faculty [*jīvitendriya*; ii. 45ab] exercises controlling power:[19]

1. with regard to "[forming an initial] connection" (*saṃbandha*) to the *nikāya-sabhāga*[20] (ii. 41a), i.e., in regard to the arising (*utpatti*) of a personal existence;
2. with regard to "supporting or maintaining" (*saṃdhāraṇa*) the *nikāyasabhāga*, i.e., in regard to the continuation (*avasthāna*) of a personal existence from birth to death.

ABB.3. *The mental faculty & the object of the controlling power;*[21] *F 105*

The mental faculty (*mana-indriya*) exercises controlling power:[22]

1. with regard to the connection at rebirth [or the first moment of the next existence] (*punarbhavasaṃbandha*), as the Sūtra explains:

   Then there occurs in the Gandharva, in the being of the intermediate existence (*antarābhava*), one or the other of two thoughts, (i) a thought associated with lust [*anunayasahagata*] or (ii) a thought associated with hostility [*pratighasahagata*]... (iii. 15);

2. with regard to (continual) domination (*vaśibhāvānuvartana*): the world, the factors (*dharma*) are subjected to thought, as the stanza says:

   The world is led by thought, is maneuvered by thought: all the factors obey this single factor, thought.[23]

C. *The five sensations, the five praxis-oriented faculties, the three pure controlling faculties & the object of the controlling power;*[24] *F 105–6*

(1) The five faculties of sensation (*vedanendriya*), i.e., the five sensations of pleasure, displeasure, satisfaction, dissatisfaction, equanimity (ii. 7), and (2) the eight controlling faculties of which the first is faith, i.e., the five (praxis-oriented) faculties of faith, vigor, mindfulness, concentration and understanding (ii. 24), and the three pure controlling faculties [*anāsravendriya*; i. 10], exercise controlling power with regard, respectively, to pollution [*saṃkleśa*] and to purification [*vyavadāna*]. <106>

1. The sensations exercise controlling power with regard to pollution (*saṃkleśa*), for the proclivities (*anuśaya*), i.e., attachment (*rāga*), etc., become attached to the sensations, and become lodged therein (*tadanuśayitvāt*).

2. Faith and the seven other controlling faculties exercise controlling power with regard to purification [*vyavadāna*], for it is thanks to them that one obtains purity.[25]

According to other masters (MVŚ, 73b6), the sensations also exercise controlling power with regard to purification, {2 b} as follows from the Sūtra:

> *sukhitasya cittaṃ samādhīyate* ["the thought of those who experience agreeable sensation gets concentrated"],[26]
>
> *duḥkhopaniṣac chraddhā* ["faith arises [having] unsatisfactoriness [for its proximate cause]"],[27]
>
> *ṣaṇ naiṣkramyāśritāḥ saumanasyādayaḥ* ["there are, because of the visible forms, etc., six sensations of satisfaction, six sensations of dissatisfaction, six sensations of equanimity, favorable to the pure and impure path"].[28]

Such is the explanation of the Vaibhāṣikas. <107>

BD. *Critique by (the Sautrāntikas); F 107*

(The Sautrāntikas[29]) criticize this explanation (ii. 2–4):

1. The sense-faculties, the eye, etc., do not exercise controlling power with regard to the protection of the person [*ātmabhāvaparikarṣaṇa*]. Here, the controlling power belongs to the consciousness (*vijñāna*), the visual consciousness, auditory consciousness, etc: it is after having distinguished that one avoids the harmful or adverse, that one takes material food.
2. That which you understand by "particular or uncommon activity of the sense-faculty" [*asādhāraṇakāraṇatva*], namely, the seeing of visible forms, etc., belongs to the consciousness (i. 42) and not to the sense-faculty.

The explanations relative to the controlling power of the other controlling faculties are equally incorrect.

AC. *BRIEF SAUTRĀNTIKA EXPLANATION OF THE CONTROLLING POWER OF EACH CONTROLLING FACULTY;*[30] *F 107–10*

Then how should one understand the controlling power of the controlling faculties?

ACA. *The six sense-faculties & their controlling power;*[31] *F 107*

2ab. The six sense-faculties [are considered as controlling faculties] because of their controlling power (1) with regard to the apperception (*upalabdhi*; i. 16a)[32] of their own particular object-referent, (2) with regard to the apprehension of all object-referents.[33]

That is to say, because of their controlling power with regard to the six consciousnesses (*vijñānakāya*).

1. The five sense-faculties, of which the first is the eye sense-faculty, exercise controlling power with regard to the five sensory consciousnesses, the visual consciousness, etc., which distinguish [*upalabdhi*] each their own particular object-referent, visible form, etc. {3 a}

2. The mental faculty (*mana-indriya*) exercises controlling power with regard to the mental consciousness (*manovijñāna*) which distinguishes all the object-referents.

It is in this way that each of these six sense-faculties is a controlling faculty.

[Objection:] – But the object-referents of the senses, visible form, etc., also exercise controlling power with regard to the consciousnesses and, therefore, should also be considered as controlling faculties.

[Answer:] – In fact, they do not exercise controlling power. By controlling power (*ādhipatya*), one understands "predominant power" (*adhikaprabhutva*). The eye exercises controlling power, for (1) it exercises this predominant power with regard to the arising of the apperception [*upalabdhi*] which apperceives visible forms, being the common cause [*sāmānyakāraṇatva*] of all the apperceptions of visible forms, whereas each visible form contributes only to the arising of a single apperception; (2) the visual apperception is sharp or obscure, strong [*paṭu*] or weak [*mandatā*], etc., according to whether the eye is strong or weak: the visible form does not exercise a similar influence. – The same comment for the other sense-faculties and their object-referents (i. 45ab). <108>

ACB. *The two sexual faculties & their controlling power;*[34] *F 108*

2cd. The two sexual faculties which have to be distinguished within the body [are considered as controlling faculties] because of their con-

trolling power with regard to (1) masculinity and (2) femininity.[35]

Separate from the controlling faculty that is called *body sense-faculty* (*kāyendriya*), two sexual faculties [are listed]. These two controlling faculties, [in terms of their intrinsic nature,] are not distinct from the body sense-faculty: they perceive tangibles. But there is a part of the body sense-faculty which receives the name of male sexual faculty or female sexual faculty because this part exercises controlling power over (1) masculinity [*puṃstva*] or (2) femininity [*strītva*].

Femininity [*strībhāva*][36] is (i) the physical form (*ākṛti*), (ii) the voice (*svara*), (iii) the movement (*ceṣṭā*), (iv) the dispositions (*abhiprāya*) proper to women. {3 b}

The same for masculinity.

Since the difference between these two natures is due to these two parts of the body, we know that these two parts exercise controlling power with regard to these two natures; they thus constitute controlling faculties.

cc. *Vitality faculty, five sensations, five praxis-oriented faculties & their controlling power;*[37] *F 108–9*

3. **(1) The vitality faculty, (2) the five sensations and (3) the five (praxis-oriented) faculties of which the first is faith are considered as controlling faculties because of their controlling power with regard, [respectively,] (1) to the duration of existence, (2) to pollution, (3) to purification.**[38]

1. The vitality faculty exercises controlling power with regard to the continuance of a personal existence from birth to death [*nikāyasabhāgasthiti*; ii. 41a]—but not, as the Vaibhāṣikas say, with regard to the connecting up (*saṃbandha*) of one personal existence with another: this connecting up depends, in fact, on the mind (*manas*)[39].

2. The five sensations exercise controlling power with regard to pollution [*saṃkleśa*], for the Sūtra[40] says: <109>

> Attachment lodges in the sensation of pleasure; hostility in the sensation of displeasure; ignorance in the sensation of equanimity.[41]

On this point (the Sautrāntikas[42]) are in accord with the Vaibhāṣikas.

3. The five (praxis-oriented) faculties of which the first is faith—(i) faith [*śraddhā*], (ii) vigor [*vīrya*], (iii) mindfulness [*smṛti*], (iv) concentration [*samādhi*], (v) understanding [*prajñā*]—exercise controlling power with regard to purification [*vyavadāna*], for, through their power, the defilements (*kleśa*) are shaken or subdued (*viṣkambhyante*) and the (noble) path is invoked (*āvāhyate*).[43]

ACD. *The three pure controlling faculties & their controlling power;* F 109–10

4. [The three pure controlling faculties, i.e.,] (1) the faculty of coming to know what is as yet unknown (*anājñātamājñāsyāmīndriya*), (2) the faculty of perfect knowledge (*ājñendriya*) and (3) the faculty of final and perfect knowledge (*ājñātāvīndriya*), are, likewise, [considered as controlling faculties] because of their controlling power (i) with regard to ascending acquisitions, (ii) with regard to *nirvāṇa*, (iii) etc.[44]

"Likewise" (*tathā*),[45] that is to say: these three are, likewise, considered as controlling faculties (*indriya*). These are the three pure controlling faculties, defined ii. 9ab.

a. The first [pure controlling faculty] exercises controlling power with regard to the acquisition of the second [pure controlling faculty].

The second exercises controlling power with regard to the acquisition of the third.

The third exercises controlling power with regard to the acquisition of *nirvāṇa*, i.e., *nirvāṇa* without remainder (*nirupadhiśeṣanirvāṇa*), for there is no *parinirvāṇa* when thought is not liberated (*vimukta*).[46] <110>

b. The word *et cetera* [*ādi*] indicates that there is another explanation:[47]

The first [pure controlling faculty] exercises controlling power with regard to the destruction [*parihāṇa*] of the defilements (*kleśa*) which are abandoned by insight into the truths (v. 4).

The second, with regard to the destruction of the defilements which are abandoned by cultivation of the truths (v. 5a).

The third, with regard to the happiness in this life (*dṛṣṭadharmasukhavihāra*), i.e., the experience (*pratisaṃvedana*) of satisfaction (*prīti* = *saumanasya*) and well-being (*sukha* = pleasure as pliancy [*praśrabdhisukha*; viii. 9b]) of the liberation from defilements (*vimukti*). (See F 112).

AD. *EXPLANATION OF THE ENUMERATION AND ORDER OF THE TWENTY-TWO CONTROLLING FACULTIES;* F 110–13

[Objection:] – Why does one enumerate [*upasaṃkhyāna*] only twenty-two controlling faculties?

If you regard as controlling faculty that which exercises "controlling power", then ignorance (*avidyā*) and the other members of dependent origination (*pratītyasamutpāda*; iii. 21) should also be enumerated among the controlling faculties, for the causes (*avidyā*, etc.,) exercise controlling power with regard to their effects (*saṃskāra*, etc.).

Likewise, [even] (1) the voice (*vāk*), (2) the hand [*pāṇi*], (3) the foot [*pāda*], (4) the anus [*pāyu*], (5) the sexual organ (*upastha*) [should be enumerated among the controlling faculties, for they] exercise controlling power (respectively) with regard (1) to speech (*vacana*), (2) to grasping [*ādāna*], (3) to walking (*viharaṇa* = *caṅkramaṇa*), (4) to excretion [*utsarga*], (5) to sensual pleasure (*ānanda*).[48]

DA. *Answer to the first part of the objection;* F 110–12

DA.1. *First opinion;*[49] F 110–11

There is no reason to add ignorance, etc., to the list proclaimed by the Fortunate One. For the enumeration [and order of the twenty-two] controlling faculties, the Fortunate One has taken into account the following characteristics:

5. **(1) The basis of thought [i.e., the six sense-faculties of consciousness]; (2) that which subdivides this basis [i.e., the sexual faculties]; (3) that which makes this basis endure [i.e., the vitality faculty]; (4) that which defiles this basis [i.e., the sensations]; (5) that which prepares the purification of this basis [i.e., the five praxis-oriented faculties]; (6) that which purifies this basis [i.e., the three pure controlling faculties]: these are all controlling faculties.**[50] {4 b}

1. The basis (*āśraya*) of thought, namely, the six sense-faculties of consciousness, the eye sense-faculty up to the mental faculty (*manas*). These are the six internal sense-spheres (*āyatana*; i. 39, iii. 22), which are the primary real entities or constituents of the sentient beings (*maula sattvadravya*).[51] <111>

2. This sixfold basis is subdivided [*vikalpa*] because of the sexual faculties.

3. This sixfold basis endures for a certain time [*sthiti*] because of the vitality faculty.

4. This sixfold basis is defiled [*saṃkleśa*] because of the five sensations.

5. The purification of the sixfold basis is prepared (*vyavadānasaṃbharaṇa*) by the five (praxis-oriented) faculties, faith, etc.

6. The sixfold basis is purified (*vyavadāna*) by the three pure controlling faculties [*anāsravendriya*].

The factors (*dharma*) which possess this characteristic of exercising controlling power with regard to the constitution, the subdivision, etc., of the sentient being, are considered as controlling faculties. This characteristic is lacking in the other factors, i.e., in the voice, the hand, etc.

ADA.2. ***Second opinion;***[52] *F 111–12*

Other masters give a different explanation [for the enumeration and order of the twenty-two controlling faculties]:

6. **Or else, there are fourteen controlling faculties [i.e., (i) 1–6, (ii) 7–8, (iii) 9, (iv) 10–14, which are, respectively,] (i) the basis of transmigration [*pravṛtti*], (ii) the arising of this basis, (iii) the duration of this basis, (iv) the enjoyment of this basis; the other controlling faculties [i.e., 15–22] have the same role [i.e., (i) basis, (ii) arising, (iii) duration, (iv) enjoyment] with regard to *nirvāṇa*.**[53]

The expression "or else" (*vā*) introduces the explanation of other masters (*aparaḥ kalpaḥ*).

1–6. The six sense-faculties (*ṣaḍāyatana*; iii. 22), from the eye sense-faculty (*cakṣur-āyatana*) up to the mental faculty (*mana-āyatana*), are the basis, the raison d'être of *saṃsāra* [*pravṛtter āśraya*].[54]

7–8. It is through the sexual faculties [*strīpuruṣa*] that the six sense-spheres (*ṣaḍ-āyatana*) arise [*utpatti*].[55]

9. It is through the vitality faculty [*jīvitendriya*] that the six sense-spheres endure (*avasthāna*).

10–14. It is through the five sensations [*vedanā*] that the six sense-spheres enjoy [*upabhoga*].

On the other hand: {5 a} <112>

15–19. The five (praxis-oriented) faculties—faith (*śraddhā*), vigor (*vīrya*), mindfulness (*smṛti*), concentration (*samādhi*), understanding (*prajñā*)—are the basis (*āśraya, pratiṣṭhā*) of *nirvāṇa* (i. 6ab).

20. *Nirvāṇa* arises (*prabhava*), appears for the first time (*ādibhāva*), through the first pure controlling faculty, the faculty of coming to know what is as yet unknown (*ājñātamājñāsyāmīndriya*).

21. *Nirvāṇa* endures [*sthiti*], develops, through the second pure controlling faculty, the *faculty of perfect knowledge* (*ājñendriya*).

22. *Nirvāṇa* is "experienced or enjoyed" (*upabhuj*; *upabhoga*) through the third pure controlling faculty, the faculty of final and perfect knowledge (*ājñātāvīndriya*), for, through this faculty, one experiences the satisfaction and well-being (*prīti-sukha*) of liberation (see F 110).

The number of the controlling faculties is thus determined, as well as the order [*anukrama*] in which the Sūtra gives them.

B. *Answer to the second part of the objection;* F 112–13

In regard to (1) the voice (*vāk*), (2) the hands (*pāṇi*), (3) the feet (*pāda*), (4) the anus (*pāya*), (5) the sexual parts (*upastha*), these are not controlling faculties:

1. the voice [*vāk*] is not a controlling faculty with regard to speech (*vacana*), since speech presupposes a certain instruction (*śikṣā*);[56]

2–3. the hands [*pāṇi*] and feet [*pāda*] are not controlling faculties with regard to grasping (*ādāna*) and walking (*viharaṇa*), for that which one calls grasping and walking is simply the hands and feet arising at a second moment in another place and with a new shape (iv. 2bd); on the other hand, one sees, as for example with snakes [*uraga*], that the hands and feet are not indispensable for grasping and walking;[57]

4. the anus [*pāya*] is not a controlling faculty with regard to the excretion of feces (*utsarga*), for heavy things (*gurudravya*) in empty space (*ākāśa* = *chidra*) always fall down; moreover, the wind (*vāyudhātu*) pushes the feces (*preraṇa*) and expels them;

5. the sexual organs [*upastha*] are not controlling faculties with regard to sensual pleasure (*ānanda*), since sensual pleasure is produced through the sexual sense-faculties.[58] <113>

If you consider the hands, feet, etc., as controlling faculties, then you should group among the controlling faculties also (i) the throat (*kaṇṭha*), (ii) teeth (*danta*), (iii) eyelids (*akṣivartman*), (iv) the joints (*aṅgulīparvan*) whose function [*kriyā*] it is, [respectively,] (i) to swallow (*abhyavaharaṇa*), (ii) to chew (*carvaṇa*); (iii) to open and close (*unmeṣanimeṣa*), (iv) to bend and extend the bones (*saṃkocavikāśa*). {5 b}

Likewise, everything that is a cause [*kāraṇa*], exercising its activity (*puruṣakāra*; ii. 58) with regard to its effect [*kārya*], would be a controlling faculty. But the name *indriya* or controlling faculty should be reserved for that which exercises controlling power (*ādhipatya*).

DETAILED EXPLANATION OF THE INTRINSIC NATURE (SVABHĀVA) OF THE TWENTY-TWO CONTROLLING FACULTIES;[59] F 113–18

We have [already] explained (1–8) the sense-faculties of consciousness and the sexual faculties (i. 9–44); (9) the vitality faculty (*jīvitendriya*) will be explained along with the formations dissociated from thought (*cittaviprayukta*; ii. 35) among which it is placed; (15–19) the five (praxis-oriented) faculties—faith, vigor, etc.—being thought-concomitants (*caitta*), will be explained with the thought-concomitants (ii. 24).

We will now explain (10–14) the faculties of sensation (*vedanendriya*; ii. 7) and (20–22) the pure controlling faculties (*anāsravendriya*; ii. 9) that are not treated elsewhere.

AEA. *The five sensations & the controlling faculties;* F 113–16

AEA.1. *Agreeable and disagreeable bodily sensation;* F 113–14

7ab. Disagreeable bodily sensation is the faculty of displeasure.[60]

"Bodily" [*kāyika*] [sensation], i.e., [sensation] "that relates to the bodies",[61] which is associated with the five sensory consciousnesses, the visual consciousness, etc.

"Disagreeable" (*aśāta*), {6 a} i.e., that which hurts (*upaghātikā*).

The sensation related to the five sense-faculties of the sensory consciousnesses and which hurts is called *faculty of displeasure* (*duḥkhendriya*). <114>

7bc. Agreeable bodily sensation is the faculty of pleasure.[62]

"Agreeable" (*śāta*), i.e., that which comforts, benefits, does good (*anugrāhikā*).

The agreeable bodily sensation is called *faculty of pleasure* (*sukhendriya*).

AEA.2. *Agreeable and disagreeable mental sensations;* F 114–15

7cd. In the third meditation, agreeable mental sensation is also (spoken of as) the faculty of pleasure.[63]

The mental [*caitasī*] sensation is the sensation associated with the mental consciousness (*manovijñāna*).

The agreeable mental sensation of the third meditation (*dhyāna*) also receives the name faculty of pleasure (*sukhendriya*). This name, everywhere else, is reserved for agreeable bodily sensation: but, in the third meditation, the bodily sensation is lacking because the five sensory consciousnesses are lacking there. Thus, when one speaks of pleasure (*sukha*) of the third meditation, one means to speak of agreeable mental sensation. (See viii. 9).

8a. Everywhere else, [i.e., in the stages lower than the third meditation,] agreeable mental sensation is [the faculty of] satisfaction.[64]

Everywhere else [*anyatra*], that is, in the stages lower than the third meditation (*dhyāna*), in the realm of desire and in the first two meditations, the agreeable mental sensation is satisfaction (*saumanasya*) or faculty of satisfaction (*saumanasyendriya*).

Above the third meditation, the agreeable mental sensation is lacking.

In the third meditation, the agreeable mental sensation is calm (*kṣema*) and peaceful (*śānta*), because the practitioners, in this meditation, are detached from joy (*prītivīta-*

rāgatvāt): thus it is [spoken of only as the faculty of] pleasure (*sukha*) and not [as the faculty of] satisfaction (*saumanasya*).[65] <115>

Below the third meditation, agreeable mental sensation is gross (*audārika*; *rūkṣa*?) and agitated because, in the stages below the third meditation, the practitioners are not detached from joy: thus it is [the faculty of] satisfaction. – Joy (*prīti*), which has a joyous exaltation (*saṃpraharṣa*) for its mode [*ākāratva*], is not distinct from satisfaction.

8bc. Disagreeable mental sensation is [the faculty of] dissatisfaction.[66]

The sensation associated with the mental consciousness and which hurts is dissatisfaction (*daurmanasya*) or the faculty of dissatisfaction [*daurmanasyendriya*].

EA.3. *Bodily and mental sensation of equanimity; F 115*

8cd. Bodily or mental intermediate sensation is [the single faculty of] equanimity, because there is no conceptualizing activity here.[67]

Intermediate [*madhya*] sensation, which is [neither agreeable or disagreeable, that is,] neither hurts nor comforts, is the "neither displeasure nor pleasure" sensation (*aduḥkhāsukhā*). This is what is called *sensation of equanimity* or *faculty of equanimity* (*upekṣendriya*).

[Question:] – Is this sensation bodily [*kāyika*] or is it mental [*caitasika*]?

[Answer:] – Whether it is bodily or mental, the intermediate sensation is sensation of equanimity. Sensation of equanimity is thus both [*ubhaya*] [i.e., bodily and mental]; nevertheless, it constitutes only one controlling faculty, because there is no conceptualizing activity (*vikalpana*) here.

EA.4. *Conceptualizing activity (vikalpana) & sensation; F 115–16*

1. There is no conceptualizing activity (*vikalpana*), intellectual operation. – Bodily or mental, sensation of equanimity is equally free from any conceptualizing element (*vikalpa* = *abhinirūpaṇāvikalpa*, conceptualizing activity consisting of defining, i. 33).

As a general rule [*prāyeṇa*],[68] agreeable or disagreeable mental sensation proceeds from a conceptualizing activity (*vikalpa*), from the conceptualizing activity of "dear" [*priya*], or "horrible" [*apriya*], etc. On the contrary, bodily sensation {6 b} is produced from an external object-field (*viṣayavaśāt*), independent of a psychological state: perfected beings (*arhat*) are alien to sympathies and antipathies, they do not conceive of the idea of "dear", the idea of "horrible", but nevertheless they are liable to bodily displeasure [*duḥkha*] and pleasure [*sukha*]. <116>

Thus we should distinguish controlling faculties relative to agreeable and disagreeable sensations [*vedanā*] according to whether these sensations are bodily or mental.

But the sensation of equanimity, even the mental one, occurs spontaneously (*svarasena, anabhisaṃskāreṇa*),[69] exactly like bodily sensation; it occurs in those who do not form any conceptualizing activity (*avikalpayatas, anabhinirūpayatas*): thus we recognize only one single controlling faculty for the two sensations of equanimity, the mental and the bodily [sensation of equanimity].

2. There is no conceptualizing activity (*vikalpana*), differentiation. – According to whether the agreeable or disagreeable sensations are bodily or mental, they hurt or comfort according to a mode of operation that is special to them, and they are not felt in the same way.

The sensation of equanimity neither hurts nor comforts; it is not differentiated; mental or bodily, it is felt in the same way.

AEB. *The three pure controlling faculties; F 116–18; AH 118; SAH 275*

AEB.1. *Nine controlling faculties in the path of insight, of cultivation, of those beyond training & the three pure controlling faculties of the noble ones;*[70] *F 116–18*

9ab. **The nine controlling faculties [i.e., the mental faculty, the sensation of pleasure, the sensation of satisfaction, the sensation of equanimity, and faith, vigor, mindfulness, concentration and understanding] in the paths (1) of insight, (2) of cultivation and (3) of those beyond training, constitute, [respectively,] three controlling faculties [for the noble ones: (1) the faculty of coming to know what is as yet unknown, (2) the faculty of perfect knowledge, (3) the faculty of completely perfect knowledge].**[71]

The (i) mental faculty, (ii) sensation of pleasure, (iii) sensation of satisfaction, (iv) sensation of equanimity, (v) faith, (vi) vigor, (vii) mindfulness, (viii) concentration and (ix) understanding (*prajñā*) constitute:

1. in the noble ones who dwell on the path of insight (*darśanamārga*), the faculty of coming to know what is as yet unknown (*anājñātamājñāsyāmi–indriya*);
2. in the noble ones who dwell on the path of cultivation of the truths (*bhāvanāmārga*), the faculty of perfect knowledge (*ājñendriya*);

3. in the noble ones who dwell on the path of those beyond training [*aśaikṣa-mārga*] (= the perfected beings [*arhat*]), the faculty of final and perfect knowledge (*ājñātāvīndriya*).[72] <117>

1. Dwelling on the path of insight[73] [*darśanamārga*], the noble ones are engaged in coming to know what is as yet unknown (*anājñātam ājñātuṃ pravṛtta*), namely, the four truths: they think "I will know". Their controlling faculty is thus called *faculty of coming to know what is as yet unknown* (*anājñātamājñāsyāmi-indriya*).[74]

2. Dwelling on the path of cultivation[75] of the truths [*bhāvanāmārga*], the noble ones no longer have anything new to know; they are perfectly knowing (*ājña*) persons. But in order to cut off the proclivities (*anuśaya*) that remain in them, they recognize again and again the truths which they already know perfectly. Their controlling faculty is called *faculty of perfect knowledge* (*ājñendriya*), the *faculty of the perfectly knowing person*, or the *perfectly knowing faculty* (*ājñam evendriyam iti vā*).

3. Dwelling on the path of those beyond training (*aśaikṣa*), {7 a} the practitioners become aware that they know: they attain the knowledge (*āva* = *avagama*)[76] that the truths are finally and perfectly known (*ājñātam iti*). Possessing finally and perfectly known knowledge (*ājñāta-āva*), they are finally and perfectly knowing persons (*ājñātāvins*), and their controlling faculty is called *faculty of final and perfect knowledge* (*ājñātāvīndriya*). – Or else, the noble ones who have the character or habit (*śīla*) to ensure or know (*avitum*) that the truth is finally and perfectly known (*ājñāta*), are finally and perfectly knowing persons (*ājñātāvin*): in fact, when the noble ones have attained (i) cognition of exhaustion (*kṣayajñāna*) and (ii) cognition of non-arising (*anutpādajñāna*) (vi. 50, 67), they know in truth:

> Unsatisfactoriness is known; I have nothing more to know,

and the rest.[77] <118>

We have explained the intrinsic natures [*svabhāva*] of the controlling faculties. We must explain their different modes [*prakārabheda*]:

A. Are the controlling faculties pure? (ii. 9bd)
B. Are they a ripened effect? (ii. 10ac)
C. [Do they have a ripened effect?] (ii. 10c–11b)
D. Are they wholesome, [unwholesome, non-defined]? (ii. 11cd)
E. To what realm do they belong? (ii. 12)
F. How are they abandoned? (ii. 13)

AF. *THE DIFFERENT MODES (PRAKĀRABHEDA) OF THE CONTROLLING FACULTIES;*[78] *F 118–31*

AFA. *Being pure (sāsrava) and being impure (anāsrava) & the controlling faculties; F 118–20*

How many are pure (*sāsrava*)? How many are impure (*anāsrava*)?

9bd. **(1) The [last] three controlling faculties are [exclusively] stainless.**

(2) [Ten controlling faculties, i.e.,] the seven material controlling faculties, the vitality faculty and the two unpleasant sensations are [exclusively] impure.

(3) Nine controlling faculties [i.e., the mental faculty, sensation of pleasure, sensation of satisfaction, sensation of equanimity and the five praxis-oriented faculties] are of two types [i.e., either pure or impure].[79]

1. The last three controlling faculties are exclusively stainless or pure (*amala, anāsrava*). Stain (*mala*) and flux (*āsrava*) are synonyms [*paryāya*].[80]

2. The material (*rūpin*) faculties are seven in number: (i–v) the five sense-faculties of the eye, etc., plus (vi–vii) the two sexual faculties, for all these seven sense-faculties are included in the aggregate of form (*rūpaskandha*). With (viii) the vitality faculty, (ix) the sensation of displeasure and (x) the sensation of dissatisfaction, ten controlling faculties in total are exclusively impure.

3. (i) The mental faculty (*manas*), (ii) the sensation of pleasure, (iii) the sensation of satisfaction, (iv) the sensation of equanimity, (v–ix) the five (praxis-oriented) faculties (faith, vigor, etc.) {7 b} constitute nine controlling faculties which can be either pure or impure.

AFA.1. *Refutation of the opinion that the praxis-oriented faculties are only pure; F 118–20*

Other masters[81] (MVŚ, 7c3) [object]: – The five (praxis-oriented) faculties are only pure, for the Fortunate One has said:

> Those in whom all these five controlling faculties, faith, etc.—to whatever degree this may be—are completely lacking, I declare them to be excluded persons [*bāhya*], belonging to the class of ordinary worldlings (*pṛthagjana*).[82]

Thus, those who possess them—to whatever degree this may be—are noble ones (*ārya*); thus they are pure. <119>

[Answer:] – This passage is not conclusive (*jñāpaka*), since the Fortunate One speaks here [in the context] of persons in whom the five "pure" (*anāsrava*) (praxis-oriented) faculties are lacking. In fact, in the passage which precedes the statement in question, the Fortunate One defines the noble ones (*āryapudgala*) according to the five (praxis-oriented) faculties.[83] Thus he refers to the five (praxis-oriented) faculties that are particular to the noble ones, i.e., the pure (praxis-oriented) faculties. Those in whom they are lacking are evidently ordinary worldlings.

Or else, if this text speaks of the (praxis-oriented) faculties in general, we would comment that there are two types of ordinary worldlings (MVŚ, 8b3): (1) those outside (*bāhyaka*), (2) those inside (*ābhyantaraka*); the first have cut off the wholesome roots [*kuśalamūla*; iv. 79], the second have not cut them off. It is in regard to the first that the Fortunate One says: "I declare them to be excluded persons, belonging to the class of ordinary worldlings."[84]

Besides, according to the Sūtra, even before setting into motion the Wheel of Dharma (vi. 54), there were in the world persons with sharp [*tīkṣṇa*], mediocre [*madhya*] or dull [*mṛdu*] controlling faculties.[85] Thus, the (praxis-oriented) faculties, faith, etc., are not necessarily and exclusively pure.

Finally, the Fortunate One has said:

> If I did not know in truth the origin [*samudaya*], disappearance [*astagama*], advantages (*āsvāda*), disadvantages (*ādīnava*), escape (*niḥsaraṇa*) in the case of the five controlling faculties, faith, vigor, etc., I would not be liberated (*mukta*), gone forth (*niḥsṛta*), separated (*visaṃyukta*), delivered (*vipraṁukta*) from the world where there are gods, Māras, {8 a} and Brahmās, from the world where there are brahmins and mendicants (*śramaṇa*); I would not reside with a thought free from mistaken views [*viparyāsa*]... .[86] <120>

Now, a similar description does not apply to pure factors (*dharma*), which are free from advantages, disadvantages, escape.

Thus the (praxis-oriented) faculties, faith, vigor, etc., can be either pure [*anāsrava*] or impure [*sāsrava*].

B. *Being a ripened effect (vipāka) and not being a ripened effect (na vipāka) & the twenty-two controlling faculties;*[87] *F 120–28*

B.1. *The vitality faculty & being a ripened effect;*[88] *F 120–24*

Among the controlling faculties, how many are a ripened (effect) (*vipāka*; ii. 57ab), how many are not a ripened (effect) [*na vipāka*]?[89]

10 a. [Vaibhāṣikas: – Only] the vitality faculty is always a ripened (effect).[90]

Only the vitality faculty [*jīvitendriya*; ii. 45ab] is always a ripened (effect).

AFB.1.1. *Stabilization and rejection of the conditioning forces of the life-force & being a ripened effect;*[91] *F 120–24*

AFB.1.1.1. *Stabilization and rejection of the conditioning forces of the life-force; F 120–21*

Objection. – The conditioning forces of the life-force (*āyuḥsaṃskāra*; see below F 122) which a perfected being (*arhat*) who is a *bhikṣu* stabilizes or causes to endure (*sthāpayati, adhitiṣṭhati*) are evidently the vitality faculty [*jīvitendriya*].[92] Of what action is the vitality faculty, thus stabilized or prolonged, the ripened (effect)?[93]

[Answer:] – According to the *Mūlaśāstra* (*Jñānaprasthāna*, 981a12):

> How do [perfected beings who are] *bhikṣus* stabilize the conditioning forces of the life-force?
>
> Perfected beings in possession of supernormal accomplishments (*ṛddhimān* = *prāptābhijñaḥ*, vii. 42), in possession of the mastery of thought (*cetovaśitva*), i.e., non-circumstantially liberated (*asamayavimukta*; vi. 56, 64), give—either to the Saṃgha or to a person [*pudgala*]—things useful to the life (*jīvitapariṣkāra*) [of a mendicant (*śrāmaṇaka*)], clothes [*cīvara*], bowls [*pātra*], etc.; after having given, {8 b} they direct their thought to their life-force [*āyuḥ*];[94] they then enter into the maximum fourth meditation (*dhyāna*; *prāntakoṭika*: "whose highest point has been pursued up to the extreme"; vii. 41); leaving this meditation, they produce thought (*citta*) and utter the words: "May the action that should produce a ripened (effect) as enjoyment (*bhogavipāka*) be transformed and produce [instead] a ripened (effect) as life-force (*āyurvipāka*)!"[95] – Then the action (giving and meditation) that should produce a ripened (effect) as enjoyment will produce a ripened (effect) as life-force. <121>

According to other masters, the prolonged life-force of the perfected beings is the ripened effect of a previous action. According to these masters, there is a remainder (*ucchesa*) of the ripened effect as life-force which should have ripened in a previous birth [*jāti*], which had been interrupted by premature death (ii. 45). It is the power of the cultivation [*bhāvanābala*] of the fourth meditation which attracts (*ākarṣaka*) this remainder and brings it about that this remainder ripens now.

How do [perfected beings who are] *bhikṣus* reject (*tyajati*, *utsṛjati*) the conditioning forces of the life-force [*āyuḥsaṃskāra*]?

Perfected beings in possession of supernormal accomplishments ... enter into the fourth meditation...; leaving this meditation, they produce thought and utter the words: "May the action that should produce a ripened (effect) as life-force be transformed and produce [instead] a ripened (effect) as enjoyment!" – Then the action that should produce a ripened (effect) as life-force will produce a ripened (effect) as enjoyment.

AFB.1.1.2. *Bhadanta Ghoṣaka: stabilization and rejection of the conditioning forces of the life-force;* F 121

[But] the Bhadanta Ghoṣaka says: It is through the power of the maximum meditation [*dhyānabala*], which these perfected beings have produced, that the fundamental material elements (*mahābhūta*) of the realm of fine-materiality are attracted and introduced (*saṃmukhībhūta*) in their bodies. These fundamental material elements are favorable to {9 a} or contrary to the conditioning forces of the life-force (*āyuḥsaṃskāra*). It is in this way that the perfected beings stabilize or reject the [conditioning forces of the] life-force.[96]

AFB.1.1.3. *(Sautrāntika:) stabilization and rejection of the conditioning forces of the life-force;* F 121

With (the Sautrāntikas[97]), we say that the perfected beings—thanks to their mastery or power in concentration (*samādhivaśitva*; *samādhiprabhāva*)—cause the momentum of the period of duration (*sthitikālāvedha*) of the fundamental material elements constituting the sense-faculties to cease [*vyāvartayante*], a momentum due to previous actions; inversely, they produce a new [*apūrva*] momentum caused by concentration [*samādhija*]. Thus the vitality faculty, in the case of the prolonged life-force of perfected beings, is not a ripened (effect). But in other cases, it is a ripened (effect).

AFB.1.1.4. *The purpose of prolonging and rejecting the conditioning forces of the life-force;* F 121–22

One question [*praśna*] leads to another.

[Question:] – For what purpose [*artha*] do perfected beings cause the conditioning forces of the life-force [*āyuḥsaṃskāra*] to endure [*adhitiṣṭhanti*]?

[Answer:] – For two purposes: (1) with a view to the benefit of others [*parahita*], (2) with a view to the longer duration of the teaching (*śāsanacirasthiti*).[98]

They see that their life-force is going to end; they see that others are incapable of assuring these two purposes. <122>

[Question:] – For what purpose do the perfected beings reject [*kṣīṇa*] the conditioning forces of the life-force?

[Answer:] – For two purposes: (1) they see that their dwelling in this world has but little use for the benefit of others, (2) they see themselves being tormented by sickness, etc.[99] As the stanza says:

> The religious life [*brahmacarya*] has been practiced well, the path has been cultivated well: they are satisfied with the destruction of the life-force, {9 b} as in the case of the disappearance of a sickness.[100]

AFB.1.1.5. *By whom, and in what place, are the conditioning forces of the life-force stabilized or rejected;* F 122

[Question:] – By whom, and in what place, are the [conditioning forces of the] life-force stabilized [*sthāpana*] or rejected [*utsarjana*]?

[Answer:] – In the three continents (*dvīpa*; iii. 53), [they are stabilized or rejected by] men or women, the perfected beings (*arhat*) of the non-circumstantially liberated (*asamayavimukta*) class who possess the maximum meditation (*dhyāna*; *prāntakoṭika*; vi. 56, 64): in fact, they possess mastery of concentration [*samādhi*] and are free from defilements [*kleśa*].[101]

AFB.1.1.6. *The difference between the conditioning forces of life (jīvita saṃskāra) and the conditioning forces of the life-force (āyus saṃskāra);*[102] F 122–23

According to the Sūtra:

> The Fortunate One, after having stabilized the conditioning forces of life (*jīvita saṃskāra*), rejected the conditioning forces of the life-force (*āyus*).[103]

[Question:] – (1) What difference is there between the conditioning forces of life and the conditioning forces of the life-force; (2) what is the meaning of the plural [*bahuvacana*] "the conditioning forces" (*saṃskāra*)?[104] <123>

[Answer:] – In regard to the first point:[105]

i. According to certain masters, there is no difference. In fact, the *Mūlaśāstra* (*Jñānaprasthāna*, 993b2; *Prakaraṇapāda*, 694a23) says:

> > What is the vitality faculty (*jīvitendriya*)? – It is the life-force (*āyus*) in the three realms (*dhātu*).

ii. According to other masters,[106] the expression "conditioning forces of the life-force (*āyuḥ-saṃskāra*)" designates the [conditioning forces of the] life-force which are the effect of actions of a previous life; the expression "conditioning forces of life (*jīvita-saṃskāra*)" designates the [conditioning forces of] life which are the effect of actions of this life (giving to the Saṃgha, etc., F 120).

iii. According to (still) other masters,[107] that by means of which the personal existence endures (*nikāyasabhāgasthiti*) is the conditioning forces of the life-force (*āyuḥ-saṃskāra*); that by means of which the life force is prolonged for a little while is the conditioning forces of life (*jīvita-saṃskāra*).

In regard to the second point:

i. The Sūtra uses the plural [*bahuvacana*] "the conditioning forces" (*saṃskāra*) because the noble ones stabilize or reject many conditioning forces. There is no advantage, in fact, in stabilizing one moment, in rejecting one moment: it is only by means of a stream of moments that the noble ones can procure the good of others; on the other hand, one moment cannot be the cause of pain.

ii. According to another opinion, the plural condemns the doctrine according to which life (*jīvita*), the life-force (*āyus*), is one single real entity (*dravya*) susceptible of duration (*kālāntarasthāvara*).[108]

iii. According to (still) another opinion,[109] the plural condemns the doctrine of the Sarvāstivādins who consider life (*jīvita*) and the life-force (*āyus*) to be a real entity [*dravya*], a factor (*dharma*). The terms *life* and *life-force* designate a number of conditioning forces (*saṃskāra*) existing simultaneously and belonging to either four or five aggregates (*skandha*) according to their realm of existence (*dhātu*). {10 a} If it were otherwise, the Sūtra would not use the expression the conditioning forces of life; it would say: "The Fortunate One, after having stabilized the lives (*jīvita*), rejects the life-forces (*āyus*)."[110]

B.1.1.7. *For what purpose does the Fortunate One stabilize and reject the conditioning forces of the life-force?*[111] *F 123–24*

[Question:] – For what purpose does the Fortunate One reject (death) and stabilize (the conditioning forces of the life-force)? <124>

[Answer:] – In order to demonstrate that he possesses mastery over death (*maraṇavaśitva*), he rejects death; in order to demonstrate that he possesses mastery over life [*jīvitavaśitva*], he stabilizes the conditioning forces of the life-force. –

He stabilizes it for a period of three months (*traimāsya*), no more, no less; for, after three months have passed, there is nothing more to do for the disciples (*vineyakārya*), and his task (*buddhakārya*) is well achieved (*subhadrāvasāna*); for, short of three months, he would leave his teaching duties unachieved.[112]

Or else,[113] in order to fulfill his statement (*pratijñātasaṃpādanārtham*):

> All *bhikṣus* who have cultivated well the four bases of supernormal accomplishments (*ṛddhipāda*; vi. 69b), if they so desire, will remain for an aeon (*kalpa*) or more than an aeon.[114]

The Vaibhāṣikas[115] say: The Fortunate One rejects or stabilizes in order to demonstrate his victory [*nirjaya*] over (1) Māra who is the aggregates [*skandhamāra*] and (2) Māra who is death [*maraṇamāra*].[116] Under the Bodhi tree [*bodhimūla*], he has already been victorious [*nirjita*] over (3) Māra who is a demon [or a son of a god] [*devaputramāra*], in the first watch of the night [*yāma*], and (4) Māra who is defilements [*kleśamāra*], in the third watch of the night (*Ekottarikā*, 39, 1).[117]

AFB.2. *Other controlling faculties & being a ripened effect (vipāka) and not being a ripened effect (avipāka);*[118] *F 124–25*

10ab. **Twelve controlling faculties [i.e., the seven material controlling faculties, the mental faculty and the four controlling faculties of sensation, but not dissatisfaction,] are of two types [i.e., sometimes being a ripened (effect) and sometimes not being a ripened (effect)].**[119]

Which twelve controlling faculties?

10bc. **[Twelve controlling faculties are of two types,] with the exception of [ten controlling faculties:] (1–8) the last eight controlling faculties and (9) dissatisfaction, [which are never a ripened (effect),] [and with the exception of (10) the vitality faculty, which is always a ripened (effect)].**[120] <125>

With the exception of the vitality faculty, which is always a ripened (effect), and the nine controlling faculties that have just been indicated (ii. 10bc) and that are never a ripened (effect), the twelve remaining controlling faculties are of two types: (i) sometimes a ripened (effect), (ii) sometimes not a ripened (effect). This refers to (1–7) the material controlling faculties, (8) the mental faculty (*mana-indriya*) and (8–12) the four sensations, the sensation of dissatisfaction [*daurmanasya*] being excluded.

1–7. The seven material controlling faculties (i.e., eye sense-faculty, ... male sexual faculty) are not a ripened (effect) [*avipāka*], insofar as they are an (effect of) accumulation (*aupacayika*; i. 37). {10 b}

In other cases, they are a ripened (effect) [*vipāka*].

8–12. The mental faculty and the four [aforementioned] controlling faculties of sensation are not a ripened (effect) (i) when they are wholesome (*kuśala*) or defiled (*kliṣṭa*), for that which is a ripened (effect) is non-defined (*avyākṛta*; ii. 57); (ii) when—still being non-defined—they arise, according to their type, either in association with modes of proper deportment (*airyāpathika*), or with skill in arts and crafts (*śailpasthānika*), or with emanations (*nairmāṇika*) (ii. 72).[121]

In other cases, they are a ripened (effect).

The last eight controlling faculties, i.e., faith, etc., the faculty of coming to know what is as yet unknown (*anājñātamājñāsyāmīndriya*), etc., are wholesome and, therefore, are not a ripened (effect).

B.3. *Dissatisfaction & being a ripened effect; F 125–27*

B.3.1. *Discussion based on scriptural authority; F 125–26*

[We could say:[122]] – But how can one affirm that [the controlling faculty of] dissatisfaction (*daurmanasya*) is never a ripened (effect) (see also iv. 58)? In fact, the Sūtra says:

> There is an action to be retributed as sensation of satisfaction (*saumanasyavedanīya*), there is an action to be retributed as sensation of dissatisfaction (*daurmanasyavedanīya*), there is an action to be retributed as sensation of equanimity (*upekṣāvedanīya*).[123]

According to the Vaibhāṣika: – The expression *daurmanasyavedanīya* should be understood not as: action to be sensed or retributed as sensation of dissatisfaction, but rather as: action with which the sensation of dissatisfaction is associated. In fact, the Sūtra says of contact (*sparśa*) that it is *sukhavedanīya*: but pleasure (*sukha*) is not a ripened (effect) of contact.[124] From all evidence, the *sukhavedanīya* contact is the contact with which the sensation of pleasure is associated. Thus the *daurmanasyavedanīya* action is action with which a sensation of dissatisfaction is associated. <126>

We respond: – You should explain the expressions *saumanasyavedanīya* and *upekṣāvedanīya* in the same way as you explain the expression *daurmanasyavedanīya*, since the three expressions appear in the same enumeration of the Sūtra. It will follow that (1) the *saumanasyavedanīya* action is an action with which the sensation of satisfaction is associated, not an action to be retributed as satisfaction; (2) that, therefore, the sensation of satisfaction is not a ripened (effect).

The Vaibhāṣika. – I have no objections [*na doṣaḥ*] to explaining the expression *saumanasyavedanīya*, either (1) as "to be retributed as satisfaction", or (2) as "with which satisfaction is associated". But the second explanation of *vedanīya* is valid only for the expression *daurmanasyavedanīya*. It refers to an action with which dissatisfaction is associated.

AFB.3.2. *Discussion based on logical reasoning; F 126–27*

We respond: – One could accept your interpretation of the Sūtra if one could solve the other issue, i.e., if it could be rationally established that dissatisfaction is not a ripened (effect).[125]

The Vaibhāṣika. – (1) Dissatisfaction is produced by a [special] imagination [*parikalpaviśeṣa*]: when one thinks of something that is undesirable [*aniṣṭa*]; (2) dissatisfaction is calmed [*vyupaśāmyate*] by a [special] imagination: when one thinks of something that one desires [*iṣṭa*]. But it is not like this with what is a ripened (effect).

We say: – But this would apply also to satisfaction, which, therefore, would not be a ripened effect.

Vaibhāṣika. – If, as you maintain, dissatisfaction is a ripened effect, then when a person has committed a mortal transgression (*ānantarya*; iv. 106) and experiences dissatisfaction with regard to it, i.e., when having regrets (*kaukṛtya*; ii. 29d), {11 a} one could say that the transgression is already, then and there, retributed [*vipakva*]: this is unacceptable (ii. 56a). <127>

[Answer:] – But you accept that satisfaction is a ripened (effect), and we would reason as you have just done: when a person has accomplished a meritorious action and experiences satisfaction from it, it is then that this action is, then and there, retributed [*vipakva*].

The Vaibhāṣika. – Persons detached from attachment (*vītarāga*) do not possess the controlling faculty of dissatisfaction;[126] but they possess the controlling faculties that are a ripened effect, the eye sense-faculty, etc.; thus the controlling faculty of dissatisfaction is not a ripened (effect).

We say: – But how could detached persons possess a satisfaction that would be a ripened (effect) in its nature? Without doubt, they possess a satisfaction that arises from meditative attainment [*samāpatti*]: but this satisfaction is wholesome [*kuśala*], and is thus not a ripened (effect). They do not possess any other.[127]

[Vaibhāṣika:] – The fact is that detached persons possess the controlling faculty of satisfaction, whatever the nature of this controlling faculty may be, whether it is or is not a ripened (effect);[128] whereas dissatisfaction never occurs among them. Thus, (we) conclude, the controlling faculty of dissatisfaction is not a ripened (effect).[129]

AFB.4. *The ripened effects of wholesome and unwholesome actions & the twenty-two controlling faculties;* *F 127–28*

1. Eight controlling faculties, i.e., (i–v) the five sense-faculties of the sensory consciousnesses, (vi) the vitality faculty, (vii–viii) the sexual faculties, are, in a fortunate plane of existence (*sugati*), the ripened (effect) of wholesome action; in an unfortunate plane of existence (*durgati*), a ripened (effect) of unwholesome action.
2. The mental faculty—in a fortunate plane of existence as in an unfortunate one—is a ripened (effect) of wholesome action or of unwholesome action.
3. The sensations of pleasure, of satisfaction and of equanimity are the ripened (effect) of a wholesome action.
4. The sensation of displeasure is the ripened (effect) of unwholesome action.[130] <128>
5. The material controlling faculties, in a fortunate plane of existence, are, we say, the ripened (effect) of wholesome action. In the case of hermaphrodites [*ubhaya-vyañjana*], in a fortunate plane of existence, the one and the other controlling faculty are the ripened (effect) of wholesome action, but the status of a hermaphrodite is attained by an unwholesome action.[131] {11 b}

AFC. *Having a ripened effect and not having a ripened effect & the twenty-two controlling faculties;*[132] *F 128–29*

Among the twenty-two controlling faculties, how many "have a ripened (effect)", are "with a ripened (effect)" (*savipāka*)? How many "do not have a ripened (effect)", are "without a ripened (effect)" (*avipāka*)?

10c–11a. **Only dissatisfaction always has a ripened (effect); ten controlling faculties, namely, (1) the mental faculty, (2–5) the four sensations (with the exception of dissatisfaction) and (6–10) faith and its following, either have a ripened (effect), [when they are unwholesome or wholesome-impure,] or do not have a ripened (effect).**[133]

i. Dissatisfaction (*daurmanasya*) always has a ripened (effect), for, on the one hand, it is never non-defined (*avyākṛta*), being the result of a [special] conceptualizing activity (*vikalpaviśeṣa*: the idea of "dear", "horrible", etc.) (ii. 8c); but, on the other hand, it is never pure (*anāsrava*), never occurs in the state of being concentrated [*asamāhitatva*].

ii. The first eight controlling faculties (i.e., the eye sense-faculty, etc., the vitality faculty, the sexual faculties) never have a ripened (effect), because they are non-defined; the last three controlling faculties (i.e., the faculty of coming to know what is as yet unknown, etc.) never have a ripened (effect), because they are pure (*anāsrava*) (iv. 60).

iii. In regard to the remaining ten controlling faculties: {12 a}

(1–4) The mental faculty and the sensations of pleasure, satisfaction and equanimity have a ripened (effect) when they are unwholesome (*akuśala*) or wholesome-impure (*kuśalasāsrava*); they do not have a ripened (effect) when they are non-defined or pure.

(5) The sensation of displeasure (*duḥkha*) has a ripened (effect) when it is wholesome or unwholesome; it does not have a ripened (effect) when it is non-defined. <129>

(6–10) Faith and the other (praxis-oriented) faculties have or do not have a ripened (effect) depending on whether they are impure or pure.

AFD. *The moral quality & the twenty-two controlling faculties;*[134] *F 129*

Among the twenty-two controlling faculties, how many are wholesome [*kuśala*], unwholesome [*akuśala*], non-defined [*avyākṛta*]?

11cd. **(1) Eight controlling faculties [i.e., faith, etc., the faculty of coming to know what is as yet unknown, etc.] are only wholesome.**

(2) Dissatisfaction is of two types [i.e., wholesome or unwholesome].

(3) The mental faculty and the sensations, with the exception of dissatisfaction, are of three types [i.e., wholesome, unwholesome, or non-defined].

(4) The other [controlling faculties, i.e., the eye sense-faculty, etc., the vitality faculty, the sexual faculties, are] of one type [i.e., non-defined].[135]

1. Eight controlling faculties, i.e., (i–v) faith, etc., (vi–viii) the faculty of coming to know what is as yet unknown, etc., are only wholesome.

2. Dissatisfaction is wholesome or unwholesome (ii. 28).

3. The mental faculty and the four [other] sensations are wholesome, unwholesome, or non-defined.

4. [The other controlling faculties, i.e., the first eight,] the eye sense-faculty, etc., the sexual faculties and the vitality faculty are non-defined.

E. *The three realms & the twenty-two controlling faculties;*[136] *F 129–30*

Among the twenty-two controlling faculties, how many belong to each of the three realms of existence [*dhātvāpta*]? {12 b}

12. **(1) In the realm of desire, the stainless or pure controlling faculties [i.e., the last three controlling faculties] are absent.**

(2) In the realm of fine-materiality, in addition, the sexual faculties and the two disagreeable sensations are absent.

(3) In the realm of immateriality, in addition, all the material controlling faculties and the two agreeable sensations are absent.[137] <130>

.1. *Realm of desire & the controlling faculties;*[138] *F 130*

With the exception of the last three controlling faculties, the stainless (*amala*), i.e., pure controlling faculties, all controlling faculties are connected with the realm of desire (*kāmāpta*; *pratisaṃyukta*): these are without connection to the realms of existence, are transcendent to the realms of existence (*apratisaṃyukta* = *adhātupatita*). Thus, nineteen controlling faculties, with the exception of the last three, are connected with the realm of desire [*apratisaṃyukta*].

.2. *Realm of fine-materiality & the controlling faculties;*[139] *F 130*

In regard to the realm of fine-materiality, by excluding in addition [to the stainless controlling faculties] (1–2) the two sexual faculties and (3–4) the two disagreeable sensations, [i.e.,] the sensation of displeasure (*duḥkha*) and the sensation of dissatisfaction (*daurmanasya*): Fifteen [of these nineteen] controlling faculties, which are common to the first two realms of existence (viii. 12ab), remain.

1–2. The sexual faculties are absent in the realm of fine-materiality:

- i. because sentient beings who are born in this realm have abandoned the desire for sexual union [*maithunadharmavairāgya*],
- ii. because these [sexual] faculties make one look ugly [*aśobhākaratva*; i. 30bd].

[Objection:] – However, the Sūtra says:

> That a woman [*strī*] is Brahmā does not happen, this is impossible. That a man [*puruṣa*] is Brahmā happens, this is possible.[140]

It seems that this Sūtra would present a difficulty.

[Answer:] – No. The sentient beings in the realm of fine-materiality are male without possessing the male [sexual] faculty. They possess, [however,] the other aspects of masculinity (*puruṣabhāva*) that one sees among males of the realm of desire, i.e., physical form [*saṃsthāna*], the sound of the voice [*svara*], [of manner of being (*ācāra*)] (ii. 2cd).

3. The sensation of displeasure (*duḥkha*, physical suffering) is absent in the realm of fine-materiality:

   i. because of the "fluidity" (*acchatva* [= translucidity, transparency] = shining, brilliance [*bhāsvara*]) of the body, from whence there is absence of displeasure produced by striking (*abhighātaja*);[141]

   ii. because of the absence of unwholesome actions liable to be retributed and thus the absence of displeasure "arisen from [the cause of] retribution" (*vipākaja*).

4. The sensation of dissatisfaction is absent:

   i. because sentient beings in the realm of fine-materiality have their life-stream penetrated by calm abiding (*śamathasnigdhasaṃtāna*);

   ii. because any cause of displeasure or irritation (*āghātavastu*[142]) is absent.[143]

AFE.3. *Realm of immateriality & the controlling faculties;*[144] *F 130*

In regard to the realm of immateriality, exclude in addition [to the three pure controlling faculties, the sexual faculties, etc.,] the five material controlling faculties (eye, etc.) (viii. 3c), the sensations of pleasure and of satisfaction. There remain [eight of the fifteen controlling faculties mentioned above, i.e.,] the mental faculty, the vitality faculty, the sensation of equanimity, faith and its following (i. 31). <131>

AFF. *The abandonment of the controlling faculties;*[145] *F 131*

Among the twenty-two controlling faculties, (i) how many are abandoned by insight into the truths [*darśanaprahātavya*]? (ii) How many by cultivation [*bhāvanā*]? (iii) How many are not the object of abandoning [*aprahātavya*]?

13. **(1) The mental faculty and three sensations [i.e., pleasure, satisfaction and equanimity] belong to three categories [i.e., (i) abandoned by insight into the truths, (ii) abandoned by cultivation, (iii) not abandoned].**

    (2) Dissatisfaction is (i) abandoned by insight and (ii) abandoned by cultivation.

(3) Nine controlling faculties [i.e., the five sense-faculties and the two sexual faculties, the vitality faculty and the sensation of dissatisfaction] are (ii) abandoned by cultivation alone.

(4) Five controlling faculties [i.e., faith, etc.] are either (ii) abandoned by cultivation or are (iii) not abandoned.

(5) [The last] three controlling faculties [i.e., the faculty of coming to know what is as yet unknown, etc.] are (iii) not abandoned.[146]

1. The mental faculty [*manas*] and the sensations of pleasure, satisfaction and equanimity are of three kinds [i.e., (i) abandoned by insight, (ii) abandoned by cultivation and (iii) not abandoned].

2. Dissatisfaction is (i) abandoned by insight and (ii) abandoned by cultivation, for, never being pure (*anāsrava*), it is always the object of abandoning.

3. The nine controlling faculties, namely, the five sense-faculties, the two sexual faculties, the vital faculty and the sensation of displeasure, are only of the class (ii) "abandoned by cultivation", for: (a) the first eight are not defiled (*kliṣṭa*); (b) the ninth does not arise from the mental faculty (*aṣaṣṭhaja* [= "arisen from the non-sixth", i.e., arisen from the other five sense-faculties]; i. 40); and (c) all [nine] are always impure.

4. The five controlling faculties of which the first is faith are not defiled, thus they are not (i) abandoned by insight; [when impure, they are abandoned by cultivation;] they can [also] be pure, thus can be (iii) "not abandoned".

5. The last three controlling faculties (the faculty of coming to know what is as yet unknown; faculty of perfect knowledge; faculty of final and perfect knowledge) {13 b} are (iii) "not abandoned", because they are pure, because factors without defects (*ādīnava, apakṣāla*?; *nirdośa*) are not to be abandoned.

[Thus the different modes (*prakārabheda*) (of the controlling faculties) have been explained.]

3. *ORIGINAL ACQUISITION (LABHA) OF THE CONTROLLING FACULTIES AT CONCEPTION & FINAL DISCARDING (TYĀGA) OF THE CONTROLLING FACULTIES AT DEATH;*[147] *F 131–34*

How many controlling faculties that are a ripened effect by nature do the sentient beings in the different realms of existence originally acquire [*prathamato labhyate*]?

14. **(1) In *kāmas*, [i.e., the realm of desire,] sentient beings acquire originally [—at conception—] two controlling faculties [i.e., the body**

sense-faculty and the vitality faculty] that are a ripened effect, exception being made for apparitional sentient beings who acquire six, seven or eight controlling faculties. <132>

(2) In *rūpas*, [i.e., in the realm of fine-materiality, sentient beings originally acquire] six controlling faculties.

(3) Above, [i.e., in the realm of immateriality, sentient beings originally acquire] one controlling faculty.[148]

The realm of desire or Kāmadhātu is called "the *kāmas*" on account of the capital role or predominance (*pradhānatva*) of the [five] objects of sense-enjoyments (*kāmaguṇa*; i. 22bd, F 43) in this realm.

The realm of fine-materiality or Rūpadhātu is called "the *rūpas*" on account of the capital role of material form (*rūpa*).[149]

The Sūtra uses this way of speaking:

> These calm liberations, beyond the material forms... .[150]

AGA. *The acquisition (lābha) of the controlling faculties at conception;*[151] *F 132–33*

AGA.1. *Realm of desire;*[152] *F 132*

In the realm of desire, (1) sentient beings who are born from a womb [*jarāyuja*], from an egg [*aṇḍaja*] and from moisture [*saṃsveda*] (iii. 8) originally, i.e., as soon as conception takes place, acquire two controlling faculties that are a ripened (effect), namely, the body sense-faculty (*kāyendriya*) and the vitality faculty (*jīvita–indriya*). It is gradually that the other controlling faculties appear in them.

[Question:] – Why are the mental faculty (*manas*) and the sensation of equanimity (iii. 42) not included?

[Answer:] – Because, at conception [*pratisaṃdhikāla*], both of them are always [*avaśya*] defiled [*kliṣṭa*]; thus, they are not a ripened effect (iii. 38).

(2) Apparitional sentient beings [*upapāduka*; iii. 9] [originally] acquire [either] six, seven or eight controlling faculties:

i. apparitional sentient beings without sex [*avyañjana*], namely, apparitional sentient beings at the beginning of the cosmic aeon (iii. 98), acquire six controlling faculties: the five sense-faculties of the sensory consciousnesses, plus the vitality faculty;
ii. apparitional sentient beings with sex [*ekavyañjana*], namely, gods (*deva*), etc., acquire seven controlling faculties;

iii. bisexual apparitional sentient beings [*ubhayavyañjana*] acquire eight controlling faculties.

[Question:] – But can an apparitional sentient being be bisexual?

[Answer:] – Yes, in the unfortunate destinies. {14 a}

A.2. *Realm of fine-materiality;*[153] *F 132*

In the realm of fine-materiality, sentient beings originally acquire six controlling faculties that are a ripened (effect), [i.e., the five sense-faculties of the sensory consciousnesses, plus the vitality faculty,] like the apparitional sentient beings without sex in the realm of desire. <133>

A.3. *Realm of immateriality;*[154] *F 133*

"Above", i.e., in the realm of immateriality. – This realm of existence is not situated above the realm of fine-materiality (iii. 3); but it is said that it is "above" (1) because it is superior (*para*) to the realm of fine-materiality from the point of view of meditative attainment [*samāpatti*]: the meditative attainments of the realm of immateriality are practiced after those of the realm of fine-materiality; (2) because the realm of immateriality outshines (*pradhānatara*) it from the point of view of its mode of existence, of the duration of its existence (*upapattitas*).

In this realm of existence, sentient beings originally acquire [only] one controlling faculty that is a ripened (effect), i.e., the vital faculty.[155]

We have explained how many controlling faculties that are a ripened (effect) by nature are acquired at conception.

B. *The discarding (tyāga) of the controlling faculties at death;*[156] *F 133–34*

[Now discarding (*tyāga*) is to be spoken of.] How many controlling faculties cease [*nirodhayati*] at death?

15a–16b. **(1) In the realm of immateriality, it is the vitality faculty, the mental faculty and the sensation of equanimity which cease for the dying person.**

(2) In the realm of fine-materiality, there are eight controlling faculties [i.e., plus the five sense-faculties of the sensory consciousnesses] which cease for the dying person.

(3) In the realm of desire, [when death takes place suddenly,] there are ten controlling faculties which cease [for the hermaphrodite]; nine controlling faculties, [for the unisexual person]; eight con-

trolling faculties, [for the being without sex]; or, when death takes place gradually, there are four controlling faculties [i.e., body sense-faculty, vitality faculty, mental faculty and faculty of equanimity] which cease. In the case of a good death, [i.e., if one's thought is wholesome at the last moment,] add five (praxis-oriented) faculties in all cases.[157]

1. For the being in the realm of immateriality—at death—three controlling faculties [i.e., vitality faculty, mental faculty, sensation of equanimity] cease at the last moment.

In the realm of fine-materiality, one has to add the five sense-faculties of sensory consciousnesses, the eye sense-faculty, etc. {14 b} In fact, the apparitional sentient beings (*upapāduka*) are born and die with all the sense-faculties (*samagrendriya*).

In the realm of desire, death takes place either (i) suddenly (*yugapat*; *sakṛt*) or (ii) gradually (*kramamṛtyu*): (i) In the first case, eight, nine or ten controlling faculties cease, according to whether the being is without sex, with sex, bisexual or hermaphroditic. (ii) In the second case, four controlling faculties, i.e., body sense-faculty, vitality faculty, mental faculty and faculty of equanimity, cease simultaneously at the last moment. These four controlling faculties do not cease separately [*pṛthak*].

2. The preceding concerns the case where the thought of the dying person is defiled (*kliṣṭa*) or unobscured-non-defined (*anivṛtāvyākṛta*). <134> If, [at the last moment,] the thought is wholesome (*kuśala*), then the five (praxis-oriented) faculties, faith, etc., should be added [to all cases] in the three realms of existence.[158]

AH. *THE OBTAINING (PRĀPTI) OF THE FRUITS OF THE RELIGIOUS PRAXIS & THE NUMBER OF CONTROLLING FACULTIES;*[159] *F 134–38*

In the exposition on the controlling faculties,[160] all the characteristics of the controlling faculties, their nature [*avasthā*] and their activities [*kāritra*], are investigated. {15 a} We ask, therefore, how many controlling faculties come into play in the obtaining [*prāpyate*] of the fruits of the religious praxis (*śrāmaṇyaphala*; vi. 52).

16cd. **One obtains [*āpti*] the two "extreme" fruits [i.e., (1) of stream enterer and (4) of perfected being] through nine controlling faculties.**

The two "intermediate" fruits [i.e., (2) of once-returner and (3) of non-returner] are obtained through seven, eight or nine controlling faculties.[161]

The "extreme" fruits are the fruits of stream-enterer (*srotaāpanna*) and of perfected being (*arhat*), for these two fruits are the first and the last [of the four] fruits.

The "intermediate" fruits are the fruit of once-returner (*sakṛdāgāmin*) and the fruit of non-returner (*anāgāmin*), for these two fruits are found between the first and the last fruit.

. *The obtaining of the extreme fruits;*[162] *F 134–35*

.1. *The obtaining of the fruit of stream enterer & the number of controlling faculties;*[163] *F 134–35*

The fruit of stream-enterer (*srotaāpanna*; vi. 35c) is obtained through nine controlling faculties: (1) the mental faculty; (2) equanimity;[164] (3–7) the five (praxis-oriented) faculties, faith, etc.; (8) the faculty of coming to know what is as yet unknown (*anājñātamājñāsyāmīndriya*), (9) the faculty of perfect knowledge (*ājña-indriya*; ii. 9ab).[165]

The faculty of coming to know what is as yet unknown constitutes the unhindered path (*ānantaryamārga*; vi. 30c); the faculty of perfect knowledge constitutes the path of liberation (*vimuktimārga*):[166] It is through these two controlling faculties that one obtains the fruit of stream-enterer, for the first induces (*āvāhaka*) the possession (*prāpti*) of disconnection from defilements (*visaṃyoga*; ii. 55d, vi. 52); the second supports and makes firm this possession (*saṃniśraya*, *ādhāra*).[167] <135>

.2. *The obtaining of the fruit of perfected being & the number of controlling faculties;*[168] *F 135*

The fruit of perfected being (*arhat*; vi. 45) is obtained through nine controlling faculties: (1) the mental faculty, (2) pleasure or satisfaction or equanimity, (3–7) the five (praxis-oriented) faculties, (8) the faculty of perfect knowledge (*ājñendriya*) and (9) the faculty of final and perfect knowledge (*ājñātavīndriya*).

Here the faculty of perfect knowledge constitutes the unhindered path (*ānantarya-mārga*); {15 b} the faculty of final and perfect knowledge constitutes the path of liberation (*vimuktimārga*).[169]

. *The obtaining of the intermediate fruits;*[170] *F 135–37*

.1. *The obtaining of the fruit of once-returner & the number of controlling faculties;*[171] *F 135*

The fruit of once-returner (*sakṛdāgāmin*; v. 36) is obtained either:

1. by the successive ones (*ānupūrvaka*; vi. 33a)—the practitioners who, before pursuing the obtaining of the fruit of once-returner, have obtained the fruit of stream-enterer; or
2. by those who are detached for the most part (*bhūyovītarāga*; vi. 29cd)—the practitioners who, before entering into the pure or supramundane path, i.e., into the direct realization of the truths (*satyābhisamaya*), have abandoned [*prahīṇa*] the first six categories [*prakāra*] of defilements of the realm of desire through the impure, mundane path: therefore, when they have achieved the path of insight into the truths, they become once-returners without beforehand having been stream-enterers.[172]

1. The successive ones (*ānupūrvaka*)—who are stream-enterers (*srotaāpanna*)—obtain the fruit of once-returner, either (a) through a mundane path [*laukika*], which does not involve the cultivation of the truths; or (b) through the pure or supramundane path (*anāsrava, lokottara*). – In the first case, [they obtain the fruit of once-returner through] seven controlling faculties: (i) the mental faculty, (ii) equanimity, (iii–vii) the five (praxis-oriented) faculties. – In the second case, [they obtain the fruit of once-returner through] eight controlling faculties: the same, plus (viii) the faculty of perfect knowledge (*ājñendriya*).

2. Those who are detached for the most part (*bhūyovītarāga*)—who are ordinary worldlings (*pṛthagjana*)—obtain the fruit of once-returner through nine controlling faculties. They should, in fact, realize the direct realization of the truths; thus [they obtain the fruit of once-returner through the just mentioned seven controlling faculties, plus] (viii) the faculty of coming to know what is as yet unknown (*anājñātamājñāsyāmīndriya*) and (ix) the faculty of perfect knowledge (*ājñendriya*), as for the obtaining of the fruit of stream-enterer (see above). <136>

AHB.2. *The obtaining of the fruit of non-returner & the number of controlling faculties;*[173] *F 136*

The fruit of non-returner (*anāgāmin*) is obtained either:

1. by the successive ones (*ānupūrvaka*), i.e., the practitioners who have already obtained the previous fruits, or
2. by those with detachment (*vītarāga*), i.e., the practitioners who, without having entered into the pure or supramundane path, have abandoned [*prahīṇa*] nine categories of defilements of the realm of desire or even the defilements of the higher stages up to and including the perception-sphere of nothingness (*ākiṃcanyāyatana*).

1. The successive ones (*ānupūrvaka*) obtain the fruit of non-returner thanks to seven or eight controlling faculties, according to whether they use the mundane path or the pure or supramundane path, as in the case when the successive ones, as mentioned above, obtain the fruit of once-returner.

2. Those with detachment (*vītarāga*) obtain the fruit of non-returner through the direct realization of the truths (*darśanamārga*), through nine controlling faculties, as in the case when those who are detached for the most part (*bhūyovītarāga*), as mentioned above, obtain the fruit of once-returner.

HB.3. *Further specifications*; F 136–37

These general explanations call for more specifications [*viśeṣa*].

1. Those with detachment (*vītarāga*) obtain the fruit of non-returner (*anāgāmin*) through "directly realizing the truths". In order to directly realize the truths, they lean [*niśritya*] either (i) on the meditative attainment of the third meditation (*dhyāna*), or (ii) on the meditative attainment of the first or of the second meditation, or (iii) on the meditative attainment of the preparatory meditation [to the first meditation] (*anāgamya*) or of the intermediate meditation (*dhyānāntara*) or of the fourth meditation: according to whether their faculty of sensation is the controlling faculty (i) of pleasure, (ii) of satisfaction, (iii) of equanimity [viii. 22b].

On the contrary, those who are detached for the most part (*bhūyovitarāga*) always obtain the fruit of once-returner with the faculty of equanimity.

2. The successive ones (*ānupūrvaka*) who endeavor to gain the fruit of non-returner in the meditative attainment of the preparatory meditation (*anāgamya*), when their (praxis-oriented) faculties are sharp [*tīkṣṇa*], start out for the last moment (i.e., the ninth path of liberation) of the preparatory meditation {16 a} and [then] enter into the first or the second meditation.

i. When they expel the defilements through the mundane path, it is then through eight and not through seven controlling faculties that they obtain the fruit: in fact, (a) the preparatory meditation, to which the penultimate moment (i.e., ninth unhindered path) belongs, involves the sensation of equanimity, and (b) the first or the second meditation, within which the last moment takes place, involves the sensation of satisfaction. The disconnection from the defilements results then from equanimity and from satisfaction; in the same way we have seen that disconnection, in the case of the stream-enterer (*srotaāpanna*), results from the faculty of coming to know what is as yet unknown (*ājñāsyāmīndriya*) and from the faculty of perfect knowledge (*ājñendriya*). <137>

ii. When they expel the defilements through the pure or supramundane path [*lokottara*], i.e., by cultivation of the truths, then the faculty of perfect knowledge (*ājñendriya*) should be added as ninth controlling faculty. The unhindered path (*ānantaryamārga*) and the path of liberation (*vimuktimārga*) are both a faculty of perfect knowledge.[174]

AHC. *Refutation of the view that the fruit of perfected being is obtained through eleven controlling faculties;*[175] *F 137–38*

17ab. **It is said that the status of the perfected being is obtained through eleven controlling faculties, because it is possible that a given person may obtain it in this way.**[176]

[Objection:] – We read in the *Mūlaśāstra* (*Jñānaprasthāna*, 994c1):

> Through how many controlling faculties is the status of the perfected being obtained? – Through eleven.

[Answer:] – In fact, the quality of the perfected being (*arhat*) is obtained [at a single time], as we have said, through just nine controlling faculties. The Śāstra answers: "Through eleven", for it does not look at the obtaining of the status of the perfected being, but at the person who obtains this status.

Noble ones can retrogress on several occasions from the status of the perfected being and can obtain it again by means of diverse meditative attainments, (1) sometimes with the faculty of pleasure (*sukhendriya*; third meditation), (2) sometimes with the faculty of satisfaction (*saumanasyendriya*; first and second meditation), (3) sometimes with the faculty of equanimity (*upkeṣendriya*; preparatory meditation, etc.). But [these] three controlling faculties never coexist.

[Objection:] – But why does the Śāstra not look at things from the same point of view when it speaks of the status of the non-returner? <138>

[Answer:] – The case is different. It does not happen that noble ones, retrogressing from the fruit of non-returner (*anāgāmin*), obtain it again by means of the faculty of pleasure (*sukhendriya*).[177] {16 b} On the other hand, persons detached [*vitarāga*] from all the defilements of the realm of desire, who have obtained the fruit of non-returner, cannot retrogress from this fruit, because their detachment [*vairāgya*] is obtained through two paths [*mārga*], i.e., produced by the mundane path [*laukika*] and confirmed by the pure or supramundane path [*lokottara*] (vi. 51).

THE NUMBER OF CONTROLLING FACULTIES WITH WHICH PEOPLE ARE ACCOMPANIED (SAMANVĀGATA);[178] *F 138–143*

With how many controlling faculties are the persons who are accompanied [*samanvāgata*] by such and such controlling faculties, accompanied? (*Jñānaprasthāna*, 6, 5; *Vibhāṣā*, 90, 2)

The twenty-two controlling faculties & the number of controlling faculties with which people are accompanied;[179] *F 138–42*

The mental faculty, the vitality faculty, the faculty of equanimity & being accompanied by three controlling faculties;[180] *F 138–39*

17cd. Those who are accompanied [*yukta*] by the mental faculty or the vitality faculty or the faculty of equanimity are necessarily accompanied by three controlling faculties.[181]

Those who are accompanied [*samanvāgata*] by one of these three controlling faculties are necessarily [*avaśya*] accompanied by the other two controlling faculties: when one of them is absent, the other two controlling faculties are absent.[182]

The accompaniment [*samanvāgama*] of the other controlling faculties is not determined [*aniyama*]. Those who are accompanied by these three controlling faculties may or may not be accompanied by the other controlling faculties.

1. Beings born in the realm of immateriality are not accompanied by the eye, ear, nose and tongue sense-faculties. {17 a}

Beings in the realm of desire cannot be accompanied by these sense-faculties: when they have not acquired [*apratilabdha*] them (at the beginning of embryonic life) or when they have lost [*vihīna*] them (blindness [*andhatva*], etc.; gradual death [*krama maraṇa*]).

2. Beings born in the realm of immateriality are not accompanied by the body sense-faculty.

3. Beings born in the realm of immateriality or in the realm of fine-materiality are not accompanied by the female sexual faculty [*strīndriya*].

Beings born in the realm of desire cannot be accompanied by it; when they have not acquired it or have lost it.

The same for the male sexual faculty [*puruṣendriya*]. <139>

4. Ordinary worldlings (*pṛthagjana*)[183] born in the fourth meditation (*dhyāna*), in the second meditation,[184] in the formless perception-spheres (*ārūpya*), are not accompanied by the faculty of pleasure.

5. Ordinary worldlings born in the fourth meditation, in the third meditation, in the formless perception-spheres, are not accompanied by the faculty of satisfaction.

6. Beings born in the realm of fine-materiality or in the realm of immateriality are not accompanied by the faculty of displeasure.

7. Detached persons (*vītarāga*) are not accompanied by the faculty of dissatisfaction.

8. Persons who have cut off the wholesome roots (iv. 79) are not accompanied by the five (praxis-oriented) faculties, faith, etc.

9. Neither ordinary worldlings nor noble ones in possession of a fruit are accompanied by the faculty of coming to know what is as yet unknown (*anājñātam-ājñāsyāmīndriya*).

10. Ordinary worldlings, the noble ones who are found in the path of insight into the truths (vi. 31ab) and perfected beings (*arhat*) are not accompanied by the faculty of perfect knowledge (*ājñendriya*).

11. Ordinary worldlings and those in training (*śaikṣa*) are not accompanied by the faculty of final and perfect knowledge (*ājñātāvīndriya*).

This enumeration allows us to determine the number of controlling faculties with which the categories of sentient beings that have not been specified are accompanied.

AIA.2. *The faculty of pleasure and the body sense-faculty & the being accompanied by four controlling faculties;*[185] *F 139*

18a. Those who are accompanied by the faculty of pleasure or the body sense-faculty are certainly accompanied by four controlling faculties.[186]

Those who are accompanied by the faculty of pleasure are [necessarily] accompanied, in addition, by (1) the vitality faculty, (2) the mental faculty, (3) the faculty of equanimity. {17 b}

Those who are accompanied by the body sense-faculty are accompanied, in addition, by the same three controlling faculties.

AIA.3. *The other sense-faculties and the faculty of satisfaction & being accompanied by five controlling faculties;*[187] *F 139*

18b. Those who are accompanied by one of the [other] sense-faculties of the sensory consciousnesses are necessarily accompanied by five controlling faculties.[188]

Those who are accompanied by the eye sense-faculty are [necessarily] accompanied, in addition, by (1) the vitality faculty, (2) the mental faculty, (3) the faculty of equanimity and (4) the body sense-faculty.

The same applies for those who are accompanied by the ear sense-faculty, etc. <140>

18c. **The same applies for those who are accompanied by the faculty of satisfaction.**[189]

Those who are accompanied by the faculty of satisfaction are [necessarily] accompanied, in addition, by (1) the vitality faculty, (2) the mental faculty, (3) the faculty of equanimity and (4) the faculty of pleasure.

[Question:[190]] – But with what kind of faculty of pleasure can beings who are born in the heaven of the second meditation (*dhyāna*) and who do not practice therein the meditative attainment of the third meditation be accompanied?

[Answer:] – They are accompanied by the faculty of defiled [*kliṣṭa*] pleasure of [the stage (*bhūmi*) of] the third meditation.

.4. *The faculty of displeasure & being accompanied by seven controlling faculties;*[191] *F 140*

18cd. **Those who are accompanied by the faculty of displeasure certainly are accompanied by seven controlling faculties.**[192]

Being accompanied by the faculty of displeasure, these sentient beings evidently belong to the realm of desire. They are necessarily accompanied by [seven controlling faculties:] (1) the vitality faculty, (2) the mental faculty, (3) the body sense-faculty and (4–7) the four controlling faculties of sensation: the faculty of dissatisfaction is absent in them since they are detached (*vītarāga*).

.5. *The two sexual faculties, the faculty of dissatisfaction, the five praxis-oriented faculties & being accompanied by eight controlling faculties;*[193] *F 140–41*

18d–19a. **Those who are accompanied by the female sexual faculty [or the male sexual faculty or the faculty of dissatisfaction or one of the (praxis-oriented) faculties] are necessarily accompanied by eight controlling faculties.**[194]

One should understand: Those who are accompanied by (1) the female sexual faculty or (2) the male sexual faculty or (3) the faculty of dissatisfaction or (4) one of the (praxis-oriented) faculties: faith, vigor, mindfulness, concentration and understanding (*prajñā*). <141>

1–2. Those who are accompanied by one sexual faculty are necessarily accompanied—in addition to this controlling faculty—by seven controlling faculties, which have been specified in ii. 18cd, since these sentient beings evidently belong to the realm of desire.

3. Those who are accompanied by the faculty of dissatisfaction are necessarily accompanied—in addition to this controlling faculty—by the same seven controlling faculties.

4. Those who are accompanied by one of the (praxis-oriented) faculties can be born in whichever of the three realms of existence; they are necessarily accompanied by (i–v) five (praxis-oriented) faculties, which always appear together, plus (vi) the vitality faculty, (vii) the mental faculty, (viii) the faculty of equanimity.

AIA.6. *The faculty of perfect knowledge, the faculty of final and perfect knowledge & being accompanied by eleven controlling faculties;*[195] *F 141*

19ab. Those who are accompanied by the faculty of perfect knowledge or the faculty of final and perfect knowledge are necessarily accompanied by eleven controlling faculties.[196]

Namely: (1) the vitality faculty; (2) the mental faculty; (3–5) the faculties of pleasure, of satisfaction, of equanimity;[197] {18 a} (6–10) the five (praxis-oriented) faculties, and (11) the eleventh, i.e., either the faculty of perfect knowledge (*ājñendriya*) or the faculty of final and perfect knowledge (*ājñātāvīndriya*).

AIA.7. *The faculty of coming to know what is as yet unknown & being accompanied by thirteen controlling faculties;*[198] *F 141–42*

19cd. Those who are accompanied by the faculty of coming to know what is as yet unknown are necessarily accompanied by thirteen controlling faculties.[199]

In fact, it is only in the realm of desire that one practices the path of insight into the truths (vi. 55). Thus those who are accompanied by this controlling faculty are beings of the realm of desire. They are necessarily accompanied by (1) the vitality faculty, (2) the mental faculty, (3) the body sense-faculty, (4–7) four controlling faculties of sensation, (8–12) the five (praxis-oriented) faculties, and (13) the faculty of coming to know what is as yet unknown (*ājñāsyāmīndriya*). They are not necessarily accompanied by the faculty of dissatisfaction or the sense-faculties of the eye, etc.; in fact, they can be "detached", in which case dissatisfaction is absent in them; they can be blind [*andha*], etc.[200] <142>

IB. *The smallest possible number of controlling faculties with which people are accompanied;*[201] *F 142–43*

With how many controlling faculties are those who are accompanied with the smallest possible number of controlling faculties accompanied?

20ab. **Sentient beings in whom the good is absent are accompanied with a minimum of eight controlling faculties, i.e., (1) body sense-faculty, (2–6) five sensations (*vid*), (7) vitality faculty and (8) mental faculty.**[202]

Beings in whom the good is absent (*niḥśubha*) are those who have cut off the wholesome roots. They necessarily belong to the realm of desire (iv. 79); they cannot be "detached". Thus they are necessarily accompanied with the enumerated controlling faculties.

"Sensation" [*vedanā*] is referred to, in the verse (*kārikā*), as *vid*. That is to say, "that which experiences or feels" (*vedayate*) by understanding it as a form of *kartari kvip*; or "sensation" [*vedana*] (*bhāvasādhana*: *auṇādikaḥ kvip*).[203] [Sensation is *vit* in the same way that *sampadana* is *sampat*.]

20cd. **In the same way, ignorant persons [i.e., ordinary worldlings] who are born in the realm of immateriality are accompanied by eight controlling faculties, namely, (1) equanimity, (2) vitality faculty, (3) mental faculty and (4–8) good controlling faculties [i.e., the five praxis-oriented faculties].**[204]

Ordinary worldlings (*pṛthagjana*) are called *ignorant persons* (*bāla*) because they have not seen the truths. {18 b} <143>

The good controlling faculties (*śubha*) are the (praxis-oriented) faculties, faith, etc. – Since it is a question of ignorant persons and since the total is eight controlling faculties, the pure controlling faculties (the faculty of coming to know what is as yet unknown, etc.) are not alluded to here by the author.

IC. *The largest possible number of controlling faculties with which people are accompanied;*[205] *F 143*

With how many controlling faculties are those who are accompanied with the largest possible number of controlling faculties accompanied?

21ac. **Hermaphrodites (*dviliṅga*) [are accompanied] with a maximum of nineteen controlling faculties, with the exception of the three stainless controlling faculties.**[206]

Hermaphrodites [*dvivyañcana*] necessarily belong to the realm of desire. These sentient beings are not "detached"; can be accompanied by the (praxis-oriented) faculties; can be accompanied by all the sense-faculties of the sensory consciousnesses. But these sentient beings are ordinary worldlings (*pṛthagjana*): thus the pure controlling faculties (the faculty of coming to know what is as yet unknown, etc.,) are necessarily absent in these sentient beings.

In the verse (*kārikā*), the pure (*anāsrava*) controlling faculties are called *stainless* [*amala*]. (1) The faculty of coming to know what is as yet unknown (*ājñāsyāmi*), (2) the faculty of perfect knowledge (*ājña*) and (3) the faculty of final and perfect knowledge (*ājñātāvin*) are pure because they are not in connection with the fluxes (*āsrava*) either due to the cognitive object or due to association (v. 17).

21cd. **Noble ones, not detached, [i.e., those in training,] can be accompanied by all the controlling faculties [i.e., with a maximum of nineteen controlling faculties], with the exception of one sexual faculty, [i.e., the male or female sexual faculty,] and two pure or stainless controlling faculties.**[207]

Noble ones (*ārya*) who are not detached (*rāgin*), thus those in training (*śaikṣa*) and not perfected beings (*arhat*), are accompanied with a maximum of nineteen controlling faculties. (1) One has to exclude either the male sexual faculty or the female sexual faculty; (2) one has to exclude the faculty of final and perfect knowledge (*ājñātāvīndriya*) in all cases; in addition, (3) [one has to exclude] the faculty of perfect knowledge (*ājñendriya*) when those in training are found in the path of insight into the truths, and (4) [one has to exclude] the faculty of coming to know what is as yet unknown (*ājñāsyāmīndriya*) when those in training are in the path of cultivation of the truths.[208] {iv. 1 a}[209]

THE WAY CONDITIONED FACTORS (SAṂSKṚTA) ARISE & FIVE-GROUP (PAÑCA-VASTU) CLASSIFICATION OF FACTORS;[210]

F 143–244

The conditioned factors[211] (*saṃskṛta*) (i. 7a), i.e., matter or form, sensation, ideation, etc., are, as we have seen, of distinct characteristics [*bhinnalakṣaṇa*]. <144> One may ask if, in the same way, they arise independently or distinctly from one another [*bhinnotpāda*]; or rather if, in certain cases, they necessarily arise together or simultaneously (*niyatasahotpāda*).

Certain conditioned factors always arise together or simultaneously.

The factors (*dharma*) are divided into five categories:[212]

I. matter or material form (*rūpa*; i. 9–14b);
II. thought (*citta*; i. 16–17);
III. thought-concomitants (*caitta*; *caitasika*) or factors (*dharma*) [or formations (*saṃskāra*)] associated with thought (ii. 23–34);
IV. formations dissociated from thought (*cittaviprayukta*) (ii. 35–48);
V. unconditioned factors (*asaṃskṛta*; i. 4–6).

I. *RŪPA* (matter or material form, 11)

1. *cakṣur-indriya* (eye sense-faculty)	6. *rūpa-artha* (visible form object-referent)
2.. *śrotra-indriya* (ear s.–f.)	7. *śabda-artha* (sound o.-r.)
3. *ghrāṇa-indriya* (nose s.–f.)	8. *gandha-artha* (odor o.-r.)
4. *jihvā-indriya* (tongue s.–f.)	9. *rasa-artha* (taste o.-r.)
5. *kāya-indriya* (body s.-f.)	10. *spraṣṭavya-artha* (tangible o.-r.)
11. *avijñapti-rūpa* (non-informative matter)	

II. *CITTA* (thought, 1)

III. *CAITTASIKA DHARMAS* (thought-concomitants, 46)

i. *mahābhūmika dharmas* (generally permeating factors, 10)

1. *vedanā* (sensation)	6. *prajñā* (understanding)
2. *cetanā* (intention)	7. *smṛti* (mindfulness)
3. *saṃjñā* (ideation)	8. *manaskāra* (mental application)
4. *chanda* (predilection)	9. *adhimokṣa* (resolve)
5. *sparśa* (contact)	10. *samādhi* (concentration)

ii. *kuśala-mahābhūmika dharmas* (wholesome permeating factors, 10)

1. *śraddhā* (faith)	6. *apatrāpya* (shame)
2. *apramāda* (diligence, heedfulness)	7. *alobha* (non-greed)
3. *praśrabdhi* (pliancy)	8. *adveṣa* (non-hatred)
4. *upekṣā* (equanimity)	9. *avihiṃsā* (non-harmfulness)
5. *hrī* (modesty)	10. *vīrya* (vigor)

iii. *kleśa-mahābhūmika dharma*s (permeating factors of defilement, 6)

1. *moha* (delusion)
2. *pramāda* (non-diligence, heedlessness)
3. *kauśīdya* (slackness)
4. *āśraddhya* (non-faith)
5. *styāna* (torpor)
6. *auddhatya* (restlessness)

iv. *akuśala-mahābhūmika dharma*s (unwholesome permeating factors, 2)

1. *āhrīkya* (non-modesty)
2. *anapatrāpya* (shamelessness)

v. *parīttakleśa-bhūmika dharma*s (factors of defilement of restricted scope, 10)

1. *krodha* (anger)
2. *upanāha* (enmity)
3. *śāṭhya* (dissimulation)
4. *īrṣyā* (jealousy, envy)
5. *pradāśa* (depraved opinionatedness)
6. *mrakṣa* (concealment)
7. *mātsarya* (avarice)
8. *māyā* (deceit)
9. *mada* (pride)
10. *vihiṃsā* (harmfulness)

vi. *aniyata dharma*-s (undetermined factors, 8)

1. *kaukṛtya* (regret)
2. *middha* (sleepiness)
3. *vitarka* (initial inquiry)
4. *vicāra* (investigation)
5. *rāga* (attachment)
6. *pratigha* (hostility)
7. *māna* (conceit)
8. *vicikitsā* (doubt)

IV. *CITTAVIPRAYUKTASAṂSKĀRA DHARMA*S (formations dissociated from thought, 14)

1. *prāpti* (possession)
2. *aprāpti* (non-possession)
3. *nikāyasabhāga* or *sabhāgatā* (group homogeneity)
4. *āsaṃjñika* (ideationlessness)
5. *āsaṃjñi-samāpatti* (attainment of non-ideation)
6. *nirodha-samāpatti* (attainment of cessation)
7. *jīvitendriya* (vitality faculty)
8. *jāti-lakṣaṇa* (characteristic of origination)
9. *sthiti-lakṣaṇa* (characteristic of duration)
10. *jarā-lakṣaṇa* (characteristic of deterioration)
11. *anityatā-lakṣaṇa* (characteristic of impermanence)
12. *nāma-kāya* (collection of names)
13. *pada-kāya* (collection of phrases)
14. *vyañjana-kāya* (collection of phonemes)

V. *ASAṂSKṚTA DHARMA*S (unconditioned factors, 3)

1. *ākāśa* (space)
2. *pratisaṃkhyā-nirodha* (cessation due to deliberation)
3. *apratisaṃkhyā-nirodha* (cessation not due to deliberation)

Fig. 1: The five-group-seventy-five-*dharma*s classification of the Sarvāstivāda

The unconditioned factors do not arise (i. 5; ii. 58) and so we do not need to occupy ourselves with them here.

THE SIMULTANEOUS ARISING (SAHOTPĀDA) OF FACTORS;[213] *F 144–244*

BAA. The simultaneous arising of atoms or molecules (*paramāṇu*); F 144

BAB. The simultaneous arising of thought, thought-concomitants and formations dissociated from thought; F 149–244

.. *The simultaneous arising of atoms or molecules (paramāṇu);*[214] *F 144–49*

We shall first study the law [*niyama*] of simultaneous arising (*sahotpāda*) of material factors (*rūpa*).

22. **In the realm of desire, (1) the molecule [*paramāṇu*, i.e., *saṃghāta-paramāṇu*][215] which does not involve sound and which does not involve any sense-faculty includes eight [kinds of] real entities [*aṣṭadravyaka*]:[216] [i.e., the four fundamental material elements and the four derivative material elements: visible form, taste, odor, tangible].[217]**

(2) When the body sense-faculty is involved in [the molecule, it includes] nine real entities.

(3) When any other sense-faculty is involved in [the molecule, it includes] ten real entities.[218] {1 b}

..1. *The meaning of the term* paramāṇu *in this context;*[219] *F 144*

By *paramāṇu* one does not understand the atom (*paramāṇu*) here in the strict sense, the real-entity atom (*dravyaparamāṇu*), the atom or monad which is a single real entity (*dravya*; i. 13), but rather the composite molecule (*saṃghātaparamāṇu*), i.e., the most subtle (*sarvasūkṣma*) among the composite matters (*rūpasaṃghāta*), since there is nothing more subtle than it among the composite matters.[220] <145>

.2. *The various numbers of real entities of the molecule in the realm of desire*[221]; *F 145–47*

1. In the realm of desire, the (composite) molecule which does not involve sound (*śabda*, *śabdāyatana*) and which does not involve any sense-faculty (*indriya*) includes eight [kinds of] real entities and not less than eight [kinds]: namely, the four fundamental material elements (*mahābhūta*, the elementary substances earth, water, fire, wind; see i. 12c) and the four derivative material elements (*bhautika*), namely, visible form (*rūpa*; i. 10a), odor, taste, tangible (see ii. 50cd: co-existent cause; see 65ab: causal relationship between fundamental and derivative material elements).

2. The (composite) molecule which does not involve sound but which involves the body sense-faculty (*kāyendriya*; *kāyāyatana*)[222] includes a ninth real entity (*dravya*), i.e., the real entity which is the body sense-faculty.

3. The (composite) molecule which does not involve sound but which involves any sense-faculty other than the body sense-faculty (sense-faculty of the eye, etc.) includes a tenth real entity, i.e., the real entity which is this other sense-faculty (eye sense-faculty, etc.), since the sense-faculties of the eye, of the ear, etc., do not exist independently from the body sense-faculty and constitute distinct sense-spheres (*āyatana*).

4. When sound is involved in the aforementioned aggregations, the total rises to nine, ten or eleven real entities: in fact, sound (*śabdāyatana*) that is produced by the fundamental material elements, which form part of the organism (*upātta*; i. 10b), does not exist independently of the sense-faculties.[223]

BAA.2.1. *Objections; F 145–47*

BAA.2.1.1. *Why are the characteristics of the four fundamental material elements not experienced at once? F 145–46*

[Objection:] – If the four fundamental material elements, the elementary substance earth, etc., are never disassociated (*avinirbhāga*) and coexist in every (composite) molecule, how is it that a given (composite) molecule is perceived either as solid [*kaṭhina*] or liquid [*drava*] or hot [*uṣṇa*] or moving [*samudīraṇa*] (i. 12d), and not as these four substances or characteristics at once? <146>

[Answer:[224]] – In a given (composite) molecule, those real entities (*dravya*, elementary substance earth, etc.) that occur most active in it (*paṭutama*, *sphuṭatama*) are perceived [on account of their power] and not the others. In the same way, when one touches a bundle of plant-stalks and needles (*sūcī-tūlī-kalāpa*),[225] one perceives (only) the needles; when one eats oversalted gruel [*saktulavaṇacūrṇa*], one perceives (only) the taste of salt. {2 a}

BAA.2.1.2. *How do we know that the molecule includes the four fundamental material elements? F 146–47*

[Objection:] – How do you know that a given (composite) molecule includes the fundamental material elements whose presence is not perceived there?

[Answer:] – All of the fundamental material elements manifest their presence through their particular efficacy, namely, supporting (*dhṛti*), cohesion (*saṃgraha*), heating or ripening (*pakti*), and expansion (*vyūhana*) (i. 12c).[226]

According to another opinion, [that of Bhadanta Śrīlābha,] the (composite) molecule includes [= consists[227] of] the four fundamental material elements, since, given the activity of certain causes [i.e., fire (*agni*), etc.] [*pratyayalābha*], solid phenomena become liquid, etc.[228] The elementary substance fire [*tejodhātu*] exists in water, since water is more or less cold,[229] which is explained through the presence of the elementary substance fire in a greater or lesser quantity.

But, we would say, that coldness is more or less intense [*atiśaya*] does not imply that there would be a mixture (*vyatibheda*; *miśrībhāva*) of a certain real entity (*dravya*), the coldness [*śīta*], with its opposite, the heat [*uṣṇa*], because sound [*śabda*] and sensation [*vedanā*], though homogeneous, each vary in intensity. <147>

According to (still) another opinion (*apara*; i.e., that of the Sautrāntikas[230]) the fundamental material elements that are not perceived in a given (composite) molecule exist in the state of seed (*bījatas*, *śaktitas*, *sāmarthyatas*), not in activity, and not in and of themselves (*svarūpatas*).[231] It is in this way that the Fortunate One was able to say (*Saṃyuktāgama*, 18, 10):

> In this piece of wood [*dāru*] there are many mineral substances [*dhātu*].[232]

The Fortunate One means that this wood contains the seeds, the potentialities (*śakti*) of many mineral substances; for gold [*suvarṇa*], silver [*rūpya*], etc., do not actually exist in the wood.

.2.1.3. *How can one establish the presence of color in wind?* F 147

(The Sautrāntikas) object again: – How can one establish the presence (*sadbhāva*) of color (*varṇa*) in wind [*vāyu*]?[233]

The Vaibhāṣikas respond: – This is [either] an object of faith (*śraddhanīya*), i.e., not of inference (*anumeya*), or else, the color exists in the wind because one perceives the odor [*gandha*] due to contact with wind and the odorous object; but odor is never dissociated [*avyabhicāra*] from color.[234]

.3. *The various numbers of real entities of the molecule in the realm of fine-materiality;*[235] F 147

We know that odor and taste are absent in the realm of fine-materiality (i. 30); thus, in regard to the (composite) molecule of the realm of fine-materiality, the numbers must be reduced. There will be six, seven and eight real entities, and when sound intervenes, seven, eight and nine real entities. We will not explain again the details which have been discussed above.

BAA.4. *The meaning of the term* dravya *in "includes eight* dravyas*";*[236] *F 147–49*

Objection: – The Vaibhāṣika says that a (composite) molecule in the realm of desire includes, at a minimum, eight *dravyas*. Should *dravya* be taken here:

1. as *dravya*s in the strict sense (*dravyam eva*), as individual real entities, as real entities which have a particular inherent characteristic [*svalakṣaṇa*],[237] or
2. as sense-spheres (*āyatana*) which can be termed *dravya*s [in the broader sense], real entities, since they each possess distinctive general characteristics [*sāmānyaviśeṣalakṣaṇa*]?[238]

1. In the first hypothesis, the proposed numbers are too small [*atyalpa*]. <148>

You say, [namely,] that the (composite) molecule includes four derivative material elements of which the first one is visible form (*rūpa*): we would thus say that then [—according to your own system—] the (composite) molecule will include not only the visible form of color (*varṇa*, the real entity blue or red, etc.) but also the visible form of shape (*saṃsthāna*, the real entity long and short, etc.) (i. 10; iv. 3c), since a number of atoms are agglomerated therein. {2 b}

[Moreover, since] the (composite) molecule [also] includes the derivative material element called *tangible* (*spraṣṭavya*), we would say further that the (composite) molecule will then be heavy or light, rough or smooth; it could be "of coldness", "of hunger", "of thirst"; it would thus include [in addition] the real entities (*dravya*), which are heaviness [*gurutva*] or lightness [*laghutva*], smoothness [*ślakṣṇatva*] or roughness [*karkaśatva*], coldness [*śīta*], hunger [*bubhūkṣā*], and thirst [*pipāsā*] (i. 10d).

Therefore, the proposed numbers are too small.

2. But if, on the contrary, the Vaibhāṣika means to take [*dravya* as] sense-spheres (*āyatana*), the numbers are too large [*atibahu*], for the fundamental material elements form part of the sense-sphere tangible [*spraṣṭavyāyatana*; i. 35a].

Therefore, it should be said that a (composite) molecule includes [only] four real entities (*dravya*), visible form, odor, taste and tangible.

The Vaibhāṣika responds. – Our definition of the (composite) molecule is good (ii. 22a). The word *dravya* is to be taken, according to the case, as both

1. real entities in the strict sense, or
2. sense-spheres (*āyatana*).

Among the eight *dravya*s of the (composite) molecule, there are:

1. four real entities properly so called: namely, the four fundamental material elements [*bhūta*], the bases and sources (*āśraya*) of derivative material elements (*bhautika*), and
2. four sense-spheres (*āyatana*): the four kinds of derivative material elements supported by the fundamental material elements: visible form (*rūpa*), odor, taste and tangible (excluding the fundamental material elements which are included within the tangible, i. 10d).

[Answer:] – This answer is not good, for each of these four derivative material elements is supported by the tetrad of fundamental material elements. The (composite) molecule will [then] include twenty *dravyas*.[239] <149>

The Vaibhāṣika replies: – No, for we look at the nature or type (*jāti*) of the fundamental material elements, i.e., solidity, etc. The nature or type of the tetrad of the fundamental material elements remains the same in that they support the derivative material element odor or the derivative material elements visible form, taste, tangible.

[Answer:] – But why do you express yourself in an ambiguous manner and use the word *dravya* in two different acceptations? Words follow the dictates of caprice, indeed one has to examine the meaning.[240]

.B. *The simultaneous arising of thought, thought-concomitants and formations dissociated from thought;*[241] *F 149–244*

[The law of the simultaneous arising of material factors has been discussed; there remains to be discussed the same with respect to the remaining factors (i.e., thought, thought-concomitants and formations dissociated from thought).]

Brief exposition;[242] *F 149–150*

23a. **Thought and thought-concomitants necessarily arise together or simultaneously.**[243]

Thought (*citta*) and thought-concomitants (*caitta*) cannot arise independently or the one without the other.

23b. **All [conditioned] factors necessarily arise with their characteristics [i.e., origination, duration, deterioration and impermanence].**[244] {3 a}

All conditioned factors (*saṃskṛta*), i.e., matter, thought (ii. 34), thought-concomitants, formations (*saṃskāra*) dissociated from thought (ii. 35), necessarily arise with their conditioned characteristics (*saṃskṛtalakṣaṇa*), i.e., origination, duration, deterioration and impermanence (ii. 46a). **<150>**

23c. Sometimes [factors arise] with possession.[245]

Among the conditioned factors, those indicative of sentient beings (*sattvākhya*, *sattvasaṃkhyāta*; i. 10) necessarily arise together with possession (*prāpti*), which relates to each one of them (ii. 37b). There is no possession of other [factors]. That is why the stanza says "sometimes" [*vā*].

Extensive exposition;[246] *F 150–244*

1. The formations associated with thought (*cittasaṃprayuktasaṃskāra*); F 150
2. The formations dissociated from thought (*cittaviprayuktasaṃskāra*); F 178–244[247]

BAB.1. *The formations associated with thought (cittasaṃprayuktasaṃskāra): forty-six thought-concomitants;*[248] *F 150–78*

1.1. Five determined kinds and one undetermined kind of thought-concomitants; F 150
1.2. Which thought-concomitants arise in association with which thought: wholesome, unwholesome, etc.? F 165
1.3. Drawing distinctions between similar thought-concomitants; F 169
1.4. Thought and thought-concomitants; F 176
 1.4.1. Mind (*citta*), mind (*manas*), consciousness (*vijñāna*): different in name but one in meaning; F 176
 1.4.2. Thought and thought-concomitants: "having a basis", etc.; F 177
 1.4.3. Thought and thought-concomitants: the five equivalences; F 178

BAB.1.1. *The five determined kinds and one undetermined kind;*[249] *F 150–65*

[Thought-concomitants (*caitta*) are mentioned.] What are thought-concomitants?[250] <151> <152>

23cd. Thought-concomitants are of five [determined] kinds: (1) the generally permeating factors; [(2) the wholesome permeating factors; (3) the permeating factors of defilement; (4) the unwholesome permeating factors; (5) the factors of defilement of restricted scope; and of one undetermined kind].[251]

Thought-concomitants are of five [determined (*niyata*)] kinds (*prakāra*) [i.e., thirty-eight thought-concomitants]:

1. generally permeating factors (*mahābhūmika*), those that accompany all thoughts (ii. 24): [ten thought-concomitants];[252]
2. wholesome permeating factors (*kuśalamahābhūmika*), those that accompany every wholesome thought (ii. 25): [ten thought-concomitants];

3. permeating factors of defilement (*kleśamahābhūmika*), those that accompany every defiled thought (ii. 26ac): [six thought-concomitants];[253]
4. unwholesome permeating factors (*akuśalamahābhūmika*), those that accompany every unwholesome thought (ii. 26cd): [two thought-concomitants];
5. factors of defilement of restricted scope (*parīttakleśabhūmika*), which have the restricted defilement for their stage (ii. 27; iii. 32ab): [ten thought-concomitants].[254]

[Thought-concomitants are of one undetermined (*aniyata*) kind: eight thought-concomitants.[255]]

3.1.1.1. *The ten generally permeating factors (mahābhūmika);*[256] *F 152–56*

3.1.1.1.a. *The meaning of the term* mahābhūmika;[257] *F 152*

Bhūmi (stage) signifies "place of movement or arising" (*gativiṣaya*; *utpattiviṣaya*). The place of arising of a factor (*dharma*) is the stage to which this factor belongs.

The "great stage" (*mahābhūmi*) [i.e., thought] is so called because it is the stage, the place of arising, of great factors [i.e., of factors of great extension, which occur everywhere]. We will call *mahābhūmika* the factor that is inherent in the great stage (*mahābhūmi*), {3 b} i.e., the factor that always occurs in any thought.[258] <153>

3.1.1.1.b. *The definitions;*[259] *F 153–55*

What are the generally permeating factors (*mahābhūmika*)?

24. (1) Sensation, (2) intention, (3) ideation, (4) predilection, (5) contact, (6) understanding, (7) mindfulness, (8) mental application, (9) resolve,[260] and (10) concentration coexist in any thought.[261]

These ten factors, according to the School [*kila*],[262] all (*samagra*) exist in any moment of thought (*cittakṣaṇa*).

1. Sensation (*vedanā*; *tshor ba*) is the three kinds of sensation or experience or affect (*anubhava*), i.e., (i) pleasant [*sukha*], (ii) unpleasant [*duḥkha*] and (iii) neither-unpleasant-nor-pleasant (i. 14).[263] <154>

2. Intention (*cetanā*; *sems pa*) is that which instigates, conditions, informs, models the thought (*cittābhisaṃskāra*; *cittaprasyanda*); it is mental action [*manaskarma*] (see i. 15; iv. 1).[264]

3. Ideation (*saṃjñā*; *'du shes*) is conceiving (*saṃjñāna*), is that which seizes or apprehends the signs [*nimitta*; male, female, etc.] of the object-field (*viṣayanimitta-grahaṇa* = *viṣayaviśeṣarūpagrāha*) (i. 14; ii. 34bd, F 177, note).[265]

4. Predilection (*chanda*; *'dun pa*) is the desire for action [*kartṛkāmatā*].[266]

5. Contact (*sparśa*; *reg pa*) is the state of contact (*spṛṣṭi*) born from the coming together (*saṃnipātaja*) of (i) the sense-faculty, (ii) the object-field [*viṣaya*] and (iii) the consciousness (*vijñāna*); in other words, it is that factor by virtue of which (*yadyogāt*) the sense-faculty, the object-field and the consciousness are as if touching one another (iii. 30).[267]

6. Understanding (*prajñā*, *mati*; *blo gros*), referred to in the stanza as *mati*, is discernment of factors [*dharmāṇāṃ pravicayaḥ*; i. 2].[268]

7. Mindfulness (*smṛti*; *dran pa*) is the not-letting-drop (*asaṃpramoṣa*) of the cognitive object (*ālambana*); a factor by virtue of which the mind (*manas*) does not forget (*vismarati*) the cognitive object, by virtue of which the mind cherishes the cognitive object so to speak [or clearly notes the cognitive object] (*abhilaṣatīva*; *abhilapatīva*).[269] (See ix, F 273–79.).

8. Mental application (*manaskāra*; *yid la byed pa*) is the tilting or orienting or alerting (*ābhoga*)[270] of thought (*cetas*): that which makes thought lean toward its cognitive object and restricts thought to the cognitive object (*ālambane cetasa āvarjanam avadhāraṇam*). (*Manaskāra* is explained as an act by the mind [*manasaḥ kāraḥ*] or, in other words, the mind [*manas*] acts in making (itself) lean toward [*manaḥ karoty āvarjayati*].) (ii, F 325–28).[271]

9. Resolve (*adhimokṣa*; *mos pa*) is the affirmation [*avadhāraṇa*] [with regard to an object], [is resolution (*adhimukti*)].[272] <155>

10. Concentration (*samādhi*; *ting nge 'dzin*) is the one-pointedness of thought (*cittaikāgratā*) toward a cognitive object (*agra* = *ālambana*; i. 33); this is the factor by virtue of which thought, in an uninterrupted stream, remains focused on a cognitive object (viii. 1).[273] <156>

BAB.1.1.1.c. *How do we know that the ten generally permeating factors coexist?*

F 156

[Question:] – How do we know that these ten thought-concomitants, having distinct characteristics [*bhinnalakṣaṇa*], coexist in one and the same thought?[274]

[Answer:] – Subtle [*sūkṣma*], surely, is the distinctive characteristic (*viśeṣa*) of thought and of thought-concomitants. It is discerned only with difficulty (*durlakṣya*) even when one limits oneself to considering each of the thought-concomitants as developing in a continuous stream [*pravāha*; *prabandha*]; how much more so when one looks at one psychological moment [*kṣaṇa*] in which they all exist together.

If the many tastes [*bahurasa*] of plants [*oṣadhi*]—tastes which we know through {4 a} a material sense-faculty—are difficult to distinguish (*duravadhāna*; *duḥpariccheda*), how much more so does this hold for non-material factors which are perceived through the mental consciousness.

B.1.1.2. *The ten wholesome permeating factors (kuśalamahābhūmika);*[275] *F 156–60*

B.1.1.2.a. *The meaning of the term* kuśalamahābhūmika;[276] *F 156*

The "stage" of wholesome factors of great extension is called *kuśalamahābhūmi*. Thought-concomitants which rise from this stage are termed the *wholesome permeating factors* (*kuśalamahābhūmika*): the factors which occur in any wholesome thought.

B.1.1.2.b. *The definitions;*[277] *F 156–60*

25. **(1) Faith, (2) diligence or heedfulness, (3) pliancy, (4) equanimity, (5) modesty, (6) shame, (7–8) two [wholesome] roots: non-greed, non-hatred, (9) non-harmfulness, and (10) vigor occur only in the wholesome thought, occur in any wholesome thought.**[278]

B.1.1.2.ba. *Faith (śraddhā);*[279] *F 156–57*

Faith (*śraddhā*; *dad pa*) is the clarification [or clearing] [*prasāda*] of thought.[280] <157>

According to another opinion,[281] it is adherence to or firm belief in [*abhisaṃpratyaya*] (1) the doctrine of the effect of actions [*karmaphala*; iv. 78b], (2) the three jewels [*ratna*; Buddha, Dharma, Saṃgha, vi. 73c], and (3) the [four] truths [*satya*].

B.1.1.2.bb. *Diligence or heedfulness (apramāda);*[282] *F 157*

Diligence or heedfulness (*apramāda*; *bag yod pa*) is the cultivation (*bhāvanā*) of wholesome factors, i.e., the acquisition [*pratilambha*] and practice [*niṣevaṇa*] of wholesome factors.[283]

Objection: – The acquisition and practice of wholesome factors is none other than the acquired and practiced wholesome factors. How can you make a separate mental factor of diligence or heedfulness?

[Answer:] – Diligence or heedfulness is the application or attention (*avahitatā*) to wholesome factors. It is said metaphorically [*upacāra*] that it is cultivation. In fact, it is the cause of the cultivation [*bhāvanāhetu*].

According to another school [*nikāya*],[284] diligence or heedfulness is the guarding (*ārakṣā*) of thought.

BAB.1.1.2.bc. *Pliancy (praśrabdhi);*[285] *F 157*

Pliancy (*praśrabdhi*; *shin tu sbyangs pa*) {4 b} is that factor through which thought is clever (*karmaṇyatā*), i.e., light or apt or versatile (*lāghava*).[286]

BAB.1.1.2.bca. *Pliancy of the body; F 157–58*

(The Sautrāntika[287] observes:) – But does the Sūtra not speak of pliancy of the body [*kāyapraśrabdhi*]?[288] <158>

[Vaibhāṣika:] – The Sūtra speaks of pliancy of the body as it speaks of bodily sensation (*kāyikī vedanā*). Any sensation is, in its nature, mental; however, the Sūtra calls *bodily* the sensation that has the five sense-faculties constituted by atoms for its basis, the sensation associated with the five sensory consciousnesses (ii. 7a). Likewise, pliancy of thought [*cittapraśrabdhi*] that depends on the five sense-faculties, pliancy of the five sensory consciousnesses, is called *pliancy of the body.*

BAB.1.1.2.bcb. *Pliancy of the body & member of enlightenment; F 158–59*

(The Sautrāntika[289] replies:) – How can the pliancy of the body [*kāyapraśrabdhi*], understood in this way, be counted among the members of enlightenment (*saṃbodhyaṅga*) (vi. 68)? In fact, (1) the five sensory consciousnesses are of the domain of the realm of desire, since they are "non-concentrated" (*asamāhita*), that is to say, since they do not occur in a concentrated state, and (2) the members of enlightenment are "concentrated" (vi. 71a). Thus, in our opinion, in the Sūtra which we have cited, the pliancy of the body is aptitude of the body (*kāyavaiśāradya*) or cleverness of the body (*kāyakarmaṇyatā*) (viii. 9).

The Sarvāstivādin: – How could the pliancy of the body, understood in this way, be a member of enlightenment? The aptitude of the body is, in fact, impure (*sāsrava*).

(The Sautrāntika:) – But it is favorable (*anukūla*) to the pliancy of thought, which is a member of enlightenment; it receives, for this reason, the name *member of enlightenment.*

The Sūtra often expresses itself in this manner. For example:

1. It teaches that joy and the factors (*dharma*) which cause the joy (*prītisthānīya*) constitute the member of enlightenment called *joy* (*prītisaṃbodhyaṅga*; vi. 71).[290]

2. It teaches that hostility and the causes of hostility (*pratighanimitta*) constitute the hindrance of malice (*vyāpādanivaraṇa*) (v. 59).[291] <159>
3. It teaches that right view (*dṛṣṭi*), right thinking (*saṃkalpa*) and right exertion (*vyāyāma*) constitute "the element of understanding" (*prajñāskandha*) (vi. 76): and yet neither thinking, which is initial inquiry (*vitarka*) in its intrinsic nature [*svabhāva*], nor exertion, which is vigor (*vīrya*) in its intrinsic nature, are [of the intrinsic nature of] understanding; but they are favorable [*anuguṇa*]) to this understanding and are, therefore, considered as [element of] understanding.[292]

[Thus,] the pliancy of the body, being a condition of pliancy of thought, is considered—like the latter, with the latter—as a member of enlightenment.

AB.1.1.2.bd. *Equanimity (upekṣa);*[293] *F 159–60*

Equanimity (*upekṣā*; *btang snyoms*) is the equivalence, balance or evenness of thought (*cittasamatā*), the factor by which thought remains equivalent, balanced or even (*sama*), free from tilting (*anābhoga*).[294]

AB.1.1.2.bda. *Equanimity & mental application; F 159–60*

(The Sautrāntika:[295]) – If every thought is associated with mental application (*manaskāra*), which is "tilting" or "orientation" or "alerting" in its nature [*ābhoga-ātmaka*], how could every wholesome thought be associated with equanimity, which is non-tilting in its nature [*anābhogātmika*]?

The Vaibhāṣika: – We have already commented on this (F 156): the specific characteristic [*viśeṣa*] of thought and of thought-concomitants is very difficult to cognize, to determine (*durjñāna*).

(The Sautrāntika:) – This is not the focus here: {5 a} it is quite unacceptable that the same thought is associated with thought-concomitants which are contradictory to each other, like tilting [*ābhog*]) and non-tilting [*anābhoga*], pleasure [*sukha*] and displeasure [*duḥkha*].[296] <160>

The Vaibhāṣika:[297] – There is tilting toward a certain cognitive object, non-tilting toward another cognitive object: thus, there is no contradiction to the coexistence of tilting and of non-tilting.

(The Sautrāntika:) – If it were like that, the associated thought-concomitants would not bear on the same cognitive object, which is contradictory to your definition of associated factors [*saṃprayukta*; ii. 34d]. For us, the factors which are contradictory, here mental application (*manaskāra*) and equanimity (*upekṣā*), and later, initial inquiry (*vitarka*) and investigation (*vicāra*; ii. 33), do not exist simultaneously but successively.

BAB.1.1.2.be. *The other wholesome permeating factors;*[298] *F 160*

5–6. We will explain modesty (*hrī*; *ngo tsha shes pa*) and shame (*apatrāpya*; *khrel yod pa*) later (ii. 32).[299]

7–8. [The two roots are] the two wholesome roots: non-greed (*alobha*; *ma chags pa*) and non-hatred (*adveṣa*; *zhe sdang med pa*) (iv. 8; viii. 29c–30a).[300] In regard to non-delusion (*amoha*), the third wholesome root, it is understanding in its nature [*prajñātmaka*]: thus it is already listed among the generally permeating factors (*mahābhūmika*).[301]

9. Non-harmfulness (*avihiṃsā*; *rnam par mi 'tshe ba*) is non-hurting or non-cruelty (*aviheṭhanā*).[302]

10. Vigor (*vīrya*; *brtson 'grus*) is the enduring energeticness of thought (*cetaso 'bhyutsāhaḥ*).[303]

Such are the thought-concomitants which are associated with any wholesome thought.

BAB.1.1.3. *The six permeating factors of defilement (kleśamahābhūmika);*[304] *F 160–64*

BAB.1.1.3.a. *The meaning of the term* kleśamahābhūmika; *F 160*

The stage of the great defilement factors (*mahākleśadharma*) is called *mahākleśa-bhūmi*. The [defiled] thought-concomitants that belong to this stage, i.e., that exist in any defiled (*kliṣṭa*) thought, are termed the *permeating factors of defilement* (*kleśa-mahābhūmika*).[305] <161>

BAB.1.1.3.b. *The definitions;*[306] *F 161*

26ac. (1) Delusion, (2) non-diligence or heedlessness, (3) slackness, (4) non-faith, (5) torpor and (6) restlessness occur always and exclusively in defiled thought.[307] {5 b}

1. Delusion (*moha*; *rmongs pa*), i.e., ignorance (*avidyā*; iii. 29), non-cognition (*ajñāna*), non-perceiving [*asaṃprakhyāna*; *mi gsal ba*; iii, F 92f.].[308]

2. Non-diligence or heedlessness (*pramāda*; *bag med pa*) is the non-cultivation [*abhāvanā*], i.e., the non-acquisition and non-practice, of wholesome factors; it is the opposite [*vipakṣa*] of diligence or heedfulness [*apramāda*].[309]

3. Slackness (*kauśīdya*; *le lo*) [is the non-energeticness of thought (*cetaso nābhy-utsāha*)]; it is the opposite of vigor [*vīrya*].[310]

4. Non-faith (*āśraddhya*; *ma dad pa*)[311] [is the non-clarity of thought (*cetaso 'prasādaḥ*)]; it is the opposite of faith [*śraddhā*].[312]

5. Torpor (*styāna*; *rmugs pa*) is the opposite of pliancy (*praśrabdhi*) (vii. 11d).[313]

It is said in the Abhidharma (*Jñānaprasthāna*, 925b10):

> What is torpor (*styāna*)? – The heaviness (*gurutā*) of the body, the heaviness of thought, the non-cleverness (*akarmaṇyatā*) of the body, the non-cleverness of thought. Bodily [*kāyika*] torpor and mental [*caitasika*] torpor are named *styāna*, torpor.

[Question:] – Now, torpor is a "mental" factor. How can it here be spoken of as bodily torpor?

[Answer:] – In the same way as there is bodily sensation [*kāyikī vedanā*; see i, F 157].

6. Restlessness (*auddhatya*; *rgod pa*), i.e., non-calmness (*avyupaśama*) of thought (vii. 11d).[314]

There are only six factors that are permeating factors of defilement (*kleśamahābhūmika*).

B.1.1.3.c. *The ten permeating factors of defilement of the Mūla Abhidharma;*[315] *F 161–64*

[Objection:] – But the *Mūla Abhidharma*,[316] on the one hand, says that there are ten permeating factors of defilement (*kleśamahābhūmika*) and, on the other hand, omits torpor (*styāna*) in its enumeration. <162>

B.1.1.3.ca. *The ten permeating factors of defilement;*[317] *F 162–63*

What are these ten [permeating factors of defilement (*kleśamahābhūmika*)]?

(1) Non-faith (*aśraddhya*), (2) slackness (*kauśīdya*), (3) forgetfulness (*muṣitasmṛtitā*), (4) distraction of thought (*cetaso vikṣepa*), (5) ignorance (*avidyā*), (6) non-introspection (*asaṃprajanya*), (7) incorrect mental application (*ayoniśomanaskāra*), (8) false resolve (*mithyādhimokṣa*), (9) restlessness (*auddhatya*), (10) non-diligence or heedlessness (*pramāda*).

[Reply:] – How foolish you are (*devānāṃpriyaḥ*)![318] {6 a} You hold on to the letter and ignore the intention (*prāptijño na tv iṣṭijñaḥ*)![319]

[Question:] – What is the intention [*iṣṭi*] here?

[Answer:] – Five of the factors mentioned in the Abhidharma as permeating factors of defilement, namely, (3) forgetfulness, (4) distraction, (6) non-introspection,

(7) incorrect mental application and (8) false resolve, have already been mentioned as generally permeating factors (*mahābhūmika*): there is no reason to name them again as permeating factors of defilement. This is just as in the case of the wholesome root non-delusion (*amoha*), which, although being a wholesome permeating factor (*kuśalamahābhūmika*), is not catalogued as such, because, being understanding (*prajñā*) in its intrinsic nature, it is classified as a generally permeating factor (*mahābhūmika*). (See below F 154, note).

(3) Forgetfulness (*muṣitasmṛtitā*), in fact, is none other than defiled [*kliṣṭa*] mindfulness (*smṛti*).[320]

(4) Distraction (*vikṣepa*; iv. 58) is defiled concentration (*samādhi*).[321]

(6) Non-introspection (*asaṃprajanya*) is defiled understanding (*prajñā*).[322]

(7) Incorrect mental application (*ayoniśomanaskāra*) is defiled mental application (*manaskāra*).[323]

(8) False resolve (*mithyādhimokṣa*) is defiled resolve (*adhimokṣa*).

This is why the *Mūla Abhidharma* counts ten permeating factors of defilement by taking into account the generally permeating factors in the state of being defiled (*kliṣṭa*).

[Question:] – Is a generally permeating factor (*mahābhūmika*) also a permeating factor of defilement (*kleśamahābhūmika*)? <163>

[Answer:] – There are four alternatives (tetralemma):

1. sensation (*vedanā*), ideation (*saṃjñā*), intention (*cetanā*), contact (*sparśa*) and predilection (*chanda*) are generally permeating factors only;
2. non-faith (*aśraddhya*), slackness (*kauśīdya*), ignorance (*avidyā*), restlessness (*auddhatya*) and non-diligence or heedlessness (*pramāda*) are permeating factors of defilement only;
3. mindfulness (*smṛti*), concentration (*samādhi*), understanding (*prajñā*), mental application (*manaskāra*) and resolve (*adhimokṣa*), [i.e., forgetfulness, distraction, non-introspection, incorrect mental application, false resolve,[324]] belong to both categories;
4. the other factors (i.e., wholesome permeating factors, etc.) are foreign to both categories.

Certain masters (MVŚ, 220a22) maintain that distraction (*vikṣepa*) is not false concentration (*mithyāsamādhi*): the alternatives or categories are then established differently; distraction is added to the second category, and concentration is taken out from the third.

B.1.1.3.cb. *The omission of torpor (styāna) in the list of the Mūla Abhidharma;*[325] *F 163–64*

As for the following remark [see above]: "The *Mūla Abhidharma* omits torpor (*styāna*) in its enumeration of the permeating factors of defilement (*kleśamahābhūmika*)", it is [nevertheless] accepted (*iṣyate*) that torpor is associated with all defilements [*kleśa*].

[Question:] – If torpor is omitted in the list, {6 b} is this my fault (*mamāparādha*) or the fault of the author of the Abhidharma (*ābhidhārmika* = *abhidharmakāra*)? <164>

The Ābhidhārmikas[326] explain the omission: – Torpor should be mentioned; it is not mentioned because it is favorable [*anuguṇa*] to concentration (*samādhi*). In fact, [we Ābhidhārmikas] declare that persons who are habitually given to torpor (*styānacarita*), i.e., dull persons, realize concentration quicker [*kṣipratara*] than persons who are habitually given to restlessness (*auddhatyacarita*), i.e., restless persons.[327]

[Objection:] – But who is dull [*styāna*] without being restless [*auddhatya*]? Who is restless without being dull? Torpor and restlessness always go together [*sahacariṣṇu*].

[Answer by the Ābhidhārmikas:] – Yes, torpor and restlessness always go together. But the term *-carita* indicates excess (*adhimātra*). The persons in whom torpor dominates are called *dull*, even though they are also restless.

[Response by the author:] – We know this as well as you; but it is because of their nature that one classifies the factors (*dharma*) in diverse categories. It is thus established that [only] six factors are permeating factors of defilement, because they alone arise with any defiled thought.

B.1.1.4. *The two unwholesome permeating factors (akuśalamahābhūmika);*[328] *F 164*

26cd. **(1) Non-modesty and (2) shamelessness occur always and exclusively in unwholesome thought.**[329]

These two factors [i.e., non-modesty (*āhrīkya*) and shamelessness (*anapatrāpya*)]—being defined below (ii. 32)—always occur in unwholesome thought. {7 a} Therefore they are called *unwholesome permeating factors* (*akuśalamahābhūmika*).[330]

B.1.1.5. *The factors of defilement of restricted scope (parīttakleśabhūmika);*[331] *F 164–65*

27. **(1) Anger (*krodha*),**[332] **(2) enmity (*upanāha*),**[333] **(3) dissimulation (*śāṭhya*),**[334]

(4) jealousy or envy (*īrṣya*),[335] (5) (depraved) opinionatedness (*pradāśa*),[336] (6) concealment (*mrakṣa*),[337] (7) avarice (*mātsarya*),[338] (8) deceit (*māyā*),[339] (9) pride (*mada*),[340] and (10) harmfulness (*vihiṃsā*),[341] etc., are the factors of defilement of restricted scope (*parīttakleśabhūmika*).[342]

BAB.1.1.5.a. *The meaning of the term* parīttakleśabhūmīka;[343] *F 164–65*

They are thus called because they have the small defilement (*parīttakleśa*) for their stage (*bhūmi*). <165> By *small defilement* (*parītta* = *alpaka*) one should understand ignorance (*avidyā*; iii. 28cd), i.e., isolated ignorance (*kevalā avidyā*) or independent ignorance (*āveṇikī avidyā*) (v. 14), not associated with attachment [*rāga*], etc.

They are conjoined with ignorance alone, (1) with the ignorance that is abandoned by the path of cultivation (*bhāvanāmārga*; *bhāvanāheya*), (2) with the ignorance that pertains to the stage of mental consciousness or mental stage [*manobhūmika*]. This is why they are called *factors of defilement of restricted scope* (*parīttakleśabhūmika*).[344]

They will be studied in the fifth chapter (v. 46ff.).

BAB.1.1.6. *The undetermined factors (aniyata);*[345] *F 165*

We have studied five categories of thought-concomitants [i.e., the generally permeating factors, the wholesome permeating factors, etc.]. There are other thought-concomitants which are undetermined (*aniyata*), which are sometimes associated with a wholesome [*kuśala*] thought, sometimes with an unwholesome [*akuśala*] or non-defined [*avyākṛta*] thought:

1. regret (*kaukṛtya*; *'gyod pa*) (ii. 28);[346]
2. sleepiness (*middha*; *gnyid*) (v. 47; vii. 11d);[347]
3. initial inquiry (*vitarka*; *rtog pa*) (ii. 33);[348]
4. investigation (*vicāra*; *dpyod pa*) (ii. 33);[349]

etc., [i.e.:[350]

5. attachment (*rāga*; *'dod chags*) (iii. 3cd; v. 2bd);[351]
6. hostility (*pratigha*; *khong khro*);[352]
7. conceit (*māna*; *nga rgyal*) (ii. 30b; v. 10ab);[353]
8. doubt (*vicikitsā*; *the tshom*)[354]]. {7 b}

.1.2. *Which thought-concomitants arise in association with which thought?*[355] *F 165–69*

.1.2.1. *Realm of desire: The five classes of thought & the number of associated thought-concomitants;*[356] *F 165–68*

[357]How many thought-concomitants [*caitta*] arise necessarily [*avaśya*] with each thought [*citta*] of each class, with the wholesome, unwholesome and non-defined thought?

There are five classes [*vidha*] of thought in the realm of desire:

1. wholesome (*kuśala*) thought constitutes one class;

2–3. unwholesome (*akuśala*) thought constitutes two classes, that is, according to whether it is:

- "independent" (*āveṇikī*), i.e., associated with ignorance (*avidyā*) alone, or
- associated with the other defilements, i.e., attachment (*rāga*), etc.;

4–5. non-defined (*avyākṛta*) thought, i.e., [thought that is] unproductive in regard to retribution, constitutes two classes according to whether it is:

- obscured (*nivṛta*),[358] i.e., associated with the afflicted view of self (*satkāyadṛṣṭi*) or with the afflicted view of holding to an extreme (*antagrāhadṛṣṭi*)[359] (v. 3), or
- unobscured (*anivṛta*), i.e., an effect of retribution (*vipākaja*), etc. (i. 37; ii. 71).[360]

.1.2.1.a. *The class of wholesome thought & the number of associated thought-concomitants;*[361] *F 165–67*

28. **Since it is always associated with initial inquiry and investigation, thought in the realm of desire, when it is wholesome, always involves twenty-two thought-concomitants [i.e., ten generally permeating factors, ten wholesome permeating factors, initial inquiry, investigation]. Sometimes regret should be added.**[362] <166>

Thought in the realm of desire is always [*avaśya*] associated with initial inquiry (*vitarka*) and with investigation (*vicāra*) (ii. 33ab). This thought, when it is wholesome, [necessarily (*avaśya*)] involves twenty-two thought-concomitants: ten generally permeating factors (*mahābhūmika*); ten wholesome permeating factors (*kuśala-mahābhūmika*); plus two undetermined factors (*aniyata*), namely, initial inquiry and investigation.

When wholesome thought involves regret (*kaukṛtya*), the total rises to twenty-three thoughts. {8 a}

BAB.1.2.1.aa. *Regret (kaukṛtya);*[363] *F 166–67*

[Question:] – What does the term *kaukṛtya*[364] signify?

[Answer:] – *Kaukṛtya* in the strict sense of the word refers to the nature of that which is badly done (*kukṛtabhāva*), but here *kaukṛtya* means a thought-concomitant which has *kaukṛtya* in the strict sense of the word for its cognitive object (*ālambana*), i.e., it means remorse (*vipratisāra*) relative to that which is badly done.

In the same way, (1) the gate of liberation (*vimokṣamukha*) which has emptiness (*śūnyatā*) or the absence of self (*ātman*) for its cognitive object is called *emptiness* (*śūnyatā*) (viii. 24–25); (2) the non-greed (*alobha*) which has the loathsome (*aśubhā*; vi. 11cd) for its cognitive object is called the *loathsome* (*aśubhā*).

In the same way, it is commonly said that the whole village [*grāma*], the whole town, the whole country [*deśa*], the whole universe has come together, designating in this way the inhabitants (*sthānin*, *āśrayin*) by the name of the habitat (*sthāna*; *āśraya*).

Kaukṛtya in the strict sense of the word, [i.e., the badly done,] is the basis, the *raison d'être* of remorse; thus remorse is termed *kaukṛtya*. For the effect receives the name of its cause, as for example, in the text: <167>

> The six sense-spheres of [the mental factor called] *contact* (*sparśāyatana*) [i.e., the six sense-faculties] are to be known as the *former action* (*paurāṇaṃ karma*).[365]

[Question:] – But how then can the regret that has an action not done [*akṛta*] for its cognitive object be designated by the name *kaukṛtya*, "regret as the badly done"?

[Answer:] – Because one says: "Not to have done this action was badly done by me", designating in this way an omission as "done", "badly done".

[Question:] – When is regret wholesome [*kuśala*]? [When is it unwholesome?]

[Answer:] – [Regret is wholesome] when it is relative (1) to an omitted wholesome action, (2) to a committed unwholesome action.

[Regret] is unwholesome when it is relative (1) to an omitted unwholesome action, (2) to a committed wholesome action.

These two kinds of regret both rest on [*adhiṣṭhāna*] the two categories of action. {8 b}

.1.2.1.b. *The two classes of unwholesome thought & the number of associated thought-concomitants;*[366] *F 167–68*

.1.2.1.ba. *Unwholesome thought associated with only ignorance or afflicted views: twenty thought-concomitants;*[367] *F 167*

29ab. **[In the realm of desire,] unwholesome thought involves twenty thought-concomitants when it is (1) independent [i.e., associated with ignorance but not associated with attachment, etc.] or (2) associated with afflicted views.**[368]

1. Independent (*āveṇika*) thought is thought associated with ignorance (*avidyā*; v. 1) [only (*kevala*)], not associated with other defilements, i.e., attachment, (*rāga*), etc.[369]

2. Unwholesome thought associated with afflicted views (*dṛṣṭi*) is thought associated with (i) false view (*mithyādṛṣṭi*) or (ii) esteeming of (such things as bad) views (*dṛṣṭiparāmarśa*) or (iii) the overesteeming of (such things as) morality and certain types of spiritual practices (*śīlavrataparāmarśa*) (v. 3); [on the other hand,] thought associated with afflicted view of self (*satkāyadṛṣṭi*) and with the afflicted view of holding to an extreme (*antagrāhadṛṣṭi*) is not unwholesome (*akuśala*), but obscured-non-defined (*nivṛtāvyākṛta*).

In these two cases, unwholesome thought involves [twenty thought-concomitants]: ten generally permeating factors (*mahābhūmika*), six permeating factors of defilement (*kleśamahābhūmika*), two unwholesome permeating factors (*akuśalamahābhūmika*), plus two undetermined factors (*aniyata*), namely, initial inquiry (*vitarka*) and investigation (*vicāra*).

Afflicted view (*dṛṣṭi*) does not count, since afflicted view is a certain understanding (*prajñā*; i. 41cd), and understanding is a generally permeating factor.[370]

.1.2.1.bb. *Unwholesome thought associated with one defilement or one subsidiary defilement or regret: twenty-one or twenty-two thought concomitants;*[371] *F 167–68*

29cd. **[In the realm of desire, unwholesome thought involves] twenty-one thought-concomitants, when it is associated [either] (1) with one of four defilements [i.e., either with attachment or hostility or conceit or doubt] [or] (2) with anger, etc. [i.e., with one of the subsidiary defilements] [or] (3) with regret.**[372]

1. Associated either with attachment [*rāga*] or hostility [*pratigha*] or conceit [*māna*] or doubt [*vicikitsā*] (v. 1), unwholesome thought involves twenty-one

thought-concomitants, the same [twenty thought-concomitants] as above, plus attachment or hostility, etc. {9 a} <168>

2. Associated with anger [*krodha*], etc., [unwholesome thought involves twenty-one thought-concomitants,] i.e., [the same twenty thought-concomitants as above,] plus one of the subsidiary defilements (*upakleśa*) enumerated above, ii. 27.

[3. Even with regret (*kaukṛtya*), (unwholesome thought involves) twenty-one thought-concomitants, regret being the twenty-first thought-concomitant.]

BAB.1.2.1.c. *The two classes of the non-defined thought & the number of associated thought-concomitants;*[373] *F 168*

30ab. **[In the realm of desire,] (1) non-defined thought involves eighteen thought-concomitants when it is obscured; (2) non-defined thought involves twelve thought-concomitants in the contrary case [i.e., when it is unobscured].**[374]

BAB.1.2.1.ca. *Obscured-non-defined thought: eighteen thought-concomitants;*[375] *F 168*

In the realm of desire, the non-defined thought, i.e., [the thought that is] unproductive in regard to retribution, is obscured [*nivṛtā*], i.e., covered by defilement (*nivṛta* = *kleśācchādita*), when it is associated (1) with the afflicted view of self (*satkāya-dṛṣṭi*) or (2) with the afflicted view of holding to an extreme (*antagrāhadṛṣṭi*). This thought involves [eighteen thought-concomitants]: ten generally permeating factors (*mahābhūmika*), six permeating factors of defilement (*kleśamahābhūmika*), plus initial inquiry (*vitarka*) and investigation (*vicāra*).

BAB.1.2.1.cb. *Unobscured-non-defined thought: twelve thought-concomitants;*[376] *F 168*

Unobscured [*anivṛtā*], non-defined [*avyākṛta*] thought involves twelve thought-concomitants: ten generally permeating factors, one initial inquiry, one investigation.

The Foreign Masters [*bahirdeśaka*] believe that regret [*kaukṛtya*] can be non-defined, for example, in a dream [*svapna*]. – Unobscured-non-defined thought associated with non-defined regret will [thus] involve thirteen thought-concomitants.

BAB.1.2.1.d. *Sleepiness (middha) & the number of associated thought-concomitants;*[377] *F 168*

30cd. **Sleepiness is not in contradiction to any category [i.e., wholesome, unwholesome or non-defined]; wherever it occurs, it increases the number by one.**[378]

Sleepiness (*middha*; v. 47, vii. 11d) can be wholesome, unwholesome, non-defined. The thought with which it is associated will thus involve (1) twenty-three thought-concomitants instead of twenty-two, (2) twenty-four thought-concomitants instead of twenty-three, (3) etc., according to whether it is (1) wholesome and free from regret, (2) wholesome and accompanied by regret, (3) etc. {9 b}

▲B.1.2.2. *The higher realms: the meditations (dhyāna) & the absence of thought-concomitants;*[379] *F 168–69*

31. **(1) In the first meditation, the unwholesome thought-concomitants, regret and sleepiness are absent; (2) beyond that, in the intermediate meditation, initial inquiry is also absent; (3) beyond that, [i.e., in the second meditation and above, up to and including the realm of immateriality,] in addition, investigation, etc., [i.e., dissimulation and deceit, are absent].**[380] <169>

1. In the first meditation (*dhyāna*):

   i. [the unwholesome thought-concomitants:] hostility (*pratigha*; v. 1); the series of anger [*krodha*], [enmity (*upanāha*), jealousy or envy (*īrṣya*), depraved opinionatedness (*pradāśa*), concealment (*mrakṣa*), avarice (*mātsarya*), harmfulness (*vihiṃsa*) (ii. 27),] with the exception of dissimulation (*śāṭhya*), pride (*mada*) and deceit (*māyā*); the two unwholesome permeating thought-concomitants (*akuśalamahābhūmika*), i.e., non-modesty [*āhrīkya*] and shamelessness [*anapatrāpya*] (ii. 32), are absent; plus
   ii. regret [*kaukṛtya*], since dissatisfaction [*daurmanasya*; ii. 8bc] is lacking, and
   iii. sleepiness [*middha*], since material food [*kavaḍīkāra āhāra*; iii. 38c] is lacking.

The other thought-concomitants of the realm of desire exist in the first meditation.[381]

2. In the intermediate meditation [*dhyānantara*], in addition, initial inquiry (*vitarka*) is absent.

3. In the second meditation (*dhyāna*) and above, up to and including the realm of immateriality, in addition, investigation (*vicāra*), dissimulation [*śāṭhya*] and deceit [*māyā*] are absent.[382] Pride (*mada*) exists in the three realms of existence (v. 53cd).

According to the Sūtra,[383] dissimulation and deceit exist up to the world of Brahmā, but not above the heavens in which the sentient beings exist in relationship [*saṃbandha*] with an assembly (*parṣad*). {10 a} Mahābrahmā, while sitting in his assembly, was asked by *bhikṣu* Aśvajit:

> Where do the four fundamental material elements [*mahābhūta*] completely disappear?

Incapable of answering, he answered deviatingly by boasting:

> I am Brahmā, the great Brahmā,[384] the Sovereign [*īśvara*], the Maker [*kartṛ*], the Creator [*nirmātṛ*], the Emanator [*sraṣṭṛ*], the Nourisher [*sṛja*], the Father of all [*pitṛbhūta*].

Later, leading Aśvajit out of the gathering, he advised him to return to the Master and to ask him.[385]

BAB.1.3. *Drawing distinctions between similar thought-concomitants;*[386] *F 169–76*

BAB.1.3.1. *The distinction between non-modesty (ahrī) & shamelessness (anapatrāpya);*[387] *F 169–71*

BAB.1.3.1.a. *Definitions; F 169–71*

We have seen how many thought-concomitants are associated with each type of thought in the three realms of existence. We have to specify [the difference] between thought-concomitants enumerated above. <170>

What is the difference [*nānākāraṇa*] between non-modesty (*ahrī*) and shamelessness (*anapatrāpya*)?

32a. Non-modesty is disrespect.[388]

Lack of respect (*agauravatā*), {10 b} i.e., lack of veneration (*apratīśatā*),[389] lack of fearful submission (*abhayavaśavartitā*) (1) with regard to the qualities [*guṇa*] (loving-kindness [*maitrī*], compassion [*karuṇā*], etc.) of oneself and others, and (2) with regard to the persons endowed with these qualities [*guṇavant*] (*ācāra-gocaragauravādisampanna*), is what is meant by *āhrīkya*, *ahrī*, a mental factor opposed to respect (*gaurava*, *sagauravatā*, *sapratīśatā*, *sabhayavaśavartitā*).

32ab. Shamelessness (*anapatrāpya* or *atrapā*) is the factor which brings it about that persons do not see the fearful consequences [*bhaya-adarśitva*] of evil.[390]

[Here] "evil" (*avadya*) means that which is condemned by the good ones [*vigarhitaṃ sadbhiḥ*].

Undesired consequences (*aniṣṭaphala*) are, in this verse (*kārikā*), called *fear* (*bhaya*), because these undesired consequences engender fear.

The condition the person is in who, when involved with evil, does not see the consequences—[more precisely,] the factor which produces this condition—is shamelessness (*anapatrāpya* or *atrapā*).

B.1.3.1.aa. *The meaning of the expression "not seeing the fearful consequences"; F 170–71*

Objection. – What do you understand by this expression "not seeing the fearful consequences" (*abhayadarśitva*)? Whether you interpret it as (1) "seeing that there are no fearful consequences" (*abhayasya darśitvam*), or as (2) "not seeing that there are fearful consequences" (*bhayasya adarśitvam*), neither of these two explanations is satisfactory. In the first case, we have a defiled understanding (*prajñā*), a wrong cognition [i.e., seeing wrongly]; in the second case, we simply have ignorance [*avidyā*] [i.e., not seeing]. <171>

[Answer:] – The expression *abhayadarśitva* signifies neither (1) seeing [*darśana*, *darśitā*; i.e., as defiled discrimination], nor (2) non-seeing [*adarśana*, *adarśitā*; i.e., as ignorance]. It describes a special factor (*dharma*) which is classified among the subsidiary defilements (*upakleśa*; v. 46), which has false view (*mithyādṛṣṭi*) and ignorance for its cause [*nimitta*], and which is called *anapatrāpya* (shamelessness) (MVŚ, 180a17).

B.1.3.1.b. *Different definitions; F 171*

According to other Masters, (1) non-modesty (*āhrīkya*) is the lack of embarrassment [*alajjana*] *vis-à-vis* oneself [*ātmāpekṣā*], when one is committing a transgression [*doṣa*]; (2) shamelessness (*anapatrāpya*) is the lack of embarrassment *vis-à-vis* others [*parāpkeṣā*], [when one is committing a transgression].[391]

[Objection:] – But in this case, how could it be possible that one considers oneself and others at the same time?

[Reply:] – We do not say that the two forms of lack of embarrassment are simultaneous [*yugapad*]:

1. there is non-modesty—an outflow of attachment (*rāganisyanda*)—when the persons do not experience embarrassment [*alajjā*] about their transgression while considering themselves;

2. there is shamelessness—an outflow of delusion (*moha*)—when they do not experience embarrassment about their transgression while considering others.

B.1.3.2. *The distinction between modesty (hrī) & shame (apatrāpya); F 171*

B.1.3.2.a. *Definitions; F 171*

(1) Modesty (*hrī*) and (2) shame (*apatrāpya*) are opposed to these two unwholesome factors (*dharma*) [i.e., non-modesty and shamelessness].[392]

Their definition, according to the first theory [F 169], is:

1. [modesty is] respect [*gauravatā*], veneration [*pratīśatā*], fearful submission [*bhayavaśavartitā*];
2. [shame is] seeing or fearing the consequences of their manifest vices [*avadye bhayadarśitā*].

[Their definition,] according to the second theory [F 171], is:

1. [modesty is] decency [or embarrassment (*lajjana*) *vis-à-vis* oneself (*ātman–apekṣā*), when one is committing a transgression (*doṣa*)];
2. [shame is] human respect [or embarrassment *vis-à-vis* others (*parāpekṣā*), when one is committing a transgression].

BAB.1.3.3. *The distinction between affection (preman) & respect (gaurava); F 171–72*

BAB.1.3.3.a. *Definitions; F 171–72*

Some believe that affection (*preman*) and respect (*gaurava*) are the same entity.

[What is the difference (*nānākāraṇa*) between affection and respect?]

32c. Affection is faith.[393]

Affection [*preman*] is of two kinds: (1) defiled (*kliṣṭa*), (2) non-defiled [*akliṣṭa*] (MVŚ, 151a8).

The first is attachment [or craving] (*rāga*; *tṛṣṇā*), for example, affection for one's wife [*dāra*] or children [*putra*].

The second is faith (*śraddhā*), for example, affection for one's teacher [*śāstṛ*], [for one's master (*guru*),] for virtuous persons [*guṇānvita*].

[Tetralemma between faith and affection:]

1. Faith may not be affection, namely, faith with regard to the truths of unsatisfactoriness and of the origin. <172>
2. Affection may not be faith, namely, defiled affection.
3. Faith may be affection, namely, faith with regard to the truths of cessation and of the path.
4. The other thought-concomitants, i.e., the factors dissociated from thought, etc., are neither faith nor affection.

According to another opinion, that is to say, ours, faith is having confidence in qualities (*guṇasaṃbhāvanā*): from this confidence arises love (*priyatā*), [which receives the name of *affection* (*preman*)]. Affection is thus not faith but the result of faith.

32c. Respect is modesty.[394]

As we have explained above (ii. 32a), respect (*gurutva*, *gaurava*) is veneration [*pratīśatā*], etc.

1. (Yet), every modesty (*hrī*) is not respect, namely, the modesty with regard to the truths of unsatisfactoriness and of the origin.[395] {11 b}

2. Modesty with regard to the truths of cessation and of the path is also respect.

According to another opinion, respect is veneration (*sapratīśatā*); from respect arises embarrassment (*lajjā*), which receives the name of *modesty* (*hrī*). Thus respect, the cause of modesty (*hrī*), is not modesty.

AB.1.3.3.b. *Tetralemma between affection & respect; F 172*

In regard to that which concerns affection [*preman*] and respect [*gaurava*], there are four alternatives (tetralemma):

1. Affection that is not respect, with regard to one's wife, one's children, one's companion in the religious life (*sārdhavihārin*), one's pupil (*antevāsin*).
2. Respect that is not affection, with regard to the master of another [*anyaguru*], to a virtuous person [*guṇānviteṣu*], etc.
3. Respect that is affection, with regard to one's master [*svaguru*], one's father, one's mother, etc.
4. Neither respect nor affection: with regard to other persons.

AB.1.3.3.c. *Affection and respect & the three realms; F 172–73*

32d. Both [i.e., affection and respect] exist in the realm of desire and the realm of fine-materiality.[396]

Affection [*preman*] and respect [*gaurava*] are absent in the realm of immateriality. <173>

[Objection:] – But you have said that affection is faith (*śraddhā*), that respect is modesty (*hrī*): now, faith and modesty are wholesome permeating factors (*kuśala-mahābhūmika*; ii. 25): thus affection and respect should exist in the realm of immateriality.

[Answer:] – Affection and respect are of two kinds: (1) relative to factors (*dharma*) or (2) relative to persons [*pudgala*]. The text refers to the second kind; the first kind exists in the three realms of existence.

BAB.1.3.4. *The distinction between initial inquiry (vitarka) & investigation (vicāra); F 173–76*

BAB.1.3.4.a. *Definitions of the Vaibhāṣikas; F 173*

33ab. Initial inquiry and investigation are grossness and subtleness of thought, [respectively].[397] {12 a}

Grossness (*audārikatā*), i.e., the gross state, of thought [*citta*], is called *initial inquiry* (*vitarka*; i. 33ab; ii, F 165).

Subtleness (*sūkṣmatā*), i.e., the subtle state, of thought, is called *investigation* (*vicāra*; ii, F 165).

BAB.1.3.4.aa. *Objections to these definitions; F 173–74*

[Objection:] – How can initial inquiry and investigation be associated (*saṃprayukta*) with thought both at the same time? Can thought be gross and subtle at the same time?

[Answer:] – According to one opinion,[398] (1) investigation is to be compared to cold water, (2) thought is to be compared to fermented curd which floats on the surface of this cold water, (3) initial inquiry is to be compared to the warmth of the light rays of the sun which shine upon the fermented curd. Because of the water and the sun, the fermented curd is not too melted [*ativilī*; *atidrava*] nor too coagulated [*atiśyā*; *atighana*]. In the same way, initial inquiry and investigation are associated (*yukta*) with a thought: thought is neither too subtle [*atisukṣma*] because of initial inquiry, nor too gross [*atyaudārika*] because of investigation.

[Reply:] – But, we would say, it follows from this explanation that initial inquiry and investigation are not grossness and subtleness of thought but the cause (*nimitta*) of its grossness, the cause of its subtleness: the cold water and the warm light rays of the sun are not the solidified state [*śyanatva*] and the fluid state [*vilīnatva*] of the ghee but the causes of these two states. <174>

Other objections are presented: – Grossness and subtleness of thought are relative [*āpekṣika*] factors. They involve many degrees: (1) [in regard to different stages,] the thought of the first meditation (*dhyāna*) is subtle in relation to the thought of the realm of desire, but gross in relation to the thought of the second meditation; (2) in regard to the same stage, the qualities and the defilements can be more or less gross or subtle, since they divide into nine categories. Thus, if initial inquiry and investigation are grossness and subtleness of thought, we would be forced to admit that they both exist up to the highest stage of the realm of immateriality.[399] But they have ceased from the second meditation onwards. – On top of that, grossness and subtleness cannot establish a specific difference (*jātibheda*): thus one cannot differentiate initial inquiry and investigation.

AB.1.3.4.b. *The definitions of (the Sautrāntika); F 174*

According to another opinion, (according to the Sautrāntika,[400]) initial inquiry and investigation are "constituents for speech" [*vāksaṃskāra*].[401] The Sūtra says in fact:

> It is after having initially inquired, after having investigated (*vitarkya*; *vicārya*) that one speaks, not without having initially inquired, not without having investigated.[402]

The constituents for speech that are gross are called *vitarkas*; {12 b} those that are subtle are called *vicāras*. [According to this explanation, by *vitarka* and *vicāra* one should not understand two distinct factors, but rather the collection of thought and thought-concomitants which provoke speech and which are sometimes gross, sometimes subtle.]

AB.1.3.4.c. *Can initial inquiry and investigation be simultaneous? F 174–76*

(The Vaibhāṣika:) – What contradiction [*virodha*] is there in the case where two factors (*dharma*)—the first (i.e., *vitarka*) being gross and the second (i.e., *vicāra*) being subtle—are associated with one and the same thought?

(The Sautrāntika:[403]) – There would not be any contradiction if these two factors had a specific difference or difference in type [*jātibheda*];[404] for example, sensation (*vedanā*) and ideation (*saṃjñā*)—although the first is gross and the second subtle (i. 22)—can coexist. But, when considering the same type [*jāti*], two states, a weak state and a strong state [*mṛdhvadhimatratā*], a gross state and a subtle state [*audārika-sūkṣmatā*], cannot coexist.

(The Vaibhāṣika:) – There is a specific difference between initial inquiry and investigation. <175>

(The Sautrāntika:) – What is this difference?

(The Vaibhāṣika.) – This difference is difficult to speak about [*durvaca*]; but it is manifested (*vyakta*) through the weakness and strength of thought (*mṛdvadhimātratā*).[405]

(The Sautrāntika:) – The weakness and strength of thought does not demonstrate the presence of two specifically different factors, since one and the same type is sometimes weak, sometimes strong.

According to another opinion—i.e., ours—initial inquiry and investigation are not associated with one and the same [*ekatra*] thought. They exist in turn.[406]

(The Vaibhāṣika would object:) – The first meditation (*dhyāna*) is connected [*yukta*] with five members (viii. 7) including initial inquiry and investigation. <176>

We answer: – The first meditation is connected with five members in the sense that five members occur in that stage, i.e., the stage of the first meditation; but a particular moment of the first meditation is connected with only four members, namely, (1) joy (*prīti*), (2) pleasure (*sukha*), (3) concentration (*samādhi*), plus (4) initial inquiry or investigation.

BAB.1.3.5. *The distinction between conceit (māna) & pride (mada); F 176*

BAB.1.3.5.a. *Definitions; F 176*

What difference [*nānākāraṇa*] is there between conceit (*māna*) and pride (*mada*)?

33b. **Conceit is elevation.**[407]

Elevation of thought (*cetasa unnatiḥ*) is in respect to others. Measuring (*mā*) the superiority in regard to qualities which one has or which one believes one has over others, one elevates oneself and depreciates others (v. 10a).

33cd. **On the contrary, pride is the exhausting oneself of the thought of those who are enamoured with their own qualities.**[408]

Because of its being enamoured [*raktasya*] with their own qualities, thought [at first] prides itself, exalts itself and [through that] abolishes or exhausts itself [*paryādāna*].[409] {13 a}

According to other masters, in the same way that wine [*madya*] produces a distinctive joyous excitement (*saṃpraharṣaviśeṣa*) called *intoxication*, so too does the attachment [*rāga*] which persons have for their own qualities.[410]

BAB.1.4. *Thought and thought-concomitants;*[411] *F 176–78*

BAB.1.4.1. *Mind (citta), mind (manas), consciousness (vijñāna): different in name but one in meaning;*[412] *F 176–77*

We have defined thought (*citta*) (i. 16) and thought-concomitants [*caitta*; ii. 23–34]. We have seen in which categories the thought-concomitants are classified, in what number they arise together, what their different characteristics are. Thought and thought-concomitants receive different names in the Scriptures.[413] [As for thought:]

34ab. **(1) Thought (*citta*), (2) mind (*manas*),[414] and (3) consciousness (*vijñāna*), these names designate the same object-referent [*ekārtha*].**[415] <177>

1. The mind is named *citta* (T. *sems*; thought) because it accumulates or collects together (*cinoti*).[416]

2. It is named *manas* (T. *yid*; mind) because it considers or thinks (*manute*).[417]

3. It is named *vijñāna* (T. *rnam par shes pa*; consciousness) because it cognizes its cognitive object (*ālambanaṃ vijānāti*).[418]

Some say:[419]

1. It is named *citta* (thought) because it is variegated (*citra*) [or is accumulated (*cita*)] with good and bad elements [*śubhāśubhairdhātubhiḥ*].[420]

2. [It is named] *manas* (mental faculty; i. 17) insofar as it is the basis [*tadevāśraya-bhūta*], i.e., of the thought that follows it.

3. [It is named] *vijñāna* (consciousness) insofar as it is based on (*āśritabhūta*) the sense-faculty and the object. {13 b}

These three names thus express different meanings, but they designate the same object-referent.

B.1.4.2. *Thought and thought-concomitants: "having a basis", etc.;*[421] *F 177–78*

34bd. (In the same way,) thought and thought-concomitants are (1) "having a basis", (2) "having a cognitive object", (3) "having an aspect or mode of activity", (4) "associated".[422]

These four different names: "having a basis", etc., [express different meanings, but] designate the same object-referent.

Thought and thought-concomitants are named:

1. "having a basis" (*sāśraya*), because they are based on sense-faculties [i.e., eye sense-faculty, etc., mental faculty];
2. "having a cognitive object" (*sālambana*; i. 34), because they seize their object-field (*viṣayagrahaṇa*);
3. "having an aspect or a mode of activity" (*sākāra*), because they take on [*ākaraṇa*] a mode or the same features [*prakāra*] according to the cognitive object [*ālambana*];[423] <178>
4. "associated" (*saṃprayukta*), i.e., equivalent and united, because they are equivalent (*sama*) with each other and not dissociated (*aviprayukta*) from each other.

B.1.4.3. *Thought and thought-concomitants: the five equivalences;*[424] *F 178*

How are they associated (*saṃprayukta*), i.e., equivalent and united?[425]

34d. **[Thought and the thought-concomitants are associated] in five ways.**[426]

Thought and thought-concomitants are associated because of five samenesses or equivalences (*samatā*):

1. equivalence with respect to basis [or sense-faculty] (*āśraya*; *rten*);
2. equivalence with respect to cognitive object (*ālambana*; *dmigs*);
3. equivalence with respect to aspect or a mode of activity (*ākāra*; *rnam pa*);[427]
4. equivalence with respect to time [of occurrence of the activity of thought and thought-concomitants] (*kāla*; *dus*);
5. equivalence with respect to the number of real entities [or the singular instance of the occurrence of a real entity or the status as real entities] (*dravya*; *rdzas*).

That is to say: the thought-concomitants (sensation, etc.) and thought are associated:

1–3. because they share the same basis, the same cognitive object and the same aspect or mode of activity;

4. because they [arise and pass away] simultaneously;
5. because, in this association, each kind is represented by only one real entity (*dravya*): only one thought can arise at any given moment, and one sensation (*ekaṃ vedanādravyam*), one ideation [*saṃjñā*], one thought-concomitant of each kind are associated with this one single thought. (See ii. 53cd).

We have explained thought and thought-concomitants in detail together with their features or categories.[428]

BAB.2. *The formations dissociated from thought (cittaviprayuktasaṃskāra): fourteen types;*[429] *F 178–244*

[The law of the simultaneous arising of the formations dissociated from thought must now be described.]

What are the formations (*saṃskāra*) dissociated from thought (*cittaviprayukta*)?

35–36a. **The formations dissociated from thought are (1) possession, (2) non-possession, (3) [group] homogeneity, (4) the state of non-ideation, (5–6) the two attainments, (7) vitality [faculty], (8–11) characteristics, (12) collection of names, etc. [*ādi*], [i.e., (13) collection of phrases, (14) collection of syllables,] and those of that type [*ca*].**[430] {14 a} <179>

.2.1. *The name "formations dissociated from thought"; F 179*

These factors (*dharma*) [or formations (*saṃskāra*)] are not associated (*saṃprayukta*; see above ii. 34d) with thought and they do not have matter or form (*rūpa*) as their intrinsic nature, but they are included within the aggregate of formations (*saṃskāra-skandha*; i. 15), hence [these formations] are called *cittaviprayukta saṃskāra* (1) because they are dissociated [*viprayukta*] from thought and (2) because, being non-material, they resemble thought [*citta*].

[The formations dissociated from thought will be discussed under seven headings:[431]]

2.2. Possession (*prāpti*; ii. 36b, 37) and non-possession (*aprāpti*; ii. 36b, 39c); F 179
2.3. Group homogeneity (*nikāyasabhāgatā*); F 195
2.4. State of non-ideation (*āsaṃjñika*); F 198
2.5. Two attainments: attainment of non-ideation (*asaṃjñisamāpatti*) and attainment of cessation (*nirodhasamāpatti*); F 200
2.6. Vitality faculty (*jīvitendriya*); F 214
2.7. Characteristics (*lakṣaṇa*): origination, deterioration, duration, impermanence; F 222
2.8. Collection of names (*nāmakāya*), collection of phrases (*padakāya*), collection of syllables (*vyañjanakāya*); F 238–44

.2.2. *Possession (prāpti) & non-possession (aprāpti);*[432] *F 179–95*

1. Definitions of possession and non-possession; F 179
2. Possible object of possession and non-possession; F 179
3. Existential status of possession and non-possession; F 181
4. Modes of possession: time periods, moral quality, realms of existence, relation to the path, etc.; F 186
5. Modes of non-possession: time periods, moral quality, realms of existence, relation to the path, etc.; F 190
6. The root-possession (*mūlaprāpti*) & the secondary possession (*anuprāpti*); F 194
7. The increasing number of possessions from moment to moment; p. 194
8. The non-material and accommodating nature of the possessions; p. 195

.2.2.1. *Definitions of possession and non-possession;*[433] *F 179*

36b. **Possession refers to (1) acquisition [*lābha*] and (2) accompaniment [*samanvaya*].**[434]

Possession (*prāpti*) is of two kinds:

1. acquisition (*lābha*; *pratilambha*) (i) of that which has not been attained (*aprāpta*) or (ii) of that which has been lost (*vihīna*) [and re-acquired];

2. accompaniment (*samanvāgama*; *samanvaya*) of that which, having [already] been attained or acquired [*pratilabdha*], has not been lost.

[It is established that] non-possession (*aprāpti*) is the opposite [*viparyaya*] [of possession].[435]

BAB.2.2.2. *Possible objects of possession and non-possession; F 179–80*

36cd. Possession and non-possession apply only (1) to the factors that fall within one's own life-stream and (2) to the two cessations [i.e., cessation due to deliberation and cessation not due to deliberation].[436] <180>

BAB.2.2.2.a. *Conditioned factors as possible objects;[437] F 180*

1. When a conditioned (*saṃskṛta*) factor (*dharma*) "falls within one's own life-stream" (*svasaṃtānapatita*), there is possession (*prāpti*) or non-possession (*aprāpti*) with respect to this factor.[438]

2. When a conditioned factor "falls within the life-stream of another person" [*parasaṃtānapatita*], there is no [possession or non-possession with respect to this factor], for no one can be accompanied by factors that fall within another life-stream.

3. When a conditioned factor "does not fall within any life-stream" [*asaṃtātipatita*; *asaṃtānapatita*], there is [likewise] no [possession or non-possession with respect to this factor], for no one can be accompanied by factors non-indicative of sentient beings (*asattvākhya*; i. 10b).[439]

BAB.2.2.2.b. *Unconditioned factors as possible objects; F 180*

As for unconditioned (*asaṃskṛta*) factors, {14 b} there is possession (*prāpti*) [and non-possession (*aprāpti*)] of the cessation due to deliberation (*pratisaṃkhyānirodha*) and of the cessation not due to deliberation (*apratisaṃkhyānirodha*) (i. 6; ii. 55).

1. All sentient beings are accompanied by the cessation not due to deliberation with respect to factors which do not arise due to an insufficiency or deficiency of conditions [*pratyayavaikalya*].

2. The Abhidharma (*Jñānaprasthāna*, 1022a) expresses itself thus:

> Who is accompanied by pure (*anāsrava*) factors[440]? – All sentient beings.

[All sentient beings] are accompanied by the cessation due to deliberation—with the exception of (i) the noble persons (*ārya*) in the first moment of the path of insight (*ādikṣaṇastha*) who are bound by all bondages (*sakalabandhana*) and (ii) the ordinary worldlings (*pṛthagjana*) who are bound by all bondages. The remaining noble ones and ordinary worldlings are accompanied by cessation due to deliberation.[441]

3. No one is accompanied by (*samanvāgata*) space (*ākāśa*). Thus there is no possession of space.

B.2.2.2.c. *Possession and non-possession come in pairs; F 180*

According to the Vaibhāṣikas, possession and non-possession are in opposition [or come in pairs]: if there is possession (*prāpti*) of a factor, there is also non-possession (*aprāpti*).[442] As this is easy to see [and an established principle (*siddhānta*)], the stanza does not speak of it in an express manner. <181>

B.2.2.3. *Existential status of possession & non-possession; F 181–86*

(The Sautrāntika[443]) denies the existence of a factor (*dharma*) called *possession* (*prāpti*).

How does the Sarvāstivādin-Vaibhāṣika establish the existence of a distinct real entity (*dravyadharma*; *bhāvāntara*)[444] called *possession* (*prāpti*)?[445]

B.2.2.3.a. *(The Sarvāstivāda:) proof based on scriptural authority & its Sautrāntika refutation; F 181*

The Sarvāstivādin: – The Sūtra (*Madhyamāgama* 49, 16) says:

> Through the arising (*utpāda*), acquisition (*pratilambha*) and accompaniment (*samanvāgama*) of the ten factors characteristic of those beyond training (*aśaikṣadharma*), noble ones become persons having abandoned five members [*pañcāṅgaviprahīṇa*].[446]

(The Sautrāntika:[447]) – If you conclude the existence of possession from this text, we would comment that one could then also be accompanied (*samanvāgama*) by (1) factors non-indicative of sentient beings (*asattvākhya*) and also (2) by factors indicative of other persons (*parasattva*); [but this goes against the rule stated in ii. 36cd], for, in fact, the Sūtra (*Cakravartisūtra*) says:

> Know, O *bhikṣus*, that the wheel-turning king (*cakravartin*) is accompanied by the seven royal treasures [*ratna*]... .[448]

Now, among these royal treasures, there are (1) the royal treasure of the wheel, (2) the royal treasure of the queen, etc.

The Sarvāstivādin: – In this text, the [non-technical] expression "is accompanied by" (*samanvāgata*) signifies "mastery over" (*vaśitva*). It is said that the wheel-turning king (*cakravartin*) enjoys mastery (*vaśitva*) over the royal treasures, for they follow his desire (*kāmacāra*). But, in the Sūtra on "the accompaniment of the ten factors of a perfected being" (*daśāśaikṣadharmasamanvāgamasūtra*), the word *accompaniment* [is used in the technical sense and] designates a distinct real entity [*dravyāntara*].[449]

BAB.2.2.3.b. *The Sarvāstivāda: proof based on logical reasoning & its Sautrāntika refutation; F 181–83*

(Sautrāntika objection:[450]) – If the word "accompaniment" (*samanvāgama*) signifies "mastery" in the *Cakravartisūtra*, {15 a} how do you ascertain that, in another Sūtra, this same word designates a possession (*prāpti*), which you maintain has an intrinsic nature [*svabhāva*]? In fact: <182>

1. this possession is not discerned or directly perceived (*prajñayate*; *pratyakṣa*), (i) as this is the case for form [*rūpa*], sound [*śabda*], etc., (ii) as this is the case for attachment [*rāga*], hatred [*dveṣa*], etc.;
2. one cannot infer [*anumāna*] the existence of possession because of its effect [or activity] (*kṛtya*), as is the case for the sense-faculties, the eye sense-faculty [*cakṣus*], etc. (i. 9): for a similar effect [or activity] is not perceived [in the case of possession].

BAB.2.2.3.ba. *Possession as the cause of the arising of factors (utpattihetu); F 182*

(The Sarvāstivādin:[451]) – Wrong [*ayoga*]! Possession [*prāpti*] has an effect [or activity]. It is the cause of the arising (*utpattihetu*) of factors (*dharma*).[452]

(The Sautrāntika:[453]) – This answer is unfortunate [for the following reasons]:

1. You maintain that one can possess the two cessations (*nirodha*); now these, being unconditioned, do not arise: only conditioned factors are "caused" (i. 7d). [Thus possession cannot be the cause of the arising of the two cessations.]

2. As for the conditioned (*saṃskṛta*) factors, there is at present, in a given person, no possession (*prāpti*) (i) of factors which this person has not yet attained [*aprāpta*],[454] nor (ii) of factors of which this person has abandoned the possession by means of changing the stage of existence (*bhūmisaṃcāra*) or by means of "detachment" [*vairāgya*]:[455] the possession of the first has never existed, whereas the possession of the second has perished. Thus how could these factors arise if the cause of their arising is possession?

(The Sarvāstivādin:) – The arising of these [conditioned] factors has for its cause the possession that arises at the same time as they do (*sahajaprāptihetuka*).

(The Sautrāntika:) – A regrettable answer! If the factors arose by virtue of possession:

1. then origination [*jāti*] and the origination-of-origination [*jātijāti*] (ii. 45c) would have no function;
2. then the factors non-indicative of sentient beings (*asattvākhya*) would not arise;
3. then how could one explain the distinction among the various grades of defilements (*kleśa*)—weak [*mṛdu*], medium [*madhya*] and strong [*adhimātra*] defilement—in the case of the persons who are bound by all bondages (*sakalabandhana*): all of these persons, in fact, possess the same possessions of all defilements of the realm of desire.[456]

[The Sarvāstivādins might reply:] – This distinction [in the various grades] proceeds from causes distinct from possession (*prāpti*)? <183>

[The Sautrāntika:] – In that case, these causes [i.e., the causes distinct from possession] are the only causes of weak, medium or strong defilement; then what would be the point of assigning possession as causes? {15 b}

B.2.2.3.bb. *Possession as the cause of the distinction between states of sentient beings (vyavasthāhetu); F 183*

The Sarvāstivādin: – Who maintains that possession (*prāpti*) is the cause of the arising (*utpattihetu*) of factors? Such is not the role that we attribute to it. For us, possession is the cause which determines the state or condition [*vyavasthāhetu*] of sentient beings.[457] Let us explain: [For argument's sake,] let us suppose the non-existence of possession (*prāpti*): what distinction could there then be between (1) the noble ones (*ārya*) at the moment in which they produce a mundane (*laukika*) thought and (2) the ordinary worldlings (*pṛthagjana*)? Now the distinction consists solely in that the noble ones, even when they have a mundane thought, are in possession (*prāpti*) of a certain number of pure factors (*dharma*).

B.2.2.3.bc. *Accompaniment and non-accompaniment as distinction in the basis or person (āśrayaviśeṣa);*[458] *F 183–85*

B.2.2.3.bca. *Accompaniment and non-accompaniment of defilements; F 183*

(The Sautrāntika:[459]) – For us, the distinction [between the noble one and the ordinary worldling] is that the first has abandoned particular defilements, while the second has not abandoned them (*prahīṇāprahīṇakleśatāviśeṣa*).

The Sarvāstivādin: – Without doubt; but if one supposes the non-existence of possession (*prāpti*), how can one say that a defilement is abandoned or not abandoned? There can only be the abandonment of a defilement through disappearance (*vigama*) of the possession of this defilement; the defilement is not abandoned as long as its possession does not disappear [*avigama*].[460]

(The Doctrine of the Sautrāntikas:[461]) – To us, [the distinction between the states of] abandonment [*prahīṇa*] and non-abandonment [*aprahīṇa*] of defilements is made in terms of a specific condition or difference in the basis or person (*āśrayaviśeṣa*; ii. 5, 6, 44d [F 211]).

1. In the case of the noble ones (*ārya*), the personal basis is totally transmuted (*parāvṛtta*), becomes different from what it was by means of the power of the path (i.e., insight into the truths, cultivation). The defilement [*kleśa*], once it has been destroyed by the power of the (noble) path, is not capable of arising further. Just as grains of rice [*vrīhī*], being burned by fire [*agnidagdha*], become different from what they were before and are no longer capable of germinating, in the same way one says that the noble ones have abandoned defilements, because their whole personal basis [*āśraya*] no longer contains the seeds or potencies (*bīja*) capable of producing the defilements.[462]

2. As for the mundane path [*laukikamārga*], this path does not completely destroy the defilements; it only damages or weakens them [*upaghāta*]: [nevertheless,] one would say that ordinary worldlings (*pṛthagjana*)—who can cultivate only the mundane path—have abandoned defilements {16 a} when their basis or person contains only the seed-states [*bījabhāva*] of the defilements damaged (*upahata*) by the mentioned path.

3. In the opposite case [*viparyaya*], when the seeds are neither burned [*agnirdagdha*] nor damaged [*anupaghāta*], one says that persons have not abandoned the defilements (*aprahīṇakleśa*). <184>

One says that persons are accompanied (*samanvāgata*) by the defilements when they have not "abandoned" them in the manner which we have just explained; one says that they are not accompanied (*asamanvāgata*) by the defilements when they have abandoned them. "Accompaniment" and "non-accompaniment" are not real entities [*dravya*], but provisional entities (*prajñapti*).

So much for that which concerns the accompaniment and the non-accompaniment of the defilements (*kleśa*).

BAB.2.2.3.bcb. *Accompaniment and non-accompaniment of wholesome factors; F 184*

As for the accompaniment and the non-accompaniment of wholesome (*kuśala*) factors (*dharma*),[463] one must distinguish [two modes (*prakāra*)]:

1. the innate wholesome factors not produced through effort (*ayatnabhāvin*), which are [referred to as] those that are acquired at birth (*aupapattika, upapattilābhika*), and
2. the wholesome factors produced [only] through effort [*yatnabhāvin*], which are [referred to as] those that are acquired through preparatory effort (*prāyogika, prayogalābhika*; ii. 71b).

1.[464] We speak of a person who has accompaniment of the first factors, [i.e., the wholesome factors not produced through effort,] when the seeds of these wholesome factors have not been damaged within the person (*āśrayasya tadbījabhāvān-upaghātāt*).
When their seeds have already been damaged [*upaghāta*], one speaks of a person who has non-accompaniment of the wholesome factors. However in actual fact, whereas the seeds of defilements can be completely destroyed (*atyantaṃ samudghāta, apoddharaṇa*), as is the case with the noble ones (*ārya*), the wholesome factors never have their roots completely cut off. This qualification has to be kept in mind when one says of the persons whose wholesome roots have been cut off (*samucchinnakuśalamūla*) by false view [*mithyādṛṣṭi*] (iv. 79–80) that they have abandoned these roots because the seed-states [*bījabhāva*] of these roots—states which belonged to the person (*āśraya; saṃtati*)—have been damaged through false view (*mithyādṛṣṭi*).

2.[465] We speak of a person who has accompaniment of the second factors, i.e., the wholesome factors produced [only] through effort: through listening, reflection, cultivation, when—these factors having arisen—one's mastery and capability (*vaśitva, sāmarthyaviśeṣa*) to make them arise [again] is not damaged.

B.2.2.3.bcc. *Accompaniment & the theory of seeds*; F 184–85

Thus, that which is understood by "accompaniment", the "fact of being endowed with" (*samanvāgama*), is not a factor constituting a distinct real entity (*nānyad dravyam*), <185> namely, the alleged possession (*prāpti*) of the Sarvāstivādins, but [seeds,[466]] a certain condition (*avasthā*) of the basis or person or name-and-form (*āśraya = nāmarūpa*), that is:

1. seeds of defiled [*kliṣṭa*] factors that are not yet uprooted (*anapoddhṛta*) by the noble path (*āryamārga*);
2. seeds of defiled factors that are not yet damaged (*anupahata*) by the mundane path (*laukikamārga*);

3. seeds of innate (*aupapattika*) wholesome [*kuśala*] factors that are not yet damaged by false view [*mithyādṛṣṭi*];
4. seeds of wholesome factors produced [only] by effort (*prāyogika, yatnabhāvin*) which are to be nourished to the point of mastery (*paripuṣṭaṃ vaśitvakāle*).[467] {16 b}

When the person (*āśraya*) is in such a state, this is called *accompaniment of defilements*, etc.

The Sarvāstivadin asks: – But what should be understood by "seed" (*bīja*)?

[Answer:] – Seed (*bīja*) is that name-and-form (*nāmarūpa*; iii. 30), i.e., the complex of the five aggregates (*skandha*), which has capability [*samartha*] in the production of its own effect either directly [*sākṣāt*] or remotely [*pāramparyeṇa*] (iii, F 81);[468] [this capability becomes effective] by means of a distinctive characteristic in the transformation of the life-stream (*saṃtatipariṇāma-viśeṣa*; see also ix, F 295f.),[469] whereby:

1. "stream" (*saṃtati*) is the conditioning forces (*saṃskāra*) of the past, present and future, having the nature of cause and effect [*hetuphalabhūta*], that constitute an uninterrupted life-stream;
2. "transformation" (*pariṇāma*) of the stream is the change (*anyathātva*) [between prior and subsequent moments] within the stream, the fact that the life-stream arises differently at each moment;
3. "distinctive characteristic" (*viśeṣa*), or the culminating point of this transformation, is that (moment of this life-stream) which is capable of producing an effect immediately [*anantara*].[470]

BAB.2.2.3.bd. *Accompaniment and non-accompaniment as consent (adhivāsana); F 185–86*

The Vaibhāṣika objects: – The Sūtra says: <186>

> Those who are accompanied by greed (*lobhena samanvāgataḥ*) are not capable of producing the four applications of mindfulness (*smṛtyupasthāna*; vi. 14).

(The Sautrāntika:[471]) – In this text, "accompanied by greed" should be understood as "consent to greed" (*adhivāsana, abhyanujñāna*), or "not rejecting greed" (*avinodana, avyupaśama*). The Sūtra does not say that the persons in whom the seeds of greed occur are, [in general,] incapable of producing the applications of mindfulness; it says that the active greed makes persons, at present, incapable of producing these spiritual practices.

B.2.2.3.be. *Summary; F 186*

To sum up, in whichever manner we might understand accompaniment (*samanvāgama*), either

1. as "cause of the arising [*utpattihetu*] of factors" (F 182), or
2. as "principle of the condition [or cause of the distinction between states] [*vyavasthāhetu*] of sentient beings" (F 183), or
3. as "special state [or distinction] in the basis or person" [*āśrayaviśeṣa*] (F 183), or
4. as "consent to" [*adhivāsana*; *avinodana*] (F 186),

accompaniment appears to us not as a real entity or real factor (*dravyadharma*), but as a provisional factor (*prajñaptidharma*).

The same holds for non-accompaniment [*asamanvāgama*], which is purely and simply the negation (*pratiṣedha*) of accompaniment.

The Vaibhāṣikas say that both, possession (*prāpti*) and non-possession (*aprāpti*), are real entities [*dravya*]. Why?

Vaibhāṣikas: – Because this is our doctrine (*siddhānta*).[472]

B.2.2.4. *Modes of possession (prāpti);*[473] *F 186–90*

[This has six topics:]

a. Time periods; F 186
b. Moral quality; F 187
c. Realms of existence; F 187
d. Relation to the path; F 188
e. Factors to be abandoned and not to be abandoned; F 188
f. Particular varieties of the time periods; F 189–90

B.2.2.4.a. *Time periods & possession;*[474] *F 186–87*

37a. **The factors of the three time periods [i.e., past, present and future factors] have, [in each case,] three varieties of possession [i.e., past, present and future possession].**[475]

Past factors can be the object of three varieties of possession, i.e., past, present, future.

The same for present and future factors.[476] <187>

[For a discussion of the exceptions to this general principle, see below F 189f.]

BAB.2.2.4.b. *Moral quality & possession;*[477] *F 187*

37b. Good [*śubha*] factors, etc., [i.e., bad (*aśubha*) factors, non-defined (*avyākṛta*) factors, have, respectively, only] good possession, etc. [i.e., bad possession, non-defined possession].[478]

Wholesome [*kuśala*], unwholesome [*akuśala*], non-defined [*avyākṛta*] factors have, respectively [*yathākrama*], [only] wholesome, unwholesome, non-defined possession.

BAB.2.2.4.c. *Realms of existence & possession; F 187*

37c. The factors connected [*āpta*] to the realms of existence [i.e., the impure factors] have possession belonging [only] to their own realm [*svadhātu*].[479]

The factors connected [*āpta*] to the realms of existence [*dhātu*] are the impure (*sāsrava*) factors. The possession of a factor of the realm of desire is, itself, [only] of the realm of desire; and so forth.

37d. The possession of factors which are not connected [*anāpta*] to the realms of existence [i.e., the possession of pure factors] has four varieties.[480]

To consider this [possession] in general (*samāsena*), the possession of these factors—the pure (*anāsrava*) factors—has four varieties: (i–iii) [the possession] is connected [*samāsa*] to (one of) the three realms, (iv) [the possession] is pure [i.e., not connected to any realm].

But it is necessary to make distinctions:

1. The possession of cessation not due to deliberation (*apratisaṃkhyānirodha*) (see ii, F 180) is connected to the realm to which the persons who attain it belong [i.e., only to the three realms].
2. The possession of cessation due to deliberation (*pratisaṃkhyānirodha*) is (i–ii) [only] connected to the realm of fine-materiality (*rūpadhātu*) and {17 b} to the realm of immateriality (*ārūpyadhātu*), (iii) is pure [i.e., not connected to any realm].[481]
3. The possession of [the truth of] the (noble) path (*mārgasatya*; vi. 25d) is only pure [i.e., not connected to any realm].[482] <188>

BAB.2.2.4.d. *Relation to the path & possession; F 188*

The possession of the factors of those in training (*śaikṣa*; vi. 45b) is [only] of those in training.

The possession of the factors of those beyond training (*aśaikṣa*) is [only] of those beyond training (*aśaikṣī*).[483]

38a. The factors belonging to those neither in training nor beyond training have three varieties of possession.[484]

These factors, i.e., the factors belonging to those neither in training nor beyond training (*naivaśaikṣanāśaikṣa*; vi. 45b)—so named because they differ from the factors of those in training and from the factors of those beyond training—are impure factors [*sāsrava*] and unconditioned factors (*asaṃskṛta*).

To consider this in general, the possession of these factors is of three varieties. But it is necessary to make distinctions:

1. The possession of the impure factors [*sāsravadharma*] is [only] of those neither in training nor beyond training (*naivaśaikṣīnāśaikṣī*);
2. Likewise, the possession of the cessation not due to deliberation (*apratisaṃkhyānirodha*) and the cessation due to deliberation (*pratisaṃkhyānirodha*) attained [*prāpta*] by [the path of] the non-noble-persons [*anārya*] [is only of those neither in training nor beyond training];[485]
3. The possession of the cessation due to deliberation, (i) when attained by the [noble] path of those in training [*śaikṣamārga*], is [only] of those in training; (ii) when attained by the [noble] path of those beyond training [*aśaikṣamārga*], is [only] of those beyond training.

B.2.2.4.e. *Factors to be abandoned and not to be abandoned & possession;* F 188–89

1. The possession of the factors to be abandoned [*heya*] either by the path of insight or by the path of cultivation is abandoned, respectively, either by the path of insight or by the path of cultivation. Thus, from the point of view of abandonment, the possession [*prāpti*] belongs to the category of these factors (ii. 13).

2. As for the factors not to be abandoned [*aheya*], their possession is differentiated [*bheda*] (as follows):

38b. The factors not to be abandoned [i.e., the pure factors] have two varieties of possession [i.e., to be abandoned and not to be abandoned].[486]

The factors not to be abandoned are pure (*anāsrava*) factors (i. 40b, ii. 13d). <189>

1. The possession of the cessation not due to deliberation (*apratisaṃkhyānirodha*) is to be abandoned by the path of cultivation (*bhāvanāheya*) [i.e., is not "not to be abandoned"].

The same for the possession of the cessation due to deliberation (*pratisaṃkhyā-nirodha*) attained by [the path of] the non-noble-persons [*anārya*].

2. But the possession of the cessation due to deliberation attained by the path of the noble ones is pure, i.e., not to be abandoned [*aheya*]. {18 a}

The same for the possession of the noble path [and of the truth of the (noble) path, i.e., it is pure and not to be abandoned].[487]

BAB.2.2.4.f. *Particular varieties of the time periods & possession; F 189–90*

BAB.2.2.4.fa. *Possession of the unobscured-non-defined factors & the time periods; F 189–90*

We have established the general principle [*utsarga*; ii. 37a]: "The factors of the three time periods have, [in each case,] three varieties of possession [i.e., past, present and future]." [Since there are exceptions (*apavāda*) to this general principle,] we must be more specific.

38cd. The possession of [unobscured,] non-defined factors arises [only] simultaneously [*sahaja*] with them, with the exception of the possession of (1–2) the two superknowledges [of seeing and hearing] and of (3) the [thought of supernormal] "emanation".[488]

The possession of unobscured-non-defined factors (*anivṛtāvyākṛta*) arises [only (*eva*)] simultaneously [*sahaja*] with those factors (*dharma*), i.e., it does not arise either prior to them [*agraja*] or subsequent to them [*paścātkālaja*]. When they are past, the possession is [only] past, when they are future, the possession is [only] future. This is due to the weakness [*durbalatva*][489] of these [unobscured-non-defined] factors.

This rule, [however,] does not apply to all of the unobscured-non-defined factors. [Exception must be made for (*varjayitvā*)] (1–2) the superknowledge of the [divine] eye and of the [divine] ear (*divyacakṣurabhijñā*, *divyaśrotrābhijñā*; vii. 45ab) and (3) the thought of emanation (*nirmāṇacitta*), which are strong (*balavat*), because they are accomplished by an extraordinary or special effort (*prayogaviśeṣa*); therefore, [even though they are included among these factors whose nature is unobscured (*anivṛta*) and non-defined (*avyākṛta*),] they have possession which arises prior to [*pūrva*], subsequent to [*paścāt*] and simultaneously with [*saha*] them.[490] <190>

Certain masters[491] maintain that the possession of the unobscured-non-defined factors of skill in arts and crafts (*śailpasthānika*) and proper deportment (*airyāpathika*) categories (ii. 72)—when they have been the object of an intense practice (*atyartham abhyastam = bhṛśam ātmanaḥ kṛtam*)—arises [not only simultaneously with] but also prior to and subsequent to them. {18 b}

3.2.2.4.fb. *Possession of the obscured-non-defined forms & the time periods; F 190*

[Does only the possession of the unobscured-non-defined factors arise simultaneously with them?]

39a. The possession of obscured, [non-defined] forms also arises [only] simultaneously with them.[492]

The possession (*prāpti*) of obscured-non-defined (*nivṛtāvyākṛta*) forms (*rūpa*) arises only simultaneously with these forms. These forms are bodily action and vocal action resulting from an obscured-non-defined thought (*kāya-*, *vāgvijñaptirūpa*). These actions, even though produced by a strong [*adhimātra*] thought, are incapable—as this thought itself—of creating the non-informative action (*avijñapti*; iv. 7a): hence they are weak [*durbala*; *daurbalya*].[493] Thus the possession of these forms arises only simultaneously with them, but not prior to or subsequent to them.

B.2.2.4.fc. *Possession of wholesome and unwholesome factors & the time periods; F 190*

Is the tri-temporal differentiation [*bheda*] of the possession (*prāpti*) of wholesome and unwholesome factors (*dharma*) subject to certain restrictions, as is the case with the possession of non-defined factors?

39b. The possession of [wholesome or unwholesome] forms within the realm of desire does not arise prior [*agraja*] to these forms [i.e., it arises simultaneously and subsequently].[494]

The possession of these wholesome [*kuśala*] or unwholesome [*akuśala*][495] forms (*rūpa*), for example, the *prātimokṣa* restraint (*prātimokṣasaṃvara*; iv. 19 and so on), does not arise prior to its having arisen. The possession arises simultaneously or subsequently, not prior.

B.2.2.5. *Modes of non-possession;*[496] *F 190–95*

[This has five topics:]

a. Moral quality; F 190
b. Time periods; F 190
c. Realms of existence; F 191
d. Relation to the path; F 191
e. Discarding of non-possession; F 193–94

BAB.2.2.5.a. *Moral quality & non-possession; F 190*

Can non-possession (*aprāpti*), like possession (*prāpti*), be good, bad, non-defined?

39c. Non-possession is [always only] undefiled and non-defined [*akliṣṭa–avyākṛta*].[497]

Non-possession is always [only] unobscured-non-defined (*anivṛtāvyākṛta*; ii. 66).

BAB.2.2.5.b. *Time periods & non-possession; F 190–91*

39d. [The factors of the] past and future time periods (*atītājāta*) [each] have three varieties of non-possession [i.e., past, present, future].[498] {19 a} <191>

The non-possession of past and future factors (*dharma*) can be past [*atīta*], future [*anāgata*] and present [*pratyutpanna*]. But one necessarily possesses the present factors: thus present factors can only have past and future [but not present] non-possession.[499]

BAB.2.2.5.c. *Realms of existence & non-possession; F 191*

40a. (1) The factors connected [*āpta*] with the realms of existence and (2) the stainless [*amala*] factors have a threefold [non-possession] [i.e., belonging either to the realm of desire, or the realm of fine-materiality, or the realm of immateriality].[500]

1. The non-possession of the factors connected to the sphere of the realm of desire belongs either to the realm of desire, the realm of fine-materiality or the realm of immateriality, according to whether the person endowed with this non-possession belongs to such and such a realm of existence.

2. The same applies to the non-possession of the pure (*anāsrava*) factors [i.e., the non-possession belongs either to the realm of desire, the realm of fine-materiality or the realm of immateriality].

BAB.2.2.5.d. *Relation to the path;*[501] *F 191–93*

In fact, non-possession (*aprāpti*) is never pure [*anāsrava*; see ii. 39c].[502]

Why?

40bc. According to the School, the non-possession of the (noble) path is referred to as the nature of an ordinary worldling.[503]

As is said in the *Mūlaśāstra* (*Jñānaprasthāna*, 928c5; MVŚ, 232b9):

What is the nature of an ordinary worldling (*pṛthagjanatva*)? – It is the non-acquisition of the noble factors (*āryadharmāṇām alābhaḥ*).

[Non-acquisition (*alābha*) means non-possession (*aprāpti*).]

Now, the nature of an ordinary worldling (*pṛthagjana*) is not pure [*anāsrava*]; thus the non-possession (*aprāpti* = *alābha*) is not pure.

B.2.2.5.da. *Three definitions of the nature of an ordinary worldling;*[504] *F 191*

Let us examine this definition:

[Question:] – When the Śāstra teaches that the nature of an ordinary worldling is the non-acquisition of the noble factors, to what noble factors does it refer? These factors begin with the receptivity to the cognition of the factors with regard to unsatisfactoriness (*duḥkhe dharmajñānakṣānti*) and include the entire pure path or noble path (vi. 25).

B.2.2.5.daa. *The definition of the ordinary worldling according to the School: "the non-acquisition of all noble factors";*[505] *F 191–92*

The Sarvāstivādin. – The Śāstra means to refer to all these factors since it does not specify any. <192>

[Reply:] – Be careful! To believe you, the persons in possession of the receptivity with regard to unsatisfactoriness (*duḥkhe kṣānti*) would be ordinary worldlings since they do not possess all the other noble factors.

The Sarvāstivādin. – The Śāstra, [when defining the nature of an ordinary worldling,] means to speak of the non-acquisition [of all or any noble factors], which is not mixed with [*vinā*] the acquisition [of any noble factor]: the persons of whom you speak, [however, i.e., the persons in possession of the receptivity with regard to unsatisfactoriness,] although they have no acquisition of the other noble factors, are not ordinary worldlings because the non-acquisition of these other [noble] factors is mixed with the acquisition of the receptivity [with regard to unsatisfactoriness] (*kṣānti*). This is quite evident, for, otherwise [*anyathā*], even the Lord Buddha, who does not have accompaniment of those [noble] factors characteristic of the "family" [*gotraka*] of the listeners (*śrāvaka*) and of the self-enlightened ones (*pratyekabuddha*) (vi. 23), would be an ordinary worldling (*anārya*).

[Reply:] – Very well. But if this were so, the Śāstra should say: "The nature of an ordinary worldling is exclusively the non-acquisition (*alābha eva*) of the noble factors [i.e., is without any acquisition of noble factors]", and not: "...the non-acquisition (*alābha*)".

The Sarvāstivādin: – The Śāstra expresses itself very well, for single words (*eka-pada*) (*Nirukta*, 2, 2) allow a restrictive meaning (*avadhāraṇāni*) so that the particle *eva* is not necessary: (for example,) *abbhakṣa* means "those who live on water alone [as food]", and *vāyubhakṣa*, "those who live on air alone [as food]". {19 b}

BAB.2.2.5.dab. *A different definition of the ordinary worldling: "the non-possession of the first stage of the path of insight and its concomitant factors";*[506] *F 92–93*

According to another opinion,[507] the nature of an ordinary worldling [*pṛthagjanatva*] is the non-acquisition [*alābha*] of the first stage of the path of insight, i.e., the receptivity to the cognition of the factors with regard to unsatisfactoriness (*duḥkhe dharmajñānakṣānti*) and its concomitant (*sahabhū*) factors [i.e., sensation, etc.] (vi. 25).

Objection: – In this hypothesis, at the sixteenth moment (*mārge 'nvayajñāna*), the noble ones would [again] become ordinary worldlings and [would no longer be] noble ones: for, in this moment, the initial receptivity (*kṣānti*) is discarded.[508]

[Answer:] – No, for the non-acquisition of the receptivity (*kṣānti*), which constitutes the nature of an ordinary worldling, has been completely [*atyanta*] destroyed [*hatatva*] in the first stage [of the path of insight].

Objection: – The receptivity in question has three varieties: (1) the receptivity of the family [*gotra*] of listeners (*śrāvaka*), (2) the receptivity of the family of self-liberated ones (*pratyekabuddha*), (3) the receptivity of the family of Buddhas (vi. 23). To which of these three varieties do you refer in your definition of the nature of an ordinary worldling?

[Answer:] – We mean to refer to all three varieties of receptivity.

[Objection:] – Be careful! Because then the Buddha, who does not possess the three varieties of receptivity, would be an ordinary worldling [*anārya*]. <193>

[Answer:] – We mean to refer to the non-acquisition of the receptivity, which is not mixed with [*vinā*] the acquisition... and so on, as above, to the examples: "those who live on water *alone*", "those who live on wind *alone*".

BAB.2.2.5.dac. *The Sautrāntika definition of the ordinary worldling: "the life-stream in which the noble factors have not yet arisen"; F 193*

[Objection:] – Then [*tarhi*] the effort [*yatna*] undertaken to avoid [*parihāra*] the [first] objection [*pūrvapakṣadoṣa*; F 192f.]: "Be careful! To believe you, the persons in possession of the receptivity with regard to unsatisfactoriness (*duḥkhe kṣānti*) would be ordinary worldlings…" is useless [*vyartha*].

[Answer:] – The good [*sādhu*] explanation is that of the Sautrāntikas.[509] For them, the life-stream which has not yet produced noble factors (*anutpannāryadharmā saṃtatiḥ*) is the nature of an ordinary worldling [*pṛthagjanatvam*].[510]

.2.2.5.e. *Discarding of non-possession;* F 193–94

How is non-possession (*aprāpti*) discarded [*vihīyate*]?

40cd. [The non-possession of a factor] is discarded (1) by the possession (*prāpti*) [of that factor] and (2) by passing to another stage.[511]

For example, the non-acquisition [*alābha*] of the noble path, which constitutes the nature of an ordinary worldling (*pṛthagjana*), is discarded [*vihīyate*] (1) when one acquires (*lābha*) the noble path,[512] (2) when one passes to another stage [*bhūmi-saṃcāra*].[513]

The same holds for the non-acquisition of the other factors.[514] <194>

.2.2.6. *The root-possession (mūlaprāpti) & the secondary possession (anuprāpti);*[515] F 190

Objection: – [According to this view,] the non-possession is discarded (*vihīyate*) first when the non-possession of the non-possession occurs [*utpadyate*], i.e., when, changing to another stage of existence, one ceases to possess the nature of an ordinary worldling; and second when the possession of the non-possession is cut off [*chidyate*], i.e., when by attaining the noble path, one cuts off the nature of an ordinary worldling. {20 a} Does this mean

1. that there is a possession (i) of the possession and (ii) of the non-possession,
2. that there is a non-possession (i) of the possession and (ii) of the non-possession?

[Answer:] – Yes: (1) of the possession (*prāpti*) and (2) of the non-possession (*aprāpti*), there is (i) a possession and (ii) a non-possession which are called, [respectively,] (i) *secondary possession* (*anuprāpti*) and (ii) *secondary non-possession* [*anu-aprāpti*]. Thus

1. the root-possession (*mūlaprāpti*) and
2. the secondary possession (*anuprāpti*) or possession of possession (*prāptiprāpti*)

are distinguished.

[Objection:] – Does this doctrine not lead to infinite regress (*anavasthā*)?[516]

[Answer:] – No, for through the power of the possession of possession (*prāptiprāpti* = *anuprāpti*), one is accompanied by the possession (*prāpti*), and *vice versa* [i.e., through the power of the possession, one is accompanied by possession of possession]. There is accompaniment of one another (*parasparasamanvāgama*).[517]

Let us explain:

When a certain factor occurs in a given person (*saṃtati*), three factors arise together, namely:

1. this factor itself, which is called *root-factor* (*mūladharma*);
2. the possession of this root-factor;
3. the possession of this possession.

The person in question is accompanied (*samanvāgata*) by the root-factor and the possession of the possession through the power of the arising of the possession.

This person is accompanied by the possession through the power of the arising of the possession of the possession.[518]

Thus, there is no infinite regress.

BAB.2.2.7. *The increasing number of possession from moment to moment;* F 194

1. At the very moment when a wholesome (*kuśala*) or defiled (*kliṣṭa*) factor[519] arises, three factors arise together, including this wholesome or defiled factor, namely: (i) the root-factor (*mūladharma*), (ii) its possession (*prāpti*), (iii) the possession of this possession (*prāpti-prāpti*).[520] <195>

2. At the following moment, six factors (*dharma*) arise together, namely: (i) the possession of the root-factor, (ii) the possession of possession of the first moment, (iii) the possession of the possession of the possession (*prāpti-prāpti*) of the first moment, plus (iii–vi) three secondary possessions (*anuprāpti*) through the power of which one is in accompaniment of the three aforementioned possessions.

3. At the third moment, eighteen factors arise together, namely, (i–ix) nine possessions (*prāpti*): the possessions of three factors produced at the first moment, the possessions of six factors produced at the second moment, plus (x–xviii) the nine secondary possessions (*anuprāpti*) through the power of which one is in accompaniment of the nine aforementioned possessions.

4. The possessions (*prāpti*) of this kind continue increasing in number from moment to moment.[521] The possessions of present and future defilements (*kleśa* and *upakleśa*), and of wholesome innate factors (*upapattilābhika*; ii. 71b) along

with the factors that are associated (*samprayukta*; ii. 53cd) and coexisting (*sahabhū*; ii. 50b) with them {20 b} arise in an infinite [*ananta*] number from moment to moment throughout beginningless and endless transmigration [*anādyanta-saṃsāra*].

B.2.2.8. *The non-material and accommodating nature of the possessions; F 195*

If one considers the life-stream of a single sentient being in the course of transmigration, [the possessions] which arise in each moment are infinite in number.

To consider the entirety of sentient beings, [the possessions] are without measure, without limit.

How wondrous it is [*bata*], [the possessions] possess a great quality [*atyutsava*]: they are [non-resistant (*apratighātin*),] non-material [*arūpiṇitva*], they give a place to one another [*avakāśamākāśe labhante*].

If they were material, the possessions of a single being could not find a place [*avakāśa*] in the universe [*ākāśa*]; not to speak of the possessions of two sentient beings! {v, 1 a}[522]

B.2.3. *Group homogeneity (nikāyasabhāgatā);*[523] *F 195–98*

1. Definition; F 196
2. The name "group homogeneity"; F 196
3. The range of the group homogeneity; F 196
4. Existential status: reasons for the group homogeneity to be a real entity; F 196
5. Discarding and acquiring the homogeneity of sentient beings; F 197
6. Five objections to the group homogeneity being a real entity; F 197
7. Discussion based on scriptural authority; F 198

B.2.3.1. *Definition;*[524] *F 195–96*

What is the [group] homogeneity (*sabhāgatā*; *nikāyasabhāga*)?

41a. [Group] homogeneity is (that which causes) the resemblance [*sāmya*] among sentient beings.[525] <196>

[Vaibhāṣikas:] – There is a real entity (*dravya*) called [*group*] *homogeneity* (*sabhāgatā*). [It is the mutual similarity [*sādṛśya*] among sentient beings,] a factor (*dharma*) by virtue of which (1) sentient beings as well as (2) the factors indicative of sentient beings (*sattvasaṃkhyāta*; i. 10) are mutually similar or homogeneous (*sādṛśya*; *sabhāga*; *sama*; *samāna*; *sadṛśa*) among themselves (MVŚ, 138a9).

BAB.2.3.2. *The name "group homogeneity"; F 196*

In the Śāstra (*Jñānaprasthāna*, etc.), this real entity is given the name *group homogeneity* (*nikāyasabhāga*):[526] the author [i.e., Vasubandhu] uses the term *sabhāgatā* [in verse 35 and 41a] for metrical reasons [*ślokabandhānuguṇyāt*].

BAB.2.3.3. *The range of the group homogeneity;*[527] *F 196*

BAB.2.3.3.a. *Homogeneity of sentient beings (sattvasabhāgatā): two types;*[528] *F 196*

The homogeneity [of sentient beings] (*sabhāgatā*) is of two kinds:

1. general or non-differentiated (*abhinna*) [homogeneity of sentient beings] and
2. particular or differentiated (*bhinna*) [homogeneity of sentient beings].

The first occurs in all sentient beings [*sarvasattva*]: by virtue of it, there is the resemblance of each sentient being [*pratisattva*] with all sentient beings. It is called [general or non-differentiated] *homogeneity of sentient beings* (*sattvasabhāgatā*).[529]

The second has innumerable varieties or subdivisions: each of these subdivisions occurs only in certain sentient beings. – Sentient beings are distinguished according to [the specificness (*pratiniyatā*) in terms of] (1) the realm of existence (*dhātu*: the realm of desire, etc.), (2) the different stages (*bhūmi*) of these realms, (3) plane of existence (*gati*; iii. 4: hell beings, etc.), (4) mode of birth [*yoni*; iii. 9: born from an egg, etc.], (5) caste (*jāti*; Brahman, etc.), (6) gender [*strīpuruṣa*], (7) status of layman (*upāsaka*) (iv. 14), of fully ordained monk (*bhikṣu*), of those in training (*śaikṣa*), of perfected beings (*arhat*), etc.[530] {1 b} This holds as well for the homogeneities (*sabhāgatā*), [i.e., they are distinguished according to the realm of existence, etc.,] by virtue of which each sentient being of a distinctive species resembles all sentient beings of this species.[531]

BAB.2.3.3.b. *Homogeneity of factors (dharmasabhāgatā); F 196*

Further, there is [also] a homogeneity with regard to factors indicative of sentient beings—[called] *homogeneity of factors* (*dharmasabhāgatā*)—which is distinguished according to the aggregate (*skandha*), sense-sphere (*āyatana*) and element (*dhātu*) [classifications]: that is, homogeneity of the aggregates (*skandhasabhāgatā*), etc., homogeneity of the aggregate of form (*rūpaskandhasabhāgatā*), etc.[532]

BAB.2.3.4. *Existential status: reasons for the group homogeneity to be a real entity; F 196*

1. If the homogeneity of sentient beings (*sattvasabhāgatā*) did not exist as a non-particular (*aviśiṣṭa*) real entity, there would be no notions (*buddhi*) or

provisional designations (*prajñapti*) "sentient beings" in general [*abhedena*], etc., in regard to sentient beings who are specified (*bhinna*) by means of mutual distinctions.

2. In the same way, it is solely by virtue of the homogeneity of factors (*dharma-sabhāgatā*) that the notions and provisional designations "aggregate", "element", etc., are justified.[533] <197>

3.2.3.5. *Discarding and acquiring the homogeneity of sentient beings; F 197*

Does it happen that one transmigrates, i.e., dies [*cyavet*]) and is reborn [*upapadyeta*], without discarding [*vijahyāt*] and without acquiring [*pratilabha*] a certain homogeneity of sentient beings (*sattvasabhāgatā*) ("humans", etc.) [i.e., without changing a certain homogeneity]?

Tetralemma (*catuṣkoṭi*) [between transmigration & changing a homogeneity]:

1. one dies in one place (the realm of desire, for example) and is reborn in the same place: the homogeneity remains the same, in spite of there being transmigration;
2. one enters into the stage in which the eventual attainment of enlightenment is assured (*niyāmāvakrānti*; vi. 26a), [i.e., the first stage of the path of insight,] by discarding the homogeneity of an ordinary worldling (*pṛthag-janasabhāgata*) and by acquiring the homogeneity of a noble one (*ārya-sabhāgatā*): there is no transmigration;
3. [both:] one dies in one plane of existence, i.e., the plane of existence of "humans" [*manuṣya*], etc., and is reborn in a different plane of existence (*gatisaṃcāra*).
4. [neither:] All other cases.

3.2.3.6. *Five objections to the group homogeneity being a real entity; F 197–98*

(The Sautrāntika[534]) does not accept the existence of the factor called [*group*] *homogeneity* (*sabhāgatā*) and presents several [i.e., five] objections.

3.2.3.6.a. *1. Objection: homogeneity of an ordinary worldling is the nature of an ordinary worldling; F 197*

If a certain real entity called *homogeneity of an ordinary worldling* (*pṛthagjana-sabhāgatā*) existed, what would be the use in assuming the nature of an ordinary worldling (*pṛthagjanatva*) consisting of the "non-acquisition of the noble factors" (see ii. 40c)? Somebody would be an ordinary worldling by means of the homogeneity of an ordinary worldling, just as somebody is a human being by means of the homogeneity of a human being (*manuṣyasabhāgatā*): for the Vaibhāṣikas do not assume a nature of a human being (*manuṣyatva*) different from the homogeneity of a human being.[535]

BAB.2.3.6.b. 2. *Objection: homogeneity cannot be known or inferred;* F 197

[Since it has no form (*arūpin*),] the world [*loka*] does not know [*paśyati*] the [group] homogeneity (*sabhāgatā*) by direct sense perception (*pratyakṣa*); one does not infer the existence of the [group] homogeneity (*paricchinatti*; *anumāna*) by an operation of understanding (*prajñā*), for the [group] homogeneity does not exercise any action by which one could know it: {2 a} nevertheless, although the world does not know anything of a homogeneity of sentient beings (*sattvasabhāgatā*), it recognizes (*pratipadyate*) the undifferentiated category of "sentient beings" (*sattvānāṃ jātyabheda*). Thus, supposing that the [group] homogeneity exists, what would be its function (*vyāpāra*)?[536]

BAB.2.3.6.c. 3. *Objection: homogeneity of insentient entities;* F 197

Why does the School not allow the homogeneity (*sabhāgatā*) to insentient entities [*asattva*], such as rice [*śāli*], barley [*yava*], mango [*māṣāmra*], bread-fruit tree [*panasa*], iron [*loha*], gold [*kāñcana*]? Yet generic [*sādṛśya*] designations or categories [*jāti*] are used in regard to them.[537]

BAB.2.3.6.d. 4. *Objection: an infinite regress results since other general group homogeneities are required;* F 197

The various kinds of [group] homogeneity (*sabhāgatā*) recognized by the School, i.e., the homogeneity of (1) sentient beings and (2) the homogeneities of the realms, of the destinies, etc., are mutually different [*anyo'nyabhinna*]. Yet then there has to be [another] general [*abhedena*] notion [*buddhi*] and provisional designation [*prajñapti*] for all of them: all are [group] homogeneities.[538] [Thus there would be the fault of an infinite regress.] <198>

BAB.2.3.6.e. 5. *Objection: the group homogeneity is nothing other than the Vaiśeṣika categories of generality or particularity;* F 198

The Sarvāstivādin champions (*dyotayati*) the doctrine of the Vaiśeṣikas. The Vaiśeṣikas accept (1) a certain category (*padārtha*) called *generality* or *universal* (*sāmānya*; *spyi*), by virtue of which there occur "common" notions and designations [*samānapratyaya*] with regard to [specific kinds of] entities [*atulyaprakāra*]; they believe also in (2) another category called *particularity* (*viśeṣa*), by virtue of which there occur "distinctive" notions and designations with regard to specific kinds [of entities].[539]

The Vaibhāṣika protests: Our theory is not to be confused with that of the Vaiśeṣikas, who believe that the universal (*sāmānya*), a single category (*padārtha*), exists in the multitude of individuals (*eko 'py anekasmin vartate*). Thus, if I would agree (*dyotita*) with the Vaiśeṣikas in terms of accepting the universal (*sāmānya*), I still condemn the interpretation which they give to it.

.B.2.3.7. *Discussion based on scriptural authority; F 198*

As for the [group] homogeneity (*sabhāgatā*), it is an individual real entity (*dravya*), for the Fortunate One, speaking of a murderer who is reborn in hell, goes on to say:

> If he comes back here and acquires the *sabhāgatā* of "humans"[*manuṣya*]... (*Madhyama*, 24, 3).[540]

(The Sautrāntika[541] answers:) – By expressing itself in this way, the Sūtra does not refer to the existence of a distinct real entity [*dravyāntara*] called [*group*] *homogeneity.* {2 b}

[Question:] – Then what does the Sūtra refer to by the term *sabhāgatā*?.

(The Sautrāntika:) – The Sūtra refers to the "conditioning forces (*saṃskāra*) of a certain nature" to which the designations "humans", etc., are provisionally applied much in the same way as homogeneity (*sabhāgatā*) is applied to rice [*śāli*], barley [*yava*] and so on.[542]

This opinion is not accepted by the Vaibhāṣika.[543]

AB.2.4. *State of non-ideation (āsaṃjñika);*[544] *F 198–200*

1. Nature & the state of non-ideation; F 198
2. Effects & the state of non-ideation; F 199
3. Location & the state of non-ideation; F 199
4. Being "with ideation" at birth and when falling from the state of non-ideation; F 199
5. Realm of desire as location of rebirth after the state of non-ideation; F 200

AB.2.4.1. *Nature & the state of non-ideation; F 198–99*

What is the state of non-ideation (*āsaṃjñika*)? <199>

41bc. **The state of non-ideation is [a factor which is able to cause] the cessation of thought and thought-concomitants [for a period of time] among [those sentient beings who are] without ideation.**[545]

For those born among the gods [*deva*] who are sentient beings[546] without ideation [*asaṃjñisattva*], there is a factor (*dharma*) called *state of non-ideation* which is able to cause the cessation [*nirodha*] of thought and thought-concomitants. This factor [is a real entity (*dravya*)] which can obstruct [*saṃnirudhyante*] future thought and thought-concomitants, and can cause them not to arise [*notpattuṃ labhante*] for a period of time [*kālāntara*],[547] like the dam which prevents the flow of the water of a river (*nadītoyasaṃnirodhavat*).[548]

BAB.2.4.2. *Effects & the state of non-ideation;*[549] *F 199*

41d. (This factor is exclusively) a ripened effect.[550]

It is exclusively [*ekāntena*] a ripened effect [*vipāka*; i. 37, ii. 57a] produced by the attainment of non-ideation (*asaṃjñisamāpatti*; ii. 42a).[551]

BAB.2.4.3. *Location & the state of non-ideation; F 199*

Where do sentient beings without ideation [*asaṃjñisattva*] abide?

41d. [Sentient beings without ideation] abide among the Bṛhatphala gods [i.e., within the fourth meditation].[552]

In the heaven of the Bṛhatphalas ["Abundant Fruit"; i.e., within the fourth meditation,] there is an elevated region [*pradeśa*] which is the abode of sentient beings without ideation; just as the abode of the Mahābrahmās—the intermediate stage (*dhyānāntarikā*) [i.e., the elevated region located between the first and second meditation]—arises in the heaven of the Brahmapurohitas (i.e., within the first meditation;[553] iii. 2c; MVŚ, 784b5).

BAB.2.4.4. *Being "with ideation" at birth and when falling from the state of non-ideation; F 199–200*

[Question:] – Do the sentient beings without ideation receive their name because they are always "without ideation" [*asaṃjñā*], or are they sometimes "with ideation" [*saṃjñā*]? <200>

[Answer:] – They are "with ideation" at birth [*upapatti*] and when falling [from this region] [*cyuti*], i.e., when dying (iii. 42; MVŚ, 784c8);[554] they are called *sentient beings without ideation* because their ideation [*saṃjñā*] is suspended for a long period of time. {3 a} When, after this long period of time, an ideation arises again, they fall, i.e., they die. As is said in the Sūtra:

> Similar to a person who wakes up after a long sleep, [those beings who have abided there for a long time,] will fall, i.e., die, when ideation arises again.

B.2.4.5. *Realm of desire as location of rebirth after the state of non-ideation; F 200*

Dying in the heaven of sentient beings without ideation, they are necessarily reborn in the realm of desire and in no other place.

1. In fact, since the power of attainment of non-ideation (*asaṃjñisamāpatti*; ii. 42a) by which these beings are born among the sentient beings without ideation has been exhausted [*parikṣaya*] and since in the course of their existence among sentient beings without ideation they were not in a position to practice again the attainment of non-ideation [to accumulate (*upacaya*) future effects], they die like arrows [*iṣu*] which, [having been shot into the air,] quickly fall to the ground when their momentum or impetus is exhausted (*kṣīnavega*).

2. On the other hand, sentient beings who will be reborn among the sentient beings without ideation necessarily possess an action the effects of which are [also] to be experienced later, i.e., in the third life-time or after [*karmāparaparyāyavedanīya*], within the realm of desire (iv. 50b), and to be experienced in the second or next life-time. This is similar to the case of sentient beings who will be reborn in Uttarakuru (iii. 90cd); they necessarily [also] possess an action the effects of which are to be experienced in a rebirth among the gods [*devopapattivedanīya*] immediately after the existence in Uttarakuru.

.2.5. *The two attainments (samāpatti);*[555] *F 200–14*

1. The attainment of non-ideation (*asaṃjñisamāpatti*); F 200
2. The attainment of cessation (*nirodhasamāpatti*); F 203
3. Summary; F 210
4. The rearising of thought after attainment; p. F 211
5. Existential status & the two attainments and the state of non-ideation; F 213–14

The *Mūlaśāstra* says:

> What are the two attainments (*samāpatti*)?[556] – The attainment of non-ideation (*asaṃjñisamāpatti*) and the attainment of cessation (*nirodhasamāpatti*).[557]

.2.5.1. *The attainment of non-ideation (asaṃjñisamāpatti);*[558] *F 200–3*

1. Nature and name; F 200
2. Location; F 201
3. The intended purpose why ordinary worldlings practice the attainment of non-ideation; F 201
4. Moral quality; F 201

5. The time of sensing the effects of the attainment of non-ideation; F 201
6. Practitioners; F 202
7. The way of acquisition; F 202

BAB.2.5.1.a. *Nature and name & the attainment of non-ideation; F 200*

What is the attainment of non-ideation (*asaṃjñisamāpatti*)?

42a. **(As the state of non-ideation [*āsaṃjñika*] is a factor (able to cause the cessation of thought and thought-concomitants,) in the same way [*tathā*], the attainment of non-ideation [is a factor able to cause the cessation of thought and thought-concomitants].**[559] **<201>**

The attainment of non-ideation is the attainment in which the practitioners are without ideation (*asaṃjñinām samāpattiḥ*) or the attainment which is without ideation [*asaṃjñā*].[560]

The phrase "in the same way" [*tathā*] indicates that this attainment, {3 b} like the state of non-ideation (*āsaṃjñika*), is able to cause the cessation of thought and thought-concomitants.

BAB.2.5.1.b. *Location & the attainment of non-ideation; F 201*

To which stage (*bhūmi*) does [the attainment of non-ideation] belong?

42b. **[The attainment of non-ideation is located] in the last [stage of] meditation.**[561]

In order to practice [*paryāpanna*] this attainment, the practitioners should enter into the [last meditation (*antyadhyāna*), i.e.,] the fourth meditation (*dhyāna*), [and in no other stage (*anyabhūmika*)].

BAB.2.5.1.c. *The intended purpose why ordinary worldlings practice the attainment of non-ideation; F 201*

For what intended purpose [*artha*] is [the attainment of non-ideation] practiced [*samāpadya*]?

42b. **[The attainment of non-ideation is practiced] with a desire for deliverance [*niḥsṛtīcchā*].**[562]

The practitioners [i.e., ordinary worldlings only] falsely claim [*manyante*] that the millennium-state of non-ideation (*āsaṃjñika*) which constitutes the [ripened] effect of the attainment of non-ideation, is true escape or deliverance [*niḥsaraṇa*]. [They practice it with a desire for liberation (*mokṣakāma*).]

3.2.5.1.d. *Moral quality & the attainment of non-ideation;*[563] *F 201*

The state of non-ideation, being a ripened effect, is necessarily morally non-defined (*avyākṛta*).

42c. (As for the attainment of non-ideation, it is) good [*śubha*].[564]

[This attainment of non-ideation is wholesome (*kuśala*)]. It produces as its ripened effect the five aggregates (*skandha*) of the gods without ideation who, as we know, are "with ideation" at birth [*upapatti*] and when falling [from this region (*cyuti*), i.e.,] when dying.

B.2.5.1.e. *The time of sensing the effects of the attainment of non-ideation; F 201*

To what category does this attainment belong from the point of view of sensing its effects?

42c. [The effects of the attainment of non-ideation] are to be experienced only in the next life.[565]

[The attainment of non-ideation is to be experienced only in the next life (*upapadya-vedanīya*).] It is not (1) to be experienced in the present life [*dṛṣṭadharmavedanīya*] nor (2) to be experienced later, i.e., in the third lifetime or after [*aparaparyāya-vedanīya*], nor (3) are its effects undetermined [*aniyata*] (iv. 50).[566]

Without doubt, the practitioners can retrogress (*parihā*) from this attainment after having produced it; but, according to the Vaibhāṣikas, they will produce it again and will be reborn among the sentient beings without ideation.[567] That is to say, the practitioners who acquire (*lābhin*) this attainment will certainly not enter into the stage in which the eventual attainment of enlightenment is assured (*niyāmāvakrānti*; vi. 26a).[568] <202>

B.2.5.1.f. *Practitioners & the attainment of non-ideation;*[569] *F 202*

42d. (This attainment is practiced by ordinary worldlings only and) not by noble ones.[570] {4 a}

Noble ones [*ārya*] see this attainment as a deep pit, a calamity (*vinipātasthāna*, i.e., *apāyasthāna*: an unfortunate rebirth state, or *giri-taṭa-vinipātasthāna*) and do not desire to enter or practice it.[571]

On the contrary, ordinary worldlings (*pṛthagjana*) identify the state of non-ideation (*āsaṃjñika*) with true liberation [*mokṣa*], they have the notion of escape (*niḥsaraṇa-saṃjñā*) in regard to it, and thus practice [*samāpadyante*] the attainment which leads to it. But the noble ones know that the impure (*sāsrava*) cannot be true liberation. Thus they do not practice this attainment.

BAB.2.5.1.g. *The way of acquisition & the attainment of non-ideation;* F 202

[Question:] – When the noble ones (*ārya*) enter [*lābha*] into the fourth meditation (*dhyāna*), do they attain [*pratilabhante*] the possession (*prāpti*) of this past and future attainment, [i.e., the attainment of non-ideation], as one attains the possession of the past and future fourth meditation as soon as one enters into the fourth meditation?[572]

[Answer:] – The non-noble-ones themselves do not attain [*pratilabhante*] the possession of the past and future attainment of non-ideation.

[Question:] – Why?

[Answer:] – [First,] since even if one would have formerly practiced it on several occasions, this attainment can be accomplished only through great efforts or great mental instigation (*mahābhisaṃskārasādhya*).[573]

42d. **([Second,] since attainment of non-ideation is not thought [*acitta*],) it is acquired belonging to one time period [*ekādhvikā 'pyate*] [i.e., the present].**[574]

One acquires (*āpyate*, *labhyate*) this attainment, not as past [*atīta*], not as future [*anāgata*], but as of a single time period [*ekakālikā*], i.e., as present time period [*vartamānakālikā*]; just as this is also the case for the *prātimokṣa* restraint (*prātimokṣasaṃvara*; iv. 35). <203>

In the second moment [*kṣaṇa*] of this attainment and in all the moments which follow the acquisition of this attainment until the moment when it comes to an end, one is accompanied [*samanvāgata*] by it as past and present. On the other hand, it is not possible to acquire the possession (*prāpti*) of this attainment while it is still future (*nānāgatā bhāvyate*) because this attainment is not thought [*acittakatva*].[575]

BAB.2.5.2. *The attainment of cessation (nirodhasamāpatti);*[576] F 203–10

1. Nature; F 203
2. Distinctions between the two attainments & modes of the attainment of cessation; F 203
   i. Intended purpose why noble ones practice the attainment of cessation; F 203
   ii. Location; F 203
   iii. Moral quality; F 203
   iv. The time of sensing the effects of the attainment of cessation; F 204
   v. Practitioners; F 204
3. The way of acquisition; F 204
4. Other similarities with and distinctions from the attainment of non-ideation; F 207
5. Retrogression; F 208

B.2.5.2.a. *Nature & the attainment of cessation;*[577] *F 203*

What is the attainment of cessation (*nirodhasamāpatti*)?[578]

43a. **The attainment which bears the name of *cessation* (*nirodha*) is also likewise, [i.e., it is a factor able to cause the cessation of thought and thought-concomitants].**[579]

Like the state of non-ideation (*āsaṃjñika*; ii. 41b) and the attainment of non-ideation [*asamjñisamāpatti*; ii. 42a], the attainment of cessation is also thus: it is a factor which is able to cause the cessation of thought and thought-concomitants.

B.2.5.2.b. *Distinctions between the two attainments & modes of the attainment of cessation; F 203–4*

What are the differences (*viśeṣa*) between the attainment of non-ideation and the attainment of cessation?

43bd. **[(1) The attainment of cessation is practiced] in order to [reach] a peaceful abode; (2) [it is] produced from [the sphere of] *Bhavāgra* [i.e., the summit of cyclic existence]; (3) [it is] good; (4) its effects are to be experienced at two [specified times, i.e., in the next life or later,] and are undetermined; (5) it is acquired by noble ones; (6) it is [only] attained through preparatory effort [*prayoga-labhya*].**[580]

B.2.5.2.ba. *The intended purpose why noble ones practice the attainment of cessation; F 203*

Noble ones (*ārya*) practice this attainment of cessation because they consider it as peaceful abode or concentration [*śāntavihāra*].[581]

As for the attainment of non-ideation, it is practiced [by ordinary worldlings] because the state of non-ideation [*āsaṃjñika*] is regarded as escape or liberation (*niḥsaraṇa* = *mokṣa*).

B.2.5.2.bb. *Location & the attainment of cessation; F 203*

[The attainment of cessation] is located in the stage [*bhūmi*] of the summit of cyclic existence (*bhavāgra*),[582] i.e., it is entered from the attainment of the perception-sphere of neither-ideation-nor-non-ideation (*naivasaṃjñānāsaṃjñāyatana*; viii. 4); whereas the attainment of non-ideation is located in the stage of the fourth meditation (*dhyāna*).

BAB.2.5.2.bc. *Moral quality & the attainment of cessation;*[583] *F 203*

[The attainment of cessation] is wholesome; it is neither non-defined [*avyākṛta*] nor defiled [*kliṣṭa*] since its originating cause is wholesome (iv. 9b). <204>

BAB.2.5.2.bd. *The time of sensing the effects of the attainment of cessation; F 204*

[The attainment of cessation] has two kinds of ripened effects [*vipāka*] which are (1) to be experienced in the next life (*upapadyavedanīya*) or (2) to be experienced later, i.e., in the third lifetime or after (*aparaparyāyavedanīya*) (iv. 50).[584]

It is also undetermined [*aniyata*], [i.e., it might never develop into a ripened effect] since the practitioners who practice it can enter *nirvāṇa* in the present existence.

[Question:] – Of what does its ripened effect consist?

[Answer:] – This attainment is able to produce the four [non-material] aggregates (*skandha*) within *bhavāgra*, i.e., in an existence in *bhavāgra* (iii. 3). {5 a}

BAB.2.5.2.be. *Practitioners & the attainment of cessation; F 204*

[The attainment of cessation] is acquired by noble ones (*ārya*) only, not by ordinary worldlings (*pṛthagjana*).[585] These latter are not capable of giving rise to it

1. because they dread annihilation (*ucchedabhīrutva*),[586]
2. because this attainment can only be given rise to by the power of the noble path: in fact, it is the practitioners for whom *nirvāṇa* is present [*dṛṣṭadharmanirvāṇa*] who are resolved with regard to this [attainment].[587]

BAB.2.5.2.c. *The way of acquisition & the attainment of cessation; F 204–7*

Although acquired by the noble ones (*ārya*), [the attainment of cessation] is not attained [*labhya*] by the mere fact of detachment (*vairāgya*). It is attained only through preparatory effort (*prayogalabhya*).

One cannot acquire [*labhyate*] this attainment as past or future, [because it is brought into existence by the power of thought (*cittabalena tadbhāvanād*)]; this point has been explained in the discussion of the attainment of non-ideation (ii. 42d).

BAB.2.5.2.ca. *The Muni & the attainment of cessation; F 204–7*

[(Question:) – Did the Fortunate One also attain (the attainment of cessation) through preparatory effort (*prāyoga*)?

(Answer:) – He did not.]

44ab. In the case of [the attainment of cessation of] the Muni, it is attained

with enlightenment (*bodhi*) and not before, for the Muni attains Bodhi in thirty-four [consecutive] moments.[588] <205>

The Lord Buddha acquires the attainment of cessation at the time when he becomes a Buddha, i.e., at the same time [*samakāla*] as the cognition of exhaustion (*kṣayajñāna*; vi. 67).[589] No quality (*guṇa*) of the Buddha is attained through preparatory effort [*prayoga*]; all of his qualities are attained by the simple fact of detachment [*vairāgya*]: as soon as he desires it, the collection of qualities appear at his will.[590]

[Objection:] – How is it that the Fortunate One, at the time of the enlightenment (*bodhi*), i.e., the cognition of exhaustion (*kṣayajñāna*), without having previously given rise to this attainment (*nirodhasamāpatti*), becomes one who is liberated through both parts (*ubhayatobhāgavimukta*), i.e., (1) liberated from the obstacle constituted by defilements (*kleśāvaraṇa*) and (2) liberated from the obstacle to meditative attainment (*samāpattyāvaraṇa*; vi. 64)?[591]

[Answer:] – He becomes one who is liberated through both parts, just as if he had previously produced this attainment, for he possesses mastery [*vaśitva*], i.e., the power to realize this attainment if he merely wishes (MVŚ, 780b26). {5 b}

B.2.5.2.caa. *The opinion of the Westerners; F 205*

The Westerners (Pāścātya)[592] claim that the Bodhisattva first gives rise to this attainment in the state of those in training [*śaikṣāvasthā*], and afterwards attains enlightenment.

Why do we not adopt this opinion? This would be to follow the *Netrīpadaśāstra* of the Sthavira Upagupta, which says: "One who, after having given rise to the attainment of cessation, gives rise to the cognition of exhaustion, should be called a Tathāgata."[593]

B.2.5.2.cab. *The opinion of the Vaibhāṣikas of Kaśmīr; F 205–7*

The Vaibhāṣikas of Kaśmīr deny that the Bodhisattva gives rise to the attainment of cessation [*nirodhasamāpatti*] before giving rise to the cognition of exhaustion (*kṣayajñāna*). <206>

The School [*kila*] maintains in fact (MVŚ, 780b10) that the Bodhisattva attains enlightenment in thirty-four [consecutive] moments, namely:

1. sixteen moments which constitute the direct realization of the truths (*satya-abhisamaya*; vi. 27), and
2. eighteen moments which constitute the abandonment of the defilements in *bhavāgra* (that is, *naivasaṃjñānāsaṃjñāyatana*) [through detachment (*vairāgya*)]: that is to say, those of the nine [moments of the] unhindered

path (*ānantaryamārga*) and nine [moments of the] path of liberation (*vimuktimārga*; vi. 44). The eighteenth moment is the cognition of exhaustion.

These thirty-four (= 16 + 18) [consecutive] moments suffice because, before entering into the direct realization of the truths, the Bodhisattva, still an ordinary worldling (*pṛthagjana*; iii. 41), has detached himself [*vītarāga*], through the mundane path, from all the stages (*bhūmi*) with the exception of *bhavāgra*. – The eighteen moments form a series in the course of (*antara*) which the noble one does not give rise to a dissimilar moment of thought [*visabhāgacitta*], i.e., a mundane, impure (*sāsrava*) thought, for example, the thought to enter into the attainment of cessation. Thus the Bodhisattva, in the state of those in training [*śaikṣa–avasthā*], i.e., before being a perfected being (*arhat*), enters the direct realization of the truths and the eighteenth moment of the abandonment of *bhavāgra*, and so does not give rise to the attainment of cessation.

Objection by the Foreign Masters (*bahirdeśaka*),[594] [i.e., Westerners]: – What fault (*doṣa*) would there be if the Bodhisattva produced this impure [*sāsrava*] thought, [i.e., the dissimilar moment of thought, in the course of these thirty-four consecutive moments]? {6 a}

[Answer:] – In this hypothesis, the Bodhisattva would veer from his intention (*vyutthānāśayaḥ syāt*) [to attain enlightenment];[595] but the Bodhisattva does not veer from his intention.

[Foreign Masters:] – It is true that the Bodhisattva does not veer from his intention [to attain enlightenment]; but this does not mean to say that he does not veer from the pure path in order to give rise to an impure thought.

[Question:] – How, in this hypothesis, would he not veer from his intention [to attain enlightenment]?

[Foreign Masters:] – He has undertaken the intention [to attain enlightenment] (*Madhyamāgama*, 56, 6):

> As long as I have not attained [*aprāpta*] the exhaustion of all fluxes [*āśravakṣaya*], I will not break [*na bhetsyāmi*] this cross-legged position [for meditation] (*utkuṭukāsana*; *paryaṅka*).[596] <207>

Now, the Bodhisattva does not veer from his intention [to attain enlightenment], for it is in a single "sitting" (*āsana*; vi. 24ab) that he completes his goal [*sarvārthaparisamāpti*].[597]

B.2.5.2.d. *Other similarities with and distinctions from the attainment of non-ideation;* F 207–8

Although the two attainments, i.e., the attainment of non-ideation and the attainment of cessation, have many distinctions [*viśeṣa*], they have this in common [*sāmya*]:

44c. Both [of these two attainments] have their basis [*āśraya*] in the realm of desire and the realm of fine-materiality.[598]

[Both of these attainments, i.e., attainment of non-ideation and the attainment of cessation, will be produced (*utpatsyate*) in the realm of desire and the realm of fine-materiality.]

To deny that the attainment of non-ideation occurs in the realm of fine-materiality is to contradict the *Mūlaśāstra*:[599] <208>

> There is a type of existence in the realm of fine-materiality which is not endowed with the five aggregates [*pañcavyavacāra*],[600] namely, (1) those of the realm of fine-materiality who [are abiding in a dissimilar moment of thought (*visabhāgacitta*) among the gods who] are "with ideation" [*saṃjñināṃ devānām*] by nature,[601] who enter into or practice (*samāpanna*) the attainment of non-ideation or the attainment of cessation,[602] {6 b} or (2) those of the realm of fine-materiality who are born among gods without ideation who have attained the state of non-ideation (*āsaṃjñika*).[603]

From this passage, it results that the two attainments are practiced by sentient beings [who have their basis] in the realm of desire and of the realm of fine-materiality [*kāmarūpāśraya*].

There is, however, this distinction [*viśeṣa*] between the two attainments:

44d. The attainment of cessation [is produced] for the first time [*āditas*] among human beings [*nṛṣu*].[604]

A person who has never produced the attainment of non-ideation can produce this attainment [for the first time in one whose basis is] either in the realm of desire or in the realm of fine-materiality; but it is necessary to be a human being [*manuṣya*] [in the realm of desire] in order to produce the attainment of cessation for the first time [*prathamatas*].

B.2.5.2.e. *Retrogression & the attainment of cessation;* F 208–10

Human beings, noble ones (*ārya*), who have produced the attainment of cessation, can retrogress from it (*parihāṇi*), can lose the possession (*prāpti*) of it, can be reborn in the realm of fine-materiality and produce this attainment there once again.

[Question:] – Can one retrogress [*parihāṇi*] from the attainment of cessation, which is similar (*sadṛśa*) to *nirvāṇa*?

BAB.2.5.2.ea. *The opinion of the Vaibhāṣikas;* F 208–9

The Vaibhāṣikas answer: – Yes; to deny retrogressing would be to contradict the *Udāyisūtra:*[605] <209>

> [Śāriputra:] O Venerable ones [*āyuṣmant*]! There are *bhikṣus* [in this world (*tatra*)] who, having perfected [*saṃpanna*] morality [*śīla*], concentration [*samādhi*], understanding [*prajñā*], are able to enter and emerge from [the cessation of ideation and sensation [*saṃjñāveditanirodha*], i.e.,] the attainment of cessation, repeatedly; [it is true that] this is possible. If they are unable to attain *ājñā* [i.e., the faculty of final and perfect knowledge][606] either in this present life or at the moment of death when their present body is broken up, they will surpass the gods who eat material food [*kavaḍīkāra*] to be reborn in a divine body produced by the mind (*manomayakāya*). {7 a} Having been reborn there, they will again repeatedly enter and emerge from [the attainment of the cessation of ideation and sensation, i.e., the attainment of cessation; [it is true that] this is possible.

This passage shows in fact that one can retrogress from the attainment of cessation (*nirodhasamāpatti*). [This is so, because,] on the one hand, Lord Buddha has explained that the "divine body produced by the mind" of which Śāriputra speaks (in this passage) is in the realm of fine-materiality.[607] On the other hand, the attainment of cessation of ideation and sensation is located only in *bhavāgra*, the highest stage of the realm of immateriality. If *bhikṣus* who have attained this attainment (*tallābhin*), would not retrogress from it, if they would not lose it, they would not be able to be reborn into the realm of fine-materiality.[608] <210>

BAB.2.5.2.eb. *The opinion of the Mahāsāṃghikas;* F 210

According to another school,[609] the attainment of cessation also belongs to the fourth meditation (*dhyāna*) and is not subject to retrogressing.

[Reply:] – This opinion is not correct. This attainment does not belong to the fourth meditation [of the realm of fine-materiality], for the Sūtra teaches that one acquires nine successive stages of meditative attainments [*anupūrvasamāpatti*].[610]

[Objection:] – How then does one explain the meditative attainment called *meditative attainment which leaps over* (*vyutkrāntaka*; viii. 18c), in which the practitioners leap over various stages of meditative attainments?

[Answer:] – The rule [*niyama*] of the successive production of meditative attainments concerns beginners.[611] Those who have acquired mastery [*vaśitva*] leap over the meditative attainments at will.

.2.5.3. *Summary; F 210–11*

.2.5.3.a. *Six distinctions; F 210-11*

There are thus (the following six) distinctions [*viśeṣa*] between the two attainments:

1. the attainment of non-ideation and
2. the attainment of cessation,

from the point of view:

i. of the stage [or location] [*bhūmi*]:

- the first is of the fourth meditation (*dhyāna*),
- the second is of *bhavāgra* (perception-sphere of neither-ideation-nor-non-ideation);

ii. of the motive or preparation (*prayoga*):

- the first proceeds from [mental application (*manasikāra*) directed toward] the notion of escape [*niḥsaraṇa*] which is falsely identified with the state of non-ideation;
- the second, proceeds from [mental application directed toward] the notion of a peaceful abode [*śāntavihāra*];

iii. of the life-stream or practitioner (*saṃtāna*) in which they occur:

- the first occurs in an ordinary worldling (*pṛthagjana*);
- the second, in a noble one (*ārya*);

iv. of the nature of their [ripened] effects [*phala*]:

- the first produces birth among those without ideation [i.e., the state of non-ideation (*asaṃjñika*)];
- the second, birth in *bhavāgra* (*Kathāvatthu*, xv. 10);

v. of [the time of] experiencing the [ripened] effects [*vedanīya*]: {7 b}

- [the effect of] the first is determined (*niyata*), is to be experienced in the next life [*upapadyavedanīya*];
- [the effect of] the second is determined in the case of a non-returner (*anāgamin*) and undetermined [*aniyata*] in the case of a perfected being (*arhat*); when it occurs, it is to be experienced in the next life [*upapadya-vedanīya*] or later, i.e., in the third lifetime or after [*aparaparyāyavedanīya*];

vi. of where they are produced for the first time [*prathamotpādana*]: <211>

- the first is produced indiscriminately within the two realms of existence [i.e., the realm of desire or the realm of fine-materiality];
- the second, only among human beings.

BAB.2.5.3.b. *Common characteristic and explanation of the name of the two attainments; F 211*

The common characteristic of these two attainments is the cessation of thought and thought-concomitants (*cittacaittānāṃ nirodhaḥ*).

[Objection:] – [If they have this common characteristic,] why is the first attainment called *attainment of non-ideation* (*asaṃjñisamāpatti*) and the second *attainment of cessation of ideation and sensation* (*saṃjñāveditanirodhasamāpatti*)?

[Answer:] – [They are so called] because the motive or preparation (*prayoga*) of the first is merely opposed (*pratikūla*) to ideation [*saṃjñā*],[612] whereas the motive or preparation of the second is opposed to both ideation and sensation (i. 21).[613] Likewise, [although] the cognition of another's mind (*paracittajñāna*; vii. 5b) bears [also] upon the thought-concomitants [i.e., sensation (*vedanā*), etc.] of another, it receives a restrictive name because its motive or preparation refers only to the thought of others.[614]

BAB.2.5.4. *The rearising of thought after the attainment; F 211–13*

In these two attainments, thought is interrupted [or stopped] [*niruddha*] for a long time (*bahukāla*).[615]

[Question:] – How then does it happen that—leaving this attainment—thought once again arises [*jāyate*], considering that thought has been interrupted [or stopped] for such a long time?[616]

BAB.2.5.4.a. *The Vaibhāṣika theory; F 211*

The Vaibhāṣikas find no difficulty in this: past factors (*dharma*; v. 25)[617] exist. Therefore, the moment of thought [just] prior to this attainment, i.e., the thought of attainment (*samāpatticitta*) or the "thought of entry into the attainment", is the condition as the equivalent and immediate antecedent (*samanantarapratyaya*; ii. 62) of the thought [just] subsequent to the attainment, i.e., the emerging-thought (*vyutthānacitta*) (MVŚ, 777b18). <212>

BAB.2.5.4.b. *(The Sautrāntika) theory; F 212*

(The Sautrāntikas[618]) reason as follows:

1. When persons are born in the realm of immateriality, form or matter (*rūpa*) is cut off [*niruddha*] for a long period of time [*cira*] (iii. 81b): if these persons are then reborn in the realm of desire or in the realm of fine-materiality, their new form does not arise from the serial continuity of form (*rūpa*) interrupted long before, but only [*eva*] from thought [*citta*].

2. Likewise, the thought emerging from the attainment does not arise from the thought [just] prior to the attainment: it arises [only] from a "body possessed with sense-faculties" (*sendriyakāya*).

This is why the ancient masters [*pūrvācārya*] say:

> Two factors (*dharma*) are one another's seeds (*anyo'nyabījaka*): these two factors are thought and the body possessed with sense-faculties.

.2.5.4.c. *The theory of Vasumitra & the debate with Ghoṣaka;* F 212–13

Vasumitra says in the treatise entitled *Paripṛcchā*:[619]

> "How is thought reborn after the attainment?" is a problem [*doṣa*] for those who claim that the attainment of cessation is without thought [*acittika*]. But I claim that this attainment is accompanied by a subtle thought [*sūkṣmacitta*; *sacittika*]. The problem does not exist for me.[620]

The Bhadanta Ghoṣaka regards this opinion as incorrect. {8 a} In fact, if any consciousness (*vijñāna*) would remain in this attainment, there would be contact (*sparśa*) through the coming together of the three [*saṃnipāta*], (1) consciousness (*vijñāna*), (2) sense-faculty [*indriya*]; (3) object-field [*viṣaya*]; due to contact, there would be sensation (*vedanā*) and ideation (*saṃjñā*) (iii. 30b). As the Fortunate One teaches:

> In dependence on the mental faculty and factors (*dharma*), mental consciousness arises; the coming together [*saṃnipāta*] of the three is contact. [With contact as their condition (*sparśapratyaya*),] there arise [at the same time] sensation, ideation, intention (*cetanā*).[621] <213>

Thus, if one accepts that thought (*vijñāna*; *citta*) persists in this attainment, sensation and ideation will not cease [*nirodha*]. But this attainment is called *cessation of ideation and sensation* (*saṃjñāveditanirodha*).

Vasumitra answers: – The Sūtra says:

> Craving [*tṛṣṇā*] has sensation as its condition [*vedanāpratyaya*].

However, even though perfected beings (*arhat*) have sensations, craving does not arise among them. The same here, i.e., not all types of contact produce sensations, and so on.

[The Vaibhāṣikas answer:] – This reasoning is not demonstrative. [Certain] Sūtra passages, in fact, explicitly qualify [contact] as follows:

> Craving arises in dependence [*pratītyotpanna*] on sensation, which (itself) has arisen (in dependence on) contact having ignorance [*avidyāsaṃsparśaja*] (iii. 27).[622]

Whereas (here) it [simply] says:

> Sensation arises in dependence on contact.

Thus we Vaibhāṣikas say that thought is interrupted in the attainment of cessation, [that the attainment of cessation is without thought (*acittika*).]

Vasumitra says: – If this attainment is completely without thought, how is it an attainment (*samāpatti*)?[623]

Vaibhāṣikas: – The attainment is thus called because it causes [*samatāpādana*] the fundamental material elements [*mahābhūta*] to be in an even state[624] that is contrary to the arising of thought. Or else, alternatively, [attainment is thus called] because the practitioners enter into an even state [of thought and thought-concomitants] (*samāgacchanti*, *samāpadyante*) through the power of the thought [of attainment (*samāpatticitta*)]: it is for this reason that the meditations (*dhyāna*), etc., are called *meditative attainments* (*samāpatti*).

BAB.2.5.5. *Existential status & the two attainments and the state of non-ideation; F 213–14*

[Question:] – Should one consider the two attainments [*samāpatti*] to be real entities (*dravyatas*, *svalakṣaṇatas*) [or provisional entities (*prajñaptitas*)]?

The Sarvāstivādin answers: – Yes, [they exist as real entities] for they obstruct the arising of thought (*cittotpattipratibandhanāt*).[625] {8 b} <214>

(The Sautrāntika[626] answers:) – No. It is not what you term *attainment* that obstructs the arising of thought; rather, it is the moment of the "thought of attainment" (*samāpatticitta*), i.e., the thought just prior to the state of attainment: for it is that very moment of thought which arises opposed [*viruddha*] to other moments of thought, that causes other moments of thought merely not to operate [*apravṛttimātra*] for a period of time [*kālāntara*]. The moment of thought just prior to attainment projects [*āpādana*] a corporeal basis (*āśraya*)[627] or life-stream (*saṃtāna*) opposed to the arising of other moments of thought. [Thus, first interpretation,] it is the state of the "mere non-operation of thought" (*apravṛttimātra*) for a certain period of time that is provisionally referred to as *attainment*, which is not a real entity (*dravyadharma*), but a provisional entity (*prajñapti-dharma*).

The Sarvāstivādin: – How can the attainment be a conditioned factor (*saṃskṛta*) if it is not a real entity?

[Answer:] – This "mere non-operation of moments of thought" did not exist before [*pūrva*] [entering] the attainment and [it will not exist after (*paścāt*) emerging from the attainment, i.e.,] when the practitioners produce again the emerging-thought (*vyutthānacitta*). One can thus, in a manner of speaking (*saṃvyavahāratas*), provisionally designate (*prajñāpyate*) it as being a conditioned factor [*saṃskṛta*] since it begins and ends.

Or [*athavā*], [second interpretation,] what we provisionally designate by the term *attainment* is the particular condition (*avasthāviśeṣa*) of the corporeal basis (*āśraya*), a condition which is projected by the moment of the thought [just prior to] attainment [in such a way that (*tathā*) (thought does not arise)].

The same holds for the state of non-ideation (*āsaṃjñika*; see ii. 41bc). The state of non-ideation is not a real entity that obstructs the arising or operation of other moments of thought [*cittapravṛttiviruddha*]; by this term we (provisionally) designate the state of non-ideation, i.e., a "mere non-operation [*apravṛttimātra*] of moments of thought", of the gods without ideation, a state which results from a certain thought.

The Vaibhāṣikas do not accept this opinion; they maintain that the state of non-ideation and the two attainments are real entities.[628]

AB.2.6. *Vitality faculty (jīvitendriya);*[629] *F 214–22*

1. Nature; F 214
2. Existential status; F 215
3. Varieties of death and their causes & the life-force (*āyus*); F 217–22

AB.2.6.1. *Nature & vitality faculty;*[630] *F 214–17*

What is the vitality faculty (*jīvitendriya*)? {9 a}

45a. The vitality (*jīvita*) is the life-force (*āyus*).[631] <215>

In fact, the Abhidharma[632] states:

> What is the vitality faculty? – The life-force [belonging to a being in any] of the three realms of existence.

What kind of factor is [referred to (*nāma*)] as life-force (ii. 10a)?

45ab. [The life-force is] the support of heat and consciousness.[633]

For, the Fortunate One said:

> When the life-force, heat and consciousness leave the human body [*kāya*], the abandoned body lies stiff, unconscious [*acetana*] like a log [*kāṣṭha*].[634]

Therefore, there exists a distinct factor (*dharma*), which is the support [*ādhārabhūta*] of heat [*ūṣman*] and consciousness [*vijñāna*], which is the cause of the duration (*sthitihetu*) of their serial continuity (*saṃtāna*) and which is referred to as life-force (*āyus*).[635]

BAB.2.6.2. *Existential status & vitality faculty; F 215–16*

(The Sautrāntika[636]) denies the existence in and of itself of the vitality faculty (*jīvitendriya*, *āyus*).

BAB.2.6.2.a. *The Vaibhāṣika reasons for the existence of the vitality faculty; F 215*

BAB.2.6.2.aa. *Heat and consciousness & the simultaneous support of the life-force itself; F 215*

(Objection by the Sautrāntika:[637]) – If the life-force is the support [*ādhārabhūta*] of heat and consciousness, by what is it itself supported?

The Vaibhāṣika: – The life-force is supported by heat and consciousness.

BAB.2.6.2.ab. *Action & the previous support of the life-force itself; F 215–16*

(Objection by the Sautrāntika:[638]) – If these three factors, i.e., life-force, heat and consciousness, mutually support one another and operate continuously (*saṃtāna-pravṛtti*) through this mutual support, how do they come to an end? Which one perishes first, the destruction of which entails the destruction of the others? For, if one of them does not perish first, these three factors will be eternal [*nitya*] and will not perish (*anivṛtti*). <216>

The Vaibhāṣika: – The life-force (*āyus*) is supported by [previous] action (*karman*), for the life-force has been projected [*ākṣipta*] through [previous] action and operates continuously as long as this projection of [previous] action entails [*anuvarttana*] it, [i.e., for the period of one lifetime].

B.2.6.2.ac. *Ripened effect & the life-force;* F 216

(Objection by the Sautrāntika:[639]) – If this is so, why do you not accept that heat and consciousness are [also] supported by [previous] action? [And if so,] why do we have to involve the life-force? {9 b}

The Vaibhāṣika: – That which is [exclusively] supported by [previous] action is, in its nature, [exclusively] a ripened effect [*vipāka*].[640] If the consciousness were [exclusively] supported by action, any consciousness, from the conception up to death, would be [exclusively] a ripened effect: this is false, [as you also accept]. Hence the necessity of the life-force (*āyus*), which is [exclusively] supported by [previous] action and is the support of heat [*ūṣman*] and consciousness [*vijñāna*].

B.2.6.2.ad. *Life-force as the support of consciousness in the realm of immateriality;* F 216

(Objection by the Sautrāntika:[641]) – Then say that action supports heat and that heat supports consciousness. The life-force is [thus] unnecessary.

The Vaibhāṣika: – The life-force (*āyus*) is necessary since, in the realm of immateriality, heat is absent. What would be the support of consciousness in the realm of immateriality if the life-force does not exist?

(The Sautrāntika:[642]) – Consciousness, in the realm of immateriality, is supported by [previous] action.

The Vaibhāṣika: – Do you have the right to change your opinion? Sometimes you assume that consciousness is supported by heat, sometimes you maintain that it is supported by [previous] action. – [643]Moreover, you have accepted this [above]: one has to avoid the consequence that any consciousness, from conception up to death, is a ripened effect. Therefore, the life-force exists, it is the support of heat and of consciousness.

B.2.6.2.b. *The Sautrāntika definition of the life-force;* F 216–17

(The Sautrāntika:[644]) – I do not [completely] deny the existence of the life-force (*āyus*). I only say that the life-force is not a distinct real entity [*dravyāntara*].

The Vaibhāṣika: – What then is the factor (*dharma*) designated by the name life-force? <217>

(The Sautrāntika:) – The life-force is the momentum or the particular capability [of the period of duration (*sthitikālāvedha;*[645] *sāmarthyaviśeṣa*) of the homogeneous collection of components (*nikāyasabhāga*)] that the action [*karman*] of a previous birth [*pūrvajanman*] [in the three realms (*traidhātuka*)] places in a being at the moment of its conception [*pratisaṃdhi*], a momentum through which, for a determined period of time, the aggregates (*skandha*) renew themselves in the homogeneous collection of components, i.e., the homogeneous stream which constitutes a personal existence (*nikāyasabhāga*; ii. 41).[646]

In the same way, a seed of grain [*sasya*; *bīja*] places a momentum or certain capability [*āvedha*] in the sprout [*aṅkura*] by which, [for a given time (*kāla*)], the plant develops to maturity [*pāka*].

In the same way, a momentum or certain capability is placed into an arrow [*iṣu*] that has been shot [*kṣipta*], which brings it about that, for a given time, it moves.[647]

BAB.2.6.2.ba. *The Vaiśeṣika theory of saṃskāra; F 217*

The Vaiśeṣika believes that a certain type of *guṇa* or "quality", called *saṃskāra* and also *vega*, *impetus*, arises in the arrow [*iṣu*]. Through the force of this quality, the arrow always moves without stopping up to the moment when the arrow falls.[648]

The *saṃskāra*, [however,] is [considered by them to be] a unity [*ekatva*];[649] on the other hand, the arrow does not encounter an obstacle: thus, no difference would be possible in the speed [*śīghra*] of the arrow;[650] moreover, the arrow will not fall (*patana*).

[Possible explanation by the Vaiśeṣika:] – The "wind" [*vāyu*] makes an obstacle [*pratibandha*] to the *saṃskāra*.

[Reply:] – Since "wind", which makes an obstacle, is the same [*aviśeṣa*], near [*samīpa*] or far [*dūra*], the arrow will either fall at first [*arvākpatana*] or will not fall [at all].

The Vaibhāṣikas maintain that the life-force (*āyus*) is a real entity.[651]

BAB.2.6.3. *Varieties of death and their causes & the life-force (āyus); F 217–22*

How death [*maraṇa*] takes place:

[Question:] – Does death take place solely through the exhaustion of the life-force (*āyuḥkṣayāt*) [or also otherwise (*anyathāpi*)]?

[Answer:] – The *Prajñaptisūtra*[652] says:

> There is (the possibility that) death results from the exhaustion of the life-force and not from the exhaustion of merit (*puṇyakṣayāt*).

Four alternatives (tetralemma between action having the life-force as ripened effect and action having enjoyment as ripened effect):

1. death through exhaustion [*paryādāna*] of [the force of] actions which have the life-force as their ripened effect [*āyurvipāka*];
2. death through exhaustion of [the force of those meritorious] actions which have enjoyment as their ripened effect [*bhogavipāka*];[653] <218>
3. death through exhaustion of [the force of] these two kinds of actions (*ubhayakṣayāt*);
4. [neither:] death through the inability to avoid unfavorable circumstances (*viṣamāparihāra*), for example, excess of food (*atyaśana*).

Death through relinquishment at will [*utsarga*] of conditioning forces of one's life-force (*āyuḥsaṃskāra*; ii. 10) should be mentioned.[654]

In the state in which the life-force is exhausted, the exhaustion of [the force of] actions which have enjoyment for their ripened effect has no further capability [*sāmarthya*] to effect death; {10 b} and reciprocally, [i.e., in the state in which enjoyment is exhausted, the exhaustion of the force of actions which have the life-force for their ripened effect has no further capability to effect death]. Therefore, the third alternative means that death occurs when the two kinds of actions are exhausted.

AB.2.6.3.a. *Untimely death & the life-force;* F 218

Untimely death (*akālamṛtyu*, *akālamaraṇa*; iii. 85c):[655]

The *Jñānaprasthāna* (997b28) says:

> Should one say: (1) the life-force continuously operates bound to or in dependence upon the life-stream [*saṃtatyupanibaddha*], or (2) the life-force abides [for the entire time determined for it], having once arisen [*sakṛd-utpanna*]?
>
> One should say:
>
> 1. the life-force of those sentient beings entangled in the realm of desire [*kāmāvacara*] who have not entered into the two attainments [i.e., the attainment of non-ideation (*asaṃjñisamāpatti*) or the attainment of cessation (*nirodhasamāpatti*)] is of the first category [i.e., it continuously operates bound to their life-stream];[656]
>
> 2. the life-force of those sentient beings entangled in the realm of desire who have entered [*samāpanna*] the attainment of non-ideation or the attainment of cessation as well as all sentient beings of the spheres of fine-materiality and immateriality [*rūpārūpyāvacara*] is of the second category,

[i.e., it should be said to abide (for the entire time determined for it), having once arisen].

What is the significance of this passage [*bhāṣita*]?[657]

[First interpretation:]

1. When the bodily basis (*āśraya*) is damaged [*upaghāta*], the life-force accordingly is damaged; (this refers to) the first case in which the life-force operates bound to or in dependence upon the serial continuity of the bodily basis (*āśrayasaṃtatipratibaddha*; *santatyadhīnatva*).

2. When the bodily basis is not capable of being damaged, the life-force abides for the entire time [determined for it] when it arose [*utpannāvasthāna*]; (this refers to) the second case in which the life-force abides [for the entire time determined for it], having once arisen.[658]

[Second interpretation:]

The Masters of Kaśmīr say that (1) the first kind of life-force (*āyus*) is "subject to having an obstacle" (*sāntarāya*); (2) the second is "not subject to having an obstacle" [*nirantarāya*].

Thus, untimely death [*akālamṛtyu*] is possible.[659] <219>

BAB.2.6.3.aa. *Intention & mortal injury;* F 219–22

[To clarify the issue of damage to the bodily basis], the Sūtra states:[660]

> There are four varieties of acquiring modes of personal existence [*ātmabhāvapratilābha*]:[661] that is to say [*tadyathā*], there is an acquiring of a mode of personal existence whereby mortal injury can occur (1) only through one's own intention [*ātmasaṃcetanā*], not through the intention of another [*parasaṃcetanā*];[662]

and so on, [i.e., (2) only through the intention of another, not through one's own intention; (3) through both; (4) through neither].

There are four alternatives (tetralemma) [between mortal injury through one's own intention (*ātmasaṃcetanā*) and mortal injury through the intention of another (*parasaṃcetanā*)]:

1. personal existence [whereby mortal injury can occur only] through one's own intention: those sentient beings of the realm of desire, namely, (i) the gods who are spoiled by amusements [*krīḍāpramoṣaka*] and (ii) the gods who are corrupted in mind with anger [*manaḥpradūṣika*],[663] who destroy their personal existence themselves {11 a} (i) by engaging in excessive

rapture [*praharṣa*] or (ii) by giving rise to excessive anger [*pradoṣa*] [and not otherwise]. Here one should also mention the Buddhas who enter into *nirvāṇa* by their own accord;

2. personal existence [whereby mortal injury can occur only] through the intention of another: those sentient beings who are in the womb [*garbha*] or in an egg [*aṇḍa*];[664]
3. personal existence [whereby mortal injury can occur] through both their own intention and the intention of another: the majority of sentient beings in the realm of desire; exception must be made for hell beings (*nāraka*), beings in the intermediate state (*antarābhavika*; iii. 12), etc.;
4. personal existence whereby neither type [of mortal injury occurs]: all sentient beings in the intermediate state [*antarābhavika*], all sentient beings of the realm of fine-materiality and of the realm of immateriality, and one part of sentient beings in the realm of desire, namely, hell beings [*nāraka*; iii. 82], inhabitants of Uttarakuru (iii. 78c), <220> those who abide in the path of insight into the truths [*darśanamārga*; vi. 28], those in the meditative attainment of loving-kindness [*maitrīsamāpatti*; viii. 29], those in the two attainments of cessation and non-ideation (ii. 42; *Kathāvatthu*, xv. 9); the sages (*rājarṣi*), i.e., the wheel-turning king (*cakravartin*) who has entered the religious life [*pravrajita*]; the messenger of the Buddha [*jinadūta*];[665] those predicted by the Buddha to live for a certain period of time:[666] Dharmila,[667] Uttara,[668] Gaṅgila,[669] and the youth (*kumāra*) Yaśas who is the son of a leading merchant [*śreṣṭhin*], Jīvaka, etc.; the Bodhisattva in his last lifetime [*caramabhavika*] and the mother [*mātṛ*] who is carrying the Bodhisattva; the wheel-turning king (*cakravartin*) and the mother who is carrying the wheel-turning king.

Objection: – The Sūtra gives an account of a question asked by Śāriputra and the answer which the Fortunate One gives to it:

> Śāriputra: "Fortunate One, who are the sentient beings who acquire a mode of personal existence (*ātmabhāvapratilābha*) not capable of having mortal injury either through their own intention or through the intention of another?"
>
> Buddha: "Śāriputra, the sentient beings who belong to the perception-sphere of neither-ideation-nor-non-ideation (*naivasaṃjñānāsaṃjñāyatana*), i.e., in the highest realm of the realm of immateriality, in *bhavāgra*." <221>

How can you say, in view of this passage, that the existence of "all" sentient beings of the realm of fine-materiality and of the realm of immateriality is not capable of having mortal injury either through their own intention or through the intention of another?

[First explanation:]

The School [*kila*; MVŚ, 772a29] gives an explanation: {11 b} – The sentient beings in the realm of fine-materiality and in the first three stages of the realm of immateriality are capable of mortal injury of their personal existence:

1. through their own intention [*ātmasamcetanā*], i.e., through the [noble] path (*āryamārga*) of their own stage [*svabhūmika*];
2. through the intention of another [*parasaṃcetanā*], i.e., through the [mundane] path [*laukikamārga*] of the preliminary concentration of the [next] higher stage [*uttarabhūmisāmantaka*] (vi. 48; viii. 22).

But, in the last stage of the realm of immateriality, neither of [these two kinds of mortal injury, that is,] (1) the [noble] path of their own stage and also (2) the [mundane] path of the [next] higher stage are possible: thus the existence of sentient beings who reside there is not subject to injury either through their own intention or through the intention of another.

[Objection:] – This answer seems weak to us; in fact, one can, in the last stage of the realm of immateriality, practice the [noble] path of the immediately lower stage [i.e., the perception-sphere of nothingness (*ākiñcanyāyatana*; viii. 20)]. Thus another explanation (*Vibhāṣā, ibid.*) must be allowed.

[Second explanation:]

In his response to Śāriputra, the Buddha, by naming the sentient beings of the perception-sphere of neither-ideation-nor-non-ideation (*naivasaṃjñānāsaṃjñāāyatana*), means [implicitly] all the sentient beings in the realm of fine-materiality (*rūpadhātu*) and in the realm of immateriality (*ārūpyadhātu*), since by naming the last one (*paryanta*) [in a series], the first [members of the series] [*ādi*] are [also implicitly] to be understood (*saṃpratyaya*). It can be shown that this is the custom:

1. Sometimes Scripture names the first term of a list the totality of which it refers to, for example:

> The first blissful birth (*sukhopapatti*; iii. 72) (within the realm of fine-materiality), namely (*tadyathā*), the Brahmakāyika gods.

One should understand [all gods belonging to the first meditation (*dhyāna*)]: "the Brahmakāyikas, the Brahmapurohitas, the Mahābrahmās".

2. Sometimes Scripture names the last term:

> The second blissful birth (*sukhopapatti*), namely (*tadyathā*), the Ābhāsvara gods.

One should understand [all gods of the second meditation]: "the Parīttābhas, the Apramāṇābhas and the Ābhāsvaras".

[Objection:] – But this explanation can [also] be challenged. In the two passages given above, the expression *tadyathā* appears, which introduces an example. It should not be translated as: "that is to say", or "namely", but as "for example". This is the rule in regard to examples, that by naming one case, all the similar cases are designated. And we accept that, in the two passages on blissful births (*sukhopapatti*), Scripture designates all the terms of the list by naming the first or the last. But as for the answer of the Fortunate One to Śāriputra [F 220], it does not contain the expression *tadyathā*. <222>

[Answer:] – The expression *tadyathā*, we say, does not introduce an example, since we encounter it in Sūtras that give a complete enumeration:

> The material sentient beings, different in body, different in ideation, namely (*tadyathā*) humans and one part of the gods… (iii. 6). {12 a}

Thus the expression *tadyathā* introduces a definition (*upadarśanārtha*). Thus the Fortunate One, in his response to Śāriputra, designates the first by naming the last, i.e., he means to speak of the two higher realms in their totality.[670]

.B.2.7. *Characteristics (lakṣaṇa);*[671] *F 222–38*

1. Nature; F 222
   - a. Four types of characteristics in Abhidharma doctrine; p. 222
   - b. Three types of characteristics in the *Trilakṣaṇasūtra*; F 223
2. Secondary characteristics (*anulakṣaṇa*) & refutation of infinite regress; F 224
3. Existential status; F 226
   - a. The *Trilakṣaṇasūtra* & its Sautrāntika interpretation as referring to a serial continuity; F 226
   - b. Provisional existence: the stream & the four characteristics; F 227
   - c. The moments; F 229
   - d. The relationship of the characterized factor (*lakṣya*) & the characteristic (*lakṣaṇa*); F 230
   - e. Objections regarding the simultaneous or successive activity/capability of the characteristics; F 231
   - f. The Vaibhāṣika reply: definition of the moment; F 232
   - g. Objections regarding the individual characteristics as causally efficient factors; F 232

h. The notions of "arisen", "the arising of form", etc. & real entities; F 235
i. Vaibhāṣika: the four characteristics as real entities & the scriptures; F 237

BAB.2.7.1. *Nature & the characteristics;*[672] *F 222–24*

BAB.2.7.1.a. *Four types of characteristics in Abhidharma doctrine;*[673] *F 222*

What are the characteristics (*lakṣaṇa*) of conditioned factors (*saṃskṛtasya*)?

45cd. The characteristics [of conditioned factors] are: (1) origination, (2) deterioration, (3) duration, (4) impermanence.[674]

These four factors (*dharma*), (1) origination (*jāti*), (2) deterioration (*jarā*), (3) duration (*sthiti*), (4) impermanence (*anityatā*), are the characteristics of conditioned factors.

The factor in which these characteristics occur is a conditioned factor (*saṃskṛta*).

The factor in which they do not occur is an unconditioned factor (*asaṃskṛta*).[675]

BAB.2.7.1.aa. *Definitions;*[676] *F 222*

1. Origination [*jāti*] is that which produces or causes conditioned factors to arise (*utpādayati; janayati*);[677]

2. duration [*sthiti*] is that which stabilizes or causes conditioned factors to perdure (*sthāpayati*);[678]

3. deterioration [*jarā*] is that which deteriorates or causes conditioned factors to decay [*jarayati*];[679]

4. impermanence [*anityatā*] is that which destroys or causes conditioned factors to perish [*vināśayati*].[680] <223>

BAB.2.7.1.b. *Three types of characteristics in the Trilakṣaṇasūtra; F 223–24*

[Objection:] – Does not the Sūtra teach the existence of [only] three conditioned characteristics (*saṃskṛtalakṣaṇa*) of the conditioned? The Sūtra says,[681] in fact:

> There are, O *bhikṣus*, three conditioned characteristics of the conditioned [*trīṇīmāni bhikṣavaḥ saṃskṛtasya saṃskṛtalakṣaṇāni*].[682] What are these three? Of the conditioned, O *bhikṣus*, (1) the arising (*utpāda*) can [also] be discerned [*prajñāyate*]; (2) the passing away (*vyaya*) can [also] be discerned, and (3) also the duration-change (*sthityanyathātva*).[683]

[See alternate translation, F 227.]

.2.7.1.ba. *Various views about the number of characteristics mentioned in the Trilakṣaṇasūtra;* F 223–24

The Vaibhāṣika: – The Sūtra should name four characteristics. The characteristic that is omitted is the characteristic of duration (*sthiti*). Strictly speaking, it uses the word *sthiti* in the compound *sthityanyathātva*, duration-change: but *sthityanyathātva* is an expression which signifies [*paryāya*] deterioration. As the Sūtra says (1) "arising" (*utpāda*) in place of "origination" (*jāti*), (2) "passing away" (*vyaya*) in place of "impermanence" (*anityatā*); in the same way, it says (3) "duration-change" (*sthityanyathātva*) in place of "deterioration" (*jarā*).

1. If the Sūtra specifies only three characteristics, this is because—with a view to arousing disgust among the faithful[684]—it points out, as the characteristics of the conditioned factor, the factors which cause it to travel through the three time periods:

   i. the power of origination causes it to pass (*saṃcārayati*) from the future into the present; {12 b}

   ii. deterioration, i.e., duration-change (*sthityanyathātva*) and impermanence (*vyaya*) causes it to pass from the present into the past, because, after deterioration, i.e., duration-change has weakened (*durbalīkṛtya*) it, impermanence finishes it (*vighātāt*). <224>

The School [*kila*] makes a comparison (MVŚ, 201b7): Let us suppose that there is a man in an inaccessible forest [*gahana*], and three enemies [*śatru*] desire to kill him. The first brings it about that this man leaves the forest; the second weakens him; the third destroys his vitality [*jīvita*]. Such is the role of the three characteristics in regard to the conditioned factor.[685]

Duration (*sthiti*), on the contrary, sustains the conditioned factor and causes it to perdure: this is why the Sūtra does not count it among the characteristics.

2. Moreover, the unconditioned factor (*asaṃskṛta*) persists eternally in its own nature (*svalakṣaṇe sthitibhāva*): the characteristic of duration is not without resemblance to the persistence of the unconditioned factor. In order to avoid any confusion, the Sūtra does not indicate duration as a characteristic of the conditioned factor.

3. Others [*anye*][686] think that the Sūtra does indeed name duration; it names it as an associate of deterioration (*jarā*), i.e., duration-change (*sthityanyathātva*), i.e., *sthiti* (duration) and *anyathātva* (change).

[Question:] – What purpose [*prayojana*] is there, would you say, in making one single characteristic of these two characteristics?

[Answer:] – Persons are attached [*saṅga*] to duration: in order to be disgusted with or not attached [*asaṅga*] to duration, the Sūtra names it together (*abhisamasya*) with deterioration, just as prosperity [*śrī*] is linked with a black ear [*kālakarṇa*] [or Śrī (the goddess of prosperity) with Kālakarṇī (the goddess of bad luck)].[687]

Conclusion: there are four characteristics.[688]

BAB.2.7.2. *Secondary characteristics (anulakṣaṇa) & refutation of infinite regress;*[689] *F 224–26*

[Objection:] – The origination, duration, etc., of any factor (*dharma*) whatsoever are also conditioned factors. They should thus arise, perdure, decay, perish; they should thus, in their turn, possess four characteristics: origination-of-origination [*jātijāti*], etc., which will be the secondary characteristics (*anulakṣaṇa*) of the factor under consideration. These secondary characteristics, being conditioned factors, have, in their turn, four characteristics. So there is the fault of infinite regress [*aparyavasāna-doṣa*].

[Answer:] – There is no infinite regress. {13 a}

46ab. **[The four primary characteristics of conditioned factors] have in their turn [secondary] characteristics termed (1) origination-of-origination, (2) duration-of-duration, [(3) deterioration-of-deterioration, (4) impermanence-of-impermanence].**[690]

The primary characteristic functions [*vṛtti*] with regard to eight factors [i.e., the principal factor, three other primary characteristics, and four secondary characteristics].

The secondary characteristic functions with regard to one factor [i.e., the primary characteristic that corresponds to it].[691] <225>

The four primary characteristics (*mūlalakṣaṇa*) are described above.

The four secondary characteristics (*anulakṣaṇa*) are (1) origination-of-origination [*jātijāti*]), (2) duration-of-duration [*sthitisthiti*], (3) deterioration-of-deterioration [*jarājarā*], (4) impermanence-of-impermanence [*anityatānityatā*].

All conditioned factors [*saṃskṛta*] are conditioned factors due to their primary characteristics; these, in their turn, are conditioned factors due to four secondary characteristics.

[Objection:] – [Then] each of the primary characteristics should have, just like the principal factor which it characterizes, four characteristics, and so forth.

[Answer:] – You do not understand the function [of the primary and secondary characteristics].

[Question: – What is this function (*vṛtti*)[692]?]

[Answer:] – It is the activity/capability [*kāritrā*] or operation [*puruṣakāra*] of the different characteristics [i.e., the primary and secondary characteristics].

When a factor (*dharma*) arises—which we will term the principal factor (*mūla-dharma*), a thought, a thought-concomitant (*caitta*)—nine factors, including itself, arise at the same time, i.e., the principal factor, four primary characteristics, four secondary characteristics.

[For example,] the first primary characteristic, the primary origination (*jāti*; *mūla-jāti*) causes (1) the principal factor, (2–4) plus three primary characteristics (duration, deterioration and impermanence), (5–8) plus four secondary characteristics to arise: in total, eight factors. (The primary origination) does not cause itself to arise: it arises through the secondary characteristic origination-of-origination (*jātijāti*). {13 b} – (i) In the same way, one hen [*kukkuṭī*] gives birth to many eggs [*apatya*], and each egg gives birth only to one chick (MVŚ, 200c19); (ii) in the same way, the primary origination (*jāti*; *mūlajāti*) causes eight factors to arise, whereas origination-of-origination causes only one factor to arise, namely, the primary origination.[693]

The same goes for the other primary and secondary characteristics. Duration-of-duration causes primary duration to perdure, (whereas primary duration) causes (1) the principal factor, (2–4) three primary characteristics and (5–8) four secondary characteristics, in which is included the duration-of-duration, to perdure.

The same for primary deterioration and primary impermanence which cause eight factors to decay and to perish, and which decay and perish themselves by means of the secondary characteristic, which corresponds to them, i.e., deterioration-of-deterioration, impermanence-of-impermanence (*jarājarā*; *anityatānityatā*). <226>

Thus the characteristics themselves have characteristics called *secondary characteristics* (*anulakṣaṇa*); they are four in number and not sixteen, and [thus] there is no fault of infinite regress [*anavasthāprasaṅga*].

.2.7.3. *Existential status & the characteristics;* F 226–38

The Sautrāntika[694] says: – All this is splitting empty space![695] Origination, duration, etc., do not exist as real entities (*na dravyataḥ saṃvidyante*) [in the way (*yathā*)[696] in which they have been discriminated (*vibhajyante*). For what reason?] We know that factors exist as real entities [*dravya*] either through (1) direct perception [*pratyakṣa*],

(2) inference [*anumāna*] or (3) scriptural authority [*āptāgama*], [as in the cases of factors such as form (*rūpa*), etc.], yet these three means of valid cognition (*pramāṇa*) are absent with respect to these characteristics.

BAB.2.7.3.a. *The Trilakṣaṇasūtra & its Sautrāntika interpretation as referring to a serial continuity; F 226–27*

The Sarvāstivādin says:[697] – But the Sūtra says:

> Of the conditioned factors, the arising can [also] be discerned (*utpādo 'pi prajñāyate*), [the passing away can also be discerned, and also the duration-change].[698]

[Reply by the Sautrāntika:[699]] – Fool! You cling to the words [*granthajñaḥ*] and miss the meaning [*na tu arthajñaḥ*]. The Fortunate One, however, said that it is the meaning [*artha*], and not the words, on which one should rely.[700] The [true] meaning of this Sūtra passage is evident:

Blinded by ignorance [*avidyāndha*], foolish people are convinced [*adhimukta*] that the uninterrupted stream (*prabandha*; *pravāha*) of conditioned forces (*saṃskṛta*; *saṃskāra*)[701] [has the nature of] self (*ātman*), of what belongs to the self [*ātmīya*], and are, therefore, obsessed [*abhiṣyvajante*] with the stream. {14 a} For the sake of removing their false conviction [*mithyādhimokṣa*] and the obsession that results from it, the Fortunate One[702]—wanting to make it clear that the stream (*pravāha*) [of conditioned forces (*saṃskāra*)] has the nature of being conditioned (*saṃskṛtatva*), i.e., of "being produced [through dependence or] through successive causes" (*pratītya-samutpannatā*)—made the following statement about the three characteristics of that which is produced through [dependence or] successive causes:

> There are three *saṃskṛta*-characteristics of the conditioned [*trīṇīmāni saṃskṛtasya saṃskṛtalakṣaṇāni*] (see F 223).[703]

It is the stream which the Fortunate One means to characterize as being conditioned, for, obviously, he does not [make this statement to] attribute the three characteristics to every single moment [*kṣaṇa*] of the serial continuity, since he [also] says that these characteristics can be discerned: Indeed, the arising [*utpāda*], passing away [*vyaya*] and duration-change [*sthityanyathātva*], [belonging to a single moment,] cannot be discerned [*prajñāyante*];[704] that which cannot be discerned does not deserve to be established as a characteristic [*lakṣaṇa*].[705] <227>

If the Sūtra uses the word *saṃskṛta* twice:[706] "There are three *saṃskṛta*-characteristics of the conditioned (*saṃskṛta*)", this is in order that one should know that these three characteristics are not (1) indications revealing the presence of a conditioned factor (*saṃskṛtāstitve lakṣaṇāni*), as in the case of seeing herons [*balākā*], which indicates that water [*jala*] must exist nearby; or (2) qualitative signs of a conditioned factor, as in the case of the signs of a maiden [*kanyālakṣaṇa*], which indicate her nature as virtuous [*sādhu*] or unvirtuous [*asādhu*]. No, these characteristics, occurring in a given entity, indicate that this given entity has the nature of being conditioned (*saṃskṛtalakṣaṇam = saṃskṛtatve lakṣaṇam*).

[Thus we will translate this canonical text (see F 223) in the following way:

> The conditioned (i.e., the serial continuity of conditioned factors) possesses three noticeable characteristics which indicate that it is conditioned, i.e., produced through successive causes. These characteristics are (1) arising, (2) duration-change, (3) passing away.]

B.2.7.3.b. *Provisional existence: the stream & the four characteristics;* F 227–29

[The Sautrāntika:[707]] – According to us, what one should understand is the following:

1. arising or origination (*utpāda*; *jāti*) is the beginning of the stream [of conditioned factors] (*pravāhasya ādiḥ*);
2. passing away or impermanence (*vyaya*; *anityatā*) is the extinction or stopping (*nivṛtti*; *uparati*) of the stream;
3. duration (*sthiti*) is the very stream continuing (*anuvartamāna*) from its beginning until its cessation;
4. duration-change (*sthityanyathātva*) or deterioration (*jarā*) is the modification of the continuous stream, the (qualitative) difference [*viśeṣa*] between its earlier and later or successive [moments].

It is by looking at it from this viewpoint—that is to say, by considering origination, impermanence, etc., as being the stream itself, the stream which is beginning, ending, prolonging itself, modifying itself (*pravāharūpa*)—that the Fortunate One said to Nanda who applies unceasingly mindfulness to his states of thought (*nityam upasthitasmṛti*):[708]

> Son of a good family [*kulaputra*], sensations are indeed well known by you as arising [*utpadyante*], as abiding [*tiṣṭhānte*], as coming to an end, disappearing or going to exhaustion [*astaṃ parikṣayaṃ paryādānaṃ gacchanti*].[709] <228>

We thus say:[710]

1. Origination [*jāti*] is the beginning of the stream [*pravāha*];
2. passing away of (the stream) [*vyaya*] is the cutting off [*uccheda*; *cheda*] [of the stream];
3. duration [*sthiti*] is the stream itself;

4. duration-change [*sthityanyathātva*] is the (qualitative) difference between earlier and later or successive (moments).

And moreover:

1. Arising (or origination) is existence following non-existence or existence that has not existed before;
2. duration is the stream [*prabandha*];
3. passing away (or impermanence) is the cutting off of the stream;
4. duration-change is considered to be the (qualitative) difference between earlier and later or successive moments of the stream.

[And:]

> Do you say—the factor (*dharma*) being momentary—that the factor would perish (immediately) if duration were absent? But, (if the factor is momentary,) it perishes spontaneously: it is useless that you attribute duration to the momentary factor.[711] <229>

Therefore, it is the stream (*pravāha*) that the Sūtra refers to when it speaks of duration, and the definition of the Abhidharma (*Prakaraṇapāda*, 694a26) is found to be justified: {15 a}

> What is duration [*sthiti*]? The conditioning forces (*saṃskāra*) arisen [*utpanna*] and not having been perished [*avināśa*].

The nature of the moment (*kṣaṇadharmatā*) cannot be "arisen and not having been perished".

[Objection:] – However, the *Jñānaprasthāna* (926b21) says:

> With respect to one thought (*ekasmin citte*),[712] what is arising [*utpāda*]? It is origination (*jāti*).
>
> What is passing away (*vyaya*)? It is death (*maraṇa*).
>
> What is duration-change (*sthityanyathātva*)? It is deterioration (*jarā*).

[Answer:] – But this passage of the Śāstra does not refer to one moment of thought but to the thought of a "homogeneous personal existence" (*nikāyasabhāgacitta*). [In a homogeneous personal existence (ii. 41) the thoughts are multiple, but this multiplicity can be designated as being one thought.]

BAB.2.7.3.c. *The moments & the four characteristics; F 229–30*

[The Sautrāntika:[713]] – However, provided that one does not consider the characteristics as distinct real entities [*dravyāntara*], these four characteristics [of the conditioned, i.e., of a stream of conditioned factors,] can also be applied to each moment (*kṣaṇa*).[714] [How is that?]

In fact,

1. arising [*utpāda*] [as applied] to each moment [refers to the fact that it] exists after not having existed (*abhūtvā bhāvaḥ*);
2. passing away (*vyaya*) [refers to the fact that] having existed, it no longer exists (*bhūtvā abhāvaḥ*);
3. duration [*sthiti*] [refers to] the connection of each prior [moment] with subsequent moments (*uttarottarakṣaṇānubandha*): in fact, the later moment resembles the previous moment, it is thus its substitute (*pratinidhībhūta*): the previous moment still exists, still abides, so to speak (*avatiṣṭhata iva*). Thus the later moment can be considered as the continuance of the previous moment;
4. duration-change (*sthityanyathātva*) [refers to] the qualitative difference (*visadṛśatva*) in this continuance or connection.

[Question:] – Then would you say that, when the successive moments arise alike (*sadṛśa*), there is no qualitative difference [*visadṛśatvā*] [i.e., no duration-change]?

[Answer:] – There is (some) qualitative difference, as this follows from the difference in the speed, slow or swift, of the falling of a *vajra* which is hurled or not hurled, which is hurled with force or without force:[715] a difference due to the transformation—different in each case—of the fundamental material elements (*mahābhūtapariṇāmaviśeṣa*) of the *vajra*. – When the factors succeed one another in a homogeneous stream, the difference is small; that is why, although they differ, they are considered to be alike. {15 b} <230>

The Sarvāstivādin objects. – Your definition (*vyavasthā*) of the characteristics does not hold for all conditioned factors. In fact, your definition of duration supposes a subsequent moment: this moment is lacking for the last moment of a sound [*śabda*] or of a flame [*arcis*], for the last moment of thought of a perfected being (*arhat*; *parinirvāṇakāla*). Thus the last moment of sound, of the flame, of the perfected being, has neither duration nor duration-change.

[Reply:] – We do not attribute duration to all conditioned factors! We say that all duration is subject to duration-change. The Fortunate One teaches three characteristics because, in certain cases (*saṃbhavaṃ prati*), there are three characteristics. But, for the last moment of the flame, there is only arising and passing away, not duration, not duration-change.

In summary, conditioned factors, (1) after not having existed, exist; (2) after having existed, exist no longer; (3) the stream of these factors is their duration; (4) the qualitative difference of the stream is their duration-change. Such is the teaching which the Fortunate One gives in the *sūtra* on the three characteristics. There is no use for distinct real entities [*dravyāntara*], origination, etc.

BAB.2.7.3.d. *The relationship of the characterized factor (lakṣya) & the characteristic (lakṣaṇa); F 230–31*

The Vaibhāṣika objects: – According to you, origination is the factor itself (*dharma*) insofar as it exists after having been non-existent. The factor which is the characterized factor (*lakṣya*) would then also be the characteristic (*lakṣaṇa*).

[Reply:] – What is wrong with that?

1. The characteristics (*lakṣaṇa*) marking a great person (*mahāpuruṣa*) are not different or distinct from the great person.

2. The dewlap [*sāsnā*], the tail [*lāṅgūla*], the hump [*kakuda*], the hoof [*śapha*], the horns [*viṣāṇa*], etc., of a cow, which are its characteristics [*gotvalakṣaṇa*], do not differ from the cow.

3. The fundamental material elements (*mahābhūta*), [earth (*pṛthivī*), etc.,] do not exist apart from their defining characteristics, solidity (*kāṭhinya*), etc. (i. 12d).

In the same way, for the Vaibhāṣika, who affirms the "momentariness" of factors (*kṣaṇikavādin*), the rising of smoke is none other than the smoke itself.[716] <231>

Let us have a closer look at this. Although I seize (*grah*) the intrinsic nature (*svabhāva*) of visible forms, etc., which are conditioned factors, as long as I do not know the fact (1) that they do not exist previously, (2) that they do not exist later, (3) that their stream transforms itself, so long do I not know their quality of being conditioned. Therefore, the quality of the conditioned does not have for its mark the quality of the conditioned, but rather the previous non-existence, etc.[717] And characteristics, [origination (*jāti*), etc.,] as distinct real entities, i.e., distinct from visible forms and other conditioned factors, do not exist.

BAB.2.7.3.e. *Objections regarding the simultaneous or successive activity of the characteristics; F 231–32*

[Objection:[718]] – Moreover, even if the characteristics were indeed distinct real entities (*dravyāntara*), [why would this nevertheless be impossible (*ayukta*)? Because] one factor (*dharma*) would have to (1) be born [*jāta*], (2) abide [*sthita*], (3) decay [*jīrṇa*] and (4) perish [*naṣṭa*] at one and the same time, [since these characteristics exist] together or simultaneously (*sahabhūta*) [with that factor].

The Sarvāstivādins in vain will maintain: – The characteristics [of the conditioned] do not perform their activity/capability at the same time (*kāritrakālabheda*); [for we Sarvāstivādins maintain]

1. that origination engenders [its activity/capability][719] when it is still future, i.e., before being born itself [*anāgatā hi jātiḥ kāritraṃ hi karoti*], and that once being born, it no longer engenders;[720]
2. that, [when a factor is already produced,] duration, deterioration and impermanence perform their activity/capability when they are present but not when they are still future;

The last three characteristics are, therefore, active in a moment when the first is no longer active, so that the four characteristics can be simultaneous without contradiction [or, it is not the case that when (a factor) is produced, it is also abiding, decaying and perishing[721]].

AB.2.7.3.ea. *The activity/capability of origination;* F 231–32

[Objection:] – Let us first look at origination, which, when it is future, engenders [its activity/capability]. One would have to examine:

1. [first (*tāvad*),] whether a future factor really exists (*dravyatas*) (v. 25 [F 50]);
2. [afterwards (*paścāt*),] whether a future factor, supposing that it does exist, can be active [*janayati*].

If origination, existing as future, engenders [its activity/capability], how can one say that it is future? <232> In fact, according to the Vaibhāṣika, the future factor is one that does not yet exercise its activity (*aprāptakāritraṃ hy anāgatam iti siddhāntaḥ*). You would have to redefine [*vaktavya*] the characteristic of the future.

On the other hand, when the factor [or the characteristic of origination] has arisen, has engendered [its activity/capability], and the operation of origination is past [or has disappeared] [*uparatakāritra*], how can you say that origination is then present? You would have to redefine the characteristic of the present.[722]

AB.2.7.3.eb. *The activity/capability of duration, deterioration, impermanence;* F 232

[Objection:] – In regard to the other characteristics, there are two possibilities, either (1) their activity/capability is exercised simultaneously [*yugapad*] or (2) their activity/capability is exercised successively [*krameṇa*].

In the first hypothesis,[723] {16 b} while duration causes a factor to perdure [*sthāpayati*], deterioration causes it to decay [*jarayati*], and impermanence causes it to perish [*vināśayati*], it would follow that the factor would abide [*sthita*], decay [*jīrṇa*] and perish [*vinaṣṭa*] at one and the same moment [*ekakṣaṇa*].

As for the second hypothesis, to accept that the activity/capability of the characteristics is not excercised simultaneously [but successively (*krameṇa*)] is to accept three moments, and this infringes upon the doctrine of momentariness [*kṣaṇikatva*].[724]

BAB.2.7.3.f. *The Vaibhāṣika reply: definition of the moment;* F 232

The Vaibhāṣika answers: – For us, the moment (*kṣaṇa*) is [precisely] the time in the course of which all these characteristics have completed their operation (*kāryaparisamāptilakṣaṇa eṣa naḥ kṣaṇaḥ*).[725]

BAB.2.7.3.g. *Objections regarding the individual characteristics as causally efficient factors;* F 232–35

BAB.2.7.3.ga. *Criticism of duration;* F 232–33

[Objection:] – In this hypothesis, explain then why duration, arising at the same time [*sahotpanna*] as deterioration and impermanence, accomplishes its operation of "causing to abide that which should abide" (*stāpyaṃ sthāpayati*) before deterioration and impermanence accomplish their operation of causing things to decay and perish.

[The Vaibhāṣikas might answer:] – Duration, being stronger, accomplishes its operation first.

We would then ask: – How is duration later weakened in such a manner that, encountering deterioration and impermanence, it decays and perishes, not alone, but with the factor (*dharma*) that it should have caused to abide?

[The Vaibhāṣikas might say:] – Duration, having achieved its task (*kṛtakṛtya*), cannot fulfill it again, in the same way that origination, having engendered [its activity/capability], no longer engenders [it].

[Answer:] – The comparison [to origination] is not appropriate:

[On the one hand,] the operation (*puruṣakāra*) of origination consists in attracting from the future the factor which origination should engender, and in causing it to enter into the present: <233> once the factor has entered into the present, origination is incapable of causing it to enter again.

On the other hand, the operation of duration is (i) to cause the factor, "which should be caused to abide" (*sthāpya*), to abide (*styāpayati*), (ii) to hinder the factor, "which the operation causes to abide", from deteriorating and perishing. Duration is capable of causing that which should be caused to abide, to abide indefinitely [*atyanta*]. Therefore, duration is capable of repeating its operation.

[We then would ask:] – Due to what obstacle or due to what adverse forces (*pratibandha*) will the activity/capability of duration cease once (the activity/capability) has begun? {17 a}

[You might say:] – The forces are deterioration and impermanence, whereby deterioration is weakening duration and impermanence then is killing it.

[We would then say:] – Since in this hypothesis deterioration and impermanence are stronger than duration, it is fitting that they exercise their activity/capability first.

Moreover, according to your conception of duration and its role, it is through the activity/capability of duration that, not only the principal factor but, moreover, deterioration and impermanence abide. Thus, when the activity/capability of duration comes to an end, the principal factor, deterioration and impermanence cease to perdure. We, [therefore,] ask: How and with regard to what object will deterioration and impermanence exercise their activity/capability of causing to decay and causing to perish?

[Furthermore,] we do not really see what deterioration and impermanence have to do. It is through duration that a factor, once arisen, does not perish for a certain time, does not perish as soon as it arises (*utpannamātra*). If duration, its task being accomplished, neglects the factor, quite certainly it will abide no longer; that is to say, it perishes by itself.

AB.2.7.3.gb. *Criticism of deterioration; F 233*

[Objection:[726]] – We could reasonably understand (1) duration and (2) impermanence in regard to a [single (*eka*)] factor: (1) "A factor, after having arisen, has not yet perished"; (2) "A factor, after having abided, perishes." – But how can one attribute deterioration to a [single] factor? Deterioration is transformation [*vipariṇāma*] [within the stream of conditioned factors], the qualitative difference [*viśeṣa*] between prior and subsequent [moments]. And yet, can one say of a [single] factor that it becomes different from itself?

> If [a factor] remains this, it is not that; if it becomes something different, it is no longer this. Thus the change of a [single] factor is impossible.[727] <234>

AB.2.7.3.gc. *Criticism of impermanence; F 234*

According to another school [*nikāyāntarīya*]:[728] – The characteristic of impermanence causes certain [material] factors (*dharma*), wood, pitcher [*ghaṭa*], etc., to perish once it has encountered the external causes of destruction [*vināśakāraṇa*], fire, hammer [*mudgara*], etc., {17 b}

[Reply:] – An absurd theory! This is like a sick person who, after having taken a laxative [*harītakī*], supplicates the gods to make it efficacious! In the logic of this system, it is the external causes of destruction which destroy, and the characteristic of impermanence is of no use.

The same school [also] assumes: – Through the virtue of their characteristic of impermanence—without foreign causes intervening—thought and thought-concomitants [*citta*; *caitta*], [the sound and the flame,] immediately perish (*kṣaṇa-nirodha*). Impermanence and duration accomplish their operation at the same time: a factor abides and perishes at the same time.

[Reply:] – This is unacceptable.

We conclude: it is with regard to the stream [*pravāha*] that the Fortunate One teaches the characteristics of the conditioned. Understood in this way, the Sūtra (ii, F 223, 227) does not lend itself to criticism:[729]

> There are three characteristics which make it clear that the conditioned is conditioned, i.e., produced through dependence… .[730]

BAB.2.7.3.gd. *Criticism of origination; F 234–35*

[Objection:] – If arising, while in its future state, is engendering [*janika*] the factor which is to be engendered [*janya*], why do not all future factors arise together or simultaneously [*yugapad*]?[731]

46cd. [Sarvāstivādin:] – Origination is able to engender that which is to be engendered, but not without the [corresponding] complete assemblage of causes and conditions.[732]

Apart from the [corresponding] complete assemblage (*sāmagrya*) of causes [*hetu*] and conditions [*pratyaya*], origination alone does not have the capability (*sāmarthya*) to engender the factor which is to be engendered. Therefore, future factors do not all arise together or simultaneously. <235>

Objection (by the Sautrāntikas:)[733] – If that is so, we observe that it is only the causes and conditions which have the capability [*sāmarthya*] to engender, and not origination, i.e., this characteristic which, [according to the Sarvāstivādins, is supposed] to accompany the factor (*dharma*) from the beginning of time and causes the factor to arise when, finally, the causes and conditions of this factor come together! [The dependence of production upon a complete assemblage of causes and condition is proven by the fact that] when there is complete assemblage of causes and conditions, the factor is produced; when there is no such complete assemblage, it is not produced: what efficacy could we attribute to origination? [Therefore, only the causes and conditions are generating.[734]] {18 a}

Reply by the Sarvāstivādin: – Do you claim to know all the factors (*dharma*) which exist? The nature of factors [*dharmaprakṛti*] is subtle [*sūkṣma*]![735] Although their reality is evident, they are unknowable.[736]

AB.2.7.3.h. *The notions of "arisen", "the arising of form", etc. & real entities; F 235–37*

[Sarvāstivādin:] – Moreover, in the absence of the characteristic "origination", the notion of "arisen" (*jātabuddhi* = *jāta iti*) would be absent.[737] And if origination is nothing other than the factor itself existing after having been non-existent, the genitive [*ṣaṣṭhīvacana*] "the arising of form" [*rūpasya utpāda*], "the arising of sensation", would not be justified; for this is tantamount to saying "the form of form" [*rūpasya rūpam*], "the sensation of sensation". – The same for duration, deterioration and passing away.

Reply by (the Sautrāntika:[738]) – This theory will lead you very far afield: in order to justify the notion of empty (*śūnya*), the notion of nonself [*anātmabuddhi*], you would [have to] accept the existence of an entity called *emptiness* [*śūnyatā*], the existence of an entity called *non-selfhood* [*anātmatva*]. And moreover, in order to establish notions [*buddhi*] such as: (1) one [*eka*], two [*dvi*]; (2) great [*mahat*], small [*aṇu*]; <236> (3) separate (*pṛthak*); (4) conjoined [*saṃyukta*]; (5) disjoined [*vyukta*]; (6) far [*para*]; (7) near [*apara*]; (8) existing [*sat*]; etc., you would [have to] accept, in conformity with the Vaiśeṣikas, the whole series of entities: (1) number (*saṃkhyā*); (2) extension (*parimāṇa*); (3) separateness (*pṛthaktva*); (4) conjunction (*saṃyoga*); (5) disjunction (*vibhāga*); (6) farness (*paratva*); (7) nearness (*aparatva*); (8) existence (*sattā*); etc. You would require "pitcher-ness" (*ghaṭatva*) in order to establish the notion of a pitcher [*ghaṭa*].

[The Sautrāntika:] – As for the genitive [*ṣaṣṭīvidhāna*], you do not accept that the intrinsic nature of form [*rūpasya svabhāva*] and form [*rūpa*] are distinct [*anya*] entities, and yet you speak of the intrinsic nature of form.

On that account [*tasmāt*], you have not established that "origination" is a distinct real entity [*dravya*]; you have not established that origination is not merely a provisional designation (*prajñāptimātra*) of the factor (*dharma*) insofar as it exists after having been non-existent.

When I want to make known to someone (*jñāpanārtham*) that a certain factor exists which, previously, did not exist, I say to them: "this factor has arisen", I designate this factor as being arisen. – Many factors, form, sensation, etc., arise, i.e., "exist after having been non-existent". Thus there are many arisings, i.e., many factors arising. Arising [*utpāda*] being multiple (*bahuvikalpa*), {18 b} with the intention to specify it so that my interlocutors know that it refers to arising having the name *form* and not to arising having the name *sensation*, I would use the genitive [*ṣaṣṭī*], "arising of form", "arising of sensation", though the arising of form is only the form arising. In the same way, one commonly says "the odor of sandalwood" [*candanasya gandha*], although sandalwood is only odor, and "the body of the torso" [*śilāputrakasya śarīra*], although the torso is only body.[739]

BAB.2.7.3.ha. *The distinction of conditioned and unconditioned factors & the existence of the characteristic "origination"; F 236–37*

Sarvāstivādin: – Since we accept the existence of the characteristic "origination", which belongs to conditioned factors and <237> does not belong to unconditioned factors, we can easily explain why unconditioned factors do not arise. But if conditioned factors arise without "origination", why do unconditioned factors, i.e., space [*ākāśa*], etc., not arise?

[Answer:] – We say that conditioned factors arise, for, after not having existed, they exist (*abhūtvā bhavanti*). But [if] the unconditioned factor is eternal [*nitya*], how could it arise? – You explain that certain factors (*dharma*), i.e., the unconditioned factors, are without the characteristic "origination", because, you say, such is the nature of factors (*dharmatā*):[740] we say that, by virtue of the nature of factors, all factors are without arising (*na sarvaṃ jāyate*).

What is more, according to you, all conditioned factors (*saṃskṛta*) equally possess the characteristic "origination" (*tulye jātimattve*), which you refuse to unconditioned factors (*asaṃskṛta*): however, you admit that certain causes are capable of producing form [*rūpa*] and incapable of producing sensation [*vedanā*]. In the same way, according to us, since conditioned and unconditioned factors are equally devoid of the characteristic "origination", all causes [and conditions] which produce conditioned factors are inefficacious with regard to unconditioned factors.

BAB.2.7.3.i. *Vaibhāṣika: the four characteristics as real entities & the scriptures; F 237–38*

The Vaibhāṣika says that the four characteristics, i.e., origination, etc., are real entities [*dravya*].[741] – Why?[742] – Should we abandon the Āgamas[743] for the reason that there are persons who object to them [*dūṣaka*]? {19 a} One does not give up sowing [barley (*yava*)] for fear of gazelles [*mṛga*], one does not give up eating sweetmeats [*modaka*] because of flies [*makṣikā*].[744] <238> One must refute the objections and hold on to the Doctrine (*doṣeṣu pratividhātavyaṃ siddhāntaś cānusartavyaḥ*).

[The characteristics have been discussed.]

AB.2.8. *Collections of names, phrases and syllables (nāmakāya, padakāya, vyañjanakāya);*[745] *F 238–43*

1. Nature; F 238
2. Existential status; F 240
   a. Objection 1: Names, phrases and syllables are material form; F 240
   b. Objection 2: Speech as articulated sound established by convention suffices; F 240
   c. Objection 3: Names cannot issue forth from speech; F 240
   d. Objection 4: Syllables do not issue forth from speech; F 241
   e. Objection 5: Present names would not designate the past and future signified; F 242
   f. Objection 6: Only syllables would suffice to exist as real entities; F 242
3. Location, range, effect, moral quality & syllables, names and phrases; F 243

AB.2.8.1. *Nature & the collections of names, phrases and syllables;*[746] *F 238–40*

What is the collection of names (*nāmakāya*), collection of phrases (*padakāya*), collection of syllables (*vyañjanakāya*)?

47 ab. (1) The collection of names, [(2) the collection of phrases and (3) the collection of syllables] are [respectively] the collections [*samukti*] of (1) ideations (*saṃjñā*), (2) sentences (*vākya*) and (3) phonemes (*akṣara*).[747]

1. By "names" or "words" (*nāman*)[748] one should understand *saṃjñākaraṇa*: "that which causes ideation to arise" [or "that which is caused by ideation"],[749] for example, the words "color", "sound", "odor", etc.

2. By "phrases" (*pada*)[750] one should understand sentences (*vākya*), phrases [long enough or] including the necessary details to bring to completion [the explication] of the signified (*yāvatārthaparisamāpti*),[751] for example the verse, "[Alas], impermanent are the conditioning forces (*saṃskāra*)..." and so on.[752] <239>

Or else, by "phrases" one should understand that which causes one to understand (*yena gamyante*) the distinctive relations (*saṃbandhaviśeṣa*) of (i) [verbal] activity [*kriyā*], (ii) quality [*guṇa*], (iii) tense [*kāla*] [of words in an expression] with regard to a certain person: for example: (i) he cooks, he reads, he goes [*pacati paṭhati gacchati*]; (ii) it is black, yellow, red [*kṛṣṇo gauro raktaḥ*];[753] (iii) he cooks, he will cook, he cooked [*pacati pakṣyati apākṣīt*].[754]

3. By "syllables" (*vyañjana*)[755] one should understand phonemes (*akṣara*; iii. 85bc), i.e., the letters (*varṇa*), vowels and consonants, for example, *a, ā, i, ī*, etc. [*ka, kha, ga*, etc.].

[Question:] – But are the phonemes not the names (*nāma*) of the [written] letters (*lipyavayava*)?

[Answer:] – One does not make or pronounce (*praṇīta*) the phonemes in order to indicate, to give an idea [*pratyāyana*] of the [written] letters; but one makes or writes [*praṇīta*] the letters in order to indicate, to give an idea of the phonemes, for, when one does not hear them [*aśrūyamaṇa*], one nevertheless comes to understand them [*pratīyeran*] through writing [*lekhya*]. Therefore, the phonemes are not the names of the [written] letters. {19 b}

[Of these, the collection of names is the collection of ideations, (the collection of phrases is the collection of sentences, the collection of syllables is the collection of phonemes).][756]

4. "Body, collection" (*kāya*), i.e., "collection" (*samukti*); *samukti*, in fact, has the meaning of "gathering" (*samavāya*), according to *Dhātupāṭha*, iv. 114.

Thus we have:

1. collection of names (*nāmakāya*) = "visual form", "sound", "odor", etc.; <240>
2. collection of phrases (*padakāya*) = "All conditioning forces (*saṃskāra*) are impermanent [*anitya*], all factors (*dharma*) are nonself [*anātman*]; *nirvāṇa* is peaceful [*śānta*]...", etc.;
3. collection of syllables (*vyañjanakāya*) = *ka, kha, ga, gha, ṅa*, etc.

BAB.2.8.2. *Existential status & the collections of names, phrases and syllables; F 240*

BAB.2.8.2.a. *Objection 1: Names, phrases and syllables are material form; F 240*

Objection by (the Sautrāntika:[757]) – Are not names, phrases and syllables (*nāman*; *pada*; *vyañjana*) "speech" (*vāc*) in their intrinsic nature [*svabhāva*] and, therefore, have sound as their nature (*śabdātmaka*)? Thus they form part of the aggregate of material form (*rūpaskandha*); they are not formations (*saṃskāra*) dissociated from thought [*cittaviprayukta*] as the Sarvāstivādin teaches.

The Sarvāstivādin: – These [three, i.e., names, phrases and syllables,] are not "speech" [*vāc*] [in their intrinsic nature]. Speech is "articulated sound" (*ghoṣa*), but an articulated sound alone (*ghoṣamātra*)—for example a cry—does not indicate and cause one to understand [*pratīyante*] the signified [*artha*].

[Question:] – What does [indicate it]?

[The Sarvāstivādin:] – It is the name (*nāman*)—issuing forth, moreover, from articulated sound [i.e., speech] (*vācam upādāya; pravartate*)—which brings to light (*dyotayati*), or indicates and causes one to understand (*pratyāyayati*), the signified.

B.2.8.2.b. *Objection 2: Speech as articulated sound established by convention suffices; F 240*

(The Sautrāntika:[758]) – What I call "speech" [*vāc*] is not articulated sound alone [*ghoṣamātra*], but rather the articulated sound which indicates or causes one to understand [*pratīyate*] the signified.

[Question: – What is the articulated sound which indicates or causes one to understand the signified?]

[Answer:] – It is the articulated sound with regard to which speakers [*vaktṛ*] have come to an agreement [*kṛtāvadhi*] that it indicates a certain signified. It is in this way that the Ancients invested the sound *go* with the power to indicate nine things [*svartha*]: {20 a}.

> The scholars [*medhāvin*] have established the sound *go* in regard to nine things: (1) speech [*vāc*], (2) cardinal region [*dig*], (3) earth [*bhū*], (4) rays of light [*raśmi*], (5) diamond [*vajra*], (6) cattle [*paśu*], (7) eye [*aksi*], (8) heaven [*svarga*] and (9) water [*vāri*].[759]

The philosopher for whom "it is the name (*nāman*) which manifests or brings to light [*dyotayati*] the signified", should accept that the sound "*go*" has been endowed, through convention, with these different acceptations. Thus, if such and such a signified is indicated to the listener by such and such a name, it is indeed articulated sound alone (*ghoṣa; śabdamātra*) that indicates the signified. What then is the use of positing the distinct entity that you call "name"?

B.2.8.2.c. *Objection 3: Names cannot issue forth from speech; F 240–41*

(The Sautrāntika) continues:[760] – [The following is not yet known: how does name (*nāma*) issue forth from "speech" (*vāc*)?] Would name be either (1) produced (*utpādya; janya*) from speech[761] or (2) manifested (*prakāśya; vyāṅgya*) from speech?[762] <241>

1. In the first hypothesis, since speech has articulated sound (*ghoṣa*) as its intrinsic nature, then any articulated sound [*ghoṣamātra*], whatever it may be, even the cry of

an animal, will "produce" name. Or if name is held to be "produced" only through an articulated sound of a particular nature [*ghoṣaviśeṣa*]—the lettered articulated sound (*varṇātmaka*)—then this particular articulated sound, being capable of "producing" name, will be quite sufficient to manifest or bring to light [*dyotaka*] the signified.

2. In the second hypothesis, this same criticism holds, by replacing the verb "to produce" with the verb "to manifest".

BAB.2.8.2.ca. *The various moments of sound do not exist in the same moment; F 241*

[Sautrāntika:[763]] – 1. But it is absurd to suppose that speech [*vāc*] "produces" [*utpāda*] name [*nāma*]. In fact, the [various moments (*sāmagrya*) of] sound [*śabda*] [which constitute a word] do not exist [as one factor] in the same moment [*kṣaṇaika-milana*], for example *r-ū-p-a*.[764] Name, [on the other hand,] which you define as one factor (*dharma*), i.e., one real entity [*ekasya*; *dravya*], cannot arise part by part [*bhāgaśas*]. Thus how does speech, when it produces name, produce it?

[Possible answer:] – The case is analogous to that of non-informative action (*avijñapti*; iv. 3d): the {20 b} last moment of informative action (*vijñapti*), i.e., bodily or vocal action, produces [*utpādayati*] non-informative action in dependence upon [*apekṣa*] past moments [of informative action].[765]

[The Sautrāntika:] – But if the last moment of the sound of speech produces [*utpāda*] name, it would suffice to hear the last sound [*śabda*] in order to understand [*pratipadyeta*] the signified.

It is not a way out to suppose (1) that speech [*vāc*] produces (*janayati*) syllables (*vyañjana*), (2) that syllables further produce name [*nāma*], (3) that name makes one understand the signified. In fact, the same objection [as above] appears: "The [various moments of] sound [which constitute a word] do not exist or meet [as one factor] in the same moment, etc."

2. For the same reason, it is absurd to suppose that speech "manifests" [*prakāśa*] name. [The (various moments of) sound [which constitute a word] do not exist or meet [as one factor] in the same moment, and one factor, i.e., one real entity, such as name, cannot arise part by part... and so on.]

BAB.2.8.2.d. *Objection 4: Syllables do not issue forth from speech; F 241–42*

[Sautrāntika:] – (The hypothesis that speech [*vāc*] produces syllables [*vyañjana*]—a hypothesis we have (above) provisionally tolerated—calls, moreover, for new comments:)

Experts apply their minds vainly but cannot find the syllables distinct from speech.[766]

Moreover, speech [*vāc*] neither (1) produces [*utpādika*] nor (2) manifests [*prakāśika*] syllables [*vyañjana*], for the same reasons which bring it about that speech neither produces nor manifests name [*nāma*; see above]: (Since speech has articulated sound as its intrinsic nature, any articulated sound alone, whatsoever it may be, would have to produce or manifest syllables. <242> Or if syllables are held to be produced or manifested only through an articulated sound of a particular nature... [*same as at the beginning of objection 3*].)

.2.8.2.e. *Objection 5: Present names would not designate the past and future signified; etc.; F 242*

But the Sarvāstivādin may assume: – Like the characteristic "origination", the name arises together with (*sahaja*) the signified [*artha*]. The question of knowing whether it is (1) produced or (2) manifested by speech, [thus] disappears.

[Reply:] – In this hypothesis, one would have no present [*vartamāna*] name designating a past [*atīta*] or future [*anāgata*] signified [*artha*].

Moreover, a father, a mother or other persons arbitrarily fix the name which is the particular name of the son, daughter, etc: how can you accept that the name, like the characteristic "origination", arises simultaneously with the signified?

Finally, unconditioned factors [*asaṃskṛtānāṃ dharmānām*] would not have a name since they do not arise: a consequence which the Sarvāstivādin cannot accept.

.2.8.2.f. *Objection 6: Only syllables would suffice to exist as real entities; F 242–43*

But the Sarvāstivādins support their claim with a text. The Fortunate One said:

> The verse [*gāthā*] is based on names, [and the poet (*kavi*) is the basis of the verse].[767]

(The Sautrāntika[768]) answers: – (1) Name (*nāman*) is a sound (*śabda*) upon which persons agree [*kṛtāvadhi*] that it indicates a certain signified [*artha*].[769] (2) Verse (*gāthā*) or phrase (*vākya*; *pada*) is a certain arrangement (*racanā*) of names: it is in this sense that, according to the Fortunate One, it is based (*saṃniśrita*) on the names. {21 a} – To assume a distinct real entity (*dravyāntara*) called *phrase* (*pada*) is a superfluous hypothesis. You might as well maintain that distinct real entities termed "a line (of ants)" [*paṅkti*] or "a succession of thoughts" [*cittānupūrvya*] exist distinct from ants [*pipīlika*] and thoughts [*citta*].[770] Assume then that the syllables alone (*akṣara*; *vyañjanamātra*), which (from our point of view) are sounds (in their intrinsic nature), exist as distinct real entities.[771] [The collection of names, etc., will be only collocations (*samūha*) of those (syllables). The designation (*prajñapti*) of that (names, etc., as distinct real entities) would thus be useless (*apārthika*).[772]]

The Vaibhāṣika: – We accept the collection of names (*nāmakāya*), the collection of phrases (*padakāya*) and the collection of syllables (*vyañjanakāya*) as [real entities (*dravya*),] as formations dissociated from thought [*viprayuktasaṃskāra*], for all factors (*dharma*) are not accessible through understanding or reasoning [*tarkagamya*].[773] <243>

BAB.2.8.3. *Location, range, effect, moral quality & syllables, names and phrases;*

F 243

One asks:

1. [Location:] With which realm of existence are the syllables, names and phrases connected [*pratisaṃyukta*]?
2. [Range:] Are the syllables, etc., [factors] indicative of sentient beings (*sattvākhya*) or non-indicative of sentient beings (i. 10b)?
3. [Effect:] Are the syllables, etc., [effects], i.e., an effect of retribution [*vipākaja*], an effect of accumulation [*aupacayika*] or an effect of equal outflow [*naiṣyandika*] (i. 37)?
4. [Moral Quality:] Are the syllables, etc., wholesome [*kuśala*], unwholesome [*akuśala*] or non-defined [*avyākṛta*]?

47cd. **(1) [The syllables, names and phrases] are connected with the realm of desire and the realm of fine-materiality; (2) they are factors indicative of sentient beings; (3) they are an effect of equal outflow; (4) they are [unobscured]-non-defined.**[774]

1. Syllables, etc., are connected [*āpta*] with two realms of existence. According to one opinion, they are also connected with the realm of immateriality, but there they are "not expressible" (*anabhilāpya, akathya*).[775] {21 b}

2. They are factors indicative of sentient beings, proceeding from the efforts [*prayatna*] of sentient beings and consisting of lettered articulated sound (*varṇa*), etc. In fact, they [manifest or bring to light [*dyotayati*] the signified, yet] accompany [*samanvāgata*] the person who speaks, not the signified which they manifest or bring to light [*dyotyate*].

3. They are an effect of equal outflow (*naiṣyandika*) [only], being produced through the homogeneous cause (*sabhāgahetu*; ii. 52); they are not an effect of retribution [*vipākaja*], since they proceed from the desire [*icchā*] of the person who speaks; they are not an effect of accumulation (*aupacayika*), since they are not material [*arūpin*].[776]

4. They are unobscured-non-defined [*anivṛtāvyākṛta*; ii. 28] [only].[777]

.2.9. *The modes of group homogeneity, possessions, characteristics, two attainments, non-possession; F 243–44*

We will explain in brief the modes, not yet indicated, of the other formations dissociated from thought [*viprayuktasaṃskāra*; ii. 35].

47d–48b. In the same way, the [group] homogeneity [(1) is connected with the realm of desire and the realm of fine-materiality; (2) is a factor indicative of sentient beings; (3) is an effect of equal outflow; (4) is unobscured-non-defined, yet] is, in addition, (5) an effect of retribution, (6) is connected with the three realms of existence.[778] <244>

"In the same way" [*tathā*], that is to say: like the syllables, names and phrases, the [group] homogeneity (*sabhāgatā*) (1) is connected with the first two spheres [*avacara*] [i.e., the realm of desire and the realm of fine-materiality], (2) is a factor indicative of sentient beings, (3) is an effect of equal outflow, (4) is unobscured-non-defined. But the [group] homogeneity is not only an effect of equal outflow: in addition, (5) it is an effect of retribution; (6) it is not only connected with the first two spheres: it is also connected with the third.

48b. Possessions are of two types [i.e., an effect of equal outflow and an effect of retribution].[779]

[Possessions (*prāpti*)] are (1) an effect of equal outflow and (2) an effect of retribution.

48c. The characteristics, [i.e., origination, deterioration, duration and impermanence, are] also [of two types, like the possessions.[780]

The characteristics [*lakṣaṇa*], origination, etc., are—like the possessions—of two types [i.e., (1) an effect of equal outflow and (2) an effect of retribution].

48cd. The two attainments and non-possession are [only] an effect of equal outflow.[781]

The two attainments without thought [*acittasamāpatti*], [i.e., the attainment of non-ideation and the attainment of cessation,] and the non-possessions [*aprāpti*; *asamanvāgama*] are an effect of equal outflow only.

As regards [all of them, i.e., the possession, the characteristics, the two attainments and non-possession,] their being connected to a realm, their being factors indicative of sentient beings or non-indicative of sentient beings], their moral quality (wholesome, etc.), the explanations have been given above. {22 a}

The characteristics coexist [*sahabhūtva*] with all conditioned factors, thus they are factors indicative of sentient beings or non-indicative of sentient beings [*sattva–asattvākhya*].

For the state of non-ideation (*āsaṃjñika*) and [vitality (*jīvita*), i.e.,] the life-force (*āyus*), see ii. 41d and 45a. {vi. 1 a}[782]

[The formations dissociated from thought have been discussed.]

CLASSIFICATION OF FACTORS ACCORDING TO CAUSES (HETU), EFFECTS (PHALA), CONDITIONS (PRATYAYA);[783] *F 244–331*

We have seen (ii. 46cd) that "origination [*jāti*] is able to engender that which is to be engendered, but not without the [corresponding] complete assemblage of causes (*hetu*) and conditions (*pratyaya*)".[784] What are the causes, what are the conditions?[785] <245>

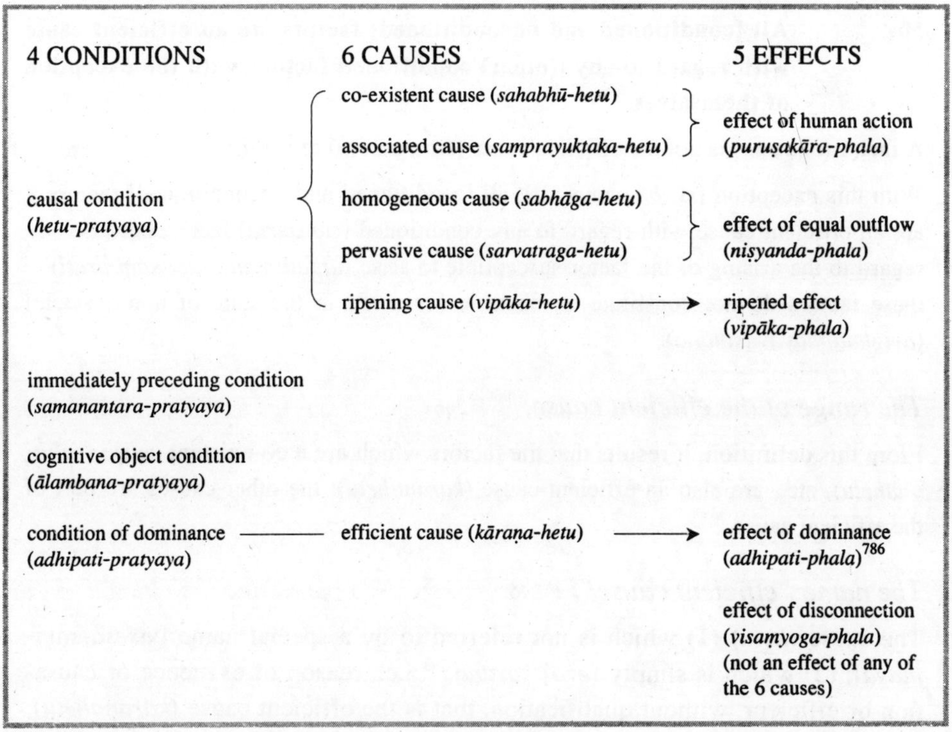

4 CONDITIONS
6 CAUSES
5 EFFECTS
co-existent cause (*sahabhū-hetu*)
associated cause (*saṃprayuktaka-hetu*)
effect of human action (*puruṣakāra-phala*)
causal condition (*hetu-pratyaya*)
homogeneous cause (*sabhāga-hetu*)
pervasive cause (*sarvatraga-hetu*)
effect of equal outflow (*niṣyanda-phala*)
ripening cause (*vipāka-hetu*)
ripened effect (*vipāka-phala*)
immediately preceding condition (*samanantara-pratyaya*)
cognitive object condition (*ālambana-pratyaya*)
condition of dominance (*adhipati-pratyaya*)
efficient cause (*kāraṇa-hetu*)
effect of dominance (*adhipati-phala*)[786]
effect of disconnection (*visaṃyoga-phala*) (not an effect of any of the 6 causes)

Fig. 1: The correlation between conditions, causes and effects[787]

A. *THE SIX CAUSES (HETU)*;[788] *F 245–75*

49. **Cause is considered as sixfold: (1) efficient cause, (2) co-existent cause, (3) homogeneous cause, (4) associated cause, (5) pervasive cause, (6) ripening cause.**[789] {1 b}

1. Efficient cause (*kāraṇahetu*; ii. 50a);
2. co-existent cause (*sahabhūhetu*; ii. 50b);
3. homogeneous cause (*sabhāgahetu*; ii. 52a);
4. associated cause (*saṃprayuktakahetu*; ii. 53c);
5. pervasive cause (*sarvatragahetu*; ii. 54a);
6. ripening cause (*vipākahetu*; ii. 54c):

these are the six types of causes [*hetu*] which the Ābhidhārmikas (*Jñānaprasthāna*, 920c5) recognize.[790] <246>

CAA. *Efficient cause (kāraṇahetu);*[791] *F 246–48*

CAA.1. *General definition;*[792] *F 246*

50a. All [conditioned and unconditioned] factors are an efficient cause with regard to any [(other) conditioned factor], with the exception of themselves.[793]

A factor (*dharma*) is not the efficient cause (*kāraṇahetu*) of itself.[794]

With this exception [*svabhāvavarjya*], all [conditioned and unconditioned] factors[795] are an efficient cause with regard to any conditioned (*saṃskṛta*) factor, because—in regard to the arising of the factor susceptible to arise (*utpattimant*; *utpādaṃ prati*)—these factors do not constitute an obstacle [or abide in the state of non-obstacle] (*avighnabhāvāvasthāna*).

CAA.2. *The range of the efficient cause;*[796] *F 246*

From this definition, it results that the factors which are a co-existent cause (*sahabhūhetu*), etc., are also an efficient cause (*kāraṇahetu*): the other causes are part of the efficient cause.[797]

CAA.3. *The name "efficient cause"; F 246*

The cause (*hetu*) (1) which is not referred to by a special name [*viśeṣa-saṃjñayā*], (2) which is simply [*eva*] *kāraṇa*,[798] i.e., reason of existence or causation or efficient, without qualification, that is the efficient cause (*kāraṇahetu*): it receives as its particular name the name which suits all causes. Compare this with the name of the sense-sphere of form [i.e., of visible form] (*rūpāyatana*; i. 24).

The efficient cause calls for the following observations.

A.4. *Clarifications to the given definition;* F 246–47

A.4.1. *The meaning of "arising (of factors)";* F 246–47

[Objection:] – The fluxes (*āsrava*) are produced among the ignorant; once the truths are known, they are not produced. In the same way, the stars (*jyotis*) are not visible when the sun [*sūrya*] shines. <247> Thus the cognition [*jñāna*] of the truths and the sun [actually] make an obstacle (*vighna*) to the fluxes, the stars. Thus it is wrong to say that all conditioned factors are an efficient cause (*kāraṇahetu*) because they do not constitute an obstacle [or abide in the state of non-obstacle] to the arising [of a factor susceptible to arise].

[Answer:] – We understand that the cognition of the truths and the light of the sun do not make an obstacle to the arising of the factor which is "arising" (*utpadyamāna*), i.e., to the factor which—its causes and conditions being completely assembled[799]—is going to exist without delay (*anantarabhāvin*).

A.4.2. *The meaning of "cause" and the two types of efficient cause;* F 247

[Question:] – Granted that it is possible to call "cause", "reason of existence", "causation", "enabling", that which is "capable" of making an obstacle [*vighnakāraṇa*] yet does not make an obstacle [*avighnakāraṇa*]. For example, villagers [*grāmīṇa*], {2 a} when their lord (*bhojaka*) does not oppress them (*anupadrotar*), say: "We are happy because of our master (*svāminā smaḥ sukhitāḥ*)."[800] But can one call that which is "incapable" of making an obstacle [and thus] does not make an obstacle a cause? [For example,]

1. *nirvāṇa* is incapable of making an obstacle to the arising of any conditioned factor, whatever it may be;[801]
2. in the same way, future factors [*anutpattidharma*] [are incapable of making an obstacle] with regard to past factors;
3. in the same way, hell beings (*nāraka*) or animals [*tiryak*] [are incapable of making an obstacle] with regard to sentient beings of the realm of immateriality.

[Thus,] with respect to making an obstacle to the arising of the conditioned factors in question, (1) *nirvāṇa*, (2) future factors and (3) hell beings are as if they did not exist (*asattulya*). Can they be considered as causes?

[Answer:] – They are causes; for, even when their lord would be incapable of harming them, the villagers would express themselves as we have said; but not about a non-existing lord.

The exposition (*nirdeśa*) which we have given of the efficient cause (*kāraṇahetu*) is a general exposition and includes (see ii. 56b):[802]

i. that which is the chief (*pradhāna*)[803] efficient cause, the efficient cause *par excellence*, and
ii. that which is the subordinate (*apradhāna*) efficient cause.

The efficient cause *par excellence* is the generative (*janaka*) cause: in this sense, the eye and the visible form [*cakṣurūpa*] are an efficient cause of the visual consciousness [*cakṣurvijñāna*]; likewise food [*āhāra*] with regard to the body [*śarīra*],[804] the seed [*bīja*], etc., with regard to the sprout [*aṅkura*], etc. <248>

Objection: – If all factors (*dharma*) are the causes of other factors because they do not make an obstacle [*anāvaraṇabhāva*], why do not all factors arise together or simultaneously [*yugapad*]?[805] When a murder [*prāṇātipāta*] is committed, why are not all sentient beings, like the murderer [*ghātaka*] himself, guilty of the transgression of murder?

[Answer:] – This objection is vain. In fact, all the factors receive the name of efficient cause because they do not make an obstacle: it is not that they are all agents (*kāraka*).

Other masters: – All efficient causes (*kāraṇahetu*) possess a real capability (*sāmarthya*) with regard to any factor (*dharma*). {2 b} For example:

1. *nirvāṇa* [is capable of indirectly producing] the visual consciousness.

[Question: – How is that?]

[Answer:] – [First,] a mental consciousness [*manovijñāna*], wholesome or unwholesome, arises having *nirvāṇa* as its cognitive object (*ālambana*; ii. 62cd); later, from this mental consciousness a visual consciousness arises; *nirvāṇa* thus has capability, indirectly [*paramparayā*], with regard to the visual consciousness.

2–3. The same argument applies to future factors [*anutpattidharma*], to hell beings [*nāraka*], etc.

[The efficient cause has been discussed.]

CAB. *Co-existent cause (sahabhūhetu);*[806] F 248–55

CAB.1. *General definition;*[807] F 248–49

50bd. **Factors which are reciprocally effects [*mithaḥphala*], for instance, (1) [fundamental material] elements (*bhūta*), (2) thought and thought-associates, (3) the characteristics [i.e., origination, etc.] and the factor they characterize, are a co-existent cause.**[808]

The factors (*dharma*) that are effects of one another [*parasparaphala*] [i.e., the effect of human action (*puruṣakāraphala*); ii. 56d, 58a] are called *co-existent cause* (*sahabhūhetu*).[809] <249>

For example, (1) the fundamental material elements (*mahābhūta*)[810] are, with one another [*anyo'nya*], co-existent causes. (2) The same also for thought [*citta*] and [the factors that are] its associates [*cittānuvartin*] (ii. 51); (3) the same also for the [four] characteristics [*saṃskṛtalakṣaṇa*], origination, etc. (ii. 45b), and the [conditioned] factor (*dharma*) they characterize [*lakṣya*].

Thus all conditioned (*saṃskṛta*) factors are part of the category of co-existent cause, [where applicable (*yathāyogaṃ*), i.e.,] in each case, the factors which are in a mutual relationship of causality must be distinguished.[811]

CAB.2. *Clarifications to the given definition;*[812] *F 249–53*

CAB.2.1. *The range of the co-existent cause; F 249*

We have reason to complete the above definition. – A factor (*dharma*) is [also considered to be] a co-existent cause (*sahabhūhetu*) of its secondary characteristics (*anulakṣaṇa*; ii. 45), [although] not being in a mutual relationship of causality [*anyo'nyaphalatva*] with them: for the secondary characteristics are not co-existent causes of their factor. This is a case to be added [*upasaṃkhyātavya*] to the definition.[813] {3 a}

CAB.2.2. *Thought-associates;*[814] *F 249–52*

CAB.2.2.1. *Range of the thought-associates;*[815] *F 249*

To what factors (*dharma*) is the name *thought-associates* (*cittānuparivartin*; *cittānuvartin*) given?

51ac. **(1) Thought-concomitants; (2) the two restraints [i.e., the restraint co-existent with meditation and pure restraint]; (3) the characteristics of thought-concomitants, of the two restraints and of thought, are thought-associates.**[816]

[The name *thought-associates* is given to]

1. all factors (*dharma*) associated with thought (*cittasaṃprayukta*; ii. 24),
2. the restraint co-existent with meditation [*dhyānasaṃvāra*] and pure restraint [*anāsravasaṃvara*] (ii. 65c; iv. 17d),[817] and
3. the characteristics, i.e., origination [*jāti*], [deterioration (*jarā*), duration (*sthiti*), impermanence (*anityatā*); ii. 45b], of all these, [i.e., (1) and (2),] and also of thought.

CAB.2.2.2. *Ten reasons why the thought-associates are termed "associates";*[818] *F 249–50*

51d. **[Thought-concomitants, the two restraints, etc., are thought-associates,] from the point of view (i) of time, (ii) of effect, [i.e., the effect of human action and the effect of disconnection,] *et cetera*, [i.e., the ripened effect and the effect of equal outflow,] and (iii) of goodness, [badness, non-definedness].**[819]

The associates are associated with thought.

CAB.2.2.2.a. *1.-4. reason: Associates from the point of view of time;*[820] *F 249–50*

In regard to "time" [*kāla*]:

i. they have the same [*eka*] arising [*utpāda*; i.e., reason 1], the same duration [*sthiti*; i.e., reason 2], the same cessation [*nirodha*; i.e., reason 3], as does thought;

ii. they are of the same [*eka*] time period [*adhvan*; i.e., reason 4] as thought.

i. When we say "the same arising…", we understand the word "same" [*eka*] in the sense of concomitance: the associates arise, perdure and perish at the same time as thought; but their arising is distinct. <250>

ii. In regard to thoughts which are not destined to arise (*anutpattidharmin*), they do not arise or perdure or perish: likewise their associates. This is why one adds: "The associates are of the same time period as thought." (Thought which is compelled not to arise is future until the moment when thought would have arisen had it arisen: its associates are then future; thought is past after the moment when thought would have perished had it arisen: its associates are then past.)[821]

CAB.2.2.2.b. *5.-7. reason: Associates from the point of view of effect;*[822] *F 250*

In regard to "effect [*phala*], *et cetera*" [*ādi*]:[823]

i. by "effect" (i.e., reason 5) one should understand the effect of human action (*puruṣakāraphala*; ii. 58ab) and the effect of disconnection (*visaṃyogaphala*; ii. 57d);

ii. by "*et cetera*" one should understand the ripened effect (*vipākaphala*; ii. 57d; i.e., reason 6) and the effect of equal outflow (*niṣyandaphala*; ii. 57c; i.e., reason 7).

[Thus,] the associates have the same effect, the same *vipāka*, the same *niṣyanda* as thought: {3 b} "same" indicates identity (*saṃkhyāne, sādhāraṇe*).

CAB.2.2.2.c. *8.-10. reason: Associates from the point of view of moral quality;*[824] *F 250*

In regard to "goodness [*śubhatā*], etc":

The associates are wholesome [*kuśala*; i.e., reason 8], unwholesome [*akuśala*; i.e., reason 9], non-defined [*avyākṛta*; i.e., reason 10], like the thought which they accompany.

Thus there are ten (i.e., 3 + 4 + 3) reasons [*kāraṇa*] by virtue of which the associates are named *thought-associates* [*cittānuparivartin*].[825]

CAB.2.2.3. *Number of associates of the most reduced thought;*[826] *F 250–52*

[Vaibhāṣikas:] – The thought for which the retinue is the most reduced (*sarvālpa citta*)[827] is a co-existent cause (*sahabhūhetu*) of fifty-eight (= 50 + 4 + 4) factors (*dharma*): namely, (1) the ten generally permeating factors (*mahābhūmika*; ii. 23) with the four characteristics for each of them [*tallakṣaṇa*]; (2) the (thought's) four characteristics [*svalakṣaṇa*] and its four secondary characteristics (*anulakṣaṇa*; ii. 46).

If, from these fifty-eight factors, the four secondary characteristics of thought are set aside—those that have no activity [*vyāpāra*] in regard to it [see F 249]—there are fifty-four factors which are a co-existent cause of this particular thought.[828] <251>

According to another opinion [*apara*], only fourteen factors are a co-existent cause of this thought, namely, the four characteristics and the ten generally permeating factors. In the same way that the (thought's) secondary characteristics have no activity in regard to thought, the characteristics of the generally permeating factors [*tallakṣaṇa*] do not have an activity in regard to thought.

The Vaibhāṣikas reject this opinion, i.e., that the forty characteristics of the generally permeating factors (*mahābhūmika*) are not a co-existent cause (*sahabhūhetu*) of thought, as being contradictory to the doctrine of the *Prakaraṇagrantha* according to which "the four characteristics, i.e., origination, deterioration, duration and impermanence, of the afflicted view of self (*satkāyadṛṣṭi*) and of the factors associated with this afflicted view (comprising the generally permeating factors), are, at the same time, an effect and a cause of the afflicted view of self".[829] <252>

Certain masters, in their reading of the *Prakaraṇagrantha*, omit the words: "and of the factors associated with this afflicted view" [*tatsaṃprayuktānāṃ ca dharmāṇāṃ*]. According to the Vaibhāṣikas of Kaśmīr, {4 a} these words figure in the text; or, when they are absent there, the context indicates that they should be supplied and that the text is incomplete.

CAB.2.3. *The relation between co-existing factors and co-existent causes: eight categories which are not co-existent causes; F 252–53*

Any factor which is a cause as a co-existent cause (*yat tāvat sahabhūhetunā hetuḥ*) is *sahabhū*, i.e., co-existing. But there are some co-existing items which are not a co-existent cause (*sahabhūhetu*):

1. the secondary characteristics [*anulakṣaṇa*] of the principal factor (*mūladharma*) are not a co-existent cause with regard to this factor (ii. 46ab; 50bd);
2. these same (secondary characteristics of the principal factor) are not co-existent causes with one another [*anyo'nya*];
3. the secondary characteristics of the thought-accompaniments are not a co-existent cause in regard to thought;
4. these same (secondary characteristics of the thought-associates) are not co-existent causes with one another;
5. derivative material elements or forms (*bhautika*; *upādāyarūpa*), i.e., blue, etc., susceptible to offering resistance (*sapratigha*) and, in addition, arisen together (*sahaja*), are not co-existent causes with one another; <253>
6. a small part [*kiṃcid*] of derivative material elements or forms not susceptible to offering resistance [*apratigha*] and, in addition, arisen together are not co-existent causes with one another; with the exception of the two restraints (see ii, F 249);
7. no derivative material element, even though arisen together with the elements (*bhūta*), is a co-existent cause in regard to the elements;
8. the possessions (*prāpti*), even when they arise with the factor to which they are related (*prāptimat*), are not a co-existent cause in regard to it.

The factors of these eight categories are co-existing factors (*sahabhū*), but are not a co-existent cause, because (i) their effect [*phala*], (ii) the ripened effect (*vipākaphala*), (iii) the effect of equal outflow (*niṣyandaphala*), are not the same [*aneka*] (see ii, F 250).

As for the possessions (*prāpti*), they do not always accompany the factor (*sahacariṣṇu*): they arise either before the factor, or after it, or at the same time (ii. 37–38).

CAB.3. *The existential status of the co-existent cause;*[830] *F 253–55*

CAB.3.1. *Sautrāntika: The co-existent cause is not established by common examples; F 253*

(The Sautrāntika[831]) criticizes the doctrine of the causality of coexistent factors:

All this may be correct (*sarvam apy etat syāt*), that "what is a co-existent cause is *sahabhū*, i.e., co-existing", and so on [see above, F 252].[832] Nevertheless, in the world, the relationship of cause and effect (*hetuphalabhāva*) is well established in certain cases: the cause is previous to the effect. It is in this way that the seed [*bīja*] is the cause of the sprout [*aṅkura*], the sprout of the stalk [*nāla*], etc. But a similar relationship is not observed between reciprocal factors. You should thus demonstrate that simultaneously arisen [things] [*sahotpanna*; LVP: *sahabhū*] can be in a relationship of cause and effect. {4 b}

B.3.2. *Proof of the simultaneity of cause and effect via two examples; F 253–54*

The Sarvāstivādin gives two examples:

1. the lamp [*pradīpa*] arises together with its radiance (*saprabha*);
2. the sprout [*aṅkura*], growing in the sunlight [*prabhā*], arises together with its shadow (*sacchāya*).

But the lamp is the cause of its radiance, the sprout is the cause of its shadow. Thus cause and effect can be simultaneous.

(The Sautrāntika:[833]) – These examples are not established.

[Regarding the first example,] we must examine (*saṃpradhāryam*) whether the lamp is the cause of its radiance, or if not, as we think, both the lamp with its radiance are the effect of the complex or assemblage [*sāmagrī*] of previous causes and conditions: oil [*sneha*], wick [*varti*], etc.[834]

In the same way, [regarding the second example,] a complex or assemblage of previous causes (seed, sunlight) is the cause of the sprout and of its shadow, of the sprout with its shadow. <254>

B.3.3. *Proof of the simultaneity of cause and effect via the definition of causality by the logicians; F 254*

The Sarvāstivādin: – The relationship of cause and effect is established by the existence and non-existence of what is called *effect*, parallel to the existence and non-existence of what is called *cause*. The definition [of causality] by the logicians (*hetu-vid*; *haituka*) is very good:

> When, due to A existing or non-existing, B (necessarily) exists or does not exist, then A is considered to be the cause and B is considered to be the effect [*yasya bhāvābhāvayoḥ yasya bhāvābhavau niyamataḥ sa hetur itaro hetumān*].

Assuming this to be the case, if we examine the factors (*dharma*) that we have defined as co-existing factors and co-existent causes (*sahabhūhetu*), we see that they all exist when one of them exists, and that none exist when one of them does not exist.[835] They are then in a mutual relationship of cause and effect [*hetuphala-bhāva*].

(The Sautrāntika:[836]) – Let us accept (for arguments sake) that, among the simultaneously arisen factors [*sahotpanna*], a factor can be the cause of another factor: [for example,] the eye sense-faculty is the cause of the visual consciousness.[837] But how could simultaneously arisen factors be causes and effects with regard to one another [*anyo'nya*] [since the visual consciousness does not become the cause of that visual faculty]?[838]

The Sarvāstivādin: – The reciprocal causality is established through the definition of causality [*kāraṇa*] which we have given: [when the one exists or does not exist, the other likewise exists or does not exist]; when thought exists, the thought-concomitants (*caitta*) exist, and *vice versa*.

(The Sautrāntika:) – Very well, but then the Sarvāstivādins should revise their system (see ii. 50bd [F 249 and 252]). In fact, (1) they have denied the mutual causality of derivative material elements (*upādāyarūpa*, *bhautika*; visible form, taste, etc.; see category 5, above F 252), although visible form never exists without (*avinābhāvin*) taste (see ii. 22); (2–3) they have denied the mutual causality of the derivative material elements and of the fundamental material elements [see category 7, F 253], and the mutual causality of the secondary characteristics and of thought [see category 1, F 252].

CAB.3.4. *Proof of the simultaneity of cause and effect via the example of the three sticks supporting one another;* F 254–55

The Sarvāstivādin. – The relationship of cause and effect in the case of coexisting factors (*sabhabhū*) such as thought and thought-concomitants, etc., is established in the same way that three sticks [*tridaṇḍa*] stay in position (*avasthāna*), [i.e.,] by supporting one another [or by their mutual power] [*anyo'nyabala*]. {5 a} <255>

(The Sautrāntika:[839]) – This new example should be examined. One wonders whether the three sticks stay in position through the power which the three sticks possess insofar as they are arisen together (*sahotpannabalena*), or rather, if the power of the complex or assemblage [*sāmagrī*] of previous causes which made them arise together does not also make them arise supporting one another.

Moreover, there are other things involved here besides the mutual power of support (*anyo'nyabala*): there is a rope [*sūtraka*], a hook [*śaṅkuka*]; there is the ground [*pṛthivī*], [which cause the sticks to stand together].

The Sarvāstivādin replies: – But the coexistent factors (*sahabhū*) have also other causes than the co-existent cause (*sahabhūhetu*), namely, the homogeneous cause (*sabhāgahetu*), the pervasive cause (*sarvatragahetu*), the ripening cause (*vipākahetu*), which have a role analogous to that of the rope, etc., [in this example]. The co-existent cause is thus established.

. *Homogeneous cause (sabhāgahetu);*[840] *F 255–67*

.1. *General definition;*[841] *F 255–257*

52a. Similar factors are a homogeneous cause.[842]

Similar (*sabhāga*; *sadṛśa*) factors (*dharma*) are homogeneous causes (*sabhāgahetu*) of factors similar [to them].

.1.1. *Same moral quality and scope & the homogeneous cause;*[843] *F 255–56*

1. The five wholesome (*kuśala*) aggregates (*skandha*) are the homogeneous causes (*sabhāgahetu*) of five wholesome aggregates, [among themselves (*anyo'nya*)].

2. When [the aggregates] are defiled (*kliṣṭa*), i.e., unwholesome (*akuśala*) and obscured-non-defined (*nivṛtāvyākṛta*), they are the homogeneous causes of defiled, [i.e., unwholesome and obscured-non-defined aggregates], [in each case, among themselves].

3. When [the aggregates] are non-defined [*avyākṛta*], i.e., unobscured-non-defined (*anivṛtāvyākṛta*), they are the homogeneous causes of non-defined [aggregates], [in each case, among themselves]. {5 b}

Nevertheless, the masters do not agree on this last point [i.e., 3.]:[844]

i. According to some, non-defined material form (*rūpa*) is the homogeneous cause of the five non-defined aggregates, but the other four aggregates, i.e., sensation, etc., are not the homogeneous causes of material form (ii. 59).[845] [This is because (the material form aggregate) is inferior (*nyūnatva*) (in nature[846] to the other aggregates).]

ii. According to others, four aggregates are the homogeneous causes (*sabhāga-hetu*) of five aggregates; but material form is not/only[847] the homogeneous cause of [the other] four aggregates.

iii. According to still others, material form is not the homogeneous cause of four aggregates and *vice versa*.[848]

4. When considering one personal existence [*nikāyasabhāga*]:

i. the first embryonic stage is the homogeneous cause of ten stages:

- the five embryonic states (*garbhāvasthā*): (1) *kalala*, (2) *arbuda*, (3) *peśin*, (4) *ghana* and (5) *praśākhā*;
- the five post-embryonic states (*jātāvasthā*): (6) *bāla* [small child under five years], (7) *kumāra* [child up to sixteen years], (8) *yuvan* [grown person], (9) *madhya* [mature person] and (10) *vṛddha* [advanced in years]. <256>

ii. The second embryonic stage is a homogeneous cause of nine stages (*arbuda*... *vārddha*), and so on. A previous moment of each stage is the homogeneous cause of the later moments of this stage. (Compare iv. 53).

When considering the stages of the next personal existence of the same type [*samānajātīya*], each of the stages of the previous personal existence is the homogeneous cause of ten stages.

5. The same holds for external (*bāhya*) entities, i.e., barley [*yava*], rice [*śāli*], etc., that is to say, the quality of a homogeneous cause remains confined in each series: barley is a similar cause of barley, not of rice.

6. (The Dārṣṭāntika[849]) denies that material form (*rūpa*) is a homogeneous cause of material form; but this contradicts the *Mahāśāstra* (*Jñānaprasthāna*, 985b14):

> The past [*atīta*] fundamental material elements (*mahābhūta*) are *hetu* and *adhipati* of the future [*anāgata*] fundamental material elements.

By *adhipati*, one should understand the condition of dominance (*adhipatipratyaya*; ii. 62d); by *hetu*, one should understand [the causal condition (*hetupratyaya*;[850] ii. 61d), i.e.,] the homogeneous cause (*sabhāgahetu*), for the other causes [of the causal condition, i.e., the co-existent cause, associated cause, pervasive cause and ripening cause,] are here evidently outside of being the cause.

CAC.1.2. *Same categories of abandonment and same stages & the homogeneous cause;*[851] *F 256–57*

[Question:] – Are all similar [*sadṛśa*] factors (*dharma*) homogeneous causes of similar factors?

[Answer:] – No.

52b. (Similar factors) belonging to a given category and a given stage (*bhū*) (are homogeneous causes only of similar factors).[852]

That is to say: the factors belonging to a given category [*nikāya*] [of abandonment; see ii. 52cd] and to a given stage (*bhūmi*) are homogeneous causes only of similar factors of their own category [of abandonment] and their own stage.

1. Factors are classed into five categories [*nikāya*] according to whether they are susceptible of being abandoned [*prahātavya*]:

i–iv. by insight [*darśana*] into each of the four truths, or
v. by cultivation (*bhāvanā*) (i. 40).

2. Factors belong to nine stages [*bhūmi*]: they are either

i. in the realm of desire, or
ii–v. in one of the four meditations (*dhyāna*), or {6 a}
vi–ix. in one of the four formless meditative attainments (*ārūpya*). <257>

1. [Thus,] (i) a factor susceptible of being abandoned by insight into the truth of unsatisfactoriness (*duḥkhadṛgheya*) is a homogeneous cause of a factor susceptible of being abandoned by insight into the truth of unsatisfactoriness, and not of the factors belonging to the other four categories; and (ii–v) so on.

2. (i) Among the factors susceptible of being abandoned by insight into the truth of unsatisfactoriness, the one belonging to the realm of desire is a homogeneous cause of a factor belonging to the realm of desire, [and not by the ones belonging to the other stages]; and (ii–ix) so on.

AC.2. *Clarifications of the given definition;*[853] *F 257–62*

The homogeneous cause has not yet been defined exactly.

AC.2.1. *Past, present and future factors & the homogeneous cause;*[854] *F 257*

52b. (In fact, only [similar] factors which have) arisen previously (are homogeneous causes).[855]

The factor—arisen [*jāta*], i.e., past [*atīta*] or present [*pratyutpanna*], and previous [*agra*], (*pūrvotpanna*; *agraja*)—is a homogeneous cause of a later [*paścima*] similar factor, arisen [*utpanna*] or not arisen [*anutpanna*]. The future factors cannot be homogeneous causes.[856]

[Question:] – On what authority is this definition based?

[Answer:] – It is based on the *Mūlaśāstra*, for the *Jñānaprasthāna* [920c15] says:

> [Question:] – What is a homogeneous cause (*sabhāgahetu*)?
>
> [Answer:] – The previously arisen (*agraja*; *pūrvotpanna*) wholesome root is a cause [*hetu*] in the quality of a homogeneous cause with regard to the later wholesome root and the factors associated with it (*tatsaṃprayukta*), of the same category and stage. In that way, the past wholesome roots are a homogeneous cause in regard to past and present wholesome roots; past and

present wholesome roots are a homogeneous cause in regard to future wholesome roots.

CAC.2.1.1. *Future factors & the homogeneous cause; F 257*

Objection. – The future factor is a homogeneous cause, for one reads in the same *Jñānaprasthāna*:

> [Question:] – Is there a time period when the factor (*dharma*) that is a cause of a certain factor, is not a cause of it?
>
> [Answer:] – Never is this factor not a cause (*na kadācin na hetuḥ*). {6 b} <258>

CAC.2.1.1.a. *First explanation: by the Vaibhāṣika; F 258*

The Vaibhāṣika: – This text does not contradict the first; for the *Jñānaprasthāna* does not refer here to that which is a cause in the quality of a homogeneous cause (*sabhāgahetu*), but rather to that which is a cause in the quality of the co-existent cause (*sahabhūhetu*), of the associated cause (*saṃprayuktakahetu*), of the ripening cause (*vipākahetu*).

CAC.2.1.1.b. *Second explanation: by the followers of the last state; F 258–59*

According to another opinion, i.e., that of the "followers of the last state" (*paramāvasthāvādin*), the answer of the *Jñānaprasthāna*: "Never is this factor (*dharma*) not a cause", refers to the homogeneous cause (*sabhāgahetu*) and is justified as follows: The future factor, in the arising state (*jāyamānāvasthā*), is certainly a homogeneous cause. Thus, taking into account the future factor in its last state, the *Jñānaprasthāna* can say that the factor is never not a cause, is always a cause, since at a certain moment of the future, it is a cause.

[Reply:[857]] – This explanation does not resolve the difficulty. In fact, if the future factor, after not having been a cause, becomes a cause by arriving at the arising state, it is not always a cause: but the *Jñānaprasthāna* says in an unrestricted way that never is this factor not a cause.

Besides, this explanation is not reconcilable with the answer that the *Jñānaprasthāna* (1026b19; MVŚ, 87a2) gives to another question:

> [Question:] – Is there a time period when the factor that is the condition as the equivalent and immediate antecedent (*samanantara*; ii. 62ab) of a certain factor is not the condition as the equivalent and immediate antecedent?
>
> [Answer:] – Yes, when it has not arisen (*yadi sa dharmo notpanno bhavati*).

Now, the case of the condition as the equivalent and immediate antecedent (*samanantara*) is analogous to that of the homogeneous cause (*sabhāgahetu*): the future condition as the equivalent and immediate antecedent, arriving at the arising state, is a condition as the equivalent and immediate antecedent. Thus, if the interpretation of the answer: "Never is this factor not a cause", in the sense of: "The future factor, in the arising state, is a homogeneous cause", is correct, the *Jñānaprasthāna*, dealing with the condition as the equivalent and immediate antecedent, should answer as for the homogeneous cause: "Never is this factor not a condition as the equivalent and immediate antecedent." But the *Jñānaprasthāna* answers: "It is not a condition as the equivalent and immediate antecedent when it has not arisen." Thus, the word "cause", in the first answer, should not be understood as homogeneous cause.

The "followers of the last state" say: – The *Jñānaprasthāna* answers the first question by saying: "Never is this factor not a cause", and the second question by saying: "It is not a cause when it has not arisen", in order to show that one can answer in two ways in order to express the same meaning (*dvimukhapradarśanārtham*). One can answer the first question as the second and the second question as the first. <259>

[Reply:[858]] – What a bizarre method of explanation! The author of the treatise [*śāstrakāra*] must truly be inept [*akauśala*]! Thus the proposed first solution [*parihāra*] is the best explanation. {7 a}

C.2.1.1.c. *Answers to various further objections; F 259–62*

[Objection:] – If the future factor (*dharma*) is not a homogeneous cause (*sabhāgahetu*), why does the *Prakaraṇapādaśāstra* teach that the future afflicted view of self (*satkāyadṛṣṭi*) has the afflicted view of self for its cause and is a cause of the afflicted view of self? We read in fact (in the cited text, p. 252 n. 2 B,1,b):

> ...with the exception of the future afflicted view of self and of the truth of unsatisfactoriness which is associated with it (*anāgatāṃ satkāyadṛṣṭiṃ tatsaṃprayuktaṃ ca duḥkhasatyaṃ sthāpyitvā*).[859]

Answer by the Vaibhāṣika: – This reading is corrupt (*vinaṣṭaka*). One should read [in its place]:

> ...with the exception of the truth of unsatisfactoriness associated with the future afflicted view of self (*anāgatasatkāyadṛṣṭisaṃprayuktam*).

To suppose that your reading is authentic, it would imply, because of the meaning that the text should express (*arthato vaivaṃ boddhavyam*), that your reading must be considered as without authority (*na tantram*), as having been determined by imitating the preceding phrase of the commentary (*bhāṣyākṣepāt*). <260>

[Objection:] – If the future factor is not a homogeneous cause, how could this commentary (*bhāṣya*) of the *Prajñapti* be explained (*kathaṃ nīyate*)?[860] This treatise says in fact:

> All factors are determined from a fourfold point of view (*catuṣke niyatāḥ*): (1) cause [*hetu*]; (2) effect [*phala*]; (3) basis (*āśraya*); (4) cognitive object (*ālambana*).[861]

The Vaibhāṣika answers: – When it says: "This factor is never not a cause of this factor", the treatise does not mean to discuss all types of causes:

1. by "cause", one should understand the associated cause (*saṃprayuktakahetu*) and the co-existent cause (*sahabhūhetu*);
2. by "effect", the effect of dominance (*adhipatiphala*) and the effect of human action (*puruṣakāraphala*) (ii. 58);[862]
3. by "basis", the six sense-faculties (the eye sense-faculty, etc.);
4. by "cognitive object", the six object-fields (*viṣaya*), i.e., visible form, etc.

[Objection:] – If the future factor (*dharma*) is not a homogeneous cause (*sabhāgahetu*), then, at first the homogeneous cause does not exist and then exists (*abhūtvā bhavati*).

[Answer:] – But this is precisely what the Vaibhāṣikas affirm! The "state (*avasthā*) of being a homogeneous cause" of the homogeneous cause is new, it exists not having existed (*abhūtvā bhavati*); however, the "real entity" (*dravya*) which is a certain homogeneous cause is not new. A future factor is not a homogeneous cause; once it has arisen, it becomes a homogeneous cause. In fact, the effect of the complete assemblage (*sāmagrya*) of causes [and conditions] is the "state" (*avasthā*) and not the "real entity" (*dravya*), the factor (*dharma*). (The future factor exists as a real entity [*dravyatas*]; the complete assemblage of the causes (and conditions) makes it pass from the future into the present, endows it with the state of the present [*vartamāna-avasthā*], and endows it, by the same fact, with the quality of homogeneous cause; see v. 25.) <261>

[Objection:] – What harm do you see in this future factor being a homogeneous cause (*sabhāgahetu*) just as it is a ripening cause (F 258; *vipākahetu*, ii. 54c)?

[Answer:] – If it were a homogeneous cause, it would have been mentioned as such in the *Jñānaprasthāna*; but the *Jñānaprasthāna*, answering the question (see above F 257): "What is a homogeneous cause?", does not say that the future wholesome roots would be a homogeneous cause with regard to future wholesome roots.

[Objection:] – We do not think that the omission of the future factor (*dharma*) in this text creates an argument against us. {7 b} This text, in fact, names only the homogeneous causes (*sabhāgahetu*) which are capable of "taking or projecting" and "giving forth" an effect (*phaladānagrahaṇasamartha*; ii. 59).

[Answer:] – No (*naitad asti*), for the effect of the homogeneous cause is the effect of equal outflow, the effect which accords with its cause (*niṣyandaphala*; ii. 57c), and this type of effect does not suit a future factor, because in the future there is no anteriority and posteriority (*pūrvapaścimatābhāvāt*). On the other hand, one cannot accept that an already arisen [*utpanna*] factor, i.e., past [*atīta*] or present [*vartamāna*], is an equal outflow [*niṣyanda*] of a future factor, in the same way that a past factor cannot be the equal outflow of a present factor, for the effect is not anterior to the cause. – Thus the future factor is not a homogeneous cause.

[Objection:] – If this is the case, then the future factor (*dharma*) would no longer be a ripening cause (*vipākahetu*; ii. 54c), for (1) the ripened effect (*vipākaphala*; ii. 56a) cannot be either simultaneous [*saha*] with or anterior [*pūrva*] to its cause; (2) the future factors do not present anteriority and posteriority [*pūrvapaścimatābhava*].

The Vaibhāṣikas answer: – The case is not the same. The homogeneous cause (*sabhāgahetu*) and its effect, which is an [effect of] equal outflow (*niṣyanda*), are similar [*sadṛśa*] factors. To suppose that they exist in the future, which lacks anteriority and posteriority [*vinā paurvāparya*], would imply that they would be mutually causes of one another [*anyo'nyahetutva*], and therefore effects of one another: now it is not acceptable that two factors would be an [effect of] equal outflow of one another [*anyo'nyaniḥṣyandatā*]. On the contrary, the ripening cause and the ripened effect are dissimilar [*bhinnalakṣaṇatva*]. [Thus,] even if anteriority and posteriority were absent [*vinā paurvāparya*], the cause remains only a [ripening] cause, the effect remains only a [ripened] effect. <262> [Therefore,] the quality of a homogeneous cause (*sabhāgahetu*) results from the state (*avasthāvyavasthita*): a future factor (*dharma*) is not a homogeneous cause; but when it enters into the present state, into the past state, it is a homogeneous cause. The quality of a ripening cause results from the very nature of the factor itself (*lakṣaṇavyavasthitas tu vipākahetuḥ*).

AC.2.2. *The stages and the impure and pure factors & the homogeneous cause;*[863] *F 262*

[Question:] – We have said that a factor (*dharma*) is a homogeneous cause (*sabhāgahetu*) of only those factors which belong to its stage [*bhū*]. Does this restriction [*niyama*] apply to all factors?

[Answer:] – This restriction applies only to impure (*sāsrava*) factors, not to pure factors [i. 5ab]: {8 a}

52cd. But the [truth of] the (noble) path [is a homogeneous cause to the truth of the (noble) path], without distinguishing the nine stages.[864]

[The reference (*adhikāra*) [in the verse] is to the homogeneous cause.]

The path is of nine stages [*bhūmi*]:

1. the preparatory meditation to the first meditation (*anāgamya*);
2. the intermediate meditation (*dhyānāntara*);

3–6. the four fundamental (*mūla*) meditations (*dhyāna*);

7–9. the three lower, fundamental formless meditative attainments (*ārūpya*; vi. 20c);

in the sense that practitioners, abiding in these nine stages of meditative states, can cultivate the path.

The factors (*dharma*) which constitute [the truth of] the path [*mārgasatya*] are a homogeneous cause of the factors which constitute [the truth of] the path, from stage to stage.

[Question: – What is the reason for this?]

[Answer:] – In fact, [the truth of] the path resides in the different stages as a guest (*āgantuka*), i.e., without forming part of the realms of existence (*dhātu*) to which the stages belong: the craving [*tṛṣṇā*] of the realm of desire, the realm of fine-materiality, the realm of immateriality, does not turn upon [the truth of] the path. [The truth of] the path—whatever the stage may be on which the practitioners rely in order to cultivate it—remains of the same nature (*samānajātīya*) [i.e., pure (*anāsravajātīya*)]; [the truth of] the path is thus a homogeneous cause of [the truth of] the path, [even though it might be of a different stage (*anyabhūmika*)].

However, the entire [truth of the] path is not a homogeneous cause of the entire [truth of the] path. One should not take into account the stage in which it is cultivated, but rather the characteristics proper to [the truth of] the path itself.

CAC.2.3. *The paths & the homogeneous cause;*[865] *F 262–64*

CAC.2.3.1. *The supramundane paths & the homogeneous cause;*[866] *F 262–64*

52d. The (noble) path is a homogeneous cause to an equal [*sama*] or superior [*viśiṣṭa*] (noble) path, [i.e., not of an inferior (noble) path, because the (noble) path is always acquired through preparatory effort].[867]

53b. **[The equal and superior factors acquired through preparatory effort are] those derived (1) from listening, (2) from reflection, [(3) from cultivation].**[873]

The factors "acquired through preparatory effort" [*prāyogika*)] are contrasted with the "innate" factors (*upapattipratilambhika*). [The factors acquired through preparatory effort] are the qualities (*guṇa*) proceeding (1) from listening (*śruta*), i.e., from the word of the Buddha [*buddhavacana*], (2) from reflection (*cintā*), (3) from cultivation (*bhāvanā*). <265>

AC.2.4.1. *The wholesome-impure factors acquired through preparatory effort and their nine modes & the homogeneous cause;*[874] *F 265*

[As for the wholesome-impure factors] acquired through preparatory effort, {9 a} they are a homogeneous cause of superior [*viśiṣṭa*] or of equal [*sama*] [factors], not of inferior [*nyūna*] [factors].

1. The factors derived from listening (*śrutamaya*) of the sphere [*avacara*] of desire are a homogeneous cause
   - i. of factors derived from listening and from reflection (*cintāmaya*) of the realm of desire;
   - ii. not of factors derived from cultivation (*bhāvanāmaya*), because these factors do not exist in the realm of desire, because a factor is a homogeneous cause of factors of the same realm of existence.

2. The factors derived from listening of the realm of fine-materiality are a homogeneous cause
   - i. of factors derived from listening and from cultivation of the realm of fine-materiality;
   - ii. not of factors derived from reflection, because these factors are absent in this realm of existence: in the realm of fine-materiality, as soon as one begins to reflect, one immediately enters into concentration (*samādhi*).

3. The factors derived from cultivation of the realm of fine-materiality are a homogeneous cause
   - i. of factors derived from cultivation of the realm of fine-materiality;
   - ii. not of factors derived from listening of the realm of fine-materiality, because these are less good.

4. The factors derived from cultivation of the realm of immateriality are a homogeneous cause
   - i. of factors derived from cultivation of the realm of immateriality;

ii. not of factors derived from listening and from reflection, because these factors are absent in this realm of existence.

Moreover, one must take into account that the factors (*dharma*) acquired through preparatory effort are of nine modes [*prakāra*]:

(1) weak–weak [*mṛdumṛdu*], (2) weak–medium, (3) weak–strong,
(4) medium–weak, (5) medium–medium [*madhyamadhya*], (6) medium–strong,
(7) strong–weak, (8) strong–medium, (9) strong–strong [*adhimātrādhimātra*].

(1) The weak-weak are a homogeneous cause of factors of nine modes; (2) the weak-medium, of factors of eight modes, with the exception of the weak-weak; and (3–9) so forth.

CAC.2.4.2. *The wholesome-impure "innate" factors and their nine modes & the homogeneous cause;*[875] *F 265*

As for the wholesome-[impure] [*kuśala*] "innate" [*upapattipratilambhika*] factors (*dharma*), the nine modes are a homogeneous cause of one another (*paraspara*).[876]

CAC.2.4.3. *The defiled factors and their nine modes & the homogeneous cause;*[877] *F 265*

As for the defiled (*kliṣṭa*) factors, the same, [i.e., their nine modes are a homogeneous cause of one another (*paraspara*)].[878]

CAC.2.4.4. *The unobscured-non-defined factors and their four kinds & the homogeneous cause;*[879] *F 265–66*

As for the unobscured-non-defined (*anivṛtāvyākṛta*) factors (*dharma*),[880] they are of four kinds (ii. 72), the subsequent one being "better" than the previous one: {9 b}

1. factors arisen from [the cause of] retribution (*vipākaja*; i. 37);
2. factors associated with the proper deportment (*airyāpathika*) of lying down [*śayana*], sitting [*āsana*], [standing (*sthiti*), walking (*caṃkramaṇa*)];
3. factors associated with skill in arts and crafts (*śailpasthānika*);
4. the thought of emanation (*nirmāṇacitta*) (vii. 48).

These four kinds are, respectively, a homogeneous cause of (1) four kinds [i.e., effect of retribution, etc.], (2) three kinds [i.e., proper deportment, etc., but not the effect of retribution], (3) two kinds [i.e., skill in arts and crafts, etc., but not effect of retribution, etc.], and (4) one kind [i.e., only the thought of emanation]. <266>

Moreover, as a thought of emanation in the realm of desire can be the result [*phala*] of each of the four meditations (*dhyāna*) (MVŚ, 89a12), there is reason to establish the same distinction here: the thoughts of emanation constitute four modes, and are—according to their mode—a homogeneous cause (1) of four modes, (2) of three modes, (3) of two modes, (4) of one mode of a thought of emanation. In fact, when being the result of a higher meditation, the thought of emanation is not a homogeneous cause of the thought of emanation that is the result of an inferior meditation: from a homogeneous cause (i.e., a thought of emanation) realized with greater effort (*ābhisaṃskārika*; *mahāyatnasādhya*) cannot proceed a factor less good [*hīyamāna*], realized with less effort [*amahāyatnasādhya*].[881]

C.2.4.5. *The pure factors;*[882] *F 266–67*

This principle being stated [ii. 52cd], the following questions (*ata evāhuḥ*) are posed and resolved:[883]

[Question:] – Is there a pure (*anāsrava*) factor (*dharma*), already arisen (*utpanna*), which is not a cause of a pure factor not destined to arise (*anutpattidharman*)?

[Answer:] – Yes. The cognition of the factors with regard to unsatisfactoriness (*duḥkhe dharmajñāna*), already arisen, is not a cause of the receptivity to the cognition of the factors with regard to unsatisfactoriness (*duḥkhe dharmajñānakṣānti*) not destined to arise. Besides, any superior (*viśiṣṭa*) factor is not a cause of an inferior (*nyūna*) factor.

[Question:] – Is there, in one life-stream [*ekasaṃtāna*], a pure factor, previously acquired (*pūrvapratilabdha*: of which one has at first attained the possession [*prāpti*]), which is not a cause of a pure factor arisen later?

[Answer:] – Yes. The future receptivities to the cognition of the factors with regard to unsatisfactoriness, [but the possession of which has been attained at the first moment of the (noble) path,] are not a cause of the cognition of the factors with regard to unsatisfactoriness already arisen. Because the effect cannot be anterior to the cause, or moreover, because the future factor is not a homogeneous cause.

[Question:] – Is there a pure factor, arisen previously, which is not a cause of a pure factor arisen later?

[Answer:[884]] – Yes. The superior (*adhimātra* = *viśiṣṭa*) factor is not a cause of an inferior [*nyūna*] factor. For example, when, after having retrogressed from a superior result, one realizes an inferior result, the superior result is not a cause of an inferior result. <267> {10 a} Besides, the possession of the cognition of the factors with regard to unsatisfactoriness, arisen previously, is not a cause of the possessions of the receptivity to the cognition of the factors with regard to unsatisfactoriness which will arise in the following moments (the moment of the subsequent receptivity to the

cognition with regard to unsatisfactoriness [*duḥkhe 'nvayajñānakṣāntikṣaṇe*], etc.), because these new possessions are less good.

[The homogeneous cause has been discussed.]

CAD. *Associated cause (saṃprayuktakahetu);*[885] *F 267–68*

CAD.1. *General definition;*[886] *F 267*

53cd. Only thought and thought-concomitants are an associated cause.[887]

Thought and thought-concomitants are an associated cause (*saṃprayuktakahetu*).

CAD.2. *Further specification of the definition;*[888] *F 267–68*

[Question:] – Is this to say that thoughts and thought-concomitants—arisen at different moments and in different life-streams [*bhinnakālasaṃtanaja*]—are among themselves [*anyo'nya*] associated causes (*saṃprayuktakahetu*)?

[Answer:] – No.

[Question:] – Would we then say that the thought and thought-concomitants (1) of the same aspect or mode of activity (*ekākāra*), i.e., having the same aspect or mode of activity [ii. 34d], of blue [*nīla*], etc., and (2) of the same cognitive object (*ekālambana*), i.e., having for their cognitive object [ii. 34d] the same blue, etc., are associated causes?

[Answer:] – No. This definition gives rise to the same criticism: thoughts and thought-concomitants of different time periods [*bhinnakāla*] and of different life-streams [*bhinnsaṃtāna*] can have the same aspect or mode of activity and the same cognitive object.

[Question:] – Would we then say that the thought and thought-concomitants of the same aspect or mode of activity and of the same cognitive object, should, moreover, be of the same time period [*ekakāla*; ii. 34d]?

[Answer:] – This still does not suffice: for different persons [*bhinnasaṃtānaja*] can see the new moon, etc. [*navacandrādi*] at the same time.

Therefore, the author adds:

53d. [Thought and thought-concomitants] which have the same basis [*samāśraya*] [are among themselves associated causes]. {10 b}

Thought and thought-concomitants which have the same [*samāna*] basis [*āśraya*; ii. 34d] are among themselves [*anyo'nya*] associated causes.

"Same" (*sama*; *samāna*) signifies undivided or non-different (*abhinna*; ii. 34d).[889] <268>

For example, a given moment (*kṣaṇa*) of the eye sense-faculty (*cakṣurindriya*) is the basis (1) of a visual consciousness, (2) of sensation (*vedanā*) and of the other thought-concomitants associated (*saṃprayukta*) with this consciousness. And likewise for the other sense-faculties up to the mental faculty (*manas*): a certain moment of the mental faculty (*manas*) is the basis (1) of a mental consciousness and (2) of the thought-concomitants associated with this consciousness.

AD.2.1.1. *The difference between the associated cause and the co-existent cause;*[890] *F 268*

[Question:] – That which is an associated cause (*saṃprayuktakahetu*) is also a co-existent cause (*sahabhūhetu*). What is the difference between these two causes?[891]

[Answer:] – 1. As for the factors [which are a co-existent cause,] they are called *co-existent cause* (*sahabhūhetu*) because they are mutually the effects of one another (*anyo'nyaphalārthena*).

[For example,] the companions in a caravan (*sahasārthika*) travel (*mārgaprayāṇa*) thanks to the support which they give one another (*parasparabalena*). In the same way, thought is the effect of the thought-concomitant, and the thought-concomitant is the effect of thought.

2. As for the factors (*dharma*) [which are an associated cause,] they are called *associated cause* (*saṃprayuktakahetu*) or mutual cause in the quality of association [*saṃprayukta*; ii. 34d], because they function identically (*samaprayogārthena*, *prayoga* = *pravṛtti*), that is to say, because they have the five samenesses or equivalences (*samatā*), [i.e., with respect to basis (*āśraya*), to cognitive object (*ālambana*), to aspect or mode of activity (*ākara*), to time (*kāla*), and to the number of real entities (*dravya*),] as defined in ii. 34.

[Thus in this case,] the travel of the companions in a caravan is assured [not only] by the mutual support which they give one another, but they use, in addition, the same food [*anna*], the same drinks [*pāna*], etc. In the same way, thought and thought-concomitants use the same basis, have the same aspect or mode of activity, etc: if even one of these five samenesses or equivalences is absent, they no longer have the same function and are not associated.[892]

[The associated cause has been discussed.]

AE. *Pervasive cause (sarvatragahetu);*[893] *F 268–70*

AE.1. *General definition;*[894] *F 268–69*

[What is the pervasive cause (*sarvatragahetu*)?]

54ab. The former [i.e., past or present] pervasive [factors] are a pervasive cause in regard to the defiled factors of their own stage.[895]

These pervasive (*sarvaga*) factors (*dharma*)—arisen previously [*pūrvotpanna*], i.e., past [*atīta*] or present [*pratyutpanna*], and belonging to a certain stage (*bhūmi*)—are the pervasive causes of later defiled [*kliṣṭa*] factors of the same stage, which are defiled (1) through their intrinsic nature [*svabhāva*], (2) through association [*saṃprayukta*] or (3) through their originating cause [*samutthāna*] (iv. 9c). We shall be studying the pervasive factors in the EXPOSITION OF THE PROCLIVITIES [*anuśaya-nirdeśa*; v. 12]. {11 a} <269>

CAE.2. *The difference between the pervasive cause and the homogeneous cause;*[896] *F 269*

The pervasive factors are only a cause of defiled factors;[897] they are a cause [*hetutva*] of defiled factors in their own category and in other categories (*nikāya*; ii. 52b): it is through the power [*prabhāva*] [of the pervasive factors] that defilements [*kleśa*] with their following (*parivāra*)—belonging [also] to categories different from [the pervasive factors]—arise (*upajāyante*).[898] They thus constitute a cause separate [*pṛthak*] from the homogeneous causes (*sabhāgahetu*).[899] (See ii. 57c).

CAE.3. *Further specification of the definition; F 269–70*

CAE.3.1. *Noble ones & the pervasive cause; F 269–70*

[Objection:] – Then would the defiled factors of noble ones [*āryapudgala*] (attachment [*rāga*], etc.) have as their cause the pervasive factors? The noble ones, however, have abandoned all pervasive factors, for these are abandoned [*prahātavya*] by insight into the truths [*darśana*].

[Answer:[900]] – The Vaibhāṣikas of Kaśmīr accept that all defiled factors have for their cause the factors abandoned by insight into the truths. Indeed the *Prakaraṇa-pāda*[901] expresses itself in these terms:

> What factors have for their cause the factors abandoned by insight into the truths? – (1) The defiled [*kliṣṭa*] factors[902] and (2) the retribution [*vipāka*] of factors abandoned by insight into the truths.
>
> What factors have for their cause non-defined (*avyākṛta*) factors? – (1) The non-defined conditioned factors (*saṃskṛta*)[903] and (2) the unwholesome (*akuśala*) factors. <270>
>
> Is there a truth of unsatisfactoriness (*duḥkhasatya*) which has for its cause the afflicted view of self (*satkāyadṛṣṭi*) and which is not a cause

of the afflicted view of self? ... *and so on until*: with the exclusion of origination-deterioration-duration-impermanence [*jāti, jarā, sthiti, anityatā*] of the future[904] afflicted view of self and of its associates [comprising the generally permeating factors], any other defiled truth of unsatisfactoriness [is a truth of unsatisfactoriness which has for its cause the afflicted view of self and is a cause of the afflicted view of self].

[Objection:] – If unwholesome (*akuśala*) factors have for their causes non-defined factors and not just unwholesome factors, {11 b} how can one explain this commentary (*bhāṣya*) of the *Prajñapti*:[905]

Is there an unwholesome factor which has for its cause only an unwholesome factor? – Yes; the first defiled intention (*cetanā*) which noble ones retrogressing from detachment [*vairāgya*] produce.[906]

Answer: – The non-defined factors, which are abandoned by insight into the truths, are a cause (i.e., pervasive cause [*sarvatragahetu*]) of this unwholesome intention. If the *Prajñapti* does not mention it, it is because it intends to name only the causes which have been abandoned.

[The pervasive cause has been discussed.] <271>

F. *Ripening cause (vipākahetu);*[907] *F 271–75*

F.1. *General definition;*[908] *F 271–75*

54cd. **[Only] (1) bad factors [which are completely impure] and (2) wholesome factors which are impure are a ripening cause.**[909]

Only (1) unwholesome [*akuśala*] factors, which are completely or necessarily [*avaśya*] impure [*sāsrava*], and (2) wholesome [*kuśala*] factors which are impure[910] are a ripening cause, because their nature is to ripen (*vipākadharmatvāt = vipaktiprakṛtitvāt*).

(3) The non-defined [*avyākṛta*] factors are not a ripening cause, because they are weak [*durbalatvāt*]; just as rotten seeds [*pūtibīja*], even though moistened [*abhiṣyandita*], do not grow [into sprouts (*aṅkura*)].

(4) The pure [*anāsrava*] factors, [although strong (*balavanto 'pi*),] are not a ripening cause because they are not moistened (*abhiṣyandita*)[911] by craving (*tṛṣṇā*); just as intact seeds (*sārabīja*), not moistened, do not grow [into sprouts]. Besides, pure factors are not bound (*pratisaṃyukta*), i.e., do not belong to any realm of existence: to which realm could the ripened effect belong that they would produce?

CAF.1.1. *The two qualities for producing a ripened effect;* F 271

The factors (*dharma*) which are neither non-defined nor pure, [i.e., the unwholesome and the wholesome-impure factors], possess the two qualities [*ubhayavidhatva*; *ubhayaprakāratva*] necessary for producing a ripened effect:

1. the proper strength [*balavat*] and
2. the moistening [*abhiṣyandita*] of craving,

just as the intact and moistened seed [has the two qualities necessary for the growth of the sprout].

CAF.1.2. *The meaning of the expression vipāka-hetu;* F 271–72

Objection. – What is the meaning of the expression *vipākahetu*? You have the choice of two interpretations of this compound: *vipākahetu* signifies either

1. cause of *vipāka* (*vipākasya hetuḥ*; i.e., as determinative compound [*tat-puruṣa*]), {12 a} or
2. cause in the quality of *vipāka* (*vipāka eva hetuḥ*; i.e., as descriptive compound [*karmadhāraya*]).

In the first case, the suffix *a* (*ghañ*) [in *vipāka*] denotes the state [*bhāva-sādhana*]: the *vipāka* (= *vipakti*) is the effect of the operation indicated by the root *vi-pac*.

In the second case, the suffix *a* [in *vipāka*] denotes the operation [*karma-sādhana*]: the *vipāka* is [the cause,] that which is ripened (*vipacyate*), i.e., the action arriving at the time when it gives forth an effect.[912]

Which of these two interpretations do you hold?

If you accept the first, how would you justify the text (*Jñānaprasthāna*, 974a26): "The eye arises from *vipāka* (*vipākajaṃ cakṣus*)"? <272>

If you accept the second, how would you justify the expression "*vipāka* of action" [*karmaṇo vipāka*]?

[Answer:] – We have shown (i. 37) that the two interpretations of the word *vipāka* are correct. (1) When one examines the effects, one must understand the word *vipāka* according to the first explanation; the meaning is: effect, retribution, ripened effect. (2) The text "The eye arises from *vipāka*" should be understood as "The eye arises from the cause of *vipāka*."

CAF.1.3. *The meaning of the compound* vi-pāka; F 272

[Question:] – What is the meaning of the compound *vi-pāka*?

[Answer:] – The prefix *vi* indicates difference. *Vipāka* is a *pāka*, i.e., an effect or maturation, dissimilar (*visadṛśa*) from its cause. [The other causes, however, have similar effects (*sadṛśaḥ pākaḥ*). (See insert in endnote.[913])]

.1.3.1. *The single ripened effect & the different numbers of aggregates as ripening cause;*[914] *F 272–73*

[Question:] – How is that?

In the realm of desire,

1. a ripening cause (*vipākahetu*) consisting of only one aggregate (*skandha*), [i.e., formations,] namely, possession (*prāpti*; ii. 36b; i.e., aggregate of formations; *pratyaya*) with its characteristics (*lakṣaṇa*; ii. 45c; i.e., aggregate of formations), produces one single effect [*ekaphala*];
2. a ripening cause consisting of two aggregates, [i.e., form and formations,] namely, bodily and vocal action [*kāyavakkarma*; i.e., aggregate of form] with their characteristics (i.e., aggregate of formations), produces one single effect;
3. a ripening cause consisting of four aggregates, [i.e., not form,] namely, thought and thought-concomitants [*cittacaitta*; i.e., the aggregates of sensation, ideation, formations and consciousness], wholesome and unwholesome [*kuśalākuśala*], with their characteristics (i.e., aggregate of formations), produces one single effect. <273>

In the realm of fine-materiality,

1. a ripening cause consisting of one single aggregate, [i.e., formations,] namely, possession [*prāpti*] with its characteristics, the attainment of non-ideation (*asaṃjñisamāpatti*; ii. 42a) with its characteristics, produces one single effect;
2. a ripening cause consisting of two aggregates, [i.e., form and formations,] namely, the informative action (*vijñapti*; iv. 2) of the first meditation (*dhyāna*) with its characteristics, produces one single effect;
3. a ripening cause consisting of four aggregates, [i.e., not form,] namely, the wholesome thought, not concentrated (*cetasyasamāhita*; for the concentrated thought always involves the form [*rūpa*] of restraint [iv. 13] and thus five aggregates), with its characteristics, produces one single effect; {13 a}
4. a ripening cause consisting of five aggregates, namely, the concentrated thought (*samāhita*) with its characteristics, produces one single effect.

In the realm of immateriality,

1. a ripening cause consisting of one single aggregate, [i.e., formations,] namely, possession [*prāpti*], the attainment of cessation (*nirodhasamāpatti*; ii. 43), with the respective characteristics, produces one single effect;
2. a ripening cause consisting of four aggregates, [i.e., not form,] namely, thought and thought-concomitants [*cittacaitta*], [wholesome (*kuśala*),] with their characteristics, produces one single effect.

CAF.1.3.2. *The single ripening cause & the different numbers of sense-spheres as ripened effect;*[915] *F 273–74*

[One sense-sphere:] – There is an action the ripened effect of which is included in one single sense-sphere (*āyatana*), **namely**, in the single sense-sphere of factors (*dharmāyatana*; i. 15): the action which has for its ripened effect the vitality faculty (*jīvitendriya*; ii. 45a).[916] In fact, the action which has for its ripened effect the vitality faculty necessarily has for its ripened effect the vitality faculty and its characteristics (ii. 45c); both form part of (1) the sense-sphere of factors.

[Two sense-spheres:] – The action which has for its ripened effect the mental faculty (*manas*) necessarily has for its ripened effect two sense-spheres, namely, (1) the sense-sphere of the mental faculty (*mana-āyatana*; i. 16b) and (2) the sense-sphere of factors (*dharmāyatana*), (which includes sensations, etc., and the characteristics which necessarily accompany the mental faculty). <274>

The action which has for its ripened effect the sense-sphere of the tangible (*spraṣṭavyāyatana*), necessarily has for its ripened effect two sense-spheres, namely: (1) the sense-sphere of the tangible and (2) the sense-sphere of factors, (which includes the characteristics of the tangible).

[Three sense-spheres:] – The action which has for its ripened effect the sense-sphere of the body (*kāyāyatana*) necessarily has for its ripened effect three sense-spheres: (1) the sense-sphere of the body, (2) the sense-sphere of the tangible, (namely, the four fundamental material elements which support the sense-sphere of the body), (3) the sense-sphere of factors, (which includes the characteristics).

In the same way, the action which has for its ripened effect either the sense-sphere of visible form (*rūpāyatana*) or the sense-sphere of odors (*gandhāyatana*) or the sense-sphere of taste (*rasāyatana*), necessarily has for its ripened effect three sense-spheres: (1) the sense-sphere of the tangible and (2) the sense-sphere of factors as above, plus, according to the case, (3) the sense-sphere of visible form or the sense-sphere of odor or the sense-sphere of taste.

[Four sense-spheres:] – The action which has for its ripened effect either the sense-sphere of the eye (*cakṣus*) or the sense-sphere of the ear (*śrotra*) or the sense-sphere of the nose (*ghrāṇa*) or the sense-sphere of the tongue (*jihvā*) necessarily has for its ripened effect four sense-spheres: (1) one of the four sense-faculties, (2) the sense-sphere of the body, (3) the sense-sphere of the tangible, (4) the sense-sphere of factors.

[Five to eleven sense-spheres:] – An action can have for its ripened effect five, six, seven, eight, nine, ten, eleven sense-spheres.[917]

Actions [*karman*], in fact, are of two types: (1) of varied effect (*vicitra*) and (2) of non-varied [*avicitra*] effect.

The same holds for [external] seeds [*bāhyabīja*], [i.e., they are of two types:] {13 b} [some external seeds, for example,] (1) lotus [*padma*], pomegranate [*dāḍima*], fig [*nyagrodha*], etc., [have varied fruits (*vicitraphala*)];[918] [some external seeds, for example,] (2) barley [*yava*], wheat [*ghodūma*], etc., [have non-varied fruits (*avicitra-phala*)].

1.3.3. *The ripened cause of one single time period and one instant & the number of time periods and moments of the ripened effect;*[919] *F 274*

It can happen that the ripened effect of an action belonging to one single time period (*ekādhvika*) belongs to three time periods (*traiyadhvika*);[920] but the reverse is not true,[921] for the effect cannot be lower than its cause (*mābhūd atinyūnaṃ hetoḥ phalam*).

The ripened effect of an action abiding for one moment (*ekakṣaṇika*) can abide for numerous moments [*bahukṣaṇika*]; but the reverse is not true, for the same reason. (MVŚ, 98a7) <275>

2. *Further specification of the definition; F 275*

2.1. *The time of the earliest occurrence of the ripened effect & the ripening cause; F 275*

The ripened effect is not simultaneous with the action that produces it, for a ripened effect is not experienced at the moment when the action is accomplished.[922]

The ripened effect does [also] not immediately (*anantara*) follow the action, for it is the condition as the equivalent and immediate antecedent (*samanantarapratyaya*; ii. 63b) which brings about (*ākarṣ*) the moment that immediately follows the action: in fact, the ripening cause depends [*apekṣā*], in order to realize its effect, on the development of the stream [*pravāha*].

CAG. *The six causes and the unconditioned factors & the three time periods;*[923] *F 275*

To which time period should a factor (*dharma*) belong in order that it might be any of these six causes? We have mentioned the rule [for the time periods (*adhvaniyama*)] implicitly [*arthatas*]; but we have not stated it in a verse (*kārikā*):

55ab. **The pervasive cause and the homogeneous cause are of two time periods [i.e., past and present]; three causes [i.e., the associated, the simultaneous and ripening causes] are of three time periods [i.e., past, present and future].**[924]

A past factor, as well as a present factor, may be a pervasive cause (*sarvatragahetu*), may function as a homogeneous cause (*sabhāgahetu*) (ii. 52b).

Factors of the past, of the present and of the future may function as an associated cause (*saṃprayuktakahetu*), a co-existent cause (*sahabhūhetu*) and a ripening cause (*vipakāhetu*).

The verse does not speak of [the rule for the time periods (*kālaniyama*) of] an efficient cause (*kāraṇahetu*; ii. 50a): (1) the conditioned factors of the three time periods may function as efficient causes; (2) the unconditioned factors are timeless [*adhvaviprayukta*].

[The causes have been discussed.]

CB. *THE FIVE EFFECTS (PHALA);*[925] *F 275–97*

A. The correspondence of the effects with the causes; F 275
   1. Relationship of the effects to the conditioned and unconditioned factors; F 275
   2. Effects which do not have a cause: the effect of disconnection (*visaṃyogaphala*); F 276
   3. Effects which do have a cause: ripened effect (*vipākaphala*), effect of dominance (*adhipatiphala*), effect of equal outflow (*niṣyandaphala*), effect of human action (*puruṣakāraphala*); F 287
B. The defining characteristics of the five effects; F 289
   1. Ripened effect (*vipākaphala*); F 289
   2. Effect of equal outflow (*niṣyandaphala*); F 290
   3. Effect of disconnection (*visaṃyogaphala*); F 291
   4. Effect of human action (*puruṣakāraphala*); F 292
   5. Effect of dominance (*adhipatiphala*); F 292
C. Two stages of causing an effect; F 293
D. The four effects of the Westerners; F 297

BA. *The correspondence of the effects with the causes;*[926] *F 275–89*

To which effect do the causes correspond? Because of which effects are (the causes) recognized as causes?

BA.1. *The relationship of the effects to the conditioned and unconditioned factors; F 275–76*

55cd. (1) Conditioned [factors] and (2) disconnection [from impure (*sāsrava*) factors] [*visaṃyoga*] "are" effects.[927]

Just as it is said in the *Mūlaśāstra*:

> What factors are an effect? (1) Conditioned [*saṃskṛta*] [factors] and (2) cessation due to deliberation (*pratisaṃkhyānirodha = nirvāṇa*).[928] <276>

Objection: – If the unconditioned [factor] [*asaṃskṛta*] "is" an effect, it should "have" a cause of which it could be said that it is the effect [*phala*]. Moreover, since you maintain that it "is" a cause (i.e., an efficient cause; ii. 50a), it should "have" an effect of which it could be said that it is the cause (*hetu*).[929]

The Sarvāstivādin answers: – The conditioned [factors] [*saṃskṛta*] alone "have" a cause, [i.e., are produced by a cause,] and "have" an effect, [i.e., produce an effect].

55d. [Sarvāstivādins:] – The unconditioned [factor] "has" neither a cause nor an effect.[930]

[Question: – What is the reason for this?]

[Answer: – The unconditioned factor "has" neither a cause nor an effect,] for one cannot attribute to it any of the six kinds of causes or any of the five kinds of effects.

BA.2. *Effects which do not have a cause: the effect of disconnection (visaṃyogaphala);*[931] *F 276–87*

BA.2.1. *The unconditioned factor which "is" an effect but does not "have" a cause; F 276–77*

BA.2.1.1. *The noble path & the effect of disconnection;*[932] *F 276–77*

[Question:] – Why can one not assume that the part of the (noble) path called *unhindered path* (*ānantaryamārga*[933]) is the efficient cause (*kāraṇahetu*) of the effect of disconnection (*visaṃyogaphala*; ii. 57d)?

[Answer:] – We have seen that the efficient cause is a cause which does not make an obstacle to the "arising" [*utpādāvighnabhāva*] [of factors susceptible to arise]; now, disconnection, being unconditioned, does not "arise". One cannot attribute to it the unhindered path (*ānantaryamārga*) as an efficient cause (*kāraṇahetu*).

[Question:] – Then how is disconnection an effect of the (noble) path? Of what is it an effect?

[Answer:] – Disconnection is the effect of the (noble) path, for it is attained due to the power [*bala*] of the (noble) path (vi. 51): in other words, it is by means of the (noble) path that practitioners attain the "possession" (*prāpti*; ii. 36cd) of disconnection. {14 b}

[Objection:] – Thus it is [only] the attaining, the possession [*prāpti*] of disconnection that is the effect of the (noble) path, and not disconnection itself [*visaṃyoga*]: for the (noble) path is capable [*sāmarthya*] with regard to the attaining of disconnection, not with regard to disconnection. <277>

[Answer:] – Wrong! There is a difference in the capability [*sāmarthya*] of the (noble) path with regard to (i) attaining [*prāpti*], on the one hand, and (ii) disconnection [*visaṃyoga*], on the other.

[Question: – How does the (noble) path have capability with regard to attaining?]

[Answer:] – The (noble) path produces attaining.

[Question: – How does the (noble) path have capability with regard to disconnection?]

[Answer:] – The (noble) path makes one attain (*prāpayati*) disconnection. Thus, although the (noble) path is not the cause of disconnection (= cessation due to deliberation), it may be said that disconnection is the effect of the (noble) path.[934]

CBA.2.2. *The unconditioned factor which "is" a cause but does not "have" an effect; F 277–78*

CBA.2.2.1. *The efficient cause and cognitive object condition & the unconditioned factor; F 277–78*

[Objection:] – Since the unconditioned [factor] (*asaṃskṛta*) does not "have" an effect of dominance (*adhipatiphala*; ii. 58d), how can one define it as an efficient cause (*kāraṇahetu*)?

[Answer:] – The unconditioned [factor] "is" an efficient cause, for it does not make an obstacle to any arising factor; but it does not "have" an effect, for, being timeless (*adhvavinirmukta*), it does not have the capability [*asamarthatva*]) of either (1) taking or projecting [*pratigrahaṇa*] or (2) giving forth [*dāna*] an effect (ii. 59ab).

The Sautrāntika:[935] – We deny that the unconditioned [factor] could be a cause. In fact, the Sūtra [or Fortunate One (*bhagavant*)] does not say that the cause can be unconditioned; it says that the cause is only [a synonym (*paryāya*) for being] conditioned:

> All causes (*hetu*), all conditions (*pratyaya*) which have for their effect the production [*utpāda*] of material form [*rūpa*], ... of consciousness [*vijñāna*], are themselves also impermanent [*anitya*].[936] Produced [*pratītyotpanna*] by impermanent causes and conditions, how could material form, ... and consciousness be permanent?

The Sarvāstivādin replies: – If the permanent [factor], the unconditioned [factor], is not a cause, it will not be a cognitive object condition (*ālambanapratyaya*; ii. 63) of the consciousness that is directed at it. {15 a}

(The Sautrāntika:[937]) – The Sūtra [passage] declares that the causes and conditions capable of producing [consciousness (*vijñana*)] are impermanent [*anitya*]. It does not say that "all" conditions (*pratyaya*) of consciousness are impermanent. The unconditioned [factor] could then be a cognitive object condition [*ālambanapratyaya*] of consciousness; for [in that case] the cognitive object condition is not generative [*janaka*]. <278>

The Sarvāstivādin: – The Sūtra says that it is the generative (*janaka*) causes [ii. 247] that are impermanent: thus the Sūtra does not deny [*pratiṣedha*] that the unconditioned [factor] may be an efficient cause (*kāraṇahetu*), that is to say, a cause which does not make an obstacle [*anāvaraṇabhāvamātra*].

(The Sautrāntika:) – The Sūtra accepts the cognitive object condition [ii. 61c]; but it does not speak of an efficient cause, "the cause which does not make an obstacle". It is thus not established that the unconditioned [factor] is a cause.

The Sarvāstivādin: – Indeed, the Sūtra does not say that that which does not make an obstacle is a cause; but it does not contradict it. Many Sūtras have disappeared.[938] How can you be assured that the Sūtra does not attribute to the unconditioned [factor] the quality of an efficient cause?

A.2.3. *Disconnection (visaṃyoga) & cessation due to deliberation (prātisaṃkhyānirodha); F 278–87*

(The Sautrāntika:[939]) – What is the factor (*dharma*) called *disconnection* (*visaṃyoga*)?

The Sarvāstivādin: – The *Mūlaśāstra* (*Jñānaprasthāna*, 923b6) says that disconnection is cessation due to deliberation (*pratisaṃkhyānirodha*; ii. 57d).

A.2.3.1. *The inexpressibility of the cessation due to deliberation & disconnection; F 278*

(The Sautrāntika:) – When I asked you [previously; i. 6] what cessation due to deliberation is, you answered: "It is disconnection"; when I ask you [now] what disconnection is, you answer: "It is cessation due to deliberation!" The two answers give a circular reasoning [*itaretarāśraya*] and do not explain the intrinsic nature of the factor, i.e., the unconditioned [factor], to which they refer. You owe us another explanation.

Sarvāstivādin: – This factor (*dharma*), in its intrinsic nature [*svabhāva*], is real but indescribable; {15 b} only the noble ones (*ārya*) "realize" it internally each for themselves [*pratyātmavedya*]. It is only possible to indicate its general characteristics by saying that there exists a real entity—distinct from others (*dravya-antara*)—which is wholesome (*kuśala*) and eternal [*nitya*], which is called *cessation due to deliberation* (*pratisaṃkhyānirodha*) and also *disconnection* (*visaṃyoga*).

CBA.2.3.2. *The definition and existential status of the three unconditioned factors; F 278–87*

CBA.2.3.2.a. *The Sautrāntika definition; F 278–79*

The Sautrāntika[940] affirms that the unconditioned [factor], i.e., the threefold unconditioned [factor] (i. 5b), is not real [*adravya*]. The three factors (*dharma*) which it refers to are not distinct and real entities [*bhāvāntara*], as are material form [*rūpa*], sensation [*vedanā*], etc.[941] <279>

1. What is called *space* (*ākāśa*) is the mere absence [*abhāvamātra*] of the tangible (*spraṣṭavya*), i.e., the absence of a resistant body (*sapratighadravya*). Persons in the dark [*andhakāra*] say that there is space when they do not encounter (*avindantaḥ*) any obstruction [*pratighāta*].[942]

2. What is called *cessation due to deliberation* (*pratisaṃkhyānirodha*) or *nirvāṇa* is—at the time of the cessation of the already arisen proclivities (*anuśaya*) and of the already arisen existence [*janman*]—the absence of arising [i.e., the non-arising (*anutpāda*)] of any other proclivities or any other existence, and that because of the power [*bala*] of understanding (*pratisaṃkhyā = prajñā*).[943] [See below the discussion of this definition.]

3. When, independent of the power of deliberation (*pratisaṃkhyā*) and because of the mere lack of causes [and conditions] [*pratyayavaikalya*], there is an absence of arising [i.e., the non-arising] of factors, this is called *cessation not due to deliberation* (*apratisaṃkhyānirodha*). For example, when premature death (*antarāmaraṇa*) interrupts the personal existence (*nikāyasabhāga*; ii. 10, 41), there is cessation not due to deliberation of the factors which would have arisen in the course of this personal existence if it had continued.[944]

CBA.2.3.2.b. *The definition by other schools; F 279–80*

According to another school [*nikāyāntarīya*]:[945]

1. cessation due to deliberation (*pratisaṃkhyānirodha*) is the future non-arising of proclivities (*anuśaya*) on account of [*sāmarthya*] understanding (*prajñā*);
2. cessation not due to deliberation (*apratisaṃkhyānirodha*) is the future non-arising of unsatisfactoriness, i.e., of existence, because of the disappearance [or lack (*vaikalya*)] of proclivities—[the cause of the arising (of unsatisfactoriness) (*utpādakāraṇa*)]—and not directly on account of understanding.[946] <280>

[The first would thus be *nirvāṇa* with remainder (*sopadhiśeṣa nirvāṇadhātu*), the second would be *nirvāṇa* without remainder (*nirupadhiśeṣa nirvāṇadhātu*).]

(The Sautrāntika:[947]) – But the future non-arising of unsatisfactoriness supposes deliberation (*pratisaṃkhyā*); it is thus included in cessation due to deliberation.

Another School [*apara*][948] defines cessation not due to deliberation as: "later non-existence (*paścād abhāva*) of the factors which have arisen, by virtue of their spontaneous [*svarasa*] cessation".[949]

[Comment:] – In this hypothesis [*kalpanā*], {16 a} cessation not due to deliberation would not be eternal (*nitya*), since it is absent (*abhāva*) as long as the factor involved (= the proclivity [*anuśaya*]) has not perished.

[Reply:] – But does cessation due to deliberation not have a certain deliberation (i.e., *pratisaṃkhyā*) for its antecedent [*pūrvakatva*]? Therefore, it too would not be eternal, for, if the antecedent were absent, the consequent would also be absent.

[Comment:] – You cannot say that cessation due to deliberation would not be eternal because it has deliberation (*pratisaṃkhyā*) for its antecedent: in fact, it does not have deliberation for its antecedent. One cannot say that deliberation is earlier, that the "non-arising [*anutpāda*] of non-arisen factors" is later. – Let us explain. The non-arising [of non-arisen factors] always exists in and of itself. (i) If deliberation is absent, the factors will arise; (ii) but if deliberation arises, the factors will absolutely the non-arising [of non-arisen factors] consists in this:

1. before this deliberation, there is no obstacle to their arising [*utpattipratibandha*];
2. given the deliberation, the factors, the arising of which has not been previously hindered (*akṛtotpattipratibandha*), do not arise.

But it does not create the non-arising.[950]

CBA.2.3.2.c. *The Sarvāstivādins: the Sautrāntika definition and the existential status of the unconditioned factors;* F 280–83

CBA.2.3.2.ca. *Refutation based on scriptural authority: Sūtra on the praxis-oriented faculties;* F 280–82

(The Sarvāstivādin refutes the Sautrāntika:[951]) – If *nirvāṇa* is simply non-arising (*anutpāda*), how can one explain the Sūtra (*Saṃyukta*, 26, 2)? <281>

> The practice [*āsevita*], the habit [*bhāvita*], the increased cultivation [*bahulīkṛta*] of the five (praxis-oriented) faculties, faith, etc., lead to the abandonment of past, future and present unsatisfactoriness.[952]

In fact, this abandonment [*prahāṇa*] is none other than *nirvāṇa*, and, [on the other hand,] it is only of a future factor (*dharma*) that one can have non-arising, not of a past or present factor.

(The Sautrāntika:[953] [1. Explanation of past and present unsatisfactoriness:]) – This Sūtra does not contradict our definition of *nirvāṇa*. In fact, by "abandonment of past and present unsatisfactoriness" one understands the abandonment [*prahāṇa*] of defilements (*kleśa*) bearing on (*ālambana*) past and present unsatisfactoriness [*duḥkha*]. Our interpretation is justified by another text (*Saṃyukta*, 3, 17): {16 b}

> Abandon predilection-attachment (*chandarāga*)[954] relative to material form (*rūpa*), sensation [*vedanā*], ... consciousness [*vijñāna*]; when predilection-attachment is abandoned, material form, ... consciousness will be abandoned and completely known (*parijñā*) by you.[955]

It is in this way that we should understand "abandonment of past and present unsatisfactoriness" of which the Sūtra on the (praxis-oriented) faculties speaks.

[2. Explanation of past and future defilement:] – If one adopts another reading of the Sūtra on the (praxis-oriented) faculties:

> The practice, [the habit, the increased cultivation] of the (praxis-oriented) faculties lead to the abandonment of past, future and present defilement (*kleśa*),

the explanation is the same.

Or rather, past defilement is defilement of the previous birth (*paurvajanmika*: *pūrve janmani bhava*); present defilement is defilement of the present birth (*aihajanmika*); it does not refer to defilement of a past or present given moment (*ekakṣaṇika*).

The same for the eighteen modes of craving (*tṛṣṇāvicarita*) (*Aṅguttara*, ii. 212): under the name *past*, one designates the modes (*vicarita*) related to past birth; under the name *present*, those related to present birth; under the name *future*, those related to future birth. <282>

Past defilements and present defilements place seed-states [*bījabhāva*] designated to produce future defilement in the present self [*saṃtati*]: when these seeds are abandoned, past and present defilement is abandoned: in the same way, one can say that action [*karma*] is exhausted when the ripened effect [*vipāka*] is exhausted.

[3. Explanation of future unsatisfactoriness and future defilement:] – As for future unsatisfactoriness, so for future defilement; that which one understands by their "abandonment" is the fact that they absolutely [*atyanta*] will not arise, in view of the absence of seed-states.

4. How otherwise is the abandonment of the past or present unsatisfactoriness understood? There is no reason to make an effort [*yatna*] in order to cause that which has ceased [*niruddha*] or that which is ceasing (*nirodhābhimukha*) to cease. {17 a}

;BA.2.3.2.cb. *Refutation based on scriptural authority: Passage on detachment; F 282–83*

The Sarvāstivādin:[956] – If unconditioned [factors] do not "exist", how can the Sūtra say:

> Among all conditioned and unconditioned factors, detachment (*virāga*) is supreme [*agra*].

How can a factor which does not exist (*asat*) be said to be supreme among the factors which do not exist?[957]

(The Sautrāntika:[958]) – We do not say that unconditioned [factors] do not exist at all. They exist actually in the manner in which we say that they exist. Let us explain:

Before sound [*śabda*] is produced, one says: "There is former non-existence of sound" [*asti śabdasya prāgabhāva*]; after sound has perished, one says: "There is later non-existence of sound" (*asti śabdasya paścād abhāvaḥ*), and yet, it is not established that non-existence [*abhāva*] exists (*bhavati*):[959] the same holds [also] for unconditioned [factors].

Although non-existent, one unconditioned [factor] is most praiseworthy [*praśasyatama*], namely, detachment (*virāga*), the absolute [*atyanta*] future non-existence of all distress [*upadrava*]. This non-existent factor is the most distinguished (*viśiṣṭa*) among the non-existent [factors]. <283> The Sūtra praises [*praśaṃsā*] it by saying that it is supreme [*agra*] so that the disciples [*vineya*] conceive joy and affection [or are enticed] [*upacchandana*] with regard to it.

CBA.2.3.2.cc. *Refutation based on logical reasoning: cessation due to deliberation is a noble truth; F 283*

The Sarvāstivādin: – If cessation due to deliberation (*pratisaṃkhyānirodha*) or *nirvāṇa* is [merely] non-existence, how can it be one of the noble truths? How can it be the third noble truth [i.e., cessation (*nirodha*)]?

[Answer:] – What should one understand by *noble truth* (*āryasatya*)? Without doubt the meaning of *satya* is: "non-erroneous" (*aviparīta*). The noble ones (*ārya*) have seen [both] that which exists and that which does not exist in a "non-erroneous" manner: in that which is unsatisfactoriness (*duḥkha*), they have seen only unsatisfactoriness; {17 b} in the non-existence of unsatisfactoriness, they have seen the non-existence of unsatisfactoriness. What contradiction do you find in the non-existence of unsatisfactoriness, i.e., cessation due to deliberation, being a noble truth?

And this non-existence is the third truth, because the noble ones have seen it and proclaim it immediately after the second [i.e., the truth of the origin (*samudaya-satya*)].

CBA.2.3.2.cd. *Refutation based on logical reasoning: Unconditioned factors are a cognitive object; F 283*

The Sarvāstivādin: – But if unconditioned [factors] are [merely] non-existents [*abhāvamātra*], then consciousness which has space [*ākāśa*] and the two cessations (*nirodha*) for its cognitive object would have a non-existent for its cognitive object.

[Reply:] – We do not see any inconvenience in this, as we shall explain in the discussion of [the existence (*astitvacintā*) of] the past [*atīta*] and future [*anāgata*] [factors] (v. 25).

CBA.2.3.2.ce. *Refutation based on protecting the Vaibhāṣika doctrine; F 283*

The Sarvāstivādin asks: – What fault [*doṣa*] do you see in maintaining that the unconditioned [factor] is a real entity [*dravya*]?

[Reply:] – What advantage [*guṇa*] do you yourself see in (maintaining that the unconditioned factor is a real entity)?

[The Sarvāstivādin:] – The advantage is that the Vaibhāṣika doctrine [*pakṣa*] is protected (*pālita*).

A.2.3.2.d. *Sautrāntika: Refutation of the unconditioned factors as a real entity; F 283–87*

A.2.3.2.da. *Refutation based on logical reasoning: direct perception and inference; F 283*

May the gods [*devatā*] take it upon themselves to protect this doctrine, if they judge it to be possible! But to maintain the distinct existence of the unconditioned [factor] amounts to affirming a non-existent factor [*abhūta*] as being a real entity. In fact, (1) the unconditioned [factor] is not known through direct perception (*pratyakṣa*), as is the case for material form [*rūpa*], sensation [*vedanā*], etc.; (2) it is not known through inference (*anumāna*) on the grounds of its activity [*karma*], as is the case for the [subtle] sense-faculties, [like the eye (*cakṣus*), etc.].

A.2.3.2.db. *Refutation based on logical reasoning: the genitive* duḥkhasya nirodhaḥ, *etc.; F 283–84*

Besides, if cessation [itself] (*nirodha*) is a distinct entity [*vastuno*], how could one justify the genitive [*ṣaṣṭhīvyavasthā*]: *duḥkhasya nirodhaḥ*, destruction or cessation of unsatisfactoriness, cessation of attachment [*rāga*], cessation of the object of the attachment? <284> – In our system, this is easy to explain: the cessation of [such and such (*amuṣya*)] an entity [*vastu*] is simply [a negation (*pratiśedhamātra*), i.e.,] the absence or non-existence of such and such an entity [*amuṣyābhāva*]. "Cessation of unsatisfactoriness" signifies "unsatisfactoriness will no longer exist". But we cannot conceive any relationship [*saṃbhandh*]) (i) of cause [*hetu*] with its effect [*phala*], (ii) of effect with its cause, (iii) of the whole [*avayavin*] with its part [*avayava*], etc., between (1) the entity, i.e., attachment, and (2) cessation conceived of as distinct entity, which would justify the genitive.[960]

The Sarvāṣtivādin answers: – We affirm that cessation is a distinct entity. {18 a} We can, however, specify cessation as being in relationship with such and such an entity (cessation of attachment [*rāga*], etc.), for one gains possession (*prāpti*; ii. 37b) of cessation at the moment when one cuts off the possession [*prāptiviccheda*] of such and such an entity [i.e., of defilements (*kleśa*)].

We reply: – But what is that which determines or specifies [*niyama*] the gaining of possession of cessation?[961]

The Sarvāstivādin. – The Sūtra speaks of the *bhikṣus* who have gained possession of *nirvāṇa* in the present life.[962] If *nirvāṇa* is non-existence, nothingness (*abhāva*), how could they gain possession of it?

(The Sautrāntika:[963]) – The *bhikṣus*, through the acquisition of the opposing force or of the counter-agent (*pratipakṣalābhena*), i.e., through the acquisition of the noble path, have attained a personality (*āśraya*) absolutely contrary [*atyantaviruddha*] [to the arising (*utpāda*)] of defilements (*kleśa*), of a new personal existence [*punarbhava*]. This is why the Sūtra says that they have gained possession of *nirvāṇa*.

CBA.2.3.2.dc. *Refutation based on scriptural authority: Saṃyukta, 13, 5; F 284–86*

Besides, we have a text [*āgama*; *Saṃyukta*, 13, 5] which shows that *nirvāṇa* is mere non-existence (*abhāvamātra*). The Sūtra says:[964] <285>

> With regard to all these kinds of unsatisfactoriness, the complete abandonment (*aśeṣaprahāṇa*), [casting aside (*pratiniḥsarga*),] expurgation (*vyantībhāva* or *vāntībhāva*), exhaustion (*kṣaya*), detachment (*virāga*), cessation (*nirodha*), appeasement (*vyupaśama*), disappearance (*astaṃgama*); the non-rebirth (*apratisaṃdhi*), non-arising (*anutpāda*), non-appearance (*aprādurbhāva*) of other kinds of unsatisfactoriness—this is peaceful (*śānta*), this is excellent (*praṇītam*), namely, the casting aside of all substratum (*sarvopadhipratiniḥsarga*), the exhaustion of craving (*tṛṣṇākṣaya*), detachment (*virāga*), cessation (*nirodha*), *nirvāṇa*.[965]

The Sarvāstivādin: – When the Sūtra says that *nirvāṇa* is non-appearance (*aprādurbhāva*) of new unsatisfactoriness, the Sūtra means to say that there is no appearance of unsatisfactoriness "in" *nirvāṇa* [*nāsmin prādurbhāva*].[966]

(The Sautrāntika:[967]) – I do not see that the locative [*saptamī*], "in *nirvāṇa*", has any force in order to establish that *nirvāṇa* is an entity. In what sense do you understand the locative *asmin*?

1. If this means to say: *asmin sati*, "*nirvāṇa* existing, there is no appearance of unsatisfactoriness", then unsatisfactoriness never would appear, for *nirvāṇa* is eternal [*nitya*].
2. If this means to say: *asmin prāpte*, "*nirvāna* being attained, there is no appearance of unsatisfactoriness", {18 b} you would have to admit that future unsatisfactoriness would not appear when the noble path—by virtue of which you suppose that *nirvāṇa* is attained—either is, or, rather, has been attained.[968] <286>

CBA.2.3.2.dd. *Refutation based on scriptural authority: Comparison with the extinction of a flame; F 286*

Therefore the comparison [*dṛṣṭānta*] of the Sūtra is excellent:

> Like the *nirvāṇa* of a flame [*pradyota*], so the liberation [*vimokṣa*] of one's thought.[969]

That is to say: just as the extinction [*nirvāṇa*] of the flame is merely the "passing away" (*aty-aya*) [or non-existence (*abhāva*)] of the flame and not a certain distinct entity, so is the liberation of the thought of the Fortunate One.

A.2.3.2.de. *Refutation based on scriptural authority (Abhidharma): the* avastuka *factors;* F 286–87

(The Sautrāntika view[970]) is also backed up by the Abhidharma where we read:

> What are the *avastuka* factors? – The unconditioned factors.

The term *avastuka* signifies ["bodiless" (*aśarīra*),] "unreal", "without intrinsic nature" [*asvabhāva*].

A.2.3.2.dea. *Vaibhāṣika: the five meanings of* vastu;[971] F 286–87

The Vaibhāṣikas do not accept this interpretation. The term *vastu*, in fact, is used in five different acceptations:

1. *vastu* in the sense of specific entity (*svabhāvavastu*), for example: "When one has attained (*pratilabh*) this *vastu* (the *aśubha*, vi. 11), one is accompanied (*samanvāgam*) by this *vastu*" (*Jñānaprasthāna*, 1026c11; MVŚ, 985a22);[972]
2. *vastu* in the sense of cognitive object of consciousness (*ālambanavastu*), for example: "All the factors are known (*jñeya*) by way of the different cognitions (*jñānena*), each knowing its particular object (*yathāvastu*)" (*Prakaraṇa*, 713c20);
3. *vastu* in the sense of "place with binding" (*saṃyojanīya*; *saṃyogavastu*),[973] for example: "Are those who are fettered to a *vastu* by the fetter [*saṃyojana*] of lust [*anunaya*] those who are fettered to this *vastu* by the fetter of hostility [*pratigha*]?" (MVŚ, 298b–c);
4. *vastu* in the sense of cause (*hetuvastu*), for example: "What are the factors endowed with a cause (*savastuka*)? – The conditioned factors [*saṃskṛta*]" (*Prakaraṇa*, 716a4);[974] {19 a} <287>
5. *vastu* in the sense of "action of taking possession" (*parigrahavastu*), for example: "*vastu* of a field [*kṣetra*], *vastu* of a house [*gṛha*], *vastu* of a shop, *vastu* of riches: abandoning the action of taking possession of these (*parigraha*), they renounce them" (MVŚ, 288b5).[975]

The Vaibhāṣika concludes: In the passage that concerns us, *vastu* has the meaning of cause; *avastuka* signifies "that which has no cause". Unconditioned [factors], although real [*dravyataḥ*], being always devoid of activity, do not have a cause which produces them, do not have an effect which they produce.

CBA.3. *Effects which do have a cause;*[976] *F 287–89*

We must explain what type of effect proceeds from each type of cause.

CBA.3.1. *The ripened effect (vipākaphala) & its cause: the ripening cause;*[977] *F 287*

56a. The ripened effect is the effect of the last cause [i.e., the ripening cause].[978]

The last cause is the ripening cause (*vipākahetu*), because the ripening cause is named last in the list (see ii, F 245). The first effect (see ii, F 275), i.e., the ripened effect (*vipākaphala*; ii. 57), is the effect of this cause.

CBA.3.2. *The effect of dominance (adhipatiphala) & its cause: the efficient cause;*[979] *F 287–88*

56b. The effect of dominance is the effect of the first cause [i.e., the efficient cause].[980] <288>

The first cause is the reason of existence or efficient cause (*kāraṇahetu*); the last effect [i.e., the effect of dominance] proceeds from it.

Because this effect is the effect of the sovereign or dominator [or predominance of the efficient cause] [*adhipatiphala*; ii. 58cd], this effect is called (1) *adhipaja*, i.e., arisen from the dominator [or predominance], or (2) *ādhipata*, i.e., appertaining to the dominator [or predominance]. The efficient cause is considered to play the part of the dominator [or predominance] (*adhipati*).

[Objection:] – But since the quality of not making an obstacle (*anāvaraṇabhāvamātrāvasthāna*; ii. 50a) suffices to constitute the efficient cause (*kāraṇahetu*), how can it be regarded as dominator [or what predominance does it have]?

[Answer:] The efficient cause is either:

1. a non-efficacious cause (*upekṣaka*)—and it is then regarded as sovereign[981] or dominator [or predominance] because of this fact itself, i.e., not making an obstacle; or rather
2. an efficacious cause (*kāraka*)—and it is then regarded as dominator [or predominance] because it is of the nature of the contributive efficacy (*aṅgībhāva*), i.e., the predominant cause (*pradhāna*), the generative cause (*janaka*). {19 b} For example, the ten sense-spheres (*āyatana*), (visual form and the eye sense-faculty, etc.,) are dominators with regard to the five sensory consciousnesses; the collective actions [*karman*] of sentient beings are dominators with regard to the receptacle world [*bhājanaloka*].[982] The ear sense-faculty, etc., also have an indirect predominance, [through

a succession,] [*pāraṃparyeṇādhipatya*] with regard to the arising of visual consciousness, for after having heard, the person experiences the desire [*kāma*] to see; and so forth. (ii. 50a)

A.3.3. *The effect of equal outflow (niṣyandaphala) & its causes: the homogeneous cause and the pervasive cause;*[983] *F 288*

56cd. The effect of equal outflow is the effect (1) of the homogeneous cause and (2) of the pervasive cause.[984]

The effect of equal outflow (*niṣyandaphala*) proceeds (1) from the homogeneous cause (*sabhāgahetu*; ii. 52) and (2) from the pervasive cause (*sarvatragahetu*; ii. 54): for the effect of these two causes is similar to its cause (ii. 57c; iv. 85).

A.3.4. *The effect of human action (puruṣakāraphala) & its causes;*[985] *F 288–89*

A.3.4.1. *The metaphorical or specialized effect of human action & its two causes;*[986] *F 288–89*

56d. The human (*pauruṣa*) [effect, i.e., the effect of human action,] is the effect of two causes [i.e., of the co-existent cause and the associated cause].[987] <289>

The effect of the co-existent cause (*sahabhūhetu*; ii. 50b) and of the associated cause (*saṃprayuktakahetu*; ii. 53c) is called *pauruṣa*, "human", i.e., effect of human action (*puruṣakāraphala*).

As the action is not distinct from the very person which does the action, "human action" (*puruṣakāra*) is the very person itself (*puruṣabhāva*). The effect of human action (*puruṣakāraphala*) can therefore be termed *human effect* (*pauruṣaṃ phalaṃ*).

[Question:] – [In our context,] what should one understand by this co-called *human action* [*puruṣakāra*]?

[Answer:] – The "activity"[988] (*kāritra*; *kriyā*; *karman*) of a factor (*dharma*) is termed its *human action* (*puruṣakāra*), because this activity is like the action of a human (*puruṣa*). In the same way, in the world, a certain plant [*oṣadhi*] is called *kākajaṅghā* ("foot of a crow") because it resembles the foot of a crow; a hero [*manuṣya*] is called *mattahastin* ("furious elephant") because he resembles a furious elephant.

A.3.4.2. *The effect of human action & the other causes; F 289*

[Question:] – Are the associated cause (*saṃprayuktakahetu*) and the co-existent cause (*sahabhūhetu*) the only causes which have an effect of human action [*puruṣakāra-phala*]?

[Answer:] – According to one opinion, the other causes also have this type of effect, with the exception of the ripening cause (*vipākahetu*). This effect arises, indeed, either simultaneous with (*sahotpanna*) or immediately following [*samanantara-utpanna*] its cause; such is not the case with the ripened effect.

According to other masters [*apara*],[989] the ripening cause also has a distant [*viprakṛṣṭa*] effect of human action, for example, the fruit [*sasya*] harvested by a farmer [*karṣaka*].

CBB. *The defining characteristics of the five effects;*[990] *F 289–93*

[Thus a factor is:

1. the effect of equal outflow (*niṣyandaphala*), because it arises similar (*sadṛśa*) to its cause;
2. the effect of human action (*puruṣakāraphala*), because it arises through the power (*bala*) of its cause;
3. the effect of dominance (*adhipatiphala*), because it arises on the grounds of the non-obstacle (*avighnabhāvāvasthāna*) of its cause.]

What are the (defining) characteristics [*lakṣaṇa*] of the various effects? {20 a}

CBB.1. *Ripened effect (vipākaphala);*[991] *F 289–90*

57ab. The ripened effect is (1) an [unobscured]-non-defined factor, (2) a factor indicative of sentient beings, (3) arising later [i.e., not at the same time, not immediately afterwards] than a [morally] determinate [action—its cause].[992]

1. The ripened effect (*vipāka*) is an unobscured-non-defined (*anivṛtāvyākṛta*) factor (*dharma*). <290>

2. Among the unobscured-non-defined factors, some are indicative of sentient beings (*sattvākhya*), others are non-indicative of sentient beings [*asattvākhya*]. Therefore, the author specifies: indicative of sentient beings, i.e., arising in the life-streams of sentient beings.

3. [Among the factors] indicative of sentient beings, [some] factors are called an *effect of accumulation* (*aupacayika*; coming from food, etc., i. 37), and an *effect of equal outflow* (*naiṣyandika*; originating from a cause which is similar to them, i. 37, ii. 57c). Therefore, the author specifies: "arising later than a [morally] determinate action":

"[Morally] determinate action" [*vyākṛta*] is so called because it produces [or is morally determined with respect to] a ripened effect [*vipākaṃ prati vyākaraṇād*];

[this determinate action] is (i) the unwholesome (*akuśala*) action and (ii) the wholesome-impure (*kuśalasāsrava*) action (ii. 54cd).

From an action of this nature there "arises later" [*uttarakāla*; *udbhava*], i.e., (i) not at the same time (*saha*) and (ii) not immediately afterwards [*antara*], the effect which one terms *ripened effect* or *matured effect* or *effect of retribution* (*vipākaphala*).[993]

[This is the defining characteristic of the ripened effect.]

B.1.1. *Difference between the ripened effect and the effect of dominance; F 290*

[Question:] – Why are the factors which are non-sentient things [*asattvākhya*], i.e., mountains, rivers, etc., not considered to be a ripened effect? Do they not arise from wholesome or unwholesome actions [*karmaja*]?

[Answer:] – Because the factors which are non-sentient things are, by nature, common [*sādhāraṇatva*], for other people are also similarly able to partake of them. But the ripened effect, by definition, is one's own [or unique or non-common] [*asādhāraṇa*], for it is not the case that another person ever experiences the ripened effect of an action which some other person has accomplished. In addition to a ripened effect, the action produces the effect of dominance (*adhipatiphala*).

[Question: – Why does another person experience the effect of dominance?] {20 b}

[Answer:] – Sentient beings partake of this effect in common because it is brought into being by the collective actions [*sādhāraṇakarmasaṃbhūtatva*] (F 288, note). <291>

B.2. *Effect of equal outflow (niṣyandaphala);*[994] *F 290–91*

57c. The effect which is similar to its cause is called *effect of equal outflow*.[995]

The factor (*dharma*) which is similar [*sadṛśa*] to its cause is the effect of equal outflow (*niṣyandaphala*). Two causes, i.e., (1) the homogeneous cause (*sabhāgahetu*; ii. 52) and (2) the pervasive cause (*sarvatragahetu*; ii. 54ab), give forth an effect of equal outflow.

B.2.1. *The difference between the pervasive cause and the homogeneous cause; F 291*

[Question:] – If the effect of the pervasive cause is an effect of equal outflow, i.e., an effect similar (*samāna*) to its cause, why not call the pervasive cause "a homogeneous cause"?

[Answer:] – The effect of a pervasive cause (*sarvatragahetu*) is always similar [*sādṛśya*] to its cause:

1. from the point of view of its stage [*bhūmi*]: the effect of the pervasive cause, like the pervasive cause, belongs to the realm of desire, etc. (ii. 52b);
2. from the point of view of its moral quality: the effect of the pervasive cause, like the pervasive cause, is defiled (*kliṣṭa*).

But it may belong to a different category [*prakāra*] than the category of its cause. By "category" (*nikāya*; *prakāra*) is meant the mode of abandonment: susceptible of being abandoned by insight into the truth of unsatisfactoriness, etc. (ii. 52b). When there is a similarity [*sādṛśya*] between the cause and the effect from this last point of view, then the pervasive cause is, at the same time, a homogeneous cause.

There are four alternatives (tetralemma) [between homogeneous cause (*sabhāgahetu*) and pervasive cause (*sarvatragahetu*)]:

1. A homogeneous cause which is not a pervasive cause: for example, the non-pervasive [*asarvatraga*] defilements (*kleśa*; attachment [*rāga*], etc.) in relation to the defilements of their own category (*nikāya*);
2. A pervasive cause which is not a homogeneous cause: the pervasive defilements in relation to a defilement of another category;
3. A pervasive cause which is at the same time a homogeneous cause: the pervasive defilements in relation to a defilement of their own category;
4. Any other factor (*dharma*) which is neither a homogeneous cause nor a pervasive cause.[996]

CBB.3. *Effect of disconnection (visaṃyogaphala);*[997] *F 291*

57d. Exhaustion [*kṣaya*] [attained] through intelligence (i.e., understanding) [*dhī*] is the effect of disconnection.[998]

Disconnection (*visaṃyoga*) or the effect of disconnection (*visaṃyogaphala*), i.e., "the effect which consists of disconnection", is exhaustion (*kṣaya* = *nirodha*) attained through understanding (*dhī* = *prajñā*). The effect of disconnection is thus the cessation due to deliberation (*pratisaṃkhyānirodha*). (See above ii, F 278). <292>

CBB.4. *Effect of human action (puruṣakāraphala);*[999] *F 292*

58ab. A [conditioned] factor is the effect of human action of the factor by the power of which it arises.[1000]

This [definition] refers to a conditioned factor (*saṃskṛta*).

Examples: 1. The concentration [*samādhi*] of the first meditation (*dhyāna*; *uparibhūmika*) is the effect of human action [*puruṣakāraphala*] of a thought in the sphere (*avacara*) of desire [*adharabhūmika*] which provokes it or prepares it (*tatprayoga-citta*); the concentration of the second meditation is the effect of human action of a thought in the sphere of the first meditation.

2. A pure [*anāsrava*] thought can be the effect of human action of an impure [*sāsrava*] factor (*dharma*), [i.e., the supreme mundane factors (*laukikāgradharma*) have for their effect the receptivity to the cognition of the factors with regard to unsatisfactoriness (*duḥkhe dharmajñānakṣānti*), vi. 25cd]. {21 a}

3. The thought of emanation (*nirmāṇacitta*) is the effect of human action (ii. 56d) of a thought in the sphere of a meditation (vii. 48).

And so on.[1001]

B.4.1. *Unconditioned factors & the effect of human action;* F 292

The cessation due to deliberation (*pratisaṃkhyānirodha*) or *nirvāṇa* is considered as an effect of human action; but the definition given in verse 58ab does not apply to cessation (*nirodha*), which, being eternal [*nitya*], does not arise. Let us say then that it is the effect of human action of the factor by the power [*bāla*] of which one attains the possession of it.[1002]

B.5. *Effect of dominance (adhipatiphala);*[1003] F 292–93

58cd. Any conditioned factor is the effect of dominance of conditioned factors, with the exception of the factors that are later than it.[1004]

B.5.1. *The difference between the effect of dominance and the effect of human action;*[1005] F 292–93

[Question:] – What difference is there between the effect of human action [*puruṣa-kāraphala*] and the effect of dominance [*adhipatiphala*])?[1006] <293>

[Answer:] – The first is connected with the agent (*kartar*); the second is connected with the agent and the non-agent.

For example, in regard to the artist [*śilpin*] who created it [i.e., the agent], the work of art [*śilpa*] is both the effect of human action and the effect of dominance; in regard to that which is *not* the artist [i.e., the non-agent], the work of art is only the effect of dominance.

CBC. *Two stages of causing an effect;*[1007] *F 293–97*

In what state (*avasthā*), i.e., in the state of past, present or future, does each of the causes (*hetu*) occur (1) when it "takes" or "projects" (*gṛhṇāti; ākṣipati*) and (2) when it "gives forth" or "produces" (*prayacchati, dadāti*) its effect?[1008]

[59.] **(1) Five causes take their effect [only when they are] in the present;**

(2) (i) two causes [i.e., the co-existent cause and the associated cause] give forth their effect in the present; (ii) two causes [i.e., the homogeneous cause and the pervasive cause] give forth their effect in the past and present; (iii) one cause [i.e., the ripening cause] gives forth its effect in the past.[1009]

CBC.1. *Definition of taking and giving forth an effect; F 293*

[Question:] – What should be understood by "taking or projecting an effect", "giving forth or producing an effect"?[1010]

[Answer:] – A factor (*dharma*) "takes" [*pratigṛhīta*] an effect when it becomes its seed-state [*bījabhāva*].[1011]

A factor "gives forth" an effect at the moment when it gives to this effect the power of arising, i.e., at the moment when—the future effect being turned toward arising, being ready to arise (*utpādābhimukha*)—this factor gives it the power which causes it to enter into the present state.

CBC.2. *The time periods & taking and giving forth an effect;*[1012] *F 293–97*

CBC.2.1. *The present & taking an effect;*[1013] *F 293–94*

59ab. **[The last] five causes take their effect [only when they are] in the present [state].**[1014]

Five causes take their effect only when they are in the present [state]: (1) when they are in the past [state], they have already taken or projected their effect [*pratigṛhītatva*]; (2) when they are in the future [state], they have no activity [*niṣpuruṣakāratva*] (v. 25).

The same holds for [the first cause, i.e.,] the efficient cause (*kāraṇahetu*); but the verse does not mention it because the efficient cause does not necessarily have an effect (*saphala*).[1015] <294>

CBC.2.2. *The present & giving forth an effect;*[1016] *F 294*

59b. **Two causes [i.e., the co-existent cause and the associated cause] give forth their effect in the present [state].**[1017]

The co-existent cause (*sahabhū*) and the associated cause (*saṃprayuktaka*) give forth their effect only when they are in the present [state]: {21 b} these two causes in fact take and give forth their effect at the same time.

BC.2.3. *The present and the past & giving forth an effect;*[1018] *F 294–97*

59c. Two causes [i.e., the homogeneous cause and the pervasive cause] give forth their effect in the past and present [state].[1019]

The homogeneous cause (*sabhāga*) and the pervasive cause (*sarvatraga*) give forth their effect when they are in the present [state] and when they are in the past [state].

[Question:] – How can they give forth their effect, i.e., the effect of equal outflow (*nisyanda*; ii. 56c), when they are in the present [state]? We have seen (ii. 52b, 54a) that they are earlier than their effect.

[Answer:] – It is said that they give forth their effect in the present [state] because they create it immediately antecedent (*samanantaranirvarttana*). When their effect has arisen, they have passed away (*abhyatīta*): they have already given it forth; they do not give forth the same effect twice.[1020]

BC.2.3.1. *Homogeneous causes not having a cognitive object;*[1021] *F 294–96*

CBC.2.3.1.a. *Wholesome homogeneous cause & taking and giving forth an effect;*[1022] *F 294–95*

It happens that, at a given moment, a wholesome (*kuśala*) homogeneous cause takes an effect and does not give forth an effect. Four alternatives (tetralemma): (1) taking, (2) giving forth, (3) taking and giving forth, (4) neither taking nor giving forth.[1023]

1. The possessions (*prāpti*) of the wholesome roots [*kuśalamūla*] abandoned at the last moment by the persons who cut off the wholesome roots (iv. 80a), take an effect, do not give forth an effect. <295>
2. The possessions of the wholesome roots acquired at the first moment by the persons who take up (*pratisaṃdadhāna*) the wholesome roots again (iv. 80c), give forth their effect, but do not take an effect.[1024]
   One should say:[1025] These same possessions, i.e., the possessions abandoned at the last moment by the persons who cut off the wholesome roots, give forth their effect but do not take their effect at the moment when these persons again take up the wholesome roots.
3. The possessions of the persons whose wholesome roots are not cut off—with the exception of the two preceding cases: (i) that of the persons who complete cutting them off, (ii) that of the persons who take up the wholesome roots again—take [an effect] and give forth [their effect].

4. In any other case, the possessions neither take nor give forth [an effect]: for example, the possessions of the wholesome roots [*kuśalamūla*] of the persons whose wholesome roots have been cut off; the possessions of the wholesome roots of a higher stage [*ūrdhvabhūmi*] by persons who have retrogressed [*parihīṇa*] from this stage: these possessions have already taken their effect, thus do not take it any longer; they do not give it forth, since the persons cannot, at the present time, have possession of these roots.

CBC.2.3.1.b. *Unwholesome homogeneous cause & taking and giving forth an effect;*[1026] *F 295–96*

In regard to the unwholesome (*akuśala*) homogeneous cause (*sabhāgahetu*), the *Vibhāṣā* establishes the same alternatives (tetralemma):

1. [Only taking:] The possessions of unwholesome factors which the persons who attain detachment from desire (*kāmavairāgya*) abandon at the last moment.
2. [Only giving forth:] The possessions which the persons who retrogress from detachment acquire at the first moment.
   One should say:[1027] These same possessions, when the persons retrogress from the detachment.
3. [Taking and giving forth:] The possessions of the persons who are not detached, with the exception of the two preceding cases. <296>
4. The possessions in any other case: for example, the possessions of the persons who are detached and not subject to retrogressing.

CBC.2.3.1.c. *Obscured-non-defined homogeneous cause & taking and giving forth an effect;*[1028] *F 296*

In regard to the obscured-non-defined (*nivṛtāvyākṛta*) homogeneous cause, {22 a} there are four alternatives (tetralemma):

1. The last possessions of obscured-non-defined factors which the noble ones who become perfected beings (*arhat*) abandon.
2. The first possessions which the retrogressed perfected beings acquire.
   To be more exact: the aforementioned possessions among the perfected beings who retrogress.
3. The possessions of the persons who are not detached from *bhavāgra*, with the exception of the two preceding cases.
4. The possessions in any other case: the possessions of the perfected beings.

BC.2.3.1.d. *Unobscured-non-defined homogeneous cause & taking and giving forth an effect;*[1029] F 296

In regard to the unobscured-non-defined (*anivṛtāvyākṛta*) homogeneous cause, when it gives forth its effect, it [also] takes it (because the unobscured-non-defined abides until *nirvāṇa*); but it can take its effect without giving it forth: the last [*carama*] aggregates (*skandha*) of the perfected beings (*arhat*) have no effect of equal outflow (*niṣyanda*).[1030]

BC.2.3.2. *Homogeneous causes having a cognitive object;* F 296–97

BC.2.3.2.a. *Wholesome and unwholesome homogeneous causes & taking and giving forth an effect;* F 296–97

We have up to now considered [the rule (*niyama*) for] the factors (*dharma*) which are not "having a cognitive object" (*sālambana*). If we consider [the rule for] thought and thought-concomitants in their successive moments [*kṣaṇaśas*; *kṣaṇānantara*], we establish the following four alternatives for the wholesome homogeneous cause:

1. [The wholesome thought] takes and does not give forth. When the wholesome thought is immediately followed by an obscured or unobscured-non-defined thought, this wholesome thought, as a homogeneous cause, takes, i.e., projects, an effect of equal outflow, namely, a future wholesome thought which is or is not destined to arise; it does not give forth an effect of equal outflow, since the thought which follows it, whether obscured-non-defined or unobscured-non-defined, is not an effect of equal outflow of a wholesome thought.
2. It gives forth and does not take. When a wholesome thought immediately follows an obscured or unobscured-non-defined thought, an earlier wholesome thought gives forth an effect of equal outflow, namely, the wholesome thought which we are considering; this earlier thought does not take an effect since it has taken it formerly. <297>
3. It takes and gives forth. Two wholesome thoughts follow one another, the first takes and gives forth an effect of uniform outflow, which is the second thought.
4. It neither takes nor gives forth. When obscured or unobscured-non-defined thoughts succeed one another, the earlier wholesome thought, as a homogeneous cause, has formerly taken its effect and later will give forth its effect; for an instant, it neither takes nor gives forth.

The alternatives regarding the unwholesome homogeneous causes could be established in a symmetrical way.

CBC.2.4. *The past & giving forth an effect;*[1031] *F 297*

59d. One cause [i.e., the ripening cause] gives forth its effect in the past [state].[1032]

The ripening cause gives forth its effect when it is in the past [state], for this effect is not simultaneous to [*saha*], nor immediately following [*samanantara*], its cause.

CBD. *The four effects of the Westerners;*[1033] *F 297*

Other masters (*anya*), i.e., the Westerners [Pāścātya] (MVŚ, 630b15), say that there are four effects which are different from the five effects that we have just mentioned:

1. effect of the base (*pratiṣṭhāphala*): {22 b} the circle of water (*jalamaṇḍala*) is the effect of the circle of wind (*vāyumaṇḍala*) (iii. 45) and so forth up to the grass (*tṛṇa*), i.e., the effect of the great earth (*mahāpṛthivī*);
2. effect of the preparatory practice (*prayogaphala*): the cognition of non-arising (*anutpādajñāna*; vi. 50), etc., is an effect of the meditation on the loathsome (*aśubhā*), etc. (vi. 11);
3. effect of a complex or complete assemblage (*sāmagrīphala*): the visual consciousness is the effect of the eye sense-faculty [*cakṣus*], of visible form [*rūpa*], of light [*āloka*] and of mental application [*manaskāra*] (*Madhyamakavṛtti*, 454);
4. effect of cultivation (*bhāvanāphala*): the emanation of thought [*cittasya nirmāṇa*; vii. 48] is the effect of meditation (*dhyāna*).

According to the Sarvāstivādins, the first of these four effects is included in the category of effect of dominance (*adhipatiphala*); the other three are included in the category of the effect of human action (*puruṣakāraphala*).

We have explained causes and effects.

CC. *TOPICS RELATED TO CAUSES AND RESULTS;*[1034] *F 297–99*

CCA. *The four categories of factors & the number of their causes;*[1035] *F 297–98*

We must now examine by how many causes the different factors (*dharma*) are produced.[1036]

From this point of view, the factors fall into four categories:

1. defiled (*kliṣṭa*) factors, i.e., (i) defilements (*kleśa*), (ii) factors associated with defilements (*saṃprayukta*) and (iii) factors having their origination in defilements (*samuttha*) (iv. 8); <298>
2. factors as ripened effect or factors arisen from the ripening cause [*vipākaja*] (ii. 54c);

3. the first pure [*prathamānāsrava*] factors, i.e., the receptivity to the cognition of the factors with regard to unsatisfactoriness (*duḥkhe dharmajñānakṣānti*; i. 38b, vi. 27) and factors coexistent with this receptivity (*kṣānti*);
4. other factors [*śeṣa*], i.e., (i) non-defined (*avyākṛta*) factors, with the exception of the factors as ripened effect, and (ii) wholesome (*kuśala*) factors, with the exception of the first pure factors.

CA.1. *Thought and thought-concomitants & the number of their causes;*[1037] *F 298*

60–61a. **Thought and thought-concomitants, [when they are] (1) defiled, (2) arisen from the ripening cause, (3) others, and (4) pure for the first time, arise from causes which remain when [the following causes] are excluded, in this order: (1) ripening cause, (2) pervasive cause, (3) these two causes [i.e., the ripening and pervasive causes], (4) these two causes [i.e., the ripening and pervasive causes] plus the homogeneous cause.**[1038]

Thought and thought-concomitants,

1. when they are defiled, arise from five causes, with the exclusion of the ripening cause; {23 a}
2. when they are a ripened effect, arise from five causes, with the exclusion of the pervasive cause;
3. when they are different from these [first] two categories and from the fourth, arise from four causes, with the exclusion of the ripening cause and the pervasive cause;
4. when they are pure for the first time, arise from three causes, with the exclusion of the aforementioned two causes [i.e., the ripening cause and the pervasive cause] and the homogeneous cause.

CA.2. *The factors which are not thought and thought-concomitants & the number of their causes;*[1039] *F 298*

61ab. **In regard to the factors which are not thought or thought-concomitants, the associated cause is further excluded.**[1040]

The factors (*dharma*) which are not thought or thought-concomitants, namely, the material factors (*rūpin*) and the formations (*saṃskāra*) dissociated from thought (ii. 35), accordingly as they fall into one of the four categories, arise from causes proper to this category, with the exclusion of the associated cause (*saṃprayuktakahetu*): [these factors,]

1. when they are defiled, arise from four causes, [i.e., with the exclusion of the ripening cause and the associated cause];
2. when they are a ripened effect, arise from four causes, [i.e., with the exclusion of the pervasive cause and the associated cause];
3. when they are different [from the first two categories and from the fourth], arise from three causes, [i.e., with the exclusion of the ripening cause, the pervasive cause and the associated cause];
4. when they are pure for the first time (pure restraint [*anāsravasaṃvara*], iv. 13), arise from two causes, [i.e., with the exclusion of the ripening cause, the pervasive cause, the homogeneous cause and the associated cause].

There is no factor which is the result of one single cause (*ekahetusaṃbhūta*): the efficient cause (*kāraṇahetu*) and the co-existent cause (*sahabhūhetu*) are never absent.[1041] {vii, 1 a}[1042] <299>

We have explained [the number (*vistara*) of] the causes (*hetu*) [of the different factors].[1043]

CD. *THE FOUR CONDITIONS (PRATYAYA)*;[1044] *F 299–331*

A. The nature of each of the four conditions; p. 300
B. Conditions & their "activities/capabilities" with regard to factors of different states; F 308
C. The different factors & the number of their conditions and causes; F 309
D. Specific explanation of the immediate condition: the causal relationships between different thoughts and different thoughts; F 315–331

What are the conditions (*pratyaya*)?

61c. The conditions, are said to be four.[1045]

[1. Causal condition (*hetupratyayatā*; ii. 61d);
2. immediately preceding condition or condition as the equivalent and immediate antecedent (*samanantarapratyayatā*; ii. 62ab);
3. cognitive object condition (*ālambanapratyayatā*; ii. 62c);
4. condition of dominance (*adhipatipratyayatā*; ii. 62d).]

[Question:] – Where is this said?

[Answer:] – In the Sūtra:

> There are four types of condition (*pratyayatās*), namely, (1) *hetupratyayatā*, (2) *samanantarapratyayatā*, (3) *ālambanapratyayatā*, (4) *adhipatipratyayatā*, i.e., that which is a condition (1) in the quality of a cause, (2) in the quality

of the immediately antecedent, (3) in the quality of a cognitive object, (4) in the quality of the dominator. <300>

By *pratyayatā* is meant "type of *pratyaya*" (*pratyayajāti*).[1046]

DA. *The nature of each of the four conditions;*[1047] *F 300*

DA.1. *Causal condition (hetupratyaya);*[1048] *F 300*

DA.1.1. *Definition;*[1049] *F 300*

What is the causal condition (*hetupratyaya*)?

61d. [If one excepts the efficient cause,] the condition which bears the name of "cause" is five causes.[1050]

If one excepts the efficient cause (*kāraṇahetu*), the five remaining causes (*hetu*) constitute the type of condition called *causal condition* (*hetupratyayatā*).

DA.2. *Condition as the equivalent and immediate antecedent (samanantarapratyaya);*[1051] *F 300–6*

DA.2.1. *Definition;*[1052] *F 300*

What is the immediately preceding condition or condition as the equivalent and immediate antecedent (*samanantarapratyaya*)?

62ab. [Only] the thought and thought-concomitants which have arisen, [i.e., past or present]—with the exception of the last [thought and thought-concomitants of the perfected being at the moment of *nirvāṇa*]—are a condition as the equivalent and immediate antecedent.[1053] {1 b}

With the exception of the final thought and the final thought-concomitants (*citta-caitta*) of the perfected being (*arhat*) at the moment of *nirvāṇa*, all thoughts and thought-concomitants which have arisen are a condition as the equivalent and immediate antecedent (*samanantarapratyaya*).

DA.2.2. *Clarification of the definition; F 300–6*

DA.2.2.1. *Clarification of equivalence, range of the condition and range of the effect; F 300–3*

[Question:] – Only thoughts [*citta*] and thought-concomitants [*caitta*] are a condition as the equivalent and immediate antecedent (*samanantarapratyaya*). Of which factors are they the condition as the equivalent and immediate antecedent?

CDA.2.2.1.a. *Clarification of equivalence* F 300–2

This type of condition is called *samanantara* because it produces equivalent (*sama*) and immediate antecedent (*anantara*) factors (*dharma*). The prefix *sam* is understood in the sense of equivalence.

Therefore,[1054] only thoughts and their thought-concomitants are a condition as the equivalent and immediate antecedent, because, with respect to the other factors, as for example the material forms (*rūpa*), there is no equivalence [*viṣamotpatti*] between cause and effect. As a matter of fact, immediately after one material form [*rūpasyānantara*] of the realm of desire, there can arise at the same time either two material forms, i.e., one of the realm of desire, the other of the realm of fine-materiality,[1055] or two material forms, i.e., one of the realm of desire, the other pure [*anāsrava*].[1056] <301> Whereas immediately after one thought [*cittānantara*] of the realm of desire there never arises at the same time one thought of the realm of desire and one thought of the realm of fine-materiality. The present operation (*saṃmukhī-bhāva*) of the material forms is confounded (*ākula*; *vyākula*): but the condition as the equivalent and immediate antecedent does not give forth a confounded effect; thus the material factors are not the condition as the equivalent and immediate antecedent.

Vasumitra says: A second material form (*rūpa*) as an effect of accumulation (*aupacayika*) can arise in the same body without the stream of a material form as an effect of accumulation being stopped [*aniruddha*]; thus material form is not a condition as the equivalent and immediate antecedent.[1057]

The Bhadanta[1058] says: The factor (*dharma*) of material form (*rūpa*) is immediately followed by more [*bahutara*] or by less [*alpatara*]. Thus it is not a condition as the equivalent and immediate antecedent. From more arises less: [for example,] when a great mass of burning straw [*palālarāśi*] becomes ash [*bhasman*]. From less arises more: [for example, when] a small seed [*vaṭanikāyāḥ*] [successively (*krameṇa*)] produces the roots of a fig tree [*nyagrodha*], the trunk, the branches and the leaves. {2 a}

Objection: – (1) When thoughts (*citta*) immediately succeed one another, do they always involve the same number of types [*jāti*] of associated thought-concomitants [*caitta*]? No. It happens that the previous thought involves a larger [*bahutara*] number of types of thought-concomitants, and the following thought, a lesser [*alpatara*] number; and *vice versa*. The thoughts, whether wholesome, unwholesome, or non-defined, succeed one another; and they do not involve the same number of associated thought-concomitants (ii. 28–30); (2) the three concentrations [*samādhi-traya*], which succeed one another, involve or do not involve initial inquiry (*vitarka*) and investigation (*vicāra*) (viii. 7). Thus, for the thought-concomitants, just as for the material factors (*dharma*), there is no equivalence (MVŚ, 52a21). <302>

[Answer:] – That is true [with regard to other types (*jātyantara*)]: there is a succession from less to more, and *vice versa* (second opinion of the *Vibhāṣā*); but only through increase or diminution of the number of types of thought-concomitants (MVŚ, 50c5). In regard to one specific type [*svajāti*], there is never a non-equivalence: more numerous sensations (*vedanā*) never arise after less numerous sensations, or *vice versa*; that is to say: a thought accompanied by one sensation is never followed by a thought associated with two or three sensations. The same holds for ideation (*saṃjñā*) and the other thought-concomitants.

DA.2.2.1.b. *Clarification of the range of the effect;*[1059] *F 302–3*

[Question:] – Is it then only in relation to its own type [*svajāti*] that what is earlier is a condition as the equivalent and immediate antecedent (*samanantarapratyaya*) of what is later? Is sensation then the condition as the equivalent and immediate antecedent of a single sensation?

[Answer:] – No. In general, earlier thought-concomitants are the condition as the equivalent and immediate antecedent of the thought-concomitants that follow, and not only of the thought-concomitants of their type. But, when considering one type, there is no succession from less to more, and *vice versa*: this justifies the expression *samanantara* or *equivalent and immediate antecedent.*

The Ābhidhārmikas who take the name of Sāṃtānasabhāgikas (MVŚ, 50c5): – Contrary to this, we maintain that a factor (*dharma*) of a specific type [*svajāti*] is the condition as the equivalent and immediate antecedent of a factor of this type only: [for example,] from thought arises thought, from sensation arises sensation, etc.

Objection: – In this hypothesis, when a defiled (*kliṣṭa* = unwholesome [*akuśala*] or obscured-non-defined [*nivṛtāvyākṛta*]) factor arises after a non-defiled [*akliṣṭa*] factor, this defiled factor will not proceed from a condition as the equivalent and immediate antecedent.

[Reply:] – It is a previously destroyed [*pūrvaniruddha*] defilement (*kleśa*) which is the condition as the equivalent and immediate antecedent of the defilement that defiles this second factor [i.e., the defiled factor mentioned in the objection]. The previous defilement is considered as immediately preceding the later defilement, even though it is separated (*vyavahita*) by a non-defiled factor, for the separation by a factor of a different nature (*atulyajātīya*) does not constitute separation. In the same way as the emerging-thought (*vyutthānacitta*) of the attainment of cessation (*nirodhasamāpatti*; ii. 43a) {2 b} has the thought-of-entry-into-attainment (*samāpatticitta*), which was previously destroyed, for its condition as the equivalent and immediate antecedent: the attainment (*samāpattidravya*) does not bring about separation. <303>

[Reply:] – We think that the theory of the Sāṃtānasabhāgikas is inadmissible; for in this theory, the pure (*anāsrava*) thought produced for the first time (i. 38b) would not have a condition as the equivalent and immediate antecedent.

CDA.2.2.1.c. *Clarification of the range of the condition;*[1060] *F 303*

The formations (*saṃskāra*) dissociated from thought (*viprayukta*; ii. 35),[1061] just as the material factors, occur confounded (*vyākula*): thus, they are not a condition as the equivalent and immediate antecedent. In fact, after a possession of the realm of desire, possessions relative to the factors (*dharma*) of the three realms of existence and to the pure factors, etc., can occur at the same time [*yugapad*].

CDA.2.2.2. *Clarification of "immediately antecedent" and the time period of the condition;*[1062] *F 303–5*

[Question:] – Why deny that future factors (*dharma*) are a condition as the equivalent and immediate antecedent?

[Answer:] – The future factors are confounded (*vyākula*): there is no anteriority, posteriority among them [*pūrvottarābhāva*] (see ii. F. 261).[1063]

CDA.2.2.2.a. *Omniscience of the Fortunate One & the confoundedness of the future factors; F 303–5*

[Question:[1064]] – How then does the Fortunate One know that such and such a future factor will arise first, such and such a factor will arise later? [For] he knows the order of the arising of all that arises until the end of time.

1. First answer.[1065] His cognition results from an inference drawn from [*sāmprata–anumāna*] (i) the past and (ii) the present:

   i. he sees the past:[1066] "From such and such a type [*evaṃjātīyaka*] of action [*karman*] arises such and such a ripened effect; from such and such a factor (*dharma*) there proceeds such and such a factor";
   ii. he sees the present: "Here is such and such a type of action: from this action will arise in the future such and such a ripened effect; here is such and such a factor: from this factor will proceed such and such a factor."

Nevertheless, the cognition of the Fortunate One is what is called *cognition resulting from a resolve* (*praṇidhijñāna*; vii. 37), and not cognition derived from inference [*ānumānika*]. By means of inference drawn from the past and the present, the Fortunate One directly sees [*pratyakṣam īkṣitvā janāti*] the factors which reside, confounded [*vikīrṇa*], in the future, and he produces this cognition: {3 a} "This person [*pudgala*], having accomplished such and such an action, will certainly receive such and such a future ripened effect."[1067] <304>

[Reply:] – To believe you, if the Fortunate One does not consider the past [*pūrvānta*], then he does not know the future [*aparānta*]. Hence he is not omniscient (*sarvavid*).

2. According to other Masters,[1068] there is a certain factor—in the life-streams of sentient beings—which is the indication (*cihna* = *liṅga*) of the effects that will arise in the future, namely, a certain formation (*saṃskāra*) dissociated from thought. The Fortunate One contemplates it [*vyavalokya*],[1069] and he knows future effects [even] without having cultivated the meditations (*dhyāna*) and the superknowledges (*abhijña*; vii. 42: cognition of death and of rebirth of sentient beings [*cyutyupapādajñāna*]) for it.

(The Sautrāntika:[1070]) – If this is the case, the Fortunate One would be an interpreter of prognostic signs [*naimittika*];[1071] he would not be a "direct seer" (*sākṣātkārin*, *sākṣāddarśin*). <305>

3. Therefore, according to the opinion of the Sautrāntikas,[1072] the Fortunate One knows all things by merely wishing [*icchāmātra*] and by knowing them directly, not by inference, not by divination. This is justified by the word of the Fortunate One (*Ekottara*, 18, 16; comp. *Dīgha*, i. 31):

> The qualities of the Buddhas, the object-field of the Buddhas [*buddhaviṣaya*], are inconceivable [*acintya*].

.2.2.2.b. *Former and later stages & the confoundedness of future factors; F 305*

[Question:] – If the future does not have anteriority and posteriority [*pūrvapaścimatābhāva*], how can one say: "Immediately after [*anantara*] the supreme mundane factors (*laukika agradharma*) only the receptivity to the cognition of the factors with regard to unsatisfactoriness (*duḥkhe dharmajñānakṣānti*) arises and not another factor" (vi. 27), and so forth until: "Immediately after the adamantine concentration (*vajropamasamādhi*) the cognition of exhaustion (*kṣayajñāna*) arises" (vi. 46c)?

The Vaibhāṣikas (MVŚ, 51b1) answer: – If the arising of this factor (*dharma*) is bound to or dependent on [*pratibaddha*] that factor, then this arises immediately after that, {3 b} just as, [for example,] a sprout [*aṅkura*] arises after the seed [*bīja*], without the condition as the equivalent and immediate antecedent intervening.

CDA.2.2.3. *Clarification of "with the exception of the last thought";*[1073] *F 305*

[Question:] – Why are the last (*carama*) thought and the last thought-concomitants of perfected beings (*arhat*) not a condition as the equivalent and immediate antecedent (*samanantarapratyaya*) (MVŚ, 50a22)?

[Answer:] – Because no [other] thought and thought-concomitant arise or continue after them.

[Objection:] – But you have given us to understand (i. 17) that by mental faculty (*manas*) is meant the thought (*citta*; *vijñāna*) which has just perished and serves as the basis of the following thought. [Now,] since no thought follows the last thought of the perfected being, this last thought should not receive either the name of mental faculty (*manas*) or the name of condition as the equivalent and immediate antecedent (*samanantarapratyaya*); and yet you consider it as being a mental faculty.

[Answer:] – The case is not the same:

1. That which constitutes the mental faculty is not the activity (*kāritra*) but the quality of being a basis (*āśraya*) for this thought, i.e., the fact of supporting the subsequent thought; whether this (latter thought) arises or does not arise is of little importance. The last thought of the perfected being (*arhat*) is a "basis": if a subsequent thought [*vijñanāntara*], which would be supported by this basis, does not arise, it is due to the absence [*vaikalya*] of other causes necessary for its arising.

2. On the contrary, that which constitutes the condition as the equivalent and immediate antecedent is the activity. Once this condition (*pratyaya*) has taken or projected [*pratigṛhīta*] an effect, nothing in the world can hinder [*pratibanddhum*] this effect from arising.

Thus, the last thought of the perfected beings is rightly called *mental faculty*, and not *condition as the equivalent and immediate antecedent.*

CDA.2.2.4. *Clarification of "immediately antecedent";*[1074] *F 305–6*

[Question:] – The factor (*dharma*) that is *cittasamanantara*, i.e., which has for its equivalent and immediate antecedent condition (*samanantarapratyaya*) a certain thought, is this factor [also] a *cittanirantara*, i.e., does it immediately follow this thought?[1075] <306>

[Answer:] – There are four alternatives (tetralemma) [between "having a condition as the equivalent and immediate antecedent" and "immediately following a thought"].

1. The thought and thought-concomitants of emerging (*vyutthāna*) from the two attainments [*samāpatti*] which are without thought [*acittakāya*; ii. 41], and all the moments [*kṣaṇa*] of these two attainments with the exception of

the first, have the thought-of-entry-into-attainment for their condition as the equivalent and immediate antecedent, and do not immediately follow this thought. (ii. 64b)

2. The characteristics (*lakṣaṇa*; ii. 45c) (i) of the first moment of these two attainments, (ii) of any thought and of any thought-concomitant of the conscious state (*sacittakāvasthā*), immediately follow a thought, but do not have a condition as the equivalent and immediate antecedent.
3. (i) The first moment of the two attainments as well as (ii) any thought and any thought-concomitant of the conscious state have the thought which they immediately follow for their condition as the equivalent and immediate antecedent.
4. The characteristics (i) of all the moments of the two attainments with the exception of the first, (ii) of the thought and thought-concomitants of emerging from the two attainments, do not have a condition as the equivalent and immediate antecedent, for they are factors dissociated from thought (*viprayukta*; ii. 35), and they do not immediately follow any thought.

[The factor that is *cittasamanantara*, i.e., which has for its equivalent and immediate antecedent condition a certain thought, is this factor also a *samāpattinirantara*, i.e., does it immediately follow the attainment? ...[1076]]

[The equivalent and immediate antecedent condition has been discussed.]

. *Cognitive object condition (ālambanapratyaya);*[1077] *F 306–7*

.1. *Definition;*[1078] *F 306*

What is the cognitive object condition (*ālambanapratyaya*)?[1079]

62c. **All [conditioned as well as unconditioned] factors are the cognitive object (*ālambana*) of consciousness [i.e., the cognitive object condition].**[1080]

All factors (*dharma*), i.e., the conditioned (*saṃskṛta*) as well as the unconditioned (*asaṃskṛta*) factors, are a cognitive object condition of thoughts and thought-concomitants (*cittacaitta*), accordingly as the case applies (*yathāyogaṃ*): for example, visual consciousness (*cakṣurvijñāna*) and the thought-concomitants, i.e., sensation, etc., associated with it, have all visible forms [*rūpa*] for their cognitive object; auditory consciousness, sounds; olfactory consciousness, odors; {4 b} tactile consciousness, tangibles. <307> [On the other hand,] mental consciousness (*manovijñāna*) and the thought-concomitants associated with it have all the factors [*sarvadharma*] for their cognitive object. [With respect to the mental faculty (*manas*), verse 62c is thus understood literally.]

CDA.3.2. *Clarification of the range of the condition;*[1081] *F 307*

When a factor (*dharma*) is the cognitive object [*ālambana*] of a thought, it cannot be that at any moment whatsoever this factor would not be a cognitive object of this thought. That is to say: even if a visible form is not seized as a cognitive object (*ālambyate*) by the visual consciousness, it is a cognitive object, for, whether it is seized or not seized as a cognitive object, its nature remains the same [*tathālakṣaṇatva*], just as fuel (*indhana*), [i.e., a piece of wood (*kāṣṭha*), etc.,] remains [in its nature] a combustible, even when it is not on fire [*anidhyamāna*].

When considering the problem from the point of view of the thought which seizes a factor (*dharma*) as a cognitive object, a threefold determination [*niyama*] is established. Thought is determined:

1. with regard to its sense-sphere (*āyatana*): for example, a visual consciousness bears only on visible form (*rūpa-āyatana*);
2. with regard to the real entity (*dravya*): a certain visual consciousness, i.e., consciousness of blue, of red, etc., bears on the blue, the red, etc. (i. 10);
3. with regard to the moment (*kṣana*): a certain visual consciousness bears on a certain moment of blue.

[Question:] – Is thought determined in the same way with regard to its basis (*āśraya*), that is to say, sense-faculty, i.e., the eye sense-faculty, etc?

Answer: – Yes.[1082] However, when present, thought is joined [*sahita*] with its basis; when past or future, it is separated [*viśliṣṭa*] from it.

According to others, when present and past, thought is joined with its basis.[1083]

[The cognitive object condition has been discussed.]

CDA.4. *Condition of dominance (adhipatipratyaya);*[1084] *F 307–8*

CDA.4.1. *Definition;*[1085] *F 307–8*

What is the condition of dominance (*adhipatipratyaya*)?

62d. **The cause called *kāraṇa* [i.e., efficient cause] is named *dominator* (*adhipa; adhipati*) [i.e., condition of dominance].**[1086]

The condition of dominance (*adhipatipratyayatā*) is none other than the cause called *reason of existence* or *efficient* (*kāraṇahetu*; ii. 50a), for the efficient cause is the condition of dominance (*adhipatipratyaya*). <308>

CDA.4.2. *Clarification of "dominance" (adhipati); F 308*

This name is justified from two points of view. – The condition of dominance, or causality of dominance, is

1. that which belongs to the greatest number of factors (*adhikaḥ pratyayaḥ*), and
2. that which is the condition for the greatest number of factors (*adhikasya vā pratyayaḥ*).

i. All factors (*dharma*) are a cognitive object condition of mental consciousness [and also a condition of dominance]. However, the factors coexisting (*sahabhū*) with a certain thought are not the cognitive object of this thought, whereas they are the efficient cause (*kāraṇahetu*) of it. Thus the factors, without exception, are a condition of dominance as efficient cause, but not as cognitive object condition.

ii. Any factor has all [conditioned] factors, with the exception of itself [*svabhāva-varjya*], for its efficient cause [or any factor is the efficient cause for all conditioned factors, with the exception of itself]. – [Could there be a factor which is not a condition in the sense of all the four conditions? Yes.[1087]] A factor is not any of the conditions of itself. – [There could also be the case that a factor is not any of the conditions of another existent (*parabhavo 'pi syāt*).] A conditioned factor (*saṃskṛta*) is not any condition of an unconditioned factor, and an unconditioned is not any condition of an unconditioned factor [*saṃskṛtamasaṃskṛtasya asaṃskṛtaṃ cāsaṃskṛtasya*].[1088]

CDB. *Conditions & their "activities/capabilities" with regard to factors of different states;*[1089] *F 308–9*

In what state (*avasthā*), i.e., past, present, or future, do the factors (*dharma*) occur with regard to which the diverse conditions exercise their "activity/capability"[1090] [*kāritra*]?

CDB.1. *The causal condition & the time periods of the factors;*[1091] *F 308–9*

Let us first examine the causal condition (*hetupratyaya*), i.e., the five causes, with the exception of the efficient cause (*kāraṇahetu*).

CDB.1.1. *The co-existent cause and the associated cause & the present factor; F 308*

63ab. **Two [of the five] causes [i.e., (1) the co-existent cause, (2) the associated cause] exercise their "activity" with regard to a perishing factor [i.e., a factor of the present].**[1092]

By "perishing" [*nirudhyamāna*], one should understand "present" [*vartamāna*]. The present factor (*dharma*) is called "perishing", "being engaged in perishing", because, having arisen, it is turned (*abhimukha*) toward its cessation [*nirodha*].

The co-existent cause (*sahabhūhetu*; ii. 50b) and the associated cause (*saṃprayuktakahetu*; ii. 53c) bring about their operation (*kāritraṃ karoti*) with regard to the present factor because they bring about their operation with regard to a factor which arises at the same time [*sahotpanna*] as they do.[1093] <309>

CDB.1.2. *The homogeneous cause, the pervasive cause and the ripening cause & the future factor;*[1094] *F 309*

63bc. Three [of the five] causes [i.e., (3) the homogeneous cause, (4) the pervasive cause and (5) ripening cause] [exercise their "activity/capability"] with regard to an arising [i.e., future] factor.[1095]

By arising factor (*dharma*), one should understand a future factor, because the future factor, not having arisen, is turned toward its arising [*utpāda*]. {5 b}

The three causes in question are the homogeneous cause (*sabhāgahetu*; ii. 52a), the pervasive cause (*sarvatragahetu*; ii. 54a), the ripening cause (*vipākahetu*; ii. 54c).

CDB.2. *The condition as the equivalent and immediate antecedent and the cognitive object condition & the time periods of the factors;*[1096] *F 309*

Concerning the other conditions:

63cd. Two other conditions [i.e., (1) the condition as the equivalent and immediate antecedent and (2) the cognitive object condition] [exercise their "activity/capability"] in reverse order, [i.e., respectively, (1) with regard to a future factor, (2) with regard to a present factor].[1097]

1. In the list of the conditions, the condition as the equivalent and immediate antecedent (*samanantarapratyaya*) comes first: it exercises its "activity/capability" as do the three causes, [i.e., the homogeneous cause, the pervasive cause and ripening cause,] namely, with regard to an arising [i.e., future] factor (*dharma*), for the thought and thought-concomitants of a given moment give up their place (*avakāśadāna*) to the thought and thought-concomitants which are arising.

2. The cognitive object condition (*ālambanapratyaya*) follows in the list: it exercises its "activity/capability" as do the two causes, [i.e., the co-existent cause and the associated cause,] namely, with regard to a perishing, [i.e., present,] factor: this perishing factor is thought–and–thought-concomitants, i.e., the subjects of

consciousness (*ālambaka*), which, in perishing, i.e., in the present, seize a present object.

B.3. *The condition of dominance & the time periods of the factors; F 309*

As for the condition of dominance (*adhpatipratyaya*), its "activity/capability" (*kāritra*) consists solely in not making an obstacle (*anāvaraṇabhāvena … avasthāna*): it does not make an obstacle either to the present factor (*dharma*), the past factor or the future factor.

[The conditions with their "activities/capabilities" (*kāritra*) have been discussed.]

C. *The different factors & the number of their conditions and causes;*[1098] *F 309–15*

Because of how many conditions do the different kinds of factors (*dharma*) arise?

C.1. *General presentation;*[1099] *F 309–13*

C.1.1. *Buddhist tradition: the arising of the world from multiple causes and conditions;*[1100] *F 309–10*

C.1.1.1. *Thought and thought-concomitants & the four conditions;*[1101] *F 309–10*

64a. **Thought and thought-concomitants arise because of four conditions:**[1102]

1. The causal condition (*hetupratyaya*) is the five causes;
2. the condition as the equivalent and immediate antecedent (*samanantarapratyaya*) is the earlier thought and thought-concomitants which have arisen not separated [*avyavahita*] by other thoughts, by other thought-concomitants; <310>
3. the cognitive object condition (*ālambanapratyaya*) is the five objects-fields [*viṣaya*] of which visible form (*rūpa*) is the first, or, in the case of mental consciousness, all factors (*dharma*);
4. the condition of dominance (*adhipatipratyaya*) is all factors, except the thought and thought-concomitants themselves [*svabhāvavarjya*] whose arising is under consideration.

DC.1.1.2. *The two attainments & the three conditions;*[1103] *F 310*

64b. **Two attainments [i.e., the attainment of non-ideation and the attainment of cessation] [arise] because of three conditions, [excluding the cognitive object condition].**[1104]

The cognitive object condition (*ālambanapratyaya*) must be excluded, because the attainment of non-ideation [*asaṃjñisamāpatti*; ii. 42] and the attainment of cessation [*nirodhasamāpatti*; ii. 43] do not seize, do not cognize a cognitive object. One has:

1. the causal condition (*hetupratyaya*) is two causes, (i) the co-existent cause (*sahabhūhetu*) (namely, the characteristics, i.e., origination, etc., [ii. 45c] of the attainment) and (ii) the homogeneous cause (*sabhāgahetu*) (namely, the earlier wholesome factors, already arisen, belonging to the [same stage or] stage of meditative attainment [*samānabhūmika*], i.e., to the fourth meditation or to *bhavāgra*, according to the case);
2. the condition as the equivalent and immediate antecedent (*samanantarapratyaya*) is the thought-of-entry-into-attainment [*samāpatticitta*] and the thought-concomitants which are associated with this thought; the thought-of-entry is not separated by any thought during all the moments of attainment;
3. the condition of dominance (*adhipatipratyaya*) is as above, [i.e., it is all factors, except the thought and thought-concomitants whose arising is under consideration].

These two attainments arise from an instigation, from an inflection, of thought (*cittābhisaṃskāraja*; *cittābhogaja*): they thus have a thought as the condition as the equivalent and immediate antecedent. They make an obstacle to the arising of thought (*cittotpattipratibandha*): thus they are not the condition as the equivalent and immediate antecedent (*samanantarapratyaya*) of the emerging-thought [*vyutthānacitta*] of the attainment, although they are immediately preceding it (*nirantara*; see ii, F 306).

CDC.1.1.3. *The other factors & the two conditions;*[1105] *F 310*

64c. **The other factors, [namely, (1) the other formations dissociated from thought and (2) the material factors, arise] because of two conditions [i.e., causal condition and condition of dominance].**[1106]

The other factors (*dharma*), namely, (1) the other formations (*saṃskāra*) dissociated from thought (*cittaviprayukta*) [—besides the two attainments discussed above—] and (2) the material factors (*rūpa*), arise because of the causal condition (*hetupratyaya*) and condition of dominance (*adhipatipratyaya*) (MVŚ, 702b21).

CDC.1.2. *Non-Buddhist tradition: the arising of the world from a single cause (ekaṃ kāraṇam); F 310–13*

All the factors (*dharma*) that arise, arise because of the five causes (*hetu*) and the four conditions (*pratyaya*) which we have just explained. <311> [Further,] the world [*jagat*] [as a whole (*sarvasya*)] does not originate from one single cause which one calls (1) God [Īśvara], (2) Self (Puruṣa), (3) Primal Source (Pradhāna) or any other name [*śabda*].[1107]

[Question:] – How do you establish this thesis?

[Answer:] – If you think that these theses are established through [various] arguments [*hetukṛta*], {6 b} you [will be forced to] give up [*vyudāsa*] your doctrine [*vāda*] that the world as a whole arises from a single cause [*ekaṃ kāraṇam*] [through the following refutation].

64d. **[The world does not arise from a single cause,] not from God [Īśvara, e.g., Mahādeva or Vāsudeva,] or from any other [single] cause, [i.e., the Self (Puruṣa), Primal Source (Pradhāna), etc.,] because there is a succession [*krama*], etc.**[1108]

That things [i.e., the world as a whole] would be produced only from a single cause, by God (Īśvara, e.g., by] Mahādeva or Vāsudeva,[1109] is inadmissible for several reasons.[1110]

CDC.1.2.1. *Refutation of various theist arguments for God being the single cause of the world; F 311–13*

CDC.1.2.1.a. *Theist argument 1: things are produced by a single cause; F 311*

The Theist: – Things [that is to say, the world as a whole] are produced by a single cause.

[Answer:] – If this were so, things would arise all at the same time [*yugapad*]: but everyone sees that they arise successively [*kramasaṃbhava*].

CDC.1.2.1.b. *Theist argument 2: Things arise successively because of the desires of God; F 311–12*

The Theist: – They arise successively because of the [power of the] desires [*chandavaśa*] of God: "May this arise now [*idānīm*]! May this perish now! May this arise and perish later [*paścāt*]!"

[Answer:] – If this were the case, then things do not arise from a single cause, because the desires (of God) are multiple [*chandabheda*; *vistara*].

Besides, these multiple desires would have to be simultaneous [*yugapad*], but since God—the cause of these desires—is not multiple [*abhinnatva*], things would all arise at the same time.

CDC.1.2.1.ba. *Theist argument 3: The desires of god are not simultaneous because there are other causes; F 311–12*

a. The Theist: – The desires of God (Īśvara) are not simultaneous, because God, in order to produce his desires, takes into account other causes [*kāraṇāntara-bhedāpekṣaṇa*].

[Answer:] – If this were so, then God is not the single cause of all things. Also, the other causes which God takes into account arise successively [*krāmītpatti*]: they depend thus on causes which are themselves dependent on other causes. There is thus the fault of infinite regress [*anavasthāprasaṅga*].

The Theist: – Let us allow that the stream of causes has no beginning [*anāditvābhy-upagama*]. {7 a}

[Answer:] – This would allow that cyclic existence (*saṃsāra*) does not have an origin. You then abandon the doctrine of a single cause in order to take sides with the Buddhist (*śākyaputrīya*) theory [*nyāya*] of causes (*hetu*) and conditions (*pratyaya*). <312>

CDC.1.2.1.bb. *Theist argument 4: God's desires are simultaneous but he desires things to arise successively; F 312*

b. The Theist: – The desires of God [*īśvaracchanda*] are simultaneous, but things [i.e., the world (*jagat*)] do not arise simultaneously [*yaugapadya*] because things arise as God desires them to arise, i.e., in succession.

[Answer:] – This is unacceptable. The desires of God remain what they are (*teṣāṃ paścād aviśeṣāt*). Let us explain. Suppose that God [simultaneously] desires: "May this arise now! May that arise later!" We do not see why the second desire, at first non-efficacious, will be efficacious later, and why, if it is efficacious later, it will not be so initially.

CDC.1.2.1.c. *Theist argument 5: The advantage of God; F 312*

[Question:] – What advantage [*artha*] does God [Īśvara] attain from this great effort by which he creates the world [*sargaprayāsa*]?

The Theist: – God creates the world for his own joy (*prīti*).

[Answer:] – He is then not God, the Sovereign (Īśvara), with regard to his own joy, since he is not able to realize it without a means (*upāya*). And if he is not Sovereign with respect to his own joy, how can he be Sovereign with respect to the world [*trailokya*]?

CDC.1.2.1.d. *Counter-argument 1: The creation of the distress of existence; F 312*

Besides, do you say that God finds joy [*prīyate*] in seeing the creatures [*prajā*] which he has created in the prey of all the distress of existence, including the tortures of the hells [*naraka*]? Homage to this kind of God! The profane stanza expresses it well: "One calls him Rudra because he burns [*nirdahati*], because he is sharp [*tīkṣṇa*], fierce [*ugra*], redoubtable [*pratāpavant*], an eater of flesh, blood and marrow [*māṃsa-śoṇitamajjād*]."[1111] {7 b}

CDC.1.2.1.e. *Counter-argument 2: The denial of the visible causes and conditions; F 312*

The followers of God [Īśvara], i.e., as a single cause of the world [*jagat*], deny visible [*pratyakṣa*] causes—causes and conditions—i.e., the efficacy (*puruṣakāra*) of the seed [*bīja*] with regard to the sprout [*aṅkura*], etc.

CDC.1.2.1.f. *Counter-argument 3: Invisibility of the activity of the (divine) cause; F 312*

If, modifying their position, the followers of God allow the existence of these causes and claim that these causes serve God as auxiliaries (*sahakārin*): this is nothing more than a pious affirmation (*bhaktivāda*), because we do not see the activity (*vyāpārādarśana*) of a (Divine) Cause next to the activity of the causes called *secondary*. <313>

CDC.1.2.1.g. *Counter-argument 4: God is not sovereign with regard to other auxiliary causes; F 313*

Besides, God would not be Sovereign with regard to [other] auxiliary causes, since these are engaged in the production of the effect through their own efficacy [*sva-sāmarthya*].

CDC.1.2.1.h. *Counter-argument 5: The creation of the world by God would not have a beginning; F 313*

Perhaps, in order to avoid the denial of causes which are visible [*pratyakṣa-puruṣakāra*], in order to avoid the [pious] affirmation of a present action by God [*īśvara*], an action which is not visible [*vyāpārādarśana*], the Theist would say that the work of God is the [first] creation [of the world] (*ādisarga*): but it would follow that creation, dependent only on God, would never have a beginning, like God himself (*anāditvaprasaṅga*). This is a consequence which the Theist rejects.

CDC.1.2.2. *Refutation of the proponents of the Self, Primal Source, etc., being the single cause of the world;* F 313

We would refute the doctrine of Self (Puruṣa), of Primal Source (Pradhāna), etc., just as we have refuted the theist doctrine, *mutatis mutandis* ("with the necessary changes"; *yathāyogam*). Thus, no factor (*dharma*) arises from a single cause.

Alas, beings are not illumined![1112] Like birds and animals, truly pitiable [*varāka*], they go from birth [*jāti*] to birth, accomplishing diverse actions; they experience the effect of these actions[1113] and falsely [*mithyā*] think [*parikalpayanti*] that God is the cause of this effect. – [1114]We must explain the truth in order to put an end to this false conception. {8 a}

CDC.2. *Specific presentation of the number of ways in which the material factors are causal conditions;*[1115] F 313–15

We have seen (ii. 64c) that the material factors (*dharma*) arise because of two conditions, i.e., causal condition (*hetupratyaya*) and condition of dominance (*adhipatipratyaya*). We must specify and see how (1) the fundamental material elements (*bhūta*; *mahābhūta*) and (2) the factors of secondary or derivative forms (*upādāyarūpa*) or derivative material elements (*bhautika*) are a causal condition, either among themselves or with one another.

CDC.2.1. *Fundamental material elements as cause of fundamental material elements;*[1116] F 313

65a. **The fundamental material elements are the cause of fundamental material elements in two ways [i.e., as homogeneous cause and co-existent cause].**[1117]

The four fundamental material elements (*bhūta*), i.e., the elementary substance earth (*pṛthivīdhātu*), etc., are causes of four fundamental material elements in the quality (1) of homogeneous cause (*sabhāgahetu*) and (2) of co-existent cause (*sahabhūhetu*). <314>

CDC.2.2. *Fundamental material elements as cause of derivative material elements;*[1118] F 314

65b. **[The fundamental material elements are the cause] of derivative material elements [i.e., visible form, taste, etc.] in five ways [i.e., in the quality of (1) generating cause, (2) reliance cause, (3) supporting cause, (4) maintaining cause and (5) growth cause].**[1119]

The four fundamental material elements are causes of derivative material elements (*bhautika*)—color, taste, etc.—in five ways [*prakāra*], "in the quality of (1) generating (*janana*) cause, (2) reliance (*niśraya*) cause, (3) supporting (*pratiṣṭhā*; *sthāna*) cause, (4) maintaining (*upastambha*) cause and (5) growth (*upabṛṃhaṇa*) cause". [It is, however, only the efficient cause (*kāraṇahetu*) which is divided in five ways.][1120]

1. Generating cause (*jananahetu*), because derivative material elements [newly] arise [*utpatti*] from [the fundamental material elements], like a child from its parents.[1121]
2. Reliance cause (*niśrayahetu*), because the derivative material elements, once arisen, come under their influence (*anuvidhā*), like monastics who rely [*niśraya*)] on their teacher (*ācārya*) and their preceptor (*upādhyāya*).
3. Supporting cause (*pratiṣṭhāhetu*), because the derivative material elements are supported (*ādhāra*) by them, like a painting [*citrakṛtya*] is supported by a wall.[1122]
4. Maintaining cause (*upastambhahetu*), because the fundamental material elements are the cause of the non-interruption [*anucchedahetu*] of the derivative material elements.
5. Growth cause (*upabṛṃhaṇahetu*; *vṛddhihetu*), because the fundamental material elements are a cause of the development of the derivative material elements. {8 b}

This means that, with regard to derivative material elements, the fundamental material elements are:

1. cause of birth (*janmahetu*);
2. cause of transformation (*vikārahetu*);
3. supporting cause (*ādhārahetu*);
4. cause of duration (*sthitihetu*);
5. cause of development (*vṛddhihetu*).

C.2.3. *Derivative material elements as cause of derivative material elements; F 314–15*

65c. **Derivative material elements are a cause of derivative material elements in three ways [i.e., in the quality of (1) co-existent cause, (2) homogeneous cause and (3) ripening cause].**

[Derivative material elements (*bhautika*) are a cause of derivative material elements] in the quality of (1) co-existent cause (*sahabhūhetu*), (2) homogeneous cause (*sabhāgahetu*) and (3) ripening cause (*vipākahetu*), not to mention the efficient cause (*kāraṇahetu*), for any factor is an efficient cause of any other factor.[1123]

1. [Co-existent cause:] The actions of body and of speech [*kāyavākkarma*] of the category described in ii. 51a, [i.e., the two restraints of the thought-associates (*cittānuparivartin*),] which are derivative material elements, are a co-existent cause. [Other derivative forms are not co-existent causes (*nānyadupādāyarūpaṃ*)].[1124] <315>

2. [Homogeneous cause:] All derivative material elements which have arisen [previously (*pūrvotpanna*)] are a homogeneous cause with regard to similar or homogeneous (*sabhāga*) derivative material elements.[1125]

3. [Ripening cause:] The actions of body and of speech are a ripening cause: the eye, etc., is produced through the ripened effect of action.[1126]

CDC.2.4. *Derivative material elements as cause of fundamental material elements; F 315*

65d. And derivative material elements are a cause of fundamental material elements in [only] one way, [i.e., as a ripening cause].[1127]

Actions of body and of speech, [being derivative material elements,] give rise to the fundamental material elements (*bhūta*) as a ripened effect: they are thus [only] a ripening cause (*vipākahetu*).

CDD. *Specific explanation of the immediate condition: the causal relationships between different thoughts and different thoughts;*[1128] *F 315–31*

We have seen that antecedent thought and thought-concomitants [*cittacaitta*] are a condition as the equivalent and immediate antecedent (*samanantarapratyaya*) of the subsequent thought and thought-concomitants. But we have not explained how many types of thought can arise immediately after each type of thought.

In order to define the rule [*niyama*], we must first establish the classification of thoughts.

CDD.1. *The twelve categories of thought;*[1129] *F 315–16*

First of all, we distinguish twelve categories [of thought (*citta*)]:

66. (1–4) The wholesome, unwholesome, obscured-non-defined, and unobscured-non-defined thought of the realm of desire. (5–10) The wholesome, obscured-non-defined, and unobscured-non-defined thought

of the realm of fine-materiality and of the realm of immateriality, [i.e., excluding the unwholesome thoughts]. (11–12) The two pure thoughts [of those in training and of those beyond training].[1130]

1–4. Four types of thought belong to the realm of desire: wholesome (*kuśala*), unwholesome (*akuśala*), obscured-non-defined (*nivṛtāvyākṛta*), unobscured-non-defined (*anivṛtāvyākṛta*).

5–10. There are three types of thought, excluding the unwholesome thought, in regard to each of the two higher realms. <316>

[In this way there are ten impure (*sānusrava*) thoughts.]

11–12. There are two pure [*anāsrava*] types of thought, i.e., that of those in training (*śaikṣa*) and that of those beyond training (*aśaikṣa*), i.e., of the perfect beings (*arhat*).

D.2. *The rules regarding combining with the twelve thoughts;*[1131] *F 316–19*

These twelve thoughts do not arise indiscriminately [*abhedena*] one after another.

D.2.1. *Combining with the ten impure thoughts of the three realms;*[1132] *F 316–19*

D.2.1.1. *Combining with the four impure thoughts of the realm of desire;*[1133] *F 316–17*

67a–68b. First, when considering the thoughts of the realm of desire, (1) immediately after the good thought, nine thoughts can arise; [on the other hand,] the good thought can arise immediately after eight thoughts.

(2) The unwholesome thought can arise immediately after ten thoughts; [on the other hand,] four thoughts can arise immediately after the unwholesome thought.

(3) The same for the obscured-non-defined thought.

(4) The unobscured-non-defined thought can arise immediately after five thoughts; [on the other hand,] seven thoughts can arise immediately after the unobscured-non-defined thought.[1134] {9 b}

D.2.1.1.a. *Combining with the wholesome thought of the realm of desire;*[1135] *F 316–17*

a. Immediately after [*anantara*] a wholesome (*kuśala*; *śubha*) thought of the realm of desire, nine [of the twelve] thoughts can arise [*utpadyante*], namely:

1–4. the four thoughts of the realm of desire;

5–6. the two thoughts of the realm of fine-materiality: a wholesome (*kuśala*) thought, when the practitioners enter into meditative attainment [*samāpatti-kāla*], an obscured-non-defined (*nivṛtāvyākṛta*) thought, when the person, dying [*nivṛta*] in the realm of desire with a wholesome thought, passes [*pratisaṃdhikāla*] into the intermediate existence of the realm of fine-materiality (iii. 38c);

7. the one thought of the realm of immateriality, which is [only] an obscured-non-defined (*nivṛtāvyākṛta*) thought, when the person, dying in the realm of desire, is reborn [*pratisaṃdhikāla*] in the realm of immateriality; [this thought of the realm of immateriality is] not a wholesome (*kuśala*) thought, because—the realm of immateriality being very distant [*ativiprakṛṣṭa*] from the realm of desire through the four kinds of distancing [*dūratā*][1136]—one cannot pass directly from the realm of desire into a meditative attainment of the realm of immateriality; <317>

8–9. the two pure thoughts—of those in training (*śaikṣa*) or of those beyond training (*aśaikṣa*)—at the entry into the direct realization of the truths (*satyābhisamaya*) (vi. 27).

b. The wholesome (*kuśala*) thought can arise immediately after [*samanantaram-utpadyate*] eight [of the twelve] thoughts, namely:

1–4. the four thoughts of the realm of desire,

5–6. the two thoughts of the realm of fine-materiality—a wholesome thought and an obscured-non-defined thought—when emerging [*vyutthānakāla*] from meditative attainment. [As for the second,] it may happen, in fact, that the practitioners, troubled (*utpīḍita*) by a defiled (*kliṣṭa*) meditative attainment, emerge from the meditative attainment: after the defiled (*kliṣṭa* = *nivṛta*) thought which is this meditative attainment, they produce a wholesome thought of a lower [*adhara*] stage [*bhūmi*], thus preventing retrogressing by having recourse [*saṃśrayaṇa*] to a wholesome lower thought (viii. 14);

7–8. two pure thoughts—of those in training or of those beyond training—when emerging from the direct realization of the truths.

CDD.2.1.1.b. *Combining with the unwholesome and the obscured-non-defined thoughts of the realm of desire;*[1137] *F 317*

a. The defiled (*kliṣṭa*) thought, i.e., the unwholesome (*akuśala*) and the obscured-non-defined (*nivṛtāvyākṛta*) thought, can arise immediately after ten [of the twelve] thoughts, i.e., excluding the two pure thoughts, because the thought-of-rebirth in the realm of desire (*pratisaṃdhikāla*) is defiled (ii. 14; iii. 38) and can follow any thought belonging to the three realms of existence.

b. Immediately after the defiled (*kliṣṭa*) thought, four [of the twelve] thoughts can arise, i.e., the four thoughts of the realm of desire. {10 a}

DD.2.1.1.c. *Combining with the unobscured-non-defined thought of the realm of desire;*[1138] *F 317*

a. The unobscured-non-defined (*anivṛtāvyākṛta*) thought can arise immediately after five [of the twelve] thoughts, namely: (1–4) the four thoughts of the realm of desire, (5) plus the wholesome (*kuśala*) thought of the realm of fine-materiality: because the thought of emanation (*nirmāṇacitta*) of the realm of desire, [being unobscured-non-defined and] having the miraculous emanation of an object of the realm of desire for its object, can immediately follow a wholesome thought of the realm of fine-materiality.

b. Immediately after the unobscured-non-defined thought, seven [of the twelve] thoughts can arise, namely:

1–4. four thoughts of the realm of desire,

5–6. two thoughts of the realm of fine-materiality, a wholesome thought (*kuśala*), because, immediately after the aforementioned thought of emanation, a wholesome thought of the realm of fine-materiality reappears, and an obscured-non-defined (*nirvṛtāvyākṛta*) thought, when a person, dying with an obscured-non-defined thought, is reborn [*pratisaṃdhikāla*] in the realm of fine-materiality, the first thought of which is necessarily obscured-non-defined (iii. 38);

7. one thought of the realm of immateriality, i.e., an obscured-non-defined thought, when a person, dying with an obscured-non-defined thought, is reborn in the realm of immateriality.]

DD.2.1.2. *Combining with the three impure thoughts of the realm of fine-materiality;*[1139] *F 317–18*

68c–69b. **[Second,] in regard to the thoughts of the realm of fine-materiality, (1) immediately after the good thought, eleven thoughts can arise; [on the other hand,] the good thought can arise immediately after nine thoughts.** <318>

(2) The obscured-non-defined thought can arise immediately after eight thoughts; [on the other hand,] immediately after the obscured-non-defined thought, six thoughts can arise.

(3) The unobscured-non-defined thought can arise immediately after three thoughts; [on the other hand,] immediately after the unobscured-non-defined thought, six thoughts can arise.[1140]

CDD.2.1.2.a. *Combining with the wholesome thought of the realm of fine-materiality;*[1141] *F 318*

a. Immediately after the wholesome (*kuśala*) thought of the realm of fine-materiality, eleven [of the twelve] thoughts can arise, except for the unobscured-non-defined (*anivṛtāvyākṛta*) thought of the realm of immateriality.[1142]

b. The wholesome thought can arise immediately after nine [of the twelve] thoughts, except for (1–2) the two defiled thoughts of the realm of desire (i.e., the unwholesome and the obscured-non-defined thoughts) and (3) the unobscured-non-defined thought of the realm of immateriality.

CDD.2.1.2.b. *Combining with the obscured-non-defined thought of the realm of fine-materiality;*[1143] *F 318*

a. The obscured-non-defined thought can arise immediately after eight [of the twelve] thoughts, except for (1–2) the two defiled thoughts of the realm of desire and (3–4) the two pure thoughts.

b. Immediately after the obscured-non-defined thought, six [of the twelve] thoughts can arise, namely, (1–3) the three thoughts of the realm of fine-materiality, (4–6) the wholesome, the unwholesome and the obscured-non-defined thoughts of the realm of desire.

CDD.2.1.2.c. *Combining with the unobscured-non-defined thought of the realm of fine-materiality;*[1144] *F 318*

a. The unobscured-non-defined (*anivṛtyāvyākṛta*) thought can arise immediately after [three of the twelve thoughts, namely,] the three thoughts of the realm of fine-materiality.

b. Immediately after the unobscured-non-defined (*anivṛtāvyākṛta*) thought, six [of the twelve] thoughts can arise, namely: (1–3) the three thoughts of the realm of fine-materiality (*rūpadhātu*), (4–5) the two defiled thoughts of the realm of desire (*kāmadhātu*) (i.e., the unwholesome [*akuśala*] and obscured-non-defined [*nivṛta-avyākṛta*] thoughts), (6) the defiled thought of the realm of immateriality (*nivṛta-avyākṛta*). {10 b}

DD.2.1.3. *Combining with the three impure thoughts of the realm of immateriality;*[1145] *F 318–19*

69c–70b. **[Third,] in regard to the thoughts of the realm of immateriality, (1) for the unobscured-non-defined thoughts as above, [i.e., the unobscured-non-defined thought can arise immediately after three thoughts; on the other hand, immediately after the unobscured-non-defined thought, six thoughts can arise].**

(2) Immediately after the good thought, nine thoughts can arise; [on the other hand,] the good thought can arise immediately after six thoughts.

(3) Immediately after the obscured-non-defined thought, seven thoughts can arise; [on the other hand,] the obscured-non-defined thought can arise immediately after seven thoughts.[1146]

D.2.1.3.a. *Combining with the unobscured-non-defined thought of the realm of immateriality;*[1147] *F 318*

a. The unobscured-non-defined (*anivṛtāvyākṛta*) thought of the realm of immateriality can arise immediately after [three of the twelve thoughts, namely,] the three thoughts of its own stage (*svabhūmika*).

b. Immediately after the unobscured-non-defined thought of the realm of immateriality, six [of the twelve] thoughts can arise, namely:

1–3. the three thoughts of this stage,
4–6. the two defiled thoughts of the realm of desire (i.e., the unwholesome and obscured-non-defined thoughts) and the one defiled thought of the realm of fine-materiality (i.e., the obscured-non-defined thought). <319>

D.2.1.3.b. *Combining with the wholesome thought of the realm of immateriality;*[1148] *F 319*

a. Immediately after the wholesome (*kuśala*) thought, nine [of the twelve] thoughts can arise, except for (1) the good thought of the realm of desire and (2–3) the unobscured-non-defined thought of the realm of desire and of the realm of fine-materiality.

b. The wholesome thought can arise immediately after six thoughts, namely:

1–3. the three thoughts of the realm of immateriality,
4. the one wholesome thought of the realm of fine-materiality,
5–6. the two pure thoughts.

CDD.2.1.3.c. *The obscured-non-defined thought of the realm of immateriality;*[1149] *F 319*

a. Immediately after the obscured-non-defined (*nivṛtāvyākṛta*) thought, seven [of the twelve] thoughts can arise, namely:

1–3. the three thoughts of the realm of immateriality,
4. the wholesome thought of the realm of fine-materiality,
5–6. the two defiled thoughts of the realm of desire (i.e., the unwholesome and obscured-non-defined thoughts),
7. the defiled thought of the realm of fine-materiality.

b. The obscured-non-defined (*nivṛtāvyākṛta*) thought can arise immediately after seven [of the twelve] thoughts, except for (1–2) the two defiled thoughts of the realm of desire, (3) the defiled thought of the realm of fine-materiality and (4–6) the two pure thoughts.

CDD.2.2. *Combining with the two pure thoughts;*[1150] *F 319*

70c–71a. **(1) The thought of those in training can arise immediately after four thoughts; [on the other hand,] five thoughts can arise immediately after the thought of those in training (*śaikṣa*).**

(2) The thought of those beyond training can arise immediately after five thoughts; [on the other hand,] four thoughts can arise immediately after the thought of those beyond training (*aśaikṣa*).[1151]

CDD.2.2.1. *Combining with the thought of those in training;*[1152] *F 319*

a. The thought of those in training—the thought belonging to the noble ones who are not perfected beings (*arhat*)—can arise immediately after four [of the twelve] thoughts, namely (1) the thought of those in training and (2–4) the wholesome (*kuśala*) thought of each of the three realms.

b. Immediately after the thought of those in training, five [of the twelve] thoughts can arise, namely, (1–4) the four thoughts which have just been named and (5) the thought of those beyond training.

CDD.2.2.2. *Combining with the thought of those beyond training;*[1153] *F 319*

a. The thought of those beyond training can arise after five [of the twelve] thoughts, (1) the thought of those in training, (2) the thought of those beyond training, (3–5) the wholesome thought of each of the three realms.

b. Immediately after the thought of those in training, four [of the twelve] thoughts can arise, (1) the thought of those beyond training and (2–4) the wholesome thought of each of the three realms.

It is according to these rules (*niyama*) that the twelve types of thought can immediately follow one another. {11 a}

ODD.3. *The twenty categories of thought;*[1154] *F 319–21*

71b–72. **The twelve types of thought make twenty thoughts: (1) by dividing the good thought of the three realms into two thoughts: the thought acquired [through preparatory effort]; the innate thought, [i.e., acquired at birth]; (2) by dividing the unobscured-non-defined thought of the realm of desire into four thoughts: the thought arisen from the ripening cause; the thought associated with proper deportment; the thought associated with skill in arts and crafts;**[1155] **<320> and the thought associated with supernormal emanations; (3) by dividing the unobscured-non-defined thought of the realm of fine-materiality into three thoughts, [i.e., the thought arisen from the ripening cause, the thought associated with proper deportment, the thought capable of creating emanations,] by excluding the unobscured-non-defined thought associated with skill in arts and crafts.**[1156]

ODD.3.1. *The divisions of the wholesome thought of the three realms;*[1157] *F 320*

The wholesome (*kuśala*) thought of each of the three realms (*dhātu*) is divided into two categories:

1. acquired through preparatory effort (*yātnika*; *prāyogika*),[1158]
2. acquired at birth or innate (*upapattilābhika*; *upapattipratilambhika*).[1159]

There are thus six types of wholesome thought corresponding to the three types of the first list.

ODD.3.2. *The divisions of the unobscured-non-defined thought of the three realms;*[1160] *F 320*

The unobscured-non-defined (*anivṛtāvyākṛta*) thought of the realm of desire is divided into four categories:

1. arisen from the ripening cause (*vipākaja*; ii. 57);
2. associated with proper deportment (*airyāpathika*): lying down [*śayana*], sitting [*āsana*], standing [*sthiti*], walking [*caṃkramaṇa*];

3. associated with skill in arts and crafts (*śailpasthānika*);[1161]
4. associated with supernormal emanations (*nairmita*; *nairmāṇika*): the thought by which the possessor of supernormal accomplishments creates visible forms [*rūpa*], etc., and which is called the *effect of superknowledge* (*abhijñāphala*; vii. 49) (see ii, F 265).

The unobscured-non-defined (*anivṛtāvyākṛta*) thought of the realm of fine-materiality is divided into three categories, since the thought associated with skill in arts and crafts (*śailpasthānika*) is lacking in this sphere.

There is no reason to divide the unobscured-non-defined thought of the realm of immateriality, since it is exclusively [an unobscured-non-defined thought] "arisen from the ripening cause".

There are thus seven types of unobscured-non-defined (*anivṛtāvyākṛta*) thought corresponding to the two unobscured-non-defined thoughts [of the realm of desire and the realm of fine-materiality] of the first list.

CDD.3.3. *Adding up the twenty categories of thought;*[1162] *F 320*

By taking into account the wholesome (*kuśala*) thoughts, we get a total of twenty (= 6 wholesome + 1 unwholesome + 3 obscured-non-defined + 8 unobscured-non-defined + 2 pure) thoughts. <321>

CDD.3.4. *Thoughts associated with modes of proper deportment, with skill in arts and crafts, with emanations; F 321*

The three unobscured-non-defined (*anivṛtyāvyākṛta*) thoughts, i.e., the thought associated with proper deportment and the following, [i.e., the thought associated with skill in arts and crafts, the thought associated with emanations,] have visible form, odor, taste and tangible for their cognitive object (*ālambana*).[1163] The thought associated with skill in arts and crafts (*śailpasthānika*), furthermore, has [also (*api*)] sound for its cognitive object.[1164]

These three unobscured-non-defined thoughts are just mental consciousnesses (*manovijñānāni*). {11 b} However, the five sensory consciousnesses precede and prepare (*prāyogika*) the thought associated with proper deportment and the thought associated with skill in arts and crafts.[1165]

According to another opinion [*apara*],[1166] there is a mental consciousness produced (*abhinirhṛta*; *utpādita*) by the thought associated with proper deportment,[1167] which has the twelve sense-spheres (*āyatana*)—from the eye sense-faculty (*cakṣurāyatana*) up to the sense-sphere of factors (*dharmāyatana*)—for its cognitive object.

CDD.4. *The rules in regard to combining with the twenty thoughts;*[1168] *F 321–24*

These twenty thoughts arise immediately after [*samanantara*] one another, in conformity with the following rules:

CDD.4.1. *Combining with the eight thoughts of the realm of desire;*[1169] *F 321–22*

Realm of desire: Eight types of thought of the sphere [*avacara*] of desire, namely:

1–2. two wholesome (*kuśala*) thoughts;
3–4. two defiled (*kliṣṭa*; i.e., unwholesome and obscured-non-defined) thoughts;
5–8. four unobscured-non-defined (*anivṛtāvyākṛta*) thoughts.

1. The wholesome thought acquired through preparatory effort (*prāyogika kuśala*):

   • "is immediately followed" [*anantara*] by ten thoughts:

   i–vii. seven thoughts of the same stage [*svabhūmika*], except for the effect of the superknowledge (*abhijñāphala*; i.e., the thought of emanation [*nirmāṇacitta*]);
   viii. thought acquired through preparatory effort (*prāyogika*) of the realm of fine-materiality;
   ix–x. thought of those in training (*śaikṣa*) and thought of those beyond training (*aśaikṣa*).

   (The wholesome thought acquired through preparatory effort:)

   "immediately follows after" [*anantara*] eight thoughts:

   i–iv. four thoughts of the same stage, i.e., two wholesome thoughts and two defiled thoughts;
   v–vi. thought acquired through preparatory effort and obscured-non-defined [*kliṣṭa*[1170]] thought of the realm of fine-materiality;
   vii–viii. thought of those in training and thought of those beyond training. <322>

2. The wholesome thought acquired at birth (*upapattilābhika kuśala*):

   • "is immediately followed" by nine thoughts:

   i–vii. seven thoughts of the same stage, except for the effect of superknowledge;
   viii–ix. the obscured-non-defined [*kliṣṭa*[1171]] thought of the realm of fine-materiality and of the realm of immateriality.

   (The wholesome thought acquired at birth:)

   • "immediately follows after" eleven thoughts:

i–vii. seven thoughts of the same stage, except for the effect of superknowledge;

viii–ix. thought acquired through preparatory effort and obscured-non-defined [*kliṣṭa*[1172]] thought of the realm of fine-materiality;

x–xi. thought of those in training and thought of those beyond training.

3–4. The unwholesome (*akuśala*) thought and the obscured-non-defined (*nivṛta–avyākṛta*) thought:

- "are followed" by seven thoughts, of the same stage, except for the effect of superknowledge.

(The unwholesome thought and the obscured-non-defined thought:)

- "follow" fourteen thoughts:

i–vii. seven thoughts of the same stage, except for the effect of superknowledge;

viii–xi. four thoughts of the realm of fine-materiality, except for the thought acquired through preparatory effort {12 a} and the effect of superknowledge;

xii–xiv. three thoughts of the realm of immateriality, except for the thought acquired through preparatory effort.

5–6. The thought arisen from the ripening cause (*vipākaja*) and the thought associated with proper deportment (*airyāpathika*):

- "are followed" by eight thoughts:

i–vi. six thoughts of the same stage, except for the thought acquired through preparatory effort and the effect of superknowledge;

vii–viii. the obscured-non-defined [*kliṣṭa*[1173]] thought of the realm of fine-materiality and of the realm of immateriality.

(The thought arisen from the ripening cause and the thought associated with proper deportment:)

- "follow" seven thoughts, of the same stage, except for the effect of superknowledge.

7. The thought associated with skill in arts and crafts (*śailpasthānika*):

- "is immediately followed" by six thoughts of the same stage, except for the thought acquired through preparatory effort and the effect of superknowledge.

(The thought associated with skill in arts and crafts:)

- "immediately follows after" seven thoughts, of the same stage, except for the effect of superknowledge.

8. The effect of superknowledge (*abhijñāphala*):

- "is immediately followed" by two thoughts, the effect of superknowledge of the same stage and the thought acquired through preparatory effort of the realm of fine-materiality.

(The effect of superknowledge:)

- "immediately follows after" two thoughts: the same thoughts.

CDD.4.2. *Combining with the six thoughts of the realm of fine-materiality;*[1174]

F 322–23

Realm of fine-materiality: six types of thought of the realm of fine-materiality, namely:

1–2. two wholesome (*kuśala*) thoughts;
3. one defiled (*kliṣṭa*; i.e., obscured-non-defined) thought;
4–6. three unobscured-non-defined (*anivṛtāvyākṛta*) thoughts.

1. The wholesome thought acquired through preparatory effort (*prāyogika kuśala*):

- "is immediately followed" by twelve thoughts:

i–vi. six thoughts of the same stage,
vii–ix. three thoughts of the realm of desire: wholesome thought acquired through preparatory effort; wholesome thought acquired at birth (*upapattilābhika kuśala*); effect of superknowledge (i.e., the thought of emanation);
x. thought acquired through preparatory effort of the realm of immateriality;
xi–xii. thought of those in training and thought of those beyond training.

(The wholesome thought acquired through preparatory effort:)

- "immediately follows after" ten thoughts:

i–iv. four thoughts of the same stage, except for the thought associated with proper deportment and the thought arisen from the ripening cause, {12 b} <323>
vi–vi. two thoughts of the realm of desire: thought acquired through preparatory effort and effect of superknowledge;
vii–viii. two thoughts of the realm of immateriality: thought acquired through preparatory effort and obscured-non-defined thought;
ix–x. thought of those in training and thought of those beyond training.

2. The wholesome thought acquired at birth (*upapattilābhika kuśala*):
   - "is immediately followed" by eight thoughts:

     i–v. five thoughts of the same stage, except for the [unobscured-non-defined] effect of superknowledge [i.e., the thought of emanation];

     vi–vii. two [defiled] thoughts of the realm of desire: unwholesome thought and obscured-non-defined thought;[1175]

     viii. obscured-non-defined thought of the realm of immateriality.

   (The wholesome thought acquired at birth:)

   - "immediately follows after" five thoughts of the same stage, except for the effect of superknowledge.

3. The obscured-non-defined (*nivṛtāvyākṛta*) thought:
   - "is immediately followed" by nine thoughts:

     i–v. five thoughts of the same stage, except for the effect of superknowledge;

     vi–ix. four thoughts of the realm of desire: two wholesome thoughts; two defiled thoughts.

   (The obscured-non-defined (*nivṛtāvyākṛta*) thought:)

   - "immediately follows after" eleven thoughts:

     i–v. five thoughts of the same stage, except for the effect of superknowledge;

     vi–viii. three thoughts of the realm of desire: thought acquired at birth; thought associated with proper deportment; thought arisen from the ripening cause;

     ix–xi. three thoughts of the realm of immateriality, except for the thought acquired through preparatory effort.

4–5. The thought arisen from the ripening cause (*vipākaja*) and the thought associated with proper deportment (*airyāpathika*):

   - "are followed" by seven thoughts:

     i–iv. four thoughts of the same stage, except for the thought acquired through preparatory effort and the effect of superknowledge;

     v–vi. two [defiled] thoughts of the realm of desire: unwholesome thought and obscured-non-defined thought;

     vii. one thought of the realm of immateriality, i.e., the obscured-non-defined thought.

(The thought arisen from the ripening cause and the thought associated with proper deportment:)

- "follow" five thoughts, of the same stage, except for the effect of superknowledge.

6. The effect of superknowledge (*abhijñāphala*; i.e., the thought of emanation [*nirmāṇacitta*]):

- "is immediately followed" by two thoughts, of the same stage, i.e., thought acquired through preparatory effort and effect of superknowledge.

(The effect of superknowledge:)

- "immediately follows after" two thoughts: {13 a} the same thoughts.

)D.4.3. *Combining with the four thoughts of the realm of immateriality;*[1176]

F 323–24

Realm of immateriality: four types of thought of the realm of immateriality, namely:

1–2. two wholesome thoughts;
3. obscured-non-defined thought;
4. thought arisen from the ripening cause.

1. The wholesome thought acquired through preparatory effort (*prāyogika kuśala*):

- "is immediately followed" by seven thoughts:

i–iv. four thoughts of the same stage;
v. thought acquired through preparatory effort of the realm of fine-materiality,
vi–vii. thought of those in training and thought of those beyond training.

(The wholesome thought acquired through preparatory effort:)

- "immediately follows after" six thoughts:

i–iii. three thoughts of the same stage, except for the thought arisen from the ripening cause;
iv. thought acquired through preparatory effort of the realm of fine-materiality,
v–vi. thought of those in training and thought of those beyond training.

ii. The wholesome thought acquired at birth (*upapattilābhika kuśala*):

- "is immediately followed" by seven thoughts:

i–iv. four thoughts of the same stage;
v. obscured-non-defined thought of the realm of fine-materiality;

vi–vii. unwholesome thought and obscured-non-defined thought of the realm of desire. <324>

(The wholesome thought acquired at birth:)

- "immediately follows after" four thoughts, of the same stage.

iii. The obscured-non-defined (*nivṛtāvyākṛta*) thought:

- "is immediately followed" by eight thoughts:

  i–iv. four thoughts of the same stage;
  v–vi. thought acquired through preparatory effort and obscured-non-defined thought of the realm of fine-materiality;
  vii–viii. unwholesome thought and obscured-non-defined of the realm of desire.

(The obscured-non-defined thought:)

- "immediately follows after" ten thoughts:

  i–iv. four thoughts of the same stage;
  v–x. thought acquired at birth, thought associated with proper deportments, thought arisen from the ripening cause of the realm of fine-materiality and of the realm of desire.

iv. The thought arisen from the ripening cause (*vipākaja*):

- "is immediately followed" by six thoughts:

  i–iii. three thoughts of the same stage, except for the thought acquired through preparatory effort;
  iv. obscured-non-defined thought of the realm of fine-materiality;
  v–vi. unwholesome thought and obscured-non-defined thought of the realm of desire. {13 b}

(The thought arisen from the ripening cause:)

- "immediately follows after" four thoughts of the same stage.

CDD.4.4. *Combining with the two pure thoughts;*[1177] *F 324*

Two pure (*anāsrava*) thoughts:

1. The thought of those in training (*śaikṣa*):

- "is immediately followed" by six thoughts:

  i–iii. thought acquired through preparatory effort of the three realms;
  iv. thought acquired at birth of the realm of desire;
  v–vi. thought of those in training and thought of those beyond training.

(The thought of those in training:)

- "immediately follows after": four thoughts:

  i–iii. thought acquired through preparatory effort of the three realms;
  iv. thought of those in training.

2. The thought of those beyond training (*aśaikṣa*):

- "is immediately followed" by five thoughts, i.e., six thoughts which follow the thought of those in training, except for the thought of "those in training".

(The thought of those beyond training:)

- "immediately follows after" five thoughts:

  i–iii. thought acquired through preparatory effort of the three realms,
  iv–v. thought of those in training and thought of those beyond training.

DD.5. *Comments about the thought acquired through preparatory effort and the innate thought;*[1178] *F 324–25*

Remarks:

DD.5.1. *Thought acquired through preparatory effort & other minds;*[1179] *F 324–25*

(1) Thought arisen through the ripening cause (*vipākaja*), (2) thought associated with proper deportment (*airyāpathika*) and (3) thought associated with skill in arts and crafts (*śailpasthānika*) arise immediately after a thought acquired through preparatory effort (*prāyogika*) of the realm of desire. For what reason is the reciprocal not true?

1. Thought arisen from the ripening cause is not favorable (*anukūla*) to a thought acquired through preparatory effort, because it is weak (*durbala*), because it develops spontaneously (*anabhisaṃskāravāhitvāt = ayatnena pravṛtteḥ*).

2–3. Thought associated with proper deportment and thought associated with skill in arts and crafts are not favorable to a thought acquired through preparatory effort, because their reason for being lies in the creation of a proper deportment or of a created thing (*īryāpathaśilpābhisaṃskaraṇapravṛttatvāt*). <325>

On the contrary, the thought of leaving (*niṣkramaṇacitta*)—that is to say, any thought, i.e., the thought arisen from the ripening cause, etc., through which the *yogins* leave the stream [*pravāha*] of the thoughts acquired through preparatory effort (*prāyogika*), such as reading, philosophical reflection, etc.—develops spontaneously (*anabhisaṃskāravāhin = anābhogavāhin*). The thought of leaving can thus immediately follow after the thought acquired through preparatory effort.

Objection. – If the thought acquired through preparatory effort does not arise immediately after the thought acquired through preparatory effort, etc., because they are not favorable to it, still less will it arise after the defiled (*kliṣṭa*) thought which is contrary (*viguṇa*) to it.

[Answer:] – The defiled (*kliṣṭa*) thought is contrary to the thought acquired through preparatory effort. However, when the practitioners get tired (*parikhinna*) of the activity (*samudācāra*) of the defilements (*kleśa*), by the very fact that the practitioners seize complete cognition (*parijñāna*) of this activity, the thought acquired through preparatory effort arises. {14 a}

CDD.5.2. *Innate thought & other thoughts;*[1180] *F 325*

The innate wholesome (*kuśala*) thought of the realm of desire is sharp (*paṭu*); it can thus arise immediately after the two pure (*anāsrava*) thoughts and also immediately after the thought acquired through preparatory effort of the realm of fine-materiality; but, as it develops spontaneously, it is not immediately followed by these same thoughts.

The innate wholesome thought of the realm of desire, being sharp, can arise immediately after the defiled (*kliṣṭa*) thought of the realm of fine-materiality; but the innate wholesome thought of the realm of fine-materiality, not being sharp, cannot arise immediately after the defiled (*kliṣṭa*) thought of the realm of immateriality.

CDD.6. *Mental application as cause of the arising of thought;*[1181] *F 325–28*

Thoughts arise immediately one after another, and they arise because of mental application (*manaskāra*; *manasikaraṇa*). We must, therefore, study mental application.

CDD.6.1. *Three types of mental application;*[1182] *F 325–28*

One can distinguish three mental applications:

1. Mental application bearing on the particular inherent characteristics (*svalakṣaṇamanaskāra*), for example, the judgments: "Material form (*rūpa*) has breaking/deterioration or obstruction (*rūpaṇa*) as its characteristic, ... consciousness (*vijñāna*) has impression or perception relative (*prativijñapti*) [to each external object-field] as its characteristic" (i. 13, 16).
2. Mental application bearing on the common characteristics (*sāmānyalakṣaṇamanaskāra*); it bears on the sixteen aspects or modes of activities [*ākāra*] of the truths, i.e., impermanent [*anitya*], etc: "The conditioned factors (*dharma*) are impermanent" (vii. 10). <326>

3. Mental application (proceeding from) resolution (*adhimuktimanaskāra*). This mental application does not bear—as the first two mental applications do—upon that which exists (*bhūtārthe*); it proceeds from resolution (*adhimukti*), i.e., from visualization (*adhimuktyā ... manaskārah*; see F 154); it governs the contemplations of the meditation on the loathsome (*aśubhā*; vi. 9),[1183] of the immeasurables (*apramāṇa*; viii. 29), of the liberations [of Ārūpya] (*vimokṣa, ārūpyavimokṣā*; viii. 32), of the perception-spheres of mastery (*abhibhvāyatana*; viii. 34), of the perception-spheres of totality (*kṛtsnāyatana*; viii. 35), etc.

DD.6.1.1. *Mental application & the noble path; F 326–28*

1. (According to the first masters quoted by the MVŚ, 53a19,) the noble path can be realized (*saṃmukhībhāva*) immediately after [any one of] these three mental applications, and, inversely, these three mental applications can be produced immediately after the noble path. This opinion is supported by the text (as translated according to these masters):

> They produce the member of enlightenment [*saṃbhodhyaṅga*] called *mindfulness* [*smṛti*] accompanied with (i.e., immediately after) [*sahāgata*] the meditation on the loathsome (*aśubhā*).[1184]

2. (According to the third masters quoted by the *Vibhāṣā*,) it is only immediately after the mental application bearing on the common characteristics (*sāmānyalakṣaṇa-manaskārānantarameva*) {14 b} that the noble path can be realized; immediately after the noble path, the three mental applications can be produced. – As for the text alleged by the first masters, it should be understood in the sense that, after having subdued thought by means of meditation on the loathsome, the practitioners are capable of producing the mental application bearing on the common characteristics, immediately after which they realize the noble path. The text is directed at this mediate action [*pāramparyamabhisaṃdhā*] related to the meditation on the loathsome and says:

> They produce the member of enlightenment called *mindfulness* accompanied with (i.e., after, although not immediately after) the meditation on the loathsome.

3. (According to the fourth masters quoted by the *Vibhāṣā*,) it is [also] only immediately after the mental application bearing on the common characteristics that the practitioners can realize the noble path; yet, immediately after the noble path, they can also only produce the mental application bearing on the common characteristics.

CDD.6.1.1.a. *The number of mental applications which can follow the noble path; F 326–28*

The author refutes the third masters:

Certainly, it can be seen that the practitioners—who have entered into the assurance of the eventual attainment of the absolute good (*samyaktvaniyāma*), into the noble path (see vi, F 180ff.), by relying on one of the three lower stages (*bhūmi*) (i.e., either preparatory meditation [*anāgamya*] or first meditation [*dhyāna*] or intermediate meditation [*dhyānāntara*])—could produce, upon leaving the noble path, a mental application bearing on the common characteristics (*sāmānyalakṣaṇamanaskāra*) of the sphere of Kāma, derived from listening and from reflection (*śrutamaya*; *cintāmaya*), because the stages in question are near; but, when the practitioners have entered into the assurance of the eventual attainment of the absolute good by relying on the second, the third or the fourth meditation, to what stage could the mental application bearing on the common characteristics belong that the practitioners would produce upon leaving the noble path? <327>

1. They would not produce the mental application bearing on the common characteristics of the realm of Kāma, because Kāma is too distanced [*ativiprakṛṣṭa*] from the higher meditations.

2. They would no longer produce the mental application bearing on the common characteristics of the stage of the three higher meditations, because they have not previously acquired this mental application (*manaskāra*), except [*anyatra*] in the course of the practice of the stages conducive to penetration (*nirvedhabhāgīya*; vi. 17: the preliminary contemplations to the entry into the noble path): but noble ones (*ārya*) cannot newly realize the stages conducive to penetration, for one cannot assume that, already possessing the fruit [*prāptaphala*], they newly realize the preparatory path [of the noble path (*tatprayoga*)].

[Reply:] – But other types [*jāti*] of mental applications bearing on the common characteristics (*sāmānyamanaskāra*) {15 a} exist that have been cultivated at the same time as the stages conducive to penetration, which are by nature stages conducive to penetration (as they bear on the truths [*saty'ālambanatva*] but differ by not bearing on the sixteen aspects): for example, seeing that: "all conditioning forces [*sarvasaṃskāra*] are impermanent [*anitya*]", "all factors [*sarvadharma*] are impersonal [*anātman*]", "*nirvāṇa* is peaceful [*śānta*]", (i.e., a generic [*sāmānya*] judgment, since it bears on all *nirvāṇa*). – It is this other type of mental application bearing on the common characteristics (*sāmānyamanaskāra*) that the practitioners manifest upon leaving the noble path.

[Answer:] – The Vaibhāṣikas do not accept this opinion, because it is illogical. [Indeed, the cultivation of the mental applications of this type is connected with the stages conducive to penetration]. (MVŚ, 53b3).

D.6.1.1.aa. *The correct doctrine; F 327–28*

(The correct doctrine is that the noble path can be followed by three categories of mental application:)

1. When one acquires the fruit [or status] of the perfected being (*arhattva*) by relying on the preparatory meditation (*anāgamya*) (MVŚ, 53b25), the thought emerging [*vyutthāna*] from the contemplation is either of this stage (i.e., preparatory meditation) or of the sphere of Kāma.

2. When one acquires the same fruit [or status] by relying on the perception-sphere of nothingness (*ākiñcanya*), the emerging-thought is either of this same stage (i.e., perception-sphere of nothingness) or of the perception-sphere of neither ideation nor of non-ideation (*naivasaṃjñānāsaṃjñāyatana*) or *bhavāgra*.

3. When one acquires the same fruit [or status] by relying on any other stage (*śeṣa*), the emerging-thought is of this other stage only [*svabhūmikameva*]. <328>

D.6.2. *The four types of mental application; F 328*

There are four types of mental application:

1. innate or natural mental application (*upapattipratilambhika*);
2. mental application derived from [listening to] the teaching (*śrutamaya*);
3. mental application derived from reflection (*cintāmaya*);
4. mental application derived from cultivation (*bhāvanāmaya*).

D.6.2.1. *The eight mental applications of the three realms; F 328*

1. [Only] three mental applications are possible in the realm of desire, i.e., the first, the second and the third, because the mental application derived from cultivation is not of the realm of desire.

2. [Only] three mental applications are possible in the realm of fine-materiality, i.e., the first, the second and the fourth, because, [the mental application derived from reflection is not of the realm of fine-materiality,] since, in this sphere, as soon as one begins cultivation or reflection (*cintā*), one enters into concentration [*samādhi*].

3. [Only] two mental applications are possible in the realm of immateriality, i.e., the first and the fourth.

There are, then, eight mental applications, i.e., three, three and two (MVŚ, 53b14).

CDD.6.2.2. *Innate mental application & the noble path; F 328*

The noble path is never produced immediately after innate or natural mental application (*upapattipratilambhika*), whatever sphere it may belong to, for the noble path requires preparatory effort (*prayogapratibaddha*). {15 b} The noble path is thus produced immediately after five mental applications: two of the realm of desire, two of the realm of fine-materiality, and one of the realm of immateriality. – But, [on the other hand,] immediately after [*anantara*] the (noble) path, the innate or natural mental application of the realm of desire can manifest [*saṃmukhībhāva*], because it is sharp (*paṭu*).

CDD.7. *Acquisition & the twelve thoughts;*[1185] *F 328–31*

How many thoughts are acquired (*lābha*; *pratilambha*) when each of the twelve types of thought (ii. 67) is manifested (*saṃmukhībhāva*)?

CDD.7.1. *Defiled thought of the three realms & acquisition of the twelve thoughts;*[1186] *F 328–29*

73ab. With the defiled thought of each of the three realms, there is, respectively, the acquisition (1) of six thoughts, (2) of six thoughts, (3) of two thoughts, [of the twelve types of thought].[1187]

CDD.7.1.1. *Definition of acquisition; F 328*

Acquisition [*lābha*] means taking possession by those who, previously, did not possess (ii. 36a).

CDD.7.1.2. *Defiled thought of realm of desire & acquisition of six of the twelve thoughts; F 328–29*

Acquisition of six [of the twelve] thoughts with the defiled thought of the realm of desire:

1. One acquires the wholesome (*kuśala*) thought of the realm of desire (a) when one takes up again the wholesome roots [*kuśalamūlapratisaṃdhāna*] by way of doubt [*vicikitsayā*],[1188] which is defiled (iv. 80c); (b) when one returns to the realm of desire by retrogressing from the higher realms (*dhātupratyāgamana*). Thought at conception [*pratisaṃdhicitta*] is necessarily defiled [*avaśyakliṣṭa*; iii. 38]; with this thought one takes possession of the wholesome thought of the realm of desire, for one did not possess it before.[1189] <329>

2–3. One acquires the unwholesome (*akuśala*) thought and obscured-non-defined (*nivṛtāvyākṛta*) thought of the realm of desire (i) when one returns to the realm of desire by retrogressing from the higher realms: for one then takes possession of whichever of these two thoughts manifests; (ii) when one retrogresses from the detachment [*vairāgya*] of the realm of desire.

4. One acquires the obscured-non-defined thought of the realm of fine-materiality when one retrogresses from the realm of immateriality into the realm of desire. With the defiled thought at conception in the realm of desire, one, in fact, takes possession of the obscured-non-defined thought of the realm of fine-materiality.

5–6. One acquires the obscured-non-defined thought of the realm of immateriality and of the thought of those in training (*śaikṣa*) when one retrogresses from the status of a perfected being [*arhattva*] by a thought of the realm of desire.

D.7.1.3. *Defiled thought of the realm of fine-materiality & acquisition of six of the twelve thoughts;* F 329

Acquisition of six [of the twelve] thoughts with the defiled thought of the realm of fine-materiality: {16 a}

One acquires (1) the unobscured-non-defined (*anivṛtāvyākṛta*) thought of the realm of desire (thought of emanation [*nirmāṇacitta*]) and (2–4) the three thoughts of the realm of fine-materiality, when one retrogresses from the realm of immateriality into the realm of fine-materiality.

One acquires (5) the obscured-non-defined (*nivṛtāvyākṛta*) thought of the realm of immateriality and (6) the thought of those in training (*śaikṣa*), when one retrogresses from the status of a perfected being [*arhattva*] by a thought of the realm of fine-materiality.

D.7.1.4. *Defiled thought of the realm of immateriality & acquisition of two of the twelve thoughts;* F 329

[Acquisition of two of the twelve thoughts] with the defiled thought of the realm of immateriality:

One acquires (1) the obscured-non-defined (*nivṛtāvyākṛta*) thought of the realm of immateriality and (2) the thought of those in training (*śaikṣa*), when one retrogresses from the status of a perfected being (*arhat*) by a thought of the realm of immateriality.

D.7.2. *Wholesome thought of the realm of fine-materiality & acquisition of three of the twelve thoughts;*[1190] F 329

73bc. **With the good thought of the realm of fine-materiality, one acquires three thoughts.**[1191]

With the wholesome (*kuśala*) thought of the realm of fine-materiality, one acquires three [of the twelve] thoughts: (1) this [wholesome] thought itself; (2–3) the unobscured-non-defined (*anivṛtāvyākṛta*) thought of the realm of desire and of the realm of fine-materiality, i.e., the thought of emanation relative to the two spheres. <330>

CDD.7.3. *The thought of those in training & acquisition of four of the twelve thoughts;*[1192] *F 330*

73cd. With the thought of those in training, one acquires four thoughts.[1193]

When one realizes the first thought of those in training (*śaikṣa*), namely, the receptivity to the cognition of the factors with regard to unsatisfactoriness (*duḥkhe dharmajñānakṣānti*; vi. 25d), one acquires four [of the twelve] thoughts:

1. the thought of those in training itself;

2–3. two unobscured-non-defined thoughts, of the realm of desire and of the realm of fine-materiality (i.e., the thoughts of emanation);

4. the wholesome thought of the realm of immateriality,

there is, by virtue of the noble path, entry into the noble path (*niyāmāvakrānti*; vi. 26a) and detachment (*vairāgya*) from the realm of desire and from the realm of immateriality.

CDD.7.4. *The other thoughts & acquisition of the twelve thoughts;*[1194] *F 330*

73d. With the other thoughts, one acquires these very thoughts.[1195]

As for the thoughts not specified above, [i.e., (1–2) the wholesome thought of the realm of desire and of the realm of immateriality, (3) the thought of those beyond training, (4–6) the unobscured thought of the three realms,] when they manifest, one acquires them by themselves.

CDD.7.5. *General statement about the three types of thought & other thoughts; F 330–31*

According to another opinion [*anya*],[1196] one can, without making a distinction [*abhedena*] between the spheres, say: {16 b}

> The wise ones [*budha*] say that one acquires nine [of the twelve] thoughts with the defiled (*kliṣṭa*) thought; one acquires six [of the twelve] thoughts with the wholesome (*kuśala*) thought; one acquires the non-defined (*avyākṛta*) thought with the non-defined thought.[1197]

D.7.5.1. *Wholesome thought & other thoughts; F 330*

Concerning the wholesome (*kuśala*) thought, one should correct this passage and read: "one acquires seven thoughts": (1) When persons take up again the wholesome roots by way of right view (*samyagdṛṣṭi*; iv. 80), they acquire the wholesome thought of the realm of desire; (2–3) when they detach themselves from the realm of desire, they acquire the thought of emanation of the realm of desire and the realm of fine-materiality, which are two unobscured-non-defined (*anivṛtāvyākṛta*) thoughts; (4–5) when they seize the concentrations [*samādhi*] of the realm of fine-materiality and the realm of immateriality, they acquire the wholesome thoughts of these two spheres; (6) by entry into the noble path [*niyāmāvakrānti*], they acquire the thought of those in training (*śaikṣa*); (7) by entry into the fruit [or status] of a perfected being [*arhattva*], they acquire the thought of those beyond training (*aśaikṣa*). <331>

D.7.5.2. *Defiled thought and the non-defined thought & other thoughts; F 331*

For the two other thoughts [*śeṣa*], [i.e., the defiled thought and the non-defined thought,] the assessment of the thoughts acquired is established according to the explanations which we have given.

D.7.6. *A stanza on acquisition of thoughts; F 331*

Here is an aide-mémoire stanza [*saṃgrahaśloka*]:

> In relation to conception, meditative attainment, detachment, retrogressing and the taking up again of the wholesome roots, one acquires thoughts which one did not possess.[1198]

* * *

This concludes the
Second Chapter (*Kośasthāna*)
called
EXPOSITION OF FACULTIES (*Indriyanirdeśa*)
in the
Abhidharmakośa-Bhāṣya.

Endnotes to Chapter Two

[1] *Lodrö Sangpo* (*LS*): As for a brief discussion of chapter 2, see Dhammajoti's *Summary*. For the structure of the first two chapters, *Dhātunirdeśa* and *Indriyanirdeśa*, see our endnote to i. 4a.

As for chapter 2, it is divided into three main sections:

1. Entitled *Indriyanirdeśa*, chapter 2 picks up the topic with which chapter 1 ends and gives a detailed discussion (= section A) of the twenty-two controlling faculties, which is clearly an insert based on the additional chapters of the AH and SAH, as can be seen from the references in the next endnote. It being an insert at the very beginning of chapter 2, could also have been the reason why Vasubandhu changed the title of the second chapter of AH, i.e., *saṃskāra* (but see here also Pu Guang's view as discussed in Dhammajoti's *Summary*, p. 7 and 15). For an overview of the main topics treated in section A, see the outline inserted into the translation.

2. Having dealt with the twenty-two controlling faculties, Vasubandhu then presents a new classification (= section B), namely, the five-group (*pañca-vastu*) classification of factors. This is introduced in the context of a discussion on the "genesis or origin" of the factors, how conditioned factors come into existence, which constitutes the beginning of the second chapter in the AH and SAH.

3. Vasubandhu's chapter 2 ends with another classification (= section C), namely, the very detailed classification of factors according to causes (*hetu*), effects (*phala*) and conditions (*pratyaya*).

[2] *LS*: AH 118, 203–6, 208–9, 237; SAH 275, 432–41, 453, 472.

[3] *LS*: SAH 433.

[4] *LS*: 1. Collett Cox summarizes Saṃghabhadra stating (Ny, 377b; EIP.VIII.676) that the twenty-two *indriyas* are "controlling faculties because they are dominant or have supreme self-mastery with regard to a certain state. Though all factors have their own dominant activity, these twenty-two are exceptionally powerful, and therefore are listed separately."

2. See also the endnotes on the controlling faculties at i. 48cd.

[5] *La Vallée Poussin* (*LVP*): *Below ad* ii. 2a, *ādhipatya* = *adhikaprabhutva*, dominant or controlling power. – Compare the explanation of the *indriyas* in *Atthasālinī*, 304, etc.

[6] *LS*: AH 203–4; SAH 433–34.

[7] *LS*: According to Dharmatrāta, it is because these five and four controlling faculties are the basis for transmigration (*saṃsāra*) that they are established as a controlling faculty. Cf. SAH.568f.

[8] *Gokhale*: [1] *caturṣv artheṣu pañcānām ādhipatyaṃ dvayoḥ kila* | *caturṇāṃ pañcaka–aṣṭānāṃ saṃkleśavyavadānayoḥ* ||

Tib.: [1] *lnga po rnam ni don bzhi la* | *dbang byed bzhi rnams gnyis la lo* | *lnga dang brgyad po de rnams ni* | *kun nas nyon mongs rnam byang la* ||

LVP: The *kārikā* ii. 1, in the *Samayapradīpikā*, omits the word *kila* by which Vasubandhu indicates that he does not share the doctrine of the School. The *kārikās* ii. 2–4, where Vasubandhu presents the doctrine of the Sautrāntikas, are omitted in the *Samayapradīpikā.*

[9] *LS*: AH 203; SAH 433.

[10] *LS*: AKB i. 19: "It is for beauty's sake that they are twofold. ... With a single [physical seat (*adhiṣṭhāna*)] of the eye or ear, or with a single nostril [*nāsikāvila*], one would be very ugly [*vairūpya*]."

[11] *LS*: Hsüan-tsang, iii, fol. 1b.

Pradhan.38.7 has *parikarṣaṇa* for LVP's reconstructed *parirakṣaṇa.*

[12] *LS*: AH 203; SAH 433.

[13] *LS*: Ibid.

[14] *LS*: Ibid.

[15] *LS*: Ibid.

[16] *LVP*: *Vibhāṣā*, 142, at the end; Buddhaghosa explains in the *Atthasālinī* (641) that the games of boys are not the games of girls, etc.

Atthasālinī, 321: "Feminine features are not the female controlling faculty; they are produced in course of process because of that faculty."

[17] *LVP*: According to the *Vyākhyā* [WOG.94.13], the Ancient Masters (*pūrvācārya*).

[18] *LS*: AH 203; SAH 433.

[19] *LS*: MVŚ, 731b23ff, gives two explanations (see DD.126) of which Vasubandhu cites the second.

[20] *LS*: Collett Cox comments (DD.130) that "the Sarvāstivāda-Vaibhāṣikas..., in particular the early Sarvāstivādins and early Sarvāstivāda-Vaibhāṣikas, use the term *nikāyasabhāga* with both the general meaning, 'homogeneous collection of components', and the more technical meaning as the dissociated factor, 'homogeneous character'. Indeed, in the Sarvāstivāda-Vaibhāṣikas' treatment of vitality, it is not clear which meaning, if either exclusively, is intended for *nikāyasabhāga.*" She further comments (DD. 109) that in the context of Vasubandhu's own definition of the vitality faculty (ii, F 216; see also ii. 3), Yaśomitra glosses the term *nikāyasabhāga* as "conditioned forces of a certain nature having the aggregate of form, and so on, as their intrinsic nature" [WOG.168.30f: ...ta eva tathābhautās saṃskārā rūpādiskandhasvabhāvā iti] and that Saṃghabhadra replaces Vasubandhu's non-technical use of *nikāyasabhāga* with "the six sense organs together with their basis".

[21] *LS*: AH 203; SAH 433.

[22] *LVP*: The mental faculty exercises controlling power with regard to defilement and purification, *Vibhāṣā*, 142, pp. 731, 732 (Bhadanta Kuśavarman); *Siddhi*, 214.

[23] *LVP*: *cittena nīyate lokaś cittena parikṛṣyate* |
ekadharmasya cittasya sarva dharmā vaśānugāḥ || [WOG.95.22f.]

Saṃyutta, i. 39.

Asaṅga (*Sūtrālaṃkāra*, xviii. 83, p. 151 ed. Lévi) shows the controlling power of thought over the condititioning forces *(saṃskāra): cittenāyaṃ loko nīyāte cittena parikṛṣyate cittasyotpannasya vaśe vartate.* (*Aṅguttara*, ii. 177).

24 *LS*: AH 204; SAH 434

25 *LVP*: Hsüan-tsang: "for all the pure factors (*dharma*) arise and develop following them".

26 *LVP*: "The thought of those who experience agreeable sensation is concentrated." Extract from the *Sūtra on the Gates of Entries into Liberation* (*vimuktyāyatana*), cited in *Vyākhyā*, p. 56 ad i. 27; *Mahāvyutpatti*, 81.

27 *LVP*: "Faith arises from unsatisfactoriness", *Saṃyutta*, ii. 31. – On the meaning of the word *upaniṣad*, "cause", see below ii. 49 (note on *hetu* and *pratyaya*), *Aṅguttara*, iv. 351 = *Suttanipāta* (*Dvayatānupassanāsutta*) (...*kā upanisā savanāya*), *Sūtrālaṃkāra*, xi. 9 (*yogopaniṣad* = having effort for its cause).

In the sense of "comparison", "approach", Pāṇini, i. 4. 79, *Vajracchedikā*, 35, 10, 42, 7 and Hoernle, *Manuscript remains*, i. p. 192 (*upaniśāṃ na kṣamate*), *Sukhāvatīvyūha*, 31, 9, *Mahāvyutpatti*, 223, 15 (or the Tibetan has *rgyu*).

In the sense of *upāṃśu*, "secret", Yaśomitra (ad ii. 49) indicates *Dīgha*, ii. 259 (*sūryopaniṣado devāḥ* = *suriyassūpanissā devā*): upaniṣacchabdas tu kadācid upāṃśau kadācit prāmukhye tadyathā sūryopanisado devā ity upāṃśuprayoga upaniṣatprayoga iti [WOG.188.17ff.]. (E. Leumann, *ZDMG*, 62, p. 101 assumes *upaniśrā* = *upanissā* = Grundlage, Nähe, or the adjective *upanissa*).

See Minaev, Zapiski, ii. 3, 277; Wogihara, *ZDMG*, 58, 454 (*dānopaniṣadā śīlopaniṣadā ... prajñayā*) and Asaṅga's *Bodhisattvabhūmi*, p. 21; S. Lévi, *Sūtrālaṃkāra*, ad xi. 9.

28 *LVP*: The Sūtra says: cakṣurvijñeyāni rūpāṇi pratītyotpadyate saumanasyaṃ naiṣkramyāśritaṃ | ...manaḥ pratītya dharmāṃś ca utpadyate saumanasyaṃ | ...daurmanasyaṃ ... upekṣā [WOG.96.7ff.]

naiṣkramya = "pure or impure path", or else, "leaving (*niṣkramaṇa*) or detachment from a sphere of existence (*dhātu*) or from *saṃsāra*". – See *also* iv. 77bc.
āśrita = "having for its object", or else, "favorable to".

We have thus: "There are, because of the visible forms, etc., six sensations of satisfaction, six sensations of dissatisfaction, six sensations of equanimity, favorable to *naiṣkramya*."

Compare *Majjhima*, iii. 218; *Saṃyutta* iv. 232; *Majjhima*, iii. 217; *Milinda*, 45 (*nekkhammasita*).

29 *LVP*: Vaṣubandhu says: "Other Masters (*apare*)...".

30 *LS*: AH 204; SAH 433–34.

31 *LS*: SAH 433.

32 *LS*: Dhammajoti comments (ADCP.55; SA.IV.262) that in this section Vasubandhu differentiates the Vaibhāṣika view, according to which the eye is an *indriya* because it exercises dominance in the seeing of visual forms, from the Sautrāntika view, according to which the dominance is with regard to the apperception of its specific object (*svārtha-upalabdhi*). See i. 42.

33 *Gokhale*: [2ab] *svārthopalabdhyādhipatyāt sarvasya ca ṣaḍindriyam* |

Tib.: [2ab] *rang gi don dang thams cad la* | *dmigs par dbang byed phyir dbang drug* |

34 *LS*: SAH 433.

35 *Gokhale*: [2cd] *strītvapuṃstvādhipatyāt tu kāyāt strīpuruṣendriye* ||

Tib.: [2cd] *mo nyid pho nyid la dbang phyir | lus las mo dang pho dbang dag |*

36 *LVP*: Compare *Dhammasaṅgaṇi*, 633, and *Atthasālinī*, 641.

37 *LS*: AH 204; SAH 434.

38 *Gokhale*: [3] *nikāyasthitisaṃkleśavyavadānādhipatyataḥ | jīvitaṃ vedanāḥ pañca śraddhādyāś c endriyaṃ matāḥ ||*

Tib.: *rigs gnas kun nas nyon mongs dang | rnam par byang la dbang byed phyir | srog dang tshor ba rnams dang ni | dad sogs dbang po lngar 'dod do ||*

39 *LS*: Dhammajoti comments (SA.IV.303): "The MVŚ explains that the dominance of the vital faculty consists in (1) enabling one to assert that a being is in possession of the faculties (*sa-indriya*), (2) sustaining the faculties.*"

* MVŚ, 731. Another view gives four aspects of its dominance: (i) in connecting up with the *nikāya-sabhāga*, (ii) in sustaining the *nikāya-sabhāga*, (iii) in fostering the *nikāya-sabhāga*, (iv) in enabling the *nikāya-sabhāga* to continue uninterrupted.

40 *LVP*: The Japanese editor refers to *Madhyamāgama*, 17, 11. – Compare *Saṃyutta*, iv, 208: *yo sukhāya vedanāya rāgānusayo so anuseti.*

41 *LVP*: sukhāyāṃ vedanāyāṃ rāgo 'nuśete | duḥkhāyāṃ dveṣaḥ | aduḥkha–asukhāyāṃ mohaḥ [WOG.95.26f.]. – By sensation of pleasure (*sukhā*), one has also to understand sensation of satisfaction (*saumanasya*)… . See ii. 7.

Compare v. 23 and 54; also *Yogasūtra*, ii. 7–8: *sukhānuśayī rāgaḥ | duḥkhānuśayī dveṣaḥ.*

42 *LS*: LVP mentions the Sautrāntikas here, but they are not explicitly mentioned in Pradhan.

43 *LVP*: In the mundane (*laukika*) path, faith and the other (praxis-oriented) faculties obstruct the defilements; in the stages conducive to penetration (*nirvedhabhāgīya*; vi. 45c), they "lead to" the (noble) path; pure, they constitute the faculty of coming to know what is as yet unknown (*anājñātamājñāsyāmi*), etc. (ii. 9b; vi. 68).

44 *Gokhale*: [4] *ājñāsyāmyākhyam ājñākhyam ājñātāvīndriyaṃ tathā | uttarottarasamprāpti-nirvāṇādyādhipatyataḥ ||*

Tib.: [4] *mya ngan 'das sogs gong nas gong | 'thob pa la ni dbang byed phyir | kun shes byed dang kun shes dang | de bzhin kun shes ldan dbang po ||*

LVP: Paramārtha and Hsüan-tsang translate the first line: "Because of their controlling power in regard to the acquisition of higher and higher paths, of *Nirvāṇa*, etc." – The Tibetan *mya ngan 'das sogs gong nas gong thob pa la ni dbang byed phyir = nirvāṇādyuttarottarapratilambhe 'dhipatyataḥ.*

Dhammasaṅgaṇi, 296, 505, 553; *Nettipakaraṇa*, 15, 60; *Compendium*, p. 177.

45 *LS*: This is the first of Kritzer's forty-four passages discussed in relation to chapter 2 (VY.36). He states that for Vasubandhu the term *tathā* means that the three mentioned controlling faculties, like the preceding nineteen, are separate controlling faculties whereas for Saṃghabhadra *tathā* should mean (Ny, 378b22-c3.): "like *strīndriya* and *puruṣendriya*, which do not exist separately from *kāyendriya*".

46 *LVP*: The faculty of final and perfect knowledge (*ājñātāvīndriya*) is mingled with the quality of a perfected being (*arhat*); it involves the cognition of exhaustion (*kṣayajñāna*) and the cognition of non-arising (*anutpādajñāna*): cognition that the defilements are destroyed and

will no longer re-arise, etc. (vi. 45; *Nettipakaraṇa*, p. 15); the perfected beings are liberated (*vimukta*) by liberation from the defilements (*kleśavimukti*) and by liberation from continued existence (*saṃtānavimukti*): they thus exercise controlling power in relation to the *parinirvāṇa* or "*nirvāṇa* without remainder" (*nirupadhiśeṣanirvāṇa*).

47 *LS*: This is the second of Kritzer's forty-four passages discussed in relation to chapter 2 (VY.38). Saṃghabhadra (Ny, 378c3–5) attributes this explanation to Vasubandhu, criticizes it (Ny, 378c5–10), "saying that it would result in many problems regarding the order of accomplishments on the Path."

48 *LVP*: Objection of the Sāṃkhyas. – *Sāṃkhyakārikā*, 34.

49 *LS*: Wangchuk Dorje and Gedun Drup attribute this opinion to the Vaibhāṣikas.

Cox summarizes Saṃghabhadra (Ny, 379a; EIP.VIII.677): "Certain other factors that have certain areas of control ... are not controlling faculties because only those factors that support, differentiate, afflict, prepare to purify, and purify perceptual consciousness are referred to as controlling faculties."

50 *Gokhale*: [5] *cittāśrayas tadvikalpaḥ sthitiḥ saṃkleśa eva ca | sambhāro vyavadānaṃ ca yāvatā tāvad indriyam ||*

Tib.: [5] *sems kyi rten dang de'i bye brag | gnas dang kun nas nyon mongs nyid | tshogs dang rnam byang ji snyed pa | dbang po dag kyang de snyed du ||*

LVP: This verse (*kārikā*) becomes verse 2 in the *Samayapradīpikā*.

51 *LVP*: We have encountered this expression, i. 35 (see also next footnote). – The six supports of the sense-faculties (*indriyādhiṣṭhāna*), that is to say, the "visible" eye, etc., and the six consciousnesses (*ṣaḍ vijñānakāyāḥ*) are also real entities of sentient beings (*sattvadravya*), but not primary (*maula*) real entities, for they depend on the controlling power of the six sense-faculties.

52 *LS*: Wangchuk Dorje and Gedun Drup attribute this opinion to the Sautrāntikas.

53 *Gokhale*: [6] *pravṛtter āśrayotpattisthitipratyupabhogataḥ | caturdaśa tathā 'nyāni nivṛtter indriyāṇi vā |*

Tib.: [6] *yang na 'jug pa'i rten dang ni | skye dang gnas dang nyer spyod las | bcu bzhi de bzhin ldog pa la | dbang po rnams ni gzhan yin no ||*

54 *LVP*: ṣaḍāyatanaṃ mūlasattvadravyabhūtaṃ saṃsaratīti *pravṛtter āśrayaḥ* [WOG.98.21f.]. – The six sense-spheres (*ṣaḍāyatana*) are essentially the sentient being who is said to transmigrate: it is thus the basis of cyclic existence.

55 *LVP*: Only two sense-spheres (*āyatana*), i.e., those of the body (*kāya*) and of the mental faculty (*manas*), exist from conception (ii. 14).

56 *LVP*: The newborn child sees, but does not speak. Speech is action (*karman*) of the tongue, which is the support (*adhiṣṭhāna*) of the tongue sense-faculty (*jihvendriya*) [cf. WOG.98.31ff.]. – For the Sāṃkhyas, the faculties of action (*karmendriya*) are, like the sense-faculties of consciousness, suprasensible substances (*atīndriya*). "Voice" is the power to speak; the "hand" is the power to grasp, etc.

57 *LVP*: You assert that snakes possess subtle (*sūkṣma*) hands and feet, yet you must prove that.

[58] *LVP*: The sexual parts (*upastha*) are conceived as distinct from the male or female sexual faculty, which is one portion, one place, of the body sense-faculty (*kāyendriyaikadeśastrī-puruṣendriyavyatiriktakalpita*).

Bliss (*ānanda*) is defiled happiness (*kliṣṭa saukhya*).

[59] *LS*: AH 118; SAH 275.

[60] *Gokhale*: [7ab1] *duḥkhendriyam asātā yā kāyikī vedanā*

Tib.: [7ab1] *lus tshor sim pa ma yin gang | sdug bsngal dbang po'i*

LVP: Compare the definitions of the *Vibhaṅga*, p. 123.

[61] *LVP*: The bodies are the eye sense-faculty and the other four sense-faculties of the sensory consciousnesses: these sense-faculties, in fact, are collections (*kāya*) or accumulations (*saṃcaya*) of atoms. The sensation that occurs in a "body", or that accompanies a "body" on which it rests, is called *bodily*. (See ii. 25, on the bodily pliancy [*praśrabdhi*].)

[62] *Gokhale*: [7b2–c1] *sukham | sātā*

Tib.: [7b2–c1] *sim pa ni | bde ba'o*

[63] *Gokhale*: [7c2–d] *dhyāne tṛtīye tu caitasī sā sukhendriyam ||*

Tib.: [7c2–d] *bsam gtan gsum pa na | sems kyi de ni bde dbang po ||*

[64] *Gokhale*: [8a] *anyatra sā saumanasyam*

Tib.: [8a] *gzhan na de yid bde ba yin |*

[65] *LVP*: Pleasure (*sukha*) is *sāta*, the agreeable, that which does good (*sātatvād hi sukham ucyate*); satisfaction, moreover, supposes joy (*prīti*). – This problem is taken up again viii. 9b.

[66] *Gokhale*: [8bc1] *asātā caitasī punaḥ | daurmanasyam*

Tib.: [8bc1] *sems kyi sim pa ma yin pa | yid mi bde ba'o*

[67] *Gokhale*: [8c2–d] *upekṣā tu madhy obhayy avikalpanāt ||*

Tib.: [8c2–d] *btang snyoms ni | bar ma'o gnyis ka'i mi rtog phyir ||*

[68] *LVP*: An exception should be made of agreeable mental sensation, which proceeds from concentration (*samādhi*) or which is a ripened effect (*vipākaphala*) (ii. 57).

[69] *LVP*: It is solely a ripened effect (*vipākaphala*) and of outflow (*naiṣyandikī*) (ii. 57c).

[70] *LS*: AH 118; SAH 275.

[71] *Gokhale*: [9ab1] *dṛgbhāvanā'śaikṣapathe nava trīṇy*

Tib.: [9ab1] *mthong bsgom mi slob lam la dgu | gsum yin*

[72] *LVP*: In fact, the group (*kalāpa*) that constitutes the three pure controlling faculties includes only seven controlling faculties, for the three sensations never coexist. When, in order to cultivate the (noble) path, practitioners abide in the first two meditations (*dhyāna*), they possess the single sensation of satisfaction (*saumanasyendriya*); they possess the single sensation of pleasure (*sukhendriya*) when they cultivate the (noble) path in the third meditation; and they possess the single sensation of equanimity (*upekṣendriya*) when they cultivate the (noble) path in the other stages (preparatory meditation [*anāgamya*], intermediate meditation (*dhyānāntara*), fourth meditation, first three formless meditative attainments [*ārūpya*]). – See ii. 16c–17b.

[73] *LVP*: The path of insight (*darśanamārga*) includes the first fifteen moments of the direct realization of the truths (*abhisamaya*), moments in the course of which one sees that which one has not previously seen (vi. 28cd). – It is exclusively pure (*anāsrava*), vi. 1.

[74] *LVP*: *aluksamāsaḥ | ākhyātapratirūpakaś cāyam ājñāsyāmītiśabdaḥ* – In the Abhidhamma, one has *anaññātaññassāmītīndriya* (*Vibhaṅga*, p. 124).

[75] *LVP*: The term *bhāvanā* has many meanings. – In the expression *bhāvanāmaya* (derived from cultivation), it is synonymous with concentration (*samādhi*). – Other exceptions are studied in vii. 27 (compare ii. 25, 2). – In the expression *bhāvanāmārga* (path of cultivation), *bhāvanā* signifies "repeated insight, cultivation".

There are two paths of cultivation (*bhāvanāmārga*):

1. Pure (*anāsrava*) or supramundane (*lokottara*) path of cultivation, which is under consideration here: this is cultivation of the truths that have already been seen in the path of insight (*darśanamārga*). This path begins with the sixteenth moment of the direct realization of the truths (vi. 28cd) and comes to an end with the acquisition of the status of a perfected being (*arhat*).

2. Impure (*sāsrava*) or mundane (*laukika*) path of cultivation; it does not have the truths for its object (vi. 49); it obstructs (*viṣkambh*) the defilements without uprooting them; it can precede and follow the path of insight.

[76] *LVP*: *Dhātupāṭha*, i. 631.

[77] *LVP*: It seems, however, that Paramārtha differs from Hsüan-tsang.

[78] *LS*: AH 205–6, 209, SAH 435–36, 439, 453.

[79] *Gokhale*: [9b2–d] *amalaṃ trayam | rūpīṇi jīvitaṃ duḥkhe sāsravāṇi dvidhā nava ||*

Tib.: [9b2–d] *gsum ni dri ma med | gzugs can srog dang sdug bsngal dag | zag dang bcas pa dgu rnam gnyis ||*

[80] *LVP*: On this topic, the Japanese editor quotes the work of Harivarman (*Nanjio* 1274).

[81] *LVP*: The Mahīśāsaka, according to the Japanese editor. The Hetuvādin and the Mahiṃsāsaka in the *Kathāvatthu*, xix. 8. – Compare ibid. iii. 6.

[82] *LVP*: *Saṃyutta*, v. 204: *yassa kho bhikkhave imāni pañcindriyāṇi sabbena sabbaṃ sabbathā sabbaṃ natthi taṃ ahaṃ bāhiro puthujjanapakkhe ṭhito ti vadāmi*. – See ii. 40bc.

[83] *LVP*: pañcemāni bhikṣava indriyāṇi | katamāni pañca | śraddhendriyaṃ yāvat prajñā-indriyaṃ | eṣāṃ pañcānām indriyāṇāṃ tīkṣṇatvāt paripūrṇatvād arhan bhavati | tatas tanutarair mṛdutarair anāgāmī bhavati | tatas tanutarair mṛdutaraiḥ sakṛdāgāmī | tatas tanutarair mṛdutaraiḥ srotaāpannaḥ | tato 'pi tanutarair mṛdutarair dharmānusārī | tatas tanutarair mṛdutaraiḥ śraddhānusārī | iti hi bhikṣava indriyapāramitāṃ pratītya phalapāramitā prajñāyate | phalapāramitāṃ pratītya pudgalapāramitā prajñayate | yasyemāni pañcendriyāṇi sarveṇa sarvāṇi na santi tam ahaṃ bāhyaṃ pṛthagjanapakṣāvasthitaṃ vadāmi [WOG.103.1ff.].

This text is cited in *Vijñānakāya*, 535b29ff., with some developments.

Compare *Saṃyutta*, v, 200.

[84] *LVP*: Compare *Sumaṅgalavilāsinī*, p. 59, on the two types of ordinary worldling (*pṛthagjana*), (1) the *andha* and (2) the *kalyāṇa*.

85 *LVP*: brahmā 'vocat | *santi* bhadanta *sattvā loke* [*jātā loke*] *vṛddhās tīkṣṇendriyā api madhyendriyā api mṛdvindriyā api* [WOG.104.4f.]. – Compare *Dīgha*, ii. 38; *Majjhima*, i, 169; *Mahāvastu*, iii, 314; *Lalita*, 395; *Divya*, 492; *Atthasālinī*, 35. – The *Kathāvatthu* cites *Dīgha*, ii. 38 (*...tikkhindriye mudindriye...*).

86 *LVP*: *Saṃyuktāgama*, 26, 4. – Compare *Saṃyutta*, v. 193 and foll. – MVŚ, 8a14.

87 *LS*: AH 206; SAH 436, 453.

88 *LS*: SAH 453.

89 *LVP*: Compare *Vibhāṅga*, p. 125; MVŚ, 741b19.

90 *Gokhale*: [10a1] *vipāko jīvitaṃ*

Tib.: [10a1] *srog ni rnam smin*

LVP: On life and death, see ii. 45.

91 *LS*: SAH 453.

92 *LS*: For a discussion of the prolongation of the life-force, see Yuichi Kajiyama's article: *Transfer and Transformation of Merits in Relation to Emptiness*, in SBP, pp. 1–20.

93 *LVP*: yad arhan bhikṣur āyuḥsaṃskārān sthāpayati taj jīvitendriyaṃ kasya vipākaḥ [WOG.105.1f.].

94 *LVP*: *tat praṇidhāya*. Commentary: *tad āyuḥ praṇidhāya cetasikṛtvā*. – MVŚ, 656b17–c3.

95 *LVP*: *yad dhi bhogavipākaṃ karma tad āyurvipākadāyi bhavatu*.

96 *LVP*: Compare the theory of the divine eye, vii, F 123.

97 *LS*: LVP mentions the Sautrāntikas here, but they are not explicitly mentioned in Pradhan.

This is the third of Kritzer's forty-four passages discussed in relation to chapter 2 (VY.42f.). Saṃghabhadra criticizes (Ny, 380c23–381a4; EIP.VIII.678) Vasubandhu's explanation.

98 *LVP*: *Vyākhyā* {WOG.105.4]: The Buddha for the benefit of others, the listener (*śrāvaka*) for the duration of the Dharma. – See Lévi and Chavannes, "Les seize Arhats protecteurs de la Loi", *J. As.*, 1916, ii. 9 and following.

99 *LVP*: *rogādyabhibhūta*; one should understand sickness (*roga*), abscess (*gaṇḍa*), thorn (*śalya*), corresponding to the threefold unsatisfactoriness, vi. 3, [i.e., unsatisfactoriness that is suffering, unsatisfactoriness that is transformation or change, unsatisfactoriness that is the fact of being conditioned].

100 *LVP*: *brahmacaryaṃ sucaritaṃ mārgaś cāpi subhāvitaḥ* |
āyuḥkṣaye tuṣṭo bhoti rogasyāpagame yathā ||

In *Milinda*, 44, the perfected being, although suffering in his body, does not enter *nirvāṇa*: *nābhinandāmi jīvitam*... .

101 *LVP*: Literally: "their life-stream is not supported by the defilements" (*kleśair anupastabdhā saṃtatih*): These are the defilements (*kleśa*) that support and make the life-stream abide. – The circumstantially liberated (*samayavimukta*) perfected beings (*arhat*) are free from defilements, but do not have mastery in concentration; those who have attained through views (*dṛṣṭiprāpta*) possess this mastery, but are not free from defilements (vi. 56).

102 *LS*: SAH 453.

[103] *LVP*: jīvitasaṃskārān adhiṣṭhāya āyuḥsaṃskārān utsṛṣṭavān [WOG.106.4].

Compare *Divyāvadāna*, 203: *atha Bhagavāṃs tadrūpaṃ samādhiṃ samāpanno yathā samāhite citte jīvitasaṃskārān adhiṣṭhāya āyuḥsaṃskārān utsraṣṭum ārabdhaḥ*. – We have the singular in *Mahāvastu*, i. 125, 19.

Dīgha, ii. 99: *yan nūnāhaṃ imaṃ ābādhaṃ viriyena paṭippaṇāmetvā jīvitasaṃkhāram adhiṭṭhāya vihareyyam*; ii. 106 ...*āyusaṃkhāram ossaji*. (Compare *Saṃyutta*, v. 152; *Aṅguttara*, iv. 311; *Udāna*, vi. 1). – Burnouf, *Lotus*, 291.

[104] *LVP*: The Pāli has the plural in other contexts, *Majjhima*, i. 295 (*aññe āyusaṃkhārā aññe vedaniyā dhammā*); *Jātaka*, iv. 215 (*āyusaṃkhārā khīyanti*).

[105] *LS*: For additional explanations, see DD.297, 303.

LVP: MVŚ, 657c10ff., enumerates fourteen opinions on this point.

[106] *LVP*: Eleventh opinion in the *Vibhāṣā*.

[107] *LVP*: Sixth opinion in the *Vibhāṣā*.

[108] *LVP*: Doctrine of the Sāṃmitīyas, according to the Japanese editor.

[109] *LVP*: Opinion of the Sautrāntikas.

[110] *LS*: Yaśomitra has [WOG.105.24]: Bhagavān jīvitāny adhiṣṭhāya āyūṃṣy utsṛṣṭavān.

[111] *LS*: SAH 453.

[112] *LVP*: According to the Japanese editor, this is the opinion of the author.

[113] *LVP*: MVŚ,657c5, the fifth of the six opinions.

[114] *LVP*: *kalpaṃ vā ... kalpāvaśeṣaṃ vā*. – That is to say, according to the very clear version of Paramārtha, "an aeon (*kalpa*) or beyond an aeon". It is usually translated: "an aeon or the remainder of an aeon" (Windisch, Rhys Davids, O. Franke). – *Dīgha*, ii. 103, 115, iii. 77; *Divya*, 201. – *Kathāvatthu*, xi. 5. – *Siddhi*, 803.

[115] *LVP*: They adopt the sixth opinion of the *Vibhāṣā*.

[116] *LS*: Jampaiyang comments (p. 289): "In Vaiśālī by blessing his life-span, the *māra* lord of Death was conquered. In Kuśīnagara by relinquishing his life-span, the *māra* of the aggregates was conquered."

[117] *LVP*: *devaputramāra, kleśamāra, maraṇamāra, skandhamāra. Dharmasaṃgraha*, lxxx; *Mahāvastu*, iii. 273, 281; *Śikṣāsamuccaya*, 198, 10; *Madhyamakavṛtti*, 49 n. 4, xxii. 10; *Bodhicaryāvatāra*, ix. 36 (the Fortunate One [*bhagavat*] is a Victor [*jina*] because he has conquered the four Māras); *Yü-chia chih-ti lun*, xxix, translated by S. Lévi, *Seize Arhats*, p. 7 (*J. As.*, 1916, ii.). In iconography (Foucher, *École des Hautes Études*, XIII, ii. 19), the Buddha is flanked by four Māras, blue, yellow, red and green. – The list of the four Māras in glossaries, Zachariae, *Göttingische Gelehrte Anzeigen*, 1888, p. 853. – See also the lists of Childers (five Māras by adding *abhisaṃskāramāra*). The *Nettippakaraṇa* distinguishes *kilesamāra* and *sattamāra* (= *devaputra*).

[118] *LS*: AH 206; SAH 436.

[119] *Gokhale*: [10a2–b1] *dvedhā dvādaśā*

Tib.: [10a2] *bcu gnyis gnyis* |

[120] *Gokhale*: [10b2–c1] *'ntyāṣṭakād ṛte* | *daurmanasyāc ca*

Tib.: [10b] *tha ma brgyad dang yid mi bde | ma gtogs pa ste*

121 *LVP*: Sensation of displeasure (*duḥkhendriya*) never arises in association with modes of proper deportment (*airyāpathika*), etc.

122 *LS*: Even though Vasubandhu plays the part of opponent in the following debate, at the end he seems to agree with the Vaibhāṣikas that dissatisfaction is never a ripened effect, which also is confirmed by iv. 57d, where he states that discontentedness is never a ripened effect.

123 *LVP*: *Ekottarāgama*, 12, 9. – The *Tipiṭaka* knows action conducive to or retributed as pleasure (*sukhavedanīya karman*) (*Aṅguttara*, iv. 382, etc.) (see iv. 45); contact (*sparśa*) conducive to or retributed as pleasure (*sukhavedanīya*), contact conducive to or retributed as dissatisfaction (*daurmanasyavedanīya*) (*Saṃyutta*, v. 211, etc.). – See iv. 57d.

124 *LVP*: According to the etymology of the author, *saumanasyavedanīya karman* signifies "action entailing satisfaction to be experienced as retribution" (*saumanasyaṃ vipākatvena vedanīyam asya*). According to the Vaibhāṣika, "action in which satisfaction should be experienced" (*saumanasyaṃ vedanīyam asmin*): this is experience through association (*saṃprayoga-vedanīyatā*; iv. 49).

125 *LVP*: *saṃprayoge 'pi na doṣo vipāke pi || agatyāpy etad evam gamyeta | kā punar atra yuktir daurmanasyaṃ na vipākaḥ* | [see WOG.107.6ff.]

126 *LVP*: According to the Sūtra, the "non-detached" have two thorns, (1) physical displeasure (*kāyika duḥkha*), (2) mental dissatisfaction (*caitasika daurmanasya*); the "detached" are free from mental dissatisfaction.

127 *LVP*: Thus detached persons do not possess all the controlling faculties (*indriya*) that are retribution.

128 *LVP*: *yādṛśaṃ tādṛśam astu* iti | aparicchidyamānam api tad asty eveti darśayati | tasy*āsti vipākāvakāśo na daurmanasyasya.* [see WOG.107.26]

129 *LS*: Since Vasubandhu states at iv. 57d that "we have established that discontentedness is never a ripened effect" (ii. 10bc), it seems that Vasubandhu agrees here with the Vaibhāṣikas. The issue is also further clarified at iv. 58cd [F 126–27], where Vasubandhu clarifies how mental trouble arises "from" the retribution of action, while its mental sensation is not retribution.

130 *LVP*: Omitted by Hsüan-tsang.

131 *LVP*: The quality of an androgyne, that is to say, the obtaining (*pratilambha*) of the two sexual faculties, is a factor (*dharma*) dissociated from thought (*viprayukta*), ii. 35.

132 *LS*: AH 206; SAH 436.

133 *Gokhale*: [10c2–11a] *tat tv ekaṃ savipākaṃ daśa dvidhā | mano'nyavittiśraddhādīny*

Tib.: [10c2–11a] *de gcig ni | rnam par smin bcas bcu rnam gnyis || yid dang tshor gzhan dad la sogs |*

LVP: This says implicitly that the first eight controlling faculties (*indriya*), as well as the last three, are always without a ripened effect. Hsüan-tsang completes the verse (*kārikā*) in order to make this point explicitly.

The verse has *tat tv ekaṃ savipākam*: *tu* in the sense of *eva*, and out of place; the meaning calls for: *tad ekaṃ savipākam eva* = dissatisfaction alone is exclusively "with a ripened effect".

134 *LS*: AH 205; SAH 435.

135 *Gokhale*: [11bd] *aṣṭakaṃ kuśalaṃ dvidhā | daurmanasyaṃ mano 'nyā ca vittis tredhā 'nyad ekadhā ||*

Tib.: [11b-d] *dge ba brgyad yid mi bde ba | rnam gnyis yid dang tshor gzhan ni | rnam gsum gzhan ni rnam pa gcig ||*

LVP: Hsüan-tsang: the last eight controlling faculties are only wholesome; dissatisfaction is wholesome or unwholesome; the mind and the other sensations are of three types; the first eight controlling faculties are non-defined only.

Although the eight controlling faculties appear at the end of the list of [twenty-two controlling faculties], here they are named first because [five of these eight] are mentioned last in the preceding verse (*kārikā*).

Compare *Vibhāṅga*, p. 125.

136 *LS*: AH 205; SAH 435.

137 *Gokhale*: [12] *kāmāptam amalaṃ hitvā rūpāptaṃ strīpumindriye | duḥkhe ca hitv ārūpyāptaṃ sukhe cā 'pohya rūpi ca ||*

Tib.: [12] *dri med ma gtogs 'dod par gtogs | pho mo'i dbang dang sdug bsngal dag | ma gtogs gzugs gtogs gzugs can dang | bde ba'ang ma gtogs gzugs med gtogs ||*

138 *LS*: AH 205; SAH 435.

139 *LS*: Ibid.

140 *LVP*: See the definition of the powers of the Tathāgata (*tathāgatabala*) in *Vibhaṅga*, p. 336: *aṭṭhānam etaṃ anavakāso yaṃ itthi sakkattaṃ kāreyya mārattaṃ kāreyya brahmattaṃ kāreyya n'etaṃ ṭhānaṃ vijjati… .*

Compare *Lotus* 407, Chavannes, *Cinq cents contes*, i, 264.

141 *LS*: Dhammajoti comments (SA.IV.192):

> Besides the non-information matter, which is unlike other matter that we encounter in phenomenal existence, the Sarvāstivāda concedes other types of special matter, such as that in the fine-material sphere and that of the intermediate beings (*antarābhava*); these kinds of matter are said to be transparent (*accha*). In fact, one reason that the faculty of suffering (*duḥkhendriya*) is absent in the beings of the fine-material sphere is that their bodies (*āśraya*) are constituted by transparent matter on account of which they are not subject to being injured. … [T]he sense faculties are said to comprise very subtle and perspicuous (*prasāda*) kinds of matter which are suprasensible (*atīndriya*), and their atoms, being transparent like crystal, are mutually non-obstructive. The MVŚ (63a) has a similar, but more illustrative description:
>
> > Because they are transparent/clear in nature, they do not mutually obstruct one another. That is to say, for such type of derived clear matter, even when a large number of them are accumulated together, there is no mutual obstruction. It is like the water in an autumn pond; on account of its clarity, even a needle that is dropped into it can be visible.

142 *LS*: Yaśomitra glosses [WOG.109.25f.]: *āghātaḥ* kopaḥ. tasya *vastu* viṣayaḥ *āghāta-vastu*.

143 *LVP*: *Dīgha*, iii. 262; *Aṅguttara*, iv. 408, v. 150.

144 *LS*: AH 205; SAH 435.

145 *LS*: AH 209; SAH 439.

146 *Gokhale*: [13] *mano vittitrayaṃ tredhā dviheyā durmanaskatā | nava bhāvanayā pañca tv aheyāny api na trayam ||*

Tib.: [13] *yid dang tshor ba gsum rnam gsum | gnyis kyis spang bya yid mi bde | dgu ni bsgom pas lnga po ni | spang bar bya min yang gsum min ||*

LVP: Compare i. 40; *Vibhaṅga*, p. 133.

147 *LS*: AH 207–8; SAH 437–38.

148 *Gokhale*: [14] *kāmeṣv ādau vipākau dve labhyete n opapādukaiḥ | taiḥ ṣaḍ vā sapta vā 'ṣṭau vā ṣaḍ rūpeṣv ekam uttare ||*

Tib.: [14] *'dod par dang por rnam smin gnyis | rnyed de rdzus te skye bas min | de yis drug gam bdun nam brgyad | gzugs na drug go gong mar gcig ||*

LVP: Compare *Kathāvatthu*, xiv. 2, *Abhidhammasaṃgaha* (*Compendium*, p. 165).

149 *LVP*: This we should understand as, "because the material forms (*rūpa*) are luminous (*accha* = *bhāsvara*) there", or else "because the material forms, not the objects of sense-enjoyments (*kāmaguṇa*), are important there". See i. 22ab, 4, a different doctrine.

150 *LVP*: ye 'pi *te śāntā vimokṣā atikramya rūpāṇy ārūpyās* te 'py anityā adhruvā anaśvāsikā vipariṇāmadharmāṇaḥ... [see WOG.111.8f.]. Compare *Saṃyutta*, ii. 123. See viii, F 140, *Majjhima*, i, 472: "A forest-dwelling bhikkhu should apply himself to those liberations that are peaceful and immaterial, transcending forms." (Bhikkhu Bodhi comments, MDB, 1270: This refers to the eight meditative attainments. As a minimum he should become proficient in the preliminary work of one meditation subject, such as a *kasiṇa*.)

151 *LS*: AH 207; SAH 437.

152 *LS*: Ibid.

153 *LS*: Ibid.

154 *LS*: Ibid.

155 *LS*: Çox summarizes Saṃghabhadra (EIP.VIII. 679): "From this it is clear that vitality exists as an actual entity: otherwise, there would be nothing upon which birth in the immaterial realm could depend."

156 *LS*: AH 208; SAH 438.

157 *Gokhale*: [15–16b] *nirodhayaty uparamann ārūpye jīvitaṃ manaḥ | upekṣām c aiva rūpe 'ṣṭau kāme daśa navā 'ṣṭa vā || kramamṛtyau tu catvāri śubhe sarvatra pañca ca |*

Tib.: [15–16b] *gzugs med dag tu 'chi ba ni | srog dang yid dang btang snyoms nyid | 'gag par 'gyur ro gzugs na brgyad | 'dod par bcu'am dgu'am brgyad || rim gyis 'chi ba dag la bzhi | dge la thams cad dag tu lnga |*

LVP: Compare *Abhidhammasaṅgaha*, *Compendium*, p. 166.

158 *LVP*: On the psychological state at death, iii. 42–43b. – In what part of the body the mental consciousness is destroyed, iii. 43c–44a. – How the vital faculties perish, iii. 44b.

159 *LS*: SAH 441.

[160] *LVP*: *indriyaprakaraṇe*. Some understand: "In the exposition that we give here of the controlling faculties"; others understand: "in the Indriyaskandhaka", the sixth book of the *Jñānaprasthāna* (Takakusu, *Abhidharma Literature*, p. 93).

[161] *Gokhale*: [16cd] *navāptir antyaphalayoḥ saptā'ṣṭanavabhir dvayoḥ* ||

Tib.: [16cd] *'bras bu tha ma gnyis dgus 'thob | gnyis ni gdun dang brgyad dang dgus* ||

[162] *LS*: SAH 441.

[163] *LS*: Ibid.

[164] *LVP*: For, at the moment when they obtain the fruit of the stream-enterer (*srotaāpanna*), the practitioners find themselves always in the state of meditative attainment called *preparatory meditation* (*anāgamya*; vi. 48), which involves the sensation of equanimity.

[165] *LVP*: The fruit of stream-enterer is obtained in the sixteenth moment of the direct realization of the truths; the first fifteen moments are *ājñāsyāmi* (the faculty of coming to know what is as yet unknown), the sixteenth is *ājña* (the faculty of perfect knowledge).

[166] *LVP*: The first moment is the unhindered path (*ānantaryamārga*); the second, the path of liberation (*vimuktimārga*); and so on. But all the moments that precede the sixteenth moment can be considered as unhindered path in relationship to this moment.

[167] *LVP*: The unhindered path (*ānantaryamārga*) destroys the defilement and leads to the possession of disconnection from the defilement: it drives out the thief. The path of liberation (*vimuktimārga*) closes the door. – The Japanese editor cites here the MVŚ, 465c9, where the Westerners, followers of a non-Kaśmīrian doctrine, are cited.

[168] *LS*: SAH 441.

[169] *LVP*: The fruit of a perfected being (*arhat*) is obtained at the moment of adamantine concentration (*vajropamasamādhi*; vi. 44cd), the unhindered path (*ānantaryamārga*), which is the faculty of perfect knowledge (*ājñendriya*). Thus the faculty of perfect knowledge is actually present. The cognition of exhaustion (*kṣayajñāna*), the path of liberation (*vimuktimārga*), which is the faculty of final and perfect knowledge (*ājñātāvīndriya*), is in the process of arising (*utpādābhimukha*). – Sensation of satisfaction, etc., according to the nature of the meditative attainment in which the practitioner realizes the adamantine concentration.

[170] *LS*: SAH 441.

[171] *LS*: Ibid.

[172] *LVP*: This doctrine of the mundane path is condemned in the *Kathāvatthu*, i. 5 and xviii. 5. – Buddhaghosa attributes it to the Saṃmitiya.

[173] *LS*: SAH 441.

[174] *LVP*: Only the successive ones (*ānupūrvaka*) change from meditational attainment, not those who are detached (*vītarāga*). The latter, in fact, if they begin the direct realization of the truths (*satyābhisamaya*) in the meditative attainment *preparatory meditation* (*anāgamya*), will not pass in the first meditation (*dhyāna*) to the sixteenth moment. What interests them is the direct realization of the truths, not the meditations with which they are familiar. On the contrary, the successive ones are interested in meditation that is new for them.

[175] *LS*: SAH 441.

[176] *Gokhale*: [17ab] *ekādaśabhir arhattvam uktaṃ tv ekasya saṃbhavāt* |

Tib.: [17ab] *bcu gcig dag gis dgra bcom nyid | 'ga' zhig srid phyir bshad pa yin |*

177 *LVP*: The non-returners (*anāgāmin*) who retrogress from the detachment of the higher stages, up to and including the second meditation (*dhyāna*), do not retrogress from the fruit of non-returner because of this: they remain non-returners, since they remain detached from the realm of desire. But they lose the fruit of non-returner when they retrogress from the detachment of the first meditation: thus retrogressed, they cannot regain the fruit through the faculty of pleasure, since this controlling faculty is of the third meditation, and the third meditation is beyond their reach.

Could it be said that they regain the fruit through the faculty of satisfaction? They could if, starting out again to gain the fruit in the meditative attainment *preparatory meditation* (*anāgamya*), they would be capable of passing, in the last moment, into the first meditation. But they cannot do that: only practitioners whose (praxis-oriented) faculties are sharp can bring about this passage, and the practitioners whom we are considering here are of weak (praxis-oriented) faculties since they have retrogressed. Only practitioners of weak faculties retrogress from a fruit.

Could it be said that, having retrogressed, practitioners can bring about the transformation of their (praxis-oriented) faculties (*indriyasaṃcāra*; vi. 41c–61b) and make them sharp? – Without a doubt, and they will obtain the fruit with eight or nine controlling faculties according to whether their path is mundane or pure, as we have said, for, in no case will they regain the fruit with the faculty of pleasure.

178 *LS*: AH 237; SAH 440, 472.

179 *LS*: SAH 440.

180 *LS*: Ibid.

181 *Gokhale*: [17cd] *upekṣājīvitamanoyukto 'vaśyaṃ trayā'nvitaḥ ||*

Tib.: [17cd] *btang snyoms dang ni srog dang ni | yid dang ldan la nges gsum ldan ||*

182 *LVP*: *na hy eṣām anyonyena vinā samanvāgamaḥ* [WOG.118.19].

183 *LVP*: The noble ones (*ārya*) possess the faculty of "pure" pleasure, for they do not lose this faculty by changing the stage (see ii, F. 141, note).

184 *LVP*: Omitted by Hsüan-tsang. – See viii. 12ab.

185 *LS*: SAH 440.

186 *Gokhale*: [18a] *caturbhiḥ sukhakāyābhyāṃ*

Tib.: [18a] *bde lus ldan la bzhi dag dang |*

187 *LS*: SAH 440.

188 *Gokhale*: [18b] *pañcabhiś cakṣurādimān |*

Tib.: [18b] *mig sogs ldan la lnga dang ldan |*

189 *Gokhale*: [18c1] *saumanasyī ca*

Tib.: [18c1] *yid bde ldan yang*

190 *LVP*: There is, in the realm of desire, the faculty of pleasure in relation to the five sensory consciousnesses; in the first meditation (*dhyāna*), the faculty of pleasure in relation to the three sensory consciousnesses (the olfactory and gustatory consciousnesses being excluded, i. 30);

in the second meditation, there is no faculty of pleasure (viii. 12); in the third meditation, the faculty of pleasure in relation to the mental consciousness (ii. 7cd). Thus, beings born in the heaven of the second meditation, if they do not cultivate the meditative attainment of the third meditation, will not possess the faculty of pleasure, since, by being reborn in [the heaven of] the second meditation, they have lost the faculty of pleasure of the lower stages. – Answer: According to Vaibhāṣika doctrine (*siddhānta*), any beings born in a lower stage possess the defiled (*kliṣṭa*) faculty of the higher stage if they have not abandoned it.

191 *LS*: SAH 440.

192 *Gokhale*: [18c2–d1] *duḥkhī tu saptabhiḥ*

Tib.: [18c2–d1] *sdug bsgnal ldan | bdun dang*

193 *LS*: SAH 440.

194 *Tib.*: [18d2–19a1] *strīndriyādimān || aṣṭābhir*

Tib.: [18d2–19a1] *mo yi dbang sogs ldan || brgyad dang*

LVP: See iv. 80a, which cites the *Jñānaprasthāna*, 997a16 and 1000c3. – *Ad* iv. 79d, the number of faculties in the first three continents (*dvīpa*).

195 *LS*: SAH 440.

196 *Gokhale*: [19a2–b] *ekādaśabhis tv ājñājñātendriyanvitaḥ |*

Tib.: [19a2–b] *kun shes ldan pa yi | dbang po ldan la bcu gcig ldan |*

197 *LVP*: How are the possessors of the faculty of perfect knowledge (*ājñendriya*), i.e., those in training (*śaikṣa*), necessarily in possession of the faculties of pleasure and of satisfaction? They can, in fact, be in the heaven of the fourth meditation or in the realm of immateriality.

The noble ones (*ārya*) necessarily obtain the faculty of satisfaction if they detach themselves from the realm of desire; they necessarily obtain the faculty of pleasure when they detach themselves from the second meditation; the same when they transmigrate (*bhūmisaṃcāra*), they do not lose the good (*śubha*) that they have obtained (according to iv. 40); they lose the good obtained when they have gained a fruit or when they perfect their (praxis-oriented) faculties (iv. 40), but this is in order to obtain the same kind of good of a higher quality.

198 *LS*: SAH 440.

199 *Gokhale*: [19cd] *ājñāsyāmīndriyopetas trayodaśabhir anvitaḥ ||*

Tib.: [19cd] *kun shes byed pa'i dbang ldan la | bcu gsum dag dang ldan pa yin ||*

200 *LVP*: But can these sentient beings be bisexual? This is difficult, since we have seen (F 105) that sentient beings without sex cannot obtain either the restraint, or a fruit, or detachment.

According to one opinion: Persons who have obtained the restraint can obtain a fruit; but these persons preserve the restraint even if they lose their sex, since the Abhidharma specifies they lose the restraint by becoming androgyne (iv. 38c) and it does not specify that they lose the restraint by losing their sex. – One can, moreover, look at gradual death: persons who have cultivated the stages conducive to penetration (*nirvedhabhāgīya*; vi. 17) could, after the loss of the sexual faculty, see the truths at the moment of death.

Second opinion: The possessors of the faculty of coming to know what is as yet unknown (*ājñāsyāmīndriya*) are never without sex. But they do not possess the female sexual faculty when they are a male, they do not possess the male sexual faculty when they are a female. Thus it cannot be said that they necessarily possess one or the other.

201 *LS*: AH 237; SAH 472.

202 *Gokhale*: [20ac1] *sarvā'lpair niḥśubho 'ṣṭābhir vinmanaḥkāyajīvitaiḥ | yukto*

Tib.: [20ab] *dge med nang na nyung ldan pa | lus tshor srog yid brgyad dang ldan |*

203 *LS*: *kvip* = *kṛt* affix zero, added to the root, used to form nouns from roots; *kartṛ* = agent; *kartṛsādhana* = an affix applied in the sense of the agent of an activity; *bhāvasādhana* = an affix applied for the formation of a word in the sense of verbal activity; *auṇādika* = an affix mentioned in the class of affixes called *uṇādi* in treatises of Pāṇini and other grammarians.

204 *Gokhale*: [20c2–d] *bālas tath ārūpya upekṣā'yurmanaḥśubhaiḥ ||*

Tib.: [20cd] *gzugs med byis ba'ang de bzhin te | btang snyoms srog yid dge rnams dang ||*

205 *LS*: AH 237; SAH 472.

206 *Gokhale*: [21ac1] *bahubhir yukta ekān na viṃśatyā 'malavarjitaiḥ | dviliṅga*

Tib.: [21ac1] *mang por ldan la bcu dgu ste | dri ma med rnams ma gtogs so | mtshan gnyis*

207 *Gokhale*: [21c2–d] *āryarāgy ekaliṅgadvyamalavarjitaiḥ ||*

Tib.: [21c2–d] *'phags pa chags bcas te | mtshan gcig dri med gnyis ma gtogs ||*

208 *LVP*: *ukta indriyāṇāṃ dhātuprabhedhaprasaṅgena* (i. 48c) *āgatānāṃ vistareṇa prabhedaḥ* [WOG.123.1f.].

209 *LS*: Hsüan-tsang, iv, fol. 1a.

210 *LS*: AH 16, 23–24, 220–21, 224; SAH 15, 54–66, 450, 453–55, 457, 484.

211 *LS*: 1. Dharmatrāta's chapter 2 of the SAH is entitled *saṃskāravarga* and, since it does not include a section dealing with the controlling faculties (*indriya*), it starts out here by contrasting the second chapter with the first chapter (SAH, p. 91), which is described as being related to the characteristics (*lakṣaṇa*) of the factors:

> That factors (*dharma*) abide in characteristic marks (*lakṣaṇa*) has already been said. The genesis of factors shall now be spoken of. It is not right that since factors are included in their specific nature (*svabhāva*), they arise through their specific power (*svabala*).

According to Dharmatrāta, the intrinsic nature of factors is weak (*durbala*) and they cannot arise through their own power or by themselves (*svabala*). All factors achieve arising through the multiple power condition (*pratyayabala*). It is compared to when a person and a boat make use of one another, and so achieve the crossing over to the other bank.

Dharmatrāta closes chapter 2 in the following way:

> *Question*: Why are these factors said to be formations?
>
> *Answer*:
>
> (96) Many factors make one factor arise. One can also make many arise. The formations formed by conditions and the forming conditions should be known as the formations.
>
> There is no factor that arises through its specific power (*svabala*): one factor arises

> because of the power of many factors; also many factors arise because of the power of one factor. This is the way all conditioned factors are. That is why it is said: "The formations formed by conditions and the forming conditions should be known as the formations."
>
> Because they are the condition for formations and because they form, formations formed by conditions are spoken of, because of being formed by conditions and because of forming formations, forming formations are spoken of.

2. Cox summarizes Saṃghabhadra (Ny, 383c; EIP.VIII.680): "All conditioned factors arise from both previous and simultaneous causes and conditions. The simultaneous arising of various conditioned factors will be presented in order to refute erroneous theories of causation. For example, some maintain that conditioned factors arise only from previous causes, or that they arise from only one cause, or that they arise from their own essential nature, or that they arise spontaneously without a cause."

212 *LS*: For the *Pañcavastuka* and its place within the first two chapters, see our endnote at the beginning of the text (i. 4). See also Frauwallner's *Pañcaskandhaka and Pañcavastuka* (SAL.135–47).

Cox writes (FCO.552–54):

> The later Sarvāstivāda fivefold taxonomy (*pañcavastuka*) is another comprehensive taxonomic system that contains both "evaluative" and "descriptive" categories, but unlike the set of 22 controlling faculties, its arrangement is not soteriologically hierarchical. Instead, it attempts to present a complete and systematic listing of all possible *dharma*s classified abstractly by distinctive intrinsic nature (*svabhāva*), without regard for the particular causal or temporal conditions of their occurrence. The previous taxonomic systems begin from specific circumstances of praxis, perception, and so forth, and present detailed descriptions of the significant activities or events (*dharma*) that interact cooperatively in those particular circumstances. The fivefold taxonomy, by contrast, takes the perspective of the *dharma*s themselves and sets out a delimited number of abstract genera that are intended to encompass every experienced event or phenomenon, or in other words every possible individual instance of a *dharma*. ...
>
> The historical development of this fivefold taxonomy has yet to be fully studied, but the categories themselves suggest certain general principles of organization and, more importantly, of progression in the interpretation of the term *dharma*. A traditional distinction between the material and the mental, typical of the older system of the five aggregates (*skandha*), is evident in the first three categories of material form, thought, and thought concomitants. But new principles of organization can also be observed that evolved from the doctrinal elaboration and resulting controversies of the early Abhidharma period.
>
> First, the distinction within the mental sphere between the two categories of thought (*citta*) and thought concomitants (*caitta*) can be seen as a natural development from the earlier distinction within the five aggregates between perceptual consciousness (*vijñāna*), identified in the new fivefold taxonomy as thought, and the other three non-material aggregates, which are subsumed and further expanded within the single

category of thought concomitants. However, this distinction between thought and thought concomitants also reflects an emphasis upon perception as the central sentient experience and a newly recognized need to isolate thought as an identifiable hub that connects the various activities constituting one sentient being and, thereby, facilitates a distinction between one sentient being and another.

Second, the new category of thought concomitants (*caitta*) comprises, according to the later, standard enumeration, 46 *dharmas* that are divided into six sub-groups according to their moral character as virtuous, unvirtuous, and so forth. In this regard, the category of thought concomitants clearly incorporates an "evaluative", soteriological purpose into the otherwise "descriptive" fivefold taxonomy.

Third, the category of dissociated forces (*cittaviprayuktasaṃskāra*) includes *dharmas* that were proposed to account for a varied range of experiential or doctrinally necessary events and is, therefore, a miscellany of *dharmas* not unified by any overall integrating principle other than dissociation from both material form and thought.

Finally, the last category of the unconditioned (*asaṃskṛta*) reflects a fundamental distinction between *dharmas* included within the first four categories that are conditioned (*saṃskṛta*), or arise and pass away through causal interaction, and *dharmas* that are not so conditioned and, therefore, neither arise nor pass away.

As for the motive and history of the five-group classification of factors, Cox states (DD.68f.): "Unlike the earlier classifications according to the five aggregates or the twelve sense spheres, which appear to have been motivated by an attempt to demonstrate non-self and impermanence, this new fivefold taxonomy reflects a concern for completeness, an interest in classification for its own sake, and a desire to demonstrate the individual, distinctive characteristic of each of the factors classified. This fivefold taxonomy is traced by the tradition to the Ābhidhārmika, Vasumitra, and indeed, it is the first topic treated in the *Prakaraṇapāda* attributed to him. Regardless of Vasumitra's actual historical contribution, the impetus for this fivefold taxonomy can in part be found in the recognition within early Sarvāstivādin Abhidharma texts of the discrete and real existence of both conditioned forces dissociated from thought and unconditioned factors as well as in the difficulty of including these two types of factors within the traditional categories."

213 *LS*: AH 16, 23–24, 220–21, 224; SAH 15, 54–66, 450, 453–55, 457, 484.

214 *LS*: AH 23; SAH 64.

In this context see also i, F 89ff. (and our endnotes), which discusses the different views on whether or not atoms touch one another and their relationship to agglomerates. Likewise see iii, F 177ff. (and our endnotes) for a discussion of the smallest unit of physical matter and the various units of space up to one league (*yojana*).

215 *LS*: Tib.: *phra rab rdul.*

216 *LVP*: On the meaning of this term, see below F 147.

LS: Tib.: *rdzas.*

217 *LS*: Discussing—in the context of the Abhidharma of the Śrāvakayāna—the general view that all entities lack a solid, permanent core, Frauwallner deals (PB.102f.) with the field of

material elements and the *aṣṭadravyaka* (i.e., the molecule "comprising eight real entities") as follows:

> In the sphere of the elements, the primary concern was with the five properties that, since ancient times, had been held to be the objects of the sense-perceptions, namely: visible form; sound; odor; taste; and tangibility. In the doctrinal discourses of the Buddha, these properties are usually mentioned alone, without reference to the [invisible] elements, since to the Buddha the external world was of interest only insofar as it affects the person and arouses sensations and passions. Now, it was explicitly taught that [visible form, etc.,] are not properties that adhere to the elements, but they are rather autonomous entities. And as the doctrine of atoms—which had been created and propagated in the meantime—was adopted, it was taught that these entities consist of atoms. The things of the external world are therefore not composed of elements but are formed from atoms of color, sound, odor, taste, and tangibility.
>
> Of course, it was also necessary to deal with the old conception of the elements, since elements—specifically the commonly known four elements of earth, water, fire, and wind—are often mentioned in the doctrinal discourses of the Buddha. What are these elements then? To explain this, one reverted to the following idea. Since the ancient times, in addition to the five properties that, as objects of the sense-perceptions, correspond to the five sense-organs, a second set of characteristic properties had been attributed to the elements. These were: solidity to earth; wetness to water; heat to fire; and motion to wind. Now it was said that the so-called *four elements* were nothing other than these same properties. With that, these four properties were classified within the *tangible* and of course the theory of atoms was also applied to them. The four elements are therefore atoms of hardness, wetness, heat, and motion.
>
> At the same time, however, according to the commonly held view, the properties of the elements never appear in isolation. The Vaiśeṣika, for example, taught that each element unites several qualities within itself, and all the other systems followed the Vaiśeṣikas in this. Opinions differed only with regard to the number and distribution of these qualities. Buddhism thus also taught accordingly that the atom-like properties of the elements never occur in isolation as single atoms, but always combined into molecules. Each molecule, to be exact, contains one property atom of each type [i.e., visible form, etc.], each of which are joined as support, so to speak, by one atom of each of the four elements. Since sound occurs only occasionally, the molecule therefore consists of a minimum of eight [types of] atoms, which may occasionally be joined by further atoms. The entire material world is built from these atoms and the diversity of individual materials derives from the predominance of this or that property atom. In this way then, against the Vaiśeṣika doctrine of the elements, Buddhism set its own doctrine, in which the concept of a [permanent] *substance* was eliminated and a loose association of autonomous property atoms took the place of [permanent] substance atoms with their numerous qualities.

As for the historical development of the Buddhist atomic theory, it is not discernable in the *sūtras*. Dhammajoti states (SA.IV.198) that it was likely adopted from outside the Buddhist schools—probably from the Vaiśeṣika (EIP.II.79–86)—and that it was at least by the time of the *Mahāvibhāṣā* articulated to a large extent in a specific Buddhist way, i.e., where atoms are seen as momentary and not permanent, etc. MVŚ, 702ab, presents the doctrine of the sevenfold incremental atomic agglomeration (see AKB iii. 85d). On the other hand, the Sarvāstivādin doctrine that a minimum of eight real entities (*aṣṭadravyaka*)—constituting the subtlest aggregate, *saṃghāta-paramāṇu*—necessarily arise simultaneously in the realm of desire was apparently articulated only after the period of the MVŚ (see SA.IV.201). As for the latter doctrine, Dhammajoti comments that "it is sufficiently clear that this 'octad molecule' does not really mean a molecule comprising eight atoms. It represents the smallest unit of matter that can be cognized by us." In this context he speaks (SA.IV.204f.) of "a contradiction that seems to have been quietly left unsettled: On the one hand, the atomic theory requires that atoms are grouped as septuplets from which matter is derived. The smallest molecule, an *aṇu*, or *saṃghāta-paramāṇu*, consisting of just seven *paramāṇu*-s is the smallest unit of matter that is perceivable—and even then not by an ordinary human being. On the other hand, a new doctrine was then articulated that a molecule that can arise in the empirical world consists of a minimum of eight substances. Taking both doctrines into consideration, one commentarial opinion, in fact, arrives at 1,379 as the number of atoms that constitute a molecule of a visible" (see AKB iii, F 148f., footnote).

218 *Gokhale*: [22] *kāme 'ṣṭadravyako 'śabdaḥ paramāṇur anindriyaḥ | kāyendriyī navadravyo daśadravyo 'parendriyaḥ* ||

Tib.: [22] *'dod na dbang po med pa dang | sgra med phra rab rdul rdzas brgyad | lus dbang lcan la rdzas dgu'o | dbang po gzhan ldan rdzas bcu'o* ||

LVP: Vasubandhu follows Dharmottara (*Nanjio* 1288), ii. 8; Upaśānta (*Nanjio* 1294), ii. 9; Dharmatrāta (*Nanjio* 1287), ii. 11: "The atoms residing in the four sense-faculties are of ten types; in the body sense-faculty, of nine types; elsewhere, of eight types, when there is odor (that is to say: in the realm of desire)." – Upaśānta: "...external, of eight types: in a stage where there is odor".

An analogous doctrine is found in the Abhidhamma of Buddhaghosa (*Atthasālinī*, 634) and in the *Compendium* (p. 164). – See above i. 13, 43c, and Th. Stcherbatsky, *The soul theory of the Buddhists*, p. 953.

219 *LS*: SAH 64.

220 *LVP*: According to Saṃghabhadra (Ny, 799a24–29): "Among the material forms (*rūpa*) that are resistent (*sapratigha*), the most subtle part, which is not susceptible of being divided again, is called *paramāṇu*; that is to say: the *paramāṇu* is not susceptible of being divided into many parts by another material form (*rūpa*) or by mind (*buddhi*). It is this *paramāṇu* that is called the *smallest material form* [or "ultimately small" among matter]; as there can be no further parts, it is given the name "smallest" [or "ultimately small"]. In the same way a moment (*kṣaṇa*) is called the *smallest unit of time* and cannot be further analyzed into half-moments (iii. 86).

An agglomeration [or multitude] of such *aṇus*, [i.e., *paramāṇus*,] that are [mutually combined and necessarily inseparable or] not susceptible of disaggregation, receives the name *saṃghātāṇu* (Dhammajoti: *saṃghāta-paramāṇu*). [See the description of the 1,379 atoms of the molecule of visible form in the footnote on page F 148.]

In the realm of desire, when sound and sense-faculty are absent, a minimum of eight real entities (*dravya*) arise together in order to constitute a *saṃghātāṇu* (Dhammajoti: *saṃghāta-paramāṇu*). – What are these real entities? – Four fundamental material elements (*mahābhūta*), four derivative material elements (*upādāya*), namely, visible form (*rūpa*), taste (*rasa*), odor (*gandha*), tangible (*spṛṣṭavya*)."

LS: LVP translates the *saṃghātaparamāṇu* as "molecule" and the *dravyaparamāṇu* as "atome ou monade", "*paramāṇu* au sense propre". In chapter 3, verse 85bc, he returns to the discussion of the *paramāṇu* as the limit or smallest unit of matter where he translates: "l'atome proprement dit (*parama-aṇu*)", which thus should refer to the *paramāṇu* as monad.

For more detail on the atom, its definition and its two types, i.e., *dravyaparamāṇu* and *saṃghātaparamāṇu*, see our endnote at iii. 85bc.

221 *LS*: AH 23; SAH 64.

222 *LVP*: The (composite) molecules that involve the body sense-faculty, the eye sense-faculty, etc., are the "atoms" that are discussed in i. 44ab.

223 *LVP*: A molecule of sound (1) produced by the hands involves the four fundamental material elements, the four derivative material elements, sound, the body sense-faculty: ten real entities; (2) produced by the tongue, eleven real entities, by adding the tongue sense-faculty whose invisible atoms are arranged on the tongue. [Note of the translator (i.e., LVP)].

224 *LS*: This is the fourth of Kritzer's forty-four passages discussed in relation to chapter 2 (VY.44f.).

Dhammajoti clarifies (SA.IV.195) that even though MVŚ, 665a, presents two answers—predominance of substance, predominance of effect—it does not comment on which view represents the orthodox Vaibhāṣika standpoint. On the other hand, Saṃghabhadra (Ny, 355b) "criticizes the Kośakāra for giving the latter view as the Vaibhāṣika view. According to Saṃghabhadra, the orthodox Vaibhāṣika view is that of predominance of substance."

As for the predominance of substance, MVŚ, 682c–683a, explicitly affirms that there can be a quantitative difference in the *mahābhūtas* without contradicting the principle of their inseparability:

> Question: Do the *mahābhūta*-s increase or decrease in substance (i.e., vary quantitatively)? ... There is a fault in either case—if they increase or decrease, how can they be inseparable? For, if in a solid substance there are more atoms of Earth (*pṛthivī-paramāṇu*) and fewer of Water, Fire and Air, the Earth atoms quantitatively intermingled with Water, etc., [accordingly as the case may be,] would be separated from the other Elements. [On the other hand,] if there is no increase or decrease, substances like water, stones, etc., ought not to differ in being solid, soft, etc.
>
> Answer: One should say that there is increase or decrease in substance among the *mahābhūta*-s. ... Although there is an increase or decrease, they are not separated, because together they perform a function by mutually supporting one another. Thus, in a solid substance, where the number of Earth atoms is greater than those of Water, Fire and Air, the Earth atoms are incapable of performing their functions in isolation from Water, etc. ... It is like the case of many villages in which there is a collective management; there is a difference in the number of villagers [among the villages],

yet [the villagers are in each case] mutually dependent and cannot be separated.

Dhammajoti comments (SA.IV.196) that "it is therefore clear that inseparability does not necessarily mean that the four Great Elements are juxtaposed. It means that the four always co-exist and are functionally interdependent. They are what the Sarvāstivādins call co-existent causes to one another. Their inseparability can be inferred from their specific characteristic and activity that can be observed in all material aggregates."

225 *LVP*: *tūlyo* vīraṇādipuṣpamūladaṇḍāḥ yāḥ siṃkā(?) iti prākṛtajanapratītāḥ [WOG.124.6f.]. – See J. Bloch, *Formation de la langue marathe*, p. 42: *siṅka* (*śikya*), "a cord to suspend objects".

LS: Tib.: *khab dang sdong bu'i tsogs.*

226 *LVP*: The elementary substance water (*abdhātu*) exists in wood (*dāru*): it is the elementary substance water that holds things together (*saṃgraha*) and that hinders them from dispersing. It is through the elementary substance fire (*tejas*) that wood matures (*pakti*) and rots. It is through the elementary substance wind that wood moves (*vyūhana*; *prasarpana*). – The elementary substance earth exists within water, since water supports (*dhṛti*) ships; etc. – See above F. 22, *Vyākhyā*, p. 34.

227 *LS*: The objection of how we know that a given composite molecule includes the fundamental material elements is addressed from the point of view of predominance of substance (= mixture) versus predominance of effect (= efficacy, intensity). Dhammajoti specifies (SA.IV.193): "Saṃghabhadra informs us [Ny, 352c.ff.] that the Sthavira Śrīlata ... denies the existence of the derived tangibles. For him they are nothing more than the specific configuration of the Great Elements. Thus, he argues, the so-called coldness is simply a designation for the state wherein the Heat Element becomes less or not predominant. Likewise, heaviness or lightness is simply a designation of the fact that there exists a bigger or smaller quantity of the Great Elements within a given form of matter."

228 *LVP*: Iron melts (becomes liquid) due to heat, thus it contains the elementary substance water; water becomes solid through coldness, thus it contains the elementary substance earth; solid bodies, rubbed one against the other, become hot, thus they contain the elementary substance fire, etc.

229 *LVP*: *apsu śaityātiśayād auṣṇyaṃ gamyate* [WOG.124.28f.].

230 *LS*: LVP mentions the Sautrāntikas here, but they are not explicitly mentioned in Pradhan. Yaśomitra labels this opinion [WOG.125.5f.] as "Sautrāntika".

231 *LS*: Tib.: *gzhan dag na re de dag las de dag sa bon gyi sgo nas yod kyi rang gi ngo bor ni ma yin te.*

The *Vyākhyā* glosses [WOG.125.7.]: *na svarūpato* na dravyataḥ ity arthaḥ.

232 *LVP*: *santy asmin dāruskandhe vividhā dhātavaḥ* [see WOG.125.9f.]. – On the meaning of *dhātu*, i. 20.

233 *LVP*: A presence that results from the definition: the molecule (*saṃghātaparamāṇu*) involves eight [kinds of] real entities.

234 *LVP*: varṇavān vāyur gandhavattvāj jātipuṣpavat [WOG.125.20]. – See also i. 13cd.

235 *LS*: AH 23; SAH 64.

[236] *LS*: SAH 64.

[237] *LVP*: yasya svalakṣaṇam asti tad dravyam [see WOG.125.31]. Blue is a real entity (*dravya*).

[238] *LVP*: sāmānyaviśeṣalakṣaṇasadbhāvāt [WOG.125.32f.]. – *Rūpa* possesses the characteristic of resistance (*rūpyate*) that is common to color and shape, to blue, etc.

LS: Dhammajoti specifies (SA.IV.203): "Does it refer to ... *āyatana*-s (i.e., *rūpa* as *rūpa-āyatana*, etc.) each possessing a distinctive common characteristic applicable to the type as a whole (e.g., all visibles are *rūpa*-s as a type—an *āyatana*)?" For the distinction between the two types of characteristics and their relativity, see the two endnotes to i. 2b (section: Etymological explanation of *dharma* and *abhi-dharma*).

[239] *LVP*: We have seen (i. 13 [F 25]) that an atom or monad never exists in an isolated state. On this point the Japanese editor cites the commentary (in six chapters) by Hui-hui. P. Pelliot has discovered this citation in T'ao 83, 5, fol. 414, where it is accompanied by a gloss that justifies the number of 1,379 atoms for the molecule of visible form, etc.

Errors excepted, here is the meaning of these glosses:

An atom never exists in an isolated state. There are, at the minimum, groups—or molecules—of seven atoms: four faces, top and bottom: six sides; the center; thus seven. To consider a molecule of derivative material form (*mahābhūtāny upādāya rūpam, bhautikaṃ rūpam*), for example, a molecule of visible form (*rūpa*) or of odor (*gandha*), there are thus seven atoms of visible form or of odor.

Each of these seven atoms is supported by complexes of seven atoms, seven atoms having the four fundamental material elements for their nature, seven atoms where the four fundamental material elements are present.

Each of these seven atoms involves four atoms, atoms of earth, of water, of fire, of wind: the atom of earth involves seven atoms of earth, etc.

Thus:

1. Seven atoms of earth, of water, of fire, of wind, in total, twenty-eight atoms, constitute one atom of four-fundamental-material-elements.

2. One atom of four-fundamental-material-elements does not exist isolated: seven of them are grouped together (7 x 28 = 196) in order to support one atom of derivative material element [196 + 1 = 197].

3. One atom of derivative material element (here, visible form) with its supports, namely, the atoms of four-fundamental-material-elements (i.e., 196 atoms), form a group with six other similar atoms: the molecule of derivative material element involves thus 1,379 atoms (7 x 197).

(But any derivative material element possesses visibility, odor, taste, tangibility. Thus this number should be multiplied by four in order to obtain the smallest part of matter existing in an isolated state, [i.e., the *saṃghatāparamāṇu*].

[240] *LVP*: *chandato hi vācām pravṛttiḥ | arthas tu parīkṣyaḥ* [WOG.126.21]. – That is to say, *chandata* icchātaḥ saṃkṣepavistaravidhānānuvidhāyino vācaḥ pravartante | *arthas tv* ābhyāṃ *parīkṣyaḥ* [see WOG.126.21].

[241] *LS*: AH 24, 220–21, 224; SAH 15–16, 54–63, 65–66, 450, 453–55, 457, 484.

See the chart of the five-group-seventy-five-*dharmas* classification of the Sarvāstivāda at ii, F 144.

In the following discussion, Vasubandhu defines all the thought-concomitants and formations dissociated from thought but does not again give a definition of thought (*citta = vijñāna*). The latter he defines at i. 16a and at various other places in the AKB. For the various ways in which he discusses thought, see our long endnote at i. 16a, which also addresses the difference in functionality between thought and thought-concomitants. By contrast, in the following expositions Vasubandhu stresses the simultaneous arising and cooperation of thought, thought-concomitants and formations dissociated from thought.

In general it can be said that within the five-group classification of factors (*pañcavastuka*)—in comparison to the older threefold classification of aggregates (*skandha*), sense-spheres (*āyatana*) and elements (*dhātu*)—the central role of thought (*citta*) is highlighted, as can be seen from the fact that thought (*citta*) is singled out, forming the second category, whereas all thought-concomitants (*caitta*) or formations associated with thought (*cittasaṃprayuktasaṃskāra*) are grouped together into the third category and all formations dissociated from thought (*cittaviprayuktasaṃskāra*) into the fourth category.

[242] *LS*: AH 16; SAH 54.

[243] *Gokhale*: [23a] *cittacaittāḥ sahā 'vaśyaṃ*

Tib.: [23a] *sems dang sems byung nges lhan cig* |

LVP: *citta = manas = vijñāna*. [See ii. 34ab].

caitta = caitasa = caitasika = cittasaṃprayukta.

LS: 1. Hirakawa (HIB.159f., 162f.) points out that the Sarvāstivādins maintained that thought-concomitants were independent entities as, for example, attachment and hostility seemed to perform such directly opposed activities that they had to be distinct *dharmas*. However, in spite of the independent entities, each person appeared to have a certain unity that marked him or her as an individual. To explain that unity, the Sarvāstivādins argued that thought (*citta*) and thought-concomitants arise at the same time and work associated (*saṃprayukta*); see the discussion of the fivefold equivalence (*samatā*), ii. 34bd, and also of the associated cause (*saṃprayuktakahetu*), ii. 53cd, which is an exemplification of the co-existent cause (*sahabhū-hetu*), ii. 50bd. But Hirakawa further points out that, as the thought and thought-concomitants arose and ceased in an instant, the theory of *saṃprayukta* still did not sufficiently explain this "certain unity" and that therefore the Sarvāstivādins described thought as a ground or base or stage (*citta-bhūmi*; see below ii, F 152: the meaning of the term *mahābhūmika*). In contrast, the Yogācārins explained this unity by postulating the store-consciousness (*ālayavijñāna*), from which both the conscious thought and its objects arose; but the Sarvāstivādins did not accept the *ālayavijñāna*.

Notice hereby that Vasubandhu, in the brief exposition here, singles out "possession" from the formations dissociated from thought. But in this context—and in terms of this "certain unity"—the Sarvāstivādins can naturally also take recourse in their doctrine of *sarvāstitva*, i.e., the tri-temporal existence of all factors (*dharma*).

2. As for the Dārṣṭāntika, Collett Cox (DD.119f.) writes:

It is far more difficult to characterize the Dārṣṭāntika psychological model because several models of psychological functioning are attributed to the Dārṣṭāntikas or to masters aligned with the Dārṣṭāntika school. For example, the **Mahāvibhāṣā* cites the Dārṣṭāntikas in general as maintaining that mental operations, or mental forces—a general term for any type of psychological event, including all thought or thought concomitants as discriminated by other schools or masters—occur only successively, and not together in one moment. The Dārṣṭāntikas are also cited as identifying certain of the discrete thought concomitants recognized by the Sarvāstivāda-Vaibhāṣikas as varieties of thought: for example, initial inquiry (*vitarka*) and investigation (*vicāra*), or volition (*cetanā*) and discernment all are identified with thought. Though the **Mahāvibhāṣā* does not describe the Dārṣṭāntikas in general as equating all thought concomitants with thought, the **Nyāyānusāra* cites the Dārṣṭāntikas as rejecting any distinct thought concomitants [Ny, 395a1ff.]. In the **Mahāvibhāṣā*, this more radical view that all thought concomitants are to be identified with thought is attributed to a master, Buddhadeva, affiliated with the Dārṣṭāntika school. His view is contrasted with that of Dharmatrāta, whose views are also often similar to those associated with the Dārṣṭāntika school. Dharmatrāta identifies thought and thought concomitants as varieties of volition (*cetanā*).[a] Like the Dārṣṭāntika view cited above that identifies both volition and discernment with thought, Dharmatrāta's view that identifies thought and thought concomitants with volition leaves open the possibility that certain thought concomitants could be recognized to exist independently of thought. Indeed, this is precisely the position that Saṅghabhadra attributes to the Dārṣṭantika master, Śrīlāta, who is said to reject all thought concomitants except for three: feelings (*vedanā*), conception (*saṃjñā*), and volition (*cetanā*).[b] Śrīlāta is described as supporting a serial model for the operation of mental forces: specifically, that the sense organ and the object-field in the first moment condition the arising of perceptual consciousness in the second moment, and the collocation of the sense organ, object-field, and perceptual consciousness, condition the successive arising of the three thought concomitants of feelings, concepts, and volition, in the third and subsequent moments [see iii, F 102–7].

[a] LS: But see more on this in our endnote to i, F 28 bottom.

[b] See Ny, 384b12. Cf. also Ny, 339b14ff., where Śrīlāta identifies the forces aggregate (*saṃskāraskandha*) with volition and explains all specific factors classed within the forces aggregate as varieties of volition.

3. As for Vasubandhu himself, Dhammajoti thinks (private communication) that he "may" have accepted most of the thought-concomitants enumerated in the AKB. See more on this in our "*kila*" endnote below (ii. 24).

244 *Gokhale*: [23b] *sarvaṃ saṃskṛtalakṣaṇaiḥ* |

Tib.: [23b] *thams cad 'dus byas mtshan nyid dang* |

245 *Gokhale*: [23c1] *prāptyā vā*

Tib.: [23c1] *thob pa'm*

246 *LS*: AH 24, 220–21, 224; SAH 15, 55–66, 450, 453–55, 457, 484.

247 *LS*: The *Avatāra* states (ESD.81): "[The conjoined conditionings (i.e., *citta-saṃprayukta-*

saṃskāra)] are said to be conjoined because of their being on a par (*samatā*) with thought in five respects, [i.e., because they both] (i) have the same basis (*āśraya*), (ii) have the same object (*ālambana*), (iii) have the same mode of activity (*ākāra*), (iv) are simultaneous, and (v) because each of them has, [in a given conjunction (*samprayoga*),] only one substance (*dravya*). [See ii. 34bd].

The disjoined conditionings are those that do not conform to the [five conditions above, and which belong to the category of neither material nor mental].

All these conjoined and disjoined conditionings are collectively named the 'aggregate of conditionings' (*saṃskāra-skandha*)."

See also ii. 34bd.

248 *LS*: AH 17–22, 217; SAH 15, 55–63, 450.

249 *LS*: AH 17, 19; SAH 55–60.

250 *LVP*: [This long endnote has three parts:]

A. The theory of thought-concomitants according to Vasubandhu, according to the Sautrāntikas.

B. *Prakaraṇapāda* and *Dhātukāya*.

C. Abhidhamma.

A. The commentary of the *Vijñaptimātraśāstra* says that the Sautrāntikas have two systems:

1. some, the Dārṣṭāntikas, maintain that only thought exists, that thought-concomitants do not exist, in agreement with Buddhadeva (see i. 35 note);

2. others admit the existence of thought-concomitants and are divided into many opinions:

i. that there are three thought-concomitants: sensation (*vedanā*), ideation (*saṃjñā*), intention (*cetanā*);

ii. that there are four thought-concomitants (by adding contact [*sparśa*]);

iii. ten thought-concomitants (the ten generally permeating factors [*mahābhūmika*]),

iv. fourteen thought-concomitants (by adding greed [*lobha*], hatred [*dveṣa*], delusion [*moha*], conceit [*māna*];

v. furthermore, certain Sautrāntikas admit all the thought-concomitants of the Sarvāstivādins.

(The information of Wassilief, p. 309, differs:

> Among the Sautrāntikas, the Bhadanta Dārṣṭāntika [i.e., "Bhadanta", i, 36] recognizes *vedanā*, *saṃjñā*, *cetanā* as real, but the Bhadanta Buddhadeva adds *sparśa* and *manasikāra*... . The Bhadanta Śrīlāta... .

Read "Bhadanta Sautrāntika" instead of Bhaṭṭopama).

See ii. 26cd; iii. 32ab.

On the problem of the thought-concomitants (*caitta*), *Kośa*, i, F 64 (footnote), viii, F 159, ix, F 252, *Siddhi*, 395; also *Compendium*, 12.

Vasubandhu presents his doctrine of the thought-concomitants in his *Pañcaskandhaprakaraṇa* (*Nanjio*, 1176; *Mdo*, 58):

> What are the thought-concomitants (*caitta*)?

The factors associated (*saṃprayukta*) with thought, namely:

1. five pervasive (*sarvaga*) [factors]: *sparśa, manaskāra, vedanā, saṃjñā, cetanā*;
2. five object-specific (*pratiniyataviṣaya*) [factors]: *chanda, adhimokṣa, smṛti, samādhi, prajñā*;
3. eleven wholesome factors: *śraddhā, hrī, apatrāpya, alobha kuśalamūla, adveṣa kuśalamūla, amoha kuśalamūla, vīrya, praśrabdhi, apramāda, upekṣā, avihiṃsā*;
4. six defilements (*kleśa*): *rāga, pratigha, māna, avidyā, dṛṣṭi, vicikitsā*;
5. the other [twenty factors] (*śeṣa*) are subsidiary defilements (*upakleśa*): *krodha, upanāha, mrakṣa, pradāśa, īrṣyā, mātsarya, māyā, śāṭhya, mada, vihiṃsā, āhrīkya, anapatrāpya, styāna, auddhatya, āśraddhya, kausīdya, pramāda, muṣitasmṛtitā, vikṣepa, asaṃprajanya*;
6. four [factors], of unstable (or undetermined) character (*gzhan du yang 'gyur ba*): *kaukṛtya, middha, vitarka, vicāra.*

B. According to the *Prakaraṇapāda* (692b20):

There are five factors (*dharma*): (1) material form (*rūpa*); (2) thought (*citta*); (3) the factors of thought-concomitants (*caittadharma*); (4) formations dissociated from thought (*cittaviprayuktasaṃskāra*); (5) unconditioned factors (*asaṃskṛta*). ...

What is thought? It is the thought (*citta*), the mental faculty (*manas*), the consciousness (*vijñāna*), that is to say, the six categories of consciousness, the visual consciousness, etc.

What are the thought-concomitants (*caitta*)? All the factors (*dharma*) associated with thought. What are these factors? Namely, *vedanā, saṃjñā, cetanā, sparśa, manasikāra, chanda, adhimukti, smṛti, samādhi, prajñā, śraddhā, vīrya, vitarka, vicāra, pramāda, apramāda, kuśalamūla, akuśalamūla, avyākṛtamūla*, all the fetters (*saṃyojana*), proclivities (*anuśaya*), subsidiary defilements (*upakleśa*), envelopments (*paryavasthāna*) (v. 47), all that is cognition (*jñāna*; vii. 1), all that is view (*dṛṣṭi*), all that is direct realization (*abhisamaya*; vi. 27), and again all the factors of this type, associated with thought, are thought-concomitants (*caitta*).

Further on (698b28 = *Dhātukāya*, 614b10):

There are eighteen elements (*dhātu*), twelve sense-spheres (*āyatana*), six aggregates (*skandha*), five appropriative aggregates (*upādānaskandha*), six elementary substances (*dhātu*), ten generally permeating factors (*mahābhūmika*), ten wholesome permeating factors (*kuśalamahābhūmika*), ten permeating factors of defilement (*kleśamahābhūmika*), ten factors of defilement of restricted scope (*parīttakleśabhūmika*), five defilements (*kleśa*), five contacts (*saṃsparśa*), five afflicted views (*dṛṣṭi*), five faculties (of sensation) (*indriya*), five factors (*dharma*), six groups of consciousness (*vijñānakāya*), six groups of contact (*sparśakāya*), six groups of sensation (*vedanākāya*), six groups of ideation (*saṃjñākāya*), six groups of intention (*cetanākāya*), six groups of craving (*tṛṣṇākāya*).

What are the eighteen elements (*dhātu*)? ...

What are the six elementary substances (*dhātu*)? Namely, the elementary substance earth... (*Kośa*, i. 28).

What are the ten generally permeating factors (*mahābhūmika*)? Namely, sensation (*vedanā*)... understanding (*prajñā*).

What are the ten wholesome permeating factors (*kuśalamahābhūmika*)? Namely, *śraddhā, vīrya, hrī, apatrapā, alobha, adveṣa, praśrabdhi, upekṣā, apramāda, ahiṃsā.*

What are the ten permeating factors of defilement (*kleśamahābhūmika*)? Namely, *aśrāddhya ... pramāda* (list cited below ii. 26ac).

What are the ten factors of defilement of restricted scope (*parīttakleśabhūmika*)? Namely, *krodha, upanāha, mrakṣa, pradāsa, īrṣyā, mātsarya, śāṭhya, māyā, mada, vihiṃsā.*

What are the five defilements (*kleśa*)? Namely, *kāmarāga, rūparāga, ārūpyarāga, pratigha, vicikitsā* (v. 1).

What are the five afflicted views (*dṛṣṭi*)? Namely, *satkāyadṛṣṭi, antagrāhadṛṣṭi, mithyādṛṣṭi, dṛṣṭiparāmarśa, śīlavrataparāmarśa* (v. 3).

What are the five contacts (*saṃsparśa*)? Namely, *pratighasaṃsparśa, adhivacanasaṃsparśa, vidyāsaṃsparśa, avidyāsaṃsparśa, naivavidyānāvidyāsaṃsparśa* (iii. 30c–31a).

What are the five faculties (of sensation) (*indriya*)? Namely, *sukhendriya, duḥkha-indriya, saumanasyendriya, daurmanasyendriya, upekṣendriya* (ii. 7).

What are the five factors (*dharma*)? Namely, *vitarka, vicāra, vijñāna, āhrīkya, anapatrāpya.* [In the *Kośa*, ii. 27, *vitarka* and *vicāra* are classified as undetermined factors (*aniyata*); ii. 26d, *āhrīkya* and *anapatrāpya* are classified as unwholesome permeating factors (*akuśalamahābhūmika*), a category pictured later, see ii. 32ab; as to the consciousness (*vijñāna*) referred to by the *Prakaraṇa* and the *Dhātukāya*, it refers without doubt to the six groups of consciousness (*vijñānakāya*).]

What are the six groups of consciousness (*vijñānakāya*)? Namely, visual consciousness (*cakṣurvijñāna*), ... mental consciousness (*manovijñāna*).

What are the six groups of contact (*saṃsparśakāya*)? Namely, contact of the eye (*cakṣuḥsaṃsparśa*), ... contact of the mental faculty (*manaḥsaṃsparśa*) (iii. 30b).

What are the six groups of sensation (*vedanākāya*)? Namely, *cakṣuḥsaṃsparśaja-vedanā*... (iii. 32a).

What are the six groups of ideation (*saṃjñākāya*)? Namely, *cakṣuḥsaṃsparśajasaṃjñā*... .

What are the six groups of intention (*cetanākāya*)? Namely, *cakṣuḥsaṃsparśajacetanā*... .

What are the six groups of craving (*tṛṣṇākāya*)? Namely, *cakṣuḥsaṃsparśajatṛṣṇā*... .

The *Dhātukāya* continues by explaining the generally permeating factors (*mahābhūmika*):

What is sensation (*vedanā*)?

See ii. 24 (F 153 note, part C).

C. *Kathāvatthu*, vii. 2–3, the Rājagirikas and the Siddhatthikas deny the association (*saṃprayoga*) of the factors (*dharma*), deny the existence of the thought-concomitants (*caitasika*); ix. 8, the Uttarāpathakas consider initial inquiry (*vitarka*) to be a generally permeating factor (*mahābhūmika*) (the technical term is missing). – *Visuddhimagga*, xiv. – *Abhidhammasaṃ-*

gaha, ii. In *Compendium*, p. 237, S.Z. Aung and C.A.F. Rhys Davids make interesting observations on the development of the doctrine of the thought-concomitants (*cetasika*).

LS: As for the historical development of the various groups of the thought-concomitants (*caitta*), see Bart Dessein's "Dharmas Associated with Awarenesses and the Dating of Sarvāstivāda Abhidharma Works" and Dhammajoti's discussion of the development of the theory of thought-concomitants (*caitasika*) (SA.IV.213–24.):

1. Reference to *cetasika/caitasika* in the *nikāya/āgama*: Dhammajoti comments that there is "no indication of the abhidharmic theory of *caitasika* in *sūtra*-s".

2. Development in the early *abhidharma* texts (*Dharmaskandha-śāstra, Saṃgītiparyāya-śāstra, Prajñapti-śāstra*): theory of *caitasika* characterized by a lack of systematization.

3. Further development in the *abhidharma* texts (from the *Dhātukāya* onwards): explicit classification of the *caittas*.

Dessein comments (p. 631) that it is the *Dhātukāya* in which the category called *mahābhūmika* appears for the first time.

251 *Gokhale*: [23c2–d] *pañcadhā caittā mahābhūmyādibhedataḥ* ||

Tib.: [23c2–d] *sems byung rnam lnga ste | sa mang la sogs tha dad phyir* ||

LS: 1. Vasubandhu's *Pañcaskandhaka* (ISBP.231) states:

> 4. What are the formations? The mental factors other than feeling and conception, and the entities that do not accompany consciousness.
>
> 4.1 What are the mental factors? Those entities that are concomitants of consciousness. What are they? Contact, attention, [...] and reflection.
>
> Among these, five are universal, five are limited to a particular object, eleven are virtues, six are [root] mental afflictions, the remaining ones are secondary mental afflictions, and four can also vary.

2. MVŚ, 220bc, lists (SA.IV.216) seven classes totaling fifty-eight *dharmas*, i.e., adding two classes:

> vi. The universal veiled-non-defined *dharma*-s (*nivṛta-avyākṛta-mahābhūmika*): *dharma*-s which exist in all *nivṛta-avyākṛta-citta*-s—*citta* conjoined with the *satkāyadṛṣṭi* and *antagrahadṛṣṭi* pertaining to the *kāmāvacara*; *citta* conjoined with all the defilements pertaining to the *rūpa*- or *ārūpya-dhātu*; all *nivṛta-avyākṛta-citta*-s existing in the mind-ground [*mano-bhūmi*] or the first five groups of consciousness.
>
> vii. The universal non-veiled-non-defined *dharma*-s (*anivṛta-avyākṛta-mahābhūmika*): *dharma*-s which exist in all *anivṛta-avyākṛta-citta*-s—whether bound to *kāma*-, *rūpa*- or *ārūpya-dhātu*; in the mind-ground or the first five groups of consciousness; whether retribution-born (*vipākaja*), pertaining to deportment (*airyapathika*), pertaining to arts and crafts (*śailpa-sthānika*) or supernormal power (lit. "fruit of higher knowledge", *abhijñā-phala* = *nairmāṇika*).

3. See AKB ii. 30ab for a discussion of the obscured and unobscured non-defined thought and thought-concomitants.

4. For the Sautrāntika explanation of the expression *mahābhūmika* and their doctrine of

the generally permeating factors (*mahābhūmika*), the wholesome permeating factors (*kuśala-mahābhūmika*), etc., see the discussion in chapter 3, F 104ff.

For Vasubandhu's position, see our endnote below.

252 *LS*: The MVŚ, 220b, explains (SA.IV.215): "The universal *dharma*-s (*mahābhūmika*): *dharma*-s which exist in all types of *citta*—whether *kliṣṭa* or *akliṣṭa*; *sāsrava* or *anāsrava*; *kuśala, akuśala* or *avyākṛta*; bound to the three realms of existence or not bound to any sphere; pertaining to the trainee (*śaikṣa*), to the non-trainee (*aśaikṣa*) or to neither; abandonable by vision (*darśana-heya*), by cultivation (*bhāvanā-heya*) or not to be abandoned (*aheya*); in the mind-ground (*mano-bhūmi*) or in the first five groups of consciousness."

253 *LS*: The MVŚ, 220 b–c, explains (SA.IV.216): "The universal *dharma*-s of defilement (*kleśa-mahābhūmika*): *dharma*-s which exist in all defiled *citta*-s—whether *akuśala* or *avyākṛta*; bound to any sphere of existence; abandonable by vision or cultivation; in the mind-ground or the first five groups of consciousness."

254 *LS*: The MVŚ, 220 b–c, explains (SA.IV.216): "The defilements of restricted scope (*parītta-kleśa-bhūmika*): *dharma*-s which exist only in a small number of defiled *citta*-s, are abandonable by cultivation and exist in only the mind-ground; 'when one arises there is necessarily not a second one, being mutually opposed'."

255 *LS*: Regarding the undetermined (*aniyata*) thought-concomitants, Dhammajoti writes (SA.IV.222f.):

> Among the extant *abhidharma* texts, AKB was apparently the first to make an explicit mention of this class. ... This class seems to be acceptable to the Vaibhāṣikas; Saṃghabhadra, for one, mentions it in the same way [Ny, 392a].
>
> Yaśomitra explains that they refer to "those which sometimes exist in a skillful, sometimes in an unskillful, sometimes in a non-defined thought. ...
>
> Yaśomitra [Vy, 132.14ff.] further remarks that by the word "etc. [i.e., *middh'ādayaḥ*; AKB ii. 27]", in Vasubandhu's prose commentary, are to be included:
>
> 1. secondary defilements (*upakleśa*) such as disgust (*arati*), yawning (*vijṛmbhikā*), exhaustion (*tandrī*), uneven consumption of food (*bhakte asamatā*) (these four together with mental sunken-ness (*cetaso līnatva*) occur in AKB [v. 59bc] as the five nourishments (*āhāra*) of torpor-sleep (*styāna-middha*); and
> 2. defilements such as greed (*rāga*), etc. "These [thought-concomitants], greed, etc., are indeterminate with regard to [their inclusion in] any of the five classes: They are not *mahābhūmika*-s because they are not found in all cases of thought; not *kuśala-mahābhūmika*-s because they are not connected with skillfulness (*kuśalatva-ayogāt*); not *kleśa-mahābhūmika*-s because they are not found in all cases of defiled thought—for greed does not exist in a mind conjoined with hostility (*sa-pratighe cetasi*) nor does hostility exist in a mind conjoined with greed (*sarāge cetasi*)" [WOG.132.15ff.].

He further quotes a stanza [WOG.132.20ff.] by *ācārya* Vasumitra which states that eight *aniyata dharma*-s are recognized—*vitarka, vicāra, kaukṛtya, middha, pratigha, śakti* (= *rāga*), *māna* and *vicikitsā*. It is to be noted that later on Pu Guang, a prominent disciple of Xuan Zang, followed this tradition and explained that the word "etc."

in the AKB stanza subsumes greed, hostility, conceit and doubt.

However, Yaśomitra here objects [WOG.132.23f.] to the number of eight, for "why are view (*dṛṣṭi*), etc., not conceded as indeterminate as well—since false view [*mithyā-dṛṣṭi*] does not arise in a thought conjoined with either hostility or doubt?"

256 *LS*: AH 17; SAH 55–56.

257 *LS*: AH 17, SAH 56.

258 *LVP*: According to the MVŚ, 80b8, cited by the Japanese editor: What is the meaning of the expression *mahābhūmikadharma*?

1. The *great* refers to thought; these ten factors are the *bhūmi*, the place of arising of thought; being the *bhūmi* of the "great", they are called *mahābhūmi*. Being *mahābhūmi* and *dharmas*, they are *mahābhūmikadharmas*.

2. Some say: Thought is great due to the superiority of its nature and of its activity; it is great and it is a *bhūmi*, thus it is called *mahābhūmi*, because it is the place that serves as basis of the thought-concomitants (*caitta*). The ten factors (*dharma*), sensation (*vedanā*), etc., because one encounters them everywhere in the *mahābhūmi*, are called *mahābhūmikadharmas*.

3. Some say: The ten factors (*dharma*), sensation, etc., occurring everywhere with thought, are called *great*; thought, being their *bhūmi*, is called *mahābhūmi*; sensation, etc., being inherent in the *mahābhūmi*, are called *mahābhūmikadharmas*.

Vasubandhu reproduces the third etymology.

We shall see (iii. 32ab [F 104f.]) that Śrīlābha does not admit this definition of the term *mahābhūmika*.

Theory of the connection (*saṃsarga*) of *paññā* and *viññāṇa*, *Majjhima*, i, 293.

259 *LS*: AH 17; SAH 55.

260 *LS*: LVP has in his volume 1: resolution (*adhimukti*) instead of resolve (*adhimokṣa*), but footnote iii, F 104 states: "One should replace *adhimukti* by *adhimokṣa* at ii, F 153, 155." Also in LVP's *Additions and Corrections* (vol. vi), he writes: "F 153: Read *adhimokṣa* and not *adhimukti*. The reading *adhimukti* seemed justified to me based on *Vyākhyā* cited vol. ii, F 154, n. 5".

261 *Gokhale*: [24] *vedanā cetanā saṃjñā chandaḥ sparśo matiḥ smṛtiḥ | manaskāro 'dhimokṣaś ca samādhiḥ sarvacetasi ||*

Tib.: [24] *tshor dang sems pa 'du shes dang | 'dun dang reg dang blo gros dran | yid la byed dang mos pa dang | ting nge 'dzin sems thams cad la ||*

LVP: [In regard to *adhimokṣa/adhimukti*, note that we adjusted the *kārikā* and its commentary, since LVP states in his footnote at iii, F 104 that one should replace *adhimukti* by *adhimokṣa* at ii, F 153, 155; but we did not adjust his footnotes.]

A. Hsüan-tsang corrects: *vedanā, saṃjñā, cetanā, sparśa, chanda, prajñā, smṛti, manaskāra, adhimukti, samādhi.*

The order of the Abhidharma (*Prakaraṇapāda, Dhātukāya*) is the following: *vedanā, saṃjñā, cetanā, sparśa, manaskāra, chanda, adhimukti, smṛti, samādhi, prajñā.*

Vasubandhu (*Pañcaskandhaka*) distinguishes five pervasive (*sarvatraga*) factors: *sparśa, manaskāra, vedanā, saṃjñā* and *cetanā*, and five object-specific (*pratiniyataviṣaya*) factors: *chanda, adhimukti, smṛti, samādhi* and *prajñā*.

The order of *Mahāvyutpatti* 104 (which reads *adhimokṣa*) differs from other sources.

The reading of *adhimukti* is confirmed by the *Vyākhyā* citing *Bhāṣya*, ii. 26ac, F 162.

B. We have inserted the essential part from the *Vyākhyā* [WOG.127.23–128.7] into the text:

> *cetanā cittābhisaṃskāra* iti. *citta*-praspandaḥ praspanda iva praspanda ity arthaḥ. *viśaya-nimitta-grāha* iti. *viṣaya*-viśeṣa-rūpa-*grāha* ity arthaḥ. *sparśa-indriya-viṣaya-vijñāna-saṃnipāta-jā spṛṣṭir* iti. *indriya-viṣaya-vijñānānāṃ saṃnipātāj* jātā *spṛṣṭiḥ*. *spṛṣṭir* iva *spṛṣṭiḥ*. yad-yogād *indriya-viṣaya-vijñānāny* anyonyaṃ spṛśantīva sa *sparśaḥ*. *dharma-pravicaya* iti. pravicinotīti *pravicayaḥ*. pravicīyante vā anena *dharmā* iti *pravicayaḥ*. yena saṃkīrṇā iva *dharmāḥ*. puṣpāṇīva pravicīyante uccīyanta ity arthaḥ. ime sāsravā ime 'nāsravāḥ. ime rūpiṇaḥ ime 'rūpiṇa iti. dharmāṇāṃ pravicayaḥ *dharma-pravicayaḥ*. pratītatvāt prajñeti vaktavye śloka-bandh'ānu guṇyena *matir* iti kārikāyām uktaṃ. *smṛtir ālambanāsampramoṣa* iti. yad-yogād *ālambanaṃ* na mano vismarati. tac cābhilapatīva. sā smṛtiḥ *manaskāraś cetasa ābhoga* iti. ālambane *cetasa* āvarjanam. avadhāraṇam ity arthaḥ. manasaḥ kāre *manaskāraḥ*. mano vā karoti āvarjayatīti *manaskāraḥ*. *adhimuktis tad-ālambanasya* guṇato *'vadhāraṇaṃ*. rucir ity anye. yathāniścayayaṃ dhāraṇeti. Yog'ācāra-cittāḥ. *samādhiś cittasyaikāgrateti*. *agram* ālambanam ity eko 'rthaḥ. yad-yogāc cittaṃ prabhandena ekatr' ālambane vartāte. sa *samādhiḥ*. yadi samādhiḥ sarva-cetasi bhavati. kim arthaṃ dhyāneṣu yatnaḥ kriyate. balavat-samādhi-niṣpādanārthaṃ. .

Here is the Tibetan version of the *Bhāṣya*:

'tshor ba ni myong ba rnam pa gsum ste | bde ba dang | sdug bsngal dang | bde ba yang ma yin sdug bsngal yang ma yin pa'o || sems pa ni sems mngon par 'du byed pa'o || 'du shes ni 'dus nas shes pa ste | yul la mtshan mar 'dzin pa'o || 'dun pa ni byed 'dod pa'o || reg pa ni yul dang dbang po dang rnam par shes pa 'dus pa las skyes pa'i reg pa'o || blo gros ni shes rab ste | chos rab tu rnam par 'byed pa'o || dran pa ni dmigs pa mi brjed pa'o || yid la byed pa ni sems kyi 'jug pa'o || mos pa ni 'dod pa'o || ting nge 'dzin ni sems rtsa gcig pa nyid do |

C. The *Dhātukāya* (614c22) gives definitions that are all in the style of the Abhidhamma. For example, concentration (*samādhi*) is defined: "The *sthiti* of thought, the *saṃsthiti*, the *abhiṣṭhiti*, the *upasthiti*, the *avikṣepa*, the *aghaṭṭana*, the *saṃdhāraṇa*, the *śamatha*, the *samādhi*, the *cittasyaikāgratā*, this is what is called *concentration*." (*Vibhaṅga*, p. 217, *Dhammasaṅgaṇi*, 11).

In the same way, sensation (*vedanā*) is *vedanā, saṃvedanā, pratisaṃvedanā, vedita*, that which will be experienced, that which is included within *vedanā*. – Mindfulness (*smṛti*) is *smṛti, anusmṛti, pratismṛti, smaraṇa, asaṃpramoṣatā ... cetaso 'bhilāpa*.

262 *LVP*: The word *kila* ["so said", "so reported"] shows that the author presents the opinion of the School (*Vibhāṣā*, 12, 10). He has explained his own doctrine in the *Pañcaskandhaka* cited in *Vyākhyā* to iii. 32 [WOG.339.7ff.,]; we will compare the definitions of this text with those of the *Twenty Verses, Siddhi* and *Abhisamayālaṃkārāloka*.

LS: See iii. 104f. for a discussion of different interpretations of the status of the generally permeating factors (*mahābhūmika*) and Vasubandhu's stance on it. Referring to iii. 104f., Kritzer comments (RCYA.135) "Vasubandhu agrees with the Vaibhāṣikas regarding the meaning of *mahābhūmika* and the simultaneity of *sparśa* and *vedanā* and disagrees with the opponent, even though he only accepts half of the Vaibhāṣikas' list of *mahābhūmikas* as being truly universal. Elsewhere [WOG.127.20–23], Yaśomitra refers to the *Pañcaskandhaka* to show the contrast between a position mentioned in the *Abhidharmakośabhāṣya* and Vasubandhu's own. For example, when Vasubandhu comments on *Abhidharmakośa* II 24, which gives the Vaibhāṣika list of *mahābhūmikas*, he uses the word *kila* to indicate that he himself does not believe that they are all present at every moment, and Yaśomitra mentions the definitions of *chanda* and *adhimokṣa* in the *Pañcaskandhaka* to illustrate that Vasubandhu really believes that they are *pratiniyata* [i.e., of limited occurence]."

Dhammajoti explains (private communication) that "although in AKB ii. 24, Vasubandhu uses '*kila*' when explaining the Vaibhāṣika view that there are ten *mahābhūmika*-s, he does not contest their realities. Saṃghabhadra (Ny, 384aff.) also does not charge that Vasubandhu denies any of them. He disputes only with Śrīlāta who asserts that there are only three *mahābhūmika*-s, denying *sparśa* and the rest as non-entities (Ny, 384b). ... [Also note that] in AKB iii. 28cd, Vasubandhu refutes the Sautrāntikas and others, and adopts the Sarvāstivāda view that *avidyā* is a distinct entity.

It is fairly safe to say that Vasubandhu accepts at least the ten thought-concomitants known as the *mahābhūmika*-s even though he may classify them somewhat differently, as in his *Pañcaskandhaka* (following Yaśomitra's suggestion): There he groups the first five as '*sarvatraga*', and the next five as '*pratiniyata*' (as in Yogācāra). In fact, if we judge by this text, he would accept most of the *caitta*-s enumerated in AKB. Note further that he describes them all as *saṃprayukta-saṃskāra*-s, conjoined with *citta*. (This remark, however, does not take into consideration the question as to whether at the time of composing the *Pañcaskandhaka* he had already held the view of *vijñaptimātra*)."

263 *LS*: Vasubandhu's *Pañcaskandhaka* (ISBP.231) states:

> 2. What is feeling? The three types of experience: pleasant, unpleasant, and neither pleasant nor unpleasant. A pleasant experience is one that you desire to be united with again when it ceases. An unpleasant experience is one that you desire to be separated from when it arises. An experience that is neither pleasant nor unpleasant is one for which you develop neither of those desires when it occurs.

Avatāra (EṢD.79): "There are three kinds of experience (*anubhava*): (i) pleasurable (*sukha*), (ii) unpleasurable (*duḥkha*) and (iii) neither pleasurable nor unpleasurable (*aduḥkha-asukha*). These are the experiencing of three results of contact (*sparśānubhavana*)."

264 *LS*: Vasubandhu's *Pañcaskandhaka* (2008) states:

> 4.1.5 *cetanā katamā | guṇato doṣato 'nubhayataś cittābhisaṃskāro manaskarma |*
>
> 4.1.5 What is volition? It is the shaping of consciousness in relation to that which is good, bad, or neither; and it is activity of the mind. ISBP.232

Ny, 384b (SA.IV.217): "*Cetanā* is that which causes *citta* to do *kuśala*, *akuśala* and *avyākṛta* [*karma*], resulting in good, bad and neutral [*vipāka*]. On account of the existence of *cetanā*, the *citta* has the activity of moving forth with regard to the object. It is like a magnet, owing to the force of which iron can move forth."

Avatāra (ESD.82): "Volition (*cetanā*) is that which renders thought [karmically] creative (*abhisaṃskāra*)—it is mental *karma*. This is also to say that it moves forth (*pra-√syand*) the thought."

[265] *LS*: Vasubandhu's *Pañcaskandhaka* (ISBP.231) states:

> 3. What is conception? The grasping of an object's sign, which is of three types: limited, great, and immeasurable.

Ny, 384b (SA.IV.218): "That which causes the determination and grasping of the diverse forms (*nimitta*) of male, female, etc., is named ideation."

Avatāra (ESD.80): "This is that which comprehends, by combining conceptually (*saṃ-√jñā*) the appearance (*nimitta*), name (*nāma*) and the signified (*artha*) [of a *dharma*]. That is, with regard to matter like blue, yellow, long and short [figures], etc.; sounds like those of a conch-shell, a drum, etc.; smells like those of gharu-wood and musk, etc., tastes like those of saltiness and bitterness, etc., tangibles like those of hardness and softness, etc., *dharma*-s like males and females, etc.—it comprehends them, [in each case], by conceptually combining together (*eka-√jñā*) their appearances, names and signification. It is the cause of reasoning (*vitarka*) and investigation (*vicāra*). Thus, this is named ideation."

[266] *LVP*: Compare *Atthasālinī*, 329: *kattukamyatā*. (See ii. 55cd and iii. 1, where predilection (*chanda*) is defined as *anāgate prārthanā*.)

LS: 1. Vasubandhu's *Pañcaskandhaka* (2008) states:

> 4.1.6 *chandaḥ katamaḥ | abhiprete vastuny abhilāṣaḥ |*
>
> 4.1.6 What is aspiration? The desire for an object that has been thought about. ISBP.232

Sthiramati, commenting on the *Pañcaskandhaka*, states (ISBP.277f.):

> The reason for saying that the object must be one that "has been thought about" is to make clear that no aspiration can develop toward something that has not been thought about. Thus, it indicates the quality that aspiration [only] occurs in relation to a particular kind of object.
>
> An entity that has been thought about is one that has been considered as a possible object for such actions as seeing, hearing, and the like. Thus, [aspiration is] a desire for and an eagerness to see, hear, etc., some particular thing.

Avatāra (ESD.82): "Predilection (*chanda*) is the liking for an undertaking (*kartu-kāmatā*). It accords with vigor (*vīrya*), [arising from the thought]: 'I will make such and such an undertaking'."

2. Dhammajoti comments (SA.IV.218) that *chanda* is the desire for action (*kartu-kāmatā*) and is indispensable for the undertaking of any action, wholesome or unwholesome. AKB v. 16 and 18ab distinguish *chanda* from desire in the bad sense of attachment (*rāga*) and craving (*tṛṣṇā*).

[267] *LS*: 1. Vasubandhu's *Pañcaskandhaka* (2008) states:

> 4.1.1 *sparśaḥ katamaḥ | trikasamavāye paricchedaḥ |*
>
> 4.1.1 What is contact? The determination that occurs upon the convergence of three. ISBP.232

Avatāra (ESD.82): "Contact (*sparśa*) is that which is born of the coming together (*saṃ-*

nipātaja) of the faculty, the object and consciousness, and which enables thought to come in contact with the object. It has the characteristic of enlivening the thought-concomitants (*caitasika-dharma-jīvanalakṣaṇaḥ*)."

2. Kritzer comments (RCYA.113) that this is Vasubandhu's clearest and most detailed description of the Sarvāstivādin definition of contact. Vasubandhu, however, does not discuss the Dārṣṭāntika position on contact here. For this and the controversy in regard to its existential status, see Vasubandhu's more detailed discussion of contact at iii. 30b–31 (F 95–101).

Dhammajoti writes (SA.IV.218): "The early Sarvāstivādin Dārṣṭāntikas deny the reality of contact, citing the *sūtra* passage which speaks of the coming together of the three—the visual faculty, the visible and the visual consciousness—as contact. So also the Sautrāntika Śrīlāta. The MVŚ compilers argue that contact is not the mere meeting of these three. They in fact serve as the conditions for the arising of a real entity called contact. Without the operation of this real force, the fact of contact among the three would be impossible." But the MVŚ, 983c–984, also distinguishes between two kinds of contact (ESD.142):

> Question: The *sparśa* conjoined with the [first] five sensory consciousnesses arises from the *indriya*, *viṣaya* and *vijñāna* [which equally exist] in the present: It is said to be a *sparśa* [born of] the coming-together of the three—this is admissible. [But in the case of] the *sparśa* conjoined with *manovijñāna*, the *indriya* is past, the *viṣaya* may be [present, past or] future, the *vijñāna* is present, how can it be said to be a *sparśa* [born of] the coming-together?
>
> Answer: There are two kinds of coming-together: (i) coming-together in the sense of co-arising and mutually not separated from each other; (ii) coming-together in the sense of not mutually contradictory, and co-operating in achieving one and the same thing.

268 *LVP*: *Pañcaskandhaka*: *upaparīkṣye vastuni pravicayo yogāyogavihito 'nyathā ca.*

LS: 1. Vasubandhu's *Pañcaskandhaka* (2008) states (ISBP.232, 235):

> 4.1.10 *prajñā katamā | tatraiva pravicayo yogāyogavihito 'nyathā ca |*
>
> 4.1.10 What is wisdom? Discrimination with respect to that same object [i.e., the object that is closely examined], whether it is generated correctly, incorrectly, or otherwise.
>
> 4.1.26 *dṛṣṭiḥ katamā | pañca dṛṣṭayaḥ – satkāyadṛṣṭir antagrāhadṛṣṭir mithyādṛṣṭir dṛṣṭiparāmarśaḥ śīlavrataparāmarśaś ca |*
>
> 4.1.26 What are views? There are five views: the perishable collection view, the view that grasps an extreme, wrong view, the consideration that views are supreme, and the consideration that morality and asceticism are supreme.
>
> 4.1.26.1 *satkāyadṛṣṭiḥ katamā | pañcopādānaskandhān ātmata ātmīyato vā samanupaśyato yā kliṣṭā prajñā |*
>
> 4.1.26.1 What is the perishable collection view? The afflicted wisdom that regards the five grasping heaps as "I" and "mine".
>
> 4.1.26.2 *antagrāhadṛṣṭiḥ katamā | tām evādhipatiṃ kṛtvā śāśvatata ucchedato vā samanupaśyato yā kliṣṭā prajñā |*
>
> 4.1.26.2 What is the view that grasps an extreme? The afflicted wisdom that, in

relation to that very [view], regards [its object] as undergoing extinction or as existing permanently.

4.1.26.3 *mithyādṛṣṭiḥ katamā | hetuṃ vāpavadataḥ phalaṃ vā kriyāṃ vā sad vā vastu nāśayato vā yā kliṣṭā prajñā |*

4.1.26.3 What is wrong view? The afflicted wisdom that denies causes, results, and actions, and rejects entities that exist.

4.1.26.4 *dṛṣṭiparāmarśaḥ katamaḥ | tām eva ca trividhāṃ dṛṣṭiṃ tadāśrayāṃś ca skandhān agrataḥ śreṣṭhato viśiṣṭataḥ paramataḥ samanupaśyato yā kliṣṭā prajñā |*

4.1.26.4 What is the consideration that views are supreme? The afflicted wisdom that regards those very three views and their basis, the heaps, as foremost, superior, most excellent, and the highest.

4.1.26.5 *śīlavrataparāmarśaḥ katamaḥ | śīlaṃ vrataṃ tadāśrayāṃś ca skandhān śuddhito muktito nairyāṇikataś ca samanupaśyato yā kliṣṭā prajñā |*

4.1.26.5 What is the consideration that morality and asceticism are supreme? The afflicted wisdom that regards morality, asceticism, and their basis, the heaps, as purifying, liberating, and conducive to deliverance.

Sthiramati, commenting on the *Pañcaskandhaka*, states (ISBP.280):

> The phrase "That same object" means the very same "object that is closely examined". Thus, wisdom is also being indicated as having a specific object, as was the case with concentration.

Avatāra (ESD.83): "Understanding (*prajña*) is the discernment (*pravicaya*) of *dharma*-s. It is the examination (*upalakṣaṇa*), as the case may be, of the following eight kinds of *dharma*-s: inclusion (*saṃgraha*), conjunction (*saṃprayoga*), endowment (*samanvāgama*), causes (*hetu*), conditions (*pratyaya*), fruitions (*phala*), specific-characteristic (*sva-lakṣaṇa*), common-characteristic (*sāmānya-lakṣaṇa*)."

2. Vasubandhu has already discussed the importance of understanding (*prajñā*) in the context of (i) the three types of Abhidharma (i. 2ab), (ii) cessation due to deliberation (*pratisaṃkhyā-nirodha*), (iii) the three types of conceptualizing activity (*vikalpa*; i. 33) and (iv) the last four controlling faculties (i. 48cd and beginning of chapter 2), i.e., the praxis-oriented faculty of understanding (*prajñendriya*) and the three pure controlling faculties: the faculty of coming to know what is not yet known (*anājñātamājñāsyāmīndriya*), the faculty of perfect knowledge (*ājñendriya*) and the faculty of final and perfect knowledge (*ājñātāvīndriya*). See in particular our endnotes to i. 2ab and 33, which list the main issues and the other main sections where *prajñā* is discussed in the AKB. Dhammajoti summarizes as follows (SA.IV.218f.):

> [Understanding (*prajñā*)], defined as the investigation of *dharma*-s (*dharmapravicaya*), is one of the most important *caitta*-s. For the Ābhidharmikas, "apart from *dharma-pravicaya* (= *prajñā*), there is no proper means for the appeasement of defilements on account of which the world wanders in the ocean of existence" [AKB i. 3]. In its pure form, it is *abhidharma per se* [i. 2a]. The specific understanding that operates in the discernment of the four noble truths in the course of spiritual progress is called discriminative deliberation (/consideration) [i. 6]. It is through this that absolute cessation of a defilement, and finally *nirvāṇa* (= *pratisaṃkhyā-nirodha*), is

> acquired. In other words, when fully perfected, *prajñā* is the perfect wisdom of a Buddha. However, in its general functioning, it may be pure or impure, right or erroneous. Thus, all views, both right or false, are *prajñā* in their essential nature. Likewise, *asaṃprajanya* [lack of proper discernment] and *akliṣta-ajñāna* [non-defiled ignorance] are also *prajñā*. *Prajñā* is in fact the *sine qua non* for the element of understanding in any perceptual process. Saṃghabhadra explains [Ny, 396a] that, among the various *caitta*-s conjoined with a *citta*, it is *prajñā* alone that has the function of being aware. It plays a predominant role in powering the mental capacity of conceptual discrimination.

In regard to *prajñā* as defilement (*kleśa*), i.e., the five afflicted views (*dṛṣṭi*), see chapter 5, particularly v, F 15–26.

269 *LVP*: See i. 33; ii, F 162; vi, F 258.

LS: 1. Vasubandhu's *Pañcaskandhaka* (2008) states (SWV.68–69):

> 4.1.8 *smṛtiḥ katamā | saṃstute vastuny asampramoṣaś cetaso 'bhilapanatā |*
>
> 4.1.8 What is recollection? The avoidance of inattentiveness toward a familiar object; a state of mental discourse. ISBP.232

Sthiramati, commenting on the *Pañcaskandhaka*, states (ISBP.279):

> The term "familiar" indicates that there can be no recollection of an object that is unfamiliar. A familiar object is one that was previously experienced.

Saṃghabhadra (Ny, 384b7f; OP.60): "Mindfulness is the cause of the notation (*abhilapana*) and non-loss (*asaṃpramoṣa*) of the object-support."

Avatāra (ESD.83): "Mindfulness (*smṛti*) is that which enables thought to remember an object clearly (*cittasyārthābhilapanā*); i.e., not to forget (*avipramoṣa*) what has been done (*kṛta*), is now being done (*kriyamāna*), or will be done in the future (*kartavya*)."

2. Vasubandhu has already discussed the importance of mindfulness (*smṛti*) in the context of the three types of conceptualizing activity (*vikalpa*; i. 33) and the last four controlling faculties (i. 48cd and beginning of chapter 2), i.e., the praxis-oriented faculty of mindfulness (*smṛti-indriya*) and the three pure controlling faculties: the faculty of coming to know what is not yet known (*anājñātamājñāsyāmīndriya*), the faculty of perfect knowledge (*ājñendriya*) and the faculty of final and perfect knowledge (*ājñātāvīndriya*). As one of the five praxis-oriented controlling faculties it is naturally also addressed throughout chapter 6 (EXPOSITION OF THE PATH AND THE PERSONS), as also within chapter 7 (EXPOSITION OF THE COGNITIONS) and chapter 8 (EXPOSITION OF THE MEDITATIVE ATTAINMENTS). Memory is discussed in chapter 9 (F 273–79). Depending on the context, in the AKB *smṛti*, *smaraṇa*, etc., are discussed and translated variously (conceptualizing activity consisting of recollecting; mindfulness; applications of mindfulness; memory; etc.): see i. 33, 48cd; v, F 6f; vi. 14ff; ix, F 273–79.

3. As for our definition here in the AKB, Jaini comments (CPBS.281f., 284):

> Vasubandhu ... defines *smṛti* as the "retention of" or "not letting drop the object" (*ālambana-asampramoṣa*). He however does not specify if the term *object* in this definition is past or present and thus leaves open the possibility that the term could be taken to mean either memory of the past or mindfulness of the present. ... [Yet] the fact that *smṛti* is found in every mental event can only lead one to conclude

> that here too the term *smṛti* is understood to mean mindfulness and not memory of the past, for the latter is not a phenomenon that occurs at all times. Vasubandhu must have perceived some anomaly here, for in this *Pañcaskandhakaprakaraṇa*, *smṛti* is not included in the group of mental factors that occur invariably, but in the next group of five factors that are found only in certain mental events (*viniyata-dharmas*). [...]
>
> We already have referred to Vasubandhu's brief definition of *smṛti* and how it was understood as mindfulness by the Vaibhāṣikas. However, in his appendix to the *Abhidharmakośabhāṣya*, called the *Pudgalaviniścaya*, Vasubandhu provides us with detailed material on *smṛti*, not as he defined it earlier as mindfulness, but as memory of the past.

4. As for the historical development of mindfulness, in his article *The four concentrations of mindfulness: on the historical development of a spiritual practice of Buddhism* (VKA265), Lambert Schmithausen comments that the four concentrations of mindfulness could be seen to function as a mirror for a great part of the Buddhist history of ideas, in which, in the course of development, nearly all dominant theories of the different directions of Buddhism are mirrored. He states that—originally being largely a formal, content-neutral training of the capacity of attentiveness—the framework of the four "concentrations of mindfulness" was, at the same time, an empty structure, which, if need be, could be filled with all kinds of possible contents and indeed also was so filled. Here we will therefore discuss *smṛti* more extensively by relying mainly on Collett Cox's article *Mindfulness and memory. The scope of smṛti from early Buddhism to the Sarvāstivāda Abhidharma.*

i. In her *Introduction* she comments that it would be tempting to distinguish two distinct functions of *smṛti* which, in various contexts, suggest themselves, namely, *smṛti* (a) as a technique central to religious praxis and (b) as an aspect of ordinary psychological processes. The first is a mode of attentiveness operative in several Buddhist models for practice and the second coincides with some of the psychological operations normally associated in the West with memory: specifically, retention and recollection. She concludes, however, that "the apparent twofold distinction in the functioning of *smṛti* does not represent a semantic bifurcation, but rather an interrelated semantic complex".

ii. *Mindfulness in Early Buddhist Scriptures*: In the first actual part of her article she investigates mindfulness in early Buddhist scriptures, where mindfulness refers "almost exclusively to techniques of religious praxis, its importance ... amply indicated by its inclusion in many of the lists of exercises or qualities that the early scriptural collections recommend as aids in abandoning all defilements and attaining enlightenment" [see vi. 67–75b]. In this context she also refers to Schmithausen's article *The four concentrations of mindfulness*, which reconstructs the original form of this practice. Schmithausen summarizes his results (VKA.265f.):

> [a] [The original form] must have consisted in a progressive training of the faculty of awareness, starting from various bodily postures as simple objects of Mindfulness, then passing over to feelings and mental states as subtler objects, and finally directed on the psychic factors (*dharmas*) responsible for bondage and release, and on the mechanism of their origination, the aim being to subjugate the bad factors and foster the good ones.

> [b] In the literary form which the four Applications of Mindfulness have found in the received *Satipaṭṭhānasutta*, the description of the Application of Mindfulness to the Body has been enlarged by the incorporation of various other spiritual practices concerned with the body, especially breath control, contemplation of the impure constituents of the body, and contemplation of corpses.
>
> The last two practices seem to reveal a tendency to choose objects of meditation because they were suited not only to train awareness, but also to inculcate the detestability and negativity of existence and thus to prepare the way for the realization of the Noble Truth of Suffering. [...]
>
> [c] The tendency to transform the four Applications of Mindfulness into forms of contemplation aimed at evaluating their objects in terms of the Buddhist analysis of existence thus virtually anticipating the realization of the Noble Truth of Suffering, is particularly in evidence in a part of a stereotyped conclusion formula which recurs at the end of each paragraph of the *Satipaṭṭhānasutta* and which admonishes that one should contemplate on the objects of meditation of the paragraph concerned as subject to origination and decay.

In the context of the early Buddhist scripture, Cox comments that the practice of mindfulness is often treated as being "tantamount to the central praxis of Buddhism: namely, as the single path leading to the ultimate soteriological goal of enlightenment and nirvāṇa". She then also addresses the operation of mindfulness and its relation to other mental functions, for example, to awareness (*samprajanya*).

iii. *Mindfulness as a Technique of Religious Praxis in Abhidharma*: In the second part of her article, Collett Cox focuses in particular on the four applications of mindfulness (see vi. 14–16), in regard to which Schmithausen continues his above summary:

> And the same tendency is systematically worked out by the Hīnayāna Schools of Abhidharma, especially by the Sarvāstivādins, who explicitly define the four Applications of Mindfulness as a spiritual exercise preparatory to the realization of the Four Noble Truths and as consisting in contemplating on their objects as impermanent, entailing suffering (*duḥkha*), and without Self.

Cox states (p. 73f.):

> The northern Indian Abhidharma texts continue the tradition of mindfulness as a technique of religious praxis, but not without significant changes in its character and operation. The four applications of mindfulness are no longer recommended as a completely independent and self-sufficient technique of praxis, but rather are included as the first four members in the standardized list of thirty-seven aids to enlightenment (*bodhipakṣya*). The thirty-seven aids are further incorporated within a new path structure [i.e., the five paths] [...] Though particularly associated with and predominant in this initial stage of praxis, the four applications, like all of the subsequent aids, nonetheless are said to characterize the entire path from their stage of predominance onward. Therefore, they continue to be practiced throughout the entire path. [...] When discussing the four applications of mindfulness, Abhidharma texts focus on three issues: [a] the nature of their respective objects; [b] the distinctive character of their mode of operation; and [c] their relation to other techniques of

religious praxis.

As for the first issue, the objects taken together are extended to encompass all possible factors (see vi. 14cd, 16).

As for the second and third, Cox comments (p. 75) that "the four applications, originally classified within the mindfulness component among the controlling factors, forces, limbs of enlightenment, and members of the eightfold noble path, are reclassified in later Abhidharma texts among the corresponding insight [*prajñā*] components" (see vi. 15ab). She then investigates the relationship between mindfulness and understanding (*prajñā*) (see vi, F 160f.). At vi, F 160f., discussing the compound *smṛtyupasthāna* (mindfulness applications), Vasubandhu presents the two alternatives, i.e., either understanding is applied through mindfulness or mindfulness through understanding. Vasubandhu opts for the second, i.e., in the operation of mindfulness, one fixes or notes (*abhilapana*) the object through mindfulness as it had been seen through understanding. This then forms the bridge to the psychological retentive, and possibly recollective, aspects of mindfulness as discussed here at ii. 24 and later in chapter 9, F 274–78.

iv. *The Development of a Psychological Description of Mindfulness in Abhidharma*: In the third part of her article, Collett Cox explains that parallel to the reinterpretation of the applications of mindfulness as varieties of understanding (*prajñā*), "there emerges a new analysis of the function of mindfulness as an ordinary psychological operation", i.e., as a thought-concomitant (*caitta*); thus mindfulness is no longer simply equated with the soteriologically oriented four applications of mindfulness. This then is also reflected in the definitions of mindfulness in which the psychological description becomes more and more the norm in Abhidharma texts. For example, the *Prakaraṇapāda* (627b23) defines mindfulness as the nonloss (or nondrifting) of mind events and the *Śariputrābhidharmaśāstra* (624a21) as retention (**smaraṇa*) and recollection (**pratisamaraṇa*, **saṃsmaraṇa*). In this context she then also explores the various connotations of *abhilapana*—which plays a key role in later Abhidharma psychological definitions of mindfulness—for which there are at least two possible derivations, each of which lending a different sense to the operation of mindfulness (p. 81):

> one derived from the root *plu*, "to float", with a privative prefix (*a-pilāpana*); the other apparently derived from the root *lap* possibly in the sense "to repeat" or, especially in the causative, "to note" with a prefix *api*, or possibly *abhi*. The derivation from the root *plu* with a privative would support the sense of "not drifting", "entering", or "fixing". The derivation from the root *lap* could have the sense of "to repeat" or, especially in the causative, "to note" [LS: causing one to be attentive to factors and to cultivate them], or possibly the sense of "to chatter" or "to express".

v. *The Psychological Operation of Mindfulness in Recollection and Memory*: Cox comments that later Abhidharma treatises furnish more information in regard to the psychological function of mindfulness as a discrete mental factor (pp. 82f.):

> This is provided in descriptions of the relation of mindfulness to other mental factors, in arguments concerning its existential status, and finally, in examinations of the events of retention and recollection, in which mindfulness plays a central role. ... [T]he operation of mindfulness and, in particular, its role in the act of recollection must be understood in terms of the general Buddhist model of psychological

> functioning. [...] There are two divergent interpretative models: that supported by the Kāśmīra Sarvāstivādins of a single mind event associated with concomitant factors; and that advanced by the Dārṣṭāntikas of a mind event followed by mental factors in a series. These two models of psychological functioning entail a radically different understanding of the operation of mindfulness and the event of recollection.

In this context, Cox explains the following (pp. 83–85):

> Mindfulness functions to cause the nonloss (*asampramoṣa*) of the object, and the fixing or noting (*abhilapana*) by the mind of the object. Such a definition is ambiguous—it could refer either to functions critical to the maintenance of meditative concentration, or to the more prosaic act of retention. However, there is some evidence to indicate that such a definition of mindfulness refers explicitly to the ordinary psychological event of recollection. In the course of a discussion on the relation between mindfulness and insight, the *Mahāvibhāṣā* presents several distinctive functions of mindfulness that relate to the event of recollection: for example, through the power of mindfulness, the object is not lost, enabling one to give rise to both specific and general activities with regard to it; or through the power of mindfulness, the practitioner thoroughly fixes or notes the object-support, and even if the object-support is forgotten, it can be recollected once again; or, mindfulness stabilizes or sustains the object-support, enabling insight to investigate it, or supports insight itself. Here mindfulness performs the functions of retention, noting or fixing, and stabilizing that are requisite for recollection.
>
> This connection between the operation of mindfulness and recollection is made explicit in an argument about the existential status of mindfulness. The argument [Ny, 389b12ff.] occurs between the Kāśmīra Sarvāstivāda-Vaibhāṣika master Saṅghabhadra, and his major opponent, Sthavira, identified as the Dārṣṭāntika master, Śrīlāta (fourth-fifth century AD). Saṅghabhadra identifies the activity of mindfulness as that of fixing or noting (*ming-chi*, **abhilapana*), which must occur when the mind cognizes any object. But Śrīlāta, who denies the separate existence of all but three mental concomitants—feelings, conception and volition—claims that mindfulness is not a separate mental factor operating on present objects in each momentary mind event. Instead, mindfulness, which for Śrīlāta means specifically memory of the past, is used merely as a provisional designation to refer to mental operations directed toward past objects. The activity of fixing or noting attributed to mindfulness by Saṅghabhadra, for Śrīlāta, is simply a feature of the operation of knowledge in general (*jñānākāra*) and does not necessitate the existence of mindfulness as a separate factor.
>
> Saṅghabhadra's response indicates that it is precisely fixing or noting, which is the distinctive activity of mindfulness, that links mindfulness to ordinary memory. [...]
>
> Thus, for Saṅghabhadra, mindfulness is not simply the recollection of past objects, but rather the activities of fixing or noting and retention as they occur with regard to every present object. Indeed, in the absence of this activity of mindfulness, which fixes or notes the present object in each and every moment, subsequent recollection would be impossible. This interpretation of the activity of mindfulness undoubtedly [is] ... completely consistent with the traditional praxis-related function of mindful-

ness, which stabilizes and attentively observes a present object without distraction.

These different views of mindfulness as functioning with regard to past or present objects reflect different views of its role in the events of retention and recollection. For those who claim that mindfulness pertains only to past objects, *smṛti* provisionally refers to the conventional experience of memory: it is the recollection of a previously experienced object. Śrīlāta, Sthiramati and Hsüan-tsang would all accept this view. Memory is then not a distinct function attributed to a discrete and actually existing mental factor. Instead, as Vasubandhu explains [at ix, F 274ff.], memory refers to a process whereby recollection arises as a result of a complex set of conditions.

For the Sarvāstivāda-Vaibhāṣikas, however, *smṛti* is a separately existing factor that operates on present objects in each and every moment; it is this present functioning of fixing or noting that enables the subsequent event of recollection. Therefore, though the Sarvāstivāda-Vaibhāṣikas would accept that the process of recollection generally occurs as Vasubandhu describes, they would not limit *smṛti* to the event of recollection.

vi. In the last part of her article, Collett Cox discusses the source of the general model of recollection accepted by both Vasubandhu and the later Sarvāstivāda-Vaibhāṣikas, namely, a passage of the *Mahāvibhāṣā* (MVB 11 T.27 55a16) where eight Buddhist and non-Buddhist theories concerning ordinary memory are refuted.

vii. Cox ends by stating:

> For Saṅghabhadra..., in accordance with Sarvāstivādin psychological analysis, mindfulness is a discrete and actually existing mental factor that arises together with each mind event. That mindfulness, which arises simultaneously with the knowledge of a prior experience, has the capability to initiate a series of mindfulness factors, one of which will arise simultaneously with the subsequent recollecting knowledge. Thus, Saṅghabhadra, like Vasubandhu, Śrīlāta and others, does assert that a successive cause and effect relation underlies the event of recollection. But, unlike them, he denies that this serial cause-and-effect relation is one simply between two moments of knowledge: one moment that grasps the original object and a subsequent one that is provisionally described as its recollection. Instead, according to Saṅghabhadra, the causal series consists of successive moments of *smṛti*, each of which is an actually existing concomitant mental factor, which appears simultaneous with mind events and performs a function essential to the process of recollection.

270 *LVP*: On *ābhoga*, see S. Lévi ad *Sūtrālaṃkāra*, i. 16, and *Muséon*, 1914.

271 *LVP*: *manaskāra = cetasa ābhoga ālambane cittadharaṇa-dharmakaḥ* (*Abhisamaya*).

LS: Vasubandhu's *Pañcaskandhaka* (2008) states:

4.1.2 *manaskāraḥ katamaḥ | cetasa ābhogaḥ |*

4.1.2 What is attention? The bending of the mind. ISBP.232

Avatāra (ESD.82): "Mental application (*manaskāra*) is that which alerts (*ā-√bhuj*) thought, i.e., it directs thought towards an object. It is also the holding in thought (*samanvāhāra*) of an object which has earlier been experienced (*pūrvānubhauta*),* etc. There are three kinds of mental application: that of a trainee (*śaikṣa*), of a non-trainee (*aśaikṣa*), and of one who is neither a trainee nor a non-trainee (*naivaśaikṣa-nāśaikṣa*). The outflow-free mental applications in the seven trainees are named mental applications of trainees. The outflow-free mental application in an *arhat* is named mental application of a non-trainee. The mental application with outflows [in an ordinary person] is named mental application neither of a trainee nor a non-trainee."

* When the mind is alerted to an object, there arises in the mind a familiar image (of a previously experienced object) which matches this object. This is the alerting of the mind.

Sthiramati (*Triṃśikāvijñaptibhāṣya*, verse 3cd; p. 20) explains (based on Jacobi's German translation, p. 16): "Attention (*manaskāra*) is (so to speak) the bending or tilting of the mind, whereby the mind (*citta*) is turned towards its cognitive object. It has for its effect that mind is held on to its object. The holding on of the mind [to its cognitive object] is due to the fact that mind is directed again and again towards its cognitive object. The effect spoken of here refers to that kind of attention which is characterized as a series [of moments] in the context of the establishment of a certain object for the mind, but not to that kind of attention which occurs in each and every moment of the mind, for the latter [kind of attention] functions in only one moment and not in another."

As for the three kinds of mental application, see ii, F 325–28.

272 *LVP*: [As already mentioned above, note that we have adjusted the *kārikā* and Vasubandhu's commentary, since LVP states in his footnote at iii, F 104, that one should replace *adhimukti* by *adhimokṣa* at ii, F 153, 155; however, we did not adjust LVP's footnotes.]

This term presents a difficulty. – *Vyākhyā* [WOG.128.2–4: *adhimuktis tadālambanasya guṇato 'vadhāraṇād* (*-ṇam* ?). rucir iti anye | yathāniścayaṃ dhāraneti yogācāracittāḥ: "*Adhimukti* is the consideration of the object from the point of view of its qualities; according to others, it is preference or inclination; according to the practitioners, it is the contemplation of the object in conformity with the decision taken." (This last point is explained *ad* ii. 72, mental application proceeding from resolution [*adhimuktimanaskāra*]).

According to the *Pañcaskandhaka* [see below], *adhimokṣa* = *niścite vastuny avadhāraṇam.*

According to the *Prakaraṇapāda*, 693a17: "What is *adhimukti*? The delectation of thought in sensation and contact."

The Tibetan version of our text, *mos pa ni 'dod pa'o*, gives: *adhimuktir icchā* or *ruciḥ* (?).

Paramārtha translates: "*Adhimukti* is a factor that brings it about that thought is sharp in regard to the characteristics of the object." – This is not a translation, but a gloss.

Hsüan-tsang translates: "*Adhimukti*, that is *neng yü ching yin-k'o.*" We can translate: "that which makes a sign of approbation with respect to the object". The expression *yin* (= *mudrā*) *k'o* (possible) is indicated by Rosenberg in several glossaries. A. Waley, who consulted the Japanese glosses, translates: "the sign of approval given to a disciple who has understood what has been taught to him". We would thus have *k'o* = *k'o-i* = "this is allowable" (A. Debesse). *Adhimukti* is the approbation of the object, the factors due to which one takes the object into consideration; it marks a first stage of mental application. – See the note of Shwe Zan Aung, *Compendium*, p. 17 and 241, on *adhimokkha*: "...the settled state of a thought...; it is deciding to attend to this, not that, irrespective of more complicated procedures as to what 'this' or 'that' appears to be".

Saṃghabhadra (384b9): Approbation (*yin-k'o*) with respect to an object is called *adhimukti*. According to other masters, *adhi* signifies superiority, dominance; *mukti* signifies liberation (*vimokṣa*). *Adhimukti* is a factor by virtue of which thought exercises its dominance over an object without any obstacle; like *adhiśīla* (higher morality). – (57b8): *Adhimukti* is a separate factor, for the Sūtra says: "Thought, because of *adhimukti*, approves (*yin k'o*) of the object." When thoughts arise, all approve (*yin*) the object; therefore, *adhimukti* is a generally permeating factor (*mahābhūmika*). – Nevertheless, the Sthavira says: "It is not established that *adhimukti* is a separate factor, for we see that its characteristic is not distinguished from that of cognition (*jñāna*): the characteristic of *adhimukti* is that thought is determined (*niścita*) with respect to its object. But this is not different from the characteristic of cognition (*jñāna*). Therefore, *adhimukti* is not a separate factor." – This is not correct, for approbation (*yin-k'o*) brings about determination.

Some say: "*Adhimukti* is determination (*avadhāraṇa, niścaya*)." This is to give to the cause of resolution (*adhimukti*) the name of its effect. – If this is the case, *adhimukti* and determination would not be simultaneous. – No: for these two mutually condition one another: because of deliberation (*pratisaṃkhyā*), approbation arises; because of approbation, determination (*niścaya*) arises. There is no contradiction: thus there is no obstacle to their being simultaneous. – If any thought includes these two, then all the categories of mind will be approbation and determination. – This objection is worthless, for it happens that, dominated by other factors, their activity is damaged: even if there would be approbation (*yin*) and determination, they are small and recognizable only with difficulty.

LS: 1. Pradhan.54.23 has *adhimokṣo 'dhimuktiḥ*.

Vasubandhu's *Pañcaskandhaka* (2008) states:

> 4.1.7 *adhimokṣaḥ katamaḥ | niścite vastuni tathaivāvadhāraṇam |*
>
> 4.1.7 What is conviction? The certitude that an object about which a determination has been made exists in just that manner. ISBP.232

Sthiramati, commenting on the *Pañcaskandhaka*, states (ISBP.278):

> The object is described as one "about which a determination has been made" in order to make clear that not all things can become the object of conviction. That is, if no determination has been reached about an object, it is not possible to [have a sense] of certitude [that it exists] in just that manner.
>
> A determination is the freedom from doubt about an object that is gained through reasoning or trustworthy scripture. It is the strong adherence by the mind to a determination that has been made about some aspect of an object, such as its impermanence or its suffering [nature]. Conviction is the [sense of] certitude that [some particular object exists] in that [very] manner and not any other.

Avatāra (ESD.83): "Resolve (*adhimukti/adhimokṣa*) is the affirmation (印可; *avadhāraṇa*) with regard to an object, i.e., it enables one to be free from diffidence with regard to an object perceived (*cittasya viṣayāpratisaṃkoca*)."

2. Dhammajoti comments (SA.IV.221) that *adhimokṣa* is not easy to translate due to its various connotations, such as: (1) affirmation/commitment/acceptance/approval; (2) decisive-

ness/determination/resolve; (3) conviction/faith; (4) liking/inclination; (5) mental freedom (resulting from the eradication of indecision).

273 *LS*: 1. Vasubandhu's *Pañcaskandhaka* (2008) states:

> 4.1.9 *samādhiḥ katamaḥ | upaparīkṣye vastuni cittasyaikāgratā |*
>
> 4.1.9 What is concentration? One-pointedness of mind toward an object that is being closely examined. ISBP.232

Sthiramati, commenting on the *Pañcaskandhaka*, states (ISBP.279):

> [The description of the object as one] "that is being closely examined" indicates [that concentration] will not [be achieved] otherwise. Thus, concentration is also being presented as a mental factor that has a specific object.

Avatāra (ESD.83): "Concentration (*samādhi*) is that which causes thought to be focused on an object. It controls the monkey-like thought (*citta*) so that it can operate (*vartate*) on a single object. The Vaibhāṣika says thus: 'Just as a snake that is confined in a bamboo pipe does not move in a crooked manner, thought, when concentrated (*samāhita*), proceeds upright'."

2. Dhammajoti comments (SA.IV.222): "Concentration may be either defiled or non-defiled; in the former case, it is also named dispersion (散亂; *vikṣepa*). Within the single moment in the cognitive process, there is always the abiding of the mind on the object, thanks to this force called concentration. But when the thought happens to be conjoined with concomitant, distraction (*auddhatya*), it is made to fluctuate with regard to the object within a series of moments. This is called dispersion, though in its intrinsic nature it is also none other than the same *dharma*, concentration [see ii, F 162]."

Vasubandhu has already discussed the importance of concentration (*samādhi*) within the context of the controlling faculties (i. 48cd and beginning of chapter 2), i.e., the praxis-oriented faculty of concentration (*samādhīndriya*) and the three pure controlling faculties: the faculty of coming to know what is not yet known (*anājñātamājñāsyāmīndriya*), the faculty of perfect knowledge (*ājñendriya*) and the faculty of final and perfect knowledge (*ājñātāvīndriya*). As one of the five praxis-oriented controlling faculties, it is addressed throughout chapter 8 (EXPOSITION OF THE MEDITATIVE ATTAINMENTS), as well as in chapter 6 (EXPOSITION OF THE PATH AND THE PERSONS) and chapter 7 (EXPOSITION OF THE COGNITIONS).

274 *LVP*: Subtlety of the mental factors, *Milinda*, 63, 87; *Atthasālinī*, 142; *Kośa*, ix, F 284.

275 *LS*: AH 19; SAH 57; AH 19; SAH 57.

276 *LS*: AH 19; SAH 57.

277 *LS*: Ibid.

278 *Gokhale*: [25] *śraddhā 'pramādaḥ praśrabdhir upekṣā hrīr apatrapā | mūladvayam ahiṃsā ca vīryaṃ ca kuśale sadā ||*

Tib.: [25] *dad dang bag yod shin tu sbyangs | btang snyoms ngo tsho shes khrel yod | rtsa ba gnyis rnam mi 'tshe dang | brtson 'grus rtag tu dge la 'byung ||*

LVP: According to the MVŚ, 220b2, and the *Prakaraṇa*: *śraddhā, vīrya, hrī, apatrapā, alobha, adveṣa, praśrabdhi, upekṣā, apramāda, avihiṃsā*. – The *Mahāvyutpatti* (104) names the third root (*amoha*) and places vigor (*vīrya*) after the roots. The *Pañcaskandhaka* also names the third root and has the same order as the *Mahāvyutpatti*, except that it places diligence or heedfulness (*apramāda*) before equanimity (*upekṣā*).

LS: Saṃghabhadra remarks (Ny, 391b; SPrŚ, 800a) that the two "*ca*" in AKB ii. 25 indicate that delight and disgust are also to be included under the *kuśalamahābhūmikas*.

The *Avatāra* (ESD.85) defines them as follows:

> Delight (**prāmodya*?, **rati*?) is gladness and inclination. Seeing the virtue in what conduces to centrifugal process (*nivṛtti-bhāgīya*), one's thought aspires for it and accords with the cultivation of the wholesome. Because of the presence of this *dharma*, one's thought rejoices in *nirvāṇa*. [The thought-concomitant] conjoined with this is named "mental application to delight".
>
> Disgust (**nirveda*? **arati*?) is repulsion (*udvega*). Seeing the faults in what conduces to the centripetal process (*pravṛtti-bhāgīya*), one's thought becomes averse to it and accords with detachment (*vairāgya*). Because of the presence of this *dharma*, one is disgusted with *saṃsāra*. [The thought-concomitant] conjoined with this is named "mental application of disgust".

Saṃghabhadra explains why they are not listed (SPrŚ, 800a; ESD.31):

> It is because the modes of activity of delight and disgust are mutually contradictory, and [hence] cannot be co-nascent, that they have not been directly indicated here [in the verse]: They do not [strictly] fulfill the condition of being *kuśalamahābhūmika* [which requires that they be co-nascent with the other *kuśalamahābhūmika*-s in all the *kuśala citta*-s].... The two "*ca*" have been mentioned in order to indicate that these two [*caitta*-s] do not operate together, being mutually contradictory in their modes of activity.

279 *LS*: AH 19; SAH 57.

280 *LVP*: *cetasaḥ prasādaḥ* [Pradhan.55.6]. – According to the *Jñānaprasthāna*, 1, 19. – In other words, faith (*śraddhā*) is the factor by which (*yadyogāt*) thought, troubled by defilements (*kleśa*) and subsidiary defilements (*upakleśa*), becomes clear: as troubled water becomes clear by the presence of a gem that purifies water (*udakaprasādakamaṇi*). We find the same example in *Atthasālinī*, 304.

See *Kośa*, vi, F 293; viii, F 158. – *Vyākhyā* [WOG.128.16ff.]: *śraddhā cetasaḥ prasāda* iti. kleśopakleśa-kaluṣitaṃ cetaḥ śraddhā-yogāt prasīdati | udaka-prasādaka-maṇi-yogād ivodakaṃ. *satya-ratna-karma-phalābhisaṃpratyaya ity apare* iti. ākāreṇa śraddhā-nirdeśaḥ. satyeṣu caturṣu ... saṃty evaitānīty *abhisaṃpratyayo* 'bhisaṃpratipattiḥ śraddha.

LS: Vasubandhu's *Pañcaskandhaka* (2008) states:

> 4.1.11 *śraddhā katamā* | *karmaphalasatyaratneṣv abhisampratyayaś cetasaḥ prasādaḥ* |
>
> 4.1.11 What is faith? Belief, aspiration, or clarity of mind toward *karma* and its results, the [Four Noble] Truths and the [Three] Jewels. ISBP.232

Avatāra (ESD.83f.): "Faith (*śraddhā*) is that which causes the clarification of thought (*cetasaḥ prasādaḥ*) with regard to its object. It is named faith on account of being receptivity based on direct realization (*abhisaṃgrahapratyaya*) to the Three Jewels, the cause-effect relationship (*hetuphala-sambandha*) and the existence (*astitva*) [of *dharma*-s]. It is a *dharma* which removes mental turbidity (*kāluṣya*). Just as a water cleansing gem (*udakaprasādakamaṇi*), when placed inside a pond, at once clarifies the turbid water; likewise, the faith-gem within the mind-pond at once gets rid of all its turbidities. Faith to the Buddha's attainment of Enlightenment, to the Dharma as being well-expounded (*svākhyāta*), to the Saṃgha as being endowed with good conduct (*supratipanna*), as well as to dependent-origination (*pratītya-samutpāda*), the true nature of *dharma* (*dharmatā*) which is not understood by the heretics (*tīrthika*)—such is the domain of activities of faith."

281 *LVP*: The explanation adopted by Vasubandhu in the *Pañcaskandhaka*.

282 *LS*: AH 19; SAH 57.

283 *LVP*: *kuśalānāṃ dharmāṇāṃ bhāvanā* [WOG.128.20f.]. – According to vii. 27, *bhāvanā* signifies acquisition (*pratilambha*), practice (*niṣevaṇa*).

LS: Vasubandhu's *Pañcaskandhaka* (2008) states:

> 4.1.19 *apramādaḥ katamaḥ | pramādapratipakṣo 'lobho yāvad vīryam, yān niśritya-akuśalān dharmān prajahāti tatpratipakṣāṃś ca kuśalān dharmān bhāvayati |*
>
> 4.1.19 What is mindfulness? The antidote to lack of mindfulness—[that is to say,] the abandoning of nonvirtuous entities together with the cultivating of those virtuous entities that are their antidotes, on the basis of the mental factors ranging from avoidance of attachment to effort.

Avatāra (ESD.84): "Heedfulness (*apramāda*) is the cultivation of the wholesome *dharma*-s (*kuśaladharma-bhāvanā*). It is opposed to heedlessness (*pramāda*), and is of the nature of guarding (*ārakṣā*) thought."

284 *LVP*: The Mahāsāṃghikas. – Diligence or heedfulness holds thought safe from the factors of pollution (*saṃkleśika*).

285 *LS*: AH 19; SAH 57.

286 *LVP*: The Abhidhamma distinguishes *passaddhi* and *lahutā* (*Dhammasaṅgaṇi*, 40–43), which the Abhidharma seems to identify. – Pliancy (*praśrabdhi*) in the meditations (*dhyāna*) is analyzed in viii. 9. – *Aṅguttara*, v, 3.

LS: Vasubandhu's *Pañcaskandhaka* (2008) states:

> 4.1.18 *praśrabdhiḥ katamā | dauṣṭhulyapratipakṣaḥ kāyacittakarmaṇyatā |*
>
> 4.1.18 What is agility? The antidote to indisposition—[that is to say,] fitness of body and mind. ISBP.233

Avatāra (ESD.84): "Calm (*praśrabdhi*) is the aptitude of the mind (*cittakarmaṇyatā*). It is opposed to torpor (*styāna*), and accords with the wholesome *dharma*-s."

287 *LVP*: According to the Japanese editor. – S. Lévi, *Sūtrālaṃkāra*, vi. 2.

288 *LVP*: The pliancy member of enlightenment (*praśrabdhisambodhyaṅga*) is twofold: (i) pliancy of thought (*cittapraśrabdhi*) and (ii) pliancy of the body (*kāyapraśrabdhi*) (*Prakaraṇapāda*, iii. 1). – *Saṃyuktāgama*, 27, 3: ...*tatra yāpi kāyapraśrabdhis tad api praśrabdhi-saṃbodhyaṅgam abhijñāyai saṃbodhaye nirvāṇāya saṃvartate | yāpi cittapraśrabdhis tad api saṃbodhyaṅgam*... . A shorter recension in *Saṃyutta*, v. 111. – In the presence of this text, says the Sautrāntika, how can you define pliancy (*praśrabdhi*) as only "the aptitude of thought"?

289 *LS*: Although not explicitly mentioned in Pradhan, LVP mentions the Sautrāntika here.

290 *LVP*: The *Vyākhyā* [WOG.129.9ff.] cites the Sūtra: tīrthikāḥ kila bhagavacchrāvakān evam āhuḥ | śramaṇo bhavanto gautama evam āha | evaṃ yūyaṃ bhikṣavaḥ pañca nīvaraṇāni prahāya cetasa upakleśakarāṇi prajñādaurbalyakarāṇi sapta bodhyaṅgāni bhāvayateti | vayam apy evaṃ brūmaḥ | tatrāsmākaṃ śramaṇasya ca gautamasya ko viśeṣo dharmadeśanāyāḥ | tebhyo bhagavatā etad upadiṣṭaṃ | pañca santi daśa bhavanti | daśa santi pañca vyavasthāpyante | ...tathā sapta santi caturdaśa bhāvanti | caturdaśa santi sapta vyavasthāpyante. – Compare *Saṃyutta*, v. 108.

291 *LVP*: The Fortunate One has said that the nine bases of pain or strife (*āghātavastu*) (*Aṅguttara*, iv. 408) are the hindrance of malice (*vyāpādanivaraṇa*).

292 *LVP*: When one regards the (noble) path as constituted by three elements, i.e., the element of morality (*śīlaskandha*), the element of concentration (*samādhiskandha*), the element of understanding (*prajñāskandha*), [then] right thinking and right exertion are classified in the element of understanding as well as right view, which, alone, is understanding (*prajñā*) in its intrinsic nature. We read in the *Prajñāskandhanirdeśa*: *prajñāskandhaḥ katamaḥ* | *samyagdṛṣṭiḥ samyaksaṃkalpaḥ samyagvyāyāmaḥ*.

293 *LS*: AH 19; SAH 57.

294 *LVP*: This is the formation of equanimity (*saṃskāropekṣā*), to be distinguished from the sensation of equanimity (*vedanopekṣā*) (i. 14; ii. 8cd) and from the equanimity of the immeasurables (viii. 29) The *Atthasālinī* (397) names ten equanimities (*upekṣā*); we find there the definition of *jhānupekkhā*: *majjhattalakkhaṇā anābhogarasā avyāpārapaccupaṭṭhānā...* (p. 174, 2).

LS: Vasubandhu's *Pañcaskandhaka* (2008) states:

> 4.1.20 *upekṣā katamā* | *sa evālobho yāvad vīryam, yān niśritya cittasamatāṃ cittaprasaṭhatāṃ cittānābhogatāṃ ca pratilabhate, yayā nirvāsiteṣu kliṣṭeṣu dharmeṣv asaṅkliṣṭavihārī bhavati* |
>
> 4.1.20 What is equanimity? Evenness of mind, inactivity of mind, and effortlessness of mind that is gained on the basis of those very same mental factors ranging from avoidance of attachment to effort. It is that [mental factor] which, having dispelled afflicted entities, remains in a state of constant adherence to those that are free from affliction. ISBP.233

Avatāra (ESD.84): "The equilibrium of thought (*citta-samatā*) is named equanimity (*upekṣā*), as it is the equanimity with regard to the aversion to the untrue and the inclination towards the true. By the force of this, the thought neither inclines towards nor turns away from the true and the untrue [respectively]; abiding in equilibrium, as a scale in perfect balance."

295 *LS*: Although not explicitly mentioned in Pradhan, LVP mentions the Sautrāntika here. This is the fifth of Kritzer's forty-four passages discussed in relation to chapter 2 (VY.46f.). Saṃghabhadra (Ny, 392b8–13) attributes this objection to Vasubandhu and "explains that, like the pair, *vīrya*, which is not resting while doing good, and *upekṣā*, which is equanimity while abstaining from doing bad, *manaskāra* and *upekṣā* are not really opposites".

Saṃghabhadra—leaving out *anābhogatā*—defines *upekṣa* as follows (Ny, 391a; ESD.149):

> *Upekṣā* is mental equilibrium (*cittasamatā*). It is opposed to *auddhatya*. Induced by conformity to what is proper, it enables *citta* not to go off the track (令心不越)—this

is the meaning of *upekṣā*. *Auddhatya*, on the other hand, is that which causes the mental disquietude which, when conjoined with it, goes off the track.

[296] *LVP*: Literally: There are factors difficult to know that can be known. [5 a] But it is quite difficult to know (or to admit) that there would be no contradiction (hostility, impossibility of coexistence) between contradictory factors: *asti hi nāma durjñānam api jñāyate | idaṃ tu khalu atidurjñānaṃ yad virodho 'py avirodhaḥ*.

[297] *LVP*: According to Hsüan-tsang and the glosses of the Japanese editor:

The Vaibhāṣika. – What contradiction is there in that mental application is the tilting of thought, that equanimity is the non-tilting of thought? In fact, we consider mental application and equanimity as distinct factors.

The Sautrāntika. – Then mental application and equanimity would not have the same object; or else, one would have to admit that all the thought-concomitants (desire, hatred, etc.) are associated.

We will encounter other factors (initial inquiry [*vitarka*], investigation [*vicāra*]) showing the same characteristic of hostility… .

[298] *LS*: AH 19; SAH 57.

[299] *LS*: Vasubandhu's *Pañcaskandhaka* (2008) states:

4.1.12 *hrīḥ katamā | ātmānaṃ dharmaṃ vādhipatiṃ kṛtvā 'vadyena lajjā |*

4.1.12 What is shame? Embarrassment about objectionable acts for reasons relating to oneself or the Dharma. ISBP.232

4.1.13 *apatrāpyaṃ katamat | lokam adhipatiṃ kṛtvā 'vadyena lajjā |*

4.1.13 What is abashment? Embarrassment about objectionable acts for reasons relating to the world. ISBP.233

Avatāra (ESD.84): "Modesty (*hrī*) is that which conforms to the proper. It is produced on account of the dominant influence of oneself and of the Dharma. It is a mental freedom (*citta-vaśitā*) opposed to the emanation of craving (*tṛṣṇā-niṣyanda*). By virtue of this, one abides respecting virtues and the virtuous.

Shame (*apatrāpya*) has the cultivation of virtues as its precondition (*guṇabhāvanā-pūrvika*). It being opposed to the emanation of delusion (*moha-niṣyanda*), one [possessing it] scorns at lowly *dharma*-s. By virtue of this, one dreads evil (*avadye bhayadarśin*)."

[300] *LS*: AKB viii. 20c–30a states that loving kindness (*maitrī*) and also compassion (*karuṇā*) are non-hatred (*adveṣa*).

Dharmatrāta states (SAH.453) that loving kindness and compassion are non-hatred "because of being the antidote (*pratipakṣa*) for hatred (*dveṣa*). Justified (*sthāna*) hatred (*dveṣa*) is cured by loving kindness; unjustified (*asthāna*) hatred is cured by compassion. Furthermore, hatred (*dveṣa*) produced for abandoning (*prahāṇa*) life (*jīvita*) of beings (*sattva*) is cured by loving kindness; hatred produced for certain punishment of beings is cured by compassion. That is why those who seek for merit can produce these unlimited ones; not those who seek for what is vicious (*doṣa*)."

[301] *LVP*: The *Pañcaskandhaka* classifies non-delusion (*amoha*) among the wholesome permeating factors (*kuśalamahābhūmika*). (In fact, understanding [*prajñā*] can be "erroneous".)

– Absence of greed (*alobha*) is the opposite of greed (*lobha*), *udvega* and *anāsakti*. – Non-hatred (*adveṣa*) is the opposite of hatred (*dveṣa*), namely, loving kindness (*maitrī*; viii. 29). – Non-delusion (*amoha*) is the opposite of delusion (*delusion*), is right thinking (*saṃyaksaṃkalpa*; vi. 69).

LS: Vasubandhu's *Pañcaskandhaka* (2008) states:

> 4.1.14 *alobhaḥ katamaḥ | lobhapratipakṣo nirvid anāgrahaḥ |*
>
> 4.1.14 What is avoidance of attachment? The antidote to attachment—[that is to say,] dissatisfaction and freedom from acquisitiveness. ISBP.233
>
> 4.1.15 *adveṣaḥ katamaḥ | dveṣapratipakṣo maitrī |*
>
> 4.1.15 What is avoidance of hatred? The antidote to hatred—[that is to say,] loving-kindness. ISBP.233
>
> 4.1.16 *amohaḥ katamaḥ | mohapratipakṣo yathābhūtasampratipattiḥ |*
>
> 4.1.16 What is the avoidance of ignorance? The antidote to ignorance—[that is to say,] the correct understanding of things as they truly are. ISBP.233

Avatāra (ESD.85): "There are three roots of wholesomeness (*kuśala-mūla*): (i) non-greed (*alobha*), a *dharma* opposed to greed (*lobha*); (ii) non-hatred (*adveṣa*), a *dharma* opposed to hatred (*dveṣa*); and (iii) non-delusion (*amoha*), a *dharma* opposed to delusion (*moha*) and having the aforementioned understanding (*prajñā*) as its specific nature (*svabhāva*). These three *dharma*-s are named the roots of wholesomeness, because they are wholesome in their specific nature, and are also productive of other wholesome *dharma*-s. 'Wholesome' means 'secure' (*kṣema*), as [what is *kuśala*] can bring about the germs of desirable (*iṣṭa*) existence and of liberation. Or again, 'wholesome' means being skilful through training (*śikṣita*), by reason of which one can, [for example], produce beautiful images. Thus, in the world people call an artist *kuśala* for producing beautiful images."

302 *LS*: Vasubandhu's *Pañcaskandhaka* (2008) states:

> 4.1.21 *avihiṃsā katamā | vihiṃsāpratipakṣaḥ karuṇā |*
>
> 4.1.21 What is avoidance of harm? The antidote to harmfulness—[that is to say,] compassion. ISBP.233

Avatāra (ESD.84): "Harmlessness (*avihiṃsā*) is the mental goodness (*citta-bhadratā*). By the force of this, one does not harm others, and becomes averse to the harmful activities in which others indulge."

303 *LVP*: Energeticness in wholesome action (*kuśalakriyā*); for energeticness in unwholesome action is not vigor (*vīrya*), but, on the contrary, slackness (*kauśīdya*). The Fortunate One said: "The vigor of persons foreign to this religion (*itobāhyaka*) is slackness (*kausīdya*)" (ii. 26a). – *Pañcaskandhaka*: "Vigor is the energeticness of thought in the wholesome, the opposite of slackness."

LS: Vasubandhu's *Pañcaskandhaka* (2008) states:

> 4.1.17 *vīryaṃ katamat | kausīdyapratipakṣaḥ kuśale cetaso 'bhyutsāhaḥ |*
>
> 4.1.17 What is effort? The antidote to laziness—[that is to say,] exertion of the mind toward virtue. ISBP.233

Avatāra (ESD.84): "Vigour (*vīrya*) has the nature of being energetic (*abhyutsāha*) in the production and cessation, [respectively], of the wholesome and unwholesome *dharma*-s. That is, it goads the thought of those sunk in the mire of transmigration (*saṃsārapaṅkanimagnasya cetaso'bhyunnatirity-arthaḥ*) to get out quickly."

Saṃghabhadra (Ny, 391b; ESD.147): "*Vīrya* is that which protects and discards, respectively, one's virtues and faults which have already arisen; and that which causes to arise and not to arise, respectively, one's virtues and faults which have not yet arisen. It is the non-slackness of the mind."

304 *LS*: SAH 58–59.

305 *LS*: As for the term *kleśa*, Dhammajoti states (SA.IV.324): "This term is understood in the sense of 'defilement' or impurity. In the Buddhist usage, the corresponding past participle, *kliṣṭa*, means 'defiled', 'soiled'. However, the primary etymological sense of 'molest' or 'be vexed' is found in the early treatises [MVŚ, 244a, 417c] and continues to be emphasized even in the late *abhidharma* treatises. Thus, the *Avatāra* defines [ESD.95] the term as follows:

> Defilements (*kleśa*) are thus named because they perturb and afflict (亂逼惱 – *kliśnantīti kleśāḥ*) the psycho-physical series. These [defilements] are none other than the proclivities [*anuśaya*].

The occurrence of this term is rare in the *sūtra-piṭaka*. Its use was historically preceded by that of *upakleśa*, although subsequently the latter generally came to be understood as 'secondary defilements'—those which proceed from *kleśa*. At this later stage, it is explained that the *upakleśa*-s [see v. 46] are also the *kleśa*, but they additionally include other defilements that are not called *kleśa*. Examples of these secondary defilements are moral immodesty, avarice, and restlessness, which are said to be emanations (*niṣyanda*) from greed (*rāga*)."

Vasubandhu devotes his entire chapter 5 to the proclivities (*anuśaya*).

306 *LS*: SAH 58–59.

307 *Gokhale*: [26ac1] *mohaḥ pramādaḥ kausīdyam āśraddhyaṃ styānam uddhavaḥ* | *kliṣṭe sad aivā*

LS: Pradhan.56.4 has *kauśīdyam*.

Tib.: [26ac] *rmongs dang bag med le lo dang* | *ma dad pa dang rmugs dang rgod* | *nyon mongs can la rtag tu 'byung* |

LVP: [*mohaḥ pramādaḥ kausīdyam āśraddhyaṃ styānam uddhatiḥ* | – *sarvadā kliṣṭe*]

Our sources give *sadā* (*rtag tu 'byung*).

308 *LVP*: According to a gloss of the Japanese editor, the path of insight expels ignorance (*avidyā*), the path of cultivation expels non-cognition (*ajñāna*), the path of those beyond training (*aśaikṣa*) expels non-perceiving (*asaṃprakhyāna*).

LS: 1. Tib.: *rmongs pa zhes bya ba ni mar rig pa ste mi shes pa dang mi gsal ba'o* ||

Yaśomitra glosses [WOG.130.15f.]: *moho nāmāvidye*ti. vidyā-vipakṣo dharmo 'nyo 'vidyeti.

2. Vasubandhu's *Pañcaskandhaka* (2008) states:

> 4.1.25 *avidyā katamā* | *karmaphalasatyaratneṣv ajñānam* | *sā punaḥ sahajā parikalpitā ca* |
>
> *rāgaḥ kāmāvacaraḥ pratigho 'vidyā kāmāvacarā – etāni trīṇy akuśalamūlāni lobho*

'kuśalamūlaṃ dveṣo mohaś ca |

4.1.25 What is ignorance? Absence of knowledge with regard to *karma* and its results, the [Four Noble] Truths, and the [Three] Jewels; moreover, it is innate and contrived.

The desire, hatred, and ignorance that occur in the desire realm are the three roots of nonvirtue—that is, the root of nonvirtue that is attachment, the root of nonvirtue that is hatred, and the root of nonvirtue that is ignorance. ISBP.234f.

Avatāra (ESD.88): "The ignorance fetter (*avidyā-saṃyojana*) is the nescience (*ajñāna*) in the three spheres. It is characterized by non-discernment. It is named *avidyā*—non-knowledge, because it is opposed to *vidyā*—knowledge; like a blind man [who is deprived of knowledge of the visible world]. This is an expression negating (*prati-√sidh*) the opposite (*pratipakṣa*). It is like calling those who are not friends (*mitra*), enemies (*a-mitra*); and words which are not true (*ṛta*), etc., untrue words (*anṛta*), etc. Ignorance itself is the fetter, therefore it is named ignorance-fetter."

Saṃghabhadra describes the characteristics of ignorance as follows (*Abhidharma-samaya-pradīpika-śāstra*, 843c–844a):

> There is a distinct *dharma* which harms the capability of understanding (*prajñā*). It is the cause of topsy-turvy views and obstructs the examination of merits and faults. With regard to *dharma*-s to be known (*jñeya-dharma*) it operates in the mode of disinclination, veiling the thought and thought-concomitants. This is ignorance.

3. Dhammajoti comments (SA.IV.336): "There has been a controversy among the Sarvāstivāda masters since the time of the MVŚ as to its exact nature, particularly as regards whether it is abandonable by vision only, or also to be abandoned by cultivation. The compilers of the MVŚ are inclined towards the former position, but apparently also tolerate the latter. There has also been a controversy as to whether the ignorance that arises with a defilement of restricted scope (*parītta-kleśa-bhūmika-dharma*; AKB ii. 27) can qualify as an 'independent ignorance'."

4. The Sarvāstivādins developed a doctrine of two types of *avidyā*, i.e., conjoined ignorance (*saṃprayukta-avidyā*) and independent ignorance (*āveṇikī avidyā*); they were already attested in the *Vijñānakāyaśāstra* and further developed in the MVŚ. See SA.IV.223f., but in particular Dhammajoti's *The āveṇikī avidyā in the Sarvāstivāda school* (2009).

5. In the latter, Dhammajoti speaks of a basic ambiguity, i.e., on the one hand, *avidyā* was generally defined as simply non-cognizance or non-discernment [see, for example, ii. 26ac], on the other, it was to be specifically associated with the non-discernment of the Four Truths [see, for example, iii, F 92], and states that this ambiguity within its definition probably led to (i) the innovation of *āveṇikī avidyā* ("independent/unique ignorance"; 不共無明; *ma rig pa ma 'dres pa*), or non-conjoined *avidyā*, which can arise as a distinctive force of ignorance in itself, as well as to (ii) the controversy whether *āveṇikī avidyā* is abandonable by insight (*darśana-heya*) only or abandonable by cultivation (*bhāvanā-heya*) as well.

6. Vasubandhu will discuss ignorance (*avidyā*) in greater detail within the context of dependent origination (*pratītyasamutpāda*) at iii. 28c–29 (F 88–94); see also iii. 21a.

As for ignorance being one of the three unwholesome roots, see iv, 8cd; but when conjoined with *satkāyadṛṣṭi* and *antagrāhadṛṣṭi*, then ignorance is not unwholesome (*akuśala*) but obscured-non-defined (*nivṛtāvyākṛta*) (see AKB ii. 30ab, iv, F 41f. and v, F 42, note; SA.IV.334). See also ESD.86.

As for ignorance being a pervasive proclivity, see v. 12.

309 *LS*: Vasubandhu's *Pañcaskandhaka* (2008) states:

> 4.1.44 *pramādaḥ katamaḥ | yai rāgadveṣamohakausīdyaiḥ kleśāc cittaṃ na rakṣati kuśalaṃ ca na bhāvayati |*
>
> 4.1.44 What is lack of mindfulness? Those forms of desire, hatred, ignorance, and laziness that do not protect the mind from the mental afflictions and do not cultivate virtue. ISBP.237

Avatāra (ESD.85): "Heedlessness (*pramāda*) is the non-cultivation of wholesome *dharma*-s (*kuśalānāṃ dharmāṇām abhāvanā*), and is opposed to the heedfulness (*apramāda*) mentioned above. It is the inability to guard thought."

310 *LS*: Vasubandhu's *Pañcaskandhaka* (2008) states:

> 4.1.43 *kausīdyaṃ katamat | kuśale cetaso 'nabhyutsāho vīryavipakṣaḥ |*
>
> 4.1.43 What is laziness? [It is] the mind's lack of exertion toward virtue; and the antithesis of effort. ISBP.237

Avatāra (ESD.85): "Slackness (*kausīdya*) is the non-energetic-ness of thought (*cetaso 'prasāda*); it is opposed to the vigour (*vīrya*) mentioned above."

311 *LVP*: The MSS. have *aśraddhya*, *aśrāddhya* and *āśraddhya*; see the *Mahāvyutpatti* of Wogihara.

312 *LS*: Vasubandhu's *Pañcaskandhaka* (2008) states:

> 4.1.42 *āśraddhyaṃ katamat | karmaphalasatyaratneṣv anabhisampratyayaś cetaso 'prasādaḥ śraddhāvipakṣaḥ |*
>
> 4.1.42 What is lack of faith? [It is] the lack of belief and lack of clarity of mind toward *karma* and its results, the [Four Noble] Truths, and the [Three] Jewels; and the antithesis. ISBP.236

Avatāra (ESD.85): "Faithlessness (*āśraddhya*) is the non-clarity of thought (*cetaso 'prasāda*). It is a *dharma* opposed to the faith (*śraddhā*) mentioned above."

313 *LS*: Vasubandhu's *Pañcaskandhaka* (2008) states:

> 4.1.40 *styānaṃ katamat | cittasyākarmaṇyatā staimityam |*
>
> 4.1.40 What is torpor? [It is] unfitness and immobility of the mind. ISBP.236

Avatāra (ESD.96): "Torpor is the lack of aptitude (*akarmanyatā*) of the psycho-physical series. It is the heaviness (*gurutā*) [of the mind and body]."

314 *LVP*: nṛtya-gīt'ādi-śṛṃgāra-veṣālaṃkārak'ādy-auddhatya-saṃniśraya-dāna-karmakaś caitasiko dharmaḥ | [WOG.130.22f.] – Comp. *Dhammasaṅgaṇi*, 429.

LS: Vasubandhu's *Pañcaskandhaka* (2008) states:

> 4.1.41 *auddhatyaṃ katamat | cittasyāvyupaśamaḥ |*
>
> 4.1.41 What is excitation? Lack of calmness in the mind. ISBP.236

Avatāra (ESD.96): "Restlessness is that which causes non-tranquility of the mind (*avyupaśama*)."

315 *LS*: SAH 58–59.

316 *LVP*: See above, F 151.

317 *LS*: SAH 58–59.

318 *LVP*: ko 'yaṃ *devānāṃpriyo* nāma | ṛjukajātīyo *devānāṃpriya* ity eke vyācakṣate | aśaṭho hi *devānāṃ priyo* bhavati | mūrkho *devānāṃpriya* ity apare | yo hīśvarāṇām iṣṭaḥ sa na tāḍanena śikṣata iti mūrkho bhavati [WOG.130.27ff.]. – The Japanese editor cites numerous glosses.

319 *LVP*: pāṭha-prāmāṇya-mātreṇa daśa kleśa-mahābhūmikāḥ prāptā ity etām eva prāptiṃ jānīte [WOG.130.25f.].

Vasubandhu reproduces the formula of the *Mahābhāṣya ad* ii. 4, 56 (episode of the grammarian and the driver of a chariot).

See S. Lévi, *JA*, 1891, ii. 549 (*Notes de chronologie indienne. Devānāṃpriya, Açoka et Kātyāyana*). – According to Kern, *Manual*, 113, the meaning of "idiot" derives from the meaning "harmless, pious": this appears to be unlikely. – See my (LVP) note in *Bulletin de l'Académie de Bruxelles*, 1923.

320 *LS*: Vasubandhu's *Pañcaskandhaka* (2008) states:

> 4.1.45 *muṣitasmṛtitā katamā* | *yā kliṣṭā smṛtiḥ kuśalasyānabhilapanatā* |
>
> 4.1.45 What is clouded recollection? [It is] afflicted recollection; and a lack of clarity with regard to virtue. ISBP.237

The *Avatāra* does not mention it.

321 *LS*: Vasubandhu's *Pañcaskandhaka* (2008) states:

> 4.1.46 *vikṣepaḥ katamaḥ* | *pañcasu kāmaguṇeṣu rāgadveṣamohāṃśiko yaś cetaso visāraḥ* |
>
> 4.1.46 What is distraction? Those forms of desire, hatred, and ignorance that cause the mind to flow outward to the five sense objects. ISBP.237

The *Avatāra* does not mention it.

322 *LS*: Vasubandhu's *Pañcaskandhaka* (2008) states:

> 4.1.47 *asamprajanyaṃ katamat* | *kleśasamprayuktā prajñā kāyavāgmanaḥpracāreṣv asaṃviditavihāritā* |
>
> 4.1.47 What is vigilance? [It is] wisdom that is concomitant with a mental affliction and [the mental factor] that causes one to engage in activities of body, speech, or mind inattentively. ISBP.237

The *Avatāra* does not mention it.

323 *LS*: As for incorrect mental application being a cause of ignorance, and *vice versa*, see iii, F 70–72.

324 *LS*: WOG.131.17f: tṛtīyā smṛty-ādayaś catvāraḥ. muṣitā-smṛty-asaṃprajanyâyoniśo-manaskāra-mithyā'dhimokṣā ity arthaḥ.

325 *LS*: SAH 58.

326 *LVP*: *evaṃ tv āhuḥ*. – *Vyākhyā*: ābhidhārmikāḥ [WOG.131.23].

I believe that with the plural (*āhuḥ*) Vasubandhu designates Dharmatrāta here—author of the *Saṃyukta-Abhidharmahṛdaya*—and his followers. This seems to result from the passages that follow (*Nanjio* 1287, chap. ii. 5 and foll. = xxiii, 12, 28b):

> The permeating factors of defilement (*kleśamahābhūmika*) have to be explained:
>
> ii. 5. *mithyādhimokṣa, asaṃprajanya, ayoniśomanaskāra, aśrāddhya, kausīdya, vikṣepa, avidyā, auddhatya, pramāda.*
>
> By false resolve (*mithyādhimokṣa*), one should understand... .
>
> ii. 6. The ten permeating factors of defilement (*kleśamahābhūmika*) are found in any defiled thought. Non-modesty (*ahrī*) and shamelessness (*atrapā*) are called *unwholesome permeating factors* (*akuśalamahābhūmika*).
>
> The ten permeating factors of defilement occur in any defiled thought. The ten factors, of which the first is false resolve (*mithyādhimokṣa*), accompany any defiled thought, sensory consciousness or mental consciousness, in the realm of desire, in the realm of fine-materiality, in the realm of immateriality. They are thus permeating factors of defilement. – Question: Torpor (*styāna*) occurs in any defiled thought: why is it not counted among the permeating factors of defilement? – Answer: Because it is favorable to concentration (*samādhi*). That is to say, persons with lethargic behavior realize concentration quickly. This is why torpor (*styāna*) is not counted in the list. – Is the factor that is a generally permeating mental factor (*mahābhūmika*) also a permeating factor of defilement? Four alternatives: 1. generally permeating factors without being a permeating factor of defilement... .

327 *LVP*: The author does not admit this opinion. Torpor (*styāna, laya*) and dissipation, defiled factors, are opposed to a "white" factor like concentration (*samādhi*).

328 *LS*: SAH 59.

329 *Gokhale*: [26c2–d] *'kuśale tv āhrīkyam anapatrapā* ||

Tib.: [26d–27a1] *mi dge la ni khrel med dang* || *ngo tsha med pa'o*

LS: Vasubandhu's *Pañcaskandhaka* (2008) states:

> 4,1.38 *āhrīkyaṃ katamat* | *svayam avadyenālajjā* |
>
> 4.1.38 What is shamelessness? Lack of embarrassment about objectionable acts for reasons relating to oneself. ISBP.236
>
> 4.1.39 *anapatrāpyaṃ katamat* | *parato 'vadyenālajjā* |
>
> 4.1.39 What is absence of abashment? Lack of embarrassment about objectionable acts for reasons relating to others. ISBP.236

Avatāra (ESD.97): "Immodesty is that which causes disrespect (*agauravatā*) to virtues and those who are virtuous. It is a *dharma* opposed to respectfulness.

Shamelessness is [that which causes] one not to see the fearful consequences of evil (*abhayadarśitva*). It is capable of leading to [rebirth in] the low planes of existence (*durgati*). [Here] evil (*avadya*) means that which is condemned by the good ones (*vigarhitaṃ sadbhiḥ*)."

330 *LVP*: According to the MVŚ, 220b4, there are five unwholesome permeating factors (*akuśalamahābhūmika*): (1) ignorance (*avidyā*), (2) torpor (*styāna*), (3) restlessness (*auddhatya*), (4) non-modesty (*ahrī*), (5) shamelessness (*anapatrāpya*). – See iii. 32ab and above at F 151.

331 *LS*: SAH 60.

332 *LS*: AKB v. 48a, defines: "Anger (*krodha*; ii. 27), the irritation (*āghāta*) of thought concerned with living beings (*sattva*) and non-living things (*asattva*), an irritation distinct [*varjita*] from malice (*vyāpāda*) and harmfulness (*vihiṃsā*)."

Vasubandhu's *Pañcaskandhaka* (2008) states:

4.1.28 *krodhaḥ katamaḥ | vartamānam apakāram āgamya yaś cetasa āghātaḥ |*

4.1.28 What is anger? Animosity of the mind toward a current source of harm that has become evident. ISBP.235

Avatāra (ESD.97): "Anger [*krodha*] is, excluding hostility and harmfulness, that which causes hatefulness (*āghāta*) with regard to the sentient and the non-sentient."

As for the difference between hostility (*pratigha*; ii. F 165) and *krodha*, Sthiramati comments, in his commentary to the *Pañcaskandhaka* (ISBP.292 and 303f.), that *pratigha* is "animosity toward sentient beings", whereby "animosity is a harshness of the mind toward sentient beings that, if you are overcome by it, will cause you to consider engaging in such wrongful conduct as killing or binding sentient beings". As for *krodha*, he comments that it "occurs only toward an object that is a source of harm in the present moment and not otherwise. The phrase 'animosity of the mind' indicates both the essential nature of this mental factor and the fact that it is associated with consciousness. Given that its nature is animosity, anger is not distinct from [the root mental affliction of] hatred [*pratigha*]; however, because the term is ascribed to a certain type of hatred that occurs in a particular circumstance, it is a form of hatred. Thus, anger is ascribed to the animosity of the mind that occurs in relation to a source of harm that is actually present. Its object can be a sentient being or something that is inanimate. Its action is to give support to such conduct as inflicting punishment and the like."

333 *LS*: AKB v. 49c–50b, defines: "Enmity (*upanāha*) is what results from the repeated thinking over of the objects of anger (*āghātavastubahulīkāra*)."

Vasubandhu's *Pañcaskandhaka* (2008) states:

4.1.29 *upanāhaḥ katamaḥ | vairānubandhaḥ |*

4.1.29 What is resentment? Adherence to enmity. ISBP.135

Avatāra (ESD.95) "Enmity (*upanāha*) is the harbouring of hatred within and not letting go of it, which results from the repeated thinking over of the objects of anger."

334 *LS*: AKB v. 49c–50b, defines: "Dissimulation (*śāṭhya*), the crookedness of thought [*citta-kauṭilya*] that brings it about that one does not express things as they are [*yathābhūtam*], either that one does not deny something when one should deny it, or that one explains something in a confused manner."

Vasubandhu's *Pañcaskandhaka* (2008) states:

4.1.35 *śāṭhyaṃ katamat | svadoṣapracchādanopāyasaṅgṛhītaṃ cetasaḥ kauṭilyam |*

4.1.35 What is guile? A deviousness of mind that adopts a means of concealing one's faults. ISBP.236

Avatāra (ESD.95): "Dissimulation (*śāṭhya*) is the crookedness of the mind (*cittakauṭilya*)."

[335] *LS*: AKB v. 47, defines: "Jealousy or envy (*īrṣya*), the anger or inner disturbance [*vyāroṣa*] of thought that is concerned with the prosperity of others [*parasaṃpatti*]."

Vasubandhu's *Pañcaskandhaka* (2008) states:

4.1.32 *īrṣyā katamā | parasampattau cetaso vyāroṣaḥ |*

4.1.32 What is envy? The complete vexation of mind at another's success. ISBP.236

Avatāra (ESD.89): "The jealousy fetter (*īrṣyā-saṃyojana*) is that by virtue of which the mind becomes unable to bear the excellences of others: When others acquire respect, offering, wealth, learning and other excellences, [a person having this fetter] becomes envious—this is the meaning of being unable to bear. Jealousy itself is a fetter, therefore it is named the jealousy-fetter."

[336] *LS*: AKB v. 49c, defines: "Depraved opinionatedness (*pradāśa*), firmly seizing or esteeming of various reproachable things (*sāvadyavastudṛḍhagrāhita*; *parāmarśa*) that brings it about that one does not accept rightful admonition [*nyāyasaṃjñapti*]."

Vasubandhu's *Pañcaskandhaka* (2008) states:

4.1.31 *pradāśaḥ katamaḥ | caṇḍavacodāśitā |*

4.1.31 What is spite? Acrimony [expressed] through heated words. ISBP.236

Avatāra (ESD.95): "Depraved opinionatedness (*pradāśa*) is the clinging to various reproachable things (*sāvadyavastu-dṛḍhagrāhitā*), as a result of which one would not accept any rightful admonition (*nyāya-samjñapti*)."

[337] *LS*: AKB v. 48a, defines: "Concealment (*mrakṣa*), hiding one's own evil or imperfections [*avadyapracchādana*]."

Vasubandhu's *Pañcaskandhaka* (2008) states:

4.1.30 *mrakṣaḥ katamaḥ | ātmano 'vadyapracchādanā |*

4.1.30 What is dissembling? Concealment of objectionable acts. ISBP.236

Avatāra (ESD.97): "Concealment (*mrakṣa*) is the hiding of one's own evil."

[338] *LS*: AKB v. 47, defines: "Avarice (*mātsarya*) (*mā mattaḥ saratu*), 'tenacity' (*āgraha*, *Mahāvyutpatti*, 109, 29) of thought [*citta*], which opposes giving [*kauśalapradānavirodhin*], whether spiritual (*dharma*) or material (*āmiṣa*) (iv. 113) (*Atthasālinī*, 373)."

Vasubandhu's *Pañcaskandhaka* (2008) states:

4.1.33 *mātsaryaṃ katamat | dānavirodhī cetasa āgrahaḥ |*

4.1.33 What is stinginess? The acquisitiveness of mind that opposes generosity. ISBP.236

Avatāra (ESD.90): "The avarice fetter (*mātsarya-saṃyojana*) is that which causes the mind to be hoarding with regard to one's own belongings and wealth. [It is the mental attitude]: 'What belongs to me must not go to others.' The avarice itself is the fetter, therefore it is named the avarice-fetter."

[339] *LS*: AKB v. 49c, defines: "Deceit (*māyā*), the factor that brings it about that one deludes others (*paravañcanā*)."

Vasubandhu's *Pañcaskandhaka* (2008) states:

> 4.1.34 *māyā katamā | paravañcanābhiprāyasyābhūtārthasandarśanatā |*
>
> 4.1.34 What is deceitfulness? The displaying of something that is untrue [in order to] deceive others. ISBP.236

Avatāra (ESD.95): "Deceptiveness (*māyā*) is the deluding of others (*paravañcana*)."

340 *LS*: AKB ii. 33cd, defines: "Pride (*mada*) is the exhausting oneself of the thought of those who are enamoured with their own qualities."

Vasubandhu's *Pañcaskandhaka* (2008) states:

> 4.1.36 *madaḥ katamaḥ | svasampattau raktasyoddharṣaś cetasaḥ paryādānam |*
>
> 4.1.36 What is [LS: pride]? [It is] the delight of someone who is infatuated with [his or her] own well-being and [a state in which] the mind is overwhelmed. ISBP.236

Avatāra (ESD.95): "Pride (*mada*) has the nature of being arrogant and caring for no-one (*cetasaḥ paryādānaṃ*), which results from an attachment to one's own physical appearance, strength, lineage, purity of precept, learning and eloquence, etc."

341 *LS*: AKB v. 49c–50b, defines: "Harmfulness (*vihiṃsā*), harming [*viheṭhana*], that finds expression in beating [*prahāra*], harsh speech [*pāruṣya*], etc., harming others."

Vasubandhu's *Pañcaskandhaka* (2008) states:

> 4.1.37 *vihiṃsā katamā | sattvaviheṭhanā |*
>
> 4.1.37 What is harmfulness? [The impulse to do] injury to sentient beings.

Avatāra (ESD.95): "Harmfulness (*vihiṃsā*) is the harming of others, as a result of which one practises the acts of beating and scolding etc."

342 *Gokhale*: [27] *krodhopanāhaśāṭhyerṣyāpradāśamrakṣamatsarāḥ | māyāmadavihiṃsāś ca parīttakleśa-bhūmikāḥ ||*

Tib.: [27a2–e] *khro ba dang | khon du 'dzin dang g.yo dang ni | phrag dog 'tshig 'chab ser sna dang | sgyu dang rgyags dang rnam 'tshe ni | nyon mongs chung ngu'i sa pa rnams ||*

LVP: Hsüan-tsang translates: "...the factors of this nature (= *iti*) are called *factors of defilement of restricted scope* (*parīttakleśabhūmika*)".

Saṃghabhadra [Ny, 392a6]: The text says: "The factors of this nature", in order to include impatience (*akṣānti*), discontent (*arati*), displeasure (*āghāta*), etc.

343 *LS*: SAH 60.

344 *LVP*: Dharmatrāta: (1) Because they are abandoned by cultivation and not by insight into the truths, (2) because they are associated with the mental consciousness and not with the other five consciousnesses, (3) because they do not arise with all thought and exist separately, they are the factors of defilement of restricted scope.

LS: The MVŚ, 220b, explains (SA.IV.223):

> Those *dharma*-s [of defilement] which obtain in some [but not all] defiled thoughts are called *dharma*-s of defilement of restricted scope. That is: the seven—anger, [enmity, depraved opinionatedness, concealment, avarice, jealousy and harmfulness]—are exclusively unskillful; dissimulation, deceptiveness and pride may be either unskillful or non-defined. Moreover, the seven, anger, etc., pertain only to the

> sensuality sphere; dissimulation and deceptiveness pertain to the sensuality sphere and the first *dhyāna*; pride pertains to all three spheres. Moreover, these ten are abandonable by cultivation only and pertain exclusively to the mental stage (*manobhūmi*). When one of them arises, there is definitely no another. Being mutually contradictory [among one another in nature], they are called *dharma*-s of defilement of restricted scope.

Yaśomitra comments on *parītta* and *alpaka* (WOG.132; SA.IV.224):

> Restricted [*parītta*] means little/minor (*alpaka*). What is that? Mere-ignorance (*avidyā-mātra*); this means solely *avidyā* (*avidyaiva kevalā*). "With that mere-ignorance" means "not with other defilements, greed, etc".

LVP has incorporated this passage of Yaśomitra into his AKB translation, i.e., the original Sanskrit (Pradhan) does not state whether *avidyā* is *āveṇikī* or not.

In this context the MVŚ reports a controversy, i.e., whether the ignorance which arises together with these restricted defilements refers to the "conjoined ignorance" (*saṃprayukta-avidyā*)—ignorance always arising in conjunction with other defilements—or to the "independent ignorance" (*āveṇikī avidyā*), which arises through its own strength. Dhammajoti discusses this controversy in his article *The āveṇikī avidyā in the Sarvāstivāda school* (2009).

1. In the latter, Dhammajoti points out that the doctrine of *āveṇikā avidyā* is not attested in the canonical texts belonging to the earlier periods, i.e., the *Dharmaskandha*, the *Saṅgīti-paryāya* and the *Prajñapti-śāstra*.

The *Vijñānakāya*, on the other hand, attests *āveṇikī avidyā* as pertaining to the four noble truths, while describing it as not being abandonable by insight (*darśana-heya*) alone but also by cultivation (*bhāvanā-heya*). The *Jñānaprasthāna*, 925c, defines it as follows (p. 7):

> What is the *āveṇikī avidyā anuśaya*?
>
> Those *avidyā*-s which are non-clarity/unclear/confused (不了; **asaṃprakhyāna/*avyakta/*mūḍha*) with regard to *duḥkha*, with regard to *samudaya*, *nirodha*, *mārga* [= the four truths].

2. The *Mahāvibhāṣā* (196c–197a) elaborates (p. 8):

> Herein, "non-clarity" signifies "being disinclined" (不欲; **na rocate*, **akāmaka*) and "being non-receptive". That is, as a result of *avidyā* veiling the *citta*, one is disinclined and non-receptive toward the Four Noble Truths, hence said to be "unclear". It is not a mere lack of understanding (非但不明). Just as a poor person who has [swallowed] bad food in his stomach, even though finding excellent food, is not inclined to consume it. Likewise is the case of an ordinary worldling (*pṛthagjana*): his *citta* being veiled by *avidyā*, when he hears the Four Noble Truths, he is not inclined toward and is not receptive to them. …
>
> Question: What is the cognitive object (*ālambana*) of this *avidyā*?
>
> Answer: The Four Noble Truths. …
>
> Comment (by the compilers of the MVŚ): This *avidyā* has as its intrinsic nature (*svabhāva*) the invariable (一向; *ekāntena*) bluntness/foolishness, invariable dullness, invariable non-clarity and invariable inconclusiveness (不決擇; **aniścitatva*) with regard to the Four Truths. …

Question: Why is this *avidyā* said to be *āveṇikī*? What does *āveṇikī* mean?

Answer: This *avidyā* arises on its own strength; it does not arise in conjunction with the other *anuśaya*-s. Hence *āveṇīkī*. It is unlike those *avidyā*-s conjoined (*saṃprayukta*) with *rāga*, etc., which arise through the strength of others.

Dhammajoti comments (p. 9) that "the consistent specification that the *āveṇikī avidyā* is the ignorance pertaining to the Four Truths would entail that it is abandoned once the practitioner enters into the *darśana-mārga*, which is the process of the direct seeing of the Four Truths, the *satyābhisamaya*", i.e., it would thus not be abandoned through cultivation (*bhāvanā-heya*). This is in fact the MVŚ compilers' own opinion, i.e., the *āveṇikī avidyā*-s are *darśana-heya* only and—besides being not conjoined with other *anuśaya*-s—they arise through their own strength. This would then also mean that the compilers' position is that the *avidyā* which arises together with *krodha*, *upanāha*, etc., having arisen through the strength of the latter, is not to be called *āveṇikī*.

3. In this context, it is worthy to mention that the MVŚ also presents a dissenting opinion—in all probability belonging to some other Sarvāstivāda masters—which comprises the following set of perspectives (p. 12): "(i) The *āveṇikī avidyā*-s are also *bhāvanā-heya*. (ii) Whereas the *darśana-heya āvenikī avidyā*-s are deluded with regard to the Four Truths, the *bhāvanā-heya āveṇikī avidyā*-s are not so deluded. (iii) Whereas the *darśanā-heya* ones arise only in the ordinary worldlings, the *bhāvanā-heya* ones can also arise in the *ārya*-s. (iv) The *darśanā-heya āveṇikī-avidyā*-s can take objects which are *sāsrava* or *anāsrava*, *saṃskṛta* or *asaṃskṛta*. The *bhāvanā-heya* ones take only *sāsrava* and *saṃskṛta* objects. (v) The *darśana-heya āveṇikī avidyā*-s arise through their own strength. The *bhāvanā-heya* ones are arisen through the strength of others."

Thus Yaśomitra's view (followed by LVP) noted above appears to be based on this second opinion in the MVŚ. It is further noteworthy that Saṃghabhadra clearly shares this view that *āveṇikī avidyā* is also *bhāvanā-heya*. He states (Ny, 613c) (p. 13):

For those who concede that there are *bhāvanā-heya āvenikī avidyā*-s, they should concede that there are *āvenikī avidyā*-s which take only *bhāvanā-heya dharma*-s as cognitive objects and are not deluded with regard to the Truths of *duḥkha* and *samudaya*, for it is illogical to speak of such an *avidyā* as taking *darśana-heya āvenikī avidyā*-s as cognitive objects. They also should concede that when an *ārya* … practices the contemplation of the True Dharma, there ought to be the *āveṇikī avidyā* which is *bhāvanā-heya*, operating in the mode of torpor and disinclination, like the case of drowsiness which obstructs the mind. Accordingly, it is known that an *ārya* in whom the *samudaya-jñāna* has arisen still has the *āveṇikī avidyā* which takes only *bhāvanā-heya dharma*-s as objects and which obstructs the contemplation of the True Dharma.

4. Both of these opinions in the MVŚ, i.e., that of the compilers and the dissenting one, appear to have been transmitted to later times, as can be seen from the following remarks from Pu Guang (T 41, no. 1821, 80a; SA.IV.224):

i. The independent ignorance in such cases of thought is so called because it is not conjoined with other defilements—both the fundamental ones such as greed (*rāga*), etc., and the secondary defilements such as anger (*krodha*), etc., and also the indeterminate ones such as regret (*kaukṛtya*)—and arises through its own strength. It is abandonable by vision [into the four truths] only.

ii. The independent ignorance includes those ignorances which are not conjoined with the fundamental defilements such as greed, etc., as well as those ignorances conjoined with anger, etc., and regret, etc.

5. As for the two *avidyās*, i.e., *saṃprayuktā avidyā* and *āveṇikī avidyā*, Dhammajoti (2009) summarizes:

> Inspired by the *sūtra* teaching that we are bound to *saṃsāra* on account of *avidyā*, the Abhidharma tradition generally continued with this interpretation of *avidyā*, and defined it principally as the ignorance or non-cognizance with regard to the Four Truths. It even underscored the central importance of *avidyā* by virtually equating it with defilement *per se*. No defilement could arise in the absence of *avidyā*. This led to the notion of "*saṃprayuktā avidyā*"—*avidyā* conjoined with the defilements.
>
> On the other hand, *avidyā* being a powerful defilement itself ought to be able to arise by its own strength, all the more so when it came to be recognized as one of the most fundamental defilements in the Abhidharma. Moreover, its specific nature and function—in addition to being merely a generic cause of defilement and *saṃsāra* ought to be properly determined. This may in fact be seen as a natural development expected in a system like Sarvāstivāda Abhidharma that attaches the greatest importance to *dharma-pravicaya* through the process of which the intrinsic characteristic of each and every real existent force in the universe is to be precisely determined. This seemed to be a major reason leading to the formulation of the doctrine of independent (*āveṇikī*) *avidyā*. This is not to say that there are two distinct *dharma*-s, one called "*avidyā*" the other, "*āveṇikī avidyā*"; rather, there are two modalities of one and the same *dharma* called "*avidyā*" whose general characteristic is non-cognizance or non-clarity.

As for the two opinions regarding *āveṇikī avidyā*, he adds:

> One major consideration between these two different camps of thought is: whether this new category, the *āveṇikī avidyā*, is to be understood more generally as the cause of spiritual ignorance to reality, or exclusively as the non-cognizance of the Four Truths.

[345] *LS*: Among the extant *abhidharma* texts, the AKB was apparently the first to make an explicit mention of this class (SA.IV.222). See our endnote at ii. 23cd.

[346] *LS*: Vasubandhu's *Pañcaskandhaka* (2008) states:

> 4.1.48 *kaukṛtyaṃ katamat | cetaso vipratisāraḥ*
>
> 4.1.48 What is regret? The mind's sense of remorse. ISBP.237

Avatāra (ESD.96): "[Properly speaking] *kaukṛtya* is the being of that which is badly done (*kukṛtabhāva*). [But] a distinct thought-concomitant, which arises by taking this *kaukṛtya* [in its proper sense] as its object (*kaukṛtyālambana*), is given the name *kaukṛtya*. Its meaning is remorse (*vipratisāra*). This is the case of giving the name of the cause to its fruit. It is just like giving the name "emptiness" (*śūnyatā*) to that which takes emptiness as its object, and "impurity" (*aśubha*) to that which takes impurity as its object. Similarly in the world, one speaks [of the inhabitants (*sthānin*)] in terms of the habitat (*sthāna*), as when one says, 'coming from all the villages, towns', [meaning the people coming from these places]. It is classified as an envelopment also only when it is defiled."

347 *LS*: Vasubandhu's *Pañcaskandhaka* (2008) states:

4.1.49 *middhaṃ katamat | asvatantravṛttiś cetaso 'bhisaṅkṣepaḥ |*

4.1.49 What is sleep? The uncontrolled contraction of the mind's activity. ISBP.237

Avatāra (ESD.96): "Drowsiness (*middha*) is the inability to sustain the psycho-physical series (*kāya-citta-saṃdhāraṇāsamartha*). It causes mental compression (*abhisaṃkṣepa*). This is classified as an envelopment only when it is defiled."

See also AKB v. 47.

348 *LS*: Vasubandhu's *Pañcaskandhaka* (2008) states:

4.1.50 *vitarkaḥ katamaḥ | paryeṣako manojalpaś cetanāprajñāviśeṣaḥ | yā cittasy-audārikatā |*

4.1.50 What is deliberation? It is a form of mental discourse that investigates; and a particular type of wisdom and volition that is a coarseness of mind. ISBP.237

Avatāra (ESD.83): "Reasoning (*vitarka*) has the characteristic of causing thought to be gross with regard to an object (*cittaudāryalakṣaṇa*). It is also named discriminative reflection (*saṃkalpadvitīyanāmā*). Struck by the wind of ideation (*saṃjñāpavanoddhata*), it operates (*vartate*) in a gross manner. It is this *dharma* which serves as the projecting cause (*pañcavijñāna-pravṛtti-hetu*) of the five consciousnesses.

349 *LS*: Vasubandhu's *Pañcaskandhaka* (2008) states:

4.1.51 *vicāraḥ katamaḥ | pratyavekṣako manojalpas tathaiva | yā cittasya sūkṣmatā ||*

4.1.51 What is reflection? It is a form of mental discourse that examines [an object] closely. It is like [the previous mental factor (i.e., *vitarka*), except that it is] a fineness of mind.

The *Avatāra* (ESD.83): "Investigation (*vicāra*) has the characteristic of causing thought to be subtle. It is this *dharma* which serves as the cause that accords with the operation of mental consciousness on its object (*manovijñāna-pravṛttyanukūla-hetu*)."

350 *LVP*: See v, F 46.

According to the Chinese. – The Japanese editor explains the final *et cetera* by attachment (*rāga*; v. 2), hostility (*pratigha*), conceit (*māna*; v. 1), doubt (*vicikitsā*).

The *Vyākhyā* reads: "regret (*kaukṛtya*), sleepiness (*middha*), etc.", and explains [WOG.132.14ff.] "etc." by: disgust (*arati*), yawning (*vijṛmbhitā*), exhaustion (*tandrī*), uneven consumption of food (*bhakte 'samatā*), etc. – It goes on: The defilements (*kleśa*), i.e., attachment (*rāga*), etc., are also undetermined, for they are not classified in any of the five categories: they are not generally permeating factors, because they do not occur in all cases of thought; they are not wholesome permeating factors, because they are not connected with the wholesome (*kuśalatva-ayogāt*); they are not permeating factors of defilement, because they do not occur in all cases of defiled thought: for there is no attachment (*rāga*) in a thought conjoined with hostility (*sapratigha*).

The Ācārya Vasumitra has written a summary mnemonic stanza (*śloka*): "The tradition (*smṛta*) is that there are eight undetermined factors (*aniyata*), namely, initial inquiry (*vitarka*), investigation (*vicāra*), regret (*kaukṛtya*), sleepiness (*middha*), hostility (*pratigha*), attachment (*sakti* = *rāga*), conceit (*māna*), doubt (*vicikitsā*)." But we (= Yaśomitra) do not admit this number eight. Why would the afflicted views (*dṛṣṭi*; v. 3a) not be undetermined? There is no false view (*mithyādṛṣṭi*) in a thought conjoined with either hostility or doubt.

351 *LS*: Vasubandhu's *Pañcaskandhaka* (2008) states:

4.1.22 *rāgaḥ kaṭamaḥ | pañcasūpādānaskandheṣu sneho 'dhyavasānam |*

4.1.22 What is desire? Strong affection for, and attachment to, the five grasping heaps. ISBP.233

Avatāra (ESD.90): "Sensuality greed is so named as it is greed (*rāga*) for sensual desire (*kāma*). This greed itself is the proclivity, therefore it is named sensual-greed proclivity. There are five of this, belonging to the five classes in the sense-sphere only, namely: the sensual-greed proclivity abandonable by insight into unsatisfactoriness (*duḥkha-darśana-prahātavya*) and so on up to that abandonable by cultivation (*bhāvanā-prahātavya*)."

352 *LS*: Vasubandhu's *Pañcaskandhaka* (2008) states:

4.1.23 *pratighaḥ katamaḥ | sattveṣv āghātaḥ |*

4.1.23 What is hatred? Animosity toward sentient beings. ISBP.234

Avatāra (ESD.87): "The hostility fetter (*pratigha-saṃyojana*) is the hatred (*dveṣa*) belonging to the five classes [of abandonables]. It is named hostility as it is characterized by the delight in harming (*āghāta*) and not being benevolent to sentient beings, etc. [It brings about the future unsatisfactoriness], just like bitter seeds. Hostility itself is the fetter, therefore it is named hostility-fetter."

353 *LS*: Vasubandhu's *Pañcaskandhaka* (2008) states:

4.1.24 *mānaḥ katamaḥ | sapta mānāḥ – māno 'timāno mānātimāno 'smimāno 'bhimāna ūnamāno mithyāmānaś ceti |*

4.1.24.1 *mānaḥ katamaḥ | hīnāc chreyān asmi sadṛśena vā sadṛśa iti yā cittasyonnatiḥ |*

4.1.24.2 *atimānaḥ katamaḥ | sadṛśāc chreyān asmi śreyasā vā sadṛśa iti yā cittasyonnatiḥ |*

4.1.24.3 *mānātimānaḥ katamaḥ | śreyasaḥ śreyān asmīti yā cittasyonnatiḥ |*

4.1.24.4 *asmimānaḥ katamaḥ | pañcopādānaskandhān ātmata ātmīyato vā samanupaśyato yā cittasyonnatiḥ |*

4.1.24.5 *abhimānaḥ katamaḥ | aprāpta uttare viśeṣādhigame prāpto mayeti yā cittasyonnatiḥ |*

4.1.24.6 *ūnamānaḥ katamaḥ | bahvantaraviśiṣṭād alpāntarahīno 'smīti yā cittasyonnatiḥ |*

4.1.24.7 *mithyāmānaḥ katamaḥ | aguṇavato guṇavān asmīti yā cittasyonnatiḥ |*

4.1.24. What is [LS: conceit]? There are seven types of pride: [ordinary] conceit, extraordinary conceit, extreme conceit, egoistic conceit, exaggerated conceit, conceit of inferiority, and wrong conceit.

4.1.24.1 What is [ordinary] [conceit]? The swelling up of the mind in which you think of someone who is inferior to you, "I am better [than him or her]", or of someone who is your equal, "I am [his or her] equal".

4.1.24.2 What is extraordinary [conceit]? The swelling up of the mind in which you think of someone who is your equal, "I am better [than him or her]", or of someone who is superior to you, "I am [his or her] equal".

4.1.24.3 What is extreme [conceit]? The swelling up of the mind in which you think of someone who is superior to you, "I am better [than him or her]".

4.1.24.4 What is egoistic [conceit]? The swelling up of the mind that originates from the mistaken notion that the five grasping heaps constitute an "I" and a "mine".

4.1.24.5 What is exaggerated [conceit]? The swelling up of the mind in which you think toward higher special attainments that you have not achieved, "I have achieved them".

4.1.24.6 What is [conceit] of inferiority? The swelling up of the mind in which you think of someone who is very much superior to you, "I am only slightly inferior to him".

4.1.24.7 What is wrong [conceit]? The swelling up of the mind in which you think, "I possess good qualities", when you are not someone who possesses good qualities. ISBP.234

Avatāra (ESD.87f.): "The conceit fetter (*māna-saṃyojana*) is the conceit in the three spheres. It is named conceit as it is characterized by mental elevation (*unnati*) when one compares one's own virtues with those of others, as in the case of an arrogant person (*stabdha-puruṣa*) depreciating others. It is further divided into seven kinds: (i) *māna*, (ii) *atimāna*, (iii) *mānātimāna*, (iv) *asmimāna*, (v) *abhimāna*, (vi) *ūnamāna*, (vii) *mithyāmāna*.

i. If, with regard to these—clan (*kula*), lineage (*gotra*), wealth (*dhana*), appearance (*varṇa*), strength (*bala*), observance of the precepts (*śīla*), learning (*bāhuśrutya*), skill in the arts and crafts (*śilpa*), etc.—others are inferior and one claims that one is superior, or others are equal to one, and one claims that one is equal; the mental elevation so produced is named *māna*.

ii. If others are equal to one, and one claims one is superior, or if others are superior and one claims one is equal; the mental elevation so produced is named *atimāna*.

iii. If others are superior, and one claims one is superior, the mental elevation so produced is named *mānātimāna*.

iv. If one clings to the five aggregates of grasping (*pañcopādāna-skandha*) as the Self (*ātman*) or what pertains to the Self (*ātmīya*), the mental elevation so produced is *asmimāna*.

v. If one has not attained the distinctive attainment (*viśeṣādhigama*) of the fruit of stream-entry (*srotaāpatti*) and one claims that one has, the mental elevation so produced is *abhimāna*.

vi. If others excel one greatly, in respect of clan and lineage, etc., and one claims that one is only a little inferior; the mental elevation so produced is named *ūnamāna*.

vii. If one claims that one has virtues when in reality one has not, the mental elevation so produced is named *mithyāmāna*.

These seven kinds of conceit are collectively named the conceit-fetter."

354 *LS*: Vasubandhu's *Pañcaskandhaka* (2008) states:

4.1.27 *vicikitsā katamā | satyādiṣu yā vimatiḥ |*

4.1.27 What is doubt? Ambivalence about the [four Noble] Truths and so forth.

Avatāra (ESD.89): "The doubt fetter (*vicikitsā-saṃyojana*) is that which causes hesitation (*vimati*) in the mind with regard to the Four Noble Truths. It is like [a man] being undecided when confronted with an intersection or a straw-man. [In the first case he is uncertain as to which is the right way to take; in the second case, he is uncertain—when seeing from afar or in darkness—as to whether it is a real man or simply a straw-man]. Likewise, there arises hesitation as to the truth or falsehood of the [Truth of] Unsatisfactoriness (*duḥkha*); etc. The doubt itself is the fetter, therefore it is named the doubt-fetter."

355 *LS*: AH, 20–22; SAH 61–63.

356 *LS*: AH 20–21; SAH 61–62.

As for Vasubandhu's discussion of *kuśala, akuśala* and *avyākṛta* in the context of the eighteen elements (*dhātu*), see i. 29c–30a; as for the number of associated thought-concomitants in regard to *kuśala, akuśala* and *avyakṛta* thoughts, see ii. 28–30d; as for the various classifications of *kuśala, akuśala* and *avyākṛta* factors, see in particular AKB iv. 8b–9c; as for the definitions of *kuśala, akuśala* and *avyākṛta* actions, see in particular AKB iv. 45ab; as for the definitions of *kuśala* and *akuśala* paths of action (*karmapatha*), see iv. 66bd.

357 *LS*: LVP has the following section after *kārikā* 28, but Pradhan places it before. I follow Pradhan since it is more conducive to headlining the text.

358 *LVP*: souillé, defiled.

359 *LVP*: Compare *Kathāvatthu*, xiv. 8.

360 *LS*: AKB ii. 71: The unobscured-non-defined (*anivṛtāvyākṛta*) thought of the realm of desire is divided into four categories:

1. arisen from the ripening cause (*vipākaja*; ii. 57);
2. associated with proper deportment (*airyāpathika*): lying down [*śayana*], sitting [*āsana*], standing [*sthiti*], walking [*caṃkramaṇa*];
3. associated with skill in arts and crafts (*śailpasthānika*);
4. associated with supernormal emanations (*nairmita*; *nairmāṇika*): the thought by which the possessor of supernormal accomplishments creates visible forms [*rūpa*], etc., and which is called the *effect of superknowledge* (*abhijñāphala*; vii. 49) (see ii, F 265).

361 *LS*: AH 21; SAH 62.

362 *Gokhale*: [28] *savitarkavicāratvāt kuśale kāmacetasi | dvāviṃśatiś caitasikāḥ kaukṛtyam adhikaṃ kva cit ||*

Tib.: [28] *'dod pa'i dge ba'i sems la ni | rtog dang dpyod dang bcas pa'i phyir | sems las byung ba nyi shu gnyis | la la dag tu 'gyod pa bstan ||*

363 *LS*: AH 21; SAH 62.

364 *LVP*: *Dhammasaṅgaṇi*, 1161; *Atthasālinī*, 784–87.

LS: See ii, F 165.

[365] *LVP*: Cf. i, F 69.

[366] *LS*: AH 20; SAH 61.

[367] *LS*: Ibid.

[368] *Gokhale*: [29ab] *āveṇike tv akuśale dṛṣṭiyukte ca viṃśatiḥ* |

Tib.: [29ab] *mi dge ba ni ma 'dres dang* | *lta dang ldan la'ang nyi shu 'byung* |

[369] *LVP*: *āveṇika = rāgādipṛthagbhūta.*

[370] *LVP*: Any view (*dṛṣṭi*) is "judgment after deliberation" (*saṃtīrikā prajñā*; i. 41cd; vii. 1).

[371] *LS*: AH 20; SAH 61.

[372] *Gokhale*: [29cd] *kleśaiś caturbhiḥ krodhādyaiḥ kaukṛtyen aikaviṃśatiḥ* ||

Tib.: [29cd] *nyon mongs bzhi dang khro sogs dang* | *'gyod pa dang ni nyi shu gcig* ||

[373] *LS*: AH 20–21; SAH 62.

[374] *Gokhale*: [30ab] *nivṛte 'ṣṭādaśā 'nyatra dvādaśā 'vyākṛte matāḥ* |

Tib.: [30ab] *bsgribs la bco brgyad lung ma bstan* | *gzhan la bcu gnyis dag tu 'dod* |

LS: As Collett Cox points out (DD.214f.), the Vaibhāṣikas propose that non-defined factors, whose moral quality is not manifest as either wholesome or unwholesome, are of two types:

1. Obscured-non-defined (*nivṛtāvyākṛta*): factors that are obscured by association with defilements (*kleśādita*), and, like unwholesome factors, they constitute an obstacle to the (noble) path. However, unlike unwholesome factors, they are incapable of producing an undesirable effect. For example, a moment of thought within the realm of desire can be obscured and non-defined in moral quality if associated with the afflicted view of self (*satkāyadṛṣṭi*) or with the afflicted view of holding to an extreme (*antagrāhadṛṣṭi*). A moment of thought within the realm of fine-materiality or the realm of immateriality can be obscured and non-defined if associated with any defilement.

2. Unobscured-non-defined (*anivṛtāvyākṛta*): factors that are certain types of form (*rūpa*), space, cessation not due to deliberation, certain dissociated factors, all ripened effects (*vipākaphala*), and moments of thought associated either with skill in arts and crafts (*śailpasthānika*) or with modes of proper deportment (*airyāpathika*), and thoughts capable of miraculous emanations (*nairmāṇika*).

See Dhammajoti's explanation of the non-defined *dharmas* in our endnote to iv. 9d (F 35).

[375] *LS*: AH 20; SAH 62.

[376] *LS*: AH 21; SAH 62.

[377] *LS*: Ibid.

[378] *Gokhale*: [30cd] *middhaṃ sarvā'virodhitvād yatra syād adhikaṃ hi tat* ||

Tib.: [30cd] *gnyid ni kun la mi 'gal phyir* | *gang la yod pa de bsnan no* ||

[379] *LS*: AH 22; SAH 63.

[380] *Gokhale*: [31] *kaukṛtyamiddhā'kuśalāny ādye dhyāne na santy ataḥ* | *dhyānāntare vitarkaś cā vicāraś cā 'py ataḥ param* ||

Tib.: [31] *de las 'gyod gnyid mi dge rnams* | *bsam gtan dang po dag na med* | *rtog pa'ang bsam gtan khyad par can* | *de yi gong na dpyod pa yang* ||

[381] *LVP*: Thought in the first meditation (*dhyāna*), when it is (1) wholesome, involves thus twenty-two thought-concomitants; (2) obscured-non-defined, it involves (i) eighteen thought-concomitants when it is independent or associated with afflicted view (*dṛṣṭi*), (ii) nineteen thought-concomitants when it is associated with attachment (*rāga*), arrogance (*māna*) or doubt (*vicikitsā*)... .

[382] *LVP*: Literally: The word "also" (*api*) shows that one has to exclude, in addition to initial inquiry (*vicāra*), dissimulation (*śāthya*) and deceit (*māyā*).

[383] *LVP*: According to the Japanese editor, *Saddharmasmṛti[upasthāna]sūtra*, 33, 10 (*Nanjio* 679, *Mdo* 24–27). – MVŚ, 670b24.

[384] *LVP*: By adding: "I am the great Brahmā", he distinguishes himself from the other Brahmās.

[385] *LVP*: Cf. *Dīgha*, i. 219ff., and *below* iv. 8a, v. 53ab.

Dīgha, i. 221f. (Transl. Walshe):

> Then, Kevaddha, the Great Brahmā, took that monk by the arm, led him aside and said:
>
> Monk, these *devas* believe there is nothing Brahmā does not see, there is nothing he does not know, there is nothing he is unaware of. That is why I did not speak in front of them. But, monk, I do not know where the four fundamental material elements cease without remainder. And therefore, monk, you have acted wrongly, you have acted incorrectly by going beyond the Blessed Lord and going in search of an answer to this question elsewhere. Now, monk, you just go to the Blessed Lord and put this question to him, and whatever answer he gives, accept it. [...]
>
> (Lord Buddha:)
>
> Where consciousness is signless, boundless, all-luminous,
> That is where earth, water, fire and air find no footing,
> There both long and short, small and great, fair and foul –
> There "name-and-form" are wholly destroyed.
> With the cessation of consciousness this is all destroyed.

[386] *LS*: SAH 59.

[387] *LS*: Ibid.

[388] *Gokhale*: [31a1] *ahrīr agurutā*

Tib.: [32a1] *ma gus ngo tsha med*

LVP: *ahrīr agurutā*. – *Jñānaprasthāna*, i. § 5 (according to Takakusu, p. 87).

[389] *LVP*: *pratīśa* = *guru*, because *śiṣyaṃ pratīṣṭaḥ*.

[390] *Gokhale*: [32a2–b] *'vadye bhayā'darśitvam atrapā* |

Tib.: [32a2–b] *khrel med* | *kha na ma tho 'jigs mi lta* |

LVP: Compare the definition of higher morality (*adhiśīla*): ...*aṇumātreṣv apy avadyeṣu bhaya-darśī*... .

[391] *LVP*: Vasubandhu, in the *Pañcaskandhaka*, adopts this definition.

LS: This is the sixth of Kritzer's forty-four passages discussed in relation to chapter 2

(VY.48): "[Vasubandhu] defends the opinion of others, saying that *āhrīkya* and *anapatrāpya* are not intended to be simultaneous. Saṃghabhadra says [393b23–25] that the objection to this opinion cited by the *sūtra*-master reflects his misunderstanding because the real problem with the opinion is that it does not treat *āhrīkya* and *anapatrāpya* as completely separate *dharmas*."

392 *LVP*: *hrī* and *apatrāpya*, see *Lalita*, 32.

See ii, F 160.

393 *Gokhale*: [32c1] *prema śraddhā*

Tib.: [32c1] *dga' dang*

LVP: *Jñānaprasthāna*, i. § 4 (according to Takakusu, p. 87).

394 *Gokhale*: [32c2] *gurutvaṃ hrīs*

Tib.: [32c2] *gus nyid ngo tsha shes* |

LVP: MVŚ, 151a15.

395 *LVP*: Since one cannot have respect with regard to impure (*sāsrava*) factors. (Note by the Japanese editor.)

396 *Gokhale*: [32d] *te punaḥ kāmarūpayoḥ* ||

Tib.: [32d] *de gnyis 'dod dang gzugs dag na* ||

397 *Gokhale*: [33ab1] *vitarkacārāv audāryasūkṣmate*

Tib.: [33a] *rtog dang dpyod pa rtshing zhib nyid* |

LVP: This definition is based on a Sūtra that is not indicated in our sources. – Cf. i. 33.

LS: As for *vitarka* and *vicāra*, see the definitions in our endnotes at ii, F 165, and also our endnotes to i. 14cd and 33.

398 *LVP*: The seventh opinion of the MVŚ, 219b3.

399 *LVP*: The argument shown in the MVŚ, 269b10, and attributed to the Dārṣṭāntikas.

400 *LS*: LVP mentions the Sautrāntikas here, but they are not explicitly mentioned in Pradhan.

401 *LVP*: That is to say, "they make speech appear" (*vāksamutthāpaka*).

402 *LVP*: *vitarkya vicārya vācam bhāṣate nāvitarkya nāvicārya* [WOG.139.10]. – Compare *Majjhima*, i. 301; *Saṃyutta* iv. 293: *pubbe kho … vitakketvā vicāretvā pacchā vācaṃ bhindati*. – On the other hand, *Vibhaṅga*, 135: *vācīsaṃcetanā = vācīsaṃkhāro*.

403 *LS*: Although not explicitly mentioned in Pradhan, LVP mentions the Sautrāntika here.

404 *LS*: Dhammajoti comments (ESD.145) that according to the Sautrāntika "*vitarka* and *vicāra* are not real entities but merely two designations for the gross and subtle states of *citta*. Their difference is one of degree, not of kind (*jātibheda*). Vasubandhu explains that their operation is not simultaneous but alternate (*prayāyeṇa*)."

405 *LS*: Saṃghabhadra writes (Ny, 394a; ESD.145):

> [Objection:] Grossness and subtleness being mutually contradictory, *vitarka* and *vicāra* should not be co-nascent in the same *citta*.
>
> [Answer:] Although the substances of the two co-exist in one and the same *citta*, the predominance of their activities differs in time. Hence they do not contradict each other. It is like equal parts of water and vinegar in combination: Although there is

> equality in substance (i.e., quantity), there is a predominance in activity [of the one over the other]. In a gross *citta*, the activity of *vicāra* is impaired as a result of the predominance of the activity of *vitarka*; so that though [the former] exists, it is difficult to detect it. In a subtle *citta*, the activity of *vitarka* is impaired as a result of the predominance of the activity of *vicāra*; so that though [the former] exists, it is difficult to detect it.
>
> One might argue that this analogy is not valid inasmuch as the activity of vinegar predominates at all times. This objection is not reasonable. I do not say definitely that the vinegar is to be compared to *vitarka* and water [to] *vicāra*; only that which predominates in activity is like vinegar: Within the *citta*, whichever of the two *dharma*-s, *vitarka* and *vicāra*, predominates in activity, is to be compared to vinegar; that whose activity is feeble is to be compared to water. Hence it is not the case that one and the same *citta* is at once gross and subtle; as *vitarka* and *vicāra*, though co-existing in the *citta*, operate at different times.

LVP adds: In the same way, attachment (*rāga*) and delusion (*moha*) are coexistent: but a person is termed "behaving through attachment" (*rāgacarita*), when attachment manifests itself... .

406 *LVP*: See viii, F 158f., for the Sautrāntika view as to whether initial inquiry (*vitarka*) and investigation (*vicāra*) are separate real entities.

Initial inquiry (*vitarka*) and investigation (*vicāra*) exist, not simultaneously, but successively (*paryāyeṇa*). What is the difference between initial inquiry and investigation? The old masters (*pūrvācārya*) say:

> What is *vitarka*? – A mental conversation (*manojalpa*) of examination (*paryeṣaka*), which has for its basis intention (*cetanā*) or the speculative consciousness (*prajñā*) depending on whether or not it involves reasoning or inference (*abhyūha*). This is the gross state of thought.
>
> What is *vicāra*? – A mental conversation of appreciation, of judgment (*pratyavekṣaka*), which has for its basis intention... .

According to this theory, *vitarka* and *vicāra* constitute two almost identical psychological complexes: they differ in that the first involves "inquiry" and the second "judgment". Some give an example: Someone examines numerous pots in order to know which one is well-baked and which one is soft: this inquiry (*ūha*) is *vitarka*; finally, this person arrives at a conclusion, "There are such a number of each category": this is *vicāra*.

The *Vyākhyā*, *ad* i. 33, cites the *Pañcaskandhaka* of Vasubandhu, which is very close to the opinion of the old masters: vitarkaḥ katamaḥ | paryeṣako manojalpaś cetanāprajñāviśeṣaḥ | yā cittasyaudārikatā | vicāraḥ katamaḥ | pratyavekṣako manojalpaś cetanāprajñāviśeṣaḥ | yā cittasya sūkṣmatā. || [see WOG.64.26ff.] The *Vyākhyā* adds [WOG.64.28]: anabhyūhāvasthāyāṃ cetanā abhyūhāvasthāyāṃ prajñeti vyavasthāpyate.

See *Dhammasaṅgaṇi*, 7–8, *Compendium*, pp. 10–11, *Milinda*, 62–63. – *Atthasālinī*, 296–97 defines initial inquiry as reasoning or deliberation (*ūhana*), and gives it as coarse (*oḷārika*), whereas investigation is subtle (*sukhuma*). – Vyāsa *ad Yogasūtra*, i. 17: *vitarkaś cittasya-ālambane sthūla ābhogaḥ | sūkṣmo vicāraḥ*; i. 42–44.

407 *Gokhale*: [33b2] *māna unnatiḥ |*

Tib.: [32b1] *nga rgyal khengs pa*

408 *Gokhale*: [33cd] *madaḥ svadharme raktasya paryādānaṃ tu cetasaḥ ||*

Tib.: [32b2–d] *rgyags pa ni | rang gi chos la chags pa yi | sems ni yongs su gtugs pa'o ||*

409 *LVP*: *paryādīyate = saṃnirudhyate*; see *Śikṣāsamuccaya*, 177, 15; *Divya*, *Sūtrālaṃkāra*, i. 12.

Definition of Saṃghabhadra: *yaḥ svadharmeṣv eva raktasya darpaś cetasaḥ paryādānaṃ kuśalānyakriyābhyupapattisaṃhāro madaḥ.*

LS: That is to say (EIP.VIII.684), due to the exhaustion caused by arrogant thoughts attached to themselves, one withdraws from the pursuit of good factors.

410 *LVP*: That is to say, pride (*mada*) is sensation, "defiled satisfaction" (*kliṣṭa saumanasya*). The Vaibhāṣika does not admit this explanation: indeed, satisfaction does not exist beyond the second meditation (*dhyāna*): now, according to v. 53c, pride exists in the three realms of existence.

411 *LS*: SAH 15, 56, 450.

412 *LS*: SAH 15.

413 *LS*: At ii. 23a, LVP footnoted:

citta = manas = vijñāna.

caitta = caitasa = caitasika = cittasaṃprayukta.

414 *LS*: For *manas*, LVP translates here "esprit" versus his usual "organe mental".

415 *Gokhale*: [34ab1] *cittaṃ mano 'tha vijñānam ekārthaṃ*

Tib.: [34ab1] *sems dang yid dang rnam shes ni | don gcig*

LVP: Compare *Dīgha*, i. 21; *Saṃyutta*, ii. 94. – Compare *Atthasālinī*, 140: "In the exposition of consciousness, consciousness (*citta*) is so called because of its variegated (*citta*) nature. Mind (*mano*) is so called because it knows the measure of an object. Mental action (*mānasa*) is just 'mind'. ... 'Heart' is the same as mind... ."

LS: 1. Vasubandhu's *Pañcaskandhaka* (2008) states:

> 5. *vijñānaṃ katamat | ālambanavijñaptiḥ | cittaṃ mano 'pi tat | citratāṃ manaḥsanniśrayatāṃ copādāya |*
>
> 5. What is consciousness? It is awareness of an object. It is also [referred to as] thought and mind, because it is diverse and because mind serves as its support.
>
> *prādhānyena punaś cittam ālayavijñānam | tathā hi tac citaṃ sarvasaṃskārabījaiḥ | tat punar aparicchinnālambanākāraṃ vijñānam ekajātīyaṃ santānānuvṛtti ca | yato nirodhasamāpattyasañjñisamāpattyāsañjñikebhyo vyutthitasya punar viṣayavijñaptyākhyaṃ pravṛttivijñānam utpadyata ālambanapratyayāpekṣaṃ prakārāntaravṛttitāṃ chinnapunarvṛttitāṃ saṃsārapravṛttinivṛttitāṃ copādāya | ālayavijñānatvaṃ punaḥ sarvabījālayatām ātmamānālayanimittatāṃ kāyālīnatāṃ copādāya | ādānavijñānam api tat kāyopādānatāṃ copādāya |*
>
> Primarily, thought is the storehouse consciousness, because that is where the seeds of all the formations are collected. Moreover, [the storehouse consciousness] does not

have a discernible object or aspect; it is of a single type; and it occurs continuously—because, after coming out of the state of composure that is a cessation, the state of composure without conception, and the state [of being born as a worldly god] that has no conception, the active forms of consciousness, which are referred to as "awareness of objects", arise again. It exists because of the occurrence of different aspects in relation to the objective condition, [because of] their occurrence after having been interrupted, and [because] *saṃsāra* is both set in motion and brought to an end. That very [consciousness] is [called] the "storehouse consciousness", because of its quality of being the storehouse and cause of [a sentient being's] individual existence, and its quality of residing in [a sentient being's] body. It is also [called] the "acquiring consciousness", because it take on [a sentient being's] embodied existence.

prādhānyena mana ālayavijñānālambanaṃ sadātmamānātmamohātmasnehādisamprayuktaṃ vijñānam ekajātīyaṃ santānānuvṛtti ca | arhattvāryamārganirodhasamāpattyavasthāṃ sthāpayitvā ||

Primarily, mind is what apprehends the storehouse consciousness as its object. It is a consciousness that is always accompanied by bewilderment toward a self, the view that believes in a self, pride toward a self, and attachment toward a self, and so on. It is of one type and it occurs continually, except when [one becomes] an Arhat, [when one has generated] the Ārya path, and [when one is absorbed in] the state of composure that is a cessation. ISBP.239f.

Avatāra (ESD.120):

(5) The specific cognition (*prativijñapti*), in a general manner, of an object-base (*viṣaya-vastu, vastu*) such as a visible, etc., [without its particular details], is named consciousness (*vijñāna*). That is, the present function [of vision, etc.] with regard to the six [external] objects of vision, etc., which arise with the accompanying assistance of the visual faculties, etc. (*indriya-sahakāra*), and which apprehend visibles and other objects only generally, are named consciousnesses.

(5.1) That which is able to apprehend the particular characteristics of [an object] is named a thought-concomitant, such as sensation, etc. Consciousness does not have this function; it serves only as the support [for the thought-concomitants]. The function of consciousness exists only in the present moment within the single moment (*kṣaṇa*) of which the specific cognition takes place.

(5.2) Consciousness also receives the names of "mind" (*manas*) and "thought" (*citta*). It is also that by which the fundamental essence of a sentient being (*mūla-sattva-dravya*) may be designated. Its function is the specific cognition of the visibles and other objects. It is divided into six types by reason of the [six] different faculties [of vision, etc., and the six] different objects. These are named visual consciousness (*cakṣur-vijñāna*), etc., up to mental consciousness (*mano-vijñāna*). The Buddha Himself has spoken of its characteristic (*lakṣaṇa*) in the *sūtra*: It is named consciousness because it cognizes discriminatively (*vijānāti*). Hence, we know that its characteristic is discriminative cognition.

2. MVŚ [371a–b] presents various distinctions (SA.IV.212):

Question: What is the difference between the three—*citta*, *manas*, *vijñāna*—mentioned in the *sūtra*?

[Answer:] There is the explanation that there is no difference—*citta* is none other than *manas*, *manas* is none other than *vijñāna*; for, although the three words are different, there is no difference in meaning... .

There is also the explanation that the three ... are also differentiated: that is, the names themselves are different... .

Furthermore, there is a difference with respect of time (*adhvan*): what is past is called *manas*; what is future is called *citta*; what is present is called *vijñāna*.

Furthermore, there is a difference with respect to designation (*prajñapti*): *citta* is designated among the *dhātu*-s; *manas*, among the *āyatana*-s; *vijñāna* among the *skandha*-s.

Furthermore, there is a difference in terms of signification (*artha*): *citta* signifies "clan" (*gotra*); *manas*, "gateway of arising'" (*āya-dvāra*), *vijñāna*, "agglomeration".

Furthermore, there is a difference in terms of activity (*kriyā*): that of *citta* is far-going (*dūragama*)...; *manas*, fore-running (*pūrvaṅgama*)...; *vijñāna*, birth-relinking (*saṃdhāna/pratisaṃdhi*)... .

Further, the activity of *citta* is being variegated (*citra*)...; *manas*, going toward... (歸趣; *gati* [?]); *vijñāna*, cognition (*vi-√jñā*)... .

Furthermore, the activity of *citta* is increasing or nourishing (滋長; *saṃcitatva*); *manas*, thinking; *vijñāna*, cognizing.

According to Venerable Parśva: the activity of *citta* is increasing and severing; *manas*, thinking and contemplating, *vijñāna*, distinguishing and comprehending. Herein, it is to be understood that what increases is the with-outflow *citta*, what severs is the outflow-free *citta*; what thinks is the with-outflow *manas*, what contemplates is the outflow-free *manas*; what distinguishes is the with-outflow *vijñāna*, what comprehends is the outflow-free *vijñāna*.

3. Waldron comments (BU.226): "In early Pāli and Abhidharma Buddhist texts, *citta*, *vijñāna*, and *manas* were said to be synonymous, but different contexts of usage evinced different ranges of meaning. [...] For the Yogācārins, however, these three terms refer to three distinct *dharmas*: *citta* refers to the *ālaya-vijñāna*, which of course accumulates pure and impure *dharmas* in the form of seeds; *manas*, from the *Mahāyānasaṃgraha* on, refers to the *kliṣṭa-manas* (as well as an antecedent *vijñāna* as the support of a succeeding one, *ṣaṇṇāmapi vijñānakāyānāmanantaraniruddhaṃ*), while *vijñāna* itself refers to the traditional classification of six forms of sensory and mental cognitive awareness (*yadālambanavijñaptau pratyupasthitaṃ*) (*Yogācārabhūmi* 11.4–8)."

416 *LVP*: Thought accumulates the wholesome and the unwholesome, such is the meaning [WOG.141.15f.]. – Tibetan: *'byed pas*: because it distinguishes. – *Atthasālinī*, 293: *ālambanaṃ cintetīti cittam.*

417 *LVP*: *mana jñāna ity asya auṇādikapratyayaḥ* (*Dhātūpāṭha*, 4, 67).

LS: Waldron comments (BU.226) on *manas* (mentation): "Derived from the Sanskrit root *man*, 'to think, believe, imagine, suppose, conjecture', *manas* is related to the Latin *mens*, 'mind, reason, intellect', and ultimately to the English 'mind, mentate', and 'to mean' (PED 515, 520; SED 783)."

418 *LS*: Dhammajoti remarks (ADCP.94): "This is emphasized by the Ābhidharmikas as an important epistemological principle: Where there is a consciousness, there necessarily is a corresponding cognitive object (*ālambana*): Consciousness cannot arise simply by itself. The Sarvāstivādins—and for that matter the Sautrāntika as well as the Yogācāra—in fact make good use of this principle. In the case of the Sarvāstivāda and the Yogācāra, consciousness and its object arise necessarily at the same time. The Sarvāstivāda invokes [the epistemological principle] to establish that past and future *dharma*-s exist; the Sautrāntika, that external reality exists; the Yogācāra, that nothing exists apart from consciousness. A corollary of this principle is that consciousness necessarily arises with a specific content, determined by the cognitive object."

419 *LS*: Gedun Drup attributes this position to the Sautrāntikas.

420 *LVP*: *citraṃ śubhāśubhair dhātubhir iti cittam* [MSS.]. The *Vyākhyā* adds [WOG.141.18]: bhāvanāsaṃniveśayogena Sautrāntika-matena Yogācāra-matena vā.

Paramārtha has read: *citaṃ śubhāśubhair dhātubhis tān vā cinotīti cittam.* – In the same way, the Tibetan translates as: "because it is accumulated (*bsags pas*) of good and bad elements (*dhātu*)."

421 *LS*: AH 18, 217; SAH 56, 450.

422 *Gokhale*: [34cd1] *cittacaitasāḥ | sāśrayālambanākārāḥ samprayuktāś ca*

Tib.: [34cd1] *sems dang sems byung dang | rten dang dmigs dang rnam bcas dang | mtshungs par ldan pa'ang*

LVP: Compare K'uei-chi, *Twenty Verses*, i, 14b.

LS: Since thought and thought-concomitants are in a reciprocal causal relationship as mutually associated causes (*saṃprayuktaka-hetu*; ii, F 267–68)—an exemplification of the co-existent cause (*sahabhū-hetu*; ii, F 248–55)—they are always conascent; they also have the same basis, share the same cognitive object, etc. Saṃghabhadra states therefore (Ny, 394c; EIP.VIII.684) that their distinction in essential nature is difficult to discern, but distinguishes them as follows: (1) thought apprehends the nature of its object in general; (2) thought-concomitants grasp the various particular characteristics of the object. See our endnote to i. 16a.

423 *LVP*: WOG.141.29–142.6: *sākārāḥ tasyaiv' ālambanasya prakāreṇa ākaraṇāt.* yena te s'ālambanā *tasyaiv' ālambanasya prakāreṇa* grahaṇāt. kathaṃ. vijñānaṃ hi nīlaṃ pītaṃ vā vastu vijānāti upalabhata ity arthaḥ. tad eva that' ālambanaṃ vastu vedanā 'nubhavati. saṃjñā paricchinatti. cetanā 'bhisaṃskarotīty evam-ādi. atha vā *tasyaiv' ālambanasya* vijñānaṃ sāmānya-rūpeṇa upalabhyatā-rūpaṃ gṛhṇāti. viśeṣa-rūpeṇa tu vedanā 'nubhavanīyatā-rūpaṃ gṛhṇāti. saṃjñā paricchedyatā-rūpaṃ gṛhṇātīty evam-ādi.

LS: 1. All *citta-caitta*s are said to be "having a mode of activity" (*sa-ākāra*; SA.IV.225), i.e., "the mode of apprehending the percept must be the same; thus, if the *citta* apprehends greenness, the *caitta*-s too apprehend likewise". Yaśomitra explains [WOG.141.29–142.6; cf. ADCP.102]:

> Because they grasp in accordance with the type of that very cognitive object. How? *Vijñāna* cognizes—that is, apperceives (*upalabhate*)—a blue or yellow entity. Like-

wise, *vedanā* feels that very object [as being pleasurable, etc.]; *saṃjñā* categorizes it; *cetanā* acts on it volitionally; etc. Or rather, *vijñāna* grasps that very object in a generic manner as a perceptible. On the other hand, in a specific manner, *vedanā* grasps it as a sensible; *saṃjñā* grasps it as a categorizable; etc.

Dhammajoti adds (private communication): "When the Sarvāstivādins say that the conjoined *citta* and *caitta*, in cognizing a blue object, share the same *ākāra*, "blue", it does not mean that blue as a color and *prajñā* as a force of understanding are the same. Of course they are different!"

2. *Controversies and difficulties*: In Sarvāstivāda Abhidharma, all *citta-caitta*s are described as *sākāra*, "with an *ākāra*", but what this term means in this context becomes not only controversial among scholars and schools but also presents difficulties or needs interpretation: How does *sākāra* apply to *prajñā* itself, which is a *caitta*? What does *sākāra* mean in the context of sensory consciousness which is devoid of *ākāra*? This can be seen or is implied, for example, in Vasubandhu's discussion at vii. 13b:

> 13b. The "aspects" or "modes of activity" are understanding.
>
> The aspects or modes of activity (*ākāra*) are mental understanding (*prajñā*; ii. 24) by nature.
>
> We would say: – But if this is so, understanding (*prajñā*), [i.e.,] that which discerns factors (*dharma*) [ii. 24], would not be "having an aspect or a mode of activity" [*sākāra*; ii. 34bd], for understanding cannot be associated (*saṃprayukta*) with [another] understanding [*prajñāntarāsaṃyoga*]. It is thus correct to say (with the Sautrāntikas) that the *ākāra* is the mode of "perception" of cognitive objects or cognitive-object–grasping–mode [*ālambanagrahaṇaprakāra*] by the thought and thought-concomitants (*cittacaitta*).

This explanation takes into account the word *ākāra* (WOG.629.6–8): One takes from *ālambana* the sound *ā*; one takes from *prakāra* the last syllable *kāra*, and one has *ākāra* by withholding *-lambanagrahanapra-*. But while all *citta-caitta*-s are said to be "*sa-ākāra*" inasmuch as all equally can grasp the object and are thus said to be "having objects (*sa-ālambana*)", for the orthodox Sarvāstivāda it is *prajñā* alone that is "called" *ākāra* (vii. 13b) on account of the fact that its mode of operation on the object is investigation or discrimination (*pravicaya, pratisaṃkhyā*). The MVŚ, 409a, states (SA.IV.269):

> Question: What is the intrinsic nature of the so-called *ākāra*?
>
> Answer: Its intrinsic nature is *prajñā*. Herein it should be understood thus:
>
> i. *prajñā* is *ākāra*; it is also what cognizes with a form (*ākārayati*) and what is cognized with a form (*ākāryate*);
>
> ii. the *citta-caitta-dharma*-s conjoined (*saṃprayukta*) with *prajñā*, while not being *ākāra*, are what cognize with a form as well as what are cognized with a form;
>
> iii. those *viprayukta-saṃskāra*-s and other existent (*sat*) *dharma*-s, while being neither *ākāra* nor what cognize with a form, are what are cognized with a form.
>
> [Omitted: Discussion of alternate views.]
>
> Question: What is the meaning of *ākāra*?

> Answer: *Ākāra* means the operation in the manner of examination/discernment (簡擇而轉; *pra-vi-√ci*) with regard to the nature of the object.

This is essentially the same as the definition given for *prajñā* at ii. 24: "the investigation or discernment of factors" (*dharma-pravicaya*), but since, as Saṃghabhadra states (Ny, 741b. ADP.8f.), "only a discriminative (*sa-vikalpaka*) consciousness is capable of grasping the specific characteristic of the object [in the form:] 'it is blue, not green', etc., ... the operation of *ākāra* pertains to the domain of mental consciousness, not to that of a sensory consciousness where *prajñā* cannot properly function", not being a view (*dṛṣṭi*), i.e., a judgment after contemplation, though being cognition (*jñāna*) (vii. 1).

Dhammajoti comments (ADP.15) that whereas the Sarvāstivāda school consistently equates *ākāra* with *prajñā* in its various texts, for the Sautrāntika and Yogācāra "*ākāra* connotes both an image/representation and a mental understanding arising in the mind—with the difference that the Sautrāntika would regard it as a correspondent to an external existent". Thus (ADP.8), the Sautrāntika stance is that "in direct perception the *ākāra* corresponds exactly to the external object. It allows no possibility of a cognitive error in a genuine *pratyakṣa* experience. However, this *ākāra* is a resemblance (*sadṛśā*) constructed by the mind." On the other hand (ADP.11), "in the Sarvāstivāda epistemological theory, the image arising in the sensory consciousness is not an *ākāra*—a mental construction by *prajñā*—but an image essentially belonging to the object, not thought. And as Pu Guang says, it arises spontaneously like a reflection in a mirror: The reflection does not belong to the mirror which is always clear by nature."

3. i. *Vasubandhu's proposal*: As we have seen above, at vii. 13b, Vasubandhu proposes (SA.IV.274) "to avoid [the] apparent contradiction by defining *ākāra* as the 'object-grasping-mode' (*ālambana-grahaṇa-prakāra*) of all the *citta-caitta*-s. In this way, *prajñā* too, as a *caitta* can be said to be 'with an *ākāra*'. Yaśomitra states that this is a Sautrāntika definition. However, if the sense of compound means a 'mode of understanding' in the perceptual process, and not an image, then it is essentially Sarvāstivāda rather than Sautrāntika. Moreover, it is noteworthy that Vasubandhu here does not contest the MVŚ statement that *ākāra* is *prajñā* and, in fact, proceeds to conclude with the same threefold classification of *dharma*-s (*ākāra*, *ākārayati*, *ākāryate*; see vii. 13d) as we have seen in the MVŚ passage quoted above. This is, however, not to say that Vasubandhu's definition of *ākāra* is identical with that of the Sarvāstivāda." Saṃghabhadra challenges Vasubandhu's proposal (Ny, 741b; SA.IV.275):

> If [the "object-grasping-mode"] refers to the different modes/species of the form of the object, then the notion that all [*citta-caitta*-s] can assume the image-form (能像) [of the object] cannot be established at all, for an object has various forms, skillful, permanent, etc. Or rather, the *rūpa-dharma*-s are to be subsumed under *ākāra*, since *rūpa-dharma*-s can also assume the images of the forms of others.
>
> If it refers to the ability to grasp the specific characteristic of the object, then *ākāra* ought not to be possible for the five [sensory] consciousnesses, since they are not capable of grasping the specific characteristic of the object—since only a discriminative (*sa-vikalpaka*) consciousness is capable of grasping the specific characteristic of the object [in the form]: "it is blue, not green", etc. However, this is not what is conceded [by his definition]. Hence [his definition] is logically invalid.

ii. *Saṃghabhadra's proposal*: Thus even though the Sarvāstivāda—when speaking of the *prajñā* which operates investigatively with regard to the object—consistently equates *ākāra* with *prajñā*, Saṃghabhadra also seems to acknowledge (ADP.12f.) that *sākāra*, in the context of *citta-caitta*s, needs interpretation in order to avoid the apparent contradiction pointed out by Vasubandhu, and he himself proposes a few of them [Ny, 741ab].

a. One proposal is that the *citta-caitta*s, including *prajñā*, are all said to be *sākāra* because they equally (*sa* = *sama*) can grasp the distinctive species of characteristic of the object, i.e., they are said to be "those which cognize with a form" (*ākārayanti*), which is synonymous with "those which grasp objects".

b. Another proposal—from the perspective that *prajñā* alone can be called *ākāra*—is that all the *citta-caitta-dharma*s "other than *prajñā*" are "said to be *sākāra* in the sense that they equally—i.e., simultaneously; not earlier, not later—with *ākāra* (= *prajñā*), operate on the object".

See further comments on *ākāra-samatā* below.

4. In this context see also Dhammajoti's discussion of "The two aspects of the notion of *ākāra* according to Pu Guang" (SA.IV.273–74). He comments (ADCP.179) that Pu Guang's explanation that *ākāra* connotes both a mode of understanding and an image is likely to have been influenced by the Sautrāntika-Yogācāra stance.

424 *LS*: AH 18, 217; SAH 56, 450.

425 *LS*: Here, within the context of the fivefold equality or sameness (*pañcadhā samatā*) among the *citta* and *caitta*s, association means simultaneous association, but, in a wider context—from the point of view of the various psychological models within the Sarvāstivāda, Dārṣṭāntika, Sautrāntika schools (see endnote to ii. 23a) and their various scholars—various meanings were given to association/conjunction (*saṃprayoga*) by the Sarvāstivāda masters themselves and others (see SA.IV.225ff; ESD.139f.). For example, Dharmatrāta, "together with other Dārṣṭāntikas, asserts that the *citta-caitta*-s arise successively, and not simultaneously, like a group of merchants who pass through a narrow road one by one. For them, *saṃprayoga* means not simultaneous association but the association or 'companionship' of two mental *dharma*-s, one immediately following the other without anything else in between the successive productions of the two." See in this context Vasubandhu's discussion of the epistemological model of Śrīlāta, in iii. 32ab (F 101–7), where he also discusses the Sautrāntika notion of arising together (*saha*) and mingled (*saṃsṛṣṭa*).

426 *Gokhale*: [34d2] *pañcadhā* ||

Tib.: [34d2] *rnam pa lnga* ||

427 *LS*: Dhammajoti comments (ADP.13):

> A sensory consciousness, being free from intellectual judgment, can be said to be devoid of *ākāra*, but this does not need to mean that in this case the condition of *ākāra-samatā* ["have the same *ākāra*"] is meaningless. Just as in the discussion above on *sākāra* as a synonym applicable to all *citta-caitta*-s including *prajñā*; likewise in this case too, *ākāra-samatā* being applicable to all conjoined *caitta*-s, cannot mean "equality in terms of *prajñā*". But it is meaningful when understood as referring to the equality/sameness of the conjoined *citta-caitta*-s (including the

mahābhūmika prajñā) in respect of the mode of apprehending the object. E.g.: all apprehend a patch of blue, etc. This is permissible by the Vaibhāṣika-s, as can be seen in Saṃghabhadra's first alternative interpretation of *sākāra* [see endnote above].

428 *LVP*: *nirdiṣṭāś cittacaittāḥ savistaraprabhedāḥ* [WOG.142.16f.]. That is to say, *saha vistaraprabhedābhyam* or *saha vistaraprabhedena*.

429 *LS*: AH 24, 220–21, 224; SAH 65–66, 453–55, 457, 484.

430 *Gokhale*: [35–36a] *viprayuktās tu saṃskārāḥ prāptyaprāptī sabhāgatā | āsaṃjñikaṃ samāpattī jīvitaṃ lakṣaṇāni ca || nāmakāyādayaś c eti*

Tib.: [35–36a] *mi ldan pa yi 'du byed rnams | thob dang ma thob skal mnyam dang | 'du shes med snyoms 'jug pa dang | srog dang mtshan nyid rnams dang ni || ming gi tshogs la sogs pa yang |*

LVP: The word *iti* indicates that one must add to this list other dissociated factors (*viprayukta*) such as schism (*saṃghabheda*; iv. 98), etc.; see ii, F 304, iv, F 206; *Siddhi*, 71; according to Saṃghabhadra, add the *houo-ho-sing*. – The *Prakaraṇa* says: *ye 'py evaṃjātīyakāḥ*: "The factors that are of this type are also 'dissociated from thought' (*cittaviprayukta*)." The same formula in the *Skandhapañcaka*.

According to the *Prakaraṇa*, the formations (*saṃskāra*) "dissociated from thought" are: (1) *prāpti*, (2) *asaṃjñisamāpatti*, (3) *nirodhasamāpatti*, (4) *āsaṃjñika*, (5) *jīvitendriya*, (6) *nikāyasabhāga*, (7) *āśrayaprāpti*, (8) *dravyaprāpti* (?), (9) *āyatanaprāpti*, (10) *jāti*, (11) *jarā*, (12) *sthiti*, (13) *anityatā*, (14) *nāmakāya*, (15) *padakāya*, (16) *vyañjanakāya* and all the other factors of this type dissociated from thought.

Possession (*prāpti*) is defined as *dharmāṇāṃ prāptiḥ*; *āśrayaprāpti* = *āśrayāyatanaprāpti*; *dravyaprāpti* (?) = *skandhānāṃ prāptiḥ*; *āyatanaprāpti* = *ādhyātmikabāhyāyatanaprāpti* (PrŚ, 694a; SA.IV.287f.):

> [What is **upadhi(/*sthāna)-pratilambha*? This is the obtaining of the abode/location of support (所依處).
>
> What is **vastu-pratilambha*? It is the obtainment of the aggregates (*skandha*).
>
> What is **āyatana-pratilambha*? It is the obtainment of the internal and external *āyatana*-s.]

Prakaraṇapāda, 694a14:

> What is possession (*prāpti*)? The possession of factors (*dharma*).
>
> What is attainment of non-ideation (*asaṃjñisamāpatti*)? The cessation of thought and thought-concomitants having for its antecedent the notion of departure attached to the abandonment of the defilement of the Śubhakṛtsnas (on the third meditation [*dhyāna*]) but not to the abandonment of the higher defilement.
>
> What is attainment of cessation (*nirodhasamāpatti*)? The cessation of thought and thought-concomitants having for its antecedent the notion of calm attached to the abandonment of the defilement of the perception-sphere of nothingness (*ākiṃcanyāyatana*).
>
> What is the state of non-ideation (*āsaṃjñika*)? The cessation of thought and thought-concomitants of sentient beings who are born among the gods without ideation

(*asaṃjñisattva*).

What is the vitality faculty (*jīvitendriya*)? The life-force (*āyus*) of the three realms (*dhātu*).

What is the group homogeneity (*nikāyasabhāga*)? The resemblance of sentient beings.

LS: 1. Vasubandhu's *Pañcaskandhaka* (2008) states:

4. *saṃskārāḥ katame | vedanāsañjñābhyām anye caitasikā dharmāś cittaviprayuktāś ca ||*

4.1 [...]

4.2 *cittaviprayuktāḥ saṃskārāḥ katame | ye rūpacittacaitasikāvasthāsu prajñapyante tattvānyatvataś ca na prajñapyante || te punaḥ katame | prāptir asañjñisamāpattir nirodhasamāpattir āsañjñikaṃ jīvitendriyaṃ nikāyasabhāgatā jātir jarā sthitir anityatā nāmakāyāḥ padakāyā vyañjanakāyāḥ pṛthagjanatvam ity evambhāgīyāḥ |*

4. What are the formations? The mental factors other than feeling and conception, and the entities that do not accompany consciousness.

4.1 [...]

4.2 What are the formations that do not accompany consciousness? They are [entities] that are nominally ascribed to a particular state of form, consciousness, or the mental factors. They are not [entities that are] ascribed to [form, consciousness, or the mental factors] themselves or to something distinct from them. What then are they? Acquirement, the state of composure without conception, the state of composure that is a cessation, the quality of having no conception, the faculty of a life force, class affiliation, birth, aging, duration, impermanence, the collection of names, the collection of assertions, the collection of syllables, the state of an ordinary being, as well as those [other entities] that are of the same kind. ISBP.231 and 237f.

Avatāra (ESD.81):

The disjoined conditionings are those which do not conform to the [five conditions: (1) having the same basis, (2) having the same object, (3) having the same mode of activity, (4) being simultaneous, and (5) each of them having only one substance, and which belong to the category of neither material nor mental]. They are [fourteen in number], namely: acquisition (*prāpti*), non-acquisition (*aprāpti*), the ideationless attainment (*asaṃjñi-samāpatti*), the cessation attainment (*nirodha-samāpatti*), ideationlessness (*āsaṃjñika*), the vital faculty (*jīvitendriya*), the group-homogeneity (*nikāyasabhāga*), production (*jāti*), duration (*sthiti*), deterioration (*jarā*), impermanence (*aniyatā*), the collection of words (*nāmakāya*), the collection of complete phrases (*padakāya*), and the collection of syllables (*vyañjanakāya*), etc.

2. As for the category of *citta-viprayukta-saṃskāra*, modern scholarship has dealt with it extensively; see in particular:

i. Collett Cox's *Disputed Dharmas. Early Buddhist Theories on Existence*, which includes an annotated translation of the "Section of factors dissociated from thought" from Saṃghabhadra's *Nyāyānusāra*.

ii. Dhammajoti's Chapter 11: "The categories of conditionings disjoined from thought"

(SA.IV.285–320).

iii. Jaini's article "The Origin and Development of the *Viprayukta-saṃskāras*" (in his CPBS.239–60) and the section "*Citta-viprayukta-saṃskāra*" in his *Abhidharmadīpa with Vibhāṣāprabhāvṛtti*, pp. 88–98.

iv. Kritzer's Chapter VI: "*Pratītyasamutpāda* and the *Cittaviprayuktasaṃskāras*" in his *Rebirth and Causation in the Yogācāra Abhidharma*, pp. 209–81, which discusses the *cittaviprayuktasaṃskāras* within the Sarvāstivāda as well as Yogācāra.

3. As for the doctrinal evolution of the category of *citta-viprayukta-saṃskāra* (SA.IV.285–91), it is not traceable to the Buddha's teachings but they were considered by the orthodox Sarvāstivādins to be an advancement regarding the understanding of conditioned factors and to be conditioned real entities themselves which are neither mental nor material in nature but which can operate on both domains. Two of them—possession (*prāpti*) and non-possession (*aprāpti*)—can operate on even the unconditioned *dharmas*. Dhammajoti comments (p. 289):

> However, it must be noted that from the beginning, even within the broad Sarvāstivāda tradition itself, this newly articulated doctrinal category known as "conditionings disjoined from thought" had not been unanimously accepted, either as regards their reality (as a *dravya* having a *svabhāva*) or as regards their total number. Thus, in the MVŚ [730b and 198b], we find that Bhadanta Dharmatrāta and the early Dārṣṭāntika masters deny the reality of the whole *viprayukta-saṃskāraskandha*. Buddhadeva considers all the conditioned *dharma*-s to be subsumable under either the Great Elements [*mahābhūta*] (as in the case of the *rūpa*) or thought [*citta*] (as in the case of the mental factors [*citta-caitta*-s]), which, of course, is tantamount to the denial of any such category as the "*dharma*-s disjoined from thought" which are conjoined neither with matter nor thought.

It was probably in the *Jñānaprasthāna* (SA.IV.287, 290) that we find the *citta-viprayukta-saṃskāras* mentioned for the first time, but it provides neither "clear definitions nor a definite list of them, but only scattered descriptions of *nikāya-sabhāgatā*, *jīvitendriya*, *jāti*, *sthiti*, *jarā*, *anityatā*, *pṛthagjanatva*, and *prāpti*". The *Dharmaskandha-śāstra* and the *Prakaraṇa-śāstra*, on the other hand, both enumerate sixteen (see LVP's endnote above), and the *Amṛtarasa-śāstra*, seventeen (adding *pṛthagjanatva*). But from the **Abhidharmahṛdaya* onward, the number seems to become more or less fixed at fourteen. Thus (DD.71) Dharmaśrī's and Upaśānta's **Abhidharmahṛdayas* as well as the **Saṃyuktābhidarmahṛdayaśāstra* propose fourteen factors by omitting from the list of sixteen (see above) the three varieties of *prāpti/pratilambha* and adding "nature of an ordinary worldling" (*pṛthagjanatva*). The AKB enumerates also fourteen but replaces *pṛthagjanatva* with *aprāpti* in its official list; the *Avatāra* gives the same fourteen, although in a different order.

4. The number of the formations dissociated from thought, however, seems never to have become absolutely fixed at fourteen in the Sarvāstivāda tradition. Vasubandhu himself ends our verse with *-ādayaś ceti*. He explains *nāmakāyādayaś*, at ii. 47ab, as collection of names (*nāmakāya*), collection of phrases (*padakāya*) and collection of syllables (*vyañjanakāya*). As for *ca iti*, Yaśomitra comments (WOG.142.29ff; SA.IV.290):

> The word *ca* [in the verse] is for the purpose of indicating those disjoined [conditionings] of a similar type that have not been [explicitly] mentioned, for, *saṃgha-*

> *bheda*, etc., are conceded as [*dharma*-s] disjoined from thought existing as real entities. This is because of the mention in the *śāstra* "and also those [disjoined conditionings] of a similar type" (see PrŚ).

And Saṃghabhadra, in the same context, states (SA.IV.290):

> -*ādaya* is meant to include the phrase-group (*pada-kāya*) and the syllable-group (*vyañjana-kāya*) as well as harmony/congruence (和合性; *sāmagrī*); *ca iti* indicates the *dharma*-s speculated by others which are none other than those of the previously [mentioned] categories: There are some who speculate that, apart from acquisition [*prāpti*], etc., there exist such [intrinsic] natures as the aggregate-acquisition (蘊得; **skandha-prāpti*), etc.

Thus Saṃghabhadra recognizes *sāmagrī* as a discrete factor, thus bringing his total number of formations dissociated from thought to fifteen. As for *saṃghabheda*, it is *asāmagrī* in its intrinsic nature.

For more detail, see SA.IV.290f. and DD.72f.

5. As for the definition and name of *citta-viprayukta-saṃskāra*, the *Prakaraṇa-śāstra* states (SA.IV.287):

> What are the *dharma*-s disjoined from thought (*citta-viprayukta-dharma*)? They are the *dharma*-s which are not thought-concomitants [*caitta*]..., i.e., [1] matter (*rūpa*), [2] the unconditioned (*asaṃskṛta*), and [3] the conditionings disjoined from thought (*citta-viprayukta-saṃskāra*).

Saṃghabhadra explains that its three components together uniquely define it as a distinct doctrinal category in the fivefold category classification of *dharmas* (Ny, 396c; SA.IV.292):

> *citta*—to signify that like thought (*citta*), these *dharmas* are not matter (*rūpa*);
>
> *viprayukta*—to signify that the thought-concomitants (*caitta*), although also not of the nature of *rūpa*, are to be excluded as they are conjoined (*saṃprayukta*);
>
> *saṃskāra*—to signify that the unconditioned (*asaṃskṛta*), although not of the nature of *rūpa* and not *saṃprayukta* with *citta*, are also to be excluded.

6. Yet despite their being a distinct doctrinal category, the activities of the formations dissociated from thought are extremely varied, which raises the question of the rationale behind this category, particularly in the light of the severe criticism from the Sautrāntikas and Vasubandhu who denied the reality of these formations, although maintaining them as conventional descriptions/designations (*prajñapti*) of phenomena. Cox comments (DD.73f.) that "like all factors (*dharma*) enumerated by the Sarvāstivāda-Vaibhāṣikas, the dissociated forces were claimed to exist as real entities (*dravya*) by virtue of their own unique intrinsic nature (*svabhāva*). The existence of these factors is proven through inference from the particular activity that each performs. Each of the dissociated forces corresponds to some doctrinally required or to some generally recognized, commonly experienced activity." Thus: "Given the diversity of activities explained and doctrinal constraints satisfied, the category of dissociated forces appears to be a derivative category with no single integrating principle. Instead, it is a miscellany containing functionally unrelated factors that are unified only by their successful operation demanding their separation from both form and thought."

As for extramural influences, in his section on the *citta-viprayukta-saṃskāras* (AD.89ff.) Jaini makes the general comment that "over a long period and particularly during the time of the *Mahāvibhāṣā*, the Ābhidharmikas were engaged in studying and criticising the doctrines of rival schools [i.e., their contemporary realists like the Sāṃkhya, Vaiśeṣika and Mīmāṃsaka, and also the Yoga school]. ... A result of these criticisms and counter-criticisms was the acceptance of not only new theories but also of new *dharmas* and novel terms in the Vaibhāṣika school." But as for specific influences, he refers only to the Vaiśeṣika category of *sāmānya* as influencing the *viprayuktasaṃskāra sabhāgatā* (see also ii. F 198).

431 *LS*: Ḍhammajoti comments (SA.IV.293) that "among these, acquisition [*prāpti*], non-acquisition [*aprāpti*] and the four characteracteristics [*lakṣaṇa*] may be said to be the ones most important doctrinally".

432 *LS*: AH 220; SAH 453.

1. To give a first impression of *prāpti* and *aprāpti*, Dhammajoti provides the following illustration (SA.IV.293):

> When a person has jealousy in him, it is because—given the required assemblage of conditions for inducing the arising of this *dharma*, jealousy—a force called acquisition [*prāpti*] is also induced to arise at the same time, by virtue of which the jealousy comes to be linked to him. This force of acquisition will continue to link the jealousy to him from moment to moment—even at those times when his mind is not occupied with this defilement but with a skillful or non-defined thought—arising and ceasing in a serial continuity of its own. It is only when he is able to develop a sufficiently strong insight as the counteragent that it comes to be delinked from him: At this moment, there arises another acquisition of another *dharma*, the acquisition of the cessation (*nirodha*) of this defilement [i.e.: to be more specific (p. 295), in the first moment known as the unhindered path (*ānantarya-mārga*), the acquisition of the defilement is severed; in the second moment known as the path of liberation (*vimukti-mārga*), the acquisition of the corresponding cessation through deliberation (*pratisaṃkhyā-nirodha*) arises]; and at the same time, the non-acquisition [*aprāpti*] of this defilement is also induced to arise, effecting the delinking. The cessation and the non-acquisition together ensure that the defilement will not arise in him any more."

We can see from this illustration that *prāpti* is the *sine qua non* for the mechanism of defilement as well as purification for the Sarvāstivādins. This is so because (SA.IV.299f.), according to their theory of tri-temporal existence (*sarvāstitva*), a defilement as a real *dharma* exists always (*sarvadā asti*) and cannot be destroyed, yet "its linkage with the practitioner effected by the corresponding acquisition [*prāpti*] can be severed by interrupting the acquisition-series. Likewise a pure *dharma* can only come to be possessed by the practitioner through the operation of an acquisition that effects the linkage."

2. Saṃghabhadra explains the two functions of *prāpti* that uniquely qualify it as an ontological entity as follows (Ny, 398b; WOG.148.22f; SA.IV.295):

> ... We know that the acquisition (*prāpti*) as acknowledged [by us] definitely possesses a [distinct] function [1] as it is the cause by virtue of which a *dharma* which has been acquired is not lost, and [2] as it is the marker of the knowledge (*jñāna-cihna*) that "this belongs to that person" (*idam asyeti*).

3. As for *aprāpti*, it is not mentioned in the official list of formations dissociated from

thought in Vasumitra's *Pañcavastuka* and also not in Dharmaśrī's and Upaśānta's **Abhidharmahṛdayas* as well as the **Saṃyuktābhidarmahṛdayaśāstra*. These texts, however, feature *pṛthagjanatva*. On the other hand, *aprāpti* is part of the official list in the *Avatāra*.

433 *LS*: AH 220; SAH 453.

434 *Gokhale*: [36b] *prāptir lābhaḥ samanvayaḥ* |

Tib.: [36b] *thob pa rnyed dang ldan pa'o* |

LVP: See i. 38cd; ii. 59b.

According to the Śāstra: *prāptiḥ katamā? yaḥ pratilambho yaḥ samanvāgamaḥ.*

The terms *lābha* and *samanvāgama* do not have the same meaning in the Abhidharma and in *Kathāvatthu*, ix. 12. – For the Theravādin, *lābha* signifies "possession", for example, the power that the noble ones possess to realize at their will such and such a meditative attainment; *samanvāgama* is understood as actual realization. – Elsewhere (iv. 4) one distinguishes *paṭilābhasamannāgama* and *samaṅgibhāvasamannāgama*, possessing potentially (*samanvāgama* of the Abhidharma), possessing actually (*saṃmukhībhāva* of the Abhidharma). – See moreover xix, 4.

LS: 1. Vasubandhu's *Pañcaskandhaka* (2008) states:

> 4.2.1 *prāptiḥ katamā* | *pratilambhaḥ samanvāgamaḥ* | *sā punar bījaṃ vaśitā saṃmukhībhāvaś ca yathāyogam* |
>
> 4.2.1 What is acquirement? [It is] obtainment and possession; moreover, according to circumstances, it is applied to [the states of] a seed, mastery, and actualization. ISBP.238

The *Pañcaskandhaka* does not have the category *aprāpti*, but has *pṛthagjanatva*, which is included in *aprāpti* at ii. 40bc.

> 4.2.14 *pṛthagjanatvaṃ katamat* | *āryāṇāṃ dharmāṇām alābhaḥ* |
>
> 4.2.14 What is the state of an ordinary being? The condition of not having achieved the qualities of an Ārya. ISBP.239

Avatāra (ESD.108 and 111f.):

> Acquisition (*prāpti*) is the cause (*kāraṇa*) which permits the affirmation: "One is in possession of a certain *dharma* (*dharmavat*)". There are three kinds of *dharma*-s: pure (*śubha*), impure (*aśubha*) and non-defined (*avyākṛta*). The pure *dharma*-s comprise faith, etc.; the impure, greed, etc.; and the non-defined, the mind of transformation (*nirmāṇacitta*), etc. One who possesses [any of] these *dharma*-s is said to be "in possession of the *dharma*". The cause of certitude for such an assertion is named acquisition (*prāpti*), obtainment (*lābha*, *pratilābha/pratilambha*), and endowment (*samanvāgama*). [...]
>
> All non-acquisitions [*aprāpti*] are of the non-veiled-non-defined nature only; unlike the case of the acquisitions described above, which are differentiated in nature.
>
> However, each of the past and future *dharma*-s has non-acquisitions belonging to the three periods of time [past, present, future]. For the present *dharma*-s, they have no present non-acquisitions, as acquisitions and non-acquisitions are contradictory to each other in nature [and hence do not co-arise]; and as it is impossible that what can

> be possessed in the present moment is not possessed. They have, however, past and future non-acquisitions.
>
> *Dharma*-s belonging to the sensuality, fine-material, and immaterial spheres, as well as the outflow-free *dharma*-s, each has non-acquisitions belonging to the three spheres. There can be no outflow-free non-acquisitions, as there is in a non-acquisition, the worldling-quality (*pṛthagjanatva*) [which is never outflow-free]. Thus it is said, [in the *Jñānaprasthāna-śāstra*]: "What is the worldling-quality? It is the non-obtainment (*alābha*) of the *dharma*-s of the Noble Ones (*āryadharma*)." Now, this non-obtainment is just a synonym for non-acquisition. Besides, all non-acquisitions being of the non-defined nature only, cannot be outflow-free.

Since Dhammajoti translates *prāpti* as acquisition and we translate *pratilambha/lābha* as acquisition, in order to avoid confusion we will replace his English renderings with the Sanskrit ones wherever it might lead to confusion.

2. As for the historical development of *prāpti*, *samanvāgama*, etc., Dhammajoti and Cox point out (SA.IV.295f; DD.79) that at the early stage *prāpti* was infrequently used in a general sense to refer to the simple act of attaining or acquiring, as, for example, "to attain a particular meditative state", and *samanvāgama* and *asamanvāgama* in the sense of continued possession or non-possession, primarily with regard to wholesome or unwholesome qualities. It was at a relatively later stage that *prāpti* came to be defined as a formation dissociated from thought, a *dharma* which effects the relation of any *dharma* to a living being (*santāna*). More specifically, it may have originated out of a pragmatic concern of the Sarvāstivādins (SA.IV.295): "It seems to have originally referred to the *prāpti* of *ārya-dharma*-s, on the basis of which the *ārya* can be properly distinguished from the ordinary worldling [*pṛthagjana*]. This stage of development may have taken place shortly after the compilation of the JPŚ and before the MVŚ", where we find the first "systematic" definitions of possession and non-possession. "The argument that the unreality of endowment [*samanvāgama*] (= *prāpti*) entails the indistinguishability of an *ārya* and an ordinary worldling is already found in the MVŚ [796c]. However, even in the later *abhidharma* texts like the AKB [ii, F 183, 191ff.], the *Abhidharmadīpa*, the *Nyāyānusāra* and the *Avatāra*, we can still sense this central concern which forms the chief argument for the necessary existence of acquisition [*prāpti*] as a real entity." For more detail, see DD.79ff.

3. As formation dissociated from thought, *prāpti* was then also distinguished from two other terms, namely, acquisition or obtainment (*pratilambha/lābha*) and accompaniment or endowment (*samanvāgama*), which were used not only as synonyms of *prāpti*, but, at the same time, also as two different cases of the latter, as can be seen in the following passage from MVŚ, 823a, which enumerates seven differences between *prāpti* and *samanvāgama* (SA.IV.296f; DD.81):

> i. Some say: The names themselves are different: one named *prāpti*, the other *samanvāgama*.
>
> ii. Some say: The acquisition of what has not been acquired is named *prāpti*; the acquisition of what has already been acquired is *samanvāgama*.
>
> iii. Some say: the acquisition at the very first instance is named *prāpti*; the subsequent repeated acquisition is named *samanvāgama*.

iv. Some say: the endowment (*sam-anu-ā-√gam*) of what has not been previously endowed is named *prāpti*; the endowment of what has already been endowed with is named *samanvāgama*.

v. Some say: What did not previously belong to one, now belongs to one—this is named *prāpti*; what has already belonged to one, now [continues to] belong to one—this is named *samanvāgama*.

vi. Some say: the acquisition at the first instance is named *prāpti*; the non-interruption of what has already been acquired is named *samanvāgama*.

vii. Some say: The initial obtaining (*pratilambha, lābha*) is named *prāpti*; the not-losing of what has already been acquired is named *samanvāgama*. Hence, whereas *prāpti* applies to the first moment, *samanvāgama* applies to both the first and subsequent moments.

These seven opinions can be divided into two basic distinctions (SA.IV.297; DD.81ff.) which either focus

a. on the stage in the temporal process of a given instance of *prāpti*—first moment or subsequently—at which a given *dharma* comes to be acquired by the individual; or

b. on the acquired *dharma* itself, i.e., on the status of a particular *dharma* vis-à-vis its prior attainment or accompaniment—whether it is acquired or possessed by the individual for the first time, or whether it is re-acquired or is being continuously possessed subsequently.

Dhammajoti comments that Vasubandhu essentially follows the first form, being based on the sixth and seventh opinion above, inasmuch as the sixth is said to refer to the first moment of *pratilambha/lābha*, "whether or not the given *dharma* is acquired for the very first time or re-obtained after having been lost".

Saṃghabhadra (Ny, 396c), on the other hand, essentially follows the second form, being based on the second opinion:

> There are two types of *prāpti*: that of what has not been previously acquired and that of what has already been previously acquired. The *prāpti* of what has not been acquired is called obtainment. The *prāpti* of what has been acquired previously is called endowment.
>
> Non-acquisition [*aprāpti*] is to be understood as opposite to this: that of what has not been previously acquired and that of what has been acquired and lost. The non-acquisition of what has not been previously acquired is called non-obtainment (*apratilambha*). The non-acquisition of what has been lost is called non-endowment (*asamanvāgama*). Thus, the nature of an ordinary worldling [*pṛthagjanatva*] is called the non-obtainment of the *ārya-dharma*-s [since a *pṛthagjana* has never yet acquired any *ārya-dharma*].

Cox comments (DD.83) that the compilers of the **Mahāvibhāṣā* do not choose one of the seven opinions offered as the correct or favored one, and that neither Vasubandhu or Saṃghabhadra provide reasons for their support of different interpretations, but Cox then links up the different interpretations by Vasubandhu or Saṃghabhadra with their different ontological models (see DD.84).

435 *LS*: Cox states that Vasubandhu's explanation is not clear here since he does not specify

the various analogous stages in the process of non-possession. Yaśomitra (WOG.143.34ff; DD.82f.), however, spells out two interpretations:

> Non-possession is of two types: (1) non-acquisition of that which has not yet been attained and (2) non-accompaniment of that which has been attained and lost.
>
> Or, (1) the first [moment] of non-possession of that which has not been attained or has been lost is non-acquisition, (2) while the non-possession of that which has not been acquired or has been lost in the second and subsequent moments is non-accompaniment.

As for Saṃghabhadra's definition of non-possession, it has been quoted above in the previous endnote. Cox comments that—although Vasubandhu does not provide a specific definition of non-possession—Yaśomitra's second definition conforms better to Vasubandhu's definition of possession and that Yaśomitra's first definition resembles Saṃghabhadra's definition of non-possession.

436 *Gokhale*: [36cd] *prāptyaprāptī svasaṃtānapatitānāṃ nirodhayoḥ* ||

Tib.: [36cd] *thob dang ma thob rang rgyud du | gtogs pa rnams kyi'o 'gog gnyis kyi* ||

LS: 1. MVŚ, 801a, states (SA.IV.294):

> There are three types of acquisition [*prāpti*]: (i) the acquisition of a conditioned *dharma*; (ii) the acquisition of a cessation through deliberation; (iii) the acquisition of a cessation independent of deliberation.
>
> i. A particular species of the acquisition of a conditioned *dharma* is specified according to that of the *dharma* acquired. A conditioned *dharma* possesses its activity that projects its own acquisition.
>
> ii. A particular species of the acquisition of a cessation through deliberation is specified according to that of the path through which [the cessation] is realized (*sākṣāt-√kṛ*). This is because a cessation through deliberation, [being an unconditioned *dharma*,] does not possess its own activity. Its acquisition is projected through the force of the path at the time when [the practitioner] is seeking its realization.
>
> iii. A particular species of the acquisition of a cessation independent of deliberation is specified according to the [practitioner's] own supporting basis (*āśraya*). This is because a cessation independent of deliberation does not possess its own activity that projects its own acquisition, and it is not sought through a path; it is in dependence on [the practitioner's] vital faculty [*jīvitendriya*] and group-homogeneity [*nikāya-sabhāga*] alone that its acquisition arises.

2. Cox writes (DD.85f: "With the development of Sarvāstivādin ontology, wherein all factors that constitute experience are separately existing, discrete, and radically momentary, accounting for the experience of connection presents a daunting challenge. Indeed, any connection between these separately existing factors would seem to be a logical impossibility. How can the apparent continuity of experience [which is not unified by any central force or 'possessing self', and our common sense notions of connection, or 'belonging to oneself'] be explained? In what sense can qualities be said to characterize, or events be said to occur within the locus of a given sentient being? And, how is the "locus of one sentient being" determined; why do separately existing factors arising in the experience of one sentient being not capri-

ciously arise in the experience of another?"

According to Cox, in early Buddhism the solution to these problems was explained on the basis of dependent origination (*pratītyasamutpāda*) (see iii. 18–38c) and, in the developed Sarvāstivādin Abhidharma theory, on the basis of the intricate interrelationships among the six causes, four conditions and five effects (see ii. 49–73). Thus why would there still be a need to insist on possession and non-possession as separately existing real entities (*dravya*)? The answer is that even though causes and conditions give rise to the particular momentary activity (*kāritra*) of the real entities that exist in the three time periods of past, present and future according to the Sarvāstivādins, it is possession and non-possession that account for the connection of a particular factor to a given life-stream (*saṃtāna*) and which thus serve to delimit the experience of each sentient being from that of other sentient beings as well as from insentient matter (see our section here). As for how possession itself, as a separately existent factor, is connected to the life-stream, see Vasubandhu's discussion, ii, F 194f., of the secondary possession or "possession of possession" (*prāptiprāpti*).

Moreover, Cox states (DD.87) that the need to posit possession and non-possession is especially evident in the case of one's relationship to cessation due to deliberation (*pratisaṃkhyānirodha*) and cessation not due to deliberation (*apratisaṃkhyānirodha*), since these two, as unconditioned factors, "have no conditioned activity and thus cannot be said to arise in the present dependent upon an assemblage of causes and conditions. Nevertheless, these two factors can be said to characterize or not characterize a given life-stream, but only insofar as they are connected to a life-stream through possession or disconnected from it through non-possession. Since possession and non-possession are themselves conditioned factors, their activities arise or pass away in dependence upon specific causes and conditions."

437 *LVP*: In myself there is possession (*prāpti*) or non-possession (*aprāpti*) relative to my defilement, to my action..., that is to say, I possess or do not possess my future or past defilement... . But there is no relation of possession or of non-possession between myself and the defilement of another.

438 *LS*: This refers to the possession of the five aggregates (including the aggregate of form) that falls into and abides in one's own life-stream.

439 *LVP*: Hairs should be regarded as "of a sentient being", since they are bound (*saṃbaddha*) to the material organs.

440 *LS*: Cox comments (DD.210) that pure factors here refer to the truth of the path and the three unconditioned factors.

441 *LVP*: The persons "bound by all the bondages" (*sakalabandhana*) are those who have not attained, through the mundane (*laukika*) path, the abandonment (= *pratisaṃkhyānirodha*) of one of the nine categories of the defilements of the realm of desire. The noble ones (*ārya*), at the first moment (*ādikṣaṇa* = *duḥkhe dharmajñānakṣānti*), have not yet attained the abandonment of the defilements to be abandoned by the (noble) path (vi. 77). – The persons who have obtained the abandonment of one category of defilement are called *ekaprakāropalikhita* (vi. 30a).

442 *LS*: The general principle is formulated by Saṃghabhadra as follows (DD.186): "If there is possession of a factor, there is also non-possession [of it]; if there is no possession of a factor, non-possession [of it] is also impossible."

[443] *LS*: Although not explicitly mentioned in Pradhan, LVP mentions the Sautrāntika here.

[444] *LVP*: *dravyadharmaḥ* = *dravyato dharmaḥ*, or else *dravyaṃ ca tad dharmaś ca sa dravyadharma*, that is to say, *vidyamānasvalakṣaṇo dharmaḥ*. – See below F 186.

[445] *LS*: This is the seventh of Kritzer's forty-four passages discussed in relation to chapter 2 (VY.50f.). He states that Saṃghabhadra (Ny, 397a12–398c1) attributes this question/challenge of the reality of *prāpti* to Vasubandhu and embarks on a long defense of the reality of *prāpti* and refutation of the *bīja* theory. He comments that the *Viniścayasaṃgrahaṇī* states that *prāpti* is only a provisional entity (*prajñapti*) and explains *prāpti* in terms of *bīja*.

MVŚ (479bc8ff., 796c10ff.) defends (DD.89) the discrete existence of accompaniment (*samanvāgama*) as a real entity by first citing several *sūtra* passages as scriptural authorities and then by offering two logical reasonings: accompaniment clearly demarcates ordinary worldlings from noble ones and provides the mechanism by which defilements can be abandoned.

[446] *LVP*: These ten factors are the eight members of the (noble) path plus right liberation (*samyagvimukti*) and right cognition (*samyagjñāna*) (*Aṅguttara*, v. 222); the five abandoned members are not the group: (1) afflicted view of self (*satkāyadṛṣṭi*), (2) overesteeming of morality and certain types of spiritual practices (*śīlavrataparāmarśa*), (3) doubt (*vicikitsā*), (4) predilection for the objects of desire (*kāmacchanda*), (5) malice (*vyāpāda*), for this group has been abandoned with the acquisition of the fruit of non-returner (*anāgāmin*), but rather the group relative to the higher spheres, (1) attachment to material form (*rūparāga*), (2) attachment to the formless (*ārūpyarāga*), (3) restlessness (*auddhatya*), (4) conceit (*māna*), (5) ignorance (*avidyā*).

[447] *LS*: Although not explicitly mentioned in Pradhan, LVP mentions the Sautrāntika here.

[448] *LVP*: *Dīgha*, iii. 59: *Dalhanemi ... sattaratanasamannāgato*.

[449] *LVP*: According to Scripture, entities (*vastu*) are either (1) existing as a real entity (*dravyasat*) or (2) existing as a provisional entity or existing as a provisional designation (*prajñaptisat*).

Saṃghabhadra refutes the Sautrāntika, Ny, 397; *Siddhi*, 54–58. – Ten factors of a perfected being, vi, F 295.

[450] *LS*: Although not explicitly mentioned in Pradhan, LVP mentions the Sautrāntika here.

[451] *LS*: 1. Notice that in the next section, the Sarvāstivādins distance themselves from this statement.

Cox comments (DD.189) that Saṃghabhadra omits this discussion and thus implicitly rejects this generative causal activity as the activity of possession.

2. Saṃghabhadra explains the two functions of *prāpti* that uniquely qualify it as an ontological entity at Ny, 397b and 398b (see introductory endnote to *prāpti* and *aprāpti* at F 179).

[452] *LVP*: The cause of the arising of a thought of desire is the "possession" of this future thought of desire.

[453] *LS*: Although not explicitly mentioned in Pradhan, LVP mentions the Sautrāntika here.

[454] *LVP*: The pure factors (*dharma*), the receptivity to the cognition of the factors with regard to unsatisfactoriness (*duḥkhe dharmajñānakṣānti*), etc.

[455] *LVP*: Respectively, the (i) non-defiled and (ii) defiled factors of the realm of desire.

456 *LS*: Cox comments (DD.213): "There would be no distinction among the various grades of defilements, since there is no distinction among grades of possession."

457 *LS*: The *Avatāra* states (ESD.108):

> [It is necessary that acquisition exists as a real entity (*dravya*)]. Were it non-existent, when defilements like greed, etc., manifest (*sammukhī-√bhū*) in a trainee (*śaikṣa*), he would not be an *ārya*, since he is then without an outflow-free mind. [Similarly], when a wholesome or non-defined mind arises in a worldling (*pṛthagjana*), he ought then to be known as one who is already detached (*vītarāga*), [i.e., an *ārya*]. Moreover, in the absence of the acquisition of Nirvāṇa, the *ārya* and the worldlings would be mutually alike, and ought to be both named "worldlings" or "*ārya*".

458 *LS*: See in the *Electronic Appendix* my *Notes on a Problem and on Two Attempts to Solve it* (2001). The problem addressed is the following (p. 3): "If the world exists only as a multitude of discrete *dharmas* which exist in the present for one fleeting shortest moment of time only and then vanish out of the present existence, then this view seems to abolish any sense of continuity and thus seems to endanger the practice of the spiritual paths and the doctrine of *karma* and seems as well to be completely counterintuitive to common experience. How can *dharmas* cause an effect after they have vanished out of the present existence? How can a tiny momentary *dharma* account for the complexities, connections and apparent continuities of our world? How do we explain our sense of individuality and distinctiveness from other persons and our sense of responsibility for our own actions?"

The *Notes* attempt to briefly summarize how the problem is approached within the Vaibhāṣika and Sautrāntika system in general, but then focus mainly on the important aspects of the functions of possession (*prāpti*) and of the theory of seeds. They are based on the chapter: "Possession and Non-possession", in Collett Cox's *Disputed Dharmas*; on the chapters: "Dharma and Dharmas", and "Doctrinal Disputes", in Edward Conze's *Buddhist Thought in India*; on Padmanabh S. Jaini's *The Sautrāntika Theory of Bīja*; on Louis de La Vallée Poussin's *Documents d'Abhidharma* (1936–1937a); on Vasubandhu's *Karmasiddhiprakaraṇa*.

459 *LS*: Although not explicitly mentioned in Pradhan, LVP mentions the Sautrāntika here.

460 *LS*: For the mechanism of defilement as well as purification within the Sarvāstivāda system, see our introductory endnote to *prāpti* and *aprāpti* (F 179). See also Cox's discussion of the function of possession and non-possession in the abandonment of defilements (DD.89–92).

461 *LS*: Although not explicitly mentioned in Pradhan, LVP mentions the Sautrāntikas here.

462 *LS*: This is the eighth of Kritzer's forty-four passages discussed in relation to chapter 2 (VY.52f.). He comments that this is one of several statements about *bīja* that Saṃghabhadra identifies (Ny, 398b21) as the opinion of Vasubandhu and that the *Viniścayasaṃgrahaṇī* "compares seeds burned by fire, which are permanently rendered unproductive, with the seeds of internal *dharmas* that have been destroyed by the *ārya*".

463 *LS*: See Jaini's section *Kuśala-dharma-bīja* (AD.111–17), where he makes the following remarks pertinent to our passage here:

> The statement of the *Kośakāra* that even a *samucchinna-kuśala-mūla* possesses a subtle element of *kuśala* is not free from contradiction. ... The Dīpakāra gives the meaning of the term *samucchinna-mūla* as understood in the Vaibhāṣika tradition,

and criticizes the theory of *bīja* as propounded by the Kośakāra.

[1] According to the Vaibhāṣikas, the *mithyā-dṛṣṭi* and the *kuśala-mūlas* each consists of three basic grades, viz., *mṛdu* (subtle or slight), *madhya* (of medium nature) and *adhimātra* (extreme). Each of these three grades is further divided into these three, e.g., *mṛdu-mṛdu … adhimātra-adhimātra.*

The *kuśala-mūlas* pertaining to the *arūpāvacara* and the *rūpāvacara* are destroyed by the *mṛdu* and *madhya mithyā-dṛṣṭis*. The *adhimātra mithyā-dṛṣṭi* destroys the *prāyogika kuśala-mūlas* pertaining to the *kāma* world, leaving in such a person only the innate or the *upapatti-lābhika* roots of good. But when a person (like Maskari Gośālīputra, for instance) comes to hold such extremely grave (*adhimātra-adhimātra*) wrong views as *nāstikavāda, ahetukavāda* or *akriyāvāda*, then he destroys even these innate and the most subtle (*upapatti-lābhika*) *kuśala-mūlas* pertaining to the *kāma loka*, whereupon he is called a *samucchinna-kuśala-mūla.*

[2] After stating this Vaibhāṣika theory of the loss of *kuśala dharmas*, the Dīpakāra turns to the Kośakāra's definition of a *samucchinna-kuśala mūla.* This he condemns as contrary to the Scriptures where it is specifically stated that the *kuśala-mūlas* are completely annihilated. He then criticizes the theory of *bīja* with the argument that the *kuśala* and *akuśala*, being incompatible like light and darkness, cannot coexist at one time. Even if they coexist, in the case of a *samucchinna-kuśala-mūla*, the *kuśala* elements are entirely lost. How can a new *kuśala* arise in this person? If it arises from the *akuśala* then one may as well argue that rice is obtained from barley seeds or that *mithyā-dṛṣṭi* is produced by right thinking. Thus the Kośakāra's theory of *bīja* and the consequent wrong definition of a *samucchinna-kuśala-mūla* do not stand the test of either the Scriptures or of reasoning [according to the Dīpakāra].

[3] The Kośakāra's definition of the term *samucchinna-kuśala-mūla* is identical with the Yogācāra definition of this term. In the *Mahāyāna-Sūtrālaṅkāra* [III. 11] only the imminent liberation of a *samucchinna-kuśala-mūla* is denied. This suggests that he may attain *parinirvāṇa* in the distant future. This would mean that according to the Yogācāras such a person is not completely devoid of a *kuśala-mūla.* The contention of the Kośakāra that the innate *kuśala-mūlas* are never entirely destroyed marks a still further departure from the orthodox Hīnayāna. It implies that unlike the *akuśala-bījas* which are completely annihilated, the elements of *kuśala* persist throughout the series of existence. This is a characteristically Mahāyānist view inasmuch as it holds an assurance of liberation even for a person like Maskarī Gośālīputra who comes to hold the gravest of wrong views.

The Kośakāra does not give further details of this incorruptible element of *kuśala.* Unlike the elements of *akuśala* which are only *sāsrava*, the *kuśala* elements are of two kinds, viz., *sāsrava* and *anāsrava.* The former pertains to the (*kuśala*) *kāma, rūpa* and *arūpa bhavas*. The *anāsrava kuśalas* are those which produce the *lokottara* (super-mundane) states like arhatship or Buddhahood. Is it possible that the incorruptible *kuśala-bīja* spoken of by the Kośakāra represents the *anāsrava-kuśala-bīja* leading to *nirvāṇa*? […]

The theory of an innate, indestructible and pure (*anāsrava*) element existing in the midst of destructible, phenomenal and impure elements shows an affinity with the Mahāyāna doctrine of *prakṛti-prabhāsvara-citta*, according to which mind is essentially and originally pure but becomes impure only by adventitious afflictions. This *prakṛti-prabhāsvara-caitta* is further described as identical with the *dharmatā*, *tathatā* and, therefore, with the *dharma-kāya* of the Buddha.

464 *LS*: This is the ninth of Kritzer's forty-four passages discussed in relation to chapter 2 (VY.54f.). Here we have one of several statements about *bīja* that Saṃghabhadra identifies (Ny, 398b21) as the opinion of Vasubandhu. As for parallels to the *Yogācārabhūmi*, Kritzer states, in regard to *samucchinnakuśalamūla*, that the *Manobhūmi* (281a22–28) specifies that the destruction of the *kuśalamūlas* does not include the destruction of their seeds.

As to whether, from Vasubandhu's point of view, *bīja* and *bīja-bhāva* are different or not, see in the context of the definition of *bīja* our endnote below (F 185).

465 *LVP*: *tair utpannais tadutpattivaśitvāvighātāt samanvāgamaḥ.*

LS: This is the tenth of Kritzer's forty-four passages discussed in relation to chapter 2 (VY.56). Saṃghabhadra (Ny, 398a22–26) claims that Vasubandhu's statement is inconsistent with his denial of the existence of future *dharmas*. Kritzer comments that the *Viniścayasaṃgrahaṇī* (587a18–19) "defines **vaśitvasamanvāgama* as follows: it is the grown (matured?) seeds that are the cause comprising the condition (*hetupratyaya*?) for the arising of good *dharmas* produced by effort and a portion of neutral *dharmas*".

466 *LVP*: "The seeds receive the name of possession (*prāpti*), at the time when they are not uprooted or damaged, where their mastery is ripened" (*anapoddhṛta-anupahata-paripuṣṭa-vaśitva-kāle bījāni prāptināma labhante*), Paramārtha, 3, p. 181b. – Hsüan-tsang: "In the person (*āśraya*), there are seeds that are not uprooted, not damaged, that have a ripened mastery: relative to this state, one uses the word possession (*prāpti*)."

467 *LS*: My translation here follows Collett Cox's translation of Vasubandhu in Saṃghabhadra's *Nyāyānusāra* (DD.189) and LVP's own correction.

468 *LS*: Yaśomitra glosses (WOG.148.1f.):

> *yan nāma-rūpaṃ phalotpattau samartham. yat* paṃca-skandh'ātmakaṃ rūpaṃ phalotpatti-samarthaṃ *sākṣād anantaraṃ* pāraṃparyeṇa *dūrataḥ.*

This is the eleventh of Kritzer's forty-four passages discussed in relation to chapter 2 (VY.58f.). Saṃghabhadra identifies it (Ny, 537b13ff.) as the opinion of Vasubandhu.

469 *LS*: This is the twelfth of Kritzer's forty-four passages discussed in relation to chapter 2 (VY.60f.). Saṃghabhadra identifies this (Ny, 398b) as the opinion of Vasubandhu.

The following longer endnote discusses the following topics: (1) historical development of the seed theory; (2) the essential characteristics of the seed theory; (3) Saṃghabhadra's two main strategies of refuting Vasubandhu's theory of seeds; (4) the relationship between *bīja* and *bījabhāva*; (5) the relationship between Vasubandhu's *bīja* theory and Śrīlāta's *anudhātu* theory; (6) further features, issues and discrepancies within the various seed theories; (7) the broader function of the seed theory within the interpretative models of Vasubandhu and the Dārṣṭāntikas or Sautrāntikas.

1. As for the historical development of the seed theory, Collett Cox explains (DD.103):

> Though it is difficult to trace the development of the seed theory prior to its use by

Vasubandhu, it does appear in the **Mahāvibhāṣā* and in the **Saṃyuktābhidharma-hṛdayaśāstra* in contexts that would appear to constitute incipient stages in its development. The earliest sources that describe in detail the dynamics of the seed theory are Vasubandhu's *Abhidharmakośabhāṣya*, and *Karmasiddhiprakaraṇa*, and Saṅghabhadra's **Nyāyānusāra*, which ascribes the seed theory to the Dārṣṭāntikas.

2. As for the seed theory itself, Dhammajoti makes the following general comments in his article "Śrīlāta's *anudhātu* doctrine" (ŚAD):

> The essential constituents of the seed theory are (i) perfuming (*vāsanā*) and (ii) a continuous process of progressive transformation in which the causal efficacy can be transmitted up to the stage when the corresponding effect is generated [i.e., *saṃtati-pariṇāma-viśeṣa*].

i. As for the first essential constituent, i.e., perfuming (*vāsanā*), he explains that "the Dārṣṭāntikas and Vibhajyavādins have transformed the original notion of its being a trace left behind by a defilement ... but in itself not of the nature of defilement, to that of causal conditioning: A *dharma*, X as the cause, 'perfumes' another *dharma*, Y as the effect, when X partly or wholly transfers its characteristic to Y or brings about a corresponding change in the latter."

ii. As for the second essential constituent, see Vasubandhu's discussion at ix, F 295f., and Dhammajoti's section 7 in his ŚAD: "Retribution-born (*vipākaja*) and retribution fruit (*vipāka-phala*)".

When discussing Vasubandhu's definition of *bīja* and *saṃtatipariṇāma-viśeṣa* in our passage here, Dhammajoti first makes the general comments (section 4) (a) that, in Vasubandhu's doctrine of the seed in the AKB, we see the seed sometimes spoken of as if it is a single entity (in which case one can speak of the "Seed"), and at other times, a plurality ("seeds"), and (b) that Vasubandhu's definition of *bīja* at ii, F 185, is rather similar to Śrīlāta's description of the pursuant element (*anudhātu*). As for the definition itself:

> And what is this so-called seed? It is that psycho-physical complex (*nāma-rūpa*) which is efficacious in generating a fruit, either directly or through a succession.

Dhammajoti comments that this definition clearly speaks of the whole causally efficacious psycho-physical complex as the seed/Seed, just as the whole causally efficacious six *āyatana*s of a person are called the pursuant element. He then quotes the following dialogue from Ny, 397b:

> [Saṃghabhadra:] What is this *nāma-rūpa*?
>
> [Sautrāntika/Vasubandhu:] The five *skandha*-s.
>
> [Saṃghabhadra:] Why do you assert that this is of the seed-nature (種子性; *bīja-bhāva*)?
>
> [Sautrāntika:] It can serve as the cause generating *dharma*-s which are skilful, etc.
>
> [Saṃghabhadra:] Do [the *skandha*-s exercise this seed-nature] [a] as a whole, or [b] individually, or [c] with respect to the specific species? Your assertion entails only these [options].
>
> [a] If [they do so] as a whole, then the seed should be a non-real (since a whole is a mere concept); it is illogical that a non-real serves as a truly existent cause.

[b] If [they do so] individually, then how can you assert that the non-defined material seeds can be the generative cause for the skilful and unskilful *dharma*-s?

[c] If [they do so] with respect to the specific species (i.e., a material seed generates a material *dharma*, etc.), then when immediately after a skilful *dharma* an unskilful *dharma* arises, or conversely—[in such a case] which serves as the seed?

[Sautrāntika:] My dear! The seed-nature is not as it is understood by you. On account of a specific volition (*cetanā-viśeṣa*) co-nascent with the preceding thought, there arises [correspondingly] a specific efficacy in the succeeding thought. This very specific efficacy in the succeeding thought is called seed. At a distinctive [culminating] point in the process of the [progressive] transformation of its serial continuity (*santati-pariṇāma-viśeṣa*), a future fruit is generated. The meaning here is as follows: in an unskilful thought, there exists a specific efficacy projected by a skilful [mental factor, which is exercised] either directly or through a succession. This serves as the seed, and immediately afterwards a skilful *dharma* comes to arise. [Likewise for the arising of an unskilful immediately after a skilful].

Cox comments (DD.95): "Since [the] seed-state [*bīja-bhāva*] is a potentiality and not an actualized event manifesting definite qualities, seed-states of any moral quality can coexist in one life-stream. Like all conditioned factors, these aggregates and their potential capability as seed-states are momentary, and this potentiality is passed along through the contiguous conditioning by which aggregates are produced in each successive moment. Thus, the actualization of a seed's potential at a later time is not the direct result of the original factor or action by which the stream of that seed-state was initially implanted. Rather, the later actualization is conditioned indirectly through the successive reproduction of the efficacy of the original action in each consecutive moment in the form of a seed-state. At a certain moment, when the appropriate causes and conditions coalesce, the seed's potential is actualized. That moment is referred to as the distinctive characteristic in the transformation of the life-stream (*saṃtatipariṇāmaviśeṣa*). By means of this process of successive transmission and transformation through which a seed develops and sprouts, Vasubandhu attempts to explain the causal efficacy of action, all varieties of causation whether homogeneous, heterogeneous, remote or immediate, and thereby all forms of apparent continuity within the life-stream."

3. Saṃghabhadra attempts to refute Vasubandhu's theory of seeds using mainly two strategies.

i. Clarification of the relationship between the seed and the life-stream: The first strategy we find in the continuation of the above dialogue (Ny, 397c; ŚAD), which goes as follows:

[Saṃghabhadra:] Now, the seed asserted by you as a specific efficacy—does it or does it not exist as an entity distinct from the skilful or unskilful thought?

[Sautrāntika:] It does not exist as a distinct entity.

[Saṃghabhadra:] [In addition to the various faults which I have pointed out regarding your theory,] it has never been observed that *dharma*-s of different species, differing in their natures, are not distinct entities.

Cox comments (DD.95): "First, Saṅghabhadra demands that the relationship between the seed and the life-stream—specifically, a given moment of thought within the life-stream—be clearly defined: that is to say, the mental and material seeds that lie dormant within the life-stream must be either identical to, or separate from, the mental and material factors constituting the life-stream at any given moment."

According to Yaśomitra (WOG.148.27–28; DD.215f.) (a) if the seed were admitted to be a distinct entity from thought, this would be tantamount to admitting possession, the formation dissociated from thought, for the dispute would then be merely a question of names, whereas (b) if the seed were not admitted to be a distinct entity from thought then there would be the fault of mixture (*sāṃkarya-doṣa*) (of the character of seed [= of the good, the bad, the impure, the pure, etc.] and the character of thought); thus he maintains (c) "that seed must be said to be neither an entity separate from thought nor an entity not separate from thought, since it has the nature of a dependent provisional entity (*upādāyaprajñaptirūpatvāt*)" (WOG.149.2–5; DD.216).

But Yaśomitra (WOG.149.4–16) also states (AD.109) that "even if a *bīja* is considered identical with *citta*, there is no fault for, a *kuśala citta* which has arisen would in that case implant its seed in a (subsequent) *citta* of its own *santāna*, the latter *citta* being either of the same kind (*kuśala*) or of the opposite kind (*akuśala*). Thereafter (*tataḥ*) the (second) *citta* would arise as qualified (determined) by the first only in accordance with the principle that a specific effect arises from a specific cause (*kāraṇa-viśeṣa*) [i.e., if the second *citta* is *anya-jātīya*, the *bīja* lies dormant].... Nor does the fact that a specific *śakti* is implanted by a *kuśala-citta* in an *akuśala-citta* entail (*iti*) that the *akuśala* becomes *kuśala* or vice versa, since it is only a specific *śakti* [i.e., it cannot produce effects which, by its very nature, it is not competent to produce] also called *bīja* or *vāsanā*. These are all synonyms."

Saṃghabhadra, on the other hand, contends (Ny, 397c; DD.95) that (a) if the seed were not admitted to be a distinct entity from thought or the life-stream, then it would not be possible to explain the succession of morally dissimilar moments of thought, whereas (b) when the seeds are considered to be merely provisional potentialities that are neither identical with nor separate from the life-stream, that this would mean to divest these seeds of any real capability.

ii. The second strategy is based on the fact that Vasubandhu does not recognize the existence of factors in the past or future, and for that matter Saṃghabhadra attacks all schools who do accept successive causation, but not *sarvāstitva*. Here (DD.95f.) "Saṅghabhadra points out that causal interaction, even between two contiguous moments, is impossible. For any given present moment, the previous moment is past and thus no longer exists; similarly, the succeeding moment, as future, does not yet exist. Since, for both the Sarvāstivāda-Vaibhāṣikas and Vasubandhu, an entity that does not exist as a real entity cannot act as a cause, Saṅghabhadra argues that Vasubandhu cannot defend causal interaction even between contiguous moments unless factors are admitted to exist in all three time periods. Thus, Saṅghabhadra concludes, Vasubandhu's theory of the contiguous transmission of a seed's potential efficacy and its eventual manifestation as a distinctive characteristic in the transformation of the life-stream is unfounded." Saṃghabhadra can thus close his discussion of the seed theory by stating (Ny, 398b15 and 398b25; DD.196f.):

> [Without accepting the existence of past and future factors,] the Dārṣṭāntikas cannot uphold change between prior and subsequent moments within a stream, conditioned forces having the nature of cause and effect within the three time periods, or the capability of producing an effect immediately. ...

> In the arguments among the various Ābhidhārmikas, the Dārṣṭāntikas often appeal to their own [theory] of seeds, and thereby, pervert the correct meaning and cause it to become unclear. There are certain masters who give different names to these seeds, each according to his own understanding. Some call them subsidiary elements (**anu-dhātu*), others call them traces (*vāsana*), still others call them capability (*sāmarthya*), or non-disappearance (*avipraṇāśa*), or accumulation (*upacaya*). Therefore, through extensive analysis of [the theory of seeds] we have [also] demolished these [other theories] and have established the correct accepted doctrine.

4. As for the relationship of *bīja* and *bījabhāva* (see above ii, F 184), Vasubandhu considers both *prāpti* and *bīja* not to be real entities (*dravya*), but see more on this below. He explains seed-state (*bījabhāva*)—in the context of discussing the latent proclivity (*anuśaya*) and envelopment (*paryavasthāna*) (v, F 6)—as "a specific power or potency (*śakti*) to produce the defilement, an ability belonging to the person under consideration (*āśraya*, *ātmabhāva*) and engendered by the previous defilement". Cox comments (DD.104) that Hyōdō (1980), pp, 69–73, "argues for a distinction in Vasubandhu's interpretation between the seeds (*bīja*), or the aggregates themselves, and the seed-state (*bījabhāva*), or the potential of those aggregates to produce an effect, a distinction not explicitly recognized by Yaśomitra or in Hsüan-tsang's translation. This distinction, Hyōdō contends, suggests that Vasubandhu recognized the actual existence of seeds, but not of the seed-state. For those like Yaśomitra who appear to identify the seed and the seed-state, both would be merely provisional. Hyōdō also suggests that this distinction between *bīja* and *bījabhāva* does not reflect the original Sautrāntika position, but rather represents Vasubandhu's own innovation within the *Abhidharmakośabhāṣya*, an innovation that results, Hyōdō claims, from Vasubandhu's assumption that causes must be real entities."

Dhammajoti reflects on Hyōdō's views and examines one of the examples put forth by Hyōdō to support his view. But while Dhammajoti acknowledges that *bīja-bhāva* is an abstract noun whereas *bīja* is a simple noun, he does not think that this necessarily must signify certain implications asserted by Hyōdō. Therefore he concludes (ŚAD):

> Xuan Zang and others have understood the *bīja* doctrine of the Sautrāntika (and it would seem also that of the early Mahāyāna Yogācāras) correctly: *bīja* is the nature of being efficacious in generating fruit, and this nature is exhibited in a sentient being's serial continuity—*bīja* is therefore interchangeable with *bīja-bhāva*; and both can be described in terms of the sentient being's psycho-physical complex.

As to their being real or not, he states that "from the Dārṣṭāntika-Sautrāntika perspective, *bīja* is not a real entity in the ordinary sense, nor is *bīja-bhāva* absolutely nothing more than a mere concept. If *bīja* and *bīja-bhāva* must be forcibly fitted into the Sarvāstivāda scheme of understanding the 'reals', then they must be said to be 'neither real nor unreal'. For this same reason, one can speak of seed/Seed in the singular when one refers to the efficacy as such, possessed by the serial continuity, or seeds in the plural when one needs to differentiate among the different specific species of efficacies."

5. As for the relationship between the *bīja* theory as expounded in the AKB and Śrīlāta's *anudhātu* theory, Dhammajoti comments (ADCP.99) that the latter may be said to be a more generalized form of the *bīja* theory, since it accounts for the continuous manifestation of the totality of a sentient being's existence—the six *āyatanas*—from one present moment to the

next, whereby the *anudhātu* is the causal efficacy within the sentient being's present serial continuity, and the next moment of the serial continuity is the effect.

6. To draw attention to further features, issues and discrepancies within the various seed theories, in the following we translate pertinent excerpts from a Yogācāra text, which accepts simultaneous causation, namely LVP's translation of Hsüan-tsang's *Siddhi* (*Ch'eng wei-shih Lun*). The excerpts deal with the characteristics of (i) the *bījas* and of (ii) the perfumable and the perfumer, within Hsüan-tsang's discussion of the *ālayavijñāna*. He states (F 96):

> a. [The *ālayavijñāna*] is actively *ālaya*, store, for it stores the *bījas* which are passively *ālaya*, being stored.
>
> b. It is passively *ālaya*, in the sense that it is "perfumed" by the *dharmas* called *saṃkleśa* [= all the impure (*sāsrava*) *dharmas* or all the *dharmas* of *saṃsāra* (*pravṛti*), i.e., not just the defiled (*kliṣṭa*) *dharmas*].

Hsüan-tsang then asks (F 100ff.):

> i. What kind of *dharma* is called *bīja*?
>
> In the *ālayavijñāna*, also called root-consciousness (*mūlavijñāna*), there occur potencies or capabilities (*śakti* or *sāmarthya*) which give rise to their effect, i.e., a present or manifest *dharma*. [The author considers the *bījas* having come to maturity, not the *bījas* in their homogeneous generation, from their origin up to the state of maturity].
>
> ii. Reality of the *bījas*.
>
> In relation to the *vijñāna*, in relation to the effect, the *bījas* are neither identical nor different. Such is, in fact, the mode of relation between the thing or intrinsic nature (*svabhāva*), *vijñāna*, and the activity (*kāritra*), *bīja*; between the cause (*hetu*), *bīja*, and the effect (*phala*), the present *dharma*.
>
> However, although not identical with the *vijñāna* and the effect, and not different from the *vijñāna* and the effect, the *bījas* are real entities (*dravyasat*). ...
>
> This is not Sthiramati's doctrine for whom the *bījas*, being neither identical to present *dharmas* nor different from them, are of "nominal existence", like the pitcher, and not real. ...
>
> iii. *Bhāgas*. ...
>
> iv. Moral type of the *bījas*.
>
> The impure *bījas*—being integrated into the *vipākavijñāna* (i.e., not having a "nature" distinct from the *vijñāna*), consequently being of the same kind—are non-defined (*avyākṛta*). Nevertheless, their causes (namely, the present *vijñānas* which perfume the *vipākavijñāna*) and their effects (namely, the present *vijñānas* which arise from the *bījas*) are good, bad. Therefore it is said that the impure *bījas* are good, bad.
>
> The pure (*anāsrava*) *bījas*—not being integrated into the *vipākavijñāna*, not being of its kind, having arisen from good causes and producing good effects—are good.

As for the characteristics of the *bījas*, Hsüan-tsang gives the following six (F 116ff.):

> i. The *bījas* are momentary (*kṣaṇika*). ...
>
> ii. The *bījas* are simultaneous (*sahabhū*) with their effect. ...

iii. The *bījas* give rise to a continuous series (*sadā-anuprabaddha* [?]). – The *bījas* are *dharmas* that—for a long period of time, of the same nature—continue in an uninterrupted series until the final stage, until the moment when the path that counteracts (*pratipakṣa*) them arises.

This definition eliminates the *Sautrāntika* doctrine for which the six *vijñānas* (the *pravṛttivijñānas*, the only *vijñānas* they accept) are *bījas*: but these *vijñānas* are variable (*vikārin*) and discontinuous and thus are out of the question. [The *rūpa* also does not answer to the definition.] ...

iv. The *bījas* are determined as to their moral type (*viniyata*). – The *bīja* possesses the capacity to give rise to a present *dharma*, good, bad, non-defined: this capacity is determined by the cause of the *bīja*, namely, the good, bad, non-defined *dharma* that perfumed-created it. ...

v. The *bījas* depend on the complex of conditions (*pratyayasāmagryapekṣa*). – In order to actualize their capacity to produce a present *dharma*, the *bījas* require the support of conditions. ...

vi. The *bījas* "lead" (*in*) to their own effect (*svaphalāvāhaka*). – Each *dharma* leads to the effect which is its own: a *bīja* of mind (*citta*) leads to mind, a *bīja* of *rūpa* leads to *rūpa*. ...

These six characteristics belong only to the "potencies" (*śaktiviśeṣa*) of the *mūla-vijñāna* or the *ālayavijñāna*. These potencies alone are truly said to be the *bījas*. – As for external seeds, rice seeds, etc., they are but a development (*pariṇāma*) of the *vijñāna* due to the potencies (or *bījas*) of the *vijñāna*. They are called *bījas* only metaphorically: they are not true *bījas*.

The *bīja*, external or internal, insofar as it engenders the near effect, the major effect, is called "generative cause" (*janakahetu*); insofar as it "projects" the distant effect, the supplementary effect (*uccheṣa*), (of such a kind that the effect does not cease immediately), it is called "projecting cause" (*ākṣepakahetu*).

As for that which is perfumable and that which perfumes, Hsüan-tsang states (F 120ff.):

In other words, (i) that in which the *bījas* can be created or nourished, (ii) that which creates or nourishes the *bījas*.

There is *vāsanā*, perfuming, creation or nourishing of the *bījas* when there is a "perfumable" and a "perfumer".

i. The perfumable must have four characteristics.

a. It endures (*āsthitasvabhāva*). – The *dharma* which, from beginning to end, continues in a series of a single type, is capable of carrying the perfume (*vāsanā*) and is perfumable. ...

b. It is indeterminate (*avyākṛtasvabhāva*). – Only the unvarying *dharma*, non-contradictory (*aviruddha*: which does not contradict either good or bad) is capable of receiving the perfume. ...

c. It is perfumable (*bhāvyasvabhāva* ?) – The autonomous *dharma* (*svatantra*), the *dharma* that is not hard like a stone. ...

d. It is in strict relationship (*saṃsṛṣṭa* ?) with that which perfumes. – The *dharma* that is simultaneous with the perfumer, in the same place, neither identical with nor separate from the perfumer. ...

The eighth *vijñāna* alone, when it is *vipāka*, shows these four characteristics, not the five thought-concomitants of the eighth and not the *pravṛttivijñāna*.

ii. The perfumer must have four characteristics.

a. Arising and ceasing (*sa-utpādanirodha*). ...

b. Being endowed with an eminent action (*adhimātrakriyā*). – The *dharma* that arises and ceases, that has great power, is capable of producing the perfume (*vāsanā*) or of perfuming (*bhāvanā*).

c. Increasing and decreasing. – The *dharma* of eminent power, able to increase and decrease, is capable of planting the perfume (*vāsanā*). ...

d. Intimately connected with the perfumed. – Same explanation as above (i.d)

Only the seven *pravṛttivijñāna*s with their thought-concomitants have an eminent action, are capable of increasing and decreasing. Having these four characteristics, they are "perfumers".

There is perfuming (*bhāvanā*) when the *vijñāna* that perfumes (= the *darśanabhāga* of one of the seven *vijñāna*s) arises and ceases at the same time as the *vijñāna* that is perfumed (= the *saṃvittibhāga* of the eighth *vijñāna*). Indeed, at this moment, *bījas* (= *vāsanā*) arise or increase in the perfumed *vijñāna* in the same way as the odor of the flower arises in the sesame seed, flower and seed arising and ceasing at the same time.

7. Although in our passage Vasubandhu discusses the seed theory within the context of possession, Cox comments (DD.96f) that this theory "has a much broader function within the interpretative models of Vasubandhu and the Dārṣṭāntikas or Sautrāntikas. The model of seeds is appealed to in all instances of general causal production: for example, the efficacy of past action; the retention and recollection of memories; the succession of dissimilar moments of thought; the arising of defilements after an interval; and the abandonment of defilements. By contrast, the Sarvāstivāda-Vaibhāṣikas use several other models in addition to possession and non-possession to account for these phenomena: namely, the six causes and four conditions; the general causal efficacy of all past factors; and unmanifest action (*avijñaptirūpa*)."

470 *LVP*: These definitions answer the questions of the Vaibhāṣika: "Is the seed a real entity (*dravya*) different from thought or not different from thought?" "Is this series a permanent (*avasthita*) real entity (*dravya*) within which different factors successively arise?" "Should the transformation (*pariṇāma*) be understood in the same way as the *pariṇāma* of the Sāṃkhyas?"

See ii. 54cd. – The doctrine of the transformation of the stream is presented again iv, F 20–22; ix, F 295f.

LS: Although a definition of the term "distinctive characteristic" (*viśeṣa*) is missing here in Pradhan, both Hsüan-tsang and Paramārtha include it in their translation. Vasubandhu, however, gives the definition of *viśeṣa* at ix, F 296, when discussing *saṃtatipariṇāmaviśeṣa* (DD.215): "[It is that] which is capable in the production of an effect immediately" (*yo anantaraṃ phalotpādanasamarthaḥ*).

471 *LS*: Although not explicitly mentioned in Pradhan, LVP mentions the Sautrāntika here.

472 *LVP*: Tibetan and Paramārtha. – Hsüan-tsang: "The two paths (doctrine of the Sautrāntikas, doctrine of the Vaibhāṣikas) are good. – How is that? – The first is not in contradiction with reasoning; the second is our system."

473 *LS*: SAH 484.

474 *LS*: Ibid.

475 *Gokhale*: [37a] *traiyadhvikānāṃ trividhā*

Tib.: [37a] *dus gsum pa yi rnam pa gsum* |

LS: The *Avatāra* (p. 109f; SA.IV.298) speaks of three kinds of *prāpti*:

1. those that arise simultaneously (*sahaja*) with the acquired *dharma* and are thus comparable to a shadow that follows the figure: this refers mostly to those of unobscured-non-defined *dharmas*;

2. those that arise prior (*agraja*) to the *dharma* to be acquired by an individual series and are thus comparable to a chief bull (*vṛṣabha*) that leads the herd, since it conduces to the arising of the *dharma*: mostly those of the wholesome *dharmas* of the realm of desire at the moment when one who has "fallen" from a higher stage and is about to be reborn (*pratisaṃdhi*) in the realm of desire.

3. those that arise subsequent (*paścātkālaja*) to the acquired *dharma* and are comparable to a calf that follows its mother, since it remains after the acquired *dharma* has ceased: mostly those of the understanding (*prajñā*) produced by listening (*śrūtamayī*), by reflection (*cintamayī*), etc., excluding the simultaneous acquisitions.

476 *LVP*: The possession (*prāpti*) of past factors (*dharma*) is:

1. either past, that is to say: "that which has arisen and has perished": the possession would be either previous to (*agraja*), or later than (*paścātkālaja*), or simultaneous (*sahaja*) with these factors;
2. or else future, that is to say: "that which has not arisen": the possession would be later than these factors;
3. or else present, that is to say: "that which has arisen and has not perished": the possession is later than these factors. And so on.

No factor is susceptible to this threefold possession (*prāpti*), for example, the possession of factors "of retribution" is only simultaneous with these factors (ii. 38c). One does not "possess" these factors before they have arisen, not after they have perished.

477 *LS*: AH 222; SAH 455.

478 *Gokhale*: [37b] *śubhādīnāṃ śubhādikā* |

Tib.: [37b] *dge la sogs kyi dge la sogs* |

479 *Gokhale*: [37c] *svadhātukā tadāptānāṃ* |

Tib.: [37c] *der gtogs rnams kyi rang khams pa* |

LVP: The impure factors are in the framework of existence, belong to the realms of existence, *dhātvāpta, dhātupatita.*

480 *Gokhale*: [37d] *anāptānāṃ caturvidhā* ||

Tib.: [37d] *ma gtogs rnams kyi rnam pa bzhi* ||

LVP: These are the *apariyāpannas* of the Abhidhamma.

[481] *LVP*: The cessation due to deliberation (*pratisaṃkhyānirodha*) or "disconnection from defilement" (*visaṃyoga*, i. 6ab; ii. 57d) can be obtained (1) by ordinary worldlings (*pṛthagjana*) or (2) by noble ones (*ārya*).

In the first case, the possession (*prāpti*) is (i) of the realm of fine-materiality or (ii) of the realm of immateriality according to whether cessation (*nirodha*) is obtained by a (mundane) path of the realm of fine-materiality or of the realm of immateriality.

In the second case, the possession is (i) of the realm of fine-materiality and pure, when cessation is obtained by a (mundane) path of the realm of fine-materiality; (ii) of the realm of immateriality and pure, when cessation is obtained by a path of the realm of immateriality; (iii) pure, when cessation is obtained by the pure path (according to the formulated principle vi. 46).

[482] *LS*: Cox comments (DD.219) that "since the truth of the path is a conditioned factor, the location of its possession is determined by its own location: that is, it is not connected to any realm. Possession not connected to any realm is then, itself, also a factor not tending toward the fluxes."

[483] *LVP*: (1) The factors of those in training (*śaikṣa*) are the pure factors of those in training (*śaikṣa*), of the noble ones who are not perfected beings (*arhat*); (2) the factors of those beyond training (*aśaikṣa*) are the pure factors of perfected beings (*arhat*).

[484] *Gokhale*: [38a] *tridhā naśaikṣā'śaikṣāṇām*

Tib.: [38a] *slob dang mi slob min gyi gsum* |

[485] *LVP*: Paramārtha: "The same for the possession (*prāpti*) obtained by non-noble-persons, of the cessation not due to deliberation (*apratisaṃkhyānirodha*) and of the cessation due to deliberation (*pratisaṃkhyānirodha*)." Hsüan-tsang: "...the possession of the cessation due to deliberation obtained by the path of the non-noble-persons".

[486] *Gokhale*: [38b] *aheyānāṃ dvidhā matā*

Tib.: [38b] *spang bya min pa'i rnam gnyis 'dod* |

[487] *LVP*: One case is not envisioned: the possession of the cessation due to deliberation, by means of the mundane path, by noble ones (*ārya*). This possession is both pure and impure, as we shall see at vi. 46.

[488] *Gokhale*: [38cd] *avyākṛtāptiḥ sahajā 'bhijñānairmaṇikād ṛte* ||

Tib.: [38cd] *lung bstan min thob lhan cig skye* | *mngon shes sprul pa ma gtogs pa* ||

[489] *LVP*: *durbalatvāt*: anabhisaṃskāravattvāt [WOG.152.8], because it is not the result of an effort.

[490] *LS*: I here follow Collett Cox's translation (DD.200).

[491] *LVP*: *Vyākhyā* [WOG.152.16f.]: The Vaibhāṣikas. – For example, Viśvakarman, the celestial artisan, possesses past, present and future skill in arts and crafts (*śailpasthānika*); the Sthavira Aśvajit possesses the modes of proper deportment (*airyāpathika*).

LS: Cox comments (DD.221) that "Viśvakarman is identified in the *Ṛgveda* as an abstract creative deity, and in the later period, becomes the divine architect and patron of the decorative and building arts" and that "Aśvajit was one of the five original disciples of the Buddha.

He so impressed Śāriputra with his deportment in begging alms that Śāriputra inquired about the doctrine of his teacher, and as a result, went to study with the Buddha."

492 *Gokhale*: [39a] *nivṛtasya ca rūpasya*

Tib.: [39a1] *bsgribs pa'i gzugs kyi'ang*

493 *LS*: According to the Vaibhāṣikas (DD.221), all material form (*rūpa*) is non-defined with the exception of (1) certain bodily or vocal informative actions (*kāyavāgvijñaptirūpa*) and (2) all non-informative actions (*avijñaptirūpa*) (i. 29f., iv. 7ab). Saṃghabhadra explains (Ny, 399a; DD.201):

> This refers only to the possession of the defiled, manifest, corporeal and vocal actions (*kliṣṭavijñaptirūpa*) within the first level of trance of the realm of form, which, as in the case of [the possession of the obscured, indeterminate factors], arises only simultaneously with [those actions]. Even though [these actions arise obscured by] excessive (*adhimātra*) defilements, since they cannot give rise to unmanifest actions (*avijñaptirūpa*), they are weak and definitely without possession [that arises] prior to or subsequent to them.

494 *Gokhale*: [39b] *kāme rūpasya nā 'grajā* |

Tib.: [39a2–b] *'dod pa na* | *gzugs kyi lngar ni skye ba med* |

495 *LS*: Pradhan.65.28 has "informative and non-informative" (*vijñaptyavijñapti*), but Hsüan-tsang uses *kuśalākuśala*. Yaśomitra glosses (WOG.152.28f): "wholesome and unwholesome, informative and non-informative form [or action]" (*kuśalākuśalasya vijñaptyavijñaptirūpasya*).

496 *LS*: SAH 454, 457, 484.

497 *Gokhale*: [39c] *akliṣṭa'vyākṛtā 'prāptiḥ*

Tib.: [39c] *ma thob ma bsgribs lung ma bstan* |

LVP: The non-possession of the defilements is not obscured, for, in this hypothesis, it would be absent in the persons liberated from defilements; it is not wholesome, for it would then have to be absent in the persons who have cut the wholesome roots. (MVŚ, 799a21).

LS: Cox comments (DD.222) that unlike possession, the moral quality of non-possession is not determined by the factors to which it is applied:

> In general, the character of non-possession is not determined by the character of the particular factor that is not possessed, because non-possession and the particular factor with regard to which it operates are contradictory. Nor is the character of the non-possession of cessation resulting from consideration determined by the path through which that cessation is attained, because its non-possession is not attained by that path. Rather, the character of non-possession is determined by the corporeal basis of rebirth (*upapattyāśraya*) or, where there is no corporeal basis, by the vitality and the homogeneous character of the sentient being who experiences it. See MVŚ 158, p. 801a13ff.

But more specifically, since non-possession is "indeterminate" (*avyākṛta*), it is not included among the factors belonging to those in training (*śaikṣa*) or those beyond training (*aśaikṣa*), which are only wholesome (*kuśala*); it is thus included with those factors belonging to those neither in training nor beyond training. On the other hand, since it is "indeterminate", i.e., not pure (*anāsrava*) or wholesome (*kuśala*), and thus to be abandoned, but "unobscured" (*anivṛta*), it is to be abandoned by the path of cultivation, since all factors that are to be abandoned by the path of insight are obscured (*nivṛta*).

498 *Gokhale*: [39d] *sā 'tītā'jātayos tridhā* ||

Tib.: [39d] *'das ma skyes kyi de rnam gsum* ||

499 *LS*: It is not possible for non-possession and possession to operate on the same factor simultaneously.

500 *Gokhale*: [40a] *kāmādyāptā'malānāṃ ca*

Tib.: [40a] *'dod sogs gtogs dang dri med kyi'ang* |

501 *LS*: AH 221; SAH 454, 457.

502 *LS*: See ii. 39c.

503 *Gokhale*: [40bc1] *mārgasyā 'prāptir iṣyate* | *pṛthagjanatvaṃ*

Tib.: [40bc] *lam ma thob pa so so yi* | *skye bor 'dod do* |

LVP: If a non-possession (*aprāpti*) could be pure, this would have to be the non-possession of pure factors; but the definition of the ordinary worldling (*pṛthagjana*) establishes that the non-possession of pure factors is not pure.

On the ordinary worldling, see i. 40, 41a; ii. 9bd; iii. 41cd, 95a; vi. 26a, 28d, 45b.

504 *LS*: AH 221; SAH 454, 457.

505 *LS*: AH 221, 224, SAH 454, 457.

506 *LS*: Ibid.

507 *LVP*: The second masters of the *Vibhāṣā*.

508 *LVP*: Compare *Kathāvatthu*, iv. 4.

509 *LS*: This is the second place in Pradhan (66.19) where the term Sautrāntika is explicitly mentioned.

510 *LS*: This is the 13th of Kritzer's forty-four passages discussed in relation to chapter 2 (VY.62f.). Saṃghabhadra (Ny, 399b10–11) identifies this passage as the opinion of Vasubandhu, and since the life-stream as a composite entity cannot be real, Saṃghabhadra (Ny, 399b11–c7) criticizes him for denying the real existence of *pṛthagjanatvam*. The *Viniścayasaṃgrahaṇī* defines *pṛthagjanatva* as a designation for the state in which the *lokottara āryadharmas* have not yet arisen. On the other hand, the denial of the *pṛthagjanatva* is already attributed to the Dārṣṭāntikas in the MVŚ, 231b26–27.

511 *Gokhale*: [40c2–d] *tatprāptibhūsaṃcārād vihīyate* ||

Tib.: [40c2–d] *de thob dang* | *sa 'phos nas ni rnam nyams 'gyur* ||

512 *LVP*: The non-possession (*aprāpti*) or non-acquisition (*alābha*) belongs to the realm of existence (*dhātu*) to which the person who is endowed with it belongs (ii. 40a). Thus a being of the realm of desire is endowed only with the status of an ordinary worldling (which is non-possession [*aprāpti*], ii. 40bc) of the realm of desire. Thus it cannot be said that, through the acquisition of the (noble) path, this being loses the status of an ordinary worldling of the sphere of the three realms. – Nevertheless, through the acquisition of the (noble) path, any status of an ordinary worldling, of whatever realm this might be, becomes impossible. Thus it

can be said that this status, under its threefold form (of the realm of desire, etc.), is abandoned, although a given being is endowed with one form only.

Two aspects of abandonment are distinguished, *vihāni* (loss) and *prahāṇa* (abandonment).

LS: The general principle here is that non-possession of a given factor is discarded by the acquisition of that factor.

513 *LVP*: Ordinary worldlings (*pṛthagjana*), detaching themselves from the realm of desire, pass into the first meditation (*dhyāna*): they lose the status of the ordinary worldling of the realm of desire, but do not, in actual fact, become noble ones (*ārya*): since another status of an ordinary worldling, of the sphere of the first meditation, appears. The same for the other stages that one ascends or descends.

LS: Saṃghabhadra states (Ny, 400a; DD.209) that "[non-possession can be discarded by passing to another stage] because non-possession operates in dependence upon the power of the corporeal basis [to which it is connected]".

514 *LVP*: By taking possession of the wholesome factors derived from listening and from reflection of the realm of desire, one loses the non-possession of these factors; by taking possession of the innate wholesome factors (ii. 71b), one loses the non-possession of the wholesome roots that have been cut off (*samucchinnakuśala*). – When, dying in the realm of desire, one is reborn in the first meditation (*dhyāna*), one loses the non-possession of the factors of the first meditation.... This theory raises delicate problems which the *Vyākhyā* summarily examines.

515 *LS*: SAH 484.

516 *LS*: In other words, each of these possessions can only be associated with the life-stream of a given sentient being through other possessions, these others through still others, and so on.

517 *LS*: Saṃghabhadra states (Ny, 400a; DD.209) in addition: "[The impossibility of infinite regress in the case of] non-possession should also be considered in accordance with [the following] principle: that is, a non-possession of the non-possession [of a particular factor] never arises simultaneously with [that original non-possession]."

518 *LVP*: Compare ii. 45cd: the play (1) of origination (*jāti*) and (2) of the origination-of-origination (*jātijāti*).

519 *LVP*: The case of the non-defined (*avyākṛta*) factor is not examined here, because one possesses this factor only at the moment when it exists (*tasya sahajaiva prāptiḥ*): the numbers differ.

520 *LVP*: The Japanese editor observes that four characteristics (*lakṣaṇa*) and four secondary characteristics (*anulakṣaṇa*) must be added (ii. 46cd) for each of these three factors; thus there are twenty-seven factors at the first moment.

521 *LVP*: At the fourth moment one possesses twenty-seven possessions (*prāpti*), namely, the possessions produced at the three preceding moments, three, six, eighteen, plus twenty-seven secondary possessions (*anuprāpti*), thus fifty-four factors. At the fifth moment, 81 [= 54 + 27] possessions and as many secondary possessions.

522 *LS*: Hsüan-tsang, v, fol. 1a.

523 *LS*: AH 220; SAH 453.

[524] *LS*: Ibid.

[525] *Gokhale*: [41a] *sabhāgatā sattvasāmyam*

Tib.: [41a] *skal mnyam sems can 'dra ba'o* |

LVP: *Prakaraṇa*, 694a23: "What is the group homogeneity (*nikāyasabhāga*)? – The commonality of nature of sentient beings."

Each sentient being possesses his or her own "sentient being" homogeneity (*sattvasabhāgatā*). Nevertheless, the "sentient being" homogeneity is said to be general because it is not differentiated. To conceive of it as unique and eternal is the error of the Vaiśeṣikas.

LS: 1. Vasubandhu's *Pañcaskandhaka* (2008) states:

> 4.2.6 *nikāyasabhāgatā katamā | yā sattvānām ātmabhāvatulyatā |*
>
> 4.2.6 What is class affiliation? The similarity in the composition of beings. ISBP.238

Avatāra (ESD.115):

> The group-homogeneity is the cause for the similarities in striving and inclination among sentient beings (*sattvānām ekārtharuciḥ sādṛṣyahetubhūta*). This is subdivided into two: (i) non-differentiated [or general] (*abhinnā*) and (ii) differentiated [or particular] (*bhinnā*).

Saṃghabhadra defines (SA.IV.300; Ny, 400a):

> There is a distinct entity called *sabhāgatā*. It is the mutual similarity (*sādṛśya*) among sentient beings. The cause of similarity (*sābhāgya-kāraṇa*) among various species of sentient beings born in the same plane of existence (*gati*), with regard to the body (*śarīra*), shape (*saṃsthana*), the [specific] functionalities of the faculties (*indriya*), and food (*āhāra*), etc., as well as the cause for their mutually similar inclinations (*ruci*), is called *nikāya-sabhāga*.

2. As for the historical development of group-homogeneity, Cox writes (DD.107f.) that the *Dharmaskandha*, *Saṅgītiparyāya* and *Jñānaprasthāna* discuss the role of homogeneity in reference to the rebirth process and list it among the causes that determine the specific rebirth state of sentient beings, but that in the later texts the role of homogeneity is expanded and given the function of determining, in addition to the specific rebirth state, also the realm, mode of birth, region, family, and distinguishing physical attributes of sentient beings; each sentient being is thus characterized by several types of homogeneous character.

3. In the Abhidharma taxonomy, group-homogeneity is included (DD.107f.) among the "formations dissociated from thought and matter" (i) because it is applied to both mental and material factors, (ii) because it cannot be assigned to more than one category.

4. As for the existential status of group-homogeneity, this is discussed by Vasubandhu in five points below, including the point of whether group-homogeneity is really needed as a distinct real entity (*dravya*) in light of the category of the nature of an ordinary worldling (*pṛthagjana*). Saṃghabhadra, in this context, adds the discussion of whether group-homogeneity is really needed in the light of the doctrine of *karma* as a cause of the similarities and dissimilarities of appearances, functionalities, etc.

Dhammajoti explains (SA.IV.301) that "in the Sarvāstivāda doctrine of *karma*, one's existence is determined by two types of *karma*. (i) The projecting (*ākṣepaka*) *karma* which results in one's being born in a particular plane of existence. This existence is designated principally by one's *nikāya-sabhāga* since 'it is only when one acquires the *nikāya-sabhāga* that one is said to be born' [Ny, 585b]. (ii) A multiplicity of completing (*paripūraka*) *karma*-s which together determine the particularities of the existence so projected. *Nikāya-sabhāga*, in acting along with the *paripūraka-karma*-s to work out these particularities, contributes to the similarities so described among members of the same species."

Saṃghabhadra therefore states (Ny, 400a; SA.IV.300):

> Just as *karma*, the *citta* and the Great Elements are all the cause for the clear matter [of which the sense organs are constituted], thus the body and shape, etc., are not caused by *karma* alone, for it is observed that the bodies and shapes [of sentient beings] are results projected (*ā-√kṣipā*) by mutually similar *karma*, [and yet] there exist differences with regard to the faculties, functionalities and food, etc. If one says that such differences result from those in the completing *karma*-s (*paripūraka-karma*), it is not reasonable, for there can be bodies and shapes which are projected by similar projecting *karma* (*ākśepaka-karma*); [but] it is on account of there being differences in the group-homogeneity that the functionalities become different. If the bodies and shapes, etc., are no more than the result of *karma*, then it would not be possible [for beings] to abandon or perform any function in accordance with their inclination.

5. Vasubandhu discusses homogeneity briefly at various other places in the AKB, mainly in regard to projecting and losing homogeneity, for example, in relation to losing restraint (*saṃvara*; iv. 38) or projecting a new birth (*janman*; iv. 95a). But as already pointed out above by Collett Cox (see endnote at ii, F 105), Vasubandhu also uses the term *nikāyasabhāga* in a non-technical sense; thus, Yaśomitra—in the context of Vasubandhu's own definition of the vitality faculty (ii, F 216)—glosses the term *nikāyasabhāga* as "conditioned forces of a certain nature having the aggregate of form, and so on, as their intrinsic nature" and that Saṃghabhadra replaces Vasubandhu's non-technical use of *nikāyasabhāga* with "the six sense organs together with their basis".

For further references see our index.

526 *LS*: Saṃghabhadra explains the compound *sabhāgatā* as follows (Ny, 400a; SA.IV.301): "*sa* (homogeneity) because of the mutual similarities in physical appearances, functionalities and inclination. *Bhāga* means cause (*nimitta*)." Cox adds (DD.235) that it "can also be interpreted as a descriptive determinative (*karmadhāraya*): that is, simply as 'similar' or 'shared' (*sa*) 'part' (*bhāga*)."

As for the compound *nikāyasabhāga*, she states (DD.234) that it is subject to several interpretations: "For example: (1) many similarities (**nikāya-samāna*) and distinctions (**bhāga*); (2) the cause of similarity (**sabhāga*) among many factors or entities (**nikāya*), or among many sentient beings (**nikāya*)."

527 *LS*: SAH 453.

528 *LS*: Ibid.

529 *LS*: The general homogeneity determines one's status as distinct from insentient matter. The *Avatāra* comments (ESD.115): "All sentient beings equally have self-attachment (*ātmasneha*), are similarly nourished by food, and have similar inclinations (*rati*)—this cause of

sameness (*samya*) is named the [general] group-homogeneity. Each [sentient being] has within him his own group-homogeneity."

530 *LVP*: By *et cetera*, one should understand: Upāsikā, Bhikṣuṇī, Naivaśaikṣanāśaikṣa, etc.

531 *LS*: The particular homogeneity determines the characteristic that defines the commonality of a particular group and distinguishes that group from others. The *Avatāra* comments (ESD.115): "Within each being [of a given category], there is a *dharma* which is the distinguishing cause (*pratiniyama-hetu*) for the similarity in striving and inclination [among members of the same category]. This is named the group-homogeneity. If this were nonexistent, there would be confusion in all the conventional usages (*loka-vyavahāra*) such as '*ārya*', 'non-*ārya*', etc."

532 *LS*: 1. The homogeneity of factors is not found in earlier Sarvāstivādin discussions of group-homogeneity, where it is used only in reference to sentient beings, and is initiated by the AKB and the **Nyāyānusāra* (DD.235).

2. Pradhan and **Nyāyānusāra* do not render "indicative of sentient beings". Cox therfore comments (DD.111) that although Saṃghabhadra's **Abhidharma-samaya-pradīpikā-śāstra* (805c10ff.) suggests that the *dharma-sabhāgatā* refers only to those aggregates and so on, that are included among factors constituting sentient beings (*sattvākhya*), it "could indicate an extension of homogeneous character beyond the realm of sentient beings. It would no longer function to explain the process of rebirth, but would refer to an abstract notion of similarity intersecting all entities, sentient and insentient alike. Indeed, Vasubandhu's intentions in suggesting this second type of homogeneous character of factors [*sabhāgatā*] are not clear."

533 *LVP*: Two readings: *evaṃ skandhādibuddhiprajñaptayo 'pi yojyāḥ* and *evaṃ dhātvādibuddhiprajñaptayo 'pi yojyāḥ*: "It is because of the homogeneity of factors (*dharmasabhāgatā*) that the elements are of the realm of desire...".

534 *LS*: Although not explicitly mentioned in Pradhan, LVP mentions the Sautrāntika here.

535 *LS*: As for the difference between *pṛthagjana-sabhāgatā* and *pṛthajanatva*, the *Avatāra* states (ESD.115):

> The cause for the homogeneity in inclination, etc., is said to be their homogeneity (*sabhāgatā*). The worldling-quality [*pṛthagjanatva*], [on the other hand,] is that which causes the doing of all unprofitable [—i.e., evil—] things (*sarvānarthakarabhūta*). ... Now, [unlike the case of the homogeneity,] it is not the case that at the times of birth and death there is the acquisition and relinquishment, respectively of the worldling-quality: [One remains a worldling in *saṃsāra* until one becomes an *ārya*]. Hence, there is a [vast] difference (*sumahāṃstadviśeṣaḥ*) between the worldling-quality and the homogeneity.

536 *LS*: As for proofs of the *sabhāgatā*, Saṃghabhadra replies (Ny, 400b; DD.232):

> One knows that [homogeneous character] has that [activity], because one observes its effect. [Thus, the activity of homogeneous character is proven through inference,] just as one knows that there was an action performed in a former life, because one observes a present effect attained through action. [The activity of homogeneous character is also proven through direct perception] because a yogic practitioner knows it through direct perception.

[537] *LS*: As for why insentient entities do not have a group-homogeneity, Saṃghabhadra presents five reasons (DD.232f.):

> [First, the Lord] did not state that grass, and so on, has a homogeneous character, because it is without the mutually respective similarity in modes of behavior [*kriyā*] and aspirations [*ruci*] [characteristic of sentient beings].
>
> [Second,] because grass, and so on, is inevitably produced only so long as it has sentient beings as its cause, it is claimed that there is homogeneous character only with regard to sentient beings.
>
> [Third, homogeneous character] is produced with actions from a previous life or effort (*prayatna*) in the present life as its cause. Since grass, and so on, has neither of these two causes—[neither action nor effort]—it is without homogeneous character. It is precisely through the existence of these two causes that the existence [of homogeneous character] as a real entity is proven.
>
> [Fourth: omitted.]
>
> [Fifth,] due to previous statements, [it is known that homogeneous character is a discrete real entity]. What was stated previously? Namely, it was stated that "even though it is observed that the body and appearance are effects projected by [previous] similar action, since there are [also] distinctions among the controlling faculties, the modes of behavior, sustenance, and so on, [one should acknowledge that these distinctions are caused by homogeneous character]".

[538] *LS*: Cox comments (DD.108f.): "In his definition of homogeneous character, Saṅghabhadra does not include an appeal to a general homogeneous character as the basis for the notion or provisional designation of the category of all sentient beings nor does he accept the need for an abstract universal concept of homogeneous character. Instead, Saṅghabhadra emphasizes the discriminating function of homogeneous character as the cause for distinctions among sentient beings. The existence of homogeneous character as a discrete factor is then inferred from this causal activity and the notion of homogeneous character in the abstract arises on the basis of its discriminating function or its observed activity as the cause of similarity among things in the same category."

[539] *LS*: 1. According to Radhakrishnan (IP), the Vaiśeṣika system takes its name from "*viśeṣa*", individuator or particularity; it emphasizes the significance of particulars or individuals and is decidedly pluralistic. It has been regarded as non-theistic. The legendary founder of the system (IP.386), "Kaṇāda, the author of the *Vaiśeṣika Sūtra* (much older than Nyāya but later than 300 B.C.), does not mention God, but later commentators felt that the immutable atoms could not by themselves produce an ordered universe unless a presiding God regulated their activities".

2. The Vaiśeṣika adopts a classification of six or seven categories (*padārtha*):

    i. real entity (*dravya*), comprising nine varieties: (*1*) earth (*pṛthivī*), (*2*) water (*āpas*), (*3*) fire (*tejas*), (*4*) air or wind (*vāyu*), (*5*) space or ether (*ākāśa*), (*6*) time (*kāla*), (*7*) spatial direction (*diś* or *dik*), (*8*) self or soul (*ātman*), (*9*) internal organ (*manas*);

    ii. quality (*guṇa*), comprising seventeen or twenty-four varieties (*1*) color (*rūpa*), (*2*) taste (*rasa*), (*3*) odor (*gandha*), (*4*) touch (*sparśa*), (*5*) number (*saṃkhyā*), (*6*) dimension or size (*parimāṇa*), (*7*) separateness (*pṛthaktva*), (*8*) contact or conjunction (*saṃyoga*), (*9*) disjunction (*vibhāga*), (*10*) farness (*paratva*), (*11*) nearness (*aparatva*), (*12*) knowledge (*buddhi* or *jñāna*), (*13*) pleasure (*sukha*), (*14*) displeasure (*duḥkha*), (*15*) desire (*icchā*), (*16*) hatred (*dveṣa*), (*17*) effort (*icchā*); (*18*) heaviness (*gurutva*), (*19*) fluidity (*dravatva*), (*20*) viscidity (*sneha*), (*21*) dispositional tendency or impetus (*vega*), (*22*) merit (*dharma*), (*23*) demerit (*adharma*), (*24*) sound (*śabda*);

iii. motion (*karma*);
iv. universal (*sāmānya*);
v. particularity (*viśeṣa*);
vi. inherence (*samavāya*);
vii. absence (*abhāva*).

3. As for *sāmānya*, Potter writes (EIP.II.133): "The fully developed Nyāya-Vaiśeṣika view of universal is that they are real, independent, timeless, ubiquitous entities which inhere in individual substances, qualities, and motions and are repeatable, i.e., may inhere in several distinct individuals at once or at different times and places. The general term used in Vaiśeṣika for such an entity is *sāmānya*. However, the initial doctrine of the school as found in the *Vaiśeṣika-sūtras* and the early commentators is substantially different from the notion just characterized."

4. In regard to the relation of the categories *sāmānya* and *viśeṣa* and the Vaibhāṣika school, Saṃghabhadra comments (Ny, 400c; DD.234):

> If the Vaiśeṣika school maintained that these two categories [of generality and of particular generalities] were not singular, were momentary and impermanent, were without support, and were distinguished [from the object to which they apply], we could accept their opinion and suffer no categorical fault (*atiprasaṅga*). The Buddha did not reject the view that the visual sense organ is able to operate with form [as its object] and suggest other interpretations, simply because the Vaiśeṣika [also] maintain [that view].

Dhammajoti adds (ESD.43) that "the concept of the Vaibhāṣika *sabhāgatā* is quite different from that of the Vaiśeṣika *sāmānya*. We must remember that *sabhāgatā* does not refer to the concept of the reality of the whole as imposed on discrete, momentary *dharma*-s. The Vaibhāṣikas themselves regard only the smallest discrete components as *paramārthasat*, and not their combination. As clearly defined in *Avatāra*, the Ny and the *Abhidharmadīpa*, *sabhāgatā* is a real entity within each sentient being, an inner force which causes the similarity in members of a group like sentient beings, human beings, etc. It is not the generality conceived as real."

[540] *LVP*: The *Vyākhyā* cites the Sūtra: prāṇātipātenāsevitena bhāvitena bahulīkṛtena (comp. *Aṅguttara*, iv. 247, etc.) narakeṣūpapadyate | *sa ced itthaṃtvaṃ āgacchati manuṣyāṇāṃ sabhāgatāṃ prāpnoti* prāṇātipātenālpāyur bhavati... [WOG.159.6ff.]. The *Daśabhūmaka* replaces the formula *sa ced* ... by *atha cet punar manuṣyeṣūpapadyate*.

Divya, 194, 30: *manuṣyāṇāṃ sabhāgatāyām upapanna iti* (*Mahāvyutpatti*, 245, 54); 122, 16: *brahmaloka-sabhāgatāyāṃ copapanno mahābrahmā saṃvṛttaḥ*. *Śikṣāsamuccaya*, 176, 9: *sa[rva]nikāyasabhāge devamanuṣyāṇāṃ priyo bhavati*.

[541] *LS*: Although not explicitly mentioned in Pradhan, LVP mentions the Sautrāntika here.

[542] *LS*: Here I follow Collett Cox's translation based on Pradhan: AKB 2.41a, p. 68.9ff: *kā*

tarhi sā. ta eva hi tathābhūtāh saṃskārā yeṣu manuṣyādiprajñaptiḥ śālyādiṣu sabhāgatāvat.

LVP translates: Par les expressions "*sabhāgatā* des hommes", etc., le Sūtra entend la similitude dans la manière d'être: de même, *sabhāgatā* du riz, du blé, des fèves, etc.

Nikāyasabhāga can also have a non-technical meaning, namely, a homogeneous collection of components or aggregates that constitutes a person. See DD.109f.

[543] *LVP*: Hsüan-tsang translates: "This is not admissible, for this is in contradiction with our system"; he omits the formula: "The Vaibhāṣikas say" (The Vaibhāṣikas say: "This is not admissible...").

[544] *LS*: AH 220; SAH 453.

1. The history of the next three formations dissociated from thought, which are states without thought (*acittaka*), shows that they have deep roots within early Buddhist and non-Buddhist meditative practice (see Bronkhorst [2000], *The Two Traditions of Meditation Ancient India*) and were elaborated within the later northern Indian Abhidharma treatises. In regard to their treatment in the *Abhidharmakośabhāṣya* and **Nyāyānusāra*, Cox explains (DD.144) that they "are both adapted from the analysis presented in the **Mahāvibhāṣā* and differ from it only in their dialogic style of explication and a lesser degree of comprehensiveness. The primary focus of these analyses is a detailed explication of the various qualities of each state according to a standard Abhidharma taxonomy of characteristics."

2. To account for the apparent disappearance of thought experienced in meditative practice, the Vaibhāṣikas enlist (i) the state of non-ideation (*āsaṃjñika*), (ii) the attainment of non-ideation (*asaṃjñisamāpatti*) and (iii) the attainment of cessation (*nirodhasamāpatti*) as real entities that induce states without thought by means of their activity of obstructing the arising of both the single thought factor (*citta*) and the simultaneous and associated thought-concomitants (*caitta*).

3. These three discrete factors are classified within the category of factors dissociated from both thought and material form since (DD.115) they induce states without thought, but are themselves not thoughts, and since they pertain to the psychic stream, and are thus not material form.

4. Whereas the state of non-ideation is an effect since it is attained through rebirth, the two states of attainment as meditative states are causes that produce an effect.

[545] *Gokhale*: [41bc] *āsaṃjñikam asaṃjñiṣu* | *nirodhaś cittacaittānāṃ*

Tib.: [41bd1] *'du shes med pa pa 'du shes* | *med par sems dang sems byung rnams* | *'gog pa'o*

LVP: *āsaṃjñikam asaṃjñisu* | *nirodhaś cittacaittānāṃ vipākas tu bṛhatphale* || – *Prakaraṇa*, 694a19. – *Dīgha*, iii. 263: *sant 'āvuso sattā asaññino appatisaṃvedino seyyathāpi devā asaññasattā*. – i. 28, iii. 33, *...saññuppādā ca pana te devā tamhā kāyā cavanti*. – One of the nine stages of sentient beings (*sattvāvāsa*), *Aṅguttara*, iv. 401; *Kośa*, iii. 6c.

LS: 1. Vasubandhu's *Pañcaskandhaka* (2008) states:

> 4.2.4 *āsañjñikaṃ katamat* | *asañjñisamāpattiphalam* | *asañjñisattveṣu deveṣūpapannasyāsthāvarāṇāṃ cittacaitasikānāṃ dharmāṇāṃ yo nirodhaḥ* |
>
> 4.2.4 What is [the quality of] having no conception? [It is] a result of the state of composure without conception; and the cessation of inconstant minds and mental fac-

tors of a being who has been born among the deities who lack conception. ISBP.238

Avatāra (ESD.113f.): "For those born among the deities who are ideationless beings (*asaṃjñi-sattveṣu deveṣūpapannānām*) there is a *dharma* named ideationlessness (*āsaṃjñika*) which causes the cessation of the thought and thought-concomitants. It is a real entity (*dravya*). It is said to be 'born of retribution' (*vipākaja*), being the retribution-fruit (*vipākaphala*) of the ideationless-attainment, and [therefore] non-defined."

2. The state of non-ideation is also further discussed at iii. 6, where it is, for obvious reasons, excluded from the stations of consciousness (*vijñānasthiti*) but included within the nine types of abiding of sentient beings (*sattvāvāsa*), planes of existence wherein sentient beings abide as they wish, i.e., in contrast to the unfortunate or lower planes of existence,

546 *LS*: Cox comments (DD.241): "Yüan-yü (Yüan-yü 9 p. 242a4ff.) observes that beings are referred to as 'sentient' because they have perceptual consciousness. Even though beings in this state of non-ideation do not have perceptual consciousness, they still have sense organs that serve as the basis for perceptual consciousness. Therefore, because they are of the same category as sentient beings insofar as they too possess this basis for perceptual consciousness, they can be referred to as 'sentient'."

547 *LS*: MVŚ, 784a24ff., identifies this period of time as 500 great aeons (*mahākalpa*).

548 *LS*: My translation here is adjusted in accord with Collett Cox's translation (DD.239).

549 *LS* SAH 453.

550 *Gokhale*: [41d2] *vipākas*

Tib.: [41d2] *rnam smin*

LS: Being a ripened effect, the moral quality of the state of non-ideation is non-defined (*avyākṛta*) (ii, F 201).

551 *LVP*: MVŚ, 615a5, five opinions.

LS: However, Saṃghabhadra explains (Ny, 400c) that the attainment of non-ideation has only the state of non-ideation and the material form of those gods as its retribution but not their group-homogeneity (*nikāyasabhāga*) and vitality (*jīvita*), which are retributed by the fourth meditation (*dhyāna*), wherein thought exists, and also not their remaining aggregates (*skandha*) which are retributed by both this attainment and the fourth meditation. During the phase where those gods are without thought (see ii. 41d), "remaining aggregates" refers to (DD.242) certain formations dissociated from thoughts other than *nikāyasabhāga* and *jīvita*—for example, since *asaṃjñisattva* is a conditioned factor, to the origination (*jāti*), deterioration (*jarā*), etc.

552 *Gokhale*: [41d3] *te bṛhatphalāḥ* ||

Tib.: [41d3] *de 'bras che* ||

553 *LVP*: The Foreign Masters claim, on the contrary, that there are nine divisions in the heaven of the fourth meditation (*dhyāna*). – On the Vṛhatphalas (Vehapphala), see Burnouf, *Introduction*, p. 614.

LS: On the specifics of the different views, see DD.242.

554 *LVP*: Opinion of the Andhakas, condemned in *Kathāvatthu*, iii. 11.

555 *LS*: AH 220; SAH 453, 455.

[556] *LVP*: On the meaning of the term *samāpatti*, see F 213.

LS: 1. As for the history of the two attainments without thought, Cox states (DD.113):

> Evidence for the practice of states of equipoise [without thought (*acittakasamāpatti*)] within the non-Buddhist Indian religious milieu is found in the canonical reports [where it is stated] that the Buddha, prior to his enlightenment, learned the meditative practice of entering the sphere of neither conception nor non-conception (*naivasaṃjñānāsaṃjñāyatana*) from the wandering ascetic, Udraka Rāmaputra. This sphere of neither conception nor non-conception is also assimilated into several early Buddhist cosmological and meditational taxonomies: for example, the nine stages of beings (*sattvāvāsa*) that include the state of non-conception as the fifth and the sphere of neither conception nor non-conception as the ninth and final stage; or, the eight liberations (*vimokṣa*) that include the sphere of neither conception nor non-conception as the seventh liberation followed by the cessation of conception and feelings (*saṃjñāveditanirodha*) as the eighth. Perhaps the most frequently encountered schema is that of the four spheres within the formless realm, which are incorporated into nine successive meditative abodes (*anupūrvavihāra*) also referred to as the nine successive states of equipoise (*anupūrvasamāpatti*): these nine states combine the four levels of trance of the realm of form, the four spheres of the formless realm, including the sphere of neither conception nor non-conception, and the cessation of conception and feelings as the ninth.

2. As for the AKB, Vasubandhu explains at iii. 6b that the two attainments and the state of non-ideation are not part of the seven stations of consciousness (*vijñānasthiti*), and this for the obvious reason that they are cut off therein. The above-mentioned nine abidings of sentient beings (*sattvāvāsa*), i.e., planes of existence wherein sentient beings abide as they wish, are discussed at iii. 6cd. In regard to the above-mentioned eighth liberation, i.e., *nirodhasamāpatti*, it is discussed at viii. 33, where its intrinsic nature as well as the thought of entry into it and the thought of leaving it are explained.

At vi. 43cd, Vasubandhu explains attainment of cessation in the context of the non-returner (*anāgāmin*) called *bodily witness* or *those who realize within their own body* (*kāyasākṣin*), "since through their body, in view of the absence of thought, they have directly realized (*sākṣātkaroti*) a factor similar to *nirvāṇa*, i.e., the attainment of cessation (*nirodhasamāpatti*)". There we also find the Sautrāntika view of attainment of cessation expressed as follows:

> When the noble ones leave the attainment of cessation (*nirodhasamāpatti*), as soon as they think: "Oh! this attainment of cessation is peaceful [*śānta*] like *nirvāṇa*!"—they acquire a calmness [*śāntatva*] of the conscious body (i.e., of the body in which the consciousness has arisen again: *savijñānakakāya*) never previously acquired. In this way, they realize directly through the body the calmness [of cessation] by virtue of two actions of realization (*sākṣātkaraṇa*): the first, the acquisition (*prāpti*)—during the attainment—of a body in accordance with cessation, the second, upon leaving the attainment, the cognition (*jñāna*) that becomes conscious of the state of the body. For the fact of "manifesting" (*pratyakṣīkāra*) is called *realization* (*sākṣātkriyā*). There is realization when one notices the calmness of the body that has again become conscious; and, from this noticing, the result is that this calmness has been acquired while the body was non-conscious.

At vi. 64ab, Vasubandhu explains attainment of cessation in the context of the perfected beings (*arhat*) called *those who are liberated through both parts* (*ubhayatobhāgavimukta*).

3. As for the term *samāpatti*, Dhammajoti explains (SA.IV.302): "The word *samāpatti* (< *sam-ā-√pad*) means attainment. In Buddhism, it means, in particular, the attainment of a meditational state. For the *abhidharma* scholiasts, it connotes an attainment in which there is complete evenness in mind and body—a connotation supposedly conveyed by the prefix *sam* taken in the sense of *samatā* ('evenness', 'equality'). ... The ideationless attainment and cessation attainment are two meditative attainments in which there is completely no mental activity at all."

Saṃghabhadra comments (Ny, 401a; DD.246):

> [The term "equipoise" (*samāpatti*) can be understood in the following way.] [The second member *-āpatti* of the compound should be understood as meaning] "to accomplish" (*niṣpatti*); [the first member *sama* or *sam*,] as "correctly" or "thoroughly". Therefore, [the state of "accomplishing correctly" or "accomplishing thoroughly"] is referred to as an equipoise. There are other masters who claim that the "appropriate" or "equilibrated" (*samatā*) "operation" [of the life-stream as a whole] is to be referred to as equipoise because that equipoise equilibrates (*samatāpādana*) thought and the four fundamental material elements (*mahābhūta*).

MVŚ, 775b23ff., states (ESD.186):

> There are two kinds of *samāpatti*: (1) that which causes the thought to be even, (2) that which causes the *mahābhūta*-s to be even. Although the *asaṃjñi*- and *nirodha-samāpatti* interrupt the even-ness of mind, causing it not to continue, they induce the even-ness of *mahābhūta*-s, causing them to manifest. Hence they are called *samāpatti*-s.

4. As for the possibility of meditative states without thought, Cox comments (DD.114f.) that while the northern Indian Abhidharma schools generally accepted this possibility and shared the enumeration of their specific qualities, "they disagreed concerning the character and functioning of such states. These disagreements can be correlated with fundamental differences of opinion on issues of ontology, causation, and psychological modeling. The primary participants in these arguments can be divided into two groups: on the one hand, the Sarvāstivāda-Vaibhāṣikas, represented by Saṅghabhadra and, in the *Abhidharmakośabhāṣya*, by Ghoṣaka; on the other hand, the Dārṣṭāntikas, who share the views of Vasumitra cited in the *Abhidharmakośabhāṣya*, the ancient masters, whom Yaśomitra identifies as the Sautrāntikas, and finally Vasubandhu."

557 *LVP*: The complete name is *saṃjñāveditanirodhasamāpatti* (attainment of cessation of ideation and sensation), see ii, F 211.

Prakaraṇa (694a19): The attainment of non-ideation (*asaṃjnisamāpatti*) is an arresting of the thought and thought-concomitants that has for its antecedent the notion of escape (*niḥsaraṇa-manasikārapūrvaka*) and which is obtained by a person freed from the defilements of the Śubhakṛtsnas and not from higher defilements.

The attainment of cessation (*nirodhasamāpatti*) is an arresting of the thought and thought-concomitants which has for its antecedent the notion of calmness and which is obtained by a person freed from the defilements of the perception-sphere of nothingness (*ākiñcanyāyatana*).

– Vasubandhu, in the *Pañcaskandhaka*, is inspired by these definitions.

558 *LS*: AH 220; SAH 453, 455.

559 *Gokhale*: [42a] *tathā 'saṃjñisamāpattir*

Tib.: [42a] *de bzhin 'du shes med snyoms 'jug* |

LS: Vasubandhu's *Pañcaskandhaka* (2008) states:

> 4.2.2 *asañjñisamāpattiḥ katamā* | *śubhakṛtsnavītarāgasya nordhvaṃ niḥsaraṇa-sañjñāpūrvakeṇa manasikāreṇāsthāvarāṇāṃ cittacaitasikānāṃ dharmāṇāṃ yo nirodhaḥ* |
>
> 4.2.2 What is the state of composure without conception? [It is] the cessation of inconstant minds and mental factors that is preceded by a form of attention that conceives of deliverance; and it is achieved by someone who has overcome desire for Complete Virtue but not for the level above it. ISBP.238

Avatāra (ESD.112):

> When one has been detached with regard to the third, but not to the fourth *dhyāna*, there is a disjoined *dharma*, named the ideationless attainment, [which can cause] the cessation of the thought and thought-concomitants of one in the stage of the fourth *dhyāna*. Although all thought and thought-concomitants have ceased when one produces this attainment; it [specifically] receives the name "Ideationless" as it is [practised] for the special purpose of eradicating ideations (*saṃjñā*). It is like the name "Knowledge of Others' Thought" [given to that knowledge specially concerned with the knowing of others' mind, even though it knows both the thought and the thought-concomitants of others].
>
> This Ideationless attainment is wholesome, and is subsumed under the fourth *dhyāna*. It is produced in the series of a non-*ārya* only, for it is produced with the thought of seeking liberation [falsely conceived as the state of ideationlessness]. The *ārya*, [on the other hand,] thinks of this state as an evil plane of existence (*apāya*) and is deeply disgusted with it. [From the point of view of retribution] it is necessarily retributed—it is retributable in the following existence only (*upapadya-vedanīya*). It is acquired by exerting effort (*prayoga-labhya*) and not by detachment (*vairāgya-labhya*).

560 *LS*: The compound *asaṃjñisamāpatti* can be interpreted either as a dependent determinative (*tatpuruṣa*) or descriptive determinative (*karmadhāraya*) (DD.246). Saṃghabhadra adds (Ny, 401a; DD. 246):

> [One might claim that since, in this equipoise, thought and all thought concomitants are extinguished, it should be referred to not simply as the equipoise of non-conception, but rather as the equipoise of no thought or thought concomitants.] [This, however, is unjustified.] [It is referred to as the equipoise of non-conception] because one produces it through aversion [specifically] to conception. Ordinary persons are not able [to produce this equipoise through] an aversion to feelings (*vedanā*) because they enter this equipoise attached to feelings.

561 *Gokhale*: [42b1] *dhyāne 'ntye*

Tib.: [42b1] *bsam gtan tha mar*

562 *Gokhale*: [42b2] *niḥsṛtīcchayā* |

Tib.: [42b2] *'byung 'dod pas* |

563 *LS*: SAH 455.

564 *Gokhale*: [42c1] *śubh*

Tib.: [42c1] *dge ba'o*

565 *Gokhale*: [42c2] *opapadyavedy aiva*

Tib.: [42c2] *skyes nas myong 'gyur nyid* |

566 *LS*: MVŚ, 774a6ff., states (DD.251) that the attainment of non-ideation (1) does not produce its effect in the present life, because this effect only takes the form of rebirth among the gods who are without ideation; (2) nor is its effect received in the third lifetime or after, since this attainment is strong and produces its effect quickly; (3) nor is its effect undetermined, because retrogression from that effect is not possible.

567 *LVP*: One does not retrogress from the attainment of non-ideation, *Vibhāṣā*, 152, p. 773c.

568 *LVP*: Through entry into assurance (*niyāma*), one obtains cessation not due to deliberation (*apratisaṃkhyānirodha*) or definitive disappearance (1) of unfortunate planes of existence, (2) of the state of non-ideation (*āsaṃjñika*), (3) of arising among the Mahābrahmas and among the Kurus, (4) of an eighth rebirth.

LS: Saṅghabhadra holds an alternative interpretation (DD.249), i.e., the effects of the attainment of non-ideation are either received in the next lifetime or are undetermined. For details see DD.249.

569 *LS*: SAH 453.

570 *Gokhale*: [42d1] *n āryasy*

Tib.: [42d1] *'phags pa'i ma yin*

571 *LS*: Cox comments (DD.252) that the noble ones compare this attainment to a deep pit to be avoided since it has as its effect the state of non-ideation and is thus said to lead to further existence in the cycle of birth and death for a period of five hundred *mahākalpa*s (see ii. 41bc).

572 *LVP*: Whoever enters into the fourth meditation (*dhyāna*) obtains at the same time the possession (*prāpti*) of all the fourth meditations that are practiced or will be practiced in the course of cyclic existence.

573 *LS*: I.e., it is not attained through mere detachment (*vairāgya*) (DD.250).

574 *Gokhale*: [42d2] *aikādhvikā 'pyate* ||

Tib.: [42d2] *dus gcig 'thob* ||

575 *LVP*: The future wholesome thought is the object of a previous possession (*prāpti*).

576 *LS*: AH 220; SAH 453, 455.

577 *LS*: SAH 453.

578 *LVP*: On the attainment of cessation (*nirodhasamāpatti*), the attainment of cessation of sensation and ideation (*saṃjñāveditanirodhasamāpatti*) (see below ii, F 211), see vi. 43cd, viii. 33a (liberations [*vimokṣa*]); *Kathāvatthu*, vi. 5, xv. 7. – In the MVŚ, 777a14, numerous opinions on this attainment: (1) for some, it is only one real entity (*dravya*), the realization of

cessation (*nirodhasākṣātkāra*); (2) for others, eleven real entities: the ten generally permeating factors (*mahābhūmika*) and cessation of thought (*cittanirodha*); (3) for others, twenty-one real entities: the generally permeating factors, the wholesome permeating factors (*kuśalamahābhūmika*) and the cessation of thought (*cittanirodha*)... .

LS: LVP writes in his *Musīla and Nārada. The Path of Nirvāṇa* (see *Electronic Appendix*), p. 212f:

> "Attainment of cessation" according to the Abhidharma or Sarvāstivādin doctrine:
>
> The "attainment of cessation" (*nirodhasamāpatti*) is a cataleptic crisis that usually lasts for seven days. It is a state similar to death. But the life-force [*āyus*] is not exhausted, warmth [*uṣman*] has not been dissipated, the sense-faculties are not fully broken but only calmed down... (*Majjhima*, I, 296 and elsewhere). – Thought and all thought-concomitants have disappeared, although the attainment is called "cessation of [two thought-concomitants, i.e., of] ideation (*saṃjñā*) and sensation (*veditā*)": the Sarvāstivādins are in conflict with several other schools on this point.
>
> It is on the level of the fourth formless meditative attainment, that is to say that the meditators can only penetrate it by emerging from this fourth meditative attainment. It therefore presupposes the prior acquisition of the eight meditative attainments.
>
> It has great benefits, notably a very great happiness of mystical order and absolute mastery over all the meditative attainments: it is the ornament and the happiness of the status of a noble one. Only the never-returners (*anāgāmin*) and perfected beings (*arhat*) have access to it. – But the formless meditative attainments and the "attainment of cessation" (*nirodhasamāpatti*) have no place in the economy of salvation.
>
> The meditators enter into the "attainment of cessation" not to enter into *nirvāṇa* and arrive at the "exit", but in order to obtain and taste the "peaceful abode" (*śāntavihāra*), or "peaceful concentration".

579 *Gokhale*: [43a] *nirodhākhyā tath aiv eyaṃ*

Tib.: [43a] *'gog pa zhes pa'ang de bzhin nyid* |

LVP: *nirodhasamāpatti*, *Siddhi*, 61, 204, 211–14, 247, 268, 283, 405–9, 751.

LS: Vasubandhu's Pañcaskandhaka (2008) states:

> 4.2.3 *nirodhasamāpattiḥ katamā | ākiñcanyāyatanavītarāgasya bhavāgrād uccalitasya śāntavihārasañjñāpūrvakeṇa manasikāreṇāsthāvarāṇām ekatyānāṃ ca sthāvarāṇāṃ cittacaitasikānāṃ dharmāṇāṃ yo nirodhaḥ* |
>
> 4.2.3 What is the state of composure that is a cessation? [It is] the cessation of inconstant minds and mental factors, as well as a portion of the constant minds, that is preceded by a form of attention that conceives of abiding [in a state of ease]; and it is achieved by someone who has overcome desire for the Sphere of Nothingness and who has set out to rise above the Peak of Existence. ISBP.238

Avatāra (ESD.112f.):

> When one has been detached with regard to the abode of no-thing-ness (*ākiṃcanyāyatana*), there is a disjoined *dharma* [which can cause] the cessation of the thought and thought-concomitants of one in [the stage of] the existence-peak. As it causes the

even (*sama*) continuation of the Great Elements, it is named the cessation-attainment (*nirodha-samāpatti*).

It belongs to the existence-peak stage, produced through exertion (*prāyogika*), and is wholesome. It is retributable in the following existence (*upapadya-vedanīya*), or in the existence after the next (*aparaparyāya-vedanīya*), or not necessarily retributable (*aniyata-vedanīya*). It is not necessarily retributable because [it is possible that] having produced this attainment, one then attains Parinirvāṇa without having acquired its retribution (*vipāka*). This attainment can effect the retribution of the four [mental] aggregates [only] in the existence-peak stage, as the latter is immaterial in nature.

Only the *ārya*-s are capable of producing this attainment, not the ordinary people, for it is produced by virtue of the *ārya*-path. The *ārya*-s, in order to dwell in bliss in the present life (*dṛṣṭa-dharma-sukha-vihārātham*), seek to produce this attainment. The worldlings, [on the other hand], dread it as [the state of] annihilation (*ucchedabhīru-tva*); and, being without the strength of the *ārya*-path, are incapable of producing it. The *ārya*-s obtain it through exertion (*prayoga*), and not by detachment. It is only in the case of a Buddha Bhagavat that its obtainment is said to be by [the mere fact of] detachment: At the very moment of obtaining the Knowledge of Exhaustion, He is already capable of producing this attainment at will—the qualities (*guṇa*) of a Buddha are not through any exertion; they appear before Him as soon as He desires them—it is [in this sense] that He is said to have obtained it.

580 *Gokhale*: [43bd] *vihārārthaṃ bhavā'grajā | śubhā dvivedyā 'niyatā c āryasy āpyā pra-yogataḥ* ||

Tib.: [43bd] *'di gnas don du srid rtse skyes | dge ba'o gnyis su myong 'gyur dang | ma nges 'phags pa'i sbyor bas 'thob* ||

581 *LVP*: *śāntavihārasaṃjñāpūrvakena manasikāreṇa. – vihāra = samādhiviśeṣa* [compare WOG.160.28f.].

LS: LVP translates and comments in his *Musīla et Nārada* (p. 25; see *Electronic Appendix*):

> "The noble ones (*ārya*) enter into this attainment by a mental application (*manasi-kāra*) that has the ideation of a peaceful abode (*śāntavihāra*) as its antecedent": that is to ṣay, with a view to enjoying the peaceful (*śanta*) abode (*vihāra*) (i.e., "excellent concentration" [*samādhiviśeṣa*]).

582 *LS*: Saṃghabhadra (Ny, 401b) explains the term "*bhavāgra*" (ESD.185):

> Because the body retributed in the *naiva-saṃjñānāsaṃjñāyatana* is by virtue of the *karma* of the highest grade, it is said to be the peak of existence or the edge of existence; just as the edge of a tree is said to be the peak/top of the tree.

583 *LS*: SAH 455.

584 *LVP*: It is "to be experienced later", when an existence in the realm of fine-materiality is interposed between the existence of the realm of desire in the course of which it is produced, and the existence of the "summit of cyclic existence" (*bhavāgra*) that is its fruit.

585 *LS*: Saṃghabhadra (Ny, 401c; ESD.186; DD.257f.) ascribes this explanation to "certain other masters", rejects it and explains (Ny, 401c; DD.257) instead that ordinary worldlings are not capable of giving rise to the attainment of cessation because they have not yet abandoned

the obstacle—pertaining to their own stage (*bhūmi*)—to the arising of the attainment of cessation, namely, the defilements of the summit of cyclic existence that are to be abandoned by the path of insight.

586 *LVP*: This attainment takes place in the plane of the "summit of cyclic existence", from which matter (*rūpa*) is absent. Ordinary worldlings (*pṛthagjana*) fear that the arresting of the thought and thought-concomitants is, under these conditions, annihilation. They do not have the same fear with respect to the attainment of non-ideation (*asaṃjñisamāpatti*), which takes place in the plane of the fourth meditation (*dhyāna*), where matter persists. In fact, the group homogeneity (*nikāyasabhāga*), the vitality faculty (*jīvitendriya*) and other formations (*saṃskāra*) dissociated from thought remain within the attainment of cessation (*nirodhasamāpatti*); but ordinary worldlings do not see them.

587 *LVP*: dṛṣṭanirvāṇasya tadadhimuktitas [WOG.161.19]. – According to a different reading, followed by the Chinese translators: *dṛṣṭadharmanirvāṇasya*.... That is to say: "The noble ones (*ārya*) intend to obtain, aim to obtain Nirvāṇa in the present life by means of this attainment, within this attainment": *dṛṣṭadharmanirvāṇasya tadadhimuktitaḥ* | dṛṣṭe janmani nirvāṇaṃ *dṛṣṭadharmanirvāṇam* | tasya *tadadhimuktitaḥ* | tad ity adhimuktiḥ *tadadhimuktiḥ* | tena vā 'dhimuktis tadadhimuktiḥ | tadadhimuktes *tadadhimuktitaḥ* | dṛṣṭe janmany etan nirvāṇam ity āryas tam adhimucyate | [WOG.161.15ff.]

588 *Gokhale*: [44ab] *bodhilabhyā muner na prāk catustriṃśatkṣaṇāptitaḥ* |

Tib.: [44ac] *thub pa'i byang chub kyis thob bya* | *dang por ma yin skad cig ma* | *sum cu rtsa bzhis thob phyir ro* |

LVP: *bodhilabhyā muner* [*na prāk catustriṃśatkṣaṇāptitaḥ* |]. See vi. 24ab. – Compare *Kathāvatthu*, i. 5, xviii. 5.

LS: See Saṃghabhadra's detailed discussion (DD.259–62) on the attainment of cessation by the Lord Buddha.

589 *LS*: AKB vi. 67ab states that the cognition of exhaustion (*kṣayajñāna*) with the cognition of non-arising (*anutpādajñāna*) is enlightenment and that by these two cognitions "one completely abandons ignorance (*aśeṣāvidyā-prahāṇāt*); by the first, one knows in all truth (*avabodha*) that the task is accomplished; by the second, one knows that the task will no longer need to be accomplished again".

590 *LVP*: The *Vyākhyā* [WOG.162.6f.] cites a stanza from the *Stotrakāra*, that is to say, of *Mātṛceṭa* (*Varṇanārhavarṇana*, 118: F.W. Thomas, *Indian Antiquary*, 1905, t. 32, p. 345): *na te prāyogikaṃ kiṃcit kuśalaṃ kuśalānuga* |

591 *LS*: Liberation through both parts is defined as liberation of thought from both (1) the obstacle of defilements (*kleśāvaraṇa*) by means of insight (*prajñā*) and (2) the obstacle to the eight liberations (*vimokṣāvaraṇa*) by means of concentration (*samādhi*). Some say that *vimokṣāvaraṇa* is the obstacle to meditative attainment (*samāpatty-avarāṇa*).

592 *LVP*: The Japanese editor cites the various interpretations of the old commentaries on the *Kośa*: The Westerners are the Sarvāstivādins of Gandhāra, or Sautrāntikas, or the masters of the land of Indhu. They are called Westerners because they are to the west of Kaśmīr, and Foreign Masters (*bahirdeśaka*) because they are outside of Kaśmīr. – See below ii, F 206, note.

593 *LVP*: *nirodhasamāpattim utpādya kṣayajñānam utpādayatīti vaktavyam tathāgata iti*

[WOG.162.19].

594 *LVP*: The Masters of the land of Indhu, of the same opinion as the Westerners.

595 *LVP*: *vyutthānāśaya* = *vyutthānābhiprāya*: "having an intention that can be discarded, that can be given up". According to another interpretation, *āśaya* = *kuśala* = *kuśalamūla*; thus: "having wholesome roots that can be discarded, that can be broken off". But the wholesome roots of the Bodhisattvas are such that once they begin to actualize, they do not stop before Bodhi has been obtained.

Vyutthāna also signifies "emerging from concentration (*samādhi*)" (*Saṃyutta*, iii. 265, etc.).

596 *LVP*: MVŚ, 204b3–c4: All the postures are good. Why does the Bodhisattva take up the squatting position? ...

597 *LVP*: Hsüan-tsang adds: "The first doctrine is the best, because this is our system."

598 *Gokhale*: [44c] *kāmarūpāśraye t ūbhe*

Tib.: [44d] *gnyis ka 'dod dang gzugs rten can |*

LVP: MVŚ, 773b11. – Three opinions: (1) only in the realm of desire, (2) also in the three lower meditations (*dhyāna*), (3) also in the fourth meditation.

According to the *Vibhāṣā*, the attainment of cessation (*nirodhasamāpatti*) cannot be extended beyond seven days-and-nights.

LS: Cox comments (DD.282) that the location of these two states of attainment and the region in which one gives rise to them must be clearly distinguished. For example, the equipoise of non-ideation is located in the fourth meditation (*dhyāna*) within the realm of fine-materiality. However, it is produced by one whose corporeal basis (*āśraya*) is located either in the realm of desire or in the realm of fine-materiality. Similarly, the attainment of cessation is located in the perception-sphere of neither-ideation-nor-non-ideation within the realm of immateriality; one enters it, however, supported by a corporeal basis in the realm of desire or in the realm of fine-materiality.

Saṃghabhadra states (Ny, 402c):

> One who has been reborn in the formless realm cannot enter the equipoise of cessation, because there is no corporeal basis [in that realm to act as the support for this equipoise]. Vitality (*jīvita*) necessarily occurs in conformity with [either] form or thought. If one who had been reborn in the formless realm were to enter the equipoise of cessation, since there would be neither form nor thought, vitality would be abandoned.

599 *LVP*: The *Jñānaprasthāna*, 1024a8, asks a fourfold question: (1) Is there an existence in the realm of fine-materiality that does not involve the five aggregates (*skandha*)? (2) Is there an existence that involves the five aggregates and is not in the realm of fine-materiality? (3) Is there an existence in the realm of fine-materiality that involves the five aggregates? (4) Is there an existence that is not in the realm of fine-materiality and that does not involve the five aggregates?

600 *LVP*: The *Jñānaprasthāna* and the *Kośa* do not use the word *skandha*, but they use a synonym, a word that the MSS of the *Vyākhyā* [WOG.163.27] transcribes indiscriminately as *vyavahāra* and *vyavacāra*. – Hsüan-tsang translates (Ch.) *hsing*, the equivalent of *saṃskāra*, as

viharaṇa, etc.; Paramārtha translates (Ch.) *p'an*, the equivalent of *nīti*, *naya*, as "to judge", "to decide". – The reading of *vyavakāra* appears certain according to the Pali sources.

1. Pali Sources. – *vokāra* = *khanda* (Childers); *Vibhaṅga*, 137: *saññābhavo asaññābhavo nevasaññānāsaññābhavo ekāvokārabhavo catuvokārabhavo pañcavokārabhavo*; Yamaka, according to *Kathāvatthu*, trans. p. 38; *Kathāvatthu*, iii. 11: if "those without ideation" possess an existence involving one *vokāra* or five *vokāras*. (Buddhoghosa explains: *vividhena visuṃ visuṃ karīyati*).

2. *Vyākhyā* [WOG.163.27f.]. – *vyavakāra* is the name that the Buddha Kāśyapa gives to the *skandhas*. – *vyavakāra* (*viśeseṇāvakāra*) signifies *savyavakāra* according to Pāṇini, v. 2, 127; thus: "that which disappoints, that which is contrary (*visaṃvādanī*) through its impermanence", a definition that suits the *skandhas* according to the stanza: "Material form (*rūpa*) is like a flake of foam..." (*Saṃyutta*, iii. 142).

3. MVŚ, 959b11. – The former Tathāgatas Samyaksaṃbuddhas call the *skandhas* by the name *vyavakāras*; but the Tathāgata Samyaksaṃbuddha Śākyamuni calls the *vyavakāras* by the name *skandhas*. The former speak of five *vyavakāras*, Śākyamuni speaks of five *upādānaskandhas* (appropriative aggregates). Here, in the Abhidharma, one speaks of an existence "with five *vyavakāras*" (*pañca-*) in order to show that the five *skandhas* of which Śākyamuni speaks are the five *vyavakāras* of which the former Buddhas speak. – Why do the former Buddhas use the term *vyavakāra*, whereas the present Buddha uses the term *skandha*? Because the Buddhas see that which is suitable to say to the faithful... . Why this expression *vyavakāra*? Because of *pravṛtti* (*saṃcāra*?): the previously arisen *skandhas* unfold because of later *skandhas*, or else, the later arisen *skandhas* unfold because of previous *skandhas*... .

601 *LS*: Cox comments (DD.282): "The sentient beings referred to here have developed moments of thought of a category dissimilar from those moments of thought characteristic of the realm of form, which tend toward the fluxes and belong to the realm of form. These dissimilar moments of thought would include, for example, thoughts that do not tend toward the fluxes (*anāsravacitta*), or moments of thought that belong to another realm. Since these dissimilar moments of thought do not belong to the realm of form, such sentient beings lack the four mental aggregates characteristic of the realm of form."

602 *LVP*: These sentient beings—being by nature with ideation—are "placed in a thought contrary to their nature" (*visabhāgacitte sthita*) when they become without ideation or non-ideational in one of the two attainments.

603 *LS*: Cox comments (DD.282): "Sentient beings born among the gods without conception have a corporeal basis within the realm of form, but lack thought and thought concomitants. Like those practicing the equipoise of non-ideation or the equipoise of cessation, these gods without conception possess only the form and the forces aggregate (or certain factors dissociated from thought)."

604 *Gokhale*: [44d] *nirodhākhyādito nṛṣu* ||

Tib.: [44e] *'gog pa dang por mi'i nang du* ||

LS: The master Pūrṇavardhana explains (Jampaiyang, p. 382):

> [*Nirodhasamāpatti*] is first generated only among humans because they have instructors and expositors and the strength of preparation. (Though) it later degenerates, it is

developed in the Form but not the Formless (Realm) because there is no support for it (there).

[*Asaṃjñisamāpatti*] is first generated in the Form Realm where one is familiar with it from beginningless *saṃsāra*.

605 *LVP*: This Sūtra was taught by Śāriputra: it bears the name Udāyin because the adversary of Śāriputra is Udāyin. – The Sanskrit edition is very close to the Pāli text. – *Madhyamāgama*, 5, 4, and *Aṅguttara*, iii. 192.

śrāvastyāṃ nidānam | tatrāyuṣmān śāriputro bhikṣūn āmantrayate sma | ih' *āyuṣmanto bhikṣuḥ śīlasampannaś ca bhavati samādhisampannaś ca prajñāsaṃpannaś ca | so 'bhīkṣṇaṃ saṃjñāveditanirodhaṃ samāpadyate ca vyuttiṣṭhate ca | asti caitat sthānam iti yathābhūtaṃ prajānāmi | sa nehaiva dṛṣṭa eva dharme pratipattyaivājñām ārāgayati nāpi maraṇasamaye bhedāc ca kāyasyātikramya devān kavaḍīkārabhakṣān anyatamasmin divye manomaye kāya upapadyate | sa tatropapanno...* [cf. WOG.164.12ff.].

Vyākhyā [cf. WOG.165.18f.]: *pratipattyaiva = pūrvam eva.*

This Sūtra is discussed at viii. 3c (thesis of the existence of material form [*rūpa*] in the realm of immateriality). – Compare *Dīgha*, i. 195; AKB viii, F 140; *Siddhi*, 407.

606 *LVP*: *ājñām ārāgayati* as in *Mahāvastu*, iii. 53, 9. – Paramārtha: "They do not obtain the faculty of final and perfect knowledge (*ājñātāvīndriya*)." Hsüan-tsang: "They do not apply themselves so as to obtain the status of a perfected being (*arhat*)...".

607 *LVP*: It is called *manomaya*, mental or produced by the mind, because it arises independently from the elements of generation; but this does not mean that it is a body produced by ideations (*saṃjñāmaya*) (*Dīgha*, i. 195), and belonging to the realm of immateriality, as Udāyin thinks.

On the "mental body" of the Bodhisattva in the *Mahāvastu*, see *Opinions sur l'histoire de la dogmatique*, p. 258.

LS: In his Hasting article MAHĀVASTU (p. 329), LVP comments: "According to the *Abhidharmakośa*, [the expression *manomaya*, 'mind-made'] means, not 'mental body', 'body formed of mind', but 'body created by the mind', without intervention of seed and blood. Such is the body of the creatures called *aupapāduka*, 'apparitional', one of whose characteristics is that, on dying, they leave no trace."

608 *LVP*: Note of the Japanese editor:

1. The gods with a "mental body" of whom the Sūtra speaks, are (i) of the realm of fine-materiality, for the Sarvāstivādin (same opinion, *Dīgha*, i. 195); (ii) of the realm of fine-materiality and of the realm of immateriality, for the Sautrāntika, (iii) the gods without ideation (Asaṃjñisattva), for Udāyin.

2. Retrogressing from the attainment of cessation, according to the Sarvāstivādin; no retrogressing, according to the Sautrāntika and Udāyin.

But according to the *Vyākhyā*, the Sautrāntika accepts the retrogressing from meditative attainment; the Sautrāntika denies, however, that the noble ones retrogress from the noble path (*āryamārga*) (*contra* the Sarvāstivādin), from which difficulties arise that the *Vyākhyā* resolves.

609 *LVP*: The Mahāsāṃghikas, etc., according to P'u-kuang, TD 41, p. 99c15.

[610] *LVP*: *Dīrgha*, 17, 11; *Dīgha*, iii. 266; *Mahāvyutpatti*, 68, 7: *navānupūrvasamāpattayas*: (1–4) the four meditations (*dhyāna*); (5–8) the four formless meditative attainments (*ārūpya*); and (9) the attainment of cessation.

[611] *LVP*: *prāthamakalpikaḥ* = āditaḥ samāpattividhāyakaḥ [WOG.166.10].

[612] *LVP*: One prepares oneself for the attainment of non-ideation (*asaṃjñisamāpatti*) by thinking: "Ideation (*saṃjñā*) is a sickness, a thorn, an abscess; this is peaceful, this is excellent, namely, the cessation of ideation."

[613] *LS*: The MVŚ, 775b9ff., states (DD.284): "Ideation and feelings are able to give rise to two types of defilements: desires and [false] views. Desires arise through the power of feelings, [false] views, through the power of conception. All defilements have these two as their head." Cox comments that "the two categories—desires and false views—represent all defilements; false views include all those defilements to be abandoned by the path of vision, and desires, those to be abandoned by the path of cultivation".

According to Saṃghabhadra (Ny, 403a), the Dārṣṭāntikas disagree and maintain (DD.267):

> In the equipoise of cessation, one only extinguishes conception and feelings [and not all other varieties of thought]. [Four reasons are given for this.] [First,] it is determined that there are no sentient beings who are without thought. [Second,] there is a distinction between the equipoise of cessation and death. [Third,] the *sūtra* states that when one enters the equipoise of cessation, perceptual consciousness is not separated from the body. [Finally,] it is said that one's life (*āyus*), warmth (*ūṣman*), and perceptual consciousness (*vijñāna*) are never separated from one another.

See Saṃghabhadra's long refutation in Ny, 403a–c (DD.267-72), which Cox summarizes as follows (EIP.VIII.692f.):

> This interpretation is unreasonable because no awarenesses and mental factors occur without identifications and feelings. ... The successive model would contradict the definitions of "awareness" and "associated mental factor".
>
> Now in response to the four reasons offered by the Dārṣṭāntika, first, the existence of sentient beings without awareness is verified by scriptural references. Second, those who have entered cessation trance are not dead because they still have vitality. Sentient beings may lack material form, as in the immaterial realm, or they may lack awareness, as in these states of trance without awareness. Third, these scriptural passages state that awareness is not separated from the body simply because awareness will be produced again in the body that serves as the corporeal basis after emerging from this trance. Fourth, the life-force, warmth, and perceptual consciousness are indeed separated from one another only in certain cases. For example, in the immaterial realm there is no warmth; similarly in the states of trance without awareness there is no perceptual consciousness.

[614] *LVP*: The preparation involves the resolution; "I will cognize the thought of another."

[615] *LVP*: The tenets (*siddhānta*) are in disagreement. (1) For the Vaibhāṣikas, etc., the two attainments and the state of non-ideation (*asaṃjñika*) are exempt of thought (*acittakāny eva...*); (2) for the Sthavira Vasumitra, etc., they are endowed with thought (*sacittakāni*) on account of a non-manifested mental consciousness (*aparisphuṭamanovijñāna*); (3) for the

Yogācārins they are endowed with thought on account of the *ālayavijñāna*. See WOG.167.5ff.

LS: As for the duration of the attainment of cessation, Saṃghabhadra says (Ny, 403c; DD.272) that it "is projected by the force [developed through] application (*prayoga*) [in practice before entering equipoise], i.e., it depends on the extent of this force.

616 *LVP*: This question is asked by the Sautrāntikas. For them, the thought that has just perished, and the thought that has perished a long time ago, are equally non-existent: however, the thought that has just perished is the cause of the thought that immediately follows it: compare the movement of the beams of a balance (*tulādaṇḍonnāmāvanāmavat*, comp. *Śālistamba* in *Bodhicaryāvatāra*, 483, 3).

617 *LS*: For the Sarvāstivādins, the arising of any consciousness depends upon the presence of three requisite conditions: an appropriate sense-faculty, which serves as the basis (*āśraya*); its corresponding object-field (*viṣaya*), which serves as the cognitive object (*ālambana*); and the condition as the equivalent and immediate antecedent (*samanantarapratyaya*), that is, the prior moment of thought.

As for the special case of the rearising in regard to the two attainments, the Sarvāstivāda-Vaibhāṣikas state that, although the activity (*kāritra*) of the thought of the moment just prior to the state without thought is past, the intrinsic nature (*svabhāva*) of it continues to exist and is capable of exerting conditioning capability (*sāmarthya*). It can be spoken of as condition as the equivalent and immediate antecedent (*samanantarapratyaya*) because it produces a subsequent factor without any similar intervening factor. Saṃghabhadra explains that *samanantara* refers simply to the fact that a subsequent factor is produced directly, i.e., without any similar intervening factor, through the power of a prior moment of thought; by contrast, "immediate succession" (*anantara*) refers to the fact that there are no intervening moments. Cf. DD.118.

618 *LVP*: *Siddhi*, 211, on the schools of the Sautrāntikas.

LS: Although not explicitly mentioned in Pradhan, LVP mentions the Sautrāntikas here.

This is the 14th of Kritzer's forty-four passages discussed in relation to chapter 2 (VY.64f.). Saṃghabhadra (Ny, 404a2–3) identifies this passage as the opinion of Vasubandhu and criticizes it (Ny, 404a3–20) along with the seed theory that underlies it.

As for parallels to the *Yogācārabhūmi*, the *Viniścayasaṃgrahaṇī* states that, "if the *indriyas* and the *mahābhūtas* that support them did not contain the seeds of consciousness and of the *caittas*, consciousness could not resume after the unconscious trances or birth in heaven".

Yaśomitra too (WOG.167.16) identifies the ancient masters (*pūrvācārya*) as the Sautrāntikas. For the identity of the ancient masters (*pūrvācārya*) as early Yogācāra masters, see Schmithausen (1987b), p. 286 (note 170); Hakamaya (1986).

As for the view presented here, Cox comments that (DD.119) "the body possessed of sense organs and thought are claimed to contain each other's seeds; therefore, thought would arise once again after an interval without thought from its own seeds latent within the corporeal basis. Specifically, prior to the arising of the state without thought, a particular moment of thought deposits its own seeds within the body; these seeds condition the body in such a way that the arising of other moments of thought is temporarily prevented. At a later time, the mental stream arises again from still other seeds of thought lying dormant within the body." Cf. Ny, 404a; DD.273f.

[619] *LVP*: The author indicates the name of the treatise because Vasumitra (termed indiscriminately as Sthavira or Bhadanta) wrote other books, the *Pañcavastuka*, etc. (WOG.167.21f.). – There is a commentary on the *Pañcavastuka* by Dharmatrāta, *Nanjio* 1283.

The Japanese editor comments that it does not refer to the Vasumitra of the *Vibhāṣā*, but to a Sautrāntika. – (See P'u-kuang, 16, 10).

LS: In our above endnote regarding the explanation of the name of the two attainments, Saṃghabhadra presented (Ny, 403a) the four Dārṣṭāntika reasons for their view that attainment of cessation only extinguishes ideation and sensation, but not all other varieties of thought. Cox writes (DD.121) that this "would leave open the possibility either that some other thought concomitants or that a subtle variety of thought remains in these states said to be 'without thought'. The latter possibility that subtle thought is not extinguished in the equipoise of non-ideation or cessation is supported by the view attributed to the Dārṣṭāntikas in the **Mahāvibhāṣā* (772c21ff., 774a14ff.). It also conforms to the view of the **Tattvasiddhiśāstra* that thought and thought concomitants are subtle and difficult to perceive in these states, which are, therefore, only provisionally described as 'without thought'. ... Śrīlāta is cited [in Ny, 420b17ff.] as suggesting that thought and thought concomitants do not arise in states said to be without thought." Cox comments (DD.119) that in the AKB these views of the Dārṣṭāntikas are represented by Vasumitra.

[620] *LVP*: MVŚ, 774a14: The Dārṣṭāntika and the Vibhajyavādin maintain that a subtle thought is not interrupted in the attainment of cessation. They say: "There are no sentient beings who are at the same time without thought and without material form (*rūpa*); nor are there persons in meditative attainment who are without thought. If the persons in meditative attainment would be without thought, the vitality faculty would be cut off; one would call these persons not *established in attainment*, but rather: *dead.*"

LS: Hirakawa explains (HIB.164) that this subtle mental consciousness (*sūkṣma-manovijñāna*) continually exists, has a minute degree of perception that makes it similar to the unconscious, is not cut off by death and thus moves on to the next life. It is said to continue to function behind man's grosser, everyday consciousness.

Schmithausen comments (AV.282f.): "Vasumitra's *citta* in *nirodhasamāpatti* is qualified as a 'not quite clear (*aparisphuṭa*) *manovijñāna*' at AKVy 167,6, but in view of the lack of any specification in AKBh this may well be a statement *expressis verbis* of what was at best implicit in Vasumitra's view. ... [W]ithin the limits of the traditional *vijnāna* system of the Sarvāstivādins and Sautrāntikas, the *citta* in *nirodhasamāpatti* could hardly be classified but as a *manovijñāna.*"

[621] *LVP*: *Saṃyuktāgama*, 11, 8; compare *Saṃyutta*, ii. 72 and the sources cited *ad Kośa*, iii. 30b.

LS: LVP translates "at the same time", which is missing in Pradhan.72.27f: *sparśapratyayā ca vedanā saṃjñā cetane 'ty uktaṃ bhagavatā.*

Saṃghabhadra adds: "No *sūtra* passage states that there is a seventh type of perceptual consciousness, thereby allowing one to claim that [some type of] perceptual consciousness is produced apart from conception and feelings." Cox comments (DD.285) that "this anticipates the later controversies concerning the nature of thought and the Yogācāra theory of the store-consciousness (*ālayavijñāna*). See Schmithausen (1987) 1: 18ff., 34ff.

[622] *LVP*: *Saṃyuktāgama*, 12, 14; *Saṃyutta*, iii. 96.

LS: According to Saṃghabhadra (DD.270), contact having ignorance (*avidyāsaṃsparśaja*) indeed gives rise to sensation and craving, but "since *arhats* are without contact having ignorance, even though they have feelings, [those feelings] do not produce craving".

[623] *LS*: As for *samāpatti*, see our general endnote to the two attainments at ii, F 200.

[624] *LVP*: *mahābhūtasamatāpādanam*. – This formula has passed into the *Mahāvyutpatti*, 68, 9.

MVŚ, 782a22: Those who are in the attainment of cessation (*nirodhasamāpatti*) cannot be burned by fire, drowned by water, wounded by the sword, or killed by another. (Compare the legends of Saṃjīva, Khāṇu-Koṇḍañña, in *Visuddhi*, xii, *JPTS* 1891, p. 112). Why do they possess this quality? Vasumitra says: because this attainment (*samāpatti*) cannot be damaged; thus they who are in it cannot be damaged. – Moreover: what one understands by *samāpatti* is that which causes the thought to be even (*sama*). Here, there is no thought (*acitta*), how can one speak of *samāpatti*? – Attainment (*samāpatti*) is of two types: (1) that which causes thought to be even; (2) that which causes the fundamental material elements to be even. Even though the two attainments interrupt the even-ness of thought, causing it not to continue, they induce the even-ness of the fundamental material elements, [causing them to manifest]. [See SA.413f.].

Also *Vibhāṣā*, 152, p. 775.

[625] *LS*: As for the Vaibhāṣika rationale as to why they maintain the two attainments and the state of non-ideation to be real entities and why they classify them among the formations dissociated from thought, see our introductory endnote to the state of non-ideation (ii, F 198).

As for them being conditioned factors (*saṃskṛta*), Cox comments (DD.115) that "like all conditioned factors, these discrete factors that induce states without thought arise and pass away in each moment and obstruct only the arising of thought in that particular moment. However, as long as the series of such factors projected by prior application continues within a given life-stream, thought will not arise." Saṃghabhadra adds (Ny, 404b; DD 275) that the duration of the attainment of the cessation is projected by the intensity of the intention (*cetanā*) of thought just prior to the attainment and that this intention determines the force of the attainment of cessation, allowing it "to diminish gradually until it reaches a state of complete extinction. When there is no [further] activity of obstruction, mental consciousness is produced once again... ." Cf. DD.275.

[626] *LS*: Although not explicitly mentioned in Pradhan, LVP mentions the Sautrāntika here.

This is the 15th of Kritzer's forty-four passages discussed in relation to chapter 2 (VY.66f.). Saṃghabhadra (Ny, 403c25–404a1) identifies this view, i.e., that the thought just prior to the state of attainment (*samāpatticitta*) obstructs the arising of thought, as the opinion of Vasubandhu and criticizes (Ny, 404a21–27) Vasubandhu's statement that something can be *saṃskṛta* while at the same time being merely provisional.

As for parallels to the *Yogācārabhūmi*, the *Viniścayasaṃgrahaṇī* states that "*asaṃjñisamāpatti* and *nirodhasamāpatti* are the mere suppression and pacification, the mere non-operation, of *citta* and the *caittas*, and that they are *prajñaptis*, not real things".

[627] *LVP*: Basis (*āśraya*) has been defined ii. 5–6; see also ii, F 183.

[628] *LVP*: Hsüan-tsang translates: "This theory is not good, for it is in contradiction with our system." – We add: "So say the Vaibhāṣikas." See above ii, F 198, note.

629 *LS*: AH 220; SAH 453.

630 *LS*: Ibid.

631 *Gokhale*: [45a1] *āyur jīvitam*

Tib.: [45a1] *srog ni tshe yin*

LVP: Buddhaghosa attributes to the Pubbaseliyas and to the Sammitiyas the doctrine which is that of the Abhidharma: the vitality faculty (*jīvitendriya*) is a *cittavippayutta arūpadhamma.* See *Kathāvatthu*, viii. 10; *Compendium*, p. 156; *Vibhāṅga*, p. 123; *Dhammasaṅgaṇi*, 19, 635; *Atthasālinī*, 644.

LS: 1. Vasubandhu's Pañcaskandhaka (2008) states:

> 4.2.5 *jīvitendriyaṃ katamat | nikāyasabhāgeṣu pūrvakarmāviddho yaḥ saṃskārāṇāṃ sthitikālaniyamaḥ |*
>
> 4.2.5 What is the faculty of a life force? [It is] the fixed period of time for the continued existence of the formations [that occur] within [various] class affiliates [of different sentient beings] that is projected by past karma. ISBP.238

Avatāra (ESD.114): "[A real entity] projected by previous *karma*, serving as the cause for the uninterrupted series of the six entrances (*āyatana*) [of the human personality], and forming the basis for the designation (*prajñapti*) of the four births and the five planes of existences—this is named the vital faculty [*jīvitendriya*]. It is also called the life-principle (*āyus*).

Thus it is said in the *abhidharma*: 'What is the vital-faculty? It is the life-principle of the three spheres of existence.' It has a substantial essence, and sustains heat (*ūṣma*) and consciousness (*vijñāna*)."

2. As for the history of *jīvita*, Cox writes (DD.125f.):

> Vitality first appears in Buddhist *sūtras* as a controlling faculty (*indriya*) within a group of three controlling faculties including also the controlling faculties of masculinity (*purisindriya*) and femininity (*itthindriya*) [e.g., *SN* 48.22 *Jīvitindriyasutta* 5: 204]. These three are also included within the established set of twenty-two controlling faculties subsequently accepted in both the northern and southern Indian Buddhist scholastic traditions. The controlling faculty of vitality appears frequently in *sūtra* references to death and the termination of a given lifetime, but its specific character and function are not examined [e.g., *MA*. 7 no. 29 p. 462b18].
>
> Early Abhidharma definitions [*Dharmaskandha*, 499a29ff., *Saṅgītiparyāya*, 368c16ff.] of the controlling faculty of vitality preserve this relation to the duration of a given lifetime. They emphasize the function of vitality as the persistence, continuation, maintenance, animation, and operation that characterize sentient beings.
>
> Other early Abhidharma treatises [*Prakaraṇapāda*, 628c19, 654a3, 694a23, 723a29ff. *Jñānaprasthāna*, 993b2ff., and *Mahāvibhāṣā*, 732b27ff.] adopt a more succinct definition, identifying the controlling faculty of vitality with the life that belongs to a being in any of the three realms (*traidhātukaṃ āyuḥ*). This early Abhidharma definition becomes the basis for the definition of vitality as a dissociated factor adopted by the later Abhidharma compendia. [...]

3. The MVŚ, 731b23ff., gives two explanations for the character and function of the vitality

faculty within the context of the controlling faculties.

In the first explanation (SA.IV.303), the dominance of the vital faculty consists in (i) enabling one to assert that a being is in possession of the faculties (*sa-indriya*), which implies that sentience is defined by the presence of the vital faculty, and in (ii) sustaining the faculties, which implies that it is the essential condition for being alive as opposed to being dead.

In the second explanation (SA.IV.317), the dominance of the vital faculty consists in (i) connecting up with the *nikāya-sabhāga*, (ii) sustaining the *nikāya-sabhāga*, (iii) fostering the *nikāyasabhāga* and (iv) enabling the *nikāyasabhāga* to continue uninterrupted. See in this context the Vaibhāṣika explanation at ii, F 105, as well as the Sautrāntika explanation at i. 3, the latter stating that the vitality faculty does not exercise controlling power with regard to the initial connection to the *nikāyasabhāga* but only with regard to the continuance of the *nikāyasabhāga* from birth to death. Cox comments (DD.131) that in the Sarvāstivāda-Vaibhāṣika treatment of vitality, it is not clear whether *nikāyasabhāga* is used in the technical sense of formation dissociated from thought or in the more general sense of *nikāyasabhāga* (see our endnote to ii. 41a); but the Sautrāntikas do not accept *nikāyasabhāga* as being a real entity.

The definition of vitality as controlling faculty is further elaborated in the later Abhidharma treatises [AKB, Ny and *Avatāra*], particularly in its technical use as being a formation dissociated from thought, where, based on certain *sūtra* passages [e.g., *Pheṇapiṇḍūpamasutta* 3: 143] (DD.127), "a sentient being is characterized by the presence of three specific components within its constitutive collocation: warmth [*ūṣman*], perceptual consciousness [*vijñāna*], and life [*āyus*]. These components distinguish, sentient beings from insentient matter and life from death within the stream of one sentient being."

Saṃghabhadra states (Ny, 404c; SA.IV.305):

> The life principle which exists as a distinct entity, capable of supporting warmth (*ūṣman*) and consciousness, is called the vital faculty. This vital faculty does not operate with only the body as its supporting basis, since the vital faculty exists in the immaterial sphere. Nor does it operate with only thought as its supporting basis, since the vital faculty also exists in one who is in the state devoid of thought. If so, with what as the supporting basis does the vital faculty operate? Its operation has the projecting *karma* in a previous life and the group-homogeneity of the present life as its supporting basis.

4. As can be seen from Saṃghabhadra's quote, these three components are discussed as being present in the vast majority of sentient states, but not in all, for example, vitality exists in sentient beings during the attainment of non-ideation, where thought and thought-concomitants are absent; it also exists in sentient beings of the realm of immateriality, where matter, i.e., warmth, is absent. Being itself neither material nor mental, it is thus included in the formations dissociated from thought.

5. As for references to vitality (*jīvita*) or life-force (*āyus*) within the AKB, we have already mentioned that Vasubandhu discussed the vitality faculty (*jīvitendriya*) within the context of the twenty-two controlling faculties at ii, F 105, and ii. 3. In this context, the vital faculty is also determined to be a ripened effect (ii. 10a), to which Vasubandhu links the discussion of:

i. the stabilization and rejection of the conditioning forces of the life-force (*āyuḥsaṃ-*

skāra), F 120;

ii. the purpose, person, place, etc., of prolonging and rejecting them, F 121;

iii. the difference between the conditioning forces of life (*jīvita saṃskāra*) and the conditioning forces of the life-force (*āyus saṃskāra*), F 122;

iv. the purpose for which the Fortunate One stabilizes and rejects the conditioning forces of the life-force, F 123.

In chapter 3, Vasubandhu discusses the vitality faculty at iii. 3cd as the basis of the mental stream in the realm of immateriality; at iii. 14 d in the context of the life expectancy of intermediate beings; and at iii. 78–85a he discusses the measurements of the life expectancy (*āyus*) of the five planes of existence, which also include a discussion (iii. 85a) of whether or not there is premature death (*antarāmṛtyu*).

At iv. 73ab, he discusses the vitality faculty in the context of killing (*prāṇātipāta*) and the vital breath (*prāṇa*), and the life-force (*āyus*), at viii. F 137f., in the context of the refutation of the hypothesis that material form as material sense-faculties exists in the realm of immateriality.

6. As for its existential status, the Vaibhāṣikas affirm it to be a real entity, whereas the Sautrāntikas deny this. For the details, see the discussion in our present section.

7. Even though the above-mentioned three specific components of heat, consciousness and life-force are central in the later Abhidharma treatises, we find (DD.127) three major issues dealt with in the AKB, Ny and *Avatāra* in their treatments of vitality, namely, (i) the possibility of states without thought, (ii) the possibility of rebirth in the formless realm and (iii) the discrimination of life from death within the stream of any given sentient being. Cox further comments (DD.130) that the lengthy discussions of the varieties of death in the AKB and Ny suggest "that the factor of vitality had become increasingly significant doctrinally as the quality that distinguishes life from death".

632 *LVP*: *Jñānaprasthāna*, 991b25 (*Indriyaskandhaka*, i), *Prakaraṇa*, 694a23.

633 *Gokhale*: [45a2–b] *ādhāra uṣmavijñānayor hi yaḥ* |

Tib.: [45a2–b] *drod dang ni* | *rnam shes rten gang yin pa'o* |

LVP: Life-force (*āyus*) and heat (*uṣman*), see AKB iii, F 107, viii, F 137; *Vibhāṣā*, p. 771a.

634 *LVP*: āyur uṣmātha vijñānaṃ yadā kāyaṃ jahaty amī |
apaviddhaḥ tadā śete yathā kāṣṭham acetanaḥ || [WOG.668.16f.]

Saṃyukta, 21, 14; *Madhyama*, 58, 4; *Saṃyutta*, iii. 143 (different readings); compare *Majjhima*, i. 296. – Cited *below ad* iv. 73ab.

635 *LVP*: MVŚ, 771a7: This Sūtra is cited by the Vibhajyavādins in order to establish that these three factors, i.e., life-force, heat and consciousness, are always united and inseparable. But Vasumitra observes that the Sūtra refers to the life-stream of a certain basis (*āśraya*).... (1) Life-force (*āyus*) forms part of the aggregate of formations (*saṃskāraskandha*), of the element of factors (*dharmadhātu*), of the sense-sphere of factors (*dharmāyatana*); (2) heat forms part of the aggregate of material form (*rūpaskandha*) and of the sense-sphere of the tangible (*spraṣṭavyāyatana*); (3) consciousness forms part of the aggregate of consciousness (*vijñānaskandha*), of seven elements (*dhātu*) and of the sense-sphere of the mental faculty (*manāyatana*): thus one should not take the Sūtra literally.

Furthermore, if these three factors would be inextricably linked, (1) there would be heat in the realm of immateriality, (2) there would be the life-force and consciousness among the non-living entities, (3) there would be consciousness in the attainment of non-ideation.

636 *LS*: Although not explicitly mentioned in Pradhan, LVP mentions the Sautrāntika here.

637 *LS*: The same as above.

638 *LS*: The same as above.

639 *LS*: The same as above.

640 *LS*: As for warmth (DD.290, 298), even though it operates continuously for the period of one lifetime, it is not exclusively a ripened effect, but rather is an effect of equal outflow (*niṣyandaphala*) "and is produced through the purely physical processes of accumulation (*aupacayika*)".

641 *LS*: Although not explicitly mentioned in Pradhan, LVP mentions the Sautrāntika here.

642 *LS*: The same as above.

643 *LVP*: Hsüan-tsang: "Moreover, this is what we have said. – What have you said? – In order to avoid this consequence... ."

644 *LS*: Although not explicitly mentioned in Pradhan, LVP mentions the Sautrāntika here.

LS: This is the 16th of Kritzer's forty-four passages discussed in relation to chapter 2 (VY.68f.). Saṃghabhadra (Ny, 404b26–c3) identifies this as the opinion of Vasubandhu and criticizes it (Ny, 404c3–22), "denying that the force referred to by Vasubandhu can continue without interruption and showing that the suggested similes are not apposite".

As for parallels to the *Yogācārabhūmi*, the *Viniścayasaṃgrahaṇī* (587a21–23 and 616a6–7) states that *jīvitendriya* (1) is the force that, due to previous *karma*, determines the duration of an *ātmabhāva* born in a particular place and (2) is explicitly stated to be a *prajñapti*.

645 *LS*: Yaśomitra glosses (WOG.169.2–3; DD.299) the compound *sthitikālāvedha* as "that particular capability (*-avedha*), which is the cause through a succession of moments (*-kāla-*) for the abiding (*sthiti-*), defined as a continuous series of aggregates" (*...sāmarthyaviśeṣaḥ. sa hi skandhaprabandhalakṣaṇāyāh sthiteḥ kṣaṇaparaṃparayā kāraṇaṃ bhavati. ata eva sthitikālāvedha ucyate*).

646 *LS*: As for the different meanings of *nikāyasabhāga*, see our endnote to ii, F 105.

Cox comments (DD.299) that Pradhan's Sanskrit edition of the AKB and both Hsüan-tsang's and Paramārtha's translations use the term *nikāyasabhāga* here. Hsüan-tsang's translation of Saṃghabhadra, on the other hand, chooses the phrase "the six sense organs together with their basis", perhaps to avoid using the term *nikāyasabhāga* in a non-technical sense and to reserve it for its technical sense as the discrete real entity posited by the Sarvāstivāda-Vaibhāṣikas.

647 *LVP*: *sasyānāṃ pākakālāvedhavat* [...] *kṣipteṣusthitikālāvedhavac ca* | [see WOG.169.5ff.]

648 *LVP*: *Vaiśeṣikadarśana*, v. 1, 16; H. Ui, *Vaiśeṣika philosophy*, p. 163. – The example of the arrow [as given above] is of no value in regard to the Vaiśeṣika who takes *vega* (impetus) as a real entity. Thus the author refutes the theory of the Vaiśeṣika.

649 *LS*: Potter remarks (EIP.II.129): "Inertia (*vega*), sometimes rendered as 'impetus', 'velocity', or even 'speed', is the quality of a moving substance which is responsible for its continuing in the same direction. There is a discrepancy between Vaiśeṣika and Nyāya on how many such inertia-qualities occur in a body moving in a line of direct flight. Seal reports that

the Vaiśeṣikas hold that there is one inertia throughout, but that Uddyotakara and the other Naiyāyikas hold that inertia, like the other qualities, is momentary and produces another one at the next moment. The Nyāya view has the advantage that acceleration and deceleration can be easily explained. The Vaiśeṣika posits that inertia loses its force as it expends energy and thus the body eventually slows down and stops."

650 *LVP*: *śīghrataratamaprāptikālabhedānupapattiḥ* [WOG.169.20].

651 *LVP*: Hsüan-tsang: "There is a real entity, the support of heat and of consciousness, called *life-force* (*āyus*): this doctrine is good." Note of the Japanese editor: The author falls into line with the Sarvāstivādin. – But one may assume that Hsüan-tsang omits the words: "The Vaibhāṣikas say: ...", since Vasubandhu, in the *Pañcaskandhaka*, adopts the Sautrāntika thesis.

LS: Cox summarizes (DD.128): "For Saṅghabhadra, the activities of animation and support, which he attributes to vitality, can be attributed to no other entity; therefore, the presence of these activities constitutes sufficient reason to justify the existence of vitality as a discrete real entity. Furthermore, vitality can function as the basis for a distinction between life and death. The occurrence of animate states without perceptual consciousness and animate states without warmth demands that death be explained, not through the termination of perceptual consciousness or warmth, but through an interruption in the stream of vitality. This separate factor of life, or vitality, whose existence is proven through its activity, characterizes all states of sentient beings including states without thought and rebirth in the formless realm; as a result, vitality must be a force dissociated from both thought and form."

652 *LVP*: *Karmaprajñāptiśāstra*, chap. xi (*Mdo* 72, fol. 240b).

653 *LVP*: On the diverse effects of action, iv. 85ff. – On enjoyment (*bhoga*), *Yogasūtra*, ii. 13.

654 *LVP*: Missing in Paramārtha. See above ii, F 122. – MVŚ, 103b3.

LS: Saṃghabhadra comments (Ny, 405a; DD.293) that this example "should not be mentioned [within the fourth alternative] because its sense is included within the first alternative".

655 *LVP*: *Vibhāṣā*, 151, p. 771.

656 *LS*: This case does not refer to sentient beings in the realms of fine-materiality and immateriality for whom the life-span is predetermined, i.e., whose life is not subject to premature mortal injury or untimely death; it also does not refer to the two states of equipoise without thought, the duration of which is determined by prior application and where untimely death is thus not possible (DD.300).

657 *LS*: This passage elucidates the last alternative of the above-given tetralemma, i.e., death through the inability to avoid unfavorable circumstances. The MVŚ, 771a23, states that untimely death is rejected by the Dārṣṭāntikas (DD.300).

As to whether or not there is a difference between the two interpretations, see DD.300–1.

658 *LVP*: [WOG.170.9ff:] This is the explanation of the Foreign Masters (Bahirdeśaka). – The explanation of the Kaśmīreans differs only in terms. Or else, the latter understand that the life-force (*āyus*) of the first category is "bound to its own stream (*svasaṃtatyupanibaddha*), but susceptible of being hindered".

659 *LVP*: According to *Kathāvatthu*, xvii, 2, the Rājagirikas and the Siddhatthikas deny premature death for the perfected beings (*arhat*; *Kośa*, ii. 10). – According to Rockhill (*Life of Buddha*, p. 189) and Wassilief, p. 244, the Prajñaptivādins deny premature death. – The *Bodhi-*

caryāvatāra (ii. 55) accepts one "natural" death (*kālamaraṇa*) and 100 premature deaths, due to each of the three humors (wind [*vāta*], bile [*pitta*], phlegm [*śleṣman*]) and to the humors joined together, which makes 404 deaths.

In addition to (1) *samucchedamaraṇa*, the death of the perfected being; (2) *khaṇikamaraṇa*, the ceaseless disappearance of factors (*dharma*) consumed by impermanence; (3) *sammutimaraṇa*, the death that one attributes to a tree, etc., the Abhidharma distinguishes (1) *kālamaraṇa* (natural death) (i) through exhaustion of merit (*puñña*), (ii) through exhaustion of one's lifetime (*āyu*), (iii) through exhaustion of both; (2) *akālamaraṇa* (premature death) due to an action that cuts off existence (*upacchedakakammanā*), in the case of Dūsī Māra, Kalabhū, etc., in the case of persons assassinated through retribution of a previous action (*Visuddhimagga*, viii, see in Warren, p. 252; *Commentaire de l'Aṅguttara*, PTS, p. 111; *Nettipakaraṇa*, p. 29; *Milinda*, p. 301). – *Abhidhammasaṅgaha, Compendium*, p. 149.

Jaina doctrine, Umāsvati, *Tattvārthādhigamasūtra*, ii. 52: *dvidhāny āyuṃsi*... .

660 *LS*: Yaśomitra suggests (WOG.170.14ff.) that this *sūtra* passage also supports the possibility of untimely death.

The translation of the following passage is based on Collett Cox's Pradhan-based translation (DD.294).

661 *LVP*: Literally: acquisition of existence (*ātmabhāvapratilambha*).

Majjhima, iii. 53 distinguishes two types of acquiring modes of personal existence, the *savyāpajjha* and the *avyāpajjha*.

662 *LVP*: *Dīgha*, iii. 231, *Aṅguttara*, ii. 159: *atth' āvuso attabhāvapaṭilābho yasmiṃ attabhāvapaṭilābhe attasaṃcetanā yeva kamati no parasaṃcetanā*... . – See *Kośa*, vi. 253, 255, 262. – *Vyākhyā*: *ātmasaṃcetanā* = ātmanā māraṇam; *parasaṃcetanā* = pareṇa māraṇam [WOG.170.15f.].

663 *LVP*: *Dīgha*, i. 19, iii. 31. – MVŚ, 997b9. There is no agreement: does this refer to the Four Kings and the Thirty-three or to other categories of gods of the realm of desire?

664 *LS*: These beings are not capable of inflicting mortal injury through their own intention (Ny, 405a).

665 *LVP*: *jinadūta*. – For example, a certain Śuka was sent by the Fortunate One to Āmrapālī; the Licchavis who were engaged in military exercises (*yogyā*), saw him and let loose a rain of arrows on him. But the messengers of the Buddha cannot be killed before having fulfilled their mission.

666 *LVP*: *jinoddiṣṭa* = iyantaṃ kālam anena jīvitavyam iti ya ādiṣṭo bhagavatā [WOG.170.24].

Perhaps one should understand: "The persons to whom the Buddha gives an order knowing that they will live long enough [to fulfill their mission]." The notes that J. Przyluski kindly gave to me on Yaśas and Jīvaka, make this version rather plausible:

"In *Mahāvagga*, i. 7, paragraph 4 is nearly incomprehensible. Yaśas cries out: 'What a danger!' and we do not know to what danger he is alluding. In the corresponding passage of the Vinaya of the Sarvāstivādins, everything is explained: At that time, Yaśas, having passed through the gate of the town, arrived close to the river Vārānasī. Then the Fortunate One was walking to the bank of the river. Yaśas, seeing the water, gave forth a cry as he had previously done. The Buddha, hearing this cry, said to the young man: 'This place has nothing to be afraid of. Cross the stream and come.' (Tōk. xvii. 3, 26[a])."

"The wife of Subhadra (comp. *Divyāvadāna*, 262–70) died before having given birth; the body was cremated but the child was not burned. The Buddha told Jīvaka to go and take the child from the middle of the flames: Jīvaka obeyed and returned without being harmed (xvii. 1, 6[a])."

667 *LVP*: Reading provided by the *Vyākhyā* [WOG.170.24]. – Tibetan: *chos len.*

668 *LVP*: Tibetan: *mchog can.*

669 *LVP*: Tibetan: *gang ga len.* – The Chinese transcriptions give Gañjila; see the failed suicide attempts of Gaṅgika, *Avadanaśataka*, 98.

670 *LVP*: The fact that the expression *tadyathā* is absent in the answer of the Fortunate One [ii, F 220] does not prove that this answer should be understood literally.

671 *LS*: AH 24; 221; SAH 65–66, 454.

672 *LS*: AH 24, 221; SAH 65, 454.

673 *LS*: Ibid.

674 *Gokhale*: [45cd] *lakṣaṇāni punar jātir jarā sthitir anityatā* ||

Tib.: [45cd] *mtshan nyid dag ni skye ba dang* | *rga dang gnas dang mi rtag nyid* ||

LVP: Paramārtha: "Moreover, there are the characteristics (*lakṣaṇa*) of the conditioned (*saṃskṛta*)...".

Hsüan-tsang: "The characteristics (*lakṣaṇa*), namely, origination, duration, deterioration, impermanence of conditioned factors (*saṃskṛta*)."

MVŚ, 198a8; *Abhidharmahṛdaya* (*Nanjio*, 1288), ii. 10.

A provisional definition of conditioned factors (*saṃskṛta*) has been given i. 7ab.

Madhyamakavṛtti, 546, *Madhyamakāvatāra*, 193: "according to the Abhidharma, the four are simultaneous". – The *Ṣaḍdarśanasaṃgraha* attributes to the Sāṃmitīyas the thesis: *catuḥkṣaṇikaṃ vastu, jātir janayati, sthitiḥ sthāpayati, jarā jarayati, vināśo vināśayati.*

LS: The following longer endnote discusses the following topics: (1) the definitions of the four characteristics in the *Pañcaskandhaka* and the *Avatāra*; (2) the general position of the four characteristics within the Sarvāstivāda teachings; (3) the history of the four characteristics and the doctrine of momentariness; (4) the reconstruction of the doctrine of momentariness via related concepts; (5) the existential status of the *saṃskṛtalakṣaṇas*; (6) selected writings from modern research.

1. *The definitions of the four characteristics in the Pañcaskandhaka and the Avatāra*:

Vasubandhu's *Pañcaskandhaka* (2008) states:

> 4.2.7 *jātiḥ katamā* | *nikāyasabhāge yaḥ saṃskārāṇām abhūtvā bhāvaḥ* |
>
> 4.2.7 What is birth? The origination of previously nonexistent formations in relation to a class affiliate.
>
> 4.2.9 *sthitiḥ katamā* | *tathaiva teṣāṃ prabandhānuvṛttiḥ* |
>
> 4.2.9 What is duration? The uninterrupted succession of [the] continuum [of the formations] in relation to [a class affiliate].
>
> 4.2.8 *jarā katamā* | *tathaiva teṣāṃ prabandhānyathātvam* |

4.2.8 What is aging? The modification of [the] continuum [of the formations] in relation to [a class affiliate].

4.2.10 *anityatā katamā | tathaiva teṣāṃ prabandhoparamaḥ |*

4.2.10 What is impermanence? The destruction of [the] continuum [of the formations] in relation to [a class affiliate]. ISBP.238–39

Avatāra (ESD.116f.):

When *dharma*-s are produced, there is a force of internal cause which makes them achieve their specific functions (*vṛtti/vyāpāra/sāmarthya*). It is this internal cause that is called the production-characteristic (*jāti-lakṣaṇa*). The causes of production of *dharma*-s are two-fold: (i) internal and (ii) external. The former is the production-characteristic and the latter comprises the six causes (*hetu*) or the four conditions (*pratyaya*). If the production-characteristic were non-existent, the conditioned *dharma*-s would be just like the [unconditioned] Space, etc., which, in spite of the assemblage of external causes and conditions, never arises. Or, [the unconditioned *dharma*-s] like Space, etc., are also capable of arising and hence become conditioned in nature. This indeed is a great incongruity. Thus, we can infer from this that there exists a distinct production-characteristic.

The cause which enables [a *dharma*] to stay temporarily, so as to be able to project a distinct fruit, is named the duration-characteristic (*sthiti*): When a conditioned *dharma* is staying temporarily, it has the power of projecting a distinct fruit. This internal cause, which enables [a *dharma*] to stay temporarily in this power of projecting a distinct fruit, is named the duration-characteristic. If this duration-characteristic were non-existent, when the conditioned *dharma*-s are staying temporarily, they ought not to be further able to project a distinct fruit. Hence, it can be inferred that there exists a distinct duration characteristic.

Deterioration (*jarā*) is that which impairs (*vi-√han*) [a *dharma*'s] efficacy of projecting fruit, rendering it incapable of further projecting another distinct fruit. If a conditioned *dharma* did not have the change—[or deterioration—] characteristic (*anyathātva-lakṣaṇa*) which impairs its activity [function/efficacy?], how is it that it does not keep on projecting one distinct fruit after another, and thus leading to *ad infinitum*? Besides, if this be the case [a conditioned *dharma*] ought not be momentary (*kṣaṇika*) in nature. Hence we can infer from this that there exists a distinct [*dharma* named] the deterioration-characteristic.

Impermanence (*anityatā*) is that which causes a present *dharma*, whose activity having been impaired [by the deterioration-characteristic] to enter into the past: There exists a distinct *dharma* named disappearance—[or impermanence—] characteristic (*vyaya-lakṣaṇa*) which causes [a *dharma*] to go from the present into the past. If this were non-existent, *dharma*-s ought not to disappear. Or, [the unconditioned *dharma*-s like] Space, etc., would also disappear [just as do the conditioned ones].

2. *The general position of the four characteristics within the Sarvāstivāda teachings*:

As for this topic, the *Avatāra* ends its discussion of them by stating (p. 118): "Thus, although the intrinsic nature (*svabhāva*) of a conditioned *dharma* always exists (*sarvadāsti*), its function is not permanent (*nitya*). It achieves its function by the force of the four characteristics, the internal causes, and the external causes." Here the four characteristics are placed within (i) the wider context of causality (see AKB ii. 49–73) and (ii) the Sarvāstivāda doctrine of existence within the three times, i.e., past, present and future entities (see AKB v. 25–27). As for the latter, Collett Cox comments (DD.361):

> Since, according to the Sarvāstivāda-Vaibhāṣikas, factors exist as real entities (*dravya*) in the three time periods, they exist even in the future time period when they have not yet been produced. Production, therefore, refers not to a factor's coming into existence, but to the arising of its activity, and when its activity arises, a factor is referred to as present. Factors are then considered to be conditioned precisely because their activity arises and passes away. Thus, for Saṅghabhadra, birth [*jāti*] does not mark the existence of a conditioned factor. According to Vasubandhu, however, factors can be said to exist only in the present time period when they acquire their own nature, which is identified by Vasubandhu with their particular activity. The arising and passing away of this nature or activity determines their existence or nonexistence and constitutes their conditioned nature.

As for the relationship of the four characteristics to (iii) the doctrine of momentariness (see ii, F 232, and further references/comments below), it is alluded to by the *Avatāra* only briefly in its discussion of *jarā* (see above) but seems to be otherwise presupposed. Rospatt introduces this doctrine at the beginning of his article *Buddhist Doctrine of Momentariness*, p. 469—without, however, at that point making the technical distinctions between the Sarvāstivāda and Sautrāntikas schools—as follows:

> Its fundamental proposition is that: everything passes out of existence as soon as it has originated and in this sense is momentary.
>
> As an entity vanishes, it gives rise to a new entity of almost the same nature which originates immediately afterwards. Thus, there is an uninterrupted flow of causally connected momentary entities of nearly the same nature, the so-called continuum (*santāna*).
>
> These entities succeed each other so fast that the process cannot be discerned by ordinary perception. Because earlier and later entities within one continuum are almost exactly alike, we come to conceive of something as a temporally extended entity even though the fact that it is in truth nothing but a series of causally connected momentary entities.
>
> According to this doctrine, the world (including the sentient beings inhabiting it) is at every moment distinct from the world in the previous or next moment. It is, however, linked to the past and future by the law of causality in so far as a phenomenon usually engenders a phenomenon of its kind when it perishes, so that the world originating in the next moment reflects the world in the preceding moment.

3. *The history of the four characteristics and the doctrine of momentariness*:

i. As for the history of impermanence (*anityatā*), Rospatt comments (IT.69) that what matters in the classical form of impermanence as old age, illness and death—as encountered by the Buddha-to-be on an excursion to a pleasure grove—is not an abstract universal law of impermanence, but the transience of life, and more concretely, that we ourselves are impermanent. Although clearly an awakening experience for the Buddha-to-be, it does not itself constitute a supramundane realization of impermanence, an insight of a higher order that liberates one from *saṃsāra* and brings about *nirvāṇa*, but forms the starting point of the entire Buddhist endeavour, i.e., right view (*samyagdṛṣṭi*) and right thinking or resolve (*samyagsaṃkalpa*) (vi., F 246) to leave home and strive for release from the cycle of death and rebirth. This is also reflected in the fact that, when the four noble truths are analyzed (see vi. 2–3; vii. 13a), impermanence is dealt with first, followed by the unsatisfactory nature of existence (*duḥkha*) and the non-existence of something to be identified as "self" or "mine" (*anātman*).

But although *anityatā* is rooted in the biological fact of the transience of life, it proved to be flexible enough to accommodate further doctrinal developments, and the soteriological need to induce a direct experience of impermanence in the present gave rise to different strategies. In this context Rospatt identifies (IT.72) (a) the relocation of death in the immediate presence—for example, when retiring to a charnel field where human corpses are discarded, so as to observe the various states of decomposition, or in the prominent practice of recollecting death (*maraṇasmṛti*; vi. 9–11)—and (b) "the shift of impermanence away from old age and death, so that the analysis of impermanence came to focus on existence within time rather than on the irreversible termination of existence", for example, when concentrating within the practice of the application of mindfulness of the body, etc. (*smṛtyupasthāna*; vi. 14–16) on the impermanent nature of existence before death.

ii. As for the doctrine of momentariness, Rospatt discusses its history in detail in his *The Buddhist Doctrine of Momentariness. A Survey of the Origins and Early Phase of this Doctrine up to Vasubandhu*. Here is its outline:

I. Exposition of the Early Phase of the Doctrine of Momentariness
   A. The Earliest Textual Evidence for the Doctrine of Momentariness
   B. The Doctrine of Momentariness in the Hīnayāna Schools
   C. The *saṃskṛtalakṣaṇas*
   D. Momentariness in the Early Yogācāra School
   E. The Various Definitions and Usages of the Term *kṣaṇa* in Buddhist Sources
II. The Origins of the Doctrine of Momentariness
   A. The Momentariness of Mental Entities
   B. The Deduction of the Momentariness of all Conditioned Entities from the Momentariness of the Mind
   C. The Deduction of Momentariness from Change
   D. The Deduction of Momentariness from Destruction
   E. The Experience of Momentariness

In regard to early Buddhism, Rospatt comments (BDM.15):

> There can be no doubt that the theory of momentariness cannot be traced back to the beginnings of Buddhism or even the Buddha himself.* It does not fit the practically orientated teachings of early Buddhism and clearly bears the mark of later doctrinal elaboration. Thus in the Nikāyas/Āgamas there are many passages which attribute duration to material and even mental entities, whereas there is, at least to my knowledge, no passage which testifies to the stance that all conditioned entities are momentary.

* LS: Yet see in this respect also Saṃghabhadra's discussion of the *Trilakṣaṇasūtra* in our

endnote at ii, F 226.

But—with the exception of two possible passages in Hsüan-tsang's translation of the *Jñānaprasthāna*, of which the second is rendered differently in Gautama Saṃghadeva's translation—Rospatt finds no relevant material regarding the doctrine of momentariness in the canonical Abhidharma works of the Sarvāstivādins either. On the other hand, since there is clear evidence for the doctrine of momentariness in the *Mahāvibhāṣa*, where the momentariness of all conditioned entities seems to be taken for granted when dealing with other issues—i.e., without treating it as a topic in its own right or without any explanation, justification or even less proof of momentariness, which seem to occur for the first time in the AKB, probably when required by the confrontation with other schools—Rospatt concludes that, even if it had played a marginal role in the *Jñānaprasthāna*, the doctrine of momentariness of all conditioned entities should be mainly postcanonic, i.e., some time between the conclusion of the Sarvāstivāda Abhidharmapiṭaka and the redaction of the *Mahāvibhāṣā*, and may have originated in the first century A.D. in the milieu of the Sarvāstivādins.

iii. a. As for the doctrine of the *saṃskṛtalakṣaṇas* within the Sarvāstivāda, Rospatt comments (BDM.46):

> That the *saṃskṛtalakṣaṇas* were originally correlated to existence over a span of time follows, [LS: among other reasons,] from the fact that the *Mahāvibhāṣā* [cf. 119a2] not only treats the *saṃskṛtalakṣaṇas* in terms of momentariness but also in terms of extended existence, though with the qualification that the *saṃskṛtalakṣaṇas* in this context are only conceptually given and not to be identified with the causally efficient *saṃskṛtalakṣaṇas* which qualify momentary conditioned entities.

Moreover (BDM.49):

> The Sarvāstivādins did not give up their doctrine of the *saṃskṛtalakṣaṇas* when they came to view all conditioned entities as momentary. This was impossible because the four *saṃskṛtalakaṇas* had become the indispensable corollary of each conditioned entity, once they had been hypostatized to causally efficient factors which account for the origination, duration, decay and annihilation of these entities. Thus the Sarvāstivādins had to carry on attributing the *saṃskṛtalakṣaṇas* to discrete conditioned entities even after the duration of these entities had been reduced to a bare moment. This meant that the operation of the four *saṃskṛtalakṣaṇas* which really requires a certain stretch of time had to be squeezed into a moment once the momentariness of all conditioned entities was espoused. ...
>
> The teaching of the Sarvāstivādins that the *saṃskṛtalakṣaṇas* of one entity all pertain to one and the same moment was already repudiated by the Dārṣṭāntikas in the *Mahāvibhāṣā* [200a4–6; cf. ii, F 231] on the grounds that these marks are incompatible with each other. This criticism was in turn rejected by the Sarvāstivādins who held that the *saṃskṛtalakṣaṇas* are, despite their simultaneity, not causally efficient at the same time [see ii, F 231, for details]. ... This still invited the charge that the qualified entity is all the same no longer momentary as it thus exists at two necessarily distinct points of time. In order to preclude this, the moment was defined as the time taken by the completion of origination and destruction [cf. ii, F 232].

b. As for the doctrine of the *saṃskṛtalakṣaṇas* within the Sautrāntikas, Rospatt comments

(BDM.60, 62):

> The Sautrāntikas shared the Sarvāstivādins' conception of the *kṣaṇa* as the smallest, indivisible unit of time, but, in contrast to the latter, solved the problem of how to squeeze a conditioned entity into an indivisible moment by adapting the mode of existence of conditioned entities to the theory of momentariness. The characteristic features, which were attributed to conditioned entities when they were still regarded as temporally extended, were not retained when their duration was reduced to a moment, but became instead assigned to chains of moments (*santāna*). This included the assignment of the *saṃskṛtalakṣaṇas*, so that origination, duration, transformation and destruction were—in accordance with the original import of the *sūtra*—related to existence over a span of time and not crammed into a moment. To do so was possible because, unlike the Sarvāstivādins, the Sautrāntikas did not accept that origination, etc., are causally efficient entities in their own right that exist apart from the thing that originates, etc. Rather than considering the marks of origination, etc., as the indispensable cause of origination, etc., they looked upon them as only conceptually given terms (*prajñaptimātra*, AKB 79,28) which express the fact that something has originated, etc. ...
>
> This correlation of the *saṃskṛtalakṣaṇas* to temporally extended phenomena accords with the original position of the Sarvāstivādins before they adopted the doctrine of momentariness.
>
> (p. 62): However, Vasubandhu also shows that it is possible to attribute the *saṃskṛtalakṣaṇas* to individual conditioned entities without accepting that these entities persist beyond origination and are subject to change. ... This characterization retains the four *saṃskṛtalakṣaṇas* only nominally (i.e., without associating with them four different states or phases), while it reduces the states of conditioned entities factually to that of existence and non-existence. It thus reflects a more radical (that is, more radical than that of the Sarvāstivādins) conception of momentariness, according to which the discrete conditioned entities neither undergo a phase of duration nor of transformation, but perish immediately after their origination. Since this destruction was not viewed as a time-demanding process, but as the simple fact that something having existed before has stopped to do so (*bhūtvābhāva*), existence was reduced by the Sautrāntikas to mere acts of originating (to flashes into existence, one might say) which do not allow for a temporal subdivision—a conception which accords with the understanding that the moment (*kṣaṇa*) is infinitesimal.

iv. With this radicalization of the instantaneous nature of existence, the doctrine of momentariness assumed its final form, presumably in the fourth century A.D.

Rospatt comments further (BM.471f.):

> Such a doctrine, fundamentally at odds with the appearance of the world, met great opposition. Initially, it was rejected by large sections of the Buddhist community, notably the Vātsīputrīyas and related schools. Later, when it had gained ground among Buddhists, it was fervently opposed by the Brahmanical schools as it contradicted their postulation of eternal entities of one sort or another (souls, atoms, primary matter, a supreme deity). This rejection made it necessary to defend the

doctrine by argumentation.

The oldest transmitted proofs of momentariness are recorded in early Yogācāra sources. They are still primarily directed against other Buddhists and derive the momentariness of all phenomena in three different ways.

First, it is presupposed that the mind is momentary—this stance is also shared by Buddhist opponents who do not accept the momentariness of matter—and on this basis it is concluded that matter, too, has to be momentary: proof from the momentariness of mind. This conclusion is based on the demonstration that mind and matter can only depend upon each other and interact as they do because they have the same duration.

Second, by referring to ageing and similar processes it is proved that everything changes all the time and thus undergoes origination and destruction at every moment. This argument rests on the presupposition that any form of transformation implies the substitution of one entity for another. This proof from change reflects the presumable doctrinal background underlying the formation of the doctrine of momentariness.

Third, it is argued that everything has to perish as soon as it has originated because otherwise it would persist eternally. This would be at odds with the law of impermanence. The argument rests on the presupposition that destruction cannot be brought about from without and that it is impossible for an entity to perish on its own account after it has persisted, as this would require a change of nature. The latter presupposition reflects the view that self-identical entities cannot change.

Vasubandhu (fourth–fifth century) marks the gradual transition between the earlier phase when the debate was still confined to Buddhism and the later phase when it was carried out between Buddhists and non-Buddhists. Vasubandhu only adopted the third type of proof, deducing momentariness from the spontaneity of destruction [see AKB iv, F 4–8]. He developed this idea further with the argument that destruction cannot be caused since, as mere nonexistence, it does not qualify as an effect. Up to the time of Dharmakīrti (c. 600–60) and to a lesser extent thereafter, this proof of momentariness, the so-called inference from perishability (*vināśitvānumāna*), dominated the controversy.

With Dharmakīrti, the doctrine entered a new phase. He developed a new type of proof, the so-called inference from existence (*sattvānumāna*), that derives the momentariness of all entities (without presupposing their impermanence) directly from the fact that they exist. On the basis of the premise that existence entails causal efficiency, Dharmakīrti demonstrates that all existing things have to be momentary as it is impossible for nonmomentary entities to function as efficient causes.

4. *The reconstruction of the doctrine of momentariness via related concepts in the AKB*:

Given that the conception of momentariness is not set forth explicitly as a topic in its own right in any of its pertinent Hīnayāna sources, it will be necessary to turn to related concepts in order to be able to arrive at a detailed reconstruction of the Sarvāstivādin's conception of momentariness.

As for the AKB, the following two references stand out (BDM.40):

i. Various definitions and usages of *kṣaṇa* (see iii. 85bc). Here is the outline related to it:

The units for calculating space (physical matter) and time; F 177

A. The smallest units of physical matter, words and time; F 177

1. Two non-computable definitions of the moment as a unit of time; F 177

1.1. Sautrāntika/Vasubandhu: Definition of the moment as a unit of "time based on characterization of the factor"; F 177

1.2. Sautrāntika/Vasubandhu: Definition of the moment as a unit of "time as an infinitesimal"; F 177

2. Vaibhāṣika: Comparison-based computable definition of time; F 178

B. The various units that measure what has been combined; F 178

1. The various units of space: Vaibhāṣika: computable definitions of the different units of space up to one league; F 178

2. The various units of time: Sarvāstivādins: computable definition of the different units of time up to the great aeon; F 179–81

ii. The well-documented treatment of the four *saṃskṛtalakṣaṇas* and the controversy on this point between the Sarvāstivādins and Sautrāntikas (i.e., our section here), which in turn has to be viewed against the background of the doctrine of *sarvāstitva* (v. 25–27 [F 49–66]).

But there are further related concepts and passages in the AKB, yet it should be kept in mind that the same term can carry different meanings according to context:

a. The mutual relationship between the four characteristics themselves as well as with the factor they characterize is discussed within the context of the co-existent cause at ii. 50bd.

b. Birth (*jāti*) and old-age-and-death (*jarāmaraṇa*) is discussed at various places within the context of dependent origination (*pratītyasamutpāda*), for example, at iii. 24cd.

c. For Vasubandhu's proof of momentariness based on the spontaneity of destruction, see iv, F 4–8.

d. Change and impermanence are discussed within the context of the four truths (*satya*) at vi. 2–3, in particular in relation to the truth of unsatisfactoriness and the three kinds of unsatisfactoriness: (a) unsatisfactoriness that is pain (*duḥkhaduḥkhatā*), (b) unsatisfactoriness that is the fact of being conditioned (*saṃskṛta*) or the unsatisfactoriness of the conditioning forces as such (*saṃskāraduḥkhatā*), (c) unsatisfactoriness that is unfavorable transformation (or change or decay) or the unsatisfactoriness based on unfavorable transformation (or change or decay) (*pariṇāmaduḥkhatā*).

e. Impermanence is also discussed at i. 2b and vii. 13a within the context of understanding (*prajñā*) and the common characteristics (*sāmānyalakṣaṇa*) or the four aspects or modes of activity (*ākāra*) of the truth of unsatisfactoriness (*duḥkhasatya*): (i) impermanent (*anitya*), (ii) unsatisfactory (*duḥkha*), (iii) empty (*śūnya*), (iv) nonself (*anātmaka*). As such it is also related with the appeasement of defilements (i. 3).

f. As for the role of impermanence within the context of the Buddhist path, see our references above ("history of impermanence") regarding the meditation on the loathsome (*aśubhā*), the application of mindfulness (*smṛtyupasthāna*) and the eightfold noble path.

g. As for whether or not momentariness can actually be experienced, see ii, F 227, and vi. 14cd.

5. *The existential status of the saṃskṛtalakṣaṇas*:

The Sarvāstivādins consider the *saṃskṛtalakṣaṇa*s to be truly existing entities and classify them within the formations dissociated from thought, but since they themselves are conditioned factors, they too have to possess their own *saṃskṛtalakṣaṇa*s. On the other hand, although the Sarvāstivādins do not contend that all conditioned entities only "exist" for a moment as the Sautrāntikas do, they consider them to be momentary in the sense that they are only "present" for a moment, namely, when they are causally efficient, whereas before this moment their intrinsic nature already exists in the future and thereafter in the past.

For the Sautrāntika view, see above (part 3.iii.b).

See naturally also Vasubandhu's discussion on this topic: ii, F 226–38.

6. *Selected writings from modern research*:

For a brief overview of modern research regarding momentariness, see BDM.4–7.

As for LVP's writings, see in the *Electronic Appendix*: (i) "Notes sur le 'moment' ou *kṣaṇa* des bouddhistes" (1934); (ii) "Documents d'Abhidharma: La controverse du temps" (1937), pp. 7–158, which includes: "Notes sur le moment (*kṣaṇa*) des Vaibhāṣikas et des Sautrāntikas", pp. 134–58.

See in particular Alexander von Rospatt's (i) *The Buddhist Doctrine of Momentariness. A Survey of the Origins and Early Phase of this Doctrine up to Vasubandhu* (1995), (ii) "Buddhist Doctrine of Momentariness" (1998), (iii) "Impermanence and Time. The Contemplation of Impermanence (*anityatā*) in the Yogācāra Tradition of Maitreya and Asaṅga" (2004).

675 *LVP*: *viparyayād asaṃskṛta iti yatraitāni na bhavanti so 'saṃskṛta iti.*

But can one not say that duration is a characteristic of the unconditioned factor? No. By characteristics, one understands real entities (*dravyāntararūpa*) distinct from the characterized factor that bring about arising, perduring, wasting away and perishing of this factor. The unconditioned factor abides but does not possess the characteristic "duration", see ii, F 224, top.

676 *LS*: AH 24; SAH 65.

677 *LS*: Saṃghabhadra defines, in his **Nyāyānusāra* (405c), origination or production (*jāti*) as follows (SA.IV.306):

> Herein, production is a distinct *dharma* which is the dominant cause of non-obstruction at the stage of arising of the conditionings (*saṃskāra*); for it induces them, enabling them to arise. "Inducing them" refers to the fact that at the time of their arising, this *dharma* serves as their condition of dominance.

Saṃghabhadra adds (DD.305): "Even though all arising of conditioned forces could be referred to as birth [*jāti*], this name 'birth' is given only to the predominant cause of non-obstruction when conditioned forces are in a state of being produced." The MVŚ, 202c–203a, explains further (SA.IV.318):

> Question: When the *saṃskṛta dharma*-s arise, do they arise on account of the fact that they are in themselves of the nature of arising (體是生法故生), or on account of being joined with *jāti-lakṣaṇa*?
>
> Answer: ... They arise on account of the fact that they are in themselves of the nature

> of arising. ... But, although they are in themselves of the nature of arising, they cannot arise without being joined with *jāti-lakṣaṇa*. ... At the time of their arising, *jāti-lakṣaṇa* is their predominant cause of production. Just as a destructible *dharma* is destroyed by a cause of destruction and an abandonable *dharma* is abandoned by a cause of abandonment; a producible *dharma* is produced by *jāti-lakṣaṇa*.

Origination operates on the *dharma* when it is in the future period. Saṃghabhadra elaborates (Ny, 411a; SA.IV.306):

> The production-characteristic serves as the conascent proximate cause (*āsanna-kāraṇa*) and produces the produced, i.e., the conditioned *dharma*-s. But [their production is not brought about by the production-characteristic alone]; this must be assisted by the assemblage of the previous causes of their own species as well as other external conditions.

See also our introductory note to the four characteristics (part 1) in regard to the consequences that would ensue, from the *Avatāra* point of view, if the origination characteristic were non-existent.

678 *LS*: Saṃghabhadra defines duration (*sthiti*) as follows (Ny, 405c; ESD.191):

> *Sthiti* is a distinct *dharma* which is the predominant cause of non-obstruction for the *saṃskṛta*-s, which have been produced but not yet destroyed, to project their own fruit.

According to the Vaibhāṣikas, if duration (*sthiti*) were non-existent, a conditioned *dharma* could not exercise its *kāritra*, i.e., its activity for projecting a *dharma*'s own effect of equal outflow (*niṣyanda-phala*) (Ny, 409c, etc.), and the *citta-caitta dharma*-s could not have any cognitive object (*ālambana*), but it is by the force of deterioration (*jarā*) and impermanence (*anityatā*) that there is not more activity after one moment (*kṣaṇa*) (MVŚ, 210c).

In regard to the term duration (*sthiti*), Saṃghabhadra elaborates (Ny, 411c; ESD.191):

> Nor do we say that the conditionings (*saṃskāra*), having been produced, stay on eternally. If so, why do you say that there is duration after the *saṃskṛta dharma*-s have been produced? By "there is duration" is meant "temporary staying": The conditionings, at the time when they are disappearing, stay temporarily; they cannot be said to stay at the time when they have disappeared or when they are being produced, as [at these times] they are without activity (*kāritra*). As we have mentioned earlier (cf. ibid., 411b), it is only at the time of disappearing that the conditionings possess the activity of projecting fruit (*phalākṣepa*).

See also our introductory note to the four characteristics (part 1) in regard to the consequences that would ensue, from the *Avatāra* point of view, if the duration characteristic were non-existent.

679 *LS*: Saṃghabhadra defines (Ny, 405c; SA.IV.307) deterioration/change (*jarā/anyathātva*) as "the cause for the conditioned (*saṃskṛta*) to be different in the subsequent [moment] from the previous [moment], in its continuation as a series". Later (Ny, 410b; DD.337) he also gives an alternate definition as the cause of the deterioration of a factor's activity:

> The Ābhidharmikas apply the term "senescence" to a factor in that state in which its intrinsic nature [is connected with] its distinctive activity, and not [when it exists

> only as] intrinsic nature. That is to say, the activity whereby a conditioned factor is able to project its own effect within its intrinsic nature is referred to as continuance; precisely the deterioration of this activity is referred to as senescence.

Cox comments (DD.371) that this alternative definition that appeals to the deterioration, decay, weakening, or injury of the activity of conditioned factors also appears in the MVŚ, 201c24ff.

See also our introductory note to the four characteristics (part 1) in regard to the consequences that would ensue, from the *Avatāra* point of view, if the deterioration characteristic would be non-existent.

680 *LS*: 1. Saṃghabhadra defines impermanence (*aniyatā*) as follows (Ny, 405c; ESD.192):

> *Aniyatā* is a distinct *dharma* which is the predominant cause for the destruction of a co-nascent *saṃskṛta* [*dharma*].

Saṃghabhadra adds (DD.306) that the suffix *tā*, or "nature", in the word *anitya-tā* has the meaning of "real entity" (*dravya*).

See also our introductory note to the four characteristics (part 1) in regard to the consequences that would ensue, from the *Avatāra* point of view, if the impermanence characteristic were non-existent.

2. This impermanence (*anityatā*) should not be confused with "impermanence" (*anityatā*) as one of the aspects or modes of activities (*ākāra*; vii. 13a) and also not with "impermanence" as one of the four common characteristics (*sāmānyalakṣaṇa*) of all conditioned factors: impermanent, unsatisfactory, empty and non-self. This is implied, for example, in Saṃghabhadra's following discussion (Ny, 412a; DD.349f.):

> Another objection has been raised [to the characteristic of desinence (*anityatā*)]: "If the characteristic of impermanence (*anityatā*) exists separately as a real entity apart from the nature [of factors as] impermanence, why isn't there also a characteristic of suffering (*duḥkha*) existing separately apart from suffering."
>
> [Saṃghabhadra's response:] Objections using examples such as these are not reasonably established. If one were to claim that [factors] exist having a nature as impermanent due to a [discrete] "characteristic of impermanence", then one could, on the basis of this claim, raise the following objection: "[Factors] should likewise exist having the nature of suffering due to a 'characteristic of suffering'." However, conditioned factors that are impermanent by nature are simply destroyed with the characteristic of desinence as their condition, just as conditioned factors that are impermanent by nature are simply produced with the characteristic of birth as their condition. What would be the use of proposing that the nature [of factors such as] suffering, similarly, has yet another "characteristic of suffering" that acts as its condition? Therefore, objections using such examples are not reasonably established. Through this [argument, in the same way] objections [using examples of] voidness and non-self are refuted.

681 *LS*: Rospatt (BDM.23) gives the following references: *Trilakṣaṇasūtra* (*AN* I 152 = T 125 607c15, *SN* III 36 = T 99 12a29–b1, *Nidānasaṃyukta*, p. 139,7–12 = T 99 83c16, cf. MPPU$_L$ III 1163, n. 1).

LVP in his *Documents d'Abhidharma*: *La Controverse du Temps* (1937; F 151f.), writes:

The moment (*kṣaṇa*) of the Sautrāntikas—i.e., the factor (*dharma*), since time does not exist in and of itself—is an infinitesimal. The factor, precisely, perishes on arising.

The moment of the Sarvāstivādins—i.e., the factor of the Sarvāstivādin—differs. The factor, once arisen, perdures for a very short time before disappearing. However, the factor is momentary.

The Sūtra, written at a time when factors were considered as impermanent (*anitya*) and not as momentary (*kṣaṇika*), says that "the conditioned factor (*saṃskṛta*) has three conditioned characteristics (*lakṣaṇa*), namely (1) arising, (2) duration-change (*sthiti-anyathātva*), (3) impermanence (*anityatā*) or cessation (*nirodha*) [*Kośa*: passing away (*vyaya*)]".

The Sarvāstivāda school teaches that the second characteristic is divided into two: duration (*sthiti*) and change (*anyathātva*). Also, it considers the characteristics as entities (*dharma*) that cause the factor to arise, perdure, perish. That is to say, the arising causes the factor to pass from the future into the present; duration maintains it... .

Does this mean that the factor is "of four moments"? This is the doctrine that a Jain source attributes to the Sāṃmitīya and we know that the scholars of Ceylon put three moments into one moment of mind. But the Sarvāstivāda doctrine, which distinguishes origination, duration and deterioration, has it that these three form only one indivisible present, a present where the before and after cannot be distinguished.

682 *LS*: Vasubandhu and Saṃghabhadra disagree (DD.356) on the interpretation of the phrase: *saṃskṛtasya saṃskṛtalakṣaṇa*, and LVP brings out this difference by providing two translations (pp. 223 and 227). Representing the Vaibhāṣika view, LVP renders: "Du conditionné, il y a, ô *bhikṣus*, trois caractères qui sont eux-mêmes conditionnés (Of the conditioned, there are, O *bhikṣus*, three characteristics which are themselves conditioned)", thus, for example, "the origination, etc., of the conditioned" was taken as a genitive, entailing that origination, etc., are something apart from the entity they refer to. Vasubandhu (ii, F 227, 234), on the other hand, understands this phrase to mean: "The conditioned (i.e., the serial continuity of conditioned factors) possesses three noticeable characteristics that indicate that it is conditioned, i.e., produced through successive causes." Thus, for him, the three characteristics that are possessed by the factor determine the quality of the factor itself as being conditioned.

683 *LVP*: This is the *Trilakṣaṇasasūtra* (see below ii, F 227). – *Saṃyuktāgama*, 12, 21; *Aṅguttara*, i. 152: *tīṇ 'imāni bhikkhave asaṃkhatassa samkhatalakkhaṇāni | katamāni tīṇi | uppādo paññāyati vayo paññāyati ṭhitassa aññathattaṃ paññāyati.* – The Sanskrit redaction has: *sthityanyathātva* (*Madhyamakavṛtti*, p. 145); *Kathāvatthu*, transl. p. 55: *ṭhitānam aññathatta.*

On *anyathābhāva*, *Saṃyutta*, ii. 274. – The Abhidhamma admits only three characteristics; certain scholars omit even duration (*sthiti*) (*Kathāvatthu*, translation, note p. 374).

For the four characteristics (*lakṣaṇa*) of the Vijñānavāda, see *Bodhisattvabhūmi*, I, xvii. § 15. (*Madhyamakavṛtti*, p. 546).

LS: The *Vyākhyā* has [WOG.171.26ff.]: *trīṇī 'māni bhikṣavaḥ saṃskṛtasya saṃskṛtalakṣaṇāni.* katamāni trīṇi. saṃskṛtasya bhikṣava utpādo 'pi prajñāyate. vyayo 'pi prajñāyate. sthityanyathātvam apīti.

Saṃghabhadra explains (Ny, 406a; DD.309) that "since the word 'also' (*api*) appears in connection with each of these [primary] characteristics, the secondary characteristics are also [implicitly] mentioned in the *sūtra* passage".

684 *LVP*: ābhiprāyiko hi sūtranirdeśo na lākṣaṇikaḥ [WOG.172.3f.].

685 *LVP*: The same comparison, with a different plot, *Atthasālinī*, 655.

686 *LS*: Although not explicitly mentioned in Pradhan, LVP mentions the Sautrāntikas here.

Rospatt (BDM.42) attributes this position to the Sarvāstivādins. He states that this position "features in the *Vibhāṣā* (150b18–22) as yet a further alternative to explain the deviation of the Abhidharmic doctrine of four *saṃskṛtalakṣaṇas* from the *sūtra*". Saṃghabhadra (Ny, 405c; DD.307) seems to be agreeing with this and explains: "The purpose of the compound is to indicate that the continuance of conditioned factors necessarily involves change. Unconditioned factors are distinguished from conditioned factors because they have continuance without change. ... One might claim that the continuance of unconditioned factors is not established, [and hence, the possibility of confusion between conditioned and unconditioned factors cannot be used as a reason why continuance is not explicitly mentioned in this *sūtra* passage]. This, however, would be unreasonable because [the continuance of unconditioned factors] is necessarily established. The fact that unconditioned factors have continuance is established precisely by establishing that there are three unconditioned factors."

687 *LVP*: *śriyam iva kālakarnīsahitām*; compare Burnouf, *Introduction*, p. 255: "The name Kālakarṇin is an epithet scornfully given by two [of the three] sons of [the very rich householder] Bhava to Pūrṇa, the son of a slave [and Bhava]. As the [three] brothers were called after their earrings, which were of wood (i.e., Dārukarṇin), of lead (i.e., Stavakarṇin), and of lac (i.e., Trapukarṇin)—[which at some point in their lives they had chosen to replace their diamond earrings, as a sign to save themselves from falling into poverty], in order to impose on Pūrṇa a name of bad omen—[the two brothers] call him "the one who has death as an earring" (Kālakarṇin). This is why the eldest brother defends him, answering that on the contrary Pūrṇa is prosperity itself."

688 *LS*: Rospatt (BDM.42) comments that "the discrepancy between the number of *saṃskṛtalakṣaṇas* in the *sūtra* and in the Abhidharma suggests that the doctrine of the *saṃskrtalakṣaṇas* cannot be traced back solely to the *Trilakṣaṇasūtra*. This impression is confirmed by the fact that the standard terms used for the *saṃskṛtalakṣaṇas* in the Abhidharma tradition of the Sarvāstivādins differ significantly from those employed in the *sūtra*. *Jāti* (= birth) is used instead of *utpāda* (= origination), *jarā* (= age) instead of *anyathātva* (= change), *anityatā* (= impermanence) instead of *vyaya* (= disappearance). The terms *jāti* and *jarā* suggest that the marks only qualify sentient existence and not conditioned entities in general as is the case in the *Trilakṣaṇasūtra*. [...] It may then be assumed that the terminology of the four *saṃskṛtalakṣaṇas* reflects two different currents, one relating them—in accordance with the *Trilakṣaṇasūtra*—to all conditioned entities, the other grasping them exclusively in terms of sentient life. ... Whereas there can be no doubt that the current relating to conditioned entities in general has its root in the *Trilakṣaṇasūtra*, it is likely that the current referring to sentient existence can be traced back to the final clause of the causal nexus (*pratītyasamutpāda*), namely that 'depending upon birth (*jāti*) there is old age (*jarā*) and death (*maraṇa*)' (*jātipratyayaṃ jarāmaraṇam*)."

689 *LS*: AH 24; SAH 65–66.

690 *LVP*: *jātijātyādayas teṣāṃ te 'ṣṭadharmaikavṛttayaḥ* |

The theory of [primary] characteristics (*lakṣaṇa*) and of secondary characteristics (*anulakṣaṇa*) is refuted by Nāgārjuna, *Madhyamaka*, vii. 1ff. See *Madhyamakavṛtti*, p. 148, on the theory of Sāṃmitīyas who admit seven [primary] characteristics and seven secondary characteristics, *utpāda*, *utpādotpāda*, etc.

691 *Gokhale*: [46ab] *jātijātyādayas teṣāṃ te 'ṣṭadharmaikavṛttayaḥ* |

Tib.: [46ab] *de dag skye ba'i skyes la sogs* | *de chos brgyad dang gcig la 'jug* |

692 *LS*: Dhammajoti comments (ESD.193) that, in our present AKB passage here, *vṛtti*, *kāritra* and *puruṣakāra* seem to be synonymous, whereas Saṃghabhadra (Ny, 409a–c; ESD.193f.) makes a distinction between *vṛtti* (功能; *gong neng*) and *kāritra* (作用; *zuo yong*):

> If a *saṃskṛta-dharma* serves as a cause for the projection of its own fruit, it is said to be [exercising its] *kāritra*. If it serves as a condition assisting [in the producing of the fruit of] a different [series], it is said to be [exercising its] function. ... Hence, there is a difference between *kāritra* and function/efficacy.

This distinction is central to Saṃghabhadra's ontological model (see v. 25–27; also ii. 59: the two stages of causing an effect). See also our endnote to ii. 231.

693 *LS*: The MVŚ, 201a, explains that origination and origination-of-origination function differently due simply to their nature (*dharmatā*). Saṃghabhadra maintains (Ny, 406a; DD.310) that even though there is no difference in terms of their intrinsic nature, the distinction between the primary and secondary characteristics is based on their respective capabilities (*sāmarthya*) and range of objects, stating that it is like the case of the five sensory consciousnesses and the mental consciousness, i.e., their intrinsic nature being the same while there is a difference in the range of their objects.

694 *LVP*: Ny, 406b16.

LS: This is the third place in Pradhan (76.23), where the term Sautrāntika is explicitly mentioned.

This is the 17th of Kritzer's forty-four passages discussed in relation to chapter 2 (VY.70f.). He comments that Saṃghabhadra (Ny, 406b16–20; DD.311f.) identifies this as the opinion of Vasubandhu and criticizes it (Ny, 406b20–29). Kritzer considers the basic positions of the Sautrāntika in the AKB and of the *Yogācārabhūmi* to be the same.

Rospatt writes that the MVŚ, 198a15–b1 discusses the different views on the ontological status of the *saṃskṛtalakṣaṇas* (BDM.44):

> As the Sautrāntikas in the AKB, the Dārṣṭāntikas opine that the *saṃskṛtalakṣaṇas* are not real entities in their own rights but only conceptually given, just like all other entities which are classified by the Sarvāstivādins as non-material factors dissociated from thought (*cittaviprayukta saṃskāra*).
>
> To the Vibhajyavādins, by contrast, the position is attributed that all *saṃskṛtalakṣaṇas* are unconditioned (*asaṃskṛta*) because only as unconditioned entities can they be potent enough to effect their function.
>
> The Dharmaguptakas held the same view with regard to the mark of destruction but

considered the marks of origination and duration as conditioned.

According to yet another stance reported in *Vibhāṣā*, the nature of the *saṃskṛta-lakṣaṇas* depends upon the entity they qualify. If they are attached to a material entity they are material, if to an entity of consciousness they have the nature of consciousness and so on.

Cox remarks (DD.148): "For Vasubandhu, the characteristics are abstractions, or provisional designations, that have no independent function. The production of each conditioned factor can be explained sufficiently through the collocation of external causes and conditions upon which it depends. The first three provisional phases of birth, continuance and senescence, Vasubandhu suggests, need no internal cause and destruction needs no cause at all. Conditioned factors are, by nature, disposed to arise and pass away and need no additional characteristics to make them do so."

695 *LVP*: *tad etad ākāśaṃ paṭyate* [WOG.173.22f.]: Space is a pure nothingness, a pure absence of any matter susceptible of resistance [*sapratighadravyābhāvamātram ākāśam*]. One cannot analyze it (*vipaṭyate, vibhidyate*).

696 *LS*: It is not that clear what the reference of *yathā* here is, but Yaśomitra (WOG.173.26ff; DD.358) identifies it as the previously described functions of the primary and secondary characteristics as applying, respectively, to eight factors and one factor.

697 *LVP*: See Saṃghabhadra's reply, Ny, 406b20 (DD.312ff.).

698 *LVP*: See F 223, note.

LS: Pradhan: *saṃskṛtasya bhikṣava utpādo 'pi prajñāyate. vyayo 'pi prajñāyate. sthityanyathātvam apīti.*

699 *LS*: This is the 18th of Kritzer's forty-four passages discussed in relation to chapter 2 (VY.72f.). He comments that Saṃghabhadra (Ny, 406c23–407b5) identifies this as the opinion of Vasubandhu and "argues at length that in fact the Buddha taught the three *saṃskṛtalakṣaṇas* with respect to the moment and not to the stream".

Ny, 407a (DD. 315):

> Now, this interpretation by [the *sūtra* master] should not [be accepted as] the meaning of the *sūtra*. First, one should not allow that there is only one arising, one passing away, and one change within the stream of conditioned forces. Further, if it were admitted [that the characteristics are to be applied to the stream of conditioned forces as a whole, and not to a single moment], it would not need to be expounded. Even if those [fools] who grasp the self had never heard [this teaching] that there is arising and passing away, and so on, in the stream of conditioned forces, they would still be capable of discerning it automatically. Since, even though they discern it, they still grasp the self, the further expounding of this teaching would be superfluous.

Ny, 407b (DD.317):

> Finally, the statement in the *sūtra*, "the arising of that which is conditioned also can be discerned, the passing away, and change in continuance also can be discerned", is made with regard to moments. The intention of this *sūtra* passage is that when the arising, and so on, of a moment is examined, it can be discerned. Therefore, the Lord made this statement in order to motivate his disciples to examine [the arising, and so

on, of each moment].

700 *LVP*: catvārīmāni bhikṣavaḥ pratisaraṇāni | katamāni catvāri | dharmaḥ pratisaraṇaṃ na pudgalaḥ | arthaḥ pratisaraṇaṃ na vyañjanam | nītārthasūtrāntaṃ pratisaraṇaṃ na neyārtham | jñānaṃ pratisaraṇaṃ na vijñānam [WOG.174.8ff.].

See the sources cited in *Madhyamakavṛtti*, 268, 598.

701 *LS*: Saṅghabhadra writes (Ny, 407c; DD.320f.):

> [S] What is specified by the term "stream of conditioned forces"?
>
> [O-V] It refers to the uninterrupted flow of conditioned factors.
>
> [S] Then, what factor constitutes its intrinsic nature?
>
> [O-V] [The stream] is a provisional factor (*prajñaptidharma*). How could one seek intrinsic nature [in it]? Rather, moments are mutually similar; they are interconnected [in a relation of] cause and effect; the conditioned forces produce effects, which occur in succession without termination; this is referred to as the stream [of conditioned forces].

702 *LS*: This is the 19th of Kritzer's forty-four passages discussed in relation to chapter 2 (VY.74f.), stating that the Buddha referred to the series and not to the moment since the arising, etc., of a moment is impossible to discern. Saṃghabhadra (Ny, 406c28–29) identifies this as the opinion of Vasubandhu and disagrees with it (Ny, 407a13–20).

But as we will see later (F 229), Vasubandhu accepts that the characteristics can also be applied to each moment, provided that one does not consider them to be distinct real entities.

703 *LS*: LVP has: "Trois *saṃkṛtalakṣaṇas* du *saṃskṛta* sont objet de connaissance."

704 *LS*: 1. Saṃghabhadra replies to Vasubandhu's statement as follows (Ny, 407b1; DD.317):

> Further, [even though the characteristics of] birth, and so on, as applied to a single moment [cannot be observed by ordinary direct perception], they can be discerned by subtle discriminative intellect: that is to say, if one closely examines the immediate succession of moments, one will be able to discern them. Subtle discriminative intellect is produced as a result of the exposition of [the teaching], and it discerns the impermanence of conditioned forces and is able to remove grasping of the self. Since this [impermanence of conditioned forces] is discerned by subtle discriminative intellect, it is unreasonable to claim that the three characteristics of arising, and so on, as applied to a single moment cannot be discerned.

2. But Vasubandhu himself also states at vi. 14cd:

> According to the School [*kila*], the application of mindfulness to the body (*kāyasmṛtyupasthāna*) is perfected [*niṣpanna*] when, being concentrated (*samāhita*), [the practitioners] see [*paśyataḥ*] the [conglomerate of] atoms [*paramāṇu*] and the successive moments (*kṣaṇa*) in the body [or see the body as atomic and momentary].

Rospatt (BDM.216), on the other hand, translates *kila* in this passage as "reportedly" and takes it to mean that "Vasubandhu indicates that his information is due to hearsay and that he himself has no direct access to such an experience". But he then also refers to our section here (F 226), commenting that "Vasubandhu even argues that the *Trilakṣaṇasūtra* cannot refer to momentary entities since their origination and so on are not cognized (according to Yaśomitra,

WOG.174,18f., because of the difficulty to ascertain a *kṣaṇa* precisely, *kṣaṇasya duravadhāra-tvāt*), whereas in the *sūtra* the origination and so on are depicted as objects of knowledge (*utpādo 'pi prajñāyate*)."

3. As for the MVŚ, it presents Bhadanta Vasumitra's view regarding "duration" (MVŚ, 201b; see LVP's *Documents d'Abhidharma*: *La Controverse du Temps*, F 155ff.):

> The characteristic "duration" during one moment is subtle, difficult to recognize, difficult to conceive (*prajñapyate*). This is why the Sūtra says that the conditioned forces do not last: the measure of one moment is known to the Buddha, it is not the domain of the Śrāvakas and Pratyekabuddhas.

Regarding the "experience of momentariness" in general, Rospatt (BDM.216) points to the paucity of pertinent textual material but then draws attention to a passage in the MVŚ, 840c21–841a11 (BDM.210f.), which, addressing the notion of death (*maraṇasaṃjñā*), teaches how the experience of momentariness can be obtained by narrowing down the span of time over which the arising and disintegration of the groups of factors constituting the person (*skandha*) is observed:

> [The yogin] contemplates that the *skandhas* (i.e., the groups of factors constituting the person) of one's lifetime arise at the time of conception (*pratisandhi*) [and] perish when old age and death are reached. Now one lifetime has numerous stages [of life] (i.e., infancy, adolescence etc.) in each of which the *skandhas* are different. Setting aside the other [states], he sees the *skandhas* of one state arising earlier and perishing later. Now one stage [of life] has numerous years in each of which the *skandhas* are different. Setting aside the other [years], he sees the *skandhas* of one state arising earlier and perishing later.
>
> > [Following this pattern, the envisaged period of time is reduced successively from a year to a season, to a month, to a day, to an hour (*muhūrta*), to a minute (*lava*), to a second (*takṣaṇa*).]
>
> Now one second (*tatkṣaṇa*) has numerous moments (*kṣaṇa*) in each of which the *skandhas* are different. Because the *kṣaṇas* [within a second] are extremely numerous, there is with regard to them a successively [more] subtle [summary] contemplation [of several *kṣaṇas*] (i.e., the number of *kṣaṇas* is gradually reduced over which the rise and fall of the *skandhas* is observed) until the *skandhas* are seen to arise in two and to perish in [the same] two *kṣaṇas*. This is called the completion of the [preparatory] practice of the viewing of origination and destruction (**udayavyayānu-paśyanāprayogasamāpti*). Immediately after this, one is able to see the *skandhas* arise in one and to perish in [the same] one *kṣaṇa*. This is called the perfection of the viewing of origination and destruction (**udayavyayānupaśyanāsiddhi*). At such a time, one says that the notion of death (*maraṇasaṃjñā*) (i.e., its contemplation) has been brought to completion, because the destruction of states is nothing but death.

Rospatt takes this section to mean that the *skandhas* are really perceived to arise and vanish every moment, and not just envisaged as doing so.

705 *LS*: *na cā 'prajñāyamānā ete lakṣaṇaṃ bhavitum arhanti*. The above translation is influenced by Collett Cox's Pradhan-based translation (DD.360).

This is the 20th of Kritzer's forty-four passages discussed in relation to chapter 2 (VY.78f.), stating that that which is not discerned should not be called a *lakṣaṇa*. Saṃghabhadra (Ny, 407b5–6) identifies this as the opinion of Vasubandhu and disagrees (Ny, 407b6–8; DD.317):

> Next, as for [the *Sūtra* master's] statement, "that which cannot be discerned should not be established as a characteristic", one cannot state unequivocally that an entity's not being discerned constitutes a sufficient reason for its not being a characteristic. Even though gross discriminative intellect cannot discern characteristics such as [the aggregate of] feelings, and so on, it is not the case that they are not characteristics. Therefore, [his] statement, "that which cannot be discerned is not a characteristic", is not reasonable.

706 *LS*: This is the 21st of Kritzer's forty-four passages discussed in relation to chapter 2 (VY.80f.). He comments that Saṃghabhadra (Ny, 407b12–14) identifies this as the opinion of Vasubandhu and disagrees with it (Ny, 407b14–24), stating that the word *saṃskṛta* is used twice in order to indicate that the characteristics and that which is characterized exist separately.

707 *LS*: This is the 22nd of Kritzer's forty-four passages discussed in relation to chapter 2 (VY.82f.). Saṃghabhadra (Ny, 407c9–11) identifies this as the opinion of Vasubandhu, who, according to Saṃghabhadra, is conforming to the accepted doctrine of the school of the Sthavira Śrīlāta. Saṃghabhadra (Ny, 407c17–408b28) refutes Vasubandhu's definitions of each of the four *lakṣaṇas* in turn.

Pradhan.77.6–8 gives: *tatra pravāhāsyādir utpādo | nivṛttir vyayaḥ | sa eva pravāho 'nuvartamānaḥ sthitiḥ | tasya pūrvāparaviśeṣaḥ sthityanyathātvam.*

708 *LS*: This is the 23rd of Kritzer's forty-four passages discussed in relation to chapter 2 (VY.84f.). Saṃghabhadra (Ny, 408b28–c5) says that the *sūtra* passage quoted by Vasubandhu does not support his view that the four characteristics are to be applied to the stream of conditioned forces as a whole, and not to a moment, since the *sūtra* passage suggests that Nanda knows past and future *dharmas*, the existence of which Vasubandhu denies.

709 *LVP*: *Saṃyukta*, 11, 14. – pravāhagatā hi *vedanās tasya viditā evotpadyante | viditā avatiṣṭhante | viditā astaṃ parikṣayaṃ paryādānaṃ gacchanti* | na kṣaṇagatāḥ kṣaṇasya duravadhāratvāt [cf. WOG.175.6ff.].

Tibetan: The *kulaputra* Nanda (Comp. *Aṅguttara*, iv. 166).

Compare *Saṃyutta*, v. 180; *Majjhima*, iii. 25 (where the Fortunate One says of Śāriputra what he says here of Nanda):

dhammā viditā uppajjanti viditā upaṭṭhahanti viditā abbhatthaṃ gacchanti.

LS: Cox comments (DD.363): "Yaśomitra (WOG.175.8ff.) explains that the feelings that are known, as mentioned in this *sūtra* passage, are those in a stream, not those of a single moment. Two reasons are given: first, a single moment is difficult to delimit (*kṣaṇasya duravadhāratvāt*)—that is, it is difficult to distinguish one moment from the next, and thereby, establish the limits of any given moment within the experience of feelings; second, feelings here must apply to a stream, since it is impossible to establish a moment that is known (*viditasya ca kṣaṇasyā 'vasthānāsaṃbhavāt*).

710 *LVP*: *'dir smras pa rgyun gyi dang po skye ba ni || chad pa 'jig pa gnas pa ste || de nyid sna phyi'i bye brag ni || gnas pa gzhan du 'gyur ba nyid || yang 'dir smras pa sngon med las byung*

skye ba ste || rgyun gnas de chad 'jig pa yin || rgyun gyis snga phyi'i bye brag ni || gnas pa gzhan du 'gyur bar 'dod || skad cig ma'i chos la ni || gnas pa med na 'jig par 'gyur || de yang 'jig 'gyur de yi phyir || de yi der rtag don med do |

> *jātir ādiḥ pravāhasya [ucchedo vyavaḥ] sthitis tu saḥ |*
> *[sthityanyathātvaṃ] tasyaiva [pūrvāparaviśiṣṭatā] ||*
> *abhūtvā bhāva utpādaḥ prabandhaḥ sthitir anityatā |*
> *taducchedo [jarā tasya pūrvāparaviśiṣṭatā] ||*
> *kṣaṇikasya hi dharmasya [sthitiṃ vinā bhaved vyayaḥ] |*
> *sa ca vyeti [svayaṃ] tasmād vṛthā tatparikalpanā ||*

Majjhima, iii. 25, contains the formula *evaṃ kila me dhammā ahutvā sambhonti* that becomes the thesis of the Sautrāntikas *abhūtvā bhāva utpādaḥ* (F 229, line 18), which we read in *Milinda*, p. 51, *ahutvā sambhoti*, and which is contradicted by the Sarvāstivādins and by *Milinda*, p. 52: *natthi keci saṃkhārā ye abhavantā jāyanti*. – Nāgasena is a Vibhajyavādin, p. 50.

<u>LS</u>: The verses are slightly different in Pradhan (77.11–14) (see RCYA.235):

> *jātir ādiḥ pravāhasya vyayaś chedaḥ sthitis tu saḥ | sthityanyathātvaṃ tasyaiva pūrva-aparaviśiṣṭatā ||*
>
> *jātir apūrvo bhāvaḥ sthitiḥ prabandho vyayas taducchedaḥ | sthityanyathātvam iṣṭaṃ prabandhapūrvāparaviśeṣa iti ||*

711 *LVP*: If one says: "It is due to duration (*sthitisadbhāvāt*) that the factor (*dharma*), once arisen, does not perish for a moment; lacking duration, even this moment would not exist"—no, for the moment exists due the causes that produce it.

If one says: "Duration welcomes, embraces (*upagṛhṇāti*) the factor engendered by causes", we ask: "If duration did not accomplish this function, what would happen?" – "The factor would not exist (*ātmasattā dharmasya na bhavet*)." – "Then say that duration engenders, not that it causes to endure."

If one says: "Duration causes the stream to continue (*avasthāpayati*)", one has to reserve the name of duration for its causes.

712 <u>LS</u>: Rospatt comments (BDM.23f.) that there is another version of the *Jñānaprasthāna* (T 1544) which reads *ekasmin kṣaṇe* instead of *ekasmiṃś citte* [as well as *anityatā* instead of *maraṇa*] and that the *Vibhāṣā* understands this passage "to teach that the three *saṃskṛta-lakṣaṇas* all occur in one moment, and explicates that this is taught in order to stop the view of others, notably the Dārṣṭāntikas, that the three *saṃskṛtalakṣaṇas* cannot exist in one moment".

713 *LVP*: Ny, 408c7.

<u>LS</u>: This is the 24th of Kritzer's forty-four passages discussed in relation to chapter 2 (VY.86f.). Saṃghabhadra (Ny, 408c7–12) identifies this as the opinion of Vasubandhu and argues (Ny, 408c12–409a2) that it leads to contradictions.

714 <u>LS</u>: Rospatt writes (BDM.42f.) that "without assenting to the hypostatization of the *saṃskṛtalakṣaṇas* to entities, the Sautrāntikas (and Yogācāras) took over the Sarvāstivādins' position that in addition to origination and destruction there are the marks of duration and change. – On a doctrinally more advanced level, however, their radical conception of momentariness according to which conditioned entities do not exist beyond origination and thus do not endure or change, prompted the position that conditioned entities are only characterized by

non-existence and an existence (or: origination) which allows for no further differentiation. This existence and non-existence are usually not identified with the canonical *saṃskṛta-lakṣaṇas*, but are instead taught to underlie them."

715 *LVP*: *kṣiptākṣiptabalidurbalakṣiptasya vajrādeś cirāśutarapātakālabhedāt* [cf. WOG.176.18ff.].

716 *LVP*: Smoke is momentary; when it "reproduces" itself in a higher place than that which it occupies at first, people say that it rises (*ūrdhvagamanākhyāṃ labhate*) and view the rising (*ūrdhvagamanatvam*) as distinct from the smoke (see iv. 2b).

717 *LVP*: *na ca saṃskṛtānāṃ rūpādīnāṃ tāvat saṃskṛtatvaṃ lakṣyate gṛhṇatāpi svabhāvaṃ yāvat prāgabhāvo na jñāyate paścāc ca saṃtateś ca viśeṣa (iti) na tenaiva saṃskṛtatvena saṃskṛtatvaṃ lakṣyate* [cf. WOG.177.26ff.].

If, seizing the intrinsic nature of visible form, one were to seize it as being conditioned (*saṃskṛtam iti*) before knowing of its previous non-existence, one could say that the conditioned is the mark of the conditioned, that the conditioned is characterized by the conditioned (*tenaiva tal lakṣitaṃ syāt*). But such is not the case.

718 *LŚ*: 1. This is the 25th of Kritzer's forty-four passages discussed in relation to chapter 2 (VY.88f.). Saṃghabhadra (Ny, 409a2–4) identifies this as the opinion of Vasubandhu and disagrees with it (Ny, 409a4–c8).

2. Saṃghabhadra, like the **Mahāvibhāṣā*, maintains that the characteristics exert their capability (*sāmarthya*) on a single factor and thus characterize each present moment, which presents the difficulty or seeming contradiction in our passage. Cox explains (DD.149):

> The **Mahāvibhāṣā* [200a9ff.] offers two solutions to this difficulty, both of which attempt to evade the contradiction by proposing a sequence in the functioning of the conditioned characteristics; that is to say, the four conditioned characteristics are said to exert their activities (**kāritra*) at different times. The solutions also demand careful consideration of the meaning of the term "momentary" [see ii, F 232].
>
> According to the first solution,[a] the characteristic of birth functions when both it and the characterized factor are about to be produced, that is, when both are future. The other three characteristics function when they and the characterized factor are about to be destroyed, that is, when they are present. Since a moment is understood, not as an absolute punctuality, but as the period from production to destruction pertaining to a single factor, the conditioned characteristics could still function within "one moment", and yet there would be no contradiction of a single factor being produced and destroyed at precisely the same time.
>
> As a second solution,[b] the **Mahāvibhāṣā* suggests that the states of production and destruction as pertaining to one factor do not constitute a single moment, and yet every moment contains all of the conditioned characteristics. That is to say, birth functions in the future time period when the factor is about to be produced; the remaining conditioned characteristics function in the present time period when that factor is about to be destroyed. Here, the **Mahāvibhāṣā* summarizes a position that would appear to suggest that each moment contains three characteristics—continuance, senescence, and desinence—of one factor together with the birth of the subsequent factor. In this way, the production and destruction of a single factor would not be simultaneous.

[a] MVŚ, 200a7–12 (BDM.50):

> So as to stop this opinion (viz. the position of the Dārṣṭāntikas that the *saṃskṛtalakṣaṇas* refer to existence over a stretch of time, MVŚ, 200a6f), it is explicated (namely in the version of the *Jñānaprasthāna* commented upon by the MVŚ, viz. T 1544, 926b20–22) that the three marks co-exist in one moment.
>
> Question: If so, then one qualified entity (*dharma*) would have to originate and decay and perish at one time.
>
> Answer: Because the time of their activity differs, [these marks] are not mutually exclusive. That is to say, when the *dharma* originates, the [mark of] origination has its activity. When the *dharma* undergoes destruction, then the [marks of] age and destruction have their activity. Even though [as] entities [they exist] simultaneously, their activity is sooner or later. That the operations of origination and destruction of one *dharma* have been completed is called "one moment". Therefore, there is no mistake [in our teaching].

[b] Rospatt translates (MVŚ, 200a12f.): "The states of origination and destruction do not occur in one moment, and yet the own-beings of the three (*saṃskṛtalakṣaṇas*) exist simultaneously in one moment."

Saṃghabhadra follows the first solution (Ny, 409a5; DD.329f.), commenting that the fault of contradictory functions—in particular that of being born and perishing—attributed to one factor in one moment is avoided since the four characteristics exist as distinct entities with their own distinctive functions quite apart from the factor that they ch acterize.

3. Collett Cox comments (DD.150f.):

> Saṅghabhadra can offer an explanation as to why production and destruction do not apply to a single factor within a single moment. But what can be done about the three characteristics of continuance, senescence, and desinence? A partial solution can be found elsewhere in the **Nyāyānusāra* [533b7ff.], where Saṅghabhadra discusses at length various interpretations of the meaning of a moment. He first states that a moment is the shortest period of time that cannot be further analyzed into prior and subsequent stages. He then adds that a moment refers to the briefest state of conditioned factors and that the present moment refers to that state in which a factor has its activity. It would then appear that the limits of a moment are the limits of a factor exerting its activity. We might then conclude that a moment does not refer to the shortest possible period of time, but rather to the period it takes to exert activity—a period that we might imagine occurs in various stages, that is, of continuance, and so on [see Sasaki (1974), 126ff.].
>
> Despite this attempted explanation, certain problems still remain. For example, how can we account for the apparent sequence in the exertion of the capability of the three conditioned characteristics? If we admit this sequence, are we not also admitting distinctions of "prior and subsequent" within one moment and, thereby, contradicting Sanghabhadra's own definition? [See Sasaki (1974), 129ff.].

Vasubandhu therefore continues this theme in subsection BAB.2.7.3 in the context of the last three characteristics.

719 *LS*: 1. Saṃghabhadra comments (Ny, 410a; DD.335) that statements like "origination per-

forms its activity when it is still future" "merely provisionally apply the term 'activity' to [what are actually] 'capabilities' functioning as immediate conditions". This might be the reason why LVP translates here *kāritraṃ hi karoti* as "engenders" ("engendre") and not as "performs its activity" ("exerce son activité") as with the other characteristics. Saṃghabhadra explains, at Ny, 409b (DD.331), the distinction between activity (*kāritra*) and capability (*sāmarthya*):

> Moreover, the states (*avasthā*) of conditioned factors are not [all] the same. In brief, there are three types: that is, distinguished [according to whether] the activity [of that conditioned factor] of projecting its own effect is not yet attained, is just attained, or has already been destroyed. Conditioned factors are, further, of two types: that is, those that exist with activity (*kāritra*) and those that exist only with intrinsic nature (*svabhāva*). The former [category] refers to the present: [that is, when a factor exists as a real entity characterized by intrinsic nature with activity]. The latter [category] refers to the past or future: [that is, when a factor exists only as a real entity characterized by intrinsic nature alone, lacking activity]. Each of these [types of conditioned factors] has two further types: that is, those whose capability (*sāmarthya*) is predominant or subordinate. That is to say, if conditioned factors are able to act as the cause in projecting their own effect (*phalākṣepa*), this [capability is predominant and] is referred to as activity (*kāritra*); if they are able to act as conditions assisting [factors] of a different category, this [capability is subordinate and] is referred to [simply] as capability (*sāmarthya*). These two types will be extensively considered in the discussion of the three time periods [Ny, 621c5ff., esp. 631c5ff; AKB v. 26 (F 55ff.)].

2. But then again, Dhammajoti comments (SA.IV.129) that "activity" is not always used in the strict technical sense which uniquely defines "present-ness": "Saṃghabhadra also claims that ... sometimes when the *abhidharma śāstra*-s are referring to a function (e.g., that of *jāti*) that serves as a proximate condition, the term *kāritra* is also used expediently". Thus this should also apply in our context to the *kāritra* as related to the other three characteristics, which is why I render *kāritra* here as "activity/capability".

Dhammajoti adds (SA.IV.129) that although in his translation of the **Nyāyānusāra* Hsüan-tsang "very consistently renders *kāritra* as *zuo yong* (作用) and as distinct from *gong neng* (功能) used for the terms denoting activities other than *kāritra*, it is important to observe that in other contexts, both in the AKB(C) and MVŚ, he is unfortunately not so consistent".

720 *LS*: Rospatt translates (BDM.51) "because [if it did so when it was already present, the *dharma* to which it is linked would be so, too, and] something having [already] originated is not originated [again]".

721 *LS*: Pradhan.78.15f. has: *na yadā jāyate tadā tiṣṭhati jīryati vinaśyati vā.* See DD.366.

Rospatt comments (BDM.50) that this view "invited the charge that the qualified entity is all the same no longer momentary as it thus exists at two necessarily distinct points of time. In order to preclude this, the moment was defined as the time taken by the completion of origination and destruction" (see below, F 232).

722 *LS*: Saṃghabhadra accuses Vasubandhu of not understanding the distinction between capability (*sāmarthya*) and activity (*kāritra*) (Ny, 409c; DD.334):

> [S] Fool! You do not understand this activity (*kāritra*). These [characteristics function as] capabilities (*sāmarthya*) and have no relation to activity. As has been previously discussed: "If conditioned factors are able to act as the cause in projecting their own effect (*phalākṣepa*), this [capability is predominant and] is referred to as activity (*kāritra*). If they are able to act as conditions assisting [factors] of a different category, this [capability is subordinate and] is referred to [simply] as capability (*sāmarthya*)." All present [factors] are able to act as the cause in projecting their own effects—[that is, they must exert their own activity]—but not all present [factors] are able to act as conditions assisting [factors] of a different category—[that is, they need not exert capability]. For example, an eye in the dark or [an eye] whose capability [of assisting] has been damaged is not capable of acting as a condition that assists in enabling visual perceptual consciousness to arise. However, its activity [of projecting its own effect] is not damaged by darkness because it is definitely able to act as a cause in projecting a future eye. In this way, there is a distinction between activity and capability.

723 *LS*: This is the 26th of Kritzer's forty-four passages discussed in relation to chapter 2 (VY.90f.). Saṃghabhadra (409c17–18) identifies this as the opinion of Vasubandhu and replies (Ny, 409c18–21; DD.333f.):

> The three [characteristics] of continuance, senescence, and desinence each give rise to their functions separately in the state in which the factor has already been produced and cause that characterized factor to have, at one time, points of dependence that are not the same. Altogether there are three [such points of dependence]. What contradiction to reason is there in an interpretation such as this?

Cox remarks (DD.368), however, that "the exact meaning of the key-phrase *so-wang*, 'points of dependence' or possibly 'desires' or 'objectives', is unclear, and as a result, the meaning of Saṅghabhadra's response is obscure".

724 *LVP*: The Vaibhāṣika is a "follower of momentariness" (*kṣaṇikavādin*): the factor abides only a moment and perishes of itself. See iv. 2b; Wassilief, p. 325. – But what should one understand by *kṣaṇa*? Here is the difficulty.

725 *LVP*: Other definitions, iii. 86a. See Index: *kṣaṇa*.

LS: 1. Pradhan has (78.24): *eṣa eva hi naḥ kṣaṇo yāvatai 'tat sarvaṃ samāpyata iti.*

LVP mentions (1937, p. 152) the version of Hiuan-tsang: *lakṣaṇakāryaparisamāptir eṣa eva hi naḥ kṣaṇaḥ*, and the version of Paramārtha: *caturlakṣaṇakāryaparisamāptir*..., and points out that Saṃghabhadra does not comment on this definition which Vasubandhu attributes to the Vaibhāṣika, the forerunner of which can be found in MVŚ, 200a7–12 (see our endnote to section BAB.2.7.3.e).

Rospatt comments (BDM.51) "that this definition of the *kṣaṇa* is difficult to reconcile with the conception of the moment as the shortest conceivable unit of time, even more so when 'duration', 'aging' and 'impermanence' are taken to occur successively".

Yaśomitra glosses (WOG.178.18ff.): *eṣa eva hi naḥ kṣaṇa* iti. *kāryaparisamāptilakṣaṇo* na tūtpattyanantaravināśalakṣaṇa ity arthaḥ, which Rospatt renders:

> "Precisely this is the moment [according to] our [understanding]" is to say that [the

moment] is characterized by the completion of what is to be done [by the *saṃskṛta-lakṣaṇas*], and that it is not characterized by [the entity's] destruction immediately after its origination.

2. Alexander Rospatt translates parts of Saṃghabhadra's exposition of *kṣaṇa* and *kṣaṇika* (Ny, 533b7–19, BDM.95; with inserts from LVP's translation in *Documents d'Abhidharma: La controverse du temps*, 1937, p. 152f.):

> What does *kṣaṇa* mean? It means the briefest [unit of] time, [a unit] that does not allow for a division into earlier and later. [– LVP: What is time? – The different states (*avasthā*) of being past, future or present. We know from that that time is a specification or distinction (*viśeṣa*) of the conditioned forces (*saṃskāra*). And the briefest state of the conditioned forces is called *moment*.]
>
> Because it is the most compressed [unit of] time it is called *kṣaṇa*. [LVP: The (word) *kṣaṇa* designates only the state of the factor endowed with activity (*sakāritrāvasthā*): thus the present]. The present entities (by contrast to past and future entities) which have [this] measure of duration (i.e., the *kṣaṇa*) are called *kṣaṇika* (momentary), as [an infant of one month is called] *māsika* (*māsa* = month and *-ika*).
>
> Or [the moment] is called *kṣaṇa* because it destroys (√*kṣaṇ* = to injure, break), that is, it functions as the cause destroying all entities (*dharma*). [*Kṣaṇa*] denotes the mark of impermanence which destroys all entities. [Because] the conditioned factors are endowed with this [mark], they are called *kṣaṇika*.
>
> Or, *kṣaṇika* is commonly (*loke*) used in the sense of "empty" (*śūnyaka*). This means that [entities] in the state of being present (rather than being past or future) are called *kṣaṇika* because they are devoid of something which would support them so that they do not perish, and hence they necessarily do not persist.
>
> Or, *akṣaṇika* is commonly (*loke*) used in the sense of not having any leisure. This means that [people] who busy themselves with other things and [thus] do not have any time for themselves are called *akṣaṇika*. Only when present (rather than past or future) do [entities] necessarily have a little time to realize their own fruit (i.e., be causally effective). Hence they are called *kṣaṇika*.
>
> [LVP: In truth, all states of the stream of conditioned factors have different times, "long minutes" (*lava*), etc. Of all times, the *kṣaṇa* is the smallest. The factor has it: thus it is called *kṣaṇika* or *momentary*.]

[726] *LS*: 1. This is the 27th of Kritzer's forty-four passages discussed in relation to chapter 2 (VY.92f.). Saṃghabhadra (Ny, 410a19–25) identifies this as the opinion of Vasubandhu and attempts to refute it (Ny, 410a25–c6) by relying on the doctrine of the tri-temporal existence and the theory of activity and capability.

2. As for deterioration, Saṃghabhadra gives two definitions (see above F 222), (1) as the cause of the distinction between consecutive moments in a stream (Ny, 405c9); and (2) as the cause of the deterioration of a factor's activity (Ny, 410b14).

As for transformation, the MVŚ, 200a29ff., distinguishes two types (DD.371):

> Transformation in intrinsic nature and transformation in activity. If one speaks in terms of transformation in intrinsic nature, one should say that the conditioned forces

are without transformation, because their intrinsic nature is without variation. If, however, one speaks in terms of transformation in activity, one should say that conditioned forces have transformation. That is to say, a factor in the future does not yet perform its activity; when it enters the present, it performs its activity; when it enters the past, its activity has ceased. Therefore, there is transformation of activity.

See BDM.55 for the discussion of various solutions offered in the **Mahāvibhāṣā* to reconcile the attribution of the characteristic of change to individual momentary entities.

727 *LVP*: *yadi sa eva nāsāv athānyathā na sa eva [hi |*
tasmāḍ ekasya dharmasya nānyathātvaṃ prasidhyati ||]

LS: The Sanskrit manuscript has a lacuna here. Rospatt (BDM.55) comments that Pradhan took over the wording from ADV 106,10f. (Vibhāṣāprabhāvṛtti on the *Abhidharmadīpa*) where the following *śloka* is cited:

tathātve na jarāsiddhir, anyathātve 'nya eva saḥ |
tasmān naikasya bhāvasya jarā nāmopapadyate ||

Rospatt translates (BDM.55):

In the case of being thus (i.e., as always), there is no ageing; in the case of difference, this one is but another [thing]. Therefore, the so-called age is not reasonable [as referring] to a single entity.

728 *LVP*: The Saṃmitīyas (see the long discussion at iv. 2c [F 4–8]).

LS: *Chü-shê-lun-chi* (T 1821) 201b22–24 (BDM.38): "The Saṃmitīyas believe that among the conditioned entities, thought-concomitants (*citta*) and mental factors (*caitta*), sound, flame, etc. are momentary. Therefore, they are necessarily without movement. The conditioned factors dissociated [from the mind] (*viprayuktasaṃskāra*), the karmic matter of manifest corporeal actions (*kāyavijñaptirūpa*), the body, mountains, wood, and so on, are not momentary (*kṣaṇika*), [but] abide for a long time."

729 *LVP*: *evam etat sūtraṃ sunītam...* [WOG.179.14].

730 *LVP*: We shall study the diverse theories relative to impermanence (*anityatva*) and to momentariness (*kṣaṇikatva*) in [my *Notes sur le moment* (*kṣaṇa*) *des Vaibhāṣikas et des Sautrāntikas* (1937; pp. 134–158)].

731 *LVP*: See above ii, F 231. Any conditioned factor is engendered through its characteristic "origination". "Origination" arises at the same time as the factor that it engenders; being "future", origination engenders it before arising itself.

732 *Gokhale*: [46cd] *janyasya janikā jātir na hetupratyayair vinā ||*

Tib.: [46cd] *rgyu dang rkyen dag med par ni | skye bas bskyed bya skyed byed min ||*

LVP: *janyasya janikā jātir na hetupratyayair vinā |*

The causes (*hetu*) and the conditions (*prayaya*) are defined at ii. 49, 61c.

733 *LVP*: The *Vyākhyā* [WOG.179.19ff,] cites the answer that the Bhadanta Anantarvarman gives to this objection: "The eye does not produce the visual consciousness without the help of light [*āloka*], etc.; but, nevertheless, it is the cause of the visual consciousness." – Answer: "We observe that the blind man does not see, that the non-blind man sees: we observe thus the efficacy of the eye. The same does not hold for origination."

Anantavarman is cited in *Vyākhyā ad* ii. 71b–72, iii. 35d and vii. 32.

LS: Although not explicitly mentioned in Pradhan, LVP mentions the Sautrāntikas here.

734 *LS*: *iti hetupratyayā eva janakā santi.*

735 *LVP*: *sūkṣmā hi dharmaprakṛtayaḥ* [cf. WOG.179.24ff.]: – The nature of thought-concomitants, i.e., of contact (*sparśa*), etc., is subtle and difficult to distinguish. – Without a doubt, replies the Sautrāntika; but the Fortunate One explained the efficacy of contact, etc: "All that which is sensation (*vedanā*), ideation (*saṃjñā*), formations (*saṃskāra*), exists because of contact..."; but he did not explain the efficacy of "origination".

736 *LS*: LVP suggests this translation in his *Additions et Corrections.*

737 *LVP*: The notion "color" has the particular inherent characteristic (*svalakṣaṇa*) of color for its object. But the notion "arisen": "the color has arisen", does not bear on the color, since one has the same notion of "origination" when it refers to sensation: "sensation has arisen". Thus the notion "arisen" bears on the action produced by a certain factor, independent of color, of sensation, and which is "origination".

738 *LS*: Although not explicitly mentioned in Pradhan, LVP mentions the Sautrāntika here.

739 *LVP*: The Buddhists (*bauddhasiddhānta*) believe that sandalwood is just the collection of odors, etc. (*gandhādisamūha*). The Vaiśeṣikas believe that sandalwood exists in and of itself; this is why the author gives the example of the torso, the example that the Vaiśeṣikas admit. – See *Madhyamakavṛtti*, p. 66; *Sāṃkhyapravacanabhāṣya*, p. 84, 148; etc.

740 *LVP*: *dharmāṇām anādikālikā śaktiḥ.*

741 *LVP*: MVŚ, 198a15: Some maintain that the conditioned characteristics of the conditioned factors (*saṃskṛtalakṣaṇa*) are not real factors, namely, the Dārṣṭāntikas, who say: "The conditioned characteristics of the conditioned factors are included in the aggregate of the formations dissociated from thought (*viprayuktasaṃskāraskandha*); the aggregate of the formations dissociated from thought is not real; thus the conditioned characteristics of the conditioned factors are not real." In order to refute their opinion... .

742 *LVP*: Hsüan-tsang: "This theory is best. Why?"

743 *LVP*: That is to say, the Abhidharmaśāstras.

744 *LVP*: We have four proverbs of the same meaning, i.e., one should not renounce a thing that is good in nature because of the defects that it presents, because of the risks that it involves.

1. *Na hi bhikṣukāḥ santīti sthālyo nādhiśrīyante.*
2. *Na ca mṛgāḥ santīti yavā* (var. *śālayo*) *nopyante.*

These two proverbs, which often go hand in hand, are studied by Col. Jacob, in *Second Handful of Popular Maxims* (Bombay, Nirṇayasāgar, 1909, p. 42, index sub voc. *na hi bhikṣukāḥ*), with the references that follow: *Mahābhāṣya*, i. 99, ii. 194, iii. 23 (Kielhorn), in the same context (*na hi doṣāḥ santīti paribhāṣā na kartavyā lakṣaṇaṃ vā na praṇeyam | na hi bhikṣukāḥ...*); Vācaspatimiśra, *Nyāyavārtikatātparyaṭīkā*, pp. 62, 441; *Bhāmatī*, p. 54; *Sarvadarśanasaṃgraha*, p. 3 of Cowell's translation. – We have to add *Kāmasūtra* (see Cat. Oxford, 216b), where the two proverbs are attributed to Vātsyāyana (indicated by Weber, *Indische Studien*, XIII, p. 326).

3. *Ato 'jīrṇabhayān nāhāraparityāgo bhikṣukabhayān na sthālyā anadhiśrayaṇaṃ doṣeṣu pratividhātavyam iti nyāyaḥ.*

Col. Jacob cites, for this third proverb, *Pañcapādikā*, p. 63 (of which the end *doṣeṣu pratividhātavyam* occurs in Vasubandhu), *Jīvanmuktiviveka*, p. 8 (which attributes the proverb to Ānandabodhācārya), and *Hitopadeśa*, ii. 50, *doṣabhīter anārambhaḥ*... .

4. *Na makṣikāḥ patantīti modakā na bhakṣyante.*

The proverb for which I have no other reference than Vasubandhu. It seems that the Buddhists, being *bhikṣus*, have substituted mendicant (*bhikṣuka*) and *sthālī* (vessel) in the proverb, making it less biting than with flies and cakes.

745 *LS*: AH 220; SAH 453.

746 *LS*: Ibid.

747 *Gokhale*: [47ab] *nāmakāyādayaḥ saṃjñāvākyā'kṣarasamuktayaḥ* |

Tib.: [47ab] *ming gi tshogs la sogs pa ni* | *ming dang ngag dang yi ge'i tshigs* |

LVP: Surendranath Dasgupta, *Study of Patañjali* (Calcutta, 1920), summarizes (pp. 192–201) the various theories of *sphoṭa*. – *Siddhi*, 68; on *sphoṭa*, Abegg, Mélanges Windisch, 1914.

LS: 1. Vasubandhu's *Pañcaskandhaka* (2008) states:

> 4.2.11 *nāmakāyāḥ katame* | *dharmāṇāṃ svabhāvādhivacanāni* |
>
> 4.2.11 What is the collection of names? The expressions [that describe] the essences of entities. ISBP.239
>
> 4.2.12 *padakāyāḥ katame* | *dharmāṇāṃ viśeṣādhivacanāni* |
>
> 4.2.12 What is the collection of assertions? The expressions [that describe] the distinguishing characteristics of entities. ISBP.239
>
> 4.2.13 *vyañjanakāyāḥ katame* | *akṣarāṇi tadubhayābhivyañjanatām upādāya* | *varṇā api te nāmapadāśrayatvenārthasaṃvarṇanatām upādāya* | *akṣaratvaṃ punaḥ paryāya–akṣaraṇatām upādāya* |
>
> 4.2.13 What is the collection of syllables? [It is the collection of] phonemes, because they are what allow both of them [i.e., the names and assertions] to become manifest. They are also the [basic] sounds [of spoken language], because meanings are communicated on the basis of names and assertions. Moreover, they are [called] "phonemes" because they cannot be replaced by any alternative form. ISBP.239

The *Avatāra* states (ESD.118f.):

> Words, phrases and syllables are those which are produced with the support of speech (*vāc*), and which cause the understanding [in each case] of the respective signified (*svārtha-pratyāyaka*), in a similar manner as knowledge (*jñāna*), manifesting with the representation/image 影像 of the signified (*artha*). These are the synonyms, respectively, for name (*saṃjñā*); sentence (*vākya*) and phoneme (*akṣara*). Just as visual consciousness, etc., are produced with eyes, etc., as their support; manifesting with the representation of the signified (*artha*), the visible, etc., and [thus] comprehend the respective objects (自境; *svārtha*). The same applies to words, etc.
>
> It is not the case that vocal sound can directly manifest the signified; [for] it cannot

be that when one utters the word "fire", one's mouth is immediately burnt! Words like fire etc., must rely on speech for their production. From these words, the signified, fire, etc., are then manifested.

By "manifesting" (*dyotayati*) is meant producing in others a comprehension (*buddhi*) of the signified to be illuminated (*dyotita*). It does not mean that [the word] unites with the signified. As sound is resistant, and as the eternal sound falsely held by the grammarians (*vaiyākaraṇena parikalpita*) is unreasonable, there cannot be any *dharma* [such as sound], apart from these three—words, phrases and syllables—which are capable of manifesting a corresponding signified. These four *dharma*-s—sound, word, the signified and knowledge—however, are similar in form, [though they are in fact distinct entities].

2. As for the history of the collections of names, of phrases and of syllables as real forces that impart significance to names, phrases and syllables—in this way making human communication possible—Jaini comments in his *The Vaibhāṣika Theory of Words and Meanings* (CPBS.202) that the Vaibhāṣika theories of words and their meanings (*artha*) can be traced back primarily to their speculations on the nature of the words of the Buddha (*buddhavacana*) (see AKB i. 25–26). Thus the *Saṅgītiparyāya* defines the teaching (*dharma*) as the three collections of name, phrase and syllable, and that which is manifested, understood, indicated, and so on, by these names, phrases and syllables is called the signified or referent (*artha*). But the intrinsic nature of *buddhavacana* was also early on a controversial topic. Yaśomitra quotes [WOG.52.15ff.] two passages from the *Jñānaprakaraṇa* (SA.IV.309):

> What is *buddha-vacana*? That which is the Tathāgata's speech, words, talk, voice, explanation, vocal-path, vocal sound, vocal action, vocal expression (*vāgvijñapti*)... .
>
> What is this *dharma* which has just been spoken of as *buddha-vacana*? The sequential arrangement, sequential establishment and sequential combination of the *nāma-kāya*, *pada-kāya* and *vyañjana-kāya*.

The preferred view of the MVŚ, 658c and 659c (SA.IV.309), explains that the first passage deals with the nature of *buddhavacana*, determining it to be vocal information (*vāg-vijñapti*), whereas the second passage deals with the function of *buddhavacana*; but the MVŚ also mentions, without rejecting it, the opinion of some who assert that *buddhavacana* has *nāma*, etc., as its nature.

Yaśomitra himself [WOG.52.10ff; CPBS.202] comments (i) that the Sautrāntikas determine *buddhavacana* to be of the nature of vocal information and hence included it in the *rūpa-skandha*, (ii) that those who maintain the category of the *viprayukta-saṃskāra*s include it in the *saṃskāra-skandha*, and (iii) that the Ābhidharmikas (but not naming them) accept both these views. Jaini thinks (CPBS.203) that the Ābhidharmikas seem "to refer to certain Vaibhāṣikas like our Dīpakāra who favoured the view that while the Buddha lived, his *vacana*s are of the nature of *nāma* as well as of *vāk* (albeit in a secondary sense) but after his death, they are only of *nāma-svabhāva*".

Saṃghabhadra does not object to either of the first two views (see endnote to i. 25).

Although the collections of names, phrases and syllables are recognized in early Sarvāstivādin Abhidharma treatises as discrete formations dissociated from thought, they are analyzed extensively only from the period of the *Vibhāṣā* compendia onward, where the focus then also shifts from the explanation of *buddhavacana* to a more abstract analysis of the nature of language and its operation. Cox comments (DD.163) that "the central problem becomes the nature of the relation between language, thought, and the world of specified referents". But even the AKB is still more concentrated on the refutation of the *nāmakāya*, etc., than on their explanation. Jaini summarizes the Vaibhāṣika and Sautrāntika positions as follows (CPBS.204):

> The Vaibhāṣika maintains that verbal sound alone is not capable of conveying any meaning. A verbal sound (*vāk*) operates on the *nāman*, and the latter conveys the meaning. Thus it is the *nāman* which gives significance to the word, which is purely material. This *nāman* is a *viprayukta-saṃskāra*. ...
>
> The Sautrāntika maintains that the *nāma-kāyas* do not play any part in conveying a meaning. It is true that all sounds or sounds alone (*ghoṣa-mātra*) do not convey a meaning. But verbal sounds (*vāk*) which are agreed upon by convention to mean a particular thing (*kṛta-saṅketa*) do convey their meanings. Since such a *saṅketa* is essential even in the assumption of the *nāma-kāya*, the latter is redundant and hence useless.

These theories of words and their meanings seem to have been influenced by the contemporary Mīmāṃsakas and the Grammarians (Vaiyākaraṇa), who had developed, respectively, their theories of eternal words and of *sphoṭa*. In this context Jaini comments that the Vaibhāṣika exposition of the *nāma-kāya* offers several points of comparison with the *sphoṭa* theory of early Grammarians (CPBS.211):

> *Sphoṭa* is defined as "the abiding word, distinct from the letters and revealed by them, which is the conveyor of the meaning" [Mādhava, *Sarvadarśanasaṅgraha*, p. 300]. The *nāma-kāya* is also distinct from letters (i.e., sound), is revealed by them, and is claimed as the conveyor of meanings. The Vaibhāṣika argument that sounds on account of their seriality cannot convey a meaning, is identical with the argument of the Sphoṭavādins against the Naiyāyikas who, like the Sautrāntika, maintained that verbal sounds (with the help of *saṅketa*) convey the *artha*. But whereas the *sphoṭa* is called a *śabda* [although not in the ordinary sense of sound] and described as one and eternal, the *nāma-kāyas* are nowhere designated as *śabda* and are declared to be many and non-eternal.

As for the Mīmāṃsaka, Cox comments (DD.160):

> Language analysis in northern Indian Abhidharma Buddhist texts appears to have originated with inquiries into the nature of the Buddha's teaching. One motive for this analysis was undoubtedly a desire to resolve the apparent contradiction between the belief in the nature of the Buddha's teaching as eternal doctrine and its phenomenal expression through speech. Early Mīmāṃsaka investigations of language also begin from a concern with the character of their basic text, specifically from a desire to validate the Vedas as the infallible repository of eternal truth and ritual authority. However, unlike the Buddhists, the Mīmāṃsakas propose that the relation between words and their referents is natural, or inborn (*autpattika*), and exists eternally quite apart from either sound or human formation.

3. As for other language-related issues in the AKB, we have already mentioned Vasubandhu's discussion of *buddhavacana* at i. 25–26, but he also discusses it briefly at i. 7cd,

when explaining ground of discourse (*kathāvastu*) as one of the synonyms for conditioned factors. The etymology of *nāman* as "that which bends" and the common meaning of *nāman*, i.e., as designation or "that which causes ideation to arise" (*saṃjñākaraṇa*), is discussed at iii. 30a in the context of explaining name-and-form, the fourth member of dependent origination (*pratītyasamutpāda*), although in the latter context *nāman* carries a different meaning than in the context of *nāmakāya*. As the smallest unit of names or words (*nāma*), the syllable (*akṣara*) is briefly discussed at iii. 85bc, and as the object-field or basis of false speech, malicious speech and frivolous speech, name or word (*nāma*) is discussed at iv. 72. The collection of names, etc., are taken up again within the context of the qualities the Buddha has in common with noble ones, namely, the four unhindered knowledges (*pratisaṃvid*; vii. 37b–40c):

i. unhindered knowledge of the (designation of the) factors (*dharma-pratisaṃvid*);
ii. unhindered knowledge of the designated thing (*artha-pratisaṃvid*);
iii. unhindered knowledge of etymology (*nirukti-pratisaṃvid*);
iv. unhindered knowledge of eloquence (*pratibhāna-pratisaṃvid*).

There is also the important passage at iii. 30cd, where Vasubandhu discusses *contact through designation* (*adhivacanasaṃsparśa*) and explains *adhivacana* as *name* (*nāma*), specifying it to be the additional cognitive object or the cognitive object (*ālambana*) *par excellence* (*adhikam*) of contact associated with the mental consciousness.

Besides *nāmakāya*, etc., language is naturally also related to sound (*śabda*); for references see our index, but also Vasubandhu's discussion of the eight types of sound, including sound of vocal informative action, at i. 10b and his discussion of sound as an atom (*paramāṇu*), as being part of the composite molecules involving sound (*saṃghātapāramāṇu*) at ii. 22.

In the context of *karma*, vocal action is discussed in general as vocal action (*vāk-karman*; iv. 2, 3d), i.e., as vocal bodily action (*vāag-vijñapti-karma*) and vocal non-informative action (*vāg-avijñapti-karma*), and more specifically as false speech (*mṛṣāvāda*), malicious speech (*paiśunya*), harsh speech (*pāruṣya*) and frivolous speech (*saṃbhinnapralāpa*) at iv. 74c–76. As for right speech (*samyagvāc*), it is discussed within the context of the eightfold noble path (iv, F 16f., 23ff; vi, F 246, 284, 291). As for voice (*vāk*) not being a controlling faculty, see ii, F 112.

At ii. 33ab [F 174], initial inquiry (*vitarka*) and investigation (*vicāra*) are discussed, from a Sautrāntika point of view, as "constituents for speech" (*vāksaṃskāra*).

As for the references to *saṃjñā*, which is closely related with *nāman*, see the references at i. 14cd and also the comments below.

4. As for examinations of language in general, Cox writes (DD.159f.):

> [The] early Buddhist and non-Buddhist investigations of language consider many of the same issues and appear to be aware of the same range of possible solutions, which were then developed in characteristic fashion within each tradition. Prominent among the issues examined are the origin of language, the nature of language in relation to sound and concept, the functional relationship among the components of language, the character of the referent of language, the mechanism by which that referent is suggested through language, and the dynamics of communication. The treatment of language in Buddhist Abhidharma materials devotes particular attention

to the nature of language and to the relation between language and its referents. The major topics in this investigation include the nature of language either as sound or as name (*nāman*), the existential status of name, and the function of name with regard to both concept [*saṃjñā*] and sound [*śabda*], specifically in manifesting the object-referent [*artha*].

5. As for *nāmakāya*, etc., being "formations dissociated from thought", Collett Cox explains (DD.163f.) that even though *nāmakāya*, etc., are closely related to sound and thus material form (*rūpa*), they can also be communicated non-verbally, i.e., they cannot be included within material form. On the other hand, even though—as objects of thought—*nāmakāya*, etc., are closely related to ideations (*saṃjñā*), since ideations are factors necessarily associated with thought they are confined to the individual mental consciousness in which they arise. Therefore, only a factor dissociated from both thought and material form could, in all these varying circumstances, support the transmission of ideations from one consciousness to another.

[748] *LS*: 1. Cox explains (DD.163) that names (i) are based upon syllables or phonemes arranged in a specific order, (ii) function to manifest the signified (*artha*) or the intrinsic nature of the signified, (iii) bear a close relation to ideation (*saṃjñā*) and (iv) enable ideations to be communicated.

2. The MVŚ, 73b2ff., states (DD.401):

> The Buddha categorized conditioned factors generally in two groups: form and not-form. Form is the form aggregate; not-form is precisely the four aggregates of feelings, and so on. The group that is not-form is referred to as name because names, which are able to manifest all factors, are included within it.

The meaning of the term *nāma*, as used in this MVŚ passage, is not the same as the meaning of the term *nāma*, as in *nāmakāya*.

[749] *LVP*: [Yaśomitra explains (WOG.181.30ff.):] The term *saṃjñākaraṇa* belongs to every-day language (*lokabhāṣā*); it is an equivalent for *nāmadheya*, name, appellation, for one says: "Devadatta is a *saṃjñākaraṇa* sound." But, here, one should understand: "That which causes ideation to arise." In fact *saṃjñā* is a mental factor (*dharma*), "ideation", "idea", "notion", or "concept" (i. 14cd); *nāman* is that which "causes", that which engenders this factor (*dharma*).

LS: 1. Cox comments (DD.164) that among the three collections, *nāmakāya* receives the greatest attention in the later Abhidharma language analyses due to its pivotal role in the relation between thought or ideations and the object-referent or meaning or signified (*artha*). Vasubandhu identifies *nāma* simply as *saṃjñākāraṇa*: *tatra saṃjñākaraṇaṃ nāma*, without giving much further explanation. In contrast to LVP who interprets *saṃjñākaraṇa* as "that which causes ideation to arise", Yaśomitra interprets [WOG.181.32ff.] *saṃjñākaraṇa* in two ways (DD.164):

> It can be understood either as a dependent determinative compound (*tatpuruṣa*): that is, "[name is] the maker of concepts", or "that by which the mental factor, concept, is made or produced" [yena saṃjñā caitasiko dharmaḥ kriyate janyate]. Or, the compound can be interpreted as a descriptive determinative (*karmadhāraya*) used exocentrically (*bahuvrīhi*): that is, "[name is] that of which the maker is concepts" [saṃjñaiva vā karaṇaṃ *saṃjñā-karaṇaṃ*]. In other words, Yaśomitra suggests a

reciprocal functioning, whereby name is either the cause of concepts, or concepts are the cause of names. P'u-kuang cites both of these interpretations and adds a third, whereby name and concept are identified with one another. However, Yaśomitra observes that name and concept must be distinct "for if name were said to be precisely concept, it would be possible for [name] to be a mental factor", and name is, instead, classified among the dissociated factors.

Saṅghabhadra explains (Ny, 413a18ff.; DD.378):

> The characteristic, name, is manifested by articulated sound (*ghoṣa*) and is [then] able to manifest the object-referent. It is a specification established in common (*kṛtāvadhi*), which both manifests that which is produced by an intention (**āśaya*) and is able to represent the intrinsic nature of object-fields (*viṣaya*) that are known, in the same way as an echo.

2. Since Vasubandhu does not elaborate much here in our sections, things have to be filled in from other sources that circle around passages based on the ideation (*saṃjñā*) section at i. 14cd, the conceptualizing activity (*vikalpa*) section at i. 33 and the above mentioned "contact through designation" (*adhivacanasaṃsparśa*) section at iii. 30cd. Dhammajoti summarizes the pith of it (ADCP.107):

> Besides *prajñā*, *saṃjñā* also is a contributing factor for the *abhinirūpaṇā*[-*vikalpa*]. This is clear from the fact that its functioning is said to involve a synthetic comprehension of appearance (*nimitta*), name (*nāma*) and signification (*artha*). Thus the *Avatāra* defines it as [ESD.80]:
>
> > This is that which comprehends, by combining conceptually (*saṃ-√jñā*) the appearance, name and the signified [of a *dharma*]. That is, with regard to matter like blue, yellow, long and short [figures], etc.; ... *dharma*-s like males and females, etc.—it comprehends them, [in each case], by conceptually combining together (*eka-√jñā*) their appearances, names and signification. It is the cause of reasoning (*vitarka*) and investigation (*vicāra*). Thus this is named ideation.
>
> It is on account of the contribution from *saṃjñā* that mental consciousness is able to operate by means of name (= *adhivacana*) which is therefore said to be the additional cognitive object (*adhikam ālambanam*) of mental contact (*manaḥ-saṃsparśa*; iii. 30cd). Saṃghabhadra comments that it is "additional" because mental consciousness takes both *nāma* and *artha* as its object, whereas the five sensory consciousnesses do not take *nāma* as their perceptual objects [Ny, 506c]. The functional difference that results from this factor of name is explained in the *Vijñāna-kāya-śāstra* as follows:
>
> > The visual consciousness can only apprehend a blue colour (*nīlam*), but not "it is blue" (*no ti nīlam iti*). Mental consciousness can also apprehend a blue colour. [But] so long as it is not yet able to apprehend its name, it cannot apprehend "it is blue". When it can apprehend its name, then it can also apprehend "it is blue" [T 26, 559b–c; cf. Ny, 342a].

Cox points out a circular process of name (*nāma*) and ideation (*saṃjñā*), and its connection with understanding (*prajñā*) (DD.165):

> For Saṅghabhadra, name and concept [*saṃjñā*] function in close connection with one another. A concept functions as an associated thought concomitant and, by definition,

acts to grasp the defining mark (*viṣayanimittodgraha*) of a perceived object-field: that is, it discriminates or determines (*pariccheda*) the particular state (*avasthā-viśeṣa*) of a given entity (*vastu*) as blue, yellow, long, and so on [see AKB i. 14d; Ny, 339a26ff; ESD.80]. This concept then applies a particular name in accordance with the determined or discriminated mark of the object-field; one identifies the object-field with a name through the operation of defining conceptual discrimination[a] (*abhinirūpaṇavikalpa*) [see AKB i. 33; MVŚ, 219b7ff; Ny, 339b29ff.]. Saṅghabhadra refers to this process of identification of an object's defining marks in his description of the activity of name as one of according with (Ch.: *sui*), summoning (Ch.: *chao*), and joining with (Ch.: *ho*) the object-referent [Ny, 413a23ff., 414b24ff]. Name thus functions bi-directionally—that is, both internally and externally: it is both held in thought prior to speech and expressed outwardly to others through speech. When a name is uttered, that name produces a concept in the consciousness of the listener. Thus, depending upon the perspective, concepts elicit names, or conversely, names elicit concepts; names and concepts, thus, function in a circular process of identification and communication.

[a] This defining conceptual discrimination (*abhinirūpaṇavikalpa*) is unconcentrated (*asamāhita*) insight (*prajñā*) that is associated with mental perceptual consciousness and is produced through hearing (*śrutamayī*) or through reflection (*cintāmayī*), and not through cultivation (*bhāvanāmayī*). It operates on an object-field in relative dependence upon its name (*nāmāpekṣā*). See MVB 42 p. 219b7ff.j

3. As for the term *artha*, Cox explains (DD.170) that it not only denotes the abstract meaning of a word, but also the object-referent to which the word refers, as, for example, when Vasubandhu refers to the object-referents of the five externally directed sense-faculties. In the context of the *Avatāra*'s discussion of *nāmakāya*, Dhammajoti comments (ESD.195): "The meaning of *artha* is as ambiguous as ever; ...we have therefore chosen the rendering 'the signified' which perhaps could cover the sense of 'meaning' as well as 'object'."

As for the existential status of *artha*, Dhammajoit comments in a private communication related to *nāmakāya* and *saṃjñā*: "One thing is clear: *artha*, whether in the sense of 'meaning' or 'object-referent', is a relative real, and not an absolute real, ... unless it means 'the object (of Reality)'. ... I.e., if *artha* means just an object in the sense of 'an external thing' such as a man, a tree, etc., that we are cognizing, then Sarvāstivāda would say that it is real—though a relative real (because it ultimately has a real existent as an *āśraya*; otherwise, no cognition at all would be possible). But if by *artha* one refers to the object qua a *svabhāva* which has manifested in the present as the perceptual object, one could say that it refers to an absolute real (*svabhāva*). In AKB i. 9ab, [for example,] the objects are clearly stated to be the sensory objects—*rūpa*, *śabda*, etc.—these are 'objects (of Reality)', i.e., real entities according to Sarvāstivāda. ... In the *Avatāra* definition, *artha* does not mean so much 'the object per se' but 'what is signified by the object'. ... *Artha* as signification is not an absolute real (not a *svabhāva*), hence one should not expect to find it among the seventy-five *dharma*-s."

750 *LS*: Saṅghabhadra explains (Ny, 413a; DD.378f.): "The characteristic, phrase, is able to explicate the object-field that is known from both a detailed and cursory perspective, [...] from the perspective of its distinctive characteristics."

751 *LVP*: This does not refer to *pada* = declined or conjugated form (Pāṇini, i. 4, 14).

752 *LVP*: The entire stanza should be considered as a *pada* [cf. WOG.182.10ff.]:

anityā vata saṃskārā utpādavyayadharmiṇaḥ |
utpadya hi nirudhyante teṣāṃ vyupaśamaḥ sukhaḥ ||

which can be explained in several ways:

1. Thesis (*pratijñā*): "The conditioning forces (*saṃskāra*) are impermanent." Reason (*hetu*): "because their nature is to arise and perish". Example (*dṛṣṭānta*): "those sentient beings, who are born and die, are impermanent".

2. Reason: "Their nature is to arise and to perish", is established by the remark: "In fact, being arisen, they die."

3. "The conditioning forces are impermanent, in other words, their nature is to arise and perish"; "because, being arisen, they perish"; "being impermanent, they are unsatisfactory, thus to stop them is happiness", this is what the Buddha wants to teach his followers.

This is the stanza that Śakra uttered at the death of the Fortunate One, *Dīgha*, ii. 157; *Saṃyutta*, i. 158; *Dialogues*, ii. 176; *Jātaka*, 94; *Madhyamakvṛtti*, p. 39; Manuscript Dutreuil de Rhins, *J. As.*, 1898, ii. 300 (p. 108); *Udānavarga*, i. 1: *Mdo*, 26, *Anityatāsūtra*; J. Przyluski, *Funérailles*, p. 9.

753 *LVP*: A type of "nominal phrase".

754 *LVP*: [WOG.182.31ff:] Name (*nāman*) makes one see (*dyotaka*) the particular inherent characteristic (*svalakṣaṇa*); phrase (*pāda*) makes one see the different relations [*saṃbandha-viśeṣa*] in which the factor whose particular inherent characteristic is known, occurs.

755 *LS*: Cox comments (DD.163): "Syllables (*vyañjana*) are defined as the basic components of language or as the smallest unit of articulation, and not, as the term *vyañjana* might suggest, as the more limited category of consonants. Syllables are then identified as phonemes (*akṣara*), which is not to suggest that they are mere vowels, but rather that syllables include consonants with an inherent vowel. These discrete syllables or phonemes then form the basis of names and phrases, and enable sounds to convey meaning to another."

Saṃghabhadra explains (Ny, 413a; DD.379):

> A syllable is able to act as the basis of that which manifests [the object-referent], because the [name and phrase] that manifest [the object-referent] depend upon and have their origin in this. [The word] "this" [in the previous sentence] is precisely this phoneme: that is to say, it causes [an utterance to be] fixed in memory [such that] there is no forgetting; or, further, it is able to preclude doubt because [name and phrase] are preserved through this [phoneme]; or it is able to preserve that [name and phrase] and transmit them to another.

He further explains (Ny, 751a10ff; DD.400): "A syllable is not able to relate directly to the object-referent; it is merely the basis of name and phrase, which specify the object-referent."

756 *LS*: Pradhan.80.19f. has *eṣāṃ ca saṃjñādīnām samuktayo nāmādikāyāḥ*.

757 *LS*: Although not explicitly mentioned in Pradhan, LVP mentions the Sautrāntika here.

This is the 28th of Kritzer's forty-four passages discussed in relation to chapter 2 (VY.94f.). Saṃghabhadra identifies (Ny, 413c11–13) this as the opinion of Vasubandhu and refutes it (Ny, 413c13–414a11) based on both scriptural authority and reasoned arguments for *nāma* being distinct from sound. Here are his reasoned arguments (SA.IV.312f.):

> Sometimes one gets the sound but not the phoneme; sometimes one gets the phoneme but not the sound. Hence we know that they differ in substance.
>
> The first case is that of hearing the sound and not comprehending the *artha*: It is observed that some people listen to others' words vaguely and then ask, "what did you say?" It is all because they have not comprehended the syllables uttered. How then can one assert that the syllables are not different from the sound?
>
> The second case is that of comprehending the *artha* without hearing the sound: It is observed that some people, without hearing the actual words spoken by others, know what they are saying by watching the movement of their lips, etc. This is all because they have comprehended the syllables uttered. This proves that the syllables must be different from the sounds.
>
> Again, it is observed in the world that people recite *mantra* silently, hence we know that the syllables of a *mantra* differ from the sound of the *mantra*.
>
> Again it is observed in the world that, of two debaters whose articulation of the sound is similar, one loses and the other wins. This cause of losing and winning must exist separately from the sound.
>
> Again as the object-domains (*viṣaya*) of the "unhindered knowledge of *dharma*-s" (*dharma-pratisaṃvid*) and "unhindered knowledge of etymological interpretation" (*nirukti-pratisaṃvid*) are different, we know that the phonemes are distinct from sound.
>
> Hence, [we may conclude from all this that] sound is merely the articulation of a language; and its form is not differentiated. The inflection therein must be made in dependence on *ka, ca, ṭa, ta, pa*, etc. The phoneme must be uttered by means of vocal sound. When the phonemes are joined together, *nāma* is produced. *Nāma* having been produced, it can illuminate the *artha*. Hence, we assert the following [causal] sequence: Vocal sound gives rise to *nāma*; *nāma* illuminates *artha*. Therefore, it is universally established that *nāma* is different from *śabda*. It should be understood here that *śabda* is that which utters and *akṣara* is that which is uttered; *artha* is neither. Thus they are established without confusion.

758 *LS*: Although not explicitly mentioned in Pradhan, LVP mentions the Sautrāntika here.

This is the 29th of Kritzer's forty-four passages discussed in relation to chapter 2 (VY.96). Saṃghabhadra identifies (Ny, 414a11ff.) this as the opinion of Vasubandhu. He insists that sound alone is not able to convey meaning but what is needed is (DD.165) the combinations of the phonemes that constitute each particular name, being established specifications (*kṛtāvadhi*) provisionally determined by consensus (*saṃketa*). He states (Ny, 414a18ff.; DD.385):

> It is precisely these names that are the specifications established [with regard to object-referents]. When speakers are about to issue forth speech, they must first reflect upon a certain specification. In this way, they are able to understand the object-referent manifested in their own speech or in the speech of others. Therefore, sound alone is not able to manifest the object-referent.

Cox comments (DD.166) that this position is in marked contrast to "the Mīmāṃsaka theory of the eternal character of language—that is, that the relation between a word and its object-referent or meaning (*śabdārthasaṃbandha*) is natural and infallible, not subject to human invention or to the vicissitudes of human intention. This rejection of the Mīmāṃsaka position is indicated in the Abhidharma classification of the name, phrase, and syllable sets as included among factors constituting sentient beings (*sattvākhya*) [see AKB ii. 47cd]."

759 *LVP*: Compare *Amarasiṃha*, iii, *Nānārthavarga*, 25.

760 *LS*: Although not explicitly mentioned in Pradhan, LVP mentions the Sautrāntika here. This is the 30th of Kritzer's forty-four passages discussed in relation to chapter 2 (VY.98). Saṃghabhadra identifies (Ny, 414a24–26) this as the opinion of Vasubandhu and rejects it, insisting that without *nāma*, the meaning of speech could not be understood. Saṃghabhadra explains his own position as follows (Ny, 414b4–9; DD.386):

> Speakers first hold the intended name in thought and only then form [the following] intention: "I will issue forth such and such a word and express such and such an object-referent to others." In this way, at a subsequent time speech is issued forth in accordance with one's intention, and phonemes are issued forth in dependence upon speech. Phonemes, further, issue forth in names, [but] only names manifest the object-referent. [The evolution of name, and so on], is reasonable, if established relying upon the perspective of this principle of successive dependence such that "speech issues forth in names and names manifest the object-referent". If name were not first held in thought, even if one were to issue forth speech, there would be no definite specification, and [this speech] would not enable others to understand the object-referent.

Cox comments (DD.403): "In this explanation, Saṅghabhadra attributes a double role to name. First, one holds a name, or a name-concept, in thought, and only then is one capable of uttering speech. Thereafter, one issues forth a verbal name. Saṃghabhadra does not explicitly propose that there are two distinct types of names: one as spoken and one as mental concept. However, the association between name and concept (*saṃjñā*) coupled with the frequent provision that name is issued forth from speech does lead to ambiguity as to the true nature of name."

761 *LVP*: That is to say: "given the voice, the word—a factor dissociated from thought—arises".

762 *LVP*: That is to say: "the word—a factor dissociated from thought—arises with the articulated sound in the process of arising: the articulated sound manifests it with a view to the designation of the object" (ghoṣeṇotpadyamānena sa cittaviprayukto dharmas utpadyate | sa taṃ *prakāśayaty* arthadyotanāya [WOG.183.26f.]).

763 *LS*: This is the 31st of Kritzer's forty-four passages discussed in relation to chapter 2 (VY.100f.). Saṃghabhadra (Ny, 415a25–b3; DD.393f.) identifies this as the opinion of Vasubandhu and claims that, since Vasubandhu does not accept past and future factors, this leads to various problems in regard to his appeal to a series of sounds as together constituting a collocation by which the signified is specified. But Saṃghabhadra also offers arguments for the existence of "name" as a "non-vocalized, meaning-bearing or object-referent-signifying unit" (DD.168) by stating (Ny, 415b; DD.394):

> Since, according to our accepted doctrine, no [factor] fails to exist in all three time periods, the last [moment (of sound)] is able to produce the name, and so on, in dependence upon prior [moments that still exist]. Even though name, and so on,

are only [actually] produced in the last moment, one cannot apprehend the object-referent by hearing only that [last moment]. This is due to the fact that one has not heard all the [prior] sounds that were issued forth in accordance with an initial consensus established in common with regard to the name, and so on. ...

764 *LS*: Yaśomitra explains (WOG.183.33ff; DD.405):

"When [speech] produces that [name], how would [speech] produce it at that time?" Thus is the meaning of the sentence. For speech that produces name would produce it [only when that speech] is present, but not all moments of the sound of speech are present at one time. For in saying the word *rūpa*, when the sound "*r*" is present, the "*ū*", "*p*", *and* "*a*" are, at that time, [still] future. When the "*ū*" is present, the sound "*r*" has [already] been uttered at that time and the "*p*" and "*a*" are [still] future. In this way, when the "*p*" and "*a*" are present successively, the others are not present at that time. Thus, speech should not produce name.

765 *LS*: "Yaśomitra (WOG.81.12ff; DD.405) explains:

When one undertakes the *prātimokṣa* vows of discipline, the manifest actions of body and speech operate, [or issue forth,] and there is no complete assemblage of those [manifest actions in a given moment]. Then, the last moment of manifest action produces the unmanifest action imparted by the *prātimokṣā* vows in dependence upon past [moments of] manifest action of body and speech. In the same way, the last moment of the sounds of speech produces name in dependence upon past [moments] of sound.

766 *LS*: Based on Pradhan, Cox translates (DD.406): "Since even those with special insight and applied thought are not able to discriminate syllables and speech from the standpoint of [their] characteristics, it is not reasonable that speech be either the producer or manifester of syllables." *vyañjanaṃ cā 'pi vāg [iti] viśiṣṭaprajñā apy avahitacetaskā lakṣaṇataḥ paricchettuṃ no 'tsahanta iti vyañjanasyā 'pi vāk nai 'vo 'tpādikā na prakāśikā yujyate.*

767 *LS*: Pradhan.81.23 has *nāmasaṃniśritā gāthā gāthānāṃ kavirāśrayaḥ.*

LVP: *Saṃyuktāgama*, 36, 27. *Saṃyutta*, i. 38: *nāmasaṃniśritā gāthā.* The *gāthā* is a "phrase" (*vākya*); it is based on the words, since it exists when the words have arisen. Therefore, word and phrase exist in and of themselves.

768 *LS*: Although not explicitly mentioned in Pradhan, LVP mentions the Sautrāntika here.

769 *LVP*: *artheṣu kṛtāvadhiḥ śabdo nāma* [WOG.185.22]. – *Mahāvyutpatti*, 245, 319, reproduces the expression *kṛtāvadhi*, *'tshams bcad pa.*

770 *LVP*: *paṅktivat*, "like the line of ants"; but, one would say, the ants that form the line exist at the same time: we shall give a new example: *cittānupūrvyavat*, "like the succession of thoughts".

771 *LS*: This is the 32nd of Kritzer's forty-four passages discussed in relation to chapter 2 (VY.102f.). Vasubandhu suggests that, for the Vaibhāṣikas, the syllables (*vyañjana*) alone should suffice to be posited as real entities. Saṃghabhadra identifies (Ny, 414b9–11) this as the opinion of Vasubandhu and replies that his position is unreasonable for three reasons (Ny, 414b11ff; DD. 387f.):

There is no [one moment of] time in which syllables operate simultaneously; a collocation [of syllables] is not reasonably established; and it is not the case that no single syllable can manifest an object-referent.

[The dependence of name, and so on, upon a collocation of syllables is analogous to the case of a tree and its shadow.] It is like a tree that is established through the combination of fundamental (*mahabhūta*) and derived material elements (*bhautika*) [and thus exists provisionally]. A shadow is not produced separately without depending upon [the tree]. Even though that shadow is issued forth in dependence upon a provisional entity, the nature of the shadow is not provisional. In the same way, many syllables gather and produce a separate name and phrase. Even though that name and phrase are issued forth in dependence upon a provisional entity—[that is, the collocation of syllables]—their nature is not provisional. ...

A single phoneme of the type [that is also a name] does not specify anything [by itself], just like a phoneme that is without an object-referent. A name arises separately taking this [single phoneme] as its condition, and only then is [that name] able to indicate the object-referent. However, just as it is difficult to distinguish two patches of light on a wall, so also is it difficult to apprehend the separateness [of two things that] are extremely close, [such as a phoneme and the name that it issues forth].

772 *LS*: This section is missing in LVP. Pradhan.81.26f. has *tatsamūhā eva nāmakāyādayo bhaviṣyantī 'ty apārthikā tatprajñaptiḥ*. See DD.404.

773 *LVP*: The factors which are of the domain of the consciousness of the Tathāgatas (*tathāgatajñānagocarapatita*) are not accessible through reasoning (*tarkagamya*).

774 *Gokhale*: [47cd1] *kāmarūpāptasattvākhyā niṣyandā 'vyākṛtās*

Tib.: [47cd1] *'dod dang gzugs gtogs sems can ston | rgyu mthun lung bstan min*

LVP: *kāmarūpāptasattvākhyāniṣyandāvyākṛtāḥ*

MVŚ, 71c25–72a29.

775 *LVP*: The phonemes, etc., are not "voice" by their nature. Nothing hinders their existence in the realm of immateriality, but, since voice is absent in this realm of existence, one cannot pronounce them there. – The Vaibhāṣika: How could you say that they exist there where they are not pronounced?

LS: Cox comments (DD.406f.) that both views are presented in the **Mahāvibhāṣā*, which seems to prefer the first interpretation, i.e., that name, and so on, are limited to the first level of meditation within the realm of fine-materiality (*rūpadhātu*), which she further specifies:

> According to this first interpretation, names, phrases, and syllables are limited to the realm of desire and the first level of trance in the realm of form because the realm to which they are connected is determined in accordance with speech. Speech, as described previously (Ny, 415a3), is produced only in dependence upon initial inquiry (*vitarka*) and investigation (*vicāra*), which are present only in the realm of desire and the first level of trance within the realm of form. Thus, if the location of name is determined in accordance with speech, it too must be limited to these two regions.

776 *LS*: Saṃghabhadra remarks (Ny, 416a; DD.408): "When it is said that name, and so on,

are produced from action, it means that they are the sovereign effects (*adhipatiphala*) produced by action."

777 *LVP*: [Saṃghabhadra comments (Ny, 416a):] The words that designate the wholesome factors are not wholesome: since a person who has cut off the wholesome roots speaking of wholesome factors, possesses (*prāpti*) the words that designate these factors.

LS: Saṃghabhadra adds (Ny, 416a11; DD.399): "[When one utters a name], one is accompanied by the name, and so on, that is able to specify [a certain factor], and not by the factor that is specified."

As for syllables, names and phrases being unobscured-non-defined, P'u-kuang (111c12ff.; DD.408) discusses:

> Why do name, and so on, not have three varieties [of moral quality—that is, virtuous, unvirtuous, and indeterminate]—in accordance with the [moral quality of] the sound [that expresses them]? One desires to issue forth verbal activity as a result of attention (*manaskāra*). Therefore, articulated sound is of three moral qualities in accordance with the [moral quality of the moment of] thought that issues forth speech. But proper attention does not project names, and so on. Therefore, they are only indeterminate.

778 *Gokhale*: [47d2–48b1] *tathā* || *sabhāgatā vipāko 'pi traidhātuky*

Tib.: [47d2–48b1] *de bzhin* || *skal mnyam rnam par smin pa'ang yin* | *khams gsum pa ste*

779 *Gokhale*: [48b2] *āptayo dvidhā* |

Tib.: [48b2] *thob rnam gnyis* |

LVP: Hsüan-tsang corrects: The possessions (*prāpti*) are of three types, i.e., "of a moment" (*kṣaṇika*; i. 38), "of equal outflow", "of retribution".

780 *Gokhale*: [48c1] *lakṣaṇāni ca*

Tib.: [48c1] *mtshan nyid rnams kyang*

781 *Gokhale*: [48c2–d] *niṣyandāḥ samāpattyasamanvayāḥ* ||

Tib.: [48c2–d] *snyoms 'jug dang* | *mi ldan pa dag rgyu mthun pa* ||

782 *LS*: Hsüan-tsang, vi, fol. 1a.

783 *LS*: AH 25–31, 48, 230, 234; SAH 25, 36, 68–88, 153–55, 232, 460–62, 465, 469, 478, 480, 525–46.

1. Dhammajoti introduces generally the topic and history of *hetu*, *pratyaya* and *phala* in the following way (SA.IV.24):

> All *dharma*-s in phenomenal existence are *pratītya-samutpanna*—dependently originated from an assemblage of conditions. In this respect, they are often called *saṃskṛta*-s, "the compounded/conditioned".
>
> In the Sarvāstivāda conception, *dharma*-s are distinct ontological entities which, in their intrinsic nature, abide throughout time, totally unrelated to one another and totally devoid of any activities [cf. MVŚ, 105c, 108c, 283b, 396a, etc.]. Given such a theory, it is of fundamental importance that the school has an articulated causal doctrine of accounting for the arising of *dharma*-s as phenomena and their dynamic

> inter-relatedness in accordance with the Buddha's teaching of *pratītya-samutpāda* [see AKB iii, F 56–119]. Moreover, for the establishment of each of the *dharma*-s as a real entity, a conditioning force (*saṃskāra*), its causal function in each case must be demonstrated. It is probably for this reason that the Sarvāstivāda was also known as Hetuvāda ["the school that expounds the causes"]—a school specifically concerned with the theory of causation. ...
>
> The Sarvāstivādins eventually articulated a doctrine of four conditions, six causes and five fruits. Significant portions of the Sarvāstivāda canonical *abhidharma* treatises are devoted specifically to these topics. Thus, the *Vijñāna-kāya-śāstra* discusses the four conditions (*pratyaya*) at length; the *Jñāna-prasthāna-śāstra* expounds on the six causes; the chapter "On *saṃgraha*, etc." of the *Prakaraṇa-pāda-śāstra* contains a total of twenty doctrinal perspectives connected with *hetu-pratyaya.*

In terms of history, Saṃghabhadra further maintains (Ny, 416b–c; SA.IV.143f; WOG.188f; see below LVP's endnote) that the doctrine of the four conditions is found in the *sūtra*-s of their school and that the six causes were not only at one time in their *Ekottarāgama*, although no longer extant, but that indications of them are scattered in the various *sūtra*-s. The MVŚ, 79a–c, states that the *sūtra*-s speak only of the four conditions while at the same not repudiating the opinions of other masters, one of which is identical with Saṃghabhadra's (ESD.200):

> These six *hetu*-s are not mentioned in the *sūtra*-s. The *sūtra*-s speak of the four *pratyayatā*-s only: viz: *hetu-pratyayatā*, etc., up to *adhipati-pratyayatā*. There are again some who say that six *hetu*-s are also mentioned in the *sūtra*-s; i.e., in the *Ekottarāgama*. A long time having passed, the particular *sūtra*-s have now been lost (*antarhita*). The Venerable Kātyāyanīputra and others, by the power of their *praṇidhi-jñāna*, perceived the *sūtra* passages which deal with the six *hetu*-s, and compiled them in their *abhidharma* treatises. Other masters say that although not all the six *hetu*-s as such are spoken of together in order, in any *sūtra*, their mention is found here and there scattered in the various *sūtra*-s. Hence these six *hetu*-s are taught by the Buddha.

Dhammajoti concludes that the doctrine of the four conditions most probably preceded that of the six causes. He then raises the question of what is the doctrinal need and significance for the six-*hetu* doctrine to be articulated in addition to the earlier four-*pratyaya* doctrine or for the elaboration of the *hetu-pratyaya* into the five *hetus* (see Fig. 1). He answers (SA.IV.145 and 164) that this Sarvāstivāda elaboration (i) shows that all real entities (*dharma*)—including both the conditioned and the unconditioned—must be shown to be causal forces, (ii) accounts for the dynamic arising and interaction of the distinct *dharma*-s that are totally unrelated in their intrinsic natures, (iii) reflects their "need to highlight the co-existent cause which exemplifies the school's fundamental principle of causality that cause and effect necessarily exist simultaneously, even though their modes (*bhāva*) of existence may differ—either past, present or future, and thus (iv) corroborates fundamentally their central doctrine of *sarvāstitva.*

2. More specifically, in regard to *dharmas* as causal forces, etc., Dhammajoti comments (SA.IV.148f.):

> In the Sarvāstivāda perspective, all *dharma*-s have always been existing. As a matter of fact, time is an abstraction on our part derived from their activities [MVŚ, 393c].

A *dharma* exists throughout time and yet is not permanent as it "courses in time" (*adhva-saṃcāra*). But as the MVŚ explains, "conditioned *dharma*-s are weak in their intrinsic nature, they can accomplish their activities only through mutual dependence":

> We declare that the causes have the activities as their fruits, not the entities in themselves (*svabhāva/dravya*). We further declare that the effects have the activities as their causes, not the entities in themselves. The entities in themselves are without transformation throughout time, being neither causes nor effects. [MVŚ, 105c]

Moreover,

> the tri-temporal *dharma*-s exist throughout time as entities in themselves; there is neither increase nor decrease. It is only on the basis of their activities that they are said to exist or not exist [as phenomena]. [MVŚ, 396a]

But, in turn, their activities necessarily depend on causes and conditions [MVŚ, 108c]:

> Being feeble in their *svabhāva*-s, they have no sovereignty (*aiśvarya*). They are dependent on others, they are without their own activity and unable to do as they wish. [MVŚ, 283b]

3. In regard to whether causes and conditions are different or not, see endnote below (F 244, bottom).

4. See Dhammajoti's detailed discussion in chapter 6: "Theory of Causality I. The Six Causes", and chapter 7: "Theory of Causality II. The Four Conditions and the Five Fruits", in his SA.IV.143–86, where he also deals in greater detail with the issue of simultaneous causation and the doctrinal importance of the co-existent cause for the Sarvāstivāda. See also his articles "The Sarvāstivāda Doctrine of Simultaneous Causality" (2000); "Sahabhūhetu, causality and *sarvāstitva*" (2002); likewise see the sections "The Middle Abhidharma Texts and the Emergence of Causal Theory" and "Conclusion" in Collett Cox's article *Dependent origination: its elaboration in early Sarvāstivādin Abhidharma texts* (1993).

784 *LS*: The *Avatāra* (ESD.116 and 120) states that the causes of origination are twofold, namely, (1) internal, i.e., the origination-characteristic (*jāti*), and (2) external, i.e., the six causes or four conditions.

But, whereas for the Sarvāstivādins the arising and ceasing of a *dharma* requires causes and conditions, for the Dārṣṭāntikas it is only the arising, i.e., not the ceasing, that requires causes and conditions.

785 *LVP*: The *Vyākhyā* [WOG.188.13ff.] makes the following remarks:

1. There is no difference between *hetu* and *pratyaya*, for the Fortunate One said: *dvau hetū dvau pratyayau samyagdṛṣṭer utpādāya | katamau dvau | parataś ca ghoṣo 'dhyātmaṃ ca yoniśo manasikāraḥ* (*Aṅguttara*, i. 87: *dve 'me bhikkhave paccayā sammādiṭṭhiya uppādāya ... parato ca ghoso yoniso ca manasikāro*).

2. *hetu, pratyaya, nidāna, kāraṇa, nimitta, liṅga, upaniṣad* are synonyms.

3. Why is a separate exposition of the causes (*hetu*) and the conditions (*pratyaya*) given? – Because (i) the exposition of the causes involves the examination of the cause as cause "not constituting an obstacle", co-existent cause, homogeneous cause, etc. (ii. 49); (ii) the exposi-

tion of the conditions involves the examination of the cause as causal (*hetu*), immediately preceding, etc., (ii. 62).

4. On *hetu* and *pratyaya*, see *Siddhi*. – The opposition of *hetu* and *pratyaya* is clear in *Kośa*, iv, F 100, 176.

LS: Dhammajoti explains (SA.IV.176) that even though the terms "cause" and "condition" were used more or less synonymously in the *sūtra-piṭaka* and there was no distinction between them articulated in the early canonical treatises of the Sarvāstivāda, it is in the MVŚ, 109b–c, that we come across various well-defined distinctions between the two:

> What are the differences between a cause and a condition? According to Venerable Vasumitra: There is no difference—a cause is a condition, a condition is a cause... . He further explains: If when this existing that exists, then this is the cause as well as the condition of that. ...
>
> In addition: [what pertains to] the same species is a cause; what pertains to a different species is a condition, e.g., fire to fire, wheat to wheat.
>
> In addition: what is proximate is a cause; what is remote is a condition. In addition: what is unique is a cause; what is common is a condition. ...
>
> In addition: what produces is a cause; what subsidiarily produces (隨能生) is a condition.
>
> In addition: what fosters its own series is a cause; what fosters another's series is a condition. ...
>
> (Also cf. opinion of *apare* in the MVŚ, 663b: "*Adhipati-pratyaya*-s are either direct or indirect, close or remote, united or not united, arising here or arising in another. Those that are direct, close, united, arising here, are called *hetu*-s. Those that are indirect, remote, not united, arising in another, are called *pratyaya*-s.")
>
> Thus, we know that although a cause and a condition do not differ in respect of substance, there is a difference in significance: a cause signifies what is proximate, a condition signifies what is remote.

For further distinctions mentioned by Saṃghabhadra, see Ny, 449c–450a (SA.IV.176f.).

786 *LS*: Dhammajoti explains (private communication) that "*adhipatiphala* is the only fruit of *kāraṇahetu*, [although the other five causes are part of the efficient cause]. But one must look into the meaning of *adhipatiphala*". He glosses (SA.IV.512): "*adhipati-phala*: 'fruit of (pre)dominance'; this is the fruit of the *kāraṇa-hetu*. The fruits of collective *karma*-s also come under this category." He comments further (SA.IV.180): "This is the most generic type of fruit, correlated to the most generic type of cause, the efficient cause." See Vasubandhu's discussion of the efficient cause (ii. 50a).

787 *LS*: In the chart note that the *samanantara-pratyaya* and *ālambana-pratyaya* have no correlatives among the six causes. Dhammajoti comments (SA.IV.145) that "this suggests that the doctrine of the four *pratyaya*-s has a wider scope than that of the six *hetu*-s".

As for the mutual inclusion or subsumption (*saṃgraha*) between the causes and the conditions, the MVŚ, 79a–b (SA.IV.171), mentions two opinions, of which the second is the one presented in the AKB:

Question: Do the causes subsume the conditions, or do the conditions subsume the causes?

Answer: They mutually subsume each other, accordingly as the case may be: The first five causes constitute the condition qua cause; the efficient cause constitutes the other three conditions.

According to some: the conditions subsume the causes, but the causes do not subsume the conditions: The first five causes constitute condition qua cause; the efficient cause constitutes the condition of dominance; the immediate condition and the condition qua object are not subsumed by any cause.

788 *LS*: AH 25, 48, 234; SAH 68–72, 74–76, 78, 469.

789 *Gokhale*: [49] *kāraṇaṃ sahabhūś c aiva sabhāgaḥ samprayuktakaḥ | sarvatrago vipāka-ākhyaḥ ṣaḍvidho hetur iṣyate ||*

Tib.: [49] *byed rgyu lhan cig 'byung ba dang | skal mnyam mtshungs par lhan pa dang | kun tu 'gro dang rnam smin dang | rgyu na rnam pa drug tu 'dod ||*

LVP: *Abhidharmahṛdaya* (*Nanjio*, 1288), ii. 11.

LS: Saṃghabhadra mentions (Ny, 416b; EIP.703f.) that the six causes are listed according to the extent of their inclusiveness: (1) the efficient cause includes all conditioned and unconditioned factors, (2) the co-existent cause includes all conditioned factors, (3–6) the homogeneous cause, associated cause, pervasive cause and ripening cause each include a portion of conditioned factors. However, an unconditioned factor is neither caused by another unconditioned factor nor by a conditioned factor, while a conditioned factor can be caused by conditioned and unconditioned factors. Further, while the homogeneous cause, the pervasive cause and the ripening cause arise prior to their effects, and the co-existent cause and the associated cause arise simultaneously with their effects, the efficient cause can arise either prior to or simultaneously with its effect.

790 *LVP*: In what Sūtra are the six types of cause (*hetu*) promulgated? In fact the Abhidharma only explains, assesses, comments on the Sūtra (sarvo hy abhidharmaḥ sūtrārthaḥ sūtranikaṣaḥ sūtravyākhyānam [WOG.188.23f.]).

The Vaibhāṣikas say that the Sūtra that dealt with this aspect has disappeared (*antarhita*). The *Ekottarāgama* enumerated the factors (*dharma*) up to the categories of 100 factors, but it no longer contains the categories above ten up to the decades (*ādaśakāt*). (See *Introduction* by La Vallée Poussin.)

But the Sūtras that characterize each type of cause (*hetu*) are not absent and the *Vyākhyā* [WOG.188f; see SA.IV.143f.] provides examples borrowed, as it seems, from Saṃghabhadra (79b16).

1. *kāraṇahetu* (efficient cause): "The visual consciousness arises due to the eye sense-faculty and visible forms" (*Saṃyutta*, iv. 87, etc.).

2. *sahabhūhetu* (co-existent cause): "These three members of the path accompany (*anuvart*) right view." "Contact is the collocation or coming together of the three, [i.e., sense-faculty, object-referent, consciousness]; sensation, ideation and intention arise together."

3. *sabhāgahetu* (homogeneous cause): "This person (*pudgala*) is endowed with wholesome factors, with unwholesome factors; his wholesome factors perish, his unwholesome factors

unfold, but there exists an accompanying (*anusahagata*) wholesome root that has not been cut off (*asti cāsyānusahagataṃ kuśalamūlam asamucchinnam*), on account of which there is the possibility of the arising of another wholesome root: this person, in the future, will become pure" (*viśuddhidharmā bhaviṣyati*; cp. *Aṅguttara*, iii. 315).

In a similar context, *Saṃyutta*, iii. 131 (compare *Kathāvatthu*, p. 215), has *anusahagata*, which Saṃghabhadra here translates exactly (*sui chü hsing*); it refers to a strong wholesome root, identified (Saṃghabhadra, 99b19) with *purāṇa-anu-dhātu* (?) (*chiu sui chieh*) of the school of the Sthavira.

But the *MSS* of the *Vyākhyā* [WOG.188.31] has *aṇusahagata* and we shall see that, in the *Bhāṣya* of iv. 79d, the Chinese version of *Jñānaprasthāna* gives the exact equivalent: *wei chü hsing*. In this passage *aṇusahagata* is the equivalent of weak-weak (*mṛdumṛdu*): "Which are the wholesome roots called *aṇusahagata*? – Those which are abandoned last when the wholesome roots are broken; those through the absence of which the wholesome roots are said to be broken." [We have seen above (ii, F 184) that, strictly speaking, the wholesome roots are never broken.]

4. *saṃprayuktakahetu* (associated cause): "That which is called *faith* (*śraddhā*), having insight (*darśana*) for its root, associated with perfect cognition (*avetyajñāna*; vi. 74c): that which those persons cognize (*vijānāti*), they penetrate it through understanding (*prajñā*; *prajānāti*)."

5. *sarvatragahetu* (pervasive cause): "For the persons who have false view (*mithyādṛṣṭi*; v. 7) the bodily actions, the vocal actions, intention, resolution (*praṇidhāna*), the *saṃskāras* that follow these actions, etc., all these factors have for their consequence unhappiness, hideousness. – Why? – Because they have a view-of-transgression (*pāpikā*), namely, false view." (Compare *Aṅguttara*, v. 212).

6. *vipākahetu* (ripening cause): "From the action done here... they savor there the retribution."

791 *LS*: AH 25; SAH 69, 78.

792 *LS*: Ibid.

793 *Gokhale*: [50a] *svato 'nye kāraṇaṃ hetuḥ*

Tib.: [50a] *rang las gzhan pa byed rgyu'i rgyu* |

LVP: *svato 'nye kāraṇahetuḥ.*

LS: The MVŚ, 104a (SA.IV.149f; ESD.199):

> What is the efficient cause?
>
> Answer: Conditioned by eye and a visible, visual consciousness arises. This visual consciousness has as its efficient cause the eye, the visible, the *dharma*-s conjoined with it, the *dharma*-s co-existent with it, as well as the ear, sound, auditory consciousness, ... the mental organ (*manas*), the mental objects (*dharma*), mental consciousness, [i.e.,] all the *dharma*-s which are material (*rūpin*), immaterial (*arūpin*), visible (*sanidarśana*), invisible (*anidarśana*), resistant (*sapratigha*), non-resistant (*apratigha*), with-outflow (*sāsrava*), outflow-free (*anāsrava*), conditioned (*saṃskrta*), unconditioned (*asaṃskṛta*), etc.—all *dharma*-s excepting itself. ... Efficient (*kāraṇa*) [here] means "being non-obstructive", "accomplishing something" (有所辦).

Avatāra (ESD.122):

> When *dharma*-s are produced, they have all *dharma*-s, excluding themselves, as their efficient causes. They are [efficient causes] either [in the sense of being] non-obstructive [to their arising] (*avighnabhāva*) or [in the sense of being] capable of producing [the *dharma*-s].

794 *LS*: Saṃghabhadra comments (Ny, 417a; EIP.VIII.704): "This is due to the fact that a factor is always an obstruction to itself, no entity is self-caused, and no entity functions with regard to itself, just as a sword does not cut itself and so on."

795 *LS*: WOG.189.17f: *sarvadharmāḥ* saṃskṛtāsaṃskṛtāḥ. – SAH 78 also has: "All factors—conditioned and unconditioned ones—are said to be the efficient cause."

796 *LS*: SAH 78.

797 *LS*: For this and the next section, cf. WOG.189.18ff.

798 *MW*: *kāraṇa*: cause, reason, the cause of anything; instrument, means; motive, origin, principle.

799 *LVP*: As soon as knowledge of the truths takes place, the causes of defilements are no longer complete, since the possession (*prāpti*) of the defilements is cut off through this knowledge.

800 *LVP*: Montaigne, iii. 9: Princes give me sufficiently if they take nothing from me, and do me much good if they do me no hurt; it is all I require of them. (Translation: John Florio)

801 *LS*: Even though the unconditioned transcend space-time and therefore are not directly involved in the cause-effect processes in phenomenal existence, they can be regarded as causes in the sense that they too function as objects of thought (see SA.IV.147).

802 *LS*: Cox summarizes Saṅghabhadra (Ny, 417a; EIP.VIII.704): "Efficient causes are of two types: (1) those that act as causes of another factor simply because they do not obstruct its arising, and (2) those that act as productive causes of another factor."

803 *MW*: *pradhāna* = chief thing or person, the most important or essential part of anything, the principal or first, chief, head of.

apradhāna = not principal, subordinate, secondary.

804 *LVP*: According to the text [WOG.190.29.]: *āhārasamudayāt kāyasya samudayaḥ*. Compare *Saṃyutta*, iii. 62.

805 *LVP*: Any cause should have an effect; kāraṇe sati kāryeṇa bhavitavyam [WOG.190.32].

806 *LS*: AH 25, 234; SAH 70, 469.

807 *LS*: AH 25; SAH 70.

808 *Gokhale*: [50bd] *sahabhūr ye mithaḥphalāḥ | bhūtavac cittacittā'nuvartilakṣaṇalakṣyavat* ||

Tib.: [50bd] *lhan cig 'byung gang phan tshun 'bras | 'byung bzhin sems kyi rjes 'jug dang | sems dang mtshan nyid mtshan gzhi bzhin* |

LVP: The suffix *vat* in the sense of *tadyathā*.

See discussion in AKB iii, F 102.

LS: Dhammajoti comments: "This is a new causal category innovated by the Sarvāstivāda. ... It is of central importance in the causal theory of the school. It became an indispensable doctrinal tool for the Yogācāra theory of cognition only (*vijñaptimātratā*)."

1. The MVŚ, 85b, states:

> Question: What is the intrinsic nature of the co-existent cause?
>
> Answer: All the conditioned *dharma*-s… .
>
> Question: What is the meaning of "co-existent" (*sahabhū*)?
>
> Answer: "Co-existent" means [i] "not mutually separated (*avinā-bhāva*)", [ii] "sharing the same effect", [iii] "mutually accordant with one another". This co-existent cause is definitely found in the three periods of times and produces the virile effect (*puruṣakāra-phala*).

According to Saṃghabhadra (Ny, 417c; SA.IV.155):

> *The co-existent* [*causes*] *are those that are reciprocally virile effects*, on account of the fact that they can arise by virtue of mutual support… . *For example: the four Great Elements are co-existent cause mutually among themselves*, … for it is only when the four different kinds of Great Elements assemble together that they can be efficacious in producing the derived matter (*upādāya rūpa*); *so also thought and the dharma-s which are thought-accompaniments*; *so also the* [*four*] *characteristics of the conditioned and the characterized* [*conditioned dharma*]. *In this way, the whole of the conditioned, where applicable* (*i.e., where a mutual causal relationship obtains*) *are co-existent causes*. (The italicized words are those also found in the AKB).
>
> Herein, the scope of the characteristics of the causes [as described by Vasubandhu] is too narrow—the thought-accompaniments and the characteristics [of the conditioned] should in each case be mentioned as co-existent causes amongst themselves. Thus, he should not have said that only those that are reciprocally the effect of one another are co-existent causes. A *dharma* and its secondary characteristics are not reciprocally effects, yet it is a [co-existent] cause of the latter [although the latter are not its co-existent cause]. … Therefore, the characteristics [of this cause] should be explained thus: Those conditioned *dharma*-s that share the same effect can [also] be considered as co-existent causes; there is no fault [in explaining thus], as it is so explained in the fundamental treatises (*mūla-śāstra*)… .

Avatāra (ESD.121):

> The conditioned *dharma*-s which are the fruits of one another, or which together bring about a common fruit are named co-existent causes—e.g., the *mahābhūta*-s; the [conditioned *dharma*-s which are] characterized (*lakṣya*) and the [four] conditioned characteristics; the thought and the thought-accompaniments (*cittānuvartin*). These are [in each case co-existent causes] for one another.

2. At AKB iii, F 102, the Vaibhāṣika also mentions the important example of the co-existent cause in the perceptual process (which is also discussed at Ny, 420c–421a and WOG.197.28ff.; cf. also i. 44cd [F 94f.]). The AKB states:

> The Vaibhāṣika: We do not deny that a cause [*kāraṇa*] sometimes precedes its effect [*kārya*]; but we affirm that the cause and the effect can be simultaneous [*sahabhāva*]: [for example,] (i) the visual sense-faculty and color, and the visual consciousness; (ii) the fundamental material elements (*mahābhūta*) and the derived material ele-

ments (*bhautika*).

3. Dhammajoti introduces the doctrinal importance of the co-existent cause within the context of Sarvāstivāda realism and as the only valid paradigm for causation. See the following longer discussion of this important topic (SA.IV.161–64):

> The doctrine of simultaneous causation lends support to the Sarvāstivāda doctrine of direct perception which, in turn, again reinforced their doctrine of pluralistic realism. This is in contrast to the Sautrāntika theory of indirect perception which eventually paves the way for the idealistic Yogācāra theory of *vijñaptimātratā.* For the Sarvāstivādins, one can be absolutely certain about the existence of external objects because our five senses directly perceive them. Thus, within a single moment of visual perception, the visual faculty, the object and the corresponding visual consciousness all arise simultaneously. All three function as co-existent causes. This is, in fact, one of Saṃghabhadra's arguments [Ny, 420c–421a] for the co-existent cause: ...
>
> But more importantly, this doctrine is indispensable for the fundamental thesis of *sarvāstitva.* Of the four major arguments put forward for the thesis—(a) *uktatvāt,* (b) *dvayāt,* (c) *sadviṣayāt,* (d) *phalāt* [AKB v. 25ab]—the first is simply an inference from the Buddha's mention of past and future objects. (c) and (d) are the only two logical arguments (*yuktitaḥ*), and (b) essentially has the same stress as (c), supported by the Buddha's own statement. (c) argues that since the object of any perception must be existent, the fact that the mind can think of past and future objects then proves the reality/existence of past and future *dharma*-s. (d) argues that past *dharma*-s must exist since a past *karma* is causally efficacious in generating a present *vipāka.* Now it must be noted that these two logical arguments cannot stand unless the simultaneous causality—in the sense that the cause and the effect must be existent at the same time—as exemplified by the *sahabhū-hetu* is conceded: Both require that the cause and the effect exist simultaneously. But it should be borne in mind that, in the Sarvāstivāda, "*existing* simultaneously" does not necessarily mean "*arising* simultaneously". When the cause and the arising effect do *arise* simultaneously—i.e., co-exist (*saha-bhū*) in the present moment—we have the case of the *sahabhū-hetu.* ...
>
> In general, if *A* causes *B*, both *A* and *B* must be existent at the same time—although they may belong to different time periods with respect to their own temporal frame of reference. That is: *A* may be past or present or future, and *B* may also be past or present or future—*but they must co-exist, although not necessarily be conascent.* To borrow Dharmatrāta's terminology, they are both existent, but not necessarily of the same "mode of existence" (*bhāva*); or in Ghoṣaka's terminology, they do not necessarily have the same "time-characteristic". Where *A* and *B* are necessarily conascent, i.e., both existing at the same *present* moment, we have the category known as the co-existent cause. In fact, in the Sarvāstivāda conception, all *dharma*-s in their essential nature have always been existent; it is only a matter of inducing their arising through causes and conditions. This is the fundamental principle underlining the Sarvāstivāda doctrine of causality. Past and future *dharma*-s are also endowed with efficacies including that of actually giving an effect, although it is only a present *dharma* that has *kāritra*—the efficacy of establishing the specific causal relationship

> with the *dharma* to be produced as its effect. ...
>
> [For Saṃghabhadra] the co-existent cause is simply a special case of simultaneous causation obtaining among the necessarily conascent *dharma*-s. The co-existent cause then actually exemplifies the general case of simultaneous causation in which a distinct *A* generates a distinct *B*—both existing simultaneously. ...
>
> The case of a homogeneous cause generating an emanation fruit as its own next moment of existence is an exception, as it involves not two ontologically distinct entities but simply the arising of a given entity itself in the next moment of its series.
>
> The Yogācāra not only accepts the Sarvāstivāda position as regards causation, but is more explicit in stating that there is no other real causality outside that represented by the co-existent and conjoined causes.

4. As can be seen from Saṃghabhadra's previously noted definition and criticism, he states that Vasubandhu's explanation is too narrow and should also include those *dharmas* that share the same effect, and in this way he is in agreement with the definition (see above) of the MVŚ. He further states (Ny, 419c; SA.IV.158):

> We do not concede that cause-effect relationship obtains reciprocally in all cases of the conascent: ... It obtains only [i] among those that share the same effect; or [ii] that are reciprocally effects; or [iii] where by the force of this, that *dharma* can arise. Such conascent [*dharma*-s] have a cause-effect relationship, [i.e., are co-existent causes].

These three cases find expression also in the three possible cases of the coexistent cause as presented in Dhammajoti's summary to his article *The Sarvāstivāda Doctrine of Simultaneous Causality* (notice: the order of the first two members is reversed):

> i. The co-nascent *dharmas* are both causes as well as effects to one another; the new *dharmas* produced in this case being these very members themselves in the reciprocal causal relationship. The co-arising of thought and mental concomitants exemplifies this situation, with the lamp-light metaphor as the typical illustration.
>
> ii. Not all the co-nascent members are reciprocally co-produced. Thus, given three (or more) members *A*, *B*, *C*, constituting the *sahabhū-hetu*, *A* and *B*, being causally coordinated, co-produce *C simultaneously*. The classical exemplification is the production of visual consciousness, conditioned by the visual faculty and visual object.
>
> iii. Two co-nascent *dharmas* may also be said to be in a *sahabhū-hetu* relationship if one is necessarily—though not reciprocally—produced by the other. Thus, a *dharma* is a *sahabhū-hetu* of the secondary characteristics, but not vice versa. This is because in the Sarvāstivāda system, a secondary characteristic is causally efficacious with regard to its corresponding primary characteristic (*mūla-lakṣaṇa*) only, not to the *dharma*.

5. The Sautrāntika rejects the Sarvāstivāda category of the co-existent cause (see ii, F 252–55). For them, a cause necessarily precedes an effect—a principle that has great significance for their theory of perception. Here Dhammajoti points out (SA.IV.159ff.) the interesting fact that even though the Sautrāntika was one of the precursors of the Mahāyāna Yogācāra, the Yogācāra itself—although holding the standpoint that only the present exists and thus

opposing the tri-temporal existence—not only takes over, without hesitation, the co-existent cause together with its subset, the associated cause (*saṃprayuktakahetu*), but considers simultaneous causation to be causality in the true sense, for apart from this simultaneous causation the other *hetu-pratyaya*s are not apperceived (*na upalabhyante*). The Yogācāra considers the *sahabhūhetu* to be an indispensable doctrinal category in their theory of *bīja*.

6. As for Vasubandhu, he seemingly accepts simultaneous causation. Dhammajoti comments (ADCP.26):

> In the AKB, Vasubandhu himself seems to be generally partisan to [the] Hīnayāna-[Sautrāntika] group. But, he too was evidently open-minded, of which fact the AKB is a testimony, and accordingly did not seem to have become exclusively partisan to the tenets of any group as such—be it those of Hīnayāna or Yogācāra Sautrāntika or Sarvāstivāda. Thus, in the context of the "what sees" debate, he seems to basically side [with] the view of Dharmatrāta; and yet at the same time probably senses the meaningfulness of the Yogācāra-Sautrāntika's concluding remark. As another illustration, Vasubandhu is known to accept some of the Sarvāstivāda *caitta*-s, and the notion of *saṃprayoga* of *citta-caitta*-s—differing from Śrīlāta. This also necessarily means that he accepts the *sahabhū-hetu* doctrine which Śrīlāta rejects. ...

809 *LVP*: One does not say that all co-existing factors (*sahabhū*) are a co-existent cause (*sahabhūhetu*). For example, derivative (*bhautika*) material form (*rūpa*), blue, etc., coexists with the fundamental material elements: but it is not a co-existent cause with them (see ii, F 253).

810 *LVP*: See i. 24; ii. 22, 65.

811 *LVP*: Any conditioned factor and its characteristics are co-existent causes (*sahabhūhetu*) among themselves; a factor is not a co-existent cause with the characteristics of another factor.

812 *LS*: AH 234; SAH 70, 469.

813 *LVP*: upasaṃkhyānakaraṇaṃ ca mahāśāstratāpradarśanārthaṃ sopasaṃkhyānaṃ hi vyākaraṇādi mahāśāstraṃ dṛśyate [WOG.191.2[1]f.].

814 *LS*: AH 234; SAH 70, 469.

815 *LS*: Ibid.

816 *Gokhale*: [51ac1] *caittā dvau saṃvarau teṣāṃ [cetaso] lakṣaṇāni ca | cittā'nuvartinaḥ.*

LS: Correction based on Pradhan.83.26: *...teṣāṃ cetaso...* . Gokhale has *...teṣāṃ saṃvarau...* .

Tib.: [51ac1] *sems las byung dang sdom gnyis dang | sems dang de dag gi mtshan nyid | sems kyi rjes 'jug*

817 *LS*: See ii. 65c: "The actions of body and of speech [*kāyavākkarma*] of the category described in ii. 51a, [i.e., the two restraints of the thought-associates (*cittānuparivartin*),] which are derivative material elements, are a co-existent cause. [Other derivative forms are not co-existent causes (*nānyadupādāyarūpaṃ*)]."

818 *LS*: SAH 70, 469.

819 *Gokhale*: [51c2–d] *kālaphalādiśubhatādibhiḥ* ||

Tib.: [51c2–d] *'dus dang ni | 'bras sogs dge la sogs pas so* ||

820 *LS*: SAH 70, 469.

[821] *LVP*: The first part of this paragraph is translated according to the *Vyākhyā*.

[822] *LS*: SAH 70, 469.

[823] *LS*: The *Vyākhyā* states (WOG.192.9f.): adhipati-phalam tu sarva-sādhāraṇatvāt na gaṇyate ("the effect of dominance, however, is not counted because it is common to all factors").

[824] *LS*: SAH 70, 469.

[825] *LVP*: The ten reasons are never gathered together. For example, in the case of the non-defined thought not destined to arise, the concomitants are concomitants due to four reasons: (1) same time, (2) same effect (i.e., of human action; *puruṣakāra*), (3) same effect of equal outflow (*niṣyanda*), (4) same status of being non-defined .

[826] *LS*: SAH 70.

[827] *LVP*: That is to say, the unobscured-non-defined thought (*anivṛtāvyākṛta*) after the second meditation (*dhyāna*); initial inquiry (*vitarka*), investigation (*vicāra*), the wholesome permeating factors (*kuśalamahābhūmika*) are absent from it.

[828] *LVP*: Thought reigns (*rājayate*) over its secondary characteristics (*anulakṣaṇa*); the latter have not acted (*vyāpāra*) on thought, as we have seen ii. 46.

[829] *LVP*: The Japanese editor refers to the *Prakaraṇa*, 745a25. – See below ii, F 259 and 269 where the same text is referred to.

The *Prakaraṇa* examines the relations between the four truths and the afflicted view of self (*satkāyadṛṣṭi*). The *Vyākhyā* gives an extract that is translated here [WOG.193.12ff.]:

A. There are four truths. Among the truths, (1) how many have the afflicted view of self for their cause without being the cause of the afflicted view of self, (2) how many are the cause of the afflicted view of self without having the afflicted view of self for their cause, (3) how many have the afflicted view of self for their cause and are at the same time a cause of the afflicted view of self, (4) how many do not have the afflicted view of self for their cause and are not the afflicted view of self?

To this question he answers: two truths do not have the afflicted view of self for their cause and are not a cause of the afflicted view of self, namely, the truth of cessation and the truth of the path; in regard to the other two truths, we have reason to distinguish.

B. The truth of unsatisfactoriness can (1) have the afflicted view of self for its cause without being a cause of the afflicted view of self, (2) have the afflicted view of self for its cause and be a cause of the afflicted view of self, (3) not have the afflicted view of self for its cause and not be a cause of the afflicted view of self: there are only three alternatives; the second (being a cause of the afflicted view of self without having the afflicted view of self for its cause) is absent.

1. Having the afflicted view of self for its cause without being a cause of the afflicted view of self: the whole truth of defiled unsatisfactoriness (i.e., all factors that are unsatisfactory and that are defiled [*kliṣṭa*]) with the exception:

   i. (a) of the past and present proclivities (*anuśaya*) that can be abandoned by insight into unsatisfactoriness, and (b) of the truth of unsatisfactoriness associated with these proclivities (for example, sensation associated with the afflicted view of self that is abandoned by the insight into unsatisfactoriness);

ii. of the future truth of unsatisfactoriness that is associated with the afflicted view of self (see ii, F 259 line 11);

iii. of the origination-duration-deterioration-impermanence of the afflicted view of self and of the factors associated with this afflicted view of self (*tatsaṃprayuktānāṃ ca dharmāṇām*: these last words are omitted in certain recensions).

2. Having the afflicted view of self for its cause and being a cause of the afflicted view of self: the truth of unsatisfactoriness that has been excluded in the preceding paragraph.

3. Not having the afflicted view of self for its cause and not being a cause of the afflicted view of self: the truth of undefiled unsatisfactoriness [i.e., the factors that are unsatisfactory but that are wholesome].

The Chinese versions, *Nanjio* 1292 (xxiii. 11, 38b10) and 1277 (10, 58b4), correspond to the preceding text. Some omissions (the phrases: "To this question, he answers" [*iti praśne visarjanaṃ karoti*] and "There are only three alternatives; the second is absent" [*trikoṭikam, dvitīyā koṭir nāsti*], are absent in them). There are significant variations in the definition of factors that have the afflicted view of self for their cause and are a cause of the afflicted view of self:

i. past and present proclivities that can be abandoned by insight into unsatisfactoriness, and the truth of unsatisfactoriness associated with these proclivities (1277: and the truth of unsatisfactoriness associated, coexistent, etc., with these proclivities);

ii. past and present pervasive (*sarvatraga*) proclivities that can be abandoned by insight into the origin, and the truth of unsatisfactoriness that is associated (1277: associated, coexistent, etc.) with them;

iii. future truth of unsatisfactoriness that is associated with the afflicted view of self;

iv. origination, etc., of the future afflicted view of self and of associated factors.

830 *LS*: See in this context Dhammajoti's article *The Sarvāstivāda Doctrine of Simultaneous Causality* (SDS), which includes translations of the definitions of the co-existent cause and associated cause of the MVŚ, AKB, *Avatāra* and the *Nyāyānusāra*. In regard to the latter it also includes a translation of the most important sections of its debate about the existential status of the co-existent cause.

831 *LS*: Although not explicitly mentioned in Pradhan, LVP mentions the Sautrāntika here.

As for Vasubandhu's position in regard to the co-existent cause, see our introductory note to the co-existent cause (above).

In the **Nyāyānusāra*, 418c, Śrīlāta—the Sautrāntika leader in Saṃghabhadra's time—presents four objections in regard to the possibility of simultaneous causality (SDS.10f.):

1. Causality among co-nascent *dharma*s cannot be established since before they arise, they have not yet come into existence; one cannot specify which *dharma*s give rise (cause) to which (effect). This would also mean that the present *dharma*s are without cause, and that we need to seek two other *dharma*s for the two co-nascent *dharma*s.

2. It is taught that where there is a cause, there is an effect. If *dharma*s in the future period can function as causes for other *dharma*s to arise, there would be the fallacy of *dharma*s arising perpetually.

3. Among two co-nascent *dharmas*—as in the case of the two horns of an ox—one cannot prove legitimately which is the cause [and] which is the effect.

4. In the world, among cases where a cause-effect relationship is universally acknowledged—such as the production of a sprout from a seed—such a simultaneous causality has never been observed.

Saṃghabhadra's detailed reply (see SDS.11–16) is primarily directed at establishing the co-existent cause: He begins with a discussion of the general characteristics or nature of causality, invoking the first part of the Buddha's statement of the principle of conditionality (see AKB iii. 81–83): "This being, that exists; from the arising of this, that arises." He then continues to answer Śrīlāta's objections one by one.

832 *LS*: Yaśomitra glosses (WOG.197.11): *sarvam apy etad syād* iti. yat tāvat *sahabhū-hetunā hetur* iti viṣṭareṇa yad uktam. See F 252.

833 *LS*: Although not explicitly mentioned in Pradhan, LVP mentions the Sautrāntika here.

834 *LS*: The Vaibhāṣika replies (Ny; SDS.15):

> This is not reasonable. For it is not perceived (*upa-√labh*) that when the lamp first arises, there is the lamp without the light. It has never been observed that a lamp exists without light [—a lamp is always that which has light]. Neither is it reasonable to claim that it is not perceived owing to the brevity of time, as it is not universally established (*prasiddha*) to be so. ...
>
> It ought not be the case that the lamp and its light are arisen by one and the same cause, as in the case of the skin, the kernel and the oil in a sesame. No [reciprocal] cause-effect relationship is observed in the combination of the skin, the kernel and the oil born of a sesame born of a common cause. In the case of the pair of the lamp and the light, it is observed in the present moment that they serve as causes which equally accord with each other, which proves the presence of causality. Hence one cannot claim that they are born of one common cause. ...
>
> If a lamp and its light were born of a common cause, then when someone covers up the lamp with something, its light—like the lamp—ought not to cease to continue. The lamp—being on a par with its light—likewise ought not to arise [anymore]. ...
>
> Hence the metaphor of the lamp and its light is universally established.

See SDS.14–16 for a translation of Saṃghabhadra's defense (presented in dialogue form by Dhammajoti) of the example of the co-nascent lamp and light.

835 *LVP*: Where one fundamental material element (*mahābhūta*) occurs, the other fundamental material elements also occur, etc.

836 *LS*: Although not explicitly mentioned in Pradhan, LVP mentions the Sautrāntika here.

837 *LVP*: I understand: "one moment (*kṣaṇa*) of the eye sense-faculty is the cause of the simultaneous visual consciousness".

838 *LS*: In this paragraph—although the AKB does later at iii, F 102—Pradhan does not mention the important example of the co-existent cause in the perceptual process (visual sense-faculty, visual object and visual consciousness), on the other hand, it occurs in both the *Vyākhyā* (WOG.197.30f.) and the **Nyāyānusāra* (420c–421a; SDS.17). Saṃghabhadra argues:

It contradicts the principle of Conditioned Co-arising (*pratītya-samutpāda*) [to hold that there are no co-nascent causes]. Thus the *sūtra* says:

> Conditioned by the visual faculty and the visual object, there arises visual consciousness.

[If the visual faculty, the visual object and the visual consciousness were not simultaneous,] then the visual faculty and visual object produced in the preceding moment ought not to be the supporting basis and the perceptual object, [respectively,] for the visual consciousness of the succeeding moment; for [in that case, the latter] exists and [the former are] non-existent. One cannot call an absolute non-existent (*atyantābhāva*) a supporting basis or a perceptual object. The same applies here: At the time when the visual consciousness arises, the visual faculty and the visual object have already ceased. This would mean that without any conditions assisting, the visual consciousness arises by itself! This is due to the fact that non-existent *dharmas* cannot serve as supporting basis, and that visual consciousness can only take a present object.

If the visual faculty, the visual object and the visual consciousness do not arise simultaneously, it would entail that the visual faculty and visual objects do not serve as conditions for visual consciousness. Or, the auditory faculty and sound, etc., would also serve as conditions for visual consciousness, being equally unrelated to visual consciousness.

If the Bhagavat says only that conditioned by the previously arisen visual faculty and the visual object, the visual consciousness arises, then he ought to say that the visual consciousness has only consciousness as its condition; because a condition of the same species [—in this case consciousness—] is a strong one, like a seed, and because a preceding consciousness serves as the equal-immediate condition (*samanantara-pratyaya*) for a succeeding consciousness. Since he does not say that visual consciousness is conditioned by consciousness, we know accordingly that in this context he speaks only of the simultaneously arisen visual faculty and visual object as the conditions for the visual consciousness.

As within the same body, no two consciousnesses arise together, he does not speak of consciousness as the condition for visual consciousness. ...

839 *LS*: Although not explicitly mentioned in Pradhan, LVP mentions the Sautrāntika here.

840 *LS*: AH 25; SAH 71.

841 *LS*: Ibid.

842 *Gokhale*: [52a] *sabhāgahetuḥ sadṛśāḥ*

Tib.: [52a] *skal mnyam rgyu ni 'dra ba'o* |

LVP: See ii. 59.

LS: 1. *Avatāra* (ESD.121):

> The *dharma*-s born anteriorily (*agraja*) and belonging to a given stage (*bhūmi*) and class (*nikāya*) are—in a similar manner to seed *dharma*-s—the homogeneous causes for the similar posterior *dharma*-s, [belonging to the same stage and class]. [Thus, a *dharma* in the sense-sphere and abandonable by insight into the truth of suffering is

the homogeneous cause only for a later *dharma* in the sense-sphere and similarily abandonable].

Saṃghabhadra defines the homogeneous cause as follows (Ny, 422a; SA.IV.152.):

> Those that can nourish and produce the emanation (*niṣyanda*) fruits, whether remote or near, are called homogeneous causes. It is to be understood that this cause obtains in the case of similar *dharma*-s with regard to similar *dharma*-s, not with regard to those of a different species.

As for "different species", Dhammajoti comments (private communication) that Saṃghabhadra proceeds to give the same examples as AKB, i.e., the five wholesome (*kuśala*) aggregates (*skandha*) are the homogeneous causes (*sabhāgahetu*) of the five wholesome aggregates, among themselves (*anyonya*), i.e., not of unskillful, etc., aggregates.

2. Cox summarizes Saṅghabhadra (EIP.VIII.706): "Homogeneous causes act to produce similar factors either immediately or remotely. 'Similar' means of the same moral quality, the same category in terms of method of abandonment, and the same stage."

3. Dhammajoti comments (SA.IV.150f.) that Saṃghabhadra does not have any objections to Vasubandhu's explanations of this cause, but that—besides the fact that the "western masters" and the Dārṣṭāntikas denied that *rūpa-dharma*-s can have a homogeneous cause—there were "other disagreements among the various Sarvāstivāda masters in terms of details concerning the nature and scope of this causal category" (see F 255), which were mostly tolerated.

843 *LS*: SAH 71.

844 *LS*: Dhammajoti comments (SA.192) that "this suggests that there were various interpretations in the Sarvāstivāda system on this cause, which were mostly tolerated". He mentions that Saṃghabhadra criticizes only the next views, i.e., "the one related to the embryonic series and the Dārṣṭāntika view that there is no homogeneous cause among the *rūpa*-s".

845 *LVP*: According to the rule "[the noble path is the homogeneous cause] to an equal or superior [noble path]" (*samaviśiṣṭayoḥ*; ii. 52d). – The four non-material aggregates (*skandha*) are "superior" (*viśiṣṭa*); material form (*rūpa*) is "inferior" (*nyūna*).

846 *LS*: Following Saṃghabhadra (Ny, 422a; SA.IV.151).

847 *LS*: Dhammajoti (SA.IV.151): "(Four are the homogeneous cause of five); [that is,] matter—being inferior in strength (勢力劣故)—is [only] the homogeneous cause of the four other aggregates." He comments that this view is not found in Pradhan, but in Hsüan-tsang's Chinese translation of the AKB. LVP, however, has: "but material form is not a homogeneous cause of four aggregates".

848 *LS*: Again, this view is not found in Pradhan. Dhammajoti translates based on Saṃghabhadra (Ny, 422a; SA.IV.151): "According to some masters: matter on the one hand, and the other four aggregates on the other, are not mutually homogeneous cause. This is because matter is 'inferior and of a different species (from the four mental aggregates)' (劣異類故)."

849 *LS*: Although not explicitly mentioned in Pradhan, LVP mentions the Dārṣṭāntika here.

Dhammajoti comments (ESD.63): "In AKB, Ny and ADV, the appellations 'Dārṣṭāntikas' and 'Sautrāntikas' are used interchangeably. The early Dārṣṭāntika in the time of MVŚ, however, were Sarvāstivādins. They broke away from the Sarvāstivāda and evolved into the Sautrāntikas around the 3rd century A.D."

According to MVŚ, 682c, both the "western masters" and the Dārṣṭāntikas deny that material form can have a homogeneous cause, but no reason for the denial is given.

Cox summarizes Saṃghabhadra (EIP.VIII.706): "The Dārṣṭāntikas claim that material form cannot act as a homogeneous cause because material form is produced and accumulated through the assistance of sufficient conditions; but this is to be rejected."

850 *LS*: See WOG.199.11ff.

851 *LS*: SAH 71.

852 *Gokhale*; [52b1] *svanikāyabhuvo*

Tib.: [52b1] *rang rigs sa pa'o*

853 *LS*: SAH 71.

854 *LS*: SAH 71.

855 *Gokhale*; [52b2] *'grajāḥ* |

Tib.: [52b2] *sngar skyes rnams* |

856 *LVP*: According to Paramārtha. – Absent in Hsüan-tsang; absent in the original.

LS: Saṃghabhadra explains (Ny, 422a; EIP.VIII.706f.) that this is so because there is no sequential ordering among future factors, that is to say: the future factor (*dharma*) has not yet performed its activity (*kāritra*), i.e., projected its own effect, but whether or not a factor has performed its activity determines the factor's state, which in turn determines the sequential ordering among factors.

857 *LS*: This is the 33rd of Kritzer's forty-four passages discussed in relation to chapter 2 (VY.104). Saṃghabhadra (Ny, 422c23–25) identifies this as the opinion of Vasubandhu and criticizes it (Ny, 422c25–423a4) on the grounds that *sabhāgahetu* actually does not resemble *samantarapratyaya*.

858 *LS*: This is the 34th of Kritzer's forty-four passages discussed in relation to chapter 2 (VY.106). Vasubandhu accuses the author of the *Jñānaprasthānaśāstra* of being bad with words. Saṃghabhadra (Ny, 423a8–9) identifies this as the opinion of Vasubandhu and defends the *Jñānaprasthāna* (Ny, 423a9–18).

859 *LVP*: According to the opponent of the Vaibhāṣika, the *Prakaraṇa* teaches that the future afflicted view of self and the factors (*dharma*) that are associated with it are at the same time the effect and the cause of the afflicted view of self. But the future afflicted view of self is neither a reciprocal (*sahabhū*) cause, nor an associated (*saṃprayuktaka*) cause, nor a ripening (*vipāka*) cause; it remains, when one does not take into account the efficient cause (*kāraṇa-hetu*), that it is a homogeneous (*sabhāga*) cause and a pervasive (*sarvaga*) cause.

For the Vaibhāṣika, the *Prakaraṇa* speaks here, not of the future afflicted view of self, but of factors (sensation, etc.) associated with this afflicted view of self: they are a cause of the afflicted view of self as a simultaneous and associated cause (*sahabhū*, *saṃprayuktaka*), and an effect of the afflicted view of self considered as simultaneous and associated cause.

We have three readings; in addition to the two readings cited here, the text: *anāgataṃ ca satkāyadṛṣṭisaṃprayuktaṃ duḥkhasatyaṃ sthāpayitvā*: "with the exception, moreover, of the truth of future unsatisfactoriness that is associated with the afflicted view of self" (see ii, F 251 [note, part B.1.b]).

mutually conjoined causes to one another? Answer: Because they are reciprocally causes, arisen through their mutual strength, mutually induced, mutually nourished, mutually strengthened, mutually dependent. This is like two bundles of straw which stay in position through mutual dependence. [Likewise,] when many ropes are combined, a huge log can be dragged; and many people can cross a big river by joining hands together. Because conditioned *dharma*-s are weak in their intrinsic nature, they can accomplish their activities only through mutual dependence. If we were to ask sensation: "Without ideation, can you [alone] sense/experience an object?" The answer would be: "No." The same questions [and answers] apply to the other thoughts and thought-concomitants as well.

**Nyāyānusāra*, 416c (SA.IV.156):

This [conjoined] cause is established because thought and thought concomitants, being conjoined, accomplish the same deed by grasping the same object.

Avatāra (ESD.121):

The thought and thought-concomitants which are mutually conjoined with one another and which apprehend a common object, are named conjoined causes—e.g., thought with sensation, etc.; sensation, etc., with [ideation], etc., sensations, etc., with thought; in each case [the mental *dharma*] cannot be [a conjoined cause] for itself.

2. As for the relationship between associated causes and co-existent causes, all associated causes are necessarily co-existent causes, but not all co-existent causes are necessarily associated causes. Or, all associated causes necessarily have the five equivalences (*samatā*; ii. 34d), but not all co-existent causes have them. For example, the fundamental material elements (*bhūta*) and the characteristics (*lakṣaṇa*), i.e., origination, etc., do not have the five equivalences and are not associated causes.

3. As for the difference between associated causes and co-existent causes—when a factor is both of these causes—see Vasubandhu's discussion and the quotes in our endnote to it.

888 *LS*: SAH 56, 75.

889 *LVP*: *Sama* can be understood as *tulya* (similar, comparable, like); this is why the author specifies.

890 *LS*: SAH 75.

891 *LVP*: MVŚ, 81b9, indicates six opinions on this point.

LS: MVŚ, 88b (SA.IV.156):

Question: What is the difference between the conjoined and the co-existent causes? Some say that there is no difference, as in one [and the same] moment, the sensation and ideation, etc., are both types of causes. Therefore, in this regard, one should say thus: Whichever are conjoined causes are also co-existent causes; some co-existent causes exist which are not conjoined causes, viz., the disjoined co-existent causes. Thus there are differences between the two causes… .

[Their differences]: conjoined causes have the sense of companionship; co-existent causes have the sense of having a common fruit.

The first means having the same supporting basis, mode of understanding and object.

The second means having the same production (*jāti*), deterioration (*jarā*), duration (*sthiti*), impermanence (*anityatā*), fruit, emanation and retribution.

The first is like holding a stick; the second is like performing an action having held the stick.

The first is like [a group of people] joining hands together; the second is like crossing a torrent having held hands together.

The first means mutually accordant with one another; the second means not being mutually apart.

**Nyāyānusāra*, 425c (SA.IV.157):

What is the difference between these two causes, i.e., the co-existent and the conjoined? To begin with, *dharma*-s that are conjoined causes are also co-existent causes. There exist *dharma*-s that are co-existent causes but not conjoined causes—viz., the [thought-]accompanying matter; *jāti*, etc.; the Great Elements. If a conjoined cause is also a co-existent cause, what, in this case, is the difference in significance between these two causes? It is not the case that the conjoined causes are none other than the co-existent causes, for these two causes differ in their significance. However, in the case where one and the same *dharma* is a conjoined cause as well as a co-existent cause, this is the difference in significance: conjoined causes signify "not mutually apart"; co-existent causes signify "having the same fruit".

Again, having the same production (*jāti*), duration (*sthiti*), etc., by virtue of the mutual strength—these are co-existent causes; grasping the same object by virtue of the mutual strength—these are conjoined causes.

According to some masters: On account of the meaning of being reciprocally fruits, the co-existent causes are established; this is like the case of fellow merchants who, mutually supported, traverse a risky road together. On account of the meaning of the fivefold equality, the conjoined cause is established; this is like those same fellow merchants having the same experience, same activities of eating, etc. Herein, they are not conjoined even when one is missing, and thus is the fact of their being reciprocally causes universally established

892 *LVP*: *yathā teṣām … samānnapānas*nānaśayanādi*paribhogakriyāyāṃ* prayogaḥ. tadvat samaprayogatvam eṣām anyonyaṃ bhavati | ata evāha | *ekenāpi hi vinā na sarve saṃprayujyante* [cf. WOG.209.26ff.].

893 *LS*: AH 25; SAH 74.

894 *LS*: Ibid.

895 *Gokhale*: [54ab] *sarvatragākhyaḥ kliṣṭānāṃ svabhūmau pūrvasarvagāḥ* |

Tib.: [54ab] *kun 'gro zhes bya nyon mongs can* | *rnams kyi rang sa kun 'gro snga* |

LS: 1. MVŚ, 80a (ESD.198):

What is *sarvatraga-hetu*? It is all the past and present *sarvatraga anuśaya*-s and their conjoined and co-existent *dharma*-s.

Avatāra (ESD.121):

The universal *dharma*-s (*sarvatraga-dharma*) born anteriorily, in a given stage, are the universal causes to the posterior, defiled *dharma*-s belonging to the same stage.

2. As for the scope of the pervasive cause, MVŚ, 90c, first presents various differing views but then specifies for the Dārṣṭāntikas, Vibhajyavādins and Vaibhāṣikas the following views (SA.IV.152f; cf. Ny, 416c):

> The Dārṣṭāntikas hold that the two defilements, i.e., ignorance (*avidyā*) and craving (*tṛṣṇā*), are universal. Their explanation is as follows: "The root of conditioned co-arising is said to be universal; ignorance is the root of the earlier part (*pūrvānta-koṭi*) of conditioned co-arising, and existence-craving (*bhava-tṛṣṇā*) is the root of the later part (*aparānta-koṭi*) of conditioned co-arising. Thus, they are universal."
>
> The Vibhajyavādins hold that five are universal: ignorance, craving, view, conceit and thought (*citta*).
>
> The Vaibhāṣika view is that three are universal: doubt (*vicikitsā*), view and ignorance, which are abandonable by vision into unsatisfactoriness, the cause of unsatisfactoriness, together with their conjoined and co-existent *dharma*-s.

AKB v. 12, states eleven pervasive proclivities: "(1–5) the five afflicted views (*dṛṣṭi*) that are abandoned by insight [into the truth] of unsatisfactoriness; (6–7) the false view (*mithyādṛṣṭi*) and the esteeming of (such things as bad) views (*dṛṣṭiparāmarśa*), abandoned by insight [into the truth] of the origin; (8–11) two doubts (*vicikitsā*) and two ignorances (*avidyā*) abandoned by insight [into the truth] of unsatisfactoriness, by insight [into the truth] of the origin".

3. As for the relationship with the homogeneous cause (*sabhāgahetu*), Dhammajoti comments (SA.IV.152): "Like the homogeneous cause, this cause as well generates an emanation fruit. From this perspective, the universal cause may be considered to be a subset of the homogeneous causes, pertaining to the defiled *dharma*-s alone. There is homogeneity between this cause and its effect in terms of stage (sense sphere, etc.) and of moral species (both are defiled). However, ... it is to be made a cause distinct from the homogeneous cause because there is no necessary homogeneity in terms of category of abandonability (*nikāya/prakāra*)." Saṃghabhadra adds (Ny, 426a) that the power of pervasive causes exceeds that of homogeneous causes since the former are able to effect factors of a category of abandonment different from their own.

[896] *LS*: SAH 74.

[897] *LS*: Pradhan.89.4f. has *kliṣṭadharmasāmanyakāraṇatvenāyaṃ*.

[898] *LVP*: (1) From the pervasives susceptible of being abandoned by insight into unsatisfactoriness proceed defilements susceptible of being abandoned by insight into the origin, of cessation and of the path, and by cultivation. (2) From the pervasives susceptible of being abandoned by insight into the origin proceed defilements susceptible of being abandoned by insight into unsatisfactoriness, of cessation and of the path, and by cultivation.

[899] *LVP*: They are called *pervasives* (*sarvaga*) because they go toward (*gacchanti*), "occupy" (*bhajante*), have for their object (*ālambante*) all [five] categories of defilements; or because they are a cause (*hetubhāvaṃ gacchanti*) of all [five] categories of defilements.

[900] *LS*: To the objection: "The afflictions of *ārya* persons are not generated from that cause because having abandoned those which are omnipresent, they do not exist", Jaimpaiyang answers: "The Vaibhāṣikas assert those are generated from the past. Thus the *Prakaraṇa*

states: ..."

901 *LVP*: See above ii, F 251.

902 *LVP*: As the text has: "the defiled factors", without specifying otherwise, this refers to defiled factors of ordinary worldlings (*pṛthagjana*) and of noble ones (*ārya*).

903 *LVP*: This refers to the non-defined conditioned phenomena (*saṃskṛta*), obscured-non-defined (*nivṛtāvyākṛta*) or unobscured-non-defined (*anivṛtāvyākṛta*), not to the two non-defined unconditioned phenomena (*asaṃskṛta*), space and cessation not due to deliberation (*apratisaṃkhyānirodha*).

904 *LVP*: The word "future" is absent in Paramārtha, and without doubt also in the original. See above ii, F 252.

905 *LVP*: According to the *Vyākhyā* [WOG.211.2ff.], the text has: *idaṃ tarhi prajñapti-bhāṣyam...* . – Hsüan-tsang translates very well: "How should one explain the *Prajñapti-pādaśāstra*?" since "this commentary (*bhāṣya*) of the *Prajñapti*" signifies "this explanation that one reads in the *Prajñapti*". – See the Tibetan version of the *Karmaprajñapti*, chap. ix. (*Mdo*. 63, fol. 229b–236a): "§ 1. Does a past intention exist that arises from a past cause, not from a future cause, not from a present cause? ... § 2. Do wholesome factors (*dharma*) exist that arise from wholesome causes? ... Do non-defined factors exist that arise from unwholesome causes? Yes: (1) the factors that are the retribution of unwholesome action; (2) the factors of the realm of desire associated with the afflicted view of self and with the afflicted view of holding to an extreme. § 3. Do wholesome factors exist that arise only from wholesome causes? Yes: the intention associated with the members of enlightenment... . Do unwholesome factors exist that arise only from unwholesome causes? ..."

We know from J. Takakusu (*JPTS* 1905, p. 77) that the *Karmaprajñapti* no longer exists in Chinese. The *Nanjio* 1317 contains the *Kāraṇaprajñapti*; the *Nanjio* 1297 contains a treatise analogous to the *Lokaprajñapti*: a summary of these two Prajñaptis may be found in *Cosmologie bouddhique*, pp. 295–350 (see *Electronic Appendix*).

906 *LVP*: *syāt | āryapudgalaḥ kāmavairāgyāt parihīyamāṇo yāṃ tatprathamataḥ kliṣṭāṃ cetanāṃ saṃmukhīkaroti*. – "At the moment when one retrogresses from detachment, the unwholesome intention of the noble ones (*ārya*) has only the unwholesome factors for its cause, the causes in the quality of the co-existent cause (*sahabhūhetu*) and of associated cause (*saṃprayuktakahetu*); the unwholesome intention does not have non-defined factors for its cause since the noble ones have abandoned the afflicted view of self and the afflicted view of holding on to an extreme" [cf. WOG.211.4ff.]: such is the interpretation of the objector.

907 *LS*: AH 25; SAH 76.

908 *LS*: Ibid.

909 *Gokhale*: [54cd] *vipākahetur aśubhāḥ kuśalāś c aiva sāsravāḥ* ||

Tib.: [54cd] *rnam smin rgyu ni mi dge dang | dge ba zag bcas rnams kho na* ||

LVP: Self-power (*svaśakti*) is absent in non-defined factors; the co-factor (*sahakārikāraṇa*) is absent in pure factors. – See iii. 36b.

LS: 1. *Avatāra* (ESD.122):

All unwholesome *dharma*-s and the wholesome *dharma*-s which are with-outflow are the retributive causes for their retribution.

2. As for the views of the different schools and the scope of the ripening cause, Dhammajoti explains (SA.IV.153):

> According to the Dārṣṭāntikas in the MVŚ, "there is no retribution cause apart from volition (*cetanā*), and no retribution fruit apart from sensation (*vedanā*)".
>
> According to others, such as the Mahāsāṃghikas, retribution causes and fruits are confined to thought and the thought-concomitants.
>
> Against these opinions, the Sarvāstivāda holds that retribution causes and fruits comprise all five *skandha*-s, that is, not only thought and the thought-concomitants but also the matter accompanying thought (*cittānuvartaka-rūpa*) and the conditionings disjoined from thought—the ideationless attainment (*asaṃjñī-samāpatti*), the cessation attainment (*nirodha-samāpatti*), all acquisitions which are *akuśala* and *kuśala-sāsrava*, and the accompanying characteristics of the conditioned (*saṃskṛta-lakṣaṇa*-s)—can constitute retribution causes [MVŚ, 96a–c]. The retributive *rūpa*-s are the bodily and vocal *karma*—both informative (*vijñapti*) and non-informative (*avijñapti*). The ideationless attainment can effect the *asaṃjñika*, that is, it can result in an existence in the ideationless realm. However, the vital faculty (*jīvitendriya*), the group-homogeneity (*nikāya-sabhāga*) and the five material faculties pertaining therein are not its retributions, but those of the *karma* in the fourth *dhyāna*. Similarly, the cessation attainment can effect the four *skandha*-s of the sphere of neither ideation-nor-non-ideation (*naiva-saṃjñā-nāsaṃjñā-āyatana*)—excepting the vital faculty and the group-homogeneity therein which are exclusively karmic fruits—as its retributions [cf. MVŚ, 15a–b]. Acquisition can effect the following as retributions: (a) matter—visual objects, sound, smell, taste; (b) thought and thought-concomitants—the three types of sensation (pleasant, unpleasant, neutral; (c) conditionings disjoined from thought—acquisition and the four characteristics of the conditioned [MVŚ, 97a, 263c].

For Śrīlāta's view of karmic retribution, see Dhammajoti's article *Śrīlāta's anudhātu doctrine.*

3. As for the relationship of the ripening cause and action according to the Vaibhāṣikas, we could formulate the following tetralemma:

i. there are factors that are only action but not a ripening cause, for example, non-defined actions;
ii. there are factors that are only a ripening cause but not action, for example, sensation associated with a wholesome intention;
iii. there are factors that are both a ripening cause and action, for example, wholesome intention (*cetanā*) or wholesome bodily and vocal action;
iv. there are factors that are neither, for example, space (*ākāśa*) or sensation associated with a non-defined intention.

4. As for further references regarding *vipākahetu* in the AKB, see in particular its entire chapter 4: *Karmanirdeśa.*

910 *LS*: The *Vyākhyā* states (WOG.211.14f.) that wholesome factors are of two modes, i.e., impure and pure: kuśalās tu dvi-prakāraḥ s'āsravā anāsravāś ceti.

911 *LVP*: *Mahāvyutpatti*, 245, 181; *Siddhi*, 488.

912 *LS*: Saṃghabhadra comments (Ny, 427b; SA.IV.154): "[*Vipāka*] may refer to the fact that the *karma* that has been done, on reaching the stage of the acquisition of the fruit, can be transformed into being capable of maturing—this [explanation] pertains to the cause [aspect of the process]."

913 *LVP*: Hsüan-tsang places some remarks here that are absent in Paramārtha:

According to the Vaibhāṣikas, the prefix *vi* indicates difference: *vipāka* signifies "a dissimilar (*visadṛśa*) effect (*pāka*)" (*Mahāvyutpatti*, 245, 182). That is to say:

1. the ripening cause (*vipākahetu*) alone gives forth only a *pāka* (effect) that is not similar to itself;
2. the co-existing (*sahabhū*), associated (*saṃprayuktaka*), homogeneous (*sabhāga*) and pervasive (*sarvatraga*) causes (*hetu*) give forth only an effect similar (*sadṛśaḥ pakāḥ*) to themselves (wholesome, unwholesome, non-defined);
3. the efficient cause (*kāraṇahetu*) gives forth a similar or dissimilar effect.

It is only the ripening cause (*vipākahetu*) that always gives forth a dissimilar effect: for the ripening cause is never non-defined and its effect is always non-defined.

[According to the Sautrāntikas,] an effect receives the name of *vipāka* under two conditions:

1. it should be produced by the last state or culminating point [i.e., distinctive characteristic] of the transformation of a stream (*saṃtānapariṇāmaviśeṣa*; see above ii, F 185);
2. it should abide more or less long [i.e., only for a limited time], because of the more or less great strength of the cause.

But the effects issued from the two causes, i.e., the co-existent cause (*sahabhūhetu*) and associated cause (*saṃprayuktakahetu*), do not show the first characteristic, for these causes project and realize their effect at the same time (ii. 59); and the effects that have issued from the three causes, i.e., efficient (*kāraṇa*), homogeneous (*sabhāga*), and pervasive (*sarvatraga*), do not show the second characteristic, for there is no limit to the repeated arising (*punaḥ punaḥ*) of these effects during the length of their cyclic existence. – Therefore the sole explanation of *vipāka* is the following: "transformation (*vipariṇāma* ?) and maturation".

LS: Pradhan has (89.26–90.4): *atha vipāka iti ko 'rthaḥ | visadṛśaḥ pāko vipākaḥ | anyeṣāṃ tu hetunāṃ sadṛśaḥ pākaḥ | ekasyobhayatheti vaibhāṣikāḥ | naiva tu teṣāṃ pāko yuktaḥ | pāko hi nāma santatipariṇāmaviśeṣajaḥ phalaparyantaḥ | na ca sahābhūsaṃprayuktahetvoḥ santatipariṇāṃaviśeṣajaṃ phalamasti | na cāpi sabhāgahetvādīnāṃ phalaparyanto 'sti | punaḥ punaḥ kuśalādyāsaṃsāraphalatvāt |*

This is the 36th of Kritzer's forty-four passages discussed in relation to chapter 2 (VY.110).

> In a discussion of the meaning of *vipākahetu*, Vasubandhu criticizes the Vaibhāṣika understanding, which, according to him, states that any cause that produces a result that is necessarily morally different from it (i.e., a good or bad cause that produces a neutral result) is *vipākahetu*. He says that this implies that the other causes give result, albeit result that is not necessarily morally different. But Vasubandhu insists that *vipāka* must be produced by *saṃtatipariṇāmaviśeṣa* and it must be 'result-bound', which Hsüan-tsang explains as limited in duration according to the strength or weakness of the cause. [...]

Saṃghabhadra [Ny, 427b18–22] identifies this as the opinion of the *sūtra*-master and criticizes [Ny, 427b22–24] Vasubandhu's representation of the Vaibhāṣika position, saying that the Vaibhāṣikas do not say that everything resulting from the six causes is *pāka*; even if they did, *pāka* would not be a synonym for *phala*, and it would not imply *vipāka*.

914 *LS*: SAH 76.

915 *LS*: Ibid.

916 *LVP*: asti karma yasyaikam eva dharmāyatanaṃ vipāko vipacyate [WOG.213.33]. – MVŚ, 97c7. (Hsüan-tsang: "the action that produces the vitality faculty, etc." By *et cetera*, one should understand either the group homogeneity (*nikāyasabhāga*) or the characteristics.)

Ācārya Vasumitra does not accept this proposition. Vitality faculty or vitality (*jīvitendriya*) is the effect of an action that projects an existence (*ākṣepakakarman*; iv. 95). (1) If retribution, which constitutes this faculty, matures (*vipacyate*) in the realm of desire, one necessarily has the body sense-faculty (*kāya-indriya*) and the vitality faculty (*jīvita-indriya*) in the first stages of embryonic life; in the last stages five other faculties (*indriya*) are added. (2) If the vitality faculty matures in the realm of fine-materiality, one has seven sense-spheres (*āyatana*); (3) in the realm of immateriality, one has the sense-sphere of the mental faculty (*mana-āyatana*) and sense-sphere of factors (*dharmāyatana*). – Yaśomitra discusses these comments and cites Saṃghabhadra [WOG.213.33ff.]. The proposition combated by Vasumitra refers to the realm of immateriality: at a certain moment, in order to be born in this realm, there is no thought (*mana-āyatana*) that is retribution.

917 *LVP*: Never twelve, for the sense-sphere of sound (*śabdāyatana*) is never retribution (i. 37bc).

918 *LS*: Yaśomitra glosses (WOG.215.9ff.): *padma-dāḍima-nyagrodh'ādīnāṃ* bījāni *vicitra-phalāni*. mūlāṃkura-nāla-pattra-keśarā-kiṃjalka-karṇikāraiś ca rūpyaṃ hi padma-bīj'ādīnaṃ. aneka-skaṃdha-śākhā-viṭapa-pattra-pallavāṃkura-puṣpa-phala-samṛddhāś ca nyagrodh'ādayaḥ pādapā jala-dharāyamāṇa dṛśyaṃte. kānicid *avicitra-phalāni. tad-yathā yava godhūm'ādīnāṃ* bījāni. eka-rūpa-phalatvāt. bīja-dharmataiṣā.

919 *LS*: SAH 76.

920 *LVP*: The retribution of a former action can have begun in the present moment, can continue in the present moment, can prolong itself in the future.

921 *LVP*: The Japanese editor gives the heroic career of the Bodhisattva as an example of a prolonged action.

922 *LVP*: *na ca karmaṇā saha vipāko vipacyate* [WOG.215.17].

923 *LS*: SAH 78.

924 *Gokhale*: [55ab] *sarvatragaḥ sabhāgaś ca dvyadhvagau tryadhvagās trayaḥ* |

Tib.: [55ab] *kun 'gro skal mnyam dus gnyis pa* | *gsum po dag ni dus gsum pa* |

LVP: Compare ii. 59.

925 *LS*: AH 226–27; SAH 73, 77–78, 153–55, 460–62, 478, 480.

Explanatory endnotes to each of the five effects will be given mainly in section CBB: "The defining characteristics of the five effects", F 289.

See also Vasubandhu's discussion as to how many of the five effects the various actions have (iv. 87–94).

926 *LS*: SAH 78, 153–55, 478.

927 *Gokhale*: [55cd] *saṃskṛtaṃ savisaṃyogaṃ phalaṃ*

Tib.: [55c] *'dus byas bral bcas 'bras bu yin* |

LVP: Disconnection (*visaṃyoga*), i.e., the effect of disconnection (*visaṃyogaphala*; ii. 57d, vi. 46), is the cessation due to deliberation (*pratisaṃkhyānirodha*) or Nirvāṇa (i. 6), one of the unconditioned factors (*asaṃskṛta*). It does "not have" a cause, and it does "not have" an effect; but it "is" a cause (*kāraṇahetu*; ii. 50a) and it "is" an effect (*visaṃyogaphala*; ii. 57d).

928 *LVP*: *Jñānaprasthāna*, 5, 4; *Prakaraṇa*, 716b9; which we can reconstruct: *phaladharmāḥ katame | sarve saṃskṛtāḥ pratisaṃkhyānirodhaś ca | na phaladharmāḥ katame | ākāśam apratisaṃkhyānirodhaḥ | saphaladharmāḥ katame | sarve saṃskṛtāḥ | aphaladharmāḥ katame | sarve 'saṃskṛtāḥ*: "What factors are an effect? All conditioned factors and cessation due to deliberation. What factors are not an effect? Space and cessation not due to deliberation. What factors have an effect? All conditioned factors. What factors do not have an effect? All unconditioned factors."

LS: The *Vyākhyā* has [WOG.216.22f.]: ākāśāpratisaṃkhyā-nirodha-varjyāḥ sarva-dharmāḥ phalam ity uktam bhavati.

929 *LS*: In regard to why disconnection does not have a cause, Saṃghabhadra answers (Ny, 429a; EIP.VIII.708f.) that disconnection is not an effect that is "produced", but rather an effect that is "attained" through the noble path that acts as homogeneous or co-existent cause for the "production" of the "possession" of this disconnection and is thus the cause of attaining this disconnection. But it is "disconnection" that is the end of the noble path and not "possession".

In regard to why disconnection does not have an effect, he answers (Ny, 429a; EIP.VIII.709) that unconditioned *dharmas* act as efficient causes (*kāraṇahetu*), however, not in the sense of "producing", but only in the sense of "non-obstructing". Future *dharmas* and unconditioned *dharmas* do not "have" an effect because they do not, like the present and past conditioned *dharmas*, have the capability of (1) taking or (2) giving forth their effects (see AKB ii. 59). Further, in the case where the unconditioned *dharmas* serve as the cognitive object of mental consciousness, they are not a productive cause.

930 *Gokhale*: [55d2] *nā 'saṃskṛtasya te* ||

Tib.: [55d] *'dus ma byas la de dag med* ||

LVP: *Milinda*, 268–71.

931 *LS*: SAH 154.

932 *LS*: Dhammajoti summarizes his discussion of cessation due to deliberation (*pratisaṃkhyānirodha*) as follows (SA.IV.484f.):

> In the Sarvāstivāda perspective, there are as many *nirvāṇa*-s or *pratisaṃkhyā-nirodha*-s as there are with-outflow *dharma*-s. These are ontologically distinct real entities. Their reality is not even dependent on the criterion of causal efficacy in the space-time dimension but on the fact that they can impact on the mental streams of

beings. Each *nirvāṇa*—via *prāpti*—acts to ensure the absolute non-arising of the defilement counteracted by the *ārya-mārga* by virtue of which the *prāpti* of the *nirvāṇa* is induced, and each is experiencible by the *ārya* as having distinct characteristics.

Nirvāṇa in the sense of the ultimate spiritual realization of the Buddhist practitioner refers to the *pratisaṃkhyā-nirodha* realized when all the *kleśa*-s and *duḥkha*-s pertaining to the three periods of time are completely abandoned (Ny, 430b). Although all practitioners acquire the same *nirvāṇa* corresponding to a given impure *dharma*, each individual's experience of *nirvāṇa* is unique by virtue of the *prāpti* that links the *nirvāṇa* to him. Acquisition (*prāpti*)—although conditioned in itself but neither mental nor material in nature—in fact plays the important role of relating the unconditioned to the conditioned. It is the *sine qua non* for man's experience of *nirvāṇa*.

933 *LVP*: The unhindered path (*ānantaryamārga*) cuts off defilement and is followed by the path of liberation (*vimuktimārga*), "the path in which defilement is already cut off", in which the practitioners take possession (*prāpti*) of disconnection, vi. 28.

934 *LVP*: Certain masters maintain that there are five types of causes:

1. *kāraka*, efficacious cause, the seed for the bud;
2. *jñāpaka*, indicating cause, smoke for fire;
3. *vyañjaka*, revealing cause, the lamp for the pot;
4. *dhvaṃsaka*, destructive cause, the hammer for the pot;
5. *prāpaka*, leading cause, chariot for a place.

On this point see *Vibhāṣā*, 16, p. 79, 2: The *Ekottara* enumerated the factors of 1 to 100; it stops now at 10; and, within 1–10, much is lost, little remains. At the *nirvāṇa* of Ānanda, 77,000 Avadānas and Sūtras, 10,000 Śāstras were lost… .

935 *LVP*: (Paramārtha differs noticeably).

Reply by the Sautrāntika: – The Sūtra speaks only of that which produces; thus the unconditioned [although non-impermanent] can be a cognitive object condition (*ālambanapratyaya*). In fact, it only says that the causal conditions (*hetupratyaya*) that produce the consciousness are impermanent; it does not say that all conditions (*pratyaya*) of the consciousness are impermanent.

Reply by the Sarvāstivādin: – Does the Sūtra not say that only the *hetu* producer is impermanent? Thus it does not deny that the unconditioned—and this by the simple fact that it does not constitute an obstacle—is the efficient cause (*kāraṇahetu*).

Reply by the Sautrāntika: – The Sūtra says that the unconditioned is a cognitive object condition; and it does not say that it is an efficient cause (*kāraṇahetu*); thus one should not define it as "cause not constituting an obstacle".

LS: This is the fourth place in Pradhan (91.15), where the term Sautrāntika is explicitly mentioned.

936 *LVP*: *ye hetavo ye pratyayā rūpasya … vijñānasyotpādāya te py anityāḥ* (*Saṃyukta*, 1, 5).

937 *LS*: Although not explicitly mentioned in Pradhan, LVP mentions the Sautrāntika here.

938 *LVP*: *sūtrāṇi ca bahūny antarhitāni* mūlasaṃgītibhraṃśāt [WOG.218.29f.].

939 *LS*: Although not explicitly mentioned in Pradhan, LVP mentions the Sautrāntika here.

940 *LS*: This is the fifth place in Pradhan (92.4), where the term Sautrāntika is explicitly mentioned.

This is the 37th of Kritzer's forty-four passages discussed in relation to chapter 2 (VY.114). Saṃghabhadra (Ny, 429a21–23) identifies this as the opinion of Vasubandhu and attempts to refute it (Ny, 429a20–21).

The denial of the *asaṃskṛtas* is already attributed to the Dārṣṭāntikas in MVŚ, 198a.

941 *LVP*: We may think that, in the pages that follow, Vasubandhu does not do full justice to the arguments of the Sarvāstivādin-Vaibhāṣika; he does not point out the texts, for example, *Udāna*, viii. 3 (*Itivuttaka*, 43, *Udānavarga*, xxvi. 21), which at least render the reality of Nirvāṇa probable. – Saṃghabhadra refutes Vasubandhu and the other masters who deny the unconditioned factors (*Nyāyānusāra*, 431b17–c2). His exposition is too long to be included here: we have provided the translation of it, at least partially, in *Documents d'Abhidharma: Textes relatifs au nirvāṇa et aux asaṃskṛtas en général* (1930) (see *Electronic Appendix*).

942 *LS*: 1. This is the 38th of Kritzer's forty-four passages discussed in relation to chapter 2 (VY.116f.). Saṃghabhadra identifies (Ny, 429a23–25) this as the opinion of Vasubandhu. Cox summarizes Saṃghabhadra (Ny, 429a27–430a7; EIP.VIII.709): "Space exists as a distinct actual entity that acts to support wind and is manifested by light. The existence of space can be inferred from these activities. Its characteristic is the nonobstruction of others, and nonobstruction by others. Further, precisely because space can serve as the supporting object in the production of the concept 'space', it can be said to exist as an actual entity. Cognition is not produced without an existent supporting object."

2. As for space, see AKB i. 5d and our endnote to it. See in particular Dhammajoti's discussion of space at SA.IV.491–96, where he also summarizes his discussion as follows:

> Not all the canonical Abhidharma treatises mention Space as an unconditioned *dharma*. [It is noteworthy that even in the *Jñānaprasthāna-śāstra* ... only the two *nirodha*-s are mentioned, but not *ākāśa*]. In the MVŚ, too, some of the Sarvāstivādin masters, like Dharmatrāta, do not accept Space as a real existent. The orthodox Sarvāstivādins, however, consistently maintain that it is a real existent, and not the mere absence of tangibles. Starting from the MVŚ, we see various arguments for and against the position that it is a real entity. A clear distinction is made in this text between the unconditioned Space on the one hand, and the conditioned space element, on the other. Vasumitra and other Ābhidharmas in the MVŚ argue that the reality of Space can not only be inferred, but actually is directly perceived since the events observed in our experience necessarily have a real causal basis—when we perceive that material things can be accommodated or that people can move about, we are actually directly perceiving a distinctive function of Space; and this distinctive function necessarily proves the existence of a distinct existent. Although Saṃghabhadra does not go so far as to assert that Space is actually directly perceived, he too argues that we can infer its reality from its observable distinctive function and characteristic (*lakṣaṇa*); and that which possesses a unique function and a unique characteristic is a uniquely real: Its function is manifested through the fact that it accommodates resistant things; its characteristic—i.e., its

observable aspect—is manifested through light. To further distinguish it as a unique existent from the space element, Saṃghabhadra articulates that whereas the space element is non-obstructive but is obstructed, Space is neither obstructive nor obstructed by other things.

943 *LVP*: *utpannānuśayajanmanirodhe pratisaṃkhyābalenānyasyā*nuśayasya janmanaś ca *anutpādaḥ pratisaṃkhyā-nirodhaḥ* [cf. WOG219.3ff.].

1. Cessation of the proclivity (*anuśaya*) is the cessation of the origin of unsatisfactoriness (*samudayasatyanirodha*, cessation of that which, in truth, is the origin of unsatisfactoriness), is *nirvāṇa* with remainder (*sopadhiśeṣanirvāṇa*).

Cessation of arising or existence (*janman*) is the cessation of unsatisfactoriness (*duḥkhasatyanirodha*, cessation of that which, in truth, is unsatisfactoriness), is *nirvāṇa* without remainder (*nirupadhiśeṣanirvāṇa*).

2. By proclivity (*anuśaya*) one should understand the traces (*vāsanā*) of the ninety-eight proclivities described in chapter 5.

LS: 1. This is the 39th of Kritzer's forty-four passages discussed in relation to chapter 2 (VY.118f.). Saṃghabhadra identifies (Ny, 429a25–26) this as the opinion of Vasubandhu. Cox summarizes Saṃghabhadra (Ny, 430a18–434b6; EIP.VIII.709): "[Cessation due to deliberation] does exist as an actual entity constituting the abandonment of all defilements of a particular category in all three time periods. Through the practice of the noble path, one first severs one's possession of a particular category of defilements; then one acquires possession of the cessation, or disconnection from this category of defilements. Therefore, one acquires possession of this cessation for each particular category of defilements that are to be abandoned."

2. As for *pratisaṃkhyānirodha*, see AKB i. 6ab and our endnote to it. See also in particular Dhammajoti's discussion of *pratisaṃkhyānirodha* at SA.IV.474–85 and the summary of his discussion of *pratisaṃkhyānirodha* (SA.IV.484f.) in our endnote to ii. 55d [F 276].

944 *LS*: 1. This is the 40th of Kritzer's forty-four passages discussed in relation to chapter 2 (VY.120f.). Saṃghabhadra identifies (Ny, 429a25–26) this as the opinion of Vasubandhu. Cox summarizes Saṃghabhadra (Ny, 430a18–434b6; EIP.VIII.710): "A mere absence is not capable of preventing the arising of a factor. Rather, cessation [not due to deliberation] must be a distinct factor attained due to a deficiency of conditions, which then itself prevents a factor from ever arising."

2. As for *apratisaṃkhyānirodha*, see AKB i. 6cd and our endnote to it. See also in particular Dhammajoti's discussion of *apratisaṃkhyānirodha* at SA.IV.485–91, where he also summarizes his discussion as follows:

> Little more than the mere mention of this cessation is found in the earlier canonical texts. Starting from the *Jñānaprasthāna*, however, we begin to find doctrinal articulations on it. This text, besides offering a definition of the cessation independent of deliberation, also distinguishes between with-outflow and outflow-free cessations independent of deliberation. In the MVŚ, [we find an] elaborate analysis—utilizing the Abhidharmic doctrinal perspectives—of its nature in comparison to those of the cessation through deliberation and the cessation of impermanence.

Moreover, already in the *Jñānaprasthāna*, we see the implication that such cessations do not exclusively pertain to mundane human experiences wherein the cognitions of certain objects are commonly missed out in the absence of the required conditions. The specific separation of such experiences from the type which are described in the *Jñānaprasthāna* as cessations of "the *dharma*-s of unsatisfactoriness in the temporal process", and specified as those of outflow-free *dharma*-s, suggests that this type of cessation can be of spiritual significance as well. This point becomes more explicit in the MVŚ which distinctly discusses the type of cessations independent of deliberation occurring every moment, of objects not cognizable by us, and also the type effecting the non-arising of the unfortunate planes of existence as a result of spiritual praxis like giving, ethical observances, etc.

Finally, whereas in the earlier canonical texts, this cessation is explained simply as being the result of the deficiency in conditions; since the MVŚ, it has been further asserted that the cessation independent of deliberation is itself a necessary contributory factor: It is a positive force—a real existent—which helps to bring about the non-arising of the object concerned. This aspect is articulately expounded by Saṃghabhadra.

945 *LVP*: The Sthaviras, according to the Japanese editor.

946 *LVP*: *anuśayapratyayavaikalyāt paścād duḥkhājātiḥ | na prajñābalat.*

947 *LS*: Although not explicitly mentioned in Pradhan, LVP mentions the Sautrāntika here.

948 *LVP*: According to the Japanese editor, the Mahāsāṃghikas.

949 *LVP*: *svarasanirodhāt*, not through the force of understanding (*prajñā*), as is the case for cessation due to deliberation (*pratisaṃkhyānirodha*).

950 *LS*: The last sentence is an addition from LVP's *Additions et Corrections*, F 145.

951 *LS*: Although not explicitly mentioned in Pradhan, LVP mentions the Sautrāntika here.

952 *LVP*: *atītānāgatapratyutpannasya duḥkhasya prahāṇāya saṃvartate* [WOG.219.29f.]. – Compare *Kathāvatthu*, xix. 1.

953 *LS*: Although not explicitly mentioned in Pradhan, LVP mentions the Sautrāntika here.

954 *LVP*: That is to say, *chanda* (predilection for future factors: *anāgate prārthanā*) and *rāga* (attachment to what one possesses: *prāpte 'rthe 'dhyavasānam*).

955 *LVP*: *yo rūpe chandarāgas taṃ prajahīta | chandarāge prahīṇe evaṃ vas tad rūpaṃ prahīṇaṃ bhaviṣyati* [cf. WOG.219f.].

Abandonment (*prahāṇa*) of material form (*rūpa*) is to be understood as unhindered path (*ānantaryamārga*); complete knowledge (*parijñā*) is to be understood as path of liberation (*vimuktimārga*; vi. 30). (Gloss by the Japanese editor).

Compare, for its doctrine, *Saṃyutta*, iii. 8.

956 *LVP*: Paramārtha, 5, p. 192a.

957 *LVP*: *Saṃyukta*, 31, 12: *ye kecid bhikṣavo dharmāḥ saṃskṛtā vā asaṃskṛtā vā virāgas teṣām agra ākhyāyate* (cited in *Vyākhyā*, iv, 127); *Aṅguttara*, ii. 34; *Itivuttaka*, § 90; *yāvatā Cundi dhammā saṅkhatā vā asaṅkhatā vā virāgo tesaṃ aggam akkhāyati.*

Detachment (*virāga*) = exhaustion of attachment (*rāgakṣaya*), cessation due to deliberation (*pratisaṃkhyānirodha*), *nirvāṇa*. – Nirvāṇa is better than cessation not due to deliberation (*apratisaṃkhyānirodha*) and space (iv. 127d).

958 *LS*: Although not explicitly mentioned in Pradhan, LVP mentions the Sautrāntika here.

959 *LVP*: We can reconstruct: *abhāvo bhavatīti na sidhyati*. – Hsüan-tsang differs: One cannot say of non-existence that it exists. The value of the verb "to be" is thus established (i.e., this verb does not signify "to exist"). It is in this way that Scripture says there are unconditioned factors.

960 *LVP*: *vastuno* (= *rāgādivastuno*) [*nirodhasya ca*] *hetuphalādibhāvāsaṃbhavāt* [WOG.221.7f.].

961 *LVP*: *Bhāṣya*: *tasya tarhi prāptiniyame* [*ko hetuḥ*]. – *Vyākhyā* [WOG.221.10ff.]: tasya nirodhasya yo 'yaṃ prāpter niyamaḥ | asyaiva nirodhasya prāptir nānyasyeti || tasmiṃ prāptiniyame *ko hetuḥ* || na hi nirodhasya prāptyā sārdhaṃ kaścit saṃbandho 'sti hetuphalādibhāvāsaṃbhavāt.

962 *LVP*: *dṛṣṭadharmanirvāṇaprāpta* [WOG.221.12f.], that is to say, "who is in Nirvāṇa with remainder" (*sopadhiśeṣanirvāṇastha*).

963 *LS*: Although not explicitly mentioned in Pradhan, LVP mentions the Sautrāntika here.

964 *LVP*: *sdug bsngal 'di ma lus par spangs pa 'byang bar 'gyur ba* (*M. Vyut.* 245, 1259) *zad pad 'dod chags dang bral ba 'gog pa rnam par zhi ba* (1260) *nub pa* (70, 4) *sdug bsngal gzhan dang nying mtshams sbyor ba med pa len pa med pa 'byung ba med pa gang yin pa 'di lta ste* | *phung po thams cad nges par spangs pa* (245, 1258) *sred pa zad pa* | *'dod chags dang 'bral ba* | *'gog pa dang mya ngan las 'das pa 'di ni zhi ba'o* | *'di ni g.ya nom pa'o* |

A variant of the end in *Mahāvastu*, ii. 285: *etaṃ śāntam etaṃ praṇītam etaṃ yathāvad etam aviparītam yam idaṃ sarvopadhipratiniḥsargo sarvasamskāraśamatho vartmopacchedo tṛṣṇākṣayo virāgo nirodho nirvāṇam*. Same text iii, 200.

Mahāvagga, third truth, 1, 6, 21.

The *Vyākhyā* [WOG.221.17] provides the first few words of the text, i.e: *yat khalv asya* [*duḥkhasya*...], and the two terms *prahāṇa* (abandonment) and *aprādurbhāva* (non-appearance). We have, *Aṅguttara*, i. 100: *parikkhaya pahāṇa khaya vaya virāga nirodha cāga paṭinissagga*; v. 421: *asesavirāga nirodha cāga paṭinissagga mutti anālaya*; *Saṃyutta*, i. 136: *sabbasaṃkhārasamatha*...; *Itivuttaka*, 51: *upadhippaṭinissagga*. – See also the Sanskrit versions of *Majjhima*, i. 497 in Pischel, *Fragments d'Idikutsari*, p. 8 (*vyantibhāva*) and *Avadānaśataka*, ii. 187 (*vāntībhāva*).

965 *LS*: Saṃghabhadra (Ny, 433a; ESD.207) replies to the Sautrāntikas as follows:

> The *sūtra* quoted cannot be used to prove that *nirvāṇa* is *abhāvamātra*. This *sūtra* speaks only with reference to the time when one enters into *nirupadhiśeṣa-nirvāṇa*: At this stage, all *upadhi*-s are completely abandoned, relinquished, etc.

966 *LVP*: [WOG.221.17ff:] In other words, *aprādurbhāva* = *nāsmin prādurbhāvaḥ*. This is the *adhikaraṇasādhana* etymology. The Sautrāntika understands *aprādurbhāva* = *aprādurbhūti* (*bhāvasādhana*).

The explanation of the Sarvāstivādin is reproduced in *Madhyamakvṛtti*, p. 525, and attributed to the philosophy which considers Nirvāṇa as a *bhāva* (mode of existence), a *padārtha* (thing) similar to a dike, which arrests the process of defilement, of action and of rebirth.

967 *LS*: Although not explicitly mentioned in Pradhan, LVP mentions the Sautrāntika here.

968 *LVP*: In fact, the path destroys the production of unsatisfactoriness (*duḥkhasamudaya*). What is the use of imagining, in regard to the path, a thing in itself called *nirodha*?

969 *LVP*: *Dīgha*, ii. 157; *Saṃyutta*, i. 159; *Theragāthā*, 906.

pajjotasseva nibbānaṃ vimokho cetaso ahū.

The Sanskrit redaction (*Avadānaśataka*, 99; *Madhyamakavṛtti*, 520; *Culva*, *Nanjio*, 118, *apud* J. Przyluski, *J. As.*, 1918, ii. 490, 509):

pradyotasyeva nirvāṇaṃ vimokṣas tasya cetasaḥ.

This happens at the moment of Nirvāṇa-without-remainder (*nirupadhiśeṣa-nirvāṇa-kāle*). – The definition *bhavanirodho nibbānam*, *Aṅguttara*, v. 9; *Saṃyutta*, ii. 116, etc.

LS: Dhammajoti comments (SA.IV.478) that the Vaibhāṣika "argues that this simile does not contradict their viewpoint: The extinction referred therein is the *anityatā-lakṣaṇa* which exists as a real *viprayukta-saṃskāradharma*, distinct from the flame. Besides, this simile is made with reference to the time of entering into the *nirupadhiśeṣa-nirvāṇa* when all remaining *upadhi*-s are completely cut off."

970 *LS*: Although not explicitly mentioned in Pradhan, LVP mentions the Sautrāntika here.

971 *LS*: SAH 478.

972 *LVP*: MVŚ, 161a10. – We read in *Prakaraṇa*, 716a3, a definition that we can reconstruct: *avastukā apratyayā dharmāḥ katame*? *asaṃskṛtā dharmāḥ* (see i. 7).

973 *LS*: Tib.: *ldan pa'i dngos po.*

974 *LVP*: This is the text cited *ad* i. 7.

975 *LVP*: The *Vyākhyā ad* i. 7 (Petrograd edition, p. 22) reproduces all these explanations.

976 *LS*: SAH 78, 153–55.

977 *LS*: SAH 78, 153.

978 *Gokhale*: [56a] *vipākaphalam antyasya*

Tib.: [56a] *rnam smin 'bras bu tha ma'i yin* |

LVP: The Japanese editor cites the MVŚ, 629c4.

The effects are of five types: 1. effect of equal outflow (*niṣyandaphala*), 2. ripened effect (*vipākaphala*), 3. effect of disconnection (*visaṃyogaphala*), 4. effect of human action (*puruṣakāraphala*) and 5. effect of dominance (*adhipatiphala*).

1. Effect of uniform outflow: the wholesome produced by the wholesome, the unwholesome produced by the unwholesome, the non-defined by the non-defined.

2. Ripened effect: the retribution (*vipāka*) is produced by wholesome or good-impure factors; the cause being wholesome or unwholesome, the effect is always non-defined. Since this effect is different from its cause and has "matured" (*pāka*), it is called *vipāka* (*visadṛśa pāka*).

3. Effect of disconnection. The unhindered paths (*ānantaryamārga*) sever defilement; they have the severing of defilement for their effect of disconnection and effect of human action; they have the path of liberation (*vimuktimārga*) for their effect of equal outflow and effect of human action; they have all the later paths, equal and superior, of their type as their effect of

[993] *LVP*: [WOG.223.31ff:] The prefix *ud* in *udbhava* signifies "later", "belatedly" (*uttarakāla*). – Concentration (*samādhi*) produces an increase of the fundamental material elements of the body: these fundamental material elements are called an *effect of accumulation* (*aupacayika*) because they arise either at the same time as the concentration, or immediately after; they are not an effect of retribution. – In the same way, the thought of emanation (*nirmāṇacitta*; i. 37, vii. 48) is non-defined, constituting a sentient being, created by a determinate action (concentration); but, arising immediately after the concentration, it is not an effect of retribution. Furthermore, the ripened effect always belongs to the same stage as the action from whence it proceeds.

[994] *LS*: AH 226; SAH 460.

[995] *Gokhale*: [57c] *niṣyando hetusadṛśo*

Tib.: [57c] *rgyu mthun rgyu dang 'dra ba'o* |

LS: 1. *Avatāra* (ESD.122):

> The homogeneous causes and the universal causes acquire thc uniform-emanation fruits (*niṣyanda-phala*; 等流果). It is said to be "uniform" (等) because the fruit is similar to the cause. It is further said to be an "emanation" (流) because it is produced from the cause. The fruit itself being the uniform-emanation, it is named a uniform-emanation fruit.

2. The Sanskrit word *niṣyanda* (*ni-√syand*) literally means "flowing forth, issuing" and Saṃghabhadra explains (Ny, 435c; EIP.VIII.710) that this effect is produced by either the homogeneous cause or the pervasive cause and that it is always similar to its causes (i) in moral quality and (ii) often in essential nature.

3. As for further references in the AKB, see i. 37–38a, which discusses and defines the effect of equal outflow (*naiṣyandika*) in the context of the eighteen elements (*dhātu*), which includes an explanation of the meaning of the term *naiṣyandika* and also determines the five sense-faculties not to be an effect of equal outflow. Further see iv. 85, which lists the various effects of equal outflow as related to each of the ten unwholesome paths of action (*karmapatha*), and iv. 87–94, which discusses the five effects in the context of the effects of various actions.

Moreover, vi. 51d discusses that "eighty-nine paths of liberation (*vimuktimārga*) are the conditioned fruits of the way of virtuous endeavor, being an effect of equal outflow (*niṣyandaphala*) and an effect of human action (*puruṣakāraphala*) of the way of virtuous endeavor".

Again, as just mentioned in more detail in our endnote to the ripened effect, Vasubandhu distinguishes (ix, F 297) the ripened effect (*vipākaphala*) and the effect of equal outflow (*niṣyandaphala*).

[996] *LVP*: The wholesome factors are not the homogeneous cause (*sabhāgahetu*) of defiled factors, etc.

[997] *LS*: AH 227; SAH 462.

[998] *Gokhale*: [57d] *visaṃyogaḥ kṣayo dhiyā* ||

Tib.: [57d] *bral ba blo yis zad pa'o* ||

LS: 1. *Avatāra* (ESD.122):

> The cessation through deliberation (*pratisaṃkhyā-nirodha*), an unconditioned, is named disconnection fruit (*visaṃyoga-phala*). [Although] it is not produced by the Path, [it is still said to be a fruit because] it is acquired by virtue of the Path, [i.e., by means of the Path, the practitioner obtains the acquisition (*prāpti*) of the disconnection]. The fruit itself being the disconnection, it is named the disconnection fruit.

2. Dhammajoti explains (SA.IV.177):

> Disconnection means disconnection from defilements. This fruit refers to the cessation through deliberation (*pratisaṃkhyā-nirodha*). However, this is not in the sense that the unconditioned *pratisaṃkhyā-nirodha* (= *nirvāṇa*), transcending temporality as it does, can be produced as an effect through a space-time causal process. It is called a "fruit" of disconnection only because it is acquired as a result of following the noble path—the path does not function as a cause as such, producing it as the effect; it only induces the arising of the acquisition (*prāpti*) of it.

3. As for further references in the AKB, see iv. 87–94, which discusses the five effects in the context of the effects of various actions.

999 *LS*: AH 227; SAH 461.

1000 *Gokhale*: [58ab] *yadbalāj jāyate yat tat phalaṃ puruṣakārajam* |

Tib.: [58ab] *gang gi stobs kyis gang skyes pa'i* | *'bras de skyes bu byed las skyes* |

LS: 1. *Avatāra* (ESD.122):

> These conjoined causes and the co-existent causes acquire the fruits of manly action (*puruṣakāra-phala*). [This fruit is so named] because by the force of this [—the manly or virile action (*puruṣakāra*)—], that [—the fruit—] is produced.

2. Dhammajoti comments (SA.IV.178) that this fruit has a rather wide scope, but that it is particularly correlated to the co-existent cause (*sabhabhūhetu*) and the associated cause (*saṃprayuktakahetu*) (see ii, F 289). AKB ii. 56d explains the terms "human" (*pauruṣa*) and "human action" (*puruṣakāra*). Saṃghabhadra distinguishes four types of effect of human action (SA.IV.178):

- i. conascent—produced by virtue of the *dharma*-s being simultaneously causes to one another;
- ii. immediate—produced in the subsequent moment by virtue of the preceding thought as the cause; e.g., the *duḥkha-dharmajñāna*, produced by the *laukikāgra-dharma*-s.
- iii. separated in time—produced mediately by virtue of successive causes in a series—e.g., a crop produced by a farmer etc.
- iv. not produced [i.e., *nirvāṇa*; see AKB ii, F 292].

3. As for further references in the AKB, see iv. 87–94, which discusses the five effects in the context of the effects of various actions, and vi. 51d, which discusses that "eighty-nine paths of liberation (*vimuktimārga*) are the conditioned fruits of the way of virtuous endeavor, being an effect of equal outflow (*niṣyandaphala*) and an effect of human action (*puruṣakāraphala*) of the way of virtuous endeavor".

1001 *LVP*: The thought at death (*maraṇacitta*) in the realm of desire, i.e., the thought of the being who dies in the realm of desire, can have, for the effect of human action, the first moment of an intermediary being in the realm of fine-materiality. – These examples show the difference between the effect of human action (*puruṣakāraphala*) and the effect of equal outflow (*niṣyandaphala*). Four alternatives (tetralemma):

1. effect of human action that is not effect of equal outflow: examples as above;
2. effect of equal outflow, the effect of the homogeneous and pervasive causes that does not immediately follow;
3. effect of equal outflow and effect of human action, parallel effect, of the same stage, follow immediately;
4. neither of the two: the ripened effect.

1002 *LS*: See Saṃghabhadra's explanations regarding this fourth type at Ny, 437a (SA.IV.179).

1003 *LS*: AH 227; SAH 461.

1004 *Gokhale*: [58cd] *apūrvaḥ saṃskṛtasy aiva saṃskṛto 'dhipateḥ phalaṃ* ||

Tib.: [58cd] *sngon byung ma yin 'dus byas ni* | *'dus byas kho na'i bdag po'i 'bras* ||

LVP: See ii. 56b and iv. 85.

LS: 1. *Avatāra* (ESD.122):

> The efficient causes acquire the fruits of dominance (*adhipati-phala*). [The word "fruit of dominance" is explained thus:] by force of this dominance (*adhipati*), that is produced. For example, the visual faculty, etc., with regard to visual consciousness, etc.; the farmer, etc., with regard to the crops, etc.—from the anterior dominance, the posterior *dharma* is produced. Being the fruit of the dominance, it is named a "fruit of dominance".

2. In the Chinese as well as in the Sanskrit, the root-verse is followed by a rephrasing of the root-verse but LVP does not translate it and instead seems to combine the two. The omitted sentence in Pradhan.96.8: *pūrvotpannādanyaḥ saṃskṛto dharmaḥ saṃskṛtasyaiva sarvasyādhipatiphalam.*

3. Dhammajoti explains (SA.IV.180):

> This is the most generic type of fruit, correlated to the most generic type of cause, the efficient cause. In terms of the *karma* doctrine of the Sarvāstivāda, the fruits commonly shared by a collection of beings by virtue of their collective *karma*-s belong to this category. Thus, the whole universe with all its planets, mountains and oceans, etc., is the result—the fruit of dominance—of the collective *karma*-s of the totality of beings inhabiting therein.

4. As for further references in the AKB, see iii. 45, which discusses *adhipatiphala* in the context of the arising of the three supporting circles (*maṇḍala*) of the receptacle world (*bhājanaloka*) and states that due to the dominance of the collective actions or the actions of all sentient beings (as effect of), there arises the circle of wind (*vāyumaṇḍala*) that rests on space (*ākāśa*).

See also iv. 1, which states that the variety of the world arises from (individual and collective) action because the "world or universe" (*lokadhātu*), which includes the *bhājanaloka*, is variegated in accordance with the beings' individual and collective *karma*. Expressed differently, it can be said that the various actions (*karma*) of sentient beings "as an efficient cause" (*kāraṇahetu*), i.e., the collective *karma*, lead to an effect of dominance (*adhipatiphala*), that is shared, though not necessarily by all beings; and that the action of an individual being "as a ripening cause" (*vipākahetu*) results, if the necessary conditions are present, in a ripened effect (*vipākaphala*) that is not shared, but individual. Moreover, see iv. 85, which lists the various effects of dominance as related to each of the ten unwholesome paths of action (*karmapatha*), and iv. 87–94, which discusses the five effects in the context of the effects of various actions.

1005 *LS*: SAH 154.

1006 *LS*: MVŚ, 106c, states (SA.IV.181):

> Question: What is the difference between a virile fruit and a fruit of dominance?
>
> Answer: That which is acquired through the exercise of an effort is a virile fruit. That which is acquired on account of non-obstruction is a fruit of dominance.... Moreover, wealth is a virile fruit in respect of the doer, and a fruit of dominance in respect of the enjoyer. Thus the fruits [of a plant] are both virile fruits and fruits of dominance in respect of the planter; [but] only fruits of dominance in respect of the enjoyer... .

1007 *LS*: SAḤ 73, 77.

1008 *LS*: Saṃghabhadra explains (Ny, 437c; EIP.VIII.710f.) that the six causes function causally in two stages:

1. Through "taking/projecting/inducing of the effect" (*ā-√kṣip*) or "grasping of an effect" (*grahaṇa/pratigrahaṇa*), which occurs only in the present time period, the cause draws out a future *dharma* preparing it for its "production" and this present activity alone is referred to as the cause's "activity" (*kāritra*). For the Vaibhāṣikas, this activity of *dharma* of grasping or projecting its own fruit—causing the arising of its following moment in its serial continuity—uniquely defines its presentness. All six causes take or draw out their effects only when they themselves are in the present time period. This step properly determines that the particular cause is causally related to its corresponding effect. Yaśomitra also explains similarly [WOG.226.12f.]:

> By "[the causes] grasp" is meant "they project". It means that they abide in the state of being a cause (*pratigṛhṇantīti*. ākṣipanti hetu-bhāvenāvatiṣṭhanta ity arthaḥ).

2. Through "giving/producing of the effect" (*phala-dāna*), which can occur in the present or past time period, the effect is made to enter into the present whereby the cause gives the effect power enabling it to arise. This is referred to as a cause's "capability" (*sāmarthya*). As this second stage cannot occur without the first stage, "this" capability cannot occur in the future time period.

1009 *LVP*: *vartamānāḥ phalaṃ pañca gṛhṇanti dvau prayacchataḥ* |
vartamānābhyatītau dvāv eko 'tītaḥ prayacchati || 59

Compare ii. 55ab.

1010 *LVP*: These definitions are given later (vi. fol. 22a7) in the original [Chinese edition]. They are placed here for the convenience of the reader.

1011 *LVP*: *tasya bījabhāvopagamanāt* [WOG.230.21]. – The factor always exists, whether it is future, present or past. We say that it seizes or projects an effect at the moment when, becoming present, it becomes the cause or seed of an effect. – The *Vyākhyā* observes that the comparison of the seed belongs to the theory of the Sautrāntikas. Also "this text is absent in certain manuscripts" (*kvacit pustake nāsty eṣa pāṭhaḥ*; WOG.230.22).

1012 *LS*: SAH 77.

1013 *LS*: Ibid.

1014 *Gokhale*: [59ab1] *vartamānāḥ phalaṃ pañca gṛhnanti*

Tib.: [59a] *lnga po da ltar 'bras bu 'dzin* |

1015 *LS*: The *Vyākhyā* glosses [WOG.226.14ff.]: *sa tu nāvaśyaṃ saphala iti nocyate.* tathā hy asaṃskṛtaṃ kāraṇa-hetur iṣyate. na cāsya phalam asti. anāgataś ca kāraṇa-hetuḥ. na ca pūrvam utpadyaṃānena dharmeṇa sa-phalaḥ.

1016 *LS*: SAH 77.

1017 *Gokhale*: [59b2] *dvau prayacchataḥ* |

Tib.: [59b] *gnyis ni rab tu 'byin par byed* |

1018 *LS*: SAH 73, 77.

1019 *Gokhale*: [59c] *vartamānā'bhyatītau dvāv*

Tib.: [59c] *da ltar gyi dang 'das pa dag* |

1020 *LVP*: On this subtle point, Saṃghabhadra, *Nyāyāvatāra*, 98a3.

1021 *LS*: SAH 73.

1022 *LS*: Ibid.

1023 *LVP*: *asti kuśalaḥ sabhāgahetuḥ phalaṃ pratigṛhṇāti na dadāti.* – According to the MVŚ, 89b13.

1024 *LVP*: The last possessions (*prāpti*) of the wholesome that are cut off, namely, the weak-weak (*mṛdumṛdu*) possessions of the wholesome roots, project their effect (*phalaparigrahaṃ kurvanti*), but do not give forth their effect (*niṣyandaphala*), since the "wholesome" moment, which they should give forth or engender (*janya*), is absent.

1025 *LVP*: Vasubandhu criticizes the doctrine of the Vaibhāṣikas. In fact, this paragraph is poorly composed (*sāvadya*): when persons take up again the wholesome roots, they acquire, tritemporally, the possession of the wholesome roots: the past possessions acquired at this moment give forth their effect, but do not seize it: for they have already seized it; but how can one say that the present possessions do not seize their effect? The proposed definition thus lacks precision. – Saṃghabhadra defends the composition of the *Vibhāṣā*.

LS: This is the 42nd of Kritzer's forty-four passages discussed in relation to chapter 2 (VY.126f.). Saṃghabhadra identifies (Ny, 438a19–20) this as the opinion of Vasubandhu and defends the Vaibhāṣika position (Ny, 438a20–25).

1026 *LS*: SAH 73.

1027 *LS*: This is the 43rd of Kritzer's forty-four passages discussed in relation to chapter 2 (VY.128f.). Saṃghabhadra identifies (Ny, 438c29–b1) this as the statement of Vasubandhu and defends the Vaibhāṣika position (Ny, 438b1–2).

1028 *LS*: SAH 73.

1029 *LS*: Ibid.

1030 *LVP*: *anivṛtāvyākṛtasya paścātpādaka* iti paścātpādakalakṣaṇaṃ vyākhyātam iti na punar ucyate [WOG.229.24ff.].

[1031] *LS*: SAH 77.

[1032] *Gokhale*: [59d] *eko 'tītaḥ prayacchati* ||

Tib.: [59d] *gcig ni 'das pas 'byin par 'gyur* ||

LVP: Vasumitra, Mahāsaṃghikas, thesis 44.

[1033] *LS*: SAH 480.

[1034] *LS*: AH 26–29; SAH 79–82.

[1035] *LS*: Ibid.

[1036] *LS*: Cox summarizes Saṃghabhadra (Ny, 436b26; EIP.VIII.711): "No factor is produced by one cause alone. The number of causes that produce any given factor is determined by that factor's essential nature as thought, material form, or dissociated from thought and material form, its moral quality, and so on. Further, although certain categories of factors may not function as certain types of causes, all classes of factors, with the exception of unconditioned factors, may function causally in more than one way. Unconditioned factors can only be comprehensive causes."

[1037] *LS*: AH 26; SAH 79.

[1038] *Gokhale*: [60–61a1] *kliṣṭā vipākajāḥ śeṣāḥ prathamāryā yathākramam* | *vipākaṃ sarvagaṃ hitvā tau sabhāgaṃ ca śeṣajāḥ* || *cittacaittās*

Tib.: [60–61a] *nyon mongs can dang rnam smin skyes* | *lhag dang dang po 'phags rim bzhin* | *rnam smin kun 'gro de gnyis dang* | *skal mnyam ma gtogs lhag las skyes* || *sems dang sems las byung ba yin* |

LVP: *kliṣṭā vipākajāḥ śeṣāḥ prathamaryā yathākramam* |
vipākaṃ sarvagaṃ hitvā tau sabhāgaṃ ca śeṣajāḥ || 60
cittacaittās [tathānye ca saṃprayuktakavarjitāḥ] |

Compare *Abhidharmahṛdaya*, ii. 12–15.

[1039] *LS*: AH 27–29; SAH 80–82.

[1040] *Gokhale*: [61a2–b] *tathā 'nye 'pi samprayuktakavarjitāḥ* |

Tib.: [61b] *mtshangs ldan ma gtogs gzhan de bzhin* |

[1041] *LS*: Saṃghabhadra comments (Ny, 61c; EIP.VIII.711) that unconditioned factors can only be efficient causes.

[1042] *LS*: Hsüan-tsang, vii, fol. 1a.

[1043] *LS*: Dharmaśri remarks (AH 29): "We have explained all the causes. Such causes were explained by the Tathāgata in order to make conversions by teaching with his power of awakenment, knowing the characteristics of all factors with certainty." See also SAH.131.

[1044] *LS*: AH 30, 230; SAH 36, 83–88, 232, 465, 525–46.

[1045] *Gokhale*: [61c] *catvāraḥ pratyayā uktā*

Tib.: [61c] *rkyen ni bzhi po dag tu gsungs* |

LVP: MVŚ, 79a26: "It is true that these six causes (*hetu*) are not mentioned in the Sūtra; the Sūtra just says that there are four *pratyayatās* (conditions)."

The Japanese editor cites the sources of the Great Vehicle, the *Nanjio* 141 (transl. Dharmagupta), *Ghanavyūha*, the *Nanjio* 140 (transl. Hsüan-tsang), the *Madhyamaka* (see *Madhyamaka-vṛtti*, p. 76).

With respect to the relation of the causes (*hetu*) and the conditions (*pratyaya*), the first masters of the MVŚ, 79ab [see SA.IV.171], say that [the four conditions and the five causes mutually subsume each other:] (1) the causal condition (*hetupratyaya*) consists of the five causes (*hetu*), with the exception of the efficient cause (*kāraṇahetu*), (2) the efficient cause consists of the other three conditions.

The second masters of the MVŚ, 79ab, say that [the conditions subsume the causes, but the causes do not subsume the conditions:] (1) the causal condition consists of five causes, and (2) the enabling cause corresponds to only the condition of dominance (*adhipatipratyaya*) [but the immediately preceding condition and the cognitive object condition are not subsumed by any cause]: this is the system adopted by Vasubandhu. [See SA.220f.].

In respect to the masters of the Great Vehicle, the homogeneous cause (*sabhāgahetu*) is at one and the same time the causal condition and the condition of dominance, whereas the other five causes are the condition of dominance.

Prakaraṇa, 712b12, enumerates four conditions (*pratyaya*). [In Devaśarman's] *Vijñānakāya*, 547b22, [ca. first century C.E., we first come across an elaborative exposition of the four conditions, when] defining them as functions of the consciousnesses (*vijñāna*) [see also Dhammajoti's translation in SA.IV.170]:

> What is the causal condition (*hetupratyaya*) of a visual consciousness? The co-existent (*sahabhū*) and associated (*saṃprayukta*) factors.
>
> What is its immediately preceding condition (*samanantarapratyaya*)? The thought and thought-concomitants to which it is equivalent and immediate antecedent, i.e., the visual consciousness that has arisen or will arise.
>
> What is its cognitive object condition (*ālambanapratyaya*)? [All the] visible forms.
>
> What is its condition of dominance (*adhipatipratyaya*)? All factors, with the exception of itself.
>
> [These are said to be the four conditions for visual consciousness… .]
>
> Of what is the visual consciousness the causal condition? Of co-existent and associated factors.
>
> Of what is it the immediately preceding condition? Of the thoughts and thought-concomitants that are equivalent and have arisen or will arise immediately after this visual consciousness.
>
> Of what is it the cognitive object condition? Of the thoughts and thought-concomitants that seize it for their object.
>
> Of what is it the condition of dominance? Of all the factors, with the exception of itself.
>
> [Just as in the case of visual consciousness, likewise are those of auditory, olfactory, gustatory, tactile and mental consciousnesses.]

The four conditions (*pratyaya*) are defined in the *Abhidharmahṛdaya*, ii. 16, as in our book: the causal condition consists of five causes; the condition of dominance corresponds to the efficient cause (*kāraṇahetu*).

For the *paccaya*s of the Abhidhamma, the *Dukapaṭṭhāna* appears as the main authority. The points of contact with the Abhidharma are numerous; the nomenclature differs; for example, the *sahajātādhipatipaccaya* is our homogeneous cause (*sahabhūhetu*). See also *Kathāvatthu*, xv. 1–2.

LS: 1. The *Avatāra* states (ESD.123):

> There are four conditions (*pratyaya*): condition qua cause (*hetu-pratyaya*), uniform-immediate condition (*samanantara-pratyaya*), condition qua object (*ālambana-pratyaya*), and condition of dominance (*adhipati-pratyaya*).
>
> Excluding the efficient cause, the other five causes are named the conditions qua cause.
>
> All past and present thought and thought-concomitants, excluding the last thought (*caramaṃ cittam*), etc., of an *arhat*, are named the uniform-immediate conditions.
>
> All *dharma*-s receive the name conditions qua object.
>
> Those [*dharma*-s] of the nature of efficient cause (*kāraṇa-hetutā*) are named conditions of dominance.

2. As for the general history of the conditions, see our introductory note to causes, effects and conditions at F 244.

3. In regard to whether causes and conditions are different or not, see endnote above (F 244, bottom).

4. As for the existential status of the conditions, Dhammajoti comments (SA.IV.146 and171) that not all Sarvāstivādins would recognize the reality of the conditions and that according to the MVŚ (47b, 283a–b, 680b, 680c, 975a, 982b) the early Dārṣṭāntikas and others deny their reality, for example, the Bhadānta Dharmatrāta declares that they are unreal, being nothing more than terminologies conceptually designated by the Abhidharma masters. On the other hand, the MVŚ compilers defend the Ābhidharmika position that they are real entities (see MVŚ 283b; SA.IV.171).

5. As for the scope of the conditions, the MVŚ, 283b, states (SA.IV.171):

> All four conditions completely subsume all *dharma*-s:
>
> the condition qua cause subsumes all conditioned *dharma*-s;
>
> the equal-immediate condition subsumes all past and present *dharma*-s other than the very last thought and thought-concomitant *dharma*-s of the past and present *arhat*-s;
>
> the condition qua object and the condition of dominance [each] subsumes the totality of *dharma*-s.

6. As for illustrations of the distinct functions of the four conditions, the MVŚ, 109a, states (SA.IV.175):

> The condition qua cause is like the seed-*dharma*.
>
> The equal-immediate condition is like a *dharma* that gives way (開導; "gives way and guides").
>
> The condition qua object is like a *dharma* walking-stick that supports.

The condition of dominance is like a *dharma* that is non-obstructive.

7. As for which of the four conditions is superior, which are inferior, the MVŚ, 703b, states:

Answer: According to some: the condition qua cause is superior, the others are inferior, for it is when there is an increase in cause that arising or ceasing occurs.

According to some: the equal-immediate condition is superior, the others are inferior, for it can give way to the gateway of the noble path.

According to some: the condition qua cause is superior, the others are inferior, for it is the support for the [arising of] thought and thought-concomitants.

According to some: the condition of dominance is superior, the others are inferior, for it does not hinder the arising and ceasing of *dharma*-s.

The correct position (如是說者): All are superior, all are inferior, for the efficacies are distinctive... .

1046 *LVP*: [WOG.232.9:] That is to say, *pratyayaprakāra*, as one says *gotā*, a type of cow.

1047 *LS*: AH 30; SAH 84–87, 525.

1048 *LS*: AH 30; SAH 87.

1049 *LS*: Ibid.

1050 *Gokhale*: [61d] *hetvākhyaḥ pañca hetavaḥ* ||

Tib.: [61d] *rgyu zhes bya ba rgyu lnga yin* ||

LS: 1. Dhammajoti comments (SA.IV.173): "This is the condition in its capacity as direct cause in the production of an effect—it is the cause functioning as the condition. In the example of the growth of a fruit plant: the condition qua cause is comparable to the seed. However, it is a common tenet of all schools of Buddhism that nothing is produced by a single cause, even though in the analysis of the causal complex, the main cause can be singled out. Of the six causes, all except the efficient cause are conditions qua cause. Strictly speaking, however, some of the efficient causes should also come under this category if they make some positive contribution in the causal process."

2. As for the scope of the causal condition, the MVŚ (283b; SA.IV.171) states that "the condition qua cause subsumes all conditioned *dharma*-s". The causal condition or condition qua cause, i.e., factors which can produce an effect, cannot include the entire category of *kāraṇahetu*, which also includes the unconditioned factors which cannot produce an effect, although being themselves a cause, namely, *kāraṇahetu* (see ii, F 277f.).

3. As for dissenting views, Saṃghabhadra states (Ny, 440b; *Śrīlāta's anudhātu doctrine*, p. 5):

[i] The Sthavira (= Śrīlāta) states that the nature of the condition qua cause (*hetupratyayatā*) is the old pursuant element [**purāṇa-anudhātu*]: the nature of being the cause, successively, in the serial continuity of a sentient being. [...]

[iii] [Saṃghabhadra:] This old pursuant element is just another name for *bīja*. ... When we examine this pursuant element, we see that it is only an empty word and [that] its intrinsic nature (體) cannot be apperceived. Thus, he (= the Sthavira) cannot claim that it is of the nature of being the cause, successively, in the serial continuity.

1051 *LS*: AH 30; SAH 84; 525.

1052 *LS*: AH 30; SAH 84.

1053 *Gokhale*: [62ab] *cittacāitta acaramā utpannāḥ samanantaraḥ* |

Tib.: [62ab] *sems dang sems byung skyes ba rnams* | *tha ma min mtshungs de ma thag* |

LS: 1. According to Dhammajoti (SA.IV.173): "A *citta* or *caitta* serves as a condition for the arising of the succeeding *citta* or *caitta*: It both gives way to and induces the arising of the next *citta-caitta* in the series. ... Moreover, Saṃghabhadra insists [Ny, 445b; see also MVŚ, 51a–b] that the notion of an equal-immediate condition necessarily entails that a subsequent thought moment can only arise upon the cessation of the preceding thought moment which thereby "makes room" for the arising of the former. ... The view of the Ābhidharmikas is given in the MVŚ [50b] as follows:

> The characteristic of the equal-immediate condition consists in its enabling the *dharma*-s that are having unique self-characteristics to arise immediately. The *dharma*-s having unique self-characteristics are the *caitta*-s, *vedanā*, *saṃjñā*, etc., and *citta*. Their self-characteristics are different individually; when they co-arise, there cannot be two [instances of them in each case].

Saṃghabhadra mentions (EIP.VIII.712) that, on the one hand, "equivalent" (see ii, F 300ff.) refers to factors of the same general category, such as sensations, ideations, and so on, and does not exclude a conditioning relationship between morally different accompanying factors of the same category, however, not in the same moment; on the other hand, "immediate antecedent" (see ii, F 303ff.) indicates that no factor of the same general category, like sensation, ideation, etc., can arise between this condition and its effect, yet factors dissociated from thought, for example, attainment of cessation (*nirodhasamāpatti*), can arise in between (see ii, F 211).

2. As for the scope of the condition as the equivalent and immediate antecedent, the Sarvāstivādins maintain that this homogeneous causality applies only to *citta-caitta*s, although not to the final *citta-caitta*s of a perfected being (*arhat*; see ii, F 305); thus, it does not apply to the domain of material form (*rūpa*), since there is no equivalence or sameness in the serial continuity of material form (see ii, F 300ff.); it also does not apply to formations dissociated from thought (see ii, F 303). The MVŚ, 52a, among other reasons mentions also the following (SA.IV.174):

> If a *dharma* is conjoined (*saṃprayuktaka*), has a supporting basis (*sāśraya*), has a mode of activity (*sākāra*), is alertive (*abhogātmaka*) and has an object (*sālambana*); then it can be established as an equal-immediate condition. This is not the case with material *dharma*-s.

In the context of *citta-caitta*s and the condition as the equivalent and immediate antecedent, see also Vasubandhu's discussion of the mental faculty (*manas*) at i. 17ab.

3. As for dissenting views, the Dārṣṭāntikas maintain (Ny, 445b and 447a; SA.IV.174) that "this category also obtains among the material *dharma*s, since the principle of the arising of the succeeding upon the ceasing of the preceding also applies—a preceding seed gives rise to a succeeding sprout; a flower gives rise to a fruit; etc. Sthavira Śrīlāta, a Sautrāntika leader also holds a similar view". See also ŚAD.22.

[1054] *LVP*: MVŚ, 52a8ff., second masters.

[1055] *LVP*: This refers to the non-informative form (*avijñaptirūpa*). When, after having undertaken the *prātimokṣa* restraint (*prātimokṣasaṃvara*) (a non-informative form in the realm of desire), persons enter into the impure meditation (*dhyāna*), they produce the meditation restraint (*dhyānasaṃvara*) (the unmanifest form in the realm of fine-materiality), whereas the non-informative form in the realm of desire continues to reproduce itself (see iv. 17bc). [Cf. WOG.232.18ff.].

[1056] *LVP*: In the case where the persons who have undertaken the *prātimokṣa* restraint (*prātimokṣasaṃvara*) enter into the pure meditation (*dhyāna*).

[1057] *LVP*: This is the second opinion presented in the *Vibhāṣā*. – When, after having eaten, the persons go to sleep or enter into concentration, the material form (*rūpa*) of accumulation produced by food and the material form of accumulation produced by sleep or by concentration (see i. 37) arise at the same time.

[1058] *LVP*: On the Bhadanta, the Sautrāntika Sthavira (WOG.232.28), see i, F 36. – Fourth opinion of the *Vibhāṣā*.

[1059] *LS*: SAH 84, 525.

[1060] *LS*: Ibid.

[1061] *LVP*: MVŚ, 52a21, two opinions. Vasubandhu presents the second.

LS: See also SAH.133.

[1062] *LS*: SAH 84.

[1063] *LVP*: The simultaneous factors presenting neither anteriority nor posteriority cannot be among themselves the condition as the equivalent and immediate antecedent (*samanantarapratyaya*).

[1064] *LVP*: Saṃghabhadra, 19, p. 444.

[1065] *LVP*: The first masters of the MVŚ, 51b15. – *atītasāmpratānumānāt* [WOG.234.4]. – Hsüan-tsang: "He infers from the past and from the present, but sees in an immediate manner."

[1066] *LVP*: *atītaṃ kilādhvānaṃ paśyati*... [WOG.234.5]. MVŚ, ibid., and 897b26.

[1067] *LVP*: Hsüan-tsang: The Fortunate One sees that from such a past action arises such an effect: from such a factor arises immediately such a factor; that, from such a present action arises such an effect: from such a factor arises immediately such a factor. Having thus seen, he is capable of knowing with regard to confounded factors of the future that such a factor will arise immediately after such a factor. Although he cognizes in this manner, it is not the cognition of inference, for the Fortunate One, inferring according to the order of arising of past and present causes and effects, then knows by direct vision of the confounded factors of the future and says: "In the future, such a being will accomplish such an action, will receive such retribution." This is the cognition resulting from a resolve (*praṇidhijñāna*), not cognition resulting from inference (*anumānajñāna*).

[1068] *LVP*: Second opinion of the MVŚ, 897b26; third opinion presented in *Nyāyāvatāra*, 444b23.

Paramārtha (194b10) differs: "There is, in the series of sentient beings, a certain factor associated with thought that is the indication of a future effect."

Nyāyāvatāra: "There is at the present time, in sentient beings, an indication of causes and future effects, similar to a prediction sign (*chāyā-nimitta*), or else, a material form (*rūpa*), or else a formation (*saṃskāra*) dissociated from thought."

"Mark, spot, stamp, sign, characteristic, symptom" (MW), indication, (Tib.) *rtags*, (Skt.) *cihna* = *liṅga*; Paramārtha and *Nyāyāvatāra*: *hsien-hsiang* = *pūrvalakṣaṇa*; Hsüan-tsang: *hsien-chao*, presage or omen.

1069 *LVP*: Japanese editor: by means of the mundane conventional cognition (*lokadhātu-saṃvṛtijñāna*; vii. 3).

1070 *LS*: Although not explicitly mentioned in Pradhan, LVP mentions the Sautrāntika here.

1071 *LVP*: Tib.: *mtshan mkhan.* – Śarad Candra suggests *gaṇaka* (= *rtsis mkhan*); rather *naimittika* (*ltas mkhan*) MVyut., 186, 123, *naimittaka*, *Divya*. – Hsüan-tsang: If that were so, the Buddha would know the future because of indications (*chan-hsiang*)... .

1072 *LS*: This is the sixth place in Pradhan (99.11), where the term Sautrāntika is explicitly mentioned.

1073 *LS*: SAH 84.

1074 *LS*: SAH 85.

1075 *LVP*: According to the MVŚ,52c12; compare *Prakaraṇa*, 764a28ff.

1076 *LS*: Vasubandhu then proceeds to describe a second tetralemma (Pradhan.99.26–100.1): *ye dharmāścittasamanantarāḥ samāpattinirantarā api te*... . See SAH.135f.

1077 *LS*: SAH 86, 525.

1078 *LS*: SAH 86.

1079 *Verdu*: EBP.77.

1080 *Gokhale*: [62c] *ālambanaṃ sarvadharmāḥ*

Tib.: [62c] *dmigs pa chos rnams thams cad do* |

LS: 1. Dhammajoti explains (SA.IV.174f.): "According to the Sarvāstivāda, cognition is cognition of an object. A cognition cannot arise by itself, without taking an object. In fact, the very possibility of a cognition presupposes a real/existent as its object. In this sense, the object serves as a condition for the cognition." That the nature of *ālambana-pratyaya*-s is determined as objects of perception even when they are not being perceived (see Ny, 448b and AKB ii, F 307), may be considered (SA.IV.175) as a definite assertion of objective realism on the part of the Sarvāstivādins. Dhammajoti adds (SA.IV.147): "In fact, the Sarvāstivādins argue they are real because they can function as objects for the generation of cognition. Indeed, it is this causal efficacy that constitutes the very mark of the existent (*sal-lakṣaṇa*) [see Ny, 621c–622a]. All existent *dharma*-s have such an efficacy, but only the present *dharma*-s have *kāritra* which is the efficacy of projecting their own fruits. – The same principle applies even in the case of the unconditioned *dharma*-s."

2. As for the scope of the cognitive object condition, since the mind can think of anything and thought can take any object, all *dharmas*—whether conditioned and unconditioned, past, present or future—can become cognitive object conditions (see our section, ii. 62c). Saṃghabhadra explains why the totality of *dharma*-s are called cognitive object condition (*ālambana-pratyaya*; Ny, 447b, SA.IV.174f.):

> The condition qua object is none other than the totality of *dharma*-s. Outside the cognitive objects of thought and thought-concomitants, there is definitely no other *dharma* that can be apperceived (*upa-√labh*). That is to say, the totality of *dharma*-s is called condition qua object because thought and thought-concomitants hold onto (*ā-√lamb*) them for their arising. Because these very cognitive objects serve as the condition for their generation, they are called conditions qua object.

As for the totality of *dharma*s, the MVŚ, 42c–43a, asks:

> If the question is posed: … "[Among the ten knowledges,] is there one that knows all *dharma*-s?" The answer is: "Yes. The conventional knowledge."
>
> If with regard to this conventional knowledge, the question is posed: "Is there a case that within two moments [of thought], all *dharma*-s are known?" The answer is: "Yes. In the first moment, this knowledge knows all [the *dharma*-s] excepting itself and those that are conjoined or co-existent with it. In the second moment, it also knows [what has existed] in the first moment, [namely] itself as well as those *dharma*-s that were conjoined or co-existent with it."

Vasubandhu further asks at vii. 18cd:

> Can one, through a single cognition, know all [individual] factors (*dharma*)? – No. However, one conventional cognition, by excluding its own complex, cognizes the rest as nonself.

See in this context also Vasubandhu's comment (F 308) that "the factors coexisting (*sahabhū*) with a certain thought are not the cognitive object of this thought, whereas they are the efficient cause (*kāraṇahetu*) of it. … [However,] a factor is not any of the conditions of itself." Thus in regard to one moment and one factor (*dharma*), the scope of the condition of dominance is wider than the scope of the cognitive object condition.

3. As for the difference and relation between cognitive object (*ālambana*), object-field (*viṣaya*) and object-referent (*artha*), see Vasubandhu's discussion and our endnotes at i. 9ab, 29bc, 34ab, 48a. As for Vasubandhu's presentation of the underlying atomic structure of the object-fields, see ii. 22. As for a discussion of epistemological, ontological and language related issues regarding cognitive objects (*ālambana*), see Vasubandhu's discussion and our endnotes at ii. 47ab and iii, F 102–7. But as already mentioned in our endnote to ii. 61c, the ontological status of the *ālambanapratyaya* is contentious among Buddhists. For example, Śrīlāta states in the *Nyāyānusāra (EIP.VIII.713):

> Śrīlāta: The external objects corresponding to the five externally directed types of perceptual consciousness cannot be their supporting object conditions, because this supporting object cannot be simultaneous with the perceptual consciousness that it produces. Mental perceptual consciousness would also be incapable of being supported by a present object. Instead, mental perceptual consciousness takes the previous objects of the five externally directed types of perceptual consciousness as its supporting object. Since this prior supporting object has already passed away, it no longer exists; nonetheless, it still may serve as a supporting object for perceptual consciousness. However, the cause for the arising of a present moment of perceptual consciousness is the prior moment of perceptual consciousness within the same stream; this causal relation between a prior and successive moment is one of recipro-

cal succession within the same stream.

Answer: Since Śrīlāta does not allow that the supporting objects of the five externally directed types of perceptual consciousness are simultaneous with their corresponding perceptual consciousness, mental perceptual consciousness cannot depend upon the supporting object of a prior moment of the five externally directed types of perceptual consciousness. Further, it is absurd to claim that even though this past object does not exist it can still serve as the supporting object for present mental perceptual consciousness; perceptual consciousness can only be supported by an existent object. Indeed, since the Dārṣṭāntikas accept the existence only of present factors and reject those of the past and future, one cannot speak of reciprocal succession. How can there be a causal relation between a nonexistent past factor and an existent present one? Therefore, supporting objects of perceptual consciousness must exist, and those of the five externally directed types of perceptual consciousness are simultaneous with their corresponding perceptual consciousness.

See in this context also Collett Cox's article *On the Possibility of a Nonexistent Object of Consciousness: Sarvāstivādin und Dārṣṭāntika theories.*

1081 *LS*: SAH 525.

1082 *LVP*: *om ity āha*. – MVŚ, 983b13.

1083 *LVP*: The first two opinions of the MVŚ, 57a14. – Third opinion: When present, past, future, thought is bound to its basis.

1084 *LS*: SAH 87.

1085 *LS*: Ibid.

1086 *Gokhale*: [62d] *kāraṇākhyo 'dhipaḥ smṛtaḥ* ||

Tib.: [62d] *byed rgyu zhes bya bdag por bshad* ||

LVP: This quarter-verse (*pāda*) is difficult to reconstruct: *kāraṇākhyo 'dhipaḥ smṛtaḥ*.

LS: 1. Dhammajoti comments (SA.IV.175): "This is the most comprehensive or generic condition, corresponding to efficient cause: It is whatever that serves as a condition, either in the sense of directly contributing to the arising of a *dharma*, or indirectly through not hindering its arising. From the latter perspective, the unconditioned *dharma*-s—although transcending space and time altogether—are also said to serve as conditions of dominance.

2. As for the scope of *adhipatipratyaya*, it is the same as that of the efficient cause (ii. 50a): "All [conditioned and unconditioned] factors are an efficient cause with regard to any [(other) conditioned factor], with the exception of themselves." This is also addressed in our section here (F 308).

1087 *LS*: *syāddharmo dharmasya caturbhirapi pratyayairna pratyayaḥ* |

1088 *LS*: LVP differs here: "Le *dharma* (*saṃskṛta*) n'est pas condition du *dharma* inconditionné, et reciproquement."

1089 *LS*: SAH 525–26.

1090 *LS*: Saṃghabhadra comments (Ny, 450a; EIP.VIII.714) that here Vasubandhu confuses a factor's activity, "which only occurs in the present and only refers to that factor's projecting its own effect, with its capability, which occurs in all three time periods and may assist in the arising of the effect of another factor". To indicate this "confusion" we will put "activity/ capability" here and in the following sections in quotation marks.

1091 *LS*: SAH 526.

1092 *Gokhale*: [63ab1] *nirudhyamāne kāritraṃ dvau hetū kurutas*

Tib.: [63ab1] *rgyu gnyis po dag 'gag pa la | bya ba byed do*

LVP: According to the MVŚ, 703a3ff.

1093 *LVP*: Hsüan-tsang: "because they bring about an effect arisen at the same time as they possess the operation".

1094 *LS*: SAH 526.

1095 *Gokhale*: [63b2–c1] *trayaḥ | jāyamāne*

Tib.: [63b2–c1] *gsum po ni | skye la'o*

1096 *LS*: SAH 525.

1097 *Gokhale*: [63c2–d] *tato 'nyau tu pratyayau tadviparyayāt ||*

Tib.: [63c2–d] *las gzhan pa yi | rkyen dag de las bzlog pa yin ||*

1098 *LS*: AH 31, 230; SAH 36, 88.

1099 *LS*: AH 31; SAH 88.

1100 *LS*: Ibid.

1101 *LS*: Ibid.

1102 *Gokhale*: [64a] *caturbhiś cittacaittā hi*

Tib.: [64a] *bzhi yis sems dang sems byung rnams |*

LVP: Compare *Abhidharmahṛdaya*, ii. 17.

1103 *LS*: AH 31; SAH 88.

1104 *Gokhale*: [64b] *samāpattidvayaṃ tribhiḥ |*

Tib.: [64b] *gsum gyis snyoms par 'jug pa gnyis |*

1105 *LS*: AH 31; SAH 88.

1106 *Gokhale*: [64c] *dyābhyām anye tu jāyante*

Tib.: [64c] *gzhan ni gnyis po dag las skye |*

1107 *LVP*: *Vyākhyā* [WOG.237.12f.]: Īśvara, Puruṣa, Pradhāna, time (*kāla*), intrinsic nature (*svabhāva*), atoms (*paramāṇu*), etc.

LS: *Siddhi*.30f. states: "[Besides the opinion that there is a God, Maheśvaradeva, seven other doctrines of non-Buddhist schools] maintain that there is one Great Brahmā (Mahābrahmā), one Time (*kāla*), one Space (*diś*), one Starting Point (*pūrvakoṭi*), one Intrinsic Nature (*svabhāva*; ?), one Ether (*ākāśa*), one Self (*ātman*). Each of these is alleged to be single, eternal, real, endowed with powers and capabilities, and able to produce all the factors (*dharma*)."

1108 *Gokhale*: [64d] *n eśvarādeḥ kramādihiḥ ||*

Tib.: [64d] *dbang phyug sogs min rim sogs phyir ||*

LVP: Compare *Bodhicaryāvatara*, ix. 119; *Ṣaḍdarśanasaṃgraha*, p. 11; *Suhṛllekha* (*JPTS*. 1886), 50, etc. – *Aṅguttara*, i, 173; Carpenter, *Theism*, 50.

In this *Siddhi*, F 30, Hsüan-tsang writes:

> According to one opinion, there is a God, Maheśvaradeva, whose nature is real, omnipresent and eternal, engendering factors (*dharma*).
>
> But, we would say: that which engenders is not eternal (e.g., earth, water, etc.); that which is not eternal is not omnipresent (*vibhu*) (e.g., a pitcher); that which is not omnipresent is not real (e.g., a pot).
>
> If Maheśvara is eternally and omnipresently endowed with powers (*śakti*, or capabilities, *sāmarthya*), he should, at all times, in all places and at the same time, produce all factors (*dharma*). If they say that Maheśvara, in order to produce the factors, depends on a desire to produce or on certain conditions, they are contradicting their doctrine of a single cause. Or else, we may say that, because Maheśvara is the eternal cause, it is false that at the time when the desire and conditions are present, that desire and conditions produce [the factors].

1109 *LS*: Burnouf (p. 573): "The Mahādeva of the Śivaites, the Vāsudeva of the Viṣṇuites, the Self (Puruṣa) or Primal Source (Pradhāna) of the Sāṃkhya."

1110 *LS*: Burnouf translates (p. 572f.) sections from Yaśomitra's *Vyākhyā* [WOG.237.21ff.]:

> Entities are neither created by God (Īśvara), or the Self (Puruṣa), or the Primal Source (Pradhāna). If, in fact, God were the single cause, whether this God were Mahādeva, Vāsudeva, or any other principle, like the Self or the Primal Source, it would be necessary, by the very fact of the existence of this cause, that the world would be created in its totality, all at once; for one cannot admit that the cause exists without its effect existing. But we see that entities come into this world successively, some from a womb, others from a sprout; from this we should conclude that there is a succession of causes, and the God is not a single cause.
>
> But, it is objected, this variety of causes is the effect of the desire of God, who has said: May this entity arise now, so that this other entity may arise later; it is in this way that the succession of entities is explained, and that it is established that God is the cause of them. To this, one replies that admitting several actions to the desire is to admit several causes; and that this destroys the first thesis, namely, that there is only a single cause.
>
> Furthermore: this plurality of causes cannot have been produced in one go, since God, the source of the distinct actions of the desire that have produced this variety of causes, is single and indivisible. Here again the objection that has been made previously reappears, namely, that it would be necessary to admit that the world has been created all at once. But the sons of the Śākyas hold to the maxim that the cycle of existence of the world has no beginning.

1111 *LVP*: Stanza (*śloka*) of Vyāsa in the *Śatarudrīya* (WOG.238.25f.). – *Mahābhārata*, vii. 203, 140; xiii. 161, 7: *yan nirdahati yat tīkṣno yad ugro yat pratāpavān | māṃsaśoṇitamajjādo yat tato rudra ucyate*. – Burnouf refers to the *Śatarudrīya* in his *Introduction*, p. 568.

1112 *LVP*: *akṛtabuddhayaḥ* = paramārthaśāstrair asaṃskṛtabuddhayaḥ [WOG.239.26f.].

1113 *LVP*: Ripened effect (*vipākaphala*) and effect of human action (*puruṣakāraphala*).

1114 *LVP*: Addition of Hsüan-tsang.

1115 *LS*: SAH 36.

1116 *LS*: Ibid.

1117 *Gokhale*: [65a] *dvidhā bhūtāni taddhetur*

Tib.: [65a] *de'i rgyu 'byung ba rnam pa gnyis* |

LVP: On the elements (*bhūta*; i. 12, ii. 22).

1118 *LS*: SAH 36.

1119 *Gokhale*: [65b] *bhautikasya tu pañcadhā* |

Tib.: [65b] *'byung las gyur pa'i rnam pa lnga* |

LVP: See AKB ii, 277, 297, *Siddhi*, 448.

1120 *LVP*: Hsüan-tsang adds that these five causes are varieties of the efficient cause (*kāraṇa-hetu*). [*LS*: Pradhan.102.26 has: *so 'yaṃ kāraṇahetureva punaḥ pañcadhā bhinnaḥ.*]

See *Vyākhyā* [WOG.29.24ff.] to AKB i. 11, where the causal relationship between the elements (*bhūta*) which form part of the person (*āśraya*) and that type of the derivative material elements (*bhautika*) which is the non-informative (*avijñapti*) is explained.

LS: MVŚ, 663a, states (ESD.131):

> Question: In what sense [is the derived matter] dependent (*upādāya*) [on the *mahābhūta*-s] (*mahābhūtāni upādāya*)? Is it in the sense of [having the *mahābhūta*-s as] cause (*hetu*), or in the sense of [having them as] conditions (*pratyaya*)? ...
> Answer: It should be said thus: it is in the sense of [having them as] cause.
> Question: These [*mahābhūta*-s], with regard to the secondary *rūpa*-s (*upādāyarūpa*), do not have [the functions of] any of the five *hetu*-s [besides being *kāraṇa-hetu* in as much as they do not hinder the arising of the *bhautika*-s], how are they the cause?
>
> Answer: Although [the meaning of] any of the five *hetu*-s, *sabhāga-hetu*, etc., are lacking, they are *hetu* in five other senses: i.e., *janana-hetu*, *niśraya-hetu*, *pratiṣṭhā-hetu*, *upastambha-hetu*, *upabṛṃhaṇa-hetu*.

Sthiramati's *Pañcaskandhaprakaraṇavibhāṣyam* states (ISBP.250):

> [The great elements] are the generating cause [*jananahetu*] [of derivative form], because [derivative form] cannot occur if [the great elements] are absent.
>
> [The great elements] are a dependence cause [*niśrayahetu*], because whatever modification [the great elements] undergo, the derivative form that is dependent on the elements undergoes a similar modification.
>
> [The great elements] are a foundation cause [*pratiṣṭhahetu*], because when the elements arise as a uniform continuum, derivative form continues to exist uninterruptedly as well.
>
> [The great elements] are a supporting cause [*upastambhathetu*] in that, by their power, derivative form does not cease to exist.
>
> They are a strengthening cause [*upabṛṃhaṇahetu*] in that when the elements become strengthened, the derivative form that is dependent on them becomes strengthened as well.

[1121] *LVP*: These definitions according to MVŚ, 663a28. – Saṃghabhadra, 452a19ff., presents other explanations, gives other examples.

[1122] *LVP*: See above ii. 59d, the effect of the base (*pratiṣṭhaphala*).

[1123] *Gokhale*: [65c] *tridhā bhautikam anyonyaṃ*

Tib.: [65c] *'byung gyur rnam gsum phan tshun du* |

[1124] *LS*: The *Vyākhyā* glosses [WOG.240.4ff.]: *kāya-karma cittānuparivarti* dhyānānasrāva-saṃvara-saṃgṛhītaṃ trividham prāṇātipātādatt'ādāna-kāma-mithy'ācāra-virati-bhedena. *vāk-karmā*pi *cittānuparivarti* dhyānānāsrava-saṃvara-saṃgṛhītam eva caturvidhaṃ. mṛṣā-vāda-paiśunya-pāruṣya-saṃbhinna-pralāpa-virati-bhedena. tad evaṃ sapta-vidhaṃ kāya-vāk-karmānyonyaṃ *sahābhū-hetuḥ*. prāṇātipāta-viratir upādāya-rūpaṃ itareṣāṃ ṣaṇṇāṃ *sahābhū-hetuḥ*. tāny api ṣaṭ tasya *sahabhū-hetur* iti sarvaṃ yojyam. *nānyad* iti. cakṣur-ādikaṃ sarvam *upādāya-rūpaṃ* prātimokṣa-saṃvar'ādi-saṃgṛhītam api yāvan nānyonyaṃ sahabhū-hetuḥ pṛthak-kalāpatvat.

[1125] *LS*: The *Vyākhyā* glosses [WOG.240.11f.]: *sabhāgasye*ti. kuśalaṃ'kuśalasya svāsaṃtānikasya kliṣṭaṃ kliṣṭasyety-ādi.

[1126] *LS*: The *Vyākhyā* glosses [WOG.240.12f.]: *yasya kāya-vāk-karmaṇa* iti. vijñapty-avijñapti-svabhāvasya samāhitasyāsamahitasya vā yathāyogaṃ.

[1127] *Gokhale*: [65d] *bhūtānām ekadh aiva tat* ||

Tib.: [65c] *'byung ba rnams kyi de rnam gcig* ||

[1128] *LS*: SAH 232, 528–46.

[1129] *LS*: SAH 528.

[1130] *Gokhale*: [66] *kuśalā'kuśalaṃ kāme nivṛtā'nivṛtaṃ manaḥ* | *rūpārūpyeṣv akuśalād anyatrā 'nāsravaṃ dvidhā* ||

Tib.: [66] *'dod yid dge dang mi dge dang* | *bsgribs pa dang ni ma bsgribs pa* | *gzugs dang gzugs med pa dag na* | *mi dge las gzhan zag med gnyis* ||

LVP: The doctrine of twelve thoughts is presented in *Vijñānakāya*, vi (fol. 54b) and in the work of Dharmatrāta, *Nanjio*, 1287, fol. 95b and following, x. 29–34: "In the realm of desire, four thoughts; in the realm of fine-materiality and the realm of immateriality, each three thoughts, also 'of those in training' (*śaikṣa*) and 'of those beyond training' (*aśaikṣa*). We will see their order of arising. In the realm of desire, the wholesome (*kuśala*) thought engenders nine thoughts and it is produced by eight thoughts... ." There follows (verses 35–46) the doctrine of twenty thoughts (*Kośa*, ii. 71b–72) that involves the presentation, in verses (*kārikā*), of the rules of the succession of thoughts. Vasubandhu contents himself *below*, as we shall see, to give a commentary (*bhāṣya*), but Yaśomitra, under the name of *saṃgrahaślokas* (summary stanzas) [WOG.245.17ff.], provides a versified redaction that perhaps preserves for us a fragment of the original text of Dharmatrāta.

[1131] *LS*: SAH 529–34.

[1132] *LS*: SAH 529–33.

[1133] *LS*: SAH 529–30.

[1134] *Gokhale*: [67–68b] *kāme nava śubhāc cittāc cittāny aṣṭabhya eva tat* | *daśabhyo 'kuśalaṃ tyasmāc catvāri nivṛtaṃ tathā* || *pañcabhyo nivṛtaṃ tasmāt sapta cittāny anantaram* |

Tib.: [67–68b] *'dod sems dge ba las sems dgu | de ni brgyad po kho na las | mi dge ba ni bcu dag las | de las bzhi ste bsgribs de bzhin || ma bsgribs pa ni lnga dag las | de las mjug thog sems bdun no |*

LVP: Compare *Kathāvatthu*, xiv. 1, where the Theravādin maintains, against the Mahāsāṃghika, that the wholesome thought cannot follow the unwholesome thought, etc.

[1135] *LS*: SAH 529.

[1136] *LVP*: 1. The four kinds of distancing (*dūratā*) are (i) basis (*āśraya*), (ii) aspect (*ākāra*), (iii) cognitive object (*ālambana*), (iv) counteragent (*pratipakṣa*):

i. The bases (or persons) (*āśraya*) of the realm of immateriality cannot "manifest" (*saṃmukhīkar*), assimilate, any factor (*dharma*) of the realm of desire, whereas sentient beings in the realm of fine-materiality can manifest, assimilate, a thought of supernormal emanation (*nirmāṇacitta*) of the realm of desire (ii. 53b).

ii. The thought of the realm of immateriality does not apply the aspects or categories (*ākāra*) of "gross" (*audārika*), etc., (vi. 49) to the realm of desire as does the thought of the realm of fine-materiality.

iii. In the same way, it does not seize the realm of desire as a cognitive object (*ālambana*).

iv. In the same way, it does not counteract the defilements of the realm of desire as do the meditations (*dhyāna*).

2. See v. 62, for a different set of four kinds of distancing: distancing (*dūratā*): (1) through difference of nature (*vailakṣaṇya*); (2) through opposition (*vipakṣatva* = *pratipakṣatva*); (3) through local separation (*deśaviccheda*); (4) through time (*kāla*).

See AKB iv, F 31; v, F 106.

[1137] *LS*: SAH 529.

[1138] *LS*: SAH 530.

[1139] *LS*: SAH 530–31.

[1140] *Gokhale*: [68c–69c1] *rūpe daś aikaṃ ca śubhān navabhyas tad anantaram || aṣṭābhyo nivṛtaṃ tasmāt ṣaṭ tribhyo 'nivṛtaṃ punaḥ | tasmāt ṣaḍ*

Tib.: [68c–69c1] *gzugs na dag las bcu gcig go | de ni dgu yi mjug thogs su || bsgribs pa brgyad las de las drug | ma bsgribs pa ni gsum las so | de las drug ste*

[1141] *LS*: SAH 530.

[1142] *LS*: LVP has Rūpadhātu, but Pradhan.204.20f., WOG.241.25, Jampaiyang and Wangchuk Dorje have Ārūpyadhātu.

[1143] *LS*: SAH 531.

[1144] *LS*: Ibid.

[1145] *LS*: SAH 532–33.

[1146] *Gokhale*: [69c2–70b] *evam ārūpye tasya nītiḥ śubhāt punaḥ || nava cittāni tat ṣaṭkān nivṛtāt sapta tat tathā |*

Tib.: [69c2–70b] *gzugs med pa'ang | de yi tshul lo dge ba las || sems dgu dag go de drug gi | bsgribs pa las bdun de de bzhin |*

1147 *LS*: SAH 533.

1148 *LS*: SAH 532.

1149 *LS*: Ibid.

1150 *LS*: SAH 533–34.

1151 *Gokhale*: [70c–71a] *caturbhyaḥ śaikṣam asmāt tu pañcā 'śaikṣaṃ tu pañcakāt* || *tasmāc catvāri cittāni*

Tib.: [70c–71a] *slob pa bzhi las de las lnga* | *mi slob pa ni lnga las so* || *de las sems ni bzhi dag go* |

1152 *LS*: SAH 533.

1153 *LS*: SAH 534.

1154 *LS*: SAH 534–37.

1155 *LVP*: Skill in the art of riding on the head of an elephant, on the back of a horse; skill in the art of archery, etc.

1156 *Gokhale*: [71b–72] *dvādaś aitāni viṃśatiḥ* | *prāyogikopapattyāptaṃ śubhaṃ bhittvā triṣu dvidhā* | *vipākajairyāpathikaśailpasthānikanairmitam* | *caturdhā 'vyākṛtaṃ kāme rūpe ṣilpa-vivarjitam* ||

Tib.: [71b–72] *bcu gnyis de dag nyi shur yang* | *gsum du skyes nas thob pa dang* | *sbyor byung dge rnam gnyis phye nas* || *rnam smin skyes dang spyod lam pa* | *bzo yi gnas dang sprul pa dang* | *'dod na lung bstan min rnam bzhir* | *gzugs na bzo ma gtogs pa'o* ||

1157 *LS*: SAH 535–36.

1158 *LVP*: That is to say, 1. derived from listening (*śrutamaya*), 2. derived from reflection (*cintāmaya*), 3. derived from cultivation (*bhāvanāmaya*). – In the realm of desire, (1.) and (2.); in the realm of fine-materiality, (1.) and (3.); in the realm of immateriality, (3.), as we have seen above at ii, F 265; compare ii, F 328.

1159 *LVP*: This is the wholesome thought (*kuśala*) of which the sentient being who has arisen in the realm of desire and the realm of fine-materiality obtains the possession (*prāpti*) at the moment of the origin of the intermediate existence (*antarābhavapratisaṃdhikṣaṇe*); at the moment of the arising, when the sentient being is reborn in the realm of immateriality.

1160 *LS*: SAH 535–36.

1161 *LVP*: A list of *śilpasthānakarmasthāna* (*Mahāvyutpatti*, 76, 5) is cited in the *Divyāvadāna*, pp. 58, 100: the art of riding on the head of an elephant, on the back of a horse, the art of archery, etc.

1162 *LS*: SAH 537.

1163 *LVP*: The visible forms, etc., (1) of the bed and of the body, etc., (2) of instruments (bow, arrow, etc.), (3) of the entity that one wants to create.

1164 *LVP*: For one apprehends the arts by listening to instruction. – The effect of retribution (*vipākaja*) is not mentioned here; thus one has the five derivative material elements (*bhautika*), visible form, etc., for one's object.

1165 *LVP*: In fact, the thought relative to walking, etc., takes place after one has seen, felt, etc. – Hsüan-tsang corrects the *Bhāṣya*: "four or five sensory consciousnesses are preparatory to the thoughts associated with the proper deportments (*airyāpathika*) and the thoughts associated with skill in arts and crafts (*śailpasthānika*) respectively". One should understand that the auditory consciousness is absent for the thoughts associated with the proper deportments.

1166 *LVP*: MVŚ, 661a16. – The Bhadanta Anantavarman (*Vyākhyā ad* ii. 46cd), in the *Explanation of the Vibhāṣā* (*Vibhāṣāvyākhyāna*) presents this opinion according to which one should admit the unobscured-non-defined thoughts (*anivṛtāvyākṛta*) not included in the abovementioned (F 320) four non-defined thoughts (*avyākṛta*), namely, the unobscured-non-defined thoughts defined vii. 51.

1167 *LVP*: Hsüan-tsang: "by thoughts associated with the proper deportments (*airyāpathika*) and thoughts associated with skill in arts and *crafts* (*śailpasthānika*)".

1168 *LS*: SAH 537–46.

1169 *LS*: SAH 538–40.

1170 *LS*: LVP has unobscured-non-defined thought of the realm of fine-materiality, but both Pradhan.106.20 and WOG.243.34 have defiled (*kliṣṭa*) thought, i.e., obscured-non-defined thought, of the realm of fine-materiality.

1171 *LS*: Again, LVP has unobscured-non-defined thought.

1172 *LS*: Again, LVP has unobscured-non-defined thought.

1173 *LS*: Again, LVP has unobscured-non-defined thought.

1174 *LS*: SAH 541–43.

1175 *LVP*: First thought of the intermediate existence (*antarābhava*) of the realm of fine-materiality.

1176 *LS*: SAH 544–45.

1177 *LS*: SAH 546.

1178 *LS*: Ibid.

1179 *LS*: Ibid.

1180 *LS*: Ibid.

1181 *LS*: SAH 232.

1182 *LS*: Ibid.

1183 *LVP*: By an effort of resolution—due to a decision—the practitioners see the body as the body really is not, namely, as being made up only of rotten bones, etc: this is the meditation on the loathsome (*aśubha*). In the same way, in the supernormal powers (*ṛddhi*; vii. 48), the practitioners imagine that the earth element is small, and that the water element is great (compare *Dīgha*, ii. 108).

LS: In the **Nyāyānusāra*, 622aff., we find a lengthy debate between the Vaibhāṣika and the Sautrāntika, represented by Śrīlāta, who claims that the following cases are examples of perception of non-existent objects (see ADCP.46f.):

1. Optical illusion of a fire-wheel (*alāta-cakra*) resulting from a whirling firebrand.
2. The cognition of the non-existent Self (*ātman*).
3. The meditational experiences, such as the all pervasiveness of a meditational object (the so-called "base of entirety", *kṛtsnāyatana*), e.g., a primary colour, that results

from resolute mental application (*adhimukti-manaskāra*). [...]

1184 *LVP*: *Saṃyuktāgama* 27, 15: *aśubhāsahagataṃ smṛtisaṃbodhyaṅgaṃ bhāvayati*. – "Mindfulness" forms a part of the (noble) path; *sahagata* (together with) signifies "immediately following".

1185 *LS*: AH 230; SAH 465.

1186 *LS*: Ibid.

1187 *Gokhale*: [73ab1] *kliṣṭe traidhāṭuke lābhaḥ ṣaṇṇāṃ ṣaṇṇāṃ dvayoḥ*

Tib.: [73ab] *khams gsum pa yi nyon mongs can | drug dang drug dang gnyis rnyed do |*

1188 *LS*: The *Vyākhyā* glosses [WOG.248.16f.]: iha *kuśala-pratisaṃdhānaṃ* samyag-dṛṣṭyā vā *vicikitsayā* vā.

1189 *LVP*: The *Vibhāṣā* discusses whether the wholesome (*kuśala*) thought of which one takes possession is innate or acquired at birth (*upapattipratilambhika*) only or acquired also through preparatory effort (*prāyogika*).

1190 *LS*: AH 230; SAH 465.

1191 *Gokhale*: [73b2–c1] *śubhe | trayāṇāṃ rūpaje*

Tib.: [73c] *gzugs skyes dge la gsum dag go |*

1192 *LS*: AH 230; SAH 465.

1193 *Gokhale*: [73c2d1] *śaikṣe caturṇāṃ*

Tib.: [73d1] *slob pa la bzhi*

1194 *LS*: AH 230; SAH 465.

1195 *Gokhale*: [73d2] *tasya śeṣite*

Tib.: [73d2] *lhag la de ||*

1196 *LS*: This is the 44th of Kritzer's forty-four passages discussed in relation to chapter 2 (VY.130). Vasubandhu comments that the wholesome thought should be presented as seven thoughts. Saṃghabhadra (Ny, 456a1) identifies this as the opinion of Vasubandhu and explains (Ny, 456a1–2) that the sixth and seventh thought are mentioned as one since they are both pure (*anāsrava*).

1197 *LVP*: This is a verse (*kārikā*) in the work of Dharmatrāta, *Nanjio* 1287, fol. 86a17: "If one acquires nine types of factors, one should know that it is with a defiled (*kliṣṭa*) thought; the wholesome (*kuśala*) thought acquires six types; the non-defined (*avyākṛta*) thought acquires the non-defined thought (transl. of Saṃghavarman). Paramārtha: "When the defiled thought is produced, one acquires, it is said, nine types of thought; with the wholesome thought...".

The *Vyākhyā* [WOG.251.17] provides the third quarter-verse (*pāda*):

> [*lābhaḥ syān navacittānāṃ kliṣṭe citta iti smṛtam* |]
> *ṣaṇṇāṃ tu kuśale citte* [*tasyaivāvyākṛtodbhave* ||]

1198 *LVP*: *upapattisamāpattivairāgyaparihāṇisu* |
kuśalapratisaṃdhau ca cittalābho [*hy*] *atadvataḥ* ||

ABOUT THE AUTHOR/TRANSLATORS

Vasubandhu (ca. 350–430 A.D.) was born in Puruṣapura in Gandhāra and is, next to Asaṅga (ca. 330–405 A.D.), his half-brother, the most famous personage of the Yogācāra school.

He originally belonged to the Śrāvakayāna school of the Sarvāstivādins and had already made a name for himself through the composition of numerous treatises when he was won over to the Mahāyāna by Asaṅga, sometime in his forties. He then with great enthusiasm put his talents to work in the service of the Mahāyāna, for which he wrote so many works that he received the name "master of a thousand doctrinal treatises". Vasubandhu counts as the great systematizer of Buddhism and is one of the six great ornaments—six great commentators of the Buddha's teaching.

Even though in the Kośa, Vasubandhu seems to be generally partisan to the "Hīnayāna"-Sautrāntikas, he too was evidently open-minded, of which fact the Kośa is a testimony, and accordingly he did not seem to have become exclusively partisan to the tenets of any group as such—be it those of Hīnayāna- or Yogācāra-Sautrāntika or Sarvāstivāda.

Vasubandhu's personage, life and dates have been a matter of great debate in modern Buddhist scholarship.

Hsüan-tsang or Xuanzang (600–664 A.D.), renowned for his sixteen-year pilgrimage to India and his career as a translator of Buddhist scriptures, is one of the most illustrious figures in the history of scholastic Chinese Buddhism.

Upon his return to China in 645, Hsüan-tsang brought back with him a great number of Sanskrit texts. In addition to his translations of the *Abhidharmakośabhāṣya* (651–654), the **Nyāyānusāra* (653–654), as well as the **Mahāvibhāṣā* (656–659), *Jñānaprasthāna* (657–660), **Abhidharmāvatāra* (658), *Prakaraṇapāda* (660) and other important Abhidharma texts, he also translated many Mahāyāna scriptures, e.g., the *Yogācārabhūmiśāstra* (646–648) and *Mahāprajñāpāramitāsūtra* (660–663), and authored the *Records of the Western Regions* (646). It is through Hsüan-tsang and his chief disciple K'uei-chi that the Fa-hsiang or Yogācāra School was initiated in China; the most important book of the school being Hsüan-tsang's *Ch'eng wei-shi lun* (*Vijñaptimātratāsiddhi*; in 659).

Louis de La Vallée Poussin (1869–1938), born in Liège (Belgium), was an indologist and specialist in Buddhist philosophy. Educated in Liège, Louvain, Paris (S. Lévy) and Leiden (H. Kern), he was a master in many languages, including Sanskrit, Pali, Chinese, Tibetan, Greek, Latin, etc., and became professor at the University of Ghent (Belgium) in 1893, a position he held until his retirement in 1929.

Hubert Durt (in *Encyclopedia of Relgion*) elaborates:

> La Vallée Poussin dedicated all the strength of his philological genius to his field and contributed to a reorientation of Buddhist studies toward the languages of northern Buddhism (Sanskrit and Tibetan) and toward Buddhist philosophy considered in its historical perspective. He produced two main types of studies: (1) scholarly editions [of Tantric texts; Mādhyamika texts; etc.] and (2) translations with exegeses. These correspond roughly to the two periods of his activity, that before and that after World War I.
>
> After World War I, La Vallée Poussin, who had in the meantime mastered the languages of the Chinese Buddhist translations, undertook the enormous enterprise of translating and critically annotating two summae of Buddhist scholastics: Vasubandhu's *Abhidharmakośa*, the masterwork of the northern Hīnayāna Abhidharma school, and Hsüan-tsang's *Vijñaptimātratāsiddhi*, the best compendium of the tenets of the Yogācāra, or Idealist, current of the Mahāyāna. For his *Abhidharmakośa* (1923–1931), La Vallée Poussin had to master the huge Kashmirian *Mahāvibhāṣā*, … . With his *Vijñaptimātratāsiddhi*: *La Siddhi de Hiuan-tsang* (1928–1929), he took the lead in the study of Idealist Buddhism, a field in which Sylvain Lévi had laid the foundation and which Paul Demiéville and La Vallée Poussin's pupil Étienne Lamotte were to continue.

Besides these two main types of studies, La Vallée Poussin produced many other writings, see our *Bibliography*. Sylvain Lévi wrote: "His work is of unrivalled magnitude." More modestly, La Vallée Poussin himself said: "Je suis l'homme du Kośa."

Gelong Lodrö Sangpo (Jürgen Balzer) — the translator — is a student of the late Ven. Trungpa Rinpoche. Born 1952 in Germany, he received his first ordination in the Karma Kagyü Sangha in 1984, France, and then moved to Gampo Abbey, Canada. From 1985–2002 he served as Secretary of *International Kagyü Sangha Association of Buddhist Monks and Nuns* and published its magazine *The Profound Path of Peace*.

He completed the traditional three year retreat in 1996 and a four year study retreat in 2003. He also served for a few years as Acting Director of Gampo Abbey. He was one of the co-founders of Nitartha Institute and is a senior teacher at the Vidyadhara Institute, the monastic college of Gampo Abbey, since its inception.

His focus of study is in the systematic traditions of Buddhist Abhidharma. In recent years, he has translated and published — under the supervision of Prof. Ernst Steinkellner — Erich Frauwallner's *The Philosophy of Buddhism* (Motilal). At present he is finalizing a translation of various books and articles by La Vallée Poussin and is also engaged in the project of translating the collected writings of Prof. Lambert Schmithausen from German into English.